*Columbia Chronologies of
Asian History and Culture*

Columbia Chronologies of Asian History and Culture

Edited by John S. Bowman

COLUMBIA UNIVERSITY PRESS

NEW YORK

COLUMBIA UNIVERSITY PRESS

Publishers Since 1893

New York

Chichester, West Sussex

Copyright © 2000 Columbia University Press

All rights reserved

Library of Congress Cataloging-in-Publication Data

Columbia chronologies of Asian history and culture / edited
by John S. Bowman.

     p. cm.

  Includes index.

    ISBN 0–231–11004–9 (cloth : alk. paper)

     1. Asia—History—Chronology.   I. Bowman, John

  Stewart, 1931–

DS33.C63 2000

950–dc21   99–047017

⊗

Casebound editions of Columbia University Press books are
printed on permanent and durable acid-free paper.

Printed in the United States of America

c 10 9 8 7 6 5 4 3 2 1

CONTENTS

CONSULTANTS AND CONTRIBUTORS

CONSULTANTS

Central Asia (Mongolia, Central Asian Republics)
MORRIS ROSSABI
Professor of History
City University of New York

China
ROBERT HYMES
Professor of Chinese History
Department of East Asian Languages and Cultures
Columbia University

Japan
HAROLD BOLITHO
Professor of Japanese History
Department of East Asian Languages and Civilizations
Harvard University

Korea
EDWARD W. WAGNER
Professor of Korean History (Emeritus)
Department of East Asian Languages and Civilizations
Harvard University

South Asia
AINSLIE T. EMBREE
Professor of History (Emeritus)
Columbia University

Southeast Asia (Indonesia, Malaysia, Myanmar, Singapore, Brunei, Philippines)
BARBARA ANDAYA
Professor, Asian Studies Program
University of Hawai'i at Manoa

Southeast Asia (Cambodia, Laos, Thailand, Vietnam)
JOHN K. WHITMORE
Adjunct Associate Professor of History and Research Associate of the Center for South and Southeast
Asian Studies
University of Michigan

CONTRIBUTING WRITERS

JOHN S. BOWMAN
Laos, Vietnam

MICHAEL GOLAY
China

MARY-ANN GALLAGHER
Cambodia, Hong Kong, Macau, Taiwan

EDWARD H. MORRIS
Korea, Central Asian Republics, Mongolia

CRISTINA PARSONS OCHAGAVIA
Brunei, Indonesia, Malaysia, Myanmar, Philippines, Singapore

EVA WEBER
Japan, Thailand

PAMELA WHITE
Bangladesh, Bhutan, India, Maldives, Nepal, Pakistan, Sri Lanka, Tibet

INDEXER

MARLENE LONDON

INTRODUCTION

Chronologies have long proved their worth—compressing masses of data that occupy many pages in standard texts, simplifying complicated material, pinning down dates that are often ignored or obscured in these same texts. There are certainly many chronologies in many books. They tend to fall into two categories. There are those for specific countries published as adjuncts to specialized histories of those countries. And then there are the big "synoptic" chronologies or timelines of the entire world's history. Each of these serves its own useful function and special public.

Yet none, it can safely be claimed, does what this one attempts—namely, to provide a chronology for all of Asia that is both specific and comprehensive. The history of each country is set forth in a detailed and sequential manner, one that is above all intended to clarify. Each of the countries or major historical/political entities of Asia (as defined: see below) gets its own full treatment. (Several of these countries have never received such an orderly treatment.) Meanwhile, each of the three largest nations—China, India, and Japan—gets separate chronologies for the many achievements in the areas of (1) arts, culture, thought, and religion, and (2) science, technology, economics, and everyday activities.

Beyond these elements, what distinguishes this work from the other available chronologies is that their entries are, at best, overly terse, and at worst, meaningful only to the initiated. Each event is simply set down as an isolated event: Individuals are not identified, places are not located, obscure words are not defined, relationships are never made clear. In this chronology, by contrast, such matters are clearly identified.

This still leaves a number of ground rules that the user of this work should know of. We discuss each of these in the pages that follow, and we advise any reader/user to consult them so as to understand the true characteristics and boundaries of this work.

ASIA AS DEFINED

We must start by declaring that ours is the historian's, not the geographer's, Asia. The geographer's Asia stretches from the eastern shores of the Mediterranean, incorporates what we know as the Middle East, winds around the southern borders of Russia and the Urals, and then sweeps across a great land mass, including many offshore islands.

The Asia of this volume includes what the specialists now designate as Central Asia, South Asia, Southeast Asia, and East Asia. It should also be admitted that there are several gray areas, countries that might have been included. The most obvious one, perhaps, is Afghanistan; but because this chronology reflects historians' views of the past, we decided that Afghanistan belongs more to the Middle East. Meanwhile, there was little debate over leaving the whole of Asiatic Russia—known as Siberia—to Russia's history.

If this seems somewhat arbitrary, it might be said that the traditional Asia of geographers is hardly less so: Why draw the boundary between Turkey and Russia? Why draw the boundary at the Urals? Why draw the line between Indonesia and New Guinea?

There remains one potentially controversial boundary we have drawn, and that is the assignment of Tibet to Central Asia. This is not intended to take a side in the ongoing dispute between China and Tibetans; it is merely intended to reflect the anthropological and cultural roots of Tibet and its distinctive history. Likewise, the decision to give Taiwan, Hong Kong, and Macau their own separate chronologies is not intended to make any political statement: this simply reflects the history of these places. In the future, their chronologies may be absorbed into China's, but for now they seem to rate their own.

DATES

Because a chronology by definition depends on dating, let us first explain some of the issues revolving around dates.

The Single Western Calendar

First came the decision to assign all dates to the traditional system and sequence employed in the Western world. Many of the countries and regions included here have their traditional calendars—the Hindu calendar, for instance, a traditional Chinese calendar, a Muslim calendar, and so forth. But because this work is clearly aimed at readers and students in the Western world and because its language, English, will mean that it is used by those already familiar with that Western outlook, we considered it totally impractical to adopt those traditional calendars. The whole point is to show relationships immediately by a common standard, which would not work if readers had to jump back and forth among these several calendars.

The B.C./A.D. System

This then raised the related question of whether to employ the traditional Western system of B.C./A.D. or to adopt other systems now being used. Increasingly more people are rejecting this system with its specific references to the Christian religion, locating all of history along a sequence that a predominantly Western religion has deemed crucial. Alternative systems, however, tend to simply substitute different terminology for those two time frames—no system generally proposed attempts to put all events on one sequence. One exception is that used by geologists and anthropologists, the BP ("before present") system, but this is used only for truly old and approximate dates. Meanwhile, some of the other systems now being used—such as BCE/CE, "before the common era"/"common era"—were considered, and one or two of our consultants did, in fact, indicate their preference for adopting one of these systems. There is also a system that employs—(for B.C.) and + (for A.D.); although neutral and even clear, the feeling is that it is not widely recognized. The fact is, though, that none of these systems really avoids dividing dates at the traditional Christian boundary; they simply change the nomenclature. Most history books being written still employ the B.C./A.D. system, so we decided to use it here.

Rounded-off Dates

We have mentioned that anthropologists have to deal with broad time frames—they often cannot be expected to know in exactly which century or decade, let alone which year, events occurred. So, too, do most historians of the ancient world; for that matter, most historians of what might be called the world's "middle ages" also deal with many approximate years. Many texts are thus filled with qualifiers such as "about 50,000 BPE" or "about 1500 B.C." or "around 1500." At the outset of this project, we found that almost all our early dates were preceded by *c.*, the traditional abbreviation for *circa*, itself a Latin word for "about." Eventually we decided that this was superfluous for all these early dates: we decided that it can be taken for granted that most dates that are rounded off in the B.C. era are just that, rounded-off approximations: 38,000 B.C., 5000 B.C., 1500 B.C., 500 B.C. So, too, are most rounded-off years well into the last few centuries. Not until we get into a country's recorded history can we be sure of exact years—although even then, this is often uncertain. So it should be understood—and we think this is fair—that the many rounded-off dates up until, say, about A.D. 1900, are just that—rounded off.

Abbreviation of circa

At times, however, we use *c.* when we have entered into the periods where specific dates are being used for surrounding historical events, and putting 1350 or 1480 might be seen as designating a specific year. So *c.* is employed to indicate that this particular date is just that—approximate and rounded off.

The Question Mark

The question mark is used in two situations. When it appears by itself, it is almost always indicating that the year of birth or death of an individual is unknown. The other use is when it follows a year or date. This is intended to indicate that (1) the exact year simply cannot be pinned down and/or (2) not all scholars can agree on this exact year; however, this is a specific year (or approximate period) that seems to be generally accepted, even if disputed by some.

Variants

We should also point out the several variants that we hope are at least consistent if not self-explanatory:

c. 1550 = the event in question occurred close to this year but cannot otherwise be pinned down

1250s = the events in question occurred during most if not all of this decade

13th century = the event occurred throughout much if not all of this century

Early 13th century = the event occurred in approximately the first third of this century

Mid-13th century = the event occurred in approximately the middle third of the century

Late 13th century = the event occurred in approximately the final third of the century

13th–14th centuries = the event occurred during a time frame that bridged these two centuries

13th and 14th centuries = the event occurred throughout much of both these centuries

Traditional and Legendary Dates

There are many dates commonly used in histories of countries that are in fact simply assigned by legend or tradition. Often these apparently specific dates have become important in the "history" of a nation or people, so we felt they must be given. But we have tried in all instances to label such dates as just that—legendary or traditional.

Dates and the World's Time Zones

When days are given (e.g., January 17, 1995) we have tried in all instances to give the date as it was in the country concerned—not necessarily the same day it is known in the West. An example: When North Korean forces crossed the 38th parallel it was about 4:00 A.M. on June 25 in Korea, but only about 3:00 P.M. on June 24 in Washington. We give the date as it fell in Korea. As it happens, almost all the locales included in this volume lie east of the Greenwich time zone, so if there is a difference in a day, it precedes the day in Western Europe or North America. A major exception to this is World War II in the Pacific, where events often occurred at times that were at an earlier hour on the same day in North America: thus Pearl Harbor occurred at 7:55 A.M. on December 7 in Hawaii when it was already 12:55 P.M. in Washington.

Discrepancies with Dates in Other Texts

All this said, there remains the problem of differences in dates in even the most respected scholarly sources. (As for more popular works, some are truly a morass of misinformation.) This proved to be one of the most challenging—and exasperating—aspects of compiling these chronologies. Some of these differences are explicitly recognized and debated by the scholars, but most of them simply sit there in the various texts as though there is no disagreement. Where these differences or discrepancies seemed vital, and we were unable to resolve them, we have tried to recognize this with a minimum of words. But ultimately, we could not record every one of the differences—this would have changed the nature of such a work. We had to settle on a single date. All we can say is that each of our consultants and contributors thought long and hard about these matters and did their best to settle on what appears to be the best one. But we do not deny that there will be many differences with other highly reputable works.

Up-to-date Dates

In all matters of history, a single discovery can upset certain accepted dates. In the case of modern Asia, this is less likely with well-recorded events, but it is certainly the case with events in the ancient and earliest periods. In general, most specialists do not rush to change or adopt dates on the basis of one or two isolated finds—they have to fit things into the whole picture. But some discoveries and announcements do seem to be incontrovertible. One such instance was announced in the final stage of this book: the finding that the early dwellers of the Zhoukoudian caves in China apparently did not make or control fires. Most of the published literature does not yet reflect this claim.

TRANSLITERATION

Another major area of problems, because so many different languages are involved in a work of this kind, is that of transliterating foreign words and names: that is, converting other alphabets and sounds into the roman alphabet that best approximates in English these many unaccustomed sounds.

Different Systems

Where there are different systems, we have used the ones recommended by our consultants—which turn out to be the ones most preferred by modern scholars. The best-known instance of these is the change in transliterating Chinese names and words. For many years, the Western world (at least in English) relied on a system named after its two nineteenth-century English proponents, Wade-Giles. Starting in the 1970s, however, English-speaking art scholars began to adopt a new system known as pinyin, and this system was soon adopted by everyone writing about China. Under pinyin, for instance, the province of Kwangtung become Guangdong.

Exceptions to the Rule

This does mean that many proper names—of individuals and places—that have long been accepted in the English language, do in fact end up looking somewhat strange or at least unfamiliar. Peiping, China, has become Beijing; Mao Tse-tung has become Mao Zedong; and so on. In general, we go along with this new system. But in a few instances, we have stayed with the traditional forms—Confucius, for instance—and especially when the traditional versions seem to be the only ones still being used in most texts.

Diacriticals

The use of diacritical symbols—those marks added to letters to indicate the special phonetic values in various languages—seemed as though it might become an especially trying or complicated issue for this work. In the end, the problem did not materialize, because our consultants accepted that these diacritical marks are not needed in a work such as this—namely, one for nonspecialists and one not designed to be read aloud. Put another way, our consultants went along with a minimalist approach.

Translations/Equivalents

We have tried to provide English translations or equivalents for at least the first time a foreign word or term or title is used. If this word does not get used again for a long time, we provide the translation again. But if the word is used in relatively close succession and/or it has passed into widespread usage (samurai, lingam), we do not provide a translation after the first use.

DISCREPANCIES IN "FACTS"

As our contributors began to examine the scholarly and authoritative texts on which they were to base their chronologies, they soon began to find countless discrepancies or differences not only among the many dates they were expected to pin down but also among some of the more general accounts, descriptions, or conclusions about events. Keep in mind that the texts they were consulting were those recommended by the scholarly authorities who served as our consultants. Our contributors did their best to sort out these problems and then to pin the events down to a specific year. And therein lies the problem, because some of these events do not easily lend themselves to one date. These were complex situations that happened in the dim past and our knowledge may be based on questionable sources. Some scholars may accentuate one aspect, some may emphasize another. They can do this in their long paragraphs, even pages, of discussion and analysis—and even then end up straddling the issue. We, conversely, were expected to reduce everything to one year. Inevitably this may have led to some simplification, probably inherent and inevitable in such a chronology with its brief entries, limited space, and blunt statements. Our consultants did their best to prevent us from being simplistic, but we plead guilty to at times having had to simplify.

That said, we labored long and hard to end up with the "truest" data. We are aware that some of our information may differ with those in other reputable sources. Allowing for some possible outright misunderstandings or errors that could creep into a work of this size, we think our information is as solid as any now generally available.

CONSULTANTS

The role of our academic consultants should be made clear. Each is a recognized authority in the area or nations whose chronologies she or he reviewed. They were consultants in the sense that they brought a sense of balance and proportion, of current and fair interpretations, of outdated claims or missing material. They approached their particular portion of the chronologies with some assurance that the contributing writers had done their work carefully. Of course the consultants were expected to catch major errors in details (and they caught many). But they cannot be held responsible for every single date and "fact": they were not asked nor expected (nor paid!) to repeat all the research, to serve as fact checkers.

OTHER ELEMENTS

Separating Arts, Culture, Thought, and Religion and Science-Technology, Economics, and Everyday Activities

For the three major countries—China, India and Japan—we provide chronologies that deal with attainments in the arts, thought, religion, and other intellectual and cultural fields, with another set of chronologies for science, technology, economics, and everyday life. There are pros and cons on both sides to this approach, and the decision to do so was not taken without considerable debate among those involved. But it was decided that although specialists in these countries' histories might find it a bit arbitrary to have such elements separated out, the individuals who might be expected to consult such a work will appreciate this approach. Most users will probably be turning to this work in search of some fairly focused information, and it seemed most helpful to separate out this specialized topics for the three main countries. In any case, it should be relatively easy and quick to move back and forth among the three sections by referring to the dates along the left margin. And finally, the index will quickly guide everyone to any and all detailed data throughout the work.

National/Independence Days

This appendix was undertaken with the thought that it would be an easily compiled and simple list of dates. In fact, it turned out to be both more difficult and informative because of the many unexplained dates and discrepancies in other sources. We have tried not only to identify the dates but also to explain their context.

Early Science and Technology in Asia

This appendix provides one accessible chronology of an increasingly important topic of history: the early achievements of Asia in the fields of science, technology, engineering, mathematics, and related fields. Its stopping at the year 1600 simply reflects what happened in world history: by that time, the Western world was moving ahead and Asia was closing itself off. In the twentieth century, of course, Asian countries joined the great international scientific-technological project; their major contributions and accomplishment are indicated in the chronologies—in the case of China, India, and Japan, the separate chronologies, in the case of other countries, their single chronology.

Asian History: A Chronological Overview

This appendix is an overview of the entire history of all of the countries and entities treated, putting their events and achievements into relation with each other country's and then in line with events and individuals elsewhere in the world.

SUMMATION

All explanations aside, we feel that our writers—with the advantage of the academic consultants to guide them away from errors and excesses—have produced the most thorough, most correct, and most accessible chronologies for these many Asian lands. As indicated above, these chronologies, unlike almost all others available, truly explain rather than assume that the user already knows the individuals and places and events. They take little for granted. They identify, locate, define, translate. In their completeness, they become true outlines of these countries' histories. And by drawing on every possible source—many of them relatively obscure—and tracking down countless discrepancies that litter even the most scholarly texts, our researchers/writers have gone beyond most standard works, actually eliminating numerous pervasive errors. To that extent, we feel that these chronologies represent true and independent contributions to the literature.

ACKNOWLEDGMENTS

The formal listing of the consultants and contributing writers (pp. vii–viii) does not begin to express the debt and appreciation the editor owes to these individuals, all of whom ended up working far beyond the literal assignments they signed on for. In addition, we would like to thank several individuals who provided special advice or help along the way: Ludwig W. Adamec of the University of Arizona, Dennis Hudson of Smith College, Peter H. Lee of the University of California at Los Angeles, and Clark Neher of Northern Illinois University. We also owe a special debt to numerous libraries, and particularly to the many librarians who helped us in tracking down often hard-to-find texts. Finally, the editor is especially indebted to several individuals who have given beyond the call of duty in seeing this work through the planning, editorial, and production stages: James Warren, the editor at Columbia University Press; Edward Knappman of New England Publishing Associates; Gregory McNamee, the manuscript editor; and most especially, Marlene London of Professional Indexing Services.

Although it is customary for the editor to take responsibility for every single error in a work, this would be presumptuous, suggesting that I could know every single "fact" in this book. Rather, what I do take responsibility for are the contents in a broader sense—decisions about what to include or not include, the failure to recognize major gaps or inconsistencies. Specialists in various areas will undoubtedly discover errors here and there; by the same token, specialists above all will know how difficult it is to get unanimity on many of these details. We can say only that all involved in this work have tried very hard to keep mistakes to a minimum.

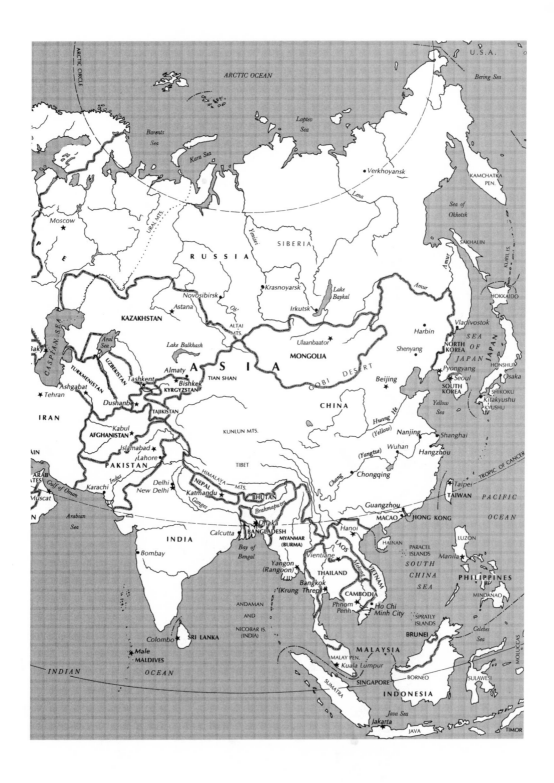

*Columbia Chronologies of
Asian History and Culture*

PART ONE

East Asia

China

POLITICAL HISTORY

PREHISTORIC AND LEGENDARY CHINA: 1,960,000–2208 B.C.

Until the late 1980s, it was believed that the first hominid (*Homo erectus*) appears in China about 800,000 B.C.; excavations at the newly discovered site of Longgupo Cave, however, found fossils, dated to between 1.96 and 1.78 million years old, that some experts claim as hominids but other see as prehominid apes. In any case, this appears to be an isolated instance, and the main focus on early hominids in China remains on the fossils found at the Zhoukoudian caves near present-day Beijing. (The fossils are still popularly known as "Peking Man.") During the next 500,000–600,000 years, this species disperses through much of central and northeastern China. Eventually this hominid species is replaced by the archaic *Homo sapiens*, which appears in China sometime after 250,000 B.C. By around 50,000 BP, *Homo sapiens sapiens* replaces previous hominids in China. By 12,000 BP, late Paleolithic people form a half dozen or more distinct cultures in China, and practices suggesting ideas of kinship, the arts, and religion develop.

China's legendary history opens around 3,000 B.C. with the advent of a series of semidivine figures who instruct the nomadic Chinese in the activities of a more sedentary civilization: fishing, hunting, farming, and trading. In China's traditional history, the Yellow Emperor of *c.* 2700 B.C., the first of the "Five Premier Emperors," used force to create a unified state; his successors are said to build on his achievement. The story of these early reigns, however, is strictly legendary, with no archaeological confirmation of any of the individuals or events. But increasingly remains of the third millennium B.C. begin to confirm at least some of the later traditions of an emerging and perhaps already distinctive form of society.

1,960,000?–1,780,000? B.C.: Hominid remains (dental fragments) in association with primitive stone tools found at Longgupo Cave near the Yangtze River in south-central China signify that hominids entered China much earlier than long thought. This species has more in common with fossils (*Homo ergaster* and *Homo habilis*) found in East Africa and is not the same as the *Homo erectus* found in China a million years later.

800,000 B.C.: A cranium of a female found near Lantian in central China is the oldest known *Homo erectus* fossil found in China.

500,000–250,000 B.C.: Hominids of the species *Homo erectus* inhabit caves at Zhoukoudian, a limestone hill on the edge of China's north-central plain about thirty miles southwest of present-day Beijing. These creatures have a brain capacity about two-thirds that of modern humans; they walk upright and make basic stone tools; whether they actually hunt animals or just scavenge for food is disputed. Similar hominids are living at numerous sites throughout eastern China during this period but little is known of their way of life except that they make crude stone tools.

250,000–50,000 B.C.: Sometime during this period, archaic *Homo sapiens* inhabit sites in various parts of China. Most modern scientists believe that fully evolved *Homo sapiens* came into China from their homeland in Africa; some believe that modern humans in China evolved from the previous *Homo erectus* living there.

50,000–12,000 B.C.: Truly modern people, *Homo sapiens sapiens*, begin to emerge and to form distinct cultures in China. They remain nomadic hunter-fisher-gatherers and depend mainly on their stone tools. During this period, these people probably evolve with many of the physical characteristics now associated with the Mongoloid people of Asia.

12,000–6000 B.C.: Scattered agricultural communities develop on the central plain of China. By 6000 B.C. at the latest, people in the Yellow River (Huang Ho) valley are cultivating millet, while people in southern China are probably beginning to cultivate rice.

5000–3000 B.C.: The Yangshao culture flourishes along the middle Yellow River. Settled communities also develop along the southeast coast and on the island of Taiwan.

In the settled farming areas below the south bend of the Yellow River, villagers live on a millet diet with supplements of game and fish. They hunt with bows and arrows, keep dogs and pigs, use hemp for fabrics.

By 5000 B.C. wet-rice cultivation is spreading along the lower Yangtze River valley, possibly introduced there from lands to the south.

4000–2000 B.C.: Perhaps overlapping and certainly ultimately succeeding the Yangshao culture, the Lungshan culture develops to the east of the Yangshao settlements. The Lungshan people exchange their goods, and this leads to some accumulation of wealth, which in turn leads to a society that appears to support more social classes, various rituals, and elaborate burials. Their towns are protected by walls of earth, suggesting some kind of conflict. At Erlitou, regarded as the first city in China, remains from about 2000 B.C. suggest an almost feudal society, possibly the basis for the Xia dynasty of Chinese myth and legend.

2852 B.C.: According to the tradition that begins in the Han dynasty, this is the date for the beginning of the legendary Age of Three Sovereigns.

2698–2599 B.C.: Han dynasty tradition claims that Xuanyuan Gongsun, the chieftain of a tribe in present-day central Henan, ascends as the Yellow Emperor, the first of those Confucius later calls the Five Premier Emperors. He is a semilegendary figure, although some historians regard him as having a historical basis.

Wherever under heaven there were people who disobeyed him, [the Yellow Emperor] would go after them; but as soon as they were pacified, he would leave them alone. He crossed mountains and opened roads, never stopping anywhere to rest for long.

Records of the Historian, by Sima Qian
(145–90 B.C.?)

2514–2437 B.C.: Han dynasty tradition claims that Zhuanxu reigns as second of the Five

Premier Emperors; he quells a rebellion of the Jiuli tribes to the south and claims dominion south of the Yangtze.

2436–2367 B.C.: Han dynasty tradition claims that Ku reigns, overseeing a period of general quiet and prosperity.

2357–2258 B.C.: Han dynasty tradition claims that Yao's long reign is marked, toward the end (*c.* 2300? B.C.), by a legendary Great Flood that inundates vast areas of the Yellow and Yangtze river valleys and causes widespread famine and political disruption.

2255–2208 B.C.: Han tradition claims that

Shun rises by virtue from humble origins to become the last of the Five Premier Emperors. During this era, the outlines of the ancient system of feudal land tenure emerge. Shun also reorganizes the bureaucracy, establishing government departments for agriculture, justice, education, public works, and other areas. Before his death, he appoints his trusted chief minister Yu as his successor.

2208 B.C.: Yu succeeds Shun and is honored as the founder of the Xia, the first dynasty of ancient China. By legend, Yu is a descendant of the Yellow Emperor.

THE THREE DYNASTIES (XIA, SHANG, ZHOU): 2208–249 B.C.

The Xia (*c.* 2200–1750 B.C.), established by the semilegendary Emperor Yu, is the first of the three ancient dynasties. Shang (*c.* 1750–1040 B.C.) and Zhou (1040–256 B.C.) follow. Historians are not entirely convinced the Xia dynasty actually exists; in any case, the three dynasties are probably not more than episodic hegemonies, historians suggest, and they likely overlap rather than succeed each other in direct line.

The Bronze Age Shang is the first of China's historic dynasties, with its first capital near present Zhengzhou and a second, later, near Anyang north of the Yellow River. Though its domain encompasses a relatively small area (parts of today's Henan, Anhui, Shandong, Hebei, and Shanxi provinces), Shang culture becomes widespread in North China and present Sichuan. A written language emerges. Royal palaces are built in the capital towns. Mansions of the wealthy class feature post and beam construction. A complex agricultural society develops. Political structures take root and society stratifies into a peasantry and an aristocracy of landowner-warriors. The first Chinese calendar comes into use. Shang artisans reach an advanced state of development in metalworking, pottery, and other crafts.

The third of the ancient dynasties, Zhou, shares a culture similar at its origins to Shang, though it develops in forms that would have been unrecognizable to rulers of the earlier dynasty. The Zhou era is the classical age of Confucius and Laozi ("the old master," by tradition the founder of Daoism). Written laws and a money economy develop. Iron implements and ox-drawn plows appear.

Zhou is a period of general political disorder and turbulence. Zhou society evolves steadily from the feudal form, with its hereditary warrior nobility, toward an independent, centralized state with armies drawn from a landed peasantry, a unification process that reaches its fulfillment in Qin. Traditional Zhou subdivisions are the Spring and Autumn (722–481 B.C.) and Warring States (403–221 B.C.) periods.

2208–*c.* 2195 B.C.: By tradition, Yu reigns for a peaceful and prosperous thirteen years. He is succeeded by sixteen kings in a dynasty that survives for nearly five hundred years.

2000 B.C.: Humans are being buried under

the foundations of important buildings on the North China plain—evidence (from modern archeological sources) of human sacrifice, probably of war captives.

1800 B.C.: The Xia dynasty comes to an end

with the reign of a degenerate king. This will become a feature of Chinese historical presentation: the last ruler of a dynasty is portrayed as corrupt, incompetent, morally bankrupt, or a combination of all three.

1760 B.C.: Tang, the virtuous first of the Shang high kings, comes to the throne; by tradition, here begins the second dynasty of ancient China.

"It is asked: Shall an army of five thousand men be raised?"

"The T'u country is pasturing on our lands, ten men."

"Will there be rain enough for the millet crop?"

Inscriptions on oracle bones, later Shang dynasty
(*c.* 1750–1040 B.C.)

1401–1374 B.C.: Pangeng reigns as Shang king; he foresees the destruction of the Shang capital at Zhengzhou by flood and moves it to a safer site at Anyang.

1122 B.C.: By tradition, the House of Zhou deposes the Shang dynasty. Modern scholars believe the Zhou triumph occurred somewhat later, probably between 1050 and 1025 B.C., when the Zhou spill out of the Wei River valley and overwhelm the Shang. The Zhou establish a new capital at present Xian.

897 B.C.: By tradition, the chieftain Feizu establishes the state of Qin in North China, with its seat on the Wei River near modern Xian.

***c.* 800 B.C.:** An estimated two hundred small lordly domains claim some form of autonomy; most of these recognize the Zhou king as feudal overlord.

With the spring days the warmth begins,
And the oriole utters its song.
The young women take their deep baskets
and go along the small paths,
looking for the tender [leaves of] mulberry trees.

The Book of Poetry, by unknown authors (end of Shang–beginning of Zhou?)

---

771 B.C.: Nomadic Rong (to the Chinese, barbarians) attacks force a weakened House of Zhou to quit its capital near present Xian and move east to Luoyang; this brings the Western Zhou subperiod to a close and inaugurates the Eastern Zhou. From this point, Zhou royal power is nominal and Zhou kings reign as figureheads.

770 B.C.: Qin becomes a full principality, beginning its rise to political prominence in North China.

722–481 B.C.: During this 240-year period, known as Spring and Autumn, as many as 170 small states coexist under nominal Zhou suzerainty. The Zhou kings rule only by default. Through alliances and wars, some states are absorbed by others.

7th century B.C.: Qin begins to gain prominence among the many Zhou states.

688 B.C.: Existence of the county as an administrative unit is first mentioned in Qin.

685–643 B.C.: Duke Huan reigns in Qi, on the eastern edge of the North China plain in present Shandong province. Qi casts coins, regulates the economy, and leads a powerful alliance of smaller states in resisting the expansion of the semibarbarian state of Chu to the south.

677 B.C.: Qin builds a new capital at Yong.

676 B.C.: Qin adopts summer sacrifice and festival of Fu.

659–621 B.C.: Duke Mu reigns in Qin. Through armed conquest, Mu extends Qin boundaries west of the Yellow River.

623 B.C.: Qin wins an important military decision over the Rong "barbarians" of the north and west; the Zhou king recognizes Qin as sovereign over the western Rong.

Confucius said: By nature men are pretty much alike; it is learning and practice that set them apart.

The Analects of Confucius, c. 551–479 B.C.

598 B.C.: County administrative organization is mentioned in the southern state of Chu.

430 B.C.: Qin repulses attack of the Rong; this is the last recorded Rong challenge to Qin.

***c.* 410 B.C.:** As Zhou dominance ebbs, a smaller number of more powerful states emerge.

403–221 B.C.: During this era, known as the Warring States period, seven major rivals jockey for supremacy. The Zhou king is no longer a real factor, as regional lords begin calling themselves kings and refuse to acknowledge the slowly dying dynasty. The rivals are organized along military lines, with important new rituals of warfare, hunting and human sacrifice. Agricultural production is on the increase during this period, partly the result of more widespread irrigation and draining. Population growth and urbanization characterize the period.

400 B.C.: The political unit known as the commandery is mentioned for the first time in the state of Wei. This large administrative unit replaces the feudal fiefs of the Zhou. The initial military purpose of the commandery is to bring frontier areas under state control. Gradually, counties become subordinate to commanderies; by the end of Zhou, ten or twelve counties will make up a commandery.

Rich is the year with much mullet and rice;
And we have tall granaries
With hundreds and thousands and millions of
* sheaves.*
We make wine and sweet spirits
And offer them to our ancestors, male and
* female;*
Thus to fulfill all the rites
And bring down blessings in full.

"Rich Year," *Book of Odes*, Zhou dynasty
(1040–256 B.C.)

---

361 B.C.: Gongsun Yang (Lord Shang) arrives in Qin and becomes chief minister.

350 B.C.: Qin moves the capital to near modern Xian.

334 B.C.: Chu conquers Yue.

326 B.C.: Qin adopts the winter festival of La.

315 B.C.: Qin captures twenty-five Rong walled towns.

256 B.C.: Qin destroys Zhou, formally ending the long-decayed Zhou dynasty.

249 B.C.: Chu conquers Confucius's home state of Lu.

QIN DYNASTY: 221–206 B.C.

Qin subdues the last of the rival Warring States during the latter decades of the third century B.C. and, as of 221 B.C., forcibly unifies China. This brief, powerful dynasty establishes an imperial system that in certain crucial respects will last, through many vicissitudes, until 1911. Qin administrators standardize weights and measures, currency and, above all, the written language. They build highway and irrigation systems, as well as a network of waterways that includes a 1,200-mile-long water transport route from the Yangtze River to Guangzhou (Canton). Joining and strengthening earlier defensive systems, they commence building the Great Wall of China. Ultimately, it will stretch 1,400 miles from southwest Gansu to southern Manchuria.

Qin rulers follow the stern militaristic tenets of the Legalist School of Shang Yang and Hanfeizi; Shang's elaborate system of rewards and punishments regulates Qin society. Law tablets unearthed in the twentieth century suggest Qin laws are harsh, though not unusually so for China at this period. Commoners are able to buy and sell land, and there is a rough equality before the law.

Qin emphasis is on obedience to the state, even over loyalty to the family. For this and other reasons, successor dynasties tend to view Qin as tyrannical and culturally backward.

3d century B.C.: Qin emerges as the most powerful of the Warring States of the North China Plain. Qin's advantage is military innovation, such as deployment of infantry in the hill country where war chariots could not operate.

Qin has the same customs as [the barbarians]. It has the heart of a tiger or a wolf. It knows nothing of traditional mores, proper relationships, and virtuous conduct.

A Wei nobleman writing to his king, 266 B.C.

---

259 B.C.: Zheng, who will become the first Qin emperor, is born.

250 B.C.: Lu Buwei, a rich merchant, rules as chancellor of Qin.

246 B.C.: Still a child, King Zheng comes to the Qin throne.

238 B.C.: Zheng reaches his majority and begins to exercise power.

237 B.C.: Zheng deposes Lu Buwei as chancellor; Lu takes poison and dies in 235.

c. 235 B.C.: The Legalist minister Li Si begins his rise to power.

230 B.C.: The rival state of Han falls to Qin.

228 B.C.: Zhao falls to Qin.

227 B.C.: An envoy from the rival state of Yan fails in an attempt to assassinate Zheng.

225 B.C.: Wei falls to Qin.

223 B.C.: Chu falls to Qin.

222 B.C.: Yan falls to Qin.

221 B.C.: Qi falls to Qin.

221 B.C.: With the defeat of the last of the other Warring States, Qin forcibly unifies China. Zheng takes the title of Qin Shi Huangdi—August Lord of Qin.

221–210 B.C.: The First Emperor, Zheng, divides the empire into thirty-six commanderies, each subdivided into counties, imposing centralized bureaucratic rule. He standardizes the Qin law code for all the empire. Capital punishments for crimes such

as rebellion and treason include prisoners' being beheaded, boiled in a cauldron, and cut in two at the waist.

220–210 B.C.: Under Meng Tian, Qin forces push the empire's borders north and northwest into modern Mongolia.

219–210 B.C.: Qin extends the empire's borders southward into the fertile, well-watered, and semi-tropical region of modern Guangdong and Guangxi provinces.

219 B.C.: The First Emperor, Zheng, sends thousands of families to colonize the Shandong peninsula on the East China coast.

c. 219 B.C.: Li Si rises to become chancellor of the left, the highest governmental post in Qin China.

216 B.C.: The principle of private land ownership is generally established throughout the empire.

211 B.C.: Qin sends thirty thousand families into the Ordos Desert to colonize the region.

July–August 210 B.C.: Emperor Zheng dies at age forty-nine while on a trip to eastern China, allegedly to seek an elixir of immortality from Daoist magicians, bringing his thirty-seven-year reign to a close. Ancient historians will portray the First Emperor as something of a barbarian, ruthless and crude, and will not be kind to his memory.

210–206 B.C.: Emperor Zheng's lavish funeral, public works, and military projects deplete imperial resources. Upon his death, the empire begins to break apart.

August–September 209 B.C.: Rebellion erupts in the state of Chu and quickly spreads to the rest of the empire.

208 B.C.: Li Si, the First Emperor's chancellor, is put to death in the central marketplace of the capital.

207 B.C.: The Second Generation Emperor kills himself and is succeeded by a son of his older brother.

January 206 B.C.: Rebels advancing from the

south sack the Qin capital, burn palaces, and put the last Qin ruler to death after a reign of only forty-six days.

202 B.C.: Four years of civil war end with the establishment of the Han dynasty on the ruins of the Qin empire.

HAN DYNASTY: 202 B.C.—A.D. 220

The Early Han emperors extend the bureaucracy. The government operates manufacturing and mining monopolies. Landed estates increase in extent; correspondingly, a part of the peasantry is impoverished. An upper class emerges as the dominant social group. Trade increases. Military initiatives push China's borders outward. The Han period sees a reasonably open society, although a wide gulf divides rulers and the ruled, rich and poor, landowners and peasants. In Later Han, new figures rise to positions of power and wealth, and great landed families are dominant.

Han is strong on ceremony and ritual. Learned men are influential at court. Early Han rulers adopt a modified Confucianism as the ideology in which state officials are to be trained. Scholars label this blend of Qin legalism and the ideas of Confucius, "Imperial Confucianism." The dynasty follows an imperial cult of ritual observance and develops the notion of humanity as part of nature. The underlying idea is that the emperor's conduct and his performance of ceremonial must be of a standard to maintain the harmony of Heaven, Earth and humankind—the balance of the cosmic forces of *yin* and *yang*. The cult emphasizes, too, the special relationship between the ruler and his ancestors.

By around 50 B.C. a period of relative decline encourages the rise of a reformist movement that calls for a return to what reformers regard as a more traditional and purer Confucianism. They see government as responsible for improving life for everyone, not just the elites. They call for the training of state officials in the unalloyed Confucian canon, establish new state cults, and attempt to abolish state monopolies. Dynastic instability and a gradual weakening of state power ends in the collapse of the Early Han dynasty in the second decade of the first century A.D. After a brief period of usurper rule and civil war, a member of the Han imperial family restores the dynasty. Buddhism makes its appearance toward the midpoint of the first century. Mass population shifts mark the last two centuries of Han primacy, with a large migratory flow from north and west to the fertile river valleys of the south. The dynasty collapses in A.D. 220.

Early Han (202 B.C.–A.D. 8)

c. **209 B.C.:** Liu Bang, who rises from peasant origins in central China, establishes the Han dynasty after leading an uprising against Qin in his native state. He will reign as the Emperor Gaodi.

8th month, 207 B.C.: Forces under Liu Bang penetrate the Qin heartland.

10th month, 206 B.C.: Liu extends his control to the Qin imperial capital.

12th month, 206 B.C.: Liu Bang's ally-turned-rival Xiang Yu, the king of Chu, enters the Qin capital and ransacks the palaces there.

Liu, now styled king of Han, opens a campaign against his former supporter and defeats three of his subkings, but fails to subdue Xiang Yu himself.

203 B.C.: Liu recovers his strength. He and Xiang Yu agree to divide China between them.

4th month, 204 B.C.: Xiang Yu besieges Liu Bang's forces and defeats them at the Han capital of Xiangyang on the Yellow River.

The common people succeeded in putting behind them the sufferings of the age of the Warring States, and ruler and subject alike sought rest in surcease of action. Punishments were seldom meted out and evildoers grew rare, while the people applied themselves to the tasks of farming, and food and clothing became abundant.

On the First Decades of the Han Dynasty, by historian Sima Qian (145–90 B.C.?)

202 B.C.: Liu Bang breaks the agreement, attacks Xiang Yu, and defeats him at Kai-xian in modern Anhui province. Xiang kills himself. Liu becomes the undisputed ruler of China and accepts the title of emperor, reigning as Gaodi until his death in 195 B.C.

202 B.C.: Gaodi declares a general amnesty and implements measures to restore law and order throughout his dominions. He shifts the capital from Luoyang to Chang'an near modern Xian. Over the next seven years he will consolidate Han power in the ten smaller kingdoms that emerge from the breakup of the Qin empire, gradually replacing their rulers with members of his family.

195–188 B.C.: Gaodi's son succeeds him as emperor, reigning as Huidi.

190 B.C.: After a five-year effort, Han military engineers complete the construction of a defensive line around the capital, Chang'an. The thirteen square miles of walls enclose the city on all four sides. Nearly fifty feet wide at the base, they are pierced by tall watchtowers.

188–180 B.C.: Empress Lu, Gaodi's widow, reigns. After her death, Han forces crush her family's bid for power.

180–157 B.C.: Wendi reigns, the first Han emperor to rule for longer than a decade.

177 B.C.: Han mobilizes to contest the invasion of the Xiongnu from their steppe empire in the Ordos region (modern Mongolia) beyond China's northern frontier. Diplomats arrange a temporary peace.

c. 170 B.C.: Two leading thinkers, Chao Cuo and Jia Yi, develop their theories of agriculture as the basis of China's economy and society. Jia Yi argues explicitly that agriculture is the nation's foundation. Chao Cuo supports farming at the expense of commerce. He also urges the Han leaders to limit the power of the subordinate kingdoms and check the incursions of the Xiongnu in the north.

168 B.C.: To ease the burden on the peasantry, government reduces the tax on produce, including grain, from one-fifteenth to one-thirtieth part.

166 B.C.: Xiongnu raiders approach the capital, Chang'an, before they are driven off.

157–141 B.C.: Wendi's son succeeds him, reigning as Jingdi. The two reigns, noteworthy for the growth of the central government, stabilize the dynasty. By 143 B.C. the empire, a highly organized bureaucratic state, comprises forty commanderies and twenty-five small kingdoms, half of them ruled by Jingdi's sons. At the end of Jingdi's reign, 90 percent of China's population works in the countryside, most as farmers. Males from the ages of twenty-three to fifty-six are liable for compulsory state service, either in the army (two years) or in a labor gang (one year).

154 B.C.: The king of Wu (eastern China) rebels; six other kings ally with him. After several months of fighting, imperial forces subdue the rebel army and crush the insurgency.

141–87 B.C.: Wudi rules, one of the longest reigns of Chinese history. Wudi, whose title means "the martial emperor," inherits an empire on a solid financial footing. By the year of his accession, Han has consolidated and expanded its central authority and established an effective tax-collecting system.

136 B.C.: Government establishes official posts for academicians who specialize in the explication of five works now to be treated as basic texts for the education of state officials: the *Book of Changes*, the *Book of*

Songs, the *Book of Documents*, the *Rites*, and the *Spring and Autumn Annals*. Thus the Confucian canon becomes the basis for training government officials.

135–119 B.C.: Han military forces respond to a succession of threats from the Xiongnu on the northwest frontier in what is today Mongolia. The invaders are driven from the borders after key victories in 121 and 119 B.C.

128 B.C.: A Han effort to establish China's authority in the Korean peninsula fails and is aborted. But Han China manages to set up a commandery in Manchuria.

124–118 B.C.: Gongsun Hong rises from pig-keeper to rule as chancellor, Han's highest office.

122 B.C.: Rebellion breaks out in the Han kingdom of Huainan and is quickly crushed. The kingdom is abolished.

Heaven is like an egg, and earth is like the yolk of the egg. Alone it dwells inside. Heaven is great and earth is small.

A *Theory of the Structure of the Universe*, by scholar
Zhang Heng (c. A.D. 120)

---

119 B.C.: The Han drives the Xiongnu north beyond the Gobi Desert. The costs of wars and rebellions are depleting the Han treasury. To pay for Wudi's initiatives, the government introduces state monopolies of salt and iron and takes other steps to bring private mining operations under state control and levies new taxes on market transactions, vehicles, and property.

111 B.C.: Han expeditionary forces conquer Guangzhou (Canton) and the provinces of Guangdong and Guangxi in southeast China and add northern Vietnam to the realm; the government establishes commanderies in the modern provinces of Yunnan and Sichuan, extending Chinese power to the southwest.

110 BC: The government creates a board to control transport and creates an important new office, superintendent of waterways and parks.

c. 110 B.C.: The Confucian scholar/statesman Dong Zhongshu (c. 175–105 B.C.) urges the emperor to curb the growth of landed estates and the concentration of great wealth.

109 B.C.: The government carries out major dike repairs to prevent flooding in the Yellow River valley.

108 B.C.: Han China resumes its effort to subdue Korea, launching two military expeditions that bring much of the peninsula under Chinese control; it sets up four commanderies in conquered Korea. The empire, divided into eighty-four commanderies and eighteen kingdoms, reaches its greatest extent of the entire Han period.

102 B.C.: A Chinese general returns from Ferghana in Central Asia with a few of the region's famous great horses. They soon become a symbol of status in imperial China.

100 B.C.: Han China tightens its hold on the provinces and the chronically turbulent frontiers. North China is virtually free of raids from beyond the borders. The government establishes control over the territory of modern Guangxi province in the south.

91–90 B.C.: With no formally nominated successor to the throne of Wudi, Han experiences a dynastic crisis.

88 B.C.: An assassination attempt on the aging Wudi fails.

March 27–29, 87 B.C.: On March 27, an eight-year-old son of Wudi and one of his consorts is nominated as heir to the throne and will rule as Zhaodi. When Wudi dies on March 29 Zhaodi succeeds as Han emperor. He reigns until 74 B.C.; real power lies in the hands of the powerful general Huo Guang.

86 B.C.: As many as thirty thousand rebels rise against Han rule in the new commanderies of the southwest. A second uprising ends in 82 B.C. with Han forces putting more than fifty thousand rebels to death.

82 B.C.: Adopting a policy of retrenchment, China begins a withdrawal from Korea.

September 10, 74 B.C.: Xuandi ascends as emperor at age eighteen, succeeding Zhaodi, who dies at twenty-two. During Xuandi's reign, which lasts until 49 B.C., reformist ideas, advanced in reaction to the exhaustion of China's resources through modernist expansion, gain ascendancy.

68 B.C.: Huo Guang, a "gray eminence" of the emperor, dies and his relatives are stripped of influence and titles; the once-powerful Huo family lapses into decline.

c. 60 B.C.: Government sets up the office of protector-general of the western regions to regulate colonial activities on the western frontier.

59–56 B.C.: The reformist Xiao Wangzhi rises to become imperial chancellor. He opposes excessive state interference in the economy and in individual lives and calls for a scaling back of China's involvement in Central Asia.

51 B.C.: Chinese diplomats conclude a peace with the Xiongnu empire on the northern frontier.

49–33 B.C.: Yuandi reigns. In his and his successor's reign, the reformists take charge. Economy in government, a loosening of controls over the daily lives of the Chinese, and military retrenchment characterize the concluding decades of the century. Reformists issue a series of eighteen amnesties during the period 48–7 B.C. and generally ease the administration of justice. They fail, however, in their efforts to restrict land holdings as a means of arresting the decline of the peasantry and tenantry.

47–44 B.C.: The government implements a series of measures to reduce spending on the imperial household, part of a general retrenchment.

46 B.C.: Chinese administration withdraws from the island of Hainan. Omens favor a move of the capital from Chang'an to Luoyang, but the notion is abandoned for the time being.

34 B.C.: Government decrees simplify and shorten judicial procedures.

33–7 B.C.: Chengdi reigns as emperor. He is said to be frivolous and selfish, a lover of low music and cockfights. He dies without producing a male heir. The half-nephew who succeeds him will rule as Aidi.

c. 30 B.C.: Treasury officials implement a new round of economy measures for the imperial household, including cuts in the budget for the upkeep of palace buildings, the abolition of the office of music, and reductions in the arms and equipment of the palace guard.

May, 7 B.C.: Aidi ascends to the Han throne.

7 B.C.: Shi Dan rises to become marshal of state. To narrow the gap between rich and poor, he calls for restrictions on the ownership of land and slaves.

5 B.C.: According to written sources, the Han civil service has a strength of 120,285 officials.

August 15, 1 B.C.: Aidi dies without an heir. The Wang family moves prominently to fill the power vacuum. The day after the emperor's death, Wang Mang continues his rise to power as the relative of a dowager empress and becomes marshal of state.

October 17, 1 B.C.: Pingdi, nine years old, ascends the throne of Han. His health is fragile throughout his brief rule and real authority lies in the hands of the regent Wang Mang. Wang looks to the early Zhou for his model or social order and justice. He attempts to redistribute land, abolish slavery, and encourage respect for the teachings of the classics.

A.D. 1–2: China retains a precarious foothold in Korea with two commanderies still intact.

September/October, A.D. 2: The world's earliest preserved census puts the population of the Han empire at 57,671,400. The heaviest population concentrations—some 44 million of the total—are in the Yellow and Huai river valleys in the north. Chengdu in modern Sichuan is China's largest city, with a population of 282,147. The capitals, Chang'an and Luoyang, have 246,200 and 195,504 inhabitants respectively. (All figures are believed to be high, especially when compared to later Chinese censuses.)

A.D. 3: Wang Mang's government carries out a reform of the schools.

February 3, A.D. 6: Pingdi dies. He is the last direct descendant of Yuandi; a succession crisis ensues. Wang Mang chooses an infant, Liu Yang, as heir apparent. Wang insinuates that the boy will lose the mandate; he thus will be the last emperor of the Early Han dynasty.

May, A.D. 6: Wang Mang declares himself acting emperor. Fabricating a genealogy, this scion of the lesser gentry will claim descent from the legendary Yellow Lord, a Han divinity. Chinese historians will regard him as a usurper.

October/December A.D. 7: Wang Mang's forces quell an uprising triggered by a provincial official who charges Wang with the murder of Pingdi.

A.D. 8–9: Wang Mang consolidates his power. He invents a series of omens that suggest the time for a dynastic change has arrived and he should become emperor.

January 10, A.D. 9: Wang Mang declares the Han dynasty at an end and proclaims himself emperor. He will rule until A.D. 23.

A.D. 9: Wang Mang orders a reorganization of the bureaucracy. He also bans the private buying and selling of slaves.

A.D. 9–11: The Xiongnu launch new raids on northern frontier. Wang Mang mobilizes a large army to confront the invaders; the show of force prevents a full-scale outbreak.

11: Heavy flooding causes great loss of life. Resulting famine destabilizes the Wang Mang regime and leads to widespread peasant unrest.

12: Political opposition forces Wang Mang to rescind measures barring the buying and selling of slaves.

14: Wang Mang's forces put down an uprising in modern Yunnan in southwest China.

18: A peasant army forms under a woman leader known as Mother Lu, and civil war breaks out in Shandong in northern China. Wang Mang mobilizes imperial forces to meet the threat.

Winter 22: The insurgent Red Eyebrows (the peasant soldiers are so called because they paint their foreheads red to distinguish themselves from government troops) defeat Wang Mang's army in Shandong.

22: The Red Eyebrows advance south toward the rich region of Nanyang in present Hunan. Rebellious forces there rise up to join the Red Eyebrows in the war against Wang Mang.

October–November, 22: Imperial forces check the rebels temporarily.

January–February, 23: Insurgent offensive resumes with a victory over Wang Mang's imperial army.

July, 23: Rebels inflict a decisive defeat on Wang Mang's army at Kunyang.

October 4, 23: Insurgents occupy the imperial capital of Chang'an and sack it. Two days later, they capture Wang Mang and behead him.

23–25: The insurgent Liu Xiu, head of a Han restoration faction, raises an independent army and enlists the peasant Red Eyebrows as allies.

August 25: Han restoration forces enter Chang'an. Liu Xiu, thirty years old, proclaims himself Son of Heaven and ascends the throne as first emperor of the Later Han.

Later Han (A.D. 25–220)

August 5, 25–May 29, 57: The first Later Han emperor, Liu Xiu, reigns as Guangwu.

November 27, 25: Guangwu enters Luoyang and makes it his capital.

March, 26: Red Eyebrow insurgents evacuate the former Han capital, Chang'an, looting palaces and tombs and partially burning the city.

October, 26–January, 27: Red Eyebrows reoccupy Chang'an briefly, then set out to try to break through the mountain barrier to the North China Plain.

March 15, 27: Imperial troops cut off the Red Eyebrow army and force its surrender.

26–30: Han campaigns subdue the Shandong peninsula. Guangwu moves to consolidate his power, but his hold is tenuous for several years. "In present times," one of his generals is heard to say, "it is not only the sovereign who selects his subjects. The subjects select the sovereign."

29: Imperial forces subdue the lower Han River valley of east-central China.

30: Outmigration from North China leads Emperor Guangwu to abolish thirty counties in the north and shrink the government bureaucracy there.

33–44: Intermittent Xiongnu raids force the withdrawal of Chinese farming communities from northern frontier regions.

34: After a long, difficult campaign, the empire pacifies northwest China.

April–May, 35: Han forces move against the last imperial rival, Gongsun Shu, on the Yangtze.

December 24, 36: Han army reaches Gongsun Shu's capital, Chengdu. Gongsun is mortally wounded in the fighting and the city surrenders the next day.

April 1, 37: Emperor Guangwu abolishes all but three of the twenty or so subordinate kingdoms. He revives them gradually, installing his sons and other near-relatives as kings. To a degree, this process stalls the concentration of imperial power.

March, 40: Aboriginal inhabitants of the Red River Valley in modern Vietnam rebel against China. Pressures of Chinese settlement in the region trigger the outbreak. The uprising is part of a pattern of uprisings—at least fifty-three between A.D. 1 and 200—on Han's southern frontier, where Chinese are migrating and intermingling with aboriginal peoples.

January–May, 43: Chinese expeditionary force crushes the Red River rebellion.

48: A violent uprising shakes northwestern Hunan and is bloodily suppressed after a campaign of several months.

57: Emperor Mingdi ascends the Han throne, succeeding Guangwu. He rules until his death in A.D. 75, a reign generally regarded as harsh and oppressive.

73: China forms an alliance with the southern Xiongnu against the rival northern federation of Xiongnu.

September 5, 75: Zhangdi ascends the throne, succeeding his father, Mingdi.

April 9, 88: Hedi becomes emperor. He is underage, and Dou Xian, a leading general and a member of the powerful Dou family, will be regent.

89: Han forces and their southern Xiongnu allies carry out a successful campaign against the northern Xiongnu. Southern Xiongnu settle permanently in northern China, driving many Chinese to the south.

92: Emperor Hedi's allies accuse Dou Xian of plotting to kill him; Dou commits suicide in prison and a number of his confederates are executed. Among the killed is Ban Gu, the historian of Han, who is implicated through his friendship with the Dou family.

92–102: Ban Chao, brother of the historian Ban Gu, is protector-general of the Western Regions covering the Silk Road to Persia and the Eastern Roman Empire. He reestablishes China's control over the insurgent west and leads an army westward to the edge of the Caspian Sea, 3,800 miles from Luoyang. He returns to China with information about Rome, the great empire of the West.

93: Tensions flare with the Xiongnu in the north. Frequent armed clashes mark Chinese-Xiongnu relations for the next century.

106: For reasons of economy the government orders a reduction of imperial palace expenses, including banquets, ballets, music, and even fodder for the palace horses. The first decades of the second century A.D. see a gradual but marked growth in power and influence of the consorts' families and the eunuchs.

February 13–September 21, 106: Shangdi, a three-month-old child, is emperor; his death touches off a brief dynastic crisis.

September 23, 106: Andi ascends the throne. He will rule until 125 and will be regarded as the least capable of all the emperors of the Han dynasty.

108 and 111: Tibetan raiders advance down the Wei River valley to the approaches of the Great Plain. These raids spur the migration of Chinese farmers southward into Sichuan and Yunnan.

125–144: Shundi reigns as emperor.

133: A severe earthquake rocks Luoyang. Some see this as an omen critical of the regime for the favoritism shown relatives, court cliques, and eunuchs.

135: Eunuchs are granted the right to adopt sons. They thus may have families that can inherit their wealth and power, which grow apace as the century advances.

137: The government puts down rebellion in Jinan in northeast China.

140: A census documents the vast changes floods, drought, famine, and war have brought about in China's population distribution since the census of A.D. 2. China's recorded population has fallen by more than 9 million over those 138 years to 48 million. By the middle of the second century, southward migration brings the north-south population closer to balance, though the north still dominates. Xiongnu and Tibetan raids have forced 6.5 million Chinese to quit the northwest—a loss of some 70 percent of the population recorded in the census of A.D. 2.

144–145: Chongdi reigns as emperor.

144–145: Rebellions break out in southeastern China; one in 145 ends with the deaths of nearly four thousand insurgents.

March 6, 145–July 26, 146: Zhidi reigns briefly as emperor and dies under murky circumstances. One account claims that he is murdered for calling one of his leading officials a bully.

August 1, 146: Huandi is emperor. He will reign until 168.

c. 150: The imperial harem numbers six thousand women. They arrive as virgins age thirteen to twenty and are selected for their beauty, bearing, and manners.

c. 150: China loses its grip on the Western Regions. Political instability disrupts trade along the Silk Road.

156: With difficulty, government forces crush a rebellion in Shandong.

156–157: Savants take an earthquake in Luoyang, a solar eclipse, and a plague of locusts as signs that heaven is displeased with the emperor and that reforms in economic policy are due.

166: A senior government official renews criticism of the dynasty for favoritism and extravagance. Interpretations of astronomical phenomena lay blame for the misconduct on the emperor and the palace eunuchs.

167: Government aids victims of a tidal wave along the east coast, distributing two thousand *cash*, a copper coin, for each victim age seven or older.

January 25, 168: Emperor Huandi dies, touching off a major political crisis. The cause is a building resentment over the power of the eunuchs. The regent Dou Wu and a group of high bureaucratic allies plot to kill the leading eunuchs.

October 24, 168: Eunuchs get wind of Dou Wu's scheme to break their power and forestall his move. The plot is aborted; Dou Wu kills himself; and the eunuchs are secure for another generation.

168–189: Lingdi reigns as emperor. The prestige of the throne ebbs during his rule, and the power of the corrupt eunuchs is nearly absolute in the palace. Many bad omens are reported during his rule: a horse gives birth to a human child; a virgin delivers a two-headed, four-armed baby; there are earthquakes, hailstorms, and caterpillar infestations. Though there are conflicts between court favorites and the bureaucrats and widespread unrest in the provinces, this is the last period of orderly government during the Han dynasty.

169–184: The era of the Great Proscription grows out of the conflict between the eunuchs and high bureaucrats. The eunuchs win the struggle and put more than one hundred of their rivals to death. Their families go under a perpetual ban of government service; the ban covers not only near relations but those who share even a great-great-grandfather with someone on the proscribed list.

178: Appointments to high office, heretofore on perceived merit except in rare instances, now go to the highest *cash* bidder. The top positions cost as much as 20 million *cash*.

184–185: The so-called Yellow Turbans rebellion rages to the south, east, and northeast of Luoyang. Several hundred thousand peasants rise up when omens and visions persuade them that the Han dynasty should be brought to an end. There is a specifically Daoist content to the rebels' ideology; rebellions such as this one are among religious Daoism's early expressions. The eunuch-dominated imperial court, too weak to react, turns to provincial warlords for protection. By February 185 the outbreak is quelled.

May–September, 189: Shaodi reigns as emperor.

May, 189: The dissident warlord Dong Zhuo advances to within eighty miles of Luoyang.

September 25, 189: Troops massacre the two thousand palace eunuchs in Luoyang. Dong Zhuo's army enters the capital and loots it.

September 28, 189: Dong Zhuo deposes Shaodi and installs his half-brother, Xiandi, on the throne. Han will soon split into as many as eight warring factions and the new emperor's reign will be nominal.

189–220: Xiandi is the Han emperor.

May 1, 190: Dong Zhuo's army burns Luoyang to the ground and shifts the imperial court to the old capital of Chang'an. Destroyed in Luoyang are the Han archives and the imperial library.

Spring 191: Under pressure from the warlords Yuan Shao and Cao Cao, Dong Zhuo retreats to Chang'an where he joins the nominal emperor, who keeps up the Han court but is without influence.

Spring 192: Dong Zhuo is killed.

August, 196: The emperor returns to a partially rebuilt Luoyang. Warlords and rebels contest control of the provinces. The empire breaks up into several parts—as many as eight distinct power centers at one point.

200: Cao Cao, with Emperor Xiandi now in his keeping, defeats his rival Yuan Shao. Over the next eight years, he establishes control over most of northeast China.

208: Cao Cao advances southward. His forces encounter the allied armies of Sun Quan and Liu Bei and are defeated at Red Cliff on the Yangtze. Sun Quan remains in control of the lower Yangtze valley. Liu Bei advances upriver to seize the rich region of Shu (modern Sichuan).

208–220: Cao Cao extends his control of north and northwest China. He resettles farmers on former Yellow Turban lands, thus helping to bring about an economic upturn after the devastation of the civil wars. The Han court remains his captive.

216: Cao Cao gives himself the title of king of Wei.

May 15, 220: Cao Cao dies. Chinese historians speculate that had he lived, his next step would have been to set himself up as emperor.

December 11, 220: Xiandi, the Han emperor, abdicates, bringing the four-hundred-year dynasty to a close. China divides into three warring kingdoms, Cao's Wei, Liu Bei's Shu Han, and Sun Quan's Wu, that vie for supremacy over the next century.

THE THREE KINGDOMS AND SIX DYNASTIES: 220–589

Turmoil marks this three and-a-half century era, a period of political and social fragmentation that corresponds roughly to the decline and fall of the Roman Empire in the west. It is the longest period of disunion in Chinese history.

The main trend of the close of the Later Han dynasty is the shift of power from the imperial court to large provincial landowners with their own courts and private armies. Three rival kingdoms, Wei, Wu, and Shu Han, temporarily survive the wreck of Later Han. The successor to Wei, the Jin, briefly reunifies the country. But it is racked by internal disorders, and the incursion of nomadic non-Chinese drives the Jin from North China. Waves of Tibetan tribes overrun northwestern China. The proto-Mongol Xianbei set up states in Gansu in the west and Hebei in the east. These intruders intermarry, adapt to Chinese ways, and rule in collaboration with the established aristocratic families. Toward the end of the fourth century, the Toba Turks found the Northern Wei dynasty with their capital at Luoyang. They provide a measure of stability and security and are able to hold North China together for a century and a half. Northern Wei institutions build, too, a framework for the eventual restoration of the empire. But for most of this nearly three-hundred-year period, China is politically divided south and north. The warlord ascendancy of Later Han forms the structure of Chinese society until the Sui/Tang reunification around 600. Chinese society and politics are strongly aristocratic in flavor, both north and south. Great families claim high offices and high status, and pass them on down the generations.

The regional dynasties of the South, one succeeding another, are at peace most of the time. Agriculture and trade flourish there. Southern rulers from their capital at Jiankang (modern Nanjing) regard themselves as more sophisticated than the barbarian northerners. From their centers on the lower Yangtze, these dynastic states push southward and colonize the aboriginal peoples in their path.

Three Kingdoms (220–265)

220: With the passing of Cao Cao, his son claims the Mandate of Heaven and founds a new dynasty, the Wei, in North China. But rivals to the south challenge this claim. Liu Bei, a member of the Han imperial family, claims from his power base of Shu (Sichuan) that he is the legitimate Han successor and declares himself emperor. Zhuge Liang, who comes down through China's history as the exemplar of the loyal and heroic government minister, becomes Liu Bei's chief administrator. On the Yangtze, Sun Quan, once allied with Liu Bei, appoints himself emperor of the third of the three kingdoms, Wu. The rival kingdoms make constant war on each other.

234: Zhuge Liang is killed campaigning with Shu Han forces in the Wei River valley. The death of this brilliant leader effectively ends the Shu Han threat to the other two kingdoms.

235–264: The Wu Kingdom contributes to the spread of Chinese culture in the south.

The immortals nourish their bodies with drugs and prolong their lives with the application of occult science, so that internal illness shall not arise and external ailment shall not enter. Although they enjoy everlasting existence and do not die, their old bodies do not change. If one knows the way to immortality, it is not to be considered so difficult.

On Immortality from Alchemy, by the religious Daoist He Gong (255–333?)

265: The Shu Han kingdom collapses. In North China, the Jin dynasty succeeds the Wei.

280: The Wu kingdom crumbles.

280–304: Jin rules a temporarily reunified empire for around a quarter century. Then non-Chinese invaders drive the Jin from North China.

Early 4th century: Waves of nomadic peoples sweep into China from the north and northwest. They establish a series of brief dynasties; warfare is constant in the north for most of the century.

312: Luoyang, the ancient capital of eastern China, falls to nomadic invaders.

Six Dynasties/Sixteen Kingdoms (317–589)

4th century: Ceaseless warfare claims tens of thousands of lives in the north and touches off a mass migration to the safer south. In the south, the Chinese push into the wilderness hinterlands from the lower Yangtze.

317–420: Span of the Eastern Jin dynasty.

386: The Northern Wei dynasty is established. Its Toba Turk rulers bring order out of chaos in northern China. They ally with powerful Chinese families with roots in the Han upper class. The great families find protection and security in the arrangement; the alien rulers tap the governing skills and general knowledge of the Chinese.

398: Northern Wei rulers order a Chinese-style capital to be built at their old Toba settlement in northern Shanxi. It is rectangular and walled on all four sides, with the traditional ancestral hall and great earth mound.

420–479: The Liu Song dynasty rules in southern China.

479–502: The Southern Qi dynasty succeeds the Liu Song.

471–499: Xiao reigns as emperor of the Northern Wei. With his Chinese allies, Xiao adopts the Chinese military organization and land-allotment procedure known as the equal-field system, which form the basis for the eventual revival of the imperial state.

495: Xiao moves the capital from northern Shanxi to the Yellow River valley.

502–557: The Liang dynasty rules in southern China.

524: The "Revolt of the Garrisons," a reaction of the steppe peoples to forced sinicization, spills onto the populous central plain of North China. The country districts are ravaged. Luoyang is attacked and more than a thousand Chinese court functionaries are massacred. Within a decade, the revolt will lead to the division of the Wei state.

534–535: Rebellion and internal division break the Northern Wei dynasty into two parts. The more economically productive, stable, densely settled and "Chinese" half, the Eastern Wei, establishes its capital at Ye in Henan. The Western Wei, still immersed in the horse-and-warrior culture of the steppes, is based on the old imperial capital at Chang'an.

543: Eastern Wei forces defeat a Western Wei army, inflicting losses of more than sixty thousand men.

546–550: To rebuild its military, once largely composed of troops drawn from the border peoples, Western Wei rulers attempt to recruit Chinese soldiers.

How may one reject [the Buddha] and refuse to learn from him? The records and teachings of the Five Classics do not contain everything. Even if the Buddha is not mentioned in them, what occasion is there for suspicion?

The Disposition of Error, a defense of the Buddha's teachings said to be by Mou Zi (probably 6th century)

548: Trouble breaks out in the placid South: The Hou Jing rebellion ravages the Yangtze provinces. Hou Jing occupies Jiankang, the Liang capital.

550: The Northern Qi state evolves out of the Eastern Wei.

550–560: Nomadic Turkish tribes assert loose control over a vast empire of Inner Asia stretching from Manchuria in the east to the Persian frontier in the west. They prosper on plunder from raids into China and on the silk routes linking China and the west.

552: Western Wei forces conquer the region of modern Sichuan on the upper Yangtze, thwarting the southern Liang kingdom's effort to establish a substate there.

552: A Liang general kills Hou Jing and crushes his rebellion. Within a few years, he will take power as the first emperor of Chen.

554: A Western Wei army attacks the temporary Liang capital at Jiangling on the central Yangtze, slaughters the city's elite, and establishes a puppet state in the region.

557–589: Along the lower Yangtze, the Chen dynasty succeeds the Liang.

557: The Northern Zhou, another offshoot of the Northern Wei dynasty, establishes a successor state to the Western Wei. Northern Zhou rulers, descendants of the military elites of the Revolt of the Garrisons of 524, restore traditional Chinese forms of government. The two former Wei states, Northern Zhou and Northern Qi, engage in a bitter rivalry for ascendancy.

557–560: Mingdi reigns as emperor of the Northern Zhou. Wudi succeeds him.

575: Northern Zhou and Chen forces agree to combine for an attack on the Northern Qi. As a reward, the Chen rulers are to be given control of the rich region between the Huai and Yangtze rivers.

577: Northern Zhou conquers Northern Qi and establishes control of all of North China, including the rich, crowded plain from the Great Wall to the Huai River valley. The Zhou then turn on their erstwhile allies of Chen, destroy the Chen forces, and tighten their hold on the provinces of the central Yangtze and Sichuan to the west.

581: A scion of the part-nomad Yang family (descendants of the Six Garrisons rebels), whose home base is the region between the ancient capitals of Luoyang and Chang'an overturns the Northern Zhou and asserts his claim to rule North China. Yang Jian will ascend the throne as the first emperor of the Sui dynasty.

SUI DYNASTY: 589–618

The Sui dynasty reestablishes China's unity. From his power base in North China, the founding emperor completes the restoration with the conquest of territory south of the Yangtze. The first Sui emperor produces a new legal code, reforms local government, unifies the bureaucracy, reorganizes the military and revives the state's finances, laying the foundations for a centralized state after three centuries of regionalism. He expands China's borders and constructs a canal system that will form the basis of Tang dynasty prosperity.

The dynasty ends abruptly, however. The second emperor reaches too far in an attempt to conquer Korea. The failed effort leads to rebellion and his loss of the Mandate.

581: Yang Jian and his allies topple the Northern Zhou dynasty and assert control over North China. Born in 541 in a Buddhist temple and raised by a nun, he is a strong, authoritarian, and successful ruler. Although a devout Buddhist in his private beliefs, Yang Jian is impatient and anti-intellectual, a man of action rather than reflection.

2d month, 581: Yang Jian takes the title of emperor, holds a dawn audience, declares an amnesty, and proclaims the dynasty of Sui. The first Sui emperor rules as Wendi.

Late summer, 581: Wendi and his henchmen murder the last of the rival Northern Zhou princes, for a total of fifty-nine executions.

When one of his Confucian advisors asks him to halt the executions, he explodes: "You bookworm. You are not fit to discuss this matter!"

582: Wendi orders a vast new capital, five miles by six, built on a site south and east of ancient Chang'an. To inaugurate his reform of the bureaucracy, Wendi orders the nomination of "the worthy and the good" for government offices. He proclaims a set of ordinances that allow for a periodic distribution of land to the peasantry as well as to nobles and others of high rank—a Northern Wei innovation the Sui extends. In the seventh month of this year, Sui also adopts new civil statutes governing bureaucratic procedures, land use, taxation, and other administrative matters.

Eastern Turks carry out large-scale raids into modern Gansu and Shanxi from their Mongolian encampments.

583: Emperor Wendi turns his attention to local government reform, abolishing all of the more than five hundred commanderies in North China. He will abolish the southern commanderies after reunification in 589. These and later measures streamline local government, reduce the number of local officials and bring the remaining ones under central government control.

3d month, 583: The Sui government moves into the partially built new capital.

587: To bring new people into government, Wendi instructs all prefectures to send three men to Chang'an annually for possible civil service appointments. After 589, the total will be nine hundred candidates a year.

587: The Sui abolishes the Liang puppet state along the central Yangtze and takes direct control of the region.

588: Emperor Wendi prepares to move on the south. He informs the Chen ruler that he is about to relieve him of his territory.

588: Sui responds to raids across the Liao River from the kingdom of Koguryo (modern Manchuria east of the Liao and the northern part of the Korean peninsula) with a seaborne punitive expedition. Chinese forces are repulsed and withdraw.

589: The Wendi emperor launches his campaign to take southern China. Sui naval forces defeat a Chen fleet on the Yangtze. Land forces advance on the capital, Jiankang, seize it, and capture the Chen ruler and his high officials for removal north to Chang'an. The provinces—the whole of eastern China south of the Yangtze—quickly fall to the Sui. China is whole again for the first time in three hundred years.

589–591: With a view to the smooth restoration of the empire, the Sui impose an easy peace. Some Chen officials retain their posts. Emperor Wendi remits all taxes in former Chen domains for ten years.

595: A civil service examination system is mentioned, possibly for the first time. The Sui refine it two years later; it is now regarded as a forerunner of the Tang and Song imperial selection system that survives until 1905.

595: Sui rulers continue the effort to demilitarize the country after generations of warfare. Wendi orders the confiscation of all weapons in the empire and bans the private manufacture of arms.

11th month, 600: Wendi deposes his eldest son and names a younger, Yang Guang, his heir apparent.

Summer 604: Emperor Wendi dies after an illness; he is possibly hastened into the afterlife by his heir. In any event, Yang Guang ascends the throne as Yangdi, the second Sui emperor. By later tradition, Yangdi is licentious, imprudent, and profligate. Yet his reign produced a greatly expanded canal system and extended China's frontiers.

604–607: Yangdi establishes an eastern capital at Luoyang. The ancient city is rebuilt and repopulated with "several tens of thousands" of rich merchant and trader families.

605: Emperor Yangdi continues his father's reform efforts by further centralizing control over the military. This gives the dynasty a firm hand on the military in interior China.

605: Khitan invaders penetrate south as far as modern Hebei before they are defeated and driven off by an Eastern Turk force under Chinese command.

606: Sui financial reforms and an improved registration system vastly increase the empire's taxable population, to 8.9 million households from only 4 million in 589.

607: Tightening his grip on power, Yangdi orders the execution of three of his critics in senior government posts.

The first full Japanese embassy to reach post-unification China arrives. Yangdi responds by sending an embassy to Japan. This will lead to a vast export of Chinese culture to Japan.

608: Sui forces rout Eastern Turk tribes in their grazing lands around Kokonor along the route to the Jade Gate and annex a large chunk of their territory to the empire.

610: Emperor Yangdi imposes a special war tax in preparation for a move on the kingdom of Koguryo.

612: The Sui assemble an army of a million soldiers near modern Beijing for the invasion of Koguryo. Chinese forces cross the Liao but are checked and forced to withdraw with heavy losses.

Early 613: A series of peasant rebellions breaks out in modern Shandong. A rebel army marches on Luoyang, the eastern capital, and besieges it.

Early summer 613: Emperor Yangdi launches a second offensive into Koguryo. Word of outbreaks at home reaches him; he detaches forces to lift the Luoyang siege and quell other disturbances, but the offensive sputters to a halt.

614: Emperor Yangdi makes a third effort to subdue Koguryo. Sui armies again cross the Liao and this time advance to the outskirts of P'yongyang, the capital. When the Koguryo king offers to submit, Chinese forces withdraw. The vassal fails, however, to turn up as required, and the emperor mulls a fourth campaign. But a spreading insurgency at home makes a resumption of the offensive impossible.

Tenth month, 614: Yangdi returns from the field, first to Luoyang, the eastern capital, then to Chang'an.

Early 615: Imperial forces scatter to quell a dozen simultaneous rebellions.

Autumn 616: Emperor Yangdi sets out by canal barge for an extended visit to his Yangtze capital, Jiangdu, which replaced the demolished Jiankang. He never returns to the North China seat of the empire.

617: Yangdi is deposed; rival rebel factions enthrone two of his grandsons. Li Yuan, a powerful Sui general, turns rebel and seizes the capital.

618: Yangdi is murdered in his bathhouse by a son of his most trusted general. A period of civil war follows his death.

TANG DYNASTY: 618–907

Tang builds on Sui foundations to consolidate and expand the imperial state, strengthening Sui law codes, tightening bureaucratic control, and building up military power. Armed expeditions into Korea, northern Vietnam, Mongolia, and Tibet extend China's influence and power. At home, the long, gradual process begins by which governance passes from powerful hereditary aristocratic families to a class of gentlemen educated in the classical tradition. Tang produces the remarkable, skilled, corrupt and ruthless Empress Wu, the only woman in China's history who rules directly as sovereign.

With the rise of the civil service comes a renewal of Confucianism. The arts flourish under the Tang dynasty; Tang poetry becomes a model for later eras. Population and economic changes further alter the north/south balance of power. The basis of prosperity is an increase in rice cultivation that population growth in the lower Yangtze valley makes possible.

Decline sets in during the latter half of the eighth century, the result of military overextension and rivalries at court. The bloody, destructive rebellion of An Lushan is ultimately crushed and Tang rule is nominally restored, but the dynasty never fully recovers. Imperial authority erodes steadily over the last 150 years of the dynasty. Corruption is widespread. Bandits ravage the countryside. During the last fifty years of Tang rule, China is essentially anarchic.

11th month, 617: With support from Turkish allies, the Sui general Li Yuan's army overruns Chang'an. The last Sui emperor's son is installed as puppet ruler.

5th month, 618: Li Yuan deposes the puppet, ascends the throne, and proclaims himself the first emperor of the new dynasty of Tang. He reigns as Gaozu.

619: The new dynasty reestablishes the "equal field" system of land tenure and allocation dating from the Northern Wei and Sui. This guarantees a fixed amount of land for every adult taxpayer and limits the total amount any individual can acquire, at least in theory: officials and aristocratic families are almost certainly excepted.

624: Gaozu defeats the last of his rivals. His authority is secure.

624: Tang issues the first set of codified statutes, modeled on the revised New Code of the first Sui emperor. They are simpler, though, and carry lighter punishments.

6th month, 626: The emperor's son seizes power in a coup, the "Incident at Xuanwu Gate," in which he kills two of his brothers, one of them the heir apparent. Gaozu hands over effective control to his ambitious son and abdicates before year's end.

The second Tang emperor rules as Taizong. The Chinese regard this reign, which lasts until 649, as a golden era. Taizong is a warrior, and he can show a foul temper. But he fosters good and honest government, is willing to listen to principled opposition, and is a patron of classical scholarship and a calligrapher of note. Opposition to his military adventures builds during the second half of his reign. The Korea campaigns are particularly unpopular because they fail while costing many lives.

627: The new emperor moves to shrink the bureaucracy, reducing the number of civil and military posts at Chang'an.

629–630: After Eastern Turk invaders approach the environs of Chang'an, Chinese forces counterattack, win a decisive victory and force the Eastern Turks to pledge allegiance to Tang.

632–635: Tang establishes control over the Central Asian oasis kingdoms beyond the northwest frontier, giving China control of the trade routes into Central Asia.

637: Taizong turns his attention to the provincial bureaucracy, personally selecting candidates for appointment as prefects.

Autumn 644: Against his chief ministers' advice, Taizong prepares an expeditionary force for an attack on the Korean kingdom of Koguryo.

Spring 645: Chinese land and naval forces invade Koguryo. The offensive stalls over the summer, however, and by the onset of the bitter Korean winter Taizong is forced to withdraw. Thousands of his troops perish in the retreat.

646: In the wake of an investigating commission's tour of the provinces, thousands of local administrators are punished for corruption and other misdeeds; seven are executed.

Early 647: A renewed attack on Koguryo is inconclusive.

649: Taizong dies; his heir ascends the throne and reigns until 683 as Gaozong.

652: Wu Zhao, the emperor's young concubine, begins her rise to power. She bears Gaozong a son.

653: A peasant woman, Chen Shuozhen, leads an uprising in modern Zhejiang province on the east coast.

Winter 655–656: The Empress Wang is deposed and Wu Zhao is elevated in her place.

657: Some 13,500 imperial bureaucrats rule a population of 45 million. A much larger bureaucracy of clerks and minor officials toils at the local level.

657: Chinese and their Uyghur allies break up the Western Turk empire. Chinese control of the north/northwest frontier region secures the trade routes leading to western Asia.

660: Gaozong suffers the first of a series of strokes that will incapacitate him for long periods. Standing in for him, Empress Wu rules effectively, despite the handicap of a powerful cultural bias against women in authority. Chinese historians will not treat her kindly; to them, she is capable of any enormity.

668: With assistance from the Korean kingdom of Silla, China defeats Koguryo at last and becomes overlord of all Korea.

669: Tang adopts new regulations intended to limit the influence of family connections on the outcome of civil service examinations. Candidates' names are to be concealed from their examiners—a requirement that will soon be dropped.

670s: Empress Wu gathers into her entourage the so-called North Gate Scholars, sages who advise her on matters of state.

674: Empress Wu presents a reformist "Twelve Point Memorial" to her husband. It calls for the promotion of agriculture, the reduction of government expenses, and promotion through the bureaucracy by talent.

675: The heir apparent, Li Hong, dies mysteriously. It is alleged that his mother the empress caused him to be poisoned.

680: The Empress Wu accuses the new heir apparent, Li Xian, of plotting rebellion against his imperial parents. She orders him banished, and he is later forced to kill himself.

681: Civil service examinations are made more difficult. Candidates must now write persuasively about political and moral problems and show they have mastered formal styles of prose and poetry. The Ministry of Rites administers exams in politics, literature, mathematics, law, and calligraphy. Of the two main degrees, *Ming Jing*, which emphasizes memorization of the Confucian classics, and *Jin Shi*, which emphasizes composition of poetry, *Jin Shi* becomes the preferred degree. Successful candidates move on to a second series of exams given by the Ministry of Personnel. These determine a candidate's placement in the bureaucracy.

December 27, 683: Emperor Gaozong dies.

December 30, 683: The heir apparent is enthroned as Zhongzong.

Winter 683: Nobles and princelings jealous of Wu begin to plot against her. Rebels seize Yangzhou on the Yangtze River and issue an anti-Wu proclamation: "With a heart like a serpent and a nature like that of a wolf, she favored evil sycophants. She has killed her own children. She is hated by the gods and by men alike; neither heaven nor earth can bear her." Troops sent from the capital quell the Yangzhou rebellion.

Early February 684: The empress, fearing a challenge to her power, forces Zhongzong from the throne and has him imprisoned. Next day, another of her sons ascends. Known as Ruizong, he is permitted no role in government.

Autumn 688: The lavish Bright Hall is completed. The building of it is a symbolic act, meant to connect Empress Wu with the imagined perfection of the early Zhou dynasty. The hall rises more than 250 feet high and is topped by Wu's symbol, a phoenix.

The princes of the Tang imperial house conspire against the Empress. She breaks up their cabal with ease and over the next eighteen months kills many members of the Li imperial family.

689: Empress Wu appears for the first time in the imperial robes and holding the jade scepter.

Late 690: Wu's high ministers urge her to take full imperial powers. Her son, Ruizong, the captive emperor, obligingly offers to abdicate in her favor. She takes title as sage and divine emperor and calls her new dynasty Zhou. The complacent Ruizong is named her successor.

Chinese sources portray the rule of the empress Wu as a carnival of corruption, license, and political terror. Networks of police spies and torturers systematically quash opposition to the empress, real and imagined. She has hundreds of her rivals murdered. Through the worst of the palace excesses, though, Tang bureaucracy functions effectively as the day-to-day governmental authority.

695–697: Mongolian Khitan, settled in the region north and east of modern Beijing and miserable in a famine year, rise in rebellion. Internal dissension rather than Chinese suppression ultimately dooms the Khitan revolt.

A lovely woman rolls up
The delicate bamboo blind.
She sits deep within,
Twitching her moth eyebrows.
Who may it be
That grieves her heart?
On her face one sees
Only the wet traces of tears.

Poem by Li Bo (Li Po) (*c.* 700–762)

698: Resurgent Eastern Turks (Tujue) raid deep into China from the northwest. They solicit Chinese support with promises to overturn the empress and restore Tang rule.

698: Empress Wu turns on Lai Junchen, a minister who had carried out a reign of terror on her behalf. The capital's population celebrates the tyrant's downfall by tearing his corpse to pieces.

705: Strengthened frontier defenses put a temporary end to large-scale raiding by the resurgent Eastern Turks.

February 22, 705: Empress Wu is forced to abdicate in favor of the legitimate heir, Zhongzong. She moves to another palace and is treated as royalty until her death later in the year.

710: Zhongzong dies, evidently poisoned by his wife. Ruizong, Wu's son, succeeds Zhongzong.

7th month, 712: With the appearance of an inauspicious comet, Ruizong abdicates. His successor, a grandson of Gaozong and Empress Wu reigning as Xuanzong, reasserts Tang control. The competence and honesty of his rule will make possible a long period of well-being and cultural renaissance.

712–755: Xuanzong rules; it is the longest reign of a Tang monarch. Known as the Enlightened Emperor, he is a poet, musician, and calligrapher of accomplishment, and a patron of the arts and of Daoism. The Chinese will look back on most of Xuanzong's reign as a time of good government, peace, and prosperity. But the mistakes and overextension of the last years will nearly bring the dynasty down.

721: A Chinese army helps forces of Gilgut repel a Tibetan invasion that would have given Tibet control of the strategically important Pamir region of Central Asia. War with Tibet will be intermittent for much of the century.

722: With its extensive borders, China carries a tremendous military burden. The empire sustains an army of more than 600,000 men.

730: Chinese military successes force Tibet to seek peace. A treaty is signed by which the Tibetan king recognizes China's suzerainty.

730–734: Natural disasters and intermittent famine blemish an era of general well-being. Grain shortages force the imperial court to move temporarily to Luoyang because Chang'an, overpeopled and difficult of access, cannot be adequately fed, especially in years of scarcity.

736: Khitan revolt in northeast China. The subordinate commander An Lushan leads a failed punitive expedition against the Khitan and is sentenced to death for his failure. He is later pardoned, however.

736–750: Peace in the west breaks down with a renewed Tibetan attack on Gilgut. Fighting, some of it heavy, all of it inconclusive, is more or less constant over the next fifteen years.

Autumn 737: The emperor promulgates a new codification of Tang law. In this revision 1,300 irrelevant articles are dropped and

2,180 are amended. It is the last systematic overhaul of the law during the Tang; the code itself will serve until the fourteenth century.

742: China's population is 48,990,880, up from 45,431,265 in 732.

The empire sustains 490,000 frontier troops with more than 80,000 cavalry horses. (The overall military establishment approaches 600,000.) Most of the frontier army is composed of long-service troops rather than conscripts or militiamen.

742–752: An Lushan wins appointment to a succession of increasingly important military commands.

745: Uyghurs in the region of modern Mongolia complete their rise to power with a decisive victory over the Eastern Turks. The Uyghurs establish their own empire that will last until 840. They maintain good political and economic relations with China during much of the period.

751: Arab forces defeat a Chinese expeditionary army at the battle of the Talas near Samarkand. This marks the high point of Chinese expansion into Central Asia.

755: An Lushan, now the adopted son of Xuanzong's favorite concubine Yang Guifei and reputed to be her lover, is denied the chief minister's post and rises in rebellion.

Late 755–early 756: An Lushan with a force of 150,000 lays waste to Hebei province and takes Luoyang. The rebel there proclaims himself Emperor of the Great Yan.

7th month, 756: The Tang heir apparent usurps the throne, designates the elderly Xuanzong "retired emperor," and ascends as Suzong.

756–762: Suzong reigns.

756: An Lushan's forces take Chang'an. The emperor flees and on the retreat is compelled to allow the murder of Yang Guifei.

757: An Lushan's son murders him and declares himself emperor.

759: Tang imperial forces retake Chang'an and Luoyang.

762–779: Daizong reigns as Tang emperor.

763: The latest Yan usurper hangs himself after a defeat and the An Lushan rebellion collapses. A precarious Tang rule is restored. Central authority is confined to four regions: the capital province, the northwest frontier zone, the lower Yangtze, and the corridor of the Grand Canal. An Lushan's uprising foreshadows the rise of independent military governors and mercenary armies.

763: Large-scale Tibetan raids penetrate deep into China. The raiders carry off thousands of prized Tang stud horses as booty.

779–805: Dezong reigns as emperor.

780: The government institutes a two-tax system, a combination of land and household levies to be collected in the summer and autumn. The land levy is according to the amount owned. The new system enables the state to collect taxes more readily. By overtaxing peasants, it also accelerates the accumulation of large land holdings, a process underway for a century or so.

Frontier drums beating alarm the travelers;
At the border the solitary cry of a wild goose.
From today the dewdrops will be white with
  frost;
In my native town the moon is shedding a
  special brightness.
All my brothers have been scattered;
Homeless, I know not whether they are alive or
  dead;
No mail is ever received, or is likely to be,
Since there is still no prospect of the war
  ending.

Poem by Du Fu (Tu Fu) (712–770)

781–786: Renewed outbreaks in the area of modern Hebei again weaken the Tang hold on China.

784: A new treaty and a redrawn border bring uneasy peace with Tibet. Both sides, however, will soon violate the truce.

791: Tibetans deal Chinese a decisive defeat and expel them from eastern Turkestan.

China will not return to the region for a thousand years.

805: Shunzong reigns briefly as emperor.

805–820: Xianzong reigns as Tang emperor.

815–817: Imperial forces subdue a military uprising in the region of modern Henan province.

820: Palace eunuchs murder Emperor Xianzong; Muzong ascends the throne. He will reign until 824.

824–826: Jingzong's brief reign ends abruptly. He possibly is a murder victim of the palace eunuchs; alternatively, he is a dabbler in alchemy and may have died of a drug overdose.

824–840: Wenzong reigns.

830: Troops of the Southern Zhao tribe storm Chengdu in Sichuan and carry off thousands of hostages.

December, 835: In the so-called Sweet Dew conspiracy, Wenzong moves to crush the palace eunuchs. They get wind of the conspiracy and foil it. In reprisal, military forces loyal to the eunuchs kill a thousand courtiers. The bloodletting continues into early 836 before the eunuchs proclaim an amnesty.

840–846: Wuzong reigns. His chief minister, Li Deyu, supervises the suppression of Buddhist, Daoist, Nestorian, Zoroastrian, and Manichaean temples and monasteries.

We have heard that up through the Three Dynasties the Buddha was never spoken of. So in this latter age it has transmitted its strange ways, instilling its infection with every opportunity, spreading like a luxuriant vine, until it has poisoned the customs of our nation.

"Edict on the Suppression of Buddhism," by the Emperor Wuzong (845)

845: Tang rulers launch a major crackdown on Buddhism. The power of the monasteries is curbed, the wealth of many larger monasteries is confiscated, and 250,000 clergy are forced to return to lay life. Within a few years, the anti-Buddhist measures will be substantially relaxed, though very little confiscated property is restored.

846–59: Xuanzong reigns. Near the end of his life, he falls into chronic illness from taking Daoist elixirs and dies at the comparatively young age of forty-nine.

859–873: Yizong reigns. Intermittent peasant uprisings and increasingly bitter rivalries between imperial courtiers and the palace eunuchs mark the reigns of Yizong and his successors.

January, 860: A small peasant uprising in modern Zhejiang province swells into a major revolt; Tang forces need six months to quell it.

861: Southern Zhao forces sack Yongzhou.

868–869: With broad peasant support, dissident army officers mutiny in Guangxi. The insurgency rages for fourteen months before imperial forces put it down.

873–888: Xizong reigns as emperor.

874: Insurgent peasants in Shandong defeat local Tang forces and advance into Henan, capturing many cities and towns.

878–884: The bandit Huang Chao, at the head of a growing gang army, ravages Guangdong, Guangxi, Hunan, and other provinces as he moves northward toward the capital.

881: Huang Chao's army of 600,000 seizes Chang'an, sacks it, and reduces it to ruins. The imperial court moves to Luoyang.

881–884: Imperial forces regroup and cut off rebels in Chang'an.

883: Zhu Wen, a bandit commander under Huang Chao, surrenders to imperial forces and is rewarded with a provincial military governorship.

884: With his retreating army cornered near Mount Taishan, Huang Chao kills himself.

885: At the head of a mercenary army, Emperor Xizong returns to Chang'an after a four-year exile. The capital is a near ruin. His stay will be temporary, however, and he has trouble paying his mercenary forces because the Tang government is no longer able to collect taxes.

888–904: Zhaozong reigns. His rule is nominal and confined to the capital district. Powerful independent military governors control central and eastern China, modern Henan, Shandong, and Anhui. In the south, in the middle and lower reaches of the Yangtze, small independent states emerge.

890–907: Zhu Wen gradually establishes control over a large area of northern China.

903: Zhu Wen leads a massacre of eunuchs in Shanxi province and in Chang'an and becomes the effective ruler of the capital.

904: Zhu Wen murders the emperor; Aizong ascends as the last Tang emperor.

907: Zhu Wen deposes Aizong and proclaims himself emperor of the Later Liang dynasty, the first of the short-lived Five Dynasties in an era of disunion.

FIVE DYNASTIES AND TEN KINGDOMS: 907–960

This brief era is a transition from the splintering of the later Tang to the reunification of most of China under the first emperors of the Song dynasty.

Five successive short-lived dynasties rule the North China plain, with the last of the five, the Later Zhou, claiming control of the largest area. Altogether, thirteen emperors reign during the fifty-three-year period. The overlapping Ten Kingdoms rule different regions of South China.

In the north, palace coups, power struggles, rebellions, raids from beyond the frontiers, and economic dislocation characterize these turbulent decades. South China is comparatively peaceful by contrast. In fact, in the South, disunion appears to have stimulated economic development.

907: Zhu Wen establishes the Later Liang dynasty in the North China plain, with its capital at Kaifeng.

907–923: The Later Liang emperors rule all or part of present Henan, Shaanxi, Shandong, Hubei, Hebei, Shanxi, Gansu, and Anhui provinces.

907–925: The former Shu kingdom controls modern Sichuan and parts of Gansu, Shaanxi, and Hubei provinces in west central China.

907–936: The Khitan people launch intermittent raids from Mongolia across China's northeastern frontier; they gradually hold and rule Chinese territory.

907–951: The kingdom of Chu rules in Hunan and part of Guangxi in South China.

907–971: The Southern Han kingdom controls parts of present Guangdong and Guangxi in South China.

907–978: The kingdom of Wuyue rules parts of modern Zhejiang and Jiangsu on the East China coast. The Northern Song eventually absorbs the kingdom.

909–945: The kingdom of Min rules modern Fujian province on the South China coast.

920: Royal forces mobilize to crush a large peasant uprising in present Henan province.

920–937: The kingdom of Wu rules in parts of present Jiangsu, Anhui, Jiangxi, and Hubei.

923: With the collapse of the Later Liang dynasty, the first emperor of the Later Tang dynasty, Li Cunxu, comes to power. The Later Tang emperors will expand their area of authority and rule from the ancient capital of Luoyang.

924–963: The kingdom of Jingnan rules part of modern Hubei. The Northern Song absorbs the little kingdom.

934–965: The Later Shu kingdom controls Sichuan and parts of Gansu, Shaanxi, and Hubei before falling to the Northern Song.

936: Shi Jingtang overthrows the Later Tang

and establishes the Later Jin dynasty. The Jin moves the capital back to Kaifeng.

937–975: The kingdom of Southern Tang rules parts of Jiangsu, Anhui, Jiangxi, Hunan, and Hubei in the Han, Gan, and Yangtze valleys.

946: A large-scale invasion of Khitan from Mongolia devastates North China. Khitan occupy Kaifeng and topple the Jin dynasty.

947–950: The Later Han dynasty, with Khitan support, briefly succeeds the Jin.

951: Guo Wei founds the Later Zhou dynasty and rules from Kaifeng. Zhou rulers manage some reforms, including reductions in rents and taxes. Criminal penalties are lightened and corrupt government officials are exposed and punished.

951–979: The Northern Han kingdom, a remnant of the Later Han, controls parts of Shanxi, Shaanxi, and Hebei in north China.

960: Later Zhou dynasty forces mobilize to meet the invading Khitan. The Zhou senior commander seizes power for himself and founds the Song dynasty. He quickly brings North China under his control and gradually absorbs the independent kingdoms to the south.

NORTHERN SONG DYNASTY: 960–1125

The three centuries of the Song dynasties form one of China's greatest ages. In an astonishing burst of creative energy, China surges to the fore in technical innovation, political theory, culture and the arts. At the same time, however, invaders from Inner Asia gradually assert political control over large sections of the country.

Rapid economic growth, both in agriculture and industry, marks the early Song period. The pace of southward migration picks up, and the Yangtze valley comes to overshadow the Yellow River valley in the north as a locus of Chinese life. Rice becomes the chief component of the Chinese diet. The Northern Song capital of Kaifeng, at the junction of the Yellow River and the Grand Canal, grows into a great trading center. Coal powers the development of iron smelting and other industries in North China. The mariners' compass for navigation is a key Song invention.

The Song era sees a reinvigoration of Confucian ideas. The spread of the printed book makes possible the expansion of education. The first Song emperors extend the examination system for the governing bureaucracy. Buddhism, as foreign and thus barbarian, wanes in influence in the upper classes (though it is still quite important on lower levels of society); the scholar Shi Jie admonishes the Chinese not to "forget their ancestors and abandon sacrifices to them, serving instead barbarian ghosts." Neoconfucian reformers become increasingly influential. Their challenges to the imperial court and the civil service to be less selfish and to reach for the highest Confucian ideals are broadly influential.

The great Song weakness is national defense. Song rulers, rising to power through scholarship rather than warfare, turn away from the aristocratic and military traditions of the steppes. Soldiers are regarded less highly even than merchants; Song uses expensive, often unreliable mercenary troops to guard its frontiers.

Over the dynasty's life, Inner Asian tribal peoples conquer large swaths of China. The Khitan Liao (907–1125) dynasty, moving into China from the grasslands to the north, opens a period of nearly five centuries of foreign rule of parts of China, though it is confined to the far north. Later, the Tangut Xia (1032–1227) from the northwest and then the Jurchen Jin (1125–1234) from eastern Manchuria incorporate Chinese territory into their empires. These dynasties adopt Chinese political customs and use Chinese bureaucrats to help them rule.

Weak defenses lead directly to the collapse of the Northern Song in 1126 and a new division of China. The vigorous Jin dynasty rules in the north as, in effect, an equal rival to China's Southern Song, whose domain is restricted to the Huai River valley southward.

907: The chieftain Abaoji becomes the un-challenged leader of the Khitan federation. The Khitan, whose original territory lay between the Manchurian forests to the east and the dry grasslands to the west, are still sem-inomadic, but they increasingly practice settled farming and weaving and produce salt and iron.

909: A Khitan army invades Hebei, defeating Chinese forces near the present city of Tian-jin.

916: After disposing of his rivals, Abaogi pro-claims himself emperor, founds the Liao dy-nasty, declares himself the equal of China's rulers, and signals his intention to gain con-trol of North China. (He reigns until 926.) Marco Polo's name for North China, Ca-thay, is a corrupted form of Khitan. From their southern capital at Beijing, the Khitan eventually will rule an empire encompass-ing Manchuria, Mongolia and a strip of North China. They will rule with Chinese help, and in the Chinese way.

926–947: Taizong is Liao emperor.

928: An independent Tangut state, the fore-runner of Xia, comes into being in northwest China.

Early 947: Khitan forces raid southward into the North China plain and occupy Kaifeng.

Fourth month, 947: Harassed by Chinese in-surgents, Liao forces withdraw from Kaifeng.

947: The Liao empire is formally subdivided into two parts for administrative purposes: the Northern, or Khitan, Division and the Southern, or Chinese, Division.

947–951: Shizong rules as Liao emperor.

951–969: Muzong reigns in Liao. He is un-distinguished, lazy, a heavy drinker; his Chi-nese subjects call him "the Sleeping Prince."

960: Later Zhou forces mobilize to drive off the Khitan invaders. Troops loyal to the Later Zhou commander Zhao Kuangyin

declare him emperor. With his brother Zhao Kuangyi, he founds the Song dynasty. Reigning until 976 as Taizu, he puts an end to two hundred years of independent re-gional armies, reorganizes the imperial forces for the task of restoring central rule, and extends imperial authority through most of China.

960: China's population approaches 80 mil-lion.

960–975: The Song dynasty conquers the states of Jingnan, Later Shu, Southern Han, and Southern Tang.

963: Song forces attack Northern Han in Shanxi. With Khitan help, the Han army turns back the invasion.

969–983: Jingzong is Liao emperor.

976: Zhao Kuangyi succeeds his brother as emperor, taking the title of Taizong. Later historians suspect him of murdering his brother to gain the throne.

977: The Song government appoints five bor-der marshals to regulate trade with Liao.

978: Wuyue falls to the Song.

Spring 979: The Song dynasty launches a new invasion of Northern Han, the last sur-viving independent Chinese state, and de-feats Han's Liao allies.

6th month, 979: Last Han forces surrender to the Song. Victorious imperial forces con-tinue the northward advance toward the Khi-tan capital at Beijing.

7th month, 979: Khitan rout Song army southwest of Beijing. Emperor Taizong is forced to retreat in a donkey cart.

979–986: Liao forces in present Hebei and Shanxi repulse recurring Song efforts to draw their state into the Chinese empire.

983–1031: Shenzong reigns as Liao emperor.

990: Liao emperor recognizes a "king of Xia."

993: Wang Xiaobo leads peasant uprising in present Sichuan. Insurgents demand redis-tribution of wealth from rich to poor.

994: Xiaobo's successor, Li Shun, takes Chengdu, asserts control of the region around it, and founds a rebel regime he calls the Great Shu.

995: Song forces crush a peasant uprising in Sichuan.

997–1067: During this middle period of Northern Song, bureaucratic corruption becomes widespread; in the northwest, Liao and the growing power of the Xia state threaten the dynasty.

997–1022: Zhenzong is Song emperor.

Summer 999: The Liao emperor mobilizes for a campaign against the Song. Over the following months, the Khitan army advances into Hebei; the offensive eventually stalls, though, and the army is recalled and disbanded.

1001–1003: Liao carries out intermittent warfare against the Song.

1004: A major Liao invasion reaches the Yellow River less than seventy miles from the Song capital at Kaifeng. It loses momentum, however, and both sides begin to talk peace. Song diplomats negotiate a treaty in which China agrees to pay an annual tribute of 100,000 ounces of silver and 200,000 bolts of silk in return for peace. Except for minor outbreaks, the treaty will hold for most of the century.

1016–1073: Lifespan of Zhou Dunyi, a leading Neoconfucian thinker.

1020: Song government encourages the expansion of schools with grants of land and books. Within eighty years the state school system supports 200,000 students.

1021: The population of Kaifeng, the Song capital, reaches 500,000 within the city walls.

1022–1063: Renzong reigns as Northern Song emperor.

1031–1055: Xingzong is Liao emperor.

10th month, 1038: The Xia ruler formally proclaims a dynasty and sends an embassy to the Song capital to announce the fact. He will reign until 1048 as Jingzong.

> *Before the rest of the world starts worrying, the scholar worries; after the rest of the world rejoices, he rejoices.*
>
> Fan Zhongyan, Confucian reformer of the Northern Song dynasty

1039–1044: Song and Xia forces clash in parts of modern Shaanxi and Gansu. Song forces suffer several major defeats and the war ends in a partial victory for the Xia, who now control large areas of north and northwest China, including the Ordos Desert region and modern Gansu and Qinghai.

1041: The Song army totals 1.25 million men. Military spending accounts for three-fourths of imperial revenues.

1042: With Song China preoccupied with the Xia war, Liao demands new territorial cessions.

1042–1043: The scholar-official Fan Zhongyan is ascendant at the Song imperial court. Fan Zhongyan undertakes to reform the civil service and local administration; he alters the examination system to emphasize application of Confucian thought to practical problems of state. He reduces labor service levies and adopts measures to improve agricultural production. He and his faction soon fall from power, however.

1043: Chinese living in the Southern Division of the Liao empire are forbidden to own bows and arrows.

1044: Northern Song ratifies revised treaty with Liao, agreeing to increase tribute of silver and silk in exchange for peace and a withdrawal of Khitan territorial demands. At the same time, Song negotiates a treaty with Xia that includes tribute payments to this rival.

1048: Yizong comes to the Xia throne as an infant.

1055–1101: Daozong reigns as Liao emperor. Early in the reign, he continues the process of sinicization of the Liao state. Among other things, he orders ritual observances to honor Confucian sages. Later, a backlash leads to anti-Chinese discrimination in the Liao domain.

1057: Ouyang Xiu directs a new brief burst of reform in Northern Song. He changes the examination system to emphasize classical learning even more strongly at the expense of literary learning.

1063–1067: Yingzong is Northern Song emperor.

1067: Shenzong succeeds Yingzong as Song emperor. He falls under the influence of the Confucian reformer Wang Anshi (1021–1086). Wang advocates greater state intervention in the economy, partly to increase state revenues and partly to reduce what he sees as abuses of private power deriving from great wealth and economic monopoly. He continues Ouyang Xiu's reform of the examination system, eliminating the literary component entirely.

1068: Shenzong backs Wang Anshi's measures to attack corruption and inequalities of wealth.

1068–1086: Huizong reigns as Xia emperor.

1069–1075: Wang Anshi's reforms, the so-called New Laws, are successively implemented in Northern Song. Some lead to social unrest; others appear to be successful. Wang Anshi sets up the loan program known as the Green Sprouts Act, enabling farmers in difficulty to borrow seed grain in the spring against the expected harvest in the autumn. He imposes price controls and extends credit to small merchants and manufacturers. Modern scholars regard Wang as a prototype of the totalitarian.

1070: Chinese in Liao are forbidden to hunt, inasmuch as hunting is viewed as a form of military training. A new law code attempts to preserve Khitan customs, but it is cumbersome and will soon be abandoned.

1076: Wang Anshi, his reforms drawing bitter opposition, resigns his imperial post. One of his leading opponents, the scholar, poet, and

painter Su Dongpo, falls too. Su, who accuses Wang of trying to force everyone to think alike, is thrown in prison and expects to be put to death.

1077: The Lu family proposes an early form of the citizens' forum that will be known as the Community Compact, which will come into widespread use during the Ming dynasty. Forum meetings discuss and adopt regulations for behavior.

1080–1084: Escaping execution, Su Dongpo is demoted from his high civil service position and exiled to the provinces.

1081–1083: Song forces attack Xia and gain ground, taking the city of Lanzhou.

1085–1100: With Shenzong's death, Zhezong reigns as Northern Song emperor.

1086: The historian Sima Guang, a conservative opponent of Wang Anshi's policies, is briefly chief imperial minister. With support from such allies as Su Dongpo, who returns to the capital on the emperor's death, he manages to overturn most of Wang Anshi's policies.

1086–1139: Chongzong reigns as Xia emperor.

1090: A visitor to the Khitan court reports that Liao law now weighs no more heavily on Chinese subjects than the Khitan tribes themselves. But he is astonished at the high level of court corruption.

1091–1093: Song renew attacks on Xia. Imperial forces again conquer territory, but are unable to consolidate their gains.

1096–1099: Intermittent fighting resumes between Song and Xia.

1100–1125: Huizong reigns as the next-to-last Northern Song emperor. A talented painter and a patron of the arts and of Daoism, he is classed a weak and indifferent ruler.

1101–1125: Tianzuo is Liao emperor.

1102: Jurchen tribes—farmers, herders, and hunters originally from the mountain forests of eastern Manchuria—raid Khitan Liao frontiers.

Autumn 1114: Jurchen pressure against Liao builds and Jurchen forces prevail in two major frontier-area battles.

1115: The Jurchen chief proclaims himself first emperor of the Jin dynasty. He reigns until 1123 as Taizu.

1117: Song diplomats agree to help the Jurchens against Liao, expecting to divide up Liao territory as a result.

1119: The Song negotiates a treaty with Xia, ending four years of costly warfare.

1120: Fang La leads brief, violent uprising in modern Zhejiang province in southeast China and raises a large army. Song forces capture and execute Fang La in 1121, and his revolt swiftly collapses.

1120: The flourishing south coastal city of Quanzhou claims a population of 500,000, including the hinterland.

Spring 1122: In alliance with the Jin, Song forces advance on Liao Beijing but fail to capture the city. A Jin army seizes the city instead.

1123: Jin diplomats negotiate a treaty with the Song by which they receive in annual tribute 200,000 ounces of silver and 300,000 bolts of silk. This is well within the capabilities of the prosperous Song Chinese, whose economy continues to boom despite nearly constant warfare along the frontiers.

1123–1135: Taizong is emperor of the Jin dynasty.

Second month, 1125: Jurchens capture Tianzuo, the last Liao emperor, bringing the dynasty to an end.

Autumn 1125: Jurchens launch full-scale war against the Song, advancing into Shanxi and Hebei on the North China plain.

Early 1126: Jurchens cross the Yellow River and threaten Song capital at Kaifeng.

1126: Huizong abdicates in favor of his son, who will rule as Qinzong.

1126–1127: Qinzong is last emperor of the Northern Song.

February 10, 1126: Jurchens lift the siege of Kaifeng after Song diplomats agree to cede large swatches of northern territory and increase annual tribute payments.

January 9, 1127: After war flares anew, the Jurchens enter Kaifeng, pillage the capital, and force the Song to abandon all of North China. With help from generals including Yue Fei (1103–1141), Prince Kang of the Song imperial family retreats southeastward and sets up a new capital in the south, first at modern Nanjing, later at Hangzhou. He will reign as Gaozong, first emperor of the Southern Song.

May 1127: Jurchens escort two former Song emperors into captivity in the north.

SOUTHERN SONG: 1127–1279

The Song imperial entourage, preferring retreat over resistance to the Manchurian Jurchens moving south from the grasslands, establishes a new court and capital at Hangzhou on the East China Sea.

Though China is again divided, what remains to the Song is vast—700,000 square miles, with a population of 60 million. The Song extends China's cultural, artistic, and technological achievement despite intermittent warfare with the neighboring Xia and Jin states. Books assume increasing importance: not only literary and philosophical works, but also practical guides to farming, childbirth, pharmacy, and Daoism.

Southern Song develops some elements of a modern economy, with paper money, credit instruments, and sophisticated foreign trade. The merchant class expands in size, wealth, and influence. China becomes a leader in maritime trade; Chinese merchant sailors ply routes to India, Arabia, and Africa. Trade among nearer neighbors is strong as well. For most of their long rivalry, commerce between the Southern Song and the Jin is uninterrupted, to both states' advantage. Tea is a major export from Southern Song.

With new strains of seed, marsh drainage, and other technological advances, rice culture flourishes in the Southern Song. Urban life develops rapidly. Industrial districts in and near Southern Song cities turn out paper, ceramics, lacquerware, and metal products. Inventors and artisans develop new armaments, particularly those using gunpowder, and advanced shipbuilding methods. China's seagoing junks, with four decks, four to six masts, and a carrying capacity of a thousand men, are the most powerful vessels of their time.

1126: China's population reaches 100 million.

1126-1138: Refugees from the north flood the Yangtze valley ahead of Jurchen invaders.

1127–1130: In North China, the Jurchens' Jin empire formally introduces a Chinese bureaucratic system, staffed largely with Chinese; for the time being, it applies only to the Jin empire's Chinese population. At the same time, the Jin rulers impose compulsory military service and raise taxes.

1127–1162: Gaozong is emperor of what we now call the Southern Song. He gradually consolidates imperial power in the Yangtze valley.

1129: Gaozong crushes a coup attempt by generals who favor a more aggressive stance against the Jurchen Jin dynasty of the north.

1130–1135: Period of intermittent warfare between Southern Song and the Jurchens. Song forces under Yue Fei recover several provinces from the Jin. The emperor restrains the general, however, in favor of buying peace with tribute.

1135: The former Song emperor Huizong dies in captivity in North China.

Yue Fei leads campaign to subdue the bandit army of Dongting Lake, pacifying the middle Yangtze region for the Southern Song.

1138–1150: Xizong rules as emperor of the Jin dynasty.

1138: Song imperial forces control most of China south of the Huai River. They establish a long-term capital at Hangzhou, a provincial city of some 200,000 known for its lake and lovely setting.

Green mountains surround on all sides the still waters of the lake. One would say, a landscape composed by a painter. Only toward the east, where there are no hills, does the land open out, and there sparkle, like fishes' scales, the bright-colored tiles of a thousand roofs.

Description of Hangzhou, the Song capital (13th century)

1139–1193: Renzong reigns as Xia emperor.

1139: Southern Song negotiators conclude a preliminary treaty with the Jin against the advice of Yue Fei, who proposes to lead an army to conquer North China and reunify the country.

The Jin introduces a new Jurchen script. For a time, three official written languages are in use in North China: Jurchen, Khitan, and Chinese.

1140: The Jin breaks the treaty and attacks Southern Song China on several fronts. Under Yue Fei, Song armies counterattack and drive back the Jin. Song forces regain some territory in Henan before the emperor orders Yue Fei to withdraw.

Summer 1140: Song armies form a defensive line along the old frontier of the Huai River.

Early 1141: Jin forces launch a new invasion. Qin Gui, a key adviser of the Emperor Gaozong, pushes strongly for peace talks. He keeps Yue Fei, the Song's best commander, in the capital, then arrests him. Allegedly in response to a Jin demand, Qin Gui arranges Yue Fei's murder in prison.

October–December 1141: Song and Jin negotiators conclude a new treaty that recognizes the division of China and, in formal terms, makes the Song a vassal of the Jin.

October 11, 1142: Jin envoy's appearance at the Southern Song court is a formal ratification of the peace accord. By terms of Qin Gui's treaty, the Southern Song cede North China to the Huai River and agree to pay a large annual tribute of silver and silk to the Jin. The Jurchens, totaling around 6 million of North China's 45 million population, will rule until 1234. They build a Chinese-style bureaucracy; many native Chinese become Jin civil servants.

1142–1143: Famine and earthquake lead to hardship, unrest, and uprisings in northwest China. Southern Song forces help Xia pacify the insurgents.

1144–1147: Confucian institutions are introduced in the Xia state. Schools, a training college for civil servants and an examination system are established. A Confucian cult is encouraged.

January 9, 1150: Court conspirators murder the violent, morbid, and paranoid Jin emperor Xizong.

1150–1161: Hailing, the leading figure in the Xizong murder conspiracy, rules the Jin. Chinese and Jurchen sources both portray him as cruel, ruthless, and homicidal. Yet he is a passionate admirer of Chinese culture, adopts such characteristic Song customs as tea-drinking and chess-playing, and further sinicizes Jin government.

1152: Hailing rebuilds Yanjing near modern Beijing, takes up residence there, and styles the city the Central Capital. In 1157, he decrees Kaifeng the southern capital.

1159–1160: The Jin mobilize for a new campaign against the Southern Song. Jin forces include 120,000 Jurchen and 150,000 Chinese conscripts; some 560,000 horses are requisitioned.

October 28, 1161: Jin army crosses the Huai River and advances toward the Yangtze.

November 26–27, 1161: Song defenders repulse the Jin army's attempt to cross the Yangtze to invade the Southern Song heartland.

December 15, 1161: Officers' cabal murders Hailing in camp near the Yangtze front. Shizong ascends the throne.

1161–1189: Reforms in education, the economy, and administration mark the long, stable reign of the Jin emperor Shizong.

Early 1162: Shizong withdraws Jin armies from the line of the Yangtze and sends a peace envoy to the Southern Song court. Border clashes continue, however.

1162: Gaozong abdicates as Southern Song emperor; his son succeeds as Xiaozong, who will rule until 1189.

1165: The Song dynasty concludes a new peace treaty with the Jin, agreeing to increase its annual tribute payments by fifty thousand ounces of silver and fifty thousand bolts of silk.

1187: The population of the Jin state is 44,705,086.

1189–1191: Guangzong rules as the Southern Song emperor.

1189–1208: Zhangzong is the Jin emperor. He is an accomplished calligrapher and patron of the arts.

1191–1192: Khitan script, still in use from the era of the Liao state, is formally abolished by the Jin.

1192: Jin army throws up defensive works on the northwestern frontier to check the growing power of the Mongols.

1193–1205: Henzong is emperor of the Xia dynasty.

1194–1224: Ningzong is emperor of Southern Song.

5th month, 1202: Jin formally adopts the Chinese legal code of the Tang dynasty.

1205: The Mongols, the new great power on the steppe, launch their first raid into Xia territory. Raiders sack fortified frontier towns and carry away livestock.

June 14, 1206: The Southern Song dynasty declares war on the Jin. The declaration asserts that the Jin has lost the Mandate of Heaven and thus the right to rule. It also calls for an uprising of Chinese within Jin borders.

1206: Temujin is enthroned as the Great Khan of the Mongols—Chinggis (Ghengis) Khan.

Autumn 1206: Jin forces repulse the Song offensive, cross the Huai River, and occupy Song strongholds in southern Shaanxi. Fighting continues intermittently through the next year.

1206–1208: Frequent Mongol raids lead Xia to seek an alliance with the Jin to the east. The Jurchens refuse to cooperate. "It is to our advantage when our enemies attack one another," the Jin prince observes. "Wherein lies the danger to us?"

1206–1211: Xianzong reigns as Xia emperor.

1207: The Jin state's population is 53,532,151; that of China as a whole, 110–120 million.

July 1208: Victorious Jin declares the war with Song at an end; the Song sends to Jin the head of the minister who started the war, Han Tuozhou.

November 2, 1208: A new peace treaty with Jin increases the Song annual tribute by 50,000 ounces of silver and 50,000 bolts of silk.

1209–1213: Wei Shao rules the Jin, but is not accorded the title of emperor.

Autumn 1209: Mongols launch major invasion of Xia territory.

1210: After a series of defeats, Xia nominally submits to the Mongols, who then turn their attention to the Jin state.

1211–1223: Shenzong is Xia emperor.

Spring 1211: Two Mongol armies push up to the Jin borders. Mongolian forces clear the mountain pass that protects Yanjing, plunder the countryside around the capital, and withdraw before winter.

1211: The Red Jacket bandit/guerrilla uprising spreads in Shandong in northeast China. It flares intermittently until 1227, when the insurgents swear fealty to the Mongols.

Spring 1213: Mongols return, raiding into Hebei, Shandong, and Shanxi.

Eighth month, 1213: The Jin ruler Wei Shao

is murdered; Xuanzong ascends the throne. He reigns until 1224.

Spring 1214: Under Mongol pressure, Jurchens shift their capital south from Yanjing to Kaifeng.

May 31, 1215: Yanjing surrenders to the Mongols.

1220–1222: Jurchen diplomatic missions seek peace with Mongols but are rebuffed.

1223–1226: Xianzong rules as emperor of the Xia.

1224–1234: Aizong—the "pitiable ancestor"—is emperor of the Jin.

1224–1264: Lizong reigns as Song emperor.

1225: Mongols invade Shandong in northeast China.

Spring 1226: Mongols launch a new invasion of Xia, overrunning most of Xia's territory. Xia emperor Xianzong is said to have died of fright.

1226–1227: Xian is the last Xia emperor. In the sixth month of 1227, Mongols besiege his capital, force him to surrender, and kill him on the spot when he does.

August 15, 1227: Chinggis [Ghengis] Khan dies. He is succeeded by his son Ogodei.

1230–1231: Mongols mount a new invasion of Jin territory.

1230: Red Jackets advance into Song territory as far as the Yangtze.

February 18, 1231: The Red Jacket leader is killed in battle with Southern Song forces; the movement collapses.

April 8, 1232: Mongols move up to walls of Kaifeng. Jin defenders use Chinese gunpowder and a weapon known as a "fire lance," probably a rocket, against the besiegers.

Summer 1232: Famine and disease spread through Kaifeng. As many as 900,000 are said to have perished within a few weeks in the capital of what some modern scholars believe is bubonic plague.

Winter 1233: Aizong slips out of stricken Kaifeng and makes his way south toward Song territory.

May 29, 1233: Kaifeng surrenders to the Mongols.

1234: Aizong commits suicide; Modi is the last Jin emperor. He falls in battle with the Mongols, bringing down the Jin state.

1237: As Mongol threat looms, Southern Song river and coastal defense navy totals twenty-two squadrons manned by 52,000 sailors.

1260s: Song reformers try to root out corruption among eunuchs, bureaucrats, and imperial relatives. This causes deep divisions in the Song court on the eve of the Mongol invasion.

1260–1261: Mongol rulers of North China send envoys to the Song court; they are rebuffed.

1264: Khubilai, grandson of Chinggis [Ghengis] Khan, ascends throne of the Great Khan of the Mongols. He moves his capital from Karakoram in Mongolia to Beijing and prepares to invade Song China.

1264–1274: Duzong is Song emperor.

1265: Mongol and Song forces clash in the western region of Sichuan.

1268: Full-scale war breaks out between the Mongols and the Southern Song. Mongol army lays siege to the Han River fortress of Xiangyang, the key to control of the Yangtze valley.

1271: Khubilai chooses a Chinese name, Yuan, for his dynasty and adopts Chinese court rituals. He departs from all precedence by not choosing his native place as the name

for the dynasty. Rather, he gave it a name with a meaning: the auspicious word *yuan*, meaning "prime."

1274–1276: Gongdi, a child, is last emperor of the Song.

March 1273: Battered by Mongol artillery hurling rocks weighing as much as a hundred pounds apiece, Song forces surrender the fortress of Xiangyang after a five-year siege.

January 1275: Mongol armies cross the Yangtze, driving the Song defenders before them. The dowager empress Xie, acting for the underage emperor, issues a call for a mass uprising against the barbarians.

December 1275: Xie sends to Mongols for peace terms, hoping to avoid a slaughter if Hangzhou, the world's largest (with 1.1 million people), richest, and most cosmopolitan city, is taken by force. The Mongol commander offers unconditional surrender.

January 1276: Mongols are given the seal of the Song dynasty and enter Hangzhou. The imperial family is taken north to Khubilai Khan's court at Beijing.

1276–1278: Mongols resume southward advance and continue their conquest, breaking up bands of increasingly demoralized Song loyalists.

March 1279: Mongols defeat the last of the loyal Song forces in a naval battle off the Guangdong coast.

YUAN DYNASTY: 1279–1368

For the first time in its long history, China is wholly under foreign domination, a division of the vast Mongol empire. Many Chinese, especially southern Chinese, despise their conquerors, though they adapt to some of their ways.

The Mongols do not force the Chinese to follow alien customs, but in some ways their rule weighs heavily. They bar the Chinese from trading in bamboo, for it could be used to fashion bows and arrows. Intermarriage is prohibited. Taxes are burdensome, and there is some expropriation of land and some forced resettlement. The economy, especially in war-ravaged (and possibly plague-decimated) North China, is badly damaged and will need decades to recover.

At times, the Yuan rulers keep Chinese out of important governmental posts. Even when they are welcomed, though, some Chinese scholars—a small but influential and much-honored minority—are reluctant to serve the new regime. With the decline in numbers of educated men entering the bureaucracy, the arts, particularly drama and painting, flourish. Some 160 complete plays survive from the Yuan era, most of them in four acts with alternate spoken passages and sung lyrics. The Chinese novel develops during this period as well.

The Mongols, brilliant conquerors, are less adept at consolidating their gains. All the same, they could claim some achievements. Advances are made in agriculture and education. Trade is promoted. Khubilai Khan extends the Grand Canal to the Yuan capital at present-day Beijing. The post road system is also extended.

In the end, the Mongols cannot hold what they seize. The first half of the fourteenth century brings a succession of severe winters, floods, famine, and plagues, calamities that uproot tens of thousands of people and prepare a fertile soil for rebellion. During the closing decades of the dynasty, the effectiveness of civil government markedly declines. The Yuan dynasty lasts less than a century.

1253–1254: Mongols under Khubilai conquer Yunnan in southwest China.

May 1261: Khubilai, now Great Khan of the Mongols, entertains proposals for governing the conquered domains of China. "If the proposals are useful, the court will liberally promote and reward the persons who make the proposals," he promises.

1267: Khubilai Khan orders the construction of a new capital at the site of modern Beijing, with avenues wide enough for cavalry to ride nine abreast.

The leading Confucian scholar Xu Heng (1209–1281) becomes chancellor of the Imperial College.

All Cathaians detested the rule of the great khan because he set over them Tartars [Mongols], or still more frequently Saracens [Arabs], whom they could not endure, for they treated them like slaves.

The Travels of Marco Polo (13th century)

1271: Khubilai Khan claims the Mandate of Heaven and decrees himself emperor of China. He takes the reign name of Shizu, calls his dynasty Yuan (meaning "prime" or "original") and establishes an imperial court in the Chinese manner. Over the next eight years, he will extend his rule to the entire country.

First month, 1274: Khubilai Khan holds first court in his new capital.

1274: Using the captured Song fleet, Mongols attempt to invade Japan. Typhoons force the fleet to return to Chinese shores.

1278–1284: Huang Hua leads an intermittent rebellion against the Yuan.

Spring 1281: Yuan invasion force of 100,000 troops, 15,000 sailors and 900 vessels lands in Japan. On August 15, a typhoon strikes Japan, destroying close to half the Yuan invasion force. The Japanese call this storm *kamikaze* (divine wind). Khubilai calls off the campaign and the survivors return to China.

Imperial forces quell a rebellion south of the Yangtze; Khubilai's troops are said to behead twenty thousand insurgents.

April 10, 1282: Dissident Chinese ambush and kill the imperial finance minister, the Muslim Ahmad. Chinese sources stigmatize Ahmad as the first of the three "villainous ministers."

May 1285: Ahmad's successor, Lu Shijung, the second of the ministerial villains, is arrested and later executed. His successor is Sangha, believed to be a Tibetan.

1286–1287: Yuan army campaigns in Annam (modern northern Vietnam). Though the fighting is inconclusive, Annam and neighboring Champa (today's southern Vietnam) agree to send tribute to the Yuan court.

1290: According to a government census, China's registered population is 58,834,711. Even though the actual population is doubtless higher, it still represents a significant decrease, especially in the north, and is largely the consequence of the Mongol invasion, war, famine, and perhaps plague.

August 1291: Sangha, the last of the three villainous ministers, is removed from office and executed.

February 18, 1294: Khubilai Khan, old, fat, and crippled with gout, dies in his palace.

May 10, 1294: Chengzong, a grandson of Khubilai, is enthroned as emperor of the Yuan dynasty. He issues an edict calling for the veneration of Confucius.

1298: Chengzong rejects a recommendation for a third attempt to invade Japan. He sends a monk on a peace mission to Japan in 1299.

Spring 1303: Imperial investigation of government corruption ends with the conviction of more than eighteen thousand officials and clerks.

1307–1311: Wuzong is Yuan emperor. His brief reign is noteworthy for the bloating of the bureaucracy and for the emperor's spending excesses.

April 1311: Renzong, the younger brother of Wuzong, ascends the Yuan throne. He will reduce expenses and attempt to shrink the bureaucracy.

1315: Yuan rulers restore China's examination system. They set quotas assuring half the degrees are awarded to Mongols and other non-Chinese candidates.

April 19, 1320: Yingzong (Shidebala to Mongolians) succeeds his father as Yuan emperor.

September 4, 1323: Disaffected Mongolian princes lead a coup that topples Yingzong; the emperor and his chief minister are murdered.

October 4, 1323: Taiding, a participant in the coup, ascends the Yuan throne. He surrounds himself with Muslim advisors; Chinese officials will have scant influence during his reign.

August 15, 1328: Taiding's death touches off the most violent succession struggle of the Yuan dynasty.

October 1328: With the ascension of Taiding's son Tianshun, civil war breaks out.

1328–1332: The war of succession rages. A rival faction installs the Mongol prince Tug Temur on the throne (1328); he abdicates in favor of his older brother, who rules briefly before he is poisoned, allegedly at Tug Temur's order; Tug Temur then regains the imperial seal and reigns as Wenzong (1329–1332). In the confusion, powerful ministers such as Bayan rise to dominance at the Yuan court.

September 2, 1332: Wenzong dies.

July 1333: Shundi (Toghon Temur to Mongolians), thirteen years old, is enthroned as the tenth (and last) emperor of the Yuan dynasty at Shangdu, the summer capital in Inner Mongolia two hundred miles north of Beijing.

1333: Bayan is named chancellor of the right, the most powerful position in Yuan China. He presides over a bureaucracy of 33,000 officials, around 30 percent of them non-Chinese. A reactionary, Bayan's expressed goal is to "impose the old regulations."

1335: Chancellor Bayan sets his reforms in motion, sharply cutting palace expenditures and reducing salt monopoly quotas. He tries to enforce a strict separatism between Mongols and Chinese. Bayan reserves most leading government positions for Mongols and other non-Chinese; he bars Chinese from owning weapons or horses; and he cancels the Confucian examination system.

March 1340: A coup removes the deeply unpopular Bayan from office. He dies in April on the journey to his place of banishment in the far south. His successor as chancellor of the right is Toghto. He reverses many of Bayan's policies, reopens top positions to Chinese candidates and restores the examination system.

June 1344: Toghto resigns as chancellor of the right. For the rest of the decade, Yuan's troubles mount: revenue shortages, floods and famine, outbreaks of piracy, and rebellions.

October 1344: Zhu Yuanzhang, born into an impoverished tenant farmer family in central Anhui province in 1328, enters a Buddhist monastery as a menial laborer after his parents die in an epidemic. He will rise from these beginnings to found the Ming dynasty.

1345–1347: Zhu Yuanzhang wanders through the Huai River valley as a mendicant monk.

August 1349: Emperor Shundi recalls Toghto to the chancellorship. He is greeted as a savior. "Toghto wants to undertake great acts and dazzle the world," a contemporary said of him. "He wants to surpass the old methods of the ancestors, and leave behind an immortal name in the historical records."

Summer 1351: Popular uprisings break out in region of the Huai River valley and rapidly spread throughout China. One major rebel group, the Red Turbans, grows out of the ardently Buddhist White Lotus Society. Liu Futong rises to prominence as a chief Red Turban leader.

April 15, 1352: Zhu Yuanzhang enlists in a Red Turban rebel group. He rises quickly through the ranks to become a trusted adviser of the Red Turban commander.

July 10, 1355: Zhu Yuanzhang leads a rebel army across the Yangtze and moves on Nanjing.

1356: Paper money ceases to circulate. Toghto's inflationary policies have made it worthless: by necessity, he prints during his last years in power vast amounts of paper currency to fund state projects and quell rebellion.

April 10, 1356: Zhu Yuanzhang enters Nanjing at the head of a triumphant Red Turban column. Yuan China is well along the way to breaking up into regional powers under warlord control.

June 11, 1358: Insurgents under Liu Futong capture Kaifeng.

January 1359: Rebels destroy the Yuan summer capital at Shangdu.

September 10, 1359: Yuan loyalist forces retake Kaifeng.

1363: Chinese warlords continue to fight each other for control of the Yangtze valley. When Liu Futong is killed in battle, Zhu Yuanzhang succeeds him as the leading insurgent commander.

September 30–October 1, 1363: Zhu's fleets win a great naval battle on the Yangtze, destroying one of his leading rivals for supremacy in the region and taking fifty thousand captives.

1366: Zhu orders the rebuilding of his stronghold of Nanjing into an imperial capital.

December 27, 1366: Zhu's forces invest fortress of Suchou on the lower Yangtze.

October 1, 1367: After a ten-month siege, Zhu's army enters Suchou, consolidating his control over the middle and lower Yangtze regions. As the last warlord standing after the civil wars of the 1360s, he prepares to lead his army north through Shandong, Henan, and Hebei.

November 13, 1367: Zhu orders invasion of the North China plain. He meets little resistance from supporters of Shundi (Toghon Temur), the Mongol/Yuan ruler.

January 23, 1368: With an offering of sacrifices to Heaven and Earth, Zhu Yuanzhang is acclaimed first emperor of the Ming dynasty. He then ascends the throne. Ruling as Taizu, the first commoner to reign in China in 1,500 years, he will restore law and order out of the chaos of the Yuan collapse.

March–April 1368: Ming forces establish control over Shandong.

April 16, 1368: Ming forces occupy Kaifeng.

May 1368: Ming army pacifies Henan.

August 15, 1368: Ming army marches on Beijing.

September 20, 1368: Ming army enters Beijing to find the Yuan court has vanished.

1370: Shundi, the last Yuan emperor, dies in Mongolia.

MING DYNASTY: 1368–1644

The first Ming emperor sets a despotic tone for the dynasty. Zhu Yuanzhang, the commoner rebel leader who seizes the throne and reigns as Taizu, casts a long shadow over the course of Chinese history. Ugly, energetic, paranoid, and despotic, he puts the stamp of capricious violence on the Ming. His limited vision—the aspect of conventional Confucianism that holds that agriculture is the source of the nation's wealth, and that trade and wealth are parasitic—contributes to China's loss of leadership in technology.

Still, China prospers for much of the 277-year Ming era—the only period from the fall of the Northern Song to the 1911 revolution during which all of the country is free of foreign rule. The population doubles during the course of the dynasty, to around 160 million. Literacy rates rise steadily. Trade revives after the first emperor's reign, and flourishes during the last century of the dynasty. Foreign trade brings in vast quantities of silver and monetarizes the economy. China's rich silks and beautiful porcelain are in demand all over the world. There is a high degree of regional economic specialization: The Yangtze delta becomes a center of cotton and silk production; Fujian in the southeast is known for tobacco and sugar cane; neighboring Jiangxi produces the best of China's porcelain.

Literature, philosophy, education, and the arts flourish. The full-length novel, which existed in the earlier Song and Yuan periods, develops during the Ming; examples (both of uncertain authorship) are *The Water Margin*, an outlaw tale set in the Song period, and *The Journey to the West*, the story of a Buddhist pilgrimage to India during the Tang dynasty. Drama and belles lettres are vigorous. Ming China has more printed books than all the rest of the world added together.

China turns inward during the Ming, with long-term consequences. Just as the Europeans launch their great voyages of exploration and discovery China, obsessed with the security problem of the northern frontier, dismantles its great seagoing fleets. Overseas trade is increasingly restricted by law. The Great Wall as it is today—brick- and stone-faced walls with watchtowers—is a product of the defensive, self-preoccupied Ming era. Its purpose, to keep the Mongols out, is an appropriate symbol for the dynasty, which tries to keep all the world at bay.

1368: The first emperor of the Ming (or "Brilliant") dynasty razes the Yuan palaces of Beijing. Taizu (also commonly known by his "reign" name, Hongwu) retains Nanjing as his capital and orders the construction of a thirty-mile network of walls to enclose the city.

Taizu moves at once to implement traditional Confucian policies. He cuts government expenditures steeply. In an effort to make the army pay for itself, he revives the old soldier/farmer system, whereby the troops are expected to produce their own sustenance. He lightens the tax burden on the peasantry and increases it for the commercial and scholarly upper classes. He promotes land reclamation projects and repairs neglected dikes and canals.

June 1370: Taizu orders restoration of the civil service recruitment examinations.

Summer 1370: Taizu orders distribution of grain in drought-stricken areas of Yellow River valley.

1371: Dissatisfied with the candidates, Taizu overturns the outcome of the recruitment examinations. "We sincerely searched for worthy men," he complains, "but the empire responded by sending empty phrasemakers." Taizu suspends the examinations for ten years.

January 19, 1371: Taizu orders an expedition against the small surviving Xia state in Sichuan.

August 3, 1371: Ming forces reach the Xia capital of Chongqing. Shortly thereafter, Chengdu falls and Sichuan is pacified.

1372: Mongols check Ming expansion north of the Great Wall.

1376: The scholar-official Ye Boju submits a memorial criticizing Taizu for harsh punishments of civil servants for minor offenses. Ye is imprisoned and dies of starvation in prison.

1380: Taizu accuses his chief minister, Hu Weiyong, of conspiring against him. He orders Hu and many of his allies summarily executed and in the purges that follow fifteen thousand are killed. During Taizu's thirty-year reign, an estimated 100,000 functionaries will perish in Taizu's purges.

With Hu's death, Taizu abolishes the chief ministers' offices and establishes six boards—Civil Office, Revenue, Rites, War, Justice, and Works—as the highest level of China's government, with each department head reporting directly to the emperor. Taizu thus becomes his own prime minister.

1381: Taizu orders the peasantry to organize in registered groups of 110 households, with single rotating households responsible for collecting the community's taxes and labor services. This is part of Taizu's effort to cut spending and reduce the imperial bureaucracy.

1381–1382: Ming invades, conquers, and annexes the provinces of Yunnan and Guizhou in southwest China.

1382: Taizu establishes a legion of personal troops known as the Embroidered-uniform Guard. Its strength will grow to 75,000 men.

September 1382: Taizu reinstitutes the civil service examination system.

May 1388: A 150,000-strong Chinese army crosses the Gobi Desert and routs the Mongols five hundred miles north of Beijing, returning with 80,000 captives and 150,000 head of livestock.

1393: A government census puts China's registered population at 60,543,812. This is an undercount, probably by more than 20 million.

1397: The final version of the Great Ming law code is compiled.

June 24, 1398: Taizu dies after an illness. Six days later, his sixteen-year-old grandson ascends the throne and rules as Huidi. He softens some of the harsher clauses of the first emperor's legal code and reduces punitively high taxes in some parts of the empire.

"One hundred eight of us, each face differing from the other, yet each face noble in its way; one hundred and eight of us, each with his separate heart, yet each heart pure as a star; in joy we shall be one, in sorrow one; our hour of birth was not one, but we will die together..." When Sunng Chiang had thus vowed, all the host together shouted assent and they said, "We would but meet again, life after life, generation after generation, forever undivided, even as we are this day!" On that day did they all mingle blood with wine and drink it and when they had drunk themselves to mighty drunkenness, they parted."

All Men Are Brothers (or *Shui Hu Chuan*), probably by Shih Nai-en and Lo Kuan Chung (14th–15th century?)

August 5, 1399: The Prince of Yan, the fourth son of Taizu (born 1360) rises in rebellion against his nephew Huidi, touching off a three-year civil war. This is in reaction to Huidi's attacks on Yan's brothers and after the emperor has made it clear that he intends to remove Yan from his position of authority.

1400: Some 200,000 Chinese military colonists resettle among the indigenous tribes of Yunnan and Guizhou.

Mid-January 1400: The Prince of Yan marches from his strongholds around Beijing southwest into Shanxi.

May 18, 1400: Yan defeats imperial forces in

a battle in which 600,000 men are said to be engaged.

Summer 1401: Yan raids Grand Canal route supplying the imperial forces.

January 1402: Yan marches south toward the imperial capital at Nanjing.

July 3, 1402: Yan's army crosses the Yangtze and approaches Nanjing.

July 13, 1402: Nanjing surrenders. Yan claims the emperor and his wife perished in a palace fire; others claim Huidi flees disguised as a Buddhist monk.

July 17, 1402: Yan ascends the Ming throne as Chengzu; he is best known by his reign title, Yongle. He carries out purges that claim tens of thousands of the second emperor's loyalists.

Emperor Yongle plans to shift the imperial capital to Beijing and demote Nanjing to the status of a secondary capital. He will mobilize hundreds of thousands of workers to build the Forbidden City—the complex of imperial palaces in the heart of the capital. He reigns until 1424.

1405–1433: The Muslim eunuch Zheng He leads a series of far-ranging overseas expeditions. The first three voyages are to India; the fourth reaches Hormuz on the Persian Gulf; and the last three touch on the coast of East Africa. Diplomacy, exploration, and trade are the purposes of the voyages. China evidently is seeking allies, along with smaller states it can draw into a tributary relationship.

The maritime exploits of Zheng He are not repeated. In fact, the Chinese fail altogether to consolidate the technical gains achieved in long-distance voyages across the open ocean.

1406: China dispatches an army to Annam (northern Vietnam) to prop up the weak Tran dynasty there.

November 19, 1406: A Chinese punitive expedition captures major towns in Annam's Red River Delta.

June 16, 1407: Chinese forces capture Annamite leaders and take them in triumph to Nanjing. Rebellions against the occupying Chinese break out at once, however, and the fighting drags on year after year.

1408: Construction of a new palace complex, eventually to be known as the Forbidden City, begins at Beijing.

1410–1424: China carries out five campaigns to disperse the Mongol tribes raiding the northern frontier. In the first campaign, Yongle leads an army of 300,000 from Beijing north to Ulaanbaatar in Mongolia.

October 28, 1420: Beijing is formally designated China's principal capital. The completed Forbidden City is a vast and dignified complex of audience halls, courtyards, palaces, pavilions, and ornamental lakes.

1422–1424: Ming forces undertake renewed campaigns against the steppe tribes of the north.

August 12, 1424: Yongle dies of an illness during the fifth and last of the Mongol campaigns, which thus end inconclusively.

September 7, 1424: Yongle's son ascends the throne. His temple name is Renzong, but he is known—as are his successors—to history more familiarly by his reign name, Hongxi.

May 29, 1425: The Hongxi emperor dies at age forty-seven. The official cause is a heart ailment.

June 27, 1425: Xuande succeeds his father as Ming emperor.

1427: China gives up its twenty-year effort to subdue Annam and withdraws. Annam agrees to nominal status as a tributary in return for China's recognition of its independence.

1428: The Xuande emperor compiles a guide to emperorship, based on Confucian principles, titled *Imperial Injunctions*.

1443–1445: Oirat Mongol tribes establish effective control of the Chinese frontier zone from Manchuria in the east to Hami at the foot of the Altai Mountains in the west.

January 31, 1435: Xuande dies of natural causes. His son, only eight years old, ascends the throne as Zhengtong. His reign sees the rise of eunuchs to positions of great power and influence.

1447: Silver miners in Zhejiang province revolt. Government forces finally quell the outbreak in August 1479.

March 1448: Tenant farmers along the Fujian-Jiangxi border rise in rebellion.

February 1449: Government forces capture Fujian peasant leaders, transport them to Beijing, and execute them. Sporadic fighting continues until 1452.

July 1449: Mongols under Esen launch a large-scale invasion of China. The emperor decides personally to lead a hastily assembled Chinese army estimated at 500,000.

September 1, 1449: Mongols defeat the Chinese at Tumu and take the Emperor Zhengtong captive.

September 15–23, 1449: Rather than ransom Zhengtong, the Ming court decides to enthrone a new emperor and defend Beijing. He is Jingtai, a half-brother of Yingzong. The lone courtier who protests is instantly put to death.

October–November 1449: Beijing withstands a brief siege before the Mongol army withdraws beyond the frontier, pillaging as it goes.

Early 1457: The captive emperor wins release from the Mongols and in a coup is restored to his throne. He reigns as Tianshun.

March 14, 1457: Jingtai, demoted to prince, dies, possibly by the hand of the palace eunuchs.

1464: Miao and Yao tribes rebel. From its origin in Guangxi province, the rebellion quickly spreads into Hunan, Guizhou, Jiangxi, and the rich urban centers of Guangdong.

February 23, 1464: Chenghua ascends the throne. He proves to be a dissolute man. His rule will be marked by a gradually worsening financial situation as tax revenues decline, and by further growth in the eunuch bureaucracy.

Late summer 1465: A Ming punitive expedition 200,000 strong takes the field and pacifies the Miao and Yao in a bloody campaign.

December 1465–January 1466: Imperial forces attack the main rebel strongholds in Big Rattan Gorge. The Yao leader and eight hundred of his followers are captured, transported to Beijing, and beheaded.

1465–1476: The Qing-Xiang uprising in the refugee wasteland of the Middle Yangtze region drags on for years. Imperial forces record initial successes, but the rebellion flares anew as famine and epidemic increase the flood of refugees. Enlightened officials finally urge a social solution to the unrest, and the region grows quiet after 1476.

The great man regards Heaven and earth and the myriad things as one body. He regards the world as one family and the country as one person. As to those who make a cleavage between objects and distinguish between the self and others, they are small men.

Inquiry on the Neo-Confucian Great Learning, by
Wang Yangming (1472–1529)

1472–1529: Lifespan of the scholar-official Wang Yangming (also known as Wang Shouren). His new form of Neoconfucian thought is widely influential—and controversial—in Ming China. He stresses the relative ease of tapping the moral principle he believes is inside everyone. His teachings provoke an outbreak of factionalism in the Ming civil service. His chief challenge to traditional Confucianism, as handed down in the works of the Song thinker Zhu Xi (1130–1200), is his rejection of the notion that moral principle and universal patterns may be understood only through careful and rational study and inquiry. Wang argues that everyone has intuitive knowledge of universal principles. Once the distorting effect of material desires is contained, buried knowledge of good rises to the surface.

In practical terms, Wang is a capable government official, often immersed in day-today affairs. He is a vigorous promoter of the Community Compact—an old idea, refurbished during the Ming, in which villages take the lead in moral renewal. This is meant to arrest the deterioration of community spirit that many scholar-officials lament.

1474: Further extension begins on what is familiarly known today as the Great Wall of China. It is a wonder of the world, but is only modestly effective as a defensive bar against invasion from the north.

1475–1476: The Miao tribe again rises in revolt. Imperial forces crush it, killing thousands.

1485: Some ten thousand eunuchs are said to be in the imperial service.

September 9, 1487: The Chenghua emperor dies. His son ascends the throne as Hongzhi eight days later.

June 19, 1505: Zhengdi ascends the Ming throne. A drunkard, he appears little interested in matters of state and his rule is torpid.

October 1511: Bandits burn a thousand imperial grain barges on the Grand Canal.

February 10, 1514: During a lantern festival in the Forbidden City, an open flame reaches gunpowder stores and touches off an explosion. The resulting fire destroys the residential palaces. Thirty thousand troops are mobilized to rebuild the palaces.

1517: First Portuguese ships reach the Pearl River estuary below Guangzhou (Canton).

January 1521: The Portuguese ambassador arrives in Beijing with the first European embassy to reach the imperial court. He finds the emperor ill, however, and fails to obtain an audience.

April 19, 1521: Zhengdi dies. A young cousin succeeds him, ascending the Ming throne on May 27 with the reign name of Jiajing. He will rule to 1567. The eleventh emperor sets up Daoist altars in his palace and obsessively prays for good fortune and a long life. He becomes addicted to Daoist aphrodisiac and fertility potions and is said to rely on divination to determine state policies. He relies heavily on the powerful and corrupt Yan

Zhu, who is his prime minister for twenty years. Recurrent revenue crises mark the reign, leaving the court and bureaucracy chronically short of resources.

1522: The "single whip" tax reform is in effect in various localities. In an effort to stimulate government revenue, it simplifies tax rates and categories of payment, often combining separate levies on a single bill, to be paid in silver.

1524: Hundreds of scholars protest at the palace gates in Beijing; the emperor orders them beaten and 134 imprisoned. Sixteen scholars die of the beatings.

July–August 1542: The Mongol leader Altan Khan launches raids into Shanxi. He captures or kills 200,000 Chinese in his path, seizes a million head of livestock, and burns thousands of dwellings.

July–November 1547: A government agency reports that piracy is out of control along China's southeast coast, especially in Zhejiang and Fujian provinces. The official charged with suppressing piracy recommends strict enforcement of the ban against overseas trading.

January 1550: Local officials in Zhejiang petition the court to ease the ban on foreign trading.

October 1, 1550: Altan Khan lays siege to Beijing and loots the suburbs, but withdraws without capturing the city.

"We shall have to see about giving you a school-name," said the Patriarch. "We have twelve words that we use in these names, according to the grade of the pupil. You are in the tenth grade." "What are the twelve words," asked Monkey. "They are Wide, Big, Wise, Clever, True, Conforming, Nature, Ocean, Lively, Aware, Perfect, and Illuminated. As you belong to the tenth grade, the word Aware must come in your name. How about 'Aware of Vacuity'?" "Splendid!" said Monkey, laughing. "From now on, let me be called 'Aware of Vacuity.'"

Journey to the West (or Monkey) by Wu Ch'eng-en
(c. 1500–1580)

April 1551: Mongols agree to cease frontier raiding in return for a guarantee of two fairs a year at which they can trade horses for tea and other goods. Six months later, when China refuses a request to trade cattle for beans and grain, the Mongols resume raiding.

1553: The Outer City is built on a site to the south of the Imperial City of Beijing.

Early 1555: Pirates attack the rich Hangzhou region and kill thousands in the city's environs. The government launches a new offensive to suppress piracy and over the next four years gradually restores control over the southeast coast.

May 1557: Fire destroys audience halls and southern ceremonial gates at the Forbidden City in Beijing.

March 1560: The Nanjing garrison revolts in protest of cuts in the troops' ration allowances. Rampaging soldiers kill the vice minister for revenue, hang his naked body from an arch, and use it for target practice. Fearing further trouble, the government allows the garrison to go unpunished.

1567: The Ming government repeals the ban on maritime trade. Portugal is permitted to establish a trading center at Macau on the south coast.

January 23, 1567: The Jiajing emperor dies. The reign of his successor, Longqing (to 1572), will be brief and colorless.

1570: China negotiates a peace treaty with the powerful Mongol raider Altan Khan, ending the incessant raiding along the northern frontier.

1573–1620: The Wanli emperor reigns. During the first years of his era, capable ministers restore the empire's finances. Later, there is deadlock between the emperor and the bureaucracy. The estimated seventy thousand eunuchs in imperial service exert great influence. Infighting among the eunuchs and the professional civil service so disgusts Wanli that he stages a sort of work stoppage: for years he refuses to see his ministers or make necessary appointments, meanwhile building up his personal fortune.

1581: Ming government again reforms tax system, decreeing a single tax for all levies, to be paid in silver.

1583: Nurhaci, born in 1552, becomes great chieftain of the fisher/hunter/farmer tribes of Jurchen stock that inhabit the hills and forests of central Manchuria (present Heilongjiang and Jilin provinces). Nurhaci organizes the entire population in military units known as banners, for the colored pennants that identify the subdivisions. He will eventually mass eight banners, as well as eight banners each of Chinese and Mongol subjects. Over a period of three decades, Nurhaci builds a powerful state on the Chinese model. After 1635 his people will be known as the Manchus.

1587: The Buddhist White Lotus sect stages an uprising in Shandong.

May 1592: Japan invades Korea with a 150,000-strong army. China mobilizes to repel the Japanese.

January 1593: A Chinese expeditionary force crosses the Yalu River. The Japanese rout the Chinese army north of Seoul and an armed truce follows.

1597–1598: Chinese and Japanese forces in Korea resume hostilities. Muskets are used extensively in these affrays, with the Japanese equipped with matchlock firearms they copy from the Portuguese. After heavy fighting with thousands of casualties, the war ends in a stalemate.

c. 1600: After decades of steady growth, China's population is an estimated 150 million.

1600: More than 700,000 Chinese colonists are settled in Yunnan and Guizhou.

October 1603: Spanish forces massacre twenty thousand Chinese colonists on Luzon in the Philippines.

1604: The Donglin Academy near Wuxi in Jiangsu province is rebuilt. Donglin becomes a center for disaffected scholar-officials troubled by the direction of the Ming. They call for a return to Zhu Xi's orthodox Confucian values unalloyed with the Buddhist elements Wang Yangming and his followers are accused of introducing.

1604: The emperor fully withdraws from affairs of state. The Ministry of Personnel reports that half the empire's magistracies are vacant, as are many other offices.

1610: With the treasury depleted by military campaigns and the heavy burden of stipends to more than twenty thousand imperial clansmen, the Ming faces bankruptcy.

1616: Nurhaci proclaims himself khan of the Later Jin—an obvious allusion to the Jurchen enemy of Song and the forerunner of the Manchu dynasty. The Later Jin succeeds the Mongols of the steppes as the preeminent threat to China's security. All men in the areas he conquers are forced as a sign of submission to adopt the Manchu hairstyle—a shaved forehead with the rest of the hair braided in a long plait.

March 26, 1619: Ming launches a punitive campaign against Nurhaci's Later Jin. It is a disaster. Within a few weeks, the Manchus win a series of battles and threaten Beijing.

April 1620: Government raises land taxes for a third time since the outbreak of war in the northeast two years earlier.

August 18, 1620: The Wanli emperor dies, ending a forty-eight-year reign. Taichang ascends the throne.

September 1620: The new emperor falls ill. On September 25 he takes a large dose of a dubious medication called red pill. He dies the next day.

October 1, 1620: Tianqi ascends as the fifteenth emperor of the Ming. He is portrayed as weak, ill-educated, and stupid, though he is said to excel at carpentry. His reign is regarded as a disaster, largely on account of his reliance on the corrupt eunuch Wei Zhongxian. The economy stagnates, and military setbacks mount.

1621: Manchus take Shenyang (Mukden) in southeastern Manchuria.

1622: Chinese subjects in Manchu-ruled Liaodong rise in rebellion. It is savagely crushed.

June 1622: White Lotus Buddhists revolt in Shandong. They block the Grand Canal, capture fifty imperial grain barges, and temporarily cut off supplies to Beijing and the Ming forces fighting in the northeast.

1624–1627: Wei Zhongxian responds to accusations of corruption from Donglin reformers with a savage crackdown; many Donglin leaders are arrested, tortured, and executed or driven to suicide, and hundreds of others are driven from public office.

1625: Chinese again rise in Liaodong. Manchu rulers suppress the rebellion by executing literati suspected of stirring unrest, and by strictly separating Manchus and Chinese.

1625: Nurhaci makes Shenyang the Manchu capital.

Spring 1626: Ming forces repulse a Later Jin offensive; Nurhaci dies of wounds; his eighth son Hong Taiji (1592–1643) succeeds him.

1626–1643: Hong Taiji rules as chieftain of the Manchus. He extends Chinese institutions and brings in Chinese to staff his bureaucracy.

September 30, 1627: The Tianqi emperor dies. His younger brother succeeds him on October 2 and reigns as Chongzhen, the last emperor of the Ming dynasty.

October 1627: The powerful eunuch Wei Zhongxian is demoted and given a minor job in the provinces. In December, fearing arrest, Wei hangs himself.

1627–1628: Severe famine causes widespread hardship in northern Shaanxi. The famine is an outgrowth of a "little ice age" that chills much of China during the first decades of the seventeenth century. Army deserters and others form gangs that ravage the Shaanxi countryside before moving on to Shanxi, Hebei, Henan, and Anhui provinces. Government seems powerless to crush the bandit gangs.

December 1629: Manchu forces pierce the Great Wall defenses and threaten Beijing.

January 14, 1630: Manchu invaders defeat Ming army only thirty miles from Beijing.

The invaders withdraw without attacking the capital, though they take and loot several important towns on their return north.

1630–1638: Peasant uprisings spread through China's heartland, rising and falling according to the Ming response. Rebels extend their operations from Shaanxi northeast into Shanxi, east into Henan, southwest into Sichuan, and southeast as far as Jiangxi.

1636: The insurgent leader Li Zicheng (1606–1645) is paramount in North China; bandit chieftain Zhang Xianzhong (1605–1647) controls much of the area between the Yellow and Yangtze rivers. Both rebel leaders are Ming army deserters.

1636: Hong Taiji of the Later Jin proclaims a new dynasty, the Qing ("pure") and takes the title of emperor.

1638: The Manchus of the Qing subdue Korea.

1642: Rebels cut Yellow River dikes; several hundred thousand people perish in flooding and subsequent famine.

April 1642: Ming defenses along the Great Wall virtually collapse under Manchu pressure. Manchu columns press their offensive in northeast China, claiming 360,000 prisoners and vast caches of spoils.

May–October 1642: Li Zicheng besieges Kaifeng. Several hundred thousand die in the city, many from starvation and disease.

1643: Zhang Xianzhong declares himself Emperor of the Great West in Chengdu in Sichuan.

Summer 1643: Li Zicheng prepares to move on Beijing.

Autumn 1643: Hong Taiji dies; his third son Fulin ascends the throne and will rule as the Emperor Shizu.

Early 1644: Li Zicheng declares himself King of the Great Shun.

April 25, 1644: The last Ming emperor hangs himself in the Imperial Hat and Girdle Pavilion in the Forbidden City palace compound. Li Zicheng's forces enter later in the day and find the emperor's corpse.

June 4, 1644: Li Zicheng abandons Beijing as the Manchus approach.

June 5, 1644: The Manchu prince Dorgon enters Beijing, marking the beginning of Manchu rule in China.

QING DYNASTY: 1644–1912

The Qing dynasty rules from 1644, but nearly a generation passes before the Manchu conquerors destroy the last of the Ming pretenders and consolidate their rule over all of China. The Manchus extend their reach with the aid of Chinese collaborators and with the tacit acceptance of most of China's people.

The required act of submission for men—the Manchu-style tonsure with the pleated braid—is humiliating, but there are compensations. The Manchus promise to preserve China's traditional beliefs and social structures. They make use of Confucian rituals and precedence. They rule in the Chinese manner, with a sort of dual Manchu-Chinese bureaucracy. By restoring and maintaining order in the countryside, they win over the powerful Chinese gentry.

The first 150 years of the Qing form a long era of stability. China expands to its present boundaries, annexing Taiwan, Chinese Turkestan, and Mongolia and claiming suzerainty over Tibet. Three capable, hard-working emperors rule for a span of more than 130 years. The first confirms Manchu rule and courts the literati and landowning gentry. The second reforms the tax system. The third, one of the most cultured of emperors, reigning for nearly sixty years, presides over what many scholars regard as the high point of traditional Chinese civilization.

By the late eighteenth century, the golden era is fast fading and the Qing's developing weaknesses are increasingly exposed to view. Qing institutions become weak and ineffective.

Factionalism and corruption spread through the bureaucracy. The army is undisciplined and sometimes incompetent. Granaries are empty and famine relief inadequate. The Grand Canal silts up. The West has caught and overtaken China in power, prosperity and technological resourcefulness. In country districts, the pressure of a rapidly rising population brings social disturbances. Deforestation and erosion cause environmental damage. With labor surpluses everywhere, wages are depressed.

The Qing state either ignores or denies its problems. The explosion of the Taiping Rebellion and two concurrent insurgencies in the mid-nineteenth century nearly destroy the Qing. Some 20 million Chinese perish in the Taiping outbreak. In the last decades of the century, the Qing tries to adapt western technology and economic practices to China's needs: railroads, telegraphs, steamships, heavy industry, specialized schools. At the same time, the encroachments of the foreign powers, especially the British, the French and the Japanese, further undermine the Qing, which seems increasingly unable to defend itself.

By 1900, despite the material gains of the Self-strengthening Movement that seeks to modernize China, the dynasty barely breathes. China is a pathetic figure, its venerable institutions incapable of confronting the challenges of modern life. Diplomacy and force impel China to grant long-term territorial leases to foreign powers. Foreign missionaries have free run of the country. Foreign businesses are allowed to open factories on China's soil. External pressures and internal rebellion bring about a final collapse.

There is no clear successor to the fallen dynasty. A long and disturbed interregnum will follow the Qing: warlord rule, ideological conflict, intellectual ferment, a devastating world war, civil war, and revolution.

June 6, 1644: A son of Hong Taiji is enthroned in the Forbidden City as boy emperor of the Qing; he ascends as Shunzhi, with Prince Dorgon as regent. Over the following months, the new rulers chase the eunuchs from the court, establish day-to-day governmental authority, confiscate vast areas of North China farmland to support their armies, and order Chinese men to cut their forelocks and start a queue.

Summer 1644: The Prince of Fu, a grandson of the Ming Emperor Wanli, is enthroned as emperor. He and his supporters move to rally resistance to the conquerors.

December 1644: The rebel leader Zhang Xianzhong proclaims a new "Great Western Kingdom" in Sichuan and rules from Chengdu.

Early 1645: Manchu forces advance southward down the line of the Grand Canal.

Spring 1645: Manchu forces pursue Li Zicheng's Great Shun Army into the mountains of frontier Jiangxi; Li dies (or is murdered) there over the summer.

May 1645: After a short siege, the Manchus take the rich commercial city of Yangzhou. In a ten-day rampage, they sack it thoroughly.

June 1645: Offering scant resistance, Nanjing surrenders to the Manchus. The Prince of Fu is captured and taken north to Beijing, where he dies the next year.

July 1645: Manchus declare any Chinese man who fails to cut his hair and start a queue within ten days will be executed. "Keep your hair and lose your head," the Chinese say, "or lose your hair and keep your head."

1646: Manchus restore national civil service examination system. As in the Ming, the system is built on memorization and analysis of orthodox Confucian texts and on a few approved commentaries (namely Zhu Xi's) on the canon.

January 1647: After withdrawing from Chengdu, which he leaves in ashes, Zhang Xianzhong is tracked and killed by Manchu forces.

January 20, 1647: Guangzhou (Canton) falls to the Manchus. Two Ming pretenders are presently caught and publicly executed in the city.

1648: Chinese troops make up three-quarters of the Manchu banner military formations. The Mongols form 8 percent of the total, the Manchus 16 percent.

1648: An uprising evicts the Manchus from Guangzhou. When Qing forces retake the city in 1650, they carry out a great massacre of the Ming defenders.

1650: With the death of the regent Dorgon, Emperor Shunzhi (born 1638) asserts his authority and rules in his own right. He studies the Chinese language and becomes an admirer of Chinese high culture. He also forms a close friendship with the Jesuit missionary Johann Schall von Bell; he appoints Schall von Bell to head the Imperial Bureau of Astronomy, a key post that oversees the calendar, always a matter of great interest to China's emperors.

1653–1659: The last known surviving grandson of the Wanli emperor, the Prince of Gui (1623–1662), is the last Ming claimant. From his base in the south, he retreats steadily westward, from Guangxi to Guizhou, Yunnan, and finally Burma.

1659: The pirate and trader Zheng Chenggong, known to the West as Koxinga, attacks Manchu Nanjing but is repulsed. When Qing forces pursue him to his stronghold of Xiamen (Amoy), he crosses the Strait of Formosa and attacks the Dutch on Taiwan.

March 1659: Remnants of the Prince of Gui's court and army cross the frontier into Burma.

1660s: Manchu consolidation involves indirect control of South China, which is left to the semiautonomous rule of the so-called Three Feudatories. They are Wu Sangui, Shang Kexi, and Geng Gimao, the three Chinese commanders who subdued most of the region for the Qing in the 1650s. Wu rules Yunnan, Guizhou, and parts of Hunan and Sichuan; Shang controls Guangdong and part of Guangxi; and Geng governs Fujian.

1661: Shunzhi dies, probably of smallpox. His son, eight years old, will succeed him as the Kangxi emperor.

December 1661: Wu Sangui leads Qing expeditionary force into Burma to track down the last Ming claimant.

February 1662: The Dutch on Taiwan surrender to Zheng Chenggong (Koxinga). He dies later in the year, but his successors build a powerful trading empire on the island. Over the next two decades 100,000 Chinese resettle in Taiwan.

January 1662: Burmese hand over the Prince of Gui and his entourage to Wu Sangui.

May 1662: The Prince of Gui and his teenage son are executed in Yunnan.

1669: Kangxi ascends as second emperor of the Qing. Only fifteen, he will rule until 1722. Kangxi is a patron of the Chinese literati. He is much interested in the Jesuits, especially for their knowledge of western science.

December 1673: The Chinese general Wu Sangui, who allied with the Manchus in their invasion of North China, leads a rebellion against the Qing. Two other so-called feudatories will follow him in rebellion. Wu proclaims a new dynasty, the Zhou, and advances northeast into Hunan.

1674: Gen Jingzhong, who succeeds his father as strongman of Fujian, rebels and leads his army northward into Zhejiang. He surrenders independently to the Qing two years later and is put to death.

1676: The third of the feudatories, Shang Zhixin (son of Shang Kexi), revolts. He marches north into Jiangxi but quickly collapses in the face of a Qing counterattack. Shang surrenders in 1677 and is executed.

1678: Wu declares himself emperor of the Zhou. He dies of dysentery later in the year, at the age of sixty-six. Qing loyalists gain momentum and push his supporters steadily westward.

Late 1670s: Powerful Zunghar Western Mongol tribes seize Kashgar, Hami, and Turfan in today's Outer Mongolia and Qinghai along the Tibetan frontier.

c. 1680: After decades of civil war, banditry, general unrest, famine, and other natural disasters, China's population is perhaps 100 million, a decrease of 50 million or more from the estimated population at the beginning of the century.

1681: Zhou resistance collapses in Yunnan; many Zhou leaders are executed. Emperor Kangxi punishes the leading rebels mercilessly, but he shows compassion for ordinary people caught up in events. With the end of the feudatories' rebellion, Qing confirms control over all of China.

July 1683: A Qing naval expedition of three hundred warships destroys Koxinga's forces in the Pescadores. Taiwan itself falls to the Qing in October and is absorbed into the empire.

1689: After a series of border clashes, Chinese and Russian envoys reach a border agreement. The Treaty of Nerchinsk will hold—today's frontier essentially follows the line fixed then.

1696: A Qing army under Emperor Kangxi defeats the Zunghars at Jao Modo beyond the Gobi Desert northwest of Beijing.

1712: The Kangxi emperor issues an edict freezing China's land tax. This effort to encourage land registration and accurate population counts has the longer-term effect of keeping the empire's tax revenues depressed.

1717: Zunghar Mongols invade Tibet. Qing responds with a counterinvasion of the mountain kingdom.

Autumn 1720: Chinese armies occupy Lhasa in Tibet, install a new Dalai Lama loyal to the Qing, and establish a permanent garrison there.

December 1722: Kangxi dies of old age in his Beijing palace. His son Yongzheng, forty-five, ascends. He is a hard worker, a devoted Buddhist, and an adherent of conservative Confucian values.

1729: Yongzheng establishes a secret office of finance to deal with important issues of state. Made up of a small group of senior officials and their secretaries, it is known to Europeans as the Grand Council.

1736–1795: Qianlong, the fourth son of Yongzheng, ascends at age twenty-five as the fourth emperor of the Qing. His is the longest reign in China's history, and an era of sustained population growth and general prosperity. China's territorial extent doubles. Qianlong is a cultured ruler. He increases the holdings of the imperial galleries; he patronizes Jesuit painters at court; he writes and publishes some 42,000 poems. Employing European architects and painters, he will build a magnificent summer palace, the Yuan Ming Yuan, on a lake on the outskirts of Beijing.

Trouble will come, however. Signs of decay are becoming apparent. Population growth puts increasing pressure on the land. Conflict with the Europeans looms. For all the glory of his reign, Qianlong postpones making hard or unpopular decisions, is perhaps incapable of making them.

1750s: Qing absorbs Muslim region of modern Xinjiang province.

1751–1784: Qianlong takes six expensive tours in the southern domains. He is said to spend more than 20 million ounces of silver during his peregrinations of 1751, 1757, 1762, 1765, 1780, and 1784.

1759: Qing forces under the Manchu bannerman Zhaohui capture Kashgar and Yarkand on the far western frontier and carry out a great slaughter of surviving Zunghar defenders. The Manchus do not permit Chinese colonization of the region, however, and they exempt Muslim men from shaving their heads and growing queues.

1774: A herbal healer named Wang Lun leads a White Lotus-inspired outbreak in Shandong. His insurgents take several towns before powerful Qing forces smother the rebellion.

1786: Triad secret societies lead uprising in Taiwan. The Triads, bandits and racketeers with an anti-Manchu political message, soon will spread to mainland South China.

December 1788: A Chinese army, campaigning in Vietnam to intervene in a dynastic conflict, enters Hanoi in triumph.

January 1789: Vietnamese counterattack drives Chinese forces back over the frontier into Guangxi. This will be the last Chinese military campaign in Vietnam until the 1970s.

1790s: The scholar-official Hong Lianji prepares a series of essays that critically consider China's problems, especially population growth that is fast outrunning production capacity.

Truth becomes fiction when the fiction's true.

The Dream of the Red Chamber (*Hung Lou Meng*), by Cao Xueqin (1792)

1792: Qing forces defeat invading Nepalese Gurkhas in Tibet. Nepal agrees to send tribute to Beijing every five years. The tribute payments will continue until 1908.

June 1793: The British Lord George Macartney's trade mission reaches Canton. His flotilla, a sixty-six-gun warship with two escorting vessels, receives permission to sail north to Tianjin, the port of entry for Beijing.

September 1793: Lord Macartney petitions the Qing court for regular (that is to say European-style) relations between the two countries. He asks for the lifting of trade restrictions and for a British resident in Beijing. Macartney is denied an audience at first, for he refuses to perform the submissive bow known as the *kowtow*. When they meet finally, Qianlong rebuffs him. The emperor shows no outward interest even in the products of English industry offered him as gifts: scientific instruments, knives, and woolen goods. "I set no value on objects strange or ingenious, and have no use for your country's manufactures," Qianlong says.

The Empire of China is an old, crazy first rate man-of-war, which a fortunate succession of able and vigilant officers has contrived to keep afloat for these one hundred and fifty years past, and to overawe their neighbors merely by her bulk and appearance.

An Embassy to China, journal of Lord George Macartney (*c.* 1793)

1796–1805: Millenarian White Lotus rebellions enflame Hubei, Sichuan, and Shaanxi provinces. By 1805, Qing punitive campaigns reduce the White Lotus army, once 100,000-strong, to scattered remnants.

1799: Qianlong dies. His favorite, the corrupt and powerful Heshen who dominates court life for the last twenty years of the reign, is arrested and forced to commit suicide.

1799–1820: Jiaqing reigns. He attacks corruption, cuts government expenses, and attempts administrative reforms. His era sees a temporary lessening of tensions with the west, as Europe is caught up in the Napoleonic Wars.

1800: China's population, rising phenomenally, passes 300 million. The lower Yangtze provinces are the most seriously overcrowded. The population of England reaches 11 million.

Needing *cash* to buy Chinese tea, the British East India Company steps up its exports of opium into the country, leading the Qing government to ban the import and domestic production of the addictive drug.

1813: Qing outlaws the smoking of opium.

An estimated 100,000 followers of the millenarian Buddhist Eight Trigrams cult rise near Beijing and capture several towns. A rebel force reaches one of the gates of Beijing before being repulsed. The outbreak claims seventy thousand lives before it is quelled.

1816: The British Lord Amherst (William Pitt) leads a trade and diplomatic mission to Beijing. He barely reaches the capital before he is turned away and humiliatingly expelled from the country.

1821–1850: Daoguang (born 1782) reigns as Qing emperor.

1826: Qing establishes a coastal patrol to cut down on opium smuggling. It soon becomes apparent that Qing naval officers will allow the trade to continue if adequately bribed.

1827: The scholar He Changling publishes his compendium of documents and commentary on Qing statecraft. This wide-ranging work considers the bureaucracy, taxes, banditry, famine relief, flood control, religion, and other matters.

1836: The emperor calls for suppression of the British-controlled opium trade.

June 15, 1836: British government appoints Charles Elliot, a former naval officer, trade commissioner for China.

January 1837: Initial results of the opium crackdown are encouraging. Officials in Guangzhou report two thousand dealers in arrest and the trade at a temporary standstill. But British traders vigorously resist efforts to shut down the fabulously profitable business.

July 10, 1838: In a memorial to the Qing court, scholar-official Lin Zexu proposes harsher punishments for opium smokers, but also a network of state sanitariums to treat addicts. At the same time, he advises a renewed crackdown on opium traders.

January–October 1839: The British opium merchant William Jardine lobbies in London for British government protection of the Guangzhou merchants. He seeks a blockade of China's ports, a new commercial treaty and the opening of new ports to western trade.

March 18, 1839: Lin Zexu is appointed imperial commissioner for suppression of the opium trade. Lin Zexu gives the Cohong merchants of Guangzhou, complicit with the British in the opium trade, three days to persuade foreign traders to hand over their opium stocks. Western houses agree to a to-

ken surrender of one thousand chests. Exasperated, Lin writes to British Queen Victoria: "Suppose there were people from another country who carried opium for sale to England and seduced your people into buying and smoking it; certainly your honourable ruler would deeply hate it and be bitterly aroused." (Opium is not illegal in Britain at this period and is widely used in the form of laudanum.)

March 24, 1839: When the foreign merchants refuse to hand over leading British opium dealer Lancelot Dent, Lin Zexu orders a halt to all foreign trade in Guangzhou. His troops blockade some 350 foreigners in their Guangzhou factories.

March 27, 1839: Charles Elliot, the British commissioner, orders the merchants to surrender their opium stocks, an estimated $9 million worth.

Mid-May 1839: Lin Zexu's crackdown nets 1,600 arrests and 35,000 pounds of opium. He eventually confiscates and destroys nearly 3 million pounds of raw opium.

July 4, 1839: Fearing arrest, the entire British community in Guangzhou is resettled in Portuguese Macau. Over the summer, Elliot sends pleas to London for assistance in the dispute.

August 24, 1839: Under Chinese pressure, Portuguese oust British merchants from Macau. They establish an outpost on sparsely peopled Hong Kong Island.

September 4, 1839: British warships destroy Chinese naval squadron at Kowloon. "Assemble yourselves," runs a Chinese proclamation. "Purchase arms and weapons; join together the stoutest of your villagers and thus be prepared to defend yourselves."

November 4, 1839: British warships fire on Chinese war junks in the Bogue (the mouth of the Pearl River at Guangzhou; Bogue is an English corruption of the Portuguese *boca tigre*, or tiger's mouth), sinking four and scattering the rest.

1840s: Triad secret society networks spread among the peasantry of the Pearl River delta of Guangdong and in the hills to the south. Large Triad bands attack South China cities; Guangzhou (Canton) is briefly threatened.

February 20, 1840: The British government names Admiral George Elliot (Charles Elliot's cousin) to command the naval task force sailing for China.

June 21, 1840: British expeditionary force of sixteen warships with 540 guns and four thousand troops in twenty-eight transports assembles off Macau. Admiral Elliot leaves four ships to blockade Guangzhou and takes the rest of the fleet north.

July 5, 1840: British bombard Zhoushan, occupy the port, and blockade nearby Ningbo on mainland Zhejiang.

August 30, 1840: With the British fleet standing off the Dagu forts guarding Tianjin, the Chinese are forced to negotiate.

January 20, 1841: The Chinese envoy Qishan and British negotiators reach agreement that gives Britain the island of Hong Kong; China agrees to pay the cost of the British expedition (six million Mexican silver dollars) and permit direct British-Chinese contacts. Both sides repudiate the tentative agreement; the Daoguang emperor is so displeased with it he orders Qishan executed.

August 10, 1841: A new British plenipotentiary, Sir Henry Pottinger, reaches Hong Kong.

June–July 1842: With reinforcements from India, British forces capture Shanghai and Zhenjiang, blocking commercial traffic on the lower Yangtze and the Grand Canal.

August 5, 1842: A British expeditionary force pushes up to the walls of Nanjing. Six days later, China again sues for peace.

August 29, 1842: The Treaty of Nanking (Nanjing) is signed aboard HMS *Cornwallis* at anchor in the Yangtze. It awards a further indemnity of 21 million ounces of silver, opens five treaty ports (Guangzhou, Xiamen, Fuzhou, Ningbo, and Shanghai), fixes a five percent tariff on imports, decrees that British subjects answer only to British law, even in disputes with Chinese, and gives

Hong Kong to Britain. The treaty is a great humiliation for China, long used to making its own decisions about the status of foreigners in the country. It sets the tone for a series of unequal treaties between China and the European powers later in the century. Daoguang accepts the treaty in September; Britain's Queen Victoria approves it in December.

Spring 1844: American and Chinese diplomats negotiate the Treaty of Wanghia, which gives the United States similar rights to Britain in China. Among other things, it opens new opportunities for American Protestant missionaries.

October 1844: France negotiates a commercial treaty with China along the lines of the British and American agreements.

1850: China's population reaches 425 million.

Thus all the people in the empire may together enjoy the abundant happiness of the heavenly father, Supreme Lord and great God. There being fields, let all cultivate them; there being food, let all eat; there being clothes, let all be dressed; there being money, let all use it, so that nowhere does inequality exist, and no man is not well fed and clothed.

The Taiping Manifesto (1850–1864)

1850–1864: The Taiping Rebellion, the greatest peasant revolt of the 19th century, sweeps China. Its leader is the charismatic Hong Xiuquan (born 1814), a Hakka (an ethnic Chinese minority of southeast China) and failed examination candidate who has come to believe he is the younger brother of Jesus. From his base in Guangxi, Hong orders his paramilitary followers to destroy temples and idols, give up alcohol and opium, and end the custom of footbinding women.

December 1850: Hong Xiuquan's militia defeats a government punitive column at Thistle Mountain.

1851–1861: Xianfeng reigns as Qing emperor.

1851: Nian rebels rise in east central China north of the Huai River. Unlike Hong Xiuquan's rebels to the south, the Nian have no direct religious affiliation or political program. Most are poor peasants, landless single men.

January 11, 1851: Hong Xiuquan declares himself king of the Heavenly Kingdom of Great Peace. His insurgent forces advance east and north, picking up adherents and weapons along the way.

July–December 1852: The Qing loyalist Zeng Guofan (1811–1872) organizes a local force, to be known as the Xiang Army, to defend his Hunan estates from the Taipings. He will become the most effective imperial commander in the rebellion.

September 1852: Taiping rebels take Changsha in Hunan.

December 1852: A Taiping army seizes Yuezhou on Dongting Lake and captures a large stockpile of arms and ammunition.

January 1853: Taiping insurgents reach Wuchang on the Yangtze, then push up to the walls of Nanjing.

March 19, 1853: Nanjing falls to Taiping rebels. They carry out a great slaughter of all Manchu survivors of the battle, including women and children.

The rebels will rule Nanjing for eleven years. They set up a government in Nanjing, call for land equalization (but do not carry it out), and propose equality between men and women. The Taiping system of civil service examinations is based on Hong Xiuquan's teachings and a Chinese translation of the Bible.

1854: Qing government establishes a foreign-staffed Inspectorate of Customs. The agency collects maritime customs that provide a steady stream of revenue for the imperial treasury.

May 1853–May 1855: A Taiping expeditionary force strikes north. After wintering over near Tianjin in 1854–1855, Taiping columns begin a slow, costly retreat southward. Qing loyalists destroy the last remnants of the insurgent expedition in the spring of 1855.

1855: Major Yellow River flooding and subsequent famine swell the ranks of the Nian rebels north of the Huai River.

1855: Muslims rise in Yunnan in the southwest, taking the city of Dali and advancing on the provincial capital of Kunming.

1856: Zhang Luoxing becomes "Lord of the Alliance" of Nian rebel groups. They raid throughout east central China from a series of moated strongholds north of the Huai.

August 1856: To forestall a suspected coup, Hong Xiquan orders the execution of Taiping leader and chief military adviser Yang Xiuqing; twenty thousand of Yang's followers are massacred.

December 1856: Qing loyalists recapture Wuchang from the Taiping rebels. By year's end, the loyalist Xiang Army regains most of Jiangxi.

December 28, 1857–January 4, 1858: The British, rebuffed in efforts to renegotiate the Treaty of Nanking of 1842, seize Guangzhou.

May 1858: British expedition takes the Dagu forts outside Tianjin, opening the way to Beijing.

July 3, 1858: British military pressure forces China to accept the Treaty of Tientsin. It protects Christianity, opens the Chinese interior to foreign travelers, extends trade up the Yangtze as far as Hankou, and establishes ten new treaty ports. Finally, the agreement stipulates that the Chinese character for *barbarian*, used to describe the British, be dropped from Chinese documents.

September 1858: Resurgent Taipings defeat the Xiang (Hunan) Army in northern Anhui.

June 1859: To enforce the Treaty of Tientsin, the British again attack the Dagu forts. They are repulsed this time with a loss of 432 killed and wounded and four gunboats sunk.

1860: The scholar Feng Guifen writes a series of essays on government and society that helps to launch the late Qing Self-strengthening Movement. He calls for the teaching of foreign languages, mathematics, and science to catch China up with the western powers. In response, the Qing establishes arsenals, shipyards, and schools that teach foreign languages and technological subjects.

1860: The Mongol general Senggelinqin leads a Qing campaign against the Nian rebels. The Nian leader Zhang Luoxing is killed in the fighting.

June 1860: Taiping columns capture Suzhou and advance eastward toward the rich lower Yangtze cities.

August 25, 1860: British and French forces enter Tianjin after seizing the Dagu forts.

September 1860: Qing authorities intercept British and French envoys traveling to Beijing. Thirty-eight Europeans are seized and twenty-five are executed. Sir Frederick Bruce, Britain's chief negotiator, orders a reinforced British-French column to march on Beijing.

October 18, 1860: Anglo-French expeditionary force occupies Beijing. On Bruce's orders, European troops burn Qianlong's elegant Summer Palace on the capital's outskirts but spare the Forbidden City. The Qing agrees to affirm the 1858 treaty. In addition, China cedes to Britain part of the Kowloon Peninsula on the mainland opposite Hong Kong and in effect legalizes the opium trade.

1861–1875: Tongzhi is the Qing emperor. He is five when he ascends the throne, and China's real rulers are his mother, the dowager empress Cixi (1835–1908), and an uncle, Prince Gong. Together with a small group of key senior officials, they carry out a series of administrative and economic reforms that shore up what appears to be a tottering dynasty.

November 11, 1861: Qing establishes the Zongli Yamen (Office for the Management of the Business of All Foreign Countries)—a forerunner of a ministry of foreign affairs. Along with attempting to manage recurring crises with the western powers, the bureau is involved in establishing foreign language schools, analyzing international law, and

studying western government forms and institutions. It also oversees and reviews all legal cases involving Chinese Christians, inasmuch as it understands that foreign powers may intervene on the converts' behalf.

1862: Muslims rise in Shaanxi and Gansu in northwest China.

January–May 1862: Taipings threaten Shanghai; the city's westerners help defend the city. Along with Zeng Guofan's Hunan columns, Qing employs a large mercenary force, the Ever Victorious Army, with a heavy complement of foreign officers; it is led first by the American adventurer Frederick Townsend Ward and later by the British Major Charles "Chinese" Gordon.

June 1862: With British and French help, Qing loyalists repulse a renewed Taiping attack on Shanghai.

June 1, 1864: Hong Xiuquan dies in the Taiping capital of Nanjing.

July 19, 1864: Zeng Guofan with his 120,000-strong Xiang Army retakes Nanjing, bringing the Taipeng rebellion to a close.

1865–1866: Revived Nian rebel armies defeat Qing loyalists in a series of battles in Hubei, Anhui, and Shandong; in one, the Mongol general Senggelinqin is killed.

January–August 1868: In a relentless campaign, Qing forces trap and crush Nian insurgent forces along the Grand Canal, then suppress the last of Nian resistance in Shandong.

1873: Qing forces retake Dali from Muslim insurgents, bringing the Yunnan rebellion to an end.

November 1873: Qing army captures Suzhou in northwest Gansu. The long Muslim rebellion in the northwest collapses.

January 1875: Emperor Tongzhi dies. His mother, the dowager empress Cixi, appoints her nephew Guangxu, three years old, as successor and continues to rule as regent. Cixi, smart and capable, is the only woman to reach a position of great power in Qing China.

1879: Zuo Zongtang leads a Qing punitive

expedition against Muslim insurgents in Xinjiang on the northwest frontier.

1880: China has diplomatic legations in London, Paris, Berlin, Madrid, Washington, Tokyo, and St. Petersburg.

1884: Xinjiang ("New Territory") is made a regular province of China.

August 22, 1884: French warships attack a Chinese fleet in Fuzhou harbor after negotiations break down over France's colonial expansion into Vietnam. Within an hour every Chinese ship—all but two are of wood—is sunk or afire and the arsenal is wrecked. More than five hundred Chinese perish.

1885: Taiwan becomes a full province of China.

1894: The reformer Sun Yat-sen (Sun Zhongshan, 1866–1925), educated in mission schools in Hawaii, offers his services to the senior scholar-official Li Hongzhang. Rebuffed, he forms the Revive China Society in Hawaii and pledges the overthrow of the Manchus.

1894: Rebellion breaks out in Korea. Both China and Japan send expeditionary forces to subdue it.

July 21, 1894: Japanese troops seize the Korean royal palace in Seoul and install a puppet regent. At sea, a Japanese warship sinks a Chinese troopship, drowning a thousand soldiers en route to Korea.

Late July 1894: Japanese defeat Chinese armies in a series of battles around Seoul and P'yongyang.

September 1894: Japanese naval forces attack Chinese fleet of two battleships and ten cruisers off the mouth of the Yalu. The Chinese admiral retreats to the strongly defended port of Weihaiwei.

October 1894: Japanese forces cross the Yalu River into Qing territory.

January 1895: Japanese column marches overland and takes the Weihaiwei forts from the landward side. The Japanese turn the fort's guns on the Chinese fleet, sinking one of the battleships and four cruisers.

April 1895: The Treaty of Shimonoseki forces

China to recognize the "independence" of Korea (Japan takes effective control of the country), pay an indemnity of 200 million ounces of silver, cede Taiwan, the Pescadores, and Liaodong in southern Manchuria, open four new treaty ports, and allow Japan to open factories in China. European protests pressure the Japanese to return Liaodong. But the Europeans seize Chinese territory for themselves: Germany in Jiaozhou in Shandong; the Russians in part of Liadong; the British in Weihaiwei and the New Territories opposite Hong Kong; and France in Guangzhou Bay.

1895–1898: Kang Youwei (1858–1927) leads a group of young reformers in protesting the treaty with Japan and in pressing the Qing government for change. They hope to extend the Self-strengthening Movement through a wide-ranging set of educational, economic, and administrative reforms. Kang attempts to meld traditional Confucian thought and modern development, arguing that the master had not resisted social and economic change. His *A Study of Confucius as a Reformer* is published in 1898.

1896: The reformer Liang Qichao (1873–1929) founds the influential journal *Chinese Progress* in Shanghai. He publishes essays arguing that China needs to adopt western political thought and institutions as well as technology.

1897: Germany occupies Jiaozhou Bay and Qingdao island off the Shandong Peninsula. Germans establish the brewery there that still makes Qingdao beer.

1898–1899: The United States tries to inaugurate an "Open Door" policy for China; with limited success, the initiative seeks to arrest the Great Powers' dividing of China into "spheres of influence."

1898: The secret society of the Harmonious Fists rises in northwest Shandong. Known in the West as the Boxers, they blame all China's ills on foreigners. Mostly young, male, and poor, they find allies among women's groups such as the Red Lanterns Shining.

March 1898: Qing court grants Russia twenty-five-year leases of the ports of Dailan and Lushun (Port Arthur) on the Liaodong Peninsula.

June–September 1898: Emperor Guangxu launches the so-called Hundred Days Reforms in government, education, commerce, and the military. He orders the examination system modernized (dropping calligraphy as an important subject, for example), the Beijing college upgraded with the addition of a medical school, mining and railroad institutes established, and military training and weaponry updated.

September 21, 1898: The dowager Cixi issues an edict announcing that the emperor has asked her to resume power. Guangxu is put under palace arrest, six leading reformers are executed without trial, and most of the reforms are canceled. Kang Youwei, absent from the capital at the time of the coup, and Liang Qichao manage to escape abroad.

Although she is a clever politician, Cixi's corruption and conservatism are perhaps exaggerated. Still, she is wholly committed to the traditional system, and particularly to her own survival in power.

Early 1899: Boxers step up attacks on Chinese Christian converts along the Shandong-Hebei border. Foreign missionaries call on Qing forces to quell the outbreaks.

June 1900: Armed Boxer groups appear in Beijing and Tianjin. Several foreign missionaries and engineers are killed. Western powers send a contingent of four hundred troops to protect foreigners in the capital.

June 17, 1900: Westerners seize the Dagu forts in preparation for the landing of a punitive expedition at Tianjin.

June 19, 1900: Boxers lay siege to the legation quarter in Beijing.

June 21, 1900: The dowager Cixi issues a proclamation against the Western powers. Boxers respond with stepped-up attacks on the missions and other foreigners. In the pro-vincial city of Taiyuan southwest of Beijing, Qing officials with Boxer sympathies round up and murder forty-four missionary men, women, and children.

August 1900: The reformer Kang Youwei launches a rising in Hubei and Anhui. His aim is to restore Guangxu as a constitutional monarch. Qing forces subdue the brief insurgency.

August 4, 1900: A multinational column of 20,800 troops (Japan, Russia, Britain, the United States, and France are represented) marches from Tianjin toward Beijing.

August 14, 1900: Western troops enter Beijing, lift the legation siege, and loot the city. The dowager and emperor flee, establishing a temporary capital at Xian in the Wei River valley.

October 1900: Sun Yat-sen's small-scale republican uprising near Guangzhou is quickly suppressed.

January 1901: From Xian, the dowager empress Cixi issues a call for reforms similar to those of 1898. In one of the most fateful changes, the Qing moves to reorganize the semi-autonomous provincial armed forces and the traditional Manchu banner formations into a "New Army" of 450,000 men modeled along western lines.

September 1901: Under duress, China signs the treaty known as the Boxer Protocol. It requires China to pay a staggering indemnity of $330 million, execute leading Boxers and their supporters, and permit foreign troops to garrison the legation quarter of Beijing.

1902–1907: From exile in Japan, Liang Qichao edits the influential reform journal *New People's Miscellany*.

June 1902: Cixi and Emperor Guangxu return to Beijing.

1903: The Japanese-educated political activist Zou Rong publishes his anti-Manchu creed, *The Revolutionary Army*. He challenges China to overthrow the Manchus and end foreign domination of the country. Zou also calls for elected legislatures, equality of women and freedoms of press and assembly. He will die of illness in a Shanghai prison in 1905.

1905: Sun Yat-sen brings several radical groups together in the Revolutionary Alliance. It follows a republican and generally socialist political line.

1905: The Qing court abolishes the examination system, the basis of traditional Chinese education.

1906: Qing establishes a Ministry of Posts and Communications. Among other things, the new bureau oversees China's growing railroad network.

1906: A summary and partial translation of Karl Marx's *Communist Manifesto* circulates in China.

September 1906: The dowager Cixi appoints a constitutional commission to tour Japan, the United States, Britain, France, Germany, Italy, and Russia and study their government structures. On return, the committee recommends imperial/parliamentary Japan as a model for China.

November 1906: Cixi issues an edict promising a constitution for China and reform of government administration. In 1908, the Qing will announce a plan to introduce constitutional government gradually over a nine-year period.

1907: Yuan Shi-kai (1859–1916), the reforming governor of Tianjin, authorizes elections for a local council.

July 1907: The Zhejiang schoolteacher Qiu Jin leads an anti-Qing rising. Captured and executed after a short trial, she becomes a revolutionary martyr.

November 1908: Emperor Guangxu and the dowager Cixi die within a day of each other. The infant Puyi (1905–1967) ascends as the tenth and last emperor of the Qing.

October 1909: China's first provincial assemblies, the product of the Qing's hesitant reforms, convene.

October 1910: Under the auspices of the Qing government, a provisional National Assembly meets in Beijing.

November 1910: Qing court agrees to speed constitutional process, announcing it will allow a fully elected national parliament to meet in November 1913.

October 9, 1911: An accidental explosion in a revolutionary bomb factory brings matters to a head in the mid-Yangtze industrial city of Hankou. Qing police raid the revolutionary headquarters and summarily execute three leaders.

October 10, 1911: A New Army unit sympathetic to the revolutionaries mutinies in Wuchang. Other units rally to its support later in the day. Next day, the revolutionary societies touch off a rising in the third of the Wuhan cities, Hanyang.

October 12, 1911: Hankou garrison mutinies.

October 22, 1911: The revolt spreads. New Army units mutiny in Shaanxi and Hunan, killing many imperial officials. By the end of October Shanxi, Jiangxi, and Yunnan provinces are in revolt.

October 30, 1911: Qing court authorizes the National Assembly to draft a constitution.

November 1911: Jiang Kanghu founds the first Chinese socialist party.

November–December 1911: Jiangsu, Sichuan, and Shandong provincial assemblies declare for the Revolutionary Alliance.

November 8, 1911: Beijing provisional National Assembly elects the Qing reformer Yuan Shi-kai premier of China.

November 11, 1911: Qing court ratifies National Assembly's appointment of Yuan Shi-kai and orders him to form a cabinet.

Early December 1911: New Army revolutionaries capture Nanjing.

December 25, 1911: Revolutionary Alliance leader Sun Yat-sen reaches Shanghai from France.

December 29, 1911: Delegates from sixteen provincial assemblies choose Sun Yat-sen as president of the provisional Republic of China.

January 1, 1912: Sun Yat-sen takes office in Nanjing. His provisional government announces China henceforth will abandon the

hai. Some 600,000 workers walk off the job. Power and telephone lines are cut and there is heavy fighting in much of the city. Some 22,000 foreign troops and police and forty-two warships guard the International Settlement.

March 22, 1927: Nationalist forces enter Shanghai.

March 23, 1927: Nationalist vanguard enters Nanjing.

March 24, 1927: Nationalist troops in Nanjing loot the British, Japanese, and American consulates, killing six foreigners. American and British warships covering the evacuation of fifty foreign nationals shell the city, killing as many as thirty-nine Chinese (the figures are disputed).

April 12, 1927: Chiang Kai-shek orders the Shanghai racketeering organization known as the Green Gang to attack union headquarters in the city. Hundreds of union leaders and other leftists are murdered over the next several weeks.

April 18, 1927: Defying the Guomindang leaders in Wuhan, Chiang Kai-shek forms a Nationalist government with himself at the head. He establishes his capital at Nanjing. The "Left" Guomindang remains in control in Wuhan.

September 1927: Communists attempt to strike back at the right-wing Nationalists with the "Autumn Harvest Uprising," a series of attacks on several Hunan towns led by Mao Zedong. They are unsuccessful. For the next three years, Chiang Kai-shek's Nationalists will hunt down Communists throughout the country.

October 1927: Mao Zedong leads a thousand survivors of the Nationalist purges and Autumn Uprising defeats into the Jinggang Mountains along the Hunan-Jiangxi border.

December 11, 1927: On orders from Stalin, the Communist Qu Qiubai (1889–1935) leads an uprising in Guangzhou (Canton). Guomindang and warlord troops crush the so-called Canton Commune after two days.

They can be divided into soldiers, bandits, robbers, beggars, and prostitutes. But they are all human beings, and they all have five senses and four limbs, and are therefore one. To the extent that they must all earn their livelihood and cook rice to eat, they are one.

Mao Zedong (1928)

Late 1928: Nationalist pressure forces Mao Zedong's little army out of the Jinggang Mountains. He resettles in a mountainous district along the Jiangxi-Fujian border and establishes the Jiangxi Soviet there, with his main base in the town of Riujin. Separate Soviets operate in remote regions of Anhui, Hubei, Hunan, Zhejiang, and Guangxi.

March 1928: Chiang Kai-shek's forces resume the Northern Expedition. He finances it largely by extortionate levies on Shanghai's Chinese industrialists.

April 1928: Nationalist columns campaign in Shandong.

May 3–11, 1928: Nationalist Chinese and Japanese forces clash around and in the Yellow River city of Jinan. The Japanese, protecting their concessions in Jinan, drive the Nationalists from the city after heavy fighting.

June 2, 1928: Zhang Zuolin, the most powerful of the northern warlords, withdraws from Beijing. Two days later, he dies when a bomb explosion wrecks his northbound train. Japanese army officers are responsible.

June 8 and 12, 1928: Nationalists occupy Beijing and Tianjin.

December 29, 1928: Zhang Xueliang, successor to his murdered father as Manchurian warlord, declares his loyalty to the Nationalist government, completing China's nominal unification. (Only four provinces, Jiangsu, Zhejiang, Anhui, and Jiangxi, are under Nationalist control.) Nanjing is declared the official capital of China.

January 1929: National Reorganization and Demobilization Conference agrees to limit China's armies to 800,000 men and cap military spending at 41 percent of the total budget.

March–May 1929: Chiang Kai-shek consolidates his power by suppressing military uprisings in Guangxi and Shandong.

July–September 1930: A bloody civil war rages between the Nanjing government and the anti-Chiang Kai-shek Northern Coalition. Chiang's forces emerge as the winner; the conflict costs 250,000 casualties on both sides.

September 18, 1931: Japanese provocateurs sabotage the South Manchurian Railway near Mukden (Shenyang) and use the incident as a pretext to occupy the city. China appeals to the League of Nations. The League recognizes China's claim, but fails to sanction Japan for the so-called Mukden Incident. By year's end, Nationalist forces have withdrawn south of the Great Wall and the Japanese are in full control of Manchuria.

January 1932: Chiang Kai-shek resumes the office of president after a temporary "retirement" from public life following the Mukden Incident. He also holds the titles of chief of the General Staff and chairman of the National Military Council.

January 29, 1932: After an exchange of fire with Nationalist troops, Japanese forces attack Shanghai. The Japanese bomb the working class district of Chapei from the air, killing many civilians.

March 1932: The deposed emperor Puyi, twenty-five, is named "chief executive" of the Japanese puppet state in Manchuria, now dubbed "Manchukuo"—Chinese for "Manchurian nation."

May 1932: Japan agrees to an armistice that ends three months of fighting around Shanghai.

July–October 1932: The third in a series of Nationalist "Bandit Suppression Campaigns" aimed at the Communists threatens Mao Zedong's Jiangxi Soviet. Nationalists launch the "3:7" program—an anti-Communist campaign three parts military and seven parts political. The political component includes local government reform, rent reduction, and food, seed, tools, and other aid to the peasantry.

January–April 1933: Japanese forces advance into Rehe province in northeast China. After weeks of hard fighting, they take complete control of the province.

February 1933: The League of Nations rejects the idea of an independent existence for Manchuria. In response, the Japanese take permanent leave of the international organization.

May 1933: Japanese troops move into Hebei province south of the Great Wall. At month's end China sues for peace. The truce negotiated at Tanggu declares northeast Hebei a demilitarized zone; the Japanese pull back to the Great Wall.

October 1933: Nationalists begin their fifth military campaign against the Communists.

1934: Chiang Kai-shek launches the Fascist-inspired New Life Movement. The object is to make the Chinese "willing to sacrifice for the nation at all times." Also on the Fascist pattern, young military academy graduates known as the Blueshirts (founded in 1932) act as a Nationalist secret police, spying on political opponents, and carrying out assassinations and lesser acts of intimidation.

Only those who readapt themselves to new conditions, day by day, can live properly. When the life of a people is going through this process of readaptation, it has to remedy its own defects, and get rid of those elements which become useless. Then we call it new life.

Chiang Kai-shek (1934)

March 1934: Puyi is installed as "emperor" of Manchukuo.

August 1934: Germany and China sign a secret military and economic aid treaty. Modern German arms and industrial capacity are to be exchanged for strategic raw materials from China.

August–September 1934: Under intense pressure from Nationalist blockade and encirclement (the 5th Bandit Suppression Campaign), Communist military leaders plan a breakout from the Jiangxi Soviet.

October 16, 1934: Some eighty thousand Communist troops and support units fight their way out of the Nationalist encirclement and begin the famous Long March, the great saga of China's Communist Party. Some twenty thousand wounded and many women and children are left behind to await Nationalist occupation.

January 7, 1935: Communists reach Zunyi in Guizhou province, where they replenish their stores from large stocks of food and clothing.

January 15–18, 1935: At the Zunyi Conference, Communist leaders analyze the Jiangxi failure. Mao Zedong is raised to full Politburo membership, an important step on his climb to complete control of the Chinese Communist Party.

May–June 1935: Communists march north into Sichuan and cross the rugged Great Snow Mountains. They reach Mougong on June 12 with around forty thousand men—half their strength at the outset of the Long March.

August–September 1935: Communist columns advance slowly through marshlands along the Qinghai/Gansu border. Exhaustion, illness, and exposure claim thousands of Long Marchers.

October 20, 1935: The Red Army, down to a strength of around eight thousand men, links up with Communist guerrillas in remote northern Shaanxi and establishes a new base at Yan'an. Thus the year-long, six-thousand-mile Long March ends. In December, Mao Zedong sums it up with these words: "It is a manifesto, a propaganda force, a seeding machine. It has proclaimed to the world that the Red Army is an army of heroes, while the imperialists and their running dogs, Chiang Kai-shek and the like, are impotent."

In Yan'an Mao formulates his theory of the peasantry rather than the proletariat as being the vanguard of revolution. He also wins a power struggle for control of the Communist Party, eliminating one rival after another.

December 9, 1935: Thousands of students rally in Beijing to protest Japanese aggression. The protests spread quickly to Nanjing, Wuhan, Shanghai, Hangzhou, and Guangzhou.

1936: A Nationalist government count puts China's population at 479,084,651.

October–November 1936: Chinese defenders repulse invasion of Japanese puppet forces in northern province of Suiyuan.

December 12, 1936: Chinese troops loyal to the Manchurian warlord Zhang Xueliang seize Chiang Kai-shek in Xian. They demand an end to the civil war and a united front with the Communists against Japan.

December 25, 1936: Chiang Kai-shek is freed after he agrees to ease military pressure on the Communists and take steps toward a united front.

July 7, 1937: Chinese troops fire on a Japanese unit near the strategic Marco Polo Bridge west of Beijing. Japan responds with an attack on the rail junction town of Wanping. The "Marco Polo Bridge Incident" will touch off a full-scale war.

July 27–31, 1937: Renewed fighting breaks out around the Marco Polo Bridge; Japanese seize control of the entire Beijing-Tianjin area.

August 14, 1937: The Chinese Nationalist air force bombs Japanese warships at anchor off Shanghai. The Nationalists miss their targets and hit the city instead, killing hundreds of civilians.

August–October 1937: In a series of fierce battles around Shanghai, Nationalists absorb 250,000 casualties—knocking more than half of Chiang Kai-shek's best troops out of action.

September 1937: As part of the united front agreement, the Red Army is redesignated the 8th Route Army and placed under nominal

Nationalist command. The Nanjing government will authorize a second Communist army, dubbed the New Fourth Army, in 1938.

November 1937: Japanese warplanes attack and sink the U.S. gunboat *Panay* as it attempts to evacuate American nationals from Nanjing.

November 11, 1937: Nationalists begin their retreat west from Shanghai.

December 13, 1937: Japanese forces enter Nanjing and launch a savage campaign of terror. At least twenty thousand women are rape victims; some 140,000 civilians and Chinese soldiers are murdered. (Some recent research suggests these figures are underestimates.) Japanese looting and arson leaves much of the city in ruins. Westerners call the seven-week rampage the Rape of Nanking.

Early 1938: Nationalist armies retreat westward up the Yangtze. As the Japanese advance, they establish puppet regimes to rule their China conquests, with Chinese collaborators in nominal authority.

May 1938: As the Japanese approach the ancient capital of Kaifeng, Chiang Kai-shek orders Yellow River dikes blown up. The demolition inundates four thousand villages, kills many peasants, and delays the Japanese advance by four months.

October 21, 1938: Japanese amphibious forces seize Guangzhou (Canton).

October 25, 1938: After months of heavy fighting, Japanese forces take Wuhan. They now control most of east China from Beijing south to Guangzhou.

December 2, 1938: The mountainous, 715-mile-long Burma Road, now the Nationalists' sole reliable supply route, officially opens. First shipments from Rangoon reach Kunming, the Yunnan capital, later in the month.

December 8, 1938: Chiang Kai-shek reaches Chongqing in Sichuan one thousand miles up the Yangtze and establishes the Nationalist capital there.

May 1939: The Japanese air force begins systematic bombing of Chongqing.

September–October 1939: With signing of the Nazi-Soviet pacts, the Soviet Union cuts off military aid to China.

1940: Communists intensify recruitment efforts in their North China strongholds. Party membership climbs to 800,000 and the Communists steadily widen their base of support among the peasantry.

1940: The United States agrees to ship one hundred P-40 fighter aircraft to the Nationalists. Former American air force officer Claire L. Chennault, an adviser to Chiang Kai-shek, recruits U.S. pilots for service in China. They will become famous as the Flying Tigers.

August 20, 1940: Communist forces launch a series of attacks against the Japanese in North China known as the Hundred Regiments Offensive. The operation is a failure. Counterattacking Japanese inflict 100,000 casualties on the Communists in September and October, devastating the region through which they pass, destroying entire villages in some instances.

January 7–13, 1941: Nationalists attack Communist New Fourth Army units south of the Yangtze. The so-called New Fourth Army Incident virtually ends the Nationalist/Communist united front against Japan. Communists withdraw and regroup north of the river. Chiang Kai-shek imposes an economic blockade, sharply restricting the flow of food and weapons to Communist forces.

August–October 1941: Japanese troops, in a North China pacification campaign, kill 4,500 villagers, burn 150,000 dwellings, and ship 17,000 Chinese to Manchuria as forced laborers.

December 1941: British Hong Kong falls to the Japanese.

February 1, 1942: Communists at Yan'an open a "Rectification Campaign" of ideological purification. Continuing into 1943, it features readings of Mao's texts, public confessions, and public humiliation of Mao's rivals such as party theorist Wang Ming. Mao's line becomes unchallengeable, any deviation from it attacked as subjective, liberal, and petty bourgeois.

April 1942: Japanese forces seize the Burmese town of Lashio, sealing off the Burma Road and cutting a vital allied supply line into China.

1943: Nationalists conscript 1.67 million men for military service. An estimated 44 percent die or desert before they join their commands.

January 1943: The Allies agree to abolish the system of extraterritoriality that for a century has denied China full control of its own affairs.

March 1943: Japanese troops round up the foreign community of Beijing, around 1,500 adults and children, for transfer to an internment camp in Shandong.

April–November 1944: Japanese forces go over to the offensive, marching south through Hunan along the Xiang River to Changsha and then onto Henyang and Guilin in Guangxi. The objective is twofold: to open a north-south overland communications corridor stretching from Korea to Vietnam, and to knock out U.S. airfields. The Ichigo Campaign, as the Japanese dub the operation, exposes the hollowness and incapacity of Chiang Kai-shek's Nationalist forces, which acknowledge taking 300,000 casualties.

June 1944: U.S. heavy bombers launch raids on Japanese targets from Chinese airfields. On June 15 the Americans bomb Japan from China for the first time, hitting a steel plant on the southern island of Kyushu.

August 1944: The U.S. observer group known as the Dixie Mission reaches the Communist bastion at Yan'an; the American high command discusses offering aid to Mao Zedong's forces.

January 1944: Americans shelve plans to aid Communist forces in the face of intense opposition from the Nationalists.

October 1944: At Chiang Kai-shek's urging,

the U.S. recalls Gen. Joseph Stilwell, America's liaison with the Nationalists since 1941. Stilwell has become an increasingly harsh critic of the Chinese generalissimo.

April 1945: Communist Party membership in North China reaches 1.2 million. The 8th Route and New 4th armies muster 900,000 men. Communists claim authority over territory with a population of 95 million.

August 8, 1945: Soviet forces advance against the Japanese in Manchuria.

August 14, 1945: After two U.S. atomic attacks on Japanese cities, Japan surrenders, bringing World War II to a close.

August–September 1945: Under an agreement with the Nationalists, United States forces occupy four key Chinese ports, Shanghai, Dagu (Tianjin), Qingdao, and Guangzhou. U.S. Marine contingents are sent to Beijing and Tianjin. A U.S. airlift moves 110,000 Nationalist troops to key cities. Japanese commanders are instructed not to surrender to Communist units. At the same time, the 100,000-strong Communist 8th Route Army under Lin Biao moves into Manchuria and occupies the region's key cities. Soviet forces in Manchuria allow Lin Biao's command access to stockpiles of Japanese arms and ammunition.

September 1945: Nationalists allow Japanese puppet government officials to retain their positions in many places, largely as a means of blocking Communist expansion. Some collaborators are given senior rank in the Nationalist army.

October 10, 1945: U.S.-sponsored negotiations between Nationalists and Communists yield a joint statement on political democracy, a unified military force, and equal legal status for all political organizations. There are, however, no mechanisms for enforcing the agreement.

November 15, 1945: Nationalists attack Communist forces in Manchuria.

Late November 1945: The U.S. ambassador to China, Patrick Hurley, resigns abruptly. He accuses American foreign service officers of favoring the Communists and undermining U.S. efforts to stabilize the Chiang Kaishek regime.

December 23, 1945: U.S. special envoy General George C. Marshall arrives in China.

January 11–31, 1946: Representatives of the Communists, the Guomindang, and other political parties meet in Nanjing for a "political consultative conference." They reach accord on constitutional government, a unified military, and a national assembly. Meantime, both sides violate the truce and military clashes are frequent. The Nationalists breach the Nanjing political agreement, reserving the presidency for Chiang Kai-shek and moving to limit the power of the Communists in the proposed new State Council.

January 13, 1946: A cease-fire negotiated by the Marshall Mission takes effect.

Spring 1946: Both sides repeatedly violate the truce in Manchuria. Communist forces resist Nationalist efforts to occupy Manchurian cities but are gradually forced to retreat to the north.

June 7, 1946: U.S. envoy Marshall negotiates a two-week cease-fire in Manchuria. The truce is extended to month's end, but the Nationalists and Communists fail to reach an accord.

July 1946: Nationalists renew the offensive in the northeast, formally opening the Chinese Civil War of 1946–1949. The Communists reorganize their forces as the People's Liberation Army.

Nationalist forces are successful in the first phase of the war. Between July 1946 and June 1947 they occupy most major cities in northeastern China, cross the Yellow River and advance into southern Shanxi, and record military gains elsewhere. In Manchuria, the Nationalists force the 8th Route Army to withdraw beyond the Sungari River to the stronghold of Harbin.

July 1946: Communist units attack a U.S. supply convoy en route from Tianjin to Beijing. Three Americans are killed, a fourth is mortally wounded, and a dozen others are injured.

Late July 1946: U.S. places embargo on shipments of war materiel to China. It will be lifted partially in October and entirely in May 1947.

October 1946: General Marshall, charging the Nationalists are using negotiations as a cover for operations against the Communists, recommends the recall of his mission.

October 10, 1946: Nationalist troops drive Communists from Kalgan in North China.

November 1946: Communist troops under Lin Biao cross the frozen Sungari River, attack the Nationalists in their winter camps, then withdraw. Lin repeats these hit-and-run tactics in January, February, and March 1947, inflicting casualties, capturing weapons stocks, and disrupting Nationalist plans for an offensive.

November 1946: Acting on its own, the Guomindang convenes a national assembly and drafts a constitution. The Communists and other political parties are not involved.

January 6, 1947: The Marshall Mission is ended. By the last day of the month, all U.S. negotiating teams are dissolved.

May 1947: Nationalist offensive begins to lose momentum. Lin Biao's 400,000-strong Communist army launches a counteroffensive against Nationalist-held cities in Manchuria, isolating the garrisons by cutting the cities' railroad links. Apathy spreads through the Nationalist ranks.

June–August 1947: Separate Communist armies cross the Yellow River and advance into Henan, Hebei, and Anhui.

April 1948: Communists recapture their old Shaanxi stronghold of Yan'an.

April 1948: Luoyang falls to the Communists. The Nationalist government's National Assembly meets to elect a president and vice president.

May 1948: Communist army surrounds Mukden (Shenyang), trapping 200,000 Nationalist troops who can be supplied only by air.

July 1948: An estimated five thousand Manchurian students in Beijing rally in protest of Nationalist policies; police open fire on the crowd, killing fourteen and wounding more than one hundred.

August 19, 1948: Chiang Kai-shek imposes a series of Financial and Economic Emergency Measures in an effort to stave off economic collapse. They limit inflation-inducing printing of banknotes, forbid wage and price increases and strikes and demonstrations, and raise taxes on commodities.

September–October 1948: Communists under Lin Biao capture Mukden and Changchun in Manchuria, killing or taking prisoner 400,000 Nationalist troops.

November 1948: A 600,000-strong Communist army masses for an attack on the railroad junction of Xuzhou in central China. The city falls after a sixty-five-day battle.

Early 1949: Nationalists prepare Taiwan as a final retreat; 300,000 troops loyal to Chiang Kai-shek are massed there.

January 14–15, 1949: Lin Biao takes Tianjin.

January 1949: Chiang Kai-shek resigns as president of Nationalist China but maintains control of the Guomindang and the armed forces.

January 22, 1949: The Nationalist commander at Beijing agrees to withdraw from the city.

January 31, 1949: Communist forces enter Beijing.

April 1949: Communists give Nationalist President Li Zongren a surrender ultimatum; he refuses to capitulate.

April 23, 1949: Nanjing falls to the Communists without a fight.

May 27, 1949: Communists take Shanghai against token resistance.

August 1949: Communist columns speed westward, taking Xian and Lanzhou.

September 1949: Beijing is again the capital of China.

October 1, 1949: Mao Zedong announces the founding of the People's Republic of China. He speaks from a reviewing stand atop the Gate of Heavenly Peace, the main entrance to the imperial palace at Beijing.

THE PEOPLE'S REPUBLIC: 1949–1998

With the Communist triumph, China again is united and free of foreign occupation. The new rulers rapidly consolidate their power; they move, too, to implement a radical vision of a new, egalitarian, and socialist society. The Communists limit the power of capitalists and landowners and begin a massive redistribution of wealth. They restrict foreign influences. They curb the press, publishers, and intellectuals. Nearly every aspect of Chinese life falls under government supervision and control. At the same time, the new government does begin to build. Within a year, China's rampant, corrosive inflation is brought under control. With Russian technical assistance, roads, railroads, bridges, electric power complexes, factories, schools, and hospitals are constructed. In the countryside, land is at first taken from the landlords and parceled out among the peasantry, then taken under state control in a vast system of collectivized agriculture.

Beginning in 1950, the Korean War draws China into the Cold War. North Korean Communists invade South Korea; the United States, fighting under the United Nations flag, pushes the invaders back to the Yalu River; Chinese "volunteers" cross the Yalu and attack the Americans. The fighting ends in a stalemate, but has long-term consequences: China and the United States are enemies, and the United States becomes the protector of Nationalist Taiwan.

Mao Zedong is China's undisputed paramount leader. In the late 1950s he launches what proves to be the terribly mismanaged and immensely destructive Great Leap Forward, a mass redeployment of the peasantry for industrial and public works projects. The result, euphemistically labeled the "Three Hard Years," is widespread famine and related calamity. Estimates of the death toll range as high as 30 million.

A few years later, Mao's revolutionary whim touches off the chaotic and devastating Cultural Revolution. Tens of thousands of radical students mobilize to form Red Guards that terrorize China at all levels. Senior government officials are taken from their homes or offices, beaten, subject to public trials and humiliations, sometimes killed. When Mao decides he has seen enough revolution and reverses course, millions of Red Guards are "rusticated"—sent into the countryside for reeducation.

With Mao's death in 1976, China enters a new phase. New leadership under the pragmatic Deng Xiaoping eases government restrictions on economic life, takes steps toward a market economy, and courts foreign investment. The collectivist agricultural policy is reversed; farmers are encouraged to grow for profit. Small private businesses spring up in the cities and, perhaps more significantly, in the countryside as well.

Rapid economic expansion brings new problems: serious ecological damage, widespread corruption, worker exploitation, unwanted foreign cultural influences, and—far worse from the leadership's perspective—an explosive demand for the loosening of political controls. The "democracy" movement spreads, a challenge to the government that ends in the 1989 massacre at Tiananmen Square that horrifies the world.

China pursues economic reform into the 1990s. The constitution is rewritten to describe China's economic system as a "socialist market economy." In 1978 there are no privately owned cars in the People's Republic; in 1993 there are 1 million. Through it all, China's Communist leadership enforces a rigid separation between economic reforms, which it consistently pursues, and political and cultural liberalization, which it ruthlessly suppresses.

September 1949: A People's Political Consultative Conference drafts a constitution for the new Communist state. Under this constitution, the rights of freedom of speech, thought, assembly, publication, and religion are guaranteed—except for "political reactionaries."

October 1949: Communist party membership approaches 4.5 million. Mao Zedong is party chairman, now the most powerful position in China. The Central Committee and the smaller Politburo coordinate government policy; real power lies with the Politburo's five-member standing committee: Mao, Liu Shaoqi, Zhou Enlai, Zhu De, and Chen Yun.

October 2, 1949: The Soviet Union recognizes the People's Republic of China.

December 16, 1949: Mao Zedong reaches Moscow, the first time in his life he has traveled outside China. Stalin ignores him at first but eventually approves a security treaty, $300 million in credits, and eventual Soviet withdrawal from Lushun (Port Arthur).

1950–1953: Communists carry out land redistribution and collectivization in South China. Around 40 percent of all cultivable land is seized and redistributed, though allotments are small, given the high rate of population to arable land: a family of five might receive one or two acres. The campaign frequently turns violent. As many as a million landlords are executed.

1950: The Soviets agree to send ten thousand technical advisers to help build heavy industrial plants in China.

January 6, 1950: Britain recognizes the People's Republic; China rejects the gesture in protest of Britain's diplomatic ties with Taiwan.

April 1950: Communist troops under Lin Biao occupy Hainan Island off the coast of southern China.

June 25, 1950: Communist North Korean columns cross the 38th Parallel into South Korea. After initial setbacks, American forces, operating under the auspices of the United Nations, drive the invaders back across the frontier and push north toward the Yalu River.

October 1950: China invades Tibet, claiming to liberate the country from imperialists.

October 19, 1950: U.S. troops take the North Korean capital, P'yongyang.

October 25, 1950: The first of an estimated 250,000 Chinese "volunteers" under Peng Dehuai cross the Yalu into North Korea. Within a few weeks, Chinese columns will drive UN forces back to the 38th Parallel and briefly occupy Seoul.

December 1950: Government freezes foreign business assets in China. On December 28 all U.S. property in China is expropriated. Many foreign businesses are pressured into selling out at low prices.

May 23, 1951: China formally absorbs Tibet.

Summer 1951: Communists move against ex-Nationalists and other "subversives" who stayed behind in China after the Liberation. Estimates of executions range into the hundreds of thousands, with an equal number of former Nationalists sent to labor camps. The campaign in Guangdong province claims to net 52,000 bandits and 89,000 other criminals; 500,000 rifles are collected. More than 28,000 are executed.

Late 1951: Communists open the Three-Anti Campaign against corruption, waste, and obstructionist bureaucracy. The targets are Communist Party members, bureaucrats, and factory and business managers.

February–June 1952: The government's Five-Anti Campaign targets capitalists suspected of bribery, tax evasion, theft, cheating on government contracts, and stealing economic information from the state. Business leaders are forced into group criticism sessions and made to confess past wrongdoing. In April in Shanghai, people's committees investigate and "criticize" seventy thousand Shanghai businessmen. On confession, they are forced to pay restitution. In practice, this often means turning over their assets to the state. The campaign tightens the Communist Party's control of business and the labor movement.

1953–1957: The government's Five-Year Plan calls for quadrupling China's steel output and doubling production of electric power and cement. Most of the plan's targets will be reached or exceeded.

1953: A census puts China's population at 582.6 million. Communist Party membership totals 6.1 million.

July 27, 1953: Armistice ends the Korean War after two years of stalemate. China's casualties are 700,000–900,000, including a son of Mao Zedong. The war deeply damages China-U.S. relations, which will take a generation to recover.

1954: Government administers China through twenty-one provinces, five autonomous regions, and two municipalities (Beijing and Shanghai). Approximately 2,200 county governments supervise 1 million Communist Party branches in towns, villages, factories, schools, and army units.

December 1954: United States and Taiwan sign mutual defense treaty.

1955: The government population registration system makes free movement difficult. Most peasants are bound to their native villages. Registration categories are hereditary (passing through the male line), so the child of a peasant has peasant registration, and so do his children.

Spring 1955: Under Foreign Minister Zhou Enlai, China takes a leading role in the Bandung Conference in Indonesia with a call for "peaceful coexistence" and African-Asian solidarity. Zhou also announces that the People's Republic would "strive for the liberation of Taiwan by peaceful means so far as it is possible."

1956: Deng Xiaoping (1904–1997) becomes general secretary of the Communist Party.

May 2, 1956: At a closed party session, Mao Zedong proposes a "Hundred Flowers Campaign" seeking criticism of the Communist Party.

1957: U.S. announces it will deploy Matador missiles in Taiwan. They are capable of delivering atomic warheads on Chinese targets.

Late April 1957: Mao overrides hardliners' opposition to launch the Hundred Flowers Campaign.

May 1–June 7, 1957: When it comes, the Hundred Flowers criticism proves far more than Mao Zedong bargained for. Student protests erupt in Beijing and many other cities. Thoroughly alarmed, Mao cancels the campaign.

June–December 1957: In the Communist Party's Anti-Rightist campaign that follows the abortive Hundred Flowers, 300,000 people are branded as rightists and subjected to various forms of persecution, including jail and exile to hard labor in the countryside.

November 2–21, 1957: Mao Zedong leads a Chinese delegation to the Soviet Union, his second and last visit there. The Soviets promise the Chinese a prototype atomic bomb and assistance in making their own. The Soviet premier Nikita Khrushchev will later withdraw the bomb offer.

Late 1957: At Mao Zedong's direction, Communist Party prepares to launch the Great Leap Forward. It opens with a new round of agricultural collectivization—the merging of large collectives into giant communes.

August 23–October 6, 1958: Chinese forces bombard the Nationalist-held islands of Quemoy and Matsu.

Our revolutions are like battles. After a victory, we must at once put forward a new task. In this way, cadres and the masses will forever be filled with revolutionary fervor, instead of conceit. Indeed, they will have no time for conceit.

Mao Zedong (1958)

Autumn 1958: With millions of farm laborers redeployed for Yellow River flood control and other large public works projects, crops are neglected and much of the harvest is left to rot in the fields.

December 1958: Mao Zedong steps down as head of state. He will be replaced in the spring of 1959 by Liu Shaoqi (1898–1969),

the author of "How to Be a Good Communist." Mao retains title of chief of the Communist Party and remains the most powerful and prestigious of China's leaders.

1959–1962: A series of poor harvests, mostly attributable to mismanagement of the Great Leap Forward (1958–1961), leads to widespread famine. As many as 30 million perish in what the government calls the "Three Hard Years" period.

March 10–23, 1959: Tibetans rise in rebellion. China quells the outbreak, but an underground insurgency continues with U.S. backing.

July 1959: In a private letter to Mao Zedong, Defense Minister Peng Dehuai sharply criticizes Great Leap Forward policies. Mao makes the letter public, denounces Peng and strips him of his posts. Lin Biao (1907–1971) succeeds Peng as defense minister. Though he supports Mao, Deng Xiaoping also questions the Great Leap Forward.

October 21, 1959: Chinese and Indian forces clash in the border region of Ladakh.

Late 1950s: Government tears down the ancient walls of Beijing to improve the flow of traffic. The area to the south of the Imperial Palace is cleared for the expansion of Tiananmen Square. A massive Soviet-style Great Hall of the People is built on one side of the square; a hundred-foot-tall Monument to the Martyrs of the People glorifies China's revolutionary heroes.

1960: Communists assign the "remolded" Puyi, the last emperor, a job in a machine repair shop at a botanical garden in Beijing.

September 1960: The Soviet Union withdraws all 1,390 advisors and technicians working in China, bringing the Sino-Soviet split, developing for two years, fully into the open.

1961: Communist Party membership rises to 17 million.

September 24, 1962: In a speech, Mao Zedong launches the Socialist Education Movement. It calls for a renewed emphasis on class warfare.

October 20, 1962: After renewed clashes in disputed frontier areas, China launches a full-scale offensive along the China-India border.

November 20, 1962: China declares a unilateral cease-fire in the Indian frontier war and withdraws from the disputed territories it had occupied.

February 1, 1964: Lin Biao launches a "learn from the army" campaign featuring Lei Feng, a selfless People's Liberation Army (PLA) soldier who is killed when a truck backs over him. The posthumous "discovery" of Lei's diary is offered as a guide for all a Communist should be.

August 6, 1964: China protests U.S. bombing of North Vietnam in retaliation for the Tonkin Gulf incidents.

October 16, 1964: China successfully tests its own atomic bomb.

June 1, 1965: Lin Biao orders all ranks and insignia abolished in the People's Liberation Army.

May 1966: With encouragement from Mao Zedong and his wife, Jiang Qing (1914–1991), radical university students in Beijing and elsewhere rise against their faculty and administration, triggering what Mao dubs the Great Proletarian Cultural Revolution.

The precipitating factor of the Cultural Revolution is Wu Han's play *The Dismissal of Hai Rui*, which is regarded as an allegorical critique of Mao. The backdrop is Mao's belief in continuing revolution, his anxiety that he is losing control of the Communist Party, and his dissatisfaction with policies that encourage private farming, incentives in industry, and other "revisions" of Marxist-Leninist doctrine. With Lin Biao, Jiang Qing, and other radical allies, he touches off a cataclysm.

May 16, 1966: The so-called 16 May Circular sets up a Cultural Revolution Group to direct the revolution. Dominated by Jiang Qing and other radicals, it reports directly to Mao. The group is charged with attacking bourgeois and revisionist ideas in the party, government, army, and cultural affairs.

May 25, 1966: Radicals at Beijing University put up a wall poster criticizing the university administration for following liberal policies. The critiques spread to campuses throughout China.

June–July 1966: Tens of thousands of students leave school to join the Red Guards. With encouragement from Jiang Qing and others, they are incited to criticize university, party, and government leaders. Party moderates try unsuccessfully to control the students through work teams sent onto the campuses (an effort Mao dubs "white terror"), and by forming their own Red Guard units in the hope of coopting the movement.

July 16, 1966: Mao Zedong, seventy years old, takes his famous Yangtze River swim, intended to show he has the health and political vigor needed to lead the Cultural Revolution.

Early August 1966: Packed with Red Guards, a hastily called meeting of the Central Committee adopts a resolution urging China's youth to criticize "those persons in authority who are taking the capitalist road."

August 18–November 26, 1966: A series of mass rallies in Beijing brings together 13 million Red Guards from throughout China. Mao himself, wearing a red armband, presides over some of the rallies. The guards are urged to attack the "four olds"—old ideas, old culture, old customs, and old habits.

Red Guards campaign against smoking, drinking, and "the bourgeois keeping of crickets, fish, cats, and dogs." Shopkeepers are coerced into adopting revolutionary names for their shops. One Red Guard group proposes that the red traffic light should henceforth signal go rather than stop. More seriously, old buildings, temples, churches, art objects, and the dwellings of "revisionists" are destroyed. Authority figures come under physical attack; thousands of intellectuals are beaten, tortured, and killed.

October–December 1966: In speeches and

editorials, the Cultural Revolution Group criticizes the Communist Party for resisting the revolution and calls for an assault on the party establishment. Red Guards are urged to target Liu Shaoqi, Deng Xiaoping, and other senior officials. Only Mao Zedong is to be exempt.

January 6, 1967: Red Guards rally in Shanghai; municipal government officials are removed from office and the radicals take over. Authorities are forced to march in the streets wearing dunce caps and carrying placards detailing their crimes; many are arrested and beaten. In similar coups elsewhere, known as the "January power seizures," Red Guards attempt to take over party organizations throughout China.

January 23, 1967: The Central Committee authorizes the Shanghai seizure of power from "capitalist roaders." At the same time, PLA units are mobilized to restore order in Shanghai and other cities.

February 1967: Mao Zedong and his allies issue a set of directives, known as the February Adverse Current, intended to curb the excesses of the Cultural Revolution. Mao criticizes the use of violence, even the dunce caps. But when senior party leaders attack the idea of the Cultural Revolution, Mao rescinds some of the crackdown measures.

June 17, 1967: China explodes its first hydrogen bomb.

On the railroad tracks we are headed for,
no sign yet of any tracks.
Where the mine I'm headed for will be drilled
nothing yet but desert land. . . .
But what isn't there will surely come to be,
our splendid dreams cannot fail.

"Far Journey," poem by Shao Yanxiang (b. 1933)

Summer 1967: Red Guards in Beijing seize Liu Shaoqi, China's head of state, and beat him in front of crowds. He will die of complications from the beatings in 1969.

July 20, 1967: PLA forces restoring order in Wuhan seize two radical Red Guard leaders. In response, Jiang Qing's Cultural Revolution Group calls on the Red Guards to take power from the "capitalist roaders" in the army. The so-called Wuhan Incident ushers in the most violent phase of the Cultural Revolution.

August 1967: Deng Xiaoping faces a Red Guard public trial. He takes off his hearing aid during the harangue. From 1968 to 1973 Deng will live quietly under house arrest in Jiangxi province.

September 1967: Mao Zedong announces a "strategic plan" to bring the Cultural Revolution he has unleashed to a conclusion.

October 17, 1967: Puyi, the last emperor, dies.

July 1968: Mao Zedong orders an end to Red Guard violence to stave off a civil war. The People's Liberation Army gradually restores order. There are purges: the investigation of the so-called May 16 Group (a radical plot said to be aimed at Zhou Enlai; it may never have existed) ends with many executions.

December 22, 1968: Mao Zedong calls for educated young people to be sent into the country—rusticated—for reeducation by peasants and workers.

March–June 1969: Russian and Chinese forces clash along their long shared border.

December 22, 1969: The United States partially lifts trade embargo on the People's Republic.

1970: China's population is 880 million, up from 630 million in 1957.

April 10–17, 1971: A U.S. table tennis team tours China. "Ping-pong diplomacy" will lead to a thaw in relations between the two countries.

July 9–11, 1971: Henry Kissinger, a senior adviser to U.S. president Richard Nixon, meets privately with Zhou Enlai to plan a Nixon visit to China. On July 15 the visit is announced.

September 13, 1971: Defense Minister Lin Biao, implicated in a mysterious plot to murder Mao Zedong, dies in the crash of an aircraft that allegedly is carrying him into exile in the Soviet Union. A longtime Mao loyalist, Lin is the former commander of victorious civil war armies and the compiler of the best-selling "little red book"—the *Quotations of Chairman Mao.*

October 25, 1971: The People's Republic of China is admitted to the United Nations; Taiwan is ousted.

February 21–28, 1972: Richard Nixon visits China.

February 28, 1972: The United States and China issue the "Shanghai Communiqué." It lays out positions of the two countries on Taiwan—China affirms Taiwan is a breakaway province it means to recover—and calls for normalization of U.S.-China relations.

March 1973: Zhou Enlai brings back into government Deng Xiaoping and other senior officials disgraced during the Cultural Revolution.

September 1973: The president of France, Georges Pompidou, is the first western European head of state to visit China.

January 1975: The rehabilitated Deng Xiaoping becomes first vice premier with day-to-day responsibility for running the country.

April 5, 1975: Chiang Kai-shek dies. His son Chiang Ching-kuo succeeds him as ruler of the Nationalist republic in Taiwan. Chiang Ching-Kuo will lift martial law, begin to open the political process, and permit visits to the mainland.

January 8, 1976: Zhou Enlai dies.

April 4–5, 1976: A mass act of homage to the late Zhou Enlai in Beijing's Tiananmen Square turns into an antigovernment rally. Hundreds of the estimated 100,000 protesters are arrested.

April 7, 1976: Mao Zedong again strips Deng Xiaoping of his offices.

September 9, 1976: Mao Zedong dies. Government declares a week-long period of mourning. Mao's successor is Hua Guofeng (born 1921).

October 6, 1976: Hua Guofeng orders the arrest of Mao's widow Jiang Qing and her radical associates Zhang Chunqiao, Wang

Hongwen, and Yao Wenyuan. Vilified as the "Gang of Four," they are accused of disrupting the economy, undermining education, and sabotaging foreign trade, among other crimes.

July 1977: Deng Xiaoping is restored to all his offices.

1978–1980: Deng Xiaoping wins a power struggle over Hua Guofeng and emerges as China's paramount leader. Deng's market-oriented economic policies trigger a boom. Average incomes will triple by the early 1990s; implementation of the "responsibility system," which turns land back to individual peasant households, will help an estimated 170 million peasants climb out of extreme poverty.

March 1978: Government announces the Four Modernizations in agriculture, industry, national defense, science, and technology. A new ten-year plan sets a target of 10 percent annual growth in industry and 4–5 percent in agriculture.

November–December 1978: The first "big character" posters calling for political freedom are pasted onto what becomes known as the Democracy Wall along the western edge of the Forbidden City in Beijing.

What is true democracy? It means the right of the people to choose their own representatives [who will] work according to their will and in their interests. Only this can be called democracy. Furthermore, the people must also have the power to replace their representatives any time so that these representatives cannot go on deceiving others in the name of the people.

"Fifth Modernization," wall poster by dissident Wei Jingsheng (Beijing, December 1978)

December 5, 1978: The electrician/dissident Wei Jingsheng (born 1949) puts up a poster calling for a "fifth modernization"—democracy. Without it, he argues, Deng Xiaoping's Four Modernizations are hollow.

December 15–22, 1978: The Central Committee announces China and the United States will establish full diplomatic relations on January 1, 1979, and exchange ambassadors on March 1, 1979. The committee also endorses the government's emphasis on economic modernization, with tentative moves toward a free market, over Maoist class warfare.

1979: Government reopens law schools (private practice of law has been banned since 1949) and reestablishes the Ministry of Justice, abolished in 1959. By 1982 5,500 lawyers are working full-time in China.

Mid-January 1979: Government begins crackdown on the Democracy Wall movement. "A few little sheets of paper and a few lines of writing, a few shouts and they're frightened out of their wits," a dissident says of the authorities.

January 28, 1979: Deng Xiaoping arrives in Washington for meetings with President Carter.

February 17, 1979: People's Liberation Army columns invade northern Vietnam in a dispute over the border and over Vietnamese involvement in Cambodia's civil war.

March 5–16, 1979: After sharp reverses, PLA forces withdraw from northern Vietnam.

March 1979: Most of the Democracy Wall leaders are in jail; Wei Jingsheng will be sentenced to fifteen years in prison.

April 1979: U.S. Congress passes the Taiwan Relations Act. It reaffirms the American commitment and guarantees a flow of defensive weaponry to Taiwan.

April 1, 1979: Government rescinds the right to hang wall posters.

November 1980: Trial of the Gang of Four (there are actually ten defendants) begins. The gang is accused of "persecuting to death" 34,800 people during the Cultural Revolution and framing and persecuting a precisely tabulated 729,511 citizens.

January 25, 1981: Gang of Four sentences are handed down: Jiang Qing and Zhang Chunqiao are condemned to death, but with a two-year stay during which they can recant and thus avoid the executioner. The others are given prison terms.

July 1981: The Communist Party Central Committee passes a preliminary judgment on Mao Zedong: he is praised for his wartime leadership and his intellectual contributions, but blamed for much of what has gone awry in China since 1956, particularly the Great Leap Forward and the Cultural Revolution. Overall, the committee concludes Mao was right 70 percent of the time, wrong 30 percent.

July 1982: Census shows China's population exceeds 1 billion. For political purposes, the count includes Taiwan, Hong Kong, and Macau.

January 25, 1983: Death sentences of Jiang Qing and Zhang Chunqiao are commuted to life imprisonment.

1984–1987: China negotiates arms agreements with Iran worth $2.5 billion and with Iraq worth $1.5 billion.

May 7, 1984: With increasing worker mobility in consequence of economic reforms making it difficult for the government to keep track of its citizens, China mandates identity cards for everyone sixteen and older.

September 26, 1984: Britain and China sign agreement for Hong Kong's reversion to Chinese sovereignty on July 1, 1997. The pact contains a guarantee of economic autonomy for the colony—the "one country, two systems" arrangement.

1985: As Sino-Soviet relations thaw, the two countries reopen consulates in Leningrad (now St. Petersburg again) and Shanghai.

April–June 1985: China moves to reduce its 4.2 million-strong armed forces by 25 percent. The People's Liberation Army reintroduces insignia of rank to distinguish officers and enlisted personnel.

1986: Taiwan legalizes political parties.

1986: China adopts a revised Code of Civil Procedure. Around twenty thousand lawyers are practicing in China.

October 12–18, 1986: Britain's Queen Elizabeth II visits China.

December 5 and 9, 1986: An estimated three thousand students at the University of Science and Technology in Hefei protest campus issues and manipulated local elections. Student protests also break out in Wuhan and Beijing.

December 19–21, 1986: Thirty thousand students, with as many non-student supporters, rally in Shanghai. Protests spread to Kunming, Chongqing, Tianjin, and Beijing.

January 1987: Communist hardliners launch a crackdown on the student protest movement. They blame physicist Fang Lizhi, writer Liu Binyan, and other older intellectuals for fanning the flames of student dissent. Fang and Liu are dismissed from the Communist Party; Fang is stripped of his teaching and research positions.

January 16, 1987: Hu Yaobang, more tolerant of dissent than other senior leaders, is made the scapegoat for the student uprising; he resigns as secretary-general of the Communist Party.

October–November 1987: The 13th Communist Party Congress reaffirms Deng Xiaoping's liberal economic policies. Deng resigns from the Central Committee, though he remains China's most powerful leader; Zhao Ziyang, a supporter of Deng's market reforms, is elected party secretary-general. Four new members, including Li Peng (born 1928) are elected to the Politburo, and Li Peng becomes acting premier.

1988: Government releases figures showing that 150,000 Communist Party members were punished in 1987 for graft or abuse of power.

January 13, 1988: Chiang Ching-kuo dies. A native Taiwanese, Lee Teng-hui, will become president of Taiwan and head of the Guomindang. Lee soon lifts all travel restrictions to the People's Republic. By May ten thousand Taiwanese a month are visiting relatives on the mainland.

April 9, 1988: Li Peng is confirmed as premier.

April 15–22, 1989: Students mass in Beijing's Tiananmen Square to honor the recently deceased Hu Yaobang. (He died of natural causes.) Student leaders demand the right of political participation, increases in education spending, and disclosure of government officials' income.

April 24, 1989: Students declare a boycott of classes. Government acts to bring nonstop Tiananmen rallies under control. Deng Xiaoping calls the protests "an episode of turmoil"—a euphemism for counterrevolution.

May 4, 1989: An estimated 100,000 students rally in Beijing to mark the seventieth anniversary of the 1919 demonstrations that launched the May Fourth Movement.

May 13, 1989: Students in Tiananmen Square begin a hunger strike. Some three thousand students will participate.

May 15, 1989: Mikhail Gorbachev arrives in Beijing, marking an end to the thirty-year Sino-Soviet split. Continuing student protests deeply embarrass the government during Gorbachev's three-day visit.

May 17, 1989: One million prodemocracy supporters rally in Beijing.

May 20, 1989: With Deng Xiaoping pressing for a hard line, the government proclaims martial law in Beijing. Premier Li Peng calls the protesters counterrevolutionaries.

May 21, 1989: A million people massing in the streets of Beijing successfully block PLA troops trying to approach Tiananmen Square.

May 29, 1989: Student protesters put up thirty-seven-foot-high foam plastic statue of the "goddess of liberty" near a giant portrait of Mao Zedong in Tiananmen Square.

June 3, 1989: Troops begin to close in on Tiananmen Square.

June 3–4, 1989: Troops and armored vehicles move against the Tiananmen Square protesters. Estimates of the dead range from one thousand to ten thousand. Li Peng and other hardliners press for the arrest and jailing of hundreds of student leaders. Fang Lizhi, Liu Binyan, and other dissidents escape into exile abroad.

Later in June the United States will suspend arms sales to China in protest of the massacre, and the World Bank will defer action on $780 million in loan requests.

June 4, 1989: PLA units kill three hundred prodemocracy protesters in Chengdu.

June 9, 1989: In a speech, Deng Xiaoping attacks the protesters and brands them as rebels. He also calls for renewed economic growth along free market lines.

January 11, 1990: Government lifts martial law in Beijing. On January 18 nearly six hundred student leaders are freed after they "confess and reform."

May 1991: Taiwan renounces the use of force to retake the Chinese mainland.

Late 1993: The dissident Wei Jingsheng is released from prison. He resumes his political activity at once and is again arrested.

May 1994: The Clinton administration acts to separate trade and human rights issues in U.S. relations with China. This opens the way for renewal of China's most favored nation trade status.

January 1995: Communist Party secretary Jiang Zemin calls for state visits, an end to hostility, and reunification of China and Taiwan. In March, the Taiwanese reject the overture.

June 16, 1995: China recalls its ambassador in protest of the U.S. decision to grant a visa to Taiwan's president.

June–August 1995: China conducts missile tests near Taiwan.

December 1995: Prodemocracy activist Wei Jingsheng is found guilty of "counterrevolution" and sentenced to fourteen years in prison.

March 1996: The National People's Congress revises China's criminal code, limiting detentions without charge to thirty days and giving defendants speedier access to lawyers. Human rights groups say the changes do not go far enough.

March 23, 1996: China conducts military exercises near Taiwan as the island turns out for its first direct presidential vote.

February 19, 1997: Deng Xiaoping, China's paramount leader, dies. He has not appeared in public since 1994. Jiang Zemin (born 1926) is president; Li Peng retains his post as premier.

July 1, 1997: Britain formally returns Hong Kong and the New Territories to China.

October 27–November 2, 1997: President Jiang Zemin visits the mainland United States (after a one-day stopover in Hawaii), the first such high-level interaction between the two countries since the events in Tiananmen Square in 1989. Although he is met by protesters at almost every occasion, President Zemin manages to win over many Americans by his benign manner and his obvious admiration for America's history.

November 16, 1997: China releases political activist Wei Jingsheng from prison and sends him at once into exile. Wei arrives in Detroit, Michigan, the next day.

1998: According to a human rights report from Amnesty International, China detained more than 200,000 people without charge and without trial in 1997. Amnesty says it has documented widespread torture in prison and police cells and unfair trials.

January 25–July 3, 1998: Returning President Jiang Zemin's visit to the United States in 1997, President William Clinton visits China and participates in official welcome ceremonies at Tiananmen Square. Although nothing substantive comes out of this meeting, it does signal a change in relations between the two countries and a willingness to forget China's past actions.

China

ARTS, CULTURE, THOUGHT, AND RELIGION

PREHISTORIC AND LEGENDARY CHINA: 1,960,000–2208 B.C.

5,000–3,000 B.C.: The Yangshao culture produces a distinctive painted pottery, reddish with black designs. Some Yangshao pottery vessels are marked with signs representing makers or owners, indicating that a form of proto-writing is emerging here.

In the settled farming areas below the south bend of the Yellow River, villagers decorate their painted pottery jars with animal and plant designs.

4000–2000 B.C.: The Lungshan culture makes a pottery that is thin, black, and burnished. At Erlitou, remains from about 2000 B.C. include palace foundations, stone carvings, bronze and ceramic ritual vessels, royal burials, and even human sacrifices.

2698–2599 B.C.: Legend credits the Yellow Emperor's recordkeeper, Cangxie, with inventing the written Chinese language.

2300–2200 B.C.: Tradition claims that the *Yaodian* (Canon of Yao), outlining the principal events of the third millennium B.C., is written down at this time, but modern scholars agree that it was written many centuries later.

THE THREE DYNASTIES (XIA, SHANG, ZHOU): 2208–249 B.C.

1700–1600 B.C.: The first bronze vessels appear. The Shang vessels are often used in sacrifices and burials. Possession of them is a sign of wealth.

1384–1111 B.C.: The Shang use oracle bones—inscribed cattle shoulder bones and turtle shells—for divination. Some 100,000 bones will be excavated at Anyang between 1927 and 1938. They reveal the earliest known written form of the Chinese language, with some 1,500 characters deciphered.

***c.* 1000 B.C.:** The Chinese written vocabulary reaches three thousand characters. The first known Chinese poetry is believed to date from the Early Zhou dynasty. Poems from the *Book of Songs* (Shijing) are sung at important court ceremonials.

c. **800–700 B.C.:** Jars made from an early form of porcelain are in use.

753 B.C.: Qin establishes its first corps of annalists to record state events.

551–499 B.C.: Lifespan of Kong Qiu; eventually the Chinese will refer to him as Kong Fuzi (Great Master Kung), but the Latinized version of this name, Confucius, is that by which he becomes known to the world at large. He is born in Lu (modern Shandong) into a family of the lower aristocracy. Longing for a return to the lost (and possibly imaginary) order and moral certainty of the Zhou, he will become China's first moral philosopher and establish a lasting form of Chinese cultural thought. For Confucius, *jen* (goodness) is the leading principle of conduct. *Yi* (righteousness, duty, justice) and *li* (etiquette or ritual) are other cardinal virtues. Government, he says, should be based on ethics, not just practical politics. Each person has a role; if each performs his role, social stability is assured. Man is perfectible, Confucius teaches, can improve, and is morally educable.

The *Analects* of Confucius are reconstructed conversations of the master with his disciples, recorded after his death. His thought will eventually be collected in the *Four Books*, the basic text of Confucianism from the Song to the twentieth century.

6th century B.C.: By tradition, the *Dao De Jing* (also known as *Classic of the Way and Its Power*) appears. Ascribed to the possibly legendary Laozi, it is regarded as the founding document of Daoism. Little is known of Laozi's life. One legend has him leaving China for the west astride a purple buffalo. In any case, his philosophical system, with its emphasis on personal spiritual freedom, is a complete contrast to and a chief rival of Confucianism. Modern scholars believe the book may have been compiled in the early third century B.C.

536 B.C.: The first certain written laws appear in the state of Cheng. Punishments for various infractions are inscribed on the sides of bronze vessels.

468–376 B.C.: Lifespan of Mozi, philosopher of the Warring States period and an early rival of Confucius. A "utilitarian" philosopher, he is interested in practical economic matters and is critical of extravagant funeral practices and other elaborate rituals. He advocates peaceful relations between competing Chinese states and decries war as wasteful.

384 B.C.: Qin officially prohibits the practice of human sacrifice.

c. **370–*c.* 300 B.C.:** The lifespan of Mengzi, known in the Western world as Mencius, the first important successor to Confucius in the same tradition; he studied with the master's grandson. The "Second Sage" extends the Confucian notion that righteousness and a sense of duty are the mark of the true ruler. He goes on to state that the ruler who neglects his responsibilities—and these include providing his subjects with adequate living conditions—forfeits the loyalty of his people; the people thus have a right to revolution. Men are born virtuous, Mencius believes; they need only to recover their lost original goodness for the evil in the world to disappear. Like the *Analects*, the *Mencius* is a record of the philosopher's conversations.

361 B.C.: Gongsun Yang (Lord Shang) is the supposed author of one of the two surviving treatises of the Legalist School of government. Legalism relies on the power of government to punish and reward, in contrast to the Confucian emphasis on ritual and the virtue of rulers.

310–220 B.C.: The lifespan of Xunzi, another important Confucian successor. His *Xunzi* is a set of essays on moral philosophy and government.

c. **310 B.C.:** The *Zhuangzi*, the second of the two founding tracts of Daoism, circulates. Its author is probably the philosopher Zhuangzi (369–286 B.C.). He argues, against Confucius, that efforts to improve the world are useless, even harmful. His philosophy emphasizes the spiritual freedom of the individual. He is a mystic, drawn to the limitless possibilities of the Dao, as opposed to the circumscribed potential of man.

280?–233 B.C.: Lifespan of Hanfeizi. A member of the Han ruling family, he is a leading theoretician of the Legalist School. The turmoil of the Warring States period underlay his argument that strict laws and harsh punishments are necessary to preserve order. He is sent to Qin as a Han ambassador, imprisoned, and poisoned, but his theories will influence the Qin state.

QIN DYNASTY: 221–206 B.C.

3d century B.C.: Qin bureaucrats extend Legalist rule. Lord Shang defined it this way: "To club together and keep your mouth shut is good; to be alienated and spy on each other is to be a scoundrel. If you glorify the good, errors will be hidden; if you put scoundrels in charge, crime will be punished."

c. 219 B.C.: The chancellor Li Si oversees simplification of written characters and makes the written language uniform throughout the empire.

c. 219 B.C.: The emperor establishes an academy of seventy scholars expert in all important areas of knowledge.

213 B.C.: The emperor orders Li Si to carry out a widespread Burning of the Books, including the archives of vanquished rival Warring States. The motive is to enforce a monopoly of learning for the imperial court; surviving material is available only to court academicians.

212 B.C.: Using forced labor, perhaps as many as 700,000 men, Emperor Zheng begins building a new throne hall and a tomb for himself in the Qin capital near modern Xian. Artists and craftsmen create some 7,500 life-size terracotta warriors to guard the burial site.

212 B.C.: Emperor Zheng orders the execution of 460 literati who question him or complain about his policies. He is alleged to have the scholars buried alive. Modern authorities doubt this version; they believe the literati were executed before burial.

July–August 210 B.C.: Many of Emperor Zheng's concubines and those who had worked on his tomb are buried with him in what is said to be one of the last recorded instances of human sacrifice in China. Also buried are the 7,500 terracotta soldiers.

HAN DYNASTY: 202 B.C.–A.D. 220

195 B.C.: A government edict establishes shrines for the worship of the emperors' ancestors.

c. 180–117 B.C.: Lifespan of the poet Sima Xiangju; he develops the new genre of poetry or rhythmic prose known as *fu*.

c. 175–105 B.C.: Lifespan of the Confucian scholar Dong Zhongshu, whose commentary on *Spring and Autumn Annals* contains an important series of short essays on political philosophy and a ruler's place in the cosmos. His thought, a synthesis of Daoism, Legalism, and Confucianism, becomes perhaps the dominant Confucian position of the early Han.

122 B.C.: Liu An, a grandson of the first Han emperor, Gaodi, dies; he is the patron of the scholars who compiled the Daoist *Huainanzi*, one of the most important philosophical works of the Early Han. The work, a collection of essays on philosophy, though Daoist in outlook, refers to other schools and aims to synthesize previous Chinese thought.

110 B.C.: Emperor Wudi sets out for the sacred Mount Tai near Confucius's birthplace to perform the *feng* and *shan* ceremonies dating from early Zhou. These rites are supposed to make him immortal and allow him to climb up to Heaven.

107 B.C.: Sima Qian (145?–90? B.C.) becomes the grand historian of Han.

c. 99–c. 85 B.C.: Sima Qian completes his history of China up to the time of Emperor Wudi (beginning 141 B.C.), the *Records of the Historian*. His *Records* contain a year-by-year chronicle, imperial genealogies, essays on important subjects such as the economy and flood control, *feng* and *shan* ceremonial, and biographical studies; they will provide the model for the dynastic histories of later periods. Sima Qian suffers castration for defending an out-of-favor soldier.

40 B.C.: Reformists move to reduce the number of religious shrines in China, partly as an economy move. These were elaborate and expensive institutions; in the reign of Xuandi (74–49 B.C.), for example, 45,000 guards were on the shrines' payroll, with another 12,000 employed as priests, cooks, and musicians.

The last four decades of the century are a period of significant change in religious observance. Many shrines are abolished. Ceremonies are simplified and made more austere. Han leaders move to restore the older gods of the Zhou dynasty. Heaven, from whom the Zhou kings believed they had been given the authority to rule, becomes the supreme deity of the state cult of Han. The emperor is the Son of Heaven. He rules by the Mandate of Heaven.

31 B.C.: Emperor Chengdi takes part in services of the cults of Heaven and Earth at new shrines in the capital, Chang'an.

26 B.C.: The emperor orders copies of literary works to be forwarded to the capital from all the commanderies and kingdoms. The purpose is to compare different versions of a text and produce a "correct" edition on silk or wooden scrolls for the imperial library.

7 B.C.: In renewed economy moves, government begins a new campaign to reduce the number of religious shrines, including the Heaven and Earth cults.

3 B.C.: In a popular surge of religious feeling, the cult of the Queen Mother of the West sweeps across China. Scholars today regard it as a response to the political and dynastic insecurity of the last years of the Early Han.

A.D. 5: Wang Mang restores the cults of Heaven and Earth. He convenes in the imperial capital of Chang'an an important scholarly conference on the classical texts, philology and divination.

48–119 or 120: Lifespan of the poet, scholar, and teacher Ban Zhao, one of a few women whose work has come down from premodern China. Her *Nu Jie* (Admonitions to Women) summarizes the Confucian feminine ideal. A good deal of her poetry survives, including the famous "Needle and Thread":

Chill autumn gleam of steel,
Fine, straight, and sharp,
You thrust your way in and gradually
  advance,
So that things far apart are all strung into
  one.

She also completes her brother Ban Gu's *History of Han*, the first work to apply Sima Qian's model to a single dynasty.

65: In concert with the continuing decay of Confucian values and a developing surge of popular religious Daoism, foreign merchants on the Silk Road introduce Buddhism to China. The Chinese are drawn to the Four Noble Truths of the Buddha, a near Indian contemporary of Confucius: Life is sorrowful; Sorrow is due to craving; Curbing craving dissolves sorrow; This is achieved through a life of discipline, meditation, and moral behavior that is fully open only to monks and wandering ascetics.

The king of Chu, half-brother of the emperor, adopts Buddhist practices—the first documented mention of Buddhism in China. A cult of the Buddha is thought to be active in the capital, Luoyang, around this time.

79: Han emperor Zhangdi convenes a conference on the correct texts and interpretations of the Confucian classics. The historian Ban Gu edits the conference report, titled *Comprehensive Discussions in the White Tiger Hall*, a landmark of Confucian scholarship.

c. 90: Buddhist monks establish a monastery at the imperial capital, Luoyang.

92: Implicated by his friendship with the Dou family in a plot against the emperor, the Han historian Ban Gu is arrested and executed.

100: A translation of the Indian Buddhist text *Sutra in Forty-two Articles* circulates in Luoyang.

2d century: Sculptors are fashioning fine bronze three-dimensional representations of familiar Han scenes. A well-known example: a Han official sits under an umbrella in a two-wheeled carriage; the horse in the shafts appears to be about to explode into a gallop.

121: China's first dictionary is presented to the emperor. It contains nine thousand characters.

160: Student population of the imperial academy, where prospective government officials are trained, reaches thirty thousand.

166: The Cult of the Buddha is formally introduced at the imperial court in Luoyang.

175–183: The authorized correct texts of the *Five Classics* and the *Analects* are engraved in stone, evidently on some forty to fifty tablets. Fragments survive today.

180: The government creates a new university styled the "School at the Gate of the Vast Capital" to train public officials.

184–215: In response to the spread of civil war in Han China, politico-religious groups flourish. Religious Daoism, with immortality as its central aim, becomes one of the two great clerical and salvationist religions of China, alongside Buddhism.

Features of the Daoist political/utopian movements that spring to life include confession of sins, good deeds such as almsgiving, abstention from alcohol, and the legend of the immaculate conception of Laozi, who is deified as the messiah of the Great Peace.

Daoist groups form protective societies in disturbed areas and carry out administrative and military as well as religious functions. The Five Pecks of Rice sect in Shanxi and Sichuan in the west, for example, establishes charity houses and other aid programs and rules effectively for four decades. In the east, the Yellow Turban rebellion rises against the imperial government in 184. While Five Pecks of Rice remains strong in the west through the end of the Han dynasty, warlords operating on behalf of the imperial court quickly subdue the Yellow Turbans and kill most of their leaders.

193: Large communities of Buddhist converts flourish in eastern China. Buddhists build a vast temple in the Chu capital of Pengcheng—it stands several stories high and can hold three thousand devotees. Later this year, the warlord Cao Cao sacks Pengcheng, driving a Buddhist community more than ten thousand strong south to the Yangtze, where the Buddha cult is thus introduced.

THREE KINGDOMS AND SIX DYNASTIES: 220–589

220–589: There is a distinct north-south split during these centuries of disunion. A southern style develops in religious observance, manners, and dress. Women are more likely to be in seclusion and concubinage in the south. Northern women have work and responsibility. Southerners cultivate rice and use sea fish; northerners tend their flocks and herds and grow millet and wheat. Southerners regard themselves as true heirs of Han civilization. Life is softer there. Northerners are a martial society, bred to warrior and hunter values; life is hard.

c. 260: The acupuncturist Huangfu Mi is in the prime of his career. He is the author of the *Classic of Acupuncture and Moxibustion*, the earliest known treatise in the field.

c. 290: The *San Guo zhi* (Record of the Three Kingdoms) is completed. It long stands as the accepted dynastic history of the period.

4th century: In a time of upheaval, Buddhism spreads rapidly throughout China, though Confucian ideas continue to shape the views of the elite on politics, society, ethics, and etiquette. Buddhism's appeal lies in its offering of consolations and magical powers; Buddhist ideas and images open up new imaginative worlds for Chinese artists and thinkers. It appeals to common people as a comfort in times of distress. Non-Chinese invaders who settle permanently among the Chinese and adopt their ways accept Buddhism too.

Buddhism becomes established in China in its Mahayana form, the Greater Vehicle, with its worship of many deities—the Buddha in various manifestations. Through translation of the sutras (traditional sermons and teachings of the Buddha and successor sages), the Chinese make major adaptations to the Buddhism of India, among them a change in the comparatively exalted position Buddhism gives to women and mothers. "The husband supports his wife," for instance, becomes "The husband controls his wife."

399–414: The Buddhist Faxian makes a long pilgrimage to India. He returns with Buddhist works that he translates for a Chinese audience.

Early 5th century: With political power shared among many competing centers, Dao popular sects remain strong in the countryside. They are descendants of the Yellow Turban and Five Pecks of Rice groups that rose in rebellion during the last decades of the Later Han dynasty.

At the same time, religious Daoism, with its emphasis on immortality, gains among the elites of south China; in the north, Kou Qianzhi attempts to establish Daoism as the state religion.

403: The argument is presented at court that Buddhist monks should be exempted from bowing to the emperor.

471–499: Xiao, emperor of the Northern Wei, pursues an aggressive sinicization policy: languages other than Chinese are prohibited at court and newcomers are ordered to adopt Chinese surnames.

Early 6th century: According to later tradition, Chan (in Japanese, Zen) Buddhism is introduced to China through Bodhidharma, an Indian sage who seeks an audience with Emperor Wudi (Liang dynasty), himself a Buddhist. Chan—the word derives from the Sanskrit for meditation—is distinctively Chinese in style. It is imparted and passed on not from a text but from an already enlightened mind, a teacher-student process that appeals to China's Confucian tradition of thinker and disciples. Bodhidharma, the Chan patriarch, enters a monastery near Luoyang and passes years in silent meditation, his face to the wall. In Chan, the goal of meditation is enlightenment, in which all illusions are cleared away and an individual becomes fully aware of wisdom. Bodhidharma leaves this summary of Chan: "A special transmission outside the scriptures; no reliance upon words or letters; direct pointing to the very mind; seeing into one's own nature."

542: Tan Luan, born in 476, patriarch of the Buddhist Pure Land sect, dies. The Pure Land scripture holds that anyone who meditates on the Buddha Amida or calls upon his name will be reborn into his paradisic Buddha-world. This will become one of the most important Chinese traditions of Buddhism in later periods.

574: Emperor Wudi (reigns 561–578) launches an effort to suppress Buddhist and Daoist religious practices in favor of Confucian ritual. Temples, scriptures, and images are destroyed in Northern Zhou and clergy are forced to return to lay life.

Sixth month, 578: With the death of Emperor Wudi, the proscription of Buddhism is relaxed to a degree.

SUI DYNASTY: 589–618

Second month, 581: Among the first acts of Emperor Wendi are the full restoration of rights to Buddhists and the rehabilitation of the Buddhist clergy. He also lifts the proscription of Daoists.

Tenth month, 581: Emperor Wendi promulgates a New Code of laws and ordinances containing 1735 articles. It eases the severe punishments of earlier codes—the severed heads of criminals are no longer to be displayed, for example. "It is Our wish that men should have no disposition to trespass and that, the state having regular punishments, they be administered in accordance with the lofty principle of no animus. Perhaps the time is not far distant when . . . they are not used."

Despite the liberal tone of his laws, Wendi himself could intervene in the harshest manner, ordering capital punishments for comparatively minor crimes. "If the Emperor was displeased with someone," one of his judges admits later, "[the courts] manipulated the procedure so that he was severely condemned."

583: Wendi also simplifies the new Sui legal code, reducing the number of laws to around five hundred. This version, a synthesis of northern and southern legal practice and tradition, helps prepare the way for reunification. The revised code contains four types of punishment: the death penalty, deportation with forced labor, forced labor only, and the bastinado (beating the soles of the feet). By tradition, the autumn equinox is the time for executions.

586: In an overture to Daoists, Wendi orders an inscribed monument to be set up at the supposed birthplace in Anhui of Laozi, whom religious Daoists claim as their spiritual ancestor. At the same time, he remains wary of Daoist subversive potential; his officials suppress alleged black magic and other dangerous practices. By the first years of the seventh century, there are 120 Buddhist establishments in the capital, to only ten Daoist.

Sixth month, 589: Wendi orders the closing of most schools teaching the Confucian curriculum.

589–591: The emperor's son, installed as the southern viceroy, conciliates Buddhists dispossessed during the upheaval to Daoists and Confucians.

c. **600:** The technique of block printing is perfected.

601: Wendi personally inaugurates a campaign to distribute Buddhist holy relics to shrines and reliquaries throughout the empire.

604: On accession, Emperor Yangdi announces that he will sponsor a revival of traditional Confucian learning.

606: The Sui initiates an effort to bring the music, instruments, and surviving performers of the era of disunion to the capital.

TANG DYNASTY: 618–907

600–700: Chinese scribes are using inked seals.

622: A river accident claims more than 80 percent of the Sui Imperial Library during its shipment from Luoyang to Chang'an. Only fourteen thousand titles survive.

624: The court astrologer Fu Yi, a nonbeliever, attacks Buddhism as foreign and urges the emperor to suppress it and force Buddhist priests and nuns to return to lay life.

Fifth month, 626: Emperor Gaozu limits the numbers of Buddhist and Daoist temples in the capital; each prefecture is allowed one temple per faith. The numbers of priests and nuns are to be reduced. Three months later, after the emperor is removed in a palace coup, the measures are withdrawn. Historians speculate that Buddhist political power may have been behind the coup, in which Gaozu's son ascends the Tang throne.

627: The new dynasty establishes a Directorate of the State University to oversee the schools. The school population rises from around four hundred to more than two thousand. Tang educational improvements draw scholars and students from the provinces to Chang'an.

628–632: Schools of calligraphy and law are founded in Chang'an.

629: Emperor Taizong orders execution as the penalty for illegal ordination of Buddhist monks. Tax evasion is usually the motive for illicit ordinations.

629–645: The Buddhist monk Xuanzang makes a pilgrimage to India. On his return, he translates Buddhist texts into Chinese and prepares an important account of his travels: *Record of the Western Regions.*

635: The Persian Olopan (or Alopen) introduces Nestorian Christianity, which has moved eastward from Syria, to China. The first Nestorian church will be built in Chang'an in 638.

637: An imperial edict gives Daoist monks and nuns preference over Buddhist clergy in court ceremonies.

638–713: Lifespan of the Buddhist patriarch Huineng, the Sixth Patriarch of Chan; he is later credited with founding the Southern School, which offers the possibility of sudden enlightenment. The sterner Northern School emphasizes gradual progress toward enlightenment through the discipline of meditation. Huineng is responsible for the *sutra* called the *Platform Sutra of the Sixth Patriarch.* In it, he suggests that no one discipline or posture will bring enlightenment. "The way is realized through the mind," he teaches. "What should it have to do with a sitting posture?"

Buddhism makes a significant contribution to Tang artistic achievement, both as an inspiration to artists and in its creation of devotional works of art such as the 97,000 Buddhist images at the Longmen Grottoes in Luoyang.

651: An Arab mission introduces Islam to China.

669–759: Lifespan of the Tang poet and landscape painter Wang Wei.

680–750: Buddhist texts are printed from wood blocks.

694: Manichaeism is introduced to China. Its adherents are known as Light Worshippers.

c. 700: A succession of Japanese embassies to China, one with as many as five hundred emissaries, send Chinese culture flowing eastward to Japan. Chinese calligraphy, Buddhist and Confucian thought, and governmental systems heavily influence Japanese institutions.

710: The historian Liu Zhiji (661–721) completes his *Understanding of History*, the first important study of historical writing in China.

711: A court memorial draws attention to how

wealthy men evade their taxes by becoming ordained Buddhist monks and novices. After an investigation in 714, thirty thousand monks and nuns are ordered returned to lay life.

712–755: Xuanzong reigns in what will be recalled as the Golden Age of the Tang dynasty. He takes an intelligent interest in poetry, historical works and religion. The era is particularly noteworthy for the poetry known as *shi*. Strict rules of rhyme and meter govern this form of short lyric poetry, which often has a strong emphasis on nature. The best-known practitioners are Wang Wei (669–759), Li Bo (*c.* 700–762), Du Fu (712–770), Pai Chui (772–846), and Gao Shi (707–765), all members of the scholar/gentry class and holders of government appointments.

Emperor Xuanzong is a patron of Daoism as well. He insists that the *Laozi*, the sacred Daoist text, be added to the curriculum in imperial civil service examinations. He and other Tang emperors are also interested in Daoism for its claims to make elixirs that confer immortality.

Eleventh month, 725: Xuanzong carries out the most significant of all state rites, the *feng* and *shan* sacrifices, on the holy mountain of Tai in Shandong.

732: Showing favoritism to the Daoists, the government orders every prefecture to establish a temple in honor of Laozi. Within a few years, Emperor Xuanzong will set up special schools in the state university for Daoist studies. At the same time, the emperor is drawn to the new Esoteric Buddhism that takes root during his reign. Doubtless part of the attraction is the use it makes of magical spells and incantations similar to those of Daoism.

768: Manichaeans are given permission to build a temple in Chang'an.

781: A stele describing the Nestorian Christian Church in China is put up in Chang'an.

c. 800–907: A new verse form, *ci*, develops, possibly from folk ballads. It is a lyric with lines of irregular length set to a melody.

835: Printing is first mentioned in literature.

843: Government moves to suppress Manichaeans.

845: Gradual pressure against Buddhist economic power builds to full-scale repression. The emperor orders the destruction of thousands of shrines, monasteries, and temples and the confiscation of vast Buddhist wealth. As many as 250,000 priests and nuns are evicted from the monasteries and forced to return to lay life; many are killed. Government officials take control of the ordination of monks as means of curbing Buddhist growth. Religious persecutions afflict the Christian community; Judaism and Islam are less troubled.

A new emperor, Xuanzong, comes to the throne in 846. He relaxes the persecutions, but some curbs remain on Buddhist temple-building and ordination.

868: The earliest extant printed book, the *Diamond Sutra*, is struck off at Dunhuang.

916: The ruler of the Khitan Liao dynasty in North China establishes the first Confucian temple in Liao.

SONG DYNASTIES: 960–1279

960–1279: During this time, a powerful, tenacious upper class of scholar-officials, the product of the expanded civil service examination system, comes to dominate Chinese life. This gentry, drawn from the landowners and degree-holders, everywhere forms a local elite, the governing link between the mass of the peasantry below and the court and high officialdom above. The gentry produces the familiar "scholar-gentleman," who carries on Chinese cultural traditions: calligraphy, landscape painting, literature, and philosophical speculation.

990–1030: The Northern Song landscape painter Fan Guan is active. His landscape masterpiece is *Travelers amid Mountains and Streams*.

c. 1010: Thirty thousand candidates take the prefectural civil service examinations each year.

c. 1050–1100: These decades mark the rise to dominance of Confucianism as an intellectual and political movement associated with reformist politics. Adherents think of themselves as reviving the Confucianism of the classical age.

c. 1050: Song China is the world's first society to make widespread use of the printed book. Paper is made from plant fibers; printing is from wooden blocks.

1051–1107: Lifespan of the Northern Song painter Mi Fei.

1055: As part of the Confucian revival, the title of Holy Duke is granted the descendants of Confucius.

1056–1057: Su Dongpo (1037–1101; born Su Shi) passes the civil service examinations, joins the bureaucracy, and enters the Song literary world. A leading Confucian opponent of Wang Anshi's New Laws of the 1070s, he is a poet, an essayist, and something of a satirist. Of his month-old boy child he writes: "All I want is a son who is doltish and dumb. No setbacks or hardships will obstruct his path to the highest courts."

1070: The leading Confucian reformer Sima Guang (1019–1086) leaves government service. He devotes nineteen years to the preparation of his chronicle of dynastic rule, *A Comprehensive Mirror for Aid in Government*, which covers 1,300 years from the late Zhou to the founding of Song, but he returns briefly to public service in the last year of his life. In this work, the scholar identifies the causes for the rise and fall of dynasties and calls for established, regular bureaucratic and court procedures to assure stabil-

ity; he argues that history teaches that repairs to the existing order are more likely to be successful than a radical overturn. He is the leader of the political opposition to the radical reformer Wang Anshi.

1075: The "Cheng Brothers," Cheng Hao (1032–1085) and Cheng Yi (1033–1107), leaders of the Neoconfucian movement, are influential. They explain the cosmos through the concepts of *li* (principle and pattern) and *qi* (vital energy and material force). Nothing, the brothers argue, can exist without both.

c. 1095: The yearly number of prefect civil service exam candidates reaches eighty thousand.

12th–13th centuries: The custom of footbinding of women, first practiced among dancers in the tenth or eleventh century, spreads to China's upper classes. The Southern Song tightly bind the feet of five- and six-year-olds to keep them from growing; the goal is to make women's movements more dainty.

1100–1126: The penultimate Northern Song emperor, Huizong, reigns as the most cultured of the Song rulers. A painter and a patron of painting, his imperial collection contains six thousand works of art. He establishes a flourishing Academy of Painting before the dynasty collapses amid the Jurchen invasion.

1130: Chan and Pure Land Buddhist sects flourish in North China state of Jin, as they do also in the Southern Song. The Jin government strictly regulates religious life. In this year, Jin rules that monks may not be ordained without government authorization.

1130–1200: Lifespan of the scholar Zhu Xi, a leading Neoconfucian. He synthesizes the major thinkers of the Neoconfucian School. He selects the *Four Books* as the essence of Confucianism: the *Analects* of Confucius himself; the book of Mencius (*c.* 370–*c.* 300 B.C.), Confucius's leading successor; the *Doctrine of the Mean*; and the *Great Learning*, chapters from one of the ancient ritual classics that he elevates to the status of an independent work. Zhu Xi's commentaries on the *Four Books* will become the official standard for civil service examinations in the Yuan dynasty and thereafter.

1138: The late emperor Huizong's Academy of Painting is reestablished on the Western Lake in the Southern Song capital of Hangzhou.

1142: National University is founded in Kaifeng; it shortly moves to Hangzhou.

1161: Monks lead uprising in modern Hebei, possibly touched off by the Jin state's repression of religion.

1163: A synagogue is built in Jin Kaifeng, probably by Jews who reach China via the caravan routes from Persia.

1188: Jin proscribes the heterodox Buddhist Dhuta sect, which had gained widespread adherence among the merchant and artisan classes.

c. **1190–1224:** Lifespan of the landscape painter Ma Yuan; he is associated with the Academy of Painting in Hangzhou.

c. **1200:** Liang Kai paints *Patriarchs of the Chan (Zen) Sect.*

1241: Emperor declares the late Confucian Zhu Xi has "illuminated the Way" and orders government students to study his commentaries on the *Four Books*.

1270: The National University in Hangzhou enrolls 1,716 students.

YUAN DYNASTY: 1279–1368

1269: Khubilai attempts to impose a universal script, based on Tibetan and consisting of a forty-one-letter alphabet. Though it is a superior script for writing premodern Mongolian, it does not displace the Uyghur script in use up until that time.

1271: The Yuan emperor adopts a new legal code, incorporating some Mongol customs. The code is comparatively lenient; capital crimes total 135, fewer than half the number in the old Song code. He also restores traditional Confucian court rituals, promotes translation of the Confucian classics into Mongolian and makes overtures to Buddhist and Daoist religious groups as well.

1274–1292: The Venetian traveler Marco Polo is resident in China. His *Travels* will introduce educated Europe to advanced Chinese civilization.

1275–1279: Mongols complete their legal classification of Chinese society with the addition of a fourth class—the newly conquered southern Chinese. The three earlier classifications, in descending order, are the Mongols, Western Asians, and Chinese and others permanently settled in North China.

1280–1354: Lifespan of the scholar-painter Zhu Wen. Finding government service under the Mongols not to his taste, he supports himself by fortunetelling.

1281: Yuan cracks down on Daoists, ordering that all Daoist texts except for the *Laozi* be destroyed.

c. **1285:** An estimated 400,000 artisans are employed in government workshops and factories.

1285: Sangha authorizes restoration of Buddhist temples and monasteries. The monk Yang Lanjianjia ransacks Song imperial tombs to raise money for the work. Yang is said to have taken 1,700 ounces of gold, 6,800 ounces of silver, 111 jade vessels, and other valuables from 101 Song tombs.

1286: Khubilai Khan recruits the brilliant Song scholar Zhao Mengfu (1254–1322), who reluctantly agrees to quit Hangzhou and journey north to Beijing. "Each person lives his life in this world according to his own times," he tells his disapproving friends. Zhao becomes a leading exponent of Confucian values at the Yuan court.

1291: With Buddhist resurgence, more than 200,000 monks serve 42,318 Buddhist temples in China.

1292: The Italian Christian missionary Giovanni Montecorvino attempts to spread Christianity in China. He will become archbishop of Beijing.

1323: Yuan adopts a new law code that incorporates new laws and regulations introduced since the beginning of the dynasty.

Spring 1329: Wenzong establishes the Academy of the Pavilion of the Star of Literature for the purpose of carrying out "tasks relating to the transmission of high culture to the Mongolian imperial establishment." Among other things, the academy is a training school for sons of high-ranking Mongols.

May 1330: Scholars of the Academy of the Pavilion begin compiling the *Grand Canon for Governing the World*, containing all major documents and laws since the founding of the Yuan dynasty; it will take thirteen months to complete.

MING DYNASTY: 1368–1644

1368: The first Ming emperor founds the imperial academy for translators. Students are drawn from the sons and relatives of government officials; local schools refer sons of commoners for study at the academy.

Taizu introduces the system of examinations known as the "eight-legged essays" for explication of the traditional Confucian canon of the *Four Books* and *Five Classics*.

1369: Taizu summons eleven Muslim astronomers to the capital to reform the Chinese calendar.

1382: The emperor Taizu, accused of favoring Buddhist teachings, orders sacrifices for Confucius throughout the empire. He evidently believes the three great teachings— Confucianism, Buddhism, and Daoism— can be synthesized into one ethical doctrine.

1407: More than two thousand scholars of the National University and the imperial Hanlin Academy finish editing and compiling a massive work that claims to incorporate the full range of classical learning. Titled the *Great Literary Repository of the Yong Le Reign*, it contains material on the classical texts, history, ritual, law, military affairs, philosophy, religion, plants and animals, medicine, astronomy, geography, and literature.

1417: The set of selections from orthodox Confucian texts known as the *Great Compendium of the Philosophy of Human Nature* is published. Together with the *Great Compendium of the Five Classics and Four Books* of 1415, it becomes the official standard of Ming learning.

1427: The emperor Xuande orders a foundry for fine bronze and copper vessels to be established. Sixty-four artisans are assigned to work there. Among other items, they cast the famous Ming incense-burners.

1436: The primer titled *Newly Compiled Four Character Glossary* is published.

1450–1457: Ming cloisonné vessels and containers feature rich blues, turquoises, and greens, with peony, lotus, and chrysanthemum decoration.

1470–1559: Lifespan of the scholar-painter Wen Zhengming. His commentary infuses meaning into the rather static scenes he paints, for example, his depiction of an ancient cypress, a symbol of endurance.

1476: Buddhism and Daoism are vigorous. One hundred thousand monks are ordained this year; by 1490 there will be five times as many monks in the empire.

***c.* 1500:** Portuguese kings begin collecting Ming porcelain.

1527–1602: Lifespan of philosopher-historian Li Zhi, heterodox author of *Book Burning, Book Holding* and other works. "Why should stress be laid on the old classics?" he asks. A liberal thinker following loosely in the tradition of Wang Yangming, he runs afoul of the Ming powers, is charged with spreading dangerous ideas, and dies in prison in his seventy-fifth year.

1552: Francis Xavier, one of the founders of the Jesuit order, dies on an island just off the Guangdong coast—his closest approach to China despite great efforts to reach the fabled empire.

1574–1646: Lifespan of Feng Menglong, author-compiler of collections of vernacular tales titled *Stories to Enlighten Men, Stories to Warn Men,* and *Stories to Awaken Men.* He peoples his sometimes comic stories with a colorful cast of robbers, nobles, monks, courtesans, and spirits.

1577: Imperial demand for high-quality porcelain peaks. The kilns at Jingdezhen in northern Jiangxi turn out 96,500 small pieces, 56,600 large pieces, and 21,600 pieces for use in sacrificial ceremonies.

1577: Alessandro Valignano, the head of the Jesuit missions in East Asia, orders that missionaries to China be fully instructed in Chinese manners and customs before they attempt to carry out their work.

1583: The Italian Jesuit missionary Matteo Ricci (1552–1610) arrives in Macau near the South China city of Guangzhou. By 1595, he has moved on to Nanjing.

1593–1657: Lifespan of Tan Qian, author of *National Deliberations,* a history of the Ming dynasty written in the form of annals.

1598: The dramatist-satirist Tang Xianzu (1550–1616) writes the *The Peony Pavilion.* That work, together with *Purple Hairpin, The Dream of Han Tan,* and *The Southern Tributary State,* are known collectively as the *Four Dreams of Linchuan* because Linchuan is the author's native county in Jiangxi province. In 1998, *The Peony Pavilion* will become the center of a controversy when Chinese officials refuse to allow it to be performed in the United States. [See June 24, 1998.]

1598: Matteo Ricci makes his first trip to Beijing.

Early 1600s: *Golden Lotus,* one of China's masterpieces of fiction, is published. An allegory of greed, the story of the hedonistic career of the scholar-official Qing Ximen, it is also a realistic portrayal of elite Chinese family life.

1602: The Dutch begin large-scale importation of Chinese porcelain. Ming kilns are best known for polychrome pieces with a blue underglaze. Such pieces are in great demand in Europe and Asia. By 1682 the Dutch United East India Company will have shipped 12 million pieces to Europe.

1601–1609: Matteo Ricci, resident in Beijing, reports on "the exceedingly large numbers of books in circulation" there compared to his native Italy and "the ridiculously low prices at which they are sold." A man of charm and wide learning, he is welcomed at the imperial court, where he preaches Christianity and lectures on Western scientific advances. He makes few converts, however, and those only among the educated elite, for the Jesuits have little influence at lower levels of the social scale.

1614: Jesuit missionaries are at work in nine of the fifteen provinces. By dynasty's end, there are an estimated 150,000 Chinese Christians.

1621: Historian Mao Yuanyi completes *A Record of Military Affairs,* a study of military theory, strategy, and campaigns throughout China's history.

1625: The unorthodox philosopher Li Zhi remains so widely read more than twenty years after his death that the emperor orders the censors to find and burn the wooden printing blocks of his works.

1638: Chen Zilong and others complete *A Collection of Essays on National Affairs during the Ming Dynasty,* a compilation of source materials on Ming history, politics, and economics.

1643: The examination system is so corrupt that first and second places in Beijing go to the highest bidders.

QING DYNASTY:1644–1912

1610–1695: Lifespan of the political philosopher-historian Huang Zongxi. A follower of the Donglin reformers of the late Ming, he writes biographies of important Ming leaders and analyses of Ming government structure, including a work titled *Cases in the History of the Ming.*

1613–1682: Lifespan of Gu Yanwu, whose wide learning, extensive travels, and empirical research inform his essays on government, ethics, economics, geography, and social relations. His work will deeply influence the *Kaozheng* scholarly movement of the eighteenth century.

1616–1705: Lifespan of the painter Zhu Da. A Ming imperial clansman, he refuses to collaborate with the Manchus, concentrating instead on his highly expressionistic paintings of birds, fish, rocks, mountains, and other natural features.

1632–1717: Lifespan of the artist Wang Hui, painter of *The Kangxi Emperor's Second Tour of the South,* 1691–1695.

1652: Xiao Yuncong paints *Reading in Snowy Mountains.*

1670: The Kangxi emperor promulgates the *Sacred Edict,* a compilation of Confucian maxims on morality, manners, and social relations.

1680: Pu Zongling (1640–1719) completes his *Strange Tales from a Lonely Studio,* a collection of five hundred stories, many with the theme of young love and many on fantastic subjects.

1688: Dramatist Hong Sheng (1645–1704) completes the *Palace of Eternal Youth,* a play set during the An Lushan rebellion of the Tang dynasty.

1691: Yuan Jiang paints *The Jiucheng Palace.*

1692: The Kangxi emperor issues an edict extending toleration to Christian converts so long as they continue to perform ancestral rites. He rescinds the edict, however, when a Vatican envoy rules against allowing Chinese Christians to perform the ancient rites.

1699: Kong Shangren (1648–1718) completes his popular drama *The Peach Blossom Fan.* Set in the Ming pretender court of the Prince of Fu, it tells the story of a Ming scholar and the woman he loves against a backdrop of court intrigue. The work becomes a favorite at the Qing court.

1724: Emperor Yongzheng bans Christianity; Jesuits are permitted only in Beijing. The ban is not enforced with violence, however. "The distant barbarians come here attracted by our culture," the emperor observes. "We must show them generosity and virtue."

1726: The massive encyclopedia titled *Complete Collection of Illustrations and Writings from Earliest to Current Times* is published. It runs to 800,000 pages and contains more than 100 million Chinese characters.

c. 1765: *Kaozheng* scholars are widely influential. Devoted to facts and rigorous in their methodology, they undertake close textual study of the Confucian classics to determine which parts of the canon are the master's and which parts are later accretions. They cast doubt on the works of once-influential Song-era interpreters such as Zhu Xi. Dai Zhen (1723–1777) is a leading *kaozheng* scholar. His later work, however, turns philosophical and speculative about human motivations and the meaning of moral action.

1768: The novel *Unofficial History of the Scholars,* an important Qing literary work, is published. It depicts the lives and struggles of the underemployed eighteenth-century educated elite.

1772–1782: As part of a vast literary compilation project that takes a decade to complete, Qianlong orders thousands of books closely examined for disparaging references to the Manchus. Some two thousand offending titles disappear entirely. The compilation, edited by Dai Zhen and known as the *Four Treasures,* is a complete anthology of the Chinese classics, histories, treatises on philosophy, and literary works. It fills 36,000 manuscript volumes.

1784–1785: The Qing government carries out a general persecution of China's small Catholic community. In 1800 the country's Catholic population is estimated at 200,000–250,000.

1792: *The Dream of the Red Chamber*, China's greatest novel, incomplete at author Cao Xueqin's death in 1763, is published. It follows the fortunes of the Jia family from wealth and power to gradual decline and final collapse.

1794–1856: Lifespan of the scholar Wei Yuan. His *Collected Writings* discusses Chinese government theory and practice. He is also the author of the *Illustrated Treatise on the Maritime Kingdoms*.

1807: Robert Morrison of the London Missionary Society (established 1795) arrives in China. Protestants find it slow going; Morrison will baptize his first Chinese convert only in 1814.

1810–1820: Li Ruzhen writes China's greatest satirical novel, *Flowers in the Mirror*. In parts of the novel gender roles are reversed and men are subjected to pain and humiliation. Li has this to say of footbinding: "Blood and flesh were squeezed into pulp and then little remained of his feet but dry bones and skin, shrunk, indeed, to a dainty size."

1819: British missionary Robert Morrison and a colleague translate the Old Testament and New Testament into Chinese.

1820s: The Xuehai Tang (the "Sea of Learning Hall") is founded in Guangzhou (Canton). It becomes an important South China center of scholarship.

1835: An American, Dr. Peter Parker, the first medical missionary sent to China, opens a hospital at Guangzhou.

1839: Thirty Catholic missionaries are at work in China. The number will more than double by 1845.

1844: Presbyterian mission school in the treaty port of Ningbo opens with an enrollment of thirty Chinese boys. The first class will graduate in 1850. Also this year, the first mission school for girls opens in Ningbo.

1850: Full translation of the Bible and a Manchu version of the New Testament circulate in China.

1850s: The Taiping Rebellion sweeps China, drawing strength from Chinese popular religion with its ghosts, spirits, and admixtures of Daoism, Buddhism, and, in the case of the Taiping leader Hong Xiuquan, Christianity.

1854: Yung Wing (1828–1912) graduates from Yale University. The first Chinese graduate of an American university, he will use his connections to import modern industrial machinery and weaponry into China from the United States.

1862: Qing reformers open an interpreters' school, teaching English and French, in Beijing. Government-sponsored language schools soon open in Shanghai, Canton, and Fuzhou.

1865: Translation of Euclid's *Elements of Geometry* is published with an introduction by the prominent reforming scholar-official Zeng Guofan.

February 1867: Beijing interpreters' school reopens as a college offering mathematics, chemistry, geology, mechanics, and international law as well as languages.

June 1870: Simmering antiforeign resentment erupts as violence in Tianjin. In the so-called Tianjin Massacre, mobs kill sixteen French missionaries and consular officials. The government tries and executes sixteen Chinese for the killings.

1879: The American Episcopal Mission founds St. John's College in Shanghai.

1890: Protestant missionaries are established in fifteen of China's sixteen provinces. By 1900 there are five hundred Protestant mission stations in the country.

1896: Two Chinese mission school graduates, given the western names of Ida Kahn and Mary Stone, return from the United States with University of Michigan medical degrees and open medical practices in China.

1896: Qing government founds Nanyang College in Shanghai.

1900: Total of Chinese Catholics reaches 700,000; there are around 100,000 Chinese Protestants.

1905: Qing abolishes the traditional Confucian examination system.

1906: Around 250 Protestant mission hospitals and dispensaries treat 2 million Chinese annually. Some 58,000 Chinese students are enrolled in Protestant mission schools.

1907: Qing approves a national system of girls' education. Within three years forty thousand girls' schools enroll 1.6 million students.

1908: The United States allocates half its Boxer indemnity, around $12 million, to train Chinese students in America. The fund will have supported 1,268 Chinese scholars by 1929.

THE REPUBLIC: 1912–1949

1904–1965: Lifespan of the painter Fu Baoshi. His works often interpret scenes from Chinese poems. His landscapes and figures celebrate China's history and scholarly tradition.

1912: Yan Fu (1854–1921), the translator of Darwin, Huxley, Spencer, and Adam Smith, is first president of the reorganized Beijing University, successor to the late Qing Metropolitan University, founded in 1898.

1915: The American Rockefeller Foundation helps establish the Beijing Union Medical College. It will become China's leading center of medical research and teaching.

1915: Chen Duxiu (1879–1942), Dean of Letters at Beijing University, founds the periodical *New Youth*, which attacks traditional Chinese thought. "We must be thoroughly aware of the incompatibility between Confucianism and the new belief, the new society, and the new state," Chen writes. In keeping with this, the magazine will abandon classical Chinese and publish in the vernacular.

1917–1926: Cai Yuanpei (1868–1948) is president of Beijing University. He upgrades the faculty, improves the curriculum, and encourages students to take "new views of the world and life." Cai will become an influential figure in the May Fourth political and cultural revival.

1919: More than 130,000 girls' schools enroll 4.5 million students.

May 1, 1919: In *New Youth*, Beijing University librarian Li Dazhao (1889–1927) publishes an introduction to Marxist theory. He will organize a Marxist study group at the university in 1921 whose attendees include Mao Zedong, a young student from rural Henan.

1920s: Lu Xun, a satirist of contemporary Chinese manners and character, is China's leading writer. Lu Xun writes in the *baihua* vernacular, following the advice of those who call for the abandonment of stilted classical literary language in favor of one accessible to ordinary people.

Lu Xun's political views turn increasingly leftist in the later 1920s, but he remains a literary independent. "Great works of literature have never obeyed any orders or concerned themselves with utilitarian motives," he remarks in 1927.

1920: Beijing University admits women students for the first time. By 1922 women students will make up 2.5 percent of the total enrollment of 35,000 in China's colleges and universities.

1922: The YMCA claims 54,000 members in thirty-six Chinese cities. China's radicals disdain the organization. "YMCAs constantly use athletics, popular education, etc. to do evangelistic work so as to smother the political thought of the youth," Shanghai radicals claim.

December 1927: The feminist writer Ding Ling publishes the story "The Diary of Miss Sophie." This hard-eyed, bleak look at emancipation—social, cultural, sexual—in Republican China will create a sensation and make its author famous. She will later become a Communist.

1928: Nationalist leader Chiang Kai-shek establishes the Guomindang Central Political Institute in Beijing for political leaders and government administrators. The course of study is nationalist and antiforeign, with a Confucian undercurrent emphasizing order, harmony, discipline, and hierarchy.

March 1928: The Crescent Moon literary society publishes the first number of its magazine. The society takes a western aesthetic view of art and artists; neither revolution nor class forms a basis for literary criticism. *Crescent Moon* writers battle polemically with the left-wing purveyors of "proletarian" literature.

1929–1937: The Academia Sinica sponsors the excavation of the heretofore legendary Shang dynasty capital at Anyang north of the Yellow River in Henan province. Archeologists unearth the foundations of fifty-three buildings, a trove of Shang bronzes, and the famous oracle bones before the Japanese invasion interrupts their work.

1930s: Cultural changes in urban China penetrate the countryside only slowly. Rural traditions remain everywhere potent: the New Year and the Lantern Festival; the springtime Qingming grave-sweeping festival (these remain popular in the cities too); and countless fairs scheduled from village to village on the birthdays of local temple gods. Along with religious observances, the fairs offer merchants shops, stalls for barbers, fortunetellers and storytellers, and livestock trading.

March 2, 1930: The League of Left-Wing Writers is established in Shanghai. Most of its writers will hew to the Communist Party line. Among the founders is the fellow traveler Lu Xun. Though a convert, he refuses to equate propaganda with literature.

October 1930: Chiang Kai-shek is baptized a Christian. His wife Soong Meiling is a graduate of Wellesley College in Massachusetts. Through his wife, Chiang makes important American connections.

1931: Pearl S. Buck, the daughter of American missionaries in China, publishes *The Good Earth*, a novel of Chinese life set in the tumultuous present. It has a great impact on Americans' views of China and its troubles. The novel sells 1.5 million copies and wins a Pulitzer Prize.

1932: Mao Dun's novel of capitalist exploitation in Shanghai, *Midnight*, is published. A committed Communist, Mao Dun (1896–1982) is a leading member of the Stalin-inspired League of Left-Wing Writers.

1932: Gao Jianfu paints *Flying in the Rain*, depicting seven biplanes aloft over a typical Chinese landscape of water, trees, and mountains.

1933: Ba Jin, the most popular novelist of the 1930s, publishes *Family*, a story of the "new youth." Its leading characters, three brothers, represent types of young activists of the May Fourth Movement.

1935: Despite the spread of coeducation in urban areas, educated women are rare in country districts; only 2 percent of women in rural China are literate, compared to 30 percent of men.

1937: The popular author Lao She's novel *Rickshaw*, exploring underclass life in Beijing, is published.

1938: Japanese occupation forces the relocation of China's universities. Nankai, National Beijing, and other institutions combine to form the National Southwest Associated University in Nationalist-held Kunming in Yunnan. By 1940, enrollment will reach three thousand.

1941: Mao Dun publishes *Putrefaction*, a political novel of the "New Fourth Army Incident" that details abuses of the Guomindang secret police.

May 2, 1942: Mao Zedong convenes the Yan'an Forum on Literature and Art, part of the Communists' ideological Rectification Campaign of 1942–1943. The forum lays down the party line on the forms and purposes of literature. The life of the people is "the sole and inexhaustible source of processed literature and art," Mao declares. He disdains traditional forms of high art, whether Chinese or foreign. "Revolutionary Chinese writers and artists must go among the masses," he says. "They must go among the masses of workers, peasants and soldiers, and into the heat of battle for a long time to come."

1943: Communist cultural commissars revamp the popular Peking opera form with a production of a work titled *Driven to Join the Liangshan Rebels*. The story is taken from a novel called *The Water Margin*, a tale of noble, protorevolutionary outlaws then a favorite work of Mao Zedong himself.

February 27, 1945: Writers and artists in the Nationalist capital of Chongqing publish a manifesto that demands an end to censorship, police spying, and war profiteering. It also seeks guarantees of personal safety, freedom of speech, and freedom to publish. The government responds with arrests; in 1946, Guomindang agents in Kunming will assassinate a poet associated with the manifesto.

1947: The popular novelist Ba Jin publishes *Cold Nights*, a work set in wartime Chongqing.

THE PEOPLE'S REPUBLIC: 1949–1998

March 1949: The Communist newspaper *People's Daily* moves to Beijing.

July 1949: First National Conference of Literature and Arts Workers meets in Beijing.

December 1949: Novelist/playwright Lao She (1899–1966, author of *Rickshaw*, 1937) returns to China after three years in the United States.

1950: Communist government establishes Institute of Archeology with permanent field stations at Anyang, Xian, and Luoyang.

October 1951: Volume 1 of *The Selected Works of Mao Zedong* is published in Beijing.

January 10, 1955: The Peking Opera Company is established.

May 25, 1955: Government dismisses the writer Hu Feng from the writer's union and other posts for "bourgeois and idealist thinking." He resists the primacy of Marxist theory in art criticism. "This weapon is frightening," he says, "because it can stifle the real feelings of creativity and art." Arrested in July and tried in secret, Hu is held in prison for most of the next twenty-four years.

1957: Mao Zedong's Anti-Rightist Campaign targets writers and artists. The journalist Liu Binyan (born 1925), who introduces the form of investigative journalism the Chinese dub "reporting literature," is among the younger victims. Older, established writers are not overlooked. During the Hundred Flowers Campaign, Ding Ling (1904–1985), author of *The Diary of Miss Sophie* and an ideologically correct, Stalin Prize-winning work of "proletarian" literature titled *The Sun Shines over the Sanggan River*, calls for the lifting of government controls on literature. In the aftermath, she is stripped of her party jobs and sent to work as a laborer on a farm near the Siberian frontier.

December 1957: Liang Bin publishes his novel *Keep the Red Flag Flying*.

March 4, 1958: *Peking Review* begins publication.

September 2, 1958: Beijing Television begins broadcasting.

March 17, 1960: Gong Pinmei, the Catholic bishop of Shanghai, is sentenced to life in prison.

Early 1960s: Government institutes the "two

track" education system, with superior schooling for talented children and lesser instruction for ordinary students. A feature is "keypoint" college preparatory schools for elite students. Mao Zedong opposes this system as "revisionist."

1961: Pan Tianshou paints *Crane and Frost Plum Together at Year's End.*

January 1961: Historian Wu Han's play *The Dismissal of Hai Rui from Office* is published. The work will be regarded as an implicit critique of Communist Party tyranny and in particular an attack on Mao Zedong.

July 1, 1961: The Museum of Chinese History and the Museum of the Chinese Revolution open in Beijing.

August 1962: The People's Literary Press publishes the fourteenth and last volume of Ba Jin's *Collected Works.*

April 1963: Jiang Qing, Mao Zedong's wife, calls for the banning of ghost plays and other traditional dramatic forms.

October 20, 1964: *The East Is Red*, a historical poem with music and dancing, is staged in Beijing.

November 1965: An article in a Shanghai newspaper attacks Wu Han's *The Dismissal of Hai Rui* as an allegorical critique of Mao Zedong. This proves to be a ranging shot in the coming Cultural Revolution.

1966–1976: Radicals target writers and artists during the Mao-inspired Cultural Revolution. The writer Ding Ling spends five years in a state prison; not even her authorship of a work titled *Songs in Praise of the Five-Year Plan* can save her. Red Guards publicly humiliate the author Ba Jin, whose novel *Family* had been a bestseller in the 1930s. Radicals forces Ba's wife to work as a streetcleaner. Red Guards drive the distinguished novelist Lao She to suicide.

June 1966: Government suspends college entrance examinations and shuts down the schools for a semester as part of the Cultural Revolution.

1967: Cultural Revolution activists dismantle the two-track education system and introduce egalitarian schooling for the masses.

July 1968: The revolutionary opera *The Red Lantern* opens in Beijing.

1972: Guan Shanyue paints *Oil City in the South*, an idealized picture of China's industrial development.

1973–1974: Government propaganda campaign attacks Confucius and Confucian thought as reactionary and praises the first emperor of Qin, Zheng, long vilified as a tyrant. Disgraced officials such as the former defense minister Lin Biao are stigmatized as "the Confuciuses of contemporary China."

April 1973: The Vienna Philharmonic Orchestra tours China. The Philadelphia Orchestra will tour the country in September.

January 14, 1974: An editorial in the *People's Daily* attacks Beethoven, Schubert, and other European composers as "bourgeois."

October 1977: College entrance examinations are restored as part of the dismantling of the Cultural Revolution education system. Decision-making is restored to academics; ideological supervision is reduced; and "quality over quantity" is sought in the schools. The latter leads to a restoration of the two-track system favoring talented students, which as Mao feared does tend to favor students of educated or high-status background.

1978: Pursuing a gradual opening to the West, China sends a first group of 480 top students to study abroad.

1979: Huang Yongyu paints *Lotus at Night.*

January 1, 1979: Publications in China using the Roman alphabet change to the pinyin system of romanization.

June 1979: The literary periodical *The Present* begins publication.

1980: Authorities ban the film *Bitter Love* on account of its "negative" message. The film tells the story of a painter and his family brutalized during the Cultural Revolution. The action signals the opening of a government campaign against "spiritual pollution," which is how the party views self-expression in the arts.

Early 1980s: The Communist leadership pursues badly needed education reform—only 14 percent of the party's 40 million members are high school graduates, a survey finds. Many Chinese students are now permitted to study abroad.

October 1, 1981: China gives salary increases to primary and secondary school teachers.

1982: Census shows illiteracy is still widespread in China; 28.2 percent of the population is classified as illiterate or semiliterate.

1982: Twenty universities and institutes offer undergraduate law studies, with two thousand students enrolled.

1983: Some eleven thousand Chinese are studying in fifty-four foreign countries at government expense; another seven thousand are paying their own way in school abroad.

July 28, 1984: At Los Angeles, China wins its first-ever Olympic gold medal, in a pistol-shooting event.

January 5, 1985: The government issues a new charter for the Chinese Writers Association that promises freedom of expression—so long as members follow party and Marxist-Leninist guidelines.

May 19, 1985: Riot erupts in Beijing after Hong Kong defeats China in a soccer match.

April 21, 1986: China mandates nine years' compulsory education in cities and other developed areas by 1990 and everywhere else by 2000.

1988: More than 7 million children drop out of China's schools—including primary schools. The State Statistical Bureau reports that 230 million Chinese are illiterate.

Spring 1988: A popular Chinese television documentary titled *River Elegy* blames China's problems on ancient traditions such as inwardness, xenophobia, and lack of curiosity about the larger world.

December 22, 1988: China's first exhibit of nude paintings opens in Beijing.

1994: Authorities ban the film *The Blue Kite*, a story of family suffering during the political upheavals of the 1950s and 1960s.

1996: China's colleges and universities enroll 3.2 million undergraduates. There are 136 million students in primary schools and 50 million in junior secondary schools.

June 24, 1998: After some weeks of negotiations, Chinese officials in Shanghai announce that they will not allow the Shanghai opera group to perform *The Peony Pavilion* at the Lincoln Center summer festival in New York City because the production is judged to be "feudal, superstitious, and pornographic." The sets and costumes may be sent because they were paid for by the Lincoln Center festival, but the singers are not allowed to leave China, thus effectively stopping the performance.

China

SCIENCE-TECHNOLOGY, ECONOMICS, AND EVERYDAY LIFE

PREHISTORIC AND LEGENDARY CHINA: 1,960,000–2200 B.C.

500,000–250,000 B.C.: It had long been widely claimed that the hominids who inhabit the caves at Zhoukoudian make and control fire in hearths, but in 1998 scientists announce that there is no evidence of a fire in the cave.

12,000–6000 B.C.: Neolithic people of China live in villages, farm, use polished stone tools, and make pottery.

5,000–3,000 B.C.: Chinese sites from as early as 5000 B.C. yield some of the oldest known evidence for keeping nonruminant animals such as pigs and chickens. By 4500 B.C. the oldest known evidence in East Asia for keeping ruminants is the bones of small and possibly domesticated cattle found in northern China.

4000–3000 B.C.: By the end of this period, copper is being used at some sites in China.

2698–2599 B.C.: According to tradition, the Yellow Emperor himself takes an interest in mathematics and astronomy and he is the patron of important texts in these fields of study.

2500 B.C.: The earliest known evidence of bronze in East Asia is found in northern China.

2357–2258 B.C.: According to tradition, during the reign of Emperor Yao important astronomical observations are made.

2255–2208 B.C.: According to Han tradition, the Emperor Shun's chief minister, Yu, tames the flood after nine devastating years with a series of permanent flood control measures: canals are dug, river channels are dredged, reservoirs are created.

THE THREE DYNASTIES (XIA, SHANG, ZHOU): 2208–249 B.C.

1500 B.C.: The Chinese are making silk about this time, the first people in the world known to do so. About this time, too, the Chinese are the first in East Asia known to use horse-drawn vehicles.

c. **1200 B.C.:** War chariots come into use in

North China military campaigns. Shang's hunter-warrior kings field armies as large as three thousand to five thousand men. These soldiers, carried into battle aboard chariots, carry spears with bronze blades, wooden bows and halberds—a wooden pole with blades affixed to the tip of the shaft.

6th century B.C.: Bronze swords appear as weapons of war, probably reaching the Chinese through contact with steppe tribes. In the next century, the crossbow, more accurate and powerful than the compound bow, will be introduced.

594 B.C.: The small state of Lu in Shandong province introduces a new system of taxation. This leads to changes in peasant-landlord relations in which the peasantry becomes more independent; at the same time, the peasant class loses some landlord protections. Some peasants are able to acquire land; others, however, are reduced to landless laborer status.

500 B.C.: Iron begins to come into use in China; its use soon spreads throughout Asia.

487 B.C.: A canal is built to link the Yangtze and Huai rivers; its purpose is military and defensive.

408 B.C.: Taxation of grain is mentioned for the first time in Qin.

400 B.C.: Animal-drawn plows gradually begin replacing hand-hoe methods of cultivation. Iron is in general use for hoes, sickles, and other agricultural tools. But it is expensive, so stone and wooden tools are still widespread.

336 B.C.: Metal currency is issued for the first time in Qin.

307 B.C.: In the state of Zhao, mounted archers to supplement infantry are used for the first time. The notion is probably borrowed from the nomadic tribes. The growing use of cavalry gives rise to an important change in dress, to trousers and tunics.

QIN DYNASTY: 221–206 B.C.

3d century B.C.: Qin's military superiority depends in part on widespread use of iron weapons. Iron tools also foster development of Qin agriculture.

This is possibly the century when the *Chou-pei Suan-chang*, China's oldest true mathematical work, is written down. Scholars believe it contains knowledge that goes back to the 12th century B.C.

246 B.C.: Work begins on the Cheng Guo Canal in southwest Qin; it eventually irrigates 465,000 acres of former wasteland.

221–214 B.C.: Meng Tian, a leading Qin general, uses 300,000 laborers to construct a defense system of packed earthen walls along the northern frontier. With much later additions, it becomes the Great Wall of China.

221–210 B.C.: The First Emperor, Zheng,

standardizes imperial weights and measures. Qin authorities demolish city walls throughout the empire and collect and destroy vast stockpiles of weapons.

220 B.C.: Construction begins on a system of imperial highways.

219 B.C.: The cutting of a mountain canal is the key link in a river network that eventually allows uninterrupted water transport from the Yangtze River to the South China port of Guangzhou (Canton).

212 B.C.: Work begins on a major highway running north from the Qin capital across the Ordos Desert and the Yellow River into modern Inner Mongolia—a total distance of more than five hundred miles. Altogether, the Qin highway network exceeds four thousand miles.

HAN DYNASTY: 202 B.C.–A.D. 200

189 B.C.: The Western Market opens in Chang'an, the Early Han capital. It becomes the principal workplace for merchants, traders, and travelers from the provinces and from Central Asia. It also is a site for divination and for such public spectacles as the execution of traitors.

139 B.C.: Zhang Qian embarks on his first journey of exploration in Central Asia. He is captured and held prisoner for ten years. He escapes and continues his wandering, giving China a new knowledge and awareness of the world to the west.

c. **120 B.C.:** Han merchants gradually develop trade routes along the Silk Road into Central Asia. They exchange Chinese silk for horses, fleece, and raw jade. Eventually wine will be imported into China from the west, and vineyards will be kept for the imperial court.

c. **120 B.C.:** Increasing contact with outlanders from India and Central Asia, with their foreign words, names, and concepts, leads to extensive additions to the Chinese written vocabulary.

115 B.C.: The government establishes an agency to regulate commodity prices.

115 B.C.: Zhang Qian sets out on his second expedition to Central Asia. He reaches Ferghana and Sogdiana and returns home with an enthusiastic report about prospects for the silk trade.

c. **115 B.C.:** State salt and iron monopolies are established.

112 B.C.: Han imposes controls on the minting of coins. The mostly copper five-*shu* piece is adopted as the standard and its manufacture restricted to government agencies. *Shu* indicates weight; five *shu* are the equivalent of three grams. Exchange value is roughly 10,000 copper coins for a 244-gram gold ingot.

104 B.C.: Zhang Qian's explorations end in the Han conquest of the kingdom of Ferghana in the northwest. Chinese traders push westward along the Silk Road to Persia.

c. **100 B.C.:** Water clocks are in use in China for marking time.

98 B.C.: Government sets up a monopoly on liquor.

81 B.C.: The emperor orders an inquiry into the causes of popular hardship. The result is a wide-ranging conference at the imperial court in which scholars debate state-run versus private enterprise, public good versus private gain. The state monopolies become a main point of contention. Confucian reformists view them as a burden on the people. Modernists see them as necessary to fund state expansion. The sessions are recorded in a remarkable document, produced some years after the conference, titled *Discourse on Salt and Iron.*

66–64 B.C.: In response to adverse portents, the government lowers the price of salt, reduces taxes, and takes other measures to ease the people's distress in a period of economic hardship.

c. **45 B.C.:** Contemporary sources mention three large textile manufactories in operation in east China, each employing several thousand workers. Most Chinese textiles are woven from hemp and silk; for the common people, garments woven coarsely from hemp are everyday wear.

44 B.C.: Reformists succeed in abolishing the state monopolies.

41 B.C.: Loss of revenue leads the state to restore monopolies on salt and iron.

30 B.C.: Heavy flooding causes widespread hardship in parts of China. Han officials respond to the disaster with new flood control programs, including dike-building and the cutting of auxiliary channels to carry off excess water.

c. **5 B.C.:** Use of the sea facilitates the unification of China and its expansion southward. A Han-era ship model found by modern archaeologists near Guangzhou (Canton) has a centered sternpost rudder, a major advance in maritime technology that will not appear in Europe for a thousand years.

1st century A.D.: Probable time when the *Chiu-chang suan-shu* (Nine Chapters on Mathematical Techniques), a classic Chinese text, is compiled. It is possibly the oldest textbook on arithmetic in existence and records knowledge probably dating back to at least the third century B.C. (for it is attributed to Chang Tsang, who lived *c.* 250–152 B.C.). It is particularly noted for its consideration of the properties and applications of the right triangle, paralleling the work of Pythagoras in some respects.

A.D. 1–2: Nearly fifty iron foundries are in operation in China north of the Yangtze. Contemporary sources suggest as many as 100,000 men work in iron and copper mines. Metalworking shops turn out farming tools; arms, including swords, spears, helmets, armor, arrowheads, and bronze triggers for crossbows; and domestic utensils such as lamps, pots, cooking stoves, and knives.

At least three government workshops are turning out fine lacquerware at this time, some of it for export. Over time, green, yellow, gold, and silver pigments supplement the basic lacquer colors of red and black.

More than thirty agencies are involved in the manufacture of salt, the essential preservative. Around a dozen works draw salt from the sea along the Shandong coast, using a system of pans or tanks for evaporation. Inland, in Manchuria and the Ordos, rock salt and brine are mined, using sophisticated engineering techniques, from deep within the earth.

c. 3–5: Major floods claim many lives, destroy crops, and alter the course of the Yellow River, touching off what will build up to a major population migration southward.

5: The government completes a new road linking the Wei River valley to today's Sichuan to the south, improving communications between the two regions.

9: Bronze footrules capable of precise measurements are in general use in the building trades.

The government of Wang Mang, who has taken power in the wake of the collapse of Early Han, introduces a new range of coins, at least twenty-eight denominations. They are minted from gold, silver, tortoise shell, cowries, and copper.

10: The government reestablishes the off-again, on-again state monopolies on liquor, salt, and iron tools. Government storehouses for grain, cloth, and silk open in five major cities as part of a price-stabilization effort. A 10 percent income tax is levied on hunters, fishermen, artisans, and merchants. Most of these practices had been tried before; modern historians regard them as a continuation of Early Han policies rather than a radical departure.

16: Wang Mang orders an executed prisoner dissected for scientific/medical research.

25: Wang Mang's new coins fail to catch on. With the advent of Later Han, the five-*shu* piece is again declared the standard.

27–c. 100: Lifespan of essayist and natural philosopher Wang Chong. He argues that disasters arise from natural causes and not the failings of rulers, and attributes belief in occult forces such as ghosts to weakness and hallucination.

30: To ease burdens on the peasantry, the first emperor of the Later Han lightens the land levy, taking only one-thirtieth part of the average harvest in tax.

c. 65: By tradition, the first suspension bridge spans the Mekong River. It carries a growing trade along the mountain road linking China and Burma.

69: Using hundreds of thousands of conscript workers, Han engineers repair dikes, build watergates, and carry out related flood-control projects.

76: Cattle epidemics devastate China's herds. A shortage of draft animals leads to significant reductions in the amount of land under cultivation and thus to food shortages.

78–139: Lifespan of Zhang Heng, scientist

and mathematician. He calculates the value of π at 3.1622—the most accurate approximation yet in China. He is best known for his invention of a seismograph.

84: To promote agriculture, government orders commanderies to recruit landless men for resettlement in fertile districts. They are to be given state-owned land and paid to farm it.

88: The government temporarily ends monopolies on iron and salt, making up the revenue shortfall by taxing private manufacturers.

92–93: Drought and locust plagues cause large crop losses. Government relief measures include dropping the tax on land and straw.

2d century: The single-wheeled barrow is in widespread use. The first steel is produced.

Large landowning families dominate agricultural life. They are responsible, in part, for significant advances in farming methods during the next century or so, particularly in irrigation technique and in the processing of grain. Iron tools are in general use on large estates, though wooden tools are still common.

101: Crop failures cause widespread hardship. In response, Han authorities cancel food and seed debts of impoverished peasants.

105: This is the traditional date given for the invention of rag paper. It may be too early a date and in any case this kind of paper did not appear suddenly. Historians suggest that paper probably found its origin in experimentation with waste silk fibers. Silk cloth and wood slips will remain the most commonly used writing materials for at least another century.

153: Famine in the aftermath of Yellow River floods and locust infestations sets hundreds of thousands of "drifting" peasants on the road. Over the next two years, overwhelmed provincial officials report large-scale starvation.

166: Greek merchant traders visit China.

190: Water engineering works, possibly a series of high water wheels, send a continuous supply of water to the city of Luoyang.

THE THREE KINGDOMS AND SIX DYNASTIES: 220–589

263: Date assigned to composition of *Hai-tau Suan-king* (Sea Island Arithmetic Classic) by Li Hui.

4th century: Constant fighting devastates the countryside and depresses trade and commerce.

c. **300:** Rag paper, an invention of the Later Han, is coming into widespread use. The first authenticated surviving pieces of paper are dated A.D. 310 and 312.

SUI DYNASTY: 589–618

581: To counter the continuing threat of nomadic invasion from the north, the Sui launches a long-term project to repair and expand the Great Wall, China's traditional line of defense. Thirty thousand workers are conscripted for the initial stages. During this short-lived dynasty, much of the wall will be rebuilt on existing foundations using traditional construction materials, pounded earth, and sun-dried brick.

581–682: Lifespan of Sun Simiao, one of China's leading pharmacologists. His *Precious Prescriptions* and *Supplement to Precious Prescriptions* cover diagnosis, treatment, and prevention of disease and record the recipes for eight hundred common drugs.

584–589: Wendi orders a canal built from Chang'an to the confluence of the Wei and Yellow rivers one hundred miles distant. The canal will speed the shipment of grain into the capital region.

585: Wendi orders a network of granaries to be built to which peasant families are to pay an average 0.7 bushels of grain a year. The system will be expanded in 596.

592: Grain and textile shortages prompt Sui officials to launch a campaign to equalize land holdings and get more land into cultivation.

605: Yangdi orders construction of the Tongji Canal linking Luoyang with Chuzhou on the Huai River. As many as a million workers are mobilized for the job. Canal building has economic, military, and political uses, all of which tend to cement unity of the empire.

607: The emperor mobilizes a million workers for a new north-south section of the Great Wall from the Ordos region to modern Shanxi province.

608: Work begins on the largest of the Sui canals, the Yongji, which runs northeast from near Luoyang to the vicinity of modern Beijing. More than a million laborers, men and women, are said to have been involved in the project.

611: Floods in the Yellow River valley cause widespread distress and attendant political unrest. Labor levies for canal building and conscription for the pending Koguryo campaign feed the discontent.

TANG DYNASTY: 618–907

624: Together with the equal field land-tenure system, the new dynasty introduces a direct tax on each adult. The tax is in three forms: grain; silk or hemp fiber or cloth; and twenty days' annual corvée, or compulsory government labor service.

624: A new waterworks system opens eighty thousand acres to cultivation in Shanxi. A transport canal will be built to carry grain produced here to the capital at Chang'an.

628: The government establishes a system of relief granaries for famine times.

639: Grain price-regulation bureaus are set up in major cities.

668–670: A series of famines and natural disasters causes widespread distress. In 670, grain is so scarce in some districts that wine brewing is prohibited.

680: As a result of poor harvests, the price of grain rises to record levels.

682: The shortage of officially minted coins is chronic. The government orders the death penalty for the counterfeiting of coin.

682–727: Lifespan of Yi Xing, the first astronomer to work out a scientific study of the meridian.

***c.* 700:** As the eighth century opens, the Tang capital of Chang'an is perhaps the world's greatest city in size, riches, and grandeur. The imperial city is meticulously laid out, with fourteen main streets running north to south and eleven running east to west. It is astonishingly diverse and cosmopolitan. People from most of the known world gather there. Exotic music, dance and acrobatics are a feature of Chang'an life. Buddhist and Daoist religious sites are numerous, of course, but there is also a mosque and a small congregation of Syrian Christians. The city maintains a fine network of parks. Though there are poorer quarters, the imperial capital is prosperous.

700–800: Fame of Tang papermaking spreads beyond China's borders. Using bast fibers, mulberry, rattan and bamboo bark, and rice or wheat stalks, artisans produce fine paper of various types and colors.

Chinese trading vessels sail regularly between Canton and the Persian Gulf.

705: Great flood devastates area of modern Hebei province and the Wei valley.

706–707: Severe drought leads to famine in Hebei and Henan.

712–713: Severe famine strikes the overpopulated, underproducing Chang'an capital region.

712–755: The reign of Emperor Xuanzong is an era of population growth, especially in the lower Yangtze basin. General prosperity is the rule for much of the reign.

714–719: Responding to natural disasters and famines, the government extends the price-regulation granary system throughout the country. Within fifteen years large surplus stocks will be available for famine relief.

733–804: Lifespan of Lu Yu, author of the *Book of Tea*, which discusses the cultivation of tea bushes and tea processing in detail. It is during this time that tea-drinking begins to become popular in China, spreading to Japan about 805.

734: Tang officials found large agricultural colonies along the northern tributaries of the Huai River in Henan for the cultivation of paddy rice. The colonies will be abandoned as unwieldy within a few years.

755: Widespread rebellion in the provinces forces the Tang to abandon its effort to control land allocation—the so-called equal field system. The result: larger landed estates, tax inequities, and a growing gap between rich and poor.

780: The government alters the tax system, imposing direct levies on the land itself rather than the occupants. This has the effect of simplifying record-keeping and collection procedures.

c. 800: Tea, in use heretofore as a medicine, is in increasingly widespread use as a beverage.

c. 810: Exchange notes—negotiable certificates merchants and traders dub "flying money"—are in circulation. They are the forerunner of banknotes.

845: An imperial report on river piracy details how bands of pirates a hundred strong cruise up and down the Yangtze, plundering settlements and market centers.

858: Tremendous floods inundate the North China plain; along the Grand Canal, tens of thousands drown.

873: A disastrous harvest fuels popular unrest. In many areas only half the crop is gathered in and famine areas face mass starvation.

SONG DYNASTIES: 960–1279

994: Liao state produces the first calendar of its own.

997: Song government mints 800 million coins a year.

11th century: China's ironworkers develop a decarbonization method for steelmaking.

Roofs that curve upward become widespread for government buildings and the houses of people of high rank.

1021–1101: Lifespan of Su Sung, astronomer and scholar-official. *Hsin I Hsiang Fa Yao*, his book on the water-powered drive mechanism for an armillary sphere and celestial

globe, reveals that the Chinese have been making clocks for some six centuries.

1031–1095: Lifespan of the scientist, scholar, and official Shen Kuo. He designs drainage and embankment systems to reclaim land for cultivation. As head of the Bureau of Astronomy, he oversees improvements to observatory instruments and more accurate calendar-making. He is also an expert in state finances. His works include the first descriptions of movable type (which he attributes to Pi Cheng, c. 1041–1048); its use will not, however, become widespread in China for another three hundred years.

1040: The Song military manual known as the *Comprehensive Essentials of the Military Classics* contains the first known written description of gunpowder.

1070s: A series of locust plagues strips North China croplands bare and leads to widespread distress.

1072: A Japanese visitor reports the price of admission to a Hangzhou bathhouse at ten *cash.* Two centuries later, Marco Polo estimates there are three thousand bathhouses in the city.

1076: A school of medicine is founded in Kaifeng; it will move to the Southern Song capital, Hangzhou, after 1126.

1078: North China produces 125,000 tons of pig iron a year.

1082–1083: A bitter winter with heavy snows in North China kills vast numbers of horses and livestock—estimates range as high as 70 percent of the total.

1085: Six billion coins are minted a year in China.

1111–1117: Imperial decrees authorize arrest of homosexual prostitutes in Kaifeng, with punishment of one hundred strokes with a rod.

1119: Chinese sources first mention the invention of the compass. The Chinese appear to have known of the magnetic compass since about 270, and some such device has probably been in use since the middle of the eleventh century.

1120: Song government collects 18 million ounces of silver in taxes.

1120s: To simplify trade and financial transactions, the Song begins issuing paper money.

1125: North China's Jin rulers decree a government monopoly on wine; private wine production is barred. The law is widely disregarded.

1126: Jin issues an edict requiring Chinese to adopt Jurchen dress and hairstyle. It is widely ignored.

1130: Chinese inventors experiment with use of gunpowder to propel projectiles out of a fire lance (*huo chiang*).

Winter 1132: Canals, lakes freeze over in Hangzhou, an unusual occurrence in the semitropical city.

June 1132: Fire consumes two miles of Hangzhou, destroying thirteen thousand homes. Fires are a recurring calamity for this densely packed city largely built of bamboo and wood.

1138: Southern Song outlaws the practice of infant abandonment and orders the establishment of foundling hospitals.

1141: Jin decrees that a male slave may buy his freedom on payment of three bolts of textiles; two bolts will purchase the freedom of a woman or child.

1149: Chen Fu's important treatise *Agriculture* contains a systematic description of paddy rice culture.

***c.* 1150:** Foreign trade has taken on great importance in Southern Song economy. Chinese merchants export silks, porcelain and copper *cash.*

***c.* 1150:** Song traders and seafarers establish China as the world's most advanced maritime nation.

1157: Jin bans the export of antiquities.

1161: Song forces fire explosive grenades from catapults in battle against the Jurchens.

***c.* 1170:** Jin emperor Shizong declares that Jurchens may no longer dress in the Chinese way or adopt Chinese names. The purpose is to preserve Jurchen customs, which seem to be dying out as most Jurchens adopt Chinese styles.

1170s: Drought and famine sweep North China.

1191: Jin rulers permit legal marriage between Jurchen and Chinese subjects.

1194: Major floods devastate large areas of the Yellow River valley in Hebei and Shandong, displacing farmers and destroying roads and bridges.

Late 12th century: In Fujian, peasant families are said to practice the custom of "bathing the infant"—the drowning of unwanted children. According to a contemporary report, "If a man should have numerous sons he brings up no more than four and keeps no more than three daughters. He claims that he has not the means for bringing up more."

13th century: By a contemporary estimate, the Chinese consume two pounds of rice per person per day.

April 15, 1208: A terrible fire rages for four days in the Southern Song capital of Hangzhou, destroying 58,000 homes. At least fifty-nine people perish in the flames; others are trampled to death in panicked attempts to flee the city.

1217: Fresh Yellow River floods inundate parts of Shandong in northeast China.

1247: Publication of *Shu-shu chiu-chang* (Mathematical Treatise in Nine Sections), an important mathematical text by Ch'in Chiu-shao.

1280: Chinese use bronze and iron mortar tubes in battle against the Mongols.

YUAN DYNASTY: 1279–1368

1261: Mongols establish the Office for the Stimulation of Agriculture to help North China's peasants recover from wartime devastation.

1270: Mongol rulers endorse the peasant village organization known as *she*, which promotes farming, land reclamation, and education.

1271: Khubilai Khan founds the Institute for Muslim Astronomy to recruit Persian and Arab astronomers to China.

February 1289: Yuan completes a 135-mile extension of the Grand Canal to Beijing.

Late 13th century: Despite political turmoil, China's economy continues to flourish. The Venetian traveler Marco Polo writes of the Yangtze valley: "I tell you that this river goes so far and through so many regions and there are so many cities on its banks that, truth to tell, in the total volume and value of the traffic on it, exceeds all the rivers of the Christians put together plus their seas." The traveler is amazed, too, by the populous and rich former Southern Song capital of Hangzhou. "Anyone seeing such a multitude would believe it impossible that food could be found to feed them all, and yet on every market day all the market squares are filled with people and with merchants who bring food on carts and boats."

1295: China has a network of 1,400 postal stations fifteen to forty miles apart; in an emergency, post riders can cover 250 miles a day.

c. 1300: Wang Zhen prepares his *Nung Shu* (Agricultural Treatise), a handbook that covers farming, forestry, animal husbandry, sericulture (silkworms), spinning, and weaving. It is especially noted for its detailed descriptions of agricultural implements, both for practical and ritual uses.

1314–1315: To increase revenue, government reestablishes state monopoly on foreign trade and adopts more aggressive tax collection policies. By 1316 widespread resistance to the tax scheme forces the Yuan to scrap the collection system.

1331–1354: An epidemic of what some scholars believe is bubonic plague devastates China. The Mongols may have transmitted it to Europe, causing the cataclysmic Black Death of 1348–1349.

1333–1334: Yellow River floods cause widespread distress.

1340s: Sections of the Grand Canal are rebuilt after heavy flood damage.

Summer 1344: Yellow River begins shifting its course, breaking through dikes and flooding vast areas. Another consequence is drought in the Huai valley region of northern Henan, Anhui, and Jiangsu provinces. Widespread epidemic and famine make this region a center of resistance to Yuan rule.

April 1351: Government announces plans to rechannel the flood-prone Yellow River. Some 170,000 troops and laborers are mobilized for the project, which is completed by year's end. In an unintended consequence, thousands of peasants concentrated for the river project join insurgent militias.

1353: In response to chronic grain shortages, government establishes state farms for rice culture in North China.

1356: Paper money ceases to circulate. Toghto's inflationary policies have made it worthless: by necessity, he prints during his last years in power vast amounts of paper currency to fund state projects and quell rebellion.

MING DYNASTY: 1368–1644

1385: High taxes and economic dislocation touch off brief uprising of 200,000 peasants in Sichuan.

1403–1419: Shipyards near Nanjing turn out two thousand vessels, including one hundred ships 370–440 feet in length.

July 1405: The Muslim eunuch Zheng He sets sail on the first of his seven voyages into what the Chinese call the "Western Oceans." The fleet, with more than 300 vessels and 27,000 men, calls at Champa, Vietnam, Java, Sumatra, Malacca, Ceylon, and South India. The largest of Zheng's vessels are nine-masted junks 440 feet long and 186 feet in the beam. Their holds are packed with silks, embroidery, and other luxuries for presentation to local potentates. On the return voyage home in 1407, Zheng engages the infamous Chinese pirate Zhen Zu off the Sumatra coast, destroys Zhen's fleet and kills five thousand of his men. Zhen himself is taken to Nanjing and executed.

July 1411: Dredging and reconstruction of the northern section of the Grand Canal begins. Some 300,000 laborers clear 130 miles of channel and build or repair thirty-eight locks so shipments of grain and materials can be sped to the new Ming capital being built at Beijing.

1413–1415: In Zheng He's fourth expedition, part of the fleet reaches Hormuz in Persia while another part touches at Somalia in East Africa and Aden on the Arabian peninsula.

July 1415: The southern section of the Grand Canal from the Yellow River to the Yangtze is completed. The canal becomes the main channel of north-south commerce.

August 1419: Zheng returns from his fourth voyage with an exotic African menagerie for the emperor: lions, leopards, zebras, rhinoceroses, and giraffes.

c. 1420: An estimated 100,000 artisans and other workers serve the Ming imperial household in Beijing.

1420: Tang Saier leads a peasant revolt in Shandong. Her forces are defeated and she is suspected of having disappeared into a nunnery. Ming authorities bring thousands of Buddhist and Daoist nuns to Beijing, but the rebel leader is never found.

1431–1433: Zheng He's seventh (and last) seaborne expedition calls at Champa, Java, Sumatra, Malacca, the Malabar Coast of India, and Hormuz on the Persian Gulf.

1439: Grand Canal and the Yellow River burst their dikes, causing massive flooding, loss of life, and famine.

1445: Famine in Shanxi sends thousands of peasants onto the roads in search of food. Some are said to sustain life on wild plants and the bark of trees.

1448: Drought and locust plagues devastate North China.

Winter 1453–1454: Bitter cold claims tens of thousands of lives. In some places snow lies deep on the ground for forty days and longer. Snows as far south as southern Hunan kill many cattle.

Late 1480s: Chronic breaks in the Yellow River dikes in Shandong cause annual flooding that costs lives and interrupts commerce on the Grand Canal.

1493–1495: Some 120,000 laborers block, channel, and dike the Yellow River to alter the main channel to the southeast. The change relieves chronic flooding and will hold until the nineteenth century.

1545: First Japanese trading fleets visit Chinese pirate anchorages off the Zhejiang coast. An important pirate-controlled private trade grows up in defiance of strict government controls on foreign contact.

April 1545: Dust storms destroy the North China winter wheat and barley crops. This comes after a long period of drought has led to widespread starvation in the northern provinces.

January 1556: Earthquake devastates large areas of Shanxi and Shaanxi provinces; 800,000 people are said to perish in the Wei River valley alone.

1559: Drought afflicts the Yangtze delta, reducing rice stocks and driving up the price of grain.

1573: With the lifting of the trade ban, Chinese merchants make contact with the Spanish in the Philippines. Within a few years, trade flourishes between China and the Americas, with Chinese silks and porcelain exchanged in vast quantities for New World silver. Much of this commerce flows through Manila, the Spanish trading center in the Philippines. Along with silver, new plants such as sweet potatoes, peanuts, and maize are introduced to China.

1574: Ming authorities put up barrier wall at Macau to keep the Portuguese colonists inside.

1578: Portuguese traders are permitted to travel up the Pearl River to do business at Guangzhou (Canton).

1593: The *Pictorial Reference Compendium* is published; it is a manual on agriculture, medicine, cooking, and other practical subjects.

1593: Construction begins on the Jia Canal, which is to run north-south, parallel to the silt-choked Grand Canal.

1599: Merchants in Linqing in Shandong province strike against high taxes and burn the Ming tax collector's office in protest.

1601: Some ten thousand porcelain workers riot in protest of imperial demands for increased production.

1604: Porcelain workers riot for higher wages.

1606: Yunnan miners joined by disaffected army officers destroy the office of the detested eunuch mining superintendent; in retaliation, a thousand miners are killed.

1609: The 110-mile-long Jia Canal opens to traffic.

1621–1627: Major fires sweep Beijing, Hangzhou, and other major cities, destroying tens of thousands of dwellings and businesses.

Winter 1628: Severe famine strikes Shanxi province; there are reports of cannibalism.

1630s: China's trade with Spain (through the Philippines) and Japan picks up substantially. By estimate, some 2 million silver pesos a year flow into China from Manila.

1635: First English trading vessels reach China.

1639: Famine, epidemics, rebellion, and banditry cause widespread suffering. A folk song of this period charges the Lord of Heaven with Dereliction of duty:

Old Skymaster,
You're getting on, your ears are deaf, your eyes
   are gone.
Can't see people, can't hear words.
Glory for those who kill and burn.
For those who fast and read the scriptures,
Starvation.

1639: Japan bans the lucrative century-old trade between Nagasaki and Macau. A short time later, the Spanish act to reduce the silver flow into Manila and thus into China. The result is a sharp curtailment of the China-Philippines trade. The silver shortage leads to deflation and serious social unrest, including tax defaults, rent riots, and the hoarding of grain.

QING DYNASTY: 1644–1912

1720: China ships 400,000 pounds of tea annually to England. Also in this year, Chinese merchants in Guangzhou (Canton) form the guild or monopolistic trade association known as the Cohong—"combined merchant companies."

1720s: With the spread of opium smoking, Qing authorities launch a crackdown on the trade. Punishment for luring someone into an opium den is strangulation. Dealers are banished to frontier military garrisons. Smokers are beaten with one hundred strokes of the rod.

1723: Eight thousand Suzhou-area silk and cotton workers (known as "calendarers") strike for higher wages. They will strike again in 1729, again with little success.

1728: A Russian-Chinese commercial treaty permits one Russian trading caravan to journey to Beijing every three years, and allows a Russian Orthodox church to operate in the capital.

1729: England exports two hundred chests of opium, each holding 130 to 160 pounds of the drug, into China. The opium trade will grow as the west tries to right the balance of trade with China: the Chinese are far less interested in western products (except for weapons and medical technology) than westerners are in China's silks, porcelain, and tea. Opium is one import the Chinese buy avidly.

c. 1750: Cotton and tobacco culture are widespread in northeast China. This is a region of small holdings, with the average family plot running to 2.5 acres and holdings greater than 20 acres uncommon. Elsewhere, New World crops such as the sweet potato, Irish potato, maize, and peanut are spreading and improving the Chinese diet.

1754: Imperial government makes the Cohong merchants liable for the behavior of foreign ships' crews ashore in Guangzhou.

1759: Qing restricts all European trade to the city of Guangzhou (Canton). Foreign merchants are confined to their own quarter of the city and are allowed to live there only during the October to March trading season.

1759: The British East India Company emissary James Flint appeals to the Qing court to lift trade restrictions and stamp out corruption in Guangzhou. Flint is arrested and jailed for three years for presenting petitions improperly and other alleged violations.

1773: Foreign encounters with China's legal system create tension. In this year, a Portuguese court in Macau finds an Englishman innocent of the charge of murdering a Chinese. Qing officials seize the acquitted man, try him in a Chinese court, and execute him. Such disputes build over the coming decades, leading to western demands that China surrender jurisdiction over western nationals in the country.

1784: First merchant vessels of the newly independent United States reach China.

1792: In Daoyi in southern Manchuria, surviving detailed demographic records show the average lifespan is around thirty-two years, mainly because of the high rate of infant mortality. Only 4 percent live beyond the age of sixty-five.

1800: China's annual exports of tea to England total 23 million pounds, worth $3.6 billion, and around a seventh of all the tea sold in China.

1800: Imports of opium from British India reach four thousand chests a year. An addiction problem becomes evident in some parts of China; by the 1820s, enough opium enters the country to feed the habits of a million addicts.

1803: Flooding silts up the Grand Canal, slowing grain shipments to the Beijing region and boosting reformers' proposals to reestablish a reliable sea transport route—a matter of recurrent debate since the Song.

1815–1850: A major outflow of silver, largely the consequence of the illicit British trade in opium, causes a long period of deflation and economic recession. Prices drop by half and more during these decades. A string of a thousand copper *cash* is roughly equivalent to one tael of silver at the close of the eighteenth century; by the 1830s the rate has fallen to 2,700 to 1.

1820s: Triad secret societies spread from Guangdong and Fujian north into the Yangtze provinces. The Triads are increasingly involved in rackets, banditry, and rebellion.

1827: During the conservative Qing dynasty, permanent widowhood comes to be exalted. By this year, so many memorial arches are being put up to honor faithful widows that the government rules only collective arches may be built.

1838: British export forty thousand chests of opium into China for a value of $18 million—making the drug the most valuable single trade commodity in the world. There are an estimated 12.5 million opium smokers in China.

1845: Serious food shortages in Beijing area lead Qing to use sea transport for grain shipments at the expense of the long-established canal routes. The shift leads to unrest among bargemen and others dependent on the canal system for their livelihoods.

1850–1900: Chinese emigration builds as the century advances. Contractors recruit Chinese laborers for Cuba, Peru, Hawaii, and Sumatra. The migrants are called coolies, from the Chinese *kuli*, meaning "bitter labor." By 1850 ten thousand Chinese are settled in Malacca (in today's Malaysia); Chinese are the dominant minority in Kuala Lumpur and Singapore.

1852: First Chinese laborers reach Hawaii. By the turn of the century 25,000 will be settled there.

Mid-1850s: Annual value of the silk trade through the treaty port of Shanghai passes $20 million. Some twenty thousand chests of illegal opium also are imported through the booming port city, which is rapidly becoming China's leading mercantile center.

1862: The scholar-official Zeng Guofan establishes the Anqing Arsenal for the manufacture of modern armaments.

August 1868: With use of machinery purchased in the West, China launches the first home-built steamship, the *Tianqi* ("the Auspicious"), at an arsenal at Shanghai.

1872: The Qing official Li Hongzhang, a modernizer, helps found the China Merchants' Steam Navigation Company. He becomes a principal shareholder in the company. Li also proposes halting construction of war junks entirely in favor of an all-steamship fleet.

1872: The *Shenbao* commercial newspaper in Shanghai hits a circulation of fifteen thousand.

1873: Half a million Chinese are settled in Singapore and vicinity.

1873: Chinese acquire United States-made Gatling machine guns for the Tianjin arsenal.

1874: A western missionary society for the suppression of footbinding is established in the coastal city of Xiamen (Amoy).

1875: An estimated 100,000 Chinese are working in Peru.

1876: China's first railway opens near Shanghai. Conservative Chinese regard railroads as disruptive and inharmonious. The provincial governor, disapproving, orders the track torn up in 1877.

1877: Qing undertakes a major expansion of the Kaiping coal mines in North China.

1880: China's first permanent railroad line opens. It connects the Kaiping mines to the port of Tianjin.

1880: Some 100,000 male Chinese are settled in the western United States, but only 3,000 Chinese women. Many migrants come as railroad workers and miners. Clashes with white Americans are frequent and sometimes violent.

1880s: China develops national cable and telegraph communications systems.

1882: United States imposes restrictions on Chinese immigration.

1890: The Hanyang Iron Works opens at Wuhan.

1890s: More than ten thousand workers are employed in modern factories in Hankou in the mid-Yangtze region. The workers suffer low wages, harsh working conditions, and substandard housing.

1893: China's urban population is 23.5 million, or 4 percent of the total population.

1896: China has 300 miles of railroad, compared to 2,300 miles in Japan, 21,000 miles in Great Britain, and 182,000 miles in the United States.

1900: An estimated 10 percent of all Chinese are opium smokers. Some 15 million are said to be addicted to the drug.

1900: More than 500,000 Chinese are settled in the Dutch East Indies (modern Indonesia).

1903: The Qing government establishes a Ministry of Commercial Affairs to promote economic development.

1903: The Shanghai Chamber of Commerce is established. It becomes a leading force in China's economy.

1905: After a decade of foreign capital infusion and construction, China's railroad network is around 4,000 miles. A north-south line links Beijing with the industrial region of Wuhan (the cities of Wuchang, Hankou, and Hanyang) on the mid-Yangtze.

June 1905: To protest U.S. Chinese exclusion policies, merchants in Guangzhou (Canton), Shanghai, Xiamen, and Tianjin launch a boycott of American goods. It is effective; normal trade will not resume until September.

1907: The Beijing Chamber of Commerce is founded. It represents around 4,500 of the capital's 25,000 commercial establishments.

1910–1911: Catastrophic flooding in the Yangtze and Huai valleys claims hundreds of thousands of lives, destroy millions of acres of crops, and send millions of refugees onto the roads in search of relief.

THE REPUBLIC: 1912–1949

1914: Young Chinese scientists trained in the United States establish the Science Society. The society's journal will become influential.

Foreign investment in China, concentrated in Shanghai and in southern Manchuria, reaches $1.61 billion. The leading investor is Britain, accounting for more than a third of the total, followed by Russia, Germany, and Japan.

1915: An American Chamber of Commerce opens in Shanghai with thirty-two members.

1916: Government sets up the Geological Survey of China. It sponsors the paleontological research that will lead to the discovery of Peking Man in 1929.

1920s: Sixty thousand rickshaw pullers are working in Beijing.

1920–1921: Severe drought leads to a devastating famine in North China. At least 500,000 die and nearly 20 million are destitute in Hebei, Shandong, Henan, Shanxi, and Shaanxi. Some villagers eat straw and leaves to survive.

1920: Some 1,700 Chinese-owned industrial enterprises employ 500,000 workers. China's railroad network totals seven thousand miles, modest for a country of such great size; China's national system, with around 3800 miles of track, employs 73,000 workers.

Nanyang Tobacco Company of Guangzhou (Canton) sells 4 billion cigarettes a year.

1922: Forty-nine new cotton mills open in China. Large modern flour mills are established around Shanghai; cigarette and paper industries flourish in the Guangzhou area. North China collieries employ fifty thousand miners.

January–March 1922: Strikes in Hong Kong and Guangzhou idle 120,000 seamen and dock workers. The strikers win pay raises and recognition of their union.

1927: Shanghai's population reaches 2.7 million.

1928: Nationalist leader Chiang Kai-shek's ally (and brother-in-law) T. V. Soong heads the newly established Central Bank of China. He launches reform efforts aimed at stabilizing China's finances.

June 9, 1928: Nationalist government founds the Academia Sinica. The academy sponsors research institutes and a National Science Council.

1930–1939: With the world's developed economies in depression, China's economy grows modestly during the decade. Output of electric power doubles. Post and telegraph services expand, regular airline routes are developed and 2,300 miles of railroad are built. Heavy taxation hinders China's growth, however. In 1936, the once prosperous Nanyang Tobacco Company turns over 39 percent of its total income to the government in taxes.

1930: Nationalists issue civil law code that gives women the right to choose their husbands, reject marriage arrangements made when they were children, and inherit family property. Such laws have little immediate impact outside the cities, however.

In Shanghai, 170,000 women are employed in cotton mills and other factories. Around 50,000 women work as prostitutes in the city.

1930: Nationalist legislature adopts a Land Law that fixes a maximum rent of 37.5 percent of the harvest; it also allows tenants of absentee landowners to buy farms they have worked for at least ten years. It is never implemented, and rents remain at the 50–75 percent level.

1931: The Nankai Institute of Economics is founded. A five-year grant from the Rockefeller Foundation in 1932 helps the institute get on its feet.

1931–1935: Falling farm prices cause widespread economic hardship—1934 prices are 58 percent below those of 1931. Natural disasters—floods, droughts, hailstorms—devastate the countryside. The 1934 rice harvest, for one example, is 34 percent below the 1931 level.

1931: A new labor law mandates equal pay for women doing the same work as men.

1931: Yangtze flooding leaves 50,000 square miles under water and creates 14 million refugees.

1934: Nationalist government bans labor unions in Henan, Hubei, Anhui, Jiangxi, and Fujian provinces.

Mid-1930s: Around nine hundred newspapers circulate in China, reaching a readership of 20–30 million.

1935: China's official unemployment figure passes 5 million.

Nationalist government surveys show that close to half of all rural householders own their own land and support their families by farming. Around a quarter—some tenants, some who own their farms—supplement their farm income with other work. The rest are classed as laborer/tenant householders who rely wholly on wage incomes.

Nationalist government issues the *fabi yuan* unit of currency.

November 1935: After two straight bad harvests, peasants in the Fuzhou area turn on their absentee landlords. When some tenants are arrested for failing to pay rent, thousands rise in protest. They destroy a police station and set fire to absentee owners' houses; clashes continue intermittently through the winter of 1936.

1936: China imposes an income tax.

Severe drought causes famine in Sichuan. Food riots break out in the cities; in Chongqing, the hungry strip the bark from the city's ornamental trees.

1937–1945: Despite wartime dislocation, Communist land policies increase agricultural production. The amount of cultivated land in targeted North China districts under Communist control doubles during this period from 8.6 million *mou* (a *mou* is a sixth of an acre) to 15.2 million *mou*.

Spring 1944: Famine strikes Henan, and tens of thousands starve to death. As Japanese forces advance, malnourished survivors attack retreating Nationalists, who continue to collect taxes and other levies during the worst months of the crisis.

September 1945–February 1947: Wholesale prices in Shanghai increase thirtyfold.

January 1946: Workers strike at the Shanghai Power Company. Forty local unions join the strike in early February, forcing the company to settle. In Shanghai alone there are more than 1,700 strikes and other labor disputes in 1946.

May 1946: The May Fourth Directive authorizes land redistribution from the well-to-do to the peasantry in areas of North China under Communist control. A complete expropriation of landlord property, including dwellings, will follow.

1946–1947: The Communists' land redistribution program sometimes turns violent, especially in northern Jiangsu, Hebei, Shandong, and Shaanxi. People are forced to make confessions of guilt for all kinds of crimes against society.

Late 1946: The unemployment rate is 30 percent in the Nationalist capital, Nanjing, and 20 percent in Guangzhou (Canton).

1947: Bubonic plague kills thirty thousand in the Manchurian industrial city of Harbin. The outbreak is traced to the Japanese release in August 1945 of flea-infested rats army researchers had used in germ warfare experiments.

February 1947: Nationalist government attempts to impose wage and price ceilings. By May, they will be lifted as unworkable.

July 1948: Nationalist government abandons the inflation-ruined *fabi yuan* currency for a new currency, the gold *yuan*. At the official exchange rate, 3 million *fabi* buy one *yuan*.

August 1948: A standard 171-pound bag of rice sells for 63 million *yuan*.

THE PEOPLE'S REPUBLIC: 1949–1998

1949–1950: The new Communist government takes over China's banks and strictly regulates the currency. A new official currency, the *renminbi* (informally, the *yuan*) is introduced. The measures dramatically lower the country's runaway inflation.

May 1, 1950: China's Marriage Reform law gives women the right to choose their marriage partners, initiate divorce, and inherit property. Several million marriages are ended by women during the law's first five years. Though the law remains on the books, the government moves to make obtaining a divorce more difficult and time-consuming.

September 29, 1952: China opens the Longhai railroad linking Jiangsu with Lanzhou in Gansu.

1953: As part of China's Five Year Plan for economic growth, workplaces are reorganized (or simply recategorized) as *danwei* (meaning units). The *danwei*, which replace companies or employers, often provide housing and social services along with employment.

1955: Government officially abolishes all wholly private business enterprises.

July 13, 1956: Baoji-Chengdu railroad opens, linking northwest China with the southwest.

April–August 1958: As part of the Great Leap Forward, the government initiates a new collectivization drive, moving to abolish private agricultural plots and merge rural collectives (production brigades and teams) into larger and larger communes.

December 1958: The Communist Party Central Committee claims 740,000 cooperatives have merged into 26,000 communes with 120 million households. The government issues inflated figures for the 1958 harvest, claiming 375 million tons of grain when the actual total is around 215 million tons. Great Leap Forward mismanagement causes massive disruption in the countryside; poor harvests and government requisitions of food trigger three years of famine that claims at least 20 million lives.

July–August 1959: Drought afflicts much of China; 30 percent of all cultivable land is affected.

November 1, 1959: China opens its first tractor factory, in Luoyang.

May 25, 1960: A Chinese expedition reaches the summit of Mount Everest.

1961: With the virtual elimination of private farming, hog production falls to 52 percent of the 1958 peak.

June 1961: Chen Yun, a senior member of the Politburo, finds the Great Leap Forward in ruins during an inspection tour of the countryside around Shanghai. He recommends restoring small private plots to peasants and reopening private rural markets.

1962: With rapid economic development, industrial products now account for 51 percent of Taiwan's exports, compared to only 7 percent in 1953.

November 9, 1962: China and Japan sign long-term trade agreement.

1963: New oilfields at Daqing in northeast China now produce two-thirds of the country's oil. This frees China from dependence on Soviet oil imports.

October 16, 1964: China explodes its first atomic bomb.

1965: Agricultural production recovers to pre-Great Leap Forward levels.

1966–1969: Taiwan develops "export processing zones" that give tax incentives and other aid to exporters of manufactured goods.

June 17, 1967: China explodes its first hydrogen bomb.

1968: Life expectancy in China is sixty years, up from forty years in 1953. This largely reflects reductions in infant mortality.

December 29, 1968: A road bridge opens over the Yangtze at Nanjing.

1969–1970: China's economy reaches full recovery after the disruptions of the Cultural Revolution. Most industries and agricultural operations reach or exceed 1966 levels.

April 24, 1970: China launches its first satellite into space.

August 16, 1972: Japanese inaugurate airline service between Japan and Shanghai.

September 9, 1972: China agrees to buy ten long-range 707 jetliners from the Boeing Company.

1973: Turning away from "self-reliance," China purchases $1 billion worth of industrial equipment—including entire plants—from the United States.

1975: The People's Republic signs a joint venture agreement with Britain's Rolls-Royce to build jet engines in China.

1975: Hu Yaobang, a protégé of Deng Xiaoping, becomes head of the prestigious Academy of Sciences in Beijing. He attempts to shield it from political interference.

July 28, 1976: A massive earthquake shatters the city of Tangshan in Hebei province. The official death toll is 242,000, with another 164,000 seriously hurt.

Late 1976: Zhao Ziyang, the Sichuan Communist Party leader, authorizes an expansion of private enterprise farming (up to 15 percent of the land in Sichuan communes). By

1979, Sichuan grain production will increase 24 percent. Similar market initiatives in industry lead to a production increase of 80 percent from 1977 to 1979.

March 1978: At a National Science Conference in Beijing, the government unveils a training program for 800,000 research workers and plans to develop new research centers.

October 12, 1978: Regular air service begins between Hong Kong and Guangzhou (Canton).

December 19, 1978: Boeing announces that China will buy three 747 jumbo jets; six days earlier, Coca Cola announced that it would build a bottling plant in Shanghai.

April 1979: China's leadership introduces "special economic zones" operating on market principles around four east coast localities: Zhuhai (near Macau), Shenzhen (opposite Hong Kong), Shantou, and Xiamen.

April 17, 1980: China enters the International Monetary Fund.

May 1980: China announces the successful launch of an ICBM with warhead delivery capability.

May 15, 1980: The World Bank admits China. The bank will approve its first loan to China the following year.

September 1980: The Communist leadership launches a strict population control program. Chinese families are encouraged to have only one child. A revised marriage law raises the legal marriage age to twenty-two for men and twenty for women. Women are encouraged to have their first—and last—child by age twenty-five. The government orders compulsory intrauterine devices for women with one child and compulsory sterilization for either husband or wife after the birth of a second child.

January 7, 1981: CAAC, China's civilian airline, begins New York-Beijing service.

July 9–14, 1981: Sichuan floods kill 700 people and leave 150,000 homeless.

1982–1992: All but a few of British Hong Kong's 3,200 toy factories relocate to mainland Guangdong, where labor costs are low and profits high.

1982: Private income accounts for nearly 40 percent of a farm family's total income, around double the proportion in 1964.

1983: China's urban population is 23.5 percent of the total, compared to 10.6 percent in 1949. Millions are flowing from the country into the towns every year.

1983: Direct foreign investment in China is estimated at $910 million.

1984: The Central Committee issues Document Number 1, which acknowledges the virtual dismantling of the system of collectivized farming and establishes what is known as the "responsibility system." In return for negotiated payments to the state, farmers may grow what they choose and keep whatever is left after they make their agreed-to deliveries. Plot assignments may be sold or inherited, though nominally the state still owns the land. The committee also extends special economic zone status to fourteen additional coastal cities and Hainan Island.

1984: Life expectancy in China is sixty-five years.

September 1, 1984: China's first nuclear reactor goes into service.

Mid-1980s: A Chinese popular joke, mocking Maoist locutions, lists the "Eight Bigs" everyone must possess: a color television, a refrigerator, a stereo, a camera, a motorcycle, a suite of furniture, a washing machine, and an electric fan.

Summer 1985: China sells two hundred military transport aircraft to private firms and provincial airlines.

In the People's Republic's worst corruption scandal to date, officials of the Hainan Island enterprise zone illegally resell $1.5 billion worth of imported motor vehicles, television sets, and video recorders.

1986: The official cost of living index rises 12 percent. Unofficially, the increase is conceded to be considerably higher.

Some 400,000 small- and medium-sized

businesses produce 40 percent of China's industrial output. Most firms are collectively owned, but a growing number are in private hands. Both types of ownership operate increasingly on market principles.

August 3, 1986: China reports the first bankruptcy case in the People's Republic's history, that of a factory in Shenyang.

September 26, 1986: The Shanghai stock exchange opens for the first time since 1949.

May 1987: Forest fires burn 2.5 million acres in Heilongjiang province in northeastern China.

1988: Strikes appear here and there. In one strike 1,100 workers in a factory making medical appliances go off the job for three months.

July 1989: Floods in Sichuan claim hundreds of lives and damage croplands; flooding in Zhejiang destroys ten thousand dwellings.

1992: Taiwan's per capita income is second only to Japan's in Asia.

1994: Construction begins on the long-planned Three Gorges Dam project on the Yangtze. Cost estimates range upward of $100 billion for what will be the largest hydroelectric project in history, creating a four-hundred-mile-long reservoir that will inundate 160 towns and force the relocation of 1.3 million people. Critics say it will severely damage the Yangtze environment.

1998: It is reported that by the end of 1997 foreign-invested companies employ some 11 percent of China's nonagricultural workforce and account for some 14 percent of the country's total annual industrial output.

January 8, 1998: The director of China's official statistics bureau announces that it is working to modernize the statistics technology and system to reflect the country's growing economy.

August 1998: Flooding from the Yangtze and its tributaries, the worst in four decades, leaves some 250 million Chinese homeless and several thousand dead.

September 1998: The latest figures from Boeing show that China has bought one-tenth of the firm's aircraft in the past three years, that one of the world's largest spare-parts centers has been established by Boeing in Beijing, and that more than one-third of the 8,500 Boeing aircraft flying around the world are equipped with parts made in China. Despite these promising statistics, China announces that it is not ready to purchase more Boeing aircraft at this time, due to the unsettled nature of the world's economies, particularly in Asia.

Japan

POLITICAL HISTORY

PALEOLITHIC ERA: 200,000?–10,500 B.C.

Some five thousand archaeological sites to date provide an understanding of Japan in the Paleolithic (Stone Age), or Pre-Ceramic era. Despite considerable debate about the length and nature of the prehistoric chronology, a number of facts emerge. Originally Japan was linked to the Asian continent by land bridges to Siberia and Korea. Over these arrived the earliest peoples in successive waves of migration. Genetic and linguistic studies indicate that these ancestors, bearing Archaic Mongoloid traits, arrived from around Lake Baikal in Russian Central Asia, and later from Southeast Asia and China by way of Korea. Most major original migrations take place by the end of the Paleolithic era; and as these peoples intermix and adapt to environmental changes, they evolve to form the modern Japanese. Today only the aboriginal peoples of the north, the Ainu of Hokkaido, and of the extreme south, the Ryukyuans of Okinawa, remain ethnically distinct, bearing close connections to the peoples of prehistoric times. These Paleolithic peoples are hunters, fishermen, and gatherers of plant foods. Inhabiting seasonal temporary settlements, they live as self-sufficient, multigenerational family groups known as bands (made up of from 20 to 150 members). They leave behind fragmentary architectural remains; increasingly complex stone tools; sporadic burials, some with grave goods; and evidence of trading networks.

200,000? B.C.: Sea recedes from the Kanto Plain around Tokyo, leaving the marine deposit known as the Shimosueyoshi Formation. From c. 130,000 to 13,000 B.C., several volcanic eruptions deposit distinct layers of ash atop the formation. This stratigraphic geological sequence will serve to date Paleolithic archaeological sites there and elsewhere in Japan, with much scholarly debate about chronology.

Crude stone tool assemblages, but no human fossil evidence, found at sites in Oita, Tochigi, and Miyagi prefectures are posited by excavators to be some 200,000 years old and to suggest the earliest immigration of *Homo erectus* to Japan.

65,000 B.C.: According to some scientists, people migrating from Mongolia and Lake Baikal in Russian Central Asia introduce new tool types, including sawtooth knives, points, and knives made of flakes.

30,000 B.C.: The Early Paleolithic era ends and the Late Paleolithic era begins.

30,000–28,000 B.C.: The earliest fragmentary human remains to date originate from this time, proving the presence of *Homo sapiens* in Japan.

28,000–18,000 B.C.: Nomads cross over to Japan by means of the Korean land bridge until the passageway is flooded.

28,000–8,000 B.C.: Important discovery of human fossil remains in Okinawa proves the existence of *Homo sapiens* in this era. To date no earlier substantial remains of hominids, such as *Homo erectus*, have been found in Okinawa.

25,000–21,000 B.C.: Sites in the southern Kanto Plain yield assemblages of pebble tools and large flake tools, including axlike tools with edge grinding (signs of repair) and knifelike tools of obsidian (volcanic glass). Paleolithic dwelling sites, often on natural terraces near streams, yield scatters of stones, remains of hearths, post holes, storage pits, and crude circles of small stone, possibly used to secure temporary animal-skin shelters.

19,000–16,000 B.C.: Peak of the last Ice Age.

Figurines found at Iwata, Honshu, dated to about 19,000 B.C., are the oldest known figurines made in Asia. Possibly as old are figurines found at Zazaragi, Honshu.

18,000 B.C.: The sea level drops and the islands of Kyushu, Shikoku, and Honshu become one land mass that may or may not still be connected to Korea by way of western Honshu. Hokkaido is linked to Siberia. Deer, elk, and mammoth roam islands. In the north, scientists have found evidence of brown bear, steppe bison, Japanese horse, Asian wild ass, and moose.

18,000–16,000 B.C.: The Japanese land mass separates completely from the Asian mainland.

18,000–9,000 B.C.: Widespread use of obsidian tools (identifiable as to exact geological source) reveals obsidian trading networks over relatively long distances.

13,000 B.C.: A gradual environmental warming trend begins, northern Pleistocene (Ice Age) animals eventually become extinct, and the human population begins steadily to increase.

13,000–11,000 B.C.: Immigrants from northeast Asia arrive in Japan by way of Hokkaido. Hokkaido excavation yields pendantlike ornaments of this era, made of material brought from the Lake Baikal region, where it has been traded for Japanese obsidian.

11,000–10,000 B.C.: Earliest pottery fragments mark the end of the Japanese Pre-Ceramic or Late Paleolithic culture.

10,500 B.C.: The bow and arrow are introduced in hunting to replace wooden spears with stone points. Spears remain in use in Hokkaido until the fifth or sixth century A.D., when they are finally replaced by the bow and arrow there.

At the end of the Paleolithic era, excavated sites indicate a settling-down process of nomadic bands in hunting camps. Burial sites with grave offerings, skilled stone toolmaking technologies, and far-reaching trade networks suggest high population density, relative complexity of social organization, and cultural exchanges with Asia.

JOMON PERIOD: 10,500–400 B.C.

The Jomon period (named after its distinctive cord-marked pottery) comprises the Mesolithic and Neolithic (transitional and late Stone Age) eras and is known for its pottery production and its highly polished stone tools. The world's oldest known pots have been excavated from Jomon sites and are unequaled in prehistoric times for aesthetic quality and variety of form and function. Makers and users of increasingly diverse stone and bone tools, the people are hunters, gatherers, and fishermen. During the period, the nomadic bands begin to inhabit villages, where they leave behind remains of ever larger ceremonial pit houses, elevated storage buildings, communal cemeteries, and ritual objects.

In an era of rich food resources, they cultivate some edible plants and discover effective processing and storage methods for nuts and other plant foods. They develop new hunting and fishing techniques as well, leaving behind evidence of fish weirs and dugout canoes. As immigrants continue to arrive from Asia, the range of trade goods and networks broadens. The bands evolve into tribal groups probably ruled by councils of elders. Jomon culture extends throughout Japan, from Hokkaido in the north to Okinawa in the south.

10,500–8,000 BC: Incipient Jomon period. Whether pottery-making originates in Japan or is brought from eastern Siberia is a subject of ongoing debate. Cord-marked pottery spreads through Honshu but does not reach Hokkaido. Habitation sites in caves and on rock shelves.

8000–5000 B.C.: Earliest form in Japan of rectangular pit houses, with earth-covered roofs, in circular arrangements. In western Japan, surface dwellings are built; from this time come the first examples of textiles in the form of twining and knitting of hemp and ramie fibers, as well as of simple embroidery. Near the end of this period pots with shell decoration appear.

7500–3500 B.C.: A dugout canoe (capable of carrying up to 1,100 pounds) and paddle from the era are found in the Torihama Shell Mound in Fukui Prefecture.

5000 B.C.: Thatched roofs are used on pit houses.

5000–3000 B.C.: Some Jomon groups begin to speak a proto-Japanese language.

5000–2500 B.C.: Regional pottery styles begin to diversify, although cord-marked pottery is still prevalent. In the Kanto region, development of pots with wavy rims or pouring spouts begins. New types of rituals objects such as figurines, earrings, and bracelets appear.

As a secondary source of food, people cultivate plants such as gourds, beans, and yams. They employ effective food processing and storage techniques, such as leaching of nuts. Acorn storage pits are dug in bogs to keep nuts over long periods. (In 1956, one such pit is found with nuts still able to sprout.)

The first contacts are made between Kyushu and the Ryukyu Islands, where distinct tropical cultures flourish, with greater dependence on vegetarian food, few if any ritual items, and unique decoration of objects.

5000–2000 B.C.: Mean environmental temperatures rise by several degrees, resulting in more abundant food resources.

4000 B.C.: Sharp rise in sea level (to 16.4 feet or 5 meters above present-day level), reducing land area but increasing the shoreline and marine food supplies. Manufacture and use of a variety of fishing implements of stone, bone, and ceramic, including hooks, weights, pumice floats, spears, and harpoons.

By this time comes the application of lacquer (from tree sap) in hues of red, black, and brown to waterproof and decorate wooden, clay, and basketware objects, including vessels, combs, and ornaments. This technique may have come from China before 5,000 B.C.

2500 B.C.: Appearance of sizable buildings (1,080 square feet, or 100 square meters) made of mud-covered walls of interlaced branches.

2500–1500 B.C.: Middle Jomon period, the most prosperous Jomon period and peak of prehistoric artistic expression, with development of sculptural "flame-style" pottery vessels, apparently for daily use. New pottery types appear, including hanging lamps, footed pots, images of natural objects, and possible winemaking vessels.

Most villages build very large communal structures (up to 2,153 square feet, or 200 square meters). Elevated houses are used for storage. Charred remains of breadlike food indicate use of grain. Communal cemeteries appear in central open squares of villages, with graves clustered possibly in family groups and probably sheltered by funerary structures. Jar burials of infants under house entrances. Evidence of hunting with traps, pits, and dogs.

Sea level begins to drop.

1500–1000 B.C.: Late Jomon period. Evidence of intervillage cooperation in use of fish weirs and of communal burials in areas surrounded by ring-shaped mounds. Development of reduction-fired black pottery.

c. **1000 B.C.:** By this millennium, Jomon people know how to cultivate dry land rice along with other plants but continue to rely mainly on hunting, gathering, and fishing.

1000–400 B.C.: Final Jomon period. Kamegaoka-style ceramics, such as shallow vessels, from Aomori Prefecture indicate new rituals. Introduction of salt production facilitates preservation of food, leads to increase in trade.

900 B.C.: Environmental cooling trend begins.

660 B.C.: Legendary date of beginning of reign of Jimmu, mythical first emperor of Japan. This ancestry for the imperial line is affirmed in A.D. 603 in the Asuka period to consolidate political power.

400 B.C.: People who cultivate rice by means of wet field methods arrive in Japan from Korea. This signals the beginning of the Yayoi period and the end of the Jomon era. In Hokkaido and northern Honshu, Jomon persists into historical times, where it is known as Epi Jomon until finally superseded by Ezo, or Satsumon, culture.

YAYOI PERIOD: 400 B.C.–A.D. 250

The Yayoi period is named after its characteristic reddish-orange, smooth pottery type, first excavated in 1884 in the Yayoi-cho district of Tokyo. The Jomon and Yayoi cultures coexist for several generations until the Yayoi emerges dominant. The major innovations of the Yayoi period come from the Asian mainland. From Korea come the techniques of wet-field rice farming, which lead to the construction of complex irrigation and drainage systems. From China come the objects and metallurgy of bronze and iron (contrary to most cultures, Japan undergoes the Bronze Age and Iron Age at about the same time). Trade and immigration bring in such goods as iron tools for agriculture and ceremonial bronze weapons, along with luxury items such as polished bronze mirrors and glass beads. Artisans arrive from the Asian mainland to introduce such crafts as bronze casting, ironmaking, glassmaking, weaving, and sophisticated woodworking techniques.

Japan becomes a highly stratified society of rulers and ruled, as rice paddies multiply and fortifications surround villages. Agriculture and warfare gradually spread throughout the country. Luxury items and rituals objects are used to indicate power in the political sphere and to indicate high status in increasingly elaborate and segregated burials. In this era of rapid social change, Japan moves from tribal society to a country of numerous regional polities, or "kingdoms," connected by ritual, trade, and competition.

400–300 B.C.: Initial Yayoi period. Rice paddy cultivation begins in early center of Yayoi culture in northwest Kyushu, the island across the strait from Korea; people begin to live in agricultural villages. The adoption of rice culture brings in from Asia new cycles of tradition, including festivals, deities, and social customs.

300–200 B.C.: Early Yayoi period. Yayoi culture extends from northwest Kyushu throughout western Japan. Fortification of villages begins in the form of moats and palisades.

c. **200 B.C.:** Korean bronze objects arrive in Japan.

100 B.C.–A.D. 100: Middle Yayoi period. Center of power moves northeast from Kyushu to Honshu's Kinai region and Nara.

Pottery is often decorated on a revolving turntable, as new types of vessels emerge, such as two-level steamers for cooking rice. Jomon deep cooking pots and large Korean storage jars are produced in great quantities.

Chinese bronze mirrors are imported to Japan where they become cult objects. Silkworm cocoons come from Korea; spinning and weaving begin with silk, hemp, and ramie.

Domestic glass production of beads begins with raw material from Korean peninsula. Domestic production of bronze objects begins, using raw material from Asia or melted-down items: production is mainly of ritual objects such as wide-bladed daggers or large decorated bells (*dotaku*). Native ironworking begins in northern Kyushu, mainly to make utilitarian objects and tools. In the following era, iron is preferred for armor and weaponry.

High sea levels flood some agricultural areas, dislocating inhabitants, and thus possibly leading to warfare. Other causes of war are competition for trade goods and routes (on which the importation of raw materials such as iron depends).

A.D. 57: According to the Chinese chronicle *Hou Han shu* (written in A.D. 445), the Han emperor Guangwu presents a gold seal to a chief from northern Kyushu. The chronicle also describes a tribute mission from Wo (or Wa, as Chinese call Japan) in this year.

100–250: Late Yayoi period. Pottery production shifts from households to specialized craft shops. Iron sickles replace stone reaping tools. The remains of a domesticated cow are found in a site from this era. A keyhole-shaped burial mound, characteristic of Kofun period, is built in the Kinai region.

c. **107:** According to the *Hou Han shu*, the king of Na in Kyushu, the southernmost island of Japan, sends tribute of 160 slaves to China.

170–180: According to the Chinese chronicle *Wei zhi* (A.D. 297), thirty chiefdoms of Wa (Japan) are at war with each other. Fighting ends when Priestess-Queen Himiko of Yamatai proves dominant and unites the chiefdoms as supreme leader.

239: According to a chronicle, Himiko sends a representative to the Chinese Wei emperor. Himiko is named Xin Wei Wo Wang (Monarch of the Wa, Friendly to Wei).

c. **250:** A group of powerful chiefs in Kinai region comes to dominate the Yayoi. Confederacies of chiefs exchange prestige goods as tokens of alliance and power. Warfare spreads over Japan as wealth concentrates increasingly in hands of a few.

KOFUN PERIOD: 250–600

The Kofun period is named after the era's mounded earth tombs, often encircled with *haniwa*, or hollow clay figures of soldiers, priests, servants, dancers, mourners, animals, houses, and boats. At times surrounded by moats, most of the ten thousand known *kofun*—round, square, and uniquely keyhole-shaped—are in the Yamato region south of Kyoto. The grandeur of these mausoleum tombs reflects the emergence of a single ruling dynasty, the Yamato court, and the move toward a unified state. Further social stratification leads to official ranking of aristocratic families, the development of a warrior elite, and craft specialization.

Overseas trade intensifies, requiring the construction of warehouses and ports, and leading to the introduction of Chinese writing and Buddhism via Korea. Buddhism transforms Japan, creating a motive for the spread of literacy, the building of architecturally impressive temples, and the manufacture of exquisite ritual objects, as well as for changes in dietary habits and funerary practices.

Toward the end of the era, as the central administrative bureaucracy grows, the Yamato rulers seek alliances with powerful local chieftains, resulting in a decrease in warfare and an advance in order and control.

c. 350: A single ruling family claims descent from the sun goddess, and the Yamato court is established in the Nara Prefecture region. The ruler is the war leader of other kingships or chiefdoms.

369: According to tradition, after Japan defeats the Korean state of Silla, the Japanese colony of Mimana is founded on the Korean peninsula.

372: According to tradition, the ruler of the Korean state of Paekche sends the Seven-Branched Sword to the king of Wa. Inscribed with the date of A.D. 369, it is now at Isonokami shrine. Sword inscriptions in Chinese characters are among the earliest examples of writing in Japan.

400–500: Middle Kofun period. About A.D. 400 the Yamato dynasty commences. They institute the *be* (specialized occupation groups) system of administration and of ranks to supervise the craft production of goods for the court. Lineage, rank, and titles remain an intense Japanese concern. The Yamato throne is passed down according to consensus of important families.

421–478: Five Yamato kings, also known as Five Kings of Wa, send tributes to the court of the Chinese Liu Song dynasty.

500–600: Late Kofun period. Horses become valued political gifts and status items; elaborate saddles and bridles, along with military weapons, are found in aristocratic burials.

507: Keitai (reigns 507–531?) ascends the throne and orders aristocratic houses to document family histories. These records are later used for the first Japanese chronicles.

512: An emissary from Paekche, Korea, requests that four districts of Mimana, or Kaya, be recognized as part of Paekche. The Yamato court finally yields.

527: The Iwai Rebellion in northern Kyushu is quickly suppressed by Yamato forces diverted from Korea. The rebel chief had refused to provide troops and supplies for the expedition against Silla, Korea.

529: Japanese commander Keno no Omi leads sixty thousand troops to Korea to try to recapture areas of Mimana taken by Silla. Failing to do so, he is recalled in disgrace and dies on the way back. In 539 Japan sends another unsuccessful expedition in aid of Paekche.

531: Henceforth, at the coronation of the emperor, in whose selection his predecessors now have more influence, the "Three Sacred Treasures"—a mirror, a sword, and carved jewels (*magatama*) — symbolize his supreme position.

c. 550: The Inland Sea area is consolidated under Yamato control to secure vital navigation routes to the Asian mainland. All regional chieftains ostensibly owe loyalty to the Yamato ruler.

554: According to a chronicle, Japan sends military aid (one thousand men, one hundred horses, and forty ships) to Paekche, threatened by the alliance of Silla and Koguryo.

c. 569: Silla has taken over all Mimana territory.

592: Assassination of Emperor Sushun (reigns 587–592) by Soga.

593: Soga Empress Suiko (reigns 593–628) ascends the throne, with nephew Prince Shotoku (574–622) ruling as regent. The first woman to occupy the throne in historic times, she uses the title *tenno*, or emperor, for the first time.

ASUKA PERIOD: 600–710

As the last stage of the Kofun period, this period takes its name from the Asuka region in southern Nara, which becomes the Yamato dynasty's capital, environs for various palaces, and site of many early Buddhist temples. Because of the written documentation that survives, Asuka is considered Japan's first historical period.

Serving as regent, Prince Shotoku implements a wide-ranging set of reforms to consolidate the power of the imperial line and to introduce Chinese-style bureaucratic administration. Also a strong patron of Buddhism, he encourages the competitive building of temples.

In mid-century begins a series of bloody succession battles, alternating with periods of rigorous reform, notably the Taika Reform, that further increase imperial power, reorganize the rank system, and expand the bureaucracy. Civil and penal codes are issued to cement internal social order, while disastrous military ventures in Korea raise fears of invasion, leading to renewed construction of defenses. Eventually diplomacy proves effective.

Japan now is a nation-state, borrowing profusely from Chinese institutional models but yet developing its own unique political ideology, worldview, and national character.

600: Japan sends its first official diplomatic delegation to China.

603: Prince Shotoku begins to transform the political landscape by introducing Chinese bureaucratic practices, with selection for office strictly by rank and then promotion by merit. Following the Korean example in the states of Paekche and Koguryo, he institutes the system of Twelve Cap Ranks, assigning hereditary royal attendants to twelve ranks marked by distinct regalia. As court officials they now are to owe loyalty directly to ruler, lessening ties to each other. The ideology of an unbroken imperial ancestry, beginning in 660 B.C. with the sun goddess, is set in place, giving supreme legitimacy to imperial lineage.

> But when those above are harmonious and those below are friendly, and there is concord in the discussion of business, right views of things spontaneously gain acceptance. Then what is there which cannot be accomplished?
>
> Seventeen-Article Constitution of Prince Shotoku (604)

604: Shotoku issues the "Seventeen Article Constitution," which seeks to codify new political institutions, including centralization of government and official retitling of ruler as *tenno* (Heavenly Sovereign). The emperor is to rule supremely and be owed complete obedience by clan leaders, as well as other subjects. Provincial governors and chieftains can no longer levy their own taxes.

607: Shotoku sends mission to the Chinese emperor, bearing a letter that for the first time describes Japan as "Land of the Rising Sun" and refers to China as "Land of the Setting Sun," thus implying relationship of equality between the two states, thereby offending the Chinese. He also sends missions in 608 and 614.

622: Shotoku dies. Not only an effective ruler but also religious and scholarly, he writes commentaries on Buddhist sutras and supports the foundation of monasteries. In the eighth century he becomes the focus of a religious cult and is held by some to be an incarnation of Buddha. (As an honored cultural icon, he will be portrayed on the modern ten thousand-yen banknote.)

645: A coup d'état overthrows oppressive Soga rulers. Successful plotter and clan chief Nakatomi no Kamatari is rewarded with the new family name of Fujiwara. Three of his granddaughters will marry into the royal family. For five hundred years Fujiwara remains the most influential family at imperial court. The capital is moved to Naniwa on Osaka Bay. Reforms from this time to the end of the century, centralizing state power on the Chinese model, collectively are referred to as the *ritsuryo* system.

646: Emperor Kotoku (reigns 645–654) issues what becomes known as Taika (Great Change) Reform edict to increase imperial power over land and manpower, to reduce influence of leading families at court, and to create an economic system to finance new political administration. Eight state ministries under the Dajokan (Grand Council of State) oversee reforms. Later, to fill bureaucratic positions, the rank system is expanded to nineteen from twelve, with appointment and promotion to be based more on merit than status.

663: In the Battle of Hakusukinoe, after two years of fighting in aid of Paekche against Silla and China on the Korean peninsula, Japan suffers its worst defeat of early times, possibly losing ten thousand men, a thousand horses, and four hundred ships. This ends Yamato aspirations for a foothold in Korea.

Following defeat, more than sixty Paekche aristocrats flee to Japan; they bring new knowledge and technology from Asia. By 684, Korean families who achieve status as important government officials are accorded the high rank of *muraji*.

668: Emperor Tenji (reigns 661–672) issues the Omi Code, a set of civil and penal laws.

670: A statewide census is carried out to facilitate taxation and military conscription. It claims some 3.5 to 5 million population, with life expectancy of twenty-eight to thirty-three years, dwelling mostly in agricultural villages.

672: After a violent civil war over succession (Jinshin Disturbance), Emperor Temmu (reigns 672–686) ascends the throne and increases power by reorganizing the rank system; he also upgrades Ise shrine, where ancestral *kami* of imperial family are worshipped. In consolidating authority, the ancient role of emperor as spiritual leader and high priest of *kami* worship supersedes his role as patron of Buddhism.

675: In an attempt to eliminate hereditary aristocratic power over land and people, Temmu calls for system of regional units (*kuni*) to be directly administered by central government. In 681 he establishes historical commission to legitimize imperial authority.

689: Based on Chinese principles and commissioned by Temmu, the Asuka-Kiyomihara Code is promulgated. Empress Jito (reigns 686–697) decrees that in each province one-quarter of all healthy males between twenty and sixty years of age are to undergo annual military training. Emperor Mommu (reigns 697–707) later increases this number to one-third and calls for each province to maintain one army corps. These measures increase power of governors, eventually lessening imperial authority.

694: The new Chinese-style capital city of Fujiwara is built north of Asuka, with a permanent palace, ministerial buildings, and a grid street plan. Ceremonial, administrative, and including Buddhist temples, the city will remain in use for only sixteen years.

c. 700: A system of eight ranks, started in 684, is codified; officials below the sixth rank cannot be promoted without special decree.

702: Emperor Mommu issues the Taiho Civil Code, which delineates duties of officials and responsibilities of state agencies. The Taiho Penal Code stays in force until 757. Both codes are based on the Asuka-Kiyomihara Code.

NARA PERIOD: 710–794

In 710 the imperial capital is moved to a new site at Nara, on the southern end of the island of Honshu. A hopeful keynote of the century is to be peace: the new capital is constructed with neither moat nor defensive walls. During this early period of what is known as Classical Japan, the country develops into a truly world-class culture. Chinese influence continues to inform the areas of politics, religion, the arts, and technology. The Chinese-style *ritsuryo* system of government prevails. In it, an authoritarian, bureaucratic, and centralized hierarchy is headed by the emperor who is served by officials appointed by him and loyal to him, and which is administered by the Dajokan (Grand Council of State) that oversees eight ministries and the provincial governors. A centralized system of census, taxation, and landholding is set in place.

As the state religion, Buddhism leads a vigorous campaign of temple-building in the capital and provinces. Nara artistic accomplishments in Buddhist-inspired architecture and statuary (known as Tempyo culture) are rivaled in the realm of letters. The early Japanese historical chronicles *Kojiki* and *Nihon Shoki*, together with the first poetry anthology, the *Man'yoshu*, appear, marking these decades as the era of the birth of Japanese literature.

Serious social and political problems underlie the glittering surface. While the land holdings of the aristocracy and religious foundations are exempt from tax, heavy state expenditures on temple-building and on the large administrative bureaucracy are financed by a severe tax burden on peasants, who are also subject to prolonged periods of labor conscription. Poverty, malnutrition, and homelessness are widespread among the lower classes. Throughout the era, often violent power struggles in court threaten to destroy government authority and destabilize the nation.

710: Imperial capital is moved from Asuka and established at Nara. Materials from Fujiwara palace structures are used to build new city of Heijokyo on site west of present-day Nara.

717: Minister Fujiwara no Fuhito begins to compile Yoro administrative codes to strengthen the bureaucracy. These are finished after his death and promulgated in 757.

724: A rebellion of the Ezo (Ainu) people in northeast Honshu is quelled after eight months with the capture of more than six hundred prisoners.

729: The powerful political figure Prince Nagaya, apparently falsely accused by the Fujiwara family of plotting rebellion, is ordered by the emperor to commit suicide.

737: An expeditionary force to Ezo territory achieves relative peace until 774. The region is overseen by the fortress at Taga and by other military outposts.

738: A law that each household must provide one able-bodied person for military service is rescinded.

740: After the death of four Fujiwara brothers from smallpox and loss of Fujiwara influence at court, Fujiwara no Hirotsugu, who has been demoted to Kyushu, assembles a rebel army of some twelve thousand to fifteen thousand soldiers there to restore Fujiwara status. A government force of seventeen thousand crushes the rebellion and executes him.

Izanagi no Mikoto and Izanami no Mikoto consulted together, saying: "We have now produced the Great-eight-island country, with the mountains, rivers, herbs, and trees. Why should we not produce someone who shall be lord of the universe?" They then together produced the Sun Goddess.

Nihongi (Chronicles of Japan) (8th century)

749: Emperor Shomu (reigns 724–749) is the first ruler to renounce the throne to become a Buddhist monk. Empress Koken (reigns 749–758) is enthroned, and she declares a new era of *Tempyo shoho,* or "Heavenly Peace and Victorious Buddhism."

750: The height of Chinese-style government in Japan, with a docile army.

757: In a failed coup d'état, government head Fujiwara no Nakamaro quells Tachibana no Naramaro's push to seize power, an ostensible attempt to improve the peasants' dismal condition.

758: Nakamaro sends officials out to hear peasants' complaints and to help the poor. He cuts the *zoyo* tax (requiring sixty labor days per year) in half and commutes debt interest. In government reforms, he renames ranks and ministries and encourages filial piety and Confucian behavior.

762: Allegedly using occult powers, Buddhist priest Dokyo cures Empress Koken of illness, apparently comes to share "the same pillow," and subsequently is elevated to high status in court.

764: Fujiwara no Nakamaro attempts a coup d'état with provincial militia and clashes with government forces, which seize and execute him. Former Empress Koken returns to the throne as Empress Shotoku (reigns 764–770). Possibly because of her behavior, she will be the last empress for eight hundred years.

765: Dokyo is appointed minister of state and in 766 is named Buddhist king (*Ho-o*), the highest positions ever held by a commoner. After Empress Shotoku's death he is exiled to the provinces.

774: Hostilities renew in Tohoku region in northeastern Honshu with a rebellion in Mutsu province. Sporadic warfare rages until 812 as the state sends out a sizable imperial expeditionary forces in 776, 788, 794, 801, and 811. Wars contribute to the national depletion of men and materiel. The heavy burden of provisioning and of the military draft on Kanto provinces leads to rising violence there.

780: Emperor Konin (reigns 770–881) downsizes the bureaucracy and sets limits on interest payments. During his reign he tries to reduce government expenditures, discipline officials and monks, and eliminate departments administering temple construction. Tax income continues to fall.

784: Following political instability, financially draining wars, and possible threat to imperial authority by powerful Nara Buddhists, Emperor Kammu (reigns 781–806) attempts to revive the *ritsuryo* system and moves capital to Nagaokakyo, west of what is now Kyoto. Building of the new city is bedeviled by bad omens, succession conspiracies, murders, and deaths from mysterious illnesses. With the posthumous promotion of murdered Prince Sawara to emperor in order to end bad luck, these troubles apparently cease. But after a decade of costly construction, the project is abandoned.

792: Government abolishes virtually all universal military conscription for provincial militia and puts an end to the border guard and capital guard system.

794: The imperial capital moves to new Heiankyo (now Kyoto) site, initiating the Heian period. The old capital city Nara eventually withers away.

HEIAN PERIOD: 794–1185

The Heian period, named after the new capital Heiankyo (Capital of Peace and Tranquillity), is regarded as the golden age of Classical Japan. In the milieu of one of the most refined courts ever, a uniquely Japanese literature bursts forth in full glory. Using the new Japanese phonetic syllabary, aristocratic women write the first known novel, *The Tale of Genji*; the quirky *Pillow Book*; and diaries that document a playful, inventive life that centers around elaborate protocol and ritual, love affairs, luxurious pomp and display, and the cult of beauty.

The emperor fades into the background as rival courtier families strive for supremacy, resulting in the Fujiwara Regency. Uncles and grandfathers rule from behind figurehead child emperors who are forced to abdicate when they become old enough to have minds of their own. The Regency gives way to a not so different *insei*, or cloister government, in which retired emperors in Buddhist monasteries rule from behind the throne. The *insei* rely more and more on rising military families to protect their interests and to maintain order in the land. With the move to Heiankyo, the overbearing Nara Buddhists are left behind, and Buddhism begins to splinter into the esoteric cults of Tendai and Shingon and the evangelical Jodo-sho, also known as the Pure Land Sect.

It is the best of times for the nobility and religious institutions, who are able to build up vast land holdings known as *shoen*, but it is the worst of times for the lower classes who suffer from exorbitant taxes, harsh landlords, famines, epidemics, and what seems like countrywide lawlessness as bands of robbers and pirates roam the provinces at will and rebel factions repeatedly challenge an ever weaker central government. It all ends in an epic civil war from which a heroic warrior family emerges, ready to take up the reins of power.

794: Heiankyo (present-day Kyoto) becomes the grand new capital, which it remains until 1868. The city is laid out in a Chinese-style grid. To eliminate the influence of Nara Buddhists, only two temples are allowed within the capital; others are to be outside the city limits.

806: The height of imperial power ends with the death of Emperor Kammu. Following succession struggles and court cabals, Fujiwara ministers and regents eventually take control.

810: In the Kusuko Incident, Emperor Heizei (reigns 806–809) decides to abdicate in favor of his younger brother Emperor Saga (reigns 809–823). Fujiwara no Kusuko, his favorite, fearing the loss of Fujiwara influence, per-

suades him to reconsider. He secretly assembles an army, but the plot is discovered, and Kusuko poisons herself. Thus the Hokke branch of Fujiwara rises to power.

811: The Tohoku people are forcibly evacuated to other provinces to break up their resistance; instead, they help spread rebellion elsewhere.

842: The Jowa Conspiracy occurs when Fujiwara no Yoshifusa seeks to eliminate the Tomo family and other rivals at court. Officials apparently unjustly accused of plotting to seat new emperor are exiled.

858: Fujiwara family dominance is complete when Fujiwara no Yoshifusa installs his grandson as Emperor Seiwa (reigns 858–876), with himself ruling as regent (*sessho*).

Seiwa is the first child emperor and first male to have a regent, while Yoshifusa is the first commoner in this position. Regency continues after Seiwa comes of age.

866: In an early case of antigovernment disorder, the Battle at Hirono River takes place when military forces of Mino and Owari provinces clash over water rights. The battle marks deteriorating social and economic conditions in the countryside.

866: In the Otemmon Conspiracy, a power struggle among court families continues when the Otemmon Gate of the imperial palace is burned. Fujiwara no Yoshifusa exploits the incident to eliminate all rivals at court.

878: A six-month revolt begins in Dewa province after a bad harvest and famine.

884: Fujiwara no Mototsune becomes regent for Emperor Koko (reigns 884–887); he takes the title of *kampaku* for the regent of an adult emperor.

887: *Ako* incident occurs when Fujiwara no Mototsune, who expects to continue as regent on accession of Emperor Uda (reigns 887–897), is instead named *ako* (the title of the ancient Chinese regent, a nominal post with no real power). He forces Uda to back down and reappoint him as *kampaku*, or regent. Only after Mototsune's death in 891 does Uda try again to free himself from the Fujiwara regency.

894: The imperial court ends official missions to China, marking the decline of Chinese influence on Japanese culture, though the Heian court continues its fascination with all things Chinese. Such arbitrary isolation creates a self-contained universe, allowing for the development of uniquely Japanese culture of arts and letters.

901: The court grants new military powers to provincial governors to quell domestic violence. The measure keeps relative peace for thirty-five years and lays the groundwork for the eventual rise of the warrior class.

903: Sugawara no Michizane (845–903), sage, government minister, and the most formi-

dable rival of Fujiwara, through Fujiwara machinations is sent away to "govern" Dazaifu in Kyushu, where he dies in exile. Later catastrophes in the capital—fires, droughts, floods, premature deaths—are attributed to his angry ghost. Twenty years after his death, Michizane is rehabilitated to his former status; seventy years later, he is elevated to prime minister. Worshipped at Shinto shrines where he is deified as Tenjin, he becomes the patron of calligraphy and poetry, of those suffering injustice, and of students preparing for exams; later he is the hero of a famous *kabuki* play.

932–941: Fujiwara no Sumitomo leads an alliance of pirates in western Japan, commanding as many as a thousand ships on the Inland Sea and inflicting violence against provincial headquarters in the form of a tax revolt as famines and epidemics spread. The imperial army and navy finally defeat pirate forces. Losing eight hundred ships and hundreds of soldiers, Sumitomo is captured and beheaded.

935–940: Warfare begins in earnest on the Kanto Plain as Taira no Masakado fights his kin in a family dispute. Despite widespread damage, the court ignores the war for four years. He eventually conquers all of the Kanto region and declares himself "new emperor." The provincial military force, under orders from the court, defeats and beheads him. This rebellion and a pirates' revolt give rise to the later Kanto independence movement led by Minamoto no Yoritomo.

He never fails
To reach the Lotus Land of Bliss
Who calls,
If only once,
The name of Amida.

Koya (10th century)

967–1068: At the height of the Heian era during the Fujiwara Regency, the hierarchy is realigned as the Fujiwara achieve supremacy by Machiavellian elimination of rival families, intermarriage with the imperial family, and forced abdications of emperors at a young age while they still are malleable. Emperors are kept busy with ritual and ceremonies while Fujiwara regents (usually their uncles and grandfathers) exercise power.

995: Fujiwara no Michinaga (966–1028) becomes head of the Fujiwara family. The greatest statesman of the era, he rules Japan for some thirty years from behind the throne during the golden age of Heian court culture. Living in greater luxury than the imperial family, he apparently is the model for the hero of the *Tale of Genji*, and he leaves behind his own diary, *Mido kampakuki*.

1019: Three thousand members of the Manchurian Jurchen tribe begin a week-long invasion of northern Kyushu, attacking a government garrison near Dazaifu. After sea battles and land fighting, the Jurchens are forced to sail back to the mainland.

1028–1031: In an alleged protest against excessive taxation, Taira no Tadatsune attacks the provincial headquarters of Awa and burns the governor to death. Before a court expedition crushes his rebellion, he ravages five provinces with a scorched-earth policy, causing the devastation of farmlands and setting back the Kanto region's economic growth by generations. Provincial disorders that follow have similar effect.

c. 1050: By the latter half of the century, the name of Heiankyo is changed to Kyoto (a word meaning "capital").

Clearly then, it is no part of the storyteller's craft to describe only what is good or beautiful. Sometimes, of course, virtue will be his theme, and he may then make such play with it as he will. But he is just as likely to have been struck by numerous examples of vice and folly in the world around him. . . . They are more important. Thus anything whatsoever may become the subject of a novel.

The Tale of Genji, by Murasaki Shikibu
(11th century)

1051–1062: In the Earlier Nine Years' War, imperial forces carry on an intermittent campaign to subdue the Abe family of Mutsu province in northeastern Honshu. The Abe invade the neighboring region and refuse to send tax revenues to court.

1068: In the absence of a Fujiwara descendant, Emperor Go-Sanjo (reigns 1068–1073) is allowed to ascend the throne. He resists Fujiwara influence to some extent, beginning the decline of Fujiwara Regency.

1081: Violent clerical demonstrations begin as some one thousand Buddhist monks from Enryakuji, two hundred of them armored and armed, move on the capital. This and subsequent protests—in 1107, 1113, 1139, 1169, and 1177—are spurred by Buddhist sectional rivalries and by opposition to court appointments and government weakness in the face of growing domestic disorder.

1087: *Insei*, or "cloister government," begins after Emperor Shirakawa (reigns 1072–1086) abdicates; it remains in effect until 1192 during the Kamakura era. While reigning emperors head the traditional court and bureaucracy, former emperors (usually emperors' fathers or grandfathers) assert control through their own retinues, with administration located in Buddhist monasteries (most emperors abdicate to become Buddhist monks in retirement). The *insei* system lasts intermittently in some form until 1840.

1129: Former emperor Shirakawa dies, leaving the imperial house in its strongest position in three hundred years.

1146: Taira no Kiyomori (1118–1181) becomes governor of the province of Aki on the western Inland Sea.

1156: In the Hogen Disturbance, after the death of retired emperor Toba (reigns 1107–1123), the faction of retired emperor Sutoku (reigns 1123–1141) tries to seize power and is crushed by the combined forces of Minamoto no Yoshitomo and Taira no Kiyomori. They support reigning emperor Go-Shirakawa (reigns 1155–1158), who retains the throne and control of the imperial house.

Real power now passes to great warrior families—the Taira, also known as Heike, and the Minamoto, also known as Genji—who begin a contest for supremacy.

1160: In the Heiji Disturbance, Minatomo no Yoshitomo seizes power with the aid of "disgruntled courtiers," imprisons Emperor Nijo (reigns 1158–1165), and makes new appointments. Taira no Kiyomori returns from pilgrimage to put down the coup; Yoshitomo is captured and killed. Thus Minamoto influence is swept from court, leaving the Taira faction firmly in control.

1167: The court orders Taira no Shigemori to "pursue and destroy" robbers in eastern Honshu and pirates in Kyushu who steal tax revenues.

1177: Regarded by court as a rustic and ruthless upstart, Taira no Kiyomori takes control of the imperial forces. Kiyomori's infant grandson will be installed as Emperor Antoku (reigns 1180–1185), consolidating Taira power.

In the Shishigatani Affair, the anti-Kiyomori faction plots to seize power but is betrayed. A second plot in 1180, led by Minamoto no Yorimasa and Prince Mochihito, ends in a losing battle at Byodo-in temple. There the wounded Yorimasa commits suicide and the prince is captured and killed, but his edict calling for a general uprising of Minamoto and their supporters against the Taira leads others to action.

1180: In the Great Civil War, also known as the Gempei War, initiated by a succession struggle, Minamoto and Taira armies begin to fight across central Japan.

April 25, 1185: By cunning, finally, the Minamoto force the Taira to sail to the western end of the Inland Sea. There, in the Battle of Dan no Ura, two navies of some one thousand ships clash, with the Minamoto emerging victorious. Taira no Kiyomori's widow, with her grandson Emperor Antoku, leaps into the sea, followed by her courtiers; other Taira are chased and killed. This battle ends Japan's Classical Age.

KAMAKURA PERIOD: 1185–1333

As the Middle Ages begin, Japan becomes one country with two systems. The emperor, his court, their way of life, and the imperial administration continue in Kyoto, while Minamoto no Yoritomo establishes his military regime, or shogunate, in Kamakura, which becomes the country's de facto capital. In effect, the provincial warrior class rises to replace the nobility in authority and power. This is the first of a series of shogunates that will rule Japan until the middle of the nineteenth century.

The goal of the shogunate is to establish law and order in the land and to create the political and judicial institutions for doing so. These changes lead to the virtual elimination of the Chinese-style *ritsuryo* system. The shogun heads a hierarchy of military vassals whom he rewards for loyal service with lands, positions, and other benefits. After Yoritomo's death, shogunal power passes to the Hojo regents, who rule from behind figurehead shoguns.

In the cultural realm, imperial courtiers turn their energies to the writing of *waka* poetry, while the literary genre of war epics becomes popular. Perhaps the period's defining trend is the adoption of Zen Buddhism by the shogunate and the spread of populist sects to commoners.

The era sees impressive advances in the areas of commerce, trade, and shipping. The landed estates known as *shoen* form the basic economic unit of feudal society. As agricultural techniques improve, some peasants begin to improve their lot. But natural disasters and excess exporting of rice lead to periodic famines. Other problems include pillaging gangs of bandits and pirates, a rise in debts and inflation, and violent factional struggles, as well as imperial attempts to wrest back power. The Mongol invasions create a sense of national purpose and unity, but also lead to developments that eventually erode the authority of the Kamakura shogunate.

1180: Minamoto no Yoritomo (1147–1199) establishes the capital of his warrior association in the remote frontier village of Kamakura in southeastern Honshu, near present-day Tokyo. With its excellent defensive position and harbor, Kamakura grows rapidly into a great government center for the *bakufu* (tent government) of the warrior class headed by the shogun, or military governor.

Yoritomo sets out to organize a regional security system that bypasses Kyoto and to guarantee the property of his followers. After a campaign to rid Kanto area of government representatives and to make some three thousand public and private officials into his vassals, he transforms the region into a personal sphere of influence. There he imposes law and order to protect equally the rights of warriors and of the nobility as landholders. His ultimate goal is peace and stability throughout the land under his control.

1184: Yoritomo establishes a board of inquiry to consider claims and lawsuits.

1185: After civil war victory, Yoritomo is granted the right by the emperor to appoint provincial constables (*shogo*) and military estate stewards (*jito*), who become most important local officials of the period. This effectively legitimizes his Kamakura government.

1189: In the Northern Campaign, Yoritomo fights the powerful Fujiwara clan of Mutsu and Dewa provinces after Yoritomo's brother Yoshitsune had escaped him by fleeing to Mutsu. There, in order to placate Yoritomo, Fujiwara Yasuhira forces Yoshitsune to commit suicide and sends his head to Kamakura. Using his brother's death as pretext for war, Yoritomo decisively defeats Fujiwara forces and brings the northern region under Kamakura control.

1192: *Gokenin* (housemen or retainers) first appear as vassals of Yoritomo. Directly answerable to the shogun, they head the hierarchy of warrior society—comprising mainly *bushi*, or *samurai* (one who waits on or attends someone)—whose leaders are holders of military commissions, family estate managers, and descendants of governors, many of them younger sons of nobility. Both *gokenin* and *samurai* are mounted warriors who control their own vassals in turn.

After Yoritomo conquers northern Honshu and leads a large army into Kyoto in a show of force, Emperor Go-Toba (reigns 1183–1198) appoints Yoritomo *sei-i tai shogun* (Great Barbarian-Subduing Generalissimo).

1199: Yoritomo is thrown from his horse and dies; he is succeeded by his sons Yoriie and then Sanetomo. Real authority passes to his widow Hojo Masako (1157–1225), who wields power as a "nun shogun," and her father Hojo Tokimasa (1138–1215), who founds a line of shogunal regents (*shikken*) who rule until the end of the era.

1203: Hojo Tokimasa becomes shogunal regent. When he plots against his daughter Masako in 1205, she exiles him to Izu. After her death, her brothers and their issue act as regent.

1219: Shogun Minamoto no Sanetomo is assassinated, ending the line of Minamoto shoguns. Infant Fujiwara prince is brought from Kyoto to become shogun, and Hojo family continues to rule as regent for figurehead child shoguns.

1221: In the Jokyo Disturbance, retired Emperor Go-Toba attempts a coup against the Hojo regent. Defeated within a month, he and two former emperors are exiled, the reigning emperor is deposed and replaced with a Kamakura choice, his followers are executed, and three thousand estates are confiscated from losers and given to Hojo vassals. The Kamakura government stations two *tandai* (shogunal deputies) in the Kyoto court to oversee all imperial activity.

1223: The first documentary mention of Japanese *wako* (pirates), who attack the Korean coast and carry out later raids in 1225, 1226, 1227, and 1263. Strong protests from the kingdom of Koryo initiate a foreign policy crisis, raising invasion fears.

1226: Initiating government by committee, Regent Hojo Yasutoki founds an eleven- to fifteen-member *Hyojosho*, or Council of State, and allows broader participation in decision-making at the highest level. He also creates the office of *rensho*, or cosigner, who must sign all important documents with the regent. This sharing of authority seeks to lessen power and succession struggles.

1232: *Goseibai Shikimoku*, a fifty-one-article legal code drawn up by the Council of State, delineates Kamakura government jurisdiction in relation to that of civil authorities and formalizes relations with vassals. Rights, duties, and responsibilities are enumerated. Code effectively sweeps away Chinese-style *ritsuryo* system.

1242: Emperor Shijo (reigns 1232–1242) dies without heir. Shogun supports as candidate Emperor Go-Saga (reigns 1242–1246). Go-Saga's princes start lengthy succession fight that ends in 1337 with establishment of northern and southern Courts.

1249: To aid the Council of State in adjudicating lawsuits, especially those concerned with land rights, shogun establishes *hikitsuke*, or high appellate court.

1263: The death of the regent Hojo Tokiyori ends the golden period of Kamakura regency.

1266: After conquering most of Korea and while preparing to invade Southern Song China, Khubilai Khan sends a letter seeking allegiance with Japan. In 1268, Mongol envoys arrive in Daifazu with documents for the emperor. The shogunate does not reply to these or subsequent envoys and prepares for war.

1272: In the Nigatsu Disturbance in Kamakura and Kyoto, a purge of those opposed to the main line of the Hojo regency is followed by the elimination of those who executed them. This marks serious instability within the shogunate.

In the sound of the bell of the Gion Temple echoes the impermanence of all things. The pale hue of the flowers of the teak-tree show the truth that they who prosper must fall. The proud ones do not last long, but vanish like a spring night's dream. And the mighty ones too will perish in the end, like dust before the wind.

Heike monogatari (Tale of the Heike), medieval epic

1274: Mongols invade Japan, landing in northern Kyushu near Hakata with ninety thousand men and nine hundred ships. Japanese are saved when a storm severely damages the invasion fleet and the Mongols leave. In 1275, the Japanese behead an emissary subsequently sent by the Mongols and plan an invasion of Korea, but do not follow through.

1281: Mongols invade again, landing near Hakata, with a much larger force — two fleets totaling some 4,000 ships and some 140,000 warriors (an army of 100,000 Chinese and 40,000 Mongols, Koreans, and Chinese). Despite Mongol tactics of massed units and bomb-tossing catapults, the Japanese fight fiercely for three months and again are saved by a typhoon.

These storms, known as *kamikaze* (divine winds), are seen as proof of heavenly protection of the homeland. The invasion leads to the construction of monumental coastal fortifications that virtually bankrupt the Kamakura shogunate. In addition, the failure to provide promised booty and rewards to warriors eventually erodes faith in the Kamakura judicial system.

1285: In the Shimotsuki Incident, a powerful group of shogunal vassals are eliminated when factionalism leads to a succession struggle. After a battle in Kamakura more than fifty combatants commit suicide, as do perhaps five hundred *gokenin* from Musashi and Kozuke provinces. This begins autocratic rule by the *tokuso*, the main line of the Hojo clan.

1293: In the Heizen Gate Disturbance, Taira no Yoritsuna, head vassal of the Hojo family, and more than ninety followers are killed by the forces of regent Sadatoki. Yoritsuna is accused of trying to make his son shogun.

1318: Emperor Go-Daigo (reigns 1318–1339) ascends the throne; in 1321 he discontinues *insei* (cloister government) and becomes active in affairs of state.

1323: Japanese *wako* (pirates) launch a large-scale raid on the Koryo coast; one hundred pirates are beheaded in Cholla province. *Wako* continue to pillage the Asian coast into the seventeenth century.

1324: In the Shocho Disturbance, a coup attempt led by Emperor Go-Daigo against the Kamakura shogunate fails.

1331: In the Genko War, Emperor Go-Daigo fails for a second time to wrest power from the shogunate. Many plotters are arrested, and he is exiled to Oki Island in 1332.

1333: Go-Daigo escapes from Oki. Meanwhile, both shogunal vassals sent to deal with his still-active supporters have grievances against the shogunal regent and change sides to support Go-Daigo. Ashikaga Takauji seizes the imperial capital, Kyoto. When the Kanto region rises in revolt, Nitta Yoshisada marches on Kamakura to burn it. This leads to the suicides of regent Hojo Takatoki and his family, thus ending the regency and the Kamakura shogunate with it.

MUROMACHI PERIOD: 1333–1573

The Muromachi period (also known as the Ashikaga period) is named for the Kyoto district of the shogun's palace. It is a time of paradox — civil wars, rebellions, and a general breakdown of the public order are accompanied by extraordinary achievements in the arts. As the shogunate moves from Kamakura to the imperial center of Kyoto and assumes much of its ceremonial monarchical aspect, its own power gradually passes from the hands of increasingly brutal or inept shoguns to those of the regional warlords, or *daimyo*. Despite often chaotic conditions, trade and commerce flourish, giving rise to an urban mercantile class, replacing agriculture as the main source of revenue and leading to the growth of such provincial cities as Sakai (Osaka), Hyogo (Kobe), and Nagasaki.

Succession disputes and quarrels between feudal groups are resolved on the battlefield or defended in massive regional castles. Rioting peasant groups periodically topple toll barricades and storm moneylenders' offices to demand debt cancellations. By the end of the Warring States era, Kyoto lies partially in ruins while its citizens seek safety in and bring high culture to other cities.

This political instability promotes unprecedented geographical and social mobility, both upward and downward, for all classes. Ironically, this milieu open to change and innovation nurtures, often through shogunal patronage and Zen influence, the emergence of *noh* performances, *renga* poetry marathons, inkbrush and decorative screen painting, austere rock gardens, the tea ceremony, and the art of flower arrangement.

Dramatically signaling the passing of the old order and the onset of the early modern order is the arrival on Japanese shores of *namban* (southern barbarians) — first the Portuguese who bring firearms and desirable trade items, and then Jesuit missionaries who introduce Christianity along with European learning.

1333–1336: In the Kemmu Restoration, Emperor Go-Daigo tries to restore direct imperial rule based on a model from five hundred years before. He grants the title of shogun to his son Prince Morinaga and appoints courtiers as military governors, but fails to reward sufficiently warriors who helped him to overthrow the Kamakura shogunate. This is a factor that causes Ashikaga Takauji to turn against him.

1336: In the Battle of Minatogawa, Takauji decisively defeats an imperial loyalist army led by Kusunoki Masashige. Takauji's samurai army forces Go-Daigo to flee with imperial regalia, initiating the period of southern and northern courts (1336–1392), or the Nambokucho era, when two emperors both claiming imperial legitimacy reign (but do not rule) in Yoshino and Kyoto, carrying on sporadic civil war.

Takauji issues *Kemmu shikimoku*, the legal code of shogunate government principles.

1336–1395: As *shugo* authority expands, *shoen* are broken up and become *chigyo* (fiefs); more powerful and autonomous *shugo daimyo* (regional warlords) emerge in provinces, with domains composed of separate fiefs. Religious institutions also become rulers of feudal domains.

1338: Installed on the Kyoto throne with his support, the child Emperor Komyo names Takauji shogun, thus beginning the 235-year Ashikaga shogunate centered in Kyoto. Descended from the Minamoto clan and related by marriage to the Hojo regents, Takauji is an able administrator who will never control all Japan, but only eight eastern provinces.

c. **1350:** *Kokujin*, or provincial landowners, begin to unite to oppose the shogun-appointed *shugo*. They also form leagues, *ikki*, with *myoshu* (independent yeoman-farmers) to oppose excesses of *shugo daimyo* greed and that of the urban elite and moneylenders.

1350–1352: In the Kanno Disturbance, Ashikaga Tadayoshi revolts against Takauji and splits the shogunate into warring factions. The two brothers eventually reconcile.

1362: Shogun Ashikaga Yoshiakira creates the position of *kanrei*, or shogun's chief minister, who presides over the shogunal council of *shugo* and conveys the shogun's orders to them for implementation. This post of *kanrei* is monopolized by three Ashikaga-related families—the Shiba, Hosokawa, and Hatakeyama.

1363: Yoshiakira persuades the powerful Ouchi and Yamana *shugo* to submit to the Ashikaga shogunate by granting them autonomy in provincial domains.

1365: Prince Kanenaga of the southern court gains control of all Kyushu. General Imagawa Sadayo wins back the northern area by 1372, but the south holds out for almost twelve years until the 1384 death of the prince.

1366: Koryo envoys ask for the suppression of pirates.

1367: After Yoshiakira dies, leaving the child Yoshimitsu as shogun, Hosokawa Yoriyuki is the shogunal regent as well as *kanrei*. Yoriyuki fosters the adoption of ceremonial ritual in the shogunate and the rise of Yoshimitsu in imperial court ranks. He tries to limit the power of the *shugo daimyo*.

1369: Ming China sends envoys to establish relations with the shogunate to end pirate activity; they do the same in 1370 and 1373. When 1378 and 1380 envoys to China are snubbed, Japan ends the attempt at diplomacy in 1383.

1370s: To limit the power of the *shugo daimyo*, Yoshimitsu insists that they reside in Kyoto in order to participate in government; there he can better monitor their activity. This contributes to the breakdown of the old order in the provinces.

1379: Yoshimitsu crushes a revolt of the Shiba, Toki, and Kyogoku families, thus frustrating the attempt of the Kanto branch of the Ashikaga clan to move power back to Kamakura.

Are we to look at flowers in full bloom, at the moon when it is clear? Nay, to look out on the rain and long for the moon, to draw the blinds and not to be aware of the passing of the spring—these arouse even deeper feelings.

Essays in Idleness, by Yoshida Kenko (14th century)

1380s: In a series of pilgrimages to provinces, Yoshimitsu aims to consolidate the loyalty of the *shugo daimyo.*

1390: Yoshimitsu defeats the rebellious Toki Yasuyuki, *shugo* of Mino and Owari. In 1391 he defeats Yamana Ujikiyo, *shugo* of eleven provinces in central Japan, reducing him to the provinces of Hoki and Tajima.

1391–1392: The Meitoku Rebellion by the Yamana family is crushed by Ouchi, reasserting shogunal authority.

1392: Yoshimitsu reconciles the northern and southern courts, with imperial regalia returned to Kyoto, where Emperor Go-Komatsu (reigns 1382–1412) rules.

1394: Yoshimitsu resigns as shogun to become *daijo daijin,* or chancellor of state, a position in the old *ritsuryo* imperial system and highest rank of the Kyoto court. This constitutes a fusion of feudal, bureaucratic, and aristocratic elements in one office. In 1395 he enters holy orders, retaining power while avoiding ceremonial aspects of office.

1397: The shogunate establishes diplomatic ties with Korea.

1399–1400: In what is known as the Oei Rebellion, Ouchi Yoshihiro plots in western Honshu against the shogun's increasingly autocratic rule. Called to Kyoto, he refuses to go, fearing assassination. Yoshimitsu uses the refusal to declare him an enemy of the shogunate. With the aid of Akamatsu, Kyogoku, and Hosokawa forces, he defeats Ouchi in a large battle at the port of Sakai (Osaka).

1401: Yoshimitsu sends an envoy to Ming China to establish diplomatic relations. He accepts Ming title of tributary "king of Japan." In his last seven years of rule, he sends at least seven tribute missions to China.

In Kyoto, *machi-gumi* (communal organizations of townsmen for internal security) emerge.

1407: Yoshimitsu has his own wife named empress dowager to succeed the late empress, and entertains the emperor as an equal. Yoshimitsu's rule marks the height of Ashikaga status and power. He dies the following year.

1408: Shogun Yoshimochi discontinues relations with Ming China.

1416–1417: The Uesugi Zensho Rebellion takes place in the Kanto region when in a succession dispute Uesugi is defeated by a coalition of three other *shugo* on the orders of the shogun. This leads to the purge of *shugo* in Kyoto, resulting in persistent political instability and loss of power for the shogun, who hereafter leaves decision-making to the *kanrei* and *shugo* cabinet.

1419: In Oei Invasion, a Korean Yi dynasty fleet attacks pirates on Tsushima.

1423: Sho Hashi completes the unification of the Ryukyu Islands, which become the Ryukyu kingdom. As an entrepôt it carries on trade with Japan, China, and Korea; in south with Annam, Siam, Malacca, Sumatra, and Java. The kingdom collapses around 1550.

1428: Ashikaga Yoshinori becomes shogun. Recklessly undermining shogunal power, he plots with vassals to betray the *shugo daimyo* and meddles in provincial and feudal matters. In major reforms of bureaucracy and military, he weakens the *kanrei* power of legislative review and expands economic policy.

The first broad popular uprising of the era, the Shocho Rebellion, takes place with a series of disturbances in Kyoto, Nara, Ise, Yoshino, Sakai, and elsewhere. During a year of national famine and epidemic, rioters demand debt-cancellation decrees (*tokusei*). They raid moneylenders' shops and burn loan contracts. As a result, the shogunate, *shugo daimyo*, and temples all agree to debt cancellations. There will be other debtors' revolts in the future.

1438: In the Eikyo Disturbance, Yoshinori exploits a potential rival to pacify the *shugo*, then pits that rival against a powerful adversary. Authority in ten Kanto provinces shifts to Uesugi from the Kanto branch of Ashikaga.

1441: In the Kakitsu Disturbance, the brutal and dictatorial Yoshinori is assassinated at a *sarugaku* performance by Harima *shugo* Akamatsu Mitsusuke, who fears confiscation of his provinces. He burns his Kyoto residence and escapes to Harima. Pursued by a punitive expedition, he commits suicide.

1454: Chaos reigns in Kyoto, with widespread thievery.

1458: Shogun Yoshimasa begins ambitious renovation of Yoshimitsu's Muromachi palace and erects a villa for his mother and a rural retreat for himself. Using the forced labor of workers and draft animals, and extracting surcharge taxes for construction, he exhibits insensitive extravagance and indifference to suffering during the famine of 1460. After his regime, Hosokawa *kanrei* (chief ministers) install and depose shoguns at their discretion.

We must distinguish in the art of the Noh between essence and performance. If the essence is a flower, the performance is its fragrance. Or they may be compared to the moon and the light which it sheds. When the essence has been thoroughly understood, the performance develops of itself.

Shikado-sho (The Book of the Way of the Highest Flower), by Zeami (15th century)

1467–1477: Onin War of the Sengoku (or Warring States) period (1467–1568) begins with a shogunal succession dispute, as rebellious vassals and armies of over 100,000

men of western Yamana and eastern Hosokawa armies battle sporadically over eleven years. Fighting rages in the Kyoto streets, leaving half of the capital in ruins, and great monuments are burned; aristocrats, merchants, and craftsmen flee to provincial cities. The war ends inconclusively, leads to decentralization of authority, breaks up *shugo* territories into smaller units, and gives rise to the ascendancy of new locally powerful military families. As *daimyo* retreat to fortress castles, peasants and villagers often are allowed a degree of self-management. Anarchy continues for a century as warlords, adventurers, religious sects, and even villages struggle for supremacy and survival in a mutual rivalry called *gekokujo* (literally, "those beneath overthrow those above").

1480s: *Shugo daimyo* withdraw from shogunal structure, emerge as *sengoku daimyo*, with greater power, including collection of taxes; regulation of markets, transportation facilities, weights and measures; enforcement of civil and penal laws; and regulation and protection of religious institutions. From 1490 to 1573 they, rather than the shogun or emperor, are in control in the country. In the 1560s some two hundred *daimyo* rule two-thirds of Japan.

Some cities and villages become semiautonomous with rule by a council of elders, as with Sakai's ten-man *egosho*.

1485: The Yamashiro *kuni ikki*, an organization of peasants and lower-rank warriors, drives out *shugo* armies, refuses to pay provincial taxes, and rules the southern part of the province until 1493.

1488: Marking the rise of popular *Ikko ikki* (single-minded league or uprising) power, *Jodo shin* sect members defeat the Kaga provincial army and establish rule there. For nearly a century they rule Kaga through priests of Honganji temple in cooperation with lesser samurai and village leaders. Uprisings spread to neighboring provinces, until a 1580 defeat by Oda Nobunaga ends their hegemony.

Who's that
Holding over four hundred provinces
In the palm of his hand
And entertaining at a tea-party?
It's His Highness
So mighty, so impressive!

Song to Hideyoshi at his shrine in Kyoto (15th–16th centuries)

1532–1536: In the Temmon Hokke Rebellion, armed members of the Nichiren Buddhist sect form the Lotus Confederation, take over the city, and refuse to pay rents and taxes in Kyoto. Finally, they are violently opposed by warrior-monks of Enryakuji temple, who destroy twenty-one main Nichiren temples and burn Kyoto's commercial center. The Nichiren flee to Sakai and build a new headquarters there.

1543: The first Europeans arrive with an accidental landfall on the island of Tanegashima of a Chinese junk carrying several Portuguese.

1553: The first of five battles of Kawanakajima takes place between warlords Uesugi Kenshin and Takeda Shingen. Minor engagements are glorified in Edo-period literature—brutal warlords are portrayed as chivalrous heroes of epic encounters.

June 12, 1560: Beginning a rise to power in Kanto region, Oda Nobunaga (1534–1582) defeats Imagawa Yoshimoto at the Battle of Okehazama. With only 2,000–3,000 soldiers he ambushes the warlord's 25,000-man army. Yoshimoto dies and his vassal Matsudaira Motoyasu (later Tokugawa Ieyasu) becomes a free agent.

1562: Nobunaga and Tokugawa Ieyasu (1543–1616) become allies.

1568: Nobunaga captures Kyoto and installs Ashikaga Yoshiaki as shogun. In 1569, Sakai submits to Nobunaga after he threatens the city with destruction when Miyoshi leaders in Sakai attack the shogun.

This begins the Shokuho regime (1568–1600), or the period between shogunates, an era of national unification and consolidation under Nobunaga and Toyotomi Hideyoshi.

January 6, 1573: Takeda Shingen defeats the army of Tokugawa Ieyasu and Oda Nobunaga at Mikatagahara, encouraging Yoshiaki to sever ties to Nobunaga.

May 1573: Nobunaga burns much of Kyoto to bring the shogun back under his control. In August he expels the shogun from Kyoto, thus ending the Muromachi period and Ashikaga shogunate.

MOMOYAMA PERIOD: 1573–1615

Also known as the Azuchi-Momoyama period, the era is named after the magnificent castles built by Nobunaga at Azuchi and by Hideyoshi at Momoyama. Although short, the period sees enormous changes. The three warlords Oda Nobunaga, Toyotomi Hideyoshi, and Tokugawa Ieyasu complete, together and individually, the unification of Japan after defeating powerful regional *daimyo* and militaristic Buddhist communities. This relatively speedy and bloody conquest is aided in part by the use of firearms introduced by Europeans. The warlords seek to consolidate their political gains by the implementation of countrywide land surveys, a reorganized tax system, and by an attempt to conquer Korea. Potential challengers to their authority are eliminated by "sword hunts" that strip all except samurai of their weapons.

The warlords begin a campaign of erecting impressive fortress castles opulently decorated inside with gold screens by top artists. Official patronage, especially under Hideyoshi, also extends to occasions of ceremonial pageantry and festivals, including dance and *noh* performances, and to the use of the tea cult as a tool of statecraft. *Kabuki* also makes its first appearance, initially as a women's performance art.

Persecution increasingly limits the activity of Christian missionaries and their converts, who come to be viewed as socially subversive. Cosmopolitanism characterizes the era as trade with Europeans, centered in Nagasaki, encompasses the Spanish, Dutch, and English, as well as the Portuguese whose exotic foods and clothing enter the vocabulary of fashionable Japanese. But this is only temporary, as internal pressures begin to threaten relations with foreigners, both religious and secular.

October 1574: Nobunaga defeats *Ikko ikki* at Ise-Nagashima. In a rise to power, he eliminates, one by one, contentious religious communities.

June 1575: In the Battle of Nagashino, Nobunaga's three thousand men using firearms are victorious over Takeda Katsuyori's cavalry, a milestone of Japan's entry into modern warfare.

1576: Nobunaga's Echizen governor conducts a "sword hunt," ordering peasants to surrender weapons, and carries out a religious inquisition.

September 10, 1580: Nobunaga burns the Osaka headquarters of Ishiyama Honganji after its surrender, concluding a ten-year campaign against the True Pure Land sect.

1580: Nobunaga destroys forts in Kansai region, orders land surveys in Yamato and Harima provinces.

April 1582: Nobunaga defeats the Takeda clan, gains power over Kanto region.

June 21, 1582: In the Honnoji Incident, wounded Nobunaga commits suicide following a surprise attack by his vassal general Akechi Mitsuhide. By now, half of Japan, including the central region and Kyoto, is under Nobunaga's control.

July 2, 1582: In the Battle of Yamazaki, Hideyoshi (1537–15,8) avenges Nobunaga's death by defeating Mitsuhide and begins his own rise to national power. As the only early Japanese leader of commoner descent, he has risen rapidly in Nobunaga's service from stable boy to *daimyo* through extraordinary talents.

July 27, 1582: Hideyoshi orders the *Taiko kenchi*, a survey of the lands and productive capacity of Yamashiro province, and a survey in 1584 of Omi province, using the new standard square measure. He moves loyal *daimyo* to strategic domains and removes potential enemies to distant sites.

As an instrument of political unification and of simplification of the land holding and taxation system, provincial land surveys through 1598 enumerate the size and yield of each rice field; guarantee tenancy of plot to actual cultivator; and set a tax rate as high as 50 percent, eliminating other taxes and dues.

1583: In the Battle of Shizugatake, Hideyoshi defeats Shibata Katsuie in a succession struggle, consolidating his supreme power over thirty of sixty provinces.

May 1584: After Tokugawa Ieyasu defeats Hideyoshi's forces at Nagakute, the campaign continues with skirmishes at Komaki.

December 16, 1584: Hostilities and succession struggle end when Hideyoshi makes peace with Oda Nobukatsu (Oda Nobunaga's son), an ally of Tokugawa Ieyasu.

April–May 1585: Hideyoshi defeats Negoro warrior-monks and gains Kii province; in July–August his troops conquer Chosokabe *daimyo* in Shikoku.

August 6, 1585: Hideyoshi is appointed *kanpaku*, or imperial regent.

January 27, 1587: Hideyoshi is appointed *Daijo daijin*, grand chancellor of state, the highest post in the *ritsuryo* system.

April–June 1587: Hideyoshi conquers Kyushu after personally leading expedition against Shimazu *daimyo* of Satsuma.

1588: Exiled Ashikaga Yoshiaki officially gives up the shogunate, marking the legal end of the Muromachi government.

Hideyoshi orders a "sword hunt" in many provinces: confiscation of weapons from all except samurai is aimed at depriving peasants, farmers, and warrior-monks of the means for armed rebellion.

August 12, 1590: With the end of the Odawara campaign, Hideyoshi defeats Go-Hojo's forces. This, along with a 1591 victory in northern Honshu, completes the unification of Japan. He moves ally and potential rival Ieyasu a safe distance to Kanto, with the marshy fishing village of Edo to be his castle town. Using landfill and waterworks construction methods, Ieyasu establishes a High City for his own fortress, samurai, vassals, and center of government, with a Low City for merchants and craftsmen who flock to the new metropolis.

February 11, 1591: Hideyoshi transfers the office of *kanpaku* (imperial regent) to his nephew and adopted son Toyotomi Hidetsugu, and himself assumes the title of *Taiko* (retired imperial regent). Juraku Palace becomes Hidetsugu's formal residence.

1592–1593: Hideyoshi invades Korea with some 250,000 men in a plan aimed at the ultimate conquest of China. Ieyasu, busy with Edo, does not participate. The Japanese are victorious until Korea seeks help from China; the Korean navy rallies, guerrillas become active, and a severe winter sets in. The war ends in an armistice that lasts until 1596, when negotiations break down.

1595: Hidetsugu commits suicide after Hideyoshi banishes him in order to clear inheritance for his own newborn son. Hidetsugu's family and retainers are massacred, and Juraku castle is torn down.

1597: The second Korean invasion begins with Japan again initially successful. After Hideyoshi's death in the following year, Japan's forces are pulled out of Korea.

September 18, 1598: Hideyoshi dies after entrusting his five-year-old son Hideyori to the five-man council of regency to assure his succession. Tokugawa Ieyasu becomes his guardian.

Hideyoshi's accomplishments are considerable—securing success as a brilliant military tactician and unifier of the nation; restoring the dignity of the imperial house; rebuilding the capital and other cities; repairing monasteries and shrines ravaged by war; and leading the nation into a lively cultural era.

October 21, 1600: In the bloody Battle of Sekigahara, Tokugawa Ieyasu defeats Ishida Mitsunari, his most dangerous enemy; the victory establishes Ieyasu's power over all Japan. He reneges on his promise to protect Hideyori's succession and consolidates power by giving eighty-seven estates confiscated from losers to his own followers. He builds a series of fortresses around Edo (Tokyo), his new capital, and strengthens his own castle there.

March 24, 1603: Ieyasu has himself named shogun.

1605: Taking the title of *ogosho* (retired shogun), Ieyasu passes the shogun post on to his son Hidetada in order to assure the continuity of the Tokugawa dynasty; he remains the power behind the figurehead.

1607: The first embassy from Korean Yi dynasty since invasions arrives in Edo to seek relations with the Tokugawa shogunate.

1609: The shogunate approves a military expedition by Shimazu family, rulers of Satsuma, against the Ryukyu Islands. In 1611 the Ryukyus become a vassal state of Satsuma.

1610: The Tokugawa allow Tanaka Shosuke to travel to New Spain (Mexico) with Rodrigo Vivero y Velasco. In 1611 Tokugawa leaders formally receive an envoy of New Spain's viceroy.

1613: Hasekura Tsunenaga leads an unsuccessful embassy to Spain's Philip III to ask for trade with New Spain.

November 1614–June 1615: In order to secure the Tokugawa shogunate, Ieyasu sets out to remove Hideyori and some ninety thousand *ronin* (masterless samurai) followers. The first siege (or winter campaign) of Hideyori's Osaka castle leads to the summer campaign (June 4, 1615) wherein the castle is overrun and Hideyori commits suicide, thus ending the Hideyoshi succession.

EDO PERIOD: 1615–1868

Named after the new shogunal capital city, the period is one of a 250-year-long, prosperous *pax Tokugawa*. Excluding Westerners from Japanese shores, the Tokugawa shoguns seek to impose social order and stability, based on Confucian principles, by means of a rigid stratification of classes and a draconian moralism that permeates nearly all areas of everyday activity. In the so-called *bakuhan* administration system, the shogun controls Edo and, nominally, some 250 *daimyo* who in turn are responsible for the governance of their own domains (*han*).

As the urban centers grow, samurai become bureaucrats; merchants and craftsmen, though low on the official social scale, flourish and form the basis of a bourgeoisie that avoids the heavy taxation that still burdens farmers. Both samurai and commoners patronize the lively Genroku artistic culture, which sees the arrival of *bunraku* puppet theater and of *haiku* poetry, and the further evolution of *kabuki* performance. Known as *ukiyo*, or "the Floating World," the licensed red-light districts and their denizens become a subject of fascination for writers and designers, who develop the colored woodblock print into a high art form.

Isolation from Westerners, interrupted occasionally by accidental or intentional intrusion of European and American vessels, is loosened as time goes on, to admit books on the sciences which become the focus of intense study by a growing phalanx of scholars, who also examine areas of Japanese culture. Meanwhile Christians are cruelly persecuted, and new Shinto utopian sects emerge.

By the middle of the nineteenth century, the shogunate is a fractured structure weakened by fiscal mismanagement. The arrival of Commodore Perry's American ships in Edo Bay to demand and get a trading agreement reopens Japan to the West. This Japanese appeasement of the foreigners provokes pro-imperial radicals into terrorism and leads to the overthrow of the Tokugawa shogunate.

1615: The shogunate issues *Buke shohatto* (ordinances relating to warrior houses): samurai are to be adept with both sword and brush, the latter referring to literacy. After nearly two hundred years of civil wars, samurai now must adapt to a peacetime existence. Their code emphasizes courage, loyalty, obedience, dignity, and willingness to sacrifice their own life in an instant. They are recognized by their assertive demeanor, two swords (a long one for fighting, a short one for committing suicide), and hair worn in a topknot with the front shaved. Forbidden to own land, they join the *daimyo* in cities and begin to work in administration.

Also issued are *Kincho narabi ni kuge shohatto* (laws governing imperial court and nobility).

1623: Becoming shogun, Ieyasu's grandson Iemitsu shapes the regime into final form by issuing directives to control all strata of society. *Daimyo* are to spend alternate time periods in Edo and in their own domains (until 1862), leaving their families hostage in Edo. The expense of maintaining two or more residences and of lengthy processions to and from Edo leaves less money for military adventurism. The shogun is to oversee their marriages and other areas of their lives; they are to communicate with the emperor only through the shogun; their households are to be under surveillance of *metsuke* (inspectors), official Tokugawa censors. Fearing dispossession of their domains, *daimyo* obey.

Villagers are to form *goningumi* (five-man groups) wherein they are mutually responsible for each other's tax payments, behavior, and religious orthodoxy.

1636: Construction of buildings on Nagasaki's artificial island of Dejima is finished; Portuguese merchants must move there from the city. In 1639 the Portuguese are banned from Japan, as are all Europeans except the Dutch, who move to Dejima.

1637–1638: In the Shimabara Rebellion, persecuted and impoverished Christians, unemployed samurai, and peasants rise up. Soon some 40,000 under Amakusa Shiro win a series of victories against *daimyo* armies from a base at Hara Castle. A shogunal force of 120,000 besieges the castle, with the Dutch helping to bombard it. After eighty days, rebels set fire to castle and all perish within. The uprising leads to 220 years of Japanese seclusion from the outside world and its pernicious influences.

Despite brutal persecution, *kakure kirishitan* (crypto-Christians) continue to worship in secret. In 1850 thousands are discovered and arrested. Anti-Christian laws remain in effect until 1872.

August 4, 1639: The shogunate's ultimate *sakoku* (exclusion policy) directive ends almost all European trade with Japan, evicts all Westerners except the Dutch.

1640: To enforce *sakoku* laws, the shogunate executes sixty-one members of a Portuguese delegation from Macau sent to protest the ban on traders.

1648: A legal code is issued to control the lives of Edo commoners. In Osaka, codes regulate urban life and commerce. In 1649 the shogunate promulgates the Keian *furegaki*: peasants are to be frugal and diligent, farmers are forbidden to drink tea or sake.

1663: In a revision to the *Buke shohatto*, warriors are banned from suicide on the death of their lord.

Summer grass
All that remains
Of warriors' dreams.

Haiku by Basho (17th century)

1680: Tsunayoshi becomes shogun, dismisses the grand councilor, and confiscates the domains of forty-six *daimyo*, beginning in 1681. In 1685 he begins to issue Edicts on Compassion for Living Things, including rules on overloading pack horses. In 1695 he orders the erection of palatial dog pounds in Edo to house some forty thousand dogs abandoned by their owners and often used for archery practice. Killing dogs is made a capital offense, convincing some that he is unbalanced.

1701–1703: In the Forty-Seven Ronin Incident, samurai pursue a vendetta to avenge their lord's death. Despite this crime, they are admired for loyalty and as exemplary self-sacrificing samurai upholding the warrior code; they are allowed to commit suicide honorably rather than be executed. Their grave, next to their master, becomes a popular pilgrimage and tourist site. This most famous event of the samurai era will be the basis for some 150 novels, plays, films, and television epics.

1716: Yoshimune becomes the eighth Tokugawa shogun and begins the Kyoho Reforms (1716–1745) upholding frugality and military spirit; mandating financial retrenchment, land reclamation, crop diversification, legal code revisions. Reforms are attempt to halt what is believed to be nation's downward spiral. He is the last great shogun; his successors tend to be figureheads manipulated by their ministers.

1738: In the largest demonstration to date, some 84,000 farmers protest in Iwakitaira.

Later protests surpass this, with 160,000 in 1754 and 200,000 in 1764. An army supplied by thirteen *daimyo* suppresses an uprising at the Ikuno silver mine.

1787–1793: Shogunal chief councilor Matsudaira Sadanobu begins the reactionary Kansei Reforms: attempts to restrict foreign trade, cancel samurai debt, restore agriculture as economic mainstay of state, and ban unorthodox teachings. He also issues severe sumptuary laws. Based on traditional Confucian theory, this policy proves economically damaging, leading to famines, uprisings, and urban violence. He resigns in 1793.

1791–1792: U.S. and Russian ships visit Japan, unsuccessfully seeking trade. During the next fifty years, repeated Western attempts are made to open relations. The shogunate's response to accidental and intentional arrivals varies. In 1806 it allows help to accidental landings, but castaways must leave; in 1825 all ships must be driven off; in 1842 the shogunate orders a return to the 1806 policy of allowing the provision of food, water, and firewood to ships.

1792–1793: An envoy from Catherine the Great, Russian navy lieutenant Adam Laksman, arrives in Hokkaido to seek the return of castaways and, unsuccessfully, to open trade relations. In 1804 an embassy by Nikolai Rezanov to Nagasaki also fails.

1799: The shogunate establishes direct control over Ezo (southern Hokkaido). In 1806 it gains power over the western region as Russian ships threaten sites in the north.

1801: After Russians introduce Russian culture and Christianity to Ainu on the Kurile Islands, the shogunate tries to win back the Ainu and drive out the Russians.

1808: In the *Phaeton* Incident, a British warship flying the Dutch flag enters Nagasaki harbor and seizes two Dutch prisoners, who are released in exchange for food and water provisions.

> *Our country, as a special mark of favor from the heavenly gods, was begotten by them, and there is thus so immense a difference between Japan and all the other countries of the world as to defy comparison. Ours is a splendid and blessed country, the Land of the Gods beyond any doubt, and we, down to the most humble man and woman, are the descendants of the gods.*
>
> *Kodo Taii* (Summary of the Ancient Way) by Hirata Atsutane (1811)

1837: In the *Morrison* Incident, a U.S. merchant ship, ostensibly trying to return castaways but actually seeking trade, is fired on when it attempts to land near Edo and later again in Kyushu's Kagoshima Bay.

In Osaka, Oshio Heihachiro heads a rebellion to seek famine relief. Ikuta Yorozu leads a similar protest. Various domains initiate reform programs.

1839: In the context of scholarly debate on the national seclusion policy, the shogunate begins attacks on Japanese specialists of *Rangaku* (Dutch studies) and *Yogaku* (Western studies). Arrested and imprisoned are Watanabe Kazan (1793–1841) and Takano Choei (1804–1850).

1841–1843: The Tempo Reforms are the most severe yet in an attempt to improve shogunal authority and the economic situation: they abolish merchant monopolies and guilds in an unsuccessful attempt to lower prices, evict *daimyo* from the region of Edo and Osaka castles, dismiss great numbers of officials, censor pornography, forcibly return peasants found in cities back to the land, and "rectify the classes" by means of extensive sumptuary laws. The reforms result in ever higher prices and are soon rescinded.

1844: In Nagasaki, a Dutch warship arrives with a letter from the king seeking trade; the shogunate refuses. As more and more foreign whaling vessels and warships enter Japanese waters, Japan begins to build up coastal defenses. Military garrisons are established at Hakodate in Hokkaido and in the Kurile Islands.

July 8, 1853: Four U.S. warships led by Commodore Matthew Perry arrive in Edo Bay to seek free trade without bloodshed. After sending a message ashore, they sail away, to return for an answer in a year. What is recognized as an ultimatum poses a dilemma for the vacillating shogunal government, and debate over a response weakens it further.

1854: Perry returns with a fleet of nine vessels, bearing gifts for the shogun, including a quarter-size railway that travels at twenty miles per hour on 350 feet of track, a telegraph with three miles of wire, two lifeboats, and lesser items. U.S. soldiers display close-order drill, firefighting, mock attack on ship, a broadside of heaviest guns, and a minstrel show, to the accompaniment of much whiskey.

The shogunate signs the Kanagawa Treaty of peace and amity with the United States, calling for two coaling stations for foreign steamships at Hakodate and Shimoda. The shogunate will also sign treaties with Great Britain (1854), Russia (1855), and the Netherlands (1856).

1856: First U.S. consul Townsend Harris arrives to conduct negotiations for 1858 Open Port Treaty: it opens Hakodate, Yokohama, Kobe, Niigata, Shimoda, and Nagasaki to American traders, with Osaka and Edo to follow. Treaty also includes extraterritoriality for foreigners, a "most favored nation" clause favoring the United States, and low tariff rates, potentially damaging Japanese economy further. In 1860 a shogunal delegation sails on an American ship to the United States to ratify the treaty. This pact sets the precedent for a series of humiliating "unequal treaties" with Westerners and leads to bitter resentment against foreigners and the shogunate, contributing to eventual open rebellion. In Chosho domain, Yoshida Shoin begins to teach imperial loyalist ideology to young samurai.

1858: Ansei commercial treaties between Japan and the United States, the Netherlands, Russia, Great Britain, and France are completed, leading to a purge of those opposed to reopening Japan to West.

1860: In the Sakuradamon Incident, shogunal advisor Ii Naosuke, who promoted the Ansei treaties, is assassinated. This begins a period of terrorist activity against foreign residents and shogunal leaders by self-styled *shishi* (men of high purpose) radicals. Their battle cry is *Sonno joi* ("Revere the Emperor, drive out the barbarian!"). Springing from southwest Japan, far from political centers, the rebellion's ultimate goals are overthrow of the shogunate in favor of emperor-headed government and national reformation. British-supplied arms will aid their struggle.

1862: In the Richardson Affair, a British merchant is murdered by Satsuma samurai; in 1863 British bombard Kagoshima in retaliation.

September 30, 1863: In a coup attempt, pro-imperial radical samurai are driven from Kyoto. In the 1864 Ikedaya Incident, they try to seize the palace and clash with shogunal police. In the Hamaguri Gomon Incident, they try to force their way into Kyoto, and an imperial court orders the shogunate to lead a punitive expedition against them into Chosho.

1864: In the Shimonoseki Bombardment, ships of Western nations retaliate against Chosho attacks on vessels passing through the strait.

1866: The Satsuma-Chosho alliance is formed against shogunate; the shogunal expeditionary army is defeated. In this year both the emperor and the shogun die.

1867: The last Tokugawa shogun, Yoshinobu, officially surrenders power and resigns from office. Rebel forces take Kyoto and Edo.

MEIJI PERIOD: 1868–1912

Meiji (Enlightened Rule) is not just the title of the era but also the name of Emperor Mutsuhito, whose reign the period encompasses. Under the slogan *Fukoku kyohei* ("Enrich the country, strengthen the military"), the leaders of the Meiji Restoration carry out a sweeping program of modernization unprecedented in Japanese history. Steps are taken to eradicate feudalism immediately, resulting in a transformation of geographical boundaries, social classes, and economic structure. Governmental reform redefines the emperor's role, produces the nation's first constitution, and sees the rise of political parties for the new parliamentary system. Giant leaps are made in the areas of education, science, technology, and commerce. The era's problems— including often violent popular unrest, financial crises, and growing militarism—cannot overshadow the remarkable successes. Industrialization on the Western model flourishes and is stimulated further by wars that gain for Japan the beginnings of a colonial empire and stature as a world power.

January 3, 1868: After military victories, the court declares imperial restoration. In October sixteen-year-old Mutsuhito selects the name Meiji (reigns 1868–1912), under which he will preside as the new emperor. Initially the government exploits his symbolic role, but later he comes to participate in decision-making. Edo is renamed first Tokei, then Tokyo. In 1869 the emperor officially moves the capital there from Kyoto.

January 27, 1868: In the Battle of Toba-Fushimi, forces claiming to represent the emperor defeat those allied to the shogunate. This begins the Boshin Civil War.

April 6, 1868: In a move to stabilize rule, the Charter Oath is issued in the emperor's name. It seeks to unify the allegiance of all classes and to open the way to social and political change. At the same time, the emperor issues *Gobo no Keiji* (Five Public Notices): upholding traditional Confucian values and banning criminal behavior, Christianity and other "heterodox" sects, injury to foreigners, and travel outside Japan. Except for the ban on injury to foreigners, the Notices are mostly ignored.

June 11, 1868: *Seitaisho*, the first constitution of the Meiji government, becomes law, granting nearly all authority to the Dajokan (Grand Council of State); the bicameral deliberative assembly will have little power.

June 27, 1869: In the Battle of Goryokaku in Ezo, *daimyo* forces led by Enomoto Takeaki surrender, ending the Boshin Civil War. With pacification of the region, the entire country comes under imperial rule. Ezo is renamed Hokkaido and the Hokkaido Colonization Office opens in 1869.

July 25–August 2, 1869: As ordered by the new government, the *daimyo* officially return *Hanseki*, or domainal registers, of land and people of 262 domains. Initially the *daimyo* are named governors of their former domains, but in July 1871 their domains are abolished. Former *daimyo* are paid off and become part of the nobility.

December 23, 1871: The Iwakura Mission sets sail from Yokohama, primarily to renegotiate "unequal treaties" of the shogunate with the West. Its diplomatic efforts rebuffed, the fifty-member group (including ambassadors, students, and baggage handlers) completes an eighteen-month tour of the United States and Europe; they bring back first-hand experience of Western industrialization to inspire Japanese modernization efforts.

January 1872: Realignment of domain boundaries results in the creation of seventy-two provincial prefectures and three urban prefectures.

April 1872: Government establishes the Army Ministry and Navy Ministry. In May 1893 the Navy General Staff is established as a separate organ of command.

January 1873: Government enacts the Conscription Ordinance of 1873, effective in April, mandating three years' compulsory military service for all males twenty years of age; this leads to antidraft rioting.

October 1873: The Dajokan separates into factions over Japanese policy toward Korea, as government rejects a military expedition against Korea after an alleged Korean insult. Some members of the losing faction found the Freedom and People's Rights Movement.

November 1873: The government organizes the Home Ministry to control social unrest, primarily among dispossessed samurai, some of whom turn to armed rebellion after the government dismantles the samurai class in 1873–1876. This ministry directs local administration and elections, police, and public works.

January 17, 1874: In a sharp critique of government policies, the Public Party of Patriots, led by Itagaki Taisuke (1837–1919) and associates, issues the Tosa Memorial, calling for the establishment of a national representative assembly.

The white snow on Fuji
Melts in the morning sun,
Melts and runs down
To Mishima,
Where Mishima's prostitutes
Mix it in their make-up.

Popular ballad (19th century)

January–February 1874: The Saga Rebellion is waged by dispossessed samurai and by a faction calling for an invasion of Korea and for a return to the feudal order. After they attack banks and government offices, they are suppressed by government forces.

May 1874: In a punitive expedition against Taiwan, following the December 1871 murder there of fifty-four shipwrecked Ryukyu Islanders, Japan's government sends a three thousand-man force that meets with strong Taiwanese resistance. China pays an indemnity and recognizes Japanese claims to the Ryukyus.

January–February 1875: In order to resolve political differences, the Osaka Conference convenes to consider establishing a representative assembly.

May 7, 1875: In the Treaty of St. Petersburg, Russia gains Sakhalin, while the Kurile Islands go to Japan. Receiving most favored nation status, Japan may fish in the Sea of Okhotsk and freely use Russian ports in the area.

June 28, 1875: Government enacts the Libel Law of 1875, together with the Press Ordinance of 1875, to control the press and limit freedom of expression in response to political activity by the Freedom and People's Rights Movement.

February 27, 1876: Japan gains "unequal privileges" in the Treaty of Kangwha with Korea. Despite Korea's tributary relation with China, the treaty recognizes Korea as an independent state, calls for diplomatic exchanges, and opens three ports to Japanese trade. The treaty is a contributing factor to the Sino-Japanese War of 1894–1895 and to the eventual Japanese annexation of Korea.

October 24, 1876: The Shinporen Rebellion by discontented samurai breaks out. It is followed by the Hagi Rebellion of October 26 and the Akizuki Rebellion of October 27.

January 29–September 24, 1877: The last and largest of former samurai disturbances is the Satsuma Rebellion by some forty thousand dissenters led by Saigo Takamori (1827–1877), originally a leader of the Meiji Restoration movement.

May 14, 1878: Six samurai conspirators from Satsuma Rebellion assassinate Home Minister Okubo Toshimichi (1830–1878), the strongest political leader of the time.

August 23, 1878: Angered by wage reductions and paltry rewards from the Satsuma Rebellion, some 260 government soldiers rise up in the Takehashi Insurrection. On October 15 fifty-three are sentenced to death and 118 banished from Tokyo. This leads the government to strengthen military discipline.

1879: The Ryukyu Kingdom is abolished, and the islands are incorporated into Japan's Okinawa Prefecture.

April 1880: A Public Assembly Ordinance is issued to control political activity: it requires registration and prior approval from police for all organizations and meetings; it also bans contact between organizations and outdoor gatherings.

Summer 1881: The Hokkaido Colonization Office scandal erupts as the agency sells off assets at very favorable rates to cronies. Public outrage forces cancellation of the sale and, in October, the resignation of finance minister Okuma Shigenobu (1838–1922). The government is forced to promise a new constitution and national assembly by 1890.

October 1881: Matsukata Masayoshi (1835–1924) becomes finance minister and starts to implement the Matsukata Fiscal Policy in order to stabilize the economy in a time of depression, bankruptcies, and inflation. By retrenchment, deflation, and currency and banking reform measures through 1885, he reestablishes confidence in the currency and banking systems. As result, from 1883 to 1890 some 368,000 peasants (or 10 percent) lose land to taxes; more lose land through mortgage foreclosures.

October 29, 1881: Leaders of the Freedom and People's Rights Movement found the nation's first national political party, Jiyoto (Liberal Party). Over the next decades numerous parties and political organizations are founded; some soon disband, while many transform or merge to form new parties.

August 30, 1882: With the Treaty of Chemulp'o, Japan receives reparations for losses of Japanese lives and property in Korea during the Imo Mutiny, when Korean troops rebel against Japanese-style modernization of the Korean army.

November 28, 1882: The Fukushima Incident is first of popular uprisings through 1884. When peasants demonstrate against high taxes and conscript labor for road construction, Jiyoto leaders are imprisoned. When a thousand peasants outside the police station demand their release, violence ensues, leading to charges of treason against fifty-eight.

September 24, 1884: In the Kabasan Incident, police and government forces suppress attempt by radical Jiyoto members to establish a more democratic government and assassinate Meiji political leaders. This and the October 31 Chichibu Incident are two of many similar events, usually with ties to the Freedom and People's Rights Movement, in the early 1880s.

December 4, 1884: In the Korean Kapsin political coup, young reformers with Japanese ties seize the royal palace and are suppressed by the Chinese garrison. The January 1885 Treaty of Seoul grants Japan an apology and reparations for the burned embassy and forty dead Japanese.

April 1885: Japan and China complete the Tientsin Convention, delineating their interests in Korea: both are to withdraw troops, neither are to send troops back without prior written notice, and Korea is to hire advisors from a third nation to train its army.

December 22, 1885: The cabinet system is adopted as the new ruling body of government, replacing the Dajokan. It is responsible only to the emperor, not the Diet, through World War II. Ito Hirobumi (1841–1907) becomes prime minister.

1885: In the Osaka Incident, Japanese Jiyoto activists plot to raise an army to invade Korea and install rebel leader Kim Okkyun in power. Police uncover the plan and arrest 130 in Osaka and Nagasaki.

October 24, 1886: In the *Normanton* Incident, British crew escape a sinking freighter, leaving twenty-three Japanese passengers to drown. The captain gets off lightly in a Yokohama British consular trial, spurring Japanese urgency to revise "unequal treaties" to abolish extraterritoriality.

December 25, 1887: The Peace Preservation Law is enacted to control rising political activism: public demonstrations and outdoor gatherings are to require police permission. The Public Order and Police Law of 1900 follows to restrain labor movements and the rights of workers.

April 30, 1888: The Privy Council, the senior consultative body to the emperor and government, is organized to ratify the Meiji constitution.

November 29, 1889: The Meiji constitution, or Constitution of the Empire of Japan, becomes effective. Influenced by the Prussian model, it defines the sovereignty of the emperor, who is served by the cabinet. The judiciary is made independent; the Diet is to initiate legislation and approve laws and the budget. Individual rights of the people are theoretically guaranteed.

November 25, 1890: The first session of the Imperial Diet, which includes the House of Peers and the House of Representatives, convenes after the first general election.

May 11, 1891: In the Otsu Incident, a Japanese policeman escorting the Russian crown prince on a tour of Japan wounds the prince in an assassination attempt. He is sentenced to life imprisonment. Speedy resolution of the diplomatic crisis is seen to demonstrate the independence of the Japanese judiciary.

July 16, 1894: In the first revision of unequal treaties, the Anglo-Japanese Commercial Treaty of 1894 does away with extraterritoriality and allows Japan partial tariff autonomy. Other Western powers sign similar pacts.

August 1, 1894: The Sino-Japanese War of 1894–1895 breaks out when Japan and China intervene in the Korean Tonghak Rebellion. Japan quickly defeats larger Chinese forces.

April 17, 1895: War ends with the Treaty of Shimonoseki. The Tripartite Intervention by Russia, France, and Germany forces Japan to give back some territory ceded by China, but Japan comes away with Taiwan, which remains a Japanese colony for the next fifty-one years. As a result of the war Japan emerges as Asia's first imperialist world power. Internally, the military gains a greater voice, foreign policy turns toward territorial expansion, and industrialization intensifies.

August 4, 1900: An Allied expeditionary force against the Boxer Rebellion in China includes some ten thousand Japanese, five thousand Russian, three thousand British, two thousand American, and eight hundred French troops.

1901: To promote Japanese expansion in Asia and to drive Russia from Manchuria (which Japan occupies in 1900), the ultranationalist Amur River Society is founded: it publishes a journal and trains and sends intelligence agents to Siberia and Manchuria.

January 30, 1902: The Anglo-Japanese Alliance, signed in London, provides for joint action in case of Russian aggression with a fourth power; it also affirms British special interests in China and Japanese interests in Korea.

February 8, 1904: The Russo-Japanese War begins as the Japanese navy attacks the Russian fleet at Port Arthur before declaring war on February 10, initiating hostilities over control of Korea and Manchuria. Japan lands troops in Korea through March and reaches Manchuria in May. Despite winning a series of battles, Japan is unable to rout Russian forces.

February 21–March 10, 1905: Japanese defeat Russians in the Battle of Mukden, but find resources depleted.

May 27–28, 1905: Japan defeats the Russian Baltic Fleet in the Battle of Tsushima, then secretly asks U.S. president Theodore Roosevelt to mediate peace. Japanese casualties reach ninety thousand.

September 5, 1905: The Treaty of Portsmouth (New Hampshire) ending the Russo-Japanese War grants Japan exclusive rights in Korea and territorial rights to Sakhalin south of the 50th parallel, as well as to the southern Liaodong Peninsula. Manchuria returns to

China, and Russia is to be paid for its lost land.

Treaty terms are protested in the Tokyo Hibiya Incendiary Incident: a mass rally and police clashes end with martial law, 350 buildings burned, seventeen dead, and some one thousand injured.

November 18, 1905: Korea becomes a Japanese protectorate under the Korean-Japanese Convention of 1905. In 1906 the office of Resident General or Japanese administrator is established in Korea.

1906: The South Manchurian Railway is founded as a semi-official Japanese company. From 1907 to 1945 it will administer railways and economic development of Manchuria.

Tea began as a medicine and grew into a beverage. . . . The fifteenth century saw Japan ennoble it into a religion of aestheticism . . . a cult founded on the adoration of the beautiful among the sordid facts of everyday existence. It inculcates purity and harmony, the mystery of mutual charity, the romanticism of the social order. It is essentially a worship of the Imperfect, as it is a tender attempt to accomplish something possible in this impossible thing we know as life.

The Book of Tea, by Okakura Kakuzo (1906)

July 24, 1907: Resident General Ito Hirobumi assumes complete control of Korean government, after forcing the abdication of King Kojong. The Korean-Japanese Convention of 1907 effectively allows Japan to control Korean internal affairs. On August 1 Ito disbands the Korean army.

1907–1908: In a so-called Gentlemen's Agreement, the governments of the United States and Japan exchange a series of six notes that spell out the U.S. ban on Japanese immigration, and the Japanese promise not to issue passports to the United States for emigrant laborers. Secrecy of the pact avoids the public humiliation of Japan.

November 30, 1908: With the Takahira-Root Agreement, the United States recognizes Japan's special interest in Manchuria while Japan recognizes U.S. interests in Hawaii and the Philippines.

October 26, 1909: A Korean nationalist assassinates Japan's Resident General, Ito Hirobumi, in Manchuria.

May 20, 1910: In the High Treason Incident of 1910, an anarchist plot to assassinate Emperor Meiji is discovered; it leads to mass arrests, several executions, and the suppression of leftists.

August 22, 1910: Japan officially annexes Korea. A treaty between Korea and Japan transforms Korea into Choson, a Japanese colony until 1945.

July 30, 1912: Emperor Meiji dies. He is succeeded by his third son Yoshihito, later called Emperor Taisho (reigns 1912–1926). On the evening of the funeral, Army General Nogi Maresuke (1849–1912) and his wife commit ritual suicide.

TAISHO PERIOD: 1912–1926

The Taisho (Great Righteousness) Period covers the reign of Emperor Yoshihito, posthumously called Emperor Taisho. Though relatively short, it encompasses important milestones. As an ally on the victorious side in World War I, Japan emerges dominant in the western Pacific sphere and as one of the Big Five powers. It expands its colonial territories, and benefits from a war-induced boom fueled in part by a shift to heavy industry in order to manufacture armaments, as well as from the withdrawal of European colonial powers that produced textiles and other vital consumer goods in East Asia.

The early postwar years see economic setbacks, with inflation and widespread rice riots.

Despite a disastrous Siberian intervention, Japan now is a major participant in international diplomatic initiatives. The Tokyo-Yokohama earthquake wreaks unprecedented destruction, but reconstruction projects help improve the economy. A significant accomplishment is the development of party government with broad popular involvement derived from the rise of an educated urban middle class and of modern mass media. But the democratic experiment is relatively short-lived, followed by a swing back toward authoritarianism and a strident nationalism.

February 11, 1913: The cabinet of Katsura Taro (1847–1913) collapses during the Taisho political crisis under pressure from the Movement to Protect Constitutional Government. This is the first time a Japanese populist movement brings down a cabinet; it opens the way for the first party-dominated cabinet in 1918.

January 21, 1914: Incriminating documents published in a London newspaper reveal the Siemens scandal, in which a German company paid kickbacks for Japanese navy contracts. Mass protests lead to the March 24 resignation of the cabinet. This is but one of a series of spectacular political scandals In Japan between 1905 and 1915.

August 23, 1914: Japan declares war on Germany, entering World War I on the side of Great Britain and the Allies. On September 2 Japan seizes German possessions on Shandong peninsula; in October, Japan ousts Germans from the Mariana, Caroline, and Marshall islands.

May 25, 1915: With the Twenty-one Demands, Japan calls for territorial and other concessions from China.

July 3, 1916: Japan and Russia sign a mutual assistance pact.

January 1917–September 1918: In a series of eight Nishihara Loans, Japan gives financial assistance to China, essentially to support a corrupt government and to finance civil war against its rivals. In return Japan gets recognition of its claims in Shandong Province and privileges in Manchuria.

November 2, 1917: With the Lansing-Ishii Pact, the United States and Japan agree to an Open Door Policy in China, and the United States recognizes Japanese special interests in China. Japan annuls the pact in 1923.

July 23–September 1918: Some 623 violent rice riots throughout Japan protest high prices caused by spiraling inflation; leads to the collapse of the Terauchi cabinet.

November 1918: As part of the Allied effort to protect military supplies in Vladivostok in the so-called Siberian Intervention during the Russian Bolshevik revolution, some seventy thousand Japanese troops settle into the Maritime Province and northern Manchuria. The other Allies withdraw in June 1920 but Japan remains, continuing to fight the Soviets until October 1922, when Japanese troops finally leave.

1918: By year's end Japan holds parts of mainland China, some of northern Manchuria, and areas in eastern Siberia.

March 1, 1919–Spring 1920: In Korea, the Samil Independence Movement begins nonviolent demonstrations, eventually involving 2 million Koreans. Violent suppression by Japan leaves 7,500 dead and 47,000 arrested.

June 28, 1919: Along with other victorious nations, Japan signs the Treaty of Versailles ending World War I. Japan gets control over the Mariana, Caroline, and Marshall islands, along with former German holdings in the Shandong peninsula.

January 16, 1920: As a permanent member, Japan attends the Paris Council meeting of the League of Nations.

February–May 1920: In the Manchurian town of Nikolaevsk near the mouth of the Amur River, several hundred Japanese residents are massacred by Bolshevik partisans during the Russian Civil War. Soviets execute the perpetrators; Japanese retaliate by occupying Sakhalin, demanding compensation. This incident delays Japanese recognition of the Soviet Union until 1925.

May 1, 1920: First May Day celebration in Japan by labor activists in Tokyo's Ueno Park.

1920: Feminist Ichikawa Fusae (1893–1981) helps found *Shin fujin kyokai* (New Women's Association), Japan's first national women's rights group. A worker for women's suffrage, she is elected to the Diet in 1953 and serves for twenty-five years.

November 4, 1921: In Tokyo an ultra-rightist radical assassinates prime minister Hara Takashi (1856–1921), the first commoner prime minister and an architect of party government.

November 1921–February 6, 1922: The Washington Conference results in the December 13, 1921, Four-Power Treaty pledging Japan, Britain, France, and the United States to mutual consultation in the Pacific region. The Nine-Power Treaty of February 6, 1922, recognizes the Open Door principle in East Asia; the Washington Naval Treaty, also of February 6, limits the ratio of naval vessels and armaments, allowing reductions by signatory nations in military expenditures.

September 1, 1923: At 11:58 AM a powerful earthquake strikes Tokyo and Yokohama. Two days of intense firestorms follow in Tokyo; 142,807 are dead or missing, 103,733 are injured, and 3,248,205 are left homeless. Ru-

mors that Korean residents are setting fires and poisoning wells lead vigilantes to massacre thousands of Koreans. Martial law is imposed; police take advantage of the chaos to kill ten labor activists in the Kameido Incident of September 4 and on September 16 kill anarchist Osugi Sakae, along with his wife and nephew. Architect Frank Lloyd Wright's Tokyo Imperial Hotel, just completed, survives tremors. (It is demolished in 1967.)

December 27, 1923: In the Toranomon Incident, a leftist radical unsuccessfully attempts to assassinate Prince Regent Hirohito.

May 26, 1924: The U.S. Immigration Act of 1925 bans further immigration from Japan. From 1868 to 1924 some 270,000 Japanese emigrate to Hawaii and the United States.

January 20, 1925: The Soviet Union and Japan sign a convention establishing diplomatic relations. In recognizing the new communist regime, Japan agrees to withdraw from northern Sakhalin while retaining partial rights to natural resources there. The Soviet Union agrees to limit communist activism in Japan.

February 20, 1925: The Universal Manhood Suffrage Law passes, laying the groundwork for the national elections of February 1928.

May 12, 1925: The Peace Preservation Law of 1925 limits freedom of assembly and speech.

December 25, 1926: Emperor Yoshihito dies, having been ill since 1921. He is succeeded by his son, Emperor Hirohito (reigns 1926–1989).

EARLY SHOWA PERIOD: 1926–1945

Showa is the period name adopted by Emperor Hirohito on his succession to the throne. Its meaning, "Enlightened Peace," is ironic in retrospect when referring to the early period. Those decades encompass some of the more warlike and violent years of the twentieth century.

As nationalist and military concerns come to preoccupy the government, its forces engage in further ventures on the Asian mainland—annexing Manchuria and part of Mongolia to set up the puppet state of Manchukuo, and entering into a second Sino-Japanese War against nationalist and communist Chinese factions. With entry into World War II, Japan's initial successes rapidly enlarge its empire in the East Asia-western Pacific sphere as it seizes colonies of the Western powers. Naval reverses at Midway change the direction of the conflict, and Japan begins a series of desperately fought battles that end in the nuclear holocaust of Hiroshima and Nagasaki. It all concludes in a humiliating defeat and occupation of the islands by the Allied powers.

May 1927: Japan and China reach accord on the March 24 Nanjing Incident, when Chinese Nationalist soldiers attacked foreign businesses and consulates, including those of Japan. Japan and the Western powers seek punishment, indemnities, and an apology.

1927–1928: Cabinet orders three Japanese expeditions to China's Shandong Province in order to block the Nationalist Chinese forces of Chiang Kai-shek. From May 1 to September 1927 four thousand troops are sent, allegedly to protect Japanese residents; they are withdrawn when Chiang stops the advance. In May 1928 Japanese and Nationalist forces clash at Jinan, with serious Chinese casualties; more Japanese troops are sent and stationed throughout Shandong Province and northern China. All forces are withdrawn when a pact is signed for the Jinan Incident.

In 1929 the text is published in Nanjing of an alleged memorandum of July 25, 1927, to Emperor Hirohito from Prime Minister Tanaka Giichi (1864–1929) outlining a plan for the conquest of Manchuria and Mongolia. Japan denies authenticity of the document.

March 15, 1928: In the March 15 Incident, mass arrests are made throughout Japan of 1,658 suspected communists in response to activities of the outlawed Japan Communist Party. The government prosecutes five hundred and exploits the situation to ban other leftist parties and organizations.

June 4, 1928: Extremist army officers of the Japanese Guandong Army in Manchuria assassinate warlord Zhang Zuolin by blowing up his train.

August 27, 1928: In Paris, an antiwar treaty known as the Kellogg-Briand Pact is signed by fourteen nations and a reluctant Japan. The agreement affects Japan's ability to intervene militarily in China and Manchuria. Later forty-eight other nations join the pact.

April 16, 1929: In the April 16 Incident, the government carries out mass arrest of some six hundred to seven hundred suspected communists. About half are tried and found guilty.

January 21, 1930: The London Naval Conference opens. A treaty signed on April 22 limits Japanese eight-inch gun cruisers; it allows 70 percent strength in other cruisers and destroyers, parity in submarines. Crisis over ratification pits Japan's naval administration against the civil government, and marks the increasing intervention of the military in national politics.

November 1930: In Tokyo, a right-wing youth shoots Prime Minister Hamaguchi Osachi (1870–1931); he dies from wounds in August 1931.

March 1931: Right-wing army officers and civilians attempt a coup d'état in order to impose military government and national reform along totalitarian lines. This March Incident is the first of a series of similar attempts, some quite violent, by military extremists to overthrow the government during this era; these attempts are kept secret by the army until the end of World War II. The slogan of right-wing extremists is "Showa Restoration."

June 25, 1931–July 2, 1932: A public trial of three hundred communists arrested for violation of the Peace Preservation Law of 1925 is staged to reveal the inner workings of the Communist Party. All are sentenced on October 29, 1932, to jail as part of the *tenko* policy of recantation and rehabilitation for "thought criminals."

September 18, 1931: In the Liutaogou Incident, Japanese military personnel detonate a bomb on the rails of the South Manchurian Railway north of Mukden, then accuse Chinese troops of the deed. Japan uses the event as a pretext to seize the Chinese garrison and Mukden.

September 1931–January 1933: Following the capture of Mukden, the Japanese Guandong Army conquers all Manchuria. This action is initially opposed by politicians and military officers in Japan.

January 28–May 5, 1932: In the Shanghai Incident, a skirmish between Chinese and Japanese troops in Shanghai follows from an incident fomented by Japanese officers, in which a Chinese mob attacked Japanese Buddhist priests. Clashes escalate to full-scale fighting until the Chinese withdraw. A truce agreement mandates a demilitarized zone and an end to a Chinese boycott on Japanese goods (in response to the Japanese conquest of Manchuria).

February 9, 1932: In the League of Blood Incident, an ultranationalist group murders a politician and industrialist; arrests uncover a list of twenty prominent assassination targets.

February 18, 1932: The Japanese Guandong Army declares the puppet state of Manchukuo, in effect until August 1945, encompassing all Manchuria and part of Inner Mongolia, with a population of some 40 million. On March 9 Puyi, the last emperor of China, is installed as ceremonial head of state while Japanese advisors hold real power.

March 27, 1933: Japan announces its withdrawal from the League of Nations after being criticized in the Lytton Commission report as the aggressor in Manchuria.

May 31, 1933: After Japanese troops move into region, the Tanggu Truce establishes an armistice, with the Great Wall as the boundary between Japanese and Chinese forces and a demilitarized zone north and east of Beijing.

December 29, 1934: Japan announces that it will withdraw (by December 1936) from the Washington Naval Treaty of 1922 and the London Naval Treaty of 1930.

June 10, 1935: In secret He-Umezu Agreement in order to ward off more aggressive

Japanese actions, China agrees to remove forces and nationalist organs from Hebei Province (including Beijing and Tianjin), to limit nationalist activity, and to ban anti-Japanese movements.

December 1935–January 15, 1936: At the second London Naval Conference, Japan seeks full parity with the U.S. and British navies. When the proposal is rejected, Japan withdraws from the conference, thus ending the system that limited naval rivalry in the Pacific for fifteen years.

1935: Champion of democratic government and retired law professor Minobe Tatsukichi (1873–1948) proposes the theory of Emperor-as-Organ-of-the-State; he is charged with a crime against the authority of the state and forced to resign from the House of Peers. The years 1935–1937 see a purge of academics and officials.

February 26–29, 1936: A military rebellion of 1,400 troops led by junior officers seizes central Tokyo, kills political leaders, and demands a new cabinet and political reforms. The trial of leaders results in executions and imprisonment.

March 9, 1936: A new cabinet is dominated by military members; it soon leads to military budget increases and greater censorship.

October 1, 1936: Japan's secret demands on China are revealed: they include Japanese advisers in the Chinese government, autonomy for five northern provinces, and tariff reductions to 1928 levels. Despite invasion threat, the Nanjing government refuses.

November 24, 1936: In the Anti-Comintern Pact, Germany and Japan agree to oppose the Soviet Union. (Italy will sign the pact on November 6, 1937.)

January 28, 1937: Nationalist and Communist Chinese agree to cooperate against the common Japanese enemy.

July 7–11, 1937: In the Marco Polo Bridge Incident, Japanese and Chinese forces clash at a bridge twelve miles southwest of Beijing. After a cease-fire, Japan mobilizes five additional divisions and on July 23 Chinese troops reenter Beijing. Thus begins the Sino-Japanese War of 1937–1945.

July 29, 1937: Japanese forces capture Beijing and Tianjin. On August 25 Japan announces a naval blockade of the entire Chinese coastline.

August–November 1937: Japanese forces attack Shanghai with a naval bombardment and 200,000-man army. Hand-to-hand combat forces the 500,000-man Chinese army into retreat.

November 3–24, 1937: The Brussels Conference seeking to end Sino-Japanese hostilities fails when Japan does not attend.

December 13, 1937: The Nationalist Chinese capital of Nanjing falls after several days fighting. A massacre ensues as some 140,000 civilians and prisoners of war die in a three-week orgy by Japanese troops of arson, looting, torture, rape, and murder. On March 30, 1940, Japanese establish a puppet Chinese government in the city.

December 15, 1937: The Popular Front Incident marks widespread repression of liberals and leftists in Japan, as government arrests left-wing socialist leaders and some four hundred others; it also dissolves left-wing political parties. In February 1938 a second wave of arrests for "obstructing the war effort" sweeps up intellectuals and university professors; many are jailed until the end of World War II.

May 5, 1938: The National Mobilization Law becomes effective, placing controls on industry, labor, contracts, prices, and the news media.

May 15, 1938: The Japanese encircle Xuzhou and capture it four days later. As Japanese pursue Chinese forces and capture large cities, Chinese guerrillas remain active in the countryside.

July 11–August 10, 1938: Clash between Japanese and Russian troops along the Manchukuo-Choson (Korea) border ends with a truce and heavy losses for the Japanese.

October 21, 1938: Japanese troops capture the major southern Chinese port city of Guang-

zhou. On October 25 five Japanese columns capture Hankou after the Nationalist government retreats to Chongqing.

November 3, 1938: Japan announces a "New Order in East Asia," a slogan that rationalizes the invasion of China.

May 2–September 15, 1939: In the Nomohan Incident, Mongolian and Japanese troops clash along the Manchuria-Outer Mongolia border; the Soviet Union sends mechanized units to aid Mongolia. They defeat the Japanese Guandong Army's 23d Division, with 17,450 Japanese casualties.

June 14, 1939: Japanese troops blockade the British and French concession in Tianjin. Britain, France, and the Soviet Union aid the Nationalist military effort.

July 1939: The National Service Draft Ordinance ensures a labor supply for strategic Japanese war industries. Some 1.6 million men and women labor draftees are joined by 4.5 million workers reclassified as draftees.

March 30, 1940: Japan installs a puppet government in China headed by Nationalist politician Wang Ching-wei.

August–November 1940: Prime Minister Konoe Fumimaro (1891–1945) tries to establish the totalitarian New Order; failure to do so reveals the vitality of the nation's political factions.

September 22, 1940: Following negotiations with the French Vichy government, Japan begins to move troops into Indochina to block supplies to Nationalist Chinese.

September 27, 1940: Japan, Germany, and Italy sign the Tripartite Pact, promising mutual military support.

October 12, 1940: The Imperial Rule Assistance Association is founded to promote goals of New Order Movement; it becomes an agent for morale and resource control during World War II as all Japanese subjects are members.

April 13, 1941: In the Soviet-Japanese Neutrality Pact, each pledges neutrality during World War II.

July 26, 1941: Because of the Japanese military occupation of Indochina, Japanese assets in the United States and Britain are frozen. The Dutch soon freeze assets in the Dutch East Indies and cancel oil contracts. These steps reduce Japanese foreign trade by 75 percent and imported oil supplies by 90 percent. To alleviate shortages, Japanese make unsuccessful diplomatic overtures to the United States on August 6.

October 16, 1941: General Hideki Tojo (1884–1948) becomes prime minister.

December 7, 1941: Following a series of unsuccessful U.S.-Japanese negotiations, planes from a Japanese naval carrier force (which set sail on November 26) carry out a surprise attack on the U.S. Pacific fleet at Pearl Harbor, Hawaii. Within the next twenty-four hours Japanese forces attack U.S. bases in the Philippines, Guam, and Midway as well as British bases in Hong Kong and Malaysia.

December 8, 1941: The United States declares war on Japan and becomes an ally of China, still mired in the Sino-Japanese War. U.S. air power will eventually help protect Chinese cities from the Japanese. A small force of Japanese land on Batan Islands, north of Luzon in the Philippines.

December 10, 1941: Japanese forces capture Guam.

December 27, 1941–April 9, 1942: Under heavy Japanese attack, U.S. authorities declare Manila an open city; it is captured on January 2, 1942, as U.S. forces retreat toward Bataan. On March 11, 1942, General Douglas MacArthur leaves the Philippines, promising to return. On April 9, 1942, Allied forces on Luzon surrender. The Japanese march 75,000 prisoners some hundred miles under horrifying conditions to a prison camp.

December 18–25, 1941: Japanese troops capture Hong Kong.

December 22–23, 1941: Japanese forces occupy Wake Island after the U.S. garrison surrenders.

January 11–March 12, 1942: Japanese forces attack and occupy the Dutch East Indies.

January 14, 1942: The United States orders alien registration; this facilitates the relocation of some 100,000 West Coast Japanese-Americans (*nisei*) to internment camps for the duration of the war.

February 8–15, 1942: Japanese troops invade Singapore, forcing the surrender of British and Australian troops. On February 19 Japanese planes bomb Darwin in a rare attack on Australia.

February 27–March 1, 1942: Japanese and Allied naval forces engage in a series of battles, with disastrous outcome for the Allies. On February 28 Japanese forces land on Java.

March 7, 1942: Japanese forces begin the occupation of New Guinea and of the Burmese city of Rangoon as British forces evacuate. On April 29 Japanese troops cut off the Burmese overland route to China.

April 18, 1942: Sixteen U.S. B-25 bombers take off from an air carrier and carry out the first raid on Tokyo and three other cities.

May 4–8, 1942: In the Battle of Coral Sea, U.S. forces inflict heavy losses on Japanese.

May 5–7, 1942: Japanese forces occupy Corregidor, off Bataan, and accept the surrender of fifteen thousand U.S. and Filipino troops.

June 3–7, 1942: Japan meets its first serious setback in the Battle of Midway, losing four carriers and many of its best pilots.

June 6–7, 1942: Japanese forces capture the Aleutian islands of Kiska and Attu off Alaska. On May 11–30, 1943, U.S. forces retake Attu; on August 15, 1943, U.S. and Canadian forces reclaim Kiska.

October 25–26, 1942: In support of their forces on Guadalcanal, Japanese and U.S. fleets fight the Battle of Santa Cruz, in which serious losses force the Japanese to draw back. In the November 13–15 naval Battle of Guadalcanal, U.S. forces gain sea control. On January 5, 1943, Japan begins to withdraw troops from the island, and on February 9 the United States recaptures it.

August 1, 1943: Japan announces the independence of Burma under a new puppet Japanese government there. British forces retake Rangoon on May 3, 1945.

August 16–23, 1943: Japanese suffer serious losses during the U.S. bombardment of their base at Wewak, New Guinea.

January 31–February 23, 1944: U.S. forces capture the Marshall Islands, first prewar Japanese domain to be seized.

February 3, 1944: U.S. battleships shell the Kurile Islands off northern Japan.

April 22, 1944: Allied forces recapture Hollandia in Dutch New Guinea.

June 15–July 9, 1944: U.S. forces recapture Saipan in the Marianas, leaving 27,000 dead Japanese.

June 18–20, 1944: In the key Battle of the Philippine Sea, Japan loses three carriers and four hundred planes. This series of Japanese losses forces Tojo to resign as prime minister on July 18.

August 10, 1944: U.S. forces retake Guam, taking fewer than a hundred Japanese prisoners from a garrison of 100,000.

October 23–26, 1944: In the Battle of Leyte Gulf, the Japanese suffer a major naval defeat; they will have to rely increasingly on suicide missions of *kamikaze* (divine wind) fighter pilots, used here for the first time. On January 9, 1945, a U.S. invasion force begins landings on Luzon; after hard fighting, it recaptures Manila on March 3.

February 16–17, 1945: U.S. bombers carry out heavy raids on Tokyo and Yokohama.

February 19–March 26, 1945: U.S. forces recapture Iwo Jima with great difficulty, gaining a base within strategic airplane range of Japan. Corregidor is retaken on February 26, with heavy Japanese losses.

March 9–10, 1945: In the Pacific war's most deadly air raid, U.S. incendiary bombs ignite a massive firestorm in Tokyo, leaving some 120,000 civilians dead.

March 18–21, 1945: A U.S. naval fleet begins the bombardment of Japan; six carriers are damaged by kamikaze pilots.

March 23–31, 1945: U.S. forces begin an attack on the Ryukyu Islands in advance of landing on Okinawa.

April 1–June 22, 1945: In the largest such operation in the Pacific, U.S. forces invade Okinawa. After almost three months, the Japanese surrender, but some 162,000 of their soldiers and civilians have been killed, and the United States has lost 12,500 soldiers.

July 5, 1945: General MacArthur announces the liberation of the Philippines.

July 26, 1945: Allies broadcast the Potsdam Declaration to Japan, calling for unconditional surrender.

August 6, 1945: A U.S. airplane drops an atomic bomb on Hiroshima, instantly killing some eighty thousand Japanese. On 9 August a second bomb is detonated over Nagasaki, killing forty thousand.

August 14, 1945: Overriding military and political leaders, Emperor Hirohito decides to end the war by submitting to unconditional surrender. After a failed last-minute attempt by some military officers to seize the emperor, on August 15 he informs the Japanese people of his decision by means of an unprecedented radio broadcast (the first time the Japanese people have heard an emperor's voice).

LATE SHOWA PERIOD: 1945–1989

The postwar era covers the second part of the Showa period, ending with Emperor Hirohito's death in 1989. The decades after World War II prove an era of remarkable change. Under the Occupation, Japan is forced to undergo far-reaching reform along democratic lines of its political, economic, and social institutions.

With the Korean War begins an industrial recovery that eventually builds Japan into a world economic superpower, known for the high quality of its automobiles and electronic consumer products. The economic miracle is accompanied by problems of environmental pollution, political corruption, student unrest and terrorism, and enormous trade surpluses. From an aloof and self-contained culture, Japan now has become a leader and partner among nations, thoroughly engaged in the international arena.

September 2, 1945: In Tokyo Bay, Japanese officials sign surrender instruments on the deck of the USS *Missouri*. With more than 2 million war dead and many cities and factories destroyed, Japan faces Allied occupation until 1952. The Supreme Commander for the Allied Powers (SCAP) is General Douglas MacArthur (1880–1969), who commands 500,000 troops and supervises military and civilian bureaucrats who dismantle the Japanese empire and war machine. The occupation repatriates 6 million Japanese military and citizens, conducts war-crimes trials and purges, and reforms through the Japanese government the nation's political and economic structure.

January 1, 1946: Emperor Hirohito delivers a New Year's message renouncing his status as a "living god."

January 4, 1946: SCAP orders a purge of the "undesirable" political elite, career military, militarists, ultra-nationalists, and business and publishing magnates from wartime positions and public office. This removal of some 200,000 allows a new generation of leaders to emerge. In spring 1946 SCAP installs Yoshida Shigeru (1878–1967), Liberal Party leader, as the new prime minister. The first postwar election takes place in April.

May 3, 1946–November 1948: A Tokyo war-crimes trial convenes to consider charges against twenty-eight political and military leaders. On December 23, 1948, wartime premier Hideki Tojo and six others are hanged. MacArthur releases the rest under amnesty. In a series of minor trials some 6,000 Japanese are tried; 920 are sentenced to death for atrocities.

May 3, 1947: A new constitution takes effect: it mandates the emperor as a symbol of state and of the unity of the Japanese people, a bicameral parliamentary government, basic civil rights, freedom of religion, and separation of church and state; it also bans gender discrimination and renounces war. Supplementary legislation extends the vote to women, lessens patriarchal authority, and revises election procedures, judiciary, and legal codes. The Local Autonomy Law gives a degree of self-government to prefectures, cities, towns, and villages.

May 3–December 1950: Following a demonstration and a series of terrorist incidents in 1949 allegedly instigated by communists, MacArthur denounces the Japan Communist Party. A "Red purge" of 1,177 government employees is followed by a purge of 10,972 private-sector workers.

June 25, 1950: The Korean War breaks out. Japan becomes a staging area and supply depot; as a partly military economy takes hold, production reaches 1936 levels by 1952. Boom conditions, inflation, and high growth prevail, leading to the economic miracle of the 1960s and 1970s.

On July 8 General MacArthur calls for the creation of a National Police Reserve of 75,000 to replace U.S. troops sent to Korea. In 1954 it is reorganized as the Self-Defense Forces under the direction of a new cabinet-level Defense Agency.

September 8, 1951: Japan signs the San Francisco peace treaty with forty-nine nations, formally ending the war: Japan loses all territory seized since 1895, agrees to pay reparations (not strictly enforced), and submits to indefinite U.S. trusteeship of the Ryukyus, including Okinawa.

April 28, 1952: Occupation formally ends and the U.S.-Japan Security Treaty takes effect: the United States maintains forces in Japan, while Japan contributes financially. U.S. military bases lead to problems with nearby Japanese who resent aircraft noise, nuclear weapons, and periodic injuries to and crimes against Japanese citizens and property by soldiers. The U.S.-Japan Mutual Defense Assistance Agreement (March 1954) will reinforce the treaty, by allowing the United States to provide military equipment and technology and Japan to develop defense industry.

April 29, 1952: Japan signs a peace treaty with China. The pact does not prevent Chinese gunboats from firing on Japanese patrols and seizing numerous Japanese fishing boats.

May 1, 1952: May Day riots express anti-U.S. feelings. More than 2,000 are injured and 1,232 are arrested.

April 27, 1953: Crown Prince Akihito arrives in England to attend the coronation of Queen Elizabeth II. Afterward he continues with a six-month world tour.

December 24, 1953: The United States returns some of the Ryukyu Islands to Japan. In 1968 the Bonin Islands are returned.

January 1954: In a shipbuilding scandal, seventy-one officials and others are arrested for bribery in exchange for contracts and subsidies; the scandal leads to the fall of the fifth Yoshida cabinet.

March 1, 1954: In the *Lucky Dragon* Incident, radioactive fallout from a U.S. atomic bomb test contaminates a Japanese fishing boat; this results in a massive outcry in Japan and the growth of the antinuclear movement. Later the United States pays $2 million compensation to Japan for damages from a series of five bomb tests. Japan protests British, Chinese, and French nuclear tests as well.

October 19, 1956: The Soviet-Japanese Joint Declaration ends state of war, restores diplomatic relations; lingering territorial issues over the Kurile Islands prevent the conclusion to this date of the official peace treaty.

December 18, 1956: Japan becomes a United Nations member.

January 19, 1960: The United States and Japan sign the Treaty of Cooperation and Security of 1960: it highlights peaceful intentions, economic cooperation, consultation before increased troop deployments. Widespread Japanese protest by peace activists over ratification leads to cancellation of planned June visit by U.S. President Eisenhower.

July 18, 1960: As Welfare Minister, Nakayama Masa is the first woman to enter the cabinet.

October 12, 1960: Chairman of the Socialist Party Asanuma Inejiro is stabbed to death by a right-wing youth at a political rally.

August 7, 1964–March 29, 1973: As the United States enters Vietnam War, Japanese economy will benefit and the government officially supports the United States. In 1965 Japanese opponents of war found the Peace for Vietnam Committee to hold teach-ins and support U.S. army deserters.

June 22, 1965: The Korea-Japan Treaty restores diplomatic relations with South Korea; supplementary agreements treat legal rights of Koreans in Japan.

October 13, 1971: Emperor Hirohito completes a goodwill tour of Europe, the first by a reigning Japanese emperor. In 1975, he will pay a similar visit to the United States.

May 30, 1972: Japanese terrorists kill twenty-four and wound seventy-six in a Tel Aviv airport attack. They are part of the Red Army Faction, formed in 1969 by dissident student members of Communist League, who advocate world revolution. In 1970–1971 they carry out bombings, robberies, and a plane hijacking in Japan. Their international activities from this date on include embassy seizures in Netherlands and Malaysia.

May 15, 1972: The United States returns Okinawa to Japan; military bases there remain the center of U.S. strategic forces in the Far East.

November 22, 1973: Japan revises its Middle East policy and recognizes Palestinian rights in response to the oil crisis, when OPEC quadruples crude-oil prices.

August 15, 1974: A diplomatic crisis ensues following the attempted murder of the South Korean president by an assassin who entered from Japan. On September 12 Japan issues a statement of "regret" and promises a full investigation.

October 8, 1974: Sato Eisaku (1901–1975) wins the Nobel Peace Prize. As Japan's longest continuously serving premier (1964–1972), he normalized relations with South Korea, oversaw the return of Okinawa, and signed the 1970 nuclear nonproliferation treaty.

February 5, 1976: The Lockheed Scandal erupts as a U.S. Senate subcommittee discovers that the aircraft corporation paid bribes and kickbacks to sell planes in Japan. Revelation of government corruption leads to the arrests of seventeen, including former prime minister Tanaka Kakuei (1918–).

September 6–November 12, 1976: A defecting Soviet pilot seeking U.S. asylum lands a MiG-25 fighter plane in Hokkaido. Japan allows the United States to inspect the plane before returning it to the USSR.

August 12, 1978: China and Japan sign the Peace and Friendship Treaty, normalizing relations and opening the way to commercial agreements.

July 24–August 26, 1982: Diplomatic crisis arises as China, Taiwan, and both Koreas protest history textbook revisions that downplay Japanese aggression of the 1930s and 1940s. Despite a Japanese promise to correct the problem, similar incidents occur in 1986 and 1988.

Later Rashomon *won the American Academy Award for Best Foreign Language Film. Japanese critics insisted that these two prizes were simply reflections of Westerners' curiosity and taste for Oriental exoticism, which struck me then, and now, as terrible. Why is it that Japanese people have no confidence in the worth of Japan? Why do they elevate everything foreign and denigrate everything Japanese? Even the woodblock prints of Utamaro, Hokusai and Sharaku were not appreciated by Japanese until they were first discovered by the West.*

Something Like an Autobiography, by Kurosawa Akira (1982)

September 6–8, 1984: When South Korea's president pays a state visit, Emperor Hirohito apologizes for harsh rule in the past.

July 6, 1988–May 29, 1989: The Recruit Scandal emerges when it is revealed that staffs of prominent politicians received gifts of stocks from the Recruit Company in 1986, from which they realized large profits. Eventually seventeen are indicted and charged with corruption.

January 7, 1989: The longest reigning emperor (sixty-two years) in recorded history, Hirohito dies. His son, Crown Prince Akihito, ascends the throne later in the day but is not formally enthroned until November 1990. Six days of national mourning follow the death, and the state funeral is held on February 24, 1989.

HEISEI PERIOD: 1989–1998

The period name of Emperor Akihito's reign, beginning in 1989, is Heisei, meaning "attainment of peace." As the century draws to a close, one of Japan's greater postwar challenges arises as internal financial problems are followed by an East Asian monetary crisis threatening massive Japanese loans in the region.

June 2, 1989: Foreign Minister Sosuke Uno is elected premier, replacing Noboru Takeshita, who resigns because of his role in the Recruit Company corruption scandal.

August 9, 1989: Sosuke Uno is himself forced to resign when he is connected to the Recruit Company's payoffs to political figures. He is replaced by former Education Minister Toshiki Kaifu.

November 12, 1990: Akihito (1933–) is formally enthroned as Japan's 125th emperor in a splendid ceremony in Tokyo.

January 17, 1991: In the Persian Gulf War, Japan refuses combat role but assists with costs; in April, it sends out minesweepers.

October 4, 1991: Premier Toshiki Kaifu announces that he will not seek reelection. On November 5 he is replaced by Kiichi Miyazawa.

January 17, 1992: Premier Miyazawa, visiting South Korea, apologizes for the Japanese army's forced use of Korean women as prostitutes, the so-called comfort women. From 1932 to 1945 the Japanese military enslaved some 200,000 Asian women, half of them Korean, as prostitutes in army brothels.

June 15, 1992: The Japanese Diet gives final approval to a bill allowing up to two thousand military personnel to be sent abroad to participate in UN peacekeeping missions. Japan's constitution forbade use of military for nondefensive purposes.

October 1992: Under the new law, the first six hundred Japanese troops arrive in Cambodia as part of UN peacekeeping operations.

June 18, 1993: The Miyazawa government falls when some of his own Liberal Democratic Party members join the opposition in a no-confidence vote. He dissolves the Diet and calls for new elections.

July 18, 1993: In the elections, the Liberal Democratic Party loses its majority in the Diet. On August 6 Morihiro Hosokawa is elected premier of a seven-party coalition, ending thirty-eight consecutive years of rule by the Liberal Democratic Party.

October 20–December 11, 1993: Empress Michiko collapses on October 20 and loses her speech faculties; by December 11 it is announced that she is beginning to recover. It is believed that her condition has been caused by the unprecedented criticism of her in the Japanese media.

April 8–June 29, 1994: Amid allegations of financial improprieties, Hosokawa resigns as premier on April 8. Tsutomu Hata is elected premier on April 25, but he resigns on June 25. On June 29, Murayama Tomiichi, leader of the Social Democratic Party, becomes the first socialist premier since 1948.

March 20, 1995: Sarin nerve gas is released in the Tokyo subway system during the morning rush hour, killing twelve and injuring over five thousand. On March 22 police raid the offices of Aum Shinrikyo, a religious cult suspected of carrying out the attack. After other raids on the cult's locations, police seize leader Asahara Shoko on May 16.

June 9, 1995: The Diet passes a resolution declaring "deep remorse" for Japan's "acts of aggression" against other Asian nations in World War II. Although appreciated, this still does not constitute a formal apology.

August 15, 1995: On the fiftieth anniversary of the end of World War II, Premier Murayama issues a "heartfelt apology" for the war; this is the first time that any Japanese leader has apologized, and it goes some way toward helping Japan to defuse its problems with South Korea, China, the Philippines, and other Asian nations.

And this is the miracle of art. For in the music or literature we create, though we have come to know despair—that dark night of the soul through which we have to pass—we find that by actually giving it expression we can be healed . . . and as these linked experiences of pain and recovery are added to one another, layer upon layer, not only is the artist's work enriched but its benefits are shared with others.

Kaifuku suru kazoku (A Healing Family), by Kenzaburo Oe (1995)

September 4, 1995–March 7, 1996: Three U.S. servicemen abduct and rape an Okinawan schoolgirl on September 4; on March 7, 1996, they are sentenced to prison by a Japanese court. The incident renews debate about U.S. bases on Okinawa; of some 44,000 U.S. troops in Japan, 26,000 are in Okinawa.

January 5, 1996: Premier Murayama resigns abruptly; on January 11, the Diet elects Ryutoro Hashimoto, leader of the Liberal Democratic Party, as premier. As a fifty-eight-year-old, Hashimoto is seen as representing a turnover to a younger, more dynamic generation of Japanese leaders.

August 14, 1996: The World War II "comfort women" issue begins to wind down with an official apology and arrangements for compensation.

September 8, 1996: In reaction to an agreement in April under which almost all U.S. military installations on Okinawa would be returned to Japan in about seven years, Okinawa holds a nonbinding referendum; 89 percent of Okinawan voters call for an immediate reduction of the U.S. military on their island. But on September 10, Premier Hashimoto offers Okinawa $45.4 million for development projects, and on September 13, the governor of Okinawa agrees to renew the lease.

December 17, 1996–April 22, 1997: In Lima, Peru, to seek the release of imprisoned compatriots, some twenty-five members of the Tupac Amaru revolutionary movement seize the Japanese ambassador's residence along with six hundred hostages, including relatives of Peru's President Alberto Fujimori, who is of Japanese ancestry. After months of frustrating negotiation, a daring military rescue of some four hundred remaining hostages takes place on live TV.

September 23, 1997: Japan and the United States announce that they have reached an agreement on a new cooperative regional security, expanding the role of Japan's forces in supporting U.S. troops in "areas surrounding Japan."

November 24, 1997: Following a series of banking and brokerage failures, Yamaichi Securities is the largest Japanese company to collapse in the postwar era. After a speculative land and stock price bubble burst in 1989, the real estate and financial services sectors have been slowly slipping into crisis. Payoff scandals, illegal trading, government protection of weak banks and brokerage houses, and the practice of shielding favored clients from investment losses *(tobashi)* magnify the situation. The monetary crisis that began in Thailand in July and spread to Indonesia, Malaysia, and South Korea follows on a Japanese lending binge in the region, thus adding further to financial woes.

Government's "big bang" financial reforms package is scheduled to take effect on April 1, 1998, but it comes too late to prevent several prominent Japanese government and business leaders from committing suicide.

July 12, 1998: In elections for the Diet that have been framed as a referendum on the ruling party's handling of Japan's financial crisis, the Liberal Democrats lose seventeen seats. On July 13, Premier Hashimoto announces that he will resign. On July 30 Foreign Minister Keizo Obuchi is named the new premier. A moderate in the old tradition of Japanese politics and with no experience in economic matters, Obuchi is not regarded by the international community as a man who will take the necessary steps to revive Japan's economy.

Japan

ARTS, CULTURE, THOUGHT, AND RELIGION

KOFUN PERIOD: A.D. 250-600

250–400: Early Kofun period. Confucian scholar Wani arrives from the Korean state of Paekche with eleven volumes of Chinese classic writings. He becomes tutor to the crown prince and becomes the first scribe. Literacy spreads very slowly at the Japanese court. In fifth- and sixth-century Japan literacy is possessed mainly by immigrant families from the Korean peninsula. Invaluable to the bureaucratic state, scribes are essential for keeping accurate records.

538 (or 552): According to tradition, Buddhism is introduced into Japan. By the end of the century it is firmly established as the official religion, politically valuable as a means to increase the authority of the rulers, and it leads to a spread of literacy. Elites vie with each other in constructing temples in the Asuka region and commissioning art works for them. Eating four-legged animals is banned for religious reasons, leading to a decrease in hunting. By the end of the century, Buddhism ends the practice of building Kofun tombs, which it sees as inappropriate. The tombs continue to be built in Kanto and Tohoku regions until the end of the seventh century.

554: In return for Japan's aid, the Korean kingdom of Paekche sends back specialists in Confucianism, Buddhism, divination, calendars, herbs, and music. Learning is apparently highly valued by Japanese of this era.

c. 585: Up to this time, inhabitants of Japan believe that malevolent native spirits (*kami*) cause calamities. With the arrival of Buddhism, they believe that plagues and disasters result from a failure to worship Buddha. Buddhism does not replace native religions of Japan and cults of sacred places and spirits centered at ancient shrine of Ise. Now known as Shinto (the way of the *kami*), these rites and shrines persist into the modern era.

ASUKA PERIOD: 600–710

604: Formally elevated to state religion, Buddhism is seen by the elite as the embodiment of advanced culture. Courtiers construct large temples where communities of priests perform ceremonies and prayers, study scriptures, and become specialists in fields of architecture, engineering, and medicine.

607: The Buddhist temple of Horyo-ji is finished near present-day Nara. Supported by Shotoku, the monastic complex of forty-five buildings features the world's oldest authenticated wooden structure and the finest surviving example of Chinese Tang period architecture in its five-story pagoda.

In the main hall, bronze statues of Shaka Trinity and the Yakushi Niyorai (Buddha of Healing) are attributed to Tori Busshi, Japan's first artist to be known by name (because he signed his works) and the era's foremost sculptor.

612: From Paekche, Korea, Mimashi arrives to open a dance school to teach *gigaku* (skill music). Performers wearing artistically expressive head-covering masks and elaborate costumes portray stock characters and beings from Buddhist and Hindu tradition in the form of ancient dance-drama. This often starts with a processional *shishi-mai*, or lion dance, still performed at folk festivals today. Popular until the seventeenth century, it has come to be performed as a mystery play in Buddhist temples.

624: The census counts forty-six Buddhist temples, with 816 monks and 569 nuns.

646: Tomb construction is restricted for the interim, leading to increased Buddhist temple construction, of which some 483 are completed by 710. In funerary practices, a ban is placed on interring valuable items in graves and practicing ecstatic grieving by self-mutilation.

672: Under Chinese influence, sibling marriages of rulers end.

681: Government issues clothing regulations containing ninety-two articles. Commoners are to wear yellow and slaves black.

693: *Toka*, a form of group dance performed by members of the Nara court, is introduced from China. Performances are usually held as a part of New Year ceremonies.

694: Empress Jito orders that copies of the Buddhist *Golden Light Sutra* be sent to provinces, to be read at the start of the first month of the year.

701: The *Gagakuryo* (Bureau of Court Music) is established on the Chinese model. *Gagaku* (elegant music), originally from the Chinese Tang dynasty, performed at court is also known as *bugaku* when accompanying dancers. *Gagaku* ensembles include flutes, various drums, and string instruments. Costumed *bugaku* dancers wear face masks of fantastic creatures with bulging eyes; they perform "Tang style," "Korean style," and "Native" pieces derived from sacred dances known as *kagura*. *Bugaku* is still performed today at shrines and imperial palace grounds by descendants of the Nara court musicians' guild.

NARA PERIOD: 710–794

712: *Kojiki* (Record of Ancient Times), written in a unique amalgam of Chinese and Japanese syntax on three scrolls, is compiled by Ono Yasumaro, who weaves together from legends and traditions a record of ancient Japanese history, intended to rival that of China. As the oldest Japanese work, it marks the debut of Japanese literature.

720: The historic thirty-volume chronicle *Nihon Shoki* or *Nihongi* (History of Japan), written in literary Chinese, is completed.

733: *Fudoki*, provincial compendia of infor-

mation about local topography, botany, zoology, origins of place names, customs,
myths, literary anecdotes, poems, and products, are completed. Except for *Izumo fudoki*, most survive only in fragments.

735: Buddhist priest and scholar Gembo (?–
746) and official Kibi no Makibi (695–775)
return from study in China. Gembo brings
back over five thousand Buddhist *sutras*;
Makibi, after study of Confucianism, ceremonial rituals, and military science, establishes a school for future government officials. A common understanding of
Confucian principles facilitates diplomatic
and other exchanges throughout East Asia.

736: The Buddhist liturgical chant, *Shomyo*,
is introduced and becomes important in the
development of Japanese music.

741: Emperor Shomu mandates a provincial
Buddhist temple system with monastery and
nunnery for each province, where prayers
and readings to protect the realm are to be
conducted. In effect, he henceforth commits substantial state resources to the spread
of Buddhism.

745: Todaiji temple, the world's largest
wooden building, is built after a smallpox
epidemic. Money for construction is raised
by the itinerant and venerated holy man Gy-
oki (668–749), also known as Japan's first
civil engineer.

751: *Kaifoso*, the first anthology of Chinese
verse (120 poems) by Japanese authors, is
published. With this, Japan becomes an active participant in Chinese civilization.

752: Shomu emerges from retirement to ded-
icate a fifty-three-foot-tall Great Buddha, the
largest bronze statue in world, at Todaiji
temple in a splendid ceremony attended by
other Asian delegations. Exquisite gifts from
the event—Persian cut-glass bowls, musical
instruments, and brocades—survive in the
Shoso-in imperial repository in Nara.

754: Chinese priest Ganjin (688–763) arrives
to teach the precepts of the Buddhist Ritsu
sect and to found, in 759, Toshodaiji as a
seminary to retrain, in the spirit of late Nara
reform, priests influenced by the decadence
of the capital.

756: Empress Komyo donates six hundred
valuable items from late Emperor Shomu's
court to Todaiji temple. Some one hundred
items form the basis of the Nara art collection in Shoso-in treasure house, built in 756.

c. 759: The oldest anthology of Japanese poems, *Man'yoshu* (Collection of Myriad
Leaves), is completed. Of 4,516 poems, most
are thirty-one-syllable *tanka*, usually linking
nature scenes and human emotions.

772: Fujiwara no Hamanari (711–790) writes
Kakyo hyoshiki (Standard Rules for the Classic Songs), the earliest book of poetry criticism.

782: *Sangaku*, theatrical entertainment including acrobatics and juggling of Chinese
origin, loses court patronage, possibly because of the earthiness of some skits. Performers become itinerant players and then
associate with Buddhist temples. *Sangaku* is
a distant ancestor of *noh* drama.

HEIAN PERIOD: 794–1185

804: During the decadence of Nara Buddhism, monks Saicho (767–822) and Kokai
(774–835) travel to China to study new forms
of Buddhism.

805: After returning from China, Saicho establishes the Tendai sect on Mount Hiei; the
temple is renamed Enryakuji after his death.
This is the first schism of Japanese Bud-

dhism. In the face of strong opposition, Saicho seeks to start a rigorous twelve-year training program for official teachers of
Buddhism. By the twelfth century, Enryakuji is immensely wealthy, with three thousand buildings, vast properties, and an army
of warrior-monks. Its position is eventually
undermined by new sects.

806: After study in China to become a master of *mikkyo* (secret teachings), a form of esoteric Buddhism developed by Indian sages, Kokai returns to start the Shingon (True Word, or Mantra) sect. In 819, he begins construction of a monastery on Mount Koya; the monastery becomes a base for teaching Shingon and training fifty monks. Shingon practices include meditation on *mandalas*, repetition of *mantras*, and use of ritual hand gestures, or *mudras*. Today the Shingon sect has some 12 million followers and twelve thousand temples.

815: According to tradition, Emperor Saga is first Japanese ruler to taste tea, brought from China by monks. At first used only medicinally until reintroduced in the twelfth century by Zen monk Eisai, it becomes favored by the upper classes.

823: Kokai is appointed abbot of Toji, the city's most important temple, by patron Emperor Saga. Considered a cultural hero, Kokai is said to have invented the *kana* syllabary, the Japanese phonetic script that advances the spread of literacy. He compiles the first Japanese dictionary and is known as calligrapher, poet, and saint who first traverses the famous Shikoku pilgrimage route of eighty-eight temples.

890: The *Catalogue of Books at Present in Japan* enumerates 1,579 titles and 16,790 volumes in total. A recent fire in the palace library has destroyed numerous others.

905: *Kokinsho*, the imperial anthology of Japanese *waka* verse, is completed. Thirty-one-syllable *waka* poems are an aristocratic genre of the Classical Age.

935: Ki no Tsurayuki writes *Tosa nikki* (Travel Diary), the first of this genre. The era is remarkable for the rise of literature in the form of *nikki* (diaries) and *monogatari* (narrative tales). *Nikki* later becomes a specialty of women writers, who use Japanese kana phonetic script (or "women's writing"), whereas men use Chinese.

938: Monk Koya (903–972) begins preaching Amida Buddhism in the Heiankyo streets.

985: Monk Genshin (942–1017) completes the religious tract *Ojo Yoshu* and spreads Amidism, or Pure Land Buddhism, among aristocrats.

1002: Lady-in-waiting to Empress Sadako, Sei Shonagon, writes the *Pillow Book*, a minor masterpiece of witty reminiscences and observations, and an important document of daily court life.

c. **1002–1019:** Lady Murasaki Shikibu writes the world's first novel and greatest Japanese classical work, *The Tale of Genji*, a lengthy and detailed account of life at the Heian court later adapted by *noh* and *kabuki* plays.

1022: Dedication of the Hojoji Monastery, constructed by Fujiwara no Michinaga, who has retired to become a Buddhist monk; it is a splendid display of his wealth and power.

1127: *Renga* or linked-verse poetry—with stanzas composed by two or more poets alternately—first appears in an imperial anthology.

1053: In the finest example of Heian architecture, the island villa of Fujiwara no Michinaga is converted by his son into the magnificent Byodo-in temple. Phoenix Hall houses gilded wooden Amida Buddha, a masterpiece of Jocho, the greatest sculptor of the age. The innovation of Jocho is to create the technique of multiblock construction, allowing mass production.

Other achievements of Heian visual arts include the invention of *maki-e* lacquer and *kirikane* gold leaf, as well as the development of *e-makimono*, or painted narrative picture scrolls: masterpieces include the *Tale of Genji Scrolls* and *Heike Nokyo*, or Lotus Sutra Scrolls.

Under warrior patronage, court culture spreads to the provinces; Hiraizumi in northern Honshu is a notable example of a place where that culture takes hold.

1175: Tendai-trained monk Honen (1133–1212) begins to preach and establishes the Jodo Shinsho (Pure Land Sect) as a mass movement. Fearing the chaos and suffering of the apocalyptic Buddhist *mappo* (End of

Law) era, its followers worship Amida Buddha, who promises rebirth in the Western Paradise. Monks Koya, Genshin, and Ryonin (1072–1132) help spread the cult to laymen.

1180–1185: The civil war of Taira and Minamoto and the Battle of Dan no Ura will inspire a lengthy medieval epic, *Heike monogatari* (Tales of the Heike), which evolves over the century from chronicles and chants by blind itinerant priests to a song accompanied by the *biwa* or lute. Possibly written in its earliest version by former courtier Yukinaga, it forms the basis of many *noh* plays.

KAMAKURA PERIOD: 1185–1333

1156–1180: New types of narrative picture scrolls emerge as work in lively realistic style is done on *Shigisan Engi* (Legends of Mount Shigi), which documents details of everyday life and actual people. Also unique is *Chojo Giga* (Frolicking Animals Scroll) which satirizes society in cartoonlike images of birds and animals.

Amida Buddhism inspires *yamato-e* scrolls that grotesquely depict hell; also depicted are other Realms of Reincarnation and the lives of saints.

1185–1333: In the samurai era the art of swordmaking is supreme, as craftsmen forge combination blades of hard and soft steel with attributes of both hammer and razor. Set into ornate handles, blades are passed down through generations as family treasures.

Under Kamakura patronage, in Seto potters begin producing glazed wares based on examples from Southern Song China.

1191: Eisai (1141–1215), founder of the Rinzai sect of Zen Buddhism, returns from four years study in China and starts to teach Zen in Japan. In 1199 he becomes abbot of the new Kamakura Monastery. Eisai plants tea seeds from China on temple grounds, begins the cultivation of tea, and introduces the Buddhist tea ritual.

With the advocacy of meditation and self-discipline as a path to enlightenment, Zen appeals to the warrior class and becomes a favored religion of the shogunate. As more masters arrive to teach Zen, it spreads to courtiers, samurai, and commoners. In the late thirteenth century a hierarchy of official Zen Buddhist monasteries is formed: *gozan* (five mountains) refers to the top-ranked temples.

1195: After destruction in the Gempei War, Todaiji is rebuilt in Nara by Amidist priest Chogen in the Daibutsu (Great Buddha) style. Works for its Great Buddha Hall are produced by the Nara family of gifted sculptors known as the Kei school. Its leaders—Unkei (1151–1223), Kaikei, and Tankei—have Jocho as their ancestor. They produce hundreds of sculptures for temples using his multiblock method.

1200: Buddhists and government join to request suppression of the Pure Land movement. The shogunate orders the expulsion of all sect priests.

1204: Major Buddhist temples unsuccessfully petition the imperial court to ban Honen's teaching of exclusive *nembutsu* (invocation of the sacred name of Amida Buddha); they fear that his doctrines undermine their own position.

1205: *Shinkokinsho*, an important imperial anthology of *waka* poetry, appears, marking the flowering of *waka* written by nobility as the imperial court loses authority. Motifs include beauties of nature, *yogen* (mystery and depth), and *sabi* (loneliness).

Poets such as Fujiwara no Teika are also scholars. Their *wagaku* (Japanese scholarship, in contrast to Chinese scholarship, or *kangaku*) focuses on *waka*-centered classical court literature and on ceremonies and ritual practices at court.

1212: Kamo no Chomei completes his masterpiece *Hojoki* (An Account of My Ten-Foot-Square Hut). The work describes how he loses his career and fortune to disasters, takes Buddhist vows, and retires to a contemplative life of mountain solitude to seek rebirth in the Pure Land of Amida.

1219–1222: An early version of *Heike monogatari* (Tales of the Heike), an account of the Gempei War, appears. An important literary genre in the Middle Ages, war tales of the era include *Hogen monogatari* (Tales of the Hogen) and *Heiji monogatari* (Tales of the Heiji).

1220: *Gukansho* (Notes on Foolish Views), an early interpretative history of Japan, appears, written by the Buddhist priest Jien (1155–1225) as partial justification for the Fujiwara Regency.

1224: Shinran (1173–1262) completes the first version of *Kyogyoshinsho*, a collection of writings marking the beginning of the Jodo Shin sect of Pure Land Buddhism.

1227: Eisai's student Dogen (1200–1253) brings the Soto sect of Zen Buddhism from China; it promotes complete equality of the sexes.

1253: Nichiren (1222–1281) establishes the populist Nichiren sect; he campaigns to make it the official state religion. Twice exiled for extremism, he predicts the Mongol invasions.

1286: Rinzai Zen master Mugaku Sogen designates as his spiritual heir Mugai Nyodai (1223–1298), the first woman Zen priest. She founds and heads Keiaiji temple and Niji *gozan* network of over fifteen subtemples.

MUROMACHI PERIOD: 1333–1573

c. 1330: Courtier Yoshida Kenko finishes his masterpiece *Tsurezuregusa* (Essays in Idleness). His impressionistic observations include nostalgia for the past, criticism of ostentation, advocacy of simplicity, and ideas on aesthetics.

Popular literature of the era includes chronicles of wars among land-holding clans highlighting heroism, treachery, murder, rape, and looting. Japanese of all classes are entertained by traditional oral narrative literature of the *etoki hoshi* (picture-explaining priests) and *Kumano bikuni* (nuns of Kumano), who use scroll paintings to tell of heroes and of themes of universal conflict.

1330s–1340s: In interior design, the *shoin* (writing hall) style emerges — features *tatami* (woven rush floor mats), *shoji* (wood-latticed paper windows), *fusuma* (sliding paper screens), *shoin* (built-in desks), split-level shelves, raised floor alcoves, and decorative platforms in a study that evolves into a reception chamber. This is the basis of modern Japanese residential design in traditional style.

1338: Kyoto replaces Kamakura as the center of Zen Buddhism. Ashikaga favor the Rinzai sect, whose *gozan* (Five Monasteries) monks serve as shogunal spiritual advisors, drafters of documents, diplomats, and tutors. Also adept at economic management, they function as moneylenders and provide revenue to the shogunate in the form of taxation, compulsory "gifts," and the purchase of licenses of appointment to abbot and other positions.

1339: The composition of *Jinno shotoki* (Chronicle of the Direct Descent of Gods and Sovereigns) by the courtier and imperial loyalist Kitabatake Chikafusa marks the Shinto revival and new research into the history of the imperial line.

In Kyoto, Muso Soseki designs Saiho-ji, Japan's first dry garden, as an aid to meditation. A priest, he is shogun Takauji's spiritual advisor, as well as a pioneer of Zen garden design using rocks and sand to suggest flowing water.

c. 1350: In Nara's Kasuga shrine, *Sarugaku no Noh* is performed by priest Kan'ami as a form of *kagura* or sacred dance. He and his son Zeami are said to have invented *noh* drama, a combination of poetic chant, mime, and slow posture dance. Zeami writes ninety plays and theorizes in twenty-one treatises on the Zen principle of "non-action" as applied to a stylized symbolic acting style. Elaborately costumed mystery plays on a bare stage treat themes of supernatural or madness, explored not by plot but by intensification of a single emotion to climax.

Day-long *noh* performances are interrupted with comic relief interludes of *kyogen*, which use satire and slapstick to poke fun at cowardly warriors, lecherous priests, shiftless servants, blind men, conniving *daimyo*, and the like.

1356: Nijo Yoshimoto and Gusai begin the compilation of the first imperially sponsored *renga* poetry collection, *Tsukubasho*. The linked-verse *renga* fad spreads from court to all levels of society.

1378: Ashikaga Yoshimitsu builds the Hana-no-Gosho (Palace of Flowers) with magnificent gardens in Kyoto's Muromachi district north of (and therefore "above") the imperial palace. As a generous patron of arts, Yoshimitsu hosts large banquets, linked-verse galas, flower viewings, and dramatic performances.

1397: Yoshimitsu begins the construction in Kyoto of the Kinkakuji, or Golden Pavilion, the ultimate in luxury and ostentation, surrounded by a large pond and set in the deer park of Kitayama estate. (Destroyed by fire in 1952, it is restored in a replica of the original.)

1434: The monks of the powerful Buddhist complex, Enryakuji, complain of actions by shogunal subordinates contrary to the interests of the monastery; this provokes a violent campaign ordered by Ashikaga Yoshinori, ending in a mass suicide of monks.

1471: Monk Rennyo begins to preach in Echizen province; the Jodo Shin sect spreads through northwestern Honshu.

Late 1400s: Shoko develops the *wachiba* tea ceremony, further perfected by Takeno Joo and Sen Rikyu. Schools are founded to teach the arts of flower arranging (*ikebana*) and of incense burning. Goto invents the metal-ornamenting craft of damascening, used on sword hilts and guards.

In an era of nostalgia, former imperial regent Ichijo Kanera is the leading scholar of *wakagu* (classical court literature and ceremony). The greatest fear of scholars during the Onin War is that books and manuscripts will be destroyed.

1477–1492: In the Higashiyama epoch, the arts of painting, architecture, and drama are generously supported by retired shogun Yoshimasa, who convokes a coterie of scholars, priests, and artists led by connoisseurs Noami, Geiami, and Soami. In 1483 Yoshimasa builds the Ginkakuji or Silver Pavilion retreat, designed in a subtle restrained style, with the first tea-ceremony room in Japan.

1495: The greatest Muromachi artist, Sessho Toyo, produces the most important work, *Haboku sansuizu* (Splashed Ink Landscape), executed in the Zen-influenced *suiboku* (water and ink) impressionistic brush-stroke manner. In the fifteenth century painting moves out of temples and becomes secular.

1505: In Kyoto, the shogunate bans *bon odori*, a simple circular dance of men and women wearing flower or tableau headdresses; it becomes popular in Momoyama era.

1536: A courtier completes the *Sanetaka ko ki* (The Record of Lord Sanetaka), a diary detailing life in Kyoto during fifty years of violence, expressing a yearning for classical culture and the values of the ancient court.

1544: In Kyoto, the shogunate unsuccessfully bans *furyo*, a lively fancy-dress dance with "varied steps and farcical postures." It becomes a fad, and in 1571 the imperial prince and shogun attend a competition of townsman groups.

August 15, 1549: Francis Xavier lands in Kagoshima with two other Jesuits and establishes Japan's first mission there, beginning the "Christian Century." Guided to Japan by the fugitive Anjiro, he is welcomed by *daimyo* (feudal lord) Ouchi and Otomo Sorin,

who hope that trade will follow. Xavier preaches against prevalent idolatry, infanticide, and sodomy. En route to India, he dies on an island off China in 1552.

1570: In a campaign against the political and military power of Buddhist sects, Nobunaga begins a ten-year war against the True Pure Land sect. In 1571 he demolishes the Tendai sect temple Enryakuji, massacring thousands of monks.

MOMOYAMA PERIOD: 1573–1615

1576: Nobunaga begins the construction of a magnificent castle at Azuchi, which in 1579 becomes his official residence. He commissions the era's greatest painter, Kano Eitoku (1543–1590), to decorate it with splendid gold screens. In 1582, it is burned down after Nobunaga's death.

1579: After the Azuchi Disputation between priests of True Pure Land and Nichiren sects, Nobunaga declares the Nichirenists to be the losers and orders three leaders executed.

The supervisor of Jesuit missions in Asia, Alessandro Valignano, arrives in Japan. In 1581 he receives from Nobunaga a gift of the Kano Eitoku scroll painting of Azuchi. Nobunaga does not convert, but many fashionable Japanese do; some minor features of the tea ceremony are said to be adaptations of Catholic sacrament.

1582: Three Christian *daimyo* send four Japanese Christian envoys to Rome's papal court; they voyage across the Pacific, cross Mexico, sail on to Spain and Italy, and return in 1590. By now, Valignano reports two hundred churches and 150,000 converts, achieved by seventy-five Jesuit priests in Japan.

1583: Hideyoshi begins the construction of Osaka castle, to be decorated by Kano Eitoku and his atelier. The Yamato tearoom is first used, with Sen Rikyu supervising.

August 6, 1585: Appointed *kanpaku* (imperial regent), Hideyoshi celebrates with a *noh* performance at the imperial palace, initiating an era of pageantry and ceremony.

March 1586: Hideyoshi displays a portable golden tearoom to the emperor at his palace.

July 1587: Alarmed by the Jesuit influence on Christian *daimyo*, Hideyoshi issues an edict forbidding forced conversion and denouncing Christianity as subversive; the next day he orders the expulsion of Jesuit missionaries. He removes Nagasaki from Jesuit control and places it under his own rule. These edicts are not enforced, but Jesuits follow his rules, especially against preaching in public.

November 1587: At Kitano shrine, Hideyoshi holds an elaborate ten-day outdoor tea ceremony to which all classes of society are invited; other events here include art exhibits, concerts, plays, and dance performances. Hideyoshi is a master of using ostentatious display to achieve his goals. He has Kano Eitoku and his atelier decorate Juraku Palace, where the emperor visits him in 1588, validating his ascension to elite status.

1588: Hideyoshi issues further anti-Christian edicts, provoked by damage to Buddhist shrines by converts and by Portuguese traders who buy and export Japanese slaves.

Work begins on Kyoto's Great Buddha Hall, ordered by Hideyoshi; a *furyo* performance danced by townsmen highlights the ceremony. The Great Buddha statue, larger than one in Nara's Todaiji, is twice damaged by earthquakes.

1589: *Yamanoue Soji ki*, a work on the *wabicha* (poverty tea) ceremony, is completed. Master potter Chojiro uses clay from near Hideyoshi's castle to make rough-style tea bowls decorated with the character *raku* (enjoyment).

In Kyoto, Hideyoshi orders brothels to be located in one licensed quarter, Nijo Yanagimachi.

1591: A Hideyoshi edict bans change of social status from samurai to farmer or merchant, or from farmer to merchant. This initiates the legal codification of social-class hierarchy.

1592: In Kyushu, Nagoya castle, Hideyoshi's headquarters for Korean invasion, is decorated by Kano Mitsunobu and Hasegawa Tohaku's atelier.

1593: The *kouta* (short song) anthology *Ryotatsu kouta sho* is issued in the first of various versions.

Hideyoshi begins to act in *noh* performances before noble audiences, using *noh* as a propaganda medium. He also commissions heroic spectacles about his own life and military victories.

1594: Hideyoshi builds Fushimi castle at Momoyama, commissioning Kano Mitsunobu and Kano Sanraku to decorate it. Accompanied by a large retinue, Hideyoshi journeys on a pilgrimage to Yoshino to view cherry blossoms. The event is celebrated with a performance of Omura Yoko's *Yoshino mode*, which glorifies Hideyoshi.

February 5, 1597: In the first violent persecution of Christians, a Hideyoshi-ordered crucifixion of twenty-six Japanese converts and foreign missionaries takes place at Nagasaki.

1598: Following the second Korean invasion, generals bring back Korean craftsmen who establish the Satsuma ware, Arita ware, and Hagi ware pottery traditions in Japan.

1599: To commemorate the deified Hideyoshi at Hokoku Jinja shrine, Kano Shosho paints the panels of *Thirty-six Poets*. His son Hideyori is honored with the dedication of one hundred *ryotatsu* songs.

1600: English sailor William Adams (1564–1620) arrives in a damaged Dutch ship. Tokugawa Ieyasu first imprisons him, then takes him on as tutor in mathematics, cartography, and gunnery. Honored with elevation to samurai rank, Adams acquires a substantial estate, takes a Japanese wife, and negotiates the opening of trade with the Dutch (1611) and English (1613).

1603: Having set up a movable-type printing press, Jesuits publish a Japanese-Portuguese dictionary; the next year, João Rodrigues issues his *Arte da Lingoa de Iapam*, an introduction to the Japanese language. They issue translations of the Bible and of the books *Imitation of Christ*, *A Guide for Sinners*, and *Aesop's Fables*.

The Portuguese also inspire fashions among the Japanese, some of whom wear capes, pantaloons, high ruff collars and rosary and crucifix accessories and play card games (*karuta*). They, too, are the source of *pan* (Portuguese bread) and *tempura* (fish or vegetables deep-fried in batter, from the Portuguese *tempero*). Portuguese and other westerners are depicted in Japanese *namban* art of the era.

This is the traditional date of the beginning of *kabuki* ("outlandish"), as female dancer Okuni mimes the male role of a rake visiting a brothel. In bawdy skits by women's troupes and by prostitutes, men (*onnagata*) often play female roles. Women's groups perform at the imperial court and tour the provinces. In 1617, the first *kabuki* theater is established in Kyoto, and the genre later becomes the sole domain of male actors.

1604: Confucian scholar Hayashi Razan enters the service of Ieyasu and establishes a school in Edo.

February 1, 1614: Prohibiting Christianity

throughout Japan, Ieyasu calls for the expulsion of 148 missionaries, deporting all (except some forty who go into hiding), along with Christian *daimyo* who refuse to recant.

Thus begins persecution in earnest. Soon Nagasaki-area Christians, including children, are put to death and tortured to make them recant.

EDO PERIOD: 1615–1868

1615: Tokugawa Ieyasu gives land at Takagamine to Hon'ami Koetsu (1558–1637), a versatile artist of the era—calligrapher, potter, designer of decorative paper (*shikishi*) and pictorial lacquerware, and connoisseur. There he founds an art colony of Lotus Conferderation members.

Under courtier patronage, he publishes *sagabon*, exquisite editions of classic Japanese literature, as well as *wakagon*, scrolls of court poetry, in collaboration with Tawaraya Sotatsu, the era's great painter of *yamato-e* (traditional Japanese) style gold screens depicting court life, and of Chinese-style brush paintings. Koetsu and Sotatsu establish the traditions of decorative style to be known as the Rimpa School. Other important schools of the era are Kano (official painters academy) and Tosa (painters to the imperial court).

1617: In Edo is established a gated and officially controlled red light district occupied by some three thousand licensed prostitutes in about two hundred houses. Similar districts are created in other cities.

1619: Persecution continues as Kyoto Christians are executed. In 1622 fifty-five Nagasaki Christians are executed; the most severe anti-Christian laws are passed in 1638. In 1665 the shogunate orders *daimyo* to carry out a yearly inquisition; it also issues regulations controlling temples and priests.

By 1641, all Japanese wives and mixed-blood children of foreigners are deported; all Japanese living abroad are forbidden to return.

1629: Women are banned from *kabuki*, which is seen as a front for prostitution. In 1652, young men's *kabuki* is banned in Edo

for similar reasons; it eventually becomes legitimate theater.

1636: At Nikko, shogun Iemitsu rebuilds Ieyasu's sumptuous mausoleum, where he is worshipped as a Shinto deity. Many important craftsmen work on the project.

1650s: In Edo, numbers of *ronin* (masterless samurai) increase and disorderly gangs disrupt the public.

1656: Leading Edo scholar Yamaga Soko (1622–1685) issues an essential work on *Bushido* (way of the warrior) and explores the philosophical basis of the samurai ethic of duty and honor.

In Edo, illegal bathhouses are popular. In 1791 the shogunate bans communal bathing by men and women in Edo public bathhouses.

1665: *Ukiyo monogatari* (Tale of the Floating World) by Asai Ryoi appears. The "floating world" of courtesans and actors becomes a popular subject for writers and artists of the era.

1666: Publication of the twenty-volume lexicon *Kimmo zui* (Illustrations and Definitions to Train the Untutored).

1682: The most famous novelist of the era, Ihara Saikaku (1642–1693), publishes *Koshoku ichidai otoko* (Life of an Amorous Man), a form of fiction known as *gesaku* (stories written for amusement). By now, some 40 percent of commoners are literate.

1683: The shogunate issues a series of sumptuary laws banning overly expensive clothing, as well as regulating food, house size, and scale of entertainments. According to Confucian principles, consumption is to be proportional to status.

1688–1704: Lively urban culture of the Genroku period flourishes with novels of Sai-kaku, plays of Chikamatsu, poems of Basho, and *ukiyo* prints. Commercial wealth en-courages an explosion of the minor arts—ceramics, lacquerware, textiles, *netsuke* (sash toggles), and *inro* (seal baskets); it allows lei-sure activities in pleasure quarters, theaters, public baths, taverns, and tea houses. De-spite the religious context, commoners at times treat pilgrimages as holiday occasions.

1689: Japan's most famous poet, Matsuo Ba-sho (1644–1694), sets out on a trip through northern Honshu, recording the journey in a travel diary, which includes what is re-garded as the first perfected *haiku*—seven-teen-syllable poems depicting vignettes from nature and their effect on the poet.

1690: In Nagasaki, German doctor Engelbert Kaempfer starts work at a Dutch trading post; he writes a two-volume *History of Ja-pan*, the century's most important European book about Japan.

1703: The debut of Chikamatsu Monzae-mon's (1653–1724) *bunraku* drama *Sonezaki shinju* (Love Suicides at Sonezaki). Re-garded as Japan's leading playwright, he writes some one hundred *bunraku* plays for two-thirds life-size puppets operated by three masked puppeteers, as well as thirty *kabuki* plays. Numerous double love-suicides among the public follow, leading to a 1723 government ban on their portrayal in litera-ture or drama.

April–May 1705: Pilgrimages to Ise draw 3.62 million. Pilgrims flock to this leading Shinto shrine throughout the Edo era.

***c.* 1718:** The influential Confucian scholar and advisor to two shoguns Ogyo Sorai (1666–1728) publishes *Rongocho* (Commen-taries on the Analects). Among other leading Confucian scholars of the era is Arai Haku-seki (1657–1725).

1722: Government bans erotic books, illus-trated by *shunga* (spring pictures); the ban results in stronger demand for such works, mostly by artist Hishikawa Moronobu (1618–

1694), the first master of the *ukiyo-e* wood-block print.

1728: Kada no Azumamaro petitions the sho-gunate to found a school of "national learn-ing," as scholars begin to reconsider ancient Japanese Shinto poetry and history in a search for canonical literature. Motoori No-rinaga (1730–1801) will cap the *kokugaku* or national learning movement with an influ-ential forty-four-volume study of *Kojiki*, the earliest Japanese classic.

1745: A Dutch-Japanese dictionary is issued by Aoki Konyo. In 1796, Inamura Sampaku and others issue the Dutch-Japanese dictio-nary *Haruma wage*.

1765: Among masters of the woodblock print, Harunobu (1724–1770) pioneers the multi-colored *nishiki-e* (brocade picture) some sev-enty years before chromolithography; Torii Kiyonobu (1752–1815) will pioneer *ukiyo-e* landscapes. Utamaro (1754–1806) depicts fe-male subjects and invents the "head and shoulders" portrait; he becomes a leading *ukiyo-e* artist. Like most artists of the era, both Harunobu and Utamaro are prolific producers of *shunga*. In reforms of 1790s and 1840s, artists of erotic and satirical prints are censored and jailed.

Other schools of the era include *Bunjin* or literati-style artists who reject academic style in favor of landscapes in the Chinese tradi-tion. Second-generation practitioners in-clude Ike no Taiga (1723–1776) and Uragami Gyokudo (1745–1820).

1776: *Kokugaku* scholar and writer Ueda Ak-inari (1734–1809) publishes *Ugetsu monoga-tari* (Tales of Moonlight and Rain), nine su-pernatural tales influenced by classical literature.

1780: Artist Shiba Kokan (1747?–1818) intro-duces the first western-style oil paintings; in 1783, he produces the first copperplate etch-ings in Japan.

1808: Shogunate orders six interpreters to study French in Nagasaki, six to study En-glish, and all to study Russian.

1811: Government establishes the Translation Office, recruits linguists to translate books from Dutch and other European languages. These works cast new light on Western international practices and lead Translation Office head Takahashi Kageyasu (1785–1829) to support the expulsion of foreign ships.

1814: A number of messianic sects based on sectarian Shinto begin to emerge: in 1814, the Kurozumikyo sect; in 1838, the Tenrikyo sect; in 1859, the Konkokyo sect.

c. 1831: *Fugaku sanjorokkei* (Thirty-six Views of Mount Fuji), a series of woodcut prints by Katsushika Hosukai (1760–1849) begins to appear; the set includes *Great Wave at Kanagawa*. The second great master of the century is Ando Hiroshige (1797–1858), who creates more than one thousand views of Edo; his best-known work is *Fifty-three Stations of the Tokaido*, depicting the route between Edo and Kyoto. Large numbers of their woodcuts are exported to the West in the 1860s, greatly influencing the French Impressionists.

1832: Publication begins of the romantic novel *Shunshoku umegoyomi* (Spring Love:

A Plum-Blossom Almanac) by Tamenaga Shunsui; with new social and psychological realism, it influences the development of the modern Japanese novel.

1840: The shogun orders the Dutch to inform him about the Opium War in China; in 1850 he sets a penalty for the unauthorized publication of news about that war. In 1843, he calls for the translation of the Dutch constitution.

1842: Scholar and writer Takizawa Bakin (1767–1848) completes his most famous work, *Nanso Satomi hakkenden* (Satomi and the Eight Dogs).

1861: Publication begins of Japan's first modern newspaper, *Nagasaki Shipping List & Advertiser* (in English). In 1862 comes the first regular Japanese-language newspaper *Kampan Batabiya Shimbun* (translated from Dutch).

1867: Publication of the first Japanese-English dictionary by the American missionary and physician James Hepburn, who uses a system of romanization developed by a collaborative group of Japanese and foreigners.

MEIJI PERIOD: 1868–1912

March 1868: As government decrees the separation of Shinto and Buddhism, Buddhist priests are to give up vows and leave Shinto shrines to return to laity. In 1870 an imperial edict makes Shinto the state religion.

1869: In Tokyo, to memorialize fallen warriors, the Shokonsha shrine is founded. Renamed Yasukuni in 1876, it will honor all war dead since 1853.

1870: Fukuzawa Yukichi (1835–1901), a leading Meiji progressive and intellectual, completes the ten-volume *Seiyo Jijo* (Conditions in the West).

Officially commoners are allowed to take surnames, intermarry with other classes, and wear clothes once exclusive to samurai.

September 1871: In a policy to equalize classes, an edict allows samurai to cut off

their topknots, abandon their swords, and enter business and farming. Nobility may wed commoners. The terms *eta* and *hinin*, formerly used to designate outcast groups, are banned.

Publication begins of *Yokohama mainchi shimbun*, the first daily newspaper in Japanese; it becomes an organ of the Freedom and People's Rights Movement.

1872: The first modern school system is mandated by the Education Order of 1872; a move to adopt a more "flexible" system is reinforced by the Education Order of 1879.

1873: The edict banning Christianity is abolished, but freedom of religion is not specifically granted.

The first baseball game in Japan is played in Tokyo, introduced by the American Horace Wilson. The first Japanese team is organized around 1880.

1874–1876: To speed modernization, government begins to hire foreign employees, including British, Germans, French, and Americans on a temporary basis to train Japanese in such areas as Western agriculture, engineering, foreign affairs, medicine, and military science. This brings to Japan such notables as Basil Hall Chamberlain, Ernest Fenollosa, and William Smith Clark.

February 1, 1874: The Meirokusha Society is founded to explore Western culture. Public lectures and a journal serve a membership of leading Japanese educators and bureaucrats.

March 1876: An edict bans the wearing of swords except on ceremonial occasions.

1877: Tokyo University is established by the unification of two older institutions.

1882: The poetry anthology *Shintaishi sho* (Collection of New-Style Poetry) is published, the first to include translations of Western poems.

1883: In Tokyo, Rokumeikan reception hall for Western-style social and entertainment events is completed. In 1890 it is transformed into Peers Hall.

July 7, 1884: The Peerage Act creates 508 new nobles, adds an elite of military and outstanding commoners. At its 1944 peak the peerage has 1,016 families; it is abolished by the 1947 constitution.

1886: Tsubouchi Shoyo (1859–1935) promotes realism, leads the modernization of Japanese literature with *Shosetsu shinzui* (Essence of the Novel).

1889: Anglican missionary John Batchelor publishes his *Ainu-English-Japanese Dictionary*.

Japan's first modern novel appears with Futabatei Shimei's publication of *Ukigumo* (Drifting Clouds), a study of an alienated hero.

October 30, 1890: The Imperial Rescript on Education is issued; a 315-word text, read aloud on special occasions, promotes Confucian virtues to unite benevolent ruler and loyal subjects. It serves as a means of political indoctrination.

1892: Prophetess Deguchi Nao (1837–1918) starts Omoto, a messianic religious movement urging world peace and universal brotherhood.

1893: After studying art in Paris, Kuroda Seiki (1866–1924) returns to bring Impressionism to Japan.

1899: In Philadelphia, educator and cultural interpreter Nitobe Inazo (1862–1933) issues *Bushido: The Soul of Japan*.

The first Japanese film premieres in Tokyo. Silent films are interpreted by *benshi*, live performers who sit by the side of the screen to read subtitles aloud; they provide full dialogue, exposition, and general commentary. Coming from traditional storytelling tradition, these "poets of darkness" usually perform to musical accompaniment.

1900: Poet Yosano Tekkan (1873–1935) starts the literary journal *Myojo* (Bright Star). Innovative and sophisticated, it becomes a sumptuous art journal.

The first Japanese woman to study abroad, Tsuda Umeko (1864–1929) founds the Tokyo Women's English School, now Tsuda College.

1901: Feminist writer and educator Yosano Akiko (1878–1942) issues a volume of *tanka* verse, *Midaregami* (Tangled Hair), four hundred poems of passion and sensuality.

December 1902: In the Textbook Scandal, publishers bribe officials to accept their books for use in schools.

1903: *Fujin no tomo* (Woman's Friend), the first women's magazine, begins publication as *Katei no tomo* (Friend of the Household).

November 1904: The socialist newspaper *Heimin shimbun*, founded in 1903, publishes the first Japanese translation of the *Communist Manifesto*; the government suspends publication.

1904: Natsume Soseki (1867–1916) completes his satirical novel *Wagahai wa neko de aru* (I Am a Cat).

British diplomat George Sansom (1883–1965) arrives. He becomes a major western interpreter of Japanese culture with the three-volume *History of Japan* (1958–1963).

October 11, 1906: A government official protests the San Francisco segregation of Japanese schoolchildren. President Theodore Roosevelt persuades the Board of Education to rescind the order.

1906: Writer Shimazaki Toson publishes *Hakai* (Broken Commandment), a realist masterpiece about a young man from an oppressed social class.

In the United States, Okakura Kakuzo (1862–1913) publishes the *Book of Tea* for a circle of Boston aesthetes; he later becomes Asian art curator at the Boston Museum of Fine Arts.

1909: In a goodwill gift, Tokyo presents more than two thousand flowering cherry trees in eleven varieties to Washington, D.C.

The Englishman Bernard Leach arrives to study Japanese pottery; his 1940 *Potter's Book* reveals Japanese glaze and kiln techniques to Western artisans.

1910: Major poet Ishikawa Takuboku (1886–1912) publishes *Ichiaku no suna* (Handful of Sand), a collection of 551 *tanka* poems.

Tono monogatari (Legends of Tono), a study of Honshu village life, is published by Yanagita Kunio (1875–1962), who develops the discipline of Japanese folklore.

1911: Initiating a feminist movement, Seitosha (Bluestocking Society) is founded as an association of "new women," including teachers, nurses, artists, and office workers.

Leading philosopher Nishida Kitaro (1870–1945) issues the book *Zen no kenkyo* (Study of Good), seeking to merge Western methodology and Buddhist tradition.

TAISHO PERIOD: 1912–1926

c. 1916: The first animated films are produced in Japan. In the 1920s, Ofuji Noburo (1900–1961) develops cut-out silhouette animation; he is the first Japanese animator to gain international fame.

1919: Director Kaeriyama Norimasa (1893–1964) produces *Sei no Kagayaki* (Glow of Life). The cinema pioneer is the first to use women actors and to film on location, as well as to experiment with editing techniques and complex stories.

January 1920: In the Morito Incident, Tokyo University professor Morito Tatsuo is imprisoned after writing a scholarly article on Kropotkin's anarchist theories. His long trial

raises the issue of academic freedom and free speech versus the government's need to suppress dangerous ideologies.

1921: Master of the "personal novel" Shiga Naoya (1883–1971) starts the serialization of his masterpiece *An'ya koro* (A Dark Night's Passing).

1926: Art historian Yanagi Muneyoshi (1889–1961) coins the term *mingei* (folk craft); he starts a movement for the study and creation of traditional decorative arts, with appreciation of regional and ethnic qualities of works in wood, bamboo, metal, paper, calligraphy, painting, and sculpture. In 1936, he helps to found the Japan Folk Craft Museum.

EARLY SHOWA PERIOD: 1926–1945

1927: Suzuki Daisetzu (1870–1966) begins publication of *Essays in Zen Buddhism* and helps to spread Zen worldwide.

1931: Director Gosho Heinosuke (1902-1981) produces Japan's first successful sound film,

Madamu to nyobo (My Neighbor's Wife and Mine).

1932: Marxist scholars begin to issue a seven-volume work on the development of Japanese capitalism.

1935: Important literary awards, the Akutagawa Prize to encourage new talent and the Naoki Prize for mature writers, are established.

1937: Ceramist Ishiguro Munemaro (1893– 1968) wins top prize at the Paris international exposition.

Novelist Nagai Kafo completes his masterpiece *Bokuto kidan* (A Strange Tale from East of the River).

1938: Ishikawa Tatsuzo's (1905–1985) novella *Ikite iru heitai* (Living Soldiers), treating the conduct of Japanese troops in Nanjing, is banned in the first test case of wartime media censorship.

LATE SHOWA PERIOD: 1945–1989

January 24, 1946: Government is ordered to ban the sale of girls by Japanese families into prostitution. In April 1958 an antiprostitution law closes brothels employing some 100,000 women.

Meanwhile, the *geisha* profession of traditional female entertainers decreases from eighty thousand in the 1920s to some ten thousand in the late 1980s.

April 23–26, 1948: Some 9,500 Koreans invade government offices in Osaka and Kobe over the issue of control of émigré schools. In March 1950, South Korea protests the required registration of 600,000 Koreans living in Japan.

September 10, 1951: *Rashomon* by Kurosawa Akira (1910–1998) wins grand prize at the Venice film festival and opens Western theaters to Japanese films. Kurosawa will receive a 1990 lifetime achievement Oscar; actor Mifune Toshiro (1920–1997) will become an international star.

1952: Sculptor-designer Isamu Noguchi (1904–1988) completes Hiroshima Peace Park bridge; he will commute between New York and Japan, eventually establishing a studio on Shikoku.

1953: Film director Ozu Yasujiro (1903–1963) completes his masterpiece *Tokyo monogatari* (Tokyo Story). Director Mizoguchi Kenji (1898–1956) completes *Ugetsu monogatari* (Ugetsu Story).

1954: Kinugasa Teinosuke's (1896–1982) film *Jigokumon* (Gate of Hell) is the first successful Japanese color film; it wins Cannes Film Festival grand prize and a 1955 Oscar. Director Tanaka Tomoyuki (1910–1997) completes the first of twenty-three Godzilla films about a lizard affected by radiation.

February 15, 1955: As a result of the 1950 Law for Protection of Cultural Assets, government designates the first Living National Treasures (men and women in traditional crafts and performing arts).

May 9–11, 1956: Mountaineer Aritsune Maki (1894–1989) leads a Japanese party in an ascent of the Himalayan peak Manaslu, the world's third highest unclimbed peak.

April 10, 1959: Crown Prince Akihito is the first of the imperial line to wed a commoner, Shoda Michiko.

1958: Seiji Ozawa (1935–) wins first prize at a French international conductors' competition; he goes on to conduct leading U.S. orchestras, becoming the chief conductor and music director of the Boston Symphony Orchestra in 1973.

1962: Avant-garde writer Abe Kobo (1924–1993) publishes *Suna no onna* (Woman in the Dunes).

October 10–24, 1964: Tokyo hosts the first Asian Olympic Games; judo, in which Japanese excel, premieres.

The Olympic Games (and, later, Expo '70) showcase the work of leading graphic artists Kamekura Yosaku and Nagaoka Shosei; the 1960s is the golden age of Japanese poster design. In 1970, Yokoo Tadanori has a solo show at New York's Museum of Modern Art.

1966: UPI news photographer Sawada Kyoichi wins a Pulitzer Prize.

1967: Composer Takemitsu Toru (1930–1996) completes *November Steps 1* for *biwa, shakuhachi,* and orchestra, commissioned by the New York Philharmonic for its 125th anniversary.

April 2, 1968–August 1969: Most of 377 universities undergo violent protests, strikes, and boycotts by students unhappy with the educational system. A promise of reform ends the upheaval.

1968: Kawabata Yasunari (1899–1972) wins Japan's first Nobel Prize for literature.

March 15, 1970: Expo '70 opens in Osaka; it is the first world's fair in an Asian city.

November 25, 1970: Writer and right-wing militarist Mishima Yukio (1925–1970) commits suicide.

1970: Japan enters the world of high fashion as Takada Kenzo (1939–) opens a Paris at-

elier. Leading designers who emerge in the 1960s and 1970s include Mori Hanae (1926–), Yamamoto Kansai (1944–), Miyake Issei (1938–), Yamamoto Yoji (1943–), and Kawakubo Rei (1942–).

January 24, 1972: In Guam, hunters find Yokoi Shoichi (1915–1997), a World War II soldier who hid in the jungle for twenty-seven years rather than suffer the shame of surrender. Welcomed home as a hero, he goes on to marry and teach thrift and survival skills. Other such soldiers are found in following years.

February 3–13, 1972: Sapporo hosts the Winter Olympic Games, the first in Asia.

1986: Architect Isozaki Arata (1931–) completes the Los Angeles Museum of Contemporary Art.

March 18, 1987: The Pritzker Prize, architecture's most prestigious award, goes to Tange Kenzo (1913–).

1987: Okamoto Ayako (1951–) is the top earner on the U.S. women's golf tour; she wins the player of the year award.

HEISEI PERIOD: 1989–1998

1989: Ito Midori is the women's figure-skating world champion; she wins a silver medal in the 1992 Winter Olympics.

May 15 and 17, 1990: At art auctions in New York, a Japanese art dealer purchases two paintings for the highest prices ever paid for any paintings; it is then revealed that he has bought them for Ryoei Saito, president of a Japanese paper manufacturing company. The top price is $82.5 million for Van Gogh's *Portrait of Dr. Gachet,* and the second highest is $78.1 million for Renoir's *Au Moulin de la Galette.*

July 12, 1991: Hitoshi Igarashi, the Japanese translator of Salman Rushdie's *Satanic Verses,* is stabbed to death, presumably by someone responding to the Ayatollah Khomeini's call for Rushdie's death because of the allegedly blasphemous nature of the novel.

1992: Ando Tadao (1941–) is the first recipient

of the new Carlsberg Architectural Prize, sponsored by the Carlsberg Breweries of Copenhagen.

1993: Maki Fumihiko (1928–) receives the Pritzker Prize for architecture.

March 23–26, 1994: In Chiba, the world figure-skating championships award top women's place to Sato Yuka.

1994: The Nobel Prize for literature goes to Kenzaburo Oe (1935–).

1995: Ando Tadao (1941–) receives the Pritzker Prize for architecture.

May 8, 1997: The Diet passes legislation that protects and promotes the culture and traditions of the Ainu ethnic minority of northern Japan. The government, however, refuses to designate the Ainu as an aboriginal people, as most anthropologists believe them to be.

May 29, 1997: The New York Yankees sign pitcher Irabu Hideki to a four-year, $12.8

million baseball contract. Other Japanese players in the United States include Hasegawa Shigetoshi, Kashiwada Takashi, and Nomo Hideo.

May 2, 1998: Hideto Matsumoto, a thirty-three-year-old rock star, hangs himself. In the following days, three of his teenage fans commit suicide.

Japan

SCIENCE-TECHNOLOGY, ECONOMICS, AND EVERYDAY LIFE

KOFUN PERIOD: A.D. 250–600

250–600: Agricultural techniques and tools evolve, with large-scale canal building and the subdivision of rice paddies, as well as the adoption of a step plow, the use of iron blades for hoes and reaping knives, and the use of horse-drawn cultivating equipment. Large manufacturing sites arise for salt production, stone beads, and ceramics, including the characteristic gray *sue* ware.

250–400: Early Kofun period. The rice basket of Japan centers on the Nara region, which grows most of the rice for the palace. Barley, millet, and wheat also are grown, probably using slash-and-burn methods. Special re-gional foods, such as trout and mushrooms, are presented as tribute to rulers.

400–500: Middle Kofun period. A specialized warrior elite emerges, as shown by iron armor, weapons, and horse gear. Numbers of craftsmen immigrate from the Korean state of Paekche. They make such luxury goods as gold jewelry, ornaments, ceramics, brocade and patterned cloth, and gilt bronze horse trappings. Large-scale canals are built to improve the irrigation of fields. Stone coffins and hollow clay figurines known as *haniwa* are made for Kofun tombs.

ASUKA PERIOD: 600–710

604: The Chinese calendar is adopted and remains in effect to *c.* 690.

646: The Taika Reform results in large-scale land surveys, the institution of a grid *(jori)* system of one-hectare square field sections, and reallocation of fields to peasants.

***c.* 660:** The Mizuochi water clock, based on a Chinese device, is erected as a two-story building in Nara Prefecture. The bell and drum are sounded to mark every thirty minutes.

683: Government orders the use of coins to facilitate financial exchanges and to stimulate the economy. The burgeoning bureaucracy requires the documentation of all transactions in the form of inscriptions on wooden tablets, or *mokkan*, later excavated in great numbers from the Fujiwara capital site.

702: Taiho statutes regulate inheritance practices: eldest sons are to inherit father's property, including chattel slaves, and one-half of the rest of the estate, with the remainder divided among brothers.

702: Standardization of weights and measures.

708: The first Japanese silver and copper coins, *wado kaihin*, are minted, following the style of Chinese Tang coins of 621. (Copper is discovered in western Japan in 707.) The minting of silver coins is halted in 709. Despite government efforts to impose the use of coins, the main media of exchange are rice, cloth, and barter. In 711, one copper coin, or *mon*, is valued at six *sho* (one *sho* equals about .72 liter) of rice.

NARA PERIOD: 710–794

723: Government allows private ownership of reclaimed lands, and farmers may leave land to heirs. Previously all rice land was in the public domain (because it used state-financed irrigation) and was reallocated every six years, according to the *Handen shoju* system. This is meant to alleviate a growing shortfall in rice production, affecting both the nutrition of the lower classes and the tax income of the state.

730: A document from Awa province shows 412 out of 414 households to be living in poverty. In Echizen province, 996 of 1,019 households are in the same condition. Large numbers of peasants run away to avoid taxes, mounting debts, and labor conscription, often becoming vagrants.

Types of conscripted labor service include up to sixty days per year of unpaid work on construction details; military service, in which soldiers have to provide their own food and weapons; palace and border guard duty for lengthy periods; and three years' work in the capital in return for exemption from most taxes and assessments. Hired workers, paid with food and money, also are used on state building projects.

735–737: A great smallpox epidemic kills 30–40 percent of the population. Over the centuries that follow, epidemics, famines, and natural disasters causing crop failures undermine the nation's social fabric, leading to a rising tide of lawlessness and provincial violence.

737: A government ban on private loans (often at rates as high as 100 percent per year) also reduces interest rates for farmers. Public lenders benefit, increasing the income of local officials.

740: In a simplification of local government, villages are abolished and replaced by towns made up of two or three villages.

743: Official permission is given for private ownership of virgin lands opened up for rice cultivation, benefiting mainly rich farmers who can afford to clear land. This eventually leads to landed estates known as *shoen*.

757: In inheritance matters, the Yoro code reduces the eldest son's share to twice that of his brothers and recognizes inheritance by daughters, who get half of what brothers do. In commoner families each member apparently gets an equal share.

HEIAN PERIOD: 794–1185

763: In the provinces, robbery and arson of government grain warehouses, often by local officials, spreads and continues into the early ninth century.

795: The rate of interest on state loans is reduced to 30 percent per year.

844: The last recorded widespread land reallocation takes place in the provinces.

950: Todaiji temple owns *shoen* in twenty-three provinces, with the total area surpassing fourteen thousand acres. With a great increase in land holdings by aristocrats and religious institutions, *shoen* virtually become manorial-style autonomous administrative and economic units, decentralizing state power.

c. 1050: Artisans, previously under patronage of court and government, begin to produce goods on their own to sell in the marketplace. This leads to formation of *za*—crafts or trade guilds of artisans, merchants, or service providers. Each *za* operates under the protection of a patron. The earliest records of *za*, connected to Todaiji temple, date from 1097.

1108: Mount Asama erupts, spreading volcanic ash across Kanto Plain, burying rice paddies, and causing great damage in Kozuke province.

1156: A major fire destroys the Great Audi-ence Hall of the imperial palace; it will not be rebuilt. Fires, accidental and intentional, are recurrent events in the capital (in 1151 and 1163) and provinces. The capital undergoes famine in 1181 and suffers earthquakes (late 1170s to early 1180s).

1179: As inflation rises and the value of money drops, court issues decree prohibiting use of Southern Song coins, which enter the country in large amounts through trade with China. (Japan has minted no money since the Nara era.) Later decrees of 1187 and 1189 ban their use only in Kyoto marketplaces. The decrees have little effect as Japanese merchants export rice, pearls, gold, mercury, sulfur, and craft items such as fans, folding screens, and scrolls. Excessive exporting to obtain coinage destabilizes the Japanese economy, and the sale of rice abroad causes periodic famine crises. Japanese continue to import coins, as well as luxury cloth, incense, Buddhist writings, calligraphy tools, and art objects of gold, silver, ivory, and precious stones.

1180–1182: A terrible famine followed by pestilence in Taira-dominated western Honshu ends fighting in the Great Civil War for two years. The situation favors the Minamoto, who have access to the agriculture of the Kanto Plain in the east, which is less affected.

KAMAKURA PERIOD: 1185–1333

1192: The imperial court issues a final ban on coin usage; by 1226, the court expresses a preference for using coins rather than cloth as the medium of exchange. By 1240 the shogunate forbids coins only in the northernmost Ou region. By the mid- to late thirteenth century, coins are the primary medium of exchange in cities, greatly facilitating financial transactions and the growth of commerce.

Early 13th century: The shogunate authorizes marketplaces in Kamakura; most regional markets operate three days per month. By the late thirteenth century independent suppliers and shops conduct business more efficiently than under the old patronage system. In the mid-thirteenth century, the shogunate organizes *za* in Kamakura.

1221: After the Jokyo Disturbance, the shogunate confiscates the land of those who participate and assigns loyal retainers to lands as *jito*, or military stewards. Thus the shogunate establishes lord-vassal relations within the proprietary rights structure of the *shoen* system. Once on the land, the *jito* seek to expand their authority.

In the early fourteenth century, relations with estate managers are formalized with *jito ukesho*, or contracts between *shoen* proprietors and *jito*, who are authorized to collect and deliver the annual tax.

1227: The shogunate orders provincial police to end the activity of *akuto* (evil bands), bandit groups that steal rice revenues, sometimes under the direction of *jito*.

1230: The shogunate bans the establishment of new *shoen*. At their height in the twelfth century, *shoen* were the nation's most important political and economic institution. With increased shogunal control, they eventually change into feudal estates controlled by the warrior class. In the fourteenth century, *shiki* (office) structure—the right to receive income from *shoen* according to one's position within the *shoen* hierarchy—weakens.

1231: A major famine ravages the country; another famine occurs in 1259.

1232: At Kamakura, the island of Wake-no-Shima is built to facilitate ship docking; it soon becomes the end of the Inland Sea route for domestic and foreign trade. To improve shipping, Asahina Canal is opened in 1241.

1239: The shogunate bans *jito* from appointing money lenders as debt collectors. Warriors take on mortgages in order to offset falling revenues and to buy luxury goods; many lose their lands as debts mount.

1252: The shogunate temporarily bans the sale of sake rice wine and destroys 32,274 sake jars in Kamakura.

1254: To limit traffic on the Inland Sea, the shogunate bans possession of more than five Chinese ships and orders the destruction of those exceeding that number. The law is meant to protect shogunal merchant ships and to increase control over trade. By late Kamakura times, the shogunate monopolizes public trading ships.

1255: A shogunal document attests to the growth of moneylenders, who usually take pawns. Most are Buddhist monks (*sanso*), shipping agents, and merchants.

1267: A decree forces lenders to accept overdue debt payments for lands already confiscated for nonpayment. The order undermines commercial contractual relationships in order to rescue shogunal retainers from financial disaster.

1279: From this year dates the oldest surviving Japanese bill of exchange, enabling its holder from Kii province to receive cash in Kamakura.

1284: The shogunate issues the Tokusei decree to cancel debts of shogunal retainers as an alternative to losing their lands to creditors, thus sacrificing justice to political expediency.

Late 13th century: Spread of *do-ikki*, associations of land cultivators and lower rank warriors, organized to obtain relief from financial hardship or redress for political grievances. With improved agricultural techniques and productivity, more peasants become independent cultivators. Their protests contribute to the weakening of the *shoen* system.

1293: An earthquake in Kamakura kills some 23,000 inhabitants.

MUROMACHI PERIOD: 1333–1573

1300s–1400s: Progress in the use of the clay-slime process for iron smelting, use of the pit saw for construction, and the use of the carpenter's plane. The manufacture of paper, silk brocade, and cotton cloth is introduced.

1342: Takauji sends a trading ship to China, uses profits to build Tenryoji temple; other "temple ships" follow.

1350s: *Za* (craft or trade guilds) appear in rural areas.

Debt cancellation and prohibition of debt cancellation are alternately mandated from this time. Both afford revenue to the shogunate, which takes a percentage of the amount owed each time.

1352: Takauji's *hanzei* (half-tax) decree reserves half of rice harvest of temples, shrines, and *shoen* for emergency military rations; it becomes a permanent source of income for military class.

1400s: Under *daimyo* (regional warlords), improved agricultural techniques include better tools, double cropping of rice and barley, new varieties of rice; use of the water wheel for irrigation, of fertilizer, and of draft animals; and the introduction of regional cash crops such as tea, flax, hemp, soybean, fruit, indigo, sesame, and cotton. Crop surpluses are often lost to debtor land confiscations.

1404: The "tally trade" pact will govern trade with China for 150 years. The system, imposed by the Chinese, limits the number of official Japanese trading missions per year. Tallies (paper certificates) carried by ships are checked against Chinese registers on arrival, providing evidence that vessels are not those of pirates or smugglers. The system is also meant to prevent Japanese dumping of goods in excess of allowable quotas.

Tally trade begins as a shogunal monopoly; it becomes a joint venture of the shogunate, temples, *daimyo*, and merchants; and finally it is controlled by Ouchi and Hosokawa,

whose rivalry leads China to end it in 1549. After that, aggressive Portuguese traders carry goods to and from Japan in competition with smugglers and pirates.

1426: Korea limits Japanese trade to official vessels traveling on ambassadorial business. Those without passports will be considered pirates. The policy is implemented by 1436. In 1443 the Kakitsu Treaty limits Japan to fifty ships per year. Japanese trade with Korea is greater than with China. Imports include tiger and boar hides, ginseng, religious articles, floral patterned woven mats, honey, and cotton cloth.

1428–1431: Famine in 1428 leads to a strike by transport workers and riots by farmers. In 1431 a major famine in Kyoto leads to the forced sale of rice. Widespread famine and plagues occur in the 1440s, 1450s, 1461, 1491–1500, and 1540.

1454: Tofukuji temple sets up a toll barrier on the highway to raise money for building a pagoda; residents tear down the barrier and burn the temple. They go on to raid Kyoto moneylenders' offices and destroy contracts. The shogunate offers partial debt cancellation.

Private toll barriers erected at fief boundaries, crossroads, and river crossings often provoke public ire. In 1459 shogun Yoshimasa uses barriers to try to create an artificial rice shortage so as to raise the selling price; he is forced to take them down after two months. In 1568 Nobunaga abolishes provincial toll barriers.

1500: The financial situation in Kyoto is abysmal, as the emperor dies and lies unburied for six months because the treasury has no funds for a funeral.

1543: Portuguese introduce matchlock muskets; in six months, Japanese are able to manufacture them. Modern firearms and cannon change the strategy of war, lead to castle-building, and allow national unification. With larger and more maneuverable ships, the Portuguese bring in glassware, clocks, eyeglasses, wool and velvet textiles, and tobacco, as well as muskets.

The shogunate borrows money from Sakai merchants, securing the loan by pledging tax revenues. A "free city," Sakai hires *ronin* (masterless samurai) for defense.

1571: As Japan's "window on the West," Nagasaki, with a good natural harbor and easily defensible, becomes a major port and center for the Portuguese, who trade mainly in Chinese silk and Japanese silver; in 1580 Jesuits are granted judicial sovereignty over the city and area.

MOMOYAMA PERIOD: 1573–1615

1580: English trading ships first arrive in Hirado, off Nagasaki.

1590: Hideyoshi orders a census on which to base a new land-holding and taxation system. Taxes henceforth are to be paid in rice, not money, to facilitate the provisioning of the army. Farmers are forbidden to neglect or abandon fields.

1591: Hideyoshi orders craftsmen and merchants to reside in towns, not villages. Each man is to follow the occupation of his father. He also takes over all gold and silver mines, mints new coins, standardizes system of weights and measures, and controls foreign trade.

1602: Driven off course by a storm, the Spanish ship *Espiritu Santo* lands in Shimizu harbor in Tosa province. Wanting trade with New Spain, Tokugawa release the crew.

1603: Nihonbashi bridge is erected in Edo. It becomes the hub of the road system and the point from which all distances are measured.

1609: Trade with Holland begins as the Dutch found a post on Hirado. Ieyasu favors trade with the Dutch and English because they are not interested in promulgating Christianity.

1613: An envoy from King James I receives permission for the English to trade with Japan. They ignore advice and choose an unsuitable site for a trading station, which they shut down after ten years.

EDO PERIOD: 1615–1868

1616: Measures to limit foreign influence begin, confining all except Chinese ships to Nagasaki and Hirado. In 1621 the shogun bans overseas travel, the construction of keeled long-distance vessels, and export of weapons. In 1635 the shogunate restricts foreign trade and ships to Nagasaki and bans Japanese from returning home from abroad (*sakoku* laws). The Dutch post on Hirado remains in operation until a total ban in 1639, when the Dutch move to Dejima.

1642: The shogunate issues regulations on village system, ordering collective organization and requiring householders to work their own land. In 1643 it prohibits the sale and purchase of farmland.

1657: In Edo, the Meireki fire burns large areas, most of Edo castle, and more than 350 shrines and temples, leaving more than 100,000 dead. The city is rebuilt with attention to disaster planning, with tiled rather than thatched roofs, open spaces as firebreaks, and earthen wall barriers. Over the centuries, some ninety serious fires occur there. In 1718, townsmen form fire brigades.

1684: In Edo, the shogunate issues codes regulating publishing.

1686: The shogunate issues regulations on trade with Korea. In 1688 China is limited to seventy ships to Nagasaki each year. In 1715 new laws limit China to thirty ships and Holland to two ships. In 1736 the Chinese are limited to twenty-five vessels, to prevent overexportation of Japanese copper.

1697: In Osaka, the Dojima rice exchange begins. In 1710, it operates with warehouse notes instead of actual grain and deals in futures.

1698: Shogun Tsunayoshi calls for the first devaluation of the currency. In the nineteenth century numerous devaluations will follow.

1707: Last eruption of Mount Fuji (as of 1998).

1719: Nishiwaka Joken writes *Chonin bukuro* (A Bagful of Advice for Merchants), followed in 1721 by *Hyakusho bukuro* (A Bagful of Advice for Farmers), which calls for literacy among farmers.

1720: Shogun Yoshimune partially ends the ban on Dutch books and allows their translation; political and religious books still are taboo. Japanese *rangaku* (Dutch learning) scholars stream to Nagasaki to study Western science and technology, including medicine, military tactics and strategy, agriculture, botany, mathematics, navigation, surveying, astronomy, cartography, ballistics, and armaments manufacture, as well as the art of vanishing-point perspective.

1724: In Edo, rice, oil, and other commodity dealers are ordered to form closed associations. In 1726 wholesalers are ordered to submit price lists and account books to the shogunate.

By now new cash crops include sugar cane and mulberry, with cotton constituting 25 percent of the produce of four provinces.

1725: The Edo population is 1.3 million (that of Kyoto is 400,000, of Osaka 300,000), with the samurai occupying two-thirds of the city area and 600,000 commoners crammed into one-eighth.

1732: In southwest Japan, a locust plague and bad weather result in the Kyoho famine. In the 1782–1787 Temmei famine, hundreds of thousands die nationwide, with reports of cannibalism. In the 1833–1836 Tempo famine some 200,000 to 300,000 perish.

1733: In the first violent public action in Edo

and other cities, *chonin* (commoners) attack the stores of rice merchants to protest high rice and commodity prices.

1750s: Merchants issue paper certificates as currency (*tegata*) backed by silver in their warehouses. In the 1660s *daimyo* began to issue paper domain money (*hansatsu*); in 1707 the shogunate banned it until 1730. Government will not print paper money until the 1860s. In 1772 the shogunate mints *nanryo nishugin* coin to increase currency in circulation.

1760s: Peasant uprisings and urban riots increase.

1774: *Kaitai shinsho*, the first complete Japanese translation of a Western anatomical text, appears.

1779: Hiraga Gennai dies; he invented a hand-cranked electric dynamo, a thermometer, and an asbestos clothmaking process and theorized about *bussangaku* (the science of production).

1783: Eruption of Mount Asama damages Kanto's rice agricultural lands, contributing to the Temmei famine and resulting in some twenty thousand deaths.

1789: Shogunal retainers are granted debt moratoriums to rescue them from destitution.

1798: Kondo Jozo explores the Kurile Islands. In 1811 Russian captain Vasilii Golovin is captured while surveying the Kuriles; he writes a widely read account of imprisonment.

1809: Establishing that Sakhalin is an island, Mamiya Rinzo finds the Tatar Strait.

1816: After seventeen years, Ino Tadataka completes the first accurate cartographic survey of all Japan.

1822: Cholera breaks out in Nagasaki and spreads to central Japan.

1823: Arriving in Nagasaki to act as physician to the Dutch, Philipp von Siebold opens a school in 1824 to teach Western medicine and science to Japanese students. In 1829, he is placed under house arrest for receiving Japanese maps and is banished, while Japanese scholars, notably Takahashi Kageyasu, are punished as spies. Siebold later writes encyclopedic works on Japanese flora and fauna.

1842: The shogunate bans domain monopolies.

Agronomist Okura Nagatsune (1768–?) begins publication of *Koeki kokusan ko* (On Increasing Profits and Productivity), the most influential farming manual in nineteenth-century Japan.

1855: In Edo, more than seven thousand die in the Ansei earthquake. In Nagasaki, a naval officer training school is founded.

1857: In Nirayama, a steel production reverberatory furnace is constructed.

MEIJI PERIOD: 1868–1912

July 1868: The first national paper currency, *Dajokan satsu*, is issued. It is not well received; new bills are issued in 1872.

1868: In Honolulu, 148 Japanese contract laborers arrive to work on Hawaiian sugar plantations. In 1869 some twenty members of the Wakamatsu colony arrive in California. A large-scale exodus begins in 1885–1886 when government eases restrictions on emigration, which is seen as a way of alleviating economic pressures. In 1899, 790 laborers sail to Peru to work on farms and by 1940 some 33,000 Japanese settle in Peru. In June 1900 the first emigrants leave Kobe for Brazil.

1870: A telegraph line unites Tokyo and Yokohama.

April 20, 1871: A government-run postal service is established between Tokyo and Osaka; it is extended in July 1872 to the rest of the country.

1871: The *yen* becomes the official monetary unit, based on the gold standard.

1872: The first national census finds the population at 33,110,825.

A railroad connecting Tokyo and Yokohama is completed; the area around the Tokyo terminal develops into the Ginza shopping and entertainment district.

To facilitate industrialization, government builds a model silk-reeling mill, with French advice and machinery, in Tomioka. In 1879 the Senju woolen mill, built with German assistance and machinery, begins operation. Most government factories prove unprofitable and are sold to private parties in the 1880s.

January 1, 1873: The Gregorian calendar is adopted.

July 28, 1873: The Land Reform Tax Law passed. It sets the tax rate at 3 percent of value and 1 percent for local surtax; evaluation is left to landowners. Peasant uprisings in Ibaraki and Mie Prefectures in 1876 result in rate reductions. In 1872 the shogunate ban on the sale and purchase of agricultural land was revoked.

1873: Iwasaki Yataro (1835–1885) founds the Mitsubishi Shokai trading company. After eliminating competitors through price cuts and well-integrated shipping routes, the company owns 80 percent of the nation's ships by 1877. It diversifies into banking, mining, insurance, iron works, and other areas. Such industrial and financial combines, or *zaibatsu*, contribute to rapid industrialization and receive favorable government treatment during the era. Other major *zaibatsu* include Mitsui (founded in 1673), Sumitomo (a seventeenth-century merchant house), and Yasuda, founded in 1880.

1875: Tokyo Meteorological Observatory is founded. In 1878, the National Astronomical Observatory is established as part of Tokyo University.

1876: American William Smith Clark arrives to serve as Sapporo Agricultural College vice president; he is credited with advising students, "Boys, be ambitious!"—a familiar Japanese slogan.

1877: In an early environmental incident, acidic pollutants from the Ashio copper mine contaminate more than fifty thousand acres of land on the Kanto Plain. Despite protests by farmers and ineffectual government controls of 1897, pollution continues until 1973 when the mine is closed. In 1974 farmers receive $7 million in damages as a result of the first successful major pollution case.

American zoologist Edward Morse arrives, organizes the Tokyo University zoology department, and introduces Darwinian theory. In the same year, he discovers the Omori Shell Mounds and conducts the first modern archaeological excavation in Japan.

1882: To halt inflation, the Bank of Japan is organized; in May 1885 it begins the issue of convertible banknotes.

June 14–16, 1886: At Amamiya silk mill, a strike by women workers is first such labor action by Japanese factory employees.

1887: Electric power first reaches Japan in the form of thermal power, which continues to predominate until 1912, even after hydroelectric power is introduced in 1890.

1888: An eruption of Bandaisan volcano results in forty-four deaths. Lava dams the Nagasegawa River to form three lakes and a swamp.

1890: Public telephone service is inaugurated in Tokyo and Yokohama.

Bacteriologist Kitasato Shibasaburo (1853–1931), together with the German scientist Emil Behring, develops serum therapies for tetanus and diphtheria. In 1892 he establishes the Institute for Infectious Diseases in Tokyo. In the 1894 Hong Kong bubonic plague, he independently identifies the bacillus.

1893: Air pollution from the Besshi copper mine pervades Ehime Prefecture.

1896: Yawata Iron and Steel Works, the nation's largest steel mill, is started by the government with the aid of German engineers. It begins operation in 1901 with iron ore from China and Korea, producing mainly military armaments and railroad equipment.

Government takes the lead in establishing basic industries—shipbuilding, mining, machine tools, cement, and glass—most of which later are given over to private control.

1897: Inventor and industrialist Toyoda Sakichi (1867–1930) designs the first Japanese power loom; in 1924 he designs an automatic power loom, at the time the most advanced in the world, which allows Japan to dominate the world silk trade in the 1920s. From his industrial research complex arise other industries, including Toyota Motor Corporation in 1933.

1907: The first experimental twelve-horsepower automobile is made. Domestic makes are produced in small numbers but cannot compete with imported cars, primarily from the United States, in the 1920s. In 1925–1926, Ford and General Motors set up plants in Japan to assemble vehicles from imported parts.

1908: Chemist Ikeda Kikunae (1864–1936) extracts monosodium glutamate (MSG) from *kombu* (kelp); this later becomes a commercial seasoning.

December 19, 1910: The first airplane flight in Japan takes place at Tokyo's Yoyogi drill ground. Production begins of foreign planes under international license; in the late 1920s, production begins of Japanese planes, primarily military craft.

March 29, 1911: The Factory Law of 1911 is the first Japanese law to protect labor in private industry: it sets the minimum child-labor age at twelve and maximum working hours at twelve, and sets guidelines for accident compensation. It is rarely enforced.

Japan's first modern labor union was founded in 1897. Trade unions organized in the 1890s, mainly on a company basis, are disbanded during World War II.

January 1912: Following an unsuccessful 1910 attempt, explorer Shirase Nobu (1861–1946) leads the first Japanese research expedition to Antarctica, landing on the continent from the Ross Sea; he names the Yamato Snow Field.

TAISHO PERIOD: 1912–1926

August 1912: Suzuki Bunji (1885–1946) and others found Yoaikai, a pioneering labor group; the name is changed to Sodomei in 1921.

1917: Physicist Honda Kotaro (1870–1954) discovers that adding cobalt to tungsten steel produces increased magnetic strength; this leads to the development of strong magnetic alloys.

1918: Pioneer geneticist Toyama Kametaro (1867–1918) dies; he improved silkworm breeds by discovering that Mendel's Law applies to insects, and applied Mendelism to eugenics.

June 25–August 9, 1921: In Kobe, a simultaneous strike at the Kawasaki and Mitsubishi shipyards is the nation's largest labor dispute to date.

1925: The first radio broadcasts begin from Tokyo Broadcasting Station, which in 1926 combines with Osaka and Nagoya stations to form *Nippon Hoso kyokai* or NHK (Japan Broadcasting Corporation), the sole public network in Japan until the end of World War II.

EARLY SHOWA PERIOD: 1926–1945

1926: Electrical engineer Yagi Hidetsugu (1886–1976) develops the Yagi-Uda antenna, the most commonly used configuration for radio and television reception.

January 1927: Government plans to redeem "earthquake bills" (loans to banks affected by Tokyo earthquake), triggering rumors of bank collapses. The Financial Crisis of 1927 ensues as thirty-seven banks are closed and the cabinet is forced to resign. As a result, five major *zaibatsu* banks come to control the nation's finances. In the same year, the Tokyo subway opens.

1928: Pioneering bacteriologist Noguchi Hideyo (1876–1928) isolates the syphilis spirochete.

March 1930: The Showa Depression of 1930–1935 begins as the stock market plummets and foreign trade declines as a result of the Japanese return to the gold standard and of the worldwide economic depression. This leads to sharp price decreases for agricultural products, bankruptcies, bank closings, business failures, 2.5 million unemployed, and violent labor disputes.

1939: Tejiro Yabuta and Hayashi extract gibberelin A from a soil fungus; this will be used as a strong growth hormone for rice.

1942: A railway tunnel under Kammon Strait, linking Honshu and Kyushu, is completed.

LATE SHOWA PERIOD: 1945–1989

1946: With World War II barely over, the Japanese Union of Scientists and Engineers is founded with the goal of reviving Japan's industries by using statistical quality control.

May 19, 1946: Before the Tokyo imperial palace some 300,000 demonstrate against food shortages. Fearing a threat to democracy, General MacArthur will ban the general strike planned for February 1, 1947, protesting labor laws of 1945–1947, which establish the rights of workers and place limits on unions.

October 21, 1946: The Diet passes a land reform bill: addressing long-time social problems, it changes the economic structure of rural Japan by ousting landlords and by facilitating land purchases by cultivators.

July 1947: General MacArthur calls for the dissolution of *zaibatsu* in an attempt to decentralize economic power. After 1952, former *zaibatsu* regroup in loose affiliations known as *keiretsu*.

December 18, 1948: To halt inflation, General MacArthur imposes Nine Principles for Economic Stabilization: these mandate balanced budget, limitation of credit, improved tax collection, wage stabilization, price controls, foreign trade controls, and a rationing system. On May 12, 1949, stock markets are allowed to reopen.

1949: Yukawa Hideki (1907–1981) is the first Japanese recipient of the Nobel Prize for physics.

1950: U.S. business consultant W. Edwards Deming (1900–1993) arrives by invitation to teach new methods of industrial quality control; his techniques aid Japan's rise to dominance. In 1951, Japan founds the Deming Prize, a competitive quality-control award. U.S. corporations will take up Deming's ideas in the 1980s in order to compete better.

April 14–December 18, 1952: A lengthy labor dispute by the Densan, or Electrical Workers' Union, results in a September strike stopping the production of electricity. Coal miners coordinate with electrical workers, beginning their own strike in October. Enforcement of the national emergency provision of the Labor Relations Adjustment Law ends both strikes in December. In 1953, the government enacts restrictions on labor actions by the electrical power and coal industries.

February 1, 1953: Television broadcasting begins; color programming starts in 1960.

1953–1960: In Minamata, industrial plant outflow poisons fish with mercury and causes nerve and mental damage to humans. The disaster leaves 1,293 official victims, 6,009 unofficial victims, and 305 dead. A similar event occurs in Niigata in 1964–1965.

June–October 1955: In the Chogoku and Kinki regions, dried milk contaminated with arsenic poisons 12,000 infants, causes serious nerve damage; 130 die. In the same year, cadmium poisoning from liquid wastes of mining and smelting operations leads to an outbreak of *itai-itai* disease.

August 1955: Japan joins GATT (General Agreement on Tariffs and Trade) and is forced to liberalize trading practices.

1955: The Sony Corporation introduces the first transistor radio to the world market; this begins growth of the Japanese consumer-electronics industry.

January 1957: As part of the International Geophysical Year, Japan establishes the Showa research station in Antarctica. On December 1, 1959, Japan signs the Antarctica Treaty, setting the region aside as a scientific preserve.

January–November 1960: In the nation's longest full-scale strike, Miike coal miners seek to uphold workers' rights.

1960: Innovative engineer Honda Soichiro (1906–1991) builds the world's largest motorcycle plant in Mie Prefecture. In 1963 he begins production of an automobile with a low pollution engine—the CVCC (combined vortex controlled combustion).

October 1, 1964: A high speed "bullet train" begins operation; traveling at an average of one hundred miles per hour, it reduces travel time from Tokyo to Osaka from 6.5 to 2.5 hours.

1965: The Nobel Prize in physics is shared by Tomonaga Shin'ichiro (1906–1979).

1967: Japan's population reaches 100,000,000.

1968: In the Kanemi oil poisoning incident, cooking oil contaminated with PCBs sickens fourteen thousand and leaves one hundred dead. Legal procedures last until 1989, when the court finds negligence, advancing the product-liability concept.

Kawasaki Heavy Industries begins work on

industrial robots. By the 1990s, Japan leads the world in robot development and usage.

Japan passes West Germany to become the world's second largest market economy.

February 11, 1970: Japan becomes the fourth nation to orbit a scientific satellite. In 1983, Japan successfully launches two communications satellites for TV broadcasting.

July 27, 1970: A Tokyo photochemical smog emergency sickens eight thousand, leading to a limited auto ban in central areas. The smog emergency of March–May 1972 provokes further demand for pollution curbs on industry. In 1971 the cabinet-level Environment Agency is organized, and in 1973 the Pollution-Related Health Damage Compensation Law passes.

1973: Esaki Reona (1925–) shares the Nobel Prize in physics.

An oil price shock leads to a greater reliance on nuclear power. By December 1989 thirty-seven reactors provide 23 percent of energy needs.

November 26–December 13, 1975: Members of the Public Corporation and National Enterprise Workers' Union (Korokyo) conduct a series of actions calling for restoration of the right to strike for public employees.

1978: Nippon Electricity Company (NEC) introduces the Voice Data Input Terminal; it can recognize 120 words spoken in groups of up to five words.

April 30, 1978: Uemura Naomi (1941–1984) is the first to reach the North Pole alone by dog sled after a fifty-four-day trek.

1979: Sony introduces the Walkman, a small portable cassette player with earphones. And in Tokyo the first commercial network of cellular telephones is set up.

April 6, 1980: The average height of Japan's current generation exceeds that of its parents by two inches (five centimeters), that of its grandparents by four inches (ten centimeters).

1980: Japan's auto production surpasses that of the United States.

1981: Fukui Ken'ichi (1918–) shares the Nobel Prize for chemistry.

Japanese scientists develop computer chips with 64 kilobits of memory. These quickly take over the market.

1982: Japan announces that it is starting a program to develop the so-called fifth generation of computers, to be based on the concept of artificial intelligence.

1984: NEC of Japan introduces the first chips with 256 kilobits of memory, four times the capacity of previous computer chips.

Japanese scientists discover an immune system suppressor in a fungus; known as FK506, it has results similar to those of cyclosporine.

1985: Seiko-Epson builds a TV set with a liquid crystal display on a two-inch screen.

April 5, 1985: Japan agrees to end all commercial whaling by March 1988.

August 12, 1985: A Japan Air Lines Boeing 747 crashes into Mount Ogura, leaving 520 dead, the country's worst single plane disaster to date.

1986: The first DAT (digital audio tape) recorders are demonstrated. At Sendai, a subway system controlled by computers using "fuzzy logic" is demonstrated.

1987: Immunologist Tonegawa Susumu (1939–) wins the Nobel Prize for Physiology and Medicine.

Nippon Telephone and Telegraph (along with IBM in the United States) introduces experimental 4- and 16-megabit chips.

Japanese companies introduce telephones on airplanes, with calls relayed by satellites.

Japanese investors purchase $26.34 billion in U.S. real estate, mostly in Hawaii, California, and New York. They go on to buy stakes in Rockefeller Center and the Chrysler Building. Sony will purchase CBS Records and Columbia Pictures.

1988: Yamaha introduces an electronic digitalized piano that uses compact discs (CDs) to direct the motion of keys.

March 13, 1988: The Seikan train tunnel from Honshu to Hokkaido, the world's longest to date, opens.

1988: Japan becomes the world's leading financial aid donor and creditor nation.

HEISEI PERIOD: 1989–1998

1989: Japan now controls about 90 percent of the world's market for 1-megabit DRAMs—dynamic random access memory chips, one of the basic components of computers. In June, seven leading U.S. computer and semiconductor firms announce that they intend to form a consortium to build DRAMs and thus challenge Japan's dominance. However, on June 22, IBM announces that it is already producing 4-megabit memory chips, instantly putting the Japanese behind in the race to make better computers. Within six months the Japanese share of the market begins to decline and the American firms decide not to form a consortium.

Japan initiates the first daily broadcasts of its analog version of high definition television (HDTV).

1990: Journalist Akiyama Toyohiro, on the Soviet *Soyuz TM-11*, is Japan's first man in space. In 1992, first astronaut Mori Mamoru travels on the U.S. *Endeavor* mission, followed by the first Japanese woman astronaut, Dr. Naito-Mukai Chiaki, aboard the *Columbia* in 1994 and by Koichi Wakata, the first astronaut to work full time in the U.S. shuttle program, on the 1996 *Endeavor* flight. In 1997, Takao Doi is first Japanese astronaut, during the *Columbia* mission, to walk in space.

December 31, 1990: After reaching an all-time high of 38,916 in December 1989, Japan's stock market Nikkei index falls to 23,838. Japan's financial troubles are traced to the threat to its oil supplies stemming from the crisis in the Persian Gulf.

1991: The Diet passes an antiracketeering law that affects sophisticated large crime syndicates known as *yakuza*, whose growth parallels and infiltrates the legitimate economy.

1993: Fujitsu announces that it is making a 256-megabit memory chip.

March 11, 1993: It is reported that of the

world's twenty-three developed countries, Japan has the lowest infant mortality rate—5 deaths per 1,000 births. (This compares to the U.S. ranking at twentieth, with 9.2 deaths per 1,000 births.)

December 14, 1993: The rice import ban is lifted; this follows several years of negotiations with the United States and other nations, seeking ways to alleviate large trade imbalances.

December 31, 1993: Japan's Nikkei stock market halts its two-year slide with the index ending the year at 17,417.

January 17, 1995: A powerful earthquake (7.2 on the Richter scale) strikes the area around Kobe; Japan's worst since 1923, it kills more than 5,000, injures more than 26,000, and leaves 300,000 homeless. The government is criticized for mishandling relief efforts.

December 31, 1995: After plunging to a new low of 15,381 in April, the Nikkei stock market index ends the year at 19,868.

January 30, 1996: Amateur astronomer Hyakutake Yuji first spots the brightest comet to approach Earth in four hundred years; it is named after him.

December 31, 1996: Japan's economy appears to be heading for a drastic downturn. Although the Nikkei stock market index remains stable at 19,361, bankruptcies are increasing, many large loans are going bad, banks and financial services are going under, and real estate and construction projects are failing.

December 31, 1997: The Nikkei stock market index collapses to a new low of 15,259; although blamed on the devaluation of its Asian neighbors' currencies, it is also due to Japan's failure to deal with its own domestic financial problems.

March 1998: Unemployment rises to 3.9 percent; although not high by many other nations' standards, this is Japan's highest since it began using the current method of calculating in 1953.

June 5, 1998: An international team of scientists led by Yoji Totsuko of the Kamioka Neutrino Observatory in Japan announces that neutrinos, subatomic particles long assumed to have no mass, do in fact have mass. This will force physicists to revise the standard model that explains particles and physical forces as the basis of all atomic physics.

Korea

EARLY HISTORY: 500,000–57 B.C.

Archaeological sites throughout Korea suggest that primitive humans inhabit the peninsula as early as 500,000 B.C. The well-excavated site at Sokchangni gives conclusive evidence of Late Paleolithic settlements, dating back to 30,000 B.C., that use a variety of crude stone tools to hunt and fish. The Ice Age and subsequent rise in sea level seem to obliterate these early populations, though some evidence may exist of late Mesolithic communities along the coast. The culture of the Neolithic Period passes through three distinct phases of development, each with its representative form of pottery. During the last of these three phases, agricultural methods are developed. As early as the ninth century B.C. northern cultures begin to use bronze in the manufacture of weapons and other items. These cultures develop a more advanced social organization that is the forerunner of the tribal federations that emerge in the fourth century B.C. Chief among these federations is Old Choson, which occupies much of the Liao and Taedong river basins. After a period of decline, Old Choson falls to Wiman, an exile from the Yan state in northern China. Wiman proves to be a strong ruler, but his ambitious program of expansion eventually brings him into conflict with the Han dynasty of China. The Han defeats Wiman Choson and establishes a protectorate over northern Korea in 108 B.C. Resistance to Chinese hegemony, however, is strong, and China reduces the territory under its active control to Nangnang (Luolang) colony with an administrative center near modern P'yongyang.

500,000 B.C.: According to radiocarbon testing of primitive tools found at Sokchangni (near Kongju) and Sangwon (near P'yongyang), the Korean peninsula begins to be inhabited about this time.

100,000–40,000 B.C.: Pre-Neanderthal and Neanderthal humans appear on the Korean peninsula. Evidence found in caves at Chommal (near Chechon) and Turubong (near Chongju) suggests a cave-dwelling culture that hunts, fishes, and gathers nuts and other vegetation. Small figurines found at these sites suggest the beginnings of an animistic faith.

30,000–20,000 B.C.: The upper layers of the Sokchangni excavation site show a more advanced culture developing on the peninsula. These people, perhaps early *Homo sapiens* of Mongoloid stock, dwell around hearths that they use for cooking and warmth; dwelling sites may have been enclosed. Like the Neanderthals, they carve figurines that suggest an animistic faith.

15,000 B.C.: Rock engravings at Sokchangni are the oldest known in East Asia.

8,000 B.C.: The beginning of Korea's Mesolithic era. Microliths found in some coastal sites suggest the existence of settlements from this time. However, as sea levels rise in the Atlantic Neolithic Period, these cultures are likely submerged.

6,000–5,000 B.C.: The first settlements of Neolithic man appear on the Korean peninsula. These settlements are confined mostly to coastal areas and are characterized by the use of a simple pottery that is either completely undecorated or adorned with short strips of clay affixed to the vessel's body. Pottery of this type is also found in Manchuria and Tsushima. This is the first of three distinctive periods of Neolithic culture in Korea. It is theorized that these three phases may correspond to three separate waves of southward migration.

4,000 B.C.: A distinctive combware pottery appears. This pottery, common to the Altaic tribes of Central Asia, is characterized by decorative strips of clay which have been wrapped around the body of the vessel in a manner evoking the scratches of a comb. The combware pottery is found mostly along the coast and near river beds, indicating that these people may depend heavily on fishing. Judging from hunting implements found at these sites, they also hunt animals such as deer and wild boar. They live in thatch huts built over a circular or square pit. These huts are clustered to form small communities.

2000 B.C.: A new type of pottery, characterized by its painted designs, appears throughout the Korean peninsula. What sort of interaction clans producing this type of pottery have with the combware clans is uncertain.

The two cultures seem to exist side by side, but ultimately the latter disappears as the former develops agricultural techniques.

2333 B.C.: According to a foundation myth recorded in the *Samguk yusa* (Memorabilia of the Three Kingdoms, 1285) and elsewhere, Tangun, a ruler born of the god Hwanung and a she-bear, founds the kingdom of Old Choson at modern P'yongyang. In the popular imagination this marks the beginning of the Korean state.

Unable to find a husband, the bear-woman prayed under an altar tree for a child. Hwanung metamorphosed himself, lay with her, and begot a son, called Tangun Wanggom. . . . In the fiftieth year of the reign of Emperor Yao, Tangun made the walled city of P'yongyang the capital and called his country Choson.

Foundation myth of Korea, from the *Samguk yusa* (Memorabilia of the Three Kingdoms), compiled by Buddhist monk Iryon (1285)

---

900 B.C.–300 B.C.: Korea's Bronze Age. An agricultural people using bronze daggers and bronze mirrors appear throughout the Sungari and Liao river basins. These people are the first Koreans to cultivate rice. Their fortified settlements, known as walled-town, or tribal, states are Korea's first organized political structures. The existence of dolmen tombs suggests a pronounced social hierarchy, inasmuch as these graves for the privileged would require an organized labor force for their construction. The culture of this period appears to be Scytho-Siberian in origin.

1122 B.C.: According to ancient Chinese texts, Kija (Viscount Chi) leads a band of Shang dynasty loyalists into Korea, and establishes a kingdom with its capital at P'yongyang.

***c.* 4th century B.C.:** Tribal federations such as Puyo, Yemaek, Old Choson, Imdun, and Chinbon emerge on the model of the

Bronze Age's walled-town state. Old Choson, the most powerful of these federations, traces its lineage to Tangun, the mythical ruler of 2333 B.C. The federation of Chin develops south of the Han River. Iron rapidly replaces bronze in the making of weapons and tools, particularly among members of the emergent ruling class. A unique heating system, called *ondol*, is also developed around this time: It consists of flues running under the floor bearing heat from a fire on one side of the house to a chimney on the other.

4th century–3d century B.C.: The three Korean Han societies emerge south of the Han River, an area once solely dominated by the Chin tribal confederation. Mahan occupies the west, Chinhan the east, Pyonhan the south of this region.

Late 4th century B.C.: The northern Chinese state of Yan invades the Liaodong Peninsula. Old Choson declines.

194–180? B.C.: Wiman, an important refugee from the Chinese state of Yen, usurps the Old Choson throne, establishes a rudimentary legal system, and greatly expands the kingdom's territory. Records kept during his reign are the first in Korea's history.

108 B.C.: The Han dynasty Emperor Wudi defeats Wiman and establishes four Chinese commanderies: Nangnang (Luolang), Chinbon (Zhenfan), Imdun (Lintun), and Hyondo (Xuantu). The Chinese do not press south of the Han River.

c. **1st century B.C.–1st century A.D.:** Three songs from Korea's earliest history have been handed down through several of Korea's histories. *Hwangjo ka* (Song of the Orioles) appears in the *Samguk sagi*, where it is given the date 17 B.C.; *Kuji ka*, or *Yong singnun ka* (Song of Welcoming the Gods) appears in the *Samguk yusa* (A.D. 42); and *Kong mudoha* (A Medley for Harp) appears in the *Haedong Yoksa*. These songs are sung at ritual occasions such as the harvest and sowing festivals, and may have been composed earlier than the 1st century B.C.

Oh lilting, joyous yellow bird!
You mate to live, and love each other;
While I, alas, unloved, unheard
Have lost my everything, sweet brother.

> *Hwangjo ka* (Song of the Orioles), believed to be
> Korea's earliest extant poem, unknown author
> (*c.* 17 B.C.)

---

82 B.C.: Due to the persistent resistance of local populations, particularly the emergent Koguryo people, the Chinese abandon outposts in Chinbon and Imdun.

75 B.C.: Chinese abandon Hyondo, leaving Nangnang as the last region directly administered by Chinese officials.

THE THREE KINGDOMS PERIOD: 57 B.C.–A.D. 668

While actively resisting Chinese sovereignty, local populations assimilate much of China's culture and adopt many of its legal and ethical precepts. Consequently, from the loose tribal organizations of the past emerge legitimate states with a highly stratified social system culminating in a monarch. By the third century A.D. Paekche in the southwest, Silla in the southeast, and Koguryo in the north emerge as the dominant kingdoms south of the Liao and Sungari rivers, while Kaya, with strong connections to Japan, occupies the peninsula's southern tip. In 313 Koguryo seizes the territory of the last remaining Chinese colony. China, however, continues to influence the political theater with diplomatic arrangements designed to keep the peninsula fragmented and susceptible to repossession. This policy backfires as Tang dynasty rulers lend their support to Silla only to witness the peninsula firmly unified under Silla governance by the end of the seventh century. During this period, Buddhism takes hold in all three kingdoms.

It combines with Confucian ideals and ancient beliefs and practices to form the fabric of Korea's national consciousness. Several of Korea's first histories, including Paekche's *Sogi* (Documentary Records) and Koguryo's *Yugi* (Extant Records), are compiled.

57 B.C.: The legendary date for the founding of the kingdom of Silla. In fact, the "kingdom" at this point consists solely of what is to be its nucleus, the walled-town state of Saro located near the Naktong River in southeast Korea.

37 B.C.: According to legend, Chumong founds the kingdom of Koguryo in a region centered on the middle Yalu and the T'ungchia River basin. The state at this juncture is probably still in transition from a loose confederation of tribes to a monarchy.

18 B.C.: According to legend, Onjo founds the kingdom of Paekche in the Mahan area of southwest Korea. However, like Silla and Koguryo, Paekche is more likely still in transition from a tribal federation to a monarchy at this juncture.

1st century A.D.: Puyo emerges as a powerful tribal federation in northern Manchuria. Its people are primarily settled along the Sungari River. Puyo rivals Koguryo to the south and forges a conciliatory policy toward China.

A.D. 30: Some Nangnang gentry lead a rebellion against the Chinese administration, but are suppressed by Chinese forces. Many seek refuge south of the Han River.

53–146: Reign of Koguryo's sixth ruler, King T'aejo. He secures the right to succession for his clan, the Ko house of the Kyeru lineage, adopts a more aggressive policy toward China, and greatly expands Koguryo's territory by subjugating the Okcho and Eastern Ye peoples who had occupied Korea's northeast littoral. A rudimentary bureaucracy centered in Kungnaesong develops at this time.

206: In an effort to check the growing power of the Korean societies south of the Han River, Chinese administrators of Nangnang establish control of the area once governed as Chinbon. The territory is called Taebang (Taifang).

234–286: Reign of King Koi, the eighth ruler of Paekche. He firmly establishes Paekche's dominance of the former Mahan area, develops a rudimentary bureaucracy centered in Hansong, and secures the right of succession for his heirs. A policy of northward expansion begins.

Mid-3d century: Kaya emerges as a kingdom with dominion over the southern tip of the peninsula.

313: Koguryo seizes the territories of China's Nangnang colony ending China's four-hundred-year presence on the peninsula.

Mid–late 4th century: Scholar Kohong writes a history of Paekche entitled *Sogi* (Documentary Records). Other histories follow including *Paekcheki* (Records of Paekche), *Paekche pon'gi* (Basic Annals of Paekche), and *Paekche sinch'an* (New History of Paekche).

346–375: Reign of King Konch'ogo, the thirteenth ruler of Paekche. He strengthens the authority of the throne and initiates a campaign of territorial expansion.

356–401: Reign of King Naemul, the seventeenth ruler of Silla. By forging close ties with Koguryo he is able to stave off the aggressive Paekche. He is the first Silla ruler to secure the right of succession to the throne for his heirs.

371: Paekche pushes north and defeats Koguryo in a battle at P'yongyang.

371–384: King Sosurium, the seventeenth ruler of Koguryo, establishes Buddhism (375) as the spiritual foundation of the state and Confucius's teachings as the legal basis. He extends the Chinese-influenced bureaucracy and commissions the *Yugi*, a history of Koguryo that has not survived.

372: Sosurium establishes T'aehak—a royal academy to train prospective government officials in Chinese language and the Confucian classics.

384: A Serindian monk named Malananda introduces Buddhism into Paekche. In the same year Mukhoja, a monk from Koguryo introduces Buddhism into Silla, but the doctrine is not accepted by the state and adherents suffer persecution.

391–412: Reign of King Kwanggaet'o, the nineteenth ruler of Koguryo. Allying himself with Silla, he embarks on a number of military campaigns that greatly enlarge Koguryo territory. Conquests include Liaodong in the west, much of Manchuria to the north, and the region between the Imjin and Han rivers formerly controlled by Paekche to the south. In addition, he routs Japanese invaders in the Silla-controlled Naktong river basin.

5th–6th centuries: Large tomb chambers are built along the Yalu River. Elaborately decorated with fresco-type murals, the tombs provide the most vivid and enduring picture of Koguryo art. The style of these paintings, particularly the use of real and fantastic animals, reflects a Central Asian influence. The scale of the tombs, which probably required a large labor force dedicated to the honor of an important person, indicates an increasingly stratified social system.

400: Japan attacks Silla. Koguryo sends assistance and the Japanese are repelled.

His gracious beneficence blended with that of August Heaven; and with his majesty military virtue he encompassed the four seas like a willow tree and swept out, thus bringing tranquillity to his rule. His people flourished in a wealthy state, and the five grains ripened abundantly. But Imperial Heaven was pitiless, and at thirty-nine he expired in majesty, forsaking his realm.

Part of an inscription on a stele dedicated to King Kwanggaet'o (391–413) of Koguryo, erected in 414

413–491: Reign of King Changsu, the twentieth ruler of Koguryo. He establishes a policy of southern expansion.

414: Stone monument consisting of 1,800 seal script characters is erected in Kungnaesong to honor King Kwanggaet'o. The monument, discovered in 1875, is one of the best preserved examples of early Korean calligraphy and relates in relative detail the various conquests of the king.

427: King Changsu moves the Koguryo capital southward from Kungnaesong to P'yongyang. The move reflects a need for an effective metropolitan center from which to govern the provinces of Koguryo's advancing southern frontier.

433: Paekche establishes an alliance with Silla against the aggressive Koguryo.

475: The Paekche capital, Hansong, falls to Koguryo troops. Paekche establishes a new capital at Ungjin, where it remains for sixty-three years.

494: Koguryo absorbs the remaining Puyo tribes in the north.

500–514: Reign of King Chijong, the twenty-second ruler of Silla. He is the first Silla ruler to adopt the Chinese title *wang* (king).

514–540: Reign of King Pophong, the twenty-third ruler of Silla. He extends territory by defeat of the Pon Kaya tribe in Naktong River basin.

520: Pophong promulgates a code of administrative law and institutes the "bone rank" system, a codification of Silla's increasingly stratified social system.

523–554: Reign of King Song, the twenty-sixth ruler of Paekche. He moves the capital to Sabi (modern Puyo) in 538 and forges close ties to the Liang dynasty in southern China and to Japan. Buddhism flourishes and is conveyed to Japan.

***c.* 527:** Silla recognizes Buddhism. Monks are accepted into highest social order (*hwarang*), and the state, hitherto the least culturally evolved of the Three Kingdoms, strengthens its stability by giving religious justification for the authority of its rulers.

539: Korea's oldest extant Buddhist image is cast in bronze. The simple figurine depicts a standing Buddha with eyes closed and one hand raised in the manner of a blessing.

Found in Koguryo, South Yonngsang province, it is unclear where the image was cast.

540–575: Reign of King Chinhong, the twenty-fourth ruler of Silla. He initiates a policy of territorial expansion.

551–554: Silla and Paekche attack Koguryo's territories along the Han River basin. Having seized upper reaches of the Han River basin, Silla turns on its ally, Paekche, in a gambit to control the entire Han region. In 554, Paekche makes a counterattack on Silla led by King Song himself. The attack fails and Song is killed.

562: Silla conquers Tae Kaya, the last of the Kaya tribes. Kaya refugees settle in Japan.

590&ndash618: Reign of King Yongsangyang, the twenty-sixth ruler of Koguryo.

598: Emperor Wendi of China begins the first of several campaigns to subdue Koguryo. Koguryo mounts a successful defense and counterattack.

612: Emperor Yangdi of China mounts a massive invasion of Koguryo. Under the leadership of General Olchi Mundok, Koguryo once again repels the invaders. The emperor launches several more campaigns (613, 614) but fails to gain any advantage. These costly military failures contribute to the downfall of the Sui in 618.

631: Koguryo completes construction of elaborate fortifications along the Liao River in an effort to discourage Chinese aggression.

632–647: Reign of Queen Sondok, the twenty-seventh ruler of Silla. During her reign the Son, or Meditation, School of Buddhism is introduced. The faith, however, remains esoteric until the ninth century and the founding of the Nine Mountain Sects of Son.

633: One of Korea's oldest extant monuments, a stone observatory called Ch'omsongdae, is erected. The observatory is evidence of an increased concern with astronomy and calendrical science.

642–655: Paekche, confident of Koguryo and Japanese support, mounts an offensive against Silla. Despite modest territorial gains, their diplomatic position vis-à-vis China is significantly weakened.

644–659: China's Tang dynasty attempts several invasions of Koguryo, but is unable to penetrate the Liao River fortifications.

660: Combined Tang and Silla forces attack Paekche and swiftly achieve complete victory. Paekche surrenders on July 18, 660.

667: The Tang-Silla alliance launches an offensive against Koguryo, whose resources have been depleted by decades of Chinese aggression.

Autumn 668: P'yongyang falls and the Koguryo kingdom comes to an end. Tang moves to establish control of the fallen Paekche and Koguryo territories. Koguryo refugees flee north to establish the kingdom of Parhae.

SILLA UNIFICATION: 670–936

Having successfully resisted Chinese maneuvers to reestablish dominance on the peninsula, Silla fixes its northern border at a line extending from the Bay of Wonsan to the Taedong River. The strength of the aristocracy weakens, which consequently alleviates tendencies towards internal strife and allows the Muyol legacy to rule uncontested for over a hundred years. Meanwhile Koguryo refugees led by Tae Choyong establish the Parhae kingdom to the north.

Assimilation of Paekche and Koguryo cultures, the continued prosperity of Buddhism, and political stability combine to have a salubrious effect on the arts in Silla. Scholars, most notably Sol Ch'ong, develop *idu*, a system of transcribing Korean phonetics using Chinese characters; *hyangga*, a genre of vernacular poetry that appeared in late Three Kingdoms Silla, flourishes;

painting and sculpture continue to develop, particularly in treatment of Buddhist themes; and porcelain begins to replace earthenware, particularly in ceremonial usage.

In the late eighth century, however, conflict arises in the aristocracy, and Silla enters a period of decline. As the authority of the throne diminishes, the power of competing aristocratic families increases. Silla attempts to gain more control of its provinces in 889 with a drive to collect taxes, but this fails as the country erupts into a series of peasant rebellions. Later Paekche and Koryo emerge from this chaos, as Silla falls back on the domain surrounding Kyongju's capital. Around this time the Khitan tribes overrun the north as members of Paekche's ruling class join the strengthening Koryo state. Silla surrenders what is left of its authority to Koryo in 935. The following year Later Paekche collapses.

c. 670: Construction begins on Anap Pond and Imhae Hall, a new residence for Silla's monarch.

671: Silla assumes control of regions once held by the Paekche kingdom. The Chinese vie for control for these same regions, but are driven back by Silla.

676: After a string of victories in the Han River basin, Silla drives the remaining Tang troops from Korean soil.

677–684?: Wonhyo (617–686) writes *Palsim suhaeng chang* (Arouse Your Mind and Practice!), a seminal article in Buddhist literature. Wonhyo's writings, particularly his numerous scriptural commentaries, exert a considerable influence on Korean, Chinese, and Japanese thought.

681–692: Reign of King Sinmun, the thirty-first ruler of Silla, a direct descendent of King Muyol. In 681, after a coup led by Kim Homdol fails, Sinmun instigates a decisive purge of all political opponents, the consequence of which is a further strengthening of royal authority.

Late 7th century—early 8th century: Scholars, most notably Sol Ch'ong (c. 660–730), develop *idu*, a system for transcribing Korean phonetics into Chinese characters.

682: Kukhak, a royal Confucian college, is founded in Silla. In 750 the name is changed to T'aehak.

685: Silla is divided into nine provinces (*chu*) to be administered by governors appointed from the aristocratic class. These governors are forced to relocate from Kyongju to the respective capitals of their provinces. The nine *chu* are Sangju, Yangju, and Kwangju from the former Silla-Kaya territories; Ungju, Chonju, and Muju from the former Paekche territories; and Hanju, Sakchu, and Myongju from the former Koguryo territories. These provinces are then divided into prefectures (*kun*) and finally counties (*hyon*).

699: In the area of southern Manchuria once dominated by the state of Puyo, the former Koguryo general Tae Choyong establishes the kingdom of Chin. He assumes the title King Ko and rules over a population that consists primarily of Koguryo (hereafter to remain the society's aristocracy) and the seminomadic Malgal people. In 713 the name of kingdom becomes Parhae.

Early 8th century: The scholar Kim Taemun writes a number of books that chronicle the development of Silla culture. None of these works is extant, but evidence exists that they contributed to the later *Samguk sagi* (Historical Records of the Three Kingdoms).

8th century–10th century: *Hyangga*, a vernacular verse genre, flourishes. Twenty-five songs of this form are extant, fourteen in the *Samguk yusa* (Memorabilia of the Three Kingdoms, 1285), and eleven devotional songs of Great Master Kyunyo in the *Knunyochon* (Life of Kyunyo, 1075).

702–737: Reign of King Songdok, a direct descendant of King Muyol and the thirty-third ruler of Silla. Conflicts with the Tang resolved, and the nobility submissive to the throne, Silla begins a period of domestic peace and cultural growth. Parhae, however, emerges as a threat to the northern border.

705: A political climate conducive to commerce helps Parhae establish diplomatic relations with Tang China.

711?: Kim Saeng, Silla's most renowned calligrapher, is born. No examples of Kim's calligraphy are extant.

721: Recognizing the threat of Parhae, Silla heavily fortifies its northern border.

722: A land distribution system called *Chongjonje* (able-bodied land) is instituted in Silla. The system, which is an adaptation of Chinese notions, allots arable land to families based on the number of males between the ages of twenty and sixty.

725: Korea's oldest extant bronze bell is cast at Sangwon Monastery on Mount Odae.

733: An alliance of Tang and Silla troops mounts an unsuccessful invasion of Parhae territories.

Mid-8th century?: A copy of the *Dharani* scripture found beneath a pagoda at Pulguk monastery (erected 751) indicates that Silla develops the art of woodblock printing around this time. The process is used to disseminate Buddhist and Confucian materials.

742–765: Reign of King Kyongdok, the thirty-fifth ruler of Silla. Although his reign marks the pinnacle of Silla prosperity, discontent among the aristocracy grows.

751: Construction of Pulguk Monastery and Sokkuram grotto. These monuments exhibit in their art an advanced religious awareness, and in their engineering a sophisticated mathematical knowledge.

765–780: Reign of King Hyegong, the thirty-sixth ruler of Silla.

768–774: Kim Taegong's plot against the throne touches off six years of political chaos, as a number of prominent nobles vie for power. Kim Yangsang emerges from the fray to seize control of the government and reduce King Hyegong to a mere figurehead.

771: Korea's largest bronze bell is cast at Pangdok Temple and dedicated to King Songdok.

780: Kim Yangsang assassinates King Hyegong and usurps the throne as King Sondok. The political stability enjoyed by Silla in the century following the rule of Muyol is never again to be attained. Intraclan struggles and decentralization of power ensue.

Late 8th century: The astronomer Kim Am writes a treatise influenced by Chinese occult arts, entitled *Tun'gap ipsong pop* (The Principles of Evading Stems).

785–798: Reign of King Wonsong, the thirty-eighth ruler of Silla. Despite the political tumult that predominates in Silla, his descendants hold the throne until 935, when the last Silla king, Ky'ongsun, surrenders to Wang Kon, the founder of the kingdom of Koryo.

788: An examination system for the selection of public officials is inaugurated in Silla. The system, like that of the Chinese, is primarily concerned with knowledge of the Confucian classics.

Early 9th century: At Porim Monastery the monk Tooi founds the Mount Kaji sect of the Son School of Buddhism. This leads to the establishment of the Nine Mountain Sects of Son.

819–830: Reign of King Son, the tenth ruler of Parhae. The kingdom reaches its height, its territory extending to the Amur River in the north, the Hamgyong region of the Korean peninsula in the south, central Manchuria in the west, and the Sea of Japan in the east.

822: Kim Honch'ang, a descendent of King Muyol, rebels against Wonsong. Despite some initial success the rebellion fails.

828: Chang Pogo establishes the Ch'onghae Garrison on Wan Island. With troops that number as many as ten thousand men he is able to subdue piracy in the area of the Yellow Sea and control trade with Japan and China. He is the most important example of the increasing independence of aristocratic families in Silla's outlying provinces.

834: In an attempt to curb the growing decadence of Silla society and its need of Chinese imports, King Hongdok issues a decree restricting ostentatious displays of wealth.

836–839: For three years after the death of King Hongdok several members of the Kim clan vie for the throne. Four kings come to the throne in three years.

839: With the support of Chang Pogo, Kim Ujing ascends to the throne as King Sinmu.

839–857: Reign of Sinmu's son King Munsong over Silla.

846: Chang Pogo is assassinated.

851: Ch'onghae Garrison is abolished.

885: Ch'oe Ch'iwon returns from China to take his place in the Silla court as an honored Confucian scholar. Upon his return he is active in criticizing the rigidity of Silla's "bone rank" system, a codification of its levels of aristocracy.

887–897: Reign of Queen Chinsong, the fifty-first ruler of Silla. She commissions the monks Taegu and Wi Hong to compile an anthology of *hyangga* (vernacular poems). Entitled *Samdae mok* (Collection of Hyangga from the Three Periods of Silla History, 888), it is no longer extant.

889: In an effort to exert a more direct control over its provinces, Silla's Kyongju court forces tax collections in all outlying areas under its dominion. This results in numerous peasant uprisings throughout the country. The first of these rebellions erupts in Pugwon in Sangju in 888.

892: Kyonhwon, a leader of peasant uprisings in Kwangju and later in Chonju, proclaims himself sole monarch over the territories in his control. He calls this kingdom Later Paekche (*Hu Paekche*) in an effort to provide legitimacy to his throne.

Late 9th century–early 10th century: Monk Toson (d. 898) systematizes a theory of geomancy that combines Daoist and Buddhist elements. Wang Kon, the founder of the Koryo dynasty (reigned 918–943), later uses Toson's principles to justify the transfer of power on the peninsula away from Kyongju to his native region of Songak. Such calculated use of geomancy becomes a common political strategy in the years of the Koryo dynasty.

901: Kungye, a former Silla prince who had emerged as a formidable commander in the peasant uprisings, proclaims himself king of a territory encompassing large parts of Kangwon, Kyonggi, and Hwanghae provinces. He calls the kingdom Later Koguryo, but later changes the name to T'aebong.

918: Wang Kon (posthumously King T'aejo) deposes Kungye as the ruler of T'aebong, moves the capital to Songak (Kaesong), and renames the kingdom Koryo. His military genius and his ability to garner support from local gentry prove instrumental in Koryo's drive to reunify the peninsula under its banner. Wang Kon establishes a conciliatory policy toward Silla and concentrates his attention on his campaign against Later Paekche.

September 20, 923–July 19, 973: Life of Great Master Kyunyo, the great practitioner of *hyangga* and devout Buddhist. Through his teachings and poems written in the vernacular he does much to popularize Buddhism.

926: The Khitan conquer the Parhae territories. Members of Parhae's ruling class flee to join the emergent Koryo kingdom.

927: Kyonhwon of Later Paekche raids Kyongju, the capital of Silla. He orders King Kyongae to commit suicide, abducts members of the royal family, and pillages the city's treasures. He is repulsed only by Wang Kon's intervention on behalf of Silla.

935: Ruling over a kingdom that in reality does not extend beyond Kyongju, Silla's last king, Ky'ongsun, surrenders his authority to Wang Kon.

936: Later Paekche collapses. Koryo remains the sole power on the peninsula.

KORYO: 918–1392

Wang Kon, posthumously known as T'aejo, establishes command of the Korean peninsula. He creates a new aristocratic order favoring former Silla aristocrats and provincial lords, but is also careful to reward the military leaders who had brought him to power. Subsequent rulers, however, gradually push aside the military elite and local magnates, and promote civil officials supportive of a strong central government. The Mongolian-Khitan invasions of the late tenth century challenge the stability of the Koryo government, but a period of prosperity follows the defeat of the Khitan in 1018. Trade flourishes, extending as far abroad as the Middle East, and a number of important scholarly works are compiled, including the *Samguk sagi* (Historical Records of the Three Kingdoms). In 1170, the discontent of military officers erupts into a series of rebellions from which Chong Chungbu emerges as leader. A succession of military dictatorships follow, notably the Ch'oe "shogunate," which rules Korea from 1196 until 1258. A new bureaucratic class, known as the *sadaebu*, or literati, emerges during military rule. It is this group of well-educated but low-level government officials that gravitate towards the Neoconfucian ideals of Ju Xi. It is also this group that is responsible for a number of developments in Korean literature, principally the *kyonggi*-style poetry and prose tales, essays, and biographies best typified by the work of Yi Kyubo. In 1231, despite a brief alliance in the struggle against the Jurchen, a Manchurian people, the Mongols turn on Koryo and demand fealty. A long, bloody war ensues, but in 1259 the court of Wonong seeks peace with the Mongols. In the fourteenth century various factions within Koryo vie with one another to fill the power vacuum left by the Mongols, whose empire rapidly declines in the later half of the century. Yi Songgye emerges from this imbroglio to usher in a new era of Korean history.

918–943: Reign of King T'aejo (Wang Kon). He adopts a lenient policy toward provincial magnates and appeases the Silla aristocracy by appointing them to high posts in the new government. He issues ten injunctions to serve as the basis of future government. In these injunctions he stresses the importance of national defense, Buddhism, unity among the aristocratic clans, and the strength of local government.

Would that all my merit
Might be passed on to others
I would like to awaken them —
Those wandering in the sea of suffering.

"Transfer of Merit," Great Master Kyunyo (10th century)

937: The Khitan, a seminomadic Mongolian people ruling over much of former Parhae, establish the Liao kingdom.

945–949: Reign of Chongjong. Hoping to transfer the capital to P'yongyang, Chongjong undertakes a massive renewal project in that city. The capital, however, remains in Kaesong.

949–975: Reign of Kwangjong.

956: Kwangjong restores all slaves to commoner status. This act increases the central government's tax base and concomitantly weakens the power of local rulers.

958: Kwangjong establishes a civil service examination system based on merit. A new bureaucratic order is established, diminishing the power of military officials, who had been instrumental in securing the supremacy of the Koryo kingdom.

975–981: Reign of Kyongjong.

976: The Stipend Land Law (*chonsikwa*) is enacted. The law provides grants of land to a few privileged members of the civil government. In 998 a comprehensive land allotment system is devised.

981–997: Reign of Songjong. Throughout his reign Songjong is particularly attentive to the views of Confucian scholars, notably Ch'oe Songno (927–989). His reforms, such as the appointment of district officials by the central government, tend to strengthen the central bureaucracy at the expense of the local aristocracy.

983: Songjong establishes twelve provinces (*mok*). The administrators of these provinces are appointed by the court in Kaesong.

983–993: The Mongolian-Khitan kingdom of Liao makes a number of attacks on Koryo's northern border, principally in 983, 985, 989, and 993. Koryo erects fortifications along the south bank of the Yalu River.

985: Envoys from Koryo travel to Beijing, China, to make a formal request for military assistance in their struggle against Liao. Faced with severe threats to its own security, the Song court refuses.

989: Just before his death Ch'oe Songno presents a twenty-eight point memorial outlining his vision of Koryo's ideal government. The memorial includes his estimation of the first five reigns of the Koryo dynasty, and his opinion of the reforms required to fulfill the promise of T'aejo.

992: The Royal Confucian Academy (Kukchagam) is established in Kaesong.

993: Koryo's commanding general So Hoi (940–998) negotiates a peace treaty with Liao. Koryo's northern boundary is recognized at the Yalu River.

994: Diplomatic relations open between Liao and Koryo. A Koryo military campaign to purge its northwest frontier of Manchurian and Jurchen tribes proves successful.

996: Coins are minted, but a money economy is slow to take root.

997–1009: Reign of Mokchong.

998: The Stipend Land Law, enacted in 976, is comprehensively revised. Under the new system, the Kaesong court allocates land to government officials in proportion to their rank. A given lot is not inheritable, but passes to the next incumbent of the position to which that lot is attached. This particular stipulation enforces the notion that all land

belongs to the king. Military officials, whose rank in this system is not high, are thereby deprived of sizable portions of land. Resentment among the military officials culminates in the coup d'état of 1014.

1009: Fearful of plots against him, Mokchong summons Kang Cho from his administrative post in the northwest. However, Kang Cho himself engineers a successful coup in which Mokchong is assassinated.

1009–1031: Reign of Hyonjong.

1010: Liao initiates a fresh attack on Koryo's northern border with the ostensible purpose of avenging the murdered Mokchong. Liao troops penetrate Koryo's Yalu fortifications and capture and execute Kang Cho. Kaesong falls. The Koryo court flees south to Naju.

1011: The process of carving woodblocks for Korea's first printing of the Buddhist canon (the *Tripitaka*) begins. The project is undertaken at the direction of the Hyonjong court in part to petition the Buddha's aid in the struggle against Liao, and in part to solidify the authority of the state religion. Son (Meditation School) documents are excluded in deference to the Kyo (Doctrinal School). The process takes seventy-seven years to complete.

c. **1014:** Hyonjong commissions Ch'oe Hang to compile a history of the Koryo kingdom from T'aejo to Mokchong.

1014: Incensed at the growing dominance of civil officials, military officers stage a successful coup d'état. Hyonjong remains the king, but the government comes under the control of Kim Hun and Ch'oe Chil, two military leaders who had taken leading roles in the coup.

1017: Silsangt'ap, a noted stupa memorializing National Preceptor Hongpop, is erected at Chongt'o Monastery.

1018: The Hyonjong court restructures local government. It divides the country into a capital region (*kyonggi*), five large administrative units (*to*), and two regions (*kye*) of particular strategic importance along the northern boundary and northeast littoral. In addition to Kaesong the court establishes P'yongyang as the western capital and Kyongju as the eastern capital. Kyongju's status as capital is later revoked in deference to a nuance of geomancy, and Hanyang (present-day Seoul) is named as the southern capital. It also creates five regional military commands (*tohobu*) and realigns the provinces (*mok*) so that they number eight. It further divides provinces into districts (*kun*), counties (*hyon*), and garrisons (*chin*).

1018: The Mongolian-Khitan troops of Liao, led by Xiao Baiya, cross into Koryo territory. The army is badly beaten at Anju by Koryo troops under the command of General Kamch'an. Lines of retreat are cut by General Minch'on. Facing complete surrender, the Khitans risk an attack on the capital. The attack fails.

1029: An outer wall around Kaesong, begun at General Kamch'an's direction, is completed.

1044: A stone wall fortifying Koryo's northern border is completed.

1046–1083: Reign of Munjong.

Mid-eleventh century: Ch'oe Ch'ung (984–1068) establishes the Nine Course Academy for the study of the Confucian classics and Chinese history. A dozen other schools modeled after Ch'oe Ch'ung's are subsequently founded. These academies are dubbed the Twelve Assemblies (*Sibi to*), and eventually supersede the prestige of the Royal Confucian Academy (*Kukchagam*).

1067: Hongwang Monastery, begun at the direction of T'aejo, is completed.

1085: Hyonmyot'ap, a noted stupa memorializing National Preceptor Chigwang, is erected at Popch'on Monastery.

1087: The first set of woodblocks for Koryo's *Tripitaka* is completed.

1090: Oich'on (1055–1101), also known as National Preceptor Taegak, publishes his *Sokchanggyong* (Supplement to the Canon), an anthology of commentaries and treatises by East Asian Buddhists not included in the *Tripitaka*. Oich'on had long championed an

extension of the predominantly Indian canon. He also strives to bring Koryo's conflicting schools of Buddhism into harmony.

1103–1122: Reign of Yejong. During his reign Yejong does much to restore the preeminence of the state academies. He establishes a scholarship foundation called the Fund for Nurturing Worthies (*Yanghyon'go*), and on the palace grounds builds academic institutes called the Ch'ongyon and the Pomun pavilions.

1104: In a move portending the ascendancy of the Jurchen, Wu Youzi attacks Koryo. He penetrates as far as Chongp'yong (Chongju).

1107: Yun Kwan leads a Koryo force across the Chongp'yong pass driving back the Jurchen. He penetrates Jurchen territory as far as Hongwon.

1108: Having driven back the Jurchen, Yun Kwan secures the northern frontier with the construction of nine fortresses, and encourages immigration as a means of establishing Koryo sovereignty. However, withering under persistent Jurchen attacks, Koryo abandons the territory.

1115: Conflict on the northern border intensifies as the Jurchen proclaim the Jin empire and begin a successful campaign against the Khitan kingdom of Liao.

1122–1146: Reign of Injong. He does much to advance the system of education, establishing schools in rural areas and dividing the Royal Confucian Academy (*Kukchagam*) into several colleges. Entrance requirements for a specific college within the National University are based on class. A number of eminent scholars emerge from the schools established by Injong, most notably the compiler of the *Samguk sagi*, Kim Pusik (1075–1151). The painter Yi Yong is thought to have painted his masterpiece, *Yesong River Scene*, during Injong's reign.

1125–1127: Having conquered Liao and China's Northern Song, the Jurchen Jin demand that Koryo acknowledge their suzerainty. Primarily due to the persuasions of Yi Changyom, the father-in-law of Injong,

Koryo capitulates, becoming in name a vassalage of the Jin empire.

1126: Learning of a plot against his life, Yi Changyom sets fire to the palace buildings, including the royal library and the national academy. Thousands of books, including early examples of woodblock printing, are lost.

1135–1136: The monk Myoch'ong proclaims a secessionist kingdom and names P'yongyang as his capital. The Kaesong court dispatches troops led by Kim Pusik, who defeats the rebel army and beheads its leaders.

1145: Injong commissions the Confucian scholar Kim Pusik to compile the *Samguk sagi* (Historical Records of the Three Kingdoms). This is the oldest extant record of Korea's history. It draws heavily on earlier historical records, the *Sogi* and the *Yugi*, that are now lost.

1146–1170: Reign of Oijong. His weakness as ruler allows top civil officials to enlarge their power at the expense of both throne and the military elite.

Mid-12th century: Koryo ceramists develop the technique of *sanggam*, a process for delineating designs using inlaying as opposed to carving or incising. The celadon porcelain of this time is generally considered among the finest ceramic art ever produced in the world. It is characterized by the simple elegance of its form and the delicacy of its colors due to the mineral nephrite, a light-green variety of jade.

1170: The military elite led by Chong Chungbu, Yi Oibang, and Yi Ko orchestrate a quick and bloody coup against the central government. Every attendant to the king and every bureaucrat in residence at the palace is killed. Oijong is spared, but exiled to Koje Island. Following the murders of Yi Ko and Yi Oibang, Chong Chungbu emerges as Koryo's despotic ruler. Military leaders establish for themselves a monopoly on government positions, thus mirroring the abuses of the supplanted civil officials.

1171–1190: Reign of Prince Ho (posthumously named Myongjong). He remains the puppet of various military dictators throughout his reign.

1172: Soldiers in the western border region (P'yongan province) rebel against local officials. This is the first in a number of popular uprisings that plague Koryo into the thirteenth century.

1173: Kim Podang leads a rebellion in the northeast but is quickly defeated.

1174: The governor of P'yongyang makes a failed attempt at secession.

Late 12th century: The monk Chinul (1158–1210) propagates the teachings of the Chogye sect of Buddhism. The Chogye sect grew out of Oich'on's efforts to fuse the Kyo and Son schools of Buddhist thought. Unlike Oich'on, however, Chinul places an emphasis on the meditation school. This break from the canon did much to foster a uniquely Korean Buddhist tradition.

1176: A peasant uprising erupts near Kongju. The rebellion spreads through Ch'ungch'ong province before it is put down by government troops. Other outbreaks occur throughout the country.

1179: General Kyong Taesong supplants Chong Chungbu as Koryo's dictator. He dies, however, not long afterward. Yi Oimin subsequently seizes power.

1182: Soldiers and government slaves rebel against local officials in Chongju. After holding the city for forty days they surrender to government troops.

1193–1202: The popular uprisings of the previous decades intensify as rebel bands join forces and set their sights beyond the seizure of local power. The first such alliance is between Kim Sami and Hyosim in the South (1193). In 1199 the rebels of Myongju (Kangnong) join forces with rebels from Kyongju. Slaves and peasants unite at Hapch'on in 1200, and in 1202 Ch'ongdo and Olchin rebels join the struggle of the Kyongju people. These uprisings are eventually suppressed by the military dictatorship of Ch'oe Ch'unghon.

1196: Ch'oe Ch'unghon (1149–1219) overthrows Yi Oimin. He purges all opposition to his rule and removes the last vestiges of authority from the throne. He and his successors rule Koryo as a sort of shogunate until 1258.

1197: Choe Ch'unghon deposes Myongjong and installs the completely submissive Sinjong (reigns 1197–1204).

1198: The would-be social reformer Manjok plots a slave rebellion within Kaesong. The plot is discovered before any uprising occurs.

Late 12th–early 13th centuries: Excluded from an active role in the military regime, several Confucian scholars devote their time to the production of Korea's first sustained narratives. A notable example of the form is Yi Kyubo's (1168–1241) *Kuk sonsaeng chon* (Story of Mr. John Barleycorn). Yi Kyubo also writes at this time the verse narrative *Tongmyong wang p'yon* (Saga of King Tongmyong), significant for its patriotic themes.

1204–1258: Despite the succession of kings Hoijong (1204–1211), Kanjong (1211–1213), and Kojong (1213–1259), power remains in the hands of the Ch'oe military regime.

1215: Mongols conquer the Jin empire; many Khitan flee into Koryo's northern regions. Koryo joins forces with the Mongols to subdue the Khitan refugees.

1219: The Khitan surrender to the Mongol-Koryo alliance at Kangdong fortress east of P'yongyang.

1231: A Mongolian army led by Sartaq invades Koryo, allegedly to revenge the murder of a Mongolian diplomat in 1225. As the Mongols advance on Kaesong, Yu Songdan (1168–1232) negotiates a peace. The Mongols leave military governors (*daruhaci*) to govern Koryo.

1232: Ch'oe U rejects the Mongol peace proposal and moves the Koryo court to Kanghwa Island, where it remains severed from contact with its ostensible subjects.

1232–1270: War with the Mongols continues.

While the court continues its residence on the well-fortified Kanghwa Island, peasants continue to resist the Mongols on the peninsula, often meeting with devastating losses.

c. 1235–1251: Seeking Buddha's aid in the struggle against the Mongols, the court on Kanghwa Island commissions woodblocks for a second Buddhist *Tripitaka*. This work, commonly known as the "Eighty Thousand *Tripitaka*" (after its still surviving woodblocks), takes sixteen years to finish and is recognized as the finest of the East Asian editions of the *Tripitaka*.

1236: *Hyangya kugop pang* (Emergency Remedies of Folk Medicine), Korea's first compilation of indigenous medical science, is published.

1249: Ch'oe U dies. In addition to his status as Korea's most powerful ruler, he was renowned as a great calligrapher, and is often referred to as one of "The Four Worthies of Divine Calligraphy." The other three are Kim Saeng (born 711?), Yu Sin (died 1104), and T'anyon (1070–1159).

The morning dew alights, the evening mist is
  there,
The angry dragon lifts his claw, the phoenix
  flies;
'Twas God who made you what you are:
Wonderful! No words can tell.

   Poem by Yi Kyubo on the calligrapher Kim Saeng
   (13th century)

1254: Jalairtai leads a decisive Mongol invasion. Over 200,000 Koryo subjects are captured, and many more perish; the Hwanyong Monastery is burned; and the woodblocks for the first *Tripitaka* are destroyed.

1258: Ch'oe Oi, the last of the Ch'oe dictators, is assassinated. Authority reverts back to the king.

1259: Wonong (reigned 1259–1274) ascends to the throne. The court decides to seek peace with the Mongols.

1270: Despite the efforts of Im Yon and his

son Im Yumu to resist surrender to the Mongols and preserve military rule, the capital returns to Kaesong, Mongol domination is accepted, and the court returns to power. A faction of the military known as the *Sambyolch'o* (Three Elite Patrols) rebels against the Mongol-Koryo state.

1271: The Mongols proclaim the Yuan dynasty and extract from Koryo a vow of loyalty, imposing severe economic levies. It becomes the practice of Koryo kings to marry Yuan princesses, take Mongol names, use the Mongol language, and dress like Mongols.

1273: The *Sambyolch'o* rebellion is put down at Cheju Island.

1274: The Mongols force Koryo to participate in its invasion of Japan. The invasion fails.

1274–1308: Reign of King Ch'ungyol. He becomes the first Koryo ruler to adopt the prefix *ch'ung*, meaning loyal (to Yuan), and abandon the suffix *jong*, meaning ancestor. He is also the first ruler to favor the Neoconfucian ideas espoused by China's Ju Xi (Chu Hsi). He establishes a national academy to foster the study of these ideas, the fundamental revolutionary aspect of which is to imbue Confucius's ethics with a spiritual justification. Buddhism and Confucianism, so long exerting a cooperative influence on national policy, are hereafter in conflict.

1281: Again the Mongols invade Japan, enlisting Koryo aid; again the invasion fails.

1285: The Buddhist monk Iryon compiles the *Samguk Yusa* (Memorabilia of the Three Kingdoms). Compared to the *Samguk Sagi* (compiled 1145), Iryon's history puts less emphasis on political events, focusing instead on the daily life and customs of ancient Korea.

1308–1313: Reign of King Ch'ungs'on. Ch'ungs'on, through his own scholarship and his encouragement of others, further propagates the Neoconfucianism of Ju Xi.

Early 14th century: A style of poetry known as *kyonggi* flourishes; it uses the Chinese language, but celebrates Korea's national heritage. (*Kyonggi* reflects the word for capital district.) It is practiced by the increasingly prominent Confucian literati, often soldiers, statesmen, and scholars. As *kyonggi* involves a rigid poetic form, it does not lend itself to romantic themes. Meanwhile *changga* ("native song") such as the *Ch'ongsan pyolgok* ("Song of Green Mountain") and *Sogyong pyolgok* ("Song of the Western Capital") develop out of the folk song tradition and are the first Korean literature in the vernacular.

1313–1330, 1332–1339: Reign of King Ch'ungsuk.

1330–1332, 1339–1344: First reign of King Ch'unghye.

1344–1348: Reign of Ch'ungmok.

1349–1351: Reign of Ch'ungj'ong.

Mid-14th century: The attacks of Japanese marauders (*waegu*) plague the coastal regions of Koryo. Threatened by economic collapse, Koryo mounts an offensive against the *waegu*. The campaign is successful and several commanders who enjoy victories, notably Ch'oe Yong and Yi Songgye, gain political prestige as well.

1351–1374: Reign of Kongmin. The strength of the Yuan greatly diminished by struggles within China, Kongmin sets about a number of reforms aimed at recovering the prior dignity of Koryo. He abolishes Mongolian military outposts, purges the government of pro-Yuan sentiment, and inaugurates a campaign to retrieve lost territory in the north.

1359–1361: A rebel band from China called the Red Turbans penetrates into northern Koryo. The court abandons Kaesong and flees to Andong. Koryo troops regroup in 1361 and vanquish the Red Turbans.

1363: Mun Ikchom (1329–1398) introduces cotton into Koryo.

1368: The Mongols are driven from China. The Ming dynasty is proclaimed, and Kongmin immediately sends envoys to Beijing to establish congenial diplomatic relations.

1374: Alarmed by the increasing liberality of

Kongmin's reforms, a faction of powerful families led by Yi Inim carries out the assassination of Kongmin. Kongmin's ten-year-old son U is placed on the throne, but power comes increasingly to lie in the hands of Yi Inim and his family.

1374–1388: Reign of King U. Throughout his reign power lies in the hands of Yi Inim. The pro-Ming policy of Kongmin is abandoned and deference returned to the Mongols.

1388: Yi Songgye deposes U and installs U's son Ch'ang on the throne. An astute statesman, Yi strengthens his position before brazenly usurping the throne for himself. One preparation for such a move is the codification of government practices along Confucian lines that Chong Tojon begins at Yi's behest in 1388. The result of these efforts are the *Choson kyongguk chon* (Administrative Code of Choson) and the *Kyongje yukchon* (Six Codes of Governance), which become the law of the land upon Yi's ascension in 1392.

1389: Yi Songgye deposes Ch'ang and establishes King Kongyang. Having curried favor with the literati in lower classes of the bureaucracy and thereby providing the ideological underpinning necessary for a new dynasty, Yi Songgye stands poised to make the decisive reforms that will close this chapter of Korea's history.

1389–1391: Yi Songgye institutes a sweeping land reform program aimed at denying prominent families the economic foundation on which to build power. The basic statute of this reform is called the Rank Land Law. Under this law all land in the Kyonggi region is allocated to both current and retired government officials in proportion to their rank. All land outside Kyonggi is annexed by the state. These reforms are by and large those counseled by a group of lower government officials faithful to the Neoconfucian ideals of Ju Xi.

1390s?: Movable metal type is used to print *Sangjongkogom yemun* (Prescribed Ritual Texts of the Past and Present). Pi Cheng of the Northern Song dynasty in China is said to have invented a movable type using clay in the eleventh century, but Koryo's use of metal type is the first in the world. (Some sources place the first Korean movable type as early as 1234.)

1392: The Supreme Council, the highest organ of the Koryo government, formally declares the end of the Koryo dynasty. Yi Songgye assumes the throne. Like the founder of the Koryo dynasty Wang Kon, he is to be posthumously titled T'aejo (the great progenitor).

EARLY CHOSON: 1392–1598

T'aejo establishes a bureaucratic order drawn along Confucian lines. The ruling class is no longer limited to members of the aristocracy as defined by Silla's bone-rank system or Koryo's hereditary tradition, but incorporates any who are able to pass the Confucian examinations and attain a government post. This newly defined ruling class is called the *yangban*, a term that refers to military and civil officials alike. Choson enjoys a flourishing of arts and culture in the years following T'aejo's reign. Improvements in printing technology allow for many newly published books, including Korea's first gazetteer, several histories, a treatise on music, and a number of works on farming. Han'gol, Korea's alphabet, is created and promulgated in 1446. This gives rise to the vernacular verse known as *sijo*, and in the mid-sixteenth century the lyrical *kasa*. In the wake of Sejo's usurpation of the throne (1455), conflict between the meritorious elite (*yangban* who had been exceptionally favored by T'aejo and subsequent rulers) and the Neoconfucian literati intensifies. Seeing a threat to the authority of the central government

Sejo launches a series of purges against the Neoconfucian literati. However, the Neoconfucians survive these purges to return to power in the reign of Sonjo (1567–1608). The Japanese ruler Toyotomi Hideyoshi invades Korea in 1592. The war lasts six years, but due to Ming assistance and the brilliant naval victories of Admiral Yi Sunsin, Choson is able to beat back the Japanese invaders and restore normal diplomatic relations.

1392–1398: Reign of T'aejo.

1394: A new palace, Kyongbok, is built in Hanyang (modern Seoul).

1395: T'aejo moves the capital from Kaesong to Hanyang.

1398–1400: Reign of Chongjong.

1400: T'aejo, still the arbiter of national policy despite his abdication, abolishes private armies and absorbs soldiers from those armies into the national army.

1400–1418: Reign of T'aejong. He initiates a severe suppression of Buddhism.

1401: Paper money is printed using mulberry bark.

1403: A foundry is established for the casting of copper type. This leads to influx of newly published books. The type is called *kyemi*, which in this context means the year 1403.

1406: T'aejong confiscates all lands held by Buddhist temples.

1418–1450: Reign of Sejong.

1419: Sejong commands Yi Chongmu to lead an attack on Tsushima. The purpose of this offensive is to completely destroy the bases from which the Japanese marauders (*waegu*) have for centuries launched their raids on the Korean peninsula.

1423: Copper coins known as the *Choson t'ongbo* (circulating treasure of the realm) are minted. However, these coins are primarily used for the purposes of tax collection. Cloth, particularly cotton, remains the main unit of exchange.

1430: The first edition of *Nongsa chiksol* (Straight Talk on Farming) is published. The book represents an attempt by the Sejong government to address problems of agriculture specific to Korea's climate. An updated edition appears in 1492.

1432: Korea's first gazetteer, *P'alto chiri chi* (Geographical Description of the Eight Provinces) is published.

1442: Choson scholars invent the world's first rain gauge.

1443: A trade agreement is reached between Choson and Japan's regional warlords, or *daimyo*. The agreement limits the number of Japanese trading ships authorized to enter Korea's ports at fifty per year.

1443–1444: A series of military campaigns against the remaining Jurchen tribes and intensified efforts of colonization secure Choson's northeast border.

1444: The Tribute Tax Law is promulgated, lowering the tax for peasant farmers to one-twentieth of a harvest as opposed to the one-tenth ordained by the Rank Land Law (1390).

1446: Sejong promulgates Han'gol, Korea's indigenous alphabet. In creating the alphabet Sejong relies on the advice of a number of scholars, most notably Song Sammun, Chong Inji, and Sin Sukchu.

1450–1452: Reign of Munjong.

1452–1455: Reign of Tanjong.

1452: Two histories of the Koryo dynasty, *Koryosa* (History of Koryo) and *Koryo sa choryo* (Essentials of Koryo History) are published.

1455: Sejo usurps the throne from the boy-king Tanjong. Many ardent scholars feel this to be an unforgivably egregious violation of Confucian principles. Their complaints, however, are met with a series of bloody purges.

1455–1468: Reign of Sejo. Sejo's principal contribution to Korea's development is his active interest in the insufficiency of Korea's legal apparatus. He begins a revision of the *Six Codes*, which is promulgated in 1471.

1456: To secure the authority of his reign, Sejo purges the *yangban* class of those individuals suspected to oppose his rule. Among those executed are the "six martyred ministers" (*sa yuksin*).

1464: Iron coins in the shape of an arrowhead are minted. However, cloth remains the principal unit of exchange.

1466: Sejo replaces the Rank Land Law with the Office Land Law, which stipulates that officials shall continue to be granted land according to their position, but that upon retirement or death that land is to be handed over to the new incumbent.

1468–1469: Reign of Yejong.

1469–1494: Reign of Songjong.

Late 15th century: Kim Sisop (1435–1493) publishes *Komo sinhwa* (New Stories of the Golden Turtle), a precursor to the vernacular fiction popularized by Ho Kyun in the late sixteenth century.

1471: The *Kyongguk taejon* (National Code) is promulgated. This compendium of laws effectively reconciles the legal inconsistencies of past reigns and served as the foundation of Korea's legal system for several hundred years. Work on this project was begun by Sejo.

1478: So Kojong compiles the *Tong munson*, an anthology of poetry and prose written by Koreans in classical Chinese.

1485: *Tongguk t'onggam* (Comprehensive Mirror of the Eastern Kingdom), a chronology of major events in Korean history stretching from Tangun to the end of Koryo, is published.

1493: *Akhak kwebom* (Canon of Music), an illustrated treatise on ceremonial music, Chinese music, and native songs, is published.

1494–1506: Reign of Prince Yonsan. Due to his tyrannical rule he never receives a posthumous title recognizing his kingship.

1498: Prince Yonsan initiates the Purge of 1498 (*muo sahwa*), in which many Neoconfucian literati held to be disloyal to the prince's rule are executed or exiled.

1504: The Purge of 1504 (*kapcha sahwa*). Prince Yonsan initiates another purge of the literati.

1506–1544: Reign of Chungjong. In reaction to the excesses of Prince Yonsan, he pro-

motes the Confucian literati, most notably Cho Kwangjo (1482–1519). As Cho Kwangjo pushes forward increasingly radical reforms, however, resentment among the meritorious elite grows.

1519: Catering to the demands of the meritorious elite, Chungjong launches a purge of the Confucian literati, including Cho Kwangjo, whom he initially endorsed.

1544–1545: Reign of Injong.

1543: Chu Sebung founds the noted Paegundong Academy, modeled on Ju Xi's Bai Lu Dong in China. Other such schools, known as *sowon*, appear with increasing frequency throughout Korea. As they insure the propagation of Confucian ideals, *sowon* prove to be an essential power base for the Neoconfucian literati.

1545: Factions struggle for power after the death of Injong. A fourth, and final, purge of the Neoconfucian literati (*olsa sahwa*) ensues.

1545–1567: Reign of Myongjong.

Mid-16th century–17th century: *Sijo* and *kasa*, two indigenous Korean verse forms, flourish. *Kasa*, a lyric verse consisting of paired lines of four syllables each, is perfected by Chong Ch'ol (1563–1593) in such works as *Kwandong pyolgok* (Song of Kangwon Scenes) and *Sa miin kok* (Mindful of My Seemly Lord). The more condensed *sijo* is shaped by Pak Illo (1561–1643) and Sin Hom (1566–1628), and perfected by Yun Sondo (1587–1671) in works such as *Sanjung sin'gok* (New Songs from My Mountain Fortress).

1556: The system by which officials are allocated land according to their position is abolished. Hereafter government officials are simply to receive a salary.

1559–1562: The height of brigand leader Im Kokchong's power.

1567–1608: Reign of Sonjo. He eschews the meritorious elite in favor of the Neoconfucian literati, who begin to dominate the political process.

1575: Traditional date assigned to the beginning of Korea's period of "factional strife" (*tangjaeng*). It is at this time that Kim Hyowon and Sim Oigyom dispute the right to a relatively minor government post. Supporters of the two politicians split into one of two factions—the Eastern (*Tong*) or Western (*So*). Rivalries of this sort are to have an increasingly deleterious effect on Korea's political stability as factions split into subfactions and points of contention compound. The private academies (*sowon*) are often closely tied to one faction or another.

1583: A Yain force led by Nit'anggae rebels in the northeast. It manages to seize Kyongwon and other garrisons before being subdued by Sin Ip.

How many friends have I, you ask?
The streams and rocks, the pines and bamboo;
Moon rising over the eastern mountain
You I welcome too.
Enough. Beyond these five companions
What need is there for more?

From *Sanjung sin'gok* (New Songs from My Mountain Fastness), by Yun Sondo (1587–1671)

Spring 1592: Having unified Japan's warring *daimyo*, Japan's ruler, Toyotomi Hideyoshi, turns his attention to expansion. His troops land at Pusan in the spring with the hope of storming through the Korean peninsula and pushing on to an invasion of Ming China.

1592–1598: The Imjin War. Hideyoshi's troops meet with much initial success. Sonjo's court abandons Seoul, flees to Oiji on the northwest border, and petitions the Ming dynasty for aid. Meanwhile, the Korean admiral Yi Sunsin achieves a number of decisive victories at sea. Admiral Yi uses in these battles armored ships of his own invention called "turtle ships" (*kobukson*); these ships are thought to be the first ironclads ever used in battle. Fierce resistance from guerrilla forces throughout the country and Ming reinforcements push the Japanese invaders south. Peace negotiations begin, but drag on for years. Hideyoshi launches a second attack in 1597, but it fails. The last Japanese troops withdraw after Hideyoshi's death in 1598.

LATE CHOSON: 1598–1910

As the seventeenth century begins, Choson is on the verge of economic collapse. Revenue to meet the costs of recovery from the Imjin War is impossible to generate as the amount of taxable land has shrunk to dangerous levels. The 1627 and 1636 Manchu invasions further weaken the economy. This dire situation is compounded by the increasing factionalism of the Confucian literati, which impedes the adoption of necessary reforms. In response to these conditions the Sirhak, or Practical Learning, School develops. In 1708 the tax code is revised to remove the burden of debt from the lower classes. The consequential growth of a money economy and a vital merchant class has a salutary effect on Choson. During the reigns of Yongjo (1724–1776) and Chongjo (1776–1800) the kingdom experiences a renaissance. Sirhak scholars produce a number of important works during this time. In the nineteenth century, however, several young kings ascend to the throne. This leads to competition for the role of regent, and factionalism once again dominates the political scene. Furthermore, Choson is slow to realize the imperative of modernization. A host of foreign powers vie for supremacy on the peninsula as Choson's rulers become mired in myopic power struggles within an increasingly powerless government. In 1910 Japan formally annexes Korea.

1606: Choson sends envoys to Japan to restore diplomatic relations.

1608–1623: Reign of Prince Kwanghae. He inherits a country ravaged by the effects of war and imperiled by the ascendancy of the Manchu in the north.

Early 17th century: Ho Kyun writes *Hong Kiltong chon* (The Story of Hong Kiltong), the first fiction of the vernacular style termed *sosol* (small talk).

1610: *Tongoi pogam* (The Exemplar of Korean Medicine) is published.

1610–1644: The first knowledge of Christianity reaches Korea when Korean envoys bring Roman Catholic works from Peking (Beijing).

1614: Yi Sugwang publishes *Chibong yusol* (Topical Discourses of Chibong). The book is often considered to be the foundation of the Sirhak School.

1616: Nurhaci leads the Manchus in a campaign against the Ming dynasty of China. The Ming court requests Choson assistance. Kwanghae reluctantly accedes, but the Korean commander, Kang Hongnip, hoping to avoid Manchu retribution, surrenders at the first opportunity.

1623–1649: Reign of Injo. He comes to power in a coup d'état engineered by the so-called Western faction.

1624: Yi Kwal, who had been instrumental in establishing Injo on the throne but had received a relatively low official post, rises in rebellion. He occupies Seoul for a time before suffering defeat at the hands of government troops. Many of his followers escape to Manchuria, where they lobby for a Manchu invasion of Choson.

1627: A Manchu force crosses the Yalu River and overwhelms the Choson defenses. Injo's court flees to Kanghwa Island. Wishing to save strength for its campaign against China, the Manchus demand allegiance but withdraw without pressing their advantage.

1631: Chong Tuwon returns from his diplomatic mission in Ming China with a number of books on astronomy and Western culture, as well as various instruments of Western invention. Although such bounty from diplomatic assignments becomes increasingly common, the Choson government remains rigid in its anti-Western policy.

1636: The Manchus again demand that Choson submit to their rule. Injo refuses, and the Manchus mount a decisive invasion of Korea. Injo swears fealty to the Manchus, who in 1644 establish the Qing dynasty (1644–1912) in China, but resentment among the Korean people toward the Manchus remains intense.

1649–1659: Reign of Hyojong.

Mid-17th century–18th century: The Sirhak school of thought flourishes. Sirhak thinkers, like their counterparts in Europe's Enlightenment, generally eschew metaphysical concerns in pursuit of a pragmatic scholarship founded upon explicit verification. Of foremost interest to Sirhak scholars is the improvement of social conditions throughout Choson. They produce a vast body of encyclopedic work on subjects as disparate as farming and Chinese classical scholarship. Perhaps the most important of Sirhak's first adherents is Yi Ik (1681–1763); his two works *Songho sasol* (Discourses of Songho) and *Kwagu-rok* (Record of Concern for the Underprivileged) provide a comprehensive treatment of many fundamental tenets of Sirhak thought and reform.

1653: A Dutch ship wrecks off Cheju Island. Among the survivors of the wreck is Hendrik Hamel, who will produce the first account of Korea to appear in the West.

A revised calendar, incorporating methods of computation gleaned from Chinese translations of Western works, is promulgated. Despite the activities of a number of distinguished Korean scholars, this is one of the only official concessions Choson makes to Western learning until the late nineteenth century.

1659–1674: Reign of Hyonjong.

1662: The Office of Embankment Works is

established to oversee improvements on Korea's irrigation system.

1674–1720: Reign of Sukchong.

1687–1688?: Kim Manjung publishes *Kuun mong* (Dream of Nine Clouds), the story of a Buddhist monk's search for enlightenment that builds on the vernacular style of Ho Kyun.

1708: The Uniform Land Tax Law (*taedong-pop*) is enacted. The law allows for tax payment in rice and lowers the rate to roughly one percent of an average harvest. An agency is created to oversee tax payments efficiently. A money economy subsequently emerges, and concomitantly a vital merchant class.

1720–1724: Reign of Kyongjong.

1724–1776: Reign of Yongjo. In an effort to curb factionalism among the literati, Yongjo adopts the "policy of impartiality" (*t'angp'yongch'aek*). The policy stipulates that official appointments should be granted in roughly equal portions to members of each of Choson's principal Confucian factions.

1728: Kim Ch'ont'aek's collection of *sijo* verse, *Ch'onggu yongon* (Enduring Poetry of Korea), appears. That Kim is a simple government clerk is indicative of the fact that literature is no longer the exclusive province of the leisured *yangban* class.

1750: Yongjo enacts the Equalized Tax Law in an effort to distribute the tax burden among artisans, merchants, and farmers. The *yangban* remains exempt.

1763: Kim Sujang's collection of *sijo* verse, *Haedong kayo* (Songs of Korea), appears. Like Kim Ch'ont'aek, Kim Sujang is a government clerk and not a member of the leisured *yangban* class.

1770: King Yongjo commissions the *Tongguk munhon pigo* (Reference Compilation of Documents on Korea), an encyclopedic chronology of Korea's geography, government, economy, and culture.

1776–1800: Reign of Chongjo. He continues the policy of impartiality. The influence of the Sirhak School reaches its height as Chongjo establishes the Kyujanggak, an institute dedicated to the fostering of scholarly work in the social sciences.

1778: An Chongbok (1712–1791) completes *Tongsa kangmok* (Annotated Account of Korean History), the finest example of the numerous historical studies undertaken with the Sirhak emphasis on detailed verification.

1784–1795: Christianity has been slowly spreading among Koreans—mostly from contacts with Roman Catholics in China. In 1784 three Koreans, Yi Songhun, Yi Pyok, and Kwon Ilsin start an informal Catholic church in Seoul. In 1785 Catholicism is officially banned by the government, and sporadic persecutions follow, but that year a Jesuit, Father Peter Grammont, enters Korea secretly and begins to baptize believers and ordain clergy. In 1795 a Chinese Catholic priest, Father Chu Mun-Mo, also enters Korea and is allowed to preach his faith. Catholicism survives and spreads as an underground religion.

1800–1834: Reign of Sunjo. Because Sunjo is only a boy of ten when he ascends the throne, his father-in-law Kim Chosun of the Andong Kim clan manages to assume control of the government. This begins the era of in-law government (*sedo chongch'i*).

1801: The Catholic Persecution of 1801. Notable Korean Catholics and the influential Chinese missionary Chou Wenmo are executed. Hwang Sayong writes his famous "silk letter" appealing to the Peking bishop for assistance. The letter, which goes so far as to suggest a large-scale invasion of Korea by Western forces, is confiscated and contributes to rising isolationist sentiment.

All government slaves are freed. The institution of private slavery remains intact.

1810–1832: A number of floods damage the harvests and intensify the economic woes of Choson. The most serious disaster strikes in 1820.

1811: Hong Kyongnae, a discontented member of the *yangban* class who had been denied a government post, leads an uprising in

P'yongan province. This rebellion, which lasts five months, becomes the rallying cry for a series of similar uprisings throughout the country.

1821: Korea's first cholera epidemic ravages the country.

1832: England becomes the first Western power to request trade with Choson. A commercial vessel lands at Ch'ungch'ongdo, but departs without success.

1834–1849: Reign of Honjong. The balance of power is transferred from the Andong Kim clan to the P'ungyang Cho clan.

Spring 1839: The Catholic Persecution of 1839 begins at the urging of Pyokp'a P'ungyang Cho.

1846: Three French warships anchor off Ch'ungch'ong Island. They forward a letter to Choson officials requesting commercial and diplomatic relations, but depart without having received a response.

1849–1863: Reign of Ch'olchong. Power returns to the Andong Kim clan.

Mid-19th century: *P'ansori*, long narratives performed by a solitary singer to an outdoor audience, flourish. Text for these one-man operas grows out of the oral folk tradition. They are first transcribed into verse, then later translated into prose that is widely read by the common people. A repertoire of twelve tales (*madang*) develops. Sin Chaehyo (1812–1884) is the most famous composer of *P'ansori*.

1857: Yu Chaegon (1793–1880) compiles *P'ungyo samson* (Third Selection of Poems of the People). The anthology is notable for its inclusion of writers from a wide range of social classes.

***c.* 1860:** Ch'oe Cheu (1824–1864) founds the *Tonghak* (Eastern Learning) church. Directing its animus at bureaucratic corruption and foreign influence, the religion spreads quickly throughout the rural communities of the three southern provinces.

Spring 1862–Spring 1863: A series of popular uprisings following the same pattern erupts throughout the country. The first is the Chinju area of K'yongsang province.

Here, as elsewhere, local populations fed up with the corruption of local officials attack and destroy government offices.

1863: Ch'oe Cheu, the founder of the Tonghak church, is executed at Taegu. However, his martyrdom results in an increase of Tonghak support.

1864–1907: Reign of Kojong. When he ascends to the throne Kojong is only twelve. His father, Hongson Taewon'gun, assumes control over the government as regent. Taewon'gun institutes a number of drastic reforms aimed at restoring power to the monarchy. Notably, he reestablishes the policy of appointing government positions based on merit, taxes the *yangban* class, and suppresses the private academies (*sowon*), which had done much to perpetuate factionalism.

1865–1867: Taewon'gun rebuilds Kyongbok Palace, which had been destroyed during the Hideyoshi invasion. The reconstruction puts an enormous strain on Choson's failing economy.

Early 1866: Taewon'gun launches another persecution of Catholicism; this continues for almost ten years.

1866: The American trading ship *General Sherman* attempts to navigate the Taedong River to P'yongyang but is burned by a mob of local people. All aboard are killed in the incident.

1866: The "Foreign Disturbance of 1866." Seeking retribution for the executions of several French missionaries, Admiral Pierre Roze leads seven French warships in an attack on Kanghwa Island. After encountering resistance from Korean troops under the command of Yang Honsu, the French withdraw.

1866: Yi Hangno (1792–1868) resigns as royal secretary and presents a memorial to the throne giving the first cogent expression to the conservative anti-Western, anti-Japanese forces that had long influenced government policy.

1871: Taewon'gun closes all but forty-seven private academies (*sowon*).

1871: The "Foreign Disturbance of 1871."

The U.S. government reacts to the *General Sherman* incident by sending Rear Admiral John Rogers on a mission to attack the Korean stronghold at Kangwha Island. The American troops retreat after sustaining heavy losses.

1873: Facing heavy pressure from the emergent Min family and disgruntled Confucian officials, Taewon'gun resigns as regent. Korea's strict isolationist policy is consequently eased.

1875: Japan sends the warship *Unyoto Kangwha* with the express purpose of generating a conflict that will stand as a justification for a future invasion. Korean troops at Ch'ojiin play into Japan's hand by firing on the ship.

February 1876: Kuroda Kiyotaka of Japan leads a force of two warships and three troop transports to Kangwha, ostensibly to seek reparation for the *Unyoto* incident of 1875. He negotiates the unequal Treaty of Kangwha (sometimes called the Treaty of Friendship). This agreement allows for Japanese settlements on the Korean peninsula, stipulates that Pusan and two other ports are to be opened for trade with Japan, and recognizes Korea's autonomy in the interest of removing China's claim to the peninsula. It also guarantees the safety of foreign (Christian) missionaries and allows them to engage in proselytizing.

1876: The *Kagok wollyu* appears. This anthology of Korean poetry, compiled by Pak Hyogwan and An Minyong, contains primarily *sijo* verse.

1880: Kim Koengjip (1842–1896) returns from Japan. He carries with him two treatises written by Chinese authors, *Chao Xian Ce Lye* (A Policy for Korea) and *Yi Yan* (Presumptuous Views). These works help generate support for a more open foreign policy.

Enlightenment entails not only learning the advanced skills of others but also preserving what is good and admirable in one's own society.

Soyu kyonmun (Travels in the West), by Yu Kilchun
(1880s)

1882: The Military Mutiny of 1882 (*imo kullan*), an attempt by conservative forces to check reform and reinstall Taewon'gun as regent, fails miserably. The Japanese demand indemnity for casualties and damages incurred by uncontrolled soldiers and negotiate the unequal Treaty of Chemulp'o (Inch'on). The Chinese capitalize on the internal chaos by sending 4,500 troops to reassert suzerainty. Taewon'gun is driven from power. Later this year, under Chinese pressure to thwart a Japanese trade monopoly, Choson signs trade agreements with the United States and Germany.

1884: Trade agreements are reached with England, Italy, and Russia.

The first Protestant missionary arrives in Korea.

December 4, 1884: Progressive forces in the government led by Kim Okkyun and assisted by the Japanese minister, Takezoe Shinichiro, stage a coup d'état. Their efforts fail as Chinese troops storm Seoul and restore Kojong to the throne.

April 18, 1885: China and Japan sign the Convention of Tientsin, which provides for the removal of all foreign troops from Korean soil. However, the Chinese commander, Yuan Shi-kai, remains in Seoul and continues to exert Chinese influence on foreign and domestic policy.

1885–1887: British forces occupy Komun Island off the southern coast of Cholla in an attempt to check Russia's growing influence in Korea. The British abandon their encampments only after receiving a formal pledge from Russia that it will seize no Korean territories.

1886: A trade agreement is reached with France.

1889: Yu Kilchun writes *Soyu kyonmun* (Observations on a Journey to the West). The book advocates Korea's modernization in emulation of the West.

February 1894–June 1894: Adherents of the Tonghak church rebel. The uprising begins in Kobu but quickly gains momentum and develops into a full-scale rebellion. Unable to suppress the peasant army, the Choson government applies to China for aid. It is quickly granted. Japan also sends troops. The Tonghak troops disperse as the government agrees to accept their proposed reforms.

July 25, 1894–April 1895: Sino-Japanese War. Again, China and Japan square off to capitalize on Korea's internal disorder. The Japanese emerge victorious and in the Treaty of Shimonoseki China repudiates its suzerainty over Korea.

July 26, 1894: The Deliberative Council (Kun'guk Kimuch'o) is formed under the direction of the Japanese. Kim Hongjip assumes a leadership role as the council initiates a number of reforms that radically restructure Korean government and society. A cabinet is installed with a prime minister overseeing seven ministries, the palace apparatus is separated from the administrative government, legal distinctions between *yangban* and commoners are erased, the eight provinces are divided into twenty-three prefectures, a Western-style judicial system is instituted, and the silver standard is adopted. Despite the good effects of these sweeping reforms, the fact they are enacted at the direction of the Japanese causes considerable resentment among the Korean people. A conspicuous defect of the reform package is its lack of attention to the improvement of Korea's military.

October 1894–January 1895: Loyal members of the Tonghak movement rise against Japanese troops throughout the country. The rebellion is effectively suppressed, but resentment of Japanese hegemony remains strong.

January 7, 1895: Fourteen articles entitled *Hongbom* (Guiding Principles for the Nation) are read at the Royal Ancestral Shrine in Seoul. These articles, sometimes referred to as Korea's first constitution, confirm the process of reform initiated in 1894 by the Deliberative Council.

October 8, 1895: In an effort to silence the pro-Russian faction within Korea's government, the Japanese minister, Miura Goro, organizes the assassination of Queen Min. King Kojong flees to the Russian legation, where he remains until February 20, 1897.

April 7, 1896: So Chaep'il's newspaper *Tongnip Sinmum* (The Independent) runs its first edition. Several days later So Chaep'il founds Tongnip Hyophoe (Independence Club), an organization dedicated to the fostering of Korean national sentiment.

1897–1904: In an effort to compete economically with Japan and thereby increase its independence, Korea rapidly industrializes. Textiles are the principle manufacture. Korea also attempts to gain control of its railroad construction, but ultimately lacks the capital.

August 1897: At the urging of So Chaep'il, Kojong changes the name of Choson to Taehan Cheguk, meaning "the Korean empire," and proclaims himself emperor.

July 1903: Russians cross the Yalu River at Yongamp'o and start a settlement.

February 1904–September 1905: Russo-Japanese War. Korea proclaims its neutrality, in spite of which Japan deploys troops in Seoul.

July 1905: The United States recognizes Japan's claim to Korea in Taft-Katsura Agreement. England follows with its recognition a month later.

September 5, 1905: Russia and Japan sign the Treaty of Portsmouth to end the Russo-Japanese War. The treaty acknowledges Japan's interests in Korea.

November 17, 1905: The Japanese force Korean officials to sign the so-called Protectorate Treaty, which stipulates that all foreign policy is to be controlled by Japanese officials residing in Korea.

1906: Yi Injik publishes *Hyol ui nu* (Tears of Blood). Written in Han'gol and depicting contemporary life, this work is the first of the so-called New Novels, which are to propel Korea's literary tradition away from antiquated themes and styles.

1907: An Ch'angho founds the Sinminhoe

(New People's Association) for the promotion of Korean independence.

June 1907: Kojong sends Yi Sangsol, Yi Chun, and Yi Wijong to the second Hague Peace Conference to protest Japan's usurpation of the Korean government. The Korean officials fail to gain any official support for their cause.

July 19, 1907: Angered at his gambit to curry international favor, the Japanese replace Kojong with his son Sunjong. This action sparks a series of anti-Japanese demonstrations.

August 1, 1907: Japan dissolves the Korean military.

1909: The Bank of Korea is established under Japanese directorship.

1909: Yi Songman (eventually to be known to the world at large as Syngman Rhee) founds the Kungminhoe, or Korean National Association, in Hawaii.

October 26, 1909: An Chunggon assassinates Ito Hirobumi, the Japanese diplomat who engineered the Japanese takeover.

August 22, 1910: Japan's resident-general forces Prime Minister Yi Wanyong to sign an annexation treaty.

August 29, 1910: Sunjong abdicates and announces Korea's submission to Japan.

JAPANESE OCCUPATION: 1910–1945

Japan establishes a colonial government headed by a governor-general and institutes a number of oppressive measures that deny all freedoms of speech and close many private schools. The remaining schools are forced to adopt a curriculum that ignores the Korean language and history and teaches the Japanese language instead. Korea's economy and infrastructure improve dramatically at this time, but the benefits of these improvements accrue primarily to the Japanese. Although overt resistance to the Japanese is punishable by imprisonment or death, resentment to colonial rule remains strong. Various underground national groups spring up. On March 1, 1919, Korea's independence movement erupts in nationwide protest. The Japanese act swiftly and violently, killing and imprisoning thousands of unarmed demonstrators. A month after the rebellion, Korean exiles in Shanghai declare a provisional government. Resistance to Japanese rule continues, but to no avail. In 1931 Japan establishes the puppet state of Manchukuo and readies for an all-out campaign against the Chinese. Consequently, programs of forced assimilation and exploitation of Korean labor and natural resources intensify. When World War II begins, Koreans are soon conscripted to fight for the Japanese. Eventually, it becomes clear that Japan is fighting a war it cannot win. The Allied nations guarantee the independence of Korea in the so-called Cairo Declaration of December 1943. On August 8, 1945, the Soviet Union declares war on Japan and sweeps through Manchuria and northern Korea. On August 15, 1945, Japan surrenders.

1912: The Japanese promulgate the land survey law, which accelerates and gives legal justification to the process, begun in 1876, of annexing Korean land. The law stipulates that land must be registered with the Land Survey Bureau or be confiscated. Because many Koreans never hear of the law or simply fail to register with it, the government is able to confiscate a large quantity of land

which it then sells extremely cheaply to Japanese.

1917: Korean activists in exile in China attend the International Socialist Congress in Stockholm and the World Conference of Small Nations in New York to promote the cause of Korean independence.

March 1, 1919: A nationwide, nonviolent demonstration is carried out in accordance with the meticulous plan of a group of some thirty patriots led by Son Pyonghoi, Yi Songhun, and Han Yongun. The demonstration begins at Seoul's T'aehwagwan Restaurant, where the group formally promulgates a "Declaration of Independence," and then spreads quickly throughout the city. Similar demonstrations in other cities get under way at the same time. The Japanese, alarmed at the scale of the movement, launch a full-scale military attack. An estimated two million people take part in 1,500 separate gatherings; according to Japanese estimates 7,509 are killed, 15,961 are injured, and 46,948 are arrested. Korean estimates are much higher.

April 1919: Although the March First Movement fails, exiles create the Taehan Minguk Imsi Chongbu (provisional government of the Republic of Korea) in Shanghai. Syngman Rhee assumes the presidency.

1919–1922: The founding of a number of literary magazines, notably *Ch'angjo* (Creation), *P'yeho* (Ruins), and *Paekcho* (White Tide), gives rise to a new literary movement. Works of this era are characterized by a direct tone and attention to life's mundane aspects.

1920: Japan's new governor-general, Saito Makoto, institutes a number of reforms known collectively as the Bunka Seiji (Cultural Policy). These reforms allow greater freedom to assemble, and ease restrictions on the press and Korean businesses. Saito also increases the size of the police force, and reorganizes Japan's colonial government for greater efficiency.

May 1922: Yi Kwangsu publishes *Minjok Kaejoron* (A Treatise on National Reconstruction), arguing for a patient approach in Korea's independence struggle.

1923: Discrimination against Koreans erupts in Japan's Kanto region. Amid the panic caused by a major earthquake, Japanese accuse Koreans of poisoning drinking wells. As many as seven thousand Koreans are murdered in retribution for this imagined crime.

April 1926: Sunjong, Korea's last sovereign, dies.

Filled with the color of grass, compounded
Of green laughter and green sorrow,
Limping along, I walk all day as if possessed by
   the spring devil:
But now these are stolen fields,
and even our spring will be taken.

"Does Spring Come to Stolen Fields?" by Yi Sanghwa
(1926)

June 10, 1926: The June 10 Independence Demonstration. As the funeral procession for Sunjong marches through Seoul, large crowds gather. Among the mourners are many students who shout anti-Japanese slogans and pass out pamphlets. Two hundred students are arrested.

1929: The workers of Wonsan go on a general strike to protest Japanese exploitation. As support for the workers spreads throughout the country, the Japanese are forced to compromise.

November 1929: The Kwangju Student Movement. The incident begins when a group of male Japanese students harasses three Korean girls. Several Korean boys lash out at the Japanese, and street fighting quickly escalates. The Japanese police intervene and arrest as many as four hundred Korean students. This incites further violence and the movement spreads to surrounding areas. 1,642 students are arrested before the violence subsides.

1931: Having established the puppet state of Manchukuo, Japan prepares to enlarge the scope of its territorial ambitions. One such preparation is increased investment in Korea's industrial development. Eventually, Korea's labor and natural resources will become an integral part of Japan's war machine.

1939: The magazine *Literature* appears. Work published in this periodical is characterized by an attention to refined language and an avoidance of political themes.

December 7, 1941: On the day of the Japanese attack on Pearl Harbor, the Korean provisional government led by Syngman Rhee declares war on Japan and begins its diplomatic campaign to garner foreign support. The Kwangbokkun (Restoration Army) is raised to aid Allied troops in their Asian operations.

December 1, 1943: The Allied powers proclaim their intention to liberate Korea from Japanese control in the so-called Cairo Declaration.

August 8, 1945: Aware of Japan's imminent defeat, and hoping to share in the spoils of victory in the Asian theater, the Soviet Union declares war on Japan. Soviet troops storm into Korea and occupy much of the north.

August 11, 1945: General Order Number 1 is drafted by the United States outlining the terms of the Japanese surrender in Korea. The order stipulates that Japanese forces north of the 38th parallel are to surrender to Soviet commanders, whereas those forces south of the parallel are to surrender to the United States.

August 15, 1945: Japan surrenders to the Allies and in so doing acknowledges Korea's autonomy.

A DIVIDED KOREA: 1945–1998

As the United States and the Soviet Union take their positions on either side of the 38th parallel, efforts to come up with a proposal for Korea's unification continue (with the conspicuous absence of a Korean delegation). When negotiations freeze, the United States-dominated United Nations and the Soviet Union square off, with each proclaiming the government of their respective spheres of influence the only legitimate government on the peninsula. U.S. and Soviet troops withdraw throughout 1948 and 1949. On June 25, 1950, the North Korean army invades South Korea. The United States quickly puts together a UN coalition army headed by General Douglas MacArthur. The Chinese become involved late in 1951, and by 1952 there is a stalemate on the 38th parallel. A peace treaty is signed on July 23, 1953, but Korea remains a divided country.

The promise of a democratic government in South Korea is never truly fulfilled as throughout the latter half of this century a succession of autocratic rulers manipulates a weak legislative body. The pattern is established by South Korea's first president Syngman Rhee and continues through Roh Tae Woo (No T'ae-u). Not until the election of Kim Young Sam in 1992 does South Korea begin to show signs of becoming a more democratic government and one eventually willing to deal with North Korea. North Korea, meanwhile, becomes one of the world's most closed nations. In 1966, after vacillating between Chinese and Russian influence, it declares itself independent and proceeds to forge its own domestic policy, characterized by reckless military spending. Kim Il Sung (1912–1994) rules until 1994 when power passes to his son, Kim Jong Il. Already barely limping by with its economic and agricultural output, North Korea is on the edge of collapsing by 1997, when the international community takes steps to buttress it, with the hope that North Korea may begin to change its ways.

September 8, 1945: U.S. forces reach Seoul. In accordance with the terms of General Order Number 1 (August 11, 1945), Soviet and U.S. forces administer two zones of occupation divided by the 38th parallel.

December 1945: By the terms of the Moscow Conference, the United States, Britain,

China, and the Soviet Union agree to govern Korea as a trusteeship for up to five years. A U.S.-Soviet Joint Commission is created to work out the terms of a unified Korean government. News of the trusteeship touches off mass protests in Korea.

March–May 1946, May–August 1947: The U.S.-Soviet Joint Commission meets, but fails to come up with a proposal for Korea's unification. The main point of contention concerns parties unfavorable to the trusteeship. The Soviets insist on barring such parties from participation in the government; the United States insists on their inclusion.

September 1946: The United Nations accepts the U.S. proposal calling for general elections in Korea.

May 10, 1948: The UN Temporary Commission on Korea oversees elections in South Korea. The Soviets bar the commission from entering the north.

July 20, 1948: Syngman Rhee is elected South Korea's first president.

August 15, 1948: The Republic of Korea (ROK) is inaugurated in the south.

August 25, 1948: Elections for North Korea's Supreme People's Assembly are held.

September 3, 1948: The constitution of the Democratic People's Republic of Korea (DPRK) is ratified by the Supreme People's Assembly in P'yongyang. Kim Il Sung is appointed premier. Six days later the new government is announced.

October 12, 1948: The USSR recognizes the Democratic People's Republic of Korea as the sole lawful government in Korea and begins to withdraw its troops.

November 1948: Rhee passes the National Security Law through the National Assembly. The law prohibits any seditious organizations, and becomes a powerful tool for the despotic Rhee, particularly in his efforts to weed out Communists in South Korea.

December 12, 1948: The UN General Assembly recognizes South Korea's National Assembly as the only lawful government in Korea.

1949: Kim Il Sung becomes chairman of the Korean Workers Party.

June 1949: The United States withdraws its troops from the peninsula, leaving behind only advisors to an undertrained and undermanned South Korean army.

June 25, 1950: North Korean troops launch a full-scale invasion of South Korea. With vastly superior weapons, and greatly outnumbering the South Korean army, the DPRK forces reach Seoul within three days.

June 26, 1950: The UN Security Council condemns the invasion and calls on its members to provide support in an effort to restore peace. This is tantamount to a declaration of war. The following day President Truman orders U.S. troops into action. U.S. forces land in Korea on July 4 and establish a defensive perimeter behind the Naktong River.

September 15, 1950: The commander of the UN troops, U.S. General Douglas MacArthur, begins his counterattack with an amphibious landing on Inch'on. The UN forces quickly push DPRK troops back to the 38th parallel.

October 7, 1950: The UN approves a resolution to permit an invasion of North Korea. UN forces take P'yongyang on October 20 and by October 26 reach the Manchurian border at the Yalu River.

Late November 1950: The Chinese intervene on behalf of the routed DPRK. They cross the Yalu River and launch a massive counteroffensive. By the end of 1952 an estimated 1,200,000 Chinese troops are involved in the fighting.

January 4, 1951: Seoul falls to the Chinese-DPRK alliance.

March 1951: UN troops regain Seoul on March 14 and by March 31 have pushed Chinese and North Korean troops back to the 38th parallel in many sectors. A stalemate ensues. The major parties begin to work for a cease-fire.

1951: Rhee creates the Liberal Party.

July 10, 1951: The first meeting of the delegates from the United States, South Korea, and North Korea takes place at Kaesong. These meetings will continue for another two years without results.

1952: Rhee forces the National Assembly to relinquish its power to elect the president. This is the first of several attempts by Rhee to frustrate democratic processes in an effort to assume a dictatorial control of the government.

July 27, 1953: An armistice ending the Korean War is signed in P'anmunjom. Basically the two Koreas return to the status quo in terms of a boundary, only now it is a heavily armed no-man's land. As called for by the armistice, representatives of the warring parties commence meetings to effect a true peace treaty, but as of 1998 they are unsuccessful.

1954: The National Assembly, now dominated by partisans of Rhee's Liberal Party, passes a measure excluding the present incumbent only from the presidential two-term limit outlined in the constitution.

1956–1966: The Sino-Soviet conflict causes confusion in North Korea's foreign and domestic policy. Ultimately, Kim Il Sung adopts a neutral stance, maintaining the independence of North Korea with respect to its feuding Communist neighbors.

December 24, 1958: Having put all opposition members of the National Assembly under restraint, Rhee's Liberal Party passes a bill to widen the application of the National Security Law and to amend the Local Self-Government Law to allow for Rhee's government to appoint heads of the local administrations.

August 1959: Cho Pongam, a popular socialist candidate for the presidency, is executed for supposed violations of the National Security Law. The execution takes place eight months before the 1960 presidential elections.

March 15, 1960: The day of the presidential elections a large student demonstration takes place in Masan. The students vehemently protest the blatant acts of election rigging undertaken by Rhee's Liberal Party. The police fire into the crowd, killing or wounding as many as a hundred demonstrators.

April 11, 1960: The body of a high school student is found in Masan harbor. Apparently the student was killed in the demonstration of March 15, and the body was deposited in the bay in order to avoid scandal. The discovery provokes more demonstrations.

April 18–26, 1960: The April Revolution. On April 18 student demonstrators in Seoul are beaten by government agents. The following day a throng of students flood into downtown Seoul and are fired upon by police. This incites more protest. On April 25 demonstrations reach their peak. When martial law troops refuse to fire upon the demonstrators, Rhee is forced to resign; he goes into exile in Hawaii.

June 15, 1960: A new constitution instituting a bicameral parliament is promulgated. South Korea's Second Republic begins.

July 29, 1960: The Korean people vote the Democratic Party to a majority in both houses. The assembly subsequently elects Yun Poson as president.

1961: The Kim regime in North Korea adopts the first of three Seven-Year Plans to revitalize a sagging economy.

May 16, 1961: Kim Jong Pil and Park Chung Hoi engineer a military coup in South Korea. Park establishes the Supreme Council for National Reconstruction (SCNR), a military junta over which he presides.

December 1962: Martial law is lifted and a constitutional referendum passes, allowing for a popularly elected president. This is known as South Korea's Third Republic.

October 15, 1963: Park Chung Hoi is elected South Korea's president.

Late 1960s: Kim Il Sung strengthens North Korea's military.

1968: North Korea seizes the U.S. electronic intelligence-gathering ship *Pueblo* and imprisons its crew for eleven months.

September 14, 1969: Park's Democratic Republican Party, dominating the National Assembly, passes a constitutional amendment allowing Park to seek a third term in 1971.

1969: Pak Kyongni publishes her multivolume novel *T'oji* (Land).

The bleak autumn wind whispered past the eaves of the shrine, the leaves rustled as they rubbed together, a nightingale cried like an elderly spinster and an owl like the ghost of an old bachelor, while the figure of the Buddha— was it no more than a lump of metal melted by a craftsman and mindlessly poured into a mold?—never spoke but only smiled.

T'oji (Land), by Pak Kyongni (1969)

October 17, 1972: Park proclaims martial law, dissolves the National Assembly, and suspends the constitution.

November 21, 1972: The Yusin Constitution is approved by public referendum. This Fourth Republic of South Korea allows for almost total control of the government by a president who is not popularly elected and who is able to appoint one-third of the National Assembly. This president is Park himself.

October 26, 1979: Kim Jae Kyu, head of the Korean Central Intelligence Agency, leads a group of men who assassinate Park and several of his guards and close associates. Choi Kyu Hah becomes the acting president and declares martial law. In December he is elected to office, promising reform. After their trial and appeals, Kim Jae Kyu and four of his accomplices are hanged on May 24, 1980.

May 14–27, 1980: A series of strikes and riots mainly arising from economic dissatisfaction have occurred around South Korea in March and April and led to increasing violence. By the first of May, the unrest has turned into political protests against the government led by students. On May 13 students at Seoul University launch a march that leads to several days of pitched battles

with the police, leaving hundreds injured. On May 17 martial law is extended across the country, and on May 18 dissident leaders Kim Dae Jung and Kim Chong Pil are arrested. This leads on May 19 to a popular uprising in Kwangju (about 165 miles south of Seoul); on May 27 troops move in and crush the uprising; the government claims that only 144 civilians have been killed, but others claim at least 475 dead.

August 27, 1980: After a series of maneuvers to control the military and other vital organs of the Korean government, such as the Korean Central Intelligence Agency, former general Chon Tuhwan is elected president by the National Council for Unification. He will be elected to the presidency by a nationwide balloting on February 11, 1981.

September 17, 1980: Kim Dae Jung, a longtime leader of the opposition to the nondemocratic governments of South Korea, is found guilty of sedition and sentenced to death. On January 23, 1981, this sentence is commuted to life imprisonment; he goes into exile in the United States in December 1982, but returns to Korea in February 1985. Although under house arrest, he will continue to lead the opposition to the government.

October 10–14, 1980: At a congress of the Korean Workers Party, Kim Il Sung appoints his son Kim Jong Il to three powerful party posts.

October 22, 1980: A new constitution is approved, ushering in Korea's Fifth Republic. Under the new constitution, a president is elected to one seven-year term.

October 9, 1983: During President Chon's visit to Burma, a bomb is set off in Rangoon, killing six high-ranking South Korean government officials, three Burmese journalists, and ten other South Koreans. (The bomb was clearly intended for Chon, who was delayed in arriving at the site.) North Korea is widely believed to be responsible for the bombing (and this will later be confirmed).

October 27, 1987: South Korea's sixth constitution is approved by national referendum; among other reforms, it limits the president's term to five years.

November 29, 1987: A South Korean Airliner is destroyed, presumably by a bomb, over the Thai-Burmese border. North Korea is widely held responsible for the event.

December 16, 1987: Factional strife amid the opposition and possible acts of vote-rigging lead to the election of Roh Tae Woo (No T'ae-u), a former general associated with corruption and crackdowns on dissidents. He will assume office on February 25, 1988.

Summer 1988: Seoul hosts the Olympic Games.

January 20, 1988: The United States imposes sanctions on North Korea for its alleged terrorist activities.

December 18, 1992: Kim Young Sam, a former dissident, is elected president of South Korea. He is sworn in on February 25, 1993.

Spring 1994: After months of crisis following reports of North Korea's nuclear program, North and South Korean leaders agree to hold an historic summit meeting on July 25. The meeting, however does not take place due the death of North Korea's Kim Il Sung.

July 8, 1994: Kim Il Sung dies. His son, Kim Jong Il, assumes day-to-day control of the country's government.

June 13, 1995: A multinational consortium, led by the United States, and North Korea announce the details of an agreement first reached in October 1994: North Korea will freeze its nuclear-weapons program in return for which it will get two nuclear reactors, made in South Korea, and supplies of fuel oil from the United States and its allies.

May 30, 1995: A South Korean fishing trawler strays into North Korean waters and its five-man crew is taken prisoner. They are not released until December 30, by which time South Korea has announced it will suspend all aid until North Korea changes its behavior.

June–July 1995: Exceptionally heavy floods are threatening the already shaky agriculture production of North Korea.

June 21, 1995: North Korea for the first time officially agrees to accept South Korea's offer of rice, thereby admitting it is having serious trouble feeding its 22 million people.

August 1995: Floods have by now devastated the grain crop in North Korea, leaving at least 100,000 homeless and causing billions of dollars in damage.

March 11–August 26, 1996: On March 11, two former presidents, Chon Tuhwan and Roh Tae Woo, are placed on trial for seizing power by violence in 1979, for financial corruption, and for their role in suppressing the prodemocracy movement. On August 26, they will be found guilty; Chon is sentenced to death and Roh is sentenced to 22.5 years in prison. On December 22, 1997, they are pardoned and released.

April 4–7, 1996: On April 4 North Korea suddenly announces it will no longer respect the demilitarized zone between the two Koreas. On April 5–7 North Korea sends troops into the zone to conduct military exercises clearly designed to taunt South Korean and U.S. forces stationed at the border. On May 14, the United States and Japan announce that they will cease sending any more food to aid North Korea.

Summer 1996: North Korea's economy deteriorates and its food crisis grows worse; it is believed that a serious famine now threatens North Korea, but it continues to act belligerently.

Mid-August 1996: Nine days of riots by mostly students in South Korea demanding reunification with North Korea leave one policeman dead and about one thousand students and police injured.

September 18, 1996: A North Korean submarine is found abandoned where it ran aground on the coast of South Korea; eventually twenty-four of its crew and passengers are killed, and one is captured alive. Although North Korea insists that this was an accident on a training exercise, it is fairly certain that many of the North Koreans were infiltrators assigned to spy on South Korea.

December 30, 1996: The U.S. government announces that for the first time North Korea is agreeing to meet with U.S. and South Korean delegates to bring about a permanent peace settlement to the Korean War.

February–April 1997: By February, North Korea is publicly admitting that it has only about half the grain it needs to feed its people; by April it reaches a new agreement with the United States, which will supply much of the grain needed.

August 5–7, 1997: After several delays, the first preliminary peace talks between North Korean, the United States, South Korea, and China are held in New York City; they break off over disagreements but the first true peace talks finally are held in Geneva, Switzerland, on December 9–10.

December 1997: The "Asian flu"—the financial and economic crisis that has been sweeping through Asia since July—takes its toll in South Korea, the eleventh largest economy in the world. Some of its largest industries are declaring bankruptcy, the stock market is collapsing, unemployment is rising. On December 3 the International Monetary Fund agrees to grant South Korea a $57 billion loan to help salvage its economy, but this comes too late for the largest of its state-owned banks, which on December 11 announces it is postponing its effort to raise $2 billion to pay its debts.

December 18, 1997: In elections held under the shadow of a collapsing economy, Kim Dae Jung, the longtime leader of the pro-democracy movement, is elected president. Even before he is sworn in on February 25, 1998, he calls for talks with Kim Jong Il of North Korea.

March 16–21, 1998: North Korea and South Korea attend the second session of the peace talks at Geneva. The results are inconclusive.

June 6–14, 1998: President Kim Dae Jung visits the United States, in part to win support for his government's policy of reconciliation with North Korea; he will try to convince the U.S. Congress to lift its economic sanctions but he gets no solid commitment.

August 31, 1998: North Korea launches a ballistic missile that crosses over Japan's territory before falling into the Pacific Ocean. North Korea claims this was a multistage rocket intended to put a satellite in orbit, but no tracking station can locate a new satellite. Although North Korea is charged with a provocative and aggressive act, it is gradually accepted that this may well have been a failed launch.

Taiwan

PREHISTORIC TAIWAN: 10,000 B.C.–A.D. 611

During what geologists call the Pleistocene Age (roughly 1.75 million years ago to 10,000 B.C.), the falling and rising of the world's sea levels left Taiwan alternately connected to and isolated from the mainland of China. Although early hominids *(Homo erectus)* are establishing themselves in parts of China during most of this time, for whatever reason none of these appear to move onto Taiwan until near the end of this period. Some scientists claim to find signs of human presence on Taiwan as early as 50,000 B.C.; if this is so, these hominids (possibly archaic *Homo sapiens*) get there by walking across a land bridge when the sea level is low. The first undisputed signs of hominids' occupation of Taiwan date from *c.* 10,000 B.C., by which time they are full-fledged *Homo sapiens*. By at least 6000 B.C. the sea level has risen to its present level, leaving Taiwan completely isolated from the mainland and with essentially its present-day physical characteristics.

Sometime thereafter—at least by about 4000 B.C.—new groups of Southern Mongoloids begin to move over to Taiwan; the main theory is that they come from southern China, although others believe that they come from the islands or mainland of Southeast Asia. In any case, from this point on the inhabitants of Taiwan pass through the cultural phases similar to those throughout East and Southeast Asia—specifically, those classed under Neolithic. Meanwhile, by at least 2800 B.C. some inhabitants of Taiwan appear to move out via boats to settle other Pacific islands, first the Philippines and then Indonesia. As a result, Taiwan remains receptive to some of the foods and other artifacts imported from their relatives around Southeast Asia and the Pacific. Taiwan, however, remains something of a backwater culture in relation to other places throughout East and Southeast Asia. Although there are legendary claims to Chinese contacts with Taiwan during the first millennium A.D., not until about A.D. 1000 will a new infusion of Chinese begin to pull Taiwan into the mainstream of Asian history.

10,000–3000 B.C.: Flaked pebble tools found at a few sites in southern and eastern Taiwan are classed as belonging to the Ch'angpinian culture (after the site on Taiwan where they are first found). Some experts regard them as similar to those of the Hoabinhian culture found throughout Southeast Asia, named after the site of Hoabinh in northern Vietnam, where the first of these distinctive tools are found. These first Taiwanese may come from the Chinese mainland opposite (about 115 miles distant) or from the Malay Peninsula or Indonesia, but little definite is known about them or how they got there; it is possible that they are the ancestors of at least some of the so-called aborigines who live on Taiwan through the twentieth century.

4500–2500 B.C.: During this period, Southern Mongoloid people make their way to Taiwan in canoes or small boats. Their exact point of origin is not certain; most likely they come from somewhere in southern China, but possibly they come from the region of Indonesia or the Malay peninsula. They speak what some label an Austric language, ancestral to the various Austronesian languages later spoken throughout much of Asia. On Taiwan they remain somewhat isolated, but they carry over the Neolithic culture that has been developing on the mainland—pottery, domesticated animals (dogs and pigs), and a diversity of tools. Although mainly relying on hunting, fishing, and the gathering of available wild foods, they may also engage in some agriculture, for by this time many Chinese are cultivating millet and rice. They also make canoes and wooden houses. During their time on Taiwan, this people's language evolves into what is sometimes classed as proto-Austronesian.

4000–2500 B.C.: On Taiwan, the most defined culture of this period is called the Ta-p'en-k'eng; it is distinguished by cord-marked and incised pottery and stone adzes; other finds that reveal some of their activities include stone net sinkers (indicative of fishing) and possibly a stone bark-cloth beater. Although some believe that the Taiwanese are cultivating millet and rice by at least 3000 B.C., there is no firm evidence for this, and stone reaping knives do not appear on Taiwan until about 2500 B.C.

3000–1500 B.C.: Some of the Austronesian people on Taiwan apparently begin to move outward, first to the Philippines and eastern Indonesia; by 1500 B.C. Austronesians are moving on to western Indonesia and Malaya and eastward to the Micronesian islands of the Pacific; by 500 B.C. they are moving still farther eastward into Polynesian islands of the Pacific. (The Austronesian speakers who remain on Taiwan are the ancestors of the 330,000 or so aboriginal peoples such as the Atayls, Amis, and Paiwans of present-day Taiwan.)

2500–500 B.C.: By 2000 B.C. the Austronesians on Taiwan are definitely cultivating such crops as millet, gourd, sugarcane, and rice. They are also becoming differentiated into several variant regional cultures, with distinctive types of pottery, adzes, projectile points, reaping knives, and houses. These cultures include the Fengpitou, the Yuanshan, and the T'ai-yuan. The numerous clay spindle whorls found indicate they make cloth.

1500–800 B.C.: One of the most ambitious sites on Taiwan of this period is at Peinan, in eastern Taiwan, where remains of a quite advanced village are found: the foundations of fifty houses with adjacent storehouses, fifteen hundred burials indicating great concern for ancestors, and fine pottery, spindle whorls, bark-cloth beaters, and fine jewelry.

1500–500 B.C.: The Austronesian people based on Taiwan (and by now also dispersed into the Philippines and Indonesia) are now engaged in a basic maritime trading economy; their navigational skills apparently enable them to move back and forth—they have added a sail to their canoe. Meanwhile, the one-time "colonists" are now introducing crops in Taiwan—domesticated chicken, coconut, breadfruit, yam, taro, banana, sago, and betel nuts (for chewing). The Taiwanese, however, still get much of their sustenance from millet and rice.

500 B.C.– A.D. 265: Little is known about Taiwan during this period. In Chinese records of the centuries before the Han dynasty (206 B.C.–A.D. 222), it is referred to as "the land of Yangchow." During the time of China's Han dynasty and the Three Kingdoms A.D. 222–265), it is called Yinchow. In any case, the Chinese of this time do not regard Taiwan as part of China, culturally or politically.

c. A.D. 230: Later Chinese historical records claim that a Chinese emperor Sun Quan sends a ten thousand-member expeditionary force to an island that may be Taiwan; in any case, nothing comes of it. Modern China will lay claim to Taiwan on the basis of this alleged expedition, but there is no official territorial claim in ancient Chinese records.

605–610: During the Sui dynasty (589–618) a Chinese emperor sends three small expeditions or missions to an island also believed to be Taiwan. Although some information

and artifacts (and several aborigines) are brought back to China, the Chinese do not appear to follow through with any political or military measures. Again, though, modern China will lay claim to Taiwan on the basis of these expeditions.

The moon is shining.
On the back of the pine tree.
The goose carries water, the duck washes
*   vegetables,*
The cook grinds grain,
The dog steps in the pestle,
The fox makes fire, the cat fries food,
The tiger goes into the mountain,
And drags down firewood;
The hen cares for the house,
Carries home my little sister

Traditional Hakka song

611–1000: Little is known about Taiwan during these centuries. Chinese records later refer to aborigines making raids on villages on the Chinese coast opposite, but nothing definite is known of what may be simply isolated acts of marauders. But it is not at all unlikely that some Chinese are making their way to Taiwan at least by the end of this period.

CHINESE AND FOREIGNERS MOVE IN: 1000–1683

The Taiwanese aborigines are pushed further into the mountains by Japanese and Chinese pirates and increasing numbers of migrants from mainland China. By the eleventh century, Hakka people, originally from the south of China near Hong Kong, have established substantial communities. Starting around the thirteenth century they are displaced from choice land by the arrival of the Fujian Chinese. The Mongol-Yuan dynasty in China, hoping eventually to conquer Japan, orders a series of expeditions to southeastern China opposite Taiwan and establishes a base on the Pescadores Islands, which lie between the Chinese coast and Taiwan. As trade develops throughout the Asian region from the sixteenth century, the island arouses the interest of Westerners. The Dutch wrest control of Taiwan from the Spanish, and rule the island as a Dutch colony. Significant Chinese settlement occurs under the Dutch, who require migrant laborers, farmers, and traders. The Dutch rule for almost four decades until they are defeated by the forces of Zheng Chenggong. Although there are some economic and social advances under the Cheng family's rule, dissension in the house of Cheng leads to a Manchu invasion. By this time there are an estimated 100,000 Chinese on Taiwan.

960–1279: The Song dynasty in China. There is little imperial interest in the Taiwan area, although it seems that Taiwanese aborigines make foraging raids along the Chinese coast. Hakka (meaning "guest") people living in southeastern China migrate to the Taiwan island. By around 1111 there are about a thousand Hakka settlements in southern Taiwan. The origins of the Hakka are obscure; they have been living in the region around Hong Kong where they retained a language and culture distinct from the Chinese. The Hakka tend to drive the aborigines back into the mountains (and later Chinese will call them *Gaoshan*, high mountains). Meanwhile, by the thirteenth century Chinese from Fujian, across the Taiwan Straits, are also beginning to come over to Taiwan.

1280–1368: The Yuan dynasty in China. These Mongol rulers with expansionist aims grow increasingly interested in the mainland and islands opposite Taiwan. In particular, the Yuan are interested in the P'eng-hu archipelago (the modern Western name is Pescadores), a cluster of islands west of Taiwan, and establish a base there. There is still confusion in court records about what the Chinese call Taiwan and whether it is confused with the Ryukyu Islands to the north. In the 1290s the Chinese send exploratory missions to an island named Liu-ch'iu, which some scholars believe was Taiwan.

You stupid Eastern barbarians! Living so far across the sea . . . you are haughty and disloyal. You permit your subjects to do evil.

Letter from Ming founder Hung-Wu to Japanese Ashikaga shogun (1380)

1430: Cheng Ho, the famous eunuch and navigator of the Ming court in China, reports to the emperor that he has discovered Taiwan, although the island can be seen from Fujian province on a clear day and has for many centuries been known to the Chinese by various names.

1514: Starting in this year, Portuguese ships based in Malacca begin to sail to China; although they make several attempts during the ensuing years, they are prevented from establishing trading posts there (until they settle on Macau in 1557). It is assumed that the sailors catch sight of the island of Taiwan, but because it is not on their maps they refer to it as *ilha formosa* (beautiful island). In 1596 the well-known Dutch navigator Jan Huyghen van Linschoten first applies this name to the island on a map seen by Europeans, so this is how it eventually comes to be known to the West.

1570: Ming dynasty court records use the name Taiwan for the first time, and the exact location of the island is documented. Some scholars believe that the name is based on the Chinese name for a people who inhabited an islet near Taiwan; others believe it is based on Chinese words for "terraced bay."

1590: By this time, Ming dynasty officials are encouraging trade and fishing vessels to go to Taiwan, and even more Chinese from southern Fujian region across the Taiwan Straits are emigrating to Taiwan in greater numbers. The Fujianese Chinese immigrants will gradually push the less affluent Hakka from the best land.

1592–1593: Japanese traders arrive in Taiwan and within a year the Japanese government is attempting to make Taiwan pay tribute to Japan. That attempt is unsuccessful.

1609–1616: The Japanese subjugate the Ryuku Islands to the north of Taiwan and subsequently try to colonize Taiwan, but this fails.

1622: The Dutch capture the P'eng-hu (Pescadores) Islands to the west of Taiwan and establish a base to control ship traffic through the Taiwan Straits.

1623–1624: In 1623 the Dutch sign a treaty with the Chinese, agreeing to withdraw from the Pescadores Islands. In exchange, they are permitted to establish posts on Taiwan and are granted other privileges. In 1624 the Dutch leave the Pescadores and move on to Taiwan, establishing their first settlement at Fort Orange, later called Fort Zeelandia, near present-day Tainan in the southwest of Taiwan.

1626: Alarmed at seeing the Dutch intruding in a part of the world they consider their monopoly, Spanish forces seize Keelung on the north coast of Taiwan; they soon expand their control across northern Taiwan.

1628–1635: In 1628 the Tokugawa shogunate orders Japanese settlers on Taiwan to withdraw; it is 1635 before the last Japanese leave. The shogunate's isolationist policies facilitate European expansion on Taiwan.

1642: Spanish settlements are captured by Dutch forces and the Spanish are driven out of northern Taiwan. Taiwan becomes a Dutch colonial enterprise ruled over by the Dutch United East India Company.

1644: Zheng Chenggong (1624?–1662, widely known in the West as Koxinga), a son of the powerful pirate-warlord Cheng Chih-lung, is appointed by the Chinese emperor to command remnants of Ming military forces against the invading Manchus. But it is too late: the Ming dynasty collapses and the Manchus establish the Qing dynasty. Operating along the southeastern coast of China, Zheng Chenggong will continue for the next seventeen years to lead the resistance against the Manchus while at the same time building his personal commercial maritime empire.

1652: In the first major anti-Western uprising in Chinese history, some fifteen thousand Chinese on Taiwan revolt against the Dutch. With the aid of two thousand aborigines, the Dutch quell the rebellion in two weeks.

1661–1662: Realizing he cannot hold out much longer against the Manchu-Qing forces, in March 1661 Zheng Chenggong (Koxinga) attacks Dutch strongholds in the south of Taiwan; the Dutch finally surrender in February 1662 and leave the island. In June 1662 Zheng Chenggong dies and is succeeded by his son, Cheng Ching. Although Cheng Ching continues to hold on to Taiwan, his rule is plagued by internal dissension for the next two decades.

1666: The first Confucian temple on Taiwan is completed. In general, the Cheng family and their fellow Ming Chinese promote Chinese culture in Taiwan.

1681: Cheng Ching dies. He is succeeded by his fifteen-year-old illegitimate son. The Manchu-Qing dynasty on mainland China, realizing that the Cheng family's hold on Taiwan is now weakened, prepares for an invasion.

For this reason we send a considerable force of ships and men to succor Formosa; in case that the great preparations of Koxinga are found to have vanished in smoke (as has often happened before), then will this fleet have been sent hither in vain.

Letter from Governor General Maatzkuiker of
Batavia to Van der Laam, commander of the Dutch
fleet (July 1680)

September 1683: The Cheng government abdicates in the face of an imminent invasion of Taiwan by Manchu forces.

THE MANCHU/QING PERIOD: 1683–1895

The Qing dynasty court records of the late seventeenth century describe Taiwan as a "frontier area." Lack of imperial interest in the region leads to inept rule by the Chinese officials sent from the mainland to govern the island. Throughout the eighteenth century, no form of central government is developed, and the officials are considered corrupt and inefficient by local settlers. Popular dissatisfaction erupts in a series of revolts against the oppression and cruelty meted out to the local citizens. By the mid-nineteenth century, Western ships are calling regularly at the island's ports and establishing a presence on the island. The Sino-French conflict in Indochina during the late nineteenth century prompts Peking (Beijing) finally to consider the strategic importance of the island. Competent officials are sent to Taiwan and the political administration is reorganized. Efficient and enlightened rule results in increased prosperity, but this comes to an abrupt end when China loses Taiwan to Japan.

1684: Taiwan is made a Chinese prefecture under the jurisdiction of Fujian province.

1684–1732: At least ten popular uprisings reflect the social and political turmoil of early Qing rule in Taiwan.

1714: Peking (Beijing) commissions three Jesuits to produce a map of Taiwan.

1729: The Qing emperor places a total ban on emigration of Chinese to Taiwan, but faced with the increasing deprivations of southeast China, many choose to emigrate illegally.

1786: A major rebellion breaks out against Chinese rule, but is rapidly crushed.

1840–1842: The First Opium War between China and Britain. The strategic importance of Taiwan is recognized as Westerners vie for trade in the wake of Chinese defeat and subsequent opening of Chinese ports to foreigners.

Late 1850s: Keelung and Tamsui on Taiwan become ports of call for Western ships. Many Western countries set up trading posts and consulates on Taiwan.

1874: A Japanese punitive expedition is sent to Taiwan to take revenge on Taiwanese aborigines who have slaughtered shipwrecked Japanese sailors. The British, nervous about a Japanese presence on Taiwan, demand that China proclaim sovereignty over the island. China is then obliged to cover the cost of the Japanese expedition and pay an indemnity for the beheaded Japanese sailors.

1875: China lifts the imperial ban on emigration of Chinese to Taiwan.

1879: Japan incorporates the nearby Ryukyu Islands and increases contact with Taiwan.

1884: The Sino-French war begins over Annam (Vietnam). The French plan to capture Taiwan in order to force Chinese capitulation.

August 1884: Liu Ming-chuan leads forces against French attempts to seize the port of Keelung.

1886: Taiwan is finally made a separate province. Liu Ming-chuan is appointed the first governor of Taiwan; he establishes a postal system and commences a railroad project.

August 3, 1894: Japan declares war against China over Korea.

April 1895: China concedes defeat by Japan. The Peace Treaty of Shimonoseki is signed, ceding Taiwan and the Pescadores Islands to Japan in perpetuity.

May 25, 1895: Local leaders in Taiwan proclaim independence and attempt to establish Asia's first republic. After five months of "pacification," the Japanese crush the new republic.

THE JAPANESE PERIOD: 1895–1945

Taiwan becomes Japan's first colonial undertaking. Government decrees are stringently enforced to establish law and order, and a system of mutual responsibility is put into effect. Agricultural productivity is increased and the economic infrastructure improved. Roads, railways and harbors are built, communications facilities upgraded, and education systems overhauled. By the 1920s Taiwan's economy is booming, diseases such as the bubonic plague have been eradicated, and industrialization is under way. However, all political decisions are made in Tokyo and administered by the colonial authorities, the local inhabitants are forced to learn Japanese at school, and little accommodation is made to local culture and customs. During the 1930s Japan grows increasingly aggressive toward China, halting the small moves toward democracy underway in Taiwan and reinstituting military rule in the area as it prepares for the conflict that becomes World War II.

June 1896: The Japanese Diet gives the Japanese governor-general in Taiwan the authority to use administrative orders in place of Japanese law to govern the land. This establishes colonial rule and prohibits local Taiwanese from benefiting from the rights accorded to Japanese citizens.

1898: Households are grouped under a system by which communities assume mutual responsibility for all wrongdoing. Harsh punishments are meted out to offenders. This applies only to Taiwanese people, and, though unpopular, the system proves very effective and is not abolished until 1945.

1903: Taiwan becomes the first electrified area outside Japan proper.

1910: Japan outlaws the practice on Taiwan of binding women's feet.

January 1920: The first major Taiwanese student organization, the Hsin Min Hui (New Citizens' Society), is founded. It is generally regarded as the precursor of all subsequent Taiwanese political organizations.

1924: The Home Rule Association of Taiwan presents a document listing twelve grievances to the Japanese colonial government.

1928: The first university is established in Taiwan.

September 1931: The Japanese occupation of Manchuria on the mainland triggers the formation of several political parties in Taiwan.

1935: In a cautious move toward democratization, Tokyo announces the establishment of elective government in Taiwan. It will, however, apply only to local government.

1936: Progress toward more democratic rule is halted as Japan heads toward war. However, Taiwan benefits from the development of heavy industry, becoming increasingly self-sufficient.

1937: Japan starts all-out aggression against China, and a new form of martial law is implemented in Taiwan.

April 1, 1938: At the Provisional National Congress of the Guomintang, the ruling Nationalist Party of China, its leader, Chiang Kai-shek, announces his intention to take back Taiwan from Japan.

1941: Japan launches its invasion of the Philippines from Taiwan, which the Japanese army calls an "unsinkable aircraft carrier."

December 1, 1943: The Cairo Declaration, signed by the Allies and China, includes a pledge to return Taiwan to the Republic of China.

July 26, 1945: The Allies sign the Potsdam Agreement, reiterating the territorial provisions of the Cairo Declaration.

BETWEEN TWO WORLDS: 1945–1998

The Chinese assume control of Taiwan, which is placed under military rule. Tensions break out between the local inhabitants and the Chinese sent over to govern. Chiang Kai-shek's Nationalist Chinese government on the mainland is defeated in 1949 and flees to Taiwan. Over the next decade, conditions on Taiwan gradually improve with a land-reform program and financial aid from the United States. The economy begins to soar and the country becomes increasingly democratized. The Nationalist Chinese claim to represent China in a world polarized into Communist and democratic blocs, but Taiwan is ousted from the United Nations as the Cold War escalates and the West seeks a rapprochement with Beijing in an attempt to balance the might of the USSR. Tensions simmer between the Republic of China in Taiwan and the People's Republic of China, which makes it clear that it intends to regain control of the island.

October 2, 1945: Taiwan officially becomes part of the Republic of China as agreed under the terms of the Cairo Declaration. It is not made a province of China as expected, but is placed under military rule. Chen Yi is appointed governor-general and supreme commander.

February 28, 1947: A Taiwanese uprising against Nationalist Chinese oppression is put down by the military, causing many deaths.

December 29, 1948: General Chen Cheng is appointed governor of Taiwan. The island is made a province and military rule dismantled in efforts to placate the outraged populace in the wake of the February massacre.

1949: As the months pass, Chiang Kai-shek's Nationalist forces are defeated by Mao Zedong's Communist forces and the Nationalists are forced to abandon the major cities on the mainland.

March 8, 1949: Chiang Kai-shek resumes presidency of the Republic of China, which he claims is now based in Taiwan. The Nationalists appoint Wu Kuo-chen governor.

December 8, 1949: The Guomintang (Nationalists), recognizing that they can no longer resist the Communists on the mainland, announce that they are relocating their capital to Taiwan. (Chiang Kai-shek arrives on Taiwan on December 10.) Martial law is applied to Taiwan by executive order. The government insists on retaining the name

"Republic of China" to underline its stated desire to regain control of mainland China.

Let's go and see the lanterns—
It's old-fashioned to wear a skirt;
Let's go and see the lanterns—
Though we're in China, lanterns were in
  Cathay.

Let's wade together through the moontide
To see the Buddhist temple afloat,

Darkly bulking over a sea
Of torches held to light the way to divinity,
Through incense-thick anachronism.

  "Lantern Festival," poem by Jung Tzu (1928–)

June 1950: Outbreak of the Korean War. The United States sends the Seventh Fleet to the Taiwan Straits to block any possible invasion by Mao's armies. Taiwan becomes synonymous with the Republic of China (as opposed to the People's Republic of China on the mainland), siding with the West and opposing communism.

1950: Taiwan, with U.S. aid, launches a highly successful land-reform program that increases agricultural production and paves the way for Taiwan's industrialization.

September 8, 1951: Under the peace treaty signed at San Francisco, Japan abandons all claims to Taiwan and the nearby Pescadores Islands.

December 1951: Taiwan's Provincial Assembly is established.

September 1953: Chiang Kai-shek extends the terms of the National Assembly, elected in 1947, until another National Assembly can be elected.

March 1954: The temporary provisions of the Constitution are indefinitely extended by the National Assembly. Chiang Kai-shek is reelected president for another six-year term.

September 3, 1954: Mainland Chinese Communist forces bombard Quemoy, the largest of the offshore islands controlled by Taiwan, but back down when the United States threatens military intervention.

January 1955: Northernmost Tache Island, held by Taiwan, falls to Communist forces. The U.S. Congress passes a resolution permitting American forces to defend Taiwan and the surrounding islands.

August 23, 1958: Mainland Chinese Communist forces fire on the offshore island of Quemoy. Once again, the threat of U.S. intervention ensures that the island remains under Taiwanese control.

March 11, 1960: The National Assembly amends the temporary provisions of the constitution to allow the president and the vice president to exceed the two-term limit. Chiang Kai-shek and Chen Cheng are reelected.

June 1960: President Eisenhower visits Taiwan. The People's Republic of China bombards Quemoy as part of a military exercise to show its disapproval of the visit.

December 1961: Taiwan's first nuclear reactor goes into operation.

February 1962: Taiwan opens its first stock exchange.

March 14, 1962: Taiwan's government announces that it does not recognize Japanese residual authority over the Ryukyu Islands.

July 1, 1964: U.S. aid to Taiwan is officially terminated. Taiwan's economy takes off to become one of the world's fastest-growing economies over the next two decades.

March 22, 1966: Chiang Kai-shek is reelected to a fourth term as president by the National Assembly.

December 3, 1966: Taiwan's first Export Processing Zone is inaugurated. Designed to encourage Western investment by reducing red tape and providing economic incentives, the zones are later emulated by other Asian countries, including China.

July 29, 1967: Compulsory education in Taiwan is extended from six to nine years.

June 25, 1968: Chiang Kai-shek's eldest son, Defense Minister Chiang Ching-kuo, is named vice premier.

1969: A U.S.-China rapprochement begins as a result of the Nixon Doctrine.

October 25, 1971: The Republic of China is expelled from the United Nations. The People's Republic of China is admitted to hold the China seat. This results in the loss of diplomatic ties between Taiwan and most of the nations with which it has had formal relations.

March 21, 1972: Chiang Kai-shek is elected to a fifth six-year term as president.

May 26, 1972: Chiang Ching-kao becomes premier.

April 5, 1975: Chiang Kai-shek dies.

May 1975: Premier Chiang Ching-kuo is elected Chairman of the Central Committee of the Guomintang (National Citizen Party). The Guomintang, now generally referred to as the KMT, was officially formed in 1919 by Sun Yat-sen in China and has been the majority party in Taiwan since the government fled to the island in 1949.

July 1976: The Republic of China Olympic Committee withdraws from the Montreal Olympic Games to protest being required to compete under the name Taiwan.

March 21, 1978: President Carter announces that the United States will cut diplomatic ties with Taiwan effective January 1, 1979. He acknowledges that there is only one China, the People's Republic of China.

April 15, 1979: The U.S. Congress passes the Taiwan Relations Act, giving Taiwan security and economic guarantees; although this is not a formal recognition of Taiwan as a sovereign nation state, its effect is much the same. Taiwan's population is now 17.1 million, and three decades of development have made Taiwan's economy one of Asia's strongest.

December 6, 1980: Supplemental national elections to the Legislative Yuan (the highest legislative organ of Taiwan) and the National Assembly, take place in what are widely regarded as Taiwan's first competitive elections. The democratization process is accelerated.

April 3, 1981: Chiang Ching-kuo is reelected Chairman of the ruling Guomintang.

December 1983: Taiwan holds its second national elections, characterized by genuine competition.

March 21, 1984: President Chiang Ching-kuo is elected to another six-year term. Lee Teng-hui is elected vice president.

September 1986: The Democratic Progressive Party (DPP) is formed.

December 1986: The first two-party elections ever held in a Chinese nation takes place in Taiwan. The Guomintang wins.

July 15, 1987: Martial law, imposed in 1949, is abolished. Martial law was never fully implemented, but the move is viewed with approval by the Western press as an indication of Taiwan's democratization.

January 13, 1988: President Chiang Ching-kuo dies. Lee Teng-hui is sworn in, becoming Taiwan's first native-born president.

March 21, 1990: Lee Teng-hui is reelected president for a six-year term and pledges democratic reform.

April 1990: The state of war with China, declared in 1949, is ended.

January 1991: The Executive Yuan (Taiwan's highest administrative body) approves a six-year development plan to improve the economic infrastructure.

December 1991: The first direct elections to the National Assembly are held. The Guomintang wins, receiving, according to some observers, a democratic mandate.

March 20, 1992: The new or Second National Assembly convenes to amend the constitution. Changes include introducing four-year terms for delegates and direct elections for the president and vice president.

July 16, 1992: The Legislative Yuan passes a statute decreeing that China is "one country, two areas" in regard to relations between Taiwan and mainland China.

December 19, 1992: The first direct elections to the Legislative Yuan are held. The ruling Guomintang wins a smaller majority of seats than expected. Disunity within the party is blamed.

January 4, 1993: President Lee Teng-hui gives the first ever State of the Nation address to the National Assembly. Shouting and fighting break out over the issue of Taiwan's independence.

February 27, 1993: President Lee Teng-hui announces that Taiwan will seek participation in the United Nations and calls for international support in this effort.

April 27, 1993: Two days of talks between representatives of China and Taiwan begin in Singapore. Four agreements are signed that specify areas of cooperation but do not address such contentious areas as sovereignty.

December 18, 1993: Officials from China and Taiwan meet in Taipei (the capital of Taiwan) to discuss improving trade and cultural links. This is the first time in forty years that an official Chinese delegation has been in Taiwan.

January 29, 1993: The ruling Guomintang wins a smaller number of seats than expected in mayoral elections marred by allegations of extensive vote-buying and violence.

February 2, 1994: Bilateral talks between China and Taiwan take place in Beijing.

August 8, 1994: A cooperation pact is signed with China. Sovereignty issues are not addressed.

September 8, 1994: The United States announces an official shift in policy toward Taiwan. The move toward a rapprochement between the United States and Taiwan angers China.

January 5, 1995: The Taiwanese cabinet approves a plan to ease a ban on direct transportation links with mainland China.

June 7–10, 1995: President Lee Teng-hui makes what is described as only a private visit to the United States, but the mainland Chinese government suspends talks with Taiwan in response.

We sincerely hope that all nations can treat us fairly and reasonably, and not overlook the significance, value, and functions we represent. Some say that it is impossible for us to break out of the diplomatic isolation we face, but we will do our utmost to demand the impossible.

President Lee Teng-hui, speech at Cornell University (June 9, 1995)

December 2, 1995: The ruling Kuomingtang loses ground to opposition parties in parliamentary elections.

March 22–27, 1996: The Dalai Lama visits Taiwan, angering the People's Republic of China.

March 23, 1996: President Lee Teng-hui wins a resounding victory in Taiwan's first democratic presidential election.

May 9, 1997: The government survives a no-confidence vote brought by opposition parties, angered by rising crime rates. A partial cabinet reshuffle ensues.

June 28, 1997: A "Say No To China" rally takes place in Taiwan three days before the transfer of Hong Kong to China.

July 1, 1997: When Hong Kong is handed over to China, Chinese Premier Li Peng declares that the "one country, two systems" policy could also work for Taiwan.

Summer 1997: The financial crisis that is spreading throughout Asia following Thailand's devaluation of its currency has some effect on Taiwan's economy.

August 21, 1997: Premier Lien Chan resigns in the face of criticism over a surge in the crime rate.

November 1997: The ruling Kuomingtang loses local elections in seven of the fifteen municipalities it had held.

January 20, 1998: The Chinese Foreign Ministry declares that China is ready to resume talks with Taiwan with no preconditions.

April 20, 1998: Thousands of Buddhists on Taiwan attend ceremonies greeting the arrival of what is regarded as a holy tooth that once belonged to Buddha.

June 30, 1998: During his visit to mainland China, U.S. President Clinton meets with a selected group of intellectuals and leaders in Shanghai and apparently spontaneously enunciates what is known as "the three no's policy": the United States would not support Taiwan independence, would not back Taiwan's efforts to enter the United Nations, and would not support the notion of two Chinas—namely, one China and one Taiwan. This is immediately met by expressions ranging from concern to criticism by Taiwanese and by some Americans, especially Republicans opposed to Clinton's policies, but Clinton and his spokesmen insist that this represents no change in U.S. policy and reiterate that the United States intends to continue supporting Taiwan under the provisions of the Taiwan Relations Act of 1979.

July 9, 1998: In an explicit follow-up to President Clinton's remarks in China about U.S. policy in regard to Taiwan, the government in Beijing urges Taiwan to "face reality" and agree to talks on an eventual reunification with China.

Hong Kong

PREHISTORIC HONG KONG

Hong Kong is a name applied to both a single island and a political entity that includes a total of 235 islands and a still larger area on the adjacent mainland, all of which the British acquired or leased in the nineteenth century. In this chronology, Hong Kong refers to this whole region. Throughout the Pleistocene Age (approx. 1.75 million years ago to 10,000 B.C.) the islands of Hong Kong are often attached directly to the mainland of China because of the low sea level; not until the world's seas rise to their present level, about 6000 B.C., did Hong Kong's islands become isolated. Although it is quite likely that some humans visited this territory earlier, the first known traces of human beings in this region date only to about 4100 B.C. What is uncertain is whether these first inhabitants originated in Southeast Asia, South China, or Taiwan. In any case, the people of Hong Kong pass through the Neolithic (New Stone) Age and Bronze Age, in both instances for the most part adopting or at least learning from the culture of peoples in southern China and Southeast Asia. Starting about 200 B.C., mainland Chinese begin to exert increasing control over southern China; not until about A.D. 220, however, do mainland Chinese appear to be becoming an active presence in Hong Kong. By about the year 400 Hong Kong seems to be involved in trade involving both China and Southeast Asia. Several bits of physical evidence during the early first millennium strongly suggest the increasing role of mainland Chinese in Hong Kong, but it will be about 800 before Hong Kong can begin to be considered as part of China. The earliest written evidence of the Chinese settlement in the Hong Kong region appears in a ninth-century poem.

4100–3000 B.C.: The oldest known evidence of human occupation in Hong Kong dates from this period, technically labeled the Middle Neolithic; it is sometimes described as that of "affluent foragers" because although these people continue to obtain most food simply by foraging, they also make quite advanced pottery and bone and shell artifacts. The first phase (Chung Hom Wan, approximately 4100–3600 B.C.) has both painted and cord-marked pottery; the second phase (Sham Wan, 3600–3000 B.C.) has finer pottery, some incised (with geometric designs) and some perforated. The main sites are on the islands of Lamma and Lantao. Other finds include stone tools—especially polished adzes. Some archaeologists see strong resemblances to the Bacsonian culture (so named after the prime site in Vietnam); others stress the strong indigenous roots of southern Chinese culture.

2800–1500 B.C.: For Hong Kong, this is the Late Neolithic period. The culture now has a strong maritime orientation—not surprisingly, in that the people live surrounded by ocean. There are indications of settlements that suggest some agriculture. The people make more sophisticated stone tools and ornamental rings from quartz and other stones; jadeite ceremonial axes (known as *yazhang*) found on Lamma and Lantao islands are almost certainly imports from China but suggest the development of ritual life; some pottery has geometric decorations; spindle whorls and net weights attest to textile industry and fishing.

1500–500 B.C.: Although most people in Hong Kong continue with their stone tools, some people begin to use copper and bronze for special weapons, tools, knives, and fish hooks. By 1300 B.C. some people on Hong Kong are casting bronze; bronze socketed axes made in bivalve molds are similar to those found in Vietnam, Cambodia, and Laos; other bronze artifacts are either of mainland Chinese import or inspiration, suggesting ties with the Red River delta in the southeast corner of China. But stone rings made of marble and agate are as much markers of this period as are bronze artifacts. There is evidently some increase in population, more people adopt rice cultivation, and domestic animals are probably being kept; but most people seem to remain tied to coastal life and little remains of permanent settlements. Burials (1000–500 B.C.) with orientation of the head to the south suggest a primitive notion of *feng shui*, the Chinese belief in geomancy.

1200 B.C.?–A.D. 200: Dating from sometime during this long period are carvings found on rocks at nine sites in Hong Kong; some of these are remote locales, others are near villages, but all are overlooking coastal water. Most of these have a sort of continuous spiral patterns, with geometric and/or zoomorphic elements. These spirals seem to link these carvings to Bronze Age artifacts dated to about 1200–400 B.C. In any case, they are not exactly like anything found either in China or anyplace else in world. It is believed that the carvings are in some way associated with rituals and religious beliefs.

The people who make them are sometimes regarded as Yueh, a somewhat vague name (sometimes spelled Yeu, Yiu, and even Viet) the Chinese applied to early inhabitants of southern China; they are a diverse people, speaking different languages and practicing different cultures, but they are most likely an Austro-Thai people and may well be ancestors of the aboriginal tribes who live in the mountains of Hong Kong as late as the nineteenth century.

221 B.C.–A.D. 220: Two Chinese dynasties—Qin (221–207 B.C.) and Han (206 B.C.–A.D. 220)—move into southern China to bring it under military control. The main point of concentration is the area around Canton (Guangzhou in Chinese), some seventy-five miles northwest of Hong Kong. The northern Chinese regard the peoples of the south practically as savages and the region as virtually a wild swamp, but the Chinese want the produce of the south—ivory, rhinoceros, pearls, medicinal drugs, and dyestuffs. There is little evidence of the Chinese presence in Hong Kong except a fair number of Han period coins, indicative of trade. It is not really known if the Chinese moved into Hong Kong with military forces, but Chinese historical texts refer to a naval battle of 120–111 B.C. and a campaign against the "barbarian Yueh," which may include inhabitants of Hong Kong.

A.D. 100–220: A brick chamber-tomb at Lei

Cheng Uk, on Kowloon peninsula—dated to about A.D. 200, the end of Han dynasty—is entirely Chinese in its design and materials. Some sixty-one pottery objects are found in this tomb as well as eight pieces of bronze. It is obvious that this is a tomb of an important person, and someone with strong links to China to the north; one surmise is that it is a memorial to a Chinese military leader in the campaigns against the Yueh. In any case, it is the oldest and strongest evidence of the Chinese presence or influence in Hong Kong.

265–907: Fine burial vases from this period found in Hong Kong are either imports or made under direct inspiration from mainland China.

300–900: A lime kiln industry flourishes in Hong Kong, particularly during the Tang dynasty (618–907); the lime is made from burning shells and coral.

?450: A Buddhist monastery at Tuen Mun, on mainland Hong Kong, claims to have been founded about this time; this is not un-reasonable, but the first written evidence of the monastery dates only from 950.

Though Tuen Mun [mountain in Hong Kong]
   is considered high,
The waves have swallowed it up.

Couplet by Han Yue, engraved on stone tablet at a
Buddhist monastery (6th century)

618–907: During the Tang dynasty Hong Kong expands its trade with Asia, particularly with Persia and India. Most of this trade passes through Canton on the Chinese mainland.

8th century: Beginning at least by this century, a settlement at Tai Bo is a major source of pearls.

9th century: The Chinese poet Han Yueh refers to Tuen Mun naval base on Hong Kong, which almost certainly serves as a customs post and guards the approach to Canton (Guangzhou).

CHINESE COLONIZATION: A.D. 907–1841

During the tenth century, the Chinese establish an Imperial Pearl Monopoly at Tai Bo. Civilians are excluded from the area until the end of the eleventh century, when the impecunious Song dynasty begins to distribute imperial property grants to influential Chinese. It is likely that another Imperial Estate exists at Kowloon, where fleeing Song emperors stay in the mid-thirteenth century. From the fourteenth century, the Chinese government pursues isolationist policies that lead to military withdrawal from the Hong Kong region. As imperial interest in the region declines, pirates increasingly terrorize the coast during the fifteenth and sixteenth centuries. Defenses are improved when the area is finally made a separate county in 1571. From the end of the eighteenth century, Western trade expands through Canton (Guangzhou) where opium is brought by the British to trade for tea. Tensions over the opium trade escalate, and erupt in the First Anglo-Chinese War (also known as the First Opium War, 1840–1842).

907–960: The Five Dynasties. The Chinese establish an Imperial Pearl Monopoly at Tai Bo in 907. Salt farms and a naval base are set up at Kowloon.

960–1279: The Song dynasty. Well-connected Chinese begin to settle in the region, apparently with imperial permission. The first temple to Tin Hua, the goddess of the fishing community, is established. An inscription at Fat Tong Mun in Hong Kong (dated to 1274) refers to the visit of a "salt field official" to the area. The last two Song emperors stay in the region during their flight from the Mongols.

1280-1368: The Yuan dynasty rules China. Little information survives about this period, although evidence suggests that the remnants of the Song court settle in the Kowloon region. Scholars believe that this area is run as a personal fief by the influential Ho family, who are granted lands in return for their support of the Yuan dynasty.

1368-1644: Ming dynasty. The imperial government responds to pirates terrorizing the region by declaring it a separate county in 1571 and appointing a senior official to restore order and improve coastal defenses.

1644: The Qing dynasty takes over China and will rule until 1912.

1661: Pro-Ming factions attack the coast, which prompts the imperial government to evacuate all citizens living within fifty *li* (about twelve miles) of the coast. Their homes and lands are burned in a bid to starve out the rebels.

1669: The coastal evacuation order is rescinded. The original Cantonese evacuees return to their former homes, although many have died from starvation. Their lands are bought by Hakka (meaning "guest") people, originally from northeast China.

1685: The British begin trading in Canton (Guangzhou).

1687: The East India Company, already in possession of the Indian Trade Monopoly, is granted monopoly over trade with China by the British government. Vast amounts of tea are imported to Britain and are paid for with silver bullion, creating a trade imbalance in China's favor.

1757: A guild of merchants called the Cohong wins exclusive right to trade with Westerners.

1759: The Chinese promulgate trading restrictions to ensure that the Western traders do not expand into other areas of China. These rules are gradually tightened to the frustration of the foreign traders.

1773: The British import opium into China in an attempt to regularize the balance of trade with China.

1793: A British mission to Peking (Beijing), led by Lord Francis Napier, fails to alleviate the trade restrictions, but establishes the British desire to occupy Hong Kong Island.

1796: An imperial edict totally bans the opium trade, which nonetheless continues to expand illegally.

March 18, 1839: Lin Zexu is appointed the Special Imperial Commissioner for the Suppression of the Opium Trade. He demands immediate surrender of all opium, which is then publicly destroyed.

September 4, 1839: As tensions mount, the British fire at a Chinese junk, touching off the First Anglo-Chinese War, known also as the First Opium War.

January 1840: War is formally declared between Great Britain and China.

BRITISH RULE: 1841–1997

Hong Kong is ceded to the British at the end of the First Anglo-Chinese War (First Opium War, 1840–1842) and quickly eclipses Macau as the foremost trading center of the region. Stonecutters Island and Kowloon are annexed to the region at the culmination of the Second Anglo-Chinese War (1856–1860). Russian and French acquisition of Chinese territories prompts Great Britain to lease the New Territories for ninety-nine years, beginning in 1898. During the latter part of the nineteenth century, the increasing demand for workers is met by regular influxes of Chinese refugees from disturbances in mainland China, but political and social reforms fail to keep up with the expanding population, causing popular dissatisfaction. Japan occupies Hong Kong briefly during World War II (1941–1945), but the British rapidly reassume control. From the 1950s, trade gives way to manufacturing and the region prospers, becoming one of the world's foremost business and financial centers. During the 1980s, the imminent expiration of the lease of the New Territories leads to negotiations for the reversion of the territory to Chinese control. In the early 1990s, attempts at democratic reform by the British Governor of Hong Kong are resisted by the Chinese government, but the handover is completed in 1997 under assurances that it will be administered as a Special Administrative Region of China.

January 20, 1841: The Chinese are defeated by the British navy in the First Anglo-Chinese War. The Treaty of Chuanbi is signed, ceding Hong Kong Island to Great Britain. However, both governments refuse to accept the terms and hostilities are renewed.

Albert is so much amused at my having got the Island of Hong Kong, and we think Victoria ought to be called Princess of Hong Kong in addition to Princess Royal.

Letter of Queen Victoria (April 13, 1841)

A barren island with hardly a house upon it.

Letter of Lord Palmerston (April 21, 1841)

1841–1842: The British occupy Hong Kong Island during the First Anglo-Chinese War.

August 29, 1842: Representatives of China and Great Britain sign the Treaty of Nanking, formally ceding Hong Kong Island to the British in perpetuity.

1852: Refugees from the Taiping Rebellion in mainland China begin to arrive in Hong Kong.

1856–1860: The Second Anglo-Chinese War (Second Opium War).

October 1860: The Treaty of Peking is signed. Great Britain acquires Kowloon and Stonecutters Island in perpetuity.

1869: The Suez Canal is opened, improving trade routes between Europe and the Far East.

July 1, 1898: The British claim that recent territorial acquisitions in China by France and Russia have caused concern over regional defense capabilities. They lease the New Territories for ninety-nine years under the Second Convention of Peking.

1908: The British government decides, despite opposition from the Hong Kong government, to close all opium-smoking parlors.

1911: Refugees flood in to Hong Kong as the Manchu dynasty is overthrown in China and the republic is established. The Chinese revolution produces a new government even more hostile to the importation of opium, and regulations are more strictly applied.

Afterward I saw the outside world, and as I began to wonder how it was that foreigners, that Englishmen could do such things as they had done, for example with the barren rock of Hong Kong.

Address at Hong Kong University by Sun Yat-sen

(1923)

May 1925–October 1926: A general strike and boycott in Hong Kong is sparked by antiforeign demonstrations in Shanghai. Fueled by anti-imperialism on the mainland, the strikes express popular indignation at the privileged status of foreigners.

December 8, 1941: The Japanese army, which has already gained control of Peking (Beijing), Tientsin (Tianjin), Shanghai, and Nanjing, mounts an attack on Hong Kong.

December 25, 1941: The British surrender Hong Kong to the Japanese. The Japanese refer to the region as "the Captured Territory of Hong Kong."

1942–1945: Trade comes to a standstill in the region and food becomes scarce.

September 15, 1945: Japan surrenders to the

Allies and the British rapidly reassume control of Hong Kong.

September 1945: The prohibition of opium is accepted by the British, and all government monopolies in Hong Kong and Singapore are abolished.

September 1949: Chinese refugees pour into Hong Kong as the Communist government is established on the mainland. The ousted Nationalist government flees to Taiwan. During the next fifty years, Hong Kong becomes one of the most prosperous, modern, and crowded cities in Asia.

April 1966: The Star Ferry Company, which runs ferries between Hong Kong Island (where many people work) and Kowloon (where many people live), decides to raise fares. This triggers violent riots expressing popular social and political dissatisfaction.

May 1967: The Cultural Revolution in China spills over into Hong Kong, and rioters protest against British rule.

March 8, 1972: China claims Hong Kong in a letter to the United Nations.

1974: Increasing numbers of Vietnamese refugees begin to arrive in Hong Kong.

March–April 1979: Hong Kong governor Sir Murray MacLehouse meets Chinese premier Deng Xiaoping, who advises the governor, "tell your investors to put their hearts at ease." However, the Chinese Foreign Minister declares that Hong Kong is part of China.

October 1980: The British government tightens up immigration laws and announces the end of the "Reach Base" policy for Chinese immigrants, which gave any Chinese person who reached the colony the right to stay.

1981: Under the terms of Britain's New Nationality Act, 2.6 million Hong Kong Chinese, erstwhile British subjects, become "Citizens of the British Dependent Territory of Hong Kong." The change in status deprives them of the right to an abode in the United Kingdom.

September 1981: British Prime Minister Margaret Thatcher visits Beijing to discuss the future of Hong Kong. She insists on the validity of former treaties but problems arise over the issue of sovereignty. The Chinese make it clear that they intend to regain the whole Hong Kong region.

December 1982: China adopts a new constitution that makes a provision for Hong Kong to be governed as a Special Administrative Region under the principle of "one country, two systems."

July 1983: Formal rounds of talks on the future of Hong Kong begin between representatives of the Chinese and British governments. The issue of sovereignty remains unresolved.

September 26, 1984: The Sino-British Joint Declaration is signed by British and Chinese prime ministers. The British government considers that governing Hong Kong Island and Stonecutter Island without Kowloon and the New Territories would be impracticable. They agree to return the whole of the Hong Kong region to Chinese control.

June 1985: The Basic Law Drafting Committee (BLDC) is set up by the Chinese to develop a constitution-like document for post-1997 Hong Kong.

September 1985: The first (indirect) elections to the Legislative Council are held. Members had hitherto been nominated.

1988: The Hong Kong government publishes a White Paper, which anticipates the first direct elections to the Legislative Council in 1991, after China has approved the Basic Law.

May–June 1989: Large public rallies are held in Hong Kong, in support of prodemocracy demonstrations in Beijing's Tiananmen Square. Over a million Hong Kong people peacefully protest the violent Chinese crackdown.

April 1990: China's National People's Congress approves the Basic Law for Hong Kong. The Basic Law will form the basis for the territory's political, economic, social, and judicial arrangements for fifty years after the handover.

April 1990: The British government announces that fifty thousand heads of household and their dependents will be granted full British national passports with the right of abode in the United Kingdom. The Chinese government says that it will refuse to accept the validity of these passports.

September 1991: Landmark direct elections are held for the Legislative Council in Hong Kong. Prodemocracy candidates win all but two of eighteen seats contested.

October 7, 1992: Governor of Hong Kong Chris Patten unveils plans for democratic reform, including expanding the voter base and instituting free elections.

December 3, 1992: Beijing threatens to abandon the Joint Declaration if Patten goes ahead with the reforms.

1993: Britain and China continue to heatedly debate the reform proposals, and the Hong Kong government implements some democratic changes.

> *The city has become*
> *adjunct to its airport.*
> *The airport has become a mere coach station*
> *for families strung out*
> *across oceans and continents.*
> "Hong Kong at the Crossroads," poem by Louise Ho
> (1990s)

December 27, 1993: In response to the governor's refusal to abandon democratic reforms, Beijing announces plans to dismantle the democratically elected Legislative Council on July 1, 1997.

May 1994: China begins issuing Hong Kong currency through the Bank of China.

1995: Legislative Council elections (four-year term) are held for the last time before Hong Kong's handover to China in 1997.

June 30, 1997: Britain's ninety-nine-year lease expires at midnight, and Hong Kong becomes a Special Administrative Region of China.

CHINESE RESTORATION: 1997–1998

The Chinese government regains control of the region and immediately dismantles the Legislative Council, replacing it with a pro-Beijing Provisional Legislature. The Asian region is in economic recession, and tourism in Hong Kong plummets. Local businesses, industry, and the Hong Kong stock market are affected by the "domino effect" of collapsing Asian currencies and banks, but by mid-1998 the region begins to show signs of stabilizing.

July 1, 1997: The Legislative Council is dissolved and replaced by a pro-Beijing Provisional Legislature. Four thousand armed troops arrive in a show of military force.

October 1, 1997: Hong Kong officially celebrates China's National Day for the first time.

October 8, 1997: Tung Chee-hwa, appointed by Beijing as the chief executive of Hong Kong, presents first State of the Territory address on the hundredth day of Chinese rule.

December 28, 1997: Hong Kong authorities begin to kill the first of some 1,400,000 million chickens suspected of harboring a

deadly avian influenza virus. Fatal to humans, the virus is suspected of killing at least twenty people before it is eliminated in March 1998. It is believed that the virus was actually introduced from the mainland.

January 12, 1998: Hong Kong's largest investment bank, Peregrine Investment Holdings, files for liquidation. Up to this point, Hong Kong seems to have been relatively unscathed by the financial crisis that is sweeping through Asia, but this now plunges Hong Kong's financial markets into a downward spiral, gradually leading to a collapse of its stock market, a rapid decline in its property values, and great pressure on its currency, the Hong Kong Dollar (HK$).

May 24, 1998: In elections to the Legislative Council, pro-democracy candidates win fourteen of the twenty directly elected seats, but the system established by the Communist government of China has held forty seats on the council for those effectively assigned by the pro-China and pro-business interests. Immediately after the election, the chief executive of the Special Administrative Region, Tung Chee-hwa, warns that there will be no acceleration of political reform.

July 6, 1998: Hong Kong formally inaugurates its new International Airport. It has cost the government HK$20 billion. In its first months it is besieged by a host of technical and logistical problems, aggravated by the increasing decline in the world's economies that translates into a decline in the trade and tourism which were expected to finance the airport.

August 14, 1998: As Hong Kong stocks and currency continue to decline in value, the government begins to purchase shares and futures with the goal of buoying the Hong Kong stock market, which has declined to a five-year low. Unemployment also hits a fifteen-year high. Defending what the free market economies see as unwarranted government intervention, Hong Kong's financial secretary, Sir Donald Tsang, claims this is called for because of "speculators who have been deploying a whole host of improper measures."

Macau (Macao)

CHINA'S MACAU

Macau is the name given to a tiny region that includes two islets (totaling only some four square miles) and a peninsula (about 2.1 square miles), the latter joined to the Chinese mainland by a narrow isthmus. Macau is some forty miles southwest of Hong Kong, and like its better known neighbor, is linked by its history to both China and the world of European colonial imperialism. Macau is literally linked to China until about 6000 B.C., when the rising sea level gives Macau its present configuration. Next to nothing is known about Macau during the prehistoric period of China and the other East Asian or Southeast Asian lands. In fact, very little is known about Macau until the coming of the Portuguese in the mid-sixteenth century. This is due probably more to the sparseness of modern archaeological research than to an absence of ancient inhabitants. It is clear, though, even without much physical or written evidence, that this territory was always part of China.

Under the Portuguese, Macau prospered as a junction for international trade, particularly between Western Europe and China; as an international port, it also became notorious for its night life, prostitution, and gambling. Although the Portuguese dominated the official and administrative affairs, it was the Chinese who gradually came to run the island's economic and social life. Seeing the handwriting on the wall, the Portuguese agreed to turn Macau back to the Chinese in 1999.

4500–3500 B.C.: During what is technically the early Middle Neolithic period in this part of the world, some inhabitants of a site on Macau known as Hac Sa Wan possess a painted pottery of a type familiar from Hong Kong during this time (where it is known as the Chung Hom Wan type).

3500–2500 B.C.: Incised pottery of the type found in Hong Kong and known as the Sham Wan phase of the Middle Neolithic is found in Macau.

1000? B.C.–A.D. 200: A number of rock carvings at Ka Ho on Coloane Islet, Macau, may be related to rock carvings on Hong Kong of this period, although there is no solid evidence of this. One of the carvings is a "chessboard" pattern and another is a more complex design that may represent boats; the carvings are accompanied by man-made pits, or small holes, cut in the rocks.

7th century–16th century A.D.: Chinese overseas trade flourishes, and it is assumed that some of this passes through Macau because of its strategic location at the mouth of the Pearl River. This also means that pirates probably use Macau as both a base and a refuge.

13th century: By this time, Macau is known as Hou Keng (Haojing) to the Chinese. During this century Chinese settlers on Macau apparently establish two temples, the Ma Kok (Mage Miu) Temple and the Kun Iam Tong (Guanyin Tang) Temple.

1276: Forces of the Southern Song dynasty of mainland China are defeated by forces of what will become known as the Yuan dynasty; the Song royal family and its loyal followers flee in two thousand junks, and a storm forces them to take refuge on the islands of Macau. The Yuan forces follow shortly but are repulsed. Supposedly the Song Chinese remain and establish the first solid Chinese settlements on Macau.

14th–15th centuries: The so-called Hoklo (boat people) Chinese begin to move onto Macau, attracted by its harbors, for they are interested in trading with southern Chinese.

1514–1553: During this period, Portuguese traders and fishermen, by now based in Malacca in Malaya, visit the Chinese mainland (1514) and try to establish a series of trading posts or fishing bases along the south coast of China. Each of these is eventually abandoned, but the Portuguese are determined to have a permanent base for their trading operations in this part of Asia.

1535–1554: The Ming Chinese establish a customs house on Macau during this time in an attempt to regulate the increasing trade along this part of China's coast. In the end, the customs house is relocated on Longbow, an island just west of Macau and also used by the Portuguese.

1552: Francis Xavier, the pioneering Catholic Jesuit missionary in Asia, dies on the island of Shangchuan (Saint John), southwest of Macau.

1553: Lionel de Souza, commander of the Portuguese enterprise in East Asia, reaches an agreement with the Chinese that allows him to establish a trading base in the area of Macau. It is not clear whether the Portuguese do establish such a base at once, although it appears that some Portuguese begin to use Macau for drying out their soaked cargo.

THE PORTUGUESE PERIOD: 1557–1999

From the 1550s, Macau rapidly becomes an important Portuguese entrepôt linking the lucrative trade routes between Europe and the Orient and enabling the Portuguese to virtually monopolize Western trade with China. Missionaries, particularly Jesuits, begin to arrive in the mid-sixteenth century, and establish several influential educational, medical and charitable institutions. By the end of the seventeenth century, Portuguese maritime preeminence has waned as a result of the loss of the pivotal port of Malacca and the Japanese ban on trade. As a result, the Chinese are able to reassert some authority in the area during the eighteenth century, and tensions develop over the trade in opium. The First Opium War (1840–1842) leads to the cession of Hong Kong Island to Great Britain; Macau is relegated to a minor commercial role. However the introduction of licensed gambling in the 1850s provides a new source of revenue. In the late twentieth century, the Macau region becomes a popular tourist destination, despite some problems with corruption and gang violence (much of it caused by the money generated by gambling casinos). Reversion of Macau to China is negotiated, and the region prepares to become a Special Administrative Region of China two years after Hong Kong is assigned the same status.

1557: This year is sometimes regarded the founding of Portugal's claim to Macau because it sees a formal and permanent agreement that replaces the verbal agreement made in 1555 between Captain-Major Lionel de Souza and Wang Po, representative of Guangdong Province and acting commander of the regional Chinese coast guard. The Portuguese agree to pay license fees, customs taxes and a yearly lease sum. (Legend claims that Portugal's great poet, Luis de Camoens, author of *The Lusiads*—the national epic based on Vasco da Gama's expedition to India—was on Macau at this time, but this is questioned by some authorities.)

Early 1560s: Increasing numbers of Christian missionaries, particularly Jesuit priests, begin to arrive in Macau, which becomes an important base for Christian evangelization throughout Asia.

1573: The Chinese construct a barrier wall at the base of the Macau peninsula, preventing access to mainland China.

January 23, 1576: The Pope declares the establishment of the Diocese of Macau.

1580: The Portuguese and Spanish crowns are united as Philip II of Spain accedes to the throne of Portugal. All Portuguese territories come under Spanish influence.

1582: Macau's first legislative body, the Municipal Senate, is formed, and the first Bishop of the Diocese is installed.

1602–1607: The Dutch, hoping to take over the lucrative Portuguese trading routes between China and Japan, make unsuccessful exploratory attacks on Macau.

June 1622: The Portuguese resist a significant Dutch invasion.

1623: Macau's first formal governor, Francesco de Mascarenhas, arrives from Portugal

and initiates major improvements to the region's defenses.

1639: The Japanese ban trade with the Portuguese, severing an important Portuguese trade route.

1640: King João IV becomes king of Portugal, ending almost a century of Spanish domination. Macau, which had pledged allegiance to the Old Royal Portuguese Crown is rewarded with the title "City of the Name of God, None Other More Loyal."

1641: The Dutch capture Malacca (in what is now called Malaysia), a Portuguese entrepôt strategically placed between Baghdad and the Spice Islands. Macau is now cut off from Goa (the capital of Portuguese India), and trade is severely disrupted.

Whosoever considers how this city of Macao fell from the peak and summit of its prosperity and ease will find that it was the turn of Fate's wheel which upset and reversed it: the present poverty being all the greater because whilst it contains so many valuable diamonds, rubies, pearls, seed-pearls, gold, silk, and musk, it is as if there were none since the inhabitants of China care nothing for such things but prize only silver which is today precisely what we lack.

João Marques Moreires (1644)

1685: An imperial directive from Peking (Beijing) allows foreign trade at all Chinese ports, including Macau, thereby ending the Portuguese monopoly on trade with China.

1688: Portuguese prominence wanes; the Chinese reassert their influence in Macau. A customs office is established and an official appointed to collect duties.

1732: A second customs house is built and a

Chinese assistant magistrate installed to exercise Chinese authority over legal affairs.

1746: Preaching Christianity to the Chinese in Macau is forbidden.

1767: The Portuguese expel the Jesuits from Macau, following suppression of the order in Portugal.

1796: An imperial edict from Peking (Beijing) places a total ban on all opium activity, but is largely ignored by the Western traders.

1808: The British occupy Macau, under pretense of protecting the area from French attack, but withdraw in late December under combined Portuguese and Chinese pressure.

1839: Lin Zexu is appointed special imperial commissioner for the suppression of the opium trade. He threatens military force if his demands are not complied with.

1844: The Portuguese government combines Timor and Solor (in what is now Indonesia) to form a single administrative Portuguese province.

1845–1849: Governor Ferreiro de Amaral is directed by Lisbon to establish Portuguese influence in the region. The Chinese are taxed and their customs houses destroyed.

August 1849: Governor Amaral is assassinated by the Chinese. The Portuguese retaliate by attacking and overwhelming the Chinese fortress of Passeleong.

1851: The Portuguese introduce licensed gambling in Macau, which becomes a major source of revenue.

1850s–1870s: Macau becomes a center for the "coolie" trade. Chinese laborers are sold and shipped overseas in appalling conditions. The trade is eventually abolished in 1873.

1862: The Treaty of Tientsin (Tianjin) recognizing Portuguese sovereignty over the region is negotiated, but the Chinese refuse to ratify it.

1888: The Luso-Chinese Treaty of Friendship is signed, confirming Portugal's administra-

tion of Macau in perpetuity, but the question of border delimitation is evaded.

There is no question that it harbors in its hidden places the riffraff of the world, the drunken shipmasters, the flotsam of the sea, the derelicts and more shameless, beautiful, savage women than any port in the world. It is hell. But to those who whirl in its unending play, it is the one haven where there is never a hand raised or a word said against the play of the beastliest emotions that ever blackened the human heart.

Cities of Sin, by Hendrik de Leeuw (1934)

1890: Portuguese integrate nearby Green Island into Macau's territory.

1928: Portugal and China sign a new Treaty of Friendship, once again avoiding the issue of border delimitation.

1937: Japan invades China as a new influx of refugees arrives in Macau from China.

1949: Victorious Communist forces establish the People's Republic of China.

---

*This city of indulgence need not fear
The major sins by which the heart is killed,
and governments are torn to pieces:
. . . nothing serious can happen here.*

"Macau," by W. H. Auden (1939)

1951: Macau joins the UN embargo on export of strategic goods to China during the Korean War and becomes an important center for gold exchange.

1955: Portugal declares Macau an overseas province, although Chinese officials consider Macau to be a Chinese territory.

November 1966–January 1967: Communist China's Cultural Revolution spills over into the region and severe rioting breaks out. The governor makes a public apology for police intervention and promises compensation.

1972: China claims Macau in a letter to the United Nations.

April 25, 1974: Military coup d'état in Portugal. The new government seeks a rapprochement with China.

1975: The Portuguese government proposes returning Macau to China, but the offer is declined. Western observers speculate that the Chinese authorities consider Macau an excellent source of foreign currency, and through it, they might quietly import precious metals and other goods from countries with which they officially have no relations.

1976: The Organic Statute (Macau's constitution) is enacted. It creates a Legislative Assembly of elected and appointed members and gives the territory increased political autonomy.

February 1979: Portugal and China sign a secret agreement. It designates Macau a "Chinese territory under temporary Portuguese administration."

February 1984: The Legislative Assembly is dissolved and reformed with equal voting rights granted to all residents.

June 30, 1986: Formal negotiations between Portugal and China on the future of Macau begin.

April 13, 1987: The Sino-Portuguese Joint Declaration is signed. Under the terms of the declaration, China will assume sovereignty of Macau on December 20, 1999. Full Portuguese citizenship rights are granted to ethnic Chinese and their descendants. The Declaration also allows for the area to be governed as a Special Administrative Region under the principle "one country, two systems," after the 1999 handover.

From our point of view, we were very glad that Portugal accepted a rather easy process for the handing over of Macau to Chinese sovereignty.

Deng Xiaoping (1987)

September 1988: A Basic Law Drafting Committee is formed to establish a constitution-like document for Macau after 1999.

February 1989: The Legislative Assembly votes to make Chinese an official language along with Portuguese.

June 1989: More than 500,000 demonstrators peaceably protest the Tiananmen Square massacre in Beijing.

September 1990: Governor of Macau Carlos Mantey Melancia resigns, stating that he is unable to cope with the corruption and administrative problems of the region.

March 31, 1993: The Basic Law (which is intended to form the basis for the territory's political, social, economic, and judicial arrangements for the next fifty years) is passed by the National People's Congress. It remains to be seen, however, whether the Chinese government will honor all of its provisions.

September 22, 1996: The last elections for the Legislative Assembly are held before the 1999 handover. Beijing announces that the new legislature will remain in office until the year 2001.

July 1997: Macau institutes tougher laws to combat gangs, for the most part fighting turf wars over the profits generated by the gambling casinos and prostitution. These gangs are known as Triads, and are estimated to have some ten thousand members. It is alleged that one reason they are able to flourish is that their leaders reside in mainland China and that members can retreat there after committing crimes. During 1997 at least 20 people are known to have been killed in Macau by gang warfare and related violence.

1998: Gang warfare becomes even more violent as three civil servants are killed and the chief of police barely escapes from a fire-bombing of his car (May 1). It is now accepted that most residents of Macau are looking forward to the Chinese taking control and enforcing law and order.

December 20, 1999: Macau becomes a Special Administrative Region of the People's Republic of China.

PART TWO

South Asia

India

POLITICAL HISTORY

PREHISTORIC SOUTH ASIA: 450,000–2600 B.C.

South Asia—the Indian subcontinent and certain adjacent lands and islands—is a vast region with great diversity in its climate, terrain, ecology, and other environmental features. Inevitably, then, it is impossible to set down generalizations that apply to the entire region. But one does hold up: there are no known fossil remains of the early hominids who most certainly are living there at least by about 450,000 B.C. (In fact, stone artifacts dating back as far as some 2,000,000 years have been found in the Pabbi Hills and Riwat in northern Pakistan, but these appear to be isolated instances.) Starting about 450,000 B.C., hominids and then archaic *Homo sapiens* living in parts of India produce a sequence of stone tools that, with several regional variants, tend to pass through much the same stages (in terms of types and techniques) as in other parts of the world during the Lower, Middle, and Upper Paleolithic periods. At some point, *Homo sapiens* appears in South Asia, but exactly who these first humans are—where they come from, their physical characteristics, etc.—is as yet unknown. By about 8000 B.C., the stone tools are also associated with rock paintings in caves and rock shelters, yet there are still no known remains of human beings. In the following millennia, communities begin to emerge throughout India, particularly in the northwest that will become Pakistan, and these gradually adopt or develop agriculture, domesticated animals, pottery, and the other elements of what is known as the Neolithic culture. The oldest human fossil remains known in South Asia are dated to about 3000 B.C., and by this time there is emerging in the Indus Valley the network of communities that will constitute the first true civilization of South Asia.

450,000–70,000 B.C.: Hominids (presumably *Homo erectus*) apparently live in parts of the Indian subcontinent, for they leave their stone tools in many sites. During this time, these tools pass through much the same stages—crude hand-held choppers to more diverse and refined tools—as those made by hominids in other parts of the world during this period. Where these hominids came from is not known—possibly from Africa, possibly from the Near East; in any case, by the end of this period, the inhabitants of

South Asia are probably like the Neanderthals of Western Europe.

70,000–35,000 B.C.: In various parts of the Indian subcontinent, stone tools of this period testify to the presence of human beings, most of whom settle in or near river valleys. In particular, at Bhimbetka, in the Vindhya Range in central India, many rock shelters and caves show signs of human occupation. Although no human fossils are as yet known, by the end of this period, these people are probably fully evolved *Homo sapiens*.

35,000–10,000 B.C.: Remains such as stone tools and animal bones at many sites around the Indian subcontinent attest to occupation by people who are most certainly *Homo sapiens*.

12,000–5000 B.C.: During this period, most people in South Asia continue to obtain nourishment by hunting, fishing, and food gathering. They probably domesticate the dog. They still depend mainly on a fairly specialized stone tool kit but also make weapons, implements, and gear of all kinds from wood and fiber.

8000 B.C.–A.D. 700: Some four hundred rock shelters in a four-square-mile area of central India centered on Bhimbetka are covered with paintings and crayon drawings (using sixteen colors); animals and human figures are the most common subjects, and the paintings tend to divide into two groups— those depicting hunters and food-gatherers, and those depicting fighters, riding on horses and elephants, and using metal weapons. Nothing certain is known about the motives of those who made them, but these paintings do not appear to have a religious or ritualistic purpose; in any case, they provide a graphic record of the way of life of the people in this part of India over many millennia.

7000–3500 B.C.: At Mehrgarh (now in west central Pakistan), people develop the earliest agricultural and pastoral community known in South Asia. These people make mud-brick houses with storage areas; next to their houses they bury their dead with elaborate beaded ornaments made of marine shells imported from the coast three hundred miles to the south and colored stones from Afghanistan and Central Asia. At first they make baskets for containers, but by about 5500 B.C. people at Mehrgarh make crude pottery, some with painted designs, as well as terracotta figurines. At least by 5000 B.C. they are cultivating barley and wheat and making small stone querns to grind grains; they are also shifting from hunting wild game to raising sheep, goats, and humped zebu, a species of cattle. Other inhabited sites in India of this period include Adamgarh, Bagor, and Koldihawa.

3500–2600 B.C.: By 3500 B.C. craftsmen at Mehrgarh are making painted pottery with the potter's wheel and high-temperature kilns. Elsewhere in India, but especially in the Indus Valley region, agriculturally based settlements are appearing; at sites such as Rehman Dheri, Naushero, and Harappa, mud-brick perimeter walls serve either as access control, fortifications, or flood protection. People are making simple huts and maintaining hearths; some make shrines for a mother goddess; some bury their dead with great care. Regional variations in cultures are emerging, as indicated by various painted designs on pottery and different types of clay figurines. Some of these places exchange food, raw materials, finished goods, and technological knowledge, and some people must be working as traders. Various specialized crafts are appearing and copper begins to be used for spearheads, arrowheads, earrings, chisels, needles, and other small objects. Most suggestive are the many seals made of bone, terracotta, and fired steatite and bearing geometric symbols; they were probably pressed on soft clay to declare ownership or just for decoration. Potters also mark their wares with symbols and people scratch graffiti on them; it is possible that this practice may serve as the basis for an early form of writing. The first examples of a distinctive Indus script are on potsherds from Harappa, dated to about 2800 B.C.

INDUS CIVILIZATION: 3000–1700 B.C.

The Indus or Harappan civilization, marked by the development of the first known cities in South Asia, is the first of India's great urban periods. Mohenjo-Daro and Harappa are among the largest and best known of the hundreds of cities, towns, and villages that support an extremely high standard of living, a network of trade routes extending to Mesopotamia and Egypt, and advanced technology.

The Harappan civilization is notable for its system of writing, city planning, advanced water systems, standard weights and measures, and fine carving. Nevertheless, this is still prehistoric India, for the Harappan script is as yet undeciphered, and the available evidence is archaeological.

Historians generally divide the Harappan civilization into three periods: Early Harappan (*c.* 3000–2600 B.C.), Mature Harappan or Urban Phase (*c.* 2600–2000 B.C.), and Late Harappan (*c.* 2000–1700 B.C.). Many sites along the Indus and Sarasvati river systems show signs of continuous occupation through these periods, but a dramatic cultural shift occurs quite suddenly *c.* 2600–2500 B.C. as Harappan cities appear. Mature Harappan culture comes to dominate almost half a million square miles straddling the modern India-Pakistan border. The largest Bronze Age civilization of the Old World, it is twice the size of contemporary Egypt or the Mesopotamian city-states and larger than modern Pakistan.

Although the Harappans gradually advance southward, this is essentially a north Indian story. Relatively little is known about the Stone Age peninsular settlements of the period, even less about the earliest settlers in eastern India.

Throughout its thousand-year history the culture displays a remarkable integrity. Modern historians have theories but no certain knowledge of the political system that creates the standardization and relative homogeneity found over such a broad geographical range, and the remarkable stability of Harappan script and city planning over many centuries. It is, however, evidently a peaceful society.

The reasons for the decline of this civilization are unclear. No evidence survives of decisive regional cataclysms or attacks. Rather, Harappan cities suffer a gradual decay of social order and degradation of their material culture, and are then abandoned. At the same time, refugees from sweeping Indo-European immigration from the northwest, and then the immigrants themselves, become predominant in northern India. The Harappans do, however, leave as permanent legacies to Indian culture their village life and ecology, ethnicity, some religious practices, costumes, artistic motifs, and possibly, in the Dravidian tongues of south India, their language.

3102 B.C.: Traditional date of the Mahabharata War (although historians trace it to war in 900 B.C.).

3000–2600 B.C.: Development of Early Harappan culture along the Indus Valley. Rapid cultural change is spurred by immigration from southern Turkmenistan into Sind and Rajasthan. Characteristic walled towns and cities are constructed throughout the Indus and Sarasvati River valleys to eastern Punjab, south as far as Kutch. Major sites include Harappa, Mohenjo-Daro, Ganweriwalla,

Kot Diji, Jalilpur, Kalibangan, Chanhu-Daro, and Amri. Many settlements, especially in Punjab and Haryana, remain stable Early Harappan cultures throughout the third millennium.

The two major ethnic groups in Early Harappan culture, presumably ancestors of present-day Indians, are people of Mediterranean type (tall frame, long head, narrow noses) and people similar to proto-Australoids (flat nose, thick lips).

2900 B.C.: The earliest known settlements in the Southern Neolithic period originate in northern Karnataka and western Andhra Pradesh, and include Brahmagiri, Tekkalakota, Utnur, Nagarajunikonda, and numerous other sites. Seminomadic pastoral culture with domesticated cattle, sheep, and goats spreads south and east throughout the peninsula during the third millennium and continues through the second millennium. Material culture includes black-on-red painted and gray pottery, stone axes and blades, and bone points.

2800–2100 B.C.: Pre-Indus culture: the earliest settlements on the subcontinent are created by seminomadic herders of Baluchistan hill cultures in the Makran and Brahui hills in present-day Pakistan. Sites include Vale of Quetta, Nal, Gumla, Kulli, Amri, and Zhob. Inhabitants of these settlements practice mixed farming, raising wheat, millet, sheep, goats, and Indian cattle. Mud-brick dwellings, stone and metal tools, terracotta and small stone objects mark the material culture of the period. Various village cultures continue largely unchanged as neighboring Harappan culture rises and flourishes for hundreds of years.

2600–2000 B.C.: Concentration of the population in cities throughout northern India marks the development of Mature Harappan culture or the Urban Phase. Some cities are built over existing settlements, whereas others are new; hundreds of sites from the period are currently known. The largest cities are Mohenjo-Daro, Harappa, Ganweriwalla,

Rakhigiri, and Dholavira. They are comparable in size—with a population of perhaps 25,000 to 30,000 each—and apparently equal in status.

2600–2000 B.C.: Mature Harappan culture expands along the Makran Coast, eastward through Punjab toward Ganges-Yamuna Doab (Rupar), and southward into Kutch and Kathiawar (Rangpur, Lothal, Somnath). Other major sites include Kalibangan and Chanhu-Daro. Hundreds of smaller towns and villages dot rivers and other trade routes in fertile agricultural areas, mostly in the Indus and Sarasvati river systems and along the coast. Harappans interact with neighboring Stone and Bronze Age settlements, though the nature of these relationships is not yet understood.

Citadels and public buildings evidence rise of civic authority in cities; however, the nature of their political or administrative systems is not yet understood, nor is the relation of cities to villages. Despite relative cultural uniformity through a large geographical area and cultural stability, Harappan civilization appears not to be governed by a centralized state; some modern historians propose a "complex chiefdom."

2500 B.C.: Traditional date of the first Indo-European, or Aryan, immigration. The term *Aryans* covers many tribes whose eastward migration lasts for centuries; their precise origin and migratory course, unclear from the archaeological record, occasion much scholarly debate, but their likeliest homeland is the southern Russian steppes. Some recent scholars question the prominent role assigned to these so-called Aryan immigrants in the subsequent development of culture in India.

2500–2000 B.C.: Bronze Age Banas Culture in fertile Rajasthan and Malwa, at fringes of Harappan civilization. Mixed agricultural settlements farm wheat, millet, rice, and cattle and use bronze much as do neighboring Harappans; but Banas people are distinguished by black and red pottery and evidently observe a different religion. The exact link between Banas and Harappan cultures is still uncertain.

2350–650 B.C.: Neolithic culture at Burzahom, Kashmir, has no Aryan or South Asian parallels. Pit dwellings and polished stone axes suggest an affinity with Central and North Asian cultures.

2000 B.C.: Peninsular settlements expand, with regional variations, in Maharashtra, Karnataka, and Tamil Nadu; major sites include Sonegaon and Chandoli. Organized into tribal chiefdoms, pastoral-agriculturalists raise varied crops (wheat, cotton, flax, millet, lentils) and domestic animals. Copper metallurgy, some craft specialization, and trade exist.

2000–1700 B.C.: Late Harappan period. Many Indus Valley cities appear to deteriorate and be abandoned. Much of population evidently migrates south and eastward, building new, smaller settlements in east Punjab and Gujarat. Among explanations proposed by modern historians for decline of Harappan civilization are invasion; disruption of agriculture and trade by changes in Indus and Sarasvati river systems; and gradual agricultural failure after centuries of intensive cultivation. Evidence fails to support any one cause.

2000–1700 B.C.: Nomadic Indo-European peoples in a great diaspora from Central Asia employ horses and superior weaponry to overrun settlements in Baluchistan hills. During the next three centuries Baluchi refugees flock into Indus cities; overpopulation coincides with breakdown of civic order and decline of civilization.

VEDIC PERIOD: 1700–600 B.C.

The defining event of this period—and one of the pivotal events of Indian history—is the great inward migration of seminomadic Indo-European tribes through the northwest frontier. Generations of scholars have not definitively settled the debate over the origins and movements of these peoples; some modern scholars deemphasize the role of the outsiders and emphasize the continuity of indigenous cultural developments.

Aryan culture represents a break with that of the indigenous people. The Aryan sacrificial religion, called Brahmanism or Vedism, pervasive in every aspect of life, is to play a key role in shaping the cultural life of the subcontinent. Its great texts—the *Vedas, Brahmanas,* and *Upanishads*—become the foundation texts for the emergence of Hinduism, one of the most profound influences on Indian history and culture.

In the absence of much contemporary archaeological or material evidence, Vedic literature is the primary historical source for the period. The texts show Vedic civilization to be the basis for classical Indian civilization, the foundation of schools of philosophy, law, ethics, and India's great Vedic sciences: math, astronomy, and medicine. Also of lasting consequence is the introduction of the Indo-Aryan language, the source of Sanskrit and many of India's numerous colloquial languages and literatures. Finally, Aryan class structure—in particular, its division into *varnas,* or castes—permanently imbeds hierarchy into Indian society.

This is northern Indian history: the immigrants spend centuries settling the Indus and Ganges regions before fanning out into eastern and south India. (Less is known of peninsular India, which remains in the Stone Age nearly to the end of the period.) Of the indigenous peoples, many Dravidians are pushed southward; others coexist with the newcomers, their cultures gradually commingling.

Newly introduced iron technology is used to clear the thick forests of the Gangetic plain for cultivation. Increased yields of plow and irrigation agriculture in turn permit a rapid expansion of population and a second period of urbanization. These occur alongside a major political change as identification with clan gives way to territorial affiliation. The regional powers and warring kingdoms that arise set the stage for many centuries of conflict.

1750–900 B.C.: Post-Urban/Post-Harappan period. The quality of material culture declines sharply in Punjab and Sind; makeshift settlements are built over earlier Harappan sites as their populations revert to village life. Some individual settlements (e.g., Cemetery H in the Indus region and successful Jhukar and Jhangar cultures in Sind; Iron Age Londo Ware settlements in Baluchistan) show local influence of distinct Harappan, Aryan, or Iranian culture. Ganges Doab is broadly settled by uniform Copper Hoard Culture.

1700–1100 B.C.: In the final movement of their great migration, Indo-European tribes calling themselves *arya* ("noble") advance from Iran into Indus River highlands and eastward along Ganges; they settle Sapta Sindhu ("Land of the Seven Rivers") region in present-day Punjab and Rajasthan.

1700–900 B.C.: Patriarchal, patrilineal family organization is permanently established in India. Supremacy of males and elders: extended families are based on male kinship and property divided among sons.

Vanquished indigenous *dasas* (an Indo-European word originally meaning "dark-skinned person" and probably referring to Harappans) and their mixed-race descendants are treated as inferiors and sometimes enslaved. By the end of the period, Vedic religion sanctions a fourth *varna* (caste): *shudras* (laborers) associated with the color black.

1500–800 B.C.: Their military superiority—horse-drawn chariots, bronze axes, and longbows—enables Indo-Europeans to conquer Harappan cities. Amid constant intertribal conflict and warfare with the indigenous people, Harappan settlements are destroyed and abandoned. Conquest and assimilation of different groups characterize Early Vedic period as coexisting Aryan and indigenous Dravidian cultures begin to converge.

> *May we enjoy the vitalizing force*
> *of God, the radiant; may he grant us wealth!*
> *He is the God who sends to rest and wakens*
> *all life that moves on two feet or on four.*
>
> Rig Veda (VI, 71), ancient Hindu religious text
> (c. 1500–1200 B.C.)

Little is known about the Indo-Europeans' political organization, but tribal groups (*janas*) are ruled by *rajas* whose primary function is leadership in war. They are advised by warriors and tribal assemblies (*sabha* and *samiti*) and supported by tribute and loot. Chiefdom gradually gives rise to hereditary kingship.

c. 1200 B.C.: Traditional date for the great Battle of Ten Kings (*Dasarajna*). Sudas, king of the Bharatas, the most powerful Indo-European clan, defeats confederated Aryan tribes led by Vishvamitra. Bharatas, Purus, and Kurus subsequently amalgamate into a single, dominant tribe, the Kuru-Pancalas.

1200–800 B.C.: Environment in the Indus system deteriorates; Post-Urban settlements are abandoned as regions in Sarasvati Valley, Saurashtra, and Maharashtra become desert. Standards of living decline in these southern areas as inhabitants revert to nomadic pastoralism.

1000 B.C.: Indo-Europeans reach the region of modern Delhi. *Aryavarta* (Land of Aryans) eventually stretches from present-day Afghanistan eastward to Ganges-Yamuna Doab. Constant warfare obtains among immigrant peoples competing for agricultural lands and forests of Aryavarta; combatants comprise foot soldiers armed chiefly with longbows.

Chief among numerous immigrant peoples is the Bharata clan. Others in north India include the Kuru-Pancalas and their major rivals in the Ganges basin, the Kasis,

Kosalas, and Videhas. Madras, Gandharas, Kekayas, and Kambojas populate the west; Magadhas, Angas, Vangas, the eastern regions.

1000–600 B.C.: Indo-Europeans occupy a huge area from the Himalayas to the Vindhya Range, from the Arabian Sea to the Bay of Bengal. Migrations into India continue through the northwest passes. Dravidians are pushed further south; some migrate to Mesopotamia. Numerous cultural and ethnic groups and warring peoples coexist, including indigenous groups (notably the Andhras) and peoples of mixed race.

1000–500 B.C.: The second great period of urbanization comes as cities arise throughout Punjab and Gangetic Plain, serving as centers for administration and artisan production. The Pandu capital at Indraprastha (ancient Delhi) and the Kuru-Pancalas capital at Hastinapura in Kurukshetra region north of Delhi are founded *c.* 1000 B.C. A major flood forces the abandonment of Hastinapura *c.* ninth century B.C.

900 B.C.: Great War in Kurukshetra depicted in *Mahabharata* ("Great Bharatha") between Kaurava (Kuru) and Pandava (Pandu) tribal alliances (the traditional date of this war is 3102 B.C.). Widely regarded as the end of an era, this war survives for thousands of years in folk memory as a war involving the whole of India.

800–550 B.C.: During the Late Vedic period, Indo-Europeans colonize a huge territory from the original Sapta Sindhu region eastward to Bengal and Orissa and southward toward Deccan. Indigenous forest-dwellers remain on margins of Aryan civilization. In a historic move, the center of power and cultural development shifts eastward from Punjab to Ganges-Yamuna Doab.

Tribal society largely gives way to geographical political organization. Most important kingdoms are those ruled by Kurus and Pancalas in upper Ganges and, to the east, by Kosalas, Kasis, and Videhas. They are surrounded by numerous small kingdoms with their own capitals and administrative structures.

EMERGENCE AND DECLINE OF EMPIRES: 600 B.C.–A.D. 300

The key political development in this period is the emergence in north India of territorial states. The many hundreds of warring groups and families of the Vedic period are now replaced by hundreds of unstable states rising and disappearing during centuries of constant warfare over territory and power. Ambiguous sources, conflicting calendars, and extreme political fragmentation make this a challenging period for historians.

The broad political outlines are known. Of the warring states, Magadha achieves supremacy throughout the north, paving the way for the great Mauryans, founders of the first pan-Indian empire. In their wake, north and south India are divided into separate kingdoms, to remain so until their reunification under the Mughals.

India's northwest frontier is invaded during these few centuries by Greeks, Persians, Scythians, Parthians, and the migrating Yuezhi, all successful in varying degrees in conquest and domination. Gradually, these foreigners are amalgamated and absorbed into existing cultural patterns.

Buddhism and Jainism arise in reaction against Brahmanism, and their scriptures and doctrines are defined. Buddhism inspires the finest art of the period—and some of the finest ever produced in India—in the form of *stupas* (reliquary shrines), rock-cut caves, and stone sculpture.

Brahmanism itself evolves into Hinduism: the great Hindu epics, *Mahabharata* and *Ramayana*, are composed, as are the *Bhagavad Gita* and the *Sutras*. The elaborate Vedic exegetical tradition begins with an explosion of texts, including pivotal works on linguistics and medicine.

Finally, India actively engages through trade, religious missions, and military encounters with Greece and Rome, West and Central Asia, Southeast Asia, and China. Villages along major trade routes become trading and manufacturing centers, prompting a second great wave of Indian urbanization. The widespread dissemination of Indian culture in Southeast Asia lays the groundwork for the establishment of Buddhism throughout eastern Asia.

c. 600 B.C.: Kosala is preeminent among sixteen great states *(mahajanapadas)* stretching across north India from present-day Afghanistan to Bengal. Some continue from the Vedic period; others are newly created in increasingly important eastern regions. These states decline after *c.* mid-4th century B.C.

6th–5th centuries B.C.: Possible date of historical events associated with *Ramayana*; Rama is generally associated with Iksvaku kings of Kosala and contemporary events in central India.

6th–5th centuries B.C.: Most north Indian states are kingdoms; about a dozen are oligarchies or republics, including the Vajjian Confederation, Videhas, and Sakyas. These have elected heads of state and supreme assemblies (sometimes numbering in the thousands) with rules governing quorums, voting, and passage of resolutions.

Late 6th century B.C.: Newly powerful kingdom of Maghada, its capital Rajagraha (present-day Rajgir), expands into the Gangetic Plain and Bengal under Bimbisara's rule (*c.* 544–493 B.C.). Magadhan hegemony in northern India continues for two centuries, its wealth based on control of Ganges trade routes and deposits of iron and copper.

And this is the Noble Truth of the way which leads to the Stopping of Sorrow. It is the Noble Eightfold Path—Right Views, Right Resolve, Right Speech, Right Conduct, Right Livelihood, Right Effort, Right Mindfulness, and Right Concentration.

Samyutta Nikaya, sermon by the Buddha
(c. 528 B.C.)

---

c. 535 B.C.: Cyrus II of Persia conquers countries in Kabul Valley and northwest India.

Persian military superiority prompts Indians to create their own cavalry; bows continue to be primary weapons. Elephants are introduced into battle, becoming as militarily important as chariots.

c. 518–507 B.C.: Darius I of Persia conquers Gandhara and areas in the mid-Indus region. Under his orders, Greek admiral Scylax explores the Indus River from Kaspapuras to the Arabian Sea, 517–515 B.C. Gandhara and lower Indus are ruled by Persian *satraps* (provincial governors) until the mid-fourth century.

Late 6th century B.C.: First mention of India in Western literature by Hecataeus of Miletus in *Periodus*. Several decades later, Herodotus gives an account of India in his *History*.

500 B.C.–A.D. 500: During this period, a series of medical texts will be compiled in India; taken together, they set forth the basic principles and practices of India's traditional Ayurvedic school of medicine.

Ayurveda means "the science of [living to an old] age" and is the name applied to the traditional science of holistic medicine practiced in India for thousands of years. It is also about this time that a collection of hymns known as the *Atharvaveda* is compiled; most of these texts are spells, many of them designed to cure diseases, thereby revealing Indians' belief that illness is caused by evil spirits.

5th century B.C.: Full emergence of territorial states ruled by kings or oligarchies with assemblies like *sabhas, parisads*. Ideas of kingship encompass hereditary succession, power, wealth, status, and elaborate and costly ceremonies. *Brahmans* and *kshatriyas* bolster royal authority, but stability is constantly threatened by factionalism.

5th century B.C.: Migrating Indo-Europeans reach south India and in centuries following assimilate with indigenous Dravidians.

c. 460 B.C.: Near the end of his thirty-year reign, Ajatasatru, son of Bimbisara and king of Magadha, conquers neighboring Kosala and Vajjian Confederation.

c. 360–330 B.C.: Mahapadma Nanda, king of Magadha, builds India's first great historical empire, reaching from Punjab east to Kalinga and south to Deccan. His army is said to number 200,000 infantry, 20,000 cavalry, and thousands of chariots and elephants.

327–326 B.C.: Alexander the Great invades northwest India with an army thirty thousand strong. Defeating Poros, king of Punjab, at great battle of Jhelum, Alexander retreats after his troops mutiny, leaving behind a weak Greek colonial administration.

c. 321–297 B.C.: Reign of Chandragupta Maurya, founder of first great Indian empire and of the Mauryan dynasty (c. 321–184 B.C.). He deposes the last Nanda king of Magadha, leads successful revolt of northwest frontier clans against Greek colonial rule, and establishes hegemony over all of north India from Afghanistan to Bengal and reaching well into Deccan. Chandragupta maintains a standing army; his campaign force is reported to number 400,000 to 600,000 infantry, 30,000 cavalry, and 9,000 elephants. He abdicates to become a monk.

Late 4th–3d centuries B.C.: Kautilya, according to Indian tradition Chandragupta's *brahman* chief minister, writes *Arthasastra*, a monumental Sanskrit work on political economy and invaluable historical source for early Indian administrative, legal, and military practice. Chandragupta's complex bureaucracy operates at national, provincial, division, district, and village levels and includes a government judiciary and secret service. His policies and institutions will remain in effect during his successors' reigns.

305 B.C.: Chandragupta repulses an incursion by the Macedonian-Greek ruler Seleucus I Nicator. In settlement, the Greeks cede a vast region along the Indus River; Hindu Kush becomes India's northwest border. Greek ambassador Megasthenes later visits Mauryan court and writes *Indika*, long the chief source of Western knowledge of India.

3d century B.C.: Under Chandragupta's rule, Mauryan capital Pataliputra (modern Patna) becomes a metropolitan city of tremendous wealth and grandeur, extends nine miles along the Ganges, moated and surrounded by massive timber palisade.

c. 297–269 B.C.: Reign of Chandragupta's son and successor Bindusara, notable for his conquest of Deccan.

c. 269–233 B.C.: Chandragupta's grandson Ashoka rules at height of Mauryan imperial power. Perhaps India's most famous ruler, he is pious, benevolent, and wise; his name is invoked to the present day as a symbol of national pride and unity.

Now the Beloved of the Gods regrets the conquest of Kalinga, for when an independent country is conquered, people are killed, they die, or are deported, and that the Beloved of the Gods finds very painful and grievous. And this he finds even more grievous—that all the inhabitants—brahmans, ascetics, and other sectarians, and householders who are obedient to superiors, parents, and elders, who treat friends, acquaintances, companions, relatives, slaves, and servants with respect, and are firm in their faith—all suffer violence, murder, and separation from their loved ones.

13th Rock Edict, by Ashoka (c. 260 B.C.)

---

c. 260 B.C.: Ashoka conquers the eastern kingdom of Kalinga (Orissa) in the only aggressive war of his reign, consolidating Mauryan rule over the entire subcontinent except Mysore. A huge toll in death and suffering leads him bitterly to regret war and adopt a policy of nonviolence; he is alleged to convert to Buddhism.

c. 256–50 B.C.: Bactrian Greeks, or Indo-Greeks, invade from their western empire and rule states of northern Indus Valley for more than a century from their capital at Bactria. The most famous Indo-Greek king is Milinda (also called Menander, reigned 155–130 B.C.), a convert to Buddhism. *Milindapanha* (*c.* 1st century B.C.), a supposed dialogue between Milinda and the Buddhist monk Nagasena, becomes a popular work of Theravada Buddhism.

c. 206 B.C.: In last Greek attempt to conquer Indian territory, Seleucid Antiochus III unsuccessfully invades the Kabul Valley.

c. 184 B.C.: Pushyamitra Sunga seizes the Mauryan throne. His dominion over north central India (to *c.* 145 B.C.) is marked by wars with northern Indo-Greeks and southern Andhras. From time of Sunga sovereignty in Gangetic basin (to *c.* 75 B.C.) and Satavahana dominion over Deccan (?30 B.C.–A.D. 250; dynastic dates are uncertain), north and south India remain politically divided until the Mughal period.

He whose mind is unperturbed in the midst of sorrows and who entertains no desires amid pleasures; he from whom passion, fear, and anger have fled away—he is called a sage of steadfast intellect. He who feels no attachment toward anything; who, having encountered the various good or evil things, neither rejoices nor loathes—his wisdom is steadfast.

Bhagavad Gita (2.55-59), traditional Hindu sacred poem c. 100 B.C.–A.D. 300)

---

c. 100 B.C.: Composition of *Manu-Dharmasastras*, the oldest and most influential version of the code of Hindu law. Based on the *Dharma Sutras* and transmitted orally, it undergoes revision for eight hundred years.

c. 100 B.C.–A.D. 70: Displaced from Central Asia by Chinese migration, the Scythians (also called Sakas) enter northern India in several separate movements. Northern Sakas under Maues (reigned *c.* 20 B.C.–A.D. 22) overwhelm the Indo-Greek empire. By the later first century B.C. Sakas are established in a large territory in the upper Indus region. Their chiefs, called *satraps*, are divided into three major groups, with capitals at Taxila, Sakala, and Mathura.

c. 90 B.C.–A.D. 65: Parthians (also called Pahlavas) push eastward from their huge West Asian empire, conquer southern Indo-Greeks, reach eastward to the lower Indus Valley.

c. 57 B.C.: First year of the Vikrama Era, one of several dozen ancient Indian eras used in dating contemporary inscriptions and documents and one of two still (in north India) in present-day use.

c. 20–5 B.C.: Reign of Kharavela, the most powerful of the Maha-Meghavahanas, dynastic rulers of Kalinga. His conquests give him dominion over nearly the whole eastern coast from Kalinga to Mysore.

1st century A.D.: The Yuezhi, Central Asian tribes, migrate through the Hindu Kush (whence their Indian name, Kushans) to northwest India and drive out Northern Sakas and Indo-Parthians. Kadphises I (reigns *c.* 15–65) founds the Kushan dynasty (to *c.* 465), which establishes capitals at Purusapura and Mathura and rules a huge north Indian empire stretching from Bactria through the upper Indus to the mid-Ganges region.

c. A.D. 60–409: Kingdoms of Western Sakas (also called Great Satraps) are established in a large region of Sind, Kutch, Kathiawar, reaching eastward nearly to Mathura. They are divided into two branches: Western Satraps in west India, their capital at Girinagara; and Ujjaini Satraps, capital at Ujjain. Most powerful of the Ujjaini Sakas is Rudradaman I (reigns *c.* 130–150).

c. 78: First year of the Saka Era, an ancient calendar still in use in south India.

Late 1st–2d centuries: Reign of Kanishka, third and greatest Kushan king (the dates of his reign are very uncertain). He conquers a huge territory reaching from the Oxus to the Ganges basin and south to Sind, Kutch, and Saurashtra, with capitals at Peshawar and Mathura; his empire coexists with many tribal states. His expeditions against China are unsuccessful.

c. 106–130: Reign of Gautamiputra Satakarni, greatest king of the Hindu Satavahana (also called Andhra) dynasty. Conquests of Western Sakas and Kushans extend his Upper Deccan kingdom from Kathiawar and southern Saurashtra all the way across the peninsula to the east coast. Styled "overlord of the Deccan," he rules from his capital at Pratisthana (modern Paithan) over a kingdom made prosperous by trade and agriculture.

NEW EMPIRES IN NORTH AND SOUTH: 300–700

This period is India's classical age. North and north central India are united for 250 years under Gupta rule in the first major empire since the Mauryas. With few exceptions, the subcontinent is otherwise occupied during the period by warring states, in later years complicated by invasions from northwest. Brief Huna (known in the West as Huns) rule in northernmost India and the Arab conquest of Sind at the end of the period herald the foreign rule to come.

Royal patronage and political stability under the Guptas promote a flowering of Sanskrit learning. Literature, art, architecture, philosophy, mathematics, and astronomy flourish. Secular Sanskrit literature enjoys its golden age as Kalidasa, generally acknowledged to be finest Indian writer of all time, and a host of other writers produce plays, poems, and prose works in popular and scholarly genres.

Underpinning this artistic efflorescence is a revival of the Hindu religion. Brahmans, gaining power and prestige through royal grants of land, embark on a program of temple building. To this period belong the first structural temples in India, embellished with representations of gods and goddesses acknowledged by most experts to be the finest Indian sculpture ever produced.

The foundation of orthodox Hinduism is laid during these centuries. The *Puranas*, elaborating the central philosophy and practice of Hinduism, take their final form. *Bhakti* cults, chief among them Vaishnavism and Saivism, bring simple devotion to the forefront of religious life, defining a new Hindu pantheon, hymnology, and worship.

c. 320: Chandragupta I (reigns *c.* 320–335), attempting to replicate Mauryan imperial glory, founds the Gupta dynasty (*c.* 320–647) in the Ganges Valley and Magadha. Alliances with neighboring Licchavis and Vakatakas cement Gupta power over north India. The old Mauryan capital of Pataliputra (modern-day Patna) becomes the Gupta capital; Saketa (modern-day Ayodhya) and Prayaga (Allahabad) are major imperial centers.

335: Death of Vakataka king Pravarasena (reigns 275–335). The Vakataka dynasty (*c.* 255–510), successors to the Satavahanas in the Deccan, reaches its greatest power during his reign; after his death the kingdom is divided among his heirs.

c. 335–376: The reign of Chandragupta's son Samudragupta is notable for the king's tireless military campaigning and expansion of empire. He conquers the entire Aryavarta, directly ruling the central Ganges Valley and exerting weaker authority over tributary states stretching northward all the way into Gandhara, Punjab, and Nepal and eastward into Assam. His expeditions into south India are unsuccessful; the Vindhya hills form the southern boundary of empire.

c. 375–414: The Gupta empire reaches its height under Chandragupta II. He imposes hegemony over the whole of north and north central India, gaining significant revenue from west coast ports. The most powerful neighboring kingdoms are Kushans to northwest, Licchavis to northeast, and Vakatakas in central Deccan. The empire declines after his reign as a result of the Guptas' decentralized administration, foreign invasions, and succession disputes.

Early 5th century: Pallavas in eastern Deccan move into vacuum left by decline of Gupta power, establish suzerainty over Karnataka and Andhra Pradesh; Kanchipuram is their capital. The Pallava dynasty (c. 300–888) becomes one of the preeminent Deccan powers, supported in large part by revenues from trade with southeast Asia.

c. **5th–6th centuries:** Compilation of *Siva-Dhanur-veda*, the great Sanskrit military classic based on the *Arthasastra*.

But what am I saying? In real truth, this bark-dress,
Though ill-suited to her figure, sets it off like an ornament.
The lotus with the Saivala entwined
Is not a whit less brilliant: dusky spots
Heighten the luster of the cold-rayed moon;
This lovely maiden in her dress of bark
Seems all the lovelier. Even the meanest garb
Gives to true beauty fresh attractiveness.

Sakuntala, a drama by Kalidasa (c. A.D. 450)

457: Skandagupta (reigns 454–467) defeats invading Hunas, but their repeated invasions from the northwest fatally weaken the Guptas.

500–550: Huna kings including Toramana (reigns 500–510) and Mihirakula (reigns 510–530) temporarily subjugate Punjab and Kashmir, extinguishing the Gupta empire. Hunas are in turn defeated (c. 550) by allied Hindu princes, and north India reverts to numerous small kingdoms. Waves of other Central Asians, including Gurjaras, Sassan-ians, and Kushans, follow into northwest India in the Hunas' wake.

c. **550:** Early Chalukya dynasty (to c. 757) founded in northern Karnataka by Pulakesin (reigns 550–566). The Chalukyas are the most powerful of the southern ruling families; different branches of the family control various areas of west and central Deccan from their centers at Aihole, Badami, and Pattadakal.

c. **556:** Simhavishnu (reigns c. 556–589) ascends Pallava throne. Northern campaigns against the Cholas, Gangas, and Chalyukas, and southern operations against the Pandyas and Cheras (Keralas) enlarge Pallava dominion to its greatest extent during his reign.

Late 6th century: Beginning of Pallava-Chalukya wars in Deccan under Chalukya kings Kirtivarman I (reigns 566–597) and Mangalesa (reigns 597–608).

c. **600–630:** Reign of greatest Pallava king, Mahendravarman I. He fights Chalukyas (608–625), turns back Harsha's Deccan invasion, and defeats neighboring Cholas, Pandyas, and Cheras.

606–647: Conquests of King Harsha of Sthanvishvara (modern-day Thaneswar), Punjab, create a new empire stretching from the Himalayas to the Vindhyas, from Gujarat to Bengal. The imperial capital of Kanyakubja (Kanauj) becomes a wealthy city. A Deccan campaign against the Chalukyas (620) fails to extend sovereignty to south India. His short-lived empire fractures after his death, and north India once again reverts to smaller kingdoms.

608–625: Chalukya-Pallava war in northeast Deccan. Pallavas extend their territory to east coast, then head south.

608–642: Reign of the greatest Chalukya king, Pulakesin II. In northern and eastern campaigns early in his reign, he extends territory to east coast, important for its trade revenues; Chalukyas dominate the northern peninsula, repulse an invasion by Harsha (620).

625–630: Chalukyas defeat Pallavas in war in south Deccan.

629–645: Xuanzang (600–664), a Buddhist pilgrim from China, travels throughout Harsha's empire as well as Pallava and Chalukya kingdoms. His *Record of Western Regions* is a valuable account of seventh-century India. Indo-Chinese religious, diplomatic, and trade exchanges are numerous during this period, and include several formal embassies from Tang emperors to Harsha's court.

630–642: Pallavas are resurgent in Chalukya war; Pallava king Narasimharvarman I (reigns *c*. 630–668) defeats Pulakesin II at the Chalukya capital at Vatapi and sacks the city. Pulakeshin II's son Vikramaditya later avenges this act by sacking the Pallava capital at Kanchi (674).

c. 650: Gurjaras, Central Asian nomads, establish themselves in Rajasthan to become the most powerful northern kingdom.

c. 650–707: Arabs conquer Sind.

655: Chalukya king Vikramaditya I defeats Pandyas and Cholas after a long war.

REGIONAL KINGDOMS: 700–1200

Regionalism is the major political theme of this period as dynastic states engage in incessant warfare. Their ruling families and armies are remarkably resilient over decades, even centuries of fighting, receding after major defeats only to regroup and reappear as major powers years later.

A few groups dominate the period: the Chalukyas and Rastrakutas in the Deccan; the Palas in the eastern region of Bengal and Bihar; and the Pallavas, Pandyas, and mighty Cholas in the peninsula. They are surrounded by hundreds of feudatories and lesser kingdoms, notably the emerging Rajput states of north and central India.

Hinduism, Jainism, Buddhism, and ancient sacrificial religions coexist, but in a great Hindu revival, Jainism and Buddhism are pushed to the periphery of the subcontinent. As Brahmanism spreads, the brahmanical priestly caste comes to occupy a preeminent position in India's social and economic hierarchy.

The artistic and cultural riches of the period are characterized, like the politics, by regional variation. Among the three most outstanding artistic achievements are the earliest of India's great structural temples, the magnificent bronze sculptures created by Chola artists, and a profusion of new vernacular languages and literatures. Intellectually, India's greatest contribution is in mathematics, undertaken in support of astronomy and representing the most advanced work in the world.

Successful Turkish invasions in the late twelfth century displace Hindu rajas across northern India and *brahmans* in power in Bengal. Northern India enters a period of Islamic rule.

8th century: In the Tamil region of Deccan, Pallavas of Kanchipuram and Pandyas of Madurai are at the height of their power. In a protracted three-way contest, the Pallavas, Pandyas, and Chalukyas struggle for supremacy.

712: The Arab conquerors of Sind (present-day western Pakistan), establish the first Islamic state in the subcontinent. Over the following decades, Arab invasions of Rajputana and Gujarat are repelled by Gurjaras; Arab traders and *sufis* (teachers) settle in India.

c. 730–750: During the reign of King Lalitaditya, Kashmir becomes the leading power in Punjab.

c. 753: In Deccan, Rastrakutas overthrow Chalukyas of Vatapi, ending their two hundred-year-old dynasty; Dandidurga founds the Rastrakuta dynasty (*c.* 753–973). After making rapid territorial gains in south India, Rastrakutas become the first Deccan kings to campaign in the north.

c. 760s: Rise of Palas as their ruler, Gopala, extends his dominion throughout Bengal, Bihar, and Assam. His successors Dharmapala (reigns *c.* 770–810) and Devapala (reigns 810–850) consolidate rule. A major northern power for several centuries (*c.* 750–1185), the Pala kingdom is known for its prosperity and cultural sophistication.

c. 780–793: Reign of Rastrakuta king Dhruva. His conquests of Gurjara-Pratihara and Pala kingdoms begin the "tripartite struggle" for control of Kanyakubja (Kanauj) and the Ganges Valley trade routes; the contest continues for more than a hundred years.

800–1200: Rise of Rajput kingdoms in central India and Rajasthan. Rulers claim to be from *kshatriya* warrior caste, and martial Rajput states fight against each other as well as the northern invaders. The four major dynasties among the many small Rajput kingdoms are Pratiharas of Kanauj, Paramaras of Malwa, Chauhans of Delhi and Ajmer, and Chalukyas of Gujarat.

c. 850: Rise of the Chola dynasty (*c.* 850–1278) in Thanjavur under King Vijayala (reigns *c.* 850–870).

c. 888: Alliance of Chalukyas and recently emerged Chola kingdom defeats Pallavas and divides their territory; six hundred-year-old Pallava dynasty gives way to Chola ascendancy in Tamil country. Chola king Parantaka I (reigns 907–953) defeats the Pandyas, Pallavas, and Sinhalese, consolidating a large southern empire from the Pennar River to Cape Comorin.

890–910: During the reign of King Mahendrapala, the Gurjara-Pratihara kingdom (*c.* 773–1027) establishes hegemony over the whole of north India with the exception of Arab-ruled Sind, Pala Bengal, and Kashmir. Pratiharas prove unable to fend off Rastrakuta attacks, however, and by the mid-tenth century north India is once again divided among warring states.

916: Indra III, king of Rastrakuta (reigns 914–927), occupies Kanyakubja, but his northern dominion is short-lived as sporadic rebellions and southern campaigns against the Cholas preoccupy the monarchy. Rastrakuta power wanes rapidly after his reign.

c. 973: From his base in Bijapur, Taila II (reigns 973–997) overthrows the Rastrakuta dynasty and founds the Later Chalukya dynasty (*c.* 973–1189). The Later Chalukyas dominate the west Deccan for two hundred years; they wage numerous military campaigns against the Cholas.

985–1014: Reign of the outstanding Chola king, Rajaraja I. He annexes northern Sri Lanka, Pandya and Chera territory, Vengi, Kalinga, the Maldives, and the Malabar Coast, creating a peninsular empire and giving the Cholas a virtual monopoly over maritime trade routes to Southeast Asia, Arabia, East Africa, and China.

c. 988–1038: Last period of Pala strength in Bihar and Bengal during reign of Mahipala.

c. 990: Sabuktagin of Ghazni, a Turkic state between Kabul and Kandahar, seizes Peshawar.

998–1030: Sabuktagin's son Mahmud of Ghazni (971–1030), one of the greatest Asian generals in history, leads some seventeen raids into northwest India; the plunder he carries away pays for the campaigns by which he creates a huge Central Asian kingdom. Known as "the Sword of Islam," Mahmud leads a Turkic cavalry armed with crossbows that overwhelms the Indians; he defeats the raja of Lahore, sacks Thaneswar (1014) and Kanauj (1018), and despoils numerous wealthy Hindu temples, including Kangra (1009), Lahore (1015), Mathura (1018), Kanauj (1019), Gwalior (1022), and Somnath (1025). He finally destroys the Pratihara dynasty (1027).

Early 11th century: Islamic scholar al-Biruni (973–1048), sent to India by Mahmud of Ghazni, spends several years in Punjab studying Sanskrit texts. His *Ta'rikh al-Hind* (Enquiry into India), a scientific exposition of Indian history, science, and culture, is a primary source for historians of the period.

1014–1044: Rajendra I ("the Great") rules at the height of Chola empire in a reign marked by far-flung warfare and conquest. He annexes Raichur Doab and southern Sri Lanka; in a famous northern campaign he marches up the east coast to defeat Palas in Bengal (1021–1022) and undertakes a victorious naval campaign against the kingdom of Srivijaya (in Malaya and Sumatra) to protect trade with China (1025).

1030: Ghaznavids conquer Punjab, establishing Islam in that province and creating a base for operations deeper into India.

1076–1147: Kalinga (Orissa) becomes a major power during the reign of Anantavarman Chodaganga, controlling the east coast between the Ganges and Godavari rivers.

Early 12th century: The Hoysala kingdom (1047–1327) rises to dominate territory west of the Chola kingdom (present-day Mysore) during the reign of Visnuvardhana. Chalukyas, Cholas, and the emerging Yadava kingdom are the Hoysalas' major rivals.

1142–1173: Reign of Kumarapala, king of Chalukyas in Gujarat. He consolidates a large Rajput confederation (until *c.* 14th century).

1175: On their first expedition into India, Ghurid Turks led by Muhammad of Ghur (reigns 1173–1206) defeat Ghazni Turks in Punjab. Ghurids gradually displace Ghazni Turks in northern India, capturing Peshawar (1179) and Lahore (1186) before turning their sights on Indian kingdoms further to the south.

Alms-giving is an ordinance of God, incumbent upon every person who is free, sane, adult, and a Muslim, provided he be possessed, in full property, of such estate or effects as are termed in the language of the law a minimum, and that he has been in possession of the same for the space of one complete year. . . . The reason why the Muslim faith is made a condition is that the rendering of alms is an act of piety, and such cannot proceed from an infidel.

Hidaya (Guidance), Islamic legal work for India by Maulana Burhan ud-din Marghinanai (*c.* 1180)

1191: Muhammad of Ghur invades Thaneswar. Rajput coalition led by Prithviraja III, king of Delhi and Ajmer, defeats the Turks at first battle of Tarain.

1192: Turkish rule in India begins after Muhammad of Ghur again invades and defeats Prithviraja III at second battle of Tarain. Ghurid general Qutb ud-Din Aibak creates the first unified empire in northern India since the Guptas; Turkish cavalry, with its modern weaponry and military tactics, overruns faction-ridden, disorganized, and poorly equipped Indian armies in a sweep through Kanauj (1193), Varanasi and Gwalior Fort (1194), Bihar (1196), and Bengal (early 1200s).

DELHI SULTANATE: 1211–1526

The Delhi sultanate is the first period in which Islamic kingdoms figure substantially in the political life of the subcontinent. By the end of the period a number of other Islamic states in addition to Delhi, including Bengal, Malwa, and Gujarat, have established independent sovereignty in northern India. Their policies are shaped by state interests rather more than by religious dogma, but the introduction of Islam to India exerts a profound influence on the social, political, and cultural life of the subcontinent that continues to the present day.

Although a number of Delhi sultans are careful to obtain patents from the eastern caliph, they are for all practical purposes sovereign, serving as military and political chiefs and courts of last appeal. Five dynasties of sultans in Delhi preside at the apex of a tiered administration:

provincial governors have a good deal of autonomy, while beneath them is the traditional local machinery of Hindu headmen and tax collectors. Successive reforms of revenue and civil administration during this period lay the groundwork for the sweeping Mughal reforms of the sixteenth century.

This is a period of personal rule, with kingdoms utterly dependent on the rulers' will and pleasure. Despite administrative reforms, no enduring governmental structure is created; every succession is a crisis, and most are settled by force. The Delhi sultans are very much warrior-kings, operating according to conventions that strike modern Western observers as savage. Enemies are routinely blinded or killed. Plunder is a common means of financing the operations of the state.

Territorial instability marks the period of the Delhi sultans. Territory is continually gained and lost through raids, warfare, internal rebellions, and land grabs in which near-family members are often the most aggressive combatants. Turkish nobles, provincial governors, and Hindus alike are in constant rebellion, and soon after the empire reaches its greatest extent in the 1330s, large independent kingdoms break away in Gujarat, Bengal, and the Deccan. At the same time, the sultans are largely successful in holding off repeated raids by Mongol hordes numbering many tens of thousands.

Although Buddhism fades from India during the time that Islam is introduced, Hinduism thrives. *Bhakti* poet-saints spread their mystical teachings from the south all the way across central and northern India; an outpouring of devotional lyrics in indigenous languages marks the beginning of India's rich regional literatures.

Islam, though present in the subcontinent for five hundred years, is now introduced to the Indian heartland not by Arabs but Turks, a historical accident with enormous cultural significance. The tastes of the Turkish sultans are tinged with Persian influence; the mosques, palaces, and tombs that they build in such numbers introduce to the subcontinent the soaring domes and arches that Mughal architects will make completely their own.

1206: The slave general Qutb ud-Din Aibak becomes the first sultan of Delhi (to 1210); he begins a long line of Turkish rulers of India. The conqueror of much of northern India and subsequently viceroy of India under Shihab ud-Din Ghuri, Qutb ud-Din succeeds to the throne after Shihab's assassination. Turkish slave officers dominate his government. In a decision with historic consequences, he fixes the capital at Delhi. He dies in a polo accident.

1210: Iltutmish (reigns 1210–1235), manumitted slave and provincial governor of Qutb ud-Din, seizes throne and founds the Mamluk, or slave-king, empire (1210–1290). An able general and administrator, he proves the greatest of early Delhi sultans: he conquers Punjab (1217), Sind (1228), and Malwa; reconquers Ranthambhor (1226) and Gwalior (1232); and deploys a large standing army

to contain constant threats and outright incursions by Chinggis Khan and neighboring Persians. His land revenue reforms, the first of several throughout the dynasty, prefigure the great administrative reforms of the Mughals.

1229: A patent from the caliph of Baghdad legitimates Iltutmish's rule. Indian Muslims, now technically part of the Abbasid caliphate, are isolated when Mongols overrun the Baghdad caliphate in 1258. The Delhi sultans manage to hold the Mongols at bay for more than a century, largely preserving India from the massacres and devastation that follow Mongol conquests elsewhere.

1236–1240: Raziyya, daughter of Iltutmish, is the only woman ever to occupy the throne of Delhi in her own right. At the head of her army, she quells rebellion in Punjab, but is deposed and executed by Turkish nobles opposed to female rule.

1266–1287: Reign of Balban. Former member of "The Forty," a famous group of Turkish slaves who dominate the government at the court of Iltutmish, and chief minister to Sultan Nasir ud-Din (reigns 1246–1266), whom he kills to gain throne. He suppresses rebellions of Turkish nobles and his own governor in Bengal, subdues Rajput chiefs, and repels a number of Mongol invasions from the northwest. Balban proclaims divine monarchy and creates a strong sultanate, exerting tight control by means of elaborate spy and police networks.

1290: The Mamluk (former slaves) dynasty is overthrown in a coup by the Khaljis, a tribe of Turks settled in northern India in wake of Turkish conquest. Khalji sultans create an Indo-Islamic state and broaden their power base by including non-Turks and Indian Muslims among government officials.

1292: Sultan Jalaluddin Khalji allows Ulgu, grandson of Hulegu, and several thousand Mongol invaders to convert to Islam and settle near Delhi. These "New Muslims" are virtually exterminated in 1311 when Ala ud-Din, discovering a conspiracy against his life, massacres them.

Early 1290s: Marco Polo is believed to land in Tamil Nadu and sail up the Malabar Coast on his return to Italy from China; his published account of India's geography, customs, and prosperity is a seminal work on India in Europe and does much to stimulate the European search for eastern trade routes.

1296: Soon after returning from his invasion of Deccan loaded with tributary gold, silver, and precious stones, Prince Ala ud-Din Khalji assassinates his uncle the sultan and assumes the throne (reigns 1296–1316). Perhaps the most outstanding of all Delhi sultans, he and his slave general Malik Kafur extend the empire across the whole of northern India with early conquests of Gujarat, Ranthambhor, Chitor, Malwa, and Maharashtra. Strict social and economic controls largely forestall rebellions.

1306: Mongols, at the zenith of their empire, are decisively defeated by Ala ud-Din after years of nearly continuous invasions. India is nearly alone among Asian states in escaping Mongol conquest and annexation.

1307–1311: In the successful Deccan campaign, Ala ud-Din defeats the Kakatiyas and Hoysalas, extends Delhi's nominal suzerainty all the way south to Cape Comorin, and takes enormous plunder. Orissa is the only major area that remains independent of Delhi rule. In the absence of a permanent administrative system, however, the Delhi sultan later loses control of much of the territory conquered in the south.

1320: Tughluqs depose the last Khalji sultan; a new dynasty is founded and order restored by Ghiyas ud-Din Tughluq (reigns 1320–1325).

1325–1351: Reign of the greatest Tughluq sultan, Muhammad bin Tughluq, who gains the throne, historians believe, after murdering his father in a staged "accident." An outstanding general, he extends the empire to its greatest extent, annexing Peshawar and the Himalayan kingdom of Nagarkot in the north, Bihar to the east, and southern states of Warangal, Ma'bar, and Dvarasamudra. The empire fractures almost immediately as rebellions (often instigated by Tughluq officials) create independent Islamic kingdoms, divisions that endure for two hundred years until the Mughal conquests. He establishes diplomatic relations with numerous other Asian states and diversifies the nobility by appointing Afghans, Persians, and Mongols.

1326–1327: Muhammad bin Tughluq founds a second administrative capital at Devagiri, the centrally located capital of the old Yadava kingdom. The city is rebuilt and a new road network constructed, including a direct route to Delhi. Renamed Daulatabad, the new capital is a failure: Delhi's ruling elite resists forced resettlement.

1333–1347: Ibn Battuta (1304–1378), the renowned scholar and traveler from Tangier, Morocco, resides in India; he spends eight years at the court of Muhammad bin Tughluq, who appoints him *qazi* (Islamic legal officer) and sends him as ambassador to China. Ibn Battuta's famous account of his 75,000-mile travels includes invaluable information on Muhammad bin Tughluq and on Indian culture and institutions.

1334–1335: A rebel sultanate founded at Ma'bar on Coromandel Coast rules for thirty years.

1336: Brothers in the sultan's service rebel, found the southern kingdom of Vijayanagar.

1337: A military expedition against Himalayan state of Qarachil ends in disaster: the entire force, numbered at 100,000 horsemen and foot soldiers, is destroyed by disease or local resistance and its equipment looted. The Delhi sultans are never again able to field a significant army, and the cost of this and other military adventures seriously depletes imperial resources.

1338: Bengal becomes independent under imperial official Fakhr ud-Din Mubarak Shah. The Ilyas Shahi (1339–1487) and Husain Shahi (1493–1538) dynasties dominate the period until Akbar's conquest (1576), creating a strong state and instilling deep roots of Islam. Awadh, suffering from overtaxation and famine, also becomes independent. Imperial minister Shams ud-Din murders Udayanadeva, last Hindu king of Kashmir, and founds independent sultanate in Kashmir (1339–1586) that survives until Akbar's annexation.

1343: The caliph of Egypt invests Muhammad bin Tughluq with sovereignty of India.

1347: Entire Deccan, including Daulatabad, frees itself from Delhi's rule with the foundation of the Bahmani kingdom.

1351–1388: Reign of Firuz Shah Tughlug in Delhi and north India. His extensive campaigns restore hegemony in the north, but he fails in repeated attempts in the 1350s to reconquer Bengal and leaves the Deccani sultanates unchallenged. He fatally weakens the army by paying troops with heritable *jagirs* (land revenues) and land grants, decreasing their dependence on and loyalty to the crown. A war of succession following his death degenerates into anarchy.

1352: The Black Death, returning back into Asia after ravaging Europe, reaches Moscow, from whence it reaches India.

1396: An independent Islamic state is created in Gujarat, the major locus of maritime trade, and survives until conquest by Akbar (1572). Notable rulers include Ahmad Shah (1411–1443), founder of the capital at Ahmadabad. In the final chaotic years of the Tughluq dynasty, Jaunpur, Malwa, and Khandesh also become important independent sultanates.

December 18, 1398: After a destructive cavalry raid through northern India, Timur (in English, Tamerlane, 1336–1405), the Mongol ruler of the huge empire of Samarkand, overruns the forces of Sultan Mahmud Tughluq and enters Delhi in triumph. He sacks the city before returning to his own empire, leaving behind him two great swaths of utter devastation and a large territory destined to suffer for a hundred years the turmoil of Turkish and Afghan clan wars, internal rebellions, and local conflicts.

The tree grows again. Fresh flowers bloom. The
  spring comes with the fragrant summer wind
  and bees are drunk. The forest of Brinda is
  filled with new airs.
Krishna has come.
On the river bank adorned with groves, new
  lovers are lost in love. Intoxicated by the
  honey of mango blossoms, kokilas freshly
  sing. The hearts of young girls are drunken
  with delight.
The forest is charged with a new flavor of love.

  Poem by Vidyapati Thakura (14th–15th centuries)

1405: The sultan of Bengal dispatches envoys to the emperor of China, initiating a series of diplomatic exchanges.

1414: Khizr Khan Sayyid, Timur's governor of Multan, besieges Delhi and assumes the throne after the death of Mahmud Tughluq.

He rules from 1414 to 1421 and founds the Sayyid dynasty (1414–1451). Weak rulers, the Sayyids never establish sovereignty beyond the Doab and Punjab, wage constant warfare with Jaunpur, and by the end of their reign are reduced to ruling over Delhi and its environs.

1451: After two unsuccessful invasions of Delhi (1441, 1447), Bahlol Lodi replaces the last Sayyid sultan, who resigns the throne; after 240 years the Turkish sultanate gives way to Afghan rule. Bahlol rules to 1489, founding the Lodi dynasty (1451–1526). A resourceful general, he restores the sultanate's fortunes and territories, subduing Jaunpur, Mewat, and the Doab. An equally forceful ruler, he promotes a new view of the king as first among equals, deriving from Afghan tribal governance, and reorganizes the imperial administration to accommodate the Afghan nobility.

1458–1511: During Mahmud Begarha's reign, Gujarat reaches height of dominion, wealth, and power, but is forced to fight an aggressive Portuguese fleet intent on controlling European trade routes. The Gujarati navy and Egyptian fleet, commanded by Turkish admiral Malik Ayaz, defeat the Portuguese off Chaul in 1508 but are themselves routed off Diu in 1509.

1459: Rao Jodha, maharaja of Marwar (reigns 1438–1488) founds a capital at Jodhpur, site of a magnificent hill fort. His seventeen sons take advantage of the weak Delhi sultanate to conquer territories contiguous to their father's. This pattern of clan members controlling small units of a single state is a characteristic of the Rajput states; it sets the stage for future Rajput conflict.

1489–1517: Reign of Sikandar Shah Lodi. A strong ruler, he restores control over nobles and reestablishes control across northern India from Punjab to Bengal. He founds a new capital on the site of modern Agra (1504) as a base for campaigns against the Rajputs.

1513: Babur, the Mongol-Turk ruler of Kabul, takes advantage of unsettled conditions in the Delhi sultanate to begin a series of exploratory raids into Punjab. He captures Kandahar in 1517. Disaffected Afghan nobles angered by the tyrannical rule of Ibrahim, the last Lodi sultan (reigns 1517–1526), invite Babur to invade.

April 19, 1526: Ibrahim is defeated and killed by Babur at the first battle of Panipat, ending the Delhi sultanate and beginning Mughal rule in India.

SOUTH INDIA: VIJAYANAGAR EMPIRE, 1336–1565

Like other medieval Indian kingdoms, Vijayanagar is a military state. Founded in the context of increased militarization of Hindu states to compete with northern sultanates, Vijayanagar engages vigorously in seemingly endless rivalries and territorial wars with its neighbors, the Bahmanis and their successor sultanates in the Deccan. Its armies number in the tens and sometimes hundreds of thousands; attacks and sieges of forts and the repeated pillage and sacking of both countryside and cities are common. Details of much of this history are obscure or only incompletely known, but Vijayanagar armies conquer an empire that at its greatest extent covers 140,000 square miles, the whole of peninsular India except for Calicut. The empire is one of the greatest states in Indian history.

Deccan geopolitics of the period is based on political and economic rather than religious rivalry. The imperial administration of Vijayanagar employs Muslims in its armies, copies the administrative and military reforms of Islamic states, permits the building of mosques and Islamic cemeteries, and contracts opportunistic alliances with neighboring sultanates; in fact, by the fifteenth century the Hindu Gajapatis of Orissa are among Vijayanagar's most implacable enemies.

The militarization introduced into the subcontinent by Islamic conquerors is partly responsible for peninsular warfare, but increasing commercialization also plays a role, for South India is a strategic and lucrative link in the far-flung and complex network of Asian and European trade. Vijayanagar's territorial reach, incorporating both east- and west-coast Deccan ports, provides vast wealth. The innumerable Arab and Persian traders and chroniclers and European visitors who contribute to Vijayanagar's cosmopolitanism are struck by the opulence of the imperial court and capital.

Under Vijayanagar rule, indigenous cultural traditions continue without interruption in south India. This period is notable for a resurgence of temple building, prompted in part by the important role temples play as political and military centers; a distinct Vijayanagar style of temple architecture evolves. The kings of Vijayanagar are also lavish patrons of learning, art, literature, and music. Their territory includes Telugu-, Kannada-, and Tamil-speaking regions. This is the golden age of Telugu literature; translations of Sanskrit religious texts into this and the other Dravidian vernaculars are a catalyst for Hindu revival.

c. **1340:** The brothers Harihara and Bukka Sangama found the Sangama (sometimes called Yadava) dynasty (to 1485) and establish an independent Hindu kingdom in central Deccan (to 1565). On his coronation day, Harihara I (reigns *c.* 1340–1356) founds the royal capital of Vijayanagar (City of Victory), from which the kingdom takes its name. Minister Anantarasa Chikka Udaiya oversees the creation of a well-organized centralized administration that survives for more than two hundred years. The empire develops a system of shared sovereignty under which kings enjoy ritual sovereignty over their southern empire, but actual local political authority is exercised by numerous ruling families *(utaiyar).* Under the *nayankara* system, military commanders are appointed *nayaka* (local governor) and granted income from estates for the purpose of raising troops; they maintain control over local chiefs.

1346: In most important of early territorial conquests, Bukka conquers and annexes neighboring Hoysala kingdom after eight years of war. By the early 1350s the Vijayanagar empire stretches across southern India from coast to coast, comprising the entire peninsula south of the Krishna and Tungabhadra rivers except for independent Calicut. Bukka is made joint ruler and heir.

1347: The neighboring Bahmani sultanate launches its first war against Vijayanagar; Bahmanis become a major rival for power in south India. Contesting Warangal, Andhra, and particularly the Raichur Doab between the Tungabhadra and Krishna rivers, the two states exist in an antagonistic relationship and are often at war.

1360–1377: During his reign, Bukka I builds his empire by conquest, annexing Tamil Madurai (1360) to the south, Raichur Doab (after war with Bahmanis, 1365), and eastern Reddi territories (1365–1370). His son Kumara Kampana conquers the sultanate of Ma'bar (1370), extending Vijayanagar dominion over the whole of south India.

1377: Bukka I's son Harihara II (reigns 1377–1404) becomes the first Vijayanagar ruler to assume the royal title *raya.* Soon after his coronation, he repels an invasion from the Bahmani sultanate, subdues a rebellion in the Tamil-speaking southern territory, and exacts tribute from Ceylon.

1380: Vijayanagar captures the important port of Goa and wrests the Konkan from Bahmanis, thereby gaining control of the west Deccan coast all the way north to Chaul (until 1470), source of rich revenues from trade. Fortified outposts are built around the peninsula.

1398–1406: A Bahmani invasion sparks eight years of war. Firuz Shah Bahmani again invades (1406) and enslaves sixty thousand Hindus.

November 7, 1406: Coronation of Devaraya I (reigns 1406–1424) after two years of civil war. He modernizes the Vijayanagar army, long at a disadvantage against more sophisticated northern weaponry and tactics, by introducing cavalry and employing Turkish archers.

1420: Italian traveler Niccolo de Conti visits Vijayanagar. His detailed written account describes Devaraya I as the most powerful king in India; he is awestruck at the splendor and wealth of the capital, covering dozens of square miles and defended by seven massive concentric fortifications. Ninety thousand soldiers are reported to be garrisoned in the city.

1424–1446: The empire achieves its largest extent during reign of Devaraya II. His army enlarged with Muslim mercenaries, he conquers eastern territories from the Krishna River to Ceylon and mounts invasions all the way south into Kerala. Imperial control of west coast ports gives the crown monopoly over trade in the vital military resource of Arabian horses.

c. 1428: Vijayanagar annexes the east-coast kingdom of Kondavidu, important for its ports. This begins a century-long conflict with the neighboring Gajapati kingdom in Orissa.

November 1442: Persian ambassador Abdur Razzaq arrives at Calicut, one of a number of small independent Hindu kingdoms on the Malabar Coast.

1443: A brother of Devaraya II treacherously murders many of Vijayanagar's nobles and princes, stabs the king, and proclaims himself *raya*. Although Devaraya survives the assault and executes its perpetrator, his kingdom is robbed of its ruling class. The Bahmanis take advantage of this weakness to invade with a force of fifty thousand cavalry and sixty thousand foot soldiers.

1463–1465: Gajapati of Orissa invade and under the superb generalship of Prince Hamvira capture a string of major eastern forts, including Udayagiri, Chandragiri, and Kanchi. They retreat after a two-year rout of Vijayanagar forces, leaving the empire severely weakened.

1470: Bahmani *wazir* Mahmud Gawan launches a Konkan campaign against Vijayanagar; he captures much of the west coast from Goa all the way north to Chaul. Efforts to retrieve Goa fail; the loss of this primary west coast port interrupts the trade in Persian and Arabian horses on which Vijayanagar's military now depends.

Life's postures, love, hate—lost to the flames;
the craving-filled kettle drum finally burst.
Lust's veil, this body, is tattered with age;
every errant shuffle is stilled.
All that lives and dies—why, they're one,
and the this and that, and haggling, are gone.
What I have found, says Kabir, is fullness itself,
A finality granted by the mercy of Ram.

From a poem by Kabir (15th century)

1470s: Saluva Narasimha, Tamil Brahman chief of Chandragiri and an extremely able general, conquers extensive territories in south India and Orissa. The newly won territory is nominally under sovereignty of Vijayanagar ruler Virupaksha II (reigns 1465–1485); in reality, by 1480 Saluva Narasimha is the preeminent power in the kingdom, effectively operating as an independent prince.

1485: Saluva Narasimha seizes a throne weakened by competing claimants (reigns 1485–1491). He thus ends the Sangama dynasty and founds the short-lived Saluva dynasty (to 1505). His campaigns rejuvenate the Vijayanagar army after years of losses and regain territory lost to Orissa and Bahmanis (whose own kingdom is approaching dissolution). The empire regains nearly the whole of its former extent in peninsular India under the regency of chief minister Narasa Nayaka, who in a remarkable streak defeats the Cheras, Cholas, Pandyas, Gajapati, and Adil Shahis.

1490: The Sultanate of Bijapur is founded. It replaces the Bahmani kingdom as Vijayanagar's primary rival. The other new Deccan sultanates, Ahmadnagar, Berar, Bidar, and Golconda, join in a tumultuous period of warfare punctuated by short-lived, quickly shifting tactical alliances.

1498: Vasco da Gama, in search of East Indian maritime trade routes, lands with four ships at Calicut (which later lends its name to major Indian export, cotton calico). His is the first European fleet to complete round-trip voyage to India. He gains Portuguese trade concessions from the *zamorin*, Calicut's ruler.

1501: In the compact of Bidar, Deccan sultanates agree to unite in war against Vijayanagar.

1505: Saluva dynasty is overthrown by Narasa Nayaka's son Vira Narasimha (reigns 1505–1509), who establishes the Tuluva dynasty (to 1542).

1505: Francisco de Almeida is appointed the first viceroy of Portuguese India (governs 1505–1509). Arriving with a fleet of twenty-one ships and a force of fifteen hundred men, he fights his way up the west coast, establishing naval supremacy as far north as Diu, Gujarat. Portuguese traders are established at Cochin (1506) and Socotra (1507).

August 8, 1509: Coronation of Vira Narasimha's half-brother Krishnadevaraya (reigns 1509–1529), who rules at the zenith of Vijayanagar's power and wealth. Soon afterward, he repulses an invasion by the confederated Deccan sultanates (1510). Krishnadevaraya pursues friendly relations with Europeans, granting Portuguese trading rights in exchange for access to trade goods, especially horses vital to his military; the second Portuguese viceroy Afonso de Albuquerque (governs 1509–1515) proposes a military alliance.

1509–1529: Krishnadevaraya curbs traditional powers of military chiefs by placing imperial forts under control of Brahman commanders and creating the *poligars*, a new military class completely dependent on the king for preferment. Muslim and Portuguese gunners are hired to defend forts, and forest tribesmen are retained as soldiers.

1512–1523: Krishnadevaraya launches a series of brilliant military campaigns against the sultanates and the Gajapati, himself leading troops in battle. He recovers the eastern provinces of Kondavidu, Warangal, and Rajamundry; secures the Raichur Doab, extending dominion northward to the Krishna River; and annexes Mysore. In a bloody war with Bijapur (1520), Vijayanagar forces sack the capital, plunder the country, and destroy the old Bahmani capital of Gulbarga.

1522: Portuguese traveler Domingo Paes visits Vijayanagar, a city of 100,000, which he describes as "the best provided city in the world" in an extensive written account of the king and his empire. Increased commercial relations bring numerous Portuguese traders and travelers to south India; their writings serve as important historical sources.

c. **1530:** Beginning of the Nayak (Naik) period of rule. The system of *nayaka*, military officers who rule as independent local powers, fills the vacuum left by the decay of imperial power, and effectively replaces the Vijayanagar kingship until the eighteenth-century Mughal annexation.

1543 or 1544: After two unsuccessful attempts to take the throne (1529, 1535), Krishnadevaraya's son-in-law Rama Raja crowns his own candidate during the war of succession. He is regent for the nominal young king Sadasivaraya (reigns until 1576). Muslims hold important offices in Rama Raja's twenty-year-long administration, including military posts; the armies of all south Indian states are by now composed of Hindus, Muslims, and European mercenaries.

1543–1562: Attempting to reverse Vijayanagar's decline, Rama Raja undertakes a series of political intrigues, alliances, and raids on Deccan sultanates. His arrogance, open contempt for neighboring Muslim princes and their ambassadors, and despoliation of their lands, coupled with his decentralization of political authority, instead ensure the destruction of his kingdom.

January 23, 1565: A Vijayanagar army said to number nearly a million men battle the combined forces of Bijapur, Ahmadnagar, Golconda, and Bidar at Talikota. The artillery of the allied force inflicts a crushing defeat: two of Vijayanagar's Muslim generals defect, Rama Raja himself is killed, and the Vijayanagar empire is destroyed. The huge capital is sacked and razed. Later Vijayanagar kings, nominally ruling until 1672 from capitals at Penukonda and Chandragiri, preside over an empire under perpetual attack by Bijapur and Golconda and disintegrating under the weight of noble factionalism, rebellions, and civil and external wars.

SOUTH INDIA: ISLAMIC STATES, 1300–1650

Islamic rule in peninsular India begins shortly after 1300, when an incursion by the Delhi sultanate brings a southward migration of Indo-Turks from the north. The Tughluq nobles who administer the provincial government soon revolt, however, and the Bahmani dynasty founds an independent sultanate in the northern Deccan at about the same time that the great Hindu state of Vijayanagar is founded to the south. In a contest more political than religious, these kingdoms fight for control of the Deccan for 150 years.

The Bahmanis solicit Muslim immigration from the Middle East, Arabia, and Persia to help administer their kingdom. Jealousies and political rivalries with the longer established Muslim population exacerbate the violence and instability endemic to the Bahmani kingdom. Around 1500, a series of successful rebellions creates five successor states governed by hereditary Muslim dynasties: the large, rich, and powerful kingdoms of Ahmadnagar, Bijapur, and Golconda and the smaller and shorter-lived kingdoms of Berar and Bidar.

Like the Bahmanis before them, the five Deccan sultanates exist in a political environment of constantly shifting alliances, rivalries, and wars. Massive armies move over the Deccan fighting for possession of forts, plundering their enemies' territory and sacking their cities. In a brief alliance, they conquer Vijayanagar in 1565. They are themselves overrun by Mughal invasion a century later.

The larger sultanates are renowned for their fabulous wealth, deriving from their diamond and gem deposits and control of interregional and international trade. Their control of ports is challenged, however, as Europeans make their first appearance in south India during this period. Portuguese navigators discover the sea route to the Indies and are followed in the early years of the sixteenth century by traders installed in west coast trading factories and protected by a formidable navy and a colonial governor. The western port of Goa, captured in 1510 to serve as the Portuguese capital, is to remain in Portugal's hands for 450 years.

The eclectic cultures of the Deccan begin percolating during this period as indigenous Marathi, Telugu, and Kannada cultures come into contact with the Arab and Persian influences brought by immigrants and, toward the end of the period, with Europeans. Each sultanate develops its own distinctive culture based on its own regional mix. The major art and architecture of the Deccan during this period are, however, Islamic. Mosques, new to peninsular India, and Islamic-style palaces and tombs are built in great numbers.

Extant architecture, sculpture, and paintings, Indian chronicles, and European travelers' accounts all attest to the opulence of medieval Deccan courts. As do their peers in medieval and early modern cultures around the world, ordinary people in the southern sultanates live in extreme poverty, subjected to ruinous taxation and arbitrary and often harsh rule.

c. 1310: Khalji general Malik Kafur conquers Deccan for the Delhi sultanate. Plunder from Madurai (1311) and elsewhere finances northerners' military campaigns. Indo-Turks rule south India in the wake of conquest.

1323: Ulugh Tughluq (the future Muhammad Shah) conquers Madurai on the Coromandel coast, beginning four hundred years of Muslim rule in parts of south India. He creates Ma'bar, a small and precarious province of the Delhi sultanate surrounded by Hindu kingdoms. After succeeding to the Delhi throne, he establishes (1327) a southern capital at the old Yadava capital of Devagiri, renamed Daulatabad.

1334: Tughluq general Jalal ud-Din Ahsan Shah rebels and founds an independent sultanate at Ma'bar (to c. 1370). It is one of many rebellions against Tughluqs that force northerners to withdraw from south India in the 1330s–1340s. The Ma'bar sultanate is noted for dynastic violence, slaughter of Hindus, and wars over trading stations with the neighboring kingdoms of Hoysala, Pandya, and Vijayanagar.

1335–1342: Widespread famines in south India.

1336: Founding of Vijayanagar empire.

1347: The governor of Gulbarga, Zafar Khan Hasan Gangu, founds the Bahmani sultanate (to 1526) after a two-year rebellion of Muslim nobles against Muhammad Shah in central Deccan. He reigns (1347–1358) as Ala ud-Din Bahman Shah. The Bahmani dynasty is particularly violent; the majority of its fourteen sultans die violently, and constant wars, massacres, and destruction characterize the period.

1347–1424: Gulbarga period of the Bahmani dynasty. Ala ud-Din's capital at centrally located Gulbarga becomes a great city.

1350: Ala ud-Din's first war against the neighboring kingdom of Warangal. His empire eventually reaches from Goa to western Warangal. He replicates the Tughluqs' administrative structure, with four provincial governors. Noble military officers administer the territories and maintain armed forces; following the Delhi sultanate's practice, local Hindu officials collect land taxes.

1358–1375: Reign of Muhammad I, son of Ala ud-Din Bahman Shah. He inaugurates a century and a half of nearly constant warfare with neighboring Vijayanagar for control of the Deccan, specifically of the well-fortified Raichur Doab between the Tungabhadra and Krishna rivers.

Late 14th–early 15th centuries: The Bahmani sultans encourage large-scale immigration of Arabs, Turks, and southern Persians to Deccan. Mostly Persian-speaking Shias, the immigrants become successful in trade and the royal army and administration, and gradually receive political preferment. Original noble settlers from Delhi sultanate fairly established in Deccan (*dakhnis*, or Deccanis), mostly Sunnis intermarried with indigenous peoples, grow resentful at political inroads of immigrants (*afaqi* or *pardesis*). The cultural and political rift between these groups is increasingly deep and bitter.

1365: Warangal cedes Golconda to the Bahmani kingdom. Bahmanis are also engaged against Reddi and Gajapati kingdoms to their east. Their armed force, largely cavalry, deploys artillery in static contests over fortified strongholds.

1378–1380: Vijayanagar takes advantage of a few years of extreme violence over Bahmani royal succession to capture Goa and other lucrative west coast ports.

1390s: Widespread famines in south India. Muhammad II Shah Bahmani (reigns 1378–1397) organizes famine relief.

1397–1422: Reign of Firuz Shah Bahmani. He expands the nobility by ennobling Hindus and granting them high office, and he himself takes wives of many nationalities. Military campaigns against Vijayanagar (1398, 1406, 1417) end in stalemate. He invades and plunders Gondwana (1412) and Warangal (1417), but is disastrously defeated at Pangal (1420) by a Vijayanagar-led coalition.

1422–1436: Reign of Firuz Shah's brother Ahmad Shah is marked by relentless military campaigns and expansionism. He visits wars, slaughter, and destruction on Vijayanagar and finally annexes Warangal (1425). He also fights against Malwa and Gujarat, successor states to the Tughluqs that are perennially contested because of their strategic location between north and south India.

1423: Famine in Deccan.

1424–1526: Bidar period of the Bahmani dynasty, so called from Ahmad Shah's transfer of the capital to Bidar.

1430–1431: Deccani officers of the Bahmani army abandon their own general, Khalaf Hasani, causing Ahmad Shah's defeat in the second Gujarati campaign. Their defection creates rivalry in aristocracy between Deccanis (Sunni Muslims long established in the Deccan) and *pardesis* (foreigners), recent immigrants from the Middle East, Arabia, and Persia who are Shias.

1436: His army now manned entirely by *pardesis*, Bahmani Shah Ala ud-Din Ahmad (reigns 1436–1458) repels northern invasion by Khandesh, a client state of Gujarat.

1446: Deccanis, now politically ascendant, treacherously persuade the sultan that *pardesis* (foreigners) are responsible for the failure of the Konkan invasion and with royal acquiescence massacre numerous *pardesis* at Chakan. After *pardesi* survivors expose the Deccanis' perfidy, the emperor punishes the Deccanis and restores *pardesis* to political favor. The Deccani-*pardesi* split becomes open hostility.

1455: Mahmud Gawan, a Persian *pardesi* in royal service, negotiates end of rebellion in Warangal, beginning a rapid political rise; he is to become one of the greatest statesmen of medieval India.

1463: Mahmud Gawan, now governor of Bijapur, is appointed *wazir* (chief minister, to 1481) of nine-year-old sultan Muhammad III Bahmani (reigns 1463–1482). Gawan proves an extremely capable ruler at the height of Bahmani power. State appointments are divided between Deccanis and *pardesis*. Government is centralized, reducing the considerable power of provincial governors; the four *tarafs* (provinces) are divided into eight, with administrative subdivision into *sarkars* and *parganas*.

c. 1470: Russian traveler Athanasius Nikitin visits Bidar; his written account describes a kingdom of tremendous luxury and wealth.

1470s: The Bahmani kingdom achieves its greatest geographical extent, stretching from the Arabian Sea to the Coromandel Coast. Military campaigns include the reconquest of much of Konkan, yielding control of the west coast trade (1470) and Goa (1475); the conquest of Rajamundry (1472) and devastation of Orissa (1478); the invasion of Karnataka (1479); and the sack of Kanchi (1481).

1472: Famine in Deccan.

April 5, 1481: Using a forged document, a Deccani party led by Nizam ul-Mulk persuades Muhammad III Bahmani to execute Mahmud Gawan for treason. During the next months, *pardesis* desert the capital in protest; the sultan dies repentant; the *nizam*, now styled Malik Naib, becomes regent for Muhammad III's son Mahmud (reigns 1482–1518) and is himself murdered in 1486. The weakened monarchy is unable to control noble factionalism and provincial rebellions; the Bahmani empire is dismembered, although the nominal sultan is enthroned until 1538.

1487–1490: Exploratory voyages by Pedro de Covilham between the Persian Gulf, India, and East Africa lead him to report to the Portuguese king that India can be reached by sea from Europe by sailing around Africa.

June 1490: Malik Ahmad Nizam ul-Mulk, son of Malik Naib, secedes from the Bahmani kingdom and founds the independent state of Ahmadnagar (to 1636) in the Marathi-speaking region of northwest Deccan. He rules as Ahmad Nizam Shah (to 1509), founding the Nizam Shahi dynasty (to 1595).

1490: Fatullah Imad ul-Mulk (d. 1504) secedes from the Bahmani kingdom, founds the Imad Shahi dynasty in the independent kingdom of Berar. This small central Deccan kingdom lies east of Ahmadnagar, which gradually annexes its territory and finally absorbs Berar outright (1574).

1490: Yusuf Adil Khan, Bahmani governor of Bijapur, secedes from the Bahmani kingdom to establish the Adil Shahi dynasty (to 1686) in the new kingdom of Bijapur in southwest Deccan. Bijapur, the southernmost of the new south Indian Islamic states, is flanked by Ahmadnagar and Vijayanagar, its two major rivals for south Indian domination.

1492: Qasim Barid, a powerful Turkish noble and superintendent of police, takes over the central government of the much-reduced Bahmani kingdom at Bidar. Although a nominal Bahmani sultan rules for thirty more years, 1492 is sometimes regarded as the founding date of the Baridi Shahi dynasty in the fifth southern sultanate of Bidar (to 1619).

Like meat-eating owls and vultures and cranes;
such are the animal bodies we bear.
Like lynxes we are, like a mongoose or fox—
They all live in homes just like ours;
All have their houses, their wives and sons—
what makes us better than they?
To fill their bodies they kill living beings
And feed on pleasures for which no one should
*   yearn.*
Sur says, unless we sing to the Lord,
We're camels and asses—that's what we are.

From the *Sursagar*, poems by Surdas (15th–16th
century)

1494: The Treaty of Tordesillas, demarcating Spanish and Portuguese spheres of influence, bars Spanish colonial expansion in the subcontinent, ensuring Portuguese domination at precisely the time European traders are establishing their first permanent settlements in southern India.

1501: Mahmud Shah Bahmani unites his *amirs* and *wazirs* in an agreement to wage annual *jihad* against Vijayanagar. The expeditions are financially ruinous.

1510: The second Portuguese viceroy, Alfonso de Albuquerque (governs 1509–1515), captures Goa from the sultan of Bijapur. Portuguese naval power is decisive in the defeat of the Ahmadnagar-Bijapur coalition. Portugal subsequently annexes further territory to the north and south of Goa, referred to as the "Old Conquests" (1543), and begins a century-long domination of the European maritime spice trade with the East Indies. Goa becomes the capital of the far-flung Portuguese empire. Portugal will hold Goa until 1962.

1512: Turkish officer Quli Qutb ul-Mulk declares an independent sultanate in the provincial capital of Golconda, and founds the Qutb Shahi dynasty (to 1687). Golconda is located in the Telugu-speaking region of east Deccan. Golconda, Bijapur, and Ahmadnagar, major successor states to the Bahmani kingdom, strike shifting tactical alliances in military campaigns against each other and Vijayanagar during next hundred years.

1527: The last Bahmani sultan, Kalimullah, flees from Bidar to Ahmadnagar. Located in the central Deccan, Bidar proves vulnerable to territorial raids by its more powerful neighbors.

January 23, 1565: A coalition of Deccan sultanates led by Ali Adil Shah I of Bijapur routs Rama Raja's forces at Talikota, ending the Vijayanagar empire. The victors' alliance is short-lived, and the sultanates are again at war within two years. Bijapur gradually extends its dominion into Vijayanagar over the next thirty years.

1571: Bijapur and Ahmadnagar sign treaties with Portugal after the sieges of Portuguese Goa and Chaul fail. Portuguese domination of sea lanes and Mughal hegemony in the north cut the Deccan off; sultans increasingly turn to local Hindus rather than Middle Eastern Muslim immigrants for administrative personnel.

1574: Ahmadnagar annexes Berar, ending the ninety-year Imad Shahi dynasty.

1590: Muhammad Quli Qutb Shah (reigns 1580–1612) founds the new capital of Golconda at Hyderabad alongside an existing fortress. Golconda, straddling major trade and military routes through the central Deccan, becomes fabulous for its wealth.

1591: Mughal emperor Akbar supports a successful coup in Ahmadnagar that installs Burhan Nizam Shah II. Wars with Bijapur, another failed attack on Portuguese Chaul (1592), and noble factionalism weaken Burhan's rule; civil war after his death (1595) brings the very successful century-long Ni-zam Shahi dynasty to an end and smoothes the path of Akbar's Deccan campaigns.

1593, 1596: Dowager queen Chand Bibi personally leads Ahmadnagar's defense against Mughal invasions, but is finally forced to cede Berar to Mughals.

1619: Bijapur annexes the sultanate of Bidar.

1626: Death of Malik Ambar, chief minister of Ahmadnagar and one of the greatest statesmen of medieval India.

1633: Mughal emperor Shah Jahan captures Daulatabad and finally annexes Ahmadnagar. The Mughal viceroy of the Deccan is installed at Aurangabad. Bijapur and Golconda, the only two remaining Deccan sultanates, become Mughal tributaries.

1646: Revolt of Shivaji against Adil Shahis marks the beginning of Maratha power in Deccan.

1656: Mughals annex Bidar, since 1619 a province of Bijapur.

1686–1687: Bijapur and Golconda, finally unable to withstand Mughal armies, are annexed by Akbar.

MUGHAL EMPIRE: 1526–1760

The Mughal dynasty (from the Persian word for Mongol, *Mughal*) originates in invasion and is driven by the idea of conquest and empire; warfare and territorial expansion are major themes of the reign. At the same time, the Mughals prove to be outstanding rulers. They succeed in imposing a strong and enduring central administration on a fragmented region previously under the sway of competing Hindu, Turkish, and Afghan chieftains and Muslim sultans. During this period the subcontinent achieves a degree of political cohesion not seen since the Gupta empire: at its height the Mughal dynasty extends this control over the whole of northern India and nearly all of the Deccan.

This is not to suggest that the empire is a tranquil one. Groups such as the Rajputs, Sikhs, and Jats (an agricultural caste), as well as members of the ruling families, are often in rebellion against the Mughals, while neighboring Afghans and Persians threaten from the northwest. After the death of the emperor Aurangzeb, the Marathas, originally in the Mughal service, create a powerful state. About this time, too, the governors of many of the provinces of the empire become virtually independent. The empire fractures without the gifted personal rule of the Great Mughals; the dynasty nominally survives until 1858, but its power ends by 1760.

Themselves Muslims, the Mughals create an elite ruling class integrated and fully reflective of the rich diversity of India's ethnic and religious groups. They rule one of the richest nations on earth, and, as their surviving art and artifacts attest, the life of the Mughal ruling class is one of ostentatious luxury. The mass of the population, however, are engaged in rural subsistence agriculture and endure lives of poverty comparable to the standard of their European counterparts.

Many of the most cherished images of India come from the artists who flourish under Mughal patronage. Architectural masterpieces like the Taj Mahal and classical Indian miniature paintings reveal at a glance a central fact of life in sixteenth- and seventeenth-century northern India: the dominant culture is Persian, with traces of the Mughals' Turkish and Mongol origins.

The Great Mughals preside over a period of great economic expansion fueled by trade. This is the period in which India meets Europe. Eager for India's cotton, sugar, indigo, and spices, the Portuguese come first, and Dutch, English, and French trading companies establish extensive operations in the subcontinent. These commercial and cultural exchanges are to have profound effects in the centuries to come.

April 21, 1526: The first Battle of Panipat, near Delhi. His men outnumbered four to one, Babur (1483–1530), the Mongol-Turk ruler of Kabul, brilliantly deploys cavalry and Turkish artillery to defeat Ibrahim, last Lodi sultan of Delhi. Ibrahim and fifteen thousand of his men are killed. The conqueror of Kandahar, Punjab, and Lahore, Babur enters Delhi and Agra as emperor of Hindustan; he establishes Mughal dynasty (to 1858) by conquest and appeals to loyalty of local *begs*, or chiefs.

One of the great defects of Hindustan being its lack of running waters, it kept coming to my mind that waters should be made to flow by means of wheels erected wherever I might settle down, also that grounds should be laid out in an orderly and symmetrical way. With this object in view, we crossed the Jun-water to look at garden-grounds a few days after entering Agra. . . . The beginning was made with the large well from which water comes for the Hot-bath, and also with the piece of ground where the tamarind-trees and the octagonal tank are now. . . . There in that charmless and disorderly Hind, plots of garden were seen laid out with order and symmetry, with suitable borders and parterres in every corner, and in every border rose and narcissus in perfect arrangement.

Memoirs of Babur (1483–1530), emperor of Hindustan (1526)

1527: Amid widespread fighting against the Portuguese, the Gujarati fleet is defeated by the Portuguese at Chaul and captured in near entirety off Bandra in 1528. The Portuguese are aggressive throughout the century, besieging coastal forts, burning coastal towns, and demanding tribute; they plunder Sind (1556). They monopolize Indian exports to Europe as well as East Indian trade, imposing marine pass rules (1559), confiscating ships and killing crews of noncomplying vessels in government-sponsored piracy.

March 16, 1527: Babur secures the throne by defeating Rana Sanga and 100,000 Rajput troops at Khanua, eliminating primary rivals in northern India. He dies in 1530 after eastern campaigns and a last great victory at the Gogra River, near Patna, in 1529, securing Bengal and Bihar.

Late 1520s–1530s: Portuguese establish numerous settlements along the west coast, with major settlements at Cochin, Diu, Bassein, and their headquarters, Goa. Their imperial strategy rejects land empire in favor of fortified factories (trading posts) and absolute control of shipping lanes by a formidable navy.

1534–1540: Succeeding his father, Humayun (reigns 1530–1540) is beset by ambitious brothers, fractious nobility, and difficulty of ruling northern India from Kabul. Campaigns across northern India fail against the Portuguese, Malwa, Bahadur Shah of Gujarat, and the rebellious Farid Khan of Bengal and Bihar. After decisive defeats at Chausa and Bilgram (1539–1540), Humayun flees to Persia, leaving Farid Khan in power. He adopts the name Sher Shah Sur.

1540–1545: In a short reign remarkable for its accomplishments, Sher Shah Sur reconquers much of Hindustan and Punjab, centralizes authority, thoroughly reforms the revenue system, and establishes silver currency: his administration lays the groundwork for a centralized northern Indian bureaucracy that Akbar is later to develop more fully. He dies besieging the Rajput stronghold of Kalinjar (1545), and rival chieftains struggle for control of his territory.

1550–1554: Giovanni Ramusio publishes the first major compendium of European travels in India. Dozens of travelers' accounts are printed in Europe during the sixteenth and seventeenth centuries.

June 23, 1555: Humayun enters Delhi in triumph to reclaim his throne after recovering Kandahar, Kabul, and Lahore with extensive military support from Persian Shah Ismail. He dies in a fall soon after his restoration.

February 1556: Humayun's young son Akbar (reigns 1556–1605) accedes at age fourteen to a crown vulnerable to hostile Afghan chiefs and the disloyalty of his own officials and relatives. Suri general Hemu occupies the Delhi throne; only Punjab province is secure. Bairam Khan, Akbar's able regent (1556–1560), defeats Hemu's 100,000-strong force at second battle of Panipat on November 5, reestablishing Mughal rule. Further campaigns in the early years of reign secure the Mughal empire over the northern provinces of Malwa (1561–1562) and Rajputana (1562–1567).

1558: Akbar reestablishes Agra as his capital.

1562: Akbar's marriage to an Ambur princess is the first of many matrimonial alliances with the great houses of the Mughals' historical enemy, the Rajputs. His wife's brother, Man Singh (1550–1614), is appointed to highest rank of civil service and becomes Akbar's chief general; such appointments integrate the imperial service and secure the loyalty of Hindu chiefs.

1563–1564: Akbar ends discrimination against Hindus by repealing pilgrimage taxes and *jizya*, the poll tax on non-Muslims. The promotion of religious toleration throughout his reign breaks with practice of some of his Muslim forebears.

1566: The king of Cannanor surrenders to the Portuguese, ending long, bloody Malabar war.

1568–1585: Akbar reconquers northern India: strategic Rajput hill forts of Chitor and Ranthambhor (1568–1569) and provinces of Rajasthan (1570), Gujarat (1572), lower Sind (1574), Bengal and Bihar (1574–1576), and Khandesh (1577). Most Rajput states become Mughal tributaries. Annexed provinces are always subject to revolts and coups, however; some areas remain in nearly continuous rebellion against the Mughals.

1571: Akbar founds a ceremonial capital at Fatehpur Sikri, west of Agra.

1573: In an episode often cited to demonstrate his military genius, Akbar leads three thousand horsemen to Ahmadabad in Gujarat, six hundred miles distant from Fatehpur Sikri, quells a rebellion, and returns to his capital in a brilliant forty-five-day operation.

1573: Akbar establishes the *mansabdar* system, tying the large bureaucracy and army into a single system. Nobles and other state officials are assigned military ranks determining their own pay (*jagirs* [assignments of land revenue] or cash) and status and the required number of troops they are responsible for supplying to the imperial army. Akbar uses imperial service as a means of political reconciliation by assigning *mansabdars* to Persians, Rajputs, others in annexed territories and creating a loyal, integrated civil service.

1578–1617: Reign of Raja Wadiyar at Mysore.

1581: First Turkey and Levant Company formed in London for overland trade to India. Ralph Fitch, John Eldred, John Newberie, and others on its first mercantile expedition reach Akbar's court in September 1585.

1584: Akbar adopts the new *Ilahi* year, a solar calendar counted in regnal years and backdated to his accession.

1585–1595: Akbar reconquers Humayun's northwestern possessions: Kabul (1585), Kashmir (1586), upper Sind (1591), Orissa (1592), Baluchistan, and Kandahar (1595). The empire is consolidated over a large area of subcontinent bounded by the Godavari River, Kabul, and Kandahar. Protection of the northwest border area from neighboring Persians and Uzbeks occupies Akbar for fifteen years.

1587: Sir Francis Drake's capture of a laden Portuguese East Indiaman yields more than £100,000 worth of Indian treasure and intelligence about the rich potential of India trade. In 1591 John Lancaster leaves Plymouth on the first English voyage to the East Indies; he lands at Cape Comorin.

Royalty is a light emanating from God, and a ray from the sun, the illuminator of the universe, the argument of the book of perfection, the receptacle of all virtues. Modern language calls this light the divine light, and the tongue of antiquity called it the sublime halo. It is communicated by God to kings without the intermediate assistance of anyone, and men, in the presence of it, bend the forehead of praise toward the ground of submission.

A'in-i-Akbari (Institutes of Akbar), political tract by Abul Fazl Allami (c. 1590)

1590: Muhammad Quli Qutb Shah, ruler of rich princedom of Golconda, founds a capital near present-day Hyderabad. Strategically sited on the trade and military routes of southern India, Golconda becomes a city of fabulous wealth.

1594–1598: Widespread famine and plague, the sixth famine in half a century. Lahore and Kashmir are severely afflicted; Akbar contributes to relief efforts.

1595–1596: Cornelis de Houtman leads the first Dutch mercantile expedition to India. Dutchman Jan Huygen van Linschoten's account of Indian navigation and commerce (published in Holland in 1596, in England in 1598) stimulates European interest in Indian trade.

1599–1602: Akbar invades Bijapur (1600), annexes Khandesh (1601), and sacks Ahmadnagar and Burhanabad; "King of the Deccan" is added to royal titles in 1602. Prince Salim (later Shah Jahangir) takes the opportunity of Akbar's absence from north India to revolt; he is pardoned.

1600: The estimated population of India is 140–150 million; some 85 percent are rural dwellers.

December 31, 1600: The East India Company (EIC) is incorporated in England with a fifteen-year monopoly of eastern trade. It comprises a group of merchants organized voyage by voyage, reliant on commercial competitiveness for success, and trading commodities in bulk. The first EIC voyages are to the East Indies.

March 20, 1602: The Dutch United East India Company (VOC) is chartered with a twenty-one-year monopoly. A government-run organization of smaller companies, its traders are backed by the Dutch army. India is targeted to supply textiles to exchange for the East Indian spices shipped by the Dutch to Europe. Sailing immediately to India, the Dutch blockade the Portuguese at Goa (1603).

1603: London merchant John Mildenhall reaches India overland; a self-appointed ambassador, he finally obtains trade privileges in Gujarat in imperial *firman* (1608).

1606: Soon after his accession, Akbar's son Jahangir (reigns 1605–1627) puts down a rebellion by his eldest son Khusrau in Lahore and executes Khusrau's supporter Sikh Guru Arjun. The Sikh community is permanently embittered. Arjun's son Hargobind (1595–1644) becomes sixth *guru* in 1606; he arms the Sikhs, fortifies their capital, and builds the Akal Takht (Immortal Throne) to symbolize their political presence.

1609: First Dutch trading post at Pulicat. Rapid multiplication of such trading posts in the 1610s–1620s contributes to VOC supremacy over EIC and other European rivals whose East India companies (e.g., French 1604, Danish 1612) are either short-lived or geographically restricted. Major Dutch trade centers include Surat, Teganapatam, Bengal, and Agra.

April 1609: William Hawkins, captain of the first EIC voyage to India, arrives at Agra carrying a letter from England's King James I. He stays at Agra for two years, but Surat merchants and Portuguese persuade Jahangir to deny England trade privileges. Competing trading powers court the emperor and provincial governors during this period trying to gain commercial advantage over rivals.

1610s: In a modest northern territorial expansion, Jahangir ends a long conflict with Mewar (1614), annexes the last Afghan territories (eastern Bengal after a five-year revolution in 1612, Orissa in 1617) and western Kutch (1618). Defeated Afghans are integrated into the Mughal nobility.

1611: Jahangir marries Nur Jahan. Promoting interests of her Persian family, she and Jahangir's second son, Prince Khurram, dominate politics for more than ten years. Jahangir, addicted to wine and opium, is politically ineffectual.

1612: The first EIC factory is founded at Surat, which becomes the most important English trading post. English posts are founded during the next twenty years at coastal and inland cities including Agra, Ahmadabad, Cambay, Broach, Nizampatam, Balasore, and Hariharpur.

1615–1618: English royal ambassador Sir Thomas Roe presses renewed negotiations at the Mughal court for a permanent commercial and friendship treaty. Prince Khurram grants trade privileges (1618) in exchange for naval support.

1616: Plague in northern India.

1620: First Danish settlement at Tranquebar.

1621: Mughals annex much southern territory after defeating confederacy of Ahmadnagar, Bijapur, and Golconda. Malik Ambar, Abyssinian slave general and chief minister and virtual ruler of Ahmadnagar, remains an irritant to Mughals, against whom he wages a long guerrilla war (1610–1629).

March 1621: Fire destroys Patna.

1622: Persian attack and capture of long-contested Kandahar (until 1637) tarnishes Mughal prestige and is a deep personal betrayal of emperor by Shah Abbas I, with whom Jahangir has exchanged numerous cordial embassies.

1623: Unsuccessful rebellion by Prince Khurram (later Shah Jahan) after breach with Nur Jahan's faction. He is pardoned.

1623: Dutch massacre of English factors at Amboyna ends British activity in Java; India becomes the focus of EIC trade.

1624: The EIC is granted power to prosecute its employees in India under English law.

March–September 1626: The emperor and Nur Jahan are seized and imprisoned for six months by her rival, Mughal general Mahabat Khan.

1628–1657: Shah Jahan's reign marks the golden period of the Mughal empire. His reign is marked by successful military campaigns in Deccan, rebellions in southern and northwestern provinces, and further territorial expansion. A quixotic campaign to recover ancestral lands in Balkh, however, fails.

1629–1636: Prince Aurangzeb's superb generalship is decisive in Mughal conquest of Deccan, a prize first sought by Akbar. Annexation of Ahmadnagar after the death of its great statesman Malik Ambar ends Nizam Shahi dynasty (1633); tributary treaty with Bijapur and Golconda (1636) grants Mughals supremacy over this vast region. As governor of Deccan (reigns 1637–1644, 1654–1658), Aurangzeb presides over years of unrest.

1630–1632: Widespread famine as drought is followed by floods; Gujarat and Deccan are devastated. Shah Jahan contributes to relief efforts.

1630s: EIC negotiations with Golconda and Portugal yield trade privileges on the Coromandel and Malabar coasts. Trade in Bengal is allowed by imperial *firman* to the EIC (1634).

1630s–1640s: Bhonsles, the most important Maratha clan, consolidate *jagirs* (land assigned to yield revenue) to expand Bijapur to south and southwest, laying the groundwork for future domination of Deccan.

June–September 1632: At war over Portuguese piracy, seizure of territory, and forced conversions in Bengal, Shah Jahan destroys the Portuguese settlement at Hugli, killing or imprisoning thousands. Fourteen thousand Indian prisoners held by the Portuguese are released.

1640: Francis Day completes the construction of Fort St. George, Madras, under a grant from the local raja.

1644: Bijapur conquers Mysore.

1646: Maratha prince Shivaji Bhonsle (1630–1680) begins operations against Bijapur. He carves out a principality by means of raids, looting, and seizure of remote hill forts; plunder and tribute finance his fiefdom. By the 1650s, he controls the Pune region, and during the following twenty years he forges a powerful Hindu kingdom from the loose Maratha federation in western and central India.

1647: Famine in Madras.

1648: Shah Jahan moves the capital from Agra to his new city of Shahjahanabad (Delhi).

February 25, 1649: Persians finally capture Kandahar and repulse all further Mughal campaigns for this strategically located province.

1651: Establishment of an EIC factory at Hugli opens the Bengali saltpeter, silk, and sugar market to the English. European trad-ing posts multiply in Bengal and Bihar and Orissa during the following decades.

1652: Venetian Niccolao Manucci (1638–1717) begins fifty years of travels through north and west India; he becomes attached to Prince Dara Shikoh's court. His published memoirs are an important source for Mughal India.

1653: Madras becomes the EIC presidency (administrative division), its capital Fort St. George.

1656–1657: Prince Aurangzeb reconquers Golconda and Bijapur to gain control of Coromandel Coast with its textiles and indigo trade.

May 1657: Maratha chief Shivaji begins a long campaign against the Mughals; he plunders Junnar, loots Ahmadnagar. He leads continual raids in Deccan, extending the Marathas' reach to the Arabian Sea coast with skillful deployment of exceptionally well trained army and (after 1659) a navy of more than four hundred vessels. An organizational genius and canny strategist, he makes—and breaks—numerous short-lived tactical alliances and treaties to achieve his ends.

July 30, 1658: Aurangzeb (reigns 1658–1707), last of the Great Mughals, assumes the throne after a two-year war of succession and imprisons his father, Shah Jahan (who dies after eight years of detention in Agra fort). In early campaigns he wins Bijapur (1660–1661, 1665–1666), and Mughal general Mir Jumla (c.1591–1663) takes Bihar and Assam (1661–1663). Under the leadership of this experienced general and provincial governor, the Mughal empire reaches its greatest extent to incorporate the whole subcontinent except Kerala.

1659: After a twelve-year war, Shivaji finally defeats Adil Shahi of Bijapur and gains control over southern Konkan. Further territorial gains in northern Konkan and large area of Karnataka enable him to create a state from old Deccan kingdoms; he continues military expeditions throughout the peninsula.

1660s–1670s: Peasant rebellions against Mughals by Mathura Jats, northwest frontier Pashtuns, Punjabi Sikhs. These groups are angered by Aurangzeb's restrictive policies toward non-Muslims, for example, his doubling of internal customs duties for Hindus to 5 percent of the value of goods (1665).

June 23, 1661: Portugal cedes Bombay to England in dowry settlement of Catherine of Braganza, bride of Charles II. Bombay is transferred to EIC (1668) and developed into the premier trading station on the west coast under the presidency of Gerald Aungier (governs 1669–1677).

1662–1663: The long Dutch-Portuguese conflict ends with the Portuguese surrender of Cochin and other ports. The Dutch become the dominant trading power in Kerala and establish Cochin as their primary East Indian port (until 1795).

1664: Shivaji plunders Surat, the greatest port in India. He is crowned raja (later maharaja, c. 1674–1680). Shivaji is Aurangzeb's nemesis. Mughal attempts to conquer or settle with him fail, although in one brief rapprochement after a defeat by Jai Singh of Ambur, Shivaji joins Mughal imperial service (1666). Shivaji again sacks Surat with fifteen thousand men (1670).

1665: After a string of major naval victories over pirates, Mughals capture Sandwip and Chittagong, havens of Feringhis, descendants of Portuguese pirates; thousands of peasants held prisoner there are freed. This victory eliminates the major threat to Bengal shipping, but pirates from other nations, especially Portugal and England, continue to harass traders.

1669: Aurangzeb, a pious, orthodox Sunni Muslim, begins persecution of Hindus at Thatta, Multan, Varanasi; he orders the destruction of Hindu temples, many of which are replaced with mosques.

1672: Chikkadevaraja Wadiyar accedes to Mysore throne (reigns 1672–1704). In a high point of the long Wadiyar dynasty, he establishes postal and police services. He accepts Mughal protection (late 1690s), but Hyderabad and local Marathas continue to vie for domination and revenues of this prosperous state.

1672–1675: Afghan revolt quelled by Mughals.

1676: Publication in France of Jean Baptiste Tavernier's *Six Voyages*, an account of his five extensive journeys through India (1630s–1660s) that becomes an important historical source.

May 1677: EIC authorizes the president of Surat to use force against Indian rulers. A six hundred-man British militia and a troop of horse are formed at Bombay.

1678: Mughals betray Rajput alliance and annex Marwar; the ensuing thirty-year rebellion ends with the restoration of Rajput independence.

1679: Aurangzeb reimposes *jizya* and other legal and economic disabilities on non-Muslims, inaugurating the enforcement of strict Islamic orthodoxy.

October 13, 1679: Twenty thousand are drowned in a storm at Masulipatam.

1681: Aurangzeb marches to Deccan, where he devotes his final twenty-six years to campaigns against Marathas. He conquers the sultanates of Bijapur and Golconda (1686–1687) and appoints imperial administrators there.

August 1683: In response to English traders' growing complaints of exactions, extortion, and other disabilities by Mughal officials and local traders in Bengal, the EIC is granted admiralty jurisdiction in India.

Late 1680s: Open conflict between local rulers and English traders. In a series of raids and attacks in Bengal, the English plunder Hugli (November 1686), sack Balasore, and attack Chittagong. Temporarily driven from Bengal, they remove to Kalikata, where they found a secure trading site at Calcutta (1690). On the west coast, the English seize Indian cargo ships, and Indian rulers imprison English officials and merchants. EIC moves its headquarters from Surat to Bombay, outside Mughal jurisdiction (May 1687).

1688: Aurangzeb captures Maratha leader, Shivaji's son Sambhaji. Sambhaji is executed and the Maratha kingdom dismantled. Marathas scatter over south India but continue to plague Mughals in a guerrilla war.

c. 1690: The tenth Sikh *guru*, Gobind Singh (fl. 1675–1708), founds *khalsa*, a militant Sikh brotherhood, an event still celebrated annually on the first of Vaisakh (April–May) in Punjab. New militarism is a direct response to Aurangzeb's orthodox zealotry. Dedicating themselves to establishing their independence of Mughal rule, Sikhs begin their transformation from a primarily religious group into a militant group in armed conflict with both Aurangzeb and Afghans.

April 1691: A *firman* from Aurangzeb grants English free trade in Bengal.

1698: Mughals take Jinji fort after the nine-year siege of Maratha leader Rajaram (reigns 1689–1700). In late Deccan campaigns led by Aurangzeb and his generals Asad Khan and Zulfiqar Khan, Mughals also take Tanjore (1694), Maratha capital Satara (1700), Tamil Nadu, and Raigarh fort (1704). *Nawab* of Arcot becomes Mughal governor of Deccan. Undaunted, Marathas turn northward, invade Gujarat and Khandesh, ravage Malwa (1705).

1698: English sea captain William Kidd, sent from London to command an expedition against Indian Ocean pirates, himself begins attacking merchant ships and taking prizes; he organizes pirates in a coastal blockade. Charged and convicted of piracy, he is hanged in England (1701).

1700: Calcutta becomes EIC presidency during the construction of Fort William there. By the early eighteenth century, then, EIC presidencies of Calcutta, Madras, and Bombay are established as the principal English trading centers; they are later to become the three great provinces of British India.

1701: An imperial *firman* awards revenue of twenty-four *parganas* near Calcutta to the English.

1702–1704: Famine kills an estimated 2 million people in Deccan.

July 3, 1703: England, Holland, and Portugal sign a treaty guaranteeing mutual safety of their trading posts in India.

1707: Aurangzeb dies in retreat from Marathas at Aurangabad, leaving weakened empire drained by decades of warfare and still harried by continual rebellions of Sikhs, Rajputs, Afghans, Jats. The *mansabdar* system begins to break down: there are insufficient *jagirs* (land grants) to pay the large numbers of imperial servants needed for Aurangzeb's Deccan wars. Mughal army retreats from Deccan.

September 1708: Merger finalized between New East India Company (chartered 1698) and EIC, with combined capitalization of £2 million. The English company wins its battle to control Bengal trade by receiving imperial grants (1716) of duty-free privileges in Bengal and right to purchase thirty-eight villages around Calcutta. EIC is now the strongest trading power in India.

1716: Mughals execute Sikh leader Banda Singh Bahadur (reigns 1708–1716), ending an eight-year-long rebellion in Punjab supported by many peasants and Himalayan Rajput chiefs. Sikhs continue their raids from base at Amritsar, however, and over next two decades create a loose confederacy of dozens of Sikh chiefdoms.

1718: Famine in Gujarat.

1719: Assuming the throne after several years of anarchy, Muhammad Shah (reigns 1719–1748) rules over dissolving Mughal empire as little more than a puppet of noble factions. His predecessors' imperial treasury is depleted, and control over the bureaucracy relinquished; many provinces achieve actual or de facto independence during his reign.

1719–1723: Reorganization of the French East India Company revitalizes this relatively small-scale enterprise, operated from factories at their Pondicherry headquarters (founded 1674), Chandranagar (1690), and Mahé (1721). French trade and political influence in India reach their height during the next two decades.

July 8, 1720: Great earthquake in Delhi.

1720–1740: Conquests of *peshwa* (chief minister) Baji Rao I create a large, powerful Maratha state from central Deccan into northern India. He appropriates enormous power, effectively replacing Raja Shahu (reigns 1708–1749) as the real authority in the Maratha empire. Baji Rao I bureaucratizes the Maratha administration on the Mughal model, systematizing the collection of tribute and taxes. Closely administering only a central area, he leaves control of most of the Maratha Confederation to subordinate chiefs of the Holkars, Bhonsles, Gaekwars, Sindhias, and other clans.

1721–1722: English-Portuguese war against Angrian-clan pirates ended by a treaty of mutual assistance against the Marathas.

1722: *Nawab* of Awadh, Sa'adat Khan, Burhan-ul-Mulk (reigns 1722–1739), establishes virtual independence from Mughals. His successor, Mughal *wazir* Safdar Jang (1739–1754), wields supreme power in the Mughal empire.

1724: Powerful Nizam ul-Mulk of Ahmadnagar, Mughal *wazir* and *subahdar* of Deccan, establishes independent kingdom of Hyderabad (reigns 1724–1748) in central and eastern Deccan. He treats with Mughals' enemies, the Marathas, and encourages their invasion of northern India in 1731. Politically enfeebled, emperor Muhammad Shah is powerless to resist when the *nizam* declares himself governor of Agra (1737).

September 24, 1726: English law enforcement is extended to India with the charter of British civil and criminal courts in Bombay, Calcutta, and Madras.

1729–1758: Rise of Travancore in Kerala during the reign of Raja Marthanada Varma. He controls pepper and other trade monopolies, encourages local Syrian Christian traders, and maintains a large army.

1730s: Malhar Rao Holkar, guerrilla fighter against *nizam* and Rajputs, leads the rise of the Holkar clan in principality at Indore by consolidating *jagirs* in central India. An important subordinate Maratha group, Holkars repeatedly raid the perennially contested province of Malwa.

1730s–1740s: Maratha campaigns under Baji Rao I and his son, Balaji Baji Rao (reigns 1740–1761). They invade Karnataka (1726), undertake northern campaigns (early 1730s), and march on Mewar and Delhi (1736). Marathas' defeat of Muhammad Shah at the Battle of Delhi in 1737 wins them Malwa province. They wage later campaigns against Konkan (1737), Bengal and Bihar (1741–1743), Rajasthan (1744–1745), and, again, northern India (1747).

1733: An English blockade forces the governor of Surat to grant more favorable treatment.

October 11–12, 1737: A cyclone and earthquake kill 300,000 people and destroy 20,000 boats at Calcutta.

1738–1739: Persian ruler Nadir Shah demonstrates the terminal weakness of the Mughal dynasty by sweeping through northern India with eighty thousand men. He takes Kandahar and in a three-month sweep (1739) takes Lahore, captures Muhammad Shah, and sacks Delhi, killing an estimated twenty thousand civilians. His plunder includes the Koh-i-Nur diamond, Shah Jahan's sumptuous Peacock Throne (later to become the symbol of the Persian monarchy), and the provinces of Kabul and Kashmir.

1739: Marathas capture Bassein fort and Chaul in war with Portuguese (1737–1741), effectively ending the Portuguese era in India. Marathas grant the EIC free trade in Deccan.

1740: Bengal becomes independent of the Mughal empire. Nawabs rule independently until the installation of a British puppet (1757).

May 1740: Nagpur ruler Raguji Bhonsle

(reigns 1727–1755) leads fifty thousand Marathas into Karnataka; defeats and kills the *nawab* of Karnataka, Dost 'Ali, at Damalcherry Pass. Marathas again invade Karnataka (December 1740), seize Trichinopoly, and capture Chanda Sahib. Raguji then turns northward, capturing Orissa (1746), repeatedly invading and plundering Bengal and Bihar and inflicting huge losses before finally wresting this rich province from the combined forces of the emperor, *peshwa*, and *nawab* of Bengal (1751).

1741–1754: As governor-general of French India, Joseph François, Marquis Dupleix, introduces European arms trade to subcontinent. His military successes lead Indian princes to pay for French training for their own troops; *sepoys* (European-trained and led Indian infantrymen) become a staple of both European and Indian armies.

1743: Nizam ul-Mulk undertakes an expedition into Carnatic. A Mughal governorship since 1712 with its capital at Arcot, Carnatic has developed into a major southern state whose wealth and proximity to Madras make it an attractive target for conquest.

1744–1748: War of Austrian Succession spills over into the First Anglo-French Carnatic War despite Dupleix's efforts to maintain neutrality in Indian territories. In major actions, French seize Madras (September 2–10, 1746); defeat English ally *nawab* Anwar-ud-din's forces at St. Thomé (November 3, 1746); unsuccessfully besiege Fort St. George (November 1746–April 1748); and repulse a British attack on Pondicherry (August–October 1748). The Treaty of Aix-la-Chapelle restoring Madras to England (1748) is the first European treaty to recognize a European nation's rights on the subcontinent.

1745: Civil war in Punjab after the Mughal governor dies. Mughal rule is thrown off in Jammu (1746), Rohilkhand (1748).

1747: Famine in Gujarat.

1748–1754: Second Anglo-French Carnatic War. The death of the *nizam* of Hyderabad (May 1748) unleashes succession crises in both Hyderabad and Carnatic. Supporting opposing factions, the English and French become embroiled in local politics; the war launches the extraordinary Indian career of young English captain Robert Clive (1725–1774). The incumbent *nawab* of Carnatic, Anwar-ud-din, is defeated and killed at the Battle of Ambur (1749) by allied forces of the French, Muzaffar Jang, and Chanda Sahib, who becomes *nawab*. Robert Clive captures Chanda Sahib's capital at Arcot and defends it against a fifty-day siege (September–October 1751). The Anglo-French treaty at Pondicherry (December 31, 1754) restores Karnatic states to native princes and pledges noninterference.

1750s: The Marathas, under the Gaekwar family, come to dominate Gujarat in 1750s by pushing back Mughal forces and consolidating *jagirs*. Gaekwar partition province with *peshwa* and establish a capital at Baroda (1766).

October 1750: *Peshwa* Balaji Baji Rao is granted supreme authority in Maratha empire under Sangola agreement with new Maratha leader Ram Raja. *Peshwa* strikes alliances with Raguji Bhonsle and other Maratha chiefs and makes Pune the seat of Maratha government. Southern campaigns (1753–1760) restore Maratha domination of Carnatic.

January 10, 1751: Rajputs massacre Marathas in Jaipur.

1752: Mughals cede Punjab to Pashtun leader Ahmad Shah Durrani (reigns 1747–1772) after his third invasion in four years. Seeking control of trade routes between India and west and central Asia, Afghans also take Kabul; they maintain a tenuous hold over the region in subsequent years, beset by fierce Sikh resistance.

May 1752: Mughals negotiate a defensive treaty assigning Marathas responsibility for defense of the empire.

1753: Awadh becomes increasingly independent from Mughals after civil war.

1754: First regular British regiment arrives in India; stationed at Madras, it replaces the EIC army as the primary British military force.

1756–1763: The Third Anglo-French Carnatic War—an extension of the European Seven Years' War—occasions fighting in India, leaving Britain the uncontested colonial power in the subcontinent. The European combatants fight a sea battle off Pondicherry (September 10, 1759); British General Eyre Coote wins the last major land battle at Wandiwash (January 22, 1760) and besieges Pondicherry for five months until the French surrender (January 15, 1761). The French East India Company is dissolved in 1769, and France's role in India effectively ends.

June 15, 1756: *Nawab* of Bengal, Siraj-ud-Daulah (reigns 1756–1757), attacks British at Calcutta after they persistently abuse trade privileges and, after the governor flees, occupies the town (June 20). Europeans are imprisoned over a hot night without water in a small room in old Fort William; many die in the so-called Black Hole of Calcutta. While numbers are contested, modern accounts usually estimate that forty-three of sixty-four European prisoners perish.

October 12, 1756: *Peshwa* signs treaty with England barring Dutch trade in Maratha dominions.

1757: Maratha-Sikh alliance drives the Pashtun governor from the Punjabi base at Lahore. Ahmad Shah Durrani, in a fourth invasion, captures and again sacks Delhi (January 23, 1757). Alamgir II formally cedes Punjab, Kashmir, and Thatta to Ahmad Shah Durrani, but Maratha armies expel Afghans (early 1758), and the war continues.

1757–1760: Robert Clive serves as EIC governor.

January 4, 1757: Clive retakes Calcutta in alliance with local Hindu merchants and *zamindars* (rent-farmers) and disaffected Muslim soldiers; he takes Chandernagar.

February 9, 1757: In the Treaty of Alinagar, Siraj-ud-Daulah concedes British terms, restoring their trading posts and permitting them to fortify Calcutta.

June 23, 1757: Battle of Plassey. Clive's three thousand troops, mostly *sepoys*, defeat Siraj-ud-Daulah's force of fifty thousand. The *Nawab* of Bengal's commanding general, Mir Ja'far, who defects to the British during battle, is installed by Clive as *nawab* (reigns 1757–1760).

1758: EIC acquires fifty-five villages near Calcutta and begins construction of a new fort there.

October 1759–February 1760: *Nizam* of Hyderabad, long pressed by Maratha armies, is defeated in *peshwa* Balaji Baji Rao's (reigns 1740–1761) Udgir campaign, losing battles at Burhanpur, Daulatabad, Ahmadnagar, and Bijapur. Marathas annex large part of Hyderabad before turning to a northern campaign.

December 1759: Clive defeats Dutch forces in Bengal.

September 27, 1760: A secret treaty with the British installs Mir Kasim as *nawab* of Bengal after Mir Ja'far is forced to resign. Clive becomes de facto ruler of Bengal.

CONTENDING POWERS: 1760–1858

The decline of Mughal power in north India is accompanied by opportunist military adventures by Marathas, Pashtuns, Iranian Safavids, Afghan Rohillas, Rajputs, and Jats, among others. The once-great Mughal empire is reduced to one among many regional kingdoms, its emperor a titular figure with no real power.

   Britain's East India Company (EIC) insinuates itself into this situation of contending powers. After assuming political control of Bengal in 1765, the EIC enters a phase of military and mercantile aggression against neighboring Indian principalities. The British make steady territorial gains through both annexations and wars. Warfare is nearly constant and ruinously expensive; mercenary armies armed with modern firearms fight over large areas. In the north, major principalities include Awadh and the new Sikh state in Punjab. In the south, Hyderabad, the Maratha Confederation, and the powerful new state of Mysore are major players. During the period the EIC also fights the French, Nepal, Afghanistan, and Persia, steadily extending and consolidating its territory.

Company Bahadur ("venerable Company"), commercially ascendant all over south and east Asia, exercises authoritarian civil, military, and judicial power in India. The stable political structure in British-governed areas is accompanied by gross corruption on the part of its employees, and is incrementally placed under the control of the British Parliament. British administration is responsible for numerous economic and social changes. The Permanent Settlement in Bengal in 1793 for the first time creates private land ownership. Indian agriculture is redirected to cash crops, supplying raw materials for British trade and industry, while the manufacturing sector is neglected to favor British manufactured goods. Late in the period, industrialization begins, in the form of railways, telegraphy, and a modern postal system.

The introduction of European—particularly British—education, law, religion, government, and philosophy sparks a backlash as Indians rediscover their own traditions. Indian opinion is divided between those who favor traditional Hindu and Islamic culture and others who embrace Western liberalism. Calcutta's Western-educated Hindu business and intellectual elite lead the vanguard for change. They come under the simultaneous sway of liberal aspirations and an entirely new concept of all-India unity that set the stage for the nationalist movements to come.

Numerous local rebellions against British rule erupt during the early nineteenth century. The whole of northern India is convulsed by the Rebellion of 1857. The proximate cause of the initial revolt by Indian soldiers in the EIC army is British disregard for Hindu and Muslim religious observances, but the consequences are much broader. After suppressing the uprising, Britain, now near the height of its colonial power, institutes direct colonial rule in India.

January 14, 1761: Ahmad Shah Durrani deploys superior Afghani cavalry and light artillery to rout the Marathas at third battle of Panipat. The Maratha force, exhausted from months of campaigns, is annihilated: 75,000 troops and camp followers are killed, 30,000 taken prisoner. Maratha political power in north India is finished; the greatly weakened *peshwa* is forced to share power with other Maratha chiefs. Ahmad Shah withdraws in March, but leaves Rohilla Afghans in control of Delhi (1761–1771).

1761: Haidar Ali usurps throne of Mysore (reigns 1761–1782). A great general, he creates a powerful south Deccan kingdom by defeating the *nawab* of Arcot, the *nizam*, and the Marathas (1764–1779) and instituting an efficient administration.

1761–1763: Marathas win two-year war with Hyderabad. Territorial gains in central India

under Treaty of Aurangabad (September 1763) position the Maratha Confederation as a major state for the remainder of the century under the leadership of Mahadji Sindhia (1727–1794). His large, modern army, based in Gwalior, proves a formidable adversary in fighting the Mughals, the British, and Gujarati and Rajasthani princes.

1763–1764: Bengal War begins with mutiny against six-year British rule (June 25, 1763). *Nawab* Mir Kasim (reigns 1760–1763) turns against his British patrons, fomenting the rebellion and ordering execution of 150 British prisoners at Patna. In retreat, the *nawab* strikes alliance with the Mughals and Shuja ud-Daula, *wazir* of Awadh (reigns 1754–1775); they are decisively defeated by the British at the Battle of Baksar (October 23, 1764).

1765: Ahalya Bai of Holkar ascends the

throne of Indore (reigns 1765–1794). Her reign is a period of unusual domestic stability and prosperity in her kingdom. The Holkar become a major branch of Maratha Confederation, vying with the *peshwa* and the Sindhias, Bhonsles, and Gaekwars for supremacy.

May 1765: Robert Clive, new governor of Bengal (reigns 1765–1767), arrives in India. He establishes a "dual system" of government in which the British exercise power through puppet *nawabs* and princes while Indians carry out local administration. Despite his attempts to end endemic corruption, EIC servants continue to intimidate and harass Indian officials, traders, and growers, extort protection money, and enrich themselves through illegal private trade. Clive's term is cut short by ill health.

August 16, 1765: The Treaty of Allahabad formalizes political settlement of the 1763–1764 Bengal rebellion. The EIC becomes *diwan* (revenue manager) of Bengal, Bihar, and Orissa, India's richest and most populous provinces, for the first time assuming political control of Indian territory. Shah Alam II establishes his capital at Allahabad. Shuja ud-Daula, restored in Awadh, becomes a British dependent.

1766–July 1769: First Mysore War. In a major battle, twelve thousand EIC troops defeat Haidar Ali's army of seventy thousand at Trincomalee (September 24, 1767), but neither force gains a permanent advantage. Haidar Ali and the British sign a treaty of mutual assistance. Neither side adheres to its provisions.

November 12, 1766: Nizam Ali (reigns 1762–1802) cedes Northern Circars, a coastal region north of Madras, giving EIC control over most of India's east coast.

1770–1771: The Great Bengal Famine kills an estimated one-third of Bengal's population as merchants profit from their substantial stores of grain.

1771: Mahadji Sindhia recovers Delhi after ten-year occupation by Rohilla Afghans.

Mughal Shah Alam II is restored and returns to Delhi under Maratha protection (January 1772). The Sindhias reign supreme in north central India for thirty years on the strength of a powerful army modernized with the help of European officers.

August 1772: As *diwan* of Bengal (and therefore the body responsible for justice), EIC reforms judicial system by installing British judges in civil and criminal courts.

1773: Under Lord North's Regulating Act, British Parliament assumes direct control of EIC's government of India in effort to control continuing chaos. A single governor-general replaces coequal governors of the three presidencies; Calcutta becomes the seat of British government in India (until 1912). EIC officials are instructed to remain politically neutral in their dealings with Indian states.

1774: Warren Hastings is named first governor-general (until 1785). A career EIC official, Hastings is the architect of British administration in India. He reforms revenue collection, slashes payments to *nawabs* and the Mughal emperor, and strictly enforces the EIC monopoly on internal trade.

1774: Madhava Rao Narayan (also called Madhava II, reigns 1774–1795), succeeds to the *peshwaship* as an infant after the murder of his father. His chief regent, Nana Phadnavis (1742–1799/1800), wields power in Pune for twenty years, directing Maratha foreign policy with consummate skill and vying with Mahadji Sindhia for supremacy within the Maratha Confederation.

April–October 1774: Rohilla War is instigated by governor of Bengal, Warren Hastings, in contravention of Regulating Act. Hastings supplies mercenaries to the *nawab* of Awadh, who invades Rohilkhand and expels twenty thousand Rohilla Afghans (April 17–23), annexing the province. Awadh, a strategically important border state, proves one of Britain's most loyal and enduring supporters among Indian principalities, but the affair becomes a major factor in Hastings's impeachment in the 1780s.

October 1774: The Supreme Court is created in Calcutta under the Regulating Act. It is empowered to apply British law to British subjects and those connected with them (the latter class is not specifically defined) in Bengal and Bihar.

December 31, 1774: British troops occupy Salsette Island off Bombay.

March 7, 1775: Under the Treaty of Surat, EIC sponsors Raghunath Rao for the *peshwaship* in exchange for a grant of Salsette and the port of Bassein. Mahadji Sindhia defeats Raghunath Rao's British-supplied army and imposes the Treaty of Purandhar (March 1, 1776), annulling the Treaty of Surat. The British install Raghunath Rao as the *peshwa*'s regent and march on Pune (November 1778). Turned back by a Maratha army of fifty thousand, British commanders concede to humiliating terms in the Convention of Wadgaon (January 1779).

March 1775: Hastings's councilor Sir Philip Francis, his political rival and *bête noir*, charges him with gross corruption. Hastings is cleared, but Francis's attacks continue for years in a relentless campaign to disgrace Hastings, greatly hampering the effectiveness of British administration.

Maharaja Nanda Kumar charges governor-general Hastings with accepting bribes. Kumar is convicted of forgery by the Supreme Court under British law and hanged at Calcutta (August 5). The proceedings are a gross abuse of new judicial powers granted by the Regulating Act: forgery is only a misdemeanor under Indian law.

January 1779–December 1782: First Anglo-Maratha War. Hastings, conscious of recent British losses in North America and determined to hold Asian colonies, deploys EIC force against Sindhia's army. The war ends inconclusively after British retreat from Wadgaon (January 12) and fight at Ahmadabad, Deeg, and Gwalior. EIC's status as a major political player in north India is rec-

ognized in Treaty of Salbai (ratified December 20, 1782).

1780–March 1784: Second Anglo-Mysore War. Haidar Ali (in alliance with the French, the *nizam*, and the Marathas) invades and occupies Karnataka, soundly defeating the British at Perambakam (September 10, 1780). A seaborne British force led by Sir Eyre Coote defeats the allies at Porto Novo (June 1, 1781) in the first of a series of victories that save Madras for Britain. Loss of French support ends Mysore threat; the Treaty of Mangalore signed by British and Mysore (March 11, 1784) restores status quo ante.

June 1781: Hastings fines raja Chait Singh of Varanasi £500,000 for failing to supply requisite cavalry. The principality, struggling from poor harvests and heavy British assessments to pay for Maratha War, rebels. The British depose the raja and annex his kingdom. The refusal or inability of impoverished kingdoms to meet enormous tax demands and their subsequent annexation by the British are frequent occurrences in coming years.

1782: Still in need of cash, Hastings presses *nawab* Asaf ud-Daula to make good arrears in Awadh's subsidy to the British. Despite earlier pledges not to invade the royal fortune, Hastings encourages the *nawab* to loot the treasuries of his mother and grandmother; the governor-general imprisons the *begum*'s ministers for a year.

Tipu Sultan (reigns 1782–1799) succeeds to the throne of Mysore after death of his father, Haidar Ali. Tipu fights against Hyderabad, the Marathas, and—especially—the British. At the same time, he develops his principality by opening diplomatic and commercial links between Mysore and Middle East, China, and France.

August 13, 1784: British prime minister William Pitt passes the India Act, strengthening parliamentary supervision over EIC's political administration of Bengal. In the new dual system of control (until 1858), EIC exercises authority only over commerce, administering political institutions under government supervision. The governor-general is made directly responsible to the Parliament. A policy of political neutrality is decreed in a further effort to end military adventurism.

1785: Mahadji Sindhia forces the emperor to name him vice-regent and deputy. Thus given command of the Mughal armies, Sindhia becomes the most powerful figure in Agra and Delhi, waging war on the Rajputs and reasserting the power of the northern Marathas against the machinations of the *peshwa*'s regent, Nana Phadnavis, in Pune.

June 1785: Hastings resigns, his tenure marred by extortion attempts and political missteps in his later years. He is succeeded as governor-general by the Marquis of Cornwallis, a British general with no experience in Asia, but with a secure reputation for probity. (He is the same Cornwallis whose surrender at Yorktown in 1781 effectively ended British rule in the American colonies.) His term (rules 1786–1793) is marked by drastic, much-needed reform of the civil service and judiciary.

1787–1795: Warren Hastings is impeached in London for military adventurism in prosecuting the Rohilla War (1774) and for soliciting bribes from Indian rulers. The impeachment derives as much from British politics as from Indian administration. Hastings is acquitted after a seven-year trial.

June 1788: Rohilla Afghan adventurer Ghulam Kadir captures the Red Fort in an attack on Delhi. He blinds Shah Alam II before being driven out by Sindhia's forces.

December 1789–March 1792: Tipu Sultan attacks the principality of Travancore (December 29, 1789), launching the Third Anglo-Mysore War against the EIC-Maratha-Hyderabad Triple Alliance. Cornwallis invades Mysore and captures the capital of Seringapatam after besieging the city (February 5, 1792). Tipu cedes most of southwestern Malabar Coast and extensive inland territory to the victors under the Treaty of Seringapatam (March 16, 1792).

May 1, 1793: Promulgation of the Cornwallis Code, with jurisdiction over Bengal. It incorporates twelve years of previous legislation and serves as the basis of British administration of India. Chief among his reforms are the separation of EIC revenue, commercial, and judicial functions, and his establishment of provincial courts of appeal in which British judges are advised by Hindu *pandits* and Islamic *qazis*. Indians are excluded from covenanted (executive) EIC positions.

March 11, 1795: The united forces of the Maratha Confederation, allied for the occasion with Tipu Sultan, attack and defeat the *nizam* at Kharda. Hyderabad, further weakened by the rebellion of one of the *nizam*'s sons, accepts harsh conditions under the treaty of peace (April 10).

April 1798: Richard Colley Wellesley, Lord Mornington, is installed as fourth governor-general (rules 1798–1805). His assignment—eliminating French-supported Marathas and Mysore—is an outgrowth of the Napoleonic Wars being fought in Europe. Major elements of Wellesley's administration are his arbitrary rule and aggressive territorial expansion. Another notable colonial legacy is his creation of a viceregal court full of British pomp and ceremony; he creates the Imperial Raj.

September 1, 1798: In the first "subsidiary alliance," Hyderabad becomes a British protectorate. Wellesley's subsidiary treaty system calls for princes to disband their own armies, pay for subsidiary British military forces stationed in their kingdoms, and accept British advisors ("residents" or "agents"). Wellesley signs one hundred such treaties in seven years. States frequently cede territory in lieu of subsidies, and large territorial concessions over the next twenty years greatly extend British dominion.

1799–1802: Ranjit Singh (reigns 1793–1839) begins his conquest of northern Sikh territories with the capture of Lahore from Afghanistan and campaigns into the northern hill kingdoms. His army of forty thousand includes many European mercenaries. Sikh power reaches its zenith during Ranjit Singh's reign. By 1809 he controls most of Punjab, consolidating his rule with Mughal administrative structures and reviving Punjabi agriculture and commerce, especially its trade in salt, grain, and textiles.

February–July 1799: The Fourth Anglo-Mysore War is the final contest between Tipu Sultan and the British. Allied British and Hyderabad troops invade Mysore (February 11); Tipu Sultan is killed defending his capital at Seringapatam (May 4). The victors partition Mysore, reducing the last fragment of the former Vijayanagar empire to a small principality ruled by the old ruling family and bound by subsidiary alliance (July 13).

March 1800: Death of Nana Phadnavis, an adroit statesman and for thirty-eight years the Marathas' chief minister. Maratha power struggle between *peshwa* Baji Rao II (reigns 1796–1818), Sindhia, and Jaswant Rao Holkar turns into civil war. The young *peshwa*, dethroned by Holkar, is nominally restored by the British under the subsidiary Treaty of Bassein (December 31, 1802) and forcibly reinstalled (May 1803) after British troops capture Pune. British authority over the Deccan is tenuous, however, and the treaty precipitates the Second Maratha War.

1801: Wellesley dethrones *nawabs* of Arcot (Karnataka) and Surat and annexes their kingdoms. A subsidiary treaty is forced on Tanjore.

November 1801: Wellesley annexes the western half of Awadh after forcing a new subsidiary treaty on the *nawab-wazir*. The British are thereby positioned for a military offensive against the Sindhias and Bhonsles.

August 1803–1805: The Second Anglo-Maratha War sets back Maratha power. The British attack the Sindhias and the Bhonsles in simultaneous invasions of Hindustan and Deccan.

August–December 1803: British Army of the Deccan under Sir Arthur Wellesley (the governor-general's brother and later famous as the Duke of Wellington) is evenly matched with Marathas, but wins battles at Ahmadnagar (August 11), Assai (September 23), and Argaon/Argaum (November 20), with a final victory at Gawilarh (December 12–15).

September–December 1803: General Gerard Lake leads Grand Army of 10,500 mostly Indian troops against 43,000 Marathas in Hindustan campaign. British take Aligarh (September 3–4) and Delhi (September 11), and destroy the Maratha army at Laswari (November 1), imprisoning the aged Mughal emperor. Defeated in the north and south, the Sindhias surrenders (December 20).

April 1804–December 1805: In a third campaign, Holkar attacks the British, killing half their force at Mokundra Pass (August 24–29, 1804); General Lake pursues him 350 miles and defeats Marathas at Farrukhabad (November 17) and at major battle and siege of Deeg (November–December 1804). Abortive British siege of Holkar's ally Bharatpur (January–April 1805) kills three thousand men. Holkar surrenders within weeks of a treaty between EIC and Sindhia (November 23, 1805).

1805: Governor-general Wellesley is recalled by EIC directors, who disapprove of his military expansionism and the high cost and logistical difficulty of administering newly acquired territories.

After 1805: *Pindaris,* outlaw bands loosely organized into raiding parties and originally attached to Maratha armies, increase in numbers as a result of demobilization after the Second Anglo-Maratha War. A heterogeneous ethnic assortment, many are Pashtuns or former Maratha soldiers.

1806: Indian EIC troops mutiny in Vellore after being ordered to replace their turbans, remove caste marks, and shave their beards.

April 15, 1809: The Treaty of Amritsar between Ranjit Singh and EIC establishes the Sutlej River as the boundary between Sikh territories and recently conquered British territories. Thus confined on their southeast frontier, the Sikhs turn instead to the northwest, conquering territory from Afghans and other tribes (1810–1820).

1810: British capture and annex the French colonial island of Mauritius (until 1968).

November 1814–October 1816: In the Gurkha War, the British send troops to stop border raids and recover territories recently annexed by the Gurkha ruler of Nepal. The British win after two difficult campaigns of mountain fighting, and under the Treaty of Sagauli (March 1816) gain some Himalayan hill stations, including Simla, later the British summer capital. Nepal retains its independence.

November 1817: Sindhia signs a subsidiary treaty with the British.

November 1817–November 1818: Third Anglo-Maratha (Pindari) War. *Peshwa* attacks British occupying his capital at Pune under terms of his subsidiary treaty. Allied forces of Sindhia and EIC, numbering 20,000, defeat a united army of *peshwa* and other Maratha clans, said to total 200,000 men. The decisive battle is fought at Mahidpur (December 21, 1817); Holkar and the Bhonsle chief of Nagpur cede territories under treaties (January 6, 1818). The British pension off Baji Rao II after his surrender (June 2, 1818), formally ending Maratha power. Except in independent Punjab and Sind, British sovereignty is secured throughout the subcontinent through the settlement, which endures until 1947.

January–April 1818: The three most important Rajput states—Mewar, Jaipur, and Marwar—sign treaties to become British tributaries. After this gain of territory by Britain, their three major cities rapidly expand and develop. Calcutta becomes the largest city in India (and in Asia), growing from some 250,000 in 1820 to 1.1 million inhabitants in 1900. Bombay has some 162,000 in 1816, 566,000 in 1849, and 776,000 in 1900.

1819: Ranjit Singh conquers Afghan province of Kashmir. He creates the first Sikh state in Punjab through further conquests of Peshawar (1821) and Ladakh (1834). Singh leads a powerful army of 100,000 Sikh warriors; a formidable strategist, he is able to keep the British at bay during the period of their greatest expansion.

1820: India's population is estimated at 134 million.

1820s: The *ryotwari* (peasant) revenue system is institutionalized throughout Bombay and Madras by Madras governor Thomas Munro (governs 1819–1827), who earlier developed the system as a civil servant in the Deccan. Unlike Permanent Settlement in Bengal, a land tax fixed on individual plots is levied directly on farmers (*ryots*) in annual assessments. As in Bengal, however, a heavy (50 percent) tax burden forces peasants to sell their land to bankers and moneylenders, this time from Madras. They become a new middle class of absentee landlords in south India.

1820s: The *mahalwari* revenue system is instituted in modern-day Uttar Pradesh by Sir Charles Metcalfe. This system recognizes traditional patterns of village joint ownership and rights in land by assessing land taxes on villages communally.

March 1824–February 1826: The First Anglo-Burmese War begins after the Burmese occupy Assam and Manipur. One-third of the 45,000-man Anglo-Indian army dies during an offensive on the Burmese capital, nearly all of them from disease. The Treaty of Yandabo (February 24, 1826) awards Britain Assam, Manipur, and Burmese coastal provinces.

1824: Indian EIC regiment mutinies at Barrackpur, near Calcutta, over conditions of Burmese War service that violate caste restrictions. Army rebellions over pay and conditions occur sporadically during the following decades.

January 18, 1826: British forces capture the fortress of Bharatpur after a two-month siege during a local succession dispute. The British kill thirteen thousand defenders and take six thousand prisoners in the operation, and themselves take heavy losses.

1830s: Grain riots occur throughout India as the domestic economy declines under the weight of extremely heavy British taxation and a worldwide slump in prices for cash crops.

1831: EIC deposes the raja of Mysore for alleged misgovernment. The British administer the province without formally annexing it until 1881. Annexations of small kingdoms continues on various pretexts; Jaintia, Cachar, and Coorg, for example, are all annexed during the early 1830s.

October 1831: Bengal's governor Lord William Bentinck and Ranjit Singh meet for discussions at Rupar on the Sutlej River and agree to open the Indus River to commerce. The British and Gaekwar conclude an Indus treaty to this effect (1832); it explicitly prohibits military transit and transport.

1833: Renewal of the EIC charter vests legislative power in India in the British Crown; the governor-general adds the title "viceroy." EIC is stripped of its remaining commercial privileges, effectively becoming the British government's political agent. The so-called Liberal Charter theoretically opens Indian civil service to Indians, a statement of principle not actually implemented for decades.

1835–1837: Thomas Babington Macaulay (1800–1859) leads Indian Law Commission review of Indian civil and criminal law and judiciary, a tangle of EIC, British government, and Bengal, Madras, and Bombay provincial codes and courts. Macaulay drafts a liberal Anglo-Indian penal code (1837, finally effected 1860–1861) enshrining freedom of the press, equal legal jurisdiction over Europeans and Indians, and Western-style educational reform.

1836: Under Act XI, "Macaulay's Black Act," Europeans are placed on equal terms with Indians under the jurisdiction of civil courts. In criminal cases, Europeans continue to be tried under Supreme Courts.

Thagi (ritual murder and robbery by highway robbers) is suppressed by a government act mandating life imprisonment for convicted offenders. Rampant in the early years of the nineteenth century, *thagi* is eliminated by the 1850s after this government eradication campaign. (*Thagi* is the source of the English word "thug.")

One means her airs and graces, but one cannot talk of them Unless one speaks of them as knives and daggers that she wields. One speaks of God's creation, but one cannot talk of it Except in terms of draughts of wine that make the senses reel.

Traditional Urdu ghazal by Ghalib (1797–1869)

1837: Accession of the last Mughal emperor, Bahadur Shah II (reigns 1837–1858), a purely titular sovereign who rules at the pleasure of the EIC.

1837–1838: Major famine in north India.

1838: The Land Owners' Society, the first all-India political organization, is founded in Calcutta to represent *zamindars'* (rent-farmers') interests.

June 1838: The Tripartite Treaty, a function of Britain's "forward policy" on India's northwest frontier, unites Britain, Ranjit Singh, and long-exiled Afghan Shah Shuja in an offensive alliance to invade Afghanistan.

1839: Civil war in Punjab among elective councils and leaders following the death of Ranjit Singh. Punjabi chiefs wage unsuccessful war on the British.

April 1839–October 1842: British invasion launches the First Anglo-Afghan War. Fifteen thousand British and Indian troops occupy Kandahar (April 1839), storm Ghazni (July 23, 1839) and capture Kabul (August 7, 1839); the British depose Shah Dost Muhammad and install puppet Shah Shuja. Afghani revolt (October–November 1841) forces British evacuation. During their retreat through the Khyber Pass on a promise of safe conduct, all but a handful of sixteen thousand British troops and camp followers are massacred (January 13, 1842). Shah Shuja is assassinated (April 1842). The British reoccupy and raze Kabul (September 15, 1842). Shah Dost Muhammad is restored (reigns 1842–1863). The fruitless British adventure in Afghanistan is estimated to have cost twenty thousand lives and £15 million.

1843: The British wage their last campaign against the Marathas, invading Gwalior during a succession dispute.

February–May 1843: In reprisal for an attack on the British residency in Hyderabad by eight thousand Baluchis (February 15), General Sir Charles James Napier launches a brutal military offensive against Sind. Outnumbered by ten to one, Napier's force slaughters twelve thousand Sindhis at Miani and Dubba. Sind is annexed in flagrant violation of British government policy.

December 1845–March 1846: The First Anglo-Sikh War is characterized by ferocious combat between two huge and powerful armies: ten thousand men are killed in a few months of fighting. The Sikhs, attacking across the Sutlej River (December 11, 1845), are routed at Mudki (December 18, 1845), Firozpur/Ferozeshah (December 21–22, 1845), Aliwal (January 28, 1846), and finally at Sobraon (February 10, 1846). Under the Treaty of Lahore (March 9, 1846), some of Britain's territorial gains are sold to Dogra prince Gulab Singh, creating the principality of Kashmir, Jammu, and Ladakh (until 1947).

December 16, 1846: Insurrection in Punjab is settled by a treaty installing a British resident in Lahore. The British sharply reduce the size of the Sikh army. Famous as fighters, Sikh soldiers later predominate in the Indian army, becoming staunch British loyalists.

1848: Governor-general Lord Dalhousie (ruled 1848–1856) first invokes the infamous "doctrine of lapse" in seizing the Maratha state of Satara. Under this doctrine (which

violates subsidiary treaties), Dalhousie directly annexes the estates of princes who die without natural heirs, disallowing the Hindu custom of adopting heirs. Other kingdoms are annexed for alleged disloyalty or misrule or debt of princes. Annexations include Sambalpur and Jaitpur (1849), Baghat (1850), Udaipur (1852), Tanjore and Jhansi (1853), and the large Maratha state of Nagpur (1854). Indian hostility to British rule intensifies.

April 1848–March 12, 1849: The Second Anglo-Sikh War begins with a Punjabi revolt in Multan (April 20, 1848). The British invade (November 9, 1848) after Sikhs ally with Punjabi rebels; a major battle is fought at Chillianwallah/Chilianwala (January 13, 1849); Sikhs are crushed in the Battle of Gujrat (February 21, 1849) before surrendering Rawalpindi (March 1849). British annex Punjab (March 12), the last major independent state in India, securing their empire over the entire subcontinent.

1851: British Indian Association is established in Calcutta. In preparation for the twenty-year review of the EIC charter in 1853, this all-India group petitions the British Parliament in London directly about deficiencies and inequities in EIC administration.

1852: The Second Anglo-Burmese War results in the loss of Lower Burma, which becomes the province of Pago.

1853: Renewal of the Company charter opens higher positions in the Indian civil service to competitive exam. Examinations are held only in England until 1921, however, effectively barring Indians; only one Indian passes the exam in its first fifteen years of open administration.

1853: John Lawrence is appointed as chief commissioner of Punjab. He founds the so-called Punjab school of British administrators by emphasizing law and order, increasing both army and police forces; it is largely due to his efforts that the Sikhs later come to the aid of the British during the Rebellion of 1857. His administration concentrates as well on public works, including the construction of roads and canals.

1853: The British pensioner *peshwa* Baji Rao II dies without biological heirs. The British abolish his title under the doctrine of lapse. The title *Nawab* of Carnatic is also abolished this year.

1855: The Sikh kingdom becomes a province of Punjab under the Treaty of Peshawar.

1855: The estimated population of India is 181 million.

1855–1856: Santal insurrection in Bihar is one of the bloodiest rebellions against British rule. Half of the thirty thousand armed rebels are killed by British troops.

1856: The General Service Enlistment Act requires Indian army recruits to serve abroad if so ordered, violating caste restrictions of many Bengalis.

Introduction of breech-loading Lee-Enfield rifles in Indian EIC regiments violates both Hindu and Muslim dietary restrictions: the cartridges, greased with pork and beef fat, must be bitten off for loading. Regiment after regiment of the 120,000 Indian troops in Bengal refuse to load their rifles and are summarily dismissed from EIC service. The intensely resentful ex-soldiers disperse to their home villages, where local mutinies and incendiary fires break out in the early months of 1857.

February 13, 1856: British annexation of the wealthy state of Awadh in violation of a fifty-year-old treaty unseats its ruler, Wajid Ali, for alleged misgovernment. His appeals to Dalhousie and the government in London are unavailing.

November 1856–April 1857: The Anglo-Persian War, undertaken after the Persian occupation of Herat, Afghanistan, is the last EIC war in India.

May 10, 1857: The Rebellion of 1857, the so-called Sepoy Mutiny, begins in Meerut, twenty-five miles northeast of Delhi. Three mutinous regiments of Indian soldiers murder several dozen British officers and other Europeans, free eighty-five of their comrades imprisoned for refusing to load the ob-

jectionable Enfield cartridges, and flee to Delhi. It is the first action in a two-year-long uprising against British rule. The Delhi garrison joins the revolt and captures the city (May 11). Europeans are killed and the Mughal heir is proclaimed Bahadur Shah II; but by November Bahadur Shah II will be captured.

June 27, 1857: Two hundred and fifty people surrender the British garrison at Kanpur after a three-week siege by Nana Sahib, adopted son of the last *peshwa*. Though promised safe conduct, they are instead massacred. Two hundred women and children captured at Kanpur are murdered on July 15.

Summer 1857: Widespread rebellion breaks out in northern provinces (centered in Delhi, Awadh, Jhansi, and Rohilkhand), with sporadic rebellions and guerrilla actions elsewhere. The insurrection cuts across many castes and ethnic and religious groups fired by grievances including land "reforms," heavy tax burdens, annexations, and wars. Both sides engage in acts of racist fury, random violence, and terrible cruelty.

July 1, 1857: After overthrowing the British in Awadh, sixty thousand rebels blockade the governor's residence in Lucknow. "Relief of Lucknow" becomes a rallying cry among the British in both England and India. Sir Henry Havelock's relief force briefly breaks through (September 25, 1857); a second relief force led by Sir Colin Campbell evacuates the garrison (November 19, 1857).

September 20, 1857: Four thousand British troops recapture Delhi after a three-month siege and six days of street fighting. In vicious British reprisals against the Delhi rebels, thousands of Indians are massacred.

December 6, 1857: Campbell's troops recover Kanpur. The British retake Lucknow (March 22, 1858), and win back Awadh and Rohilkhand.

April–June 1858: At the end of Sir Hugh Rose's central Indian campaign, Nana Sahib's general Tantia Topi and Laksmi Bai, dowager *rani* of Jhansi, surrender at Gwalior (June 17–20, 1858). Sporadic fighting continues for another year before the British completely pacify the country. The rebellion costs the British government £36 million, a year's worth of Indian revenue.

August 2, 1858: The Government of India Act replaces EIC's authority with British Crown rule.

September 1858: The 350-year-old Mughal dynasty is finally extinguished with the exile of Bahadur Shah II to Burma and the murder of his sons in reprisal for the Kanpur massacre.

BRITISH INDIA: 1858–1947

The beginning of this period is shaped by traumatic memories of the Rebellion of 1857–1858. India is placed under Crown rule and comes under the sway of a series of British viceroys of varying quality and understanding of India, but all exercising significant power in their brief terms. Britain, at the height of imperial glory, becomes an entrenched colonial power, developing its famously complex, self-perpetuating imperial bureaucracy and for many years excluding Indians from meaningful participation in their own governance.

Imperial exigencies profoundly shape India's development. External security concerns lead to repeated military aggression and territorial annexation to the north and northeast until about 1900. Britain builds many thousands of miles of railways, roads, and communications lines, vital to the maintenance of military control but also constituting a valuable national legacy. The economy, by contrast, is allowed to develop under a system of laissez-faire; cotton, jute, tea, and steel are all major industries.

British education, administration, philosophy, and legal and political traditions throw up enormous challenges to the newly emerging educated Indian elite to create a place for their own culture in the modern world. Numerous religious and social reform movements arise that seek to reconcile India's ancient religions with modern society and to modernize caste, marriage and inheritance customs, and the position of women. Modern literature flourishes in India's many vernacular languages.

Politics, particularly nationalist politics, builds on these regional social and religious reform movements. New political movements are led largely by professionals educated at the new universities in Bengal, Bombay, and Madras. Their work is supported by regional political organizations, newspapers, and new communications networks. An All-India political organization, the Indian National Congress, emerges in 1885. It is destined to play a major political role for more than a century.

World War I proves to be a catalyst for nationalist activity. India's huge wartime sacrifice—more than a million troops are shipped abroad, and they suffer heavy casualties—raises Indians' political aspirations and forces Britain to promise self-government. Mahatma Gandhi takes to the national stage after 1920, uniting social, religious, and political reformers and leading the nation through numerous local actions and three great civil disobedience campaigns.

Nationalist efforts barely unite a patchwork of castes and religions, and communal violence erupts repeatedly as political constituencies maneuver for constitutional, social, and religious accommodations. Opposition to British rule gains momentum, however, and the incremental political reforms introduced by the government in 1909, 1921, 1935, and 1937 fail to stem the nationalist tide. Indians' full appreciation of their own sacrifices for the Allied cause in World War II makes independence inevitable.

Sectarian strife intensifies as planning proceeds for independence. Efforts at political compromise are finally abandoned as all parties recognize that partition must inevitably accompany a constitutional settlement. In the traumatic transition from the Indian Empire to the independent states of India and Pakistan, millions of people are displaced in one of the world's largest ever migrations. One million people die in unchecked communal violence. The period thus ends as it began, with national trauma, as India enters independence.

November 1, 1858: Transfer of the governance of India to the British Crown is announced by royal proclamation at grand *durbar* at Allahabad. For nearly ninety years, India will be ruled by a British viceroy subject to the oversight of the British Parliament and a British secretary of state.

1858–1862: The first viceroy, Lord Canning, revokes Dalhousie's doctrine of lapse, renounces further territorial annexations, and pledges nonintervention in religion and autonomy of 560 principalities. Headquartered at Calcutta and Simla, he presides over 1,500-member Indian Civil Service (ICS); it develops into the famous imperial bureaucracy and sets the standard for other British colonial administrations.

1858–1863: The army is thoroughly reorganized to increase the ratio of British to Indian forces, restrict artillery to British troops, and favor Indians from loyalist areas (especially Gurkhas and Sikhs). One-third of Indian government's annual expenditure is for military funding.

July 8, 1859: The British government formally announces the end of the Rebellion of 1857.

1860: Military raids against the Waziris, a people in near-constant rebellion in Punjab.

1860: Landless Tamils emigrate as indentured laborers to South African sugar plantations hit by abolition of slavery in British colonies. They are followed by numerous "passenger Indians," merchants and shopkeepers; Indians become a significant community in South Africa. Indentured emigration continues until 1911.

1860: The Indian Penal Code and Criminal Procedure Code (1861) are enacted after years of work by the Law Commission. They replace a patchwork of Islamic law, haphazard British regulations, and judicial rulings with a uniform system of criminal law.

1860–1861: Major famine in northern India.

Famines kill nearly one million people in Orissa (1865–1867) and hundreds of thousands in northwest and central India (1868–1870).

1861: Indian Councils Act enlarges the Viceroy's Executive Council and Legislative Council with appointed Indian advisors selected from landed gentry. Provincial legislative councils with restricted powers are reestablished in Madras and Bombay and later formed in Bengal (1862), Northwest Provinces (1886), and Punjab (1898). The Central Provinces is created from territories in Bengal and the Northwest Provinces.

1862: In accordance with the 1861 Indian High Courts Act, High Courts are created in Calcutta, Bombay, and Madras out of old Supreme Courts of Judicature and Sadar courts of appeals.

1862: Annexation of Lower Burma.

December 1863: The Indian army crushes a revolt against Western rule by the militant Islamic Wahabi movement on the northwest frontier; the Wahabi headquarters at Malka is destroyed.

1864: Satyendranath Tagore, the first Indian to compete in the Indian Civil Service exams in London, begins his thirty-four-year government career. Indianization proceeds very slowly: by 1887, only a dozen Indians have joined the civil service.

1864: Cyclone kills tens of thousands in Calcutta and Madras.

1864–1869: During his tenure, Viceroy Sir John Lawrence applies the principles of the "Punjab school" of administration throughout India; government expands education and public works including sanitation and irrigation projects, roads, and railways.

January–November 1865: The Bhutan War begins with a British invasion after numerous border disputes; Bhutan becomes a British protectorate (1866), extending imperial power in the eastern Himalayas.

1867: Poona Sarvajanik Sabha is founded. This unofficial representative body becomes the major political organization in the Deccan.

1871: The first general census produces unreliable figures; a modern retrospective estimate of population is 206 million.

1872: Taxpayers are enfranchised to elect half of Bombay's corporation (local government), first local body with wide powers of decision-making and authority to tax and distribute funds. Beginning of Indian engagement in political arena, public accountability of government. Representative local government is established in Calcutta in 1876.

February 8, 1872: Viceroy Lord Mayo (governs 1869–1872) is murdered by a transported Afghan convict while visiting an Andaman Islands prison settlement.

1873–1874: Major famine in Bengal and Bihar.

1874: Assam is administratively detached from Bengal to become its easternmost province. Its border with Burma undergoes continual readjustment over the following decades.

April 1875: Reversing 1858 nonintervention policy, British try, depose, and deport premier Hindu prince and longtime British ally Malhar Rao, Gaekwar of Baroda, for "notorious maladministration." They install and supervise a successor government.

May–June 1875: Riots in Pune and Ahmadnagar (the so-called Deccan riots). Impoverished and heavily in debt, peasants attack and plunder usurious moneylenders.

1875–1877: Rise of nationalist organizations in Bengal; founders are mostly moderate university-educated reformers schooled in British political and legal traditions. They include the Indian League, founded in Calcutta by journalist Shishir Kumar Ghose (1840–1911) on September 25, 1875; the Indian Association, founded by Surendranath Banerjea (1848–1925), the editor of *Bengalee*, on July 26, 1876; the National Moham-

medan Association, founded by Sayyid Amir Ali, in 1877. Moderates dominate the nationalist movement's first twenty years.

1876: The British garrison the Baluchistan capital of Quetta after nearly twenty years of internal strife. Baluchistan is annexed (1887).

1876–1878: Great famine throughout subcontinent kills an estimated 5 million people.

January 1, 1877: British Queen Victoria is proclaimed empress of India at the great Delhi *durbar*. She never visits India, now known as the Indian Empire.

March 14, 1878: The Vernacular Press Act, hurriedly passed to suppress opposition to Afghan War, proscribes seditious writing in vernacular languages; English-language publications are exempted. The Act mobilizes nationalists. It is repealed in 1882.

April 1878: British government orders Indian troops to Malta and Cyprus to counter Russian expansion in Turkey. The Indian army is deployed repeatedly throughout the last half of century to fight British wars in China, Southeast Asia, Persia, and Africa. Nationalists unite in opposition.

November 1878–September 1880: The Second Anglo-Afghan War. Provoked by the *amir*'s perceived pro-Russian stance, the Indian army invades (November 21, 1878) and overwhelms Afghans. A treaty is signed at Gandamak (June 1879). The new British resident and staff are murdered in Kabul (September 1879), however, prompting savage British reprisals. The Indian army crushes the Afghani revolt at the Battle of Kandahar (August–September 1880) to end the war. Afghanistan becomes a quasi-protectorate of Britain, but the expense and brutality of the war bring down Disraeli's government in London and end Lord Lytton's viceregency.

February 23, 1879: Independent radical nationalist Vasudev Balvant Phadke (1845–1883) leads the first of a number of Deccan raids. He incites and trains *dacoits* (brigands) to revolt against British rule, leaving a swath of plunder and destruction before he is tried and transported (November 1879).

December 24, 1879: Resolution for Statutory Civil Service, issued by Viceroy Lord Lytton (governs 1876–1880), opens high ICS positions to Indians by nomination. Intended to draw loyalist Indian aristocrats into the administration, the program is largely a failure.

1880s: Self-rule movement in Maharashtra led by Bal Gangadhar Tilak (1856–1920), India's first revolutionary nationalist. As editor of Marathi-language Pune newspapers *Kesari* and *Mahratta*, he appeals to orthodox Hinduism and Maratha history to stir popular resistance to the British government.

1881: The first reliable census reports India's population as 250 million.

March 18, 1881: Mysore, under direct British administration for fifty years, is restored to its ruling family. The new maharaja, Chama Rajendra Wodeyar IX, immediately institutes first representative assembly in any princely state. Legislative councils are also established in Travancore (1888) and Hyderabad (1893). Despite political and other reforms in these and a few other progressive princely states, notably Baroda and Cochin, the majority of principalities remain autocratic and socially and economically backward.

May 1882: Lord Ripon's Resolution on Local Self-Government provides for partly elected representational government in municipalities and districts. They control budgets for education, medical relief, and local works. These bodies train generations of Indian political leaders.

1883: The Famine Code enacts recommendations of viceregal Famine Commission of 1880, specifies procedures for famine detection and relief. Further famine commissions revise the code (1897, 1900).

January 30, 1883: The Ilbert Bill on Criminal Jurisdiction, empowering Indian judges to try Europeans, is introduced to the Legislative Council, setting off a year of intense public debate in India and Britain. A racist campaign by the 50,000-strong British-born civilian community in India forces liberal viceroy Lord Ripon (governs 1880–1884) to reverse the policy. A compromise passed in January 1884 allows Europeans to demand a European jury. Retired English civil servant Allan Octavian Hume (1829–1912) subsequently calls on Indians to unite in a patriotic nationalist organization, a summons that results in the formation of the All-India National Congress (1885).

December 28–30, 1883: Surendranath Banerjea's Indian Association convenes the All-India National Conference in Calcutta to discuss public affairs. It is the first such nonelected assembly and a forerunner of Indian National Congress, with which it merges (1885).

May 16, 1884: Madras Mahajan Sabha (Great People's Society), founded in Madras, is the outgrowth of several decades of regional political organization. It convenes India's first regional political conference (December 1884–January 1885).

November 1885: The Third Anglo-Burmese War erupts after years of boundary and commercial disputes. An amphibious force of nearly thirteen thousand Indian army troops under General Harry Prendergast advances up Irrawaddy River (November 9); Burmese King Thibaw surrenders at Mandalay (November 28). Upper Burma is annexed as an Indian province (May 1886); widespread Burmese rebellion continues until *c.* 1915.

December 28–30, 1885: First meeting of the All-India National Congress in Bombay launches the first great nationalist movement. Under first president W. C. Bonnerjee, seventy-three delegates call for more Indian participation in government, less military spending and foreign adventurism, reduced "home charges" (the Indian government's annual payments to Britain for salaries and pensions of India Office officials). Meeting annually, the Congress rapidly becomes largest and most powerful political force in India. It follows a loyalist course until the 1930s.

1886–1887: Recommendations of the Public Services (Aitchison) Commission result in the creation of a locally recruited provincial civil service in order to engage more Indians in government service. The age limit for ICS candidates is raised in 1892 and again in 1906 to benefit Indian candidates, but by 1909, only sixty of 1,142 ICS officers are Indian.

1889: Suspecting the maharaja of Kashmir of intrigue with Russia, the British secure his resignation and establish regency, bringing Kashmir under increased British control.

1890: Sikkim becomes a British protectorate.

March 1891: British invade northeastern principality of Manipur after a coup, remove royal family, and install client government. Manipur is annexed.

1892: Second Indian Councils Act expands Imperial and Provincial Legislative Councils, adding indirectly elected Indian representatives. Legislative Councils have only a consultative role, but educated Indians for the first time have representation in provincial and national government. Muslims petition for representation on Imperial Legislative Council (1893).

1894–1899: Viceroy Lord Victor Alexander Elgin's tenure is marked by military expeditions against numerous rebellious tribes along northwest frontier; troops are dispatched to Chitral (1895), Tirah (1896), and the Khyber Pass (1897–1898). Sixty thousand Indian army troops are eventually deployed to pacify the region.

1896: Bubonic plague appears in Bombay, arriving aboard ships from China. It becomes endemic throughout the subcontinent within a few years, causing millions of deaths. Widespread famine (1896–1900) kills more than 750,000 people; government relief is slow and inadequate. India's population drops between 1895 and 1905.

1896: Demarcation of the Indo-Afghan border after three years' work by British official Sir Mortimer Durand.

1896: The first significant emigration of Indian laborers to East Africa; the Indian community in Kenya, Tanzania, and Uganda eventually numbers in the hundreds of thousands.

June 22, 1897: Two days after B. G. Tilak lectures on the *Bhagavad Gita*'s condoning of violence, one of his protégés assassinates a British official in Pune. It is India's first act of nationalist terrorism. Tilak is convicted of sedition (September 1897).

1901: Creation of the separate Northwest Frontier Province along the strategically important Indo-Afghan border, designed by Viceroy Lord Curzon (governs 1899–1905) as a counterweight to frontier risings and Russian influence in Central Asia. The United Provinces of Agra and Oudh is created (1902).

November 5, 1902: After forty years of direct British administration of Berar, a mortification to the *nizam* of Hyderabad, a treaty reaffirms the *nizam*'s sovereignty of Berar, but grants the British a lease in perpetuity. The *nizam* eventually cedes Berar (1936).

1903–1904: British army officer and explorer Sir Francis Younghusband leads a British expedition to Tibet. He imposes a trade treaty on the Dalai Lama and recognizes Chinese sovereignty over Tibet.

July 20, 1905: Without prior public consultation, government formally announces that Bengal is to be partitioned, creating a new majority Muslim province in East Bengal and Assam (capital Dacca). Widely denounced, the plan fuels Hindu nationalist revolt. Mass rallies, petitions, and direct action draw millions into politics for the first time and rejuvenate Congress as a popular party.

August 7, 1905: The *Swadeshi* ("of our own land") movement is begun by Surendranath Banerjea and other Bengali nationalists in protest against impending partition. Boycott of British imports is the heart of their strategy; their public cloth-burnings, demonstrations, and strikes are repressed by police. *Swadeshi* becomes an all-India movement, remaining especially strong in Bengal; it is later integral to Gandhian activism.

October 16, 1905: Bengal is partitioned. In addition to spurring Hindu nationalism, the newly created province of East Bengal is a catalyst for Muslims' political cooperation and, eventually, development of the Islamic separatist movement.

1906: The "extremist" faction in Congress is led by three leaders of the militant wing of the emerging nationalist movement: B. G. Tilak, Bengali editor Bipin Chandra Pal (1858–1932), and Lala Lajpat Rai (1865–1928), leader of Arya Samaj. They promote *swadeshi*, boycott, and mass action rather than political cooperation with the British.

October 1, 1906: Simla Deputation. In anticipation of constitutional reform, Muslim leaders headed by Aga Khan III successfully lobby Viceroy Lord Minto (governs 1905–1910) for separate Muslim electorates and weighted political representation.

December 26, 1906: Under the leadership of a moderate president, the "Grand Old Man" Dadabhai Naoroji (1825–1917), a session of Congress at Calcutta endorses the *swadeshi* movement, calls for national education, and adopts *swaraj* (self-government) as a national goal.

December 30, 1906: The All-India Muslim League is founded at Dacca under presidency of Viqar-ul-Mulk (1841–1917). Aga Khan is a moving force behind its creation. A small, elite organization of British loyalists from northern India, the Muslim League repudiates the *swadeshi* movement and concentrates in its early years on winning fair representation for Muslim interests in India.

1907–1910: The British government assumes and ruthlessly enforces emergency powers, enacting Seditious Meetings Act (May 11, 1907), Newspapers (Incitement to Offences) and Explosive Substances Acts (June 8, 1908), and Press Act (1910). Rights of assembly and the press are sharply restricted and the right to trial by jury withdrawn. The legislation is used to prosecute nationalists; opposition leaders including Ajit Singh, Lala Lajpat Rai, and B. G. Tilak are imprisoned or deported and numerous organizations and newspapers are suppressed.

August 28, 1907: John Morley, secretary for India in the British cabinet (1905–1910), pushes through the Council of India Act authorizing appointment of the first Indians to the Secretary of State's Council.

December 26–27, 1907: Indian National Congress session at Surat is marked by a deep disagreement between Moderates (evolutionary reformers under Gopal Krishna Gokhale [1866–1915] and Surendranath Banerjea) and Extremists (New Party delegates led by Tilak, Ghose, Pal), who want outright boycott of British administration. The meeting ends in chaos with exclusion of the Extremists, and Congress is split for nine years.

April 30, 1908: First act of nationalist terrorism in Bengal as a bomb kills two Britons. Terrorism in Bengal and Maharashtra reaches a peak in 1908–1910.

May 25, 1909: Morley-Minto Reforms are embodied in third Indian Councils Act, pushed through by Morley, who is determined to provide better government in India. Provincial Legislative Councils are enlarged; Indian representatives for the first time form majorities. The restricted franchise includes separate Muslim electorates. Satyendra Prasanna Sinha (1864–1928) becomes the first Indian appointed to the viceregal Executive Council.

1909: After the first-ever legislative elections in India, 135 Indian representatives join legislative councils. The Muslim League, with no national organization or platform, fares poorly in balloting.

1911: A census reports India's population as 303 million.

December 12, 1911: At a magnificent coronation *durbar* in Delhi, Britain's King George V announces the annulment of the 1905 Bengal partition and redrawing of the northeast provinces as Bengal (capital Calcutta), Assam (Shillong), and Bihar and Orissa (Patna). The seat of government is shifted from Calcutta to the old Mughal capital of Delhi.

December 23, 1912: Viceroy Henry Hardinge (governs 1910–1916) is seriously injured in an assassination attempt at the state entry into the new capital at Delhi.

March 22, 1913: The Muslim League adopts a goal of self-government, a policy shift that attracts a progressive younger membership, including Muhammad Ali Jinnah (1876–1948), a liberal Bombay attorney and former Congress activist.

November 1, 1913: Overseas Indians found the Ghadar (Mutiny) Party, a San Francisco–based revolutionary Sikh organization pledged to overthrow the British *raj* from abroad by supplying arms and men. Twenty-nine of its leaders are convicted in San Francisco (November 1917) for violating U.S. neutrality.

July 3, 1914: The Simla Convention, signed by Britain and Tibet, fixes India's northeast frontier and assigns substantial new territory to Assam. Never ratified by China, disputed border proves constant bilateral irritant.

August 4, 1914: India is swept into World War I as Britain declares war on Germany. The war delays planned political reform in India, with unintended and long-lasting consequences.

September 22, 1914: Madras is bombarded by a German cruiser.

September 29, 1914: Three hundred and seventy-six Indians (including 346 Sikhs), refugees from Hong Kong, Shanghai, and Yokohama denied admission to Canada, arrive in India after months at sea in appalling conditions aboard a Japanese freighter, *Komagata Maru*. Refusing a government order to go directly to Punjab, they are attacked by soldiers and police; several dozen Sikhs are killed or disappear and the rest are arrested. The incident lends momentum to revolutionary Ghadar Party, established throughout Punjab by 1915.

October 1914: Major deployments of Indian army troops to all theaters of war. They suffer heavy losses on the European Western Front, 1914–1915, and throughout the war in occupied German East Africa.

1915: The Defense of India Act enacts broadly framed wartime martial law. Extraordinary government powers of arrest, detention, and censorship are used to suppress political dissent, particularly in Punjab and Bengal.

January 9, 1915: Mohandas Gandhi (1869–1948) returns from twenty years' struggle against discriminatory legislation affecting the Indian community in South Africa, where he has developed the philosophy and practice of civil disobedience.

February 15–18, 1915: The Fifth Light Infantry, an Indian Muslim battalion, mutinies at the British garrison in Singapore. Many European officers and civilians are killed before the revolt is quelled and the battalion disbanded.

April 1915–January 1916: Indian infantry and mountain forces are among the quarter-million troops killed in the British debacle at Gallipoli.

December 1, 1915: The Provisional Government of India is declared in Kabul by an anti-British faction. Raja Mahendra Pratap assumes the presidency but is unable to generate international recognition.

April 28, 1916: Borrowing an Irish organizational title, Tilak founds the Home Rule League in western India. British-born theosophist Annie Besant (1847–1933) independently founds a Home Rule League in Madras in September. Popularist publicity and the programs of Home Rule Leagues help sustain nationalist sentiment.

April 29, 1916: The British commander surrenders to the Turks at Kut-el-Amara, Iraq, after five months' siege, handing over six thousand Indian prisoners of war. Thousands of Indian troops die from lack of food, equipment, and medicines in the campaign for Baghdad because of Indian army incompetence. British minister for India Austen

Chamberlain resigns in disgrace. The force that finally captures Baghdad (March 1917) includes 100,000 Indians.

December 1916: Jinnah and Tilak agree to the historic Lucknow Pact (formally, the Congress-League Scheme of Reforms). It is a joint demand for dominion status within the British empire, with separate electorates and parliamentary self-government. Their political rapprochement is short-lived.

December 1916: Extremists reconcile with Congress after a nine-year split; Annie Besant, an ardent nationalist and outstanding orator, is the first woman to serve as Congress president (1917).

1917–1918: Gandhi's first victories with indigo growers and textile workers in Champaran and Ahmadabad cement his reputation as charismatic leader with mass appeal and effective nonviolent methods of forcing social change. Training thousands of followers and appealing to mass of population, he comes to have vast influence in shaping the movement for independence.

January 1917–October 1918: Indian forces play a major role in the Allied offensive against the Turks in Palestine.

August 20, 1917: The new secretary of state for India, Edwin S. Montagu (1917–1922), announces a turning point in imperial policy: Britain's commitment to associate Indians in all branches of the administration with a view to "responsible government in India as an integral part of the Empire."

1918: Indians are made eligible for the King's Commission, but Indianization of the officer corps is slow: by 1928, only seventy-seven officers of the Indian army are Indian.

1918–1919: Twelve to fourteen million South Asians perish in a flu epidemic.

July 8, 1918: Publication of Report on Indian Constitutional Reform (also called Montagu-Chelmsford Reforms or Montford Report) by E. S. Montagu and Viceroy Lord Chelmsford (governs 1916–1921). It calls for self-government as far as possible at the local level; a transition to self-government at the

provincial level; and dyarchy (shared rule) at the national level, with most important ministries reserved to British administrators.

November 1, 1918: The All-India Moderate Conference is convened in Bombay under Surendranath Banerjea to unite in support of the Montford Report, which the Extremist-dominated Congress opposes. T. B. Sapru and M. R. Jayakar form Liberal Party, which enjoys a brief electoral success in the 1920s.

November 11, 1918: Armistice with Germany ends World War I. During the war, 1.4 million Indian volunteers have been sent overseas, constituting 17 percent of the British armed forces. More than 70,000 have suffered combat casualties; 61,000 have died. Fully half these men are from Punjab, a province with 7 percent of India's population.

1919–1920: Sir S. P. Sinha becomes the first Indian parliamentary undersecretary of state for India in London. Raised to the British peerage, he shepherds the Government of India Act through the House of Lords.

1919–1924: The Khilafat Movement supports the imperial claims of the Ottoman caliph (*khalifa*), whose empire was dismembered after World War I. Gandhi advises on their program of noncooperation, beginning with all-India *hartal* (work stoppage, August 1, 1920). Twenty thousand participate in ill-fated *hijrah* (flight) from Sind and Peshawar to Afghanistan (1920). The movement lasts until Turkey's Kemal Ataturk announces secular reforms and abolishes the caliphate (1924).

March 18, 1919: The Rowlatt Acts (or "Black Acts") extend wartime martial law provisions and tighten press restrictions for three years. Passed to deal with political dissidents, they pass over the united opposition of E. S. Montagu and Indian members of the Imperial Legislative Council. Deeply disillusioned with renewed racial discrimination after wartime sacrifices, Jinnah and other Indian legislators resign in protest. The Acts spur a great postwar wave of nationalism. They are withdrawn in 1922.

April 6, 1919: A one-day all-India *hartal* (work stoppage) is called by Gandhi to protest the Rowlatt Acts.

April 10, 1919: Two Punjabi nationalist leaders are summarily deported; when their followers protest at Lahore, British troops open fire, killing unarmed demonstrators. Enraged survivors attack British residents and a bank.

April 13, 1919: The Amritsar Massacre. Obeying their British officer's command, Indian soldiers fire for ten minutes into a dense crowd of unarmed holiday celebrants at Jallianwala Bagh, a walled public square in Amritsar, killing 379 people and wounding 1,208. Punjab's governor, Sir Michael O'Dwyer, defends the action, declares martial law, and engages in a period of intense repression and degradation of Indians. Millions of disillusioned loyalists join the nationalist movement; Gandhi's *satyagraha* (noncooperation) campaign attracts an ever larger number of adherents.

May 3–28, 1919: Third Anglo-Afghan War. Afghan King Amanullah invades India, but is quickly defeated by superior weaponry (including bombs, planes, radio) of British Indian troops. The Treaty of Rawalpindi (August 8) establishes mutual independent relations. Pashtun incursions are frequent, however, from 1920 to 1925.

June 28, 1919: India signs the Treaty of Versailles, ending World War I and becoming a founding member of the League of Nations. The first Indian signatory is Maharaja Ganga Singh of Bikaner (reigns 1887–1943).

September 1919: A special open session of Congress at Calcutta attracts five thousand delegates who vote Gandhi's agenda to win *swaraj* (self-government): a complete boycott of British imports and institutions (schools, courts, elections) designed to halt the machinery of the British *raj*. Congress, hitherto a relatively small, elite association, now comes under Gandhi's control and be-

gins to mobilize the masses. Crossing boundaries of region, caste, and religion, it becomes India's first national movement.

December 23, 1919: The Government of India Act enacts the Montagu-Chelmsford Reforms of 1917–1918, effective January 1, 1921. A bicameral central legislature is established and the franchise broadened, with separate communal and special-interest electorates. Most radical is the devolution of some powers to provinces and, at provincial level, the institution of dyarchy (dual authority): Indian autonomy over "transferred" departments (education, health, and agriculture), with others (irrigation, revenue, and justice) "reserved" to British officials. The Act inaugurates a period of significant political development at the provincial level.

1920: Lord Sinha, appointed governor of Bihar and Orissa, becomes the first Indian to head a province.

1920: Tilak founds the Congress Democratic Party. Akali Dal (Party of Immortals) is founded by Tara Singh (1885–1967), politicizing Sikhs. Many other political parties are created during the 1920s and 1930s, most existing for brief periods in unstable alliances.

August 1, 1920–February 1922: Gandhi leads the first national *satyagraha* movement. Its centerpiece is mass nonpayment of land taxes (which supply half of government revenue). Sixty thousand people are imprisoned in its first year. This first mass antigovernment campaign crosses class, provincial, and sectarian lines, forging a national ideology and interregional political links.

November 1920: The *satyagraha* movement affects national elections for Central Legislative Assembly as many Congress members refuse to run and voters stay away from polls: Tilak's Democratic Party is the beneficiary.

December 1920: Fourteen thousand delegates to Congress, representing a wide social and political spectrum (including many Muslims), approve Nagpur Resolution supporting national *satyagraha* campaign. Gandhi pledges *swaraj* (self-government) by December 31, 1921, an unrealistic promise that he is later forced to retract.

1921: A census reports India's population as 318.9 million, a rise of 54 percent during the previous half century. Falling death rates and rising birth rates create a population explosion: 352.8 million in 1931; 389 million in 1941.

April 8, 1921: Council of State and Central Legislative Assembly are inaugurated. Chamber of Princes is established, an advisory body that formally but ineffectually brings princes into the political process.

August 1921: Moplah rebellion in Malabar: Muslim peasants in this historically rebellious region revolt against Hindu landlords, killing Europeans and Hindus and forcing conversions. British military response leaves more than 2,000 dead and 45,000 in prison, but riots continue along the Malabar Coast for several years.

November 17, 1921: An all-India *hartal* (work stoppage) greets the arrival of the British Prince of Wales; the Non-Cooperation Movement boycotts the state visit. Forty thousand Indians are jailed within the month.

February 7, 1922: Widespread violence, especially Chauri-Chaura massacre (the murder of twenty-two policemen, February 5), leads Gandhi to call off the *satyagraha* campaign, which is judged a failure. He calls instead for simple hand spinning, weaving *(khadi)*, and village-based social programs. Gandhi is arrested and imprisoned for incitement (March 10); he removes himself from political activity until 1929.

August 2, 1922: British prime minister Lloyd George delivers his famous "steel frame" speech in Parliament. He describes British civil servants as the steel frame of the colonial structure, and claims, "Britain will in no circumstances relinquish her responsibilities to India." This statement is widely interpreted as a repudiation of 1919 reforms.

1923: As one of the liberalization measures of Viceroy Lord Reading (rules 1921–1926), ICS entrance exams are held for the first time in New Delhi as well as London. Indianization proceeds rapidly; Indian civil servants outnumber British by 1940.

1923: National elections for Central Legislative Assembly give the Swaraj Party (founded 1922) the most seats in a splintered field. Swarajists, a Congress activist group led by Motilal Nehru (1861–1931) and C. R. Das (1870–1925), succeed for only a few years before their movement declines.

August 1923: The All-India Hindu Mahasabha, an organization founded in 1915 to promote Hindu interests, enters the national political arena under the presidency of Madan Mohan Malaviya. A session at Varanasi attracts 1,500 delegates from a wide range of Hindus. The party is unsuccessful electorally but remains politically active until the 1940s.

1924–1926: Communal violence escalates. Hundreds are killed or injured in Hindu-Muslim rioting in Malabar and northern cities, including Delhi and Calcutta.

December 1924: The Muddiman Committee, investigating the effects of 1919 legislative reforms, issues a divided report. The Indian Minority Report criticizes the concept of dyarchy and recommends major changes.

1925: The Sikh Gurdwara Act, passed after five years of conflict between government and Sikhs, places all Punjabi *gurdwaras* (Sikh temples) under the authority of a central committee. This de facto structure of self-government survives to the present day.

1926: Swarajists and Nationalists dominate elections for the Central Legislative Assembly. Results show a steady rise in voter participation among the 3.7 percent of the population holding a franchise.

1927: The opposition British Labour Party calls for full dominion status for India.

1927: Jawaharlal Nehru (1889–1964), the son of Motilal Nehru, attends an anti-imperialism conference in Brussels.

1927: The Madras session of Congress declares the goal of independence, not dominion status.

1928: Gandhi leads a local *satyagraha* campaign of farmers at Bardoli, Gujarat, against tax increases. Its success proves the power of civil disobedience to force change.

1928–1929: Terrorist activity increases in Bengal and northern India. Revolutionary Surya Sen leads an attack on Chittagong armory in September 1928; he is executed in 1933. Bhagat Singh, a Hindustani socialist, bombs the Assembly Hall, Delhi, on April 8, 1929; he is executed in 1931. Large bomb factories are discovered in north India.

February 3, 1928: The Simon Commission, a British parliamentary group directed to evaluate the Montagu-Chelmsford Reforms, arrives in India and is met with an all-India *hartal* (work stoppage). Thousands of Indians demonstrate against the commission's all-British composition; Congress, Jinnah, and other Indian leaders boycott its work. The conservative reform advocated in the Simon Report (June 1930) is overtaken by events.

August 28–31, 1928: The All-Parties Conference at Lucknow accepts the Nehru Report, written by Motilal Nehru and T. B. Sapru as a draft constitution for the federally organized, self-governing dominion of India. Congress also accepts the Report (henceforth known as Nehru Constitution), but Muslim cooperation ends when Jinnah walks out of a meeting in December after failure to agree on political representation for Muslims. He joins Aga Khan III's All-Parties Muslim Conference, committed to separate Muslim electorates.

August 30, 1928: Radical dissidents led by Jawaharlal Nehru and militant Bengali leader Subhas Chandra Bose (1897–1945) break away from Congress to form the socialist Independence for India League, calling for outright independence. Gandhi returns to active politics to heal the rift.

March 20, 1929: Thirty-one "communists" (many of them nationalists or trade unionists) are arrested for treason. Their trial (the so-called Meerut Conspiracy Case) becomes a cause célèbre, and the verdicts, finally issued in January 1933, are suspended. The Communist Party is outlawed in July 1934.

March 29, 1929: Jinnah leads the All-Parties Muslim Conference to adopt "Fourteen Points" outlining minimum Muslim political demands, which include separate electorates.

October 31, 1929: The Irwin Declaration, issued by the viceroy, commits the British government for the first time to dominion status for India. It announces a Round Table Conference to begin discussions on constitutional issues.

November 2, 1929: An "All Parties Manifesto" accepting the Irwin Declaration is approved by various parties, including Congress.

December 29–31, 1929: Under the leadership of Jawaharlal Nehru, representing the young left wing of the party, the Lahore session of Congress rejects the Irwin Declaration and Nehru Constitution. The manifesto calls instead for *purna swaraj* (full independence), civil disobedience, and boycott of the proposed Round Table Conference. Congress is rejuvenated as a national political force.

1930: Under the leadership of the "Frontier Gandhi," Abdul Ghaffar Khan, Muslim Pashtuns in the Northwest Frontier Province participate in a national civil-disobedience action. Thousands of his Khudai Khidmatgars (Red Shirt Volunteers) are arrested and the movement outlawed. Indian Muslims elsewhere do not support noncooperation.

January 26, 1930: Purna Swaraj (Complete Independence) Day is declared by Congress. A resolution demanding "complete freedom from the British" is read in all villages and towns. This date will later be celebrated in independent India as Republic Day.

March 12–April 5, 1930: The second national civil disobedience movement (to 1934) begins with Gandhi's salt march to the Gujarat coast. At Dandi (April 5) he defies the government salt monopoly by producing natural sea salt; millions of Indians follow his example. (The salt tax is the third-largest source of government revenue.) This symbolically powerful action is supported by widespread strikes, boycotts, nonpayment of taxes, and raids on government salt depots; Gujarat and Bombay are centers of revolt. The sixty thousand to ninety thousand political arrests include Jawaharlal and Motilal Nehru, Gandhi, and the Congress Working Committee.

November 12, 1930–January 19, 1931: The First Round Table Conference on Reforms meets in London to hammer out constitutional formula for Indian federation. Delegates include Aga Khan III, Jinnah, Indian princes, and British representatives. Congress boycotts the conference; most of its leaders are in jail.

1930: At annual Muslim League conference at Allahabad, president Sir Muhammad Iqbal (1877–1938) first publicly calls for autonomous Islamic state within Indian federation, encompassing the 70 million Muslims of northwest India. (*Pakistan*, "Land of the Pure," is first proposed as name for Islamic nation by Muslim students in England, 1933.) The majority of Muslims, however, are uninterested in partition; Muslim League continues its leading role in negotiating constitutional settlement.

1930–1932: No Rent campaigns in Gujarat, United Provinces, and Bengal.

1930s: Amid worldwide economic depression, hundreds of thousands of overseas Indians return from Burma, Malaya, and Ceylon.

March 5, 1931: Gandhi-Irwin Pact signed. Government recognizes *swadeshi* movement in exchange for the suspension of civil disobedience campaign. Congress agrees to participate in the Round Table Conference.

September 7–December 1, 1931: Gandhi is Congress's sole representative at the Second Round Table Conference in London; Iqbal, Jinnah, and Aga Khan III also attend, as do untouchables leader Bhimrao Ramji Ambed-

kar (1891–1956) and Sikh Master Tara Singh. Little is accomplished; Hindu-Muslim differences are intractable and Indian princes at odds. In a U.S. radio broadcast, Gandhi appeals for international support for Indian aspirations.

1932: Aden is annexed to India as part of Britain's colonial empire.

January 4, 1932: Gandhi is jailed after resumption of the civil disobedience campaign. Eighty thousand political prisoners are jailed in the early months of the year. Viceroy Lord Freeman Willingdon's government assumes draconian powers; Congress, peasant associations (*kisan sabhas*), and other organizations are outlawed.

August 16, 1932: British prime minister Ramsay MacDonald unveils the Communal Award, extending separate electorates to Sikhs, Christians, Anglo-Indians, Scheduled Castes ("untouchables"; Gandhi's term for them is "Harijans," children of God), Europeans, regional and special interest groups. A hunger strike by Gandhi in Yervada Jail forces negotiation of the Pune Pact (signed September 24), creating reserved legislative seats for the Scheduled Castes.

August 17–November 7, 1932: Delegation from the India League in London visits India to assess the political situation. Its report is a detailed indictment of the government's "reign of terror" in repressing the civil disobedience campaign.

November 7–December 24, 1932: The Third Round Table Conference in London fails once again to bridge differences between Indian National Congress and Muslim League leaders. Minor outcomes include the creation of the new provinces of Orissa and Sind (effected 1936).

1933: The Royal Indian Air Force is formed. The Royal Indian Navy is created in 1934.

January 16, 1934: Great earthquake in Bihar.

1934: Officially contesting Central Legislative Assembly elections for the first time, Congress wins a majority of seats. Indian women vote for the first time.

Consciously or unconsciously we are acting non-violently towards one another in daily life. All well-ordained societies are based on the law of non-violence. I have found that life persists in the midst of destruction and, therefore, there must be a higher law than that of destruction. Only under that law would a well-ordered society be intelligible and life worth living. And if that is the law of life, we have to work it out in daily life. Wherever . . . you are confronted with an opponent, conquer him with love. In a crude manner, I have worked it out in my life. That does not mean that all my difficulties are solved. I have found, however, that this law of love has answered as the law of destruction never does.

Young India, by Mahatma Gandhi (October 1, 1933)

August 2, 1935: British Parliament passes the Government of India Act. The franchise is extended sixfold, to 30 million; provincial self-government is mandated; dyarchy is instituted at the federal level, extending Indian authority; the Federation of India is created, an elaborate association of British provinces, principalities, and Congress-administered areas. The federation blueprint angers Congress and Muslim League by ignoring the work of the three Round Table Conferences; it is only partly implemented.

1936: The All-India Kisan Sabha, a national federation of peasant associations, is founded. It forms part of an emerging socialist movement in the 1930s led by Jawaharlal Nehru and S. C. Bose.

1936: B. R. Ambedkar founds the Independent Labour Party in Bombay to pursue the fight for full equality by members of the Scheduled Castes.

February 20, 1937: Completion of the first general elections to Provincial Legislative Assemblies under the 1935 Act; 15.5 million of the 30.1 million eligible voters participate. Congress wins 70 percent of the popular vote. The Muslim League, poorly organized on a national basis, fares badly.

April 1, 1937: The Indian constitution takes force. India is administratively reorganized into eleven provinces (Northwest Frontier, Punjab, Sind, Bombay, Central Provinces, Uttar Pradesh, Bihar, Bengal, Assam, Orissa, and Madras). Provincial self-government is instituted, with Congress assuming control of seven provinces. Women and untouchables are enfranchised. Federal Court created. Burma and Aden become separate British colonies.

October 1937: Spurred by failure in elections and Jinnah's leadership, the Muslim League begins period of resurgence. Jinnah spends the next ten years uniting factions in order to make Muslims a genuine political force and leads the drive toward Muslim partition.

1939: Congress fractures in leadership struggle between Gandhi and S. C. Bose. Bose resigns the Congress presidency (April 29, 1939) and forms the radical Forward Bloc at Calcutta.

September 3, 1939: Britain declares war on Germany. Without consultation, viceroy Lord Linlithgow (governs 1936–1943) pronounces India at war. Remembering the experience of World War I, Congress demands a statement of Britain's postwar "goals and ideals."

October 17, 1939: The Viceroy's Statement on War Aims and the War Effort repeats the British goal of Indian dominion status, but states that the 1935 Government of India Act may be amended after the war. Unsatisfied, Congress resigns its provincial ministries during the following weeks and (November 23) reiterates its demand for independence.

December 22, 1939: The Muslim League celebrates a Day of Deliverance from the Congress *raj* and does not oppose the British war effort.

December 27, 1939: The first Indian troops reach France.

1940: Indians for the first time outnumber Europeans in the Indian Civil Service.

March 19–20, 1940: Congress, meeting in Ramgarh, demands independence and constituent assembly, committing to a campaign of civil disobedience.

March 23, 1940: At a 100,000-strong meeting in Lahore, the Muslim League adopts the goal of an independent Pakistan. Fazlul Huq, Bengal's premier, is instrumental in forging the Lahore Resolution (later called Pakistan Resolution) calling for independent states in India's Muslim-majority northwestern and eastern regions. Gandhi strongly opposes partition; Congress, which still claims to represent all Indians, elects Muslim Maulana Azad as its president in 1940. One-nation versus two-nation polemics dominate Indian public life until independence.

July 2, 1940: S. C. Bose is arrested and his Forward Bloc banned. Bose escapes to Germany (1941) and in daily broadcasts originating there urges revolution against British rule. Terrorist violence occurs throughout World War II against British targets in Bengal.

August 8, 1940: Viceroy Linlithgow's "August Offer" proposes broader Indian representation on the Executive Council, a constituent assembly after the war, and protection for the political representation of Muslims and other minorities. Congress and the Muslim League reject the offer.

September 1940–May 1943: Four Indian army divisions arrive in North Africa; they play a major role in the Allied victory at El Alamein (October 23–November 3, 1942).

October 17, 1940: Congress launches its third great civil disobedience campaign, individual *satyagraha* against the war (to 1942). Gandhi's chief disciple Vinoba Bhave, Jawarharlal Nehru, and twenty thousand others are arrested and sentenced after declaring their intention to resist the war; thousands of *satyagrahis* remain in jail until December 1941.

January–May 1941: Two Indian army divisions are deployed against Italian forces in East Africa.

August 14, 1941: Announcement of the Atlantic Charter, a document agreed to by Prime Minister Churchill and President Roosevelt affirming self-government and national self-determination for all peoples. On September 9 Churchill announces in the British House of Commons that the Charter does not apply to the British empire.

December 7, 1941: Japan bombs Pearl Harbor and rapidly takes control in the Pacific theater of war. Sixty thousand Indian troops become prisoners of war when British stronghold of Singapore falls to Japanese (February 15, 1942). Japan's advance in the Pacific forces Britain to negotiate independence with India, which has assumed vital strategic importance to the Allies.

1942: Akali Dal demands a separate Azad (Free) Punjab.

1942–1943: Famine in Bengal is caused primarily by wartime dislocations, black marketeering, administrative incompetence, and the decision to give troop movements precedence over shipment of relief supplies. Between 1 million and 3 million people starve.

March 23–April 12, 1942: With Japanese invasion of India an imminent danger, Sir Stafford Cripps leads First Cabinet Mission to India. In exchange for wartime support, he offers (March 29) a constituent assembly and full dominion status after the war, with freedom to withdraw from the Commonwealth. In April, Jinnah, Gandhi, and Congress all reject the offer, which Gandhi is later to call "a postdated check on a bank that was failing."

April 6, 1942: First Japanese bombing of India. Calcutta is bombed (December 20, 1942).

May 1942: Burma falls, trapping ninety thousand Indian residents. Thousands die trying to flee back to India. Indian troops are heavily engaged in southeast Asia for the duration of the war.

August 8, 1942: Congress adopts a "Quit India" movement and sanctions mass civil disobedience. Their demand for outright and unconditional British withdrawal from India is effectively a declaration of war against the government. Congress is outlawed and its leaders arrested.

August 11–September 1942: The "Quit India" movement proceeds despite the incarceration of Congress leaders. Rejecting Gandhian nonviolence, it is marked by widespread violence, arson, and murder, mostly in terrorist attacks on government buildings and railways. Amid ensuing riots, 1,000 are killed (nearly all Indians), 3,000 injured by official count (other estimates put deaths at 10,000); 60,000 arrests are made in last months of 1942. British deploy their huge wartime armed force (including bombs) to crush the rebellion.

June 1943: Field Marshall Archibald Wavell is appointed viceroy (1943–1947). India is placed under direct rule for the duration of the war as the government takes over provincial rule.

September 1943–May 1945: Three Indian divisions participate in the Allied campaign in Italy.

October 21, 1943: In Japanese-occupied Singapore, S. C. Bose proclaims the Provisional Government of Azad (Free) India and declares war on the United States and Britain. He leads an Indian National Army of forty thousand men, including Indian prisoners of war freed for the purpose and residents of Malaya. Seven thousand INA members invade Assam in cooperation with the Japanese (March–May 1944) before being driven back. Bose surrenders in Rangoon (May 4, 1945).

December 1943: The Muslim League, meeting at Karachi, adopts the slogan "Divide and Quit," committing itself to partition.

May 6, 1944: Gandhi is released from prison on medical grounds and immediately begins pursuing political settlement of independence.

September 3, 1944: Sikh "protest day."

September 9–27, 1944: Jinnah and Gandhi meet to explore settlement based on partition, a position opposed by most Hindu organizations. Their talks fail, but strengthen political prestige of Jinnah and Muslim League.

May 7, 1945: Germany surrenders.

June 14, 1945: Wavell proposes to establish transitional government of India with British restricted to positions of viceroy and commander-in-chief, the Executive Council otherwise to comprise Indians. Congress leaders are released from jail (June 15).

June 25–July 14, 1945: Twenty-one political leaders meet at the Simla Conference to consider Wavell's proposal. They disagree over the representation of Muslims and Scheduled Castes, preventing the formation of an interim government.

July 1945: Clement Attlee forms a new Labour government in London. The new administration is anxious for quick withdrawal from India, which it views as a drain on Britain.

August 15, 1945: Japanese surrender ends World War II. Indian armed forces, numbering 205,000 in October 1939, now total nearly 2.5 million. India has suffered more than 24,000 deaths, 54,000 injuries, and thousands more missing in action.

September 20–23, 1945: The Congress Committee, led by Gandhi and Nehru, again rejects British terms for self-government and demands British withdrawal from India.

November–December 1945: Indian National Army officers, on public trial in Delhi for wartime treason, become national heroes; Congress and Muslim League hail them as patriots. They receive suspended sentences in an atmosphere of heightened nationalist pride.

December 1945–January 1946: In elections for the Constituent Assembly, Congress wins 90 percent of the general seats; the Muslim League wins all thirty seats reserved for Muslims. The results demonstrate both the broad popular base of support for Congress and the emergence of the Muslim League as a powerful political force.

February 18–23, 1946: Royal Indian Navy in

Bombay harbor mutinies over pay and racial discrimination. Subsequent police strikes in Malabar and Bihar demonstrate the increasingly shaky loyalty of local law enforcement authorities.

March 23–June 29, 1946: The second British Cabinet Mission visits India seeking constitutional formula for Indian independence. Cabinet Mission Plan (May 16) proposes a three-tier federal structure with substantial provincial autonomy and provisions for partial Muslim self-government. It rejects partition.

June–July 1946: Congress, Muslim League, and Sikhs all reject Cabinet Mission Plan. The Muslim League calls (July 27) for "direct action"—work stoppages, strikes, demonstrations. Jinnah proclaims, "We bid goodbye to constitutional methods."

August 16, 1946: Muslim League's "Direct Action Day" turns into the "Great Killing" in Calcutta, where in three days of civil war 4,000 people are killed, 15,000 injured, and 100,000 made homeless. The Muslim League is accused of abetting the anti-Hindu frenzy of murder, looting, and arson.

September 2, 1946: Nehru forms an interim government at Wavell's invitation. After weeks of boycott, Jinnah allows five Muslim League members to join the cabinet (October 13), but they refuse to acknowledge Nehru's leadership and adopt obstructionist tactics.

Late 1946–1947: Sectarian violence spreads across India, especially in Bengal, Bihar, and Punjab. Bodies pile up in the streets of India's cities as Hindus and Muslims engage in a year of bloody communal clashes. Gandhi walks through strife-torn provinces exhorting reconciliation of Hindus and Muslims and reciting prayers from the Koran.

December 3–6, 1946: Talks in London in December among Jinnah, Nehru, Wavell, and the British government break down.

December 9, 1946: The first session of the Constituent Assembly in Delhi is boycotted by the Muslim League.

February 20, 1947: British prime minister Attlee commits Britain to quit India in June 1948. Lord Mountbatten is appointed viceroy to oversee the transfer of power.

March–July 1947: After the resignation of Khizr Hayat Khan's shaky coalition government in Punjab, the province is rocked for four months by violence, murders, arson, and pillage. Violence spreads to the Northwest Frontier Province and Delhi.

March 23–April 2, 1947: The Inter-Asian Relations Conference convened by Nehru draws representatives of twenty-eight African and Asian countries to Delhi. It is the beginning of a unified voice for developing nations.

March 24, 1947: Lord Mountbatten is sworn in as India's last viceroy. Soon realizing that the political situation is explosive, he shortens the timetable for British withdrawal.

April 20, 1947: Nehru publicly accepts partition. Amid much public debate on the division of Bengal and Punjab, V. K. Menon crafts a compromise constitutional formula.

June 3, 1947: Formal announcement in British House of Commons of a plan to partition the subcontinent into India and Pakistan at independence (June 3d Plan). Britain will withdraw in August.

July 18, 1947: George VI signs the Indian Independence Act, proclaiming creation of the independent dominions of India and Pakistan at midnight, August 14–15, 1947. Borders are to be drawn and imperial assets divided within a month.

July–August 1947: An estimated twelve million people migrate across the future borders between India and Pakistan. Inadequately policed, this profound social upheaval is made even more terrifying by murder, stealing, and rape. Muslim refugees on their way from India to Pakistan, Hindus, and Sikhs traveling into India are slaughtered. It is estimated that half a million people are killed.

REPUBLIC OF INDIA: 1947–1998

At midnight on August 14–15, 1947, the Republic of India is born. Under the terms of independence, the subcontinent is partitioned. The new government of India, led by the brilliant and charismatic prime minister Jawaharlal Nehru, declares its intention to recreate the nation as a modern socialist, secular state. His Congress Party dominates Indian politics, and his legacy of strong, centralized rule is continued by his daughter, Indira Gandhi, whose premiership ("Indira Raj") is characterized by a tremendous concentration of government power.

Directing a centrally planned economy, Nehru issues a series of Five-Year Plans outlining an ambitious program designed to revolutionize agriculture and industry. The Green Revolution of the 1960s and high technology are outstanding successes. The early years of independence are also years of profound social reforms. Hindu women and the Scheduled Castes ("untouchables") gain equal rights under the law; education is democratized and nationalized. But India's ancient legacy of landlordism, poverty, illiteracy, and communal division is deeply embedded, and progress is uneven. Village life continues to be characterized by technological underdevelopment; urban poverty becomes a serious issue as millions flock to cities seeking economic opportunity.

The drawing of boundaries between India and Pakistan in 1947 provokes a refugee crisis of epic proportions as an estimated 10 to 15 million people cross Indo-Pakistani borders. Within fifteen years, India fights three border wars with Pakistan and one with China. India's historic ethnic and cultural diversity challenges the new political nation. After popular protests in the late 1950s, old British administrative territories are replaced with linguistically defined regions, but communal strife continues to be a strong, sad theme in Indian national life.

As the leader of the second-largest country in the world during the dangerous years of the Cold War, Nehru designs a foreign policy based on nonaggression and nonalignment. He leads the nonaligned movement among Third World nations. A period of alliance with the West to counter the emerging power of neighboring China gives way to a position of independent strength as India becomes a nuclear and economic world power. With a population projected to exceed one billion early in the twenty-first century and endemic poverty a persistent problem, India's task is to capitalize on the economic and cultural promise of its rich history.

August 15, 1947: At midnight on August 14–15, India gains independence from Great Britain as a dominion of the British Commonwealth. Jawaharlal Nehru marks the occasion with his famous "Tryst with Destiny" speech to the Constituent Assembly. Sind, Northwest Frontier Province, West Punjab, and East Bengal are separated as independent Pakistan. All of India's 550 principalities except Hyderabad and Junagadh (both with Muslim rulers and majority Hindu populations) plus Kashmir join the dominion in which their territory lies, setting the stage for a period of territorial fighting and border re-

adjustment. Nehru is appointed prime minister; the Earl of Mountbatten, the last British viceroy, is named governor-general. Post of deputy prime minister is created for Vallabhbhai Patel (1875–1950), who further distinguishes himself as India's first home minister.

August 1947: One of largest migrations in history begins as millions of Hindus and Sikhs leave West Punjab, now Pakistan, to cross into India as Muslims in Indian territory cross into Pakistan. Government control on both sides of the border is seriously threatened; six weeks of massacres, looting, and arson result in estimated half a million deaths. Ten to fifteen million people become refugees.

Long years ago, we made a tryst with destiny, and now the time comes when we shall redeem our pledge, not wholly or in full measure, but very substantially. At the stroke of the midnight hour, when the world sleeps, India will awake to life and freedom. A moment comes, which comes but rarely in history, when we step out from the old to the new, when an age ends, and when the soul of a nation, long suppressed, finds utterance. It is fitting that at this solemn moment we take the pledge of dedication to the service of India and her people and to the still larger cause of humanity.

Speech to India's Constituent Assembly by
Jawaharlal Nehru (August 14, 1947)

1947: The new Indian government invades and takes Junagadh after *nawab* elects to join Pakistan. *Nizam* of Hyderabad, hoping to remain independent, is given a year to consider his choice.

1947: Gandhi promotes nonviolent end to communal rioting in Bihar and Bengal by walking barefoot throughout the provinces.

October 26, 1947: Maharaja Hari Singh of Kashmir, a Hindu hoping to keep his largely Muslim state independent of both India and Pakistan, accedes to India in exchange for military assistance. A crisis ensues. Muslims in southwest Kashmir revolt, aided by Pashtun tribesmen from Pakistan; Indian troops are airlifted in. Three days of heavy fighting subsides into two-year-long First (and undeclared) Indo-Pakistani War. Kashmir is to prove the most persistent and intractable of India's territorial disputes.

Early January 1948: Gandhi fasts for a week in protest against riots and violence and against Congress's treatment of Muslims and inaction on Kashmiri refugees.

January 30, 1948: Gandhi is assassinated in Delhi at a daily public prayer meeting in his garden, allegedly by a member of a rightist

Hindu paramilitary organization. Nehru mourns, "The light has gone out of our lives."

June 21, 1948: Chakravarti Rajagopalachari becomes first Indian governor-general (1948–1950).

September 15–17, 1948: One month after expiration of *nizam*'s one-year grace period, government of India takes over Hyderabad. The *nizam*, desirous of remaining independent or joining Pakistan, is forced instead to surrender and accede to India (November 1949).

January 1, 1949: UN-sponsored cease-fire in Kashmir, now partitioned. Cease-fire line (agreed July 29) gives Pakistan control over western province of Azad (Free) Kashmir, India control in east; this de facto border remains in place as further negotiations fail to reach agreement. A plebiscite over Jammu (southern Kashmir) promised for 1953 is never held.

1949: Creation of the Dravida Munnetra Kazhagam (DMK, Dravidian Progressive Federation), founded by C. N. Annadurai. Calling for recognition of Dravidian cultural traditions and radical land reform, it becomes the dominant political force in southern India.

November 26, 1949: Adoption of a new constitution drafted by the Constituent Assembly. Federal structure divides functions between central and state governments modeled on the British parliamentary system. Members of the Rajya Sabha (Council of State) are elected by state legislatures; the more powerful Lok Sabha (House of the People) is popularly elected. The prime minister is the political leader, with the elected president as head of state.

1949: At a meeting hosted by Nehru, fifteen African and Asian nations condemn Dutch "police action" in Indonesia. It is the first of many such means by which Nehru promotes his vision of a unified Third World voice and developing nations in international affairs.

January 26, 1950: Sovereign democratic Republic of India is born as a new federal constitution takes effect. The last principalities are incorporated. A secular state, India is the world's largest democracy, with a universal adult franchise covering 173 million voters. Rajendra Prasad assumes the presidency (1950–1962); Jawaharlal Nehru becomes prime minister, leader of the Lok Sabha. Nehru (1889–1964), popularly called Panditji, is a brilliant and charismatic leader with a socialist vision for India; he becomes the architect of early Five-Year Plans, the industrialization of India, and a foreign policy of nonalignment.

1951: Census records India's population at 356.9 million.

1951: Founding of conservative Hindu nationalist party, Bharatiya Jan Sangh (Indian People's Party). It is the forerunner of the Bharatiya Janata Party (BJP) that will be formed in 1980.

June 3, 1951: Massive Socialist Party demonstration in Delhi against government policies on housing and food.

March 1, 1952: Nehru's Congress Party sweeps the first general elections in the new republic; 105 million voters participate. Rajendra Prasad is elected president (May). The Congress Party will dominate India's government until 1977.

1953: The state of Madras is divided on a linguistic basis into the states of Tamil Nadu (Land of the Tamils) and Andhra Pradesh (Telugu-speaking). Monsoons fail for a second year; famine is averted with imported grain.

February 15, 1954: Kashmir's assembly ratifies accession to India.

April 29, 1954: Nonaggression treaty with China, tacitly endorsing the Chinese occupation of Tibet. Chinese alliance is central to Nehru's foreign policy; Nehru and China's Chou En-lai exchange visits during the year. *Panch shila* (five principles) govern Nehru's foreign policy and vision for solidarity among developing countries: "mutual respect" for territory and sovereignty; nonaggression; noninterference in one another's internal affairs; equality and mutual benefit; peaceful coexistence.

December 1954: Congress formally adopts its goal of a "socialistic pattern of society," in line with Nehru's desire to create a secular, neutral, socialist state.

Winter 1955: Chinese troops cross-border incursion into Uttar Pradesh; they withdraw after Indian protest.

April 1955: Nehru and Nasser of Egypt are motive forces behind historic meeting of twenty-nine nonaligned nations at the Bandung Conference in Indonesia. Nehru's cultivation of nonalignment during the Cold War makes India eligible for technical and economic aid from both the Eastern and Western blocs.

June 1955: Nehru visits the USSR; Khrushchev visits India in November.

1956: Passage of the Hindu Code Bill replaces the existing patchwork of laws with a uniform code mandating sex and caste equality for all Hindus.

1956: The Linguistic States Reorganization Act is implemented. Boundaries in southern India are redrawn to reflect linguistic regions, including Malayalam-speaking Kerala and Kannada-speaking Karnataka (Mysore).

1956: India, Burma, Ceylon, and Indonesia demand withdrawal of foreign troops from Egypt after the Suez Crisis. Nehru is frequently at the diplomatic forefront of conflicts affecting Third World nations, including the Korean War and the Algerian civil war.

May 28, 1956: France cedes its remaining settlements to India.

1957: Congress sweeps the second general elections throughout India except for Kerala, where a communist government is formed.

1959: Conservative Swatantra (Freedom Party) is founded. Its central doctrine is laissez-faire.

April 3, 1959: Fleeing persecution in Chinese-occupied Tibet, the Dalai Lama and thousands of followers seek asylum in India and establish a government-in-exile at Dharmsala.

Late 1959: Cross-border incursions, skirmishes between Indian and Chinese troops. The "cartographic war" continues for several years as the difficulty of surveying mountainous border regions produces conflicting maps and territorial claims.

1960: Nehru visits Pakistan.

May 1, 1960: After several years of often violent agitation, the linguistically based states of Maharashtra (Marathi-speaking) and Gujarat (Gujarati-speaking) are created from the old British state of Bombay. Nehru refuses to sanction a separate Punjabi-speaking Sikh state despite continuing agitation.

1961: Census records population at 435.5 million.

December 17, 1961: In line with Nehru's aggressive "forward policy," the Indian army invades remaining Portuguese settlements at Goa, Damao, and Diu (other attempted invasions since the mid-1950s have failed). Government terms the invasion a "police action."

1962: The third general elections give Congress overwhelming majorities in national and state legislatures.

1962: Goa is annexed.

October 20, 1962: War breaks out between India and China over rival claims to territory in area of Aksai-Chin, in Jammu-Kashmir, and in the Northeast Frontier Agency. Chinese troops advance before unilaterally withdrawing (November 20). An informal truce follows; China retains selected frontier areas, and borders remain undefined. Nehru's faith in Asian unity, solidarity among nonaligned nations, and nonaggression in foreign affairs is shattered.

1962–1965: The manifest weakness of the Indian military, exposed by the Chinese invasion, weakens India's long-standing policy of neutrality, but India receives military aid from the USSR as well as the United States and Britain. Indian army troop strength is doubled to 900,000. Ten new mountain divisions are trained for operations in contested northern frontier regions.

December 1, 1963: Nagaland, partitioned off from Assam, is declared a separate state after fifteen years of agitation for independence. Northeast region continues to be troubled by tribal separatism.

1964: Home Minister G. L. Nanda launches an anticorruption drive.

May 27, 1964: Nehru dies of a heart attack. He is succeeded by Lal Bahadur Shastri, a skillful leader in both domestic and international affairs.

January–June 1965: Two thousand cease-fire violations are reported in Kashmir; India charges Pakistan with guerrilla infiltration, while Pakistan ascribes the unrest to an indigenous revolt.

April 1965: U.S.-equipped Pakistani troops fire on Indian guards along contested border and easily penetrate Indian territory in western Rann of Kutch. Two weeks of fighting are ended by arrival of monsoons. The Commonwealth and United Nations press for a cease-fire (agreed to on June 30). A UN commission is charged with establishing the Indo-Pakistani border.

September 1–25, 1965: The Second Indo-Pakistani War is fought after a month of cross-border operations. It begins with a major Pakistani invasion of Jammu; fighting is widespread in Kashmir and Punjab for several weeks as air strikes target Lahore, Delhi, and Karachi. Limited in duration by a U.S.-British arms embargo on both combatants, the war kills twenty thousand, mostly civilians, and ends inconclusively with Indian forces circling Lahore. The United Nations negotiates a cease-fire (September 27).

1965: Monsoons fail; famine threatens. 1966–1967 is time of further drought.

The Bow Bazaar house. Central, an idol in the shape of an umbrella stand. Hung with folded, black umbrellas like the offerings of pilgrims and worshippers. On either side of it, the reception arranged by the heads of this many-headed family. In the small of my back, I feel a surreptitious push from Jiban and am propelled forward into the embrace of his mother who is all in white and smells of clean rice and who, while placing her hand in blessing, also pushes a little harder than I think necessary, and still harder, till I realize what it means, and go down on my knees to touch her feet.

Voices in the City, by Anita Desai (1965)

January 4–10, 1966: Prime minister Shastri and Pakistani president Muhammad Ayub Khan meet at the historic Tashkent Summit, sponsored by the USSR. The Declaration of Tashkent pledges "normal and peaceful" relations, restoration of economic and trade ties, and diplomatic resolution of disputes. Territorial sovereignty is restored to status quo ante, and troops are withdrawn to their prewar positions.

January 11, 1966: Prime minister Shastri dies of a heart attack, provoking a Congress Party succession crisis.

January 19, 1966: Nehru's daughter, Indira Gandhi (1917–1984), the relatively inexperienced leader of the Congress's left wing, becomes prime minister. She proves a powerful and ambitious ruler; her appropriation of power and autocratic method of wielding it make her long premiership (governs 1966–1977, 1980–1984) controversial among both contemporaries and later historians.

January 26, 1966: In her Independence Day address, Prime Minister Gandhi pledges to build on her father's legacy and pursue the principles of the Tashkent Agreement. She also announces a major grain deal with the United States. Fourteen million tons of American wheat are imported in 1966–1967.

March 1966: Indira Gandhi visits the United States, where she secures a major commitment of American loans and credits for implementation of the Fourth Five-Year Plan (1966–1971).

July 1966: Continuing her father's policy of nonalignment, Gandhi visits the USSR and calls on Third World nations to help end the Vietnam War.

November 1, 1966: After a summer of escalating Sikh separatist campaigns, Punjab is divided into two states: Sikh, Punjabi-speaking Punjab in northwest; and Hindu, Hindi-speaking Haryana to southeast. They share the new capital of Chandigarh.

February 1967: Congress suffers huge losses in general elections, losing numerous state assembly seats and control of six states; Gandhi's Lok Sabha majority, two hundred when she took office, is reduced to fifty. The electorate is disenchanted with stalled development and weak economy—most especially the recent devaluation of the rupee.

1967: Election of the first Muslim president, Zakir Husain (governs 1967–1969).

1967: The Naxalite communist faction leads a peasant occupation of land in the antilandlord movement in North Bengal.

April 1967: U.S. resumption of arms shipments to Pakistan sparks an arms race on the subcontinent.

September 1967: Indo-Chinese border clashes along the Sikkim-Tibet frontier.

1968: India declines to sign the international Nuclear Non-Proliferation Treaty; Gandhi cites inadequate guarantee of Indian security. Both India and Pakistan persist in refusing to sign this treaty despite international appeals to them to do so.

July 1969: At the Congress convention at Bangalore, Gandhi announces an aggressive socialist initiative including the nationalization of banks, limits on personal income and corporate profits, and land reform. Besides signaling a more aggressive pursuit of economic development, these measures indicate the prime minister's intention of wresting control of Congress from the conservative old guard of her father's era.

July 19, 1969: Three days after taking personal charge of finance portfolio, Gandhi nationalizes fourteen major banks, including the Central Bank and Bank of India. This move marks the beginning of the "Indira Raj," a period of near-absolute rule by the prime minister.

November 12, 1969: The Indian National Congress splits. The prime minister leads the "New Congress," or Congress (I). She forges a left-wing coalition including communists, DMK, and militant Sikh party Akali Dal. Old Congress, led by Morarji Desai, joins forces with Swatantra and Jan Sangh members of parliament to create formal political opposition, which gathers little support.

1970: India cedes Chandigarh, the shared capital of Punjab and Haryana, to Punjab after the fast-unto-death of Darshan Singh Pheruman and threatened self-immolation of Sant Fateh Singh. Transfer of the capital, postponed after Hindu Jats in Haryana demand compensation, is never implemented.

June 1970: Gandhi continues to strengthen her power by taking over the Home Ministry and cabinet portfolios for atomic energy and planning.

1970: 100,000 refugees stream into West Bengal in the wake of devastating floods in East Pakistan, adding to political tensions. Presidential rule is declared.

September 7, 1970: After failing to secure parliamentary enactment, government issues presidential order revoking pensions and privileges of former maharajas. The Supreme Court declares the decree unconstitutional (December 15). Amid further governmental disarray—some ministers distance themselves from Gandhi's land reforms—Gandhi calls new elections.

March 1–10, 1971: Congress sweeps the fifth general election, fought on its promise to eliminate poverty but widely regarded as a vote on Indira Gandhi's controversial leadership. The result is interpreted as public endorsement of Gandhi's plans to lower unemployment, clear slums, reform land tenure, build public housing, and reduce poverty and economic inequality. Stiff taxes are levied on wealth and corporate profits, but are largely evaded.

March 31, 1971: India appeals for UN intervention in the week-old Bangladeshi war of independence, which is creating an unmanageable refugee crisis. Nearly 1 million refugees cross the border from East Pakistan during April; by the end of December, nearly 10 million impoverished refugees have arrived in India, posing a crushing financial and logistical burden. Pakistan accuses India of supporting the war in Bangladesh; Indian troops do in fact help equip and train the Bangladeshi insurgents.

August 9, 1971: In light of continuing U.S. support of Pakistan and its own need to secure protection from China, India shifts its great power orientation and signs a twenty-year treaty of friendship with the Soviet Union.

December 1971: Former maharajas' government allowances and privileges are finally abolished by constitutional amendment.

December 3–17, 1971: Third Indo-Pakistani War coincides with the final phase of the Bangladeshi war of independence. Provoked by India's aid to Bangladeshi rebels, Pakistan strikes Indian air bases and invades Kashmir and East Pakistan. Superior Soviet-equipped Indian forces overrun Pakistani forces in the east, while holding off Pakistani attacks in its own western territory. Indian forces take Dhaka (December 16); a cease-fire is agreed to the following day. Indira Gandhi wins a major geopolitical victory. Bangladesh achieves independence and refugees are speedily repatriated.

1971: Decennial census records India's population at 548.2 million.

January 1972: Reorganization of northeastern India results in creation of four new states (Meghalaya, Tripura, Manipur, Himachal Pradesh), bringing total to 21.

March 19, 1972: Treaty of friendship is signed with independent Bangladesh.

Early 1972: India begins atomic weapons development.

April 1972: Supreme Court confirms legality of the twenty-fourth constitutional amendment (passed August 1971) allowing parliament to alter "fundamental rights" promised in the constitution.

July 2, 1972: Simla Agreement signed by India and Pakistan renounces the use of force to settle disputes and restores status quo before the Third Indo-Pakistani War, save that Bangladesh is now an independent state.

April 8, 1973: India assumes administrative control of the protectorate of Sikkim at its ruler's invitation following two weeks of antigovernment unrest there.

1974: Massive protests and student strikes in Bihar and Gujarat against government corruption and high inflation created by two years of regional drought and worldwide oil price shocks of 1973–1974. Violence, strikes, and sit-ins are widespread as Indians protest persistent poverty, widespread corruption and almost universal tax evasion by the ruling classes, a huge black market economy, and assassination of officials. J. P. Narayan calls for "total revolution"; Morarji Desai undertakes two fasts-unto-death in protest at corrupt Congress ministry in Gujarat.

February 1974: Desai and Narayan join opposition parties across the political spectrum from communists to the extreme right wing to form Janata Morcha (People's Front). The opposition is united in condemning what it views as Indira Gandhi's autocratic leadership.

May 18, 1974: India becomes the world's sixth nuclear power with a successful underground nuclear explosion in Rajasthan.

1975: Sikkim becomes India's twenty-second state.

March 6, 1975: 100,000 demonstrators march in Delhi to protest the Gandhi government.

June 11, 1975: Gandhi is convicted of campaign fraud in the 1971 election. She disregards mandatory six-year bar from political office, refusing to relinquish premiership.

June 25, 1975: Janata Morcha, recent victor in Gujarat elections, stages huge antigovernment rally in Delhi. Narayan urges national campaign of *satyagraha* (civil disobedience) in protest against official corruption and Gandhi's remaining in office. Senior government ministers urge her resignation pending appeal of her conviction.

June 26, 1975: Gandhi declares a national emergency, suspending civil rights, imposing press censorship, and reserving to herself almost absolute powers (until 1977). Political opposition is banned: Desai, Narayan, and thousands of other political opponents are jailed or placed under house arrest. Constitutional amendments are passed barring legal challenges to the emergency and granting top government officials immunity from prosecution for official acts. Gandhi's so-called Disciplined Democracy lasts two years, causing an international furor as India abandons democratic principles and institutions for autocratic rule.

July 21, 1975: Gandhi's government announces the Twenty-Point Program of economic reforms designed to lower inflation, implement radical rural land reform, and step up enforcement of tax collection. The measures produce economic gains and lower inflation. A cult of personality forms around the prime minister; the president of Assam, Dev Kant Barooah, makes his famous pronouncement that "India is Indira, and Indira is India," while a poster campaign proclaims, "She saved India!"

February 1976: Opposition DMK ministry in Tamil Nadu is toppled by central government on grounds of corruption and its leaders jailed. In March, Janata Morcha ministry cedes power to Congress after losing a vote of confidence.

April 16, 1976: Relations with Pakistan are normalized for the first time since the 1971 war.

January 18, 1977: The Emergency is suddenly canceled, political prisoners freed, and opposition parties restored. Parliamentary elections delayed from 1976 are called for March. Desai and Narayan quickly recreate opposition Janata Morcha. Jagjivan Ram (1908–1986), leader of *dalits* (literally "oppressed," a term used for the "untouchables" from the 1970s) resigns his defense portfolio and founds Congress for Democracy, which allies with Janata.

February 1977: Janata coalition defeats Gandhi at polls by making election a referendum on Emergency. Congress is defeated for the first time in India's history, winning less than one-third of Lok Sabha. Indira and Sanjay Gandhi both lose in their "safe" Uttar Pradesh districts; many of their supporters are also ousted.

1977: Morarji Desai, aged eighty, becomes India's fourth prime minister (governs 1977–1979). He presides over a government occupied by factionalism and uncertainty over succession to the aging leadership. His laissez-faire government allows the resurgence of corruption, smuggling, black marketeering, tax evasion, and high inflation.

November 19, 1977: Cyclone and flood in Bay of Bengal leave seven thousand to ten thousand dead in Andhra Pradesh.

December 1978: Desai makes charges against Indira Gandhi, reelected in November to Lok Sabha as a member of Congress (I) [for Indira] Party; she is expelled from the legislature and jailed for a week. This persecution proves a serious political miscalculation; widespread national demonstrations are held in Gandhi's support.

1979–1980: Under pressure from decades of immigration from Bangladesh, northeastern states are rocked by violent protests. The Assamese Liberation Army engages in a *satya-graha* campaign to eject 5 million Bengali immigrants. Mizo, Bodo, other tribal peoples, largely of Burmese, Mongol, and Sino-Tibetan descent, organize and agitate for independence. The central government responds with military force and creation of another small state, Mizoram (1987).

July 19, 1979: Weakened by defections of left-wing parties and others frustrated by governmental ineffectualness, Desai resigns in the face of certain loss in a vote of no confidence in Lok Sabha. Y. B. Chavan and Charan Singh fail in turn to form lasting administrations, signaling the end of Janata as political force.

December 1979: The USSR invades and occupies Afghanistan in guerrilla war against fundamentalist Muslim *mujahedeen*. India refuses to condemn the invasion in the United Nations on the grounds that the Soviets were invited in by the communist government of Afghanistan.

1980: India acquires intermediate nuclear missile technology.

January 6, 1980: Gandhi resumes premiership after Congress (I) decisively wins seventh national elections on the platform, "Elect a Government That Works!" Her son and heir apparent Sanjay Gandhi, leader of the Youth Congress, wins his first parliamentary seat; a large number of his hand-picked Congress (I) candidates are also swept into office. While being groomed to succeed his mother, Sanjay Gandhi has himself attracted much criticism for overseeing programs of aggressive slum clearance and forced sterilization, and has been charged with personally profiting from a state industrial venture.

June 1980: Sanjay Gandhi dies at age thirty-four while piloting his stunt plane. His brother Rajiv (1944–1991), a commercial pilot with no political experience, stands for his seat and takes on his political role.

1981: Census reports India's population at 690.2 million.

November 1981: Skirmishes occur along

Indo-Pakistani border amid bilateral tensions over continuing U.S. military aid to Pakistan and Pakistan's nuclear weapons program.

1982: Nominated by Gandhi, Zail Singh (governs 1982–1987) becomes the first Sikh elected president. His election fails to conciliate Sikh separatists.

1982: A year after Indira Gandhi rejects Sikh demands for political control of Punjab, a conference of Sikhs declares holy war on Indian government. Movement for independent Sikh Khalistan (Land of the Pure) escalates acts of terrorism and killings in Punjab, Haryana, and New Delhi. Punjabi separatist agitation is spearheaded by followers of young fundamentalist, Sant Jarnail Singh Bhindranwale (1947–1984). They are armed with weapons diverted from the flow of arms through Pakistan to rebels in the war in Afghanistan.

Early 1984: Bhindranwale occupies the Golden Temple in Amritsar and demands constitutional recognition of Sikhs and special status for their holy city. Many die in ensuing Hindu-Sikh violence.

June 5–6, 1984: Indian army storms the Golden Temple in "Operation Bluestar." Two days of terrible fighting leaves hundreds dead and destroys some of the temple buildings. Sikh unrest continues.

Summer 1984: Seeking to maintain strong central control, Gandhi orders the deposition of Kashmir's chief minister, Farooq Abdullah, the most popular public figure in that state. In August, she orders the ouster of Andhra's chief minister, N. T. Rama Rao.

October 31, 1984: Indira Gandhi is assassinated in her garden by two of her Sikh bodyguards seeking revenge for the assault on the Golden Temple in Amritsar in June. Her son Rajiv Gandhi, despite his political inexperience, is immediately sworn in as prime minister (governs 1984–1991). Hindus avenging Mrs. Gandhi's death rampage through Delhi: anti-Sikh rioting, arson, and murder kill thousands and wreak vast de-struction of property before the army is finally called out on 3 November. Civil liberties groups later charge that the violence was organized by Congress (I) and tacitly sanctioned by police and army; a 1987 government investigation is inconclusive.

December 3, 1984: Massive chemical leak from Union Carbide insecticide-manufacturing plant in Bhopal, Madhya Pradesh, kills 2,800 and injures hundreds of thousands of others in the worst industrial accident in history. A $470 million settlement is negotiated between the Indian government and the company, and criminal charges are filed against Union Carbide (July 1992).

December 24, 1984: Running a "Remember Indira" campaign, Rajiv Gandhi leads Congress (I) to landslide victory in eighth national elections. A handsome and popular politician, he represents a new political and cultural generation of upwardly mobile, technically educated Indians impatient with India's ancient traditions and famously convoluted bureaucracy. He promises to free private enterprise by deregulation, cut taxes on wealth and inheritance, and solve long-simmering regional disputes.

1985: Accords signed by Rajiv Gandhi with Asom Gana Parishad (Assam People's Party) and Mizo National Front give provincial parties political control in eastern regions. These accords produce renewed threats of communal violence against Muslim immigrants from Bangladesh.

June 23, 1985: In an attack thought to be the work of Sikh terrorists, an Air India plane en route from Toronto to London is destroyed by a bomb, killing 329 people. A second bomb intended for an Air India flight kills two baggage handlers at Tokyo's main airport. Sikh terrorism will continue to be a major problem in India, with thousands of victims claimed over the years.

July 1985: Punjab Accord signed by Rajiv Gandhi and Akali Dal leader H. S. Longowal makes long-sought concessions to Sikhs and finally transfers Chandigarh to Punjab.

Longowal is assassinated by Sikh terrorists weeks later, and the accord is never implemented. Terrorist and Disruptive Activities [Prevention] Act (1985), intended to combat Punjabi terrorism by broadening government's powers of detention, is in force for ten years.

December 1985: Rajiv Gandhi cosponsors founding of the South Asian Association for Regional Cooperation (SAARC), a seven-nation forum for the peaceful resolution of disputes. Members are India, Pakistan, Sri Lanka, Bangladesh, Bhutan, Nepal, and Maldives.

1986: Mizoram and Arunachal Pradesh become states.

April 30, 1986: Two thousand police and troops storm Golden Temple, Amritsar, to expel Sikh rebels who have declared an independent Khalistan. The government assumes direct rule of Punjab (May 1987) to try to control continuous guerrilla warfare by Sikh separatists. Sikhs holding the temple surrender after another Indian attack (May 1988).

1987: Finance minister V. P. Singh investigates tax evasion by leading companies and families. He is transferred to Ministry of Defense, where he continues his anticorruption crusade. The campaign contributes to Rajiv Gandhi's growing unpopularity.

1987: In an agreement with Sri Lanka, India agrees to stop sheltering and training Tamil separatists in Tamil regions of India, and promises Indian Peace-Keeping Force (IPKF) to disarm Tamil forces in Sri Lanka. India is forced to withdraw the IPKF (1989–1990) after its troops are drawn into combat.

November 1989: Beset by corruption scandals and popular unhappiness with price hikes, Rajiv Gandhi's Congress Party loses the ninth national elections. A fragile right-wing/communist anticorruption coalition assumes power under the premiership of V. P. Singh.

January 1990: Explosions and border skirmishes in Jammu and Kashmir after months of increased violence, strikes, and terrorism led by Kashmir Liberation Front (KLF) and dozens of other groups in Srinagar. During the following years, governor's rule is declared, local officials suspended, martial law and curfews imposed. Despite the presence of more than half a million Indian troops, the largest anywhere since World War II, fundamentalists seeking independence or union with Pakistan continue their terrorist campaign; an estimated forty thousand Kashmiris die in the violence from 1989 to 1994.

August 7, 1990: V. P. Singh's coalition government announces implementation of the 1980 Mandal Commission recommendation to increase share of government jobs reserved to low-caste people ("backward classes") to 27 percent. High-caste students and professionals mount demonstrations and legal challenges; the controversy brings down Singh's government on November 7.

October 30, 1990: Thousands of preventive arrests fail to avert a mass gathering of Hindus, including the leader of a government coalition party, at Babri Masjid in Ayodhya, Uttar Pradesh. This mosque was built by Babur, who reigned from 1527 to 1530, on the supposed birthplace of Rama, a holy Hindu site; demonstrators want to replace the mosque with a temple to Rama.

November 7, 1990: With resignation of V. P. Singh, Chandra Shekhar, leader of a group of dissident Socialists, is invited to become prime minister. But he serves only with the support of Rajiv Gandhi and will be forced to resign in March 1991.

November 27, 1990: Government places Assam under direct rule to curb continuing separatist violence by Bodo tribesmen; the insurgency continues.

1991: Indian troops join the UN observer mission during the Persian Gulf War.

January 27, 1991: "No attack" nuclear treaty with Pakistan, first proposed in 1985 and signed December 1988, takes effect.

May 21, 1991: Rajiv Gandhi is assassinated by a Tamil suicide bomber in Tamil Nadu while campaigning during national elections, ending the Nehru dynasty that has dominated Indian politics since independence. Congress Party is returned to government in the final rounds of elections (June 12 and 15) thanks to a "sympathy vote," while losing support in the northern heartland, the Gandhis' traditional stronghold. Gandhi is succeeded as Congress Party president by party elder P. V. Narasimha Rao, former disciple of Mahatma Gandhi and Nehru and a cabinet minister in Indira and Rajiv Gandhi's administrations.

July 24, 1991: Addressing an economic crisis, the government abandons its long-held policy of central economic planning.

1992: Exposure of a $2 billion bank and securities fraud by brokers and bankers. A 1994 government report blames both government and financial institutions.

A UN report names India as Third World's biggest buyer of conventional arms during the previous five years: military purchases totaled $12.2 billion.

December 6, 1992: Hindu extremists destroy the Babri Masjid mosque in Ayodhya, setting off the worst nationwide communal violence since independence. An estimated 1,200 people are killed, 5,000 injured. A government White Paper (February 1993) blames state governments for mismanaging the crisis; four state governments are replaced by President's rule. After years of official inquiries, dozens of senior Hindu political and religious leaders are charged with conspiracy (September 1997).

September 7, 1993: In a landmark agreement signed in Beijing by prime ministers Rao and Li Peng, India and China agree on bilateral troop reductions along their common border pending a final boundary agreement.

January 31, 1995: An Amnesty International report charges Indian government with thousands of illegal executions in Kashmir since 1990 in repressing separatist move-

ment. International Commission of Jurists report (March 2, 1995) accuses Indian security forces of torturing prisoners in Kashmir and alleges Pakistani government complicity in separatist terrorism there.

June 3, 1995: Mayawati, sworn in as chief minister of Uttar Pradesh, becomes the first *dalit* ("oppressed," or untouchable) to head a state government.

July 28, 1995: Bombay's name is changed to Mumbai (Bambai in Hindi) following a decision by the state government of Maharashtra.

Early 1996: Greatest corruption scandal in India's history breaks with revelation of Delhi businessman's payment of $18 million in bribes since 1990 to Congress Party and Bharatiya Janata Party leaders. Several dozen politicians are charged; seven cabinet ministers resign.

April–May 1996: Congress Party is routed in general elections, winning its lowest-ever share (28 percent) of the vote. Rao resigns as prime minister (May 10) and, after being charged with corruption (June), resigns as Congress Party president (September 21) and parliamentary leader (December 19).

May 16–28, 1996: Atal Bihari Vajpayee, leader of the Bharatiya Janata Party, serves as prime minister after no party wins a majority in the elections. Although Vajpayee himself is regarded as a moderate, his party is perceived as anti-Muslim and almost aggressively nationalist. Realizing he could not win a vote of confidence on May 28, Vajpayee resigns and a coalition of centrists, leftists, and regional parties takes over.

August 20, 1996: India's veto of long-negotiated draft Comprehensive Nuclear Test Ban Treaty prevents its formal adoption by UN Conference on Disarmament. The veto is overridden by the UN General Assembly and signed by five nuclear-weapons powers (the United States, Russia, Britain, France, and China) on September 24, 1996. India and Pakistan refuse to sign, citing the advantage it offers nations with nuclear capability, and thus prevent the treaty's enactment into international law. India's veto is held responsible for its failure to win a two-year UN Security Council seat (October 1996).

1997: India's estimated population exceeds 1 billion.

April 1997: Inder Kumar Gujral becomes prime minister after a year of political instability, leading to the possibility of warmer relations with Pakistan.

June 1997: India commences talks with Pakistan in effort to resolve their long-standing issues.

July 25, 1997: Former cabinet minister and ambassador K. R. Narayan becomes first *dalit* president of India.

September 22, 1997: In a UN speech, India's prime minister Inder Kumar Gujral calls for negotiations with Pakistan on a mutual non-aggression pact and for UN monitoring of the Indo-Pakistani border.

February–March 1998: Results from the general election are inconclusive. Rajiv Gandhi's widow, Sonia Gandhi, an Italian, is persuaded to campaign for the Congress Party without herself standing for election; despite their loss at the polls, she is appointed party president on April 6.

March 19, 1998: Atal Bihari Vajpayee takes over as prime minister and forms a coalition government dominated by Hindu nationalists. Although this marks a remarkable comeback for Vajpayee, who was forced to resign after only thirteen days as prime minister (May 16–28, 1996), many observers worry about his government's possible policies in regard to India's Muslims, Pakistan, and nuclear weapons.

May 11–13, 1998: India conducts five underground nuclear tests, its first since 1974, and for the first time acknowledges itself to be a nuclear state. Pakistan responds by conducting its first nuclear test on May 28.

India

ARTS, CULTURE, THOUGHT, AND RELIGION

INDUS CIVILIZATION: 3000–1700 B.C.

3000 B.C.: Early Baluchistan settlements worship fertility goddess; the bull is also associated with religion.

3000–2600 B.C.: Symbolism in Early Harappan culture provides evidence of intellectual developments. Incised and painted marks on pots are currently interpreted as identifying owners. Religious symbols include buffalo and *Bos indicus* (Indian cattle) heads, *pipal* foliage.

2600–2000 B.C.: Inscriptions on seals, pottery, and household goods employ earliest system of writing on subcontinent. Although pictographic script, containing hundreds of symbols, is still undeciphered, it represents a lingua franca in use throughout the Mature Harappan civilization; current scholarly opinion assigns language to early Dravidian family.

The finest artworks of the Harappan civilization are small, square stamp seals, finely carved of steatite and polished. These usually incorporate an inscription and a mythic or real animal (bull, zebu, rhinoceros) or geometrical motifs. Individuals typically use them to mark ownership or seal packages; some, evidently of religious significance, serve as amulets. Stone carving and sculpture are to endure as India's most important art forms.

A new kind of finely decorated pottery heralds the arrival of the Mature Harappan period. Floral, geometric, or fish-scale designs are painted in overall designs on mass produced, wheel-thrown redware. Terracotta is also used to fashion expressive human and animal figurines. Sculptures of stone and high-quality bronze include animals and human and divine figures, the most famous being a Mohenjo-Daro bronze of a naked dancing girl. No evidence of monumental sculpture or painting survives from the Harappan culture.

Religion is pervasive in Mature Harappan civilization, although no temples are built. Terracotta mother-goddess figures are ubiquitous, as are depictions of tree spirits and stone and phallic representations resembling later Siva *lingam*. Rituals are associated with animal sacrifice, public wells and baths (including Mohenjo-Daro's famous Great Bath), and burials. Bulls, tigers, and elephants have ritual significance.

Harappans wear diverse ethnic styles of

dress, mostly unstitched garments. Men and women both wear strips of cloth draped and tied around the waist or used as shawls and wraps. Women ornament themselves with elaborate hairstyles and much jewelry, including bangles, earrings and nose orna-ments, and strings of beads worn around neck and waist.

Harappan pastimes include dice (the earliest known anywhere in the world), hopscotch, marbles, and other toys.

2000–1500 B.C.: Indo-Aryan develops in Harappan region as a distinct language.

VEDIC PERIOD: 1700–600 B.C.

1700–900 B.C.: Numerous dialects of Old Indo-Aryan, the musical, highly inflected language spoken by migratory Indo-European tribes (they are illiterate), spread through northern India and become commingled with local languages. Dravidian languages survive further southward as indigenous peoples migrate into the peninsula.

Aryan society is marked by three-class social structure: *brahmans* (priests); *kshatriyas* (warrior-rulers who become landowners, military leaders, nobles); and *vaishyas* (ordinary clan members). These classes, or *varnas* (literally, colors), are associated with white, red, and brown respectively, perhaps deriving from skin tones, and institute a long Indian history of hierarchy and color. Modern scholars disagree whether the Indian caste system derives from the Aryan *varna* or *jati* (kinship group).

Ethnically heterogeneous, Indo-European immigrants nevertheless develop religious practices and ideas that become widely accepted. As Aryan language and social ideas are assimilated, Aryan religion, too, becomes mingled with traditional practices. The Vedic religion, also called Brahmanism, is pantheistic; gods personify natural forces and include Agni (fire), Indra (war), Varuna (cosmic order), and Surya (sun). Its central rite is the fire sacrifice, performed by *brahmans* closely identified with ruling *kshatriyas*. Religious observances incorporate music and dance.

Pastimes include chariot racing, wrestling, hunting, animal fights, gambling, music (lutes, flutes, harps, drums accompany songs), and dancing. There is widespread use of wine and the intoxicants *soma* (used in important religious rites) and *sura*.

1500–1000 B.C.: *Rig Veda* (Knowledge of Prayers), the oldest and most sacred part of the Vedas, is composed and compiled over generations. It includes tales of Vishnu and Siva. The oldest religious text in the world and chief text of orthodox Hinduism, its thousand hymns are transmitted orally by priests until first recorded *c.* 600 B.C. *Rig Veda* is composed in the Vedic language, Old Indo-Aryan, largely in the Sapta Sindhu region; besides its religious and literary value, it is an important source for north Indian history.

1000 B.C.: Development of sacrificial Brahmanistic rituals emphasizes correct performance.

1000–500 B.C.: The second great period of urbanization in the Gangetic region is now identified by two stages of fine pottery production: Painted Grey Ware (*c.* 1000–450 B.C.) and Northern Black Polished Ware (*c.* 600–200 B.C.). Culture is also characterized by production of burnt brick, bone and ivory carvings, and worship of mother goddess.

800–600 B.C.: Religious texts basic to Hindu doctrine proliferate; they are the intellectual precursors of Buddhist and later Indian philosophy. Continuous revision makes these works difficult to date precisely. Their language, Late Vedic, shows the convergence of Indo-Aryan and indigenous languages.

Later Vedic *samhitas* (collections of poems and songs) include: (1) *Samaveda* (hymns; chanting style invented this period is still in present-day use); *Yajurveda* (ritual formulas); *Atharvaveda* (magic charms and spells). (2) *Brahmanas*: prose works explaining procedures for and meanings of increasingly complex rituals, the preserve of *brahmans*. (3) *Aranyakas* (Forest Texts): discourses on mystical significance of ritual sacrifice, written by sages living contemplative lives in the forest.

800–550 B.C.: So-called Brahmana Period: Sacrificial rituals become increasingly elaborate and widely practiced. As repositories of ritual texts, chants, and performance practice, priests monopolize magical powers and interpretation of *dharma* (religious law); often, in concert with rajas, they appropriate tremendous power and wealth.

8th century B.C.: Collection of history and traditions, later incorporated in epics and *Puranas*, are attributed to Lomaharsana.

700 B.C.: Religious, philosophical, and social reaction against orthodox sacrificial Brahmanism germinates in the Gangetic plain, particularly among *kshatriyas*. Mysticism and meditation fundamental to this movement are to become central to Indian religious thought and practice: new doctrine leads to rise of hermits, itinerant mendicants, ascetics (*munis*), who gradually supplant *brahmans* as holders of spiritual knowledge.

700–500 B.C.: Composition of the *Upanishads*, abstract philosophical works completing Vedic canon and forming foundation texts of classical Hindu philosophy; they introduce central concepts including *atman* (individual soul) and *brahman* (world soul), transmigration of souls, and *karma* (moral causation). Of many so-called Upanishads, various religious traditions recognize ten to eighteen as revealed scripture. Teachings based on these works are called *Vedanta* (end, or culmination, of the Vedas).

EMERGENCE AND DECLINE OF EMPIRES: 600 B.C.–A.D. 300

600–200 B.C.: Sutra Period. Aphoristic supplements to Vedic texts, sutras in the aggregate comprise a sort of encyclopedia on Vedic customs and law. They are numerous, their relationship complex, and exact dates of composition uncertain. They are grouped into six major divisions of *Vedangas* (branches of learning): *Chandas Sutras* (prosody); *Siksa Sutras* (phonetics); *Nirukta Sutras* (etymology); *Vyakarana Sutras* (grammar); *Jyotisa Sutras* (astronomy); *Kalpa Sutras* (ritual), in turn divided into *Srauta-* (ritual sacrifice), *Grihya-* (domestic ceremonial), *Dharma-* (civil code) *Sutras*.

c. 563 B.C.–483 B.C.: Probable lifespan of Siddhartha Gautama, the Buddha (traditional dates 623–544/543 B.C.). He achieves enlightenment at Bodh Gaya, in present-day Bihar, and after *c.* 528 B.C. lives as an itinerant preacher, rejecting Vedic and Brah-

manic authority. Based in northern provinces, where a number of anti-Brahmanic sects are fermenting, Buddhist monasticism introduces celibacy, discipline, yogic practice, and begging to Indian religious life. Survival of the sect is problematic at Buddha's death, for he leaves no written teachings.

c. 540–468 B.C.: Probable lifespan of Vardhamana Mahavira (traditional dates 600–528 B.C.), the twenty-fourth and final Jain *tirthankara* (ford-maker), a line of great teachers given the title of *jina* (spiritual victor). Through his preaching in north India, Jainism is established as major religion. Adherents, mostly *kshatriya* merchants and landowners, are found throughout subcontinent by the third century B.C. Jainism takes as central the ethical precept of *ahimsa* (nonharming); its practices of asceticism, fasting, and vegetarianism become important strands in Indian spiritual life and in the twentieth century are central to the philosophy of Mahatma Gandhi.

500 B.C.: Yaska's *Nirukta*, an etymological study of archaic Vedic. Linguistics, essential to the study of Vedic texts, is the earliest Indian science to be systematized. Panini's *Astadhyayi*, a scientific grammar of classical Sanskrit regarded as one of the greatest linguistics texts ever written, contains four thousand *sutras*. Its completeness and the large exegetical literature it inspires (the greatest being Patanjali's *Mahabhashya*, 2d century B.C.) halt the natural development of Sanskrit and perpetuate its position as the preeminent language of Indian learning and literature for another two thousand years.

500 B.C.–A.D. 1000: Prakrits, vernacular dialects used for everyday speech, evolve from Old Indo-Aryan languages during what is sometimes called the Middle Indo-Aryan Period of language development. Among the most important of the early Prakrits are Pali (the language of Buddhist scriptures), Maharashtri, Magadhi, and the Ardhamagadhi, or half-Magadhi, adopted by Jains.

c. 484 B.C.: Death of Makkhali Gosala. He dissolves a long association with Mahavira to found the heterodox Ajivika sect, a rival to Buddhism and Jainism based on strict determinism and extreme self-mortification. The sect flourishes in Gujarat *c.* 4th–2d centuries B.C. under Mauryan patronage.

c. 480 B.C.: First Buddhist Council held at Rajagraha soon after Buddha's death to recite his teachings for accurate oral transmission of doctrine. Second Buddhist Council meets at Vaishali *c.* 380 B.C. amid deepening rifts over monastic discipline.

400 B.C.: Composition in Pali of *Tipitaka*, the oldest complete Theravada Buddhist scriptural canon. It includes Buddha's teachings and *Jakatas*, five hundred stories that form the basis of Buddhist iconography. *Tipitaka* is codified *c.* 250 B.C. and first recorded in Ceylon *c.* 100 B.C. (It will become more widely known by its Sanskrit title, *Tripitaka*.)

400–100 B.C.: Composition of the *Ramayana*, traditionally attributed to the poet-sage Valmiki and regarded as the first literary poem in Sanskrit. Siva here emerges as a separate, powerful god. A verse epic of the life of Prince Rama and his wife Sita, *Ramayana* is considered by some writers as an allegorical treatment of Aryans' conflict with and ultimate conquest of indigenous peoples on the jungle frontier *c.* 6th–5th centuries B.C.

400 B.C.–A.D. 400: Composition of the *Mahabharata*, India's great folk epic of the Bharata War *c.* 900 B.C. This encyclopedic Sanskrit work, the world's longest poem, mixes historical figures and legend in a profusion of poems, myths, and legends elaborated by centuries of oral transmission and augmentation. Together with *Ramayana*, it is a seminal work of Indian culture.

c. 321–184 B.C.: Mauryan court life is rich and luxurious. Imperial clothing incorporates gold and pearls, buildings are carved and gilded, decorated with large terracotta figures. Primary royal sport is hunting. Animal fights (bulls, elephants, rhinoceroses) are also popular.

300 B.C.: Writing down of the *Dhammapada*, which contains the true teachings of the Buddha, recorded by his disciples. A popular and enormously influential text in Pali verse, it is a foundation text of Theravada Buddhism.

Composition of fables known as *Panchatantra*. These Sanskrit verses are transmitted orally until being recorded *c.* 4th century A.D. Their subsequent translation into Arabic and Persian reaches a wide audience, and they exert a profound influence on world literature.

300 B.C.–A.D. 200: Old Tamil Period, also called the Sangam Age. Earliest Tamil inscriptions date *c.* 3d century B.C. Early Tamil literary works, mostly poems dealing with love and war, are the earliest in any Dravidian language and comprise an outstanding classical literature; works of 470 poets are compiled in anthologies collectively called *sangam*. The corpus includes *Ettuttogai* (Eight Anthologies), *Pattuppattu* (Ten Songs), *Padirruppattu* (Ten Tens), and a set of eighteen works including the famous *Tirukkural*. This last work—sometimes known as the *Tiruvalluvar* (after its otherwise unknown author) and sometimes called merely the *Kural* or *Kurral* (after the short couplets that make up the work)—is a collection of moralistic aphorisms.

c. 269–233 B.C.: Buddhism is the overriding influence on Ashoka's reign after his conversion *c.* 260 B.C. While also supporting Jains and Ajivikas, he promulgates Buddhist teachings of righteousness, compassion, reverence and makes the first recorded pilgrimage to Buddhist holy sites *c.* 249 B.C. Buddhism's rise into a major world religion is attributed to Ashoka's dispatching of missionaries to south India, Ceylon, the Himalayas, and Southeast Asia.

Throughout the Mauryan kingdom, Ashoka and later rulers erect thousands of *stupas*, monasteries, and monumental freestanding stone pillars incised with lengthy Buddhist inscriptions, the majority erected along major trade and pilgrimage routes. The excavation of chambers in living rock to be used for meditation or religious retreat (most famously the Barabar Caves, Bihar) begins a thousand-year-long Indian tradition.

Ashoka's edicts are the earliest extant written materials of Indian history and a rich source of religious and political information. Incised on rocks, cave walls, and pillars throughout the vast empire, these edicts promulgate *dharma* (law), the Buddhist code of conduct. Mostly in the Magadhi language, the majority are recorded in Brahmi, the earliest and most widely used of south Asian scripts.

Artistic revival under the Mauryans of stone sculpture, little practiced since the Indus civilization but reemerging in sophisti-

cated form: naturalistic, well-proportioned forms are distinguished by "Mauryan polish." The finest examples of Mauryan art are symbolic carved capitals and animals crowning Ashokan pillars (the lion capital near Sarnath is now India's national emblem). *Yaksi* and *yaksa* figures (female and male earth-spirits) and terracotta plaques are common. Buddhist iconography is created.

253? B.C.: Third Buddhist Council, summoned by Ashoka to Pataliputra to consider doctrine; according to tradition, the Council also completes the *Tipitaka* (or *Tripitaka*).

3d–2d centuries B.C.: Badarayana's *Uttaramimamsa Sutras* (also called *Vedanta Sutras* or *Brahma Sutras*), simplified version of Brahmanic teachings prepared in response to growing heterodox movements. It is a central Vedanta text.

2d–1st centuries B.C.: Rebuilding of the great *stupa* at Sanchi: the original Ashokan *stupa* is doubled in size to 120 feet in diameter, enclosed by a stone railing and *toranas* elaborately carved with religious narratives and cosmological symbolism. *Stupas*, the most characteristic Buddhist and Jain art form from Ashoka onward, are the earliest surviving religious architecture in India. During this period, clockwise circumambulation of *stupas* becomes central to Buddhist devotional rites.

200 B.C.–A.D. 200: Numerous cave temples are excavated from rock cliffs for religious retreat and meditation; frequently painted or carved, they develop into a major art form. Among the earliest examples are the Sungadynasty caves at Bhaja, Maharashtra; the finely carved Chera-dynasty cave temple at Udayagiri-Khandgiri, Orissa; and the earliest caves at Ajanta, West Deccan.

2d century B.C.–1st century A.D.: Emergence of Mahayana (great vehicle) Buddhism. Although this differs from the earlier Theravada (way of the elders; also called Hinayana, or lesser vehicle) school in points of fundamental doctrine and in having its own, Sanskrit scriptures, the two Buddhist schools continue to coexist as broad and sometimes overlapping movements.

2d century B.C.–3d century A.D.: A major southern school of art flourishes under Satavahana patronage at Amaravati, in modern-day Andhra Pradesh. Great *stupas* and some of India's finest sculptures are produced, generally in limestone or marble, and carved with tremendous vitality, complexity, and flow. Major Buddhist sites at Nagarjukonda and Amaravati, where magnificent *stupa* is completed *c.* A.D. 200. This school greatly influences Southeast Asian art.

150 B.C.: A great flowering of Buddhist art, particularly of stone sculpture, comes under the Sunga and Satavahana dynasties. Relief carvings on balustrades and *toranas*, or gateways, at monastery at Bharhut, Madhya Pradesh, are outstanding examples of Sunga art. Images include complex narrative reliefs, iconic representation of deities, symbolic representations of Buddha. Sunga art is also notable for terracotta figures, often *yaksis* and *yaksas* or monumental Buddhas.

100 B.C.–A.D. 300: Probable writing down of the *Bhagavad Gita*, the central Hindu text of devotion and social ethics in which the god Krishna occupies the central role. It is incorporated in the *Mahabharata* (sixth book) and becomes a central text of Vedanta.

100 B.C.–A.D. 400: Composition in south India of *Prajnaparamita Sutras*, a central text on enlightenment and one of the earliest scriptures of Mahayana Buddhism.

1st century B.C.: The Saka is the first dynasty known to employ Sanskrit as the official language of government.

1st century B.C.–1st century A.D.: Composition of *Natyashastra*, earliest and most comprehensive treatise in voluminous Indian literature on theater, dance, and music. Attributed to Bharata, it sets out rules for dramatic composition, grammar of classical dance, and aesthetic theory of *rasa* (wholeness) that are followed by generations of writers and performers.

Early 1st century A.D.: The Karle cave temple in Maharashtra contains a fine example of a rock-cut *chaitya* hall (cave used for purposes of worship). This vaulted, apsidal sanctuary is cut 124 feet deep into living rock and contains elaborately carved columns along its nave, a forty-five-foot vaulted ceiling, and a *stupa*.

1st century A.D.: Asvaghosha, a Mahayana Buddhist scholar and saint and the earliest known poet and dramatist of classical Sanskrit literature, flourishes at Kanishka's court at Peshawar. He helps to establish the canon of Mahayana Buddhism. His great literary work is *Buddhacarita*, an epic treatment of Buddha's life.

***c.* 50:** According to the tradition of the Syrian Christian Church of Kerala, St. Thomas undertakes a Christian mission to India. Church tradition also suggests that Thomas visits court of Parthian Gondophares during his reign (*c.* A.D. 20–50) in Punjab.

***c.* 78:** According to tradition, a fourth and final Buddhist Council, summoned to Kashmir by Kanishka and dominated by Theravada followers, authorizes commentaries on the Buddhist canon. Kanishka, a Buddhist convert, sends Buddhist missionaries to Central Asia and China during his reign (the traditional Chinese date is 217 B.C.).

***c.* 79:** Jains split into Svetambara (white-clad) and Digambara (sky-clad, or naked) sects in the first of many such schisms; the sects have different scriptures and cosmology.

1st–2d centuries: Under the influence of Mahayana Buddhism, the earliest anthropomorphic representations of Buddha appear. Appearing more or less simultaneously in Gandhara and Mathura, they already incorporate the elongated earlobes, third eye, and cranial protuberance that are to become conventions in depicting Buddha.

2d century: Height of Gandharan, or Indo-Greek, art in the northwest, especially Peshawar and Taxila, under Kushan imperial and noble patronage. Unique in the long history of Indian art, works exhibit Buddhist content and classical Greco-Roman modeling and costume. Sculptures predominate, usually of gray schist—statues, portraits, narrative relief carvings, Mahayana saints and *bodhisattvas* (enlightened beings who devote themselves to the improvement of humans) are common. Gandharan-style art is produced in some peripheral territories for six centuries.

150–250: fl. Nagarjuna, a Buddhist philosopher under the patronage of Kanishka; works attributed to him (which may be the work of several conflated authors) underpin the Madhyamika (Middle Path) school of Mahayana Buddhism and enter the Tibetan and Chinese Buddhist canons.

2d–early 3d centuries: Compilation of *Sattasai* (also called *Gathasaptasati*) important early Prakrit anthology of seven hundred erotic hymns in the Maharashtri dialect, attributed to but more probably sponsored by Satavahana king Hala.

2d–3d centuries: Mathura is the center of the finest Kushan dynasty art production. Sculpture is purely indigenous in style, with soft, rounded figures, chiefly of red sandstone; both religious and secular figures are sensuously, even voluptuously rendered. *Yaksis, bodhisattvas*, ancient fertility goddesses alike are incorporated into Buddhist iconography. Patrons are typically monks or nuns.

3d century: Vajrayana (Thunderbolt, or Diamond Vehicle), an esoteric and Tantric aspect of Mahayana Buddhism, spreads from its point of origin in eastern India. Within a few centuries, its exacting yogic and ritual practices are established strains of both Buddhism and Hinduism.

c. 300: Composition of Patanjali's *Yoga Sutras*, a classical treatise on yoga.

3d–4th centuries: fl. Bhasa, Sanskrit dramatist and author of thirteen plays, most based on *Mahabharata* and *Ramayana*. Among them are the oldest Sanskrit dramas to survive intact.

NEW EMPIRES IN NORTH AND SOUTH: 300–700

Early 4th century: The *Puranas* (Ancient Tales), a massive compendium of tales based on earlier material, undergoes substantial revision. The new version of this central text, an encyclopedia of legends, myths, and customary observances, reflects elevation of Vishnu and and Siva. Of its eighteen *mahapuranas* the Vaishnava *Bhagavata Purana* achieves the widest popularity.

4th century: *Panchatantra*, the oldest collection of Sanskrit fables, is first recorded after five hundred years of oral transmission.

4th century: Sudraka writes *Mricchakatika* (The Little Clay Cart), a ten-act Sanskrit play beloved for its earthy social realism. Sanskrit drama, an upper-class Gupta diversion, is generally associated with religion and romance; Sudraka breaks with convention in lacing his love story with such unromantic subjects as gamblers, murder, and the mud and filth of city life.

4th–6th centuries: Gupta sculpture, known for its elegance and simplicity, is classical period of plastic art in India. It refines earlier Kushan conventions, depicting gods and goddesses and narrative legends and myths. Sarnath and Mathura are major centers for production of sculpture. Artists in Sarnath, Uttar Pradesh, specialize in Buddhist temple sculpture; the simple, serene style developed there is to exert profound influence on sculpture in central and eastern India and southeast Asia. Workshops in Mathura, by contrast, produce images for Buddhists, Jains, Vaishnavites, and Saivites alike; much of their work is exported.

Late 4th century: Rise of Vaishnavism, the religion of most of the Gupta emperors. This sect introduces the elaboration of *avatars* (incarnations) of deities and the cult of Vishnu's consort Lakshmi. Saivism is the most important among other sects that emerge in Hindu resurgence under Gupta rule.

399–414: Faxian, a Buddhist monk and the first Chinese pilgrim to India, spends more than ten years seeking Buddhist texts in north India and Ceylon. His chronicle of Buddhist India is a major historical source for the Gupta age.

c. **400:** Asanga founds Yogacara, the second great school of Mahayana Buddhism stressing meditation and the practice of yoga. Monastic Hinayana Buddhism continues to be practiced as well, particularly in north India.

c. **5th century:** Vatsyayana writes *Kamasutra*, classic manual on art and technique of love. In addition to erotic practice, the work considers at length the life of a sophisticated citizen (*nagaraka*).

Early 5th century: Kalidasa, India's greatest classical poet and dramatist, is one of the "nine gems" at the court of Chandragupta II. His major plays include *Sakuntala* (the name of the heroine), *Meghaduta* (The Cloud Messenger), and two of the six Sanskrit *mahakavyas* (great poems), *Kumarasambhava* and *Raghuvamsa*.

The first Hindu structure temple is constructed at Sanchi. Its basic form is a simple flat-roofed shrine room and porch with carved pillars and doors. As structure temples develop, cave temples continue to be built, copied from Buddhist prototypes and in some cases created in remodeled Buddhist *caitya* halls.

5th century: The fifth and lowest social class of "untouchables," *panchamas*, mentioned theoretically in early Vedic works, is institutionalized in Indian society. *Panchamas* are required to live apart from main settlements; they perform occupations regarded as unclean, for example, sanitation and work involving dead human beings or animals.

Compilation of the first Tamil grammar, *Tolkappiyam*.

453 or 456: Jain canon is finalized at Second Council at Valabhi. Jainism coexisting with Brahmanism, Vaishnavism, Saivism, and Buddhism, is strongest in Karnataka, Gujarat, and Rajasthan.

Late 5th century: The earliest Gupta cave paintings are executed at the Bagh caves in western Malwa, a monastic settlement consisting of a series of ten carved and painted rock-cut sanctuaries. Ajanta cave temples enter their final phase (until the early 7th century): twenty-four of Ajanta's thirty halls date from the period, with walls, ceilings, columns painted with anthropomorphic Buddhist images and narratives, especially from *Jakata* tales. Painted caves widespread, probably executed by professional artists.

5th–6th centuries: The great Buddhist university and monastery at Nalanda in Bihar (founded several centuries earlier) flourishes, teaching both Mahayana Buddhist doctrine and Vedic disciplines to students from as far away as China. Buddhism comes under increasing pressure from new *bhakti* religions.

6th century: Tiruvalluvar composes his *Kural*, sometimes called "the Tamil *Veda*" and regarded as one of south India's greatest literary treasures.

Bharavi writes the Sanskrit *mahakavya* (great epic) *Kiratarjuniya*.

The earliest, greatest Tamil epic, *Silappadikaram*, is written by Jain monk Ilango; another of the five great Tamil epics, *Manimekhalai*, is written by Sathanar, a Buddhist.

c. **535–550:** The Siva cave-temple is excavated on Elephanta Island, Bombay. Its huge sculptures, including a triple-headed Siva, date from the late 8th century.

c. **578:** Rich shrines to Siva and Vishnu are created at the Badami cave-temples in Karnataka. These caves, containing the earliest major program of Hindu mythological sculpture, are prototypes for later temples, which are filled with sculpted and carved images as image worship becomes central to Hindu practice.

Late 6th–8th centuries: Mahayana Buddhism is carried to Ceylon, Tibet, China, Japan, and Southeast Asia by missionaries including Bodhidharma (*c.* 480–520), Padmasambhava, and Kukai.

Saiva cave-temples are built at Ellora in Maharashtra and at Aurangabad.

6th–9th centuries: Development and spread of *bhakti* (devotional worship). Vaishnavism and Saivism are spread by *bhaktas*, wandering teachers, seers, and saints from south India who teach and sing their devotional poetry throughout India. Sri Nathamuni compiles *Nalayira Prabandham*, four thousand hymns of the twelve Vaishnavite *Alvars*, including Nammalvar and Sri Andal. Saivite hymns of Sambandar, Appar, Tirumular, Sundarar, and other *Nayanars* (devotees of Siva) are collected by Nambi-Andar-Nambi into eleven *Tirumurais*. Both collections achieve scriptural status. Vaishnavism and Saivism form the foundation of orthodox Hinduism, which gradually displaces Buddhism and Jainism.

c. 600: The bodhi tree at Bodh Gaya, site of the Buddha's enlightenment, is cut down; a Hindu shrine is erected. Enormous brick Mahabodhi temple is built there (late 6th–7th centuries).

c. 600–630: Pallava king Mahendravarman I is converted by Appar from Jainism to Saivism. His capital at Kanchi becomes a Saivite center, and Saivite temples are erected throughout his kingdom. The royal conversion is a blow to Jainism in south India.

606–647: King Harsha, a great patron of learning, is himself a noted poet: three Sanskrit plays are ascribed to him: *Nagananda* (The Happiness of Serpents), *Priyadarsika* (The Beautiful Lover), and *Ratnavali* (The Pearl Necklace).

Harsha's court poet Bana writes *Harsha-carita*, a Sanskrit prose romance on his patron's reign. Despite its epic literary treatment, it is regarded as the first biography in India.

7th century: Rise of the Sakti cult in east India introduces worship of female principle to Hinduism. Reviving worship of the mother goddess from old fertility cults, the Sakti cult is closely associated with Saivism and prefigures the creation of consorts for male gods.

Buddhism is declining, with a rise of heterodox cults. According to tradition, a conference convened by Harsha at Kanauj is attended by thousands of kings, priests, and representatives of various Buddhist cults.

Casting of life-size statue of Buddha at Sultanganj, Bihar, indicates a thriving tradition of metalwork.

c. 625: First written mention of chess (Sanskrit *chaturanga*). Game pieces are based on the four branches of the Indian army.

632: Death of Muhammad, founder of Islam.

c. 650: Magha composes the Sanskrit *mahakavya Sisupalavadha*.

c. 660–710: fl. Dandin, an outstanding writer of Sanskrit prose. His works include *Dasakumaracarita* (The Adventure of Ten Princes), a picaresque prose romance of city life, and *Kavyadarsa*, a major treatise on Sanskrit poetics.

c. 670: Finest group of Pallava Hindu mythological carvings is executed at Mamallapuram temples, an unfinished but grand complex of sculpted cliffs, rock-cut shrines and caves, and structural temples (c. 630–728). Another outstanding example of south Indian temple-building is Kailasanatha temple at Kanchipuram (c. 700–728).

REGIONAL KINGDOMS: 700–1200

Early 8th century: Tantric Buddhist missionaries Vajrabodhi and Amogavajra visit China. After the eighth century, Tantric Buddhism is firmly established from Bengal into north India, Nepal, Tibet, China, Japan, and Southeast Asia. It greatly influences

Hindu and Buddhist ritual and artistic production.

8th century: Composition of Kutulaha's *Lilavati*, an early novel in Prakrit verse. Novels, written in verse or prose and usually mixing historical subjects with fantasy and fiction, are a popular secular genre of the time.

The *Jivaka-Cintamani*, regarded as one of the greatest Tamil literary works, is composed by Tiruttakkadeva.

The Arab conquest of Sind (712) brings Islam to the subcontinent. The new religion slowly becomes established through colonization and forced conversion.

730: Death of the Sanskrit dramatist Bhavabhuti, author of the court comedy *Malatimadhava* and two plays based on the *Ramayana*.

Mid-8th century: Period of the first large temples in India begins. Hundreds of temples are built in Orissa; the primary sites include Bhubaneshwar (major temples include Lingaraja and Rajarani [*c.* 1000] and Puri (Jagannatha shrine).

750–1150: Buddhism flourishes in east India under Pala patronage. The Palas found new universities at Vikramasila and Paharpur, endow a great Buddhist university at Nalanda.

c. **775:** Kailasa temple, Ellora, is founded under Rastrakuta patronage. Sacred to Siva, it is a freestanding monolithic structure carved out of a volcanic hill and richly sculpted inside and out with huge devotional figures.

c. **788–820:** Saivite philosopher Sankara further develops Vedanta. He travels throughout India, publicly propounding his monistic doctrine of Advaita and founding four seminaries modeled on Buddhist organization to propagate his teachings. His work shapes the philosophy and practice of Hinduism for centuries and is instrumental in driving Buddhism out of India.

9th century: Kamban writes his Tamil *Ramayana*, a classic of Indian literature.

The earliest surviving classic of Kannada literature, a treatise on poetics entitled *Kavirajamarga*, indicates that this vernacular

has been a well developed literary language for several hundred years.

Composition of *Bhagavata Purana*, a primary Vaishnavite text. Dozens of vernacular translations popularize this Sanskrit work, and its glorification of Krishna is to exert an enormous influence on Hindu practice and Indian culture.

c. **900:** fl. Rajasekhara, Sanskrit dramatist and lyric poet. His *Balaramayana* has been described as perhaps the longest play ever written.

c. **950–1050:** Construction of the temple complex at Khajuraho, Madhya Pradesh. Most of the more than eighty temples built around the lake are in *nagara* (northern) "temple-mountain" style, a tall square tower surmounting the main cell. Richly decorated with carving, painted plastered surfaces, and precious metals and gems, they are known for their exceptionally fine sculpture.

10th century: Zoroastrian refugees from religious persecution in Persia arrive and settle in Gujarat. They are the ancestors of modern-day Parsis (Persians).

10th–11th centuries: Compilation of *Charyapadas*, a collection of mystical songs that is the oldest literary work in a north Indian vernacular. Used by *bhakti* preachers, vernaculars such as Hindi, Oriya, Gujarati, Bengali, Marathi, Urdu, Kannada, and Telugu are gradually replacing Prakrit and Sanskrit as literary vehicles. Emerging languages are still fluid and closely related; several vernaculars claim *Charyapadas* as an ancestral work.

10th–12th centuries: Ranna, Pampa, and Ponna, the "three gems" of early Kannada literature, flourish, writing *campu*, a genre combining prose and verse.

c. **1000:** The greatest Chola temple is constructed at Thanjavur (Tanjore). Dedicated to Siva, it is typical of *dravida* (southern) style, its two hundred-foot pyramidal tower topped with a massive domed capstone. Profusely decorated with sculpture and wall paintings, *dravida* temples are distinguished by massive *gopuram* (gateways). Other outstanding examples include the Chola temples at Rajarajesvara and Gangaikondacolapuram.

Abhinavagupta writes monumental esthetic treatise in Sanskrit; it contains classic exposition of metaphysical basis of Hindu art.

1000–1250: Emergence of the new artistic genre of miniature painting. The paintings illustrate Buddhist and Jain manuscripts from Nepal, Gujarat, and eastern India as well as Hindu manuscripts from Rajasthan, Delhi, and Jaunpur. They are linear and flat in style and use a limited, bright palette.

c. 1031: A magnificently carved Jain temple in honor of Adinatha is completed at Mount Abu, four hundred miles northeast of Bombay. Jain temples differ in design from Hindu temples mainly by incorporating a large number of cells to hold sacred images. Jain temple building reaches its peak *c.* 1000–1400; other major temple sites include Satrunjaya and Girnar.

c. 1050: fl. Somadeva II, author of the huge compendium of folktales *Kathasaritsagara*.

c. 1070–1100: fl. Bilhana, Sanskrit poet of Kashmir whose works include *Vikramankadevacarita*, a life of Chalukya king Vikramaditya VI. Typical of local dynastic histories first produced during the period, it combines historical and legendary material in a finely crafted poetic narrative.

11th century: Nannaya begins translation of *Mahabharata* as a Telugu *champu* (it is completed by others in succeeding centuries). The work helps prompt a Hindu renaissance in the Telugu-speaking region.

11th–12th centuries: Bronze sculpture in the Chola kingdom, ranked by art historians among the finest works of art ever produced, reaches the height of elegance and refinement. Most are Saivite and Vaishnavite icons, ranging from a few inches high to life size; among the best known is the image of Siva as Lord of the Dance, one leg raised in front of him and encircled by fire. Chola sculptures are to exert a profound influence on Sinhalese and Southeast Asian art.

1137: Death of philosopher Ramanuja, founder of Srivaishnava sect. His works create a philosophical underpinning for the *bhakti* movement.

1159–1192: fl. Chand Bardai. His *Prithvirajarasau*, a long Hindi poem celebrating Prithviraja, last Hindu king of Delhi, is one of the earliest literary works written in a north Indian vernacular.

Late 12th century: Basava founds Virasaivism, popular Siva cult in Karnataka and Andhra. Also known as Lingayats, his *bhakti* sect flourishes under Chalukya patronage, ousting Jains from the region. Simple prose sermons (*vachanas*) by him and his followers become Kannada literary classics.

Jayadeva's operatic drama *Gita-Govinda* is composed at court of Sena kings of Bengal. Like other court literature, it is written in Sanskrit. Through linked songs and narrative, it celebrates the love of Krishna and his consort Radha; she becomes a favorite deity in Bengal thanks to the popularity of this work.

1173: Death of Hemachandra, an early Jain scholar at the court of Chalukya king Kumarapala, whom he converts to Jainism. Jainism flourishes under royal patronage at the Gujarati court; many temples and shrines are built in the region, and Jains are for centuries prominent in Rajput kingdoms in administration, military, and trade.

1197, 1203: The Muslim-Ghurid sack of monasteries at Nalanda and Vikramasila helps seal the end of Buddhism in India, brought about not only by the Mamluk destruction of their monasteries and libraries, but also by influences including the growth of popular *bhakti* sects; the decline of royal patronage on which monastic Buddhism depends; and the gradual assimilation of Buddhism into Hinduism. By the thirteenth century, Buddhist monks disperse to Tibet, Nepal, and southern India.

1198: Completion of first mosque in Delhi, Quwwat al-Islam Mosque.

12th–13th centuries: *Vasara* style of architecture develops in Deccan under Hoysala patronage. Temples at Halebid, Belur, and Somnathpur typify this style, characterized by squat, star-shaped structures with dense ornamental surface carving.

DELHI SULTANATE: 1211–1526

1197?–1276: Lifespan of Madhva, a philosopher.

Early 13th century: Persian is introduced as the official administrative language during the reign of Iltutmish, helping to unify conquered territories.

Early 13th century: Construction of late period Jaina temples in Rajasthan at Ranakpur, Mt. Abu, Jarsalmer, and elsewhere. They are built of sandstone and white marble, their interiors decoratively carved to translucent thinness.

The *bhakti* movement spreads northward from Karnataka, established in Maharashtra by Virasaivas, poet-saints, before being carried to northern India and Bengal. *Bhakti* devotional hymns, orally transmitted rhymed religious lyrics, are the major Hindu literary vehicle of period. Hindu mystics and Sufis share aversion to ritual, emphasizing personal devotion and love of God and use of poetry and song in religious practice; their relations are cordial, and much interchange of religious practice occurs.

1225: Qutb Minar, a detached, 238-foot minaret, is erected at Delhi, possibly to commemorate a Turkish victory (it towers imposingly over the Delhi plain). The Delhi sultans are great builders. They introduce minarets, domes, arches, portals, and ornamentation with calligraphic and geometrical designs.

1235: Death of Shaikh Mu'in ud-Din Chishti (born 1142). The Chistiya order founded by him, devoted to music, poetry, and the care of the poor, is the first and most important major Sufi order in India (*sufis* are Muslim mystics). His tomb at Ajmer becomes a Sufi pilgrimage site. Muslim scholars and Sufis pour into northern India ahead of the Mongol advance across Central Asia, bringing not only Islam, but Persian literature and science; they congregate in Bengal, from whence Islam is later carried to Southeast Asia.

1246–1266: Historian Minhaj ud-Din Siraj, author of *Tabakat-i-Nasiri*, history of the slave kings, holds high office at court of Nasir ud-Din. Historical writing, a major Islamic literary genre, flourishes in India during the Delhi sultanate and Mughal periods, introducing methodology different from traditional spiritual historical writing of Hindus.

c. 1250: Surya Temple is built at Konarak during reign of Ganga King Narasimhadeva (reigns 1238–1264). Based in design on the sun god's chariot, it is the last great Hindu temple built in north India. Kalinga (Orissa) temples, distinctive masses of richly ornamented and sculpted spires, reach their zenith during this period. Other famous examples include Ananta Vasudeva Temple (1278) and Vakeshvara Temple (*c.* 1300–1350), Bhubaneshwar.

1258 onward: Mongol invasions in Central Asia and the Near East produce a flood of refugee Muslim scholars, princes, writers, and artists. Balban's court becomes a haven for these immigrants and the sultan an enthusiastic patron of their culture. Persian ideas of divine kingship and decorous, highly ceremonial behavior at court also influence his reign.

1275–1296: Jnaneshvara, the foremost Maharashtrian poet-saint, writes enduring works of poetry and philosophy during his brief life. He is the first and widely regarded as the greatest Marathi poet; he writes his masterwork *Jnaneshvari* (1290), a poetical-philosophical commentary on the *Bhagavad Gita*, at the age of fifteen.

1295: Plunder of the famous Hindu temple at Somanatha during a Turkish raid into Gujarat.

13th–14th centuries: Urdu language develops as the medium for Turkish soldiers to communicate with local populations (*ordu*: Turki "army," "camp"). An amalgam of Turki, Persian, and the Hindi dialects around Delhi, Urdu combines Arabic script with largely Hindi grammar. It becomes widespread in northern India and later develops into a literary language.

14th century: The Kashmiri poet-saint Lal Ded flourishes. She abandons her husband and lives as a wandering ascetic. Her preaching and *bhakti*, written in the Kashmiri *vakh* form, popularize Saivism.

The most notable architectural achievements of the period are mosques. Among the greatest is the fortress-like Kalan Masjid (completed 1387) at Delhi.

Ramananda, the foremost north Indian *bhakti* leader and preacher in Hindi, preaches a message of inclusion and universalism, welcoming women and *shudras* (peasants) into his congregations; he inspires an enormous Hindi *bhakti* literature devoted to Rama.

1311: Alai Darwaja is built near Qutb Minar in Delhi. This fine gateway to the Quwwat al-Islam mosque complex, constructed for Ala ud-Din Khalji, incorporates a true arch and dome and is typical of early Indo-Muslim architecture in its use of red sandstone and marble and its calligraphic decoration.

1321: Tughluqabad founded at Delhi. The fort constructed there is the most famous Tughluq site still standing.

1325: The poet-musician Amir Khusrau (born 1253) dies after serving seven Delhi sultans. An Indian-born Sufi, he is a master Persian lyricist, author of extremely influential *ghazals* (a type of lyric couplet) and the epic *Khamsa*. An accomplished musician as well, he is reputed to have invented the *qawwali* (Indo-Muslim religious repertoire), of which his are the earliest surviving compositions.

***c.* 1325:** Ghiyas ud-Din Tughluq's tomb is built at Delhi. Tombs are new to India, for indigenous religions practice cremation. This structure demonstrates the military influence common to much Tughluq architecture, but borrows from the Khaljis the red sandstone and marble facing that Mughals will later develop into a rich architectural tradition.

1325–1351: Muhammad bin Tughluq, known for his love of philosophy and his broad intellectual sympathies, cultivates Jains and *yogis* at his court and is famous for participating in celebrations of the Hindu Holi festival, a holiday on which caste and gender distinctions are set aside and revelers throw colored water at one another. Arab travelers report the existence in Delhi of one thousand colleges and two thousand centers for mystics during his reign.

1341: Muhammad ibn Badr Jajarmi composes *Mu'nis al-Ahrar*.

1350–1550: Jain painting, a major indigenous painting tradition centered on Gujarat and Rajasthan, reaches its greatest refinement. Recognizable by the angular bodies and protruding eyes of their human figures, these paintings typically illustrate sacred Jaina texts such as the *Kalpa sutra*.

1351–1388: Firuz Shah Tughluq, himself an architect and engineer, is a notable builder: he founds Firuzabad, the fifth city at Delhi, and, according to his autobiography, builds thirty towns, one hundred each of palaces, tombs, and dams, and two hundred inns. Jaunpur (1359), a garrison town, is built in a distinctive massive architectural style and becomes a center of learning. Hisar-i Firuza (modern Hisar), built in the desert, is an ambitious project requiring much hydraulic engineering. After the fourteenth century an Indo-Muslim architectural style develops, fusing Turkish, Persian, and indigenous styles.

1356: Completion of Zia ud-Din Barani's *Tarikh-i-Firoz Shahi*, an account of the Delhi sultans.

15th century: Ironically, clan warfare and political chaos of the late sultanate produce a permanent legacy of fine architecture. Notable mosques include Atala Masjid (1408) and Jami Masjid (1438) at Jaunpur and the magnificent congregational Jami Masjid at Mandu (completed 1454). The Lodi sultans are known for their magnificent tombs.

1400: India's Muslim population is estimated at 3.2 million (1.8 percent of the population, up from 0.2 percent in 1200). Muslims comprise 10 percent of the population by 1535. Conversion, not immigration, is the major source of this increase. Sufism, with its popular appeal, is key to the spread of Islam in India: Hindus from the lowest and urban artisan castes convert in greater numbers than their higher-caste coreligionists.

c. **1400–1450:** At the same time that some Hindu temples in Gujarat are razed at the order of Ahmad I (1414), Gujarati architecture achieves great refinement under the patronage of Ahmad and his successors, continuing indigenous traditions while borrowing Persian raised domes and love of interior light and space. The new capital of Ahmadabad, an Islamic fortified city with strong Indian features, is the most important architectural center and becomes a city of tremendous wealth and power. Mahmud Begarha (reigns 1458–1511), another outstanding Gujarati builder, founds Janagadh and the new capital at Champaner.

1469–1539: Lifespan of Guru Nanak, the founder of the Sikh (meaning "disciple") religion. As a young man working as an accountant for a Muslim governor, he has a mystical experience that convinces him to set out and preach the need to live a life of prayer and service. Sikhism believes in one God; rejects the rituals, idols, priests, temples and mosques, and all such trappings of other religions; and stresses the need to seek union with God through service as well as prayer. It also stresses the tradition of the *guru*, the teacher, who provides knowledge of the essentials of the faith. There have been ten major gurus including Nanak, whose teachings are recorded in the *Adi Granth*. Although Nanak had called for pacifism, Sikhs will take up arms to defend themselves against Muslim persecutions and will eventually become famed soldiers in the Indian army.

SOUTH INDIA: VIJAYANAGAR EMPIRE, 1336–1565

1330s–1350s: Brothers Sayana and Madhava flourish under the patronage of Vijayanagar *rayas* as government ministers and Sanskrit scholars. Sayana's extensive Vedic commentaries, written under royal commission, contribute to a Hindu revival. As minister of Harihara I and Bukka I, Madhava is a chief architect of the Vijayanagar state; he is also a spiritual leader, philosopher, and author of Sanskrit verse.

1340s–1360s: Telugu poet Nachana Somana flourishes under the patronage of Bukka I, like other *rayas* a great patron of learning.

His major work is *Uttara-harivamsha*, based on the *Ramayana*.

1343: Completion of the city of Vijayanagar. The capital of an extremely prosperous state, it becomes one of the richest cities in the world, remarkable for its architectural grandeur, huge palaces, monumental gateways, and temples. Its population grows to an estimated half million people. Vijayanagar's material opulence and rich markets are a source of wonder to travelers.

1350s–1370s: Bukka I decrees that all religions are equal.

14th–15th centuries: Creation of *vachana sastra*, body of literature of some two hundred writers. These Kannada-dialect translations from Sanskrit, written by Virasaivas poet-saints, are important in dissemination of Hindu religious texts. Greatest poet is Naranappa (Kumaravyasa), translator of *Mahabharata*; other seminal translations include Narahari's *Torave Ramayana*, Vithalanatha's *Bhagavata Purana*.

Early 15th century: Arunagiri, outstanding *bhakti* poet, composes more than four thousand Tamil hymns to Muruga. He performs them at temples; more than a thousand are collected in *Tiruppugazh*.

1406–1424: Under Devaraya I, Vijayanagar becomes the premier south Indian center of learning and art. In his Pearl Hall, he showers artists, writers, and philosophers with gold and precious gems. Srinatha, called the "poet-emperor," serves as Devaraya II's court poet and travels widely, entering literary and poetry contests in Hindu courts all over south India. Like other Telugu writers of the period, his work consists largely of vernacular translations of Sanskrit texts. His near-contemporary Potana (1450–1510) produces the first Telugu translation of *Bhagavatam*. Annamacharya (1424–1503) is regarded as the father of the Telugu devotional lyric.

1424–1446: Devaraya II permits the construction of mosques and cemeteries in his empire.

Mid-15th century: Development of the distinctive "Vijayanagar temple style": religious complexes include a sanctuary; a separate "thousand-pillared" pavilion *(mantapa)*, the columns densely decorated with sculpture and carving; and shrines for deities' consorts. Enclosing walls incorporate towering gateways *(gopuras)* with tiers of carving; those at Kanchi temple are 188 feet (ten stories) high. Famous examples include Vitthala, Krishna, Ramachandra, Virupaksha temples in Vijayanagar and temples in Tadpatri and Lepakshi, south Andhra.

15th–16th centuries: Distinct regional cultures and languages flourish in period of political disunity. Literary flowering in indigenous languages owes much to rise of Vaishnava *bhakti*; the verse often blends religious and erotic elements. Mirabai (1498–1565), a princess of Mewad, is revered for her *padas*, intensely emotional lyrics devoted to God. The devotional verse celebrating the love of Radha and Krishna written by Vidypati (fl. 15th century), recited in both worship and dance, is important in Maithili, Hindi, and Bengali literatures.

c. 1479–1531: Vaishnavite philosopher Vallabhacharya founds Vallabh Sampraday, a Mathura sect. It is continued by a hereditary succession of leaders.

1485–1532: Chaitanya, Bengali mystic believed to be incarnation of Krishna, preaches in Orissa, Deccan, and elsewhere, spreading loving worship *(bhakti)* of Krishna. He attracts a huge number of followers of all castes and religions. His life and teachings start the Neo-Vaishnava movement and inspire a large body of biographical and devotional literature. (The modern-day Society for Krishna Consciousness follows his teachings.)

1486–1517: Man Singh Tomar, raja of Gwalior, builds magnificent palace (the only pre-Mughal palace to survive to the present day). His consort Mrignayana, a great patron of music, attracts musicians from all over India.

16th century: Brahmans wield enormous power in Vijayanagar. Hindu rites are elaborated with the addition of dance, drama, and music. Temples are community political and military centers—monastic orders *(mathas)* are close allies of local rulers—and sometimes incorporate schools and hospitals.

Early 16th century: Thunchat Ezhuttacchan (literally "father of letters"), a Kerala poet, writes in the relatively new Dravidian vernacular of Malayalam. He invents *kilippattu*, a melodious narrative form that becomes the basis of traditional Malayalam verse. His translations of Sanskrit texts, especially *Ramayana*, are read to large audiences.

1509–1529: King Krishnadevaraya is a great builder. He builds a new city at Nagalpur and palaces and outstanding temples throughout south India.

Golden age of Telugu literature. The *prabhanda*, tightly organized metrical stories based on *Puranas*, is a major genre. Among its most celebrated practitioners are Krishnadevaraya's court poet, Alasani Peddana *(Manu Charita)*; Timmana *(Parijatapaharanam)*; and the king himself *(Amuktamalyada)*.

1510: Franciscans construct the first European church in India at Portuguese Cochin.

1518: Death of the poet-saint Kabir. A low-caste weaver, he challenges traditional religious and social orthodoxy by denying the truth of both Hindu and Islamic beliefs, preaching instead a religion of love and devotional worship *(bhajan)*. His works are compiled in 1504 as *Kabir granthavali*.

c. 1550: Lakshmisha translates *Jaimini Bharata*, one of the most popular works of Kannada literature.

1564: Death of the poet-saint Purandaradasa,

founder of Karnatak musical system, one of India's major classical musical traditions. More than a thousand of his Kannada *kirtana*, devotional songs, still survive; they form the earliest surviving body of Dravidian-language *bhakti*.

1580: Death of Pingala Surana, author of *Kalapurnodaya*, an innovatory novel in Telugu verse. Other important contemporary Telugu writers include Ramaraja Bhushana and Venkatakavi. After the fall of Vijayanagar, Tanjore and Madurai are major Telugu cultural centers under the patronage of Nayak rulers.

c. 1590: Construction of the great temple at Srirangam, Tamil Nadu, a famous example of baroque splendor as Vijayanagar temple architecture spreads throughout Karnataka and Tamil Nadu under Nayak patronage. Notable contemporary temples in Tamil Nadu include Vellore, Kanchipuram, and Tiruvannamalai. The seventeenth-century Minakshi Sundareshvara Temple at Madurai, its "thousand-pillared hall" crowded with carvings of gods, mythical characters, donors, and animals, is one of the largest in India.

SOUTH INDIA: ISLAMIC STATES, 1300–1650

c. 1295–1325: Khalji invasions from the north bring Islam and Islamic cultural influences to northern Deccan. Establishment of the first major Muslim settlements in south India (excepting long-established coastal traders).

Early 14th century: Burhan al-Din (dies 1340) brings the Chishtiya order of Sufism from north to south India. Sufism is instrumental in the peaceful promulgation of Islam in the peninsular region. The population of the area, however, remains largely Hindu.

c. 1367: Completion of the Jami Masjid, a mosque unique in India in its Saracenic design, at Gulbarga. Mosques, palaces, pavilions, and tombs are built in first Bahmani

capital at Gulbarga as Bahmanis interrupt indigenous Deccani artistic traditions by introducing Islamic influences from the Delhi sultanate, Central Asia, and Persia.

1397–1422: High period of southern Islamic culture during the reign of Firuz Shah Bahmani, the most learned of the scholarly Bahmani sultans; Firuzabad is a great center of Islamic culture. In the late Gulbarga period (1347–1424), many fine buildings are constructed at the capital, among them Firuz Shah's own tomb at Haft Gumbaz and the shrine of fifteenth-century Sufi saint Gesudaraz.

15th century: The Dakhni language, early form of Urdu, develops in central and south

India. In addition to its borrowings from indigenous Dravidian languages, Urdu is further enriched as Muslim poets incorporate Persian and Arabic vocabulary and verse forms.

1472–1473: Mahmud Gawan's great *madrasa* (Islamic theological college) is founded in Bidar. It becomes center of Islamic scholarship, and is also renowned for its fine Persian architecture incorporating minarets, domes, and tiled facades. Mahmud Gawan is the greatest builder of the Bidar period (1424–1526), when the second Bahmani capital is filled with new mosques, palaces, shrines, and royal tombs.

1490–1686: Adil Khan's capital at Bijapur becomes a major Islamic cultural center. Bijapur is one of the richest south Indian states; among the architectural treasures of its capital are Mihtar Mahal, Jami Masjid, and Gol Gumbad, the tomb of Muhammad Adil Shah (reigns 1627–1656), featuring one of the largest domes in the world at the time of its construction. Bijapur is one of a number of major urban centers in south India during the period: its population eventually reaches half a million.

Early 16th century: Shiism, introduced to southern India by *pardesis*, becomes influential in south Muslim sultanates: Golconda's rulers are Shias, as are some rulers of Ahmadnagar (1509–1553) and Bijapur (*c.* 1510–1534, 1558–1582).

Portuguese intermarriage with local population (a deliberate policy of Viceroy Albuquerque to produce loyalists) produces a new ethnic group, Goans, or Luso-Indians. Lasting cultural influences include minority Catholic population as well as foods such as potatoes, tomatoes, and chilies.

1565: The loss of royal patronage after the fall of Vijayanagar induces artists and artisans to migrate to the rich courts at Bijapur and Golconda, where they develop distinctive schools of painting. Bijapur becomes India's second most important artistic center after Delhi thanks to patronage of Ibrahim Adil

Shah II (reigns 1579–1627). His painters employ Persian style and striking use of color in sensitive depictions of the private lives of royalty.

Late 16th century: The earliest Deccani school of painting, noted for its superb portraiture, flourishes in Ahmadnagar under patronage of Husayn Nizam Shah I (reigns 1554–1565), Murtaza I (reigns 1565–1588), and Burhan II (reigns 1591–1595).

The third major Deccani school of painting develops in Golconda, one of the world's richest cities. This style is notable for crowded compositions incorporating elaborate surface pattern and something of the luxuriant flavor of Hindu sculptural forms. Qutb Shahi sultans are lavish patrons of scholars and poets as well as painters. They also sponsor large-scale agriculture and irrigation projects and much building. Golconda's distinctive architectural style typically sets large domes on square, plain bases.

1591: Construction of Char Minar (Four Minarets) in the center of Hyderabad. This huge and elaborate four-arched gateway, supporting an elevated mosque, becomes the symbol of Hyderabad.

***c.* 1591–1596:** Sayyid Ali Tabataba writes *Burhan i Ma'asir,* a dynastic history of the Bahmanis and Nizam Shahis.

1624: Death of Sufi Ahmad Sirhindi (born 1564), an adherent of the austere reformist Naqshbandi sect recently introduced into India. He is the author of a celebrated collection of letters that is extremely influential in the development of Islamic thought in India.

***c.* 1635–1659:** fl. Kshetrayya, a musician in the Carnatic tradition whose peripatetic career takes him to the courts of Golconda, Tanjore, and Madurai. He is a composer of devotional and erotic Telugu lyrics in *pada* form, designed to be performed through both song and dance. His work becomes the oldest continuously performed repertory in India.

MUGHAL EMPIRE: 1526–1760

***c.* 1520–1529:** Composition of Babur's remarkable autobiographical *Babur-nama*, a Turkish-language classic.

1526–1530: Turkish language, customs, and culture (love of horses, pleasure gardens, love of symmetry and formal design, public architecture) are imported to India by Babur's court.

***c.* 1538–1545:** Sher Shah's magnificent tomb at Sasaram, Bihar, is one of the crowning achievements of Indo-Muslim architecture. Though brief, his reign is responsible for use of indigenous architectural tradition.

1540–1549: Humayun's Persian interregnum is decisive, for he is an aesthete and a great lover of nature and art and deeply absorbs Persian culture during his residence. Persian is dominant Mughal cultural influence and lasting legacy to Indian architecture, literature, gardens, manners, and dress. Persian language becomes widespread in imperial circles.

1541–1545: First great wave of Christian missionary activity is launched as the first Jesuit in India, the Spaniard Francis Xavier (1506–1552, canonized 1622), founds the mission to Coromandel and Malabar coasts' fishermen. In their zeal to win Christian converts, priests frequently take part in the government of Portuguese India.

1549: Mughal school of painting founded as Humayun brings Persian court masters Mir Sayyid Ali and Abd al-Samad to his court in exile in Kabul. They accompany him to Delhi (1555), where they train more than a hundred Indian artists in the imperial atelier, Persianizing indigenous Islamic, Hindu, and Jain traditions of miniature painting. Great Hindu artists include Daswanth, animal painter Miskin, and Basawan.

Mid-16th century: Thousands of devotional hymns to Krishna written in *bhakti* tradition are compiled in *Sursagar*, attributed to Surdas (1479–1584). Another famous *bhakti* poet is the mystic Dadu Dayal (1544–1603). Surdas writes in Braj-bhasha, which becomes the leading literary dialect of Hindi for two hundred years.

Akbar names as first poet laureate Ghazali Mashhadi (1526–1572), one of a flood of expatriate Persian poets and intellectuals who enjoy munificent imperial patronage at the Mughal courts. Persian is the lingua franca of Mughal political life, and the ancient art of Persian poetry thus enjoys a final flowering in India. Faizi (1547–1595), second laureate and most famous Persian poet of his age, is Indian-born.

1550s–1590s: The Deccani school of painting flourishes under the patronage of the courts of Bijapur, Ahmadnagar, and Golconda. A favored genre, *ragamala*, comprises cycles of paintings based on musical *ragas* and *raginis*, scales or modes associated with emotions, moods, seasons, or times of day.

1551: Death of Kadi Kadan, author of mystical verse in Sindhi and an early, influential exponent of vernacular religious literature.

1556: Portuguese missionaries employ the first printing press in India to print Christian tracts in vernacular languages. Many missionaries study indigenous languages: Portuguese Henry Henriquez becomes known as a scholar of Tamil after publishing the first Catholic works in that language.

1560: Portuguese impose the Inquisition in the archbishopric (since 1557) of Goa.

1562: Tansen, a renowned court musician in his native Gwalior, is invited to Akbar's court at Delhi. The palace here is the first Indian building to incorporate a formal garden in the Persian style, a hallmark of Mughal architecture. Architecture is the major art form of the Mughal dynasty: the *mansabdar* system enriches an aristocracy that, because offices and properties are not hereditary, has no incentive to save; instead, nobles spend lavishly on the mosques, tombs, summer houses, gardens, rest houses of the Mughal architectural renaissance.

1572: Luiz Vas de Camoens publishes *Os Lusiadas*, the great Portuguese national epic celebrating Da Gama's voyage to India in 1498.

c. **1572–1602:** Akbar grants the Jesuits permission to practice their faith; their first wave of church-building includes churches at Lahore, Agra, and Hugli.

1574: Tulsidas (1532–1623), regarded as the greatest Hindi poet, begins writing his masterwork, *Ramacaritmanas*. It presents Rama as a supreme deity accessible to all through devotional worship, and provides north Indian Hindus with a vital wellspring of cultural identity in this period of Muslim rule. The Awadhi, or eastern Hindi dialect in which it is written creates the basis for modern Hindi.

Late 16th century: Mughals introduce backgammon to India. Other amusements include chess and cards; wrestling, hunting, and animal fights; and polo—Akbar invents an illuminated polo ball for night play. Emperors and courtiers also indulge freely in wine and opium.

1577: Sikhs' holy city of Amritsar is founded by Ramdas, fourth *guru*.

1579: Akbar's "infallibility decree" declares him supreme arbiter of religious affairs.

October 24, 1579: Jesuit Thomas Stephens, the first known English settler in India, arrives at Goa (he dies there in 1619). To encourage conversions, he translates Christian material into Marathi Purana form (published 1616). Stephens's grammar of Konkani will be published posthumously in 1640 and will be instrumental in preserving the language of Goa.

1580–1582: The first Jesuit mission at Agra by Akbar's invitation. Prints presented to the emperor introduce European art to Mughal court painters, who begin incorporating European motifs and illusionist techniques into their work.

1582: Akbar promulgates a new syncretistic faith, *Din-i Ilahi* (Divine Faith), the fruit of seven years of talks with Hindus, Jains, Parsis, Buddhists, and Jesuits at his famous religious assembly, Ibadat Khanah (House of Worship). Orthodox Muslims unite in opposition to this heresy, which attracts few adherents and ends with Akbar's reign. A man of broad intellectual curiosity, Akbar insists throughout his reign on religious tolerance, promoting a policy of *sulh-i kull* (universal peace).

Persian is declared the administrative language of the empire.

c. **1585:** Akbar begins commissioning translations of Sanskrit Hindu texts into Persian for use by Mughal officials (incidentally making these texts accessible to European scholars). Numerous calligraphic manuscripts of literary and religious texts, fables, and Islamic and dynastic histories are brilliantly illustrated by court painters. Portraiture also flourishes: Akbar and, later, Jahangir flout Islamic restrictions on figural representations, borrowing statues and designs depicting animals and people from Rajput art.

1590: Death of Urfi Shirazi, the poet credited with introducing *sabk-i Hindi*, the formalistic "Indian style," into the Persian poetry of India. His finest work is in the genre of *qasidas*, a rhymed lyric poem.

1590s: Flowering of Islamic historiography, one of the major literary genres of the period. Akbar orders the composition of *Tarikh-i alfi* (A History of [the First] Thousand Years [of Islam]); important histories of India are written by Abd al-Kadir Bada-uni (1540–1615) and Nizam al-Din Ahmad al-Harawi (1549–1594).

1599: Synod of Diamper compels Syrian Christians in Kerala to submit to the authority of Rome. Violent reaction against forced Latinization results in a break with the Roman church (1653–1661).

Early 17th century: Rejecting Akbar's heresies, Sufi saint Shaikh Ahmad Sirhindi (1564–1624) seeks to restore Islamic orthodoxy among the Mughal nobility. His teachings will later influence Aurangzeb.

1601: *Akbar-nama*, the official chronicle of Akbar's reign and an outstanding history of the period, is composed by the emperor's confidant and court historian Abu'l Fazl Allami (1551–1602). This and his *A'in-i Akbari* (Institutes of Akbar), a statistical gazetteer of imperial administration, are important models for Mughal chroniclers and sources for later historians.

1604: Traditional date of compilation of Sikh scripture *Adi Granth* by fifth *guru*, Arjun. Its hymns are written in Hindi, Hindi-Marathi, and Punjabi. A shrine to house this sacred text is built at the Golden Temple in Amritsar.

1605–1622: Jahangir records the first seventeen years of his reign in his autobiographical *Tuzuk-i Jahangiri*; the chronicle is completed by others. Biography is an important Mughal literary genre; another well-known example is Shah Nawaz Khan's biographical encyclopedia of Mughal nobility.

May 20, 1606: Arrival at Goa of Italian Jesuit Roberto de Nobili (1577–1656). Founding his mission at Madura, he expands missionaries' activity from the coasts to the interior. His belief in presenting Christianity in indigenous cultural forms leads him to learn Tamil and Sanskrit and to adopt Indian dress and diet.

***c*. 1610:** Muhammad Qasim Hindushah Firishta (*c*. 1550–1623), the leading historian of Ibrahim Adil Shah's court at Bijapur, completes *Gulistan-i Ibrahimi*, the greatest chronicle of Islamic India.

1610s: Mughal painting reaches its zenith under Jahangir, a great connoisseur and outstanding patron of painting. As a young prince, Jahangir had founded his own atelier; under the supervision of master Aqa Riza, his artists develop a new, naturalistic style distinctive for its subdued palette, psy-

chologically expressive portraiture, and outstanding natural history painting. Leading artists include Aqa Riza's son Abu'l-Hasan, nature painter Mansur, portraitists Manohar and Bishndas, and mannerist Farrukh Beg. Albums of portraits and pictorial records of imperial activities are favored genres.

1615–1616: Deaths of Indian Persian poets Malik Qummi and Zuhuri, the most outstanding among many poets at the court of Adil Shah II at Bijapur, the southern center of Persian letters.

1627: Death of Jahangir's poet laureate Talib Amuli (1590–1627), author of delicate *ghazals*. Among other best known contemporary poets writing in Persian are Muhammad Husain Naziri Nishapuri (dies 1612) and Kalim.

***c*. 1630:** Bihari Lal (1559–1663), a Hindi poet at the Jaipur court, compiles an anthology of his work, *Satsai*. Comprising only 713 couplets, the work is celebrated for its economy of thought and beauty of expression. Enormously popular, it is illustrated by many Punjabi court painters.

Tukaram (1608–1649), a low-caste poet-saint of Maharashtra, begins his vast output of *abhangas*, spiritual lyrics, still sung by pilgrims to Pandharpur, while Muktesvara (1609–1690) is known for colloquial narratives based on epics and Puranas. Hindu devotional poetry flourishes in many regions during the period.

1632: Shah Jahan orders the destruction of Hindu temples: seventy-six are leveled at Varanasi.

1632–1647: The Taj Mahal is erected in Agra as a tomb for Shah Jahan's favorite queen, Mumtaz Mahal (1592–1631).

1634: The Peacock Throne, a potent symbol of Mughal wealth created of diamonds, rubies, emeralds, and gold, is completed for Shah Jahan after seven years' work. Royal treasury is depleted by outlays for Shah Jahan's lavish monuments, artistic commissions, and jewel collection, regarded as the finest in the world.

1638–1648: In a further display of imperial

splendor, Shahjahanabad, a new capital, is built at Delhi; it serves as the seat of Indian government for two hundred years. Shah Jahan's reign is the golden age of Mughal mosque architecture: in Shahjahanabad are built both the Moti Masjid (Pearl Mosque) and the congregational Jami Masjid, the largest mosque in India. During this period, too, Akbar's forts at Lahore and Agra are renovated in marble.

1641–1642: Ali Mardan Khan, a noble Persian defector to the Mughal court, designs Shah Jahan's major garden, Shalimar Garden at Lahore. Formal Persian gardens, first introduced to India by Babur and integral to Mughal architectural design, typically incorporate symmetrically arranged watercourses, pools, terraces, and avenues, often in traditional *char bagh* (four quarters) plan.

1656: The Koh-i Nur diamond is found at Kolhapur and presented to the emperor.

1670s: Development of the classical Carnatic style of music. Tanjore becomes a leading center of music under the patronage of the Bhonsle kings.

1672: Completion of *Fatawa-i Alamgiri*, the great six-volume digest of Sunni laws compiled by Indian theologians at Aurangzeb's behest. Islamic studies flourish under Aurangzeb's patronage; Gujarat and Golconda are also centers of Arabic scholarship during this period.

1673–1674: Aurangzeb builds the congregational Badshahi Mosque at Lahore. A devout and ascetic Muslim, he dismisses court artisans whose work is inconsistent with Islamic teachings, maintaining the great Mughal tradition of artistic patronage only in the construction of mosques. Artistic achievement declines rapidly during his reign. His enforcement of Islamic law includes suppression of drinking, gambling, and sexual immorality.

1675: Aurangzeb executes Sikh Guru Tegh Bahadur (reigns 1644–1675) for refusing to convert to Islam, resulting in enduring Sikh enmity toward the Mughals.

1676: Death of Mirza Muhammad Ali Sa'ib (1601–1676), outstanding Persian poet of the century at the court of the governor of Kashmir.

1694: Aurangzeb founds a Sunni theological institution at Farangi Mahal, Lucknow. The college is to produce many famous scholars and politicians in the nineteenth and twentieth centuries.

17th–18th centuries: Development in Kerala of *kathakali*, stylized dance-drama. *Attakhattas*, stories written for these performances, become a literary genre in their own right; Unnayi Varyar is the most famous practitioner.

1705: The first Protestant mission in India is founded by Danish Lutherans at Tranquebar.

1707: Death of Vali, the first major Urdu poet; his *Diwan* (1720) ushers in a literary revolution. Siraj-ud-Din (1715–1763) is another early Urdu poet. After this generation, Urdu replaces Persian as India's major literary language among Muslims.

1708: Assassination of Guru Gobind Singh at Nander. He is the last living Sikh guru; authority passes to Sikh scripture and community.

1721: Death of Mirza Abdul Qadir Bidil of Patna, who with Nasir Ali Sirhindi (dies 1697) represents the pinnacle of the "Indian style" of Urdu poetry.

1732: Muhammad Hashim Khafi Khan's *Muntakhab al-Lubab*, a history of Hindustan from 1519 to 1718, is published. Its independence of imperial patronage makes it particularly valuable as an impartial historical source.

1734: Death of most popular poet-saint of late Mughal period, Gujarati poet Premanand (1636–1734). His best known long poem, *Kumvarbainu Mameru*, is based on life of fifteenth-century Gujarati poet-saint Narasingh Mehta.

1739: Sack of Delhi by Nadir Shah results in destruction of much Mughal art. Artists and writers quit the capital to join provincial courts. The new cultural centers include Murshidabad, Lucknow, and Hyderabad.

1741: Pope Benedict XIV's bull prohibits "prevaricating sophistry" in India; Jesuit influence begins permanent decline.

CONTENDING POWERS: 1760–1858

18th century: With Mughal decline, northern Indian artists, artisans, musicians, and poets disperse to other courts. Regional courts take over artistic patronage from Mughals, for example, the Maratha state of Thanjavur, notable for literature (in Tamil, Telugu, Sanskrit, Marathi), painting, and music (creating the Karnatak classical genre). Proliferation of provincial courts results in new mobility, as experienced Indian scribes, administrators, and soldiers find employment in centers such as Lahore and Hyderabad.

In Bengal by the end of this century the words of the songs by *bauls* are being written down. A *baul* is a religious nomad who wanders through the countryside of Bengal (and later Bangladesh) and composes or repeats songs, mostly of a spiritual nature; he is supported either by patrons or by donations from individual listeners.

1718–1775: Lifespan of Ramprasad Sen, Bengali poet famed for his *sakta* songs: Saktism is a cult devoted to the worship of Kali, Siva's consort.

1764: The Golden Temple at Amritsar (1588), the holiest shrine of the Sikhs, is rebuilt by Ranjit Singh. The heavy Islamic influence of its design is typical of Sikh architecture.

1775: *Nawab* Asaf ud-Daula moves the capital of Awadh to Lucknow, which becomes the subcontinent's largest, grandest city. He builds the great vaulted and galleried Bara Imambara (1784), designed by Kifayut Ali, for performance of Shiite Muharram rites. Islamic and neoclassical European styles are both represented in an elegant architectural renaissance, and fuse into the extreme hybrid "nawabi" style in buildings like Claude Martin's famous mansions, Farhad Baksh (1781) and Constantia (1795).

1780–1782: The first English-language newspaper in India, James Augustus Hickey's weekly *Bengal Gazette*, is published. It is closed down after repeated journalistic attacks on government and public figures. English-language papers, generally produced by and for the British, also appear in Madras (1785) and Bombay (1789).

1781: Calcutta Madrasa, or Muhammadan College, is founded by Warren Hastings to teach Arabic, Persian, and Islamic law; his promotion of Oriental scholarship serves the East India Company's administrative needs. A Sanskrit college is founded at Varanasi (1791) to teach Hindu religion, literature, and law. A Sanskrit college is also founded in Calcutta (1823).

1784: Sir William Jones, a scholar of Indic culture, founds the Asiatic Society of Bengal in Calcutta to promote research in oriental studies. This scholarly association is instrumental in spreading knowledge of Indian history, antiquities, and languages throughout Europe.

1784: Mir Hasan (1727–1786) completes his masterwork *Sihrul Bayan*, an Urdu *masnavi* (verse romance). The rise of Urdu as a primary literary language owes much to Sauda (1713–1781), poet laureate at Delhi and other northern courts, an extremely versatile writer best known as a satirist. Their contemporary Mir (1722–1810), a court poet at Lucknow called Khuda-e Sukhan (literally, "poetry's God"), is the preeminent writer of Urdu *ghazals* and writes the first Urdu autobiography.

1798: The Society for Promoting Christian Knowledge posts its first missionary to Calcutta.

1799: Government imposes censorship on

newspapers to control dissemination of information about wars.

Late 18th–early 19th centuries: The court at Lucknow becomes a premier musical center. Development of new forms there: classical *kathak* (dance), and improvisational Hindi song form, *thumri*, invented at court of Wajid Ali Shah (reigns 1847–1856).

Golden age of Karnatak music, one of the major classical schools. Telugu vocal tradition spreads throughout the south as musicians from Tanjore migrate to the Travancore court at Trivandrum, Mysore, and other princely courts. Among the most influential are Tyagaraja (1767–1847), best known for his popular Telugu *kirtanam* to Rama, and his contemporaries Muttuswami Diksitar (1775–1835), Syama Sastri (1762–1827), and his son Subbaraya Sastri (1803–1862).

1800: College of Fort William, Calcutta, is founded by governor-general Wellesley with an ambitious curriculum designed to teach Indian languages and customs to civil servants; it is the first British post-secondary institution in India.

William Carey establishes his mission and printing press at Serampore, near Calcutta. Head of the Bengali and Sanskrit department at Fort William College, he prints 212,000 items in forty languages over the next thirty years, including vernacular texts, dictionaries, grammars, translations of Sanskrit and Western religious works, and scientific linguistic studies.

1810: Publication of the first modern Hindi prose work, Lalluji Lal's (1763–1835) *Prem Sagar*. Sadal Misra, his colleague at Fort William College, writes another Hindi classic, *Nasiketopakhyan*.

1813: Renewal of the East India Company charter for the first time allocates a small annual budget for higher education (which is not spent). The charter also officially permits the activities of Christian missionaries in the subcontinent. As an adjunct to their proselytizing, Christian missionaries introduce Western-style education; missionary schools proliferate over the next decade.

1815–1830: The Bengal Renaissance begins in the ferment of European ideas, the Orientalist education movement, and consequent debate between Orientalists and Anglicists. The Bengal Renaissance is led by Ram Mohan Roy (1772–1833) of Calcutta, a critic of popular Hinduism who promotes a synthesis of historical Indian culture and newly imported British ideas.

1816: The Hindu College, Calcutta, is founded, the center of Western education for the Indian elite. Two dozen similar institutions open in Calcutta alone within the next twenty years. The teaching of English becomes widespread in private institutions founded by Indians and British. Modernizing Indians embrace Western science, math, philosophy, history, and literature.

1818: Three Bengali journals are founded. Intended to be instructional, they disseminate knowledge of the rest of the world and stimulate development of Bengali as a literary language. Dozens of periodicals in other vernaculars follow, including Persian, Urdu, Gujarati (1822), and Marathi (1831). There is an explosion of vernacular publishing in the 1830s–1840s.

1818: The first public library in India opens in Calcutta, housing more than eleven thousand volumes.

1819: Death of Mrityunjay Vidyalankar (1762–1819), the "father of Bengali prose." Encouraged by William Carey and influenced by modern European literary forms, Vidyalankar and contemporaries such as Ramram Basu and Rajiblochan Mukherji forge Bengali prose into India's first great modern vernacular literature. English and Bengali literature are seminal influences on other vernaculars.

H. H. Wilson, a British employee at the Calcutta mint and leading Orientalist, compiles and publishes the first Sanskrit-English dictionary.

1820: First published collection of Nazir of

Agra (1740–1830), naturalist poet of everyday Indian life who writes in colloquial Urdu.

October 1821: Founding of Poona Sanskrit College, offering a traditional Hindu curriculum. Unlike Calcutta, Bombay continues strong support of traditional vernacular education alongside new Western-style educational institutions.

March 17, 1823: In a seminal act of political protest, Ram Mohun Roy and five others formally protest press restrictions under the new Press Ordinance.

February 18, 1824: Court of Directors Despatch, influenced by James Mill, recommends on utilitarian grounds the promotion of Western education in India.

1828: Brahmo Samaj (Society of Brahma) is founded in Calcutta by progressive Hindu reformers. Its members oppose *sati* (ritual immolation of Hindu widows on dead husband's funeral pyres) and polygamy and strongly endorse women's rights.

1829: In the first of a series of British-imposed social reforms, Bengal's governor Lord William Bentinck abolishes *sati* (the burning of a widow with her husband's corpse); at first the ban is in Bengal only but in 1830 it is extended to Bombay and Madras. The British also ban child sacrifice and discourage infanticide. Hindus and Europeans alike decry government interference in orthodox religious practices, but Bentinck's Age of Reform (1828–1835) is regarded as his most important legacy to India. Bentinck serves as governor-general of all India 1833–1835.

1829–1847: Reign of Swathi Thirunal, maharaja of Travancore. A scholar and poet in seven languages, he presides over a culturally rich court, patronizing among others the Malayalam *kathakali* poets Irayimman Thampi and Vidwan Koithampuran. The maharajas of Travancore and Cochin champion Western education in south India by supporting mission schools.

1830: Death of Bapu Chhatre (1788–1830), teacher and seminal writer of Marathi literature, including a Marathi translation of *Aesop's Fables*. His near-contemporary Dadoba Panduran Tarkhadkar (1814–1882) compiles a Marathi grammar (1836), among many other works.

1830s: Bengal radicals advocate the Europeanization of Indian culture. They are mostly educated at Hindu College, mentored by teacher and poet Henry Louis Derozio (1809–1831), and influenced by British nationalism. Calcutta emerges as the home of India's intellectual vanguard.

1835: Macaulay's *Minute on Education* recommends that the government advance Western education in India and establishes English as the medium of higher education. Macaulay argues that Indians desire instruction in English, rather than Sanskrit or Arabic, in order to have access to Western knowledge.

English formally replaces Persian as the official language of government and courts. The use of Persian rapidly declines among Indian Muslims, although Arabic continues to be used in composing works of Islamic theology.

March 7, 1835: Bentinck incorporates Macaulay's recommendations in a resolution committing the government to promote "European literature and science." In a defeat for the Orientalists, English-language instruction replaces Sanskrit and Arabic at the university level, a policy decision with enormous consequences for Indian culture and politics.

June 1835: Calcutta Medical College is founded. Calcutta's first hospital is built (1838). Medical colleges are also founded in Bombay (1845), Madras (1851), and Lahore (1860).

August 3, 1835: The New Press Law guarantees freedom of the press.

1838: The English-language *Bombay Times*, forerunner of the *Times of India*, begins publication.

1849: Hindu Girls' School, Calcutta, is the first such institution in India. Girls' education lags behind boys' until the government takes direct control of schools later in the century.

1850: Civil Disabilities Removal Act is passed, allowing Christian converts to inherit property. Deeply unpopular, it is widely seen by Indians as part of coordinated British assault on Hinduism and Islam.

1853: The first nationalist newspaper, the English-language *Hindoo Patriot* is founded in Calcutta. Edited by Harischandra Mukherji, it becomes a leading journal.

July 19, 1854: Sir Charles Wood's *Despatch on Education* articulates the framework for a comprehensive publicly funded educational system from primary through university level. The creation of new middle schools and universities, the education of girls, and teacher training are key elements in the plan.

1856: Remarriage of high-caste Hindu widows is legalized in contravention of age-old custom. The Bengali scholar and reformer Isvarchandra Vidyasagar (1820–1891) is at the forefront of the campaign to institute this social reform; the movement becomes an important model for reformers.

1857: Universities are incorporated in Calcutta, Bombay, and Madras under terms of Universities Act (1856). With faculties of arts and sciences, engineering, law, and medicine, they are examining bodies modeled on the University of London; post-secondary instruction takes place in colleges.

BRITISH INDIA: 1858–1947

November 1, 1858: Queen Victoria's Proclamation promises that people of "whatever race or creed may be impartially admitted to offices in our service," and pledges to respect "ancient rights and usages in India."

1861: The blank-verse epic *Meghanad-badh Kavya*, the masterwork of Michael Madhusudan Datta (1824–1873), is published. India's first great modern poet, Datta writes in Bengali, the first vernacular language to enjoy a modern literary renaissance. He is regarded as the creator of modern Bengali drama.

1865: Publication of *Durgeshnandini*, the first of Bankim Chandra Chatterjee's (1838–1894) many novels. The quality and popularity of his historical and social fiction, written in Bengali and based on English novelistic tradition, establishes the novel as a major Indian literary form.

1867: Prarthana Samaj (Prayer Society), Hindu social reform movement in Maharashtra, is founded in Bombay. It focuses especially on improving status of women and untouchables and modernizing marriage laws. One of its founders is Mahadev Govind Ranade (1842–1901), a rigorous critic of child marriage, the seclusion of women, and widow remarriage and perhaps the greatest reformer of the century.

1867: A conservative Islamic theological seminary is founded at Deoband by Muhammad Qasim Nanautavi. An important center of Islamic scholasticism, it trains generations of Muslims and inspires the founding of similar orthodox institutions across north India. Urdu is popularized through its use as the medium of instruction.

1867: The Indian Museum, Calcutta, is founded. It opens to the public in 1878.

1867–1880: Hindu Mela, an annual fair promoting Hindu culture and national identity, is held at Calcutta.

1869: Death of Ghalib (1797–1869), considered the greatest Urdu poet of all time, a writer also of Persian verse and a renowned prose stylist. His work modernizes and broadens the subject matter of traditional genres. Muhammad Ibrahim Zauq (1789–1894) is another renowned Urdu writer of the period.

1870: The Aligarh Movement, a loyalist Islamic reform movement, is founded by Sayyid Ahmad Khan (1817–1898). In seeking to marry Western learning with traditional Islamic values, the Aligarh Movement draws the opposition of Deoband Muslims; these groups form the basis of two major strands of politics among Indian Muslims.

1870: Rajkumar College is founded at Rajkot to provide English education to Indian princes, stalwart allies of the British. Other princes' colleges include Mayo College, Ajmer (1872) and Aitcheson College, Lahore (1886).

1871: The Indian Reform Association is founded by Keshub Chandra Sen (1838–1884), a leading social and religious reformer and leader of Brahmo Samaj. The association sponsors women's and workers' education, temperance, and charity.

1872: After ten years of activism in north India, anti-Muslim attacks by fundamentalist Sikh Kukas in eastern Punjab become violent. Kuka (or Namdhari) movement is outlawed, its founder Ram Singh (1826–1885) arrested, and other leaders executed.

July 1872: Intercaste marriages and widow remarriage, long forbidden by Hindu doctrine, are legalized.

1873: Satyashodak Samaj (Truth-Seeking Society) is founded at Pune by Jotirao Phule. This influential anti-Brahman movement, aiming to democratize Hinduism for the lower classes, is later to be revived in the 1920s.

1874: Death of Ramalinga Swamigal (1823–1874), leading Tamil poet, whose nearly one thousand devotional hymns are collected in *Tiruarutpa*. Modern Tamil pioneer is Arumuga Navalar (1822–1876), Madras writer and publisher of Tamil works.

B. C. Chatterjee composes *Bande Mataram* (Hail to Thee, Mother). Set to music by Rabindranath Tagore, it becomes the anthem of Congress and thus of Indian nationalism.

1875: Arya Samaj is founded at Bombay by Dayananda Saraswati (1824–1883) as a vehicle for Hindu renewal. Arya Samaj, with 100,000 members by 1900, is particularly successful in north India and Punjab. The organization founds numerous Dayanand Anglo-Vedic (DAV) schools and colleges. Saraswati's "back to the Vedas" message emphasizes caste reform and equal rights for women; many are attracted back to observant Hinduism and ritually reconverted by *suddhi* (purification). Saraswati's preaching in Hindi does much to spread this vernacular.

1877: The Mohammedan Anglo-Oriental College (now Aligarh Muslim University) is founded by Sayyid Ahmad Khan. Designed to reconcile modern Western learning and traditional Islamic scholarship, it becomes north India's foremost Islamic educational institution, and educates founders of Muslim League and Pakistan.

The Birdwood Survey reports the existence of nearly two hundred vernacular newspapers. Leading Bengali journals include *Amrita Bazar Patrika* and *Bengalee*. *Mahratta* and *Kesari*, influential nationalist organs in Maharashtra, are founded in January 1881. Vernacular languages and journals are central to religious and cultural revival and political education; in some cases (Utkal movement in Orissa, Telugu speakers of Andhra), they underpin provincial separatist movements.

1881: Giris Chandra Ghosh (1844–1912) publishes the first of the forty plays that will establish his reputation as the greatest Bengali dramatist.

1882: Founding of the University of Punjab, the first in northern India. The University of Allahabad is founded in 1887.

Hunter Educational Commission endorses an 1854 policy favoring Western education and recommends the development of a grant-supported private system of schools.

Most of its recommendations are adopted in 1884. Numerous educational institutions are subsequently established, and education of women and untouchables increases; by 1901, however, only 9.8 percent of males and 0.7 percent of females are literate, while few untouchables are educated at all.

October 24, 1884: M. G. Ranade founds Deccan Education Society, Bombay. Indigenous educational institutions are founded in Deccan by Vishnu Krishna Chiplunkar (1850–1882), Gopal Ganesh Agarkar (1856–1895), and others during the 1880s, notably New English School (1880), Fergusson College (1885).

1885: Death of Harish Chandra, father of modern Hindi literature, at age thirty-five. A versatile and prolific writer under the pseudonym Bhartendu, he is especially known for dramatic works.

c. 1885–1920: Classical period of Marathi literature, second great vernacular corpus. Major dramatists include Annasaheb Kirloskar, Govind Ballal Deval, K. P. Khadilkar, S. K. Kolhatkar. Foremost Marathi poet is Krishnaji Keshav Damle (1866–1905). Hari Narayan Apte (1864–1919), first major Marathi novelist, writes social and historical fiction.

1886: Death of Ramakrishna (born 1834). A Calcutta mystic and charismatic spiritual leader, he exercises tremendous influence on educated young Bengali reformers.

1887–1901: Govardhanram N. Tripathi (1855–1907), a major Gujarati writer, publishes his classic social novel *Saraswatichandra*. Other pioneering Gujarati authors include Narmad (1834–1886), the father of modern Gujarati prose, a scholar and the author, in addition to literary works, of the first Gujarati dictionary (1873); and poet Dalpatram (1820–1898), whose works, performed orally, treat modern secular themes.

December 1887: The Indian National Social Conference is created as an annual national forum for discussion on reform issues including polygamy, child marriage, *purdah* (secluding women), and widow remarriage.

M. G. Ranade lays the theoretical basis for this secular humanist organization.

1889: The Ahmadi sect, an Islamic movement regarded as heretical by orthodox Muslims, is founded at Qadiyan, Punjab, by Ghulam Ahmad, who claims to be the successor to the Prophet Muhammad.

1891: The Age of Consent Act, the first social reform act in thirty-five years, raises the age of consent from ten to twelve. The issue sparks national controversy over the power of the British government to legislate private behavior. Some progressive princely states including Mysore, Travancore, and Baroda also outlaw child marriage.

1893: Altaf Hussain, called Hali (the Modern One), calls for a new Urdu poetics. His critique of the Urdu poetic tradition specifically targets the ancient *ghazal* form. Hali (1837–1914) is considered the great poet of the Muslim revival. Muhammad Shibli Numani (1857–1914) is at the forefront of reforming Urdu prose.

As part of the Hindu nationalist revival, B. G. Tilak revives the Ganapati Festival in Pune, the annual ten-day celebration of Ganesh, the elephant-headed Hindu god. He also inaugurates the annual Shivaji festival, Raigad (1895–1896). Both are enthusiastically embraced throughout Maharashtra, where they boost the cause of Maratha nationalism.

May 5, 1897: Swami Vivekananda (1863–1902), a disciple of Ramakrishna, founds the Ramakrishna Mission at his monastery in Belur, Bengal. Dedicated to famine and plague relief, the mission spreads throughout India after his death. Vivekananda's U.S. and European tours (including participation at the World Parliament of Religions in Chicago, 1893) do much to spread appreciation of Hinduism in the West.

1900: To combat Hindus' conversion to other faiths, Arya Samaj begins a reform program of reconversion by means of the *suddhi* (purification) ritual. Arya Samaj membership reaches nearly one million by 1931.

1904: The Indian Universities Act, landmark legislation, authorizes universities to appoint professors and lecturers, transforming them from ineffectual examining bodies into teaching institutions.

1905: Lord Curzon appoints the first Director General of Archaeology, which leads in turn to the accidental discovery of Mohenjo-Daro (1921). A lover of Indian history, Curzon passes laws protecting historic monuments and funds restoration at Agra and Delhi.

1907: Englishwoman Annie Besant (1847–1933) assumes presidency (until 1933) of Theosophical Society, headquartered in Adyar, Madras. It appeals particularly to Western-educated Indians and is an important force for reforms concerning education and women.

1910: The Department of Education is created. In a great universities movement after 1913, postgraduate education is initiated (1914) and teaching and residential universities are founded throughout the subcontinent. Universities are founded among many other cities at Patna, Lucknow, Varanasi, Delhi, Mysore, Hyderabad, and Pune.

1912: Maithili Saran Gupta (1886–1964), one of the founders of modern Hindi literature, achieves fame with his great nationalist poem *Bharat Bharati*.

1913: Rabindranath Tagore (1860–1941) wins the Nobel Prize for literature. His body of work in all genres, especially lyric verse and short fiction, anchors the Indian literary renaissance with its synthesis of Western and Indian influences.

The first feature film in India is produced: *Rajah Harishandra*, directed by D. G. Phalke. He founds a studio in Bombay, which with Madras becomes an important center of film production.

1913–1930: The new capital of New Delhi is built to a classic European city plan designed by British architects Sir Edward Lutyens and Sir Herbert Baker. Council House opens January 18, 1927.

March 23–24, 1918: Major political leaders renounce the practice of untouchability at the first All-India Depressed Classes Conference.

1922: Bengali Kazi Nazrul Islam (1899–1978), "Rebel Poet" and author of politically charged secular poetry, publishes *Agnivina*, one of his best-known collections.

1923: Sir Muhammad Iqbal (1877–1938), one of the literary giants of the twentieth century, publishes *Bang-i-Dira*, a collection of Urdu poems. He soon afterward embarks on a long and distinguished political career.

1923–1947: Period of the Kallol movement, a modernist revolt of progressive Bengali writers. One of the leading figures is the poet Jivanananda Das (1899–1954).

July 1924: Bhimrao Ramji Ambedkar (1891–1956) founds the Depressed Classes Institute in the Deccan.

1929: The Female Inheritance and Age of Consent Acts take force, enabling women to inherit property and raising the age of marriage to fourteen for girls and eighteen for boys. The Right to Property Act (1937) extends inheritance rights to Hindu widows.

1931: Production of *Alam Ara*, the first Indian talkie. Its formula of song and dance sets the standard for India's most popular film genre. Advent of sound splits film industry into sectors producing national films (in Hindi and Hindustani), and regional (vernacular) films, of which Bengal is the most important market.

September 30, 1932: All-India Untouchability League formed. Temple Entry Movement (1932–1933). Hindu leaders abolish public prohibitions on untouchables, but legislation ending legal disabilities on untouchables fails to pass.

1935: Publication of *Godan*, the most famous work of Premchand (1880–1936), the foremost Urdu and Hindi novelist. Pioneer of social fiction, he writes of village life, at first in Urdu, after 1916 in Hindi.

1936: Progressive Writers' Movement is launched. This movement, favoring concrete social realism, reaches its zenith in

1947 and produces its greatest achievements in fiction.

1937: Congress-run provinces institute experimental Basic Education, stressing crafts and practical skills rather than traditional education.

REPUBLIC OF INDIA: 1947–1998

1947: English and Hindi, written in *devanagari* script, are designated joint national languages for purposes of legislation and law. Fourteen major regional languages are also official languages; their territories are not reflected in provincial borders, and linguistic agitation goes on for some years.

1951: Foreign modernist architects are commissioned to build new capital cities. Le Corbusier begins designing new Indian Punjabi capital of Chandigarh (City of Silver, 1951–1964), while Louis Kahn designs Sher-e-Bangla-Nagar complex, home of the National Assembly in Dhaka (1962–1970). Their work inaugurates an era of modern architecture in India.

1955: The Hindu Marriage Act raises the marriage age to fifteen for women (keeping eighteen for men); Hindu women are granted the right of divorce. Hindu Succession Act (1956) grants women rights of inheritance equal to men's.

The first film in the *Pather Panchali* trilogy (1955–1959) by director Satyajit Ray (1921–1992) is released. India's film industry, centered on Bombay ("Bollywood") is one of the world's largest producers of feature-length films.

1959: Government endorses family planning.

1961: Census shows gains in education during 1950s: the literacy rate has risen to 23.7 percent (12.8 percent for women). The Third Five-Year Plan (1961–1965) aims to further constitution's goal of universal compulsory elementary education.

The Dowry Prohibition Act is passed, banning the effective selling of brides by demands for dowries.

1963: Parliament approves retention of English as one of India's official languages.

1965: Regular television broadcasts begin, six years after experimental introduction of the technology. Radio and television broadcasting are government monopolies.

Vishnu Dey, one of the leading modern poets, wins Bangladesh's national Academy Award.

Final third of the 20th century: There is a striking flowering of Indian writers who compose their works in English and thus attain both international critical and popular acceptance. Among them are: R. K. Narayan (1906–), whose distinguished career spans the century, and who writes realistic fiction set in the imaginary town of Malgudi (e.g., *The Vendor of Sweets*, 1967) (his favorite theme is traditional versus modern India); V. S. Naipaul (1932–), essayist and novelist (e.g., *A Wounded Civilization*), a Trinidadian of Indian descent, controversial satirist, and critic of what he sees as stagnation of Indian culture; Anita Desai (1937–), a resident of the United States, whose novels usually deal with Indian women's struggles in a repressive society; and Salman Rushdie (1947–), who lives in Britain but writes mostly of the Indian subcontinent, and whose novel *Midnight's Children* (1981) is a picaresque fiction of India since independence.

1979: Mother Teresa (dies 1997), founder of the Missionaries of Charity, Calcutta (1948) and winner of the first Templeton Prize for Progress in Religion (1973), wins the Nobel Peace Prize. Numerous international trips during her later years make her a beloved and widely admired figure around the world.

February 14–24, 1989: On February 14 Iran's Ayatollah Khomeini issues a *fatwa*, or religous edict, that calls on Muslims to kill Salman Rushdie because his latest novel, *The Satanic Verses* (1988), is said to blaspheme the Islamic faith. Rushdie was born (1947) in Bombay, India, to Muslim parents, who moved to Pakistan in 1964; he emigrated to England in 1965 and writes his novels in English. He goes into hiding in England. On February 24 some ten thousand Muslims demonstrate in Bombay, and twelve people are killed when police open fire; in 1991, the Japanese translator of *Satanic Verses* is killed, and in 1991 and 1993 two other people involved with publishing the work are attacked. The *fatwa* is formally lifted on September 24, 1998, but individual Muslims continue to threaten Rushdie's life.

1991: The Places of Worship Bill prohibits the conversion of mosques to Hindu temples.

1995: The literacy rate of Indians over fifteen reaches 52 percent, up from 34 percent in 1970.

India

SCIENCE-TECHNOLOGY, ECONOMICS, AND EVERYDAY LIFE

INDUS CIVILIZATION: 3000–1700 B.C.

3000 B.C.: In Baluchistan, localized cultures are distinguished by various types of tools, implements, pottery, and burial customs.

3000–2600 B.C.: Early Harappan settlements live by traditional subsistence agricultural and pastoral economy. Plows are employed in a field pattern still used in modern-day Punjab. Industries include copper toolmaking and production of stone blades from cores. Economic specialization rises as factory towns such as Lewan and Taraki Qila produce tools and beads.

Gradual cultural convergence among Early Harappan communities over an enormous geographical range results in a transition to the relatively homogeneous urban Harappan culture. Some sites exhibit characteristics of mature Harappan cities: massive mud brick city walls; city planning, with separate citadel and residential districts; water storage systems; multiroomed houses. Tools include plows and grinding stones.

2600–2000 B.C.: Harappan farmers practice mixed farming on floodplains using irrigation and inundation techniques. Barley, wheat, millet, peas, sesame, and perhaps rice are major crops, produced in surplus quantities. The land tax is paid in grain. Livestock includes humped cattle, sheep, goats, buffalo, and pigs.

Sophisticated, uniform urban planning in the Mature Harappan period (about ten known sites are classified as cities). Cities are sited adjacent to rivers and oriented north-south. A citadel is built on a massive mound to west, surrounded by public buildings (assembly halls, baths and other ritual spaces); a "lower city" to the east contains a residential/commercial quarter (including warehouses and workshops). The citadel and lower city are fortified with mud or baked brick walls. Streets follow grid plan with broad main streets. Cities are periodically rebuilt, always to same plan; Mohenjo-Daro has ten layers.

Occupational specialization accompanies social classification among the Harappans: potters, dyers, metal- and shell-workers, and beadmakers are concentrated in separate quarters of towns, living in barrack-like housing.

Harappans invent the most sophisticated

sewage system of any known ancient culture: the standard urban design incorporates excellent public water supply, drainage, and sewage systems. Public and private wells are numerous. Urban houses contain bathrooms with brick drains; covered sewers in streets lead to soak pits. Cesspits are common in rural settlements.

Harappans develop an advanced brickmaking technology: kiln-baked bricks are produced to standard measurements in the 1:2:4 proportion still favored today. Mature Harappan buildings use baked brick with timber components; larger houses are two stories.

Harappans manufacture tools, utensils, jewelry, furniture, and toys from ceramic, stone and semiprecious stones, wood, shell, ivory, and copper; carnelian beads are a notable product. Metalworkers master hammering, casting, and chiseling techniques; metal vessels and figurines are technically outstanding. Bronze and copper are fashioned into weapons, tools, and utensils.

Further economic specialization as individual Harappan communities become centers of trade, mining, agriculture, or craft production. Trade with Central Asia and the Arabian peninsula develops.

Well-organized storage and land and water transport supply Harappan cities with agricultural products. Pack animals such as bullocks and asses, river boats, and two-wheeled bullock carts are used for haulage. Maritime and overland trade routes are well established to Baluchistan, Mesopotamia, the Persian Gulf, West and Central Asia, and peninsular India. Grain, wood, cotton, ivory beads, and tools are exported in exchange for shells, stones, silver, copper, woolen textiles,

and food. Harappan towns and cities are clustered along trade routes; coastal sites, evidently ports or trading posts, abound from Gujarat all the way to the modern-day border between Pakistan and Iran.

Late 3rd millennium B.C.: Construction of water storage tanks for irrigation, invented in Ceylon, reaches India and spreads throughout the subcontinent.

2000 B.C.: First cultivation of cotton. Advent of spinning, dying, and weaving cotton; raw cotton is brought for processing in cities. Indians are first to use cotton for clothing; cotton manufacture remains India's major industry for millennia.

Early 2nd millennium B.C.: Neolithic South Indian communities domesticate cattle.

2000–1700 B.C.: Gradual economic breakdown throughout Harappan territory.

1900 B.C.: As the power of Harappan cities declines, cultural uniformity gives way to regionalization. Many elements of Harappan art and technology are preserved, but as Aryan ideas and culture replace Indus culture, urban civilization, writing, stamp seals, and some specialized crafts disappear.

1750–900 B.C.: Post-Urban/Post-Harappan Period. The quality of material culture declines sharply in Punjab and Sind; makeshift settlements are built over earlier Harappan sites as their populations revert to village life. Some individual settlements (e.g., Cemetery H in the Indus region and the successive Jhukar and Jhangar cultures in Sind, Iron Age Londo Ware settlements in Baluchistan) show the local influence of distinct Harappan, Aryan, or Iranian culture. Ganges Doab is broadly settled by uniform Copper Hoard Culture.

VEDIC PERIOD: 1700–600 B.C.

1600–1400 B.C.: Period I, Malwa Occupation, in south Indian villages, is characterized by rectilinear wattle-and-daub thatched dwellings with hearths and plaster floors. The sec-

ond millennium B.C. in south Deccan is the Southern Neolithic: nomadic cattle herders, wattle-and-daub structures with thatched roofs, agriculture, pastoralism, megalithic graves, monuments. Malwa Culture agricultural settlements spread slowly eastward, reaching Ganges Doab and western Bengal *c*. 10th century B.C.

1500 B.C.: Rice cultivation is widespread over Kathiawar and peninsular India.

1500–800 B.C.: Indo-European immigrants are seminomadic Bronze Age warriors and cattle herders. During early Vedic period, they develop settled agricultural-pastoral communities with wood or reed dwellings. Cows, not yet sacred, are dominant commodity, come to be used as currency (cattle breeding is also extensive in south India), while horses, sheep, and goats are also bred.

Skilled copper- and bronze-workers produce weaponry and tools, including harpoons and axes. Other crafts include carpentry, smithing, tanning, spinning, and weaving. By the end of the period, specializations include chariot- and rope-making, dying, and fabrication of armor; specialized merchants and moneylenders also appear.

1400–1000 B.C.: Period II, Early Jorwe Period, in south Indian villages. Its culture—small dwellings, distinctively shaped pots, jar burials—blends characteristics from the northwest (Iran-influenced), northeast (Southeast Asia and China-influenced), and earlier Malwa cultures.

c. **1325–1000 B.C.:** Bronze Age in much of the peninsula.

c. **1200–1100 B.C.:** Iron technology introduced into northern India is employed initially for weapons and horse harnesses. Iron technology spreads eastward and southward *c*. 1000–500 B.C.

12th century B.C.: Lagadha writes *Vedanga Jyotisa* (Vedic Astronomical Auxiliary), astronomical computations for Vedic ritual calendar. The need for accurate calendars to time Brahmanical rituals propels development of astronomy into a major Indian science. Numerous astronomical texts, both mystical and empirical, appear in the following centuries.

1000–700 B.C.: Period III, Later Jorwe Period, in south Indian villages, characterized by round dwellings. Evidence of structures of specialized craftspeople (e.g., goldsmiths).

800 B.C.: Maritime trade with Babylon.

800–500 B.C.: Iron technology makes possible the clearing of the dense forests of the Gangetic plain, apparently by slashing and burning, then using iron axes and ox-drawn plows. Development of irrigation, cultivation of rice follow; rice is important crop in grain-based late Vedic agriculture. Plow and irrigation agriculture increase crop yields, allowing expansion of the population.

Sulbasutras, the earliest known works of Indian mathematics, describe exact measurement and construction of sacrificial altars and incorporate basic theories of plane geometry and algebraic solutions; they demonstrate the practical, computational nature of Indian mathematics.

EMERGENCE AND DECLINE OF EMPIRES: 600 B.C.–A.D. 300

?c. 600 B.C.: Possibly the time of a legendary figure in Indian medicine, Susruta. (Others date him anywhere from 1000 B.C. to A.D. 900.) He is said to have taught medicine at Varanasi, India, where he specialized in surgery and operated on cataracts. He is credited with having composed or edited the *Susrutasamhita*, the oldest and the seminal book on surgery in early India (although the extant written versions date from many centuries later). Amazingly modern in some of the instruments, diagnoses, and procedures it describes, it is also one of the major texts of the Indian school of Ayurvedic medicine. *Ayurveda* means "the science of [living to an old] age" and is the name applied to the traditional science of holistic medicine practiced in India for thousands of years. It is also about this time that a collection of hymns known as the *Atharvaveda* is compiled; most of this text are spells, many of them designed to cure diseases, thereby revealing Indians' belief that illness is caused by evil spirits.

500 B.C.: Increased trade in the Ganges Valley ushers in a second period of urbanization as towns develop at administrative and craft centers along rivers and highways. Major trade routes connect Ganges region with Punjab and Taxila; Deccan and west coast; Ganges delta and east coast ports.

Moated and fortified cities of second urbanization are sophisticated and crowded urban spaces, with large avenues, palaces, public buildings, houses, shops, religious sites, parks, and gardens. Houses, constructed of wattle and daub with thatched roofs, are frequently several stories high, with balconies, screened windows, and ogee-shaped dormers.

Silver and copper bent-bar and punch-marked coinage, issued in the northwest, soon spreads to the Ganges plain and remains current for several centuries.

Iron weaponry is prevalent. Unique manufacturing technique of melting in crucibles produces Indian *wootz* steel famous for its quality. Extensive exports of raw steel to Damascus, where it is made into highly prized light, curved "Damascus" swords.

500 B.C.–A.D. 500: During this period, a series of medical texts is compiled in India; taken together, they set forth the basic principles and practices of India's traditional Ayurvedic school of medicine.

500–150 B.C.: Clan ownership of land gives way to individual land holding; settled agrarian economy develops along with concepts of land and private property. Wealthy landowners employ slaves and hired laborers.

3rd–2nd centuries B.C.: The cotton industry flourishes. By the turn of the millennium, dyed cotton from southern India—Indians are noted dyers—is the prominent trade commodity with Rome.

c. **269–233 B.C.:** Ashoka's paternalistic government promotes social order by building shaded roads, wells, and rest houses for travelers. The state also enforces ethical and religious laws and supervises liquor, gambling, and prostitution.

During Ashoka's reign, the first nine Hindu numerals (they have no symbol for zero at this time) are inscribed in some of his decrees, the so-called rock edicts. Although these digits will evolve in their appearance considerably over the centuries, they will be taken over by the Arabs in Baghdad late in the 8th century. These digits will then become the basis of modern Western numerals.

2nd century B.C.–2nd century A.D.: The Kushan and Satavahana dynasties are financed partly by trade revenues. Both have extensive trade contacts throughout the Middle East and Asia. Ports line both coasts of the peninsula; sailing times to the West are considerably shortened by the recognition in the mid-1st century A.D. of the seasonal pattern of Indian Ocean monsoons. Indian exports include spices, cotton, indigo, wood, grain, ivory, pearls and precious stones, iron, and copper.

2nd century B.C.–3rd century A.D.: Urbanization in south India; rise of specialized crafts and guilds during the Satavahana dynasty.

1st century A.D.: Kushans' Hellenic-style gold coinage, standard for centuries, shows royal portraits on obverse and deities on reverse, surrounded by inscriptions.

A.D. 77: Completion of the Greek geographer Pliny's *Natural History*, containing much information about India. Greek descriptions of Indian geography and navigation, abundant in the early centuries A.D., include Strabo's *Geography* and Arrian's *Indica*.

1st–2nd centuries: Kanishka's court physician Caraka revises ancient Vedic medical texts, which then become known as the *Caraka Samhita*, oldest classical Ayurvedic medical text still in present-day use.

Early centuries A.D.: *Siddhanta* period of

Indian astronomy. Texts lay a rationalistic, mathematical basis for the science and they include twelve-sign zodiac, calculation of planetary movements and lunar phases, and accurate predictions of eclipses.

2nd century: Many Indian cultures and dynasties since at least the 4th millennium B.C. have stored and used monsoon rains for irrigation, but Chola hydraulic engineering is outstanding. Cholas are identified with weir *(anicut)* technology, their most famous construction being Kaveri Anicut on Kaveri River, a massive earthwork three hundred meters long, twelve to eighteen meters wide, and five meters high.

2nd–6th centuries: Indians establish trading stations on the Malay Peninsula; colonies spread across Southeast Asia, disseminating Indian culture—particularly Buddhism—to the rest of Asia.

NEW EMPIRES IN NORTH AND SOUTH: 300–700

4th century: Gupta silver and gold coinage achieves extremely high artistic and technical standard; coins feature Sanskrit legends and royal portraits. Coins minted by Samudragupta (reigns *c.* 335–376) in particular are regarded as works of art.

4th–5th centuries: The famous iron pillar at Mehrauli in Delhi is cast, the quality of its iron unsurpassed. Advanced metallurgists create a number of large iron objects; steel becomes a major industry in the 1st millennium A.D.

***c.* 350–400:** *Surya Siddhanta*, seminal astronomical work of northern India, includes references to trigonometric functions. This work is revised during succeeding centuries, taking final form in the *c.* 10th century A.D.; it forms the foundation of medieval Indian astronomy and is the basis for the Hindu calendar, developed in Nepal.

***c.* 500:** Mathematician and astronomer Aryabhata the Elder writes the *Aryabhatiya*, a scientific astronomical treatise, thereby founding India's Aryabhatan school of astronomy. His astronomical discoveries include earth's rotation on its axis and the length of the solar year. The first Indian to treat mathematics as a science separate from astronomy, he uses decimal place-value system, calculates a fairly accurate value of π, and works with a sine-based trigonometry.

***c.* 550:** Mathematician and astronomer Varahamihira recognizes zero. Sixth-century Indian mathematics also recognizes irrational and negative numbers. Mathematics flourishes under the Guptas.

595: The earliest recorded appearance in India of mathematical notational system of nine digits plus zero in an inscription in Gujarat.

7th century: Indians are the first to use symbols for unknown quantities, permitting the development of algebra.

628: Brahmagupta (born 598), mathematician, astronomer, and founder of second major school of astronomy, composes treatise *Brahmasphutasiddhanta*. An Arab translation of his work (*c.* 800) introduces Indian mathematics and astronomy to the West.

REGIONAL KINGDOMS: 700–1200

***c.* 773:** Developed and long used in India, the nine-digit system of numerical notation, including zero, is carried to Baghdad. The system appears in an Arab text *c.* 820, reaches widespread use in Islamic world by the late eleventh century and subsequently in Europe, where they are mistakenly called "Arabic" numerals.

11th century: Cholas maintain extensive trade with China; the export of Chinese spices to Europe is a major imperial revenue source.

1018–1060: Reign of Bhoja, king of Malwa. An architect and engineer, he is known among other achievements for the 250-square-mile reservoir he constructs at Bhojasagara, which survives for four hundred years.

1114–1185: Lifespan of mathematician and astronomer Bhaskara II, the author of the major Indian treatise *Siddhantasiromani*, an early precursor of differential calculus. His analysis of indeterminate equations will not be rediscovered by European mathematicians for six hundred years. Mathematics is the greatest intellectual achievement of medieval India.

DELHI SULTANATE: 1211–1526

Early 13th century: Sound silver coinage issued by Iltutmish is a model for later sultans.

13th century: The first manufacture of white paper in India. It replaces palm leaves as a common writing and painting medium around 1350.

13th century: Turkish rulers of India (mamluks) import the Turkish system of slavery, an institution used to create a professional governing class. Variously purchased or taken as prisoners of war or to discharge debts, slaves are often trained as military commanders, for which posts they may rise to the highest ranks of government. A number of Delhi sultans are to come from this class.

Late 13th century: A wave of Muslim immigrants includes many scientists who introduce Islamic texts, instruments, and methods, many with Greek origins. Islamic astronomers bring astrolabes, astronomical tables; Greco-Arab mathematical and astronomical texts including Ptolemy and Euclid are translated into Persian; Greco-Arab medical practices are added to those of indigenous Ayurvedic physicians.

1296–1316: Taxation of land reaches peak of 50 percent during the reign of Ala ud-Din Khalji. He imposes sumptuary laws and rigidly enforces price controls on commodities including grain, cloth, horses, and slaves.

1320–1325: Ghiyas ud-Din Tughluq promotes agriculture and irrigation projects, develops postal system, and creates poor-relief system.

1329–1330: In addition to small silver and gold coins, Muhammad bin Tughluq introduces copper or brass token currency on Chinese model. The new coinage is a spectacular failure because of widespread counterfeiting, and the entire issue is redeemed at face value at enormous loss to the imperial treasury (1332).

1350s: Firuz Shah undertakes an ambitious canal-building program for irrigation and military purposes.

Late 14th century: A trade route is established via Tabriz to the port of Hormuz, opening an overland/sea route to Europe for Central and Western Asian commerce. Indian merchants establish a large international market for exports of cottons, gems, carpets, and leather goods.

SOUTH INDIA: VIJAYANAGAR EMPIRE, 1336–1565

***c.* 1340–1356:** The reign of Harihara I, founder of the Vijayanagar Empire of southern India with the support of his four brothers, Hari-

hara I establishes several of the mainstays of this empire. It is relatively centralized, but the land, both the home territory and the various conquered territories, is assigned to military commanders or local landowners. They collect heavy taxes from farmers as well as from many activities and transactions, including foreign trade; they retain some of the taxes and send the rest to the central government.

Late 14th century: Harihara II's annexation of west coast ports (including Bhatakal, Barakuru, and Mangaluru) places the empire at the center of an extensive international trade network reaching all the way from western Iberia and west Africa to China and Indonesia. India is the world's major supplier of pepper and sandalwood, exported in exchange for gold, silver, arms, and horses. Malabar's coastal waters yield pearls, and the region specializes in cutting and polishing precious stones. Luxury goods from all over Europe, north Africa, and Asia abound in Vijayanagar's markets.

1403: Compilation of the *Venvaroha*, a handbook for calculating lunar positions, the most popular work of Madhava of Sangamagrama (*c.* 1340–1425), astronomer, mathematician, and founder of the late Aryabhata or Kerala school of mathematics. Some of his calculations of infinite series are unknown in Europe until the seventeenth century. His followers in the Kerala school include Nilakantha Somayaji (1444–1545) and Acyuta Pisarati (*c.* 1550–1621). Traditional Hindu culture and science flourish in Vijayanagar while Islamic rule interrupts their development in north India.

Early 16th century: Superior naval power wins Portuguese monopoly of maritime commerce. Their control of trade in the Arabian and Persian horses vital to Indian armies puts them in a powerful negotiating position with Vijayanagar kings, with whom their relationship is generally cordial: flourishing trade is in the interest of both powers.

SOUTH INDIA: ISLAMIC STATES, 1300–1650

15th century: A famous hospital is built at Bidar, where Hindu and Muslim physicians serve all comers.

MUGHAL EMPIRE: 1526–1760

1540–1545: Sher Shah builds an extensive network of roads in north India and restores the ancient pilgrimage route, which still survives as the Grand Trunk Road. His coinage, based on the silver standard rupee, will later be adopted by Akbar and his successors.

Late 16th century: Rapid expansion of trade with Europe and Middle East. Gujarat (Surat) and Bengal (Hugli) remain major Indian ports. The two major land trade routes go via Kandahar and Kabul. Major exports include cotton and indigo from Gujarat, spices from Malabar, sugar from Bengal and Madras, saltpeter, silk, and rice from Bengal; India receives gold, silver, and copper in return. Most cargo is transported by sea through the west coast port of Surat; lighter luxury items (gold, ivory, silks) travel by camel over northwest passes.

1570 onward: Akbar's building program includes much infrastructure. Road and bridge network begun by Babur and Sher Shah is expanded to connect capital to vital trade routes in Bengal and Gujarat, Uttar Pradesh, and Kabul. Numerous roadside wells, storehouses for merchants' cargoes, and bazaars are also constructed.

1577: *Kalimah*, the Muslim creed, is removed from national coinage. During Akbar's reign the silver rupee replaces the copper *tanka* as the major unit of currency. Mughal coinage, famous for purity, uniformity, and design, reaches its zenith under Jahangir.

1580: Akbar's minister Todar Mal builds on short-lived reforms begun by Sher Shah and undertakes a twenty-year overhaul of the imperial revenue system. Innovations include accurate surveys of national agricultural production and fixed revenue assessments (*zabt*) payable in cash and based on average historical yields and prices.

1584: Akbar replaces the Muslim lunar calendar with the *fasli*, a solar calendar for revenue and administrative purposes; the "divine era" so inaugurated is backdated to begin with his accession.

Late 16th century: Akbar introduces the Persian technique of weaving pile carpets; India becomes famous for intricate floral designs and invents pictorial carpets as Agra, Fatehpur Sikri, Lahore become centers of manufacture. The Mughal emperors surround themselves with luxurious goods: in addition to artists and weavers, imperial workshops employ thousands of jewelers, carvers, stonecutters, calligraphers, bookbinders, and other artisans.

Political unification, greatly increased trade, and linkage by roads and waterways help make Lahore, Delhi, Agra, and Ahmadabad leading commercial cities. They benefit from the lavish consumption and artistic patronage of the Great Mughals and other nobles; contemporary travelers often remark on the extraordinary prosperity and luxury of Indian cities.

17th century: The Indian economy is basically self-sufficient. Agriculture is the largest sector, followed by textiles. Agriculture, as a source of taxes, is vital: but 30 percent of tax revenues flow to the nobility, so spending on luxury items, noble retinues, and artistic patronage forms a disproportionately large part of the economy. Celebrated diamond and ruby mines are developed in Golconda.

Trade allows the development of a commercial economy and a large, prosperous merchant class. Specialized sectors of haulers, shippers, agents, bankers, brokers, and insurers evolve. Cash economy develops, with specialized money-lending, commodity production, and grain wholesaling sectors. Uniform imperial copper coinage (*dams*) and bills of exchange (*hundis*) gain widespread commercial use.

Cotton cloth, the most important single item of trade, finds a global market ("Indian cotton is king"). Fashionable Europeans throughout the century buy calico and Indian cottons for furnishings and clothing.

1623: First exports of tobacco, introduced by the Portuguese at the end of the sixteenth century. Cotton, sugar cane, opium, and indigo are major cash crops.

1670: English exports and investment in India total £303,000.

1700: In first of many such bans, England prohibits importation of Indian textiles. The East India Company reroutes Indian textiles to Europe, substitutes China tea as major import into England.

Early 18th century: Weakening of central government authority permits the rise of rich merchant and warrior classes among provincial Hindus; *zamindars'* (rent-farmers') holdings become permanent.

Pune becomes the banking and financial center of Maratha kingdom; banking branches into Gujarat, Ganges, southern India. A sophisticated trade and banking network is created throughout the Deccan. Agricultural development pushes southward into Maratha territory.

1720: First bank established in Bombay.

1720–1745: British exports to India increase from total of £578,155 in goods and £2,770,238 in bullion (1720–1725) to £1,105,750 in goods and £2,529,108 in bullion (1740–1745).

1724–1735: Sawai Jai Singh II, maharaja of Jaipur (1688–1743), builds five astronomical observatories across northern India comprising huge precision stone and masonry instruments of his own design. He employs dozens of astronomers, commissions translations of scientific works and research trips to Europe, and publishes accurate tables based on years of observations.

Mid-18th century: Mughal economic power is eroded by the Afghan settlement in Rohilkhand as Afghans divert trade from the traditional Mughal commercial strongholds of Delhi, Agra, and Bengal.

CONTENDING POWERS: 1760–1858

1764–1777: James Rennell, surveyor-general of Bengal, completes the first survey of Bengal. He publishes a Bengal atlas (1788), and the first modern map of India in his *Memoir of a Map of Hindoostan* (1783).

1765: The British acquisition of Bengal, the richest of Indian provinces, allows Europeans and Indian associates to skim off huge fortunes through trade monopolies, corruption, extravagant gift-giving, and high permanent assessments on *zamindars*. EIC officials returning to England with fortunes made in India are derisively referred to as "nabobs," from the Hindi word for high government official.

1780: The EIC gains the monopoly on opium trade. Indian agriculture shifts to cash crops grown for export under British coercion late in the eighteenth century; opium, traded for China tea for the English market, rapidly becomes EIC's most profitable Indian commodity. By the early nineteenth century opium is second only to the land tax as the EIC's largest source of revenue in India.

1793–c. 1830: The rules of Britain's so-called Permanent Settlement disrupt traditional patterns of agriculture and village life in Bengal. The first generation of Muslim *zamindars* ("rent-farmers"—that is, people given the right to collect the rents for land) put much land into agricultural production, creating increases in population and wealth, but the *zamindars* cannot meet steep British revenue assessments; by 1820 they are forced to sell more than one-third of the land in Bengal to pay their arrears. The land is bought by Calcutta's new banking and business elites, who thereby form a new class of Hindu middle-class landowners.

1813: The EIC loses its India trade monopoly. Within the next twenty years, Bengal's handloom cotton industry is destroyed by cheap imports of British machine-loomed cotton, creating widespread poverty and social displacement. Textile exports to Britain nearly disappear.

1817: A program begins of rebuilding and reopening old canals on Jumna, long silted up; much of north India is brought under irrigation.

1820: Coal mining begins in Raniganj, Bengal. Bengal coal fields are heavily exploited by mid-century, partly in response to demands from newly built railways.

1828: Dwarkanath Tagore of Calcutta (1794–1846) becomes the first Indian director of a bank; he founds the Union Bank in 1829. A pioneering industrialist, he amasses a business empire in indigo, jute, silk, mining, and sugar.

1833: In its renewal of the East India Company charter, the British parliament abolishes EIC's trading rights. Large numbers of European planters and merchants subsequently establish businesses in India to take advantage of new commercial opportunities.

1834: Governor-general Bentinck imports tea seeds and specialist labor from China and initiates Indian cultivation of tea on government-owned plantations in Assam (1836). Domestic Indian tea shortly comes under cultivation as well. Exports to Britain begin in the late 1830s, and tea is a major export industry by the end of the century.

1836: Reconstruction of the Grand Trunk Road, the central highway across India, begins.

1836–1854: Major irrigation works in Madras

on the Coleroon, Godavari, and Krishna rivers. The 525-mile-long Ganges Canal dates to the same period. Extensive construction of canals for irrigation and navigation during the century create a network of major routes for inland water transport.

1843: Ten years after its abolition in Britain's African and West Indian colonies, slavery is outlawed in British India.

1847: The Civil Engineering College is founded at Roorkee, Northwestern Provinces. Engineering colleges are founded in Calcutta (1856) and Pune and Madras (1858).

1849: After annexation, Punjab is developed through a model public works program constructing roads, bridges, and irrigation systems. Irrigation greatly increases agricultural yields, making the province particularly profitable.

April 16, 1853: Great Indian Peninsular Line, the first railway in India, begins passenger service between Bombay and Thana. Governor-general Dalhousie's plans to modernize India rest on the construction of communications and transport networks, specifically, the creation of railways, telegraph, and postal systems. His proposal for three major rail lines connecting Madras, Bombay, and Calcutta (April 1853) is the genesis of India's extensive railway network.

1853: The first successful cotton mill opens in Bombay. The cotton industry industrializes in a rapid period of growth during the rest of the decade.

1854: A cheap, efficient national postal system is introduced. Reaching the remotest villages, it stimulates the political unification of India and the growth of literacy and education.

The Assam Clearance Act offers large tracts of land to Europeans intending to grow tea for export; within twenty years, Indian tea production increases thirty-fold, spreading eventually to the Punjab, Mysore, and Darjeeling.

1854: The first mechanized jute mill in India opens at Serampore. Exported to Dundee, Scotland, since 1838, jute becomes a major industry with the development of large-scale production to replace Russian supplies interrupted by the Crimean War. The first modern cotton mill also dates from this year.

March 24, 1854: Transmission from Agra to Calcutta of the first telegraph message in India. Dalhousie personally plans the route. This technology is to prove invaluable in Britain's management of the Crimean War and the Rebellion of 1857.

After 1854: Karachi is developed into a major city after British annexation of Sind, serving as army headquarters and major entrepôt for Indus, Punjab, and Afghanistan trade, especially exports of wheat and cotton.

BRITISH INDIA: 1858–1947

1858–1880: In the wake of the Rebellion of 1857, £150 million of British capital flows into India for investment in technology and agriculture; British priorities are military control, foreign trade, and famine relief. Rapid construction of railways (from 200 miles in 1858 to 8,500 miles in 1880) creates the first integrated railway system in Asia. Advanced transport is the catalyst for the development of the cotton, iron, steel, and coal industries.

1859: Completion of the Bari Doab Canals in Punjab, the first stage of the world's largest integrated irrigation system. Irrigation and better transport to port cities hastens the agricultural shift from food to cash crops, preventing domestic agriculture from alleviating repeated famines.

The Bengal Rent Act is India's first right of occupancy law. It prohibits excessive rents and curbs landlords' powers, but fails to establish real security of tenure.

1859–1860: Government fiscal reforms include imposition of an income tax and creation of paper currency. Customs duty is levied to retire the ruinous government debt from the Rebellion.

Indigo growers in Bengal and Bihar strike against mistreatment by their European bosses in the "Blue Mutiny," the first of a series of such uprisings.

1860s–1870s: After the Crimean War (1853–1856) deprives Britain of raw hemp, a jute industry rises in Bengal to supply mills in Dundee, Scotland, becoming a major national industry. Exports, only 20,000 metric tons in 1849, reach 128,000 tons in 1863; 312,000 tons in 1871; and 526,000 tons in 1882. India eventually supplies two-thirds of the world's jute.

March 1, 1865: The first telegraph line to Europe opens. By 1880, less than thirty years after the laying of the first telegraph line, internal cables stretch twenty thousand miles, creating a revolution in communications.

1869: The Suez Canal opens, reducing passage between India and Britain from three months to three weeks. India is brought into closer contact with Western cultural and economic influences.

1870s: Tea plantations extend beyond Assam and Bengal into south India. European planters and traders of tea and coffee (its culture introduced in subcontinent in 1830) rapidly expand production in climate of increased infrastructure investment. Tea exports nearly triple from 1875 to 1885 as India displaces China as Britain's major supplier of tea. Blight destroys India's fledgling coffee industry in the 1890s; it does not recover for fifty years.

1870–1890: Artificially boosted by an embargo on the Confederacy during the American Civil War (1861–1865), the Indian cotton market collapses after the war, exports dropping by half between 1865 and 1866. Viceroy Lytton overrules his Legislative Council to abolish cotton duties in 1879. The move favors mechanized Lancashire cotton mills and worsens the Indian economy in these years of crop failures and famine.

1881: The Factory Act, one of Ripon's reforms, regulates child labor and conditions of factory workers. Further Factory Acts (1891, 1911, 1922, 1934) regulate working hours and mandate other improvements.

November 24, 1882: The 500-mile-long Sirhind Canal opens.

1883: The Famine Code establishes procedures for the detection and relief of famines with grain shipments, relief, and work programs.

1885: The Bengal Tenancy Act, passed after twelve years of agitation by tenant farmers, for the first time establishes tenants' right of occupancy and provides a means of equitable settlement of tenant-landlord disputes.

1885: The first meeting of Indian National Congress demands reduction of "home charges": as much as 50 percent of Indian government revenue is remitted to London to administer the India Office and meet other British charges. Dadabhai Naoroji is the prime exponent of the economic-drain argument, which holds that India's poverty is due to British charges, exploitation, and plunder of India's precious metals and raw materials.

1887: The huge Empress Cotton Mill is established in Nagpur by Jamshed Tata (1839–1904), a Parsi industrialist of Bombay. Bombay has eighty power mills by the early 1890s. By 1900 Bombay and Ahmadabad, emerging as industrial centers, are centers of this important export commodity. Tata's fortune in cotton mills helps to found India's greatest commercial dynasty; Tata enterprises largely underpin India's industrial development.

Early 1890s: A slump in the international silver market leads to a 50 percent devaluation of the rupee, resulting in economic depression and loss of foreign investment capital. The cotton import duty is reimposed in 1894, prompting retaliatory British imposition of a tax on Indian textiles.

1892: Sir Prafulla Chandra Ray (1861–1944), professor of chemistry at Calcutta, founds the Bengal Chemical and Pharmaceutical Works, the basis of India's large chemical industry.

1895: Jagadis Chandra Bose (1858–1937), professor of physics at Calcutta, wins international renown for his pioneering work on short radio waves; he is later known for work in biophysics.

1897: British physician Ronald Ross, an employee of the Indian Medical Service (1881–1899) whose researches are, however, largely self-financed, discovers that malaria is carried by mosquitoes. He wins the Nobel Prize (1902).

1904: The Cooperative Society Act provides for the creation of urban and rural credit societies. More than eight thousand cooperative societies are formed by 1912, easing the shortage of affordable credit in the agricultural sector.

1905–1910: Boycott of British goods is a bonanza for domestic manufacturers of cotton, sugar, metal, and other goods.

1908: The Calcutta Stock Exchange is founded.

1911: Jamshed Tata's son Dorabji Jamsetji Tata opens India's first steel mill at Jamshedpur in Bihar. Largely spurred by Allied military requirements during World War I, it becomes the British Empire's largest steelmaking complex. The steel industry undergoes enormous growth during and after World War I; production rises from 63,000 metric tons in 1913 to 192,000 tons in 1918 and 583,000 tons in 1927.

1914–1918: Disruptions to international trade during World War I cause shortages in India of imported commodities and food (exacerbated by large exports of wheat to Britain), inflation, speculation, and profiteering. Nearly £150 million of Indian government revenues are diverted to the war effort. Domestic industries, however, develop to compensate for lost imports.

1920: Meghnad Saha (1894–1956) publishes pioneering work on thermal ionization in the interstellar atmosphere that will become the basis of modern astrophysics.

More than a million workers participate in two hundred short strikes protesting working conditions. The All-India Trade Union Congress holds its first meeting in Bombay under Lala Lajpat Rai's presidency in October 1920. Labor unions flourish in the 1920s, supported by such legislation as the Workmen's Compensation Act (1923) and Trade Unions Act (1926), which recognizes the right to strike.

1920s–1930s: As it is elsewhere, the global postwar economic depression is severe in India, especially in the huge agricultural sector dependent on raw materials exports. Agricultural depression sends many to cities in search of (nonexistent) jobs. But this period also sees second great wave of industrialization for domestic consumption in the sugar, steel, cotton, paper, and cement industries protected by tariffs on imports.

1924: The method of quantum statistical mechanics by Satyendra Nath Bose (1894–1974), Calcutta physicist, is published by Einstein. It becomes known as "Bose-Einstein statistics," and the particle "boson" is later named for him.

1928–1929: Peak year for strikes. The Indian Trade Disputes Act and Public Safety Act (1929) aim to reduce labor unrest.

1929–1933: Severe economic depression. Protective tariffs are placed on selected industrial sectors, including iron, steel, and textiles.

1930: Sir Chandrasekhara Venkata Raman (1888–1970) wins the Nobel Prize for physics for his 1928 discovery of the "Raman effect," changes in light wavelengths on which spectroscopy technology is based. He founds the Indian Academy of Sciences (1934).

1932: Sukkur Barrage and Canals, Sind, is the final major work of a massive irrigation project in the Indus Valley. Sind and Punjab are showcases of irrigation technology: 88 percent and 58 percent of cultivated land respectively is under irrigation in these provinces by 1938–1939.

1935: The Reserve Bank of India is founded and assumes responsibility for currency and foreign exchange policy.

1939–1945: The Indian economy booms during World War II. It is a period of rapid industrial growth, especially of steel, cotton, paper, and cement, though much of the output of war industries and agricultural sector is swallowed up by Allied armies and inflation. The pharmaceutical, chemical, and light engineering sectors are developed. Domestic manufacture of bicycles, railroad engines, automobiles begins. The balance of payments shifts for the first time ever to India's favor as the country provides millions of pounds' worth of war materiel and supplies.

REPUBLIC OF INDIA: 1947–1998

1947: India enters independence as one of the world's poorest countries and with a population of 350 million. The average life expectancy is thirty-two years, half that of industrialized nations, and tuberculosis is common. Literacy rates are low. Much of India's progress during the next half-century occurs in health and education. Much of Punjab's rich wheat production has been lost to Pakistan. Millions of refugees need aid and resettlement, but resources to help them are lacking. India remains a net food importer for twenty years.

1948: *Bhoodan* (gift of land) movement initiated by Vinoba Bhave, disciple of Gandhi. Bhave walks from village to village soliciting gifts of land from wealthy landowners so he can deed it in turn to landless laborers. A million acres are transferred nationwide in the first decade.

January 26, 1950: The constitution abolishes discrimination on the basis of untouchability, but provides no mechanism for enforcing the right of this 60 million-member minority. In 1955 the Untouchability (Offenses) Act will establish university, hiring, and legislative quotas for backward castes and legal remedies for discrimination against them.

1951–1955: The First Five-Year Plan calls for rebuilding railroads, agricultural development through irrigation and canals, and boosting consumer-goods manufacturing sector. Agricultural production increases by 25 percent over the five years of the plan.

1952: With Ford Foundation support, government launches Community Development and Rural Extension Program, sending college students and technical experts into villages to support self-help agricultural, water, and educational initiatives.

1953: Air India is nationalized. It becomes a major international carrier.

1956–1961: The Second Five-Year Plan continues drive for food production, concentrates on industry and mining of iron and coal. The Five-Year Plans are extremely successful: industrial production doubles from 1955 to 1964. Production of electricity quadruples from 1950 to 1960, and triples from 1960 to 1970.

April 1, 1957: Adoption of decimal currency.

1957: Completion of the sixteen-mile-long Hirakud Dam on the Mahanadi River, the longest dam in the world.

1958: India's first nuclear reactor, its technology developed jointly with Canada, goes online.

1959–1964: Nationwide introduction of *Panchayati Raj* (government by village councils), adapting traditional *panchayats* into a three-tiered system devolving local responsibility for economic development.

1960: The Indus Waters Treaty is signed with Pakistan for development of Indus waters.

1961: The first ten years of planned economy result in an increase in food-grain production from 51 million tons to 82 million tons. The population grows from 360 million to 440 million during the period.

1961–1966: The Third Five-Year Plan focuses on heavy industries and makes India world's seventh-ranked industrial nation. Iron, steel, electricity, cement, fertilizer, and consumer goods industries receive $5 billion in aid from the Aid India Consortium (the United States, Britain, Canada, France, West Germany, and Japan). Industrial development is rapid during these years: steel production, 1,732 metric tons in 1955, and 3,286 tons in 1960, nearly doubles again to 6,470 tons in 1965.

1962: Adoption of the metric system of measurement.

1965: Introduction of dwarf Indica high-yield rice. The "Green Revolution" of the late 1960s vastly increases grain production by introduction of high-yield Mexican wheat, Taiwanese and Philippine rice, and chemical fertilizers. Wheat is the star performer, production nearly doubling in the twenty years after 1969. Major wheat-growing areas in Punjab and western Uttar Pradesh benefit economically: Punjab, with the largest per capita income, has the highest standard of living in the country.

June 1966: Devaluation of the rupee from 4.76 to 7.50 per U.S. $1 dents government's popularity. Economy is further weakened by war with Pakistan and poor monsoons.

1969: The first nuclear reactors are completed at Trapur.

Life expectancy at birth reaches fifty-one years, a rise of nineteen years in the twenty-two years since India gained independence.

1970: The revised Fourth Five-Year Plan, issued after postponements, calls for increased funding for agriculture and a substantial government commitment to family planning.

1970s: Sanjay Gandhi oversees two major governmental programs, both controversial. The family planning program, encouraging two-child families, is locally and sometimes harshly implemented; revelations of abuses (1977) lead to its collapse, overall decline in use of birth control, and a return to higher birthrates.

Early 1970s: The global oil shock hits India and contributes to a rate of inflation among the highest in the world and a deterioration in the balance of trade.

1970s: A slum-clearance program in Delhi lacks adequate plans for resettlement of those evicted; many lower-class Congress supporters are alienated. Population growth of major cities during the 1960s and 1970s outstrips provision of infrastructure and services: over these twenty years the population of Calcutta, India's largest city, increases from 4.4 million to 9.2 million, Bombay from 4.2 million to 8.2 million, and Delhi from 2.1 million to 4.9 million.

June 1, 1972: The Space Commission and Department of Space are created by government resolution. The space program is centered on the multipurpose Indian National Satellite System (INSAT) and the Indian Remote-sensing Satellite System (IRS); India becomes a world leader in the application of satellite technology to socioeconomic development in, for example, managing natural resources and forecasting natural disasters.

1974: The Fifth Five-Year Plan aims boldly at "removal of poverty" and "attainment of economic self-reliance" through continued high investment in industry and further huge increases in grain production. Trade increases rapidly from the mid-1970s: total value of exports nearly doubles from 1975 to 1980, from 36.4 billion to 66 billion rupees, as imports more than double from 53.4 billion to 111 billion rupees.

May 18, 1974: The first Indian underground test of a nuclear device.

1975: Emergency years see significant rises in productivity, capital investment, and industrial growth.

April 19, 1975: First Indian satellite launched, named *Aryabhata* after the fifth-century astronomer. Indian satellites will be launched from foreign bases until 1980.

1977: Eradication of smallpox is declared.

1979–1980: *Satyagraha* (noncooperation) campaign closes down new oil fields in Assam, threatens foreign exchange earnings by important regional tea and jute industries. (Cotton, tea, rice, jute are still India's major exports.)

July 1980: India becomes the world's sixth country to launch its own satellites with the successful launch of the *Rohini* satellite.

1980s: Industrial growth continues at an astonishing rate, with industrial production up 80 percent overall from 1980 to 1988. The electricity and natural gas industries grow exponentially: electricity production doubles during these eight years (India also jointly develops several major hydroelectric projects with Bhutan). Steel production is up nearly 40 percent. Trade continues to boom, with the value of exports in 1980–1988 rising from 66 billion to 185 billion rupees, as imports increase from 111 billion to 267 billion rupees.

1982: Indian scientific expedition to Antarctica.

1984: Rajiv Gandhi implements probusiness policies based on the U.S. model of development. He promotes high-tech imports and foreign investment; India subsequently becomes a world leader in training computer technicians.

Rakesh Sharmi becomes the first Indian in space as part of a Soviet team.

1986–1990: Life expectancy at birth reaches fifty-eight years, according to UN figures.

1989: Test launch of the intermediate-range ballistic missile *Agni*.

1990s: Government statistics indicate that nearly 350 million of India's 960 million people live in poverty.

July 1991: Government abandons centralized planning and announces plans to reform trade and industry and liberalize the economy. This "structural reform," designed to address among other problems a foreign exchange and foreign debt crisis, is backed by International Monetary Fund and World Bank loans, but is domestically unpopular.

1992: Second-generation INSAT-2A is the first Indian-made communications satellite to be placed in orbit. The first Indian-built submarine, INS *Shalki*, is commissioned.

February 27, 1993: In order to promote exports, the rupee is allowed to float in trade dealings. Full convertibility is extended to other sectors of the economy in subsequent years.

May 11–13, 1998: India conducts five underground nuclear tests, its first since 1974, and for the first time acknowledges itself to be a nuclear state. (Pakistan will respond by conducting its first nuclear test on May 28.)

Pakistan

Until independence in 1947 and partition from India, the provinces of Pakistan are politically conjoined with the Indian empires of the subcontinent. Consequently, the long history of what will become the state of Pakistan belongs to the chronology of India and includes such phases as the ancient Harappan civilization of the Indus Valley, the rise of Sikhism in Punjab, the Delhi sultanate and Mughal periods, the nationalist movement, and other events before independence.

Pakistan's history since independence is politically tumultuous. The military vies for power with the civil authorities; civilian and, frequently, military governors-general, then prime ministers compete with the legislature for authority, and prime ministers arrogate dictatorial powers. Martial law is several times declared, and the country is for twenty years directly under military power, governed by generals Ayub Khan and Zia after military coups. Corruption and nepotism are rife.

Relations with India after independence are for the most part tense, occasionally erupting into open warfare: Pakistan fights, and loses, three wars with India. It is the Cold War, however, that dominates foreign relations until the 1990s. Pakistan allies itself with U.S.-led Western nations that funnel a large amount of advanced weaponry into the country to counter the USSR, particularly after the Soviet invasion of neighboring Afghanistan in 1979. At the same time, Pakistan pursues a vigorous nuclear program, refusing to sign international treaties and citing its need to match India's nuclear capability. This culminates in Pakistan's first successful nuclear bomb test in 1998.

August 14, 1947: Pakistan is born as provinces of British India with a large Islamic population (Sind, North West Frontier Province, Baluchistan, and parts of Punjab and Bengal) are partitioned into an independent nation of 32.5 million. Pakistan itself is geographically split, its western and eastern wings separated by the thousand-mile expanse of northern India; until 1959, its capital is Karachi, on the Arabian Sea coast in West Pakistan. Muhammad Ali Jinnah (dies September 1948), leader of the Muslim

League and the architect of Muslim separatism, becomes governor-general.

Are the wise men of Europe who have hung
Their ring in the nose of Greece and Hindustan:
is this their civilizations' highest rung—
A childless woman and a jobless man?

"A Question," poem by Allama Muhammad Iqbal
(1930s)

August 1947: One of largest migrations in history begins as millions of Hindus and Sikhs leave West Punjab, now Pakistan, to cross into India as Muslims in India territory cross into Pakistan. Government control on both sides of the border is seriously threatened; six weeks of massacres, looting, and arson result in estimated half a million deaths. Ten to fifteen million people become refugees.

September 30, 1947: Pakistan joins the United Nations.

October 26, 1947: Maharaja Hari Singh of Kashmir, a Hindu hoping to keep his largely Muslim state independent of both India and Pakistan, accedes to India in exchange for military assistance. A crisis ensues. Muslims in southwest Kashmir revolt, aided by Pashtun tribesmen from Pakistan; Indian troops are airlifted in. Three days of heavy fighting subsides into the two-year-long First (and undeclared) Indo-Pakistani War. Kashmir is to prove the most persistent and intractable of India's territorial disputes.

June 1949: The Awami (People's) League is founded by Husain Shahid Suhrawardy as an alternative to the Muslim League; its aim is to extend the political base to non-Muslims. The Awami League is to become East Pakistan's leading political party.

September 7, 1950: The Constituent Assembly presents a report on the constitution. Its failure to agree on the terms of a new constitution reflects the political instability that afflicts Pakistan from the outset; the government fails to secure public confidence or support.

It is extremely difficult to appreciate why our Hindu friends fail to understand the real nature of Islam and Hinduism. They are not religions in the strict sense of the word, but are in fact different and distinct social orders, and it is a dream that the Hindus and Muslims can ever evolve a common nationality, and this misconception of one Indian nation has gone far beyond the limits and is the cause of most of your troubles and will lead India to destruction if we fail to revise our notions in time.

Presidential address to the Muslim League by
Quaid-i-azam Muhammad Ali Jinnah (March 1940)

February 23, 1951: The Rawalpindi Conspiracy, a planned coup against the government and commander-in-chief General Muhammad Ayub Khan, is exposed.

October 18, 1951: Assassination of prime minister Liaquat Ali Khan (governs 1947–1951) at a public meeting in Rawalpindi.

February 21, 1952: Riots in East Bengal's capital, Dhaka, follow the rejection of Bengali as an official national language coequal with Urdu and English. Several dozen protesters are killed, and the date is henceforth commemorated as Martyrs Day in East Pakistan. In West Pakistan, communal tensions exist among Baluchis, Pashtuns, and Muhajirs, Urdu-speaking immigrants from the 1947 partition.

November 2, 1953: The Constituent Assembly votes to declare Pakistan an Islamic republic.

1953–1954: U.S. military alliance with Pakistan.

March 5, 1954: Pakistan joins the Southeast Asia Treaty Organization (SEATO).

March 19, 1954: United Front coalition crushes Muslim League in East Pakistan elections on a twenty-one-point platform advocating provincial autonomy and official status for Bengali. Abdul Kasem Fazlul Haq forms a short-lived government in Dhaka in April; the central government arrests him for treason and imposes direct rule (until 1956).

May 19, 1954: Pakistan and the United States sign a mutual defense treaty.

June 7, 1954: Inauguration of Pakistan International Airlines.

September 22, 1954: The Constituent Assembly votes to curtail the power of the governor-general, whose plans for the administrative merger of the four western provinces (Punjab, North-West Frontier Province, Sind, and Baluchistan) are unpopular and who has dismissed a number of provincial and national officials.

October 24, 1954: The governor-general declares a state of emergency; the cabinet and Constituent Assembly are dissolved. The Supreme Court later upholds their dissolution.

1955: Pakistan is a founding member (with Turkey, Iraq, Iran, and Britain) of the Middle East Treaty Organization. This mutual security alliance, later known as Central Treaty Organization (minus Iraq and plus the United States, 1959–1979) is designed to counter Soviet influence in the Middle East.

September 30, 1955: The four western provinces are abolished and replaced with the single administrative unit of West Pakistan. East Bengal is renamed East Pakistan.

1955–1960: The first of a series of economic Five-Year Plans. Industrialization proceeds rapidly; using 100 as base index of industrial production in 1955, industrial production index reaches 147 by 1960 and 265 by 1964. Other early priorities in the planned economy include development of natural gas and electrical power industries; generation of electrical power increases nearly tenfold during the 1950s, another sixfold during the 1960s.

March 23, 1956: The first constitution takes effect. Pakistan becomes an Islamic republic. Legislative seats are evenly divided between eastern and western wings of the country. The date will be celebrated annually hereafter as Pakistan Day.

October 28, 1958: Martial law administrator General Ayub Khan exiles President Iskander Mirza (rules 1956–1958) and assumes the presidency (1958–1969) three weeks after Mirza's declaration of martial law. Ayub Khan's major achievement is land reform designed to end traditional feudal patterns of land ownership.

1959–1967: Construction of a new capital at the northern city of Islamabad, planned and designed by leading international architects, including Louis I. Kahn (National Assembly Building). The northern city of Rawalpindi serves as provisional capital during these years.

September 19, 1960: Pakistan and India sign the Indus Waters Treaty.

March 2, 1961: The Muslim Family Laws Ordinance regulates marriage and divorce.

March 23, 1962: Ayub Khan promulgates second constitution, ending martial law. He assumes presidency, an office granted enhanced powers by the new constitution.

March 2, 1963: Pakistan and China sign a border agreement in Beijing. The Chinese alliance is intended to counterbalance India's relationship with the Soviets.

Life is beautiful.
It will not remain so forever.
As the waters have gone to the sea,
And the flowers have gone with the spring
So will joys depart.

From a poem by Ai Li (1908–)

December 25, 1963: The Fundamental Rights Bill passes National Assembly; civil rights become legally enforceable.

1964: Introduction of television.

August 29, 1964: Pakistan's first submarine is delivered by the United States.

1965: Reported opening of the first nuclear reactor in Pakistan. Foreign Minister Zulfikar Bhutto promises, "If India builds the bomb, we will eat grass or leaves, even go hungry. But we will get one of our own."

1965: Monsoons fail; famine threatens. The years 1966–1967 will be a time of further drought.

January 1, 1965: In the first presidential election under the 1962 constitution, Ayub Khan, running as a Muslim League candidate, narrowly defeats Combined Opposition Party's Fatima Jinnah, Muhammad Ali Jinnah's sister.

January–June 1965: Two thousand cease-fire violations are reported in Kashmir; India charges Pakistan with guerrilla infiltration, while Pakistan ascribes the unrest to an indigenous revolt.

February 16, 1965: At a meeting of opposition parties, Rahman presents Six-Point Program, a plan for federal system with provincial control of taxes, currency, trade, and militia—in effect, independence for East Pakistan.

April 1965: U.S.-equipped Pakistani troops fire on Indian guards along contested border and easily penetrate Indian territory in western Rann of Kutch. Two weeks of fighting are ended by arrival of monsoons. The Commonwealth and United Nations press for a cease-fire (agreed June 30). A UN commission is charged with establishing the Indo-Pakistani border.

September 1–25, 1965: The Second Indo-Pakistani War is fought after a year of violence in Kashmir and a month of cross-border operations. It begins with major Pakistani invasion of Jammu; fighting is widespread in Kashmir and Punjab for several weeks as air strikes target Lahore, Delhi, and Karachi. Limited in duration by a U.S.-British arms embargo on both combatants, the war kills twenty thousand, mostly civilians, and ends inconclusively with Indian forces circling Lahore. The United Nations negotiates a cease-fire (September 27), but Pakistan is clearly the loser. Pakistan's government declares a national emergency (lasting until 1985). The arms embargo on combatants imposed during the war will last ten years.

January 4–10, 1966: Pakistani president Muhammad Ayub Khan and Indian prime minister Shastri meet at the historic Tashkent Summit, sponsored by the USSR. The Declaration of Tashkent pledges "normal and peaceful" relations, restoration of economic and trade ties, and diplomatic resolution of disputes. Territorial sovereignty is restored to status quo ante, and troops are withdrawn to their prewar positions.

1966: The Awami League, headed by Sheikh Mujibur Rahman, proclaims the Six-Point Program as the basis for Pakistan's constitution.

1967: Pakistan adopts the metric system.

November 30, 1967: The Pakistan People's Party (PPP) is formed in Lahore under the chairmanship of Zulfikar Ali Bhutto.

1968: Agreement with India over disputed territory in the Rann of Kutch.

Pakistan declines to sign the international Nuclear Non-Proliferation Treaty, citing the necessity of maintaining a balance of power in the subcontinent. Both India and Pakistan persist in refusing to sign this treaty despite international appeals to them to do so.

March 25, 1969: Ayub Khan is forced to resign after years of opposition to his rule. He turns the presidency over to General Agha Muhammad Yahya Khan (rules 1969–1971). Yahya Khan immediately abrogates the constitution, dissolves legislative assemblies, and reimposes martial law, but political parties are restored and elections scheduled for 1970.

November 12, 1970: A cyclone and tidal wave kill hundreds of thousands of people in East Pakistan.

December 7, 1970: Awami League wins 160 of 162 National Constituent Assembly seats from East Pakistan, giving Rahman overall parliamentary majority. He prepares to form a government and push through the Awami League federalist platform. Bhutto refuses to participate in Awami League government. The political cleft precipitates a crisis; demonstrations in East Pakistan become violent.

March 25, 1971: Yahya Khan declares an emergency in East Pakistan, bans Awami League, and arrests Rahman. Pakistan's army attacks Bengali separatists demonstrating in East Pakistan.

I remember,
Dacca, March 1971,
Sabir, friend and brother
your gray eyes suddenly become sombre
foreseeing
a universal blood dance
a universal blight that
amputees inflict on themselves
you saw it all
the lost cause, the awesome response
yet you smiled
the secret smile of the soldier
knowing
that darkness will descend
and eternal glory be won.

Poem by Akbar S. Ahmed (1972)

April 17, 1971: Nationalist leaders in East Pakistan declare independence as the state of Bangladesh. A million Bengalis flee to India in April, where they establish a government in exile and a national army (Mukti Bahini). During the nine-month civil war, 300,000 people are killed. Ten million refugees cross the border to India.

August 9, 1971: India signs treaty with the Soviets in geopolitical realignment that prompts a counterbalancing U.S. foreign policy "tilt" toward Pakistan.

December 3–17, 1971: The Third Indo-Pakistani War coincides with the final stage of the Bangladeshi war of independence. Provoked by India's aid to Bangladeshi rebels, Pakistan strikes Indian air bases and invades Kashmir and East Pakistan. Superior Soviet-equipped Indian forces overrun Pakistani forces in the east, while holding off Pakistani attacks on western Indian territory.

December 16, 1971: Pakistan surrenders Dhaka to Indian army; India declares cease-fire (December 17). East Pakistan achieves independence as the state of Bangladesh; refugees in India are quickly repatriated. The outcome is a major geopolitical victory for Indira Gandhi. The peace accord signed at Simla (July 2, 1972) provides for repatriation of ninety thousand prisoners of war.

December 20, 1971: Yahya Khan's government collapses. Zulfikar Ali Bhutto becomes president of Pakistan (president 1971–1973, prime minister 1973–1978). One of his first acts is to free Rahman after a huge public rally in Karachi (January 3, 1972). Bhutto pursues a domestic policy of "Islamic socialism" and improves relations with India, other Islamic states, and the United States.

1973–1974: Revolt in Baluchistan is subdued by large-scale bombing by Pakistani and Indian forces.

April 10, 1973: Passage of the third constitution, framed by National Assembly, establishes the federal republic and invests the prime minister with executive power. Urdu becomes Pakistan's official language.

1974: Heavy industries and banks are nationalized.

February 22, 1974: Pakistan recognizes Bangladesh. Prime minister Bhutto hosts a meeting of thirty-seven Islamic countries in Lahore.

March 7, 1977: General elections called by Bhutto, who is seeking popular mandate, are contested by nine-party opposition coalition. Bhutto's PPP wins amid charges of vote-rigging.

July 5, 1977: Coup by army chief of staff General Muhammad Zia ul-Haq. He unseats prime minister Bhutto, suspends the constitution, and declares martial law (its imposition is later upheld by the Supreme Court). He assumes a so-called caretaker presidency (September 16, 1978, until 1988) with sweeping powers; during his administration political parties are banned, their leaders arrested, and censorship enforced. Elections, though periodically promised, are delayed until 1985.

September 16, 1977: Bhutto, charged with conspiracy to murder a political opponent, is arrested. The Lahore High Court unanimously finds him guilty and sentences him to death (March 18, 1978).

January 1, 1978: Eleven thousand political prisoners jailed by Bhutto's government are released and the Hyderabad Special Tribunal is dissolved. Results of a government investigation into Bhutto's misdeeds during the 1977 election are published in July.

1979: Opening of Khunjerab Pass on Karakoram Highway, North-West Frontier Province, provides an all-weather highway through the Himalayas to China.

February 10, 1979: Provincial high courts are supplemented with *sharia* (Islamic law) benches of Muslim *qazis* (chief judges) to rule on Islamic law.

March 12, 1979: Pakistan quits the Western-oriented Central Treaty Organization (CENTO).

April 4, 1979: Zulfikar Ali Bhutto is hanged despite international appeals for clemency.

November 1979: The U.S. embassy in Islamabad is sacked; Pakistani authorities decline to intervene.

December 27, 1979: The USSR invades Afghanistan, beginning a nineteen-year-long war as Afghan rebels fight the Soviet-controlled government in Kabul. By August 1981, 2.3 million registered Afghan refugees from the fighting, mostly Pashtuns, have crossed the border into Pakistan, where they are housed in tent encampments in North-West Frontier Province and Baluchistan. The influx, reaching 3.5 million refugees at its peak, imposes an immense economic burden on Pakistan.

1980s: The United States steps up arms sales to Pakistan; Afghani fundamentalist rebels (*mujahedeen*) operate from border camps inside Pakistan, supplied with U.S. antiaircraft weapons and other arms funneled through Pakistani political organizations. The increase in weaponry available in Pakistan militarizes domestic communal violence.

March 7, 1980: Founding of Islamic University, Islamabad.

June 3, 1980: Measures announced to bring the legal code into line with *sharia*, the code of Islamic law, include reforms of education, banking, and the judiciary.

1981: A census records Pakistan's population as 84,254,000, up from 65,309,000 in 1971 and 42,880,000 in 1961.

February 7, 1981: Nine opposition parties join to found the Movement for the Restoration of Democracy (MRD), which demands Zia's resignation, the lifting of martial law, and free multiparty elections.

November 11, 1981: Zia formally submits an offer made verbally in September for a "no war" pact with India. The offer comes amid increased border incidents and the controversial purchase of F-16 fighters from the United States, which increases economic and military aid to Pakistan throughout the early 1980s to counter Soviet military assistance to India.

March 11, 1983: Signing of accord with India for cultural and economic cooperation.

September 28–October 2, 1983: Opposition boycotts the first local elections in Sind and Punjab since the 1977 coup. Widespread clashes and thousands of arrests mar the campaign.

December 1984: Refugees from the war in Afghanistan number 2.5 million, posing severe economic and logistical problems. Afghani resistance to the Soviet occupation is headquartered at Peshawar and armed by the United States and Pakistan until Pakistan stops supporting Afghani *mujahedeen* (*c.* 1991).

December 19, 1984: In a national referendum on Zia's presidency that is widely believed to be rigged, a huge majority of voters endorse his program of Islamization and the extension of his term of office. MRD boycotts the election.

January 1, 1985: Non-Islamic banking is abolished.

February 25, 1985: General election for National Assembly proceeds despite opposition boycott. Constitution is restored (March 10) and on April 10 Muhammad Khan Junejo forms the first civilian cabinet in eight years; it will last until 1988.

December 8, 1985: Pakistan is a founding member of the South Asian Association for Regional Cooperation (SAARC).

December 30, 1985: Restoration of the constitution. Martial law and the twenty-year-long national emergency are lifted. Despite the installation of a civilian government, Zia retains power.

August 14, 1986: MRD demands new general elections. Opposition parties hold rallies throughout the year despite government ban on demonstrations; four hundred opposition leaders are arrested, including PPP leader Benazir Bhutto, daughter of Zulfikar Ali Bhutto.

December 14–15, 1986: One hundred and fifty people are killed in the worst ethnic riots in Karachi since independence. Serious communal violence between Pashtuns and Muhajirs again breaks out in July 1987, April–May and October 1988, and May 1990.

1988: Pakistan, Afghanistan, the United States, and the Soviet Union sign an agreement pledging Soviet withdrawal from Afghanistan.

May 29–31, 1988: Zia dismisses Prime Minister Muhammad Khan Junejo (rules 1986–1988) for alleged corruption, dissolves national and provincial assemblies, and calls for new elections. The Supreme Court later rules the dissolution unconstitutional (March 10, 1989).

June 15, 1988: Zia declares *sharia* to be the supreme law of Pakistan.

August 17, 1988: President Zia, the U.S. ambassador, and a number of senior army officers are killed when their airplane crashes.

November 16, 1988: PPP wins 92 of 207 contested National Assembly seats in the first free general election in ten years. Benazir Bhutto becomes prime minister (December

2, until 1990), the first woman to head a modern Islamic state.

December 29–31, 1988: At private meetings during SAARC summit, Bhutto and Rajiv Gandhi of India sign bilateral agreements on cultural exchanges, taxation, and nuclear security.

February 5, 1989: Official announcement of first successful test of long-range missile (first reported by *New York Times*, May 1988).

May 22, 1989: Government commits to a twenty-year plan to develop nuclear power plants. Despite government's public insistence that Pakistan is pursuing only peaceful uses of nuclear technology, international concern persists that the technology will be used to produce bombs.

October 1, 1989: Pakistan rejoins the Commonwealth of Nations seventeen years after quitting to protest Bangladesh's independence.

January 1990: Explosions and border skirmishes in Jammu and Kashmir after months of increased violence, strikes, and terrorism. Pakistani-backed fundamentalists seeking independence or union with Pakistan continue their terrorist campaign; more than half a million Indian troops are deployed. An estimated forty thousand Kashmiris die in the violence from 1989 to 1994.

August 6, 1990: President Ghulam Ishaq Khan dismisses Prime Minister Benazir Bhutto and dissolves the National Assembly. The courts uphold her removal; she is later charged with abuse of power, corruption, and nepotism. Bhutto's PPP loses every province to the Islamic Alliance, a rightist coalition, in October 24 elections.

October 1990: The U.S. Congress suspends military and economic aid to Pakistan because of continued nuclear weapons development. Delivery of $370 million worth of military equipment, including twenty-eight F-16 fighters, is blocked. The Agency for International Development (USAID) announces in December 1991 that it will also stop aid to Pakistan.

1991: Pakistan leads South Asia with a growth in GDP of 6.7 percent.

February 1991: The foreign secretary admits that Pakistan has capability of producing nuclear weapons, but denies any intention of testing a bomb or exporting nuclear weapons technology.

1991: Pakistan sends ten thousand troops to join the international coalition against Iraq during the Persian Gulf War.

September 1992: Floods kill two thousand people.

October 6, 1993: Running on an anticorruption program, Benazir Bhutto is narrowly elected to a second term as prime minister (rules 1993–1996). It is the fourth change of government in a year characterized by power struggles between Prime Minister Nawaz Sharif and President Ghulam Ishaq Khan.

1994: Benazir Bhutto and her brother, Mir Murtaza, have been in competition over who should head their father's Pakistan People's Party. Realizing that Benazir has no intention of yielding power, by June Murtaza forms a faction with his supporters.

December 3, 1994: Pakistan and China agree to strengthen financial and technical cooperation in heavy industry, engineering, and power generation.

December 17, 1994: The UN General Assembly approves a resolution sponsored by Pakistan and Bangladesh calling for nuclear-weapon-free zone in South Asia.

March 2, 1995: An International Commission of Jurists report upholds Indian allegations of Pakistan government's complicity in Muslim separatist terrorism in Kashmir.

April 11–13, 1995: Prime Minister Bhutto visits Washington; top agenda items include nuclear proliferation, the blocked delivery of F-16 fighters, and the alleged supply of M-11 missiles to Pakistan by China. U.S. military aid to Pakistan, suspended since 1990, is resumed in October.

September 6, 1995: Several thousand people

protesting Pakistani support for the Taliban militia attack Pakistan's embassy in Kabul.

September 20, 1996: Benizar Bhutto's brother, Mir Murtaza, and seven of his bodyguards are killed in a twenty-minute gun battle with the police in Karachi. The police claim they were fired on first. Murtaza had made so many political enemies that it is never established just who was behind his death.

September 24, 1996: China, France, Russia, the United Kingdom, and the United States sign the UN draft Comprehensive Nuclear Test Ban Treaty despite India's veto. India and Pakistan both refuse to sign, preventing its enactment into international law.

November 5, 1996: Benazir Bhutto is removed as prime minister by President Farooq Leghari on charges of economic mismanagement and corruption. An interim government is installed. Benazir's husband Asif Ali Zardari is immediately imprisoned and charged with conspiring in the murder of her brother, Mir Murtaza (September 20, 1996).

1997: Pakistan's estimated population is 132 million, projected to reach 259 million by 2030. (Pakistan would then be the world's fourth-largest country.)

February 3, 1997: Turnout is low in the fourth general election in nine years, with only 25 percent of voters coming to the polls. Nawaz Sharif's Pakistan Muslim League (PML-N) wins 134 seats to PPP's 18, even capturing seats in Bhutto's stronghold of Sind.

1998: Throughout 1998, Benazir Bhutto, her jailed husband, Asif Ali Zardari, and her mother, Nusrat Bhutto, find themselves fighting charges that they accepted millions of dollars in kickbacks in government contracts and engaged in shady business and real estate deals; eventually it is alleged that the family took some $1.5 billion. On April 28, the government freezes the family's accounts and assets. On September 2, the Swiss government issues an indictment charging Benazir Bhutto with money laundering through Swiss banks. In June, a Pakistan court begins hearing the charges.

April 6, 1998: Pakistan conducts the first successful test of the surface-to-surface *Ghauri* missile, capable of penetrating deep into Indian territory.

May 28, 1998: Pakistan announces it has tested five nuclear devices, thus making its the world's seventh nuclear power. Pakistan justifies its action on the grounds that India has tested nuclear devices on May 11 and 13. When the international community expresses its disapproval—including the U.S.

imposition of economic sanctions—Pakistan's President Rafiq Tarar immediately declares a state of national emergency.

September 22–October 5, 1998: On September 22 Asif Ali Zardari, Benazir Bhutto's husband, is charged with corruption. On October 5 Bhutto is formally charged with corruption. Through all the months that she has been under investigation, Benazir Bhutto has been free to play an active role in opposing the government and even to travel, all the while claiming that all charges are politically motivated.

Bangladesh

The early history of Bangladesh falls within the chronology of India, where until 1947 it is effectively the easternmost province, known as East Bengal. Upon the partition of India and Pakistan in that year, Islamic East Bengal becomes the eastern wing of Pakistan. (The East Pakistan period [1947–1971] is dealt with in the chapter on Pakistan, and includes the years of struggle for independence.)

East Pakistan achieves independence as Bangladesh (Land of the Bengalis) only after a civil war and the intervention of India in 1971. The country's first prime minister, Sheikh Mujibur Rahman, almost immediately imposes martial law, and the political history of Bangladesh is an unhappy narrative of dictatorship punctuated by coups, assassinations, and brief experiments in constitutional democracy. Underneath it all lies a country constantly struggling with the relentless pressures of its natural environment, its population, and its poverty.

December 1970: Elections are held throughout Pakistan to choose an assembly that will write a new constitution. The Awami League, the party based in East Pakistan and led by Sheik Mujibar Rahman, wins a majority and calls for self-government of East Pakistan.

The road to you is blocked
By temples and mosques.
I hear your call, my lord,
But I cannot advance—
Masters and teachers bar my way. . . .

Spiritual song by Madan Baul (19th century)

March 1, 1971: Determined not to let the Awami League have its way, Pakistan's president Yahya Khan postpones the first meeting of the newly elected assembly. Demonstrations begin to unsettle East Pakistan.

March 25, 1971: Yahya Khan declares an emergency in East Pakistan, bans the Awami League, and arrests Rahman. Pakistan's army attacks demonstrating Bengali separatists in East Pakistan. Civil war breaks out.

March 26, 1971: A group of Bangladeshi nationalists make a covert radio broadcast in East Pakistan calling for independence from Pakistan. This event will be observed as Bangladesh's Independence Day.

April 17, 1971: Nationalist leaders in East Pakistan declare independence as the state of Bangladesh. A million Bengalis flee to India in April, where they establish a government in exile and a national army (Mukti Bahini). During the nine-month civil war, 300,000 people are killed. Ten million refugees cross the border to India.

December 3–17, 1971: The Third Indo-Pakistani War coincides with final stage of the Bangladeshi war of independence. Provoked by India's aid to Bangladeshi rebels, Pakistan strikes Indian air bases and invades Kashmir and East Pakistan. Superior Soviet-equipped Indian forces overrun Pakistani forces in the east while holding off Pakistani attacks on western Indian territory.

December 4, 1971: The assembly dominated by the Awami League adopts a new constitution for an independent Bangladesh.

December 16, 1971: Pakistan surrenders Dhaka to the Indian army; on December 17 India declares a cease-fire. December 16 is hereafter celebrated annually as Victory (or National) Day as East Pakistan achieves independence as the state of Bangladesh; refugees in India are quickly repatriated. The outcome is a major geopolitical victory for Indira Gandhi. A peace accord signed at Simla (July 2, 1972) provides for the repatriation of ninety thousand prisoners of war. Dhaka, capital of the former East Pakistan, becomes the capital of the new nation, renamed Dacca. Bangladesh faces endemic poverty and food shortages and enormous destruction from its nine-month war for independence.

January 10, 1972: Freed from prison in West Pakistan, Sheikh Mujibur Rahman returns to Dacca. He is sworn in as prime minister (1972–1975) and issues an interim constitution.

1972: Banks and Pakistani-owned industries are nationalized. The national currency, the *taka*, is introduced, replacing the rupee.

December 16, 1972: The constitution of independent Bangladesh takes effect, instituting parliamentary democracy and enacting

principles of *Mujibbad* (Mujibism): nationalism, secularism, democracy, and socialism.

March 1973: The Awami League wins 292 of 300 seats in first general election to Jatiya Sangsad (parliament). The centerpiece of Rahman's program of socialist legislation is the rapid nationalization of industries. His administration is hampered by corruption, inefficiency, and the lack of experienced civil servants.

1974: The first national census records the population at 76,398,000.

February 22, 1974: Pakistan formally recognizes Bangladesh as an independent state.

July–August 1974: Hundreds of thousands of people are killed as heavy monsoons and flooding leave 40 percent of the country under water.

September 17, 1974: Bangladesh joins the United Nations.

December 28, 1974: After months of political chaos, Rahman declares a state of emergency and suspends the constitution.

January 25, 1975: Rahman amends the constitution, abolishes parliament, and assumes near-total power in his own hands as president. Political parties except the Awami League are outlawed on February 25.

June 6, 1975: Opposition parties are outlawed: Rahman's new party, Bangladesh Krishak Sramik Awami League (BAKSAL), is the sole legitimate political entity.

August 15, 1975: In the so-called majors' plot, disaffected army officers assassinate Rahman and his family and install Khandakar Mushtaque Ahmed as president (rules August–November 1975). BAKSAL is disbanded.

November 3–7, 1975: An attempted coup by Rahman adherents fails.

1976: Tribal peoples in the southeastern Chittagong Hill Tracts, mostly Buddhists of Tibetan descent, begin a guerrilla campaign against government resettlement of Bengali Muslims in the hill region. The army and Muslim settlers are targeted and 3500 people killed in a campaign that continues until the late 1990s.

April 21, 1977: Major General Ziaur Rahman (Zia), chief martial law administrator and a key figure in suppressing the November 1975 rebellion, becomes president (rules 1977–1981). His presidency is ratified in an uncontested referendum on May 30.

April 1978: Zia lifts the ban on political parties and creates an independent judiciary.

June 3, 1978: At the head of the new Jatiyatabadi Ganotantrik Dal (JAGODAL, National Democratic Party), Zia is elected president with 76.7 percent of the votes. He promulgates the 19-Point Program promoting self-sufficiency; its chief goals are to increase food production and promote family planning.

February 18, 1979: Zia's party, now named the Bangladesh Nationalist Party (BNP), wins 207 of 300 parliamentary seats in a general election, handily defeating the Awami League (39) and the newly resurrected Muslim League (20).

April 6, 1979: Martial law is revoked and the constitution restored.

Where the mind is without fear and the head is held high;
Where knowledge is free;
Where the world has not been broken up into fragments by narrow domestic walls;
Where words come out from the depth of truth;
Where tireless striving stretches its arms toward perfection;
Where the clear stream of reason has not lost its way into the dreary desert sand of dead habit;
Where the mind is led forward by thee into everwidening thought and action—
Into that heaven of freedom, my Father, let my country awake.

Poem by Rabindranath Tagore (1912)

May 30, 1981: President Zia, along with two aides and six bodyguards, is assassinated in an attempted coup by disgruntled army officers. By June 1 the government announces that the rebellion is crushed. On September 23 twelve officers are executed.

March 24, 1982: Zia's successor, Abdus Sattar (rules 1981–1982), is ousted in a bloodless coup by army chief of staff Hussain Muhammad Ershad (rules 1982–1990), who establishes martial law, suspends the constitution (until November 1986), and outlaws political parties. His administration is marked by Islamization and an anticorruption drive.

October 7, 1982: A border agreement is signed with India.

1983: Dacca is renamed Dhaka.

February 14–15, 1983: Student protests sparked by a new Arabic language requirement in schools turn into riots against martial law.

October 14, 1984: Amid an opposition campaign of general strikes and demonstrations, 2 million people demonstrate in Dhaka against Ershad's martial law regime and demand a neutral caretaker government until elections are held.

January 16, 1985: Ershad appoints a new "non-political" cabinet and announces the restoration of political rights (rescinded in March).

March 21, 1985: Ershad's presidency (assumed June 1984) is ratified in a referendum widely felt to be rigged. Parliamentary elections scheduled for April 6 are canceled after a boycott by opposition parties.

May 24–25, 1985: Eleven thousand people are killed and hundreds of thousands left homeless by a severe cyclone and tidal wave.

December 8, 1985: Bangladesh is a founding member of the South Asian Association for Regional Cooperation (SAARC).

May 7, 1986: Amid charges of fraud, the general election is swept by Ershad's Jatiya (National) Party. The Awami League coalition, led by Rahman's daughter Sheikh Hasina Wazed, wins one hundred seats, while BNP, led by Zia's widow, Khaleda Zia, boycotts the election. Ershad is reelected president in October.

November 10, 1986: The 1972 constitution is restored and martial law revoked.

August 1987: Flooding after heavy monsoons leaves 24 million people homeless or without food. Two million houses are destroyed.

November 10, 1987: "Siege of Dhaka." The political opposition attempts to close down government with a massive demonstration in the capital, the culmination of a year of anti-Ershad protests and strikes (including national strikes in February, June, and July). Five thousand people are arrested. A state of emergency is declared (November 27). Ershad dissolves parliament and frees jailed opposition leaders (December 6).

March 3, 1988: The Jatiya Party is returned with an overwhelming majority in a general election boycotted by the opposition and marked by flagrant election fraud. Four days of demonstrations and strikes follow the announcement of the results.

June 7, 1988: Islam is established as the state religion by a constitutional amendment after the opposition walks out of the Jatiya Sangsad in protest.

Late August–early September 1988: In the worst monsoon flooding in forty years, three-quarters of Bangladesh is inundated. Three thousand people die, and 25 million, one-quarter of the population, are left homeless. A major cyclone and tidal wave on December 2 causes thousands more deaths and adds millions more to the numbers of homeless.

December 4, 1990: Ershad resigns after eight weeks of violent protests against his eight-year dictatorship. He is arrested on December 12 for corruption, abuse of power, and nepotism. He is jailed for successive convictions on firearms and financial charges (1991, 1995).

February 27, 1991: A general election returns the BNP to power. Khaleda Zia, widow of President Zia, becomes prime minister on March 20.

April 30, 1991: A severe cyclone and tidal wave leave millions homeless. The official death toll is 140,000.

Mid-September–October 1993: Islamic extremists threaten to put Taslima Nasreem on trial for her book *Lajja* (Shame), which they claim includes blasphemous elements such as depicting Muslims attacking a Hindu family. After reports of death threats and that a price has been placed on her head, a court orders police protection. When the government files a case charging her with blasphemy in 1994, she flees; on her return in September 1998, the government puts out a warrant for her arrest.

December 23, 1994: Opposition members of parliament resign en masse in an effort to force elections. Widespread strikes and violent demonstrations occur throughout 1995 in protest at the perceived corruption of the Zia government.

March 27, 1996: Rising protests against her government force Khaleda Zia to resign and agree to new elections.

Far and near,
repeatedly,
houses and cities
crumble;
there a hamlet collapses
with a crash.
After millennia
on this earth,
the shadows we cast
are of fear
and death, of loss
and bewilderment.

From a poem by Jivanananda Das (1940s)

June 12, 1996: Khaleda Zia and her BNP are defeated in elections. In a massive turnout, the Awami League is returned to power; Sheikh Mujibur Rahman's daughter, Sheikh Hasina Wazed, becomes prime minister (June 23). Her administration promotes foreign investment and oil and gas exploration.

December 12, 1996: In a major diplomatic

breakthrough, Bangladesh and India sign the Ganges Water Treaty, a thirty-year agreement to share water.

1997: Bangladesh's population is estimated at 125.3 million.

June–September 1997: Strikes and demonstrations protest the government's tough policies on the work week, pay, and related issues. The BNP continues to fuel the unrest and calls for railroad and road blocks.

October 5, 1997: Angry at the BNP's role in protests, the government arrests three of its prominent leaders.

November 2, 1997: To protest the government's actions, the 116 BNP members of parliament walk out.

March 2, 1998: Three BNP members of parliament sign a memorandum of understanding with the Awami League and on March 9 return to parliament.

April 21, 1998: Khaleda Zia and her family are formally charged with corruption.

Bhutan

An independent Himalayan kingdom throughout its recorded history, Bhutan is remarkable for the continuity of its culture over two and a half thousand years. Bhutan becomes a Buddhist kingdom in the eighth century, when Tantric Buddhism is introduced by the Indian saint Padmasambhava. Neither the Hinduism of neighboring India nor the Islamic influence that permeates so much of Central and South Asia penetrates here (although the Nepalese who will enter Bhutan in later centuries do bring Hinduism with them).

The father of the modern nation is a seventeenth-century monk, Ngawang Namgyal, who calls his territory Drukyul (Land of the Thunder Dragon) after his own Drukpa Kagyupa Buddhist sect. (Drukyul remains the traditional name of the country; Bhutan is used only in English-language foreign correspondence.) This *Drukpa*, the name of the sect, comes to refer to the Bhutanese people themselves.

Traditional culture has been nurtured in Bhutan by both choice and geography. Its civilization develops in the Inner Himalaya, a central region of cultivable valleys protected to the north by the forbidding High Himalaya and to the south by the jungles of the Himalaya foothills. Foreign relations are confined to its nearest neighbors, most especially Bhutan's huge northern neighbor, Tibet, but also Sikkim and northern India. The British presence in India results in Bhutan's being a British protectorate for nearly a century.

In Bhutan's Lamaist theocracy, monks *(lamas)* are both religious and political leaders. Not until the early twentieth century, after half a century of civil war, does Bhutan establish a hereditary monarchy, and the nation achieves full autonomy only in 1935. The third king, Jigme Dorji Wangchuk, sets Bhutan on the road to constitutional monarchy in the 1950s, creating a national assembly and setting in motion a multitude of social and economic reforms designed to modernize an ancient land.

2000 B.C.: Although little is known about who made them, stone tools and weapons, megaliths, and remains of large stone structures found in Bhutan suggest that some people are living here by this time.

c. **500 B.C.–A.D. 600:** The state of Lho Mon (southern darkness), or Monyul (dark land), in the southern lowlands of present-day Bhutan, is inhabited, some scholars believe, by the Monpa, a fierce mountain tribe. Their religion is Bon, shamanistic and nature-worshipping.

7th century: Introduction of Buddhism by Tibetan King Srongsten Gampo. He constructs temples in the region called *Bhota* (present-day Bhutan) at Bumthang and Kyichu.

747: Indian monk Padmasambhava (Bhutanese name Guru Rimpoche), arrives at invitation of a local king. He converts the kings of Khempalung and Sindhu and, headquartered in Bumthang, founds the Nyingma, or Red Hat, sect of Mahayana Buddhism.

9th century: Development of small independent kingdoms with rulers called *debs*. Dzongkha-speaking Tibetan *lamas* and members of Tibetan-Mongol military expeditions settle in Bhutan. Descendants of these Bhutia immigrants form the majority of Bhutan's present-day population; Dzongkha, the primary language of Bhutan, uses Tibetan script.

11th century: In a second wave of Buddhism, Tibetan Buddhists flow into Bhutan. They establish Tibetan-style religious feudalism: lamas exercise both temporal and spiritual power, ruling over estates in western Bhutan.

Early 13th century: Drukpa Kagyupa, a Red Hat order of Tibetan Buddhism, is introduced by Tibetan lama Phajo Drugom Shigpo, one of numerous monks fleeing the domination of the Gelugpa (Yellow Hat) sect in Tibet. Drukpa Kagyupa is to become the dominant form of Buddhism and state religion in Bhutan.

Early 15th century: *Shabdrung* (spiritual ruler) Thangtong Gyalpo (1385–1464) repulses invasions by Tibetan rulers. The iron chain suspension bridges he builds help link major valleys into a trade network.

16th century: First issue of copper coinage in Bhutan.

1450–1521: Lifespan of Pemalingpa, a greatly revered Buddhist in Bhutan.

1616–1629: Ngawang Namgyal (1594–1651), a Tibetan monk, arrives in Bhutan in flight from the Dalai Lama. In 1629 he founds his first *dzong* (fortified monastery) at Simthoka. After defeating rival religious leaders, he assumes the title *shabdrung* (this office, the spiritual head of government, is sometimes called *dharma raja*). He is Bhutan's first great national figure. The head of civil government (called *deb raja* or *druk desi*) in a dual system of governance is also generally a monk. Appointed provincial governors *(penlops)* maintain armed forces and fight off repeated attacks from Tibet.

1629–1651: Ngawang Namgyal constructs dozens of *dzongs* in western valleys and calls his country Drukyul (Land of the Thunder Dragon) after his Drukpa Kagyupa school of Buddhism. These massive sloping stone structures serve both as monastic communities and civil administrative centers. The term *Drukpa* comes to refer also to the people of Inner and High Himalaya. His legal code, *Tsa Yig*, is based on Buddhist *dharma* (religious law) and remains in force until the 1960s.

Late 1600s: Although dead, Ngawang Namgyal is claimed for more than fifty years to be in spiritual retreat as regents try to identify a legitimate claimant to the throne.

1728–1730: Civil war over the *shabdrung's* succession ends with a Tibetan invasion of its weakened neighbor. Tibet imposes suzerainty over Bhutan, which thereby falls under the ultimate control of the Chinese emperor. But neither China nor Tibet ever exercises executive power in Bhutan.

1772: Bhutanese forces invade the neighboring Indian state of Cooch Bihar, a Bhutanese dependency, during a succession dispute. A British force expels the Bhutanese. A peace treaty signed at Fort William, Calcutta, April 25, 1774, is followed by British commercial missions to Bhutan.

19th century: Foreigners popularize the name Bhutan, probably derived from the Sanskrit term *Bhotanta* (end of *Bhot*, or Tibet; an alternate origin is *Bhu-uttan*, highlands).

1826–1842: Armed cross-border raids by the local population in Athara (Eighteen)

Duars, fertile areas bordering Bengal and Assam in northeast India. After a series of incursions by both sides (1828–1836), the British government in India annexes Assam Duars (1841). Bhutan relinquishes some of its Bengal Duars (1842).

1862: Bhutanese forces seize property, money, and prisoners in raids in Sikkim and Cooch Bihar. Sir Ashley Eden, sent to negotiate return of British citizens and property (January 1864), is insulted by a *penlops* (governor) and, in an act unprecedented in diplomatic annals, signs an agreement under duress with the note, "under compulsion."

December 1864–November 1865: War over the Duars. After decades of border raids and tensions, British army invades and in five months defeats Bhutan. Under the Treaty of Sinchula (November 11, 1865), Bhutan becomes a quasi-protectorate of Great Britain and cedes its southeastern frontier territories: Bengal and Assam Duars and the territory of Devangiri.

1882–1885: Ugyen Wangchuk, a provincial governor, has been fighting various rivals; during these years he emerges victorious and ends up the effective ruler of a united Bhutan.

Late 19th century: The British encourage large-scale immigration of Nepalese into southwestern Bhutan to cultivate the Duars. The new Hindu minority is not assimilated with the Bhutanese.

1903–1904: Ugyen Wangchuk, reversing a thousand years of close association with Tibet, accompanies Sir Francis Edward Younghusband's British military expedition to Lhasa. He is instrumental in mediating the Anglo-Tibetan Convention of 1904.

December 17, 1907: Half a century of civil war ends with election of Ugyen Wangchuk as first hereditary monarch (rules 1907–1926), ending the three hundred-year-old *shabdrung* system. The date is hereafter celebrated as National Day. The new Druk Gyalpo (dragon king) consolidates absolute power with administrative appointments of family members and close associates. His reforms include Western-style schools and improved communications networks.

January 8, 1910: By the Treaty of Punakha, Bhutan becomes a full British protectorate, placing its foreign policy under control of British government of India. Britain pledges not to interfere in Bhutan's internal affairs.

August 1926: Coronation of the second king, Jigme Wangchuk (reigns 1926–1952). He continues his father's modernization of education, health care, and roads.

August 2, 1935: (British) Government of India Act recognizes Bhutan's autonomy from British India and Indian princely states.

August 8, 1949: Treaty of Friendship with India reaffirms the 1910 pact by acknowledging Bhutan as a protectorate of the new Indian republic. Devangiri territory is returned to Bhutan.

October 27, 1952: Coronation of the third king, Jigme Dorji Wangchuk (reigns 1952–1972). He directs a modernization program funded by Indian foreign aid.

1951: Bhutan closes its northern border after the Chinese occupation of Tibet.

1953: Jigme Dorji creates the Tshogdu (National Assembly). In the absence of a written constitution, the royal enabling decree for the Constitution of the National Assembly, is Bhutan's primary legal document.

1959: Nepalese immigration is banned after a decade of large inflows. Discrimination against the Nepalese minority is widespread.

1961–1966: The First Five-Year Development Plan focuses on road-building. Subsequent Five-Year Plans target education, health care, agriculture, and electric power. India provides technical and financial aid.

1962: Thimphu in western Bhutan is designated the national capital, replacing the tradition of locating the capital wherever the king is resident.

Bhutan lifts its self-imposed isolation by joining its first international organization, the Colombo Plan for Asian and Pacific development. The first official postal service inaugurated; sales of commemorative stamps come to be a major source of foreign exchange.

April 5, 1964: Assassination of Jigme Palden Dorji, prime minister and brother-in-law of the king, in political factionalism. An attempted assassination of the king fails in July 1965.

1968: The king renounces his power of veto (which has never been used) and creates the Council of Ministers, Bhutan's first cabinet. The High Court (Thimkhang Gongma) is created and empowered to review the king's decisions. The Bank of Bhutan is founded as a central bank and charged with supervising the transition from a barter to a monetary economy.

1969: Census reports Bhutan's population as just over one million.

June 1969: Under a constitutional amendment proposed by the king, the Tshogdu gains full sovereignty. The monarch, stripped of his power, is subject to periodic votes of confidence by the legislature.

September 21, 1971: Bhutan is admitted to the United Nations. Its sovereignty is broadened, its association with India redefined as a "special relationship."

July 24, 1972: Accession of the fourth king, Jigme Singye Wangchuk (reigns 1972–). His reign is notable for broadening political participation without, however, instituting political parties or national elections.

1974: Introduction of the *ngultrum* as the standard unit of currency. In an effort to expand its economy, Bhutan is opened to tourism.

1979: Refugees who do not agree to take citizenship are expelled from the country.

December 8, 1985: Bhutan is a founding member of the South Asian Association for Regional Cooperation (SAARC). As part of Bhutan's seeking international contacts, diplomatic relations are established through the 1980s with a number of countries, including Japan (1986) and Sri Lanka (1987).

August 1986: The government news bulletin, *Kuensel*, is transformed into the country's first national newspaper; weekly editions are published in Dzongkha, Nepali, and English.

1988: Growing concerns about increased proportion of Nepalese population and loss of traditional culture leads to adoption of policy of *Driglam Namzha* (national customs and etiquette), which mandates Dzongkha-language education in schools and the wearing of national dress on holidays. The teaching of Nepali in state schools is discontinued.

1988: A census records 100,000 illegal Nepalese immigrants in southern Bhutan; the government begins large-scale deportations. Other Nepalese emigrate voluntarily. The Nepalese proportion of Bhutan's population, 40 percent in 1990, is estimated at 28 percent only a few years later; the forced migration causes a refugee crisis in Nepal.

July 2, 1990: Exiled opposition leaders petition the king for democratic government. Meanwhile, antigovernment terrorists are becoming active while ethnic Nepalese clash with the Bhutanese army.

December 1992: Amnesty International publishes a report detailing both the Bhutanese government's human rights violations against the Nepalese and its efforts to improve its human rights record.

January 7, 1993: Bhutan and India agree to joint construction of one of Asia's largest dams on Sankosh River, a $760 million project.

October 7, 1993: After mediation by SAARC, Bhutan agrees to sign an agreement with Nepal, promising to settle the status of the 100,000 or so Bhutanese refugees of Nepalese origin who are in refugee camps in Nepal.

1994–1998: Despite the agreement signed in October 1993, Bhutan and Nepal cannot agree on the exact status and treatment of the refugees. The refugees still stranded in Nepal continue to demand that they be allowed to return to Bhutan and continue with their own culture.

1997: Estimates of Bhutan's population range from 600,000 to 1.8 million. Although modernization is taking place in some areas, the traditional culture remains dominant. Weaving, for instance, is a fundamental part of Bhutanese life; elaborate patterns and some of the most sophisticated weaving techniques in the world transform cotton, silk, and wool; weaving skills and connoisseurship are widespread; the products are used for clothing, gift-giving, and even as currency.

Maldives

The Republic of Maldives is a maritime nation encompassing some 1,200 small, flat, largely coral islands in nineteen atolls stretching across five hundred miles in the Indian Ocean southwest of India; its own official name is Divehi Raajje (Island Kingdom). Only some 250 of the islands are inhabited. The islands' geographical position largely determines their economic and cultural development. Unable to produce enough food to feed its people, Maldives is throughout its long history dependent on trade, and its location on major maritime trade routes allows Egyptian, Arab, Chinese, and European traders in turn to leave their marks.

Little is known of the earliest history of the islands, but the ancestors of the present-day population are agreed to be Dravidians (from southern India) and Sinhalese (from Sri Lanka). From the early centuries of the Christian era, Maldives is an independent state. Unusual for South Asia, it is never truly occupied or long directly governed by colonial powers, which are perhaps deterred by the notoriously pestilential conditions caused by a chronically polluted water supply.

Replacing Buddhism in the twelfth century, Sunni Islam remains the state religion to the present day. The sultanate established in the twelfth century survives well into the twentieth. It finally gives way to a centralized presidency that continues Maldives' history of authoritarianism.

The nation's self-imposed political isolation is broken only in the 1960s, when Maldives begins to join international organizations and tourism brings the modern world to the islands. Modernization is undertaken at about the same time, with education, health programs, and communications arriving late in the twentieth century.

2000 B.C.: The Maldive Islands are located on Egyptian, Mesopotamian, and Indus civilization trading routes. The first settlers are the legendary Redin, a seafaring, sun-worshipping people.

c. **5th–4th centuries B.C.:** Probable date of settlement by Dravidian-speaking people from Kerala, south India; they introduce Buddhism, which is well established by the fourth century A.D. They are followed by

Sinhalese immigrants from present-day Sri Lanka, whose Indo-Aryan language, Divehi (literally, "island language"), replaces Dravidian.

4th century A.D.: The earliest apparent recorded mention in Western world of Maldives: Ammianus Marcellinus tells of the Roman emperor Julian's receiving an ambassador *"ab Divis."*

9th century: Arrival of the Arabs, the last major immigrant group. The kingdom is five hundred miles in extent, from Maliku ("Minicoy" in atlases) in the north to Addu in the south. Its capital is the central island of Male.

10th century: Middle Eastern and Chinese traders are regular visitors to Maldives. The economy is trade-dependent; Maldives imports grain and textiles that islands cannot produce in exchange for fish (especially dried "Maldive fish" exported to Ceylon), coconuts, ambergris, and the cowrie shells used as currency throughout Asia.

1153: The last Buddhist king is converted to Sunni Islam and founds the sultanate (until 1932). He rules as Sultan Muhammad al Adil. Maldives never institutes a secular legal system, but enforces *sharia* (Islamic law).

1153: Hukuru Miskit is built at Male; despite extensive later restoration and additions, the mosque remains the islands' most important architectural site. Many Buddhist sites are destroyed in the early years of Islamic rule.

1343–1346: North African traveler Ibn Battuta serves as Maldivian *qazi* (chief justice); his subsequent written account of the islands comments on the unusual freedom given women there.

1558–1573: The Portuguese, engaged in conflict with the suzerain of Maldives (the Mamale of Kannanur, India), occupy Male.

1573: The Portuguese are expelled in a popular revolt led by Maldivian hero Muhammad Bodu Takurufanu, an event subsequently celebrated as National Day. He founds a new dynasty (reigns 1573–1584). Kannanur retains control over Maliku.

When the month of Ramadan ended, the Wazir sent me a robe and we went out to the musalla; the road by which the Wazir would pass from his house was decorated and spread with cloths and strings of cowries were placed right and left of it. Every one of the amirs and principal men who had a house on his way had planted beside it little coco-palms, areca trees, and bananas and had stretched from one tree to the next cords from which he hung green nuts. The owner of the house would then stand beside its door and, as the Wazir passed, would throw down in front of him a piece of silk or cotton cloth, which his slaves picked up together with the cowries placed along the road.

Ibn Batuta (1304–1377)

1602: Frenchman François Pyrard is shipwrecked on the islands. Imprisoned in Male for five years, he learns Divehi and after escaping back to France publishes his *Voyages* (1611), a detailed account and long the most authoritative work on the country. Pyrard reports economic specialization, with separate atolls producing lace, stone carvings, metalwork, jewelry, lacquerwork, and elaborately woven grass mats.

1645: Government sends tribute to the governor of Ceylon; it is henceforth paid annually to the Dutch and (after 1796) British governors until Ceylon's independence (1947). Maldives is, however, still governed locally under traditional Islamic rule.

1725: Composition begins of an Arabic history (*tarikh*) of the sultanate from 1153 to 1821. It is supplemented by some Maldivian chronicles (*Radavali*).

November 1879: The Archeological Commissioner of Ceylon, H. C. P. Bell, visits Maldives. He writes an important report on the islands (1881), and after subsequent visits researching ancient Buddhist sites (1920, 1922), an authoritative work on the islands (published posthumously, 1940).

1887: The British declare Maldives a protectorate (until 1965); they control foreign relations and defense, but respect local Islamic governance.

1924: The first formal schools open in Male. Despite the subsequent spread of public education, the majority of students continue to attend communal or private Islamic schools.

1932: Nobles force King Muhammad Sams ud-Din Muhammad Iskandar (reigns 1903–1935) to accept a constitution. Monarchical power is replaced by oligarchical rule; the sultanate becomes elective.

1939–1945: British eastern fleet is based at Addu atoll during World War II.

1953: Former prime minister Muhammad Amin Didi declares the First Republic and assumes the presidency. He reforms education and promotes women's rights, but the republican experiment is short-lived. A conservative opposition overthrows him and restores the monarchy (Sultan Muhammad Farid Didi, reigns 1954–1968).

1956: A British plan to reestablish its wartime naval base in Addu atoll generates public controversy. After prime minister Ibrahim Nasir (rules 1958–1968) calls for reconsideration of terms with the British, separatists favoring the base declare the United Suvadivian Republic in the southern atolls (1959–1962).

1960: After a century of domination of foreign trade, Gujarati Borah merchants (Indian Muslims) are expelled by Nasir's government, which takes over control of this sector.

1962: Voice of Maldives, a government radio station, is established.

1963: Maldives joins the Colombo Plan promoting development in Pacific countries.

July 26, 1965: Britain recognizes the independence of the Maldive Islands.

September 21, 1965: Maldives joins the United Nations.

March 1968: A national referendum approves replacement of the sultanate with the Second Republic.

November 11, 1968: Prime Minister Nasir proclaims the Republic of Maldives (Divehi

Jumhuriya). November 11 is henceforth celebrated annually as Republic Day. A new constitution provides for centralized presidential government. Political parties are banned. Nasir, regarded as the father of the country, is elected president (rules 1968–1978) by the Majlis (citizens' council). He appoints Ahmed Zaki prime minister (the premiership becomes an elective office in 1972).

1972: Maldives opens to tourism, which with fishing becomes one of the nation's most important industries.

March 1975: President Nasir arrests and exiles Prime Minister Zaki, apparently to eliminate an increasingly popular political rival, and abolishes the premiership.

March 29, 1976: The last British troops leave their naval base on Addu atoll.

1977: Government announces the romanization of Divehi script. The experiment is a failure; in 1979 the traditional Thaana script is restored. It is based on Sanskrit and Sinhala and is written from right to left.

December 1977: The first accurate census reports a population of 142,832.

1978: President Nasir is accused of corruption in office and flees to Singapore. He is later found to have appropriated millions of dollars from the national treasury.

1978: Government television station begins broadcasts.

November 11, 1978: Maumoon Abdul Gayoom, former minister of transport, takes office after his election as president (rules 1978–); he will be reelected at five-year intervals (until by the late 1990s he is the longest serving head of state in Asia). Maldives subsequently joins the International Monetary Fund and World Bank.

1980: Creation of the High Court; judges are appointed by the president.

1981: The Maldives Monetary Authority is created as the nation's first central bank.

July 1982: Maldives joins the Commonwealth of Nations, assuming full membership in June 1985.

December 8, 1985: Maldives becomes a founding member of South Asian Association for Regional Cooperation (SAARC).

1986: India signs a treaty pledging capital for public projects in Maldives.

November 3–4, 1988: An armed force estimated between 150 and 200 come ashore and enter the capital, Male, in an attempted coup. Most of the men are mercenaries, Tamils from Sri Lanka, and the attempted coup seems to be led by Abdullal Luthufi, a Maldivian businessman based in Sri Lanka. For a few hours, the force appears to be taking control, but at the request of President Gayoom 1,600 Indian paratroopers fly in and soon drive the coup forces out. About seventy of them get to sea with about thirty hostages, but the ship is captured on November 8. This is the third attempted coup by political opposition since 1980.

August 12–September 16, 1989: On August 12, after a trial of those captured in the attempted coup, sixteen of the leaders are given the death sentence and fifty-nine others get prison terms. On September 16, however, President Gayoom announces that the death sentence is commuted to life imprisonment.

1990: International reports warn that if global warming continues, rising ocean levels may submerge Maldives within a century. Most of the islands are little more than six feet above sea level.

August 29, 1994: Japan announces that it will extend a grant-in-aid of up to 100 million yen to help the Maldives purchase rice.

1996: Maldives has been committed to developing tourism since the early 1970s, and by the end of this year it is revealed that tourism contributes some 20 percent of the country's gross domestic product and 70 percent of its foreign exchange. Seventy-four previously uninhabited islands have been turned into resorts since 1973, and seventy more islands are to be offered to developers. At least 350,000 tourists are arriving each year. Although the government is conservative and Islamic-based in its domestic programs—for example, no Maldivians may work at the bars serving liquor to foreigners—it adopts liberal policies toward foreign investors in tourism and related infrastructure.

1997: Maldives' population is estimated at 280,000, up from some 240,000 in 1993. Its quickly increasing population is putting severe demands on land, housing, water, and all resources.

November 27, 1997: Maldives adopts a new constitution that for the first time will allow more than one candidate to run for the presidency.

May 8, 1998: Hilton International opens a US$17 million resort hotel on two adjacent islets, Rangali and Rangali Finolhu.

Nepal

The central Himalayan kingdom of Nepal (Nepal Adhirajya), bounded on three sides by India and the other by Tibet, is inextricably linked with its larger neighbors. Little is known of its prehistory, but in the earliest centuries of the Christian era, a population thought to be descended from northerners is subjugated by the Indian Licchavis dynasty.

India is the source of the strands of monastic Buddhism and Hindu kingship that intertwine in the Newar culture of the Kathmandu Valley principalities. Repeated Indian migrations—of monks, Rajasthani princes, and Maithili fleeing the Islamic invasions of India—reinforce Hindu influence throughout medieval Nepal during the Malla dynasty.

Not until the eighteenth century is Nepal expanded to its present extent by the conquests of its national hero, Prithvi Narayan. The national identity he forges is based squarely on ancient traditions of Hinduism and monarchy. The century-long autocratic rule of the prime ministerial dynasty known as the Ranas is similarly steeped in ancient traditions; Nepal's modernization only begins after their overthrow in 1951.

Nepal's traditional isolation from foreigners is partly geographical and partly self-imposed. The geopolitical reality of colonial rule in India leads Nepal in the mid-nineteenth century to ally itself with Great Britain, a policy decision with enormous repercussions.

During the twentieth century Nepal dispatches many thousands of Gurkha soldiers to fight in the British and Indian armies in two world wars. Postwar Indian independence, new international organizations, the pressing need for modernization, and a difficult transition from absolute monarchy to a modern parliamentary democracy dominate Nepalese history during the last half of the century.

c. 563 B.C.?: Siddhartha Gautama, the Buddha, a member of the Sakya clan, is born at Lumbini in the Terai, the flat strip of Nepal that borders India.

500 B.C.: About this time significant immigration of Indo-Aryan Khasa peoples into western Nepal pushes the indigenous Tibeto-Burman Kirata people into the eastern Terai. The economy of both kingdoms is based on trade.

3d century B.C.: Buddhism, established in Kathmandu Valley, introduces elements that become central to Nepalese culture, including architectural forms such as *stupas* (Buddhist temples) and such ideas as the king as upholder of cosmic law.

Early centuries A.D.: Population is largely Newars, speaking a Tibeto-Burman language and supposed by some scholars to have originated from the north. Waves of immigration from India bring Indian religion, culture, and art, historically the strongest influence on Nepalese culture. Stone sculptures of *bodhisattvas* (enlightened beings) and *yaksas* (attendant deities) are created in the great central Kathmandu Valley, referred to in ancient texts as *Nepala mandala.*

c. 400–750: The first Nepalese state is ruled by the Licchavi dynasty, descended from a north Indian clan and almost certainly speaking an early form of Newari. Both Hinduism and Buddhism are brought from India and flourish.

This is the golden age of Nepalese culture under the Licchavis and is heavily influenced by north Indian Kushana models. Sanskrit is the official administrative and literary language. Monasteries, *stupas, lingam* shrines containing phallic representations of Siva, palaces, *stelae* (pillars), and fountains are constructed in Nepal and spread to Tibet. Traders, missionaries, and pilgrims spread Buddhism from Nepal throughout Asia.

723: Traditional date for the founding of Kathmandu. The city is known until the sixteenth century as Kantipur (City of Glory).

c. 750–1200: Nepal is ruled by Bhauttas, Palas, and Karnatas during the "Transitional" or Thakuri period. Many monasteries are built in the tenth to twelfth centuries to house monks fleeing from Islamic invaders in India.

879: Beginning of *Nepala Samvat*, the Newari national era (until the 18th century).

1200–1769: Rule of Malla kings. *Malla* designates a person of great power; the first so called is Ari Malla (reigns 1200–1216). Kathmandu remains the political and economic center, but a separate Malla dynasty rules at Jumla in northwest Nepal.

1345–1346: The Sultan of Bengal raids the Kathmandu Valley, destroying every major Buddhist shrine.

c. 1382–1395: Reign of Jayasthiti Malla, who unites the Malla kingdoms of Kathmandu Valley and codifies a legal system based on ancient *dharma* (religious law).

14th century: Newari, an old language based on Gurkhali in common use in the Kathmandu Valley, develops into a literary language. The Khas language spreads through western regions, eventually evolving into Nepali. Maithili, the language introduced by Indian refugees in the fourteenth century, flourishes in the south.

1428–1482: The Malla kingdom achieves its greatest extent during the reign of Yaksha Malla. After his death, however, the empire is divided among his sons into the constantly warring kingdoms of Kathmandu, Patan, and Bhadgaon.

16th century: The Malla empire in the far west disintegrates into *baisi*, twenty-two kingdoms. In the near west emerges a confederation of *chaubisi*, twenty-four kingdoms. They are ruled by Rajasthani princes fleeing the Mughal conquests of India. They introduce Hindu influences and Indian dress and administration. Members of the *kshatriya* (warrior) caste, they also bring firearms, artillery, and their own martial culture. It is a period of constant conflict and political turmoil.

16th–17th centuries: The Late Malla period is the high point of Newar architecture. Extremely wealthy, the Malla kings are great patrons of art and drama and builders of stupas, temples, and palaces. Later Malla kings include Pratapa Malla (reigns 1641–1674), the "poet-king" of Kathmandu; Sri Nivasa (reigns 1661–1684), the builder of Darbar Square, Patan; and Bhupatindra Malla of Bhadgaon (reigns 1696–1722).

April 3, 1743: Prithvi Narayan Shah, a descendant of Rajasthani kings, becomes raja of the small hill-kingdom of Gorkha (reigns 1743–1775), founding the Shah dynasty (which survives to the present day).

1760s: Prithvi Narayan, one of the great figures of Nepalese history, uses advanced Indian weaponry to conquer the Newar kingdoms and create the modern kingdom of Nepal. (1768 is traditionally regarded as the year of unification.) He himself takes the ancient three capitals: Kathmandu, Patan, three miles to the southeast, and Bhadgaon, nine miles eastward (1768–1769). He isolates Nepal, expelling foreigners and missionaries, and pursues a cautious foreign policy, famously describing Nepal as a "yam between [the] two boulders" of China and British India.

1775–1805: The militarized kingdom of Gorkha reaches its greatest extent during military campaigns of Prithvi Narayan's successors, stretching from the Sutlej to the Tista rivers. Their armies briefly occupy Tibet (1788–1792).

1806–1837: During the tenure of Bhimsen Thapa, a minister wielding absolute power, Gorkha kings are virtually prisoners in their own palace. Bhimsen Thapa and Queen Tripurasundari (reigns 1806–1832) reportedly murder more than ninety political enemies at court.

I saw Balaju today at this age
And I write
It's the paradise of earth.
Birds that serenade around perching over the
    creepers
Bring you the ecstasy by their melodies;
Nothing would be like it
If I could compose a poem sitting here;
On top of that,
If I could make a lovely damsel dance here
I know, I would drag the paradise
Down to this place.

Poem by Bhanu Bhata (1814–1869)

1814–1816: The Anglo-Nepali War ends Nepalese expansionism. Some 48,000 British and Indian troops attack across Nepal's east and west frontiers, overwhelming a well-armed and well-trained but much smaller Nepalese army. Treaty of Sagauli deprives Nepal of one-third of its territory, fixing borders that survive to the present day. A British Resident is stationed in Kathmandu; otherwise Nepal is closed to foreigners. In the wake of the war, the British employ Nepalese warriors in the Indian army. ("Gurkha" is British version of Gorkha.)

1837: King Rajendra Bikram Shah Dev (reigns 1816–1847) comes of age, ousts Minister Bhimsen Thapa, and establishes independent royal rule. Royal, noble, and priestly factions engage in endless court intrigues and political assassinations; Nepal has eight governments in nine years.

September 14, 1846: At an emergency meeting summoned by Queen Rajyalakshmi in the state *Kot* (armory), the entire Council of State—Nepal's aristocracy—is murdered. The Kot Massacre is an event with enormous national consequences.

September 15, 1846: Jung Bahadur Kunwar, commander of the guard during the Kot Massacre, is appointed prime minister (rules 1846–1877) and begins a purge of his political enemies. Queen Rajyalakshmi and her family are exiled, King Rajendra deposed, and heir apparent Surendra installed as figurehead king (reigns 1847–1881) with the title *maharajadhiraj* (great king of kings). Thousands from the nation's leading families flee Nepal.

1854: Inspired by a trip to France and England (1850–1851), Jung Bahadur introduces a new legal code, *Muluki Ain*, and introduces European art, architecture, and fashions. He allies himself with Britain, the strongest world power and de facto ruler of India; Nepal supplies troops to the British side during the Sepoy Mutiny (1856–1857).

1855–1856: War with Tibet after trade disputes secures Nepalese trading facilities in Lhasa, the Tibetan capital.

August 1856: The king is forced to grant Jang extraordinary political and judicial powers under the title of maharaja. Jang establishes the offices of both prime minister and maharaja as hereditary, with separate lines of succession residing in his own family, now named Rana (ruled 1856–1951).

1914–1918: Nepal commits sixty thousand Gurkha troops to the British and Indian armies during World War I.

1918–1929: Prime Minister Chandra Shamsher (rules 1901–1929) founds Nepal's first college, Tri-Chandra College (1918) and introduces social reforms including the abolition of slavery (1920) and *sati* (widow-burning) (1929).

1923: A treaty of friendship with Britain recognizes Nepal's wartime contribution by confirming its independence.

1934: Great Nepal-Bihar earthquake, the worst in modern history. Its death toll is never established with certainty.

1935: The Nepal Praja Parishad (Nepal People's Council, NPC), Nepal's first political party, is founded by exiles in India with close ties to the Indian nationalist movement. A plot by Tribhuvan Bir Bikram Shah Dev (rules 1911–1955) and the NPC against the Rana regime is discovered (1940), and four NPC leaders are executed.

1939–1945: Without signing a formal declaration of war, Nepal contributes 120,000 Gurkha troops to the British and Indian armies during World War II.

January 1947: The Nepali National Congress is founded by Nepalese exiles in India. In March 1950 the group adopts armed revolution as its goal.

January 1948: The Government of Nepal Act, Nepal's first constitution, is promulgated, creating a bicameral parliament and High Court and vesting executive power in the prime minister. Ranas oppose the constitution; political struggle between the Ranas and the king continues for several years.

In our hands the workbroom
the dust of the road.
Inside, our lovely truths
keep opening and opening.

Age after age we wept
tears of servitude.
We offered up our souls
scorning our flesh.

From "Sweeper," poem by Laxmi Prasad Devkota
(c. 1950)

1950: Treaties of friendship and trade with India lay the foundation for Nepal's foreign policy. Economic policy is detailed in the first of a series of Five-Year Plans.

November 6, 1950: King Tribhuvan Bir Bikram is deposed by the government and takes refuge in the Indian embassy in Kathmandu. He then goes into exile in Delhi, India.

November 11, 1950–January 16, 1951: The opposition Congress leads a promonarchist revolution that forces Maharajah Mohan Shumshere Jung Bahadur Rana to resign as prime minister (November 13), thus ending the century-old monopoly of his family. The Rana family pledges to restore the king and hold elections.

February 15, 1951: After negotiations have guaranteed his role, the king returns to Kathmandu.

February 18, 1951: Restored to his throne, King Tribhuvan appoints members of the opposition Congress Party to the cabinet and creates a parliamentary monarchy. Years of instability follow, with factionalism rife between the king and political parties. The government survives coup attempts in April 1951 and January 1952.

July 31, 1950: The India-Nepal Peace and Friendship Treaty is signed.

August 13, 1952–April 13, 1953: With the country in a state of unrest, the king suspends parliamentary power.

May 29, 1953: Sherpa mountaineer Tenzing Norgay reaches the summit of Mount Everest with British climber Edmund Hillary; their British expedition is the first to ascend the world's highest peak. Sherpas, members of a Bhotia people who live in the high mountains of eastern Nepal, are skilled mountaineers and frequently support European expeditions.

1955: Mahendra Bir Bikram Shah Dev ascends the throne (reigns 1955–1972). A national police force is created.

December 14, 1955: Nepal joins the United Nations.

1956–1961: First of a series of Five-Year Plans that promote development, focusing on road-building, education, health, and agriculture, and aiming at universal provision of "basic needs" by the end of the century. Agricultural development of the Terai is particularly targeted through resettlement programs.

1959: Founding of Tribhuvan University in Kathmandu.

February 12, 1959: The king introduces a constitution providing for parliamentary government, with substantial power reserved to the monarch.

February 18, 1959: The first general election gives Nepali Congress an overwhelming parliamentary majority. February 18 is subsequently celebrated as Democracy Day. Bisheshwar Prasad Koirala forms the first popularly elected government. He undertakes land reforms and establishes relations for the first time with the major world powers.

June 28, 1960: In a serious border incident, China attacks Nepalese troops, but later apologizes for "carelessness."

December 15, 1960: In what is a royal coup, King Mahendra assumes direct rule, abrogating constitution and dissolving parliament. The prime minister is imprisoned for eight years. Press censorship is imposed on political news (until 1990). Political parties are banned (January 5, 1961). Many Nepali Congress leaders go into exile in India, where they begin launching violent raids.

1961: A treaty with China for the first time contains a detailed delimitation of the common border.

1962: *Muluki Ain*, a new legal code, ends caste and sex discrimination, permits divorce, and guarantees the right to trial.

December 16, 1962: Mahendra's second constitution (the "Panchayat Constitution") creates four tiers of *panchayats* (councils) from village level to the Rashtriya Panchayat (National Assembly). In this "party-less democracy," political parties are banned, and only local councils are directly elected. The monarchy remains absolute. Nominally outlawed, political parties operate openly, and numerous demonstrations over the years protest the constitution.

January 31, 1972: Birendra Bir Bikram Shah Dev (reigns 1972–) ascends the throne (although he is not formally crowned until February 24, 1975). His appeal for Nepal to be declared a "zone of peace" (1975) is repudiated by India, which regards Nepal as a vital buffer with China, but the goal becomes a cornerstone of Nepalese foreign policy.

King Birendra asked that Nepal be recognized as a "zone of peace." He asked that Nepal's freedom and independence not be "thwarted by the changing flux of time when understanding is replaced by misunderstanding, when conciliation is replaced by belligerency and war." The King insisted that his request for this "zone of peace" was not prompted by "fear or threat from any country or quarter." But he did refer to Nepal's "concern . . . to preserve our independence—a legacy handed down to us by history." Nepal took pride in having "close and cordial ties of understanding" with its neighbors. "If our relations with India have been deep and extensive, our relations with China have been equally close and friendly, consistently marked by understanding of each other's problems and aspirations."

Coronation address by King Birendra Bir Bikram
Shah Dev (February 25, 1975)

April 1979: Student demonstrations turn into antimonarchy riots.

May 2, 1980: In a national referendum, Nepalese vote 2.4 million to 2 million to retain the *panchayat* system rather than reintroduce multiparty democracy. The closeness of the result is a clear indication of popular desire for reform.

1981: A census reports the population at 15,023,000, up more than 50 percent in the past twenty years.

May 9, 1981: First direct elections to Rashtriya Panchayat; political parties boycott the poll.

December 8, 1982: Birendra opens Nepal's largest ever development project, a hydroelectric power plant at Kulekhani.

June 20, 1985: After months of demonstrations against the twenty-five-year ban on political parties, bombs explode in the royal palace, National Assembly, and other public buildings in Kathmandu. It is the first terrorist attack ever in Nepal. Fourteen hundred people are arrested. A *satyagraha* (noncooperation) campaign for multiparty democracy launched by the Nepali Congress on May 23 is called off.

July 16, 1985: Seventh Five-Year Plan calls for a shift from agriculture, long Nepal's economic bedrock, to small and cottage industries.

December 8, 1985: Nepal is a founding member of the South Asian Association for Regional Cooperation (SAARC). SAARC's permanent secretariat is located in Kathmandu.

1986: First television broadcasts.

May 12, 1986: The second general election is boycotted by the Nepali Congress.

May 31, 1986: In a signal of economic independence, the Nepalese rupee is unlinked from the Indian rupee after thirty years.

1988–1990: Tens of thousands of Nepalese immigrants in Bhutan return to Nepal, fleeing nationalist policies and a poor economy. Many are forced to live in border refugee camps, posing a severe economic burden.

August 21, 1988: A major earthquake along the southern border with Bihar kills 650 people and injures thousands.

March 24, 1989–June 1990: India closes all but two border crossings with Nepal after a trade and transit treaty expires, blocking the flow of tourists and oil and gas shipments.

February 18, 1990–April 19, 1990: Democratic revolution. Despite the preventive arrest of 700 activists, 200,000 march in a Democracy Day rally in Kathmandu (February 18). General strikes follow.

April 8, 1990: King Birendra restores political parties.

April 16, 1990: Birendra amends the 1962 constitution to accommodate multiparty democracy and dissolves parliament.

November 8, 1990: A new constitution is adopted, replacing the *panchayat* system with constitutional monarchy and creating a bicameral parliament with a House of Representatives and National Council. Multiparty democracy is restored after a thirty-year ban on political parties. The constitution mandates universal suffrage and guarantees civil rights, curtails royal power, and creates an independent judicial system.

May 12, 1991: Congress wins the first multiparty general election. Communists make a surprisingly strong showing, however, and political factionalism results in the formation of four governments within the next six years.

May 26, 1991: Nepali Congress secretary Girija Prasad Koirala becomes prime minister after the general election and forms the first independent government since 1962. The government initiates economic reforms of privatization and promotion of foreign trade and investment.

October 7, 1993: An agreement is signed with Bhutan on refugees from that country, their numbers grown from 77,000 in January 1993 to more than 100,000. By 1995, however, their numbers are only slightly reduced, to 85,000.

November 15, 1994: In the elections for the

House of Representatives, the United Communist Party of Nepal (UCPN) wins 88 of the 205 seats. On November 29, Man Mohan Adhikari is sworn in as the country's first communist prime minister. He pledges not to let communism overwhelm the country's democratic traditions and pledges to encourage business.

June 13–September 10, 1995: King Birendra dissolves parliament and calls for new elections. He is supported by the communists but opposed by the opposition parties. On August 28, the country's Supreme Court rules that parliament must be reinstated. The unrest continues and on September 10

prime minister Adhikari resigns; a coalition government, led by Sher Bahadur Deuba, takes over.

1996: Protests, strikes, and financial scandals continue to keep Nepal in a state of unrest.

1997: Nepal's estimated population is 23.1 million.

March 6, 1997: Deupa's coalition government fails to satisfy the electorate and he resigns, to be replaced by another coalition government.

April 12, 1998: King Birendra appoints Girija Prasad Koirala, leader of the New Congress Party, as prime minister; he is sworn in on April 15.

Sri Lanka (Ceylon)

Called Lanka in the *Ramayana*, the island of Sri Lanka has a 2,500-year-long history combining two major cultural strands. The Indo-Aryan Sinhalese who originally settle the island are joined before the beginning of the Christian era by Tamils from South India. Despite the early and strong historical link with India, reinforced by periodic invasions from across the straits separating them, Sri Lanka develops a distinctive culture.

Indian missionaries convert the Sinhalese to Buddhism in the third century B.C. The great ancient and medieval civilizations of Sri Lanka, their capitals of Anuradhapura and Polonnaruva resplendent with *stupas* (Buddhist shrines), temples, and palaces, are Buddhist kingdoms. The large Tamil minority practices Hinduism.

Sri Lanka's early civilizations are based on agriculture made possible by some of the most advanced hydraulic engineering in the ancient world. From the earliest period, the island's economy is also dependent on trade. The European trading nations that administer the island during the five hundred-year-long colonial period—Portuguese, Dutch, and British in turn—leave a legacy of social and political institutions to the island they call Ceylon.

Among the most valuable colonial legacies is a peaceful transition to independence in 1948. Another is the well-functioning multiparty democracy that during the succeeding half-century makes Sri Lanka a political model for developing nations.

Beginning in the late 1970s, Sri Lanka is afflicted by communal violence as separatist Tamils wage a terrorist war for independence. Tens of thousands of people are killed and the political and economic life of the nation consumed in an apparently unbreakable cycle of violence.

70,000–26,500 B.C.: There is apparently continuous occupation of Sri Lanka from at least 70,000 B.C. on, although there are no human fossils from this time, only stone tools.

26,500–8500 B.C.: The oldest directly dated occupation site in Sri Lanka is a cave site of Batadomba-lena, with microlithic artifacts. At least fifty other sites on Sri Lanka dating from somewhat later during this time frame also yield stone tools and remains of plants and animals indicative of human exploitation of natural resources.

10,000–100 B.C.: Little is known of the people except that they make stone tools.

5000–500 B.C.: Balangoda culture spreads across the island.

2500 B.C.: The first storage tanks (later called *eri*) are built for irrigation.

500 B.C.?: Indo-Aryans from north India, the "People of the Lion" and ancestors of the Sinhalese, settle in the dry north-central region. (The traditional date, according to the *Mahavamsa*, is 543 B.C., Year 1 of the Buddhist Era).

5th century B.C.–A.D. 500: Sophisticated engineering, particularly the discovery of outlet-valve technology, underpins the development of one of world's greatest ancient hydraulic civilizations. Kings Panduwasa and Pandukabhaya are two of the earliest builders of massive earthen "tanks" linked by canals. This monumental irrigation system allows the cultivation of rice in the arid northern and southern plains.

3d century B.C.: Indian emperor Ashoka's missionary son Mahinda converts Sinhalese king Devanampiya Tissa (reigns 250–c. 207 B.C.) to Buddhism. The king founds a monastery at Mahavihara. Theravada Buddhism becomes the state religion; royal patronage embeds it deeply in Sinhalese culture.

c. 3d century B.C.–mid-13th century A.D.: The island's magnificent Buddhist kingdoms produce the classical age of Sinhalese civilization. Three major cultural areas are the kingdoms of Rajarata in the north, including the wealthy and cosmopolitan cities Anuradhapura and Polonnaruva; western Dakkinnadesa, its capital Kandy; and Rohana in the south.

c. 100 B.C.–a.d. 300: Second stone-age period.

1st century B.C.: Rohana prince Dutthagamani expels Tamil general Elara, the Chola ruler of Anuradhapura, after a fifteen-year war. Anuradhapura becomes the most powerful city-state of Sri Lanka.

Ruanwaeli Dagoba Anuradhapura: Hail! The great King Gajabahu Gamini Abhaya, grandson of King Wahaba, son of King Tisa, having restored the Dakshina Abhaya and other wiharas [rock temples] and having protected them, made them inhabited, having strengthened the faith, having repaired the dilapidated buildings, after having given the wiharas, he gave to the priesthood the enjoyment of the four pratyayas.

Inscription on cave rock in Sri Lanka (1st–3d century A.D.?)

4th century A.D.: Arrival on the island of the Tooth Relic, believed to be the tooth of the Buddha. It is Sri Lanka's greatest treasure; the shrine housing it accompanies the Royal Palace.

5th century: The militarily aggressive south Indian (Tamil) states of Pandyas, Pallavas, and Cholas begin repeated attacks on Sri Lanka, at times ruling island kingdoms. The kingdoms of India and Sri Lanka become politically entwined over the following centuries, and south India profoundly influences Sinhalese art and architecture.

c. 496: The "cloud maidens" are painted in the caves of Sigiriya.

6th century or later: Compilation by Buddhist monks of *Mahavamsa* (Great Genealogy), Pali chronicle of the island's history through the 1st century A.D. Based on fourth-century sources, the work is the beginning of the world's second-oldest continuous written history.

7th century: Development of irrigation technology using stone dams and sluices.

1070: Vijayabahu I of Rohana (reigns 1070–1110) expels the Tamil Cholas from their seventy-five-year rule over Rajarata and during a long reign rebuilds Buddhist temples destroyed by the Hindu occupiers.

Mid-12th century: Parakrama Samudra, a massive artificial lake and the greatest irrigation work on the island, is completed during reign of Parakramabahu I "the Great" (reigns 1153–1186). His capital at Polonnaruva becomes one of the greatest ancient capitals of the world during his reign.

Late 12th century: The brahmanic legal system of King Nissankamalla (reigns 1187–1197) requires for the first time that the monarch be Buddhist. It also institutes hereditary castes in Sri Lanka's ancient occupation-based caste system, under which the *Goyigama*, originally agriculturalists, become the Sri Lankan elite.

Those who increase the wealth they have inherited from their ancestors and enjoy greater prosperity than their ancestors are known as atijata *or the best sons. As for me, I inherited the one kingdom of Maya, that my father left me, and have now under my sway all three kingdoms. I have killed or chased away from the country all the Tamils that he was unable to subdue. . . . I have taken unto myself queens from India and received all kinds of treasure as tribute from them. . . . I united church and state. My children, as a result of all these achievements I have become an* atijata *son to my parents. Do you also become* atijata *sons to me.*

"The Abdication of King Parakramabahu II," from *Mayurapada Buddhaputra Pujavaliya*, a history of medieval Sri Lanka (1266)

13th century: Compilation of the *Culavansa* (Lesser Genealogy), a continuation of the *Mahavamsa* attributed to the monk Dhammakitti and completed by others through the eighteenth century. These chronicles are regarded as an unrivaled source for ancient and medieval South Asian history.

c. 1200–1600: Hydraulic civilizations decline, beset by succession conflicts. Cultural center shifts from irrigated rice regions to the rain-fed southwest of the island, where an economy develops based on trade, especially of cinnamon. Muslim traders settle in coastal enclaves.

1371: The kingdom of Kotte is founded in southwest Sri Lanka (until 1597).

14th–early 15th centuries: The first Tamil kingdom in the island, founded in Jaffna at far north, reaches the peak of its power. It remains independent until 1620.

1469: The kingdom of Kandy is founded in the central highlands (until 1815).

1505: Portuguese sailors given trade privileges at Colombo fortify their factory. They increasingly interfere in local politics, finally sponsoring a puppet king in Kotte (1521). The Portuguese call the island Cilao.

1521–1594: The kingdom of Sitawake controls most of the island and vigorously opposes the encroaching Portuguese; it collapses suddenly after the death of the king.

1592: Kandy becomes the royal capital. The Tooth Relic accompanies the court to the city; the Temple of the Tooth Relic (Dalada Maligawa), built to house it, becomes Sri Lanka's holiest shrine.

1597: Portuguese take possession of Kotte under the terms of King Dharmapala's will, later annexing Jaffna (1619); Portuguese captains-general eventually govern more than half the island. They introduce Christianity (the Catholicism they bring remains the dominant Christian denomination in Sri Lanka). Portuguese is widely spoken, and many islanders adopt Portuguese surnames. They decisively shift the economy to dependence on export trade.

1639–1640: Dutch defeat Portuguese to win control of east and west coasts of Sri Lanka. They capture Colombo (1656) and Jaffna (1658). Dutch governors enforce a trade monopoly and codify law, incorporating the Tamil legal code in the laws of Jaffna.

1796: British conquer ruling Dutch; a British governor takes control of the island they call Ceylon. Formal cession under the Peace of Amiens (1801) makes the island Britain's first Crown colony (until 1948).

March 15, 1815: The annexation of Kandy to the Crown colony after British invasion brings Sri Lanka under single rule.

1827: British introduce coffee cultivation. Coffee replaces spices as major export commodity; migrant Tamil laborers are recruited from Tamil Nadu in south India to work plantations. Cultivation reaches its peak in the 1870s before a blight destroys the industry.

1831–1832: The Colebrooke Report, issued by the British Colebrooke-Cameron Commission (1829–1833), recommends imposition of a uniform system of trade, economy, administration, education, and justice throughout the country. The reforms it advocates lay the groundwork for the modern state of Sri Lanka.

1833: The Charter of Justice codifies many of the Colebrooke recommendations, mandating a laissez-faire economy and land reform, establishing Executive and Legislative Councils, establishing English schools, and opening the civil service to Sri Lankans. The English-educated elite created by these reforms·form the basis of Sri Lanka's nationalist movement.

1841: Ceylon Bank is founded to finance the expansion of agriculture.

Mid-19th century: A new elite based on plantation agriculture and trade develops, with English habits. Their nationalism, based on Buddhism and largely conservative, is reformist in nature.

***c.* 1880–1910:** Three major cash crops—tea, rubber, and coconuts—come to dominate the plantation system of agriculture introduced by the British in the 1830s. (They remain the mainstay of Sri Lanka's present-day economy.) British recruit a large number of resident Tamils as permanent labor force on tea and rubber plantations.

1910: Election of the first Sinhalese member of the Legislative Council.

1919: Ceylon National Congress is founded by Sinhalese and Tamil political organizations.

1931: Constitutional reform based on Donoughmore Commission recommendations (1927) creates a strong representative legislative body. The first elections with universal suffrage are held.

1942–1945: Sri Lanka becomes a base of British naval operations and headquarters of the South-East Asia Command during World War II.

July 1944: The Soulbury Commission on constitutional reform recommends protectorate status for Sri Lanka. The Sinhalese argue for full independence.

February 4, 1948: Ceylon achieves independence. Don Stephen Senanayake, leader of the United National Party (UNP) is the nation's first prime minister at the head of a British-style parliamentary system of government (rules 1947–1952). February 4 is hereafter celebrated annually as Independence and National Day.

April 11, 1956: S. W. R. D. Bandaranaike, the founder (1951) of the opposition Sri Lanka Freedom Party (SLFP) and elected on a divisive "Sinhala Only" platform after an emotional campaign, takes office as prime minister (1956–1959). The Official Language Act (1956) makes Sinhala the official language; this ˙and other aggressively Sinhalese policies discriminate against the Tamils in employment and deeply alienate the Tamil community. Tamil campaigns for recognition provoke further anti-Tamil measures.

1958: Hundreds of people are killed in national communal riots.

September 26, 1959: Assassination of Prime Minister Bandaranaike by a Buddhist monk.

Why strive so hard
To escape
The clutches of Death.
It is no use.
That you call death and
try to escape from
is but the shadow of Death.
The real Death is Life itself.

Death, impassive as the Himalayas,
Stands beside you.

From a poem by Siri Gunasinghe (*c.* 1955)

July 22, 1960: Sirimavo Bandaranaike succeeds her husband as prime minister (rules 1960–1965, 1970–1977, 1994–), becoming the world's first female head of a democratic government. She continues her late husband's socialist policies under the umbrella of a "Common Programme." She carries out his mandate to promote Sinhalese interests, making no room for those of the Tamils. Sinhala is made the sole official language (1961).

1965: The UNP wins general election. Prime Minister Dudley Senanayake's administration (1965–1970) mitigates strict Sinhalese policies of its predecessors, for example, by permitting the use of Tamil for official purposes in Tamil-speaking regions (1966). The UNP loses office in a general election swept by United Front coalition of opposition parties, including communists.

1971: National uprising led by Marxist Janatha Vimukthi Peramuna (JVP). The People's Liberation Front is suppressed.

May 22, 1972: A new constitution declares the newly named Democratic Socialist Republic of Sri Lanka (Sri Lanka Prajathanthrika Samajavadi Janarajaya). The country is a member of the Commonwealth. Sinhala is codified as the official language.

1972: The Land Reform Act limits individual holdings to twenty-five acres of paddy land, fifty acres of other land.

1975: Nationalization of banks and plantations.

1977: Mrs. Bandaranaike is turned out of office after losing general election in a UNP landslide. She is subsequently convicted of abuse of power. The National Assembly amends the constitution (October 4) to provide for a centralized French-style presidential government.

August 16, 1978: Adoption of a new constitution, promulgated by President J. R. Jayewardene of the UNP (rules 1978–1989). The National State Assembly is renamed Parliament. Freedom of speech and civil rights are guaranteed. Buddhism is declared the "fore-most" religion, Sinhala the official language, and Tamil a national language. Jayewardene wins reelection under the new constitution, but his reforms fail to stop escalating Tamil separatist unrest.

1979: The Prevention of Terrorism Act grants extraordinary military and police powers. Intended to be temporary, it is permanently enacted as terrorism continues.

1981: The political capital is moved to the Colombo suburb of Sri Jayawardhanapura.

August 12, 1981: Former prime minister Sirimavo Bandaranaike survives a bomb attack that injures dozens of others and ignites communal rioting. A national state of emergency is imposed for five months.

July 24–31, 1983: Civil war begins. Tamil guerrillas ambush and murder thirteen Sinhalese soldiers in Jaffna and the Sinhalese offer reprisals, unleashing the worst ethnic violence since independence and leaving nearly a thousand dead and one hundred thousand refugees in Colombo. A state of emergency is declared and lasts five years. The Tamil insurgents' primary groups—the Liberation Tigers of Tamil Eelam (LTTE), known as the "Tamil Tigers," and the Eelam People's Revolutionary Liberation Front (EPRLF)—seek an independent Tamil Eelam (Precious Land) in the north of the island. The JVP is also rejuvenated. Their guerrilla campaign of terrorism, ambushes, raids, and bombs will continue, with interruptions for talks and cease-fires, for more than sixteen years and claim an estimated sixty thousand lives. Several hundred thousand Tamil civilians flee the island during the next decade.

January 10, 1984: "Amity talks" begin in Colombo between Tamils and Sinhalese, producing an abortive proposal to increase Tamil political power. India sponsors another round of talks in 1985.

December 8, 1985: Sri Lanka is a founding member of the South Asian Association for Regional Cooperation (SAARC).

May 14, 1985: In the first attack in a Sinhalese

province, Tamil separatists kill 150 civilians in the sacred Buddhist city of Anuradhapura. Talks between the government and Tamils in Thimphu, Bhutan, in July–August break down over political recognition of Tamils; mediation by India in the spring of 1986 also fails, as do many subsequent efforts at negotiation. Colombo is first targeted in terrorist bombings April–May 1986.

December 1986: The Jayewardene Plan proposing broad devolution of power to the provinces fails. The president launches a military campaign against the north in February 1987.

Spring 1987: Major terrorist attacks against civilians (April 17 and 21) create a crisis. Government launches Operation Liberation, a major offensive against Jaffna (May 26). India intervenes in the insurgency with a small but symbolic airdrop of humanitarian aid to Tamils under siege in Jaffna (June 4).

July 29, 1987: Indo-Sri Lankan Accord promises political reform in Tamil regions in return for disarming of Tamil rebels. An Indian Peacekeeping Force is deployed in Jaffna to supervise disarmament, but proves deeply unpopular. This and subsequent cease-fires and agreements fail to hold. Sinhalese terrorists attack parliament on August 18. The presence of Indian troops in Sri Lanka, who become drawn into the conflict and eventually number seventy thousand, infuriates citizens of both countries; troops withdraw beginning June 1988, and the last Indian forces leave March 24, 1990. This and subsequent cease-fires and agreements fail to hold.

December 19, 1988: Presidential election is won by former prime minister Ranasinghe Premadasa (rules 1978–1988 as prime minister, 1989–1993 as president). Some 750 people die in three months of election-related violence.

February 5, 1989: One thousand people are killed, including fourteen candidates, in violence surrounding the first parliamentary elections in eleven years. Premadasa's UNP wins a majority. His government's pursuit of peace includes programs to reduce poverty.

June 18, 1990: The government declares all-out war after Tamil Tigers break a year-old cease-fire in a week of violence that kills hundreds of people. Three thousand people are killed in the next three months.

May 21, 1991: Indian prime minister Rajiv Gandhi is assassinated by Tamil rebels.

May 1, 1993: President Premadasa is assassinated by Tamil rebels in Colombo, a week after the murder of the opposition leader, Lalith Athulathmudali.

October 23, 1994: Tamils assassinate the opposition presidential candidate, Gamini Dissanayake.

August 16, 1994: After seventeen years in power, the UNP is defeated in elections by the People's Alliance coalition.

November 9, 1994: Chandrika Bandaranaike Kumaratunga is elected president. She promises to end the violence raging throughout Sri Lanka and appoints her mother, Sirimavo, prime minister.

December 5–6, 1995: After a long campaign against the Tamil Tigers, government forces capture Jaffna, held by the rebels since 1990. Half a million residents flee the city in the last month of fighting. Feeling confident with this victory, the government promises amnesty if the Tamils will lay down their arms, but this is quickly rejected. On December 10 government forces resume their offensive.

April 8, 1996: President Chandrika Bandaranaike Kumaratunga declares a nationwide state of emergency as necessary to preserve order. The government then launches another military offensive against the Tamils and the fighting rages throughout the year.

July 10, 1997: Because the government forces have made some headway against the Tamils, the state of emergency is lifted in large areas of the country.

August 26, 1997: President Chandrika Bandaranaike Kumaratunga launches a campaign to gain support for a new constitution that will devolve more administrative autonomy to the Tamils' territory in the northeast. The Tamils, however, reject this plan.

1998: As the rebellion continues, government forces and the Tamils continue to suffer high casualties. The Tamils employ suicide bombers who take a terrible toll among civilians.

January 25, 1998: The sacred Temple of the Tooth Relic at Kandy, Sri Lanka's holiest Buddhist shrine and a UNESCO World Heritage Site, is bombed by the Tamil Tigers. The Liberation Tigers of Tamil Eelam (LTTE), their official organization, is now officially outlawed.

PART THREE
Southeast Asia

Brunei

EARLY EVIDENCE: 7TH–14TH CENTURIES A.D.

As an Islamic state, Brunei traces its early history to its first Muslim ruler; earlier history is entwined with myth and legend, making it difficult to reconstruct a chronology linking the present-day dynasty to an early kingdom. Although transliteration from the Chinese can pose a problem in identifying place names, the most reliable source for early dating is to be found in Chinese records based on the reports of official court envoys as well as merchants and travelers. There is some evidence that an early mainland kingdom called Funan may be linked to the later kingdoms of Brunei. From as early as the fifth century, the north coast of Borneo has been a stopping-off point on the maritime trade route between China and Indonesia. Trading of camphor and cowries, products for which northwest Borneo is known, are useful references for placing historical records in the area that is now Brunei. Following the emergence of the state called P'o-ni by the Chinese, which is possibly linked to earlier kingdoms, more reliable traces are made.

A.D. 630: Chinese sources describe a kingdom named P'o-li, which some scholars place in northwest Borneo.

680s: There is evidence of possible settlement along the Bay of Brunei at this time; the settlement becomes known as P'o-ni or Fo-ni in Chinese.

8th century: Chinese coins dating from this time are found at Kota Batu, near Brunei's present-day capital.

835: Records of trade in camphor suggest that northwest Borneo may have connections with Srivijaya at this time.

c. 987: P'o-ni, which in the seventeenth century the Chinese call Bun-lai, and is most likely Brunei, is described as an independent state at this time in an Arabic journal.

13th century: By this time P'o-ni has a large fleet, trades in camphor, and possibly extends its influence to the Sulu archipelago and the Philippines.

1365: According to the *Negarakertagama*, the Javanese court poem of this time, Burun-geng (Brunei) is a tributary state of the Javanese Majapahit empire.

1369: P'o-ni is sacked by Sulu raiders but remains under Majapahit control.

EARLY SULTANATES: 15TH–19TH CENTURIES

The Portuguese conquest of Malacca and the relocation of the Muslim court to Johor, on the southern tip of the Malay Peninsula, bring Brunei into contact with the Islamic kingdom; at this time there are also ties to the Philippines and contact with traders from throughout Southeast Asia. Although there are Muslim tombstones in Brunei dating from the thirteenth century, it is uncertain at what time Brunei officially converts to Islam. The first sultanate of Brunei under Sultan Mohammed (Alak Betatar) is described in the *Shaer Awang Semaun*, the Brunei foundation myth, in which Alak Betatar's lineage is traced to legendary origins.

By the sixteenth century Brunei is a large kingdom covering most of North Borneo and extending as far as the Philippines. Its domination of trade in the area is challenged in the seventeenth century by Sulu, an island sultanate to the north in what is now the southern Philippines, that gains control over much of Brunei's territory. The sultanate is weakened by civil war and threat from the Sulu kingdom; Brunei loses its prominence as a trading port and its territory is reduced to the area of Brunei Town.

1515: According to the Portuguese traveler Tomé Pires's account in the *Suma Oriental* (1563), Sultan Mohammad (Alak Betatar) becomes the first sultan of Brunei and embraces Islam at this time. Other sources, including the present-day Brunei Historical Centre, push this date back by two centuries.

July 1521: A Spanish delegation lands at Muara, observing a brick fort and bronze and iron cannons.

16th century: Sultan Sharif Ali builds mosques and establishes the Islamic legal system in Brunei. Trade with Portuguese Malacca, as well as the Philippines, thrives.

The king again sent three very ornamented prahus, which came playing pipes and drums and cymbals, and going round the ships, their crews saluted us with their cloth caps, which hardly covered the tops of their heads. We saluted them, firing the bombards without stones. . . . They said that their king was well pleased that we should make provisions here of wood and water, and that we might traffic at our pleasure with the islanders.

The Voyage of Magellan, by Antonio Pigafetta (1525)

Late 16th century: Hassan, ninth sultan of Brunei, creates an effective administrative system and resists European expansion. Brunei's influence spreads along the coastal areas of present-day Sabah and Sarawak, and to islands beyond Borneo.

April 1578: Having captured Sulu and the Philippines, and at odds with the Brunei aristocracy established there, Spain enters the Bay of Brunei at Muara and takes the capital. Sultan Abdul Kahar and his son Saiful Rijal retreat. An illness causes the departure of the Spanish forces; Abdul Kahar dies and Sultan Saiful Rijal returns to the capital to rebuild and rearm it against the attacks that are to continue until 1645.

Mid-1600s: Sultan Mohammed Ali is murdered and civil war ensues, with Sulu intervention.

1768: Date of a British report stating that Brunei had been engaged in an extended civil war; scarcity of information from this time suggests that turmoil continued through the end of the century.

1776: Reports indicate that Brunei is a thriving commercial port, inviting British protection against the Sulu threat.

EUROPEAN PRESENCE: 1839–1984

Brunei, which lacks agricultural or mineral resources, has little to interest the European trading companies and colonizing nations engaged in commerce throughout Southeast Asia in the early nineteenth century. British adventurer Captain James Brooke arrives in North Borneo, takes a part of Sarawak and all of the Limbang River, reduces the Brunei kingdom, and divides it in two. Brooke establishes himself as the first White Raja of Sarawak, a title that remains in the family until 1951. As the area of North Borneo is divided up and contested, the Brunei sultanate welcomes British protection. After the Japanese occupation during World War II, Brunei continues to resist both cutting ties with England and joining a federation with other north Borneo states or Federation of Malaysia with Indonesia, Sabah, and Sarawak. This sense of protected independence has paid off; the struggling state is transformed when its oil fields are developed.

1830: Sarawaks rebel against Pengiran Makota, the Bruneian chieftain overseeing mining in Sarawak.

1839: James Brooke arrives in Sarawak; Brunei's chieftain Pengiran Muda Hassim requests his assistance in quashing rebellion. In return, Brooke requests governorship of Sarawak.

July 1842: Brunei Sultan Omar Ali Saifuddin II (reigns 1828–1852) cedes part of Sarawak and its dependencies to James Brooke.

October 1843: With a show of force, Brooke backs Pengiran Muda Hassim in a Bruneian dynastic rivalry; Sultan Omar offers the island of Labuan, at the entrance to Brunei Bay, to Britain.

Late 1845: Sultan Omar orders the assassination of Hassim and his allies.

July 1846: Brooke and Admiral Sir Thomas Cochrane attack Brunei Town by sea and depose the sultan. Omar is reinstated after pledging loyalty to Queen Victoria; he gives Britain the right to suppress piracy off Borneo and confirms the cession of Labuan to Britain on December 18.

1847: Treaty between Britain and Brunei gives Britain control over Brunei's trade.

August 1861: James Brooke acquires for Sarawak the coastal region west of Bintulu from Brunei's Sultan Abdul Munim (reigns 1852–1885).

1865: Sultan Munim grants a ten-year lease of much of present-day Sabah to U.S. business interests, resulting in the formation of the American Trading Company of Borneo, which fails in 1866.

1868: Charles Brooke succeeds James Brooke as Raja of Sarawak and continues a policy of expansionism.

It is not given to the cleverest and most calculating of mortals to know with certainty what is in their interest: yet it is given to quite a lot of simple folk to know every day what is their duty.

Sultan Omar (19th century)

1877: Anglo-Dutch business interests purchase American concessions in Sabah from Sultan Munim as well as from Sulu, which also claims it; the area eventually comes under British control as British North Borneo, then becomes a Malaysian state.

September 17, 1888: In order to stem further cession of Bruneian territory, Sultan Hassim Jalilul Alam Aqamaddin (reigns 1885–1906) signs a Protectorate Agreement with Britain. (Supplements to this agreement will be signed on December 3, 1905, and January 2, 1906.) Internal affairs are not interfered with and independence is recognized.

March 17, 1890: The Limbang River, which flows into Brunei Bay, is claimed for Sarawak by Charles Brooke. Britain agrees to cede the river; Sultan Hassim refuses and Brunei receives no cession fees. Trade is directed elsewhere.

1900: Brunei's chief employer is the Island Trading Syndicate factory, which produces *kachu* (cutch), a tanning dye extracted from the bark of mangrove trees; by 1904 this resource is depleted and trees must be purchased from Sarawak.

1906: A treaty states that at the death of Sultan Hassim, a British Resident is appointed to Brunei to assist in administration and offer protection. Under the residency of Malayan Consul Malcolm Stewart Hannibal McArthur, economic and governmental reforms that provide the foundations for modernization of Brunei are introduced.

1917: Death of Charles Brooke; Raja Vyner Brooke is his successor.

April 1929: The British Malayan Petroleum Company (PMPC), a subsidiary of Royal Dutch Shell, succeeds in finding oil at the Seria oil field. The nearby settlement of Kuala Belait is developed by the BMPC to provide facilities for the immigrant populations employed by this new industry.

1931–1933: Vyner Brooke transfers to Brunei rights to Muara, Pulau Berembang, and Kota Batu.

1935: By this time, Brunei is the British Commonwealth's third-largest oil producer.

December 16, 1941: Brunei is invaded by Japanese troops at Kuala Belait; Britain had destroyed oil field and port installations to deny Japan oil facilities. Japan drills new wells and develops a naval base.

June 10, 1945: Allied forces land at Labuan; Brunei Town is captured in three days, and the British Military Administration is established.

September 6, 1946: Sultan Ahmad Tajuddin (reigns 1924–1950) takes over the administration of Brunei; he pledges loyalty to Britain and accepts a new Resident.

1948: The governor of the British colony of Sarawak is appointed High Commissioner of Brunei.

1950: Sultan Omar Ali Saifuddin III (reigns 1950–1967) succeeds his brother Ahmad Tajuddin. Omar Ali negotiates favorable terms in oil revenues and taxation to finance Brunei's modernization.

January 1956: Pro-independence Partai Rakyat Brunei (PRB) is formed under A. M. Azahari.

September 19, 1959: A written constitution is drawn up. Britain withdraws its Resident but retains control of Brunei's defense, internal security, and foreign affairs.

August 31, 1962: The PRB wins a landslide victory in the first general election. Sultan Omar, who desires to maintain ties with Britain in a gradual approach to independence, bans the PRB.

December 8, 1962: Revolt is launched with the backing of the Communist North Kalimantan National Army; Omar puts down the rebellion in four days with assistance of the British Army's Gurkhas, who remain in Brunei. On December 20 a state of emergency is declared. It will remain in place until well after independence.

1963–1965: Indonesian president Sukarno launches war (*Konfrontasi*) against Malaysia; Brunei offers base of operations for British troops combating Indonesian soldiers in northern Borneo.

August 1966: Partai Barisan Kemerdekaan Rakyat is formed by a merger of all political parties. The PBKR demands independence from Britain.

October 4, 1967: To avoid instituting democratic changes pledged to Britain after independence, Sultan Omar Ali abdicates in favor of his son, Hassanal Bolkiah, who is at school in Britain.

August 1968: Coronation of Hassanal Bolkiah, the twenty-ninth sultan of Brunei.

1971: A British-Bruneian treaty provides a limited British military presence; Brunei gains full control over internal affairs and remains

British protectorate. British Gurkha troops are stationed in Brunei and British administrators hold government posts.

1973: Liquefied natural gas is produced at Lumut plant.

November 1977: A UN resolution calls for Britain to facilitate free elections and the return of political exiles in Brunei.

January 1979: Treaty of Friendship and Co-operation is drawn up with Britain, providing for independence in five years.

January 1982: The Internal Security Act allows for political detentions and the curtailment of political activities without trial in a reinforcement of the state of emergency proclaimed in 1962.

INDEPENDENCE: 1984–1998

Since its independence from Britain, Brunei has thrived on its oil and natural gas reserves, which comprise a major share of Brunei's export earnings; it is the world's second largest producer of liquefied natural gas. Brunei Shell Petroleum, 50 percent of which is owned by the government, is the nation's largest company. QAF Holdings, an investment company in which the sultan's brother has a majority interest, is second. On a much smaller scale, there is an industry of brass workers practicing traditional lost-wax casting techniques to produce cannons, guns, and gongs for ceremonial and decorative use.

In this oligarchy, the sultan is prime minister as well as minister of finance and domestic affairs; his brothers are ministers of foreign affairs and culture. Most important government positions are held by members of the royal family.

January 1, 1984: Brunei becomes an independent nation ruled by Sultan Hassanal Bolkiah as its "democratic" monarch. The Gurkha troops remain to guard the Seria oil field at a cost of £3 million a year to Brunei; the sultan may use the troops for defense from external aggression. Hassanal pledges to lift the state of emergency that has been in place since 1962, step down as prime minister, and hold a general election.

January 1984: Brunei joins the Association of Southeast Asian Nations (ASEAN).

February 23, 1984: With leaders from seventy countries in attendance, Brunei conducts ceremonies observing its independence. (This day will henceforward be observed as National Day.)

May 1985: The Brunei National Democratic Party (BNDP), with Malay-only membership, is formed with government restrictions placed on its activities.

1986: The Brunei National Solidarity Party (BNSP), a multiracial offshoot of the BNDP, is formed.

January 27, 1988: Hassanal bans the BNDP and arrests its leader; the BNSP disbands.

1988: The Royal Brunei Malay Regiment in charge of national security purchases $400 million of military equipment. Defense is the government's largest expense.

1988: Brunei University opens; the government discourages students from studying abroad in an effort to limit foreign influences and promote Malay-Islamic culture.

1990: Eight detainees from the revolt of 1962 are released.

1991: Logging firms, which produce timber for domestic use only, are required to halve their tree-felling. Commercial logging has remained minimal and the development of ecotourism is being considered in forests that are used primarily for jungle-warfare training.

September 1992: Brunei is one of four new nations admitted to the Nonaligned Movement, a group of fifty-three Third World nations that holds its tenth summit this year in Jakarta, Indonesia.

December 18, 1995: Brunei signs an ASEAN pact declaring the area from Myanmar to Indonesia a nuclear-free zone.

February 26, 1997: Prince Jefri Bolkiah, the youngest brother of the sultan of Brunei, resigns as finance minister amid rumors of disagreements with the sultan over the handling of Brunei's vast wealth.

March 3, 1997: A complaint filed in the U.S. federal court in Los Angeles by a former Miss America charges that in 1996 she had been hired to make a promotional appearance in Brunei for the sultan. Once there, she alleges, her passport was taken from her and she was held prisoner for thirty-two days while she was expected to entertain at a discotheque for Asian men, some of whom subjected her to sexual harassment. Although this case will be dismissed in 1998, the American media will find other young women who have similar tales. The sultan and his court will deny all such claims.

February–April 1998: Forest fires that have been razing thousands of acres in Indonesia are casting a blanket of thick smog over Brunei along with other parts of the island of Borneo.

July 31, 1998: Prince Jefri Bolkiah, a younger brother of the sultan, is removed from control of the nation's investment arm and telecommunications empire by the sultan. This follows rumors that have been circulating throughout Southeast Asia for many weeks that the conglomerate he controlled has suffered major financial losses.

September 19, 1998: Queen Elizabeth II of Great Britain visits Brunei and inspects a parade honoring the alliance between Brunei's armed forces and the Brigade of Nepali Gurkhas, stationed here under a 1983 agreement with London to protect Brunei's oil fields.

Cambodia

PREHISTORIC CAMBODIA: 14,000 B.C.–A.D. 150

No evidence yet exists for the presence of early hominids in Cambodia, as it does for Indonesia and China, but it is known that by at least 38,000 B.C. *Homo sapiens* is moving through or into Cambodia. Exactly where these first inhabitants came from is not known for sure; whether from Malaysia or Indonesia, Vietnam or China, or some other region, they are probably not a Mongoloid people but are instead Australo-Melanesians, the short, darker people who inhabit parts of Southeast Asia at this time. Certainly other peoples moved into Cambodia in the ensuing millennia, and again their exact origins are not known. By about 13,000 B.C. the inhabitants of Cambodia are beginning to participate in the cultural developments occurring around them in Southeast Asia; they will continue to do so for the next thirteen thousand years. Cambodians will later fill in these early years with myths, legends, and folktales about their fabulous ancestors, but archaeologists and historians are not able to do much better when it comes to details. It is believed that the direct ancestors of today's Khmer arrive in Cambodia only about 200 B.C., and not until about the first century A.D. do the Khmer people of Cambodia appear to set themselves apart from the Funanese and Chams who live around the delta region of the Mekong River. By the end of the first century A.D. much of southern Cambodia will fall under the influence of the Funanese, and it is as the kingdom of Funan that Cambodia first enters history.

13,000–4000 B.C.: The earliest known culture in Cambodia is the Hoabinhian, so named after the site in northern Vietnam where it was first discovered, Hoa Binh. This Hoabinhian culture, which is found across much of Southeast Asia, west to Burma, and north into southern China and possibly to Taiwan, is best distinguished by its tools: flat river pebbles of varying shapes but usually about fist size, flaked on one or both sides but with cutting edges around their entire circumference. The Hoabinhians forage and hunt for most of their food; although not agriculturists, they may have taken some trouble to encourage such native plants as yams and taro.

4000–1500 B.C.: Mongoloid people make their way into Cambodia during this period and mix with the earlier Australo-Melanesian people. They build houses on wooden piles, hunt and fish, and cultivate native fruits and root crops. The first known pottery in Cambodia appears about 4000 B.C., from which time it continues to be made in a variety of types. By the end of this period, the inhabitants of Cambodia have domesticated pigs and water buffalo and are cultivating rice. It appears that the residents of Cambodia retain many links with their neighbors, from whom they have drawn for many of their cultural advances. Sites in Cambodia possibly inhabited by the end of this period include several around Tonle Sap, the great lake of central Cambodia; the best known of these is Samrong Sen.

1500–500 B.C.: People in Cambodia are making use of an increasingly more elaborate material culture. By at least 1000 B.C. they are making bronze artifacts using sandstone molds, probably under the influence of the more advanced bronze workers of Thailand and Vietnam. Samrong Sen, near Tonle Sap, is one of the major sites for bronze finds of this period (and copper deposits are found nearby).

500–200 B.C.: At least by the end of this period, people known as Khmer seem to be moving into modern Cambodia. Nothing certain is known of their origins, but it appears that they are moving south from Thailand's Khorat Plateau and seeking the fertile Mekong valley. Whoever they are, they speak a Mon-Khmer language that is closely related to the Austroasiatic languages spoken by most Vietnamese and by peoples in Laos, Thailand, Burma, Malaysia, and India.

200 B.C.–A.D. 100: Towns with earthen moats and ramparts like those found in Thailand are also found in the Siem Reap plain of central Cambodia and most likely date from this period. Bronze flasks and bells dating to early first millennium A.D., probably made under the influence of the Vietnamese Dong Son culture, are found in Cambodia. During this time, three different peoples are residing in southern Indochina—the Khmer, Funanese, and Chams. By about A.D. 100 the Funanese establish the kingdom of Funan (as it is known by the Chinese sources) and assert their rule over much of southern Cambodia, linked as it is to the sea routes.

FUNAN PERIOD: A.D. 150–550

Khmer legend claims that in the first century A.D. an Indian Brahman named Kaundinya married a local princess of divine extraction and founded the state of Funan in the general area of the Mekong basin. This myth of origin is documented by Chinese records which provide most of the written history of this period. These Chinese historians recognize a single kingdom that they name Funan, although most scholars now believe that Funan consisted of a number of principalities, or chiefdoms, without a fixed political or ritual center. It has been conjectured that the Funanese are at the head of a loose confederation of states along the coast of the Gulf of Siam similar to that at Oc Eo. Excavation of the coastal city of Oc Eo has yielded religious artifacts, building foundations, and objects of diverse geographical origin, including Roman coins dating from the mid-second century. These findings suggest a large and thriving city strategically situated at the junction of important maritime trading routes between China and India and drawing on a well-managed rice hinterland. Inland Khmers bring forest goods from the interior to trade. In the third century the Kingdom of Funan appears for the first time in Chinese records, which describe the visit of two envoys of the Wu ruler in China, K'ang T'ai and Zhu Ying. These envoys confirm that the Funanese are experienced maritime navigators and builders of large ships who trade with India, China and, indirectly, Rome. During the fourth century, the process of Indianization broadens, perhaps influenced by waves of traders and pilgrims. Temples of brick and stone honor the Hindu gods Siva and, to a lesser extent, Vishnu; the Funanese are also touched by Buddhism. It appears that Oc Eo goes into decline during the fourth century, when an all-sea route is pioneered between India and China via the Strait of Malacca. By the end of the sixth century, this has become the preferred route, and Funan's economy, essentially based on trading and oriented toward the sea, declines. In the late sixth century, Funan disappears from Chinese records and is replaced by the region called Chenla by Chinese historians.

225: Chinese records mention the Kingdom of Funan for the first time and describe the visit to the court of Funan by two envoys from the Wu ruler in China, K'ang T'ai and Zhu Ying.

243: A mission is sent from the Funan court to the capital of the Wu kingdom in the south of China.

357: An embassy is sent to the court of the Eastern Chin dynasty ruling southern China. They bring elephants as gifts; these are deemed dangerous and ordered to be returned.

478: A trade mission returning from China with the Indian monk Nagasena is shipwrecked and forced to journey overland. It is attacked by Chams from the neighboring kingdom, called Lin-yi in Chinese historical records.

484: Nagasena is given a commission by the court of Funan to return to the Chinese court with gifts (including two ivory models of Buddhist shrines) and complaints about the Chams. Nagasena reports to the Chinese court that the state religious cult in Funan is addressed to Siva, but that Buddhism is also important.

539: A Funanese embassy to China reports that Funan possesses a hair relic of the Buddha. This illustrates the importance of Buddhism in Funan, which is also evident in the nature of the gifts offered to the Chinese court.

6th century: The number of Sanskrit inscriptions recording some of the pious activities of sixth-century royalty increases during this period. According to Chinese records, Funan is defeated by the neighboring kingdom of Chenla; in any case, Funan disappears from Chinese records and is replaced by Chenla.

CHENLA PERIOD: 550–802

According to Chinese annals, the vassal state of Chenla rebels and overcomes Funan. Scholars no longer believe that one unified political bloc replaced another, as suggested by the Chinese records, and posit instead that Chenla consists of a number of Khmer principalities jostling for hegemony. It seems likely that Chenla's preeminence during this period is geographical rather than political, and reflects a shift away from international maritime trade toward an emphasis on rice cultivation. From the late sixth century, conquerors from the mid-Mekong region concentrate their ambitions in northern Cambodia, suggesting that the significance of rice cultivation is becoming more apparent. It appears that the wealth of these new kingdoms derives primarily from wet-rice agriculture, which requires more labor and less land than the dry rice cultivation of previous centuries. Inscriptions indicate that a number of royal lines exist simultaneously during this period, and it seems likely that allegiance to a sovereign state must, in many cases, be in name only. King Bhavavarman, flourishing in the latter half of the sixth century, establishes a capital at Bhavapura and a kingdom around the Tonle Sap (Great Lake). His brother and eventual successor, Mahendravarman, conquers lands extending into northeast Thailand before returning to Bhavapura, where he endows a number of shrines containing *lingam* (the phallic symbol of the Hindu god Siva) along the Mekong River. Isanavarman, probably a descendant of Mahendravarman, flourishes during the 620s and inscriptions attest to conquests across much of Cambodia. During the late seventh century, it appears that some Malay kingdoms to the south (the Malay Peninsula and Sumatra) inherit the former commercial sphere of Funan and lay claim to sovereignty of the area. Toward the end of the eighth century a Khmer prince appears in this capital region and heads north, conquering and unifying Cambodian lands.

612: The first inscription in the Khmer language, heavily influenced by Sanskrit vocabulary, is carved at Angkor Borei. The number of inscriptions increases rapidly from this date.

Late 6th century: According to later inscriptions, King Bhavavarman flourishes. He establishes a capital city at Bhavapura, the site of which is still debated, although it seems that his kingdom is probably confined to an area bordering the Tonle Sap.

c. 600: Mahendravarman, brother of Bhavavarman, returns to Bhavapura where he erects a number of shrines containing *lingams* along the Mekong River. He extends his kingdom into part of the former territory of Funan and sends an embassy to China.

620s: The reign of Isanavarman is attested by fourteen inscriptions. By 628 he is no longer mentioned; it is likely that he is either dead or his dominions are crumbling.

657: Jayavarman I, who comes from the area northeast of Tonle Sap, is known to have been ruling. He establishes his capital, Purandarapura, at a site identified with Ak Yum (west of Phnom Bakheng at the center of the future site of Angkor).

706: According to Chinese sources, the kingdom of Chenla splits into two parts at this point: Land Chenla in the north and Water Chenla in the south. This division is said to have remained in effect until 838, but modern scholars dispute these records as too simplistic; it seems more likely that Chenla in fact consisted of several political entities.

638: Four embassies from the northwest of the Khmer territory are sent to Chinese courts. Various kings are mentioned in the inscriptions.

c. 777: Jayavarman II, perhaps an exiled Khmer prince, appears in lands apparently held by Malay states in the southeast of Cambodia at the end of the eighth century. In his northward progress he unites a number of different principalities under his rule and promotes an ideal of Khmer unity. Eleventh-century inscriptions say that his task is not only to unite Khmers, but also to rebut claims made over them by a king of Java.

KHMER EMPIRE: 802–1431

From the beginning of the ninth century, Jayavarman II establishes a new unified and independent Khmer state and locates his capital near the northwest shore of the Tonle Sap. He is consecrated as a *devaraja* (god-king), instituting the belief system by which Khmer kings are linked to the gods. In the late ninth century his successor Indravarman I constructs a vast artificial irrigation system that insures the kingdom's economic prosperity, based on wet-rice agriculture. His son, Yasovarman I, extends the Khmer empire and establishes his capital at Yasodharapura, precursor of Angkor. He is responsible for the construction of the first temple mountain, which symbolizes Mount Meru, home of the gods in Hindu mythology, and becomes characteristic of Khmer architecture during the Angkor period. In the mid-tenth century, Rajendravarman II restores Angkor after a period of neglect and inaugurates institutions of centralized government, by which ancient principalities are absorbed and administrative divisions standardized. During the twelfth century, the Angkor Empire reaches its apogee under Suryavarman II, who expands the empire into much of modern Cambodia, Thailand, and Laos. He cultivates diplomatic relations with the Song court in China, promotes trade, and undertakes a massive construction program that includes the great temple complex of Angkor Wat. His reign is followed by a period of unrest plagued by military incursions from the neighboring kingdom of Champa, which eventually sacks Angkor in 1177. At the end of the twelfth century, Jayavarman VII, an adherent to Mahayana Buddhism, expels the Chams and restores the empire. He is responsible for an enormous number of religious constructions, hospitals and an intricate road network linking the outer reaches of the empire. In the thirteenth century, a great number of Khmer people convert to Theravada Buddhism, although the Chinese envoy, Chou Ta-kuan (Zhou Daguan), reports at the end of the thirteenth century that Hindu cults are still approved religions at the Angkor court. During the fourteenth century Thai invasions become increasingly troublesome, and the hydraulic irrigation system that had underpinned Khmer economic prosperity falls into disrepair. By the early fifteenth century the site of Angkor has become increasingly difficult to defend against Thai invaders, and in 1431 Angkor is sacked. Economic priorities change as the agrarian economy gives way to an emphasis on wealth generated by maritime trade and commerce. The center of the Khmer polity shifts south to the area surrounding Phnom Penh, near the confluence of the Mekong River and the Tonle Sap.

c. 770–c. 834: Reign of Jayavarman II. Although historians used to date his reign from 802–850, it now seems necessary to set it earlier. Jayavarman II appears in the southeast of Cambodia at the end of the eighth century and progresses northwest, bringing different kingdoms under his rule. He establishes a series of capitals north of the Tonle Sap before settling at Hariharalaya (eight miles to the southeast of the present-day provincial capital of Siem Reap), which remains the Khmer capital for most of the ninth century.

802: This date is traditionally accepted as the formal consecration of the *devaraja* (god-king) Jayavarman II as "universal monarch" in a ceremony conducted by Brahmans of the Saivaite sect. The king and his kingdom are brought under the protection of Siva with whom the king is explicitly linked. This belief system, by which Khmer kings are believed to be directly linked to the gods, is developed by subsequent kings. This date is now being questioned as modern scholars believe the ceremony took place as early as 770.

c. 877–889/890: Reign of Indravarman I. Under Indravarman I the great religious foundations typical of the Angkor period start to appear. He is also responsible for vast irrigation projects, including reservoirs, necessary for wet-rice cultivation and for feeding temple moats.

His rule was like a crown of jasmine on the lofty heads of the kings of China, Champa and Java.

Inscription describing the reign of King Indravarman I (reigned c. 877–899/890)

879: The Preah Ko monument is consecrated at Indravarman's capital of Hariharalaya.

This group of five tower shrines inaugurates the Roluos style of architecture. It contains three images of Siva and three of the Goddess and is dedicated to Indravarman's predecessors, performing the double function of honoring the deities and legitimizing his reign. The inscription for Preah Ko suggests that unspecified contenders had been subdued in order for Indravarman to become king.

881: A *lingam* (originally a phallic symbol, but which becomes an abstract representation of the god Siva during the Angkor period) is consecrated on the five-tiered pyramid of Bakhong, which is intended to serve as the king's sarcophagus. This is the first state shrine set on a pyramid, which will become the hallmark of the Angkor kingdom.

c. 889/890–c. 910/912: Reign of Yasovarman I. He establishes a new capital, Yasodharapura, at what will become the site of Angkor. The first temple-mountain is constructed on the summit of a natural hill at the center of the city, Phnom Bakheng, and is an explicit representation of Mount Meru, home to the gods in Hindu cosmology, with five terraces symbolizing the five peaks of the holy mountain. Other temple mountains at Phnom Krom and Phnom Bok follow. He is also responsible for the construction of the great reservoir known as the Eastern Baray, and inscriptions attest to the vast extent of his dominion. The increasing number of references to "Kambuja-desa" (Cambodia) in inscriptions during this period suggests that the notion of a unified state is becoming an accepted concept as well as an ideal. During his reign several sanctuaries are built in Angkor, as well as about a hundred monasteries worshipping the three main cults of Siva, Vishnu, and the Buddha throughout the realm, each monastery apparently serving as a royal outpost.

893: Consecration of Lolei, a temple dedicated to Yasovarman's ancestors in Hariharapura and constructed on an island in the great reservoir created by his father.

c. 944–968: Reign of Rajendravarman II. He restores Yasodharapura as the capital and constructs a number of temples and shrines. He extends the borders of the empire once again, and invades the heartland of the rival Cham empire to the east. Under Rajendravarman II, teams of officials are appointed to administer the provinces, instituting an early form of central government and consolidating the power of Angkor.

Rajendravarman's brilliance burned the enemy kingdoms, beginning with Champa.

Inscription describing the rule of Rajendravarman II
(reigned c. 944–968)

---

c. 950: Khmer legend claims that Rajendravarman II captures a golden statue as a trophy from the Chams.

c. 953: Consecration of the East Mebon temple-mountain, which rises from the artificial lake known as the Eastern Baray.

961: Consecration of Pre Rup temple.

c. 968–c. 1000: Reign of Jayavarman V. He accedes to the throne as a child. His guru (teacher), Yajuavaraha, holds enormous power, reflecting the increasingly strong influence of priestly families at this time. The monks and priests, often well-born, are experts in the literature of high culture, largely responsible for education and often functioning as advisers to the king or government. The Banteay Srei shrine is founded at this time. Jayavarman's death is followed by a period of confused conflict among rival claimants to the throne.

c. 1002–1050: Reign of Suryavarman I. He vanquishes all other claimants to the throne. Under his leadership, the Khmers expand to the north and west and regional capitals are established at Sukhothai and Phimai (now Thailand) with road networks to connect the empire. Territorial expansion brings increased economic prosperity and trade, which in turn stimulates urbanization. The landowning system is elaborated and rice cultivation developed. He brings religious foundations (including their treasures and manpower) under the control of a government-supervised system dominated by state temples endowed by the king. Four *lingam* shrines facing north, south, east, and west attest to the extent of the king's dominions. The Ta Keo temple is probably constructed around this time. It is notable for being the first temple built of sandstone, more durable and workable than materials formerly used.

c. **1010:** Suryavarman I fights his way to the capital.

1011: A stone inscription attests to an oath of allegiance to Suryavarman I sworn to by about four hundred of his officials.

1050–*c.* 1066: Reign of Udayadityarman II. He is guided by a powerful guru (teacher), Divakarapandita. The king is responsible for the creation of the massive temple-mountain Phnom Baphuon, and he revives the *deva-raja* (god-king) cult. He probably also creates Angkor's largest irrigation project (although it is sometimes attributed to Suryavarman I) known as the Western Baray; a mile and a half wide and eight miles long, it is still used to irrigate twenty-eight square miles today.

1052: An inscription at Sdok Kak Thom shrine reveals the history of a priestly family. It records the endowments of temples in new territories and illustrates how a growing population expands into new areas as part of a state-sponsored system. The district is first granted by the king's decree; temples are then founded, each with a stone *lingam* marking a sacred shrine. A community of servants and bonded labor is then granted by benefactors to supply the temple's needs, creating a settlement.

c. **1066–*c.* 1080:** Reign of Harsavarman III. Little is known about this king, although, according to Chinese sources, Angkor and Champa are required by China to help fight Vietnam.

c. **1080–*c.* 1107:** Reign of Jayavarman VI. He is probably responsible for the great religious foundations at Phimai (now in Thailand)

that honor Hindu and local territorial gods, but are particularly influenced by Buddhism. He establishes a new royal line, but the period is marked by division and great unrest. He is succeeded by his elder brother, about whom little is known.

c. **1113–1150:** Reign of Suryavarman II (although inscriptions date his reign to 1102). Angkor reaches the peak of its glory under Suryavarman II. His military conquests enable him to expand the empire once again and place his own choice on the throne of the rival kingdom of Champa (to the east). The relative peace which ensues allows him to encourage trade and marks a period of greater involvement with the outside world. Embassies are sent to the Chinese court, and Suryavarman II is honored by the Chinese emperor Gaozong for his support of the Song court, fleeing from northern invaders. An impressive hydraulic-irrigation system is created and hydraulic cities are established at a distance from Angkor for the first time. A number of important sanctuaries are created during his reign, including Beng Mendelea, Banteay Smare, and the Preah Pithu temple group. A vigorous revival of Visnu-ism on the Indian subcontinent coincides with the building and dedication of the celebrated Angkor Wat. It is conjectured that Suryavarman II dies after a campaign in Vietnam in the 1150s, but there is no evidence to confirm this.

1116, 1120: The Angkor court sends embassies to China.

c. **1150:** Completion of Angkor Wat. This temple complex, dedicated to Vishnu, is estimated to have taken about thirty years to construct and is the most spectacular surviving monument to the Angkor empire. Spread over five hundred acres, it is an enormous representation of Mount Meru, home of the gods in Hindu cosmology. It is surrounded by a moat representing the ocean encompassing the world in Hindu mythology; this moat is bridged by a causeway in the form of a snake, which rears up to form a fan of snake heads, a distinctive feature of Khmer architecture at this period. The world's largest relief sculpture adorns the walls of the outer galleries depicting the Hindu creation myth, the Churning of the Sea of Milk. The complex faces west, in the direction of the setting sun, which seems to suggest a funerary function. The moats and waterways make a significant contribution to the hydraulic resources of the area.

c. 1150–c. 1165: Reign of Yasovarman II. The absence of inscriptions and questionable legitimacy of rulers seems to indicate that this is another period of unrest and dissension. It seems likely that Yasovarman II came to a violent end at the hands of one of his officials, who then proclaimed himself king.

c. 1165–1177: Reign of Tribhuvaniditya. This period remains obscure. The reign of Tribhuvaniditya is ended when a Cham fleet makes its way unexpectedly to the Tonle Sap and scores a rapid and decisive victory that gives power (briefly) at Angkor to the Cham ruler, Jaya Indravarman IV.

1181–c. 1218: Reign of Jayavarman VII. After four years of fighting, he expels the Chams. He may have been about sixty years old at the time of his accession. The empire is stabilized and expanded into parts of Laos, Thailand, and Champa. He is a follower of Mahayana Buddhism, which becomes the new state religion, although Hindu cults are still approved. He is responsible for a vast number of religious constructions including Banteay Srei, Srah Srang, Ta Prohm, and the famous Bayon temple. He institutes an extensive public works program, which includes hospitals, rest-houses, and a network of roads. The end of his reign is obscure.

1186: Dedication of Ta Prohm (Ancestor Temple) in which Jayavarman VII honors his mother in the guise of Prajnaparamita, the goddess of wisdom, conceived metaphorically as the mother of the Buddha.

They eat from bowls and vases of gold. From that comes the proverb of rich Chenla. The people are in fact rich. The weather is always hot. Neither ice nor snow is found there.

Those who have many slaves have more than a hundred; those who have only a few from ten to twenty; only the very poor have none at all.

Memorials on the Customs of Cambodia, by Chou Ta-kuan (late 13th century)

1191: Khmer forces capture the Cham capital. Also in this year, the Preah Khan (Sacred Sword) temple is dedicated. The inscription states that it has been built on the site of an important victory over the Chams, but no other evidence has been found to support this claim. The shrine contains a carved portrait of Jayavarman's father with traits of the Buddha. The Neah Po'on temple is probably also completed around this time.

1190s: A number of changes are made to the Bayon temple during its construction, indicating ideological shifts and uncertainty. The temple is covered with bas-reliefs depicting historical Cambodian events rather than the usual Hindu or Buddhist myths, but is perhaps most famous for the hundreds of gigantic carved faces that adorn it and that have given rise to the expression "the Angkor smile."

c. 1243–1295: Reign of Jayavarman VIII. He sponsors the last known royally endowed temple, the Mangalartha. His reign shows some evidence of resurgent Hinduism; a number of Buddhist temples are defaced.

1285: Consecration of the Mangalartha temple.

c. 1295–1308: Reign of Indravarman III. Indravarman is host to the Chinese envoy, Chou Ta-kuan, whose *Memorials on the Customs of Cambodia* provide an invaluable source of contemporary information. Thai forces repeatedly attack the northwest region of Cambodia. Subsequent records become increasingly obscure, but it seems the great dynasties of Angkor have come to an end.

14th century: Principalities such as Sukothai and Lovo, which formerly sent tribute to the Angkor court, now proclaim themselves independent. The Thais grow increasingly aggressive and establish a new capital at Ayudhya. Cambodian political influence diminishes and the emphasis on trade rather than agrarian subsistence increases.

1353: Thai forces sack Angkor.

1371–1419: More than a dozen tributary missions are sent from Cambodia to China, indicating that trade is being expanded and that the Thais are being kept temporarily at bay.

1431: Angkor is again sacked by the Thais. Thai aggression and the increasing importance of maritime trade drive the population south toward the vicinity of Phnom Penh.

He removed the august statues of the Buddha made of gold, silver, bronze and precious stones, as well as a number of statues of the August Bull and other animals.

Description in Cambodian chronicles of the Thai king's removal of statues after the sacking of Angkor, 1431

CONTESTED CAMBODIA: 1431–1863

In the early fifteenth century, Angkor is abandoned for a new capital further south at Phnom Penh, far from marauding Thais and advantageously situated for riverine trade. Angkorean institutions such as temple-building, inscriptions, and irrigation works fade as trade is expanded both at sea and with neighboring trading cities such as Ayudhya in Thai territory. In the mid-sixteenth century the capital is moved north of Phnom Penh to Lovek, where increasing numbers of foreigners, traders, and Spanish and Portuguese missionaries arrive. Lovek falls to the Thais in the late sixteenth century, opening up an era of Thai domination. Vietnamese Nguyen overlords gain control of the Mekong Delta from the beginning of the seventeenth century, cutting Cambodia off from the lucrative maritime trade routes. For most of the eighteenth century Cambodia is subject to Thai influence, but King Chan initiates a pro-Vietnamese policy from the beginning of the nineteenth century, triggering a struggle for control of Cambodia by its two more powerful neighbors. The Vietnamese eventually emerge victorious and attempt to impose vigorous controls on the Cambodians. During the 1830s Cambodia is almost unrecognizable as a distinct nation. Rebellion erupts in 1840 when Cambodia's queen is arrested. Once again, the Thais and Vietnamese scrabble for control of the contested Cambodian territories, until King Duang is finally consecrated under joint Vietnamese and Thai protection. He initiates negotiations with the French, who are expanding into Vietnam, but his death precipitates another succession crisis. Duang's successor, Norodom, reopens negotiations with the French, and Cambodia becomes a French protectorate in 1863.

1444: A new capital is established at Phnom Penh, well situated for trade at the confluence of the Mekong river and the Tonle Sap.

1556–1557: The Portuguese missionary Gaspar da Cruz visits the Cambodian court. He leaves after a year, unable to make converts (which he blames on royal interference in everyday life), but provides the first European eyewitness account of Cambodia.

1563: *Suma Oriental*, including the account of the Portuguese Tomé Pires's travels between 1512 and 1515, is published in Venice. Pires is the first European to write about Cambodia.

1569: Burmese sack the Thai capital of Ayudhya.

1580s: Thais regain strength and prepare for another invasion of Cambodian territory.

1577–1578: Inscriptions at Angkor Wat indicate that partial restoration under royal patronage is carried out. A Portuguese explorer, Diego da Couto, reports some forty years later that a king of Cambodia had stumbled across the ruins of Angkor while on an elephant hunt. However, this story is not confirmed by other sources.

1587: Thais unsuccessfully lay siege to Lovek, which has become the new capital in the mid-sixteenth century.

1590s: Around this period, European sources state that the Cambodian King Sattha changes his policy toward Western missionaries, who are now allowed to preach.

1593: King Sattha sends gifts of rice to the Spanish governor-general in Manila, seeking protection against the threatening Thais. Before the Spanish can respond, the king and his youngest son flee to southern Laos, leaving another son to defend Lovek.

1594: Lovek falls to the Thais: a new era of Thai domination lasts for almost two hundred years.

1620s: Vietnamese colonize much of the Mekong Delta.

1626: Nguyen overlords in southern Vietnam break with the northern Le dynasty.

1640s: Malayo-Cham faction domination culminates with Khmer Muslim rule on throne.

1650s: Large numbers of foreigners reside in Phnom Penh, including Spanish and Portuguese missionaries and traders from Europe, Southeast Asia, the Persian Gulf, and Japan. Vietnamese depose the Muslim king and take him to Vietnam.

c. 1700: By this time Vietnamese control of the Mekong basin is squeezing Cambodia out of the lucrative trading routes on the Gulf of Siam.

1767: The Thai capital of Ayudhya falls to Burmese army.

1768: The Thai king and his court seek asylum in Cambodia. A new Thai dynasty begins under an erstwhile regional overlord named Taksin who attempts to reestablish Thai hegemony over Cambodia.

1768–1772: Thai armies attack overland to Angkor while naval attacks destroy several coastal villages along the Gulf of Siam.

1772: Phnom Penh is burned down.

1779: The Thai protégé, Prince Eng, aged seven, is placed on the Cambodian throne at Udong (near Phnom Penh), the new capital.

The rich must protect the poor, just as clothing protects the body.

Traditional Cambodian proverb

1782: The Thai king is deposed by his own minister of war.

1780s: The heir to the Nguyen throne, fleeing the Tay Son rebellion, seeks asylum in Bangkok, paving the way for a Thai/Vietnamese rapprochement.

1790: Eng is anointed in Bangkok.

1794: Eng returns to Cambodia under Thai protection. Cambodian chronicles treat this as an event of miraculous significance. The Thais grant the provinces of Siem Reap and Battambang to Baen, a former official who had been governing Cambodia for the Thais. No details about the transfer have been discovered but it seems that Baen is not required to provide Eng with troops and has to send tributary gifts—usually wild cardamom—to Bangkok.

1796: Eng builds his palace at Udong and visits Bangkok on a tributary mission.

1797: At the beginning of this year, Eng dies. The next ten years until the coronation of Ang Chan in 1806 are poorly documented. It seems that the king, while a young prince, became alienated from the Thai court. He begins to formulate a pro-Viet policy.

1808: After this date all foreigners wishing to

visit Phnom Penh require Vietnamese permission.

1809: Death of the Thai king, Rama I. Cambodia becomes increasingly alienated from Bangkok.

1811–1812: Several military campaigns between the Thais and the Vietnamese in Cambodian territory are indecisive.

1812: The Cambodian capital is moved back to Phnom Penh.

1816: The Cambodians attempt to regain the northwestern provinces given to Baen. They are unsuccessful, but this marks the last attempt before the 1960s of a formally constituted Cambodian army to take offensive action against foreign troops.

1817: Vietnamese officials recruit several thousand Viets and about a thousand Cambodians to excavate the Vinh Te Canal, which runs for about twenty-five miles between the Gulf of Siam and the fortified citadel of Chandoc in Vietnamese territory.

Workers were divided into groups. One Vietnamese marched at the head of each group, another at the back, and a third in the middle. The Vietnamese would beat the Cambodians on the back to make them busy. . . . Everyone was exhausted and covered with mud.

Cambodian chronicles describing working conditions during the excavation of the Vinh Te Canal, c. 1820

1820–1821: An anti-Thai rebellion breaks out at Ba Phnom, led by a former monk named Kai. He and his supposedly invulnerable supporters move north, attacking Viet military posts. A mixed Cambodian-Vietnamese force sent against him fails, but the rebels are finally defeated by a purely Vietnamese force near Kompong Cham. The leaders are executed in Saigon and many followers are beheaded in Phnom Penh.

1830–1831: Thais make tentative military probes into western Cambodia.

1832–1833: A revolt breaks out in Phnom Penh over the Vietnamese emperor's decision to replace his viceroy's entourage with officials loyal to him. When news of the rebellion reaches the Thai king he assembles an expeditionary force, hoping to reinstate Im and Duang, brothers of the Cambodian King Chan. The Vietnamese abandon Phnom Penh and Chan is sent into exile. A Thai commander named Bodin occupies the capital but is forced to withdraw in the face of Cambodian opposition to Im and Duang. The brothers are given ambiguous control of the contested provinces of Battambang and Siem Reap in the northwest.

1834: King Ang Chan returns to his battered capital under strict Vietnamese control and supervision. General Truong Minh Giang, who had defeated a serious rebellion in Saigon, is put in charge of consolidating Vietnamese control of Cambodia.

1835: Early in the year, Ang Chan dies after a month's illness. With no sons, it is agreed that the second daughter, Princess Mei, will accede to the throne as her elder sister is suspected of being pro-Thai.

Late 1830s: Giang pursues a policy of Vietnamization in Cambodia. He attempts to mobilize and arm the Khmer, to increase Vietnamese colonization of the region, and to "reform" the habits of the people.

December 1839: Prince Im defects to Phnom Penh with several thousand men under the mistaken belief that he was to be given the Cambodian throne by the Vietnamese. He is arrested by Giang and taken to Saigon and Hue.

1840: Vietnamese emperor Minh Mang decrees that all Cambodian land is to be measured anew and that records be maintained regarding rainfall, granaries, and irrigation works. The Vietnamese are to take over administration of the provinces themselves, and a new, more extensive taxation system is instituted.

June 1840: Princess Mei and her sisters are demoted to minor roles in the Vietnamese civil service by Emperor Minh Mang. The six highest-ranking *okya* (Cambodian officials) are secretly placed under arrest and taken to Saigon, along with the royal regalia necessary for legitimizing a new ruler, passed to Mei by her father.

August 1840: Princess Mei and her sisters are arrested in Phnom Penh.

September 1840: A wide-ranging anti-Vietnamese rebellion breaks out with the support of the *okya*.

Early 1841: Emperor Minh Mang dies following an accident. The new Vietnamese emperor, Thieu Tri, is less committed to victory in Cambodia, and the rebellion, already losing momentum, collapses.

1840s: Battles between Thais and Viets in Cambodia continue with the advantage alternating between the two sides.

We are happy killing Vietnamese. We no longer fear them; in all our battles we are mindful of the three jewels [of Buddhism]: the Buddha, the law, and the monastic community.

Rebel quoted in Cambodian chronicles during the rebellion against Vietnam in 1841

1844: Bodin is forced to abandon Phnom Penh when the Vietnamese try to reinstate Princess Mei as Cambodia's legitimate queen. Thai forces congregate near Udong.

1845: Negotiations for a cease-fire are opened. Emperor Thieu Tri is no longer interested in Cambodia, and a form of joint vassalage ensues.

April 1848: Prince Duang is anointed by Thai and Cambodian Brahmans in Udong and ascends the Cambodian throne at the age of

fifty-two. A brief Cambodian renaissance takes place; temples are restored and literature revived. He is careful to perform the rituals that his subjects associate with the welfare of the kingdom.

Mid-1850s: King Duang, encouraged by the French missionary Monsigneur Jean Claude Miche, writes to the French government seeking "friendship"—a euphemism for protection.

1856: A French diplomatic mission with a draft treaty of cooperation fails to reach the Cambodian court.

1860: Duang dies, and the nation is plunged into a series of civil wars.

1861: Duang's designated heir Norodom is forced to flee Cambodia, unable to rule.

All that can be said respecting the present Cambodians is that they are an agriculture people, among whom a certain taste for art still shows itself in the carved work of the boasts belonging to the better classes, and their chief characteristic is unbounded conceit.

Travels in Siam, Cambodia and Laos, by Henri Mouhot (1858–1860)

1862: Norodom returns to Cambodia with Thai support. However, frustrated with Thai interference, Norodom reopens negotiations with the French, who have established themselves in Saigon.

August 1863: A delegation of French naval officers concludes a treaty with Norodom, and Cambodia becomes a French protectorate in return for timber concessions and mineral exploration rights.

THE FRENCH PROTECTORATE: 1863–1953

King Norodom is forced to submit to ever-tighter French controls throughout the final years of the nineteenth century. The French reforms trigger widespread rural uprisings, which are firmly put down by French military forces. After the accession of King Sisowath in 1904, Cambodia enters a period of increased economic prosperity and relative calm, although peasant rebellion breaks out intermittently in response to heavy tax burdens. Anticolonial feeling escalates during the 1930s, which coincides with the increasing popularity of the emerging Communist Party of Indochina. When Japanese forces occupy Indochina during World War II, the Vichy French administration is left in place. They appoint Prince Sihanouk, a nineteen-year-old schoolboy, king in 1941. The French administration is suddenly imprisoned on the eve of the Japanese surrender and Cambodian independence is briefly declared. However, the French rapidly reassume control after the Japanese defeat in 1945 but make some concessions towards establishing Cambodia as an autonomous state within the French Union. The Khmer Issarak (Khmer Freedom) movement gains momentum, and King Sihanouk dissolves the National Assembly when it becomes too troublesome. He effectively introduces martial law and embarks on a Royal Crusade for Independence. With the war escalating in Vietnam, the French finally concede Cambodian independence in 1953.

Mid-1864: The Thais and the French agree to cosponsor Norodom's coronation. For the last time, Thais choose the titles of a Cambodian king. Thai influence in Cambodia begins to wane from this point.

1866: On French advice, Norodom transfers the capital to Phnom Penh.

1866, 1870: Dynastic and millenarian revolts break out against Norodom's rule; French troops have difficulty putting down the insurrections.

June 1884: The French pressure King Norodom into agreeing to a series of wide-reaching reforms: these include the abolition of slavery, the institution of land ownership, and the establishment of French *résidents* (overseers) in provincial cities. These reforms break with over a thousand years of Cambodian tradition and enrage the elite.

Early 1885: Rebellion erupts throughout Cambodia under several leaders. The French, mistrustful of Norodom, enter into negotiations with his half-brother, Prince Sisowath, who attempts to quell the uprising with little success.

July 1886: After a year and a half of rebellion and discontent, the French are forced to seek the help of King Norodom, who proclaims that if the rebels lay down their arms the French will respect Cambodian customs and laws.

1886: The treaty encasing the unpopular reforms is ratified, but the French have learned to be cautious, and the reforms are not put into effect until twenty years later, after the death of Norodom.

1890s: During this period of French consolidation throughout Indochina, taxes are brought under their control and King Norodom's powers are gradually eroded. By 1894 there are ten French residences in the Cambodian *sruk* (provinces) who voice complaints about Cambodian torpor and corruption. The French make no secret of their preference for Prince Sisowath, who is formally promised the throne in 1897, and encourage Norodom's addiction to opium. Norodom's son, Prince Yakanthor, is exiled to Algeria for agitation.

1897: The French *résident supérieur*, Huynh de Verneville, cables Paris to say that Norodom is no longer capable of ruling. Paris concurs and de Verneville is given the power to issue royal decrees, appoint officials, and collect indirect taxes.

1904: Norodom dies and Sisowath comes to the throne.

1906: Coronation of Prince Sisowath. He immediately departs on a tour of France, which coincides with Franco-Thai negotiations for the return of the provinces of Battambang and Siem Reap.

April 1907: Agreement is reached on the retrocession of the provinces of Battambang and Siem Reap. The ruins of Angkor Wat are returned to Cambodian control, as well as the prosperous rice-growing region of Battambang.

1909: A copy of the Cambodian translation of sacred Buddhist writings is deposited at a temple at Angkor Wat. For the next sixty years Cambodian monarchs frequently visit the site and sponsor religious ceremonies there.

1914: Outbreak of World War I in Europe. France floats war loans to which local people throughout Indochina are required to subscribe.

November 1915: Some three hundred peasants petition King Sisowath to reduce their taxes. The king meets the delegation and makes vague promises of action.

Early 1916: Delegations of increasing numbers of peasants arrive to petition the King for a reduction in taxes, and scattered incidents throughout the provinces culminate in several deaths. The French are frightened by the speed and efficiency with which the peasantry have mobilized, and consequently increase their control over the next decade.

1916–1925: Cambodia enters a period of increased economic prosperity; the first Cambodian rice mills are inaugurated and Cambodia begins exporting high-quality rubber. Roads and railways are built, but the profits fail to trickle down to the peasantry and the period is marked with constant rural rebellion and disorder. No money is spent on education or medical services, and electricity and running water are virtually unknown outside Phnom Penh.

April 18, 1925: Feliz Louis Bordez, French *résident* of Kompong Chhnang, is beaten to death by local villagers. He had achieved rapid promotion owing to his improvements of tax-collection procedures. Angered by the failure of a village to make payments, he visited the village himself, handcuffed the culprits, and threatened to imprison them, but was set on by the crowd, to the horror of the French community.

December 1925: The trial of Bordez's killers begins. Anticolonial feeling increases.

1927: Sisowath dies and is succeeded by King Monivong.

1930: Vietnamese communist movements unite as the Indochina Communist Party (ICP). There are no Cambodian members until 1932.

1936: The first Khmer-language newspaper, named *Nagarra Vatta* (Angkor Wat), appears. For the first time, Cambodians can read about world events in their own language. The paper provides a focus for an increasing sense of nationalism.

June 1940: Overrun by the German forces, France signs an armistice with Germany. The effect on France's colonial empire in Indochina will be that the French there are forced by their German masters to cooperate with the Japanese.

December 1940: The first local Khmer Issarak (Khmer Freedom) Committee, dedicated to Cambodian independence, is established.

1941: Japanese occupying forces flood into Indochina. Vichy French retain administrative control and are left virtually undisturbed by the Japanese. Thais attack French positions in Laos and Cambodia, regaining control of much of northwest Cambodia.

1941: King Monivong dies and is succeeded by his nineteen-year-old grandson Sihanouk, a high school student in Saigon whom the French consider to be pliable.

July 1942: Following an ill-advised demonstration in Phnom Penh, several prominent Khmer are imprisoned and *Nagarra Vatta* newspaper is shut down.

March 13, 1945: The Japanese pressure King Sihanouk to abrogate treaties with the French and declare Cambodian independence. (He actually declares an independent Kampuchea, using the original Khmer word for the kingdom of Kambuja, which had become transformed into Cambodia by Westerners.) Sihanouk subsequently forms a new government, placing himself at the head of a group of the pro-French elite.

September 1945: On the eve of their surrender, the Japanese install a new government under Son Ngoc Thanh, a former editor of *Nagarra Vatta*. His short-lived government will give form to the Cambodian sense of nationalism.

October 15, 1945: The French resume control of Cambodia after the Japanese surrender; the country is flooded with French troops and Son Ngoc Thanh is forced to go into exile in France.

January 4, 1946: A Franco-Cambodian agreement is signed, recognizing Cambodia as an autonomous state within the French Union. Cambodians are granted control of all services dealing with purely Cambodian interests.

March 1946: The Democratic Party, Cambodia's first political party, is formed. It reveals an increasing sense of nationalism and the desire for modernization.

September 1, 1946: The Democratic Party, moderate nationalists led by their founder, Prince Sisowath, gains victory in elections to the Cambodian Constituent Assembly.

July 15, 1947: King Sihanouk approves Cambodia's first constitution.

February 1, 1948: A Khmer Issarak Committee is formed in western Cambodia. Although the first Issarak group had been formed in 1940, it failed to make progress in the Cambodian fight for independence.

September 18, 1948: Under French pressure, King Sihanouk dissolves the Cambodian National Assembly when the Democrats' support for the increasingly troublesome Issarak party brings them into conflict with French authorities. He forms a new government of conservative ex-Democrats.

November 8, 1949: War between the French and the Vietminh intensifies in Vietnam; the increasingly pressured French decide to allow Cambodian independence and a treaty is signed making Cambodia an independent state within the French Union.

April 19, 1950: The United Issarak Front (UIF) is founded under the leadership of Son Ngoc Minh, a former monk (whose real name is Achar Mean) now a key figure in the communist movement. This is the most important move to date toward a unified pro-Vietnamese revolutionary movement in Cambodia. In Paris, disaffected Khmer students, including Ieng Sary and Soloth Sar (eventually to be known as Pol Pot) form the revolutionary Marxist Circle.

August 11, 1951: Democrats win another large victory in elections to the National Assembly; the right-wing Khmer Renovation Party under Lon Nol also gains representation.

September 30, 1951: In the wake of the dissolution of the Indochina Communist Party, the Khmer People's Revolutionary Party is formed.

October 29, 1951: Son Ngoc Thanh, the nationalist leader who ruled briefly in 1945, is brought back from exile in France. Thousands arrive to greet him at the airport.

January–February 1952: Thanh tours the provinces, testing the political waters and downplaying the importance of the monarchy, which infuriates Sihanouk. Soon after, Thanh founds a newspaper called *Khmer Krom* (Cambodians Awake).

March 9, 1952: Son Ngoc Thanh flees Phnom Penh and sets up a guerrilla base on the Thai border. By this time, however, Communist-controlled guerrilla bands are estimated to control one-sixth of Cambodian territory.

January–June 1953: King Sihanouk, in an effort to call attention to his country's situation, travels to France and other countries on a "royal crusade for independence," warning Western leaders that Issarak rebellion is being fanned by France's behavior. On April 17 he gives an interview in New York City and calls for complete independence. By May he is back in Cambodia.

June 15, 1953: Sihanouk dissolves democratic government as nationalist and communist antigovernment activity increases and goes into exile to a villa at Siem Reap, near the Angkor temples, in another attempt to force France to capitulate.

July 3, 1953: France declares it is ready to

grant full independence to Cambodia, Vietnam, and Laos. Determined to make sure of their intentions, Sihanouk insists that this include the control of national defense, police, the courts, finances. France agrees.

Mid-October 1953: A military agreement is signed between King Sihanouk and French officials transferring the remaining attributes of de facto independence to the Cambodian

government. The king is granted authority over Cambodia's armed forces, judiciary, and foreign affairs, although the French retain their economic hold over the country.

November 8–9, 1953: On November 8 Sihanouk returns to Phnom Penh. The next day, at a parade for the withdrawing French troops, Sihanouk declares full independence for Cambodia.

INDEPENDENT CAMBODIA: 1954–1998

The Geneva Conference opens in 1954. King Sihanouk is accorded international recognition and promises free elections. He abdicates in favor of his father in 1955 and his party wins a massive victory in the elections of that year. By the early 1960s, war is escalating in neighboring Vietnam and the Cambodian Communist Party has reorganized, gaining new adherents. A government crackdown on the left follows the 1962 elections to the National Assembly and many left-wing intellectuals, including Pol Pot, flee to guerrilla positions along the Vietnamese border. In 1970, a coup led by Lon Nol deposes Sihanouk and establishes the Khmer Republic. A State of Emergency is declared as Communist forces, dubbed the Khmer Rouge, gain much of the country. In 1975 the Khmer Rouge gain control of Phnom Penh and announce the "Year Zero." All urban civilians are immediately evacuated to form cooperatives in demarcated rural zones; private property, religion and traditional customs are abolished. Hard agricultural labor, starvation rations, and brutal purges result in the deaths of perhaps a fifth of Cambodia's population. Tensions with Vietnam develop; its forces invade Cambodia and establish the pro-Hanoi People's Republic of Kampuchea in 1979. Prince Sihanouk forms an alliance with the Khmer Rouge and the Khmer People's National Liberation Front to oppose Vietnamese occupation. Guerrilla warfare continues throughout the 80s although talks among all opposing factions begin in 1988, culminating in an agreement in 1991. Two years later, the Republican government, led by Hun Sen, is defeated in elections by the Funcinpec Party led by Sihanouk's son, Norodom Ranariddh. Ranariddh is overthrown in a brutal coup in 1997 by Hun Sen. The influence of the Khmer Rouge diminishes, hastened by senior-level defections from their ranks. In April 1998 the death of Pol Pot is announced. Hun Sen wins the elections in July 1998.

April 26–July 21, 1954: The Far Eastern Conference is held in Geneva, Switzerland. On July 20 France agrees to recognize the absolute independence of Cambodia (as well as of Vietnam and Laos) and accords King Sihanouk international recognition as the sole legitimate authority in Cambodia. He promises to institute democratic elections in 1955.

September 8, 1955: The Southeast Asia Treaty Organization (SEATO) is formed at the instigation of the United States; Sihanouk refuses to join.

March 2, 1955: King Sihanouk abdicates in favor of his father, Norodom Suramarit, in order to avoid constitutional restraints on his political actions. Soon after, Prince Sihanouk establishes the Sangkum Reastr Niyum (People's Socialist Community).

May 1955: Sihanouk, as prime minister, signs a military aid agreement with the United States, angering the governments of North Vietnam and China.

September 1955: Sihanouk's Sangkum Party wins a massive victory in the elections for the National Assembly. Although pronounced correct by international observers, there are widespread rumors of fraud and voter intimidation.

April 1956: At the Sangkum Conference, the left-wing Pracheachon Party offers to enter into a coalition with the Sangkum.

1958: Sangkum candidates win another resounding victory in elections for the National Assembly. Some left-wing intellectuals are brought into the cabinet.

April 1960: King Norodom Suramarit dies. Sihanouk is named head of state without ascending the throne.

September 1960: The Cambodian Communist Party reorganizes as the Worker's Party of Kampuchea. Soloth Sar (later to be known as Pol Pot) is appointed to the Central Committee.

1962: Sihanouk gains another victory in the National Assembly elections. With the escalation of war in Vietnam, his government cracks down on the left. Many left-wing intellectuals flee the capital and establish bases along the Vietnamese/Cambodian border.

November 6, 1963: After Ngo Dinh Diem's assassination in Saigon, Sihanouk discontinues all U.S. aid projects, exacerbating anti-government feeling among the peasants.

May 1965: Sihanouk, who has repeatedly proclaimed Cambodia's neutrality, breaks off diplomatic relations with the United States when the fighting intensifies in Vietnam. He also allows the North Vietnamese to use Cambodia to transport material and base troops fighting in the South for the first time.

November 11, 1966: Elections to the National Assembly bring in conservatives; Lon Nol, commander of Cambodia's army, is appointed prime minister.

April 1967: A full-scale rural revolt erupts in Samlaut, northwest Cambodia. The uprising is savagely repressed by Lon Nol, and another wave of prominent leftists in the government flee to join the guerrillas.

January 1968: The Tet offensive and U.S. aid operations in South Vietnam push increasing numbers of Communists into Cambodian "sanctuaries."

March 1969: The United States secretly begins to bomb Communist sanctuaries in Cambodia.

January 1970: Sihanouk travels to France.

March 8, 1970: Protests against the Vietnamese National Liberation Front (NLF) erupt in the border province of Svey Rieng.

March 11, 1970: Mobs sack the North Vietnamese and South Vietnamese embassies in Phnom Penh.

March 13, 1970: As Sihanouk leaves for Moscow, Lon Nol issues an ultimatum demanding that all Vietcong and North Vietnamese troops be withdrawn from Cambodia before dawn on March 15.

March 18, 1970: A motion withdrawing confidence in Sihanouk is passed at a joint session of the National Assembly and the Royal Council. Shortly before leaving Moscow for Beijing, Sihanouk is informed of his deposition.

March 19, 1970: A state of emergency is declared, granting Lon Nol full powers.

March 20, 1970: South Vietnamese troops, accompanied by ethnic Khmer troops and U.S. Special Forces advisors, enter Cambodia, forcing a Communist retreat.

March 23, 1970: Sihanouk announces the formation of the National United Front of Kampuchea (NUFK), allied to North Vietnam, with forces consisting largely of the Communists his army had previously struggled to destroy.

March 26, 1970: Mass demonstrations break out, some overtly pro-Sihanouk, but all are brutally repressed by the army. Hundreds are killed and thousands arrested.

April 20, 1970: Lon Nol sends a personal letter to U.S. President Richard Nixon, urgently appealing for military aid. The U.S. military prepares for a full-scale incursion into Cambodia.

April–June 1970: A joint U.S.-South Vietnamese force launches an offensive into eastern Cambodia, preceded by waves of B-52 bombers dropping hundreds of tons of bombs. The invasion achieves nothing; the rural population and the American people are appalled by the brutality.

May 1970: Sihanouk announces formation of a Government-in-Exile, the Royal Government of the National Union of Kampuchea.

October 1970: Lon Nol's government declares the establishment of the Khmer Republic.

October 1971: Lon Nol declares a state of emergency as revolutionary forces gain control of much of the country. The National Assembly is deprived of its legislative powers and transformed into the Constituent Assembly. Lon Nol assumes the titles of President of Republic and President of the Council of Ministers.

June 1972: Lon Nol is formally elected as president in Cambodia's first presidential election, which is condemned as fraudulent.

January 27, 1973: The Paris Agreements on "ending the war and restoring peace in Vietnam" are signed by opposing sides.

February 1973: The National United Front of Kampuchea rejects the Republican offer to enter into peace talks; the United States decides to embark on a bombing campaign, although the B-52 raids begun in 1969 have never really ceased.

May 1973: The "Democratic Revolution" begins in Communist-controlled regions: land is collectivized, people relocated, political study sessions instituted, and traditional customs and religious rites are abolished.

August 15, 1973: Bombing and U.S. military operations in Indochina stop.

March 1975: Communists break through Republican lines to the outskirts of Phnom Penh.

April 1, 1975: Lon Nol flees to Hawaii.

April 17, 1975: The Republican army formally surrenders to the Khmer Rouge. Within hours of victory, all civilians are ordered to evacuate the city.

January 5, 1976: The constitution of Democratic Kampuchea is promulgated; it guarantees no human rights and abolishes private property, organized religion, and family-oriented agricultural production.

March 1976: Elections are held to a newly created 250-seat Assembly.

April 1976: Sihanouk is forced to resign as head of state and is placed under house arrest. Khieu Samphan is named president and Soloth Sar (who now takes on the *nom de guerre* Pol Pot) becomes prime minister.

April 1977: Cambodia escalates border raids against Vietnam as the anti-Vietnamese contingent of the Communist Party becomes increasingly influential.

September 1977: Pol Pot finally reveals the existence of the Communist Party of Kampuchea behind the government front, as well as his position as secretary.

October 1977: Vietnam, alarmed by the Democratic Kampuchea-Beijing alliance, responds to Cambodian border incursions by launching a major offensive into Cambodia.

January 3, 1977: Cambodia rejects a Vietnamese proposal to withdraw both forces five kilometers from the border and negotiate a truce.

April–May 1978: Eastern Zone dissidents are executed by Pol Pot's followers in a far-reaching purge; tens of thousands are slaughtered, although some escape to Vietnam, including Hun Sen.

December 1978: Leading survivors of the Eastern Zone purge form the Cambodian National United Front for National Salvation (CNUFNS).

December 25, 1978: Vietnamese and CNUFNS forces mount a major offensive on several fronts against Cambodia.

January 7, 1979: Phnom Penh is abandoned to the Vietnamese forces. The Khmer Rouge government retreats to the Thai border and sets up resistance bases.

January 19, 1979: The pro-Hanoi People's Republic of Kampuchea is declared.

February 17–March 16, 1979: China launches a punitive attack on North Vietnam for its invasion of Cambodia.

March 18, 1979: Vietnam and Cambodia sign a twenty-five-year Treaty of Peace, Friendship and Cooperation.

April 1979: Cambodian refugees begin to flood into Thailand. Thousands are forcibly repatriated and die of starvation or landmine explosions.

August 18, 1979: Pol Pot and Ieng Sary are tried in absentia on charges of genocide. They are sentenced to death by a government tribunal.

August 21, 1979: The Khmer Rouge form a new Patriotic and Democratic Front of the Great National Union of Kampuchea in order to attract wider support.

September 19, 1979: Former prime minister Son Sann establishes the Khmer People's National Liberation Front to oppose the Vietnamese occupation as well as the possible return to power of Pol Pot's forces.

September 1979: Cambodia's UN seat is awarded to the Khmer Rouge.

October 1979: Emergency food aid from the West finally begins after the government of the People's Republic of Kampuchea agrees to allow border distribution.

October 14, 1980: The UN General Assembly votes to continue recognizing the exiled regime of Democratic Kampuchea.

March 25, 1981: Prince Sihanouk announces the formation of the National United Front for a Cooperative, Independent, Neutral and Peaceful Cambodia, to oppose the Vietnamese-backed government in Phnom Penh.

June 1981: The National Assembly approves a draft constitution and chooses members of the new Council of State and Council of Ministers.

July 1981: The International Conference on Kampuchea, convened by the United Nations, opens in New York.

September 4, 1981: The three major resistance leaders—Sihanouk, Son Sann, and Khieu Samphan—agree on joint action against the Vietnamese-backed regime in Phnom Penh.

December 7, 1981: The Khmer Rouge announces the abolition of the Communist Party of Kampuchea. Few observers believe this has actually occurred.

June 1982: The two anti-Communist Cambodian resistance groups and the Khmer Rouge sign an agreement establishing a tripartite Coalition Government of Democratic Kampuchea to oppose the Vietnamese-backed regime, with Prince Sihanouk as president, Son Sann as prime minister, and Khieu Samphan as vice-president.

May 20, 1983: The PRK marks a "National Day of Hatred" to commemorate the atrocities of the Pol Pot government.

Late May 1983: Vietnamese arrest and purge more than three hundred PRK officials, including some members of the security police, in an attempt to control subversion.

July 1983: PRK Foreign Minister Hun Sen criticizes a communiqué issued by the sixteenth ASEAN conference of foreign ministers, especially a Thai demand that the People's Army of North Vietnam troops be withdrawn thirty kilometers from the border as a condition for talks.

October 1983: The CGDK is seated as the representative of Cambodia at the United Nations. For the first time since Democratic Kampuchea was ousted from power in Cambodia, Vietnam does not force a vote on a credentials challenge.

January 1984: At a press conference Hun Sen rejects any kind of reconciliation with Sihanouk or Son Sann.

September 23, 1984: U.S. President Reagan meets with Sihanouk and Son Sann in New York after his address to the UN General Assembly.

January 1985: Hun Sen is elected premier at the PRK National Conference in Phnom Penh.

August 1985: Vietnam announces its intention to withdraw all forces from Cambodia by late 1990.

1987: Hun Sen and Sihanouk meet in France.

July 1988: The first face-to-face talks among

all opposing Cambodian factions are held at the Jakarta Informal Meeting (JIM 1).

February 1989: Jakarta Informal Meeting 2 convenes.

April 1989: Vietnam announces its decision to withdraw all forces from Cambodia by late September.

April 30, 1989: The country's name reverts to Cambodia.

May 1989: Hun Sen and Sihanouk meet in Jakarta.

1990: The five permanent members of the UN Security Council put forward a plan calling for the creation of a Supreme National Council (SNC) to be composed of six representatives of the guerrillas, two from each faction.

May 1991: A formal cease-fire is finally adopted.

October 23, 1991: An agreement is at last signed and formally accepted on all sides. The plan calls for each army to demobilize 70 percent of its troops. The interim functioning of the government is to be handled by the United Nations until elections can be held in 1993.

November 1991: The United Nations begins the massive task of repatriating nearly 370,000 refugees from the camps in Thailand. The Khmer Rouge become increasingly intransigent.

December 1992: The Khmer Rouge begins a campaign of harassment directed at UN peacekeepers, who are on several occasions kidnapped and shot.

April 1993: Khmer Rouge officials close their offices in Phnom Penh and withdraw from the peace process. They claim that millions of Vietnamese are still in the country illegally.

May 23, 1993: The Funcinpec Party headed by Sihanouk's son, Norodom Ranariddh, wins 58 of 120 seats in elections. The Phnom Penh government, led by Hun Sen, wins 51 seats.

June 21, 1993: Hun Sen finally concedes defeat. Fearing that the country will become

ungovernable, Hun Sen and Ranariddh agree to work together as joint prime ministers.

September 24, 1993: Sihanouk signs a new constitution with limited powers and once again assumes the position of king of Cambodia.

August 1996: Ieng Sary defects from the Khmer Rouge to the government in exchange for amnesty, taking many of his soldiers with him.

June 1997: Ranariddh, in an apparent attempt to bolster his position before the 1998 elections, negotiates with members of a Khmer Rouge faction who have reportedly arrested Pol Pot.

July 7, 1997: A coup led by Hun Sen overthrows Norodom Ranariddh, who flees to Bangkok. At least forty of Hun Sen's political opponents are executed and American aid is temporarily frozen.

July 25, 1997: A Western journalist is invited to witness a dramatic show trial of Pol Pot in the northern Cambodia jungle.

March 30, 1998: Prince Norodom Ranariddh returns to Cambodia under a Japanese-brokered peace plan that calls for free elections on July 26.

April 15, 1998: Pol Pot dies. A Thai military team determines that a heart attack was the probable cause of death.

There was no sadness or sorrow expressed at the cremation. We are actually happy because we will be spared further international criticisms because of Pol Pot.

Non Nou, Pol Pot's former Khmer Rouge jailer, describing the cremation of Pol Pot on April 17, 1998

July 26–September 1, 1998: Elections take place on July 26, but it takes many days for the counting to produce results. By August 3 it is clear that Hun Sen and his party have a plurality, with 41 percent of the vote. The opposition charges fraud, but most international observers report that the elections seem fair (although it is believed that some two hundred people on all sides have been beaten or murdered during the campaign). Hun Sen's victory is officially confirmed on September 1, but he is unable to convince the two leading opposition parties to form a three-party coalition because they contend that Hun Sen intends to hold all major cabinet posts for his party.

September 5–17, 1998: Hun Sen and the two main opposition leaders, Prince Ranariddh and Sam Rainsay, meet at Siem Reap under the sponsorship of King Sihanouk but are unable to reach an agreement on how to proceed. By this time there are frequent demonstrations in Phnom Penh by those claiming that Hun Sen won by fraud. Police crack down with increased force, and four people are confirmed dead, another eighteen are claimed to have been killed, and scores are injured. Finally the leaders of the various parties ask their supporters to cease such demonstrations.

September 24, 1998: The new National Assembly is sworn in on the steps of Angkor Wat. The leaders of the major parties have still not agreed on how to form a government.

Indonesia

PREHISTORIC INDONESIA: 1,800,000–2000 B.C.

During what geologists call the Pleistocene epoch (approximately 1,800,000 to 8000 B.C.), much of the earth is drastically affected by glacial cycles. These are intermittent periods of about 100,000 years (punctuated by shorter interglacial periods), when so much of the earth's water is locked up in ice sheets that it exposes large areas of land today totally under water or protruding as islands. In particular, the alternately rising and lowering sea level covers or exposes the continental shelf (known as the Sunda Shelf) that connects western Indonesia to the Malay peninsula. During those phases when there are land bridges, many animals—including early hominids (possibly the first *Homo erectus* in Asia) and the orangutan—are able to make their way down into territory as remote as Java and Sumatra. By about 18,000 B.C. the sea level begins to rise, until by about 6000 B.C. it has left the islands and land configurations of Southeast Asia much as they are today. Meanwhile, *Homo sapiens* has emerged in Indonesia about 40,000 B.C., and during the next several thousand years these humans pass through several cultural stages, distinguished primarily by their various stone tools. By about 3000 B.C. the complex of achievements known as the Neolithic culture begins to emerge in Indonesia.

1,800,000–1,200,000 B.C.: A few scholars assign to this time the earliest hominid fossils (probably *Homo erectus*) found at Mojokerto (Perning), eastern Java, and Sangiran, east-central Java, but most do not accept such an early date.

1,200,000–750,000 B.C.: Most scholars date to this time the earliest fossil hominid finds in Java. Included among them is the first *Homo erectus* fossil, found in Java in 1891 by Eugene Dubois, a Dutch anatomist, and dated to about 800,000 B.C. The *Homo erectus* whose fossils are found on Java over the years is often known as Java Man.

750,000–100,000 B.C.: Some experts believe that simple stone tools found in several of the Indonesian islands were made by *Homo erectus*, at least during the latter part of this period. (Archaeologists call the time from about 500,000 to 15,000 B.C. the Paleolithic or Old Stone Age.)

100,000–40,000 B.C.: Fossil finds (known as

Solo Man because the sites are near the Solo River) from northeast-central Java sites such as Ngandong, Sambungmacan, and Ngawi, appear to be *Homo erectus*, but some may be *Homo sapiens*. In both cases there continues to be disagreement among scholars as to whether they are direct descendants of immigrants from Africa or whether they evolved in Asia independently. Stone tools begin to appear at several Indonesian sites.

40,000–2000 B.C.: By this time *Homo sapiens* is clearly moving into Indonesia and throughout adjacent islands; the earliest cave dwellings date from this time. Scholars do not agree on all the details, but it appears that two main population groups are present in Indonesia: first the Australoid (or Australo-Melanesian), and, certainly by about 2000 B.C., the Southern Mongoloid. Although there is some intermixture, the Australoids are in general being isolated or pushed to the fringes of the region while the Southern Mongoloids become the more numerous and dominant people.

38,000–2000 B.C.: In Indonesia, remains (usually stone tools, shell middens, and animal bones) attest to human occupation: in eastern Sabah (northeastern Borneo) between 28,000 and 5,000 B.C.; in Sulawesi between 27,000 and 2000 B.C.; in Timor and Flores between 11,000 and 2000 B.C.; and in Java, probably between 5000 and 2000 B.C. Throughout this time, almost all of these people survived on an economy built on hunting and food gathering.

8000–2000 B.C.: Named after Hoa Binh, a site in North Vietnam where the tool assemblage was first discovered, "Hoabinhian" refers to distinctive flaked pebble tools and the associated peoples and cultures found at sites across much of Southeast Asia—from Burma in the west, across Thailand and Malaysia, and even into southern China (and possibly Taiwan). The oldest are dated to about 16,000 B.C. In Indonesia, the only known Hoabinhian sites are in the northeastern Sumatran highlands and date to no earlier than 8000 B.C., suggesting that this area of Indonesia is culturally linked to the Malay Peninsula and the mainland. Because of the large shell middens (refuse heaps) associated with these Sumatran sites, it is believed that these people had a way of life dependent on coastal as well as inland food gathering and hunting; but some probably also took steps to protect and encourage indigenous food sources such as forest tubers and fruit trees.

EARLY EVIDENCE: 2000 B.C.–A.D. 500

By about 2000 B.C. new migrants appear to be moving into some of the islands of Indonesia, pushing aside most of the earlier inhabitants. These new people, of Mongoloid stock, probably came from Taiwan and/or southern China (and possibly via the Philippines). They carried an agricultural economy, introduced pottery, and had some new tools including stone adzes. About 1500 B.C. systematic clearance of forests begins to emerge on Java and Sumatra, indicating agriculture. The cultivation of crops involves more settled and populous communities, although there is little clear archaeological information on societal developments in Indonesia before the first millennium A.D., when influences from India are recorded. Throughout this period, Indonesia remains an essentially fragmented region inhabited by small, dispersed villages with little more than basic subsistence economies; but there presumably are some local chieftains, and burial remains of the last few hundred years of this period suggest hierarchies of wealth and power. Especially along the coasts, contacts and trade with foreigners will begin to draw the Indonesians into a more ambitious world. There is some evidence of contact with Indian traders by as early as the third century B.C., but it will be several centuries before there appear to be small states developing from commerce with India; isolated evidence of direct contact with China also dates from about this time, but full contact does not commence until several centuries later.

2000–500 B.C.: In various Indonesian islands (Borneo, Sulawesi, Timor, Talaud Islands, the Moluccas), about 2000 B.C. there appear the first signs of the Neolithic cultural complex: cultivated plants (rice possibly by 2500 B.C., then millet possibly by 2000 B.C.), tubers (such as taro), fruit-bearing trees (such as bananas), pig husbandry, and pottery.

500–200 B.C.: Perhaps by 500 B.C., certainly by 200 B.C., metalworking—with copper, bronze (including bronze casting), and iron—is being introduced into Indonesia, most likely from Vietnam.

3d century B.C.: Possible beginning of contact with India.

2d century B.C.: Bronze and copper artifacts (numerous drums, a statuette, a lidded vessel) of the Dong Son style (so named after the type site in northern Vietnam) appear in Java, Sumatra, and southern Moluccas; most likely these are imported from Vietnam, although some may have been made locally. There are indications of an advancing maritime technology during this century.

200 B.C.–A.D. 200: Some pottery dating from China's Han dynasty is found in southern Sumatra.

200 B.C.–A.D. 300: Indian influence is suggested by shards of Indian Rouletted Ware, now believed to date from this time; these are found at burial sites at Buni in northwest Java and at Sembiran in northeast Bali. Glass beads found at several Indonesian burial sites are also presumed to be of Indian origin. Such remains suggest the presence of Indian traders in Indonesia several hundred years before this is documented in Sanskrit writings and temples constructed in the Indian style.

At several sites in Indonesia, the dead are buried in large jars, usually placed in caves.

Early centuries A.D.: Around Pagaralam, on the Pasemah Plateau in southern Sumatra, large stone monuments include underground burial chambers, some with wall paintings, and carvings of humans and animals. Other elaborate funerary objects (carved sarcophagi, iron and bronze objects, beads) are found on Java and Bali. Although such finds suggest the existence of a stratified society, the exact dates remain in dispute and some of the finds probably come from still later centuries. Local metalworking centers are also appearing in parts of Indonesia.

A.D. 400: Chinese Buddhists begin sea travel to India via Indonesia by this time; the Strait of Malacca becomes the preferred trade route from China to India.

EARLY KINGDOMS: 500–1377

Buddhism and Hinduism, brought to Indonesia from India, provide a cultural basis for the governments formed by rulers of the early kingdoms that rise and fall between the sixth and fourteenth centuries. Inland agrarian communities develop a sedentary agriculture technology and practice wet rice cultivation; coastal settlements, especially in northeastern Java and in Sumatra, carry on overseas trade. In Java, the predominance of land cultivation creates an agrarian society ruled by a courtly hierarchy that oversees the large peasant population and the distribution of goods. Although it is believed that villagers practice predominantly traditional religious ritual, the influence of India manifests itself in many ways. Sanskrit inscriptions found far from trade routes suggest the presence of Brahmans or local scholars with some knowledge of India in some royal courts, primarily on Java, where Siva worship is taught to the ruling elite. Sanskrit literature is believed to provide religious and legal guidelines for the formation of the early kingdoms of the archipelago, but with considerable adaptation to local conditions. Hindu structure and ritual influence is concentrated at the courts.

The pre-Islamic Majapahit state is generally viewed as a high point of Indonesian unification during this period. Both Buddhism and Saivite Hinduism are practiced, but the first significant Chinese settlements date from this time and there is evidence of Muslim presence at court. The Majapahit state, which thrives on a rich agricultural economy using irrigation technology, establishes an efficient administration to govern the large population that flourishes in eastern Java; vassalage is claimed over Brunei and other areas in Sumatra. But the hegemony is challenged by the Muslim commercial center of Malacca, under a shadowy figure known as Paramesvara, on the Malay Peninsula. The ports of northern Java, where Muslim communities of sea traders develop and where rulers convert to Islam, have strong economic and religious links to Malacca, contributing to the decline of Majapahit and furthering the Islamization of Indonesia.

While old Malay and indigenous cultural forms are preserved in the remote interiors of Sumatra and Borneo, Indian culture is more strongly reflected in the artistic production of Java, Bali, in coastal areas of Sumatra, and the Malay peninsula. In these areas traditional artistic forms are influenced by the *Mahabharata* and the *Ramayana*, the great epics of ancient India. The *wayang kulit*, or shadow theater using flat leather puppets, is a traditional Javanese art form that at this time draws on stories from the Indian epics. Javanese literature, written in old Javanese (*kawi*), flourishes. The integration of Hindu and Indonesian cultures that takes place during the era of the early kingdoms provides a foundation for political and social structure on the archipelago.

6th–7th centuries: Chinese chronicles from this time reveal the influence of Buddhism in Indonesia. Hierarchical states are beginning to develop.

8th century: The Kingdom of Mataram, founded by Sanjaya (reigns 732–760), is a Javanese agrarian state with a large population. Mataram gains power over smaller states and rules central Java, parts of Sumatra, and Bali. The state thrives on inland agriculture. Siva worship is practiced.

8th century: The Srivijaya kingdom of Sumatra, centered in Palembang, thrives on maritime trade. One of the major schools of Buddhism, Mahayana Buddhism, is practiced.

Late 8th century–late 9th century: The Buddhist kingdom of Sailendra flourishes in Java until the mid-ninth century, gaining control over both Mataram and Srivijaya kingdoms. Mahayana Buddhism is practiced. Boro-

budur, the Mahayana Buddhist temple complex known for its immense *stupa*, or dome-shaped shrine, is built by Sailendra rulers on the Kedur plain near Jogakarta in central Java. The temple represents a synthesis of Buddhist belief and indigenous ancestor worship.

9th to late 12th century: Sailendra rulership extends to the Malay Peninsula, western Java, and Sumatra. Palembang (southeastern Sumatra), an area apparently under Sailendra, controls international trade routes.

Late 9th century: Practice of Shaivite Hinduism returns under Mataram rulership of King Pikatan (reigns 838?–851?).

Late 9th or early 10th century: The monuments of Prambanan, dedicated to Siva, Vishnu, and Brahma, are built by Pikatan.

929–947: Mataram King Sindok (reigns 929–947) extends the region of wet-rice irrigation to the Brantas river valley in eastern Java.

Hindu influences on art, religion, and government are progressively localized. Coastal cultivation and sea trade develop.

1016: There are indications of some kind of military disaster in Java, possibly related to rivalry with Srivijaya.

1019: Airlangga (reigns 1019–1042) establishes his kingdom over the greater part of Java. With its political center at Kediri, it becomes a densely populated agricultural area and extends influence into Bali. Siva and Buddha are worshipped at court, and commoners practice a mix of Indian religious influences and traditional religion. The arts, adapting Indian themes, flourish. Airlangga divides his kingdom in two parts along the Brantas River forming the kingdoms of Kediri and Janggala for his sons.

1025: First raid by Cholas, Tamils from the south of India. Palembang is plundered and the capital is moved to Jambi. Further raids reduce the power of Srivijaya.

1222: Kediri falls and the Singasari dynasty is founded by Ken Angrok (reigns 1222–1227) near the present-day city of Malang. The fall of Kediri is later chronicled in the *Parataron* (Book of Kings). Angrok unites the divided Airlangga kingdom.

Late 13th century: Muslim foreign traders, long transients in Indonesia, now begin to establish trading posts.

1268: Kertanagara (reigns 1268–1292), Kediri prince and last ruler of the Singasari dynasty, extends the empire in east Java and seeks to establish Javanese supremacy over Srivijaya on Sumatra.

1292: As the Mongols are invading Indonesia, Kertanagara is slain by a rival Kediri prince who has captured the capital.

1293: After the Kediri rebels are suppressed and the Mongols are repulsed, Prince Vijaya, known as Kertarajasa (reigns 1293–1309) and son-in-law of Kertanagara, establishes the Javanese kingdom of Majapahit; the kingdom expands and becomes a major political and cultural influence on the archipelago.

1309: Kertarajasa is succeeded as Majapahit ruler by his son-in-law Jayanagara (reigns 1309–1328). Several rebellions ensue.

1319: A Kediri prince leads revolt and seizes the capital; Jayanagara flees under the protection of Gajah Mada (reigns 1330–1364), who returns to retake the capital and restore the king to power. Gajah Mada is made minister.

1320–1370: At the height of the Majapahit reign, the Panataran temple is built near Bitar.

1328–1350: After death of Jayanagara, Kertanagara's daughter is regent for Hayam Wuruk, her son; Gajah Mada is chief minister of state. Majapahit claims authority over much of the archipelago, including Bali, Sumatra, and Borneo.

1350: Hayam Wuruk (reigns 1350–1389) ascends to throne as Rajasanagara; Gajah Mada continues as his powerful minister.

1364: Death of Gajah Mada. Rajasanagara gains full power; territorial expansion and flowering of literary and cultural expression characterize his reign.

1365: *Nagarakertagama*, an epic poem and court chronicle composed by Buddhist monk Prapanca in praise of Rajasanagara, celebrates the kingdom of Majapahit.

Already the Prince had climbed into the jewel-singhasana [lion-throne palanquin], radiant, sparkling. Shoddhodani [Siddhartha Buddha] in the body was His aspect, just coming out of Jinapada [the Buddha's estate], splendid. Evidently Tripuraharendra was she who entered into the Presence at His side, beautiful, imposing, for equally superlatively well made was their attire, being humans preeminent, magnificent.

Nagarakertagama, epic poem by Rakawi Prapanca
of Majapahit (1365)

1377: Majapahit sends punitive raid against Palembang. There are indications that Majapahit vassal Parameswara subsequently flees to Malacca, where he establishes a thriving port that controls trade in the Strait of Malacca and challenges Majapahit hegemony.

RISE OF ISLAMIC KINGDOMS: 1290–1682

Islam develops in Indonesia as a result of both the conversion of indigenous populations exposed to Islam and the arrival and assimilation of Muslim foreigners, Chinese and Indian as well as Arab. The expansion of Malacca, a developing Muslim trading empire on the Malay Peninsula founded in about 1400, is considered instrumental in the spread of Islam throughout the archipelago. East Javanese traders supply food products to Malacca and keep a strong presence there. Indian Muslim communities of sea traders develop, and merchants convert to Islam to receive preferred treatment. There is also evidence of the adoption of Islam by Javanese courtiers; some historians propose that Sufi mystics were influential in the process. The inland state of Mataram adapts Islam to the existing belief system and establishes hegemony in central and eastern Java. Malay language and culture spread with the establishment of sultanates in coastal communities. Historians view the process as a slow cultural absorption in which traditional Hindu-Javanese beliefs and customs are accommodated. In the sixteenth century, Portugal's conquest of Malacca on the Malay Peninsula, and the religious corruption and heavy-handed attempts to promote Christianity along the sea trading routes it controls, serve to strengthen Islamic unity and resistance in Indonesia. On the western coast, Banten is a Muslim agricultural state, and Demak is a major Muslim port on the north coast. Muslim scholars hold important positions at court. Aceh, on the northern tip of Sumatra, is a center of religious study and controls much of Sumatra as well as some states on the Malay Peninsula. The Islamization that evolves at this time is a process that has continued into the modern era.

1290s: Pasai, formerly Samudra, and Perlak adopt Islam and develop as small trading kingdoms on the north coast of Sumatra.

1292: Marco Polo visits Sumatra on his voyage home to Italy by ship from China.

1360s: Conquest of Pasai by Majapahit; under new rulership, Pasai becomes a major commercial center of the Strait of Malacca.

1377: Majapahit attacks Palembang, and Prince Parameswara flees, eventually arriving in Malacca, on the Malay Peninsula, where he establishes a port that becomes a thriving state.

1389: Ascension of Majapahit King Vikramawardhana (reigns 1389–1429), bringing a period of decline, famine, and civil war.

1404–1406: Civil wars and the emergence of the state of Malacca undermine Majapahit stability. Malacca comes to control the strait and international trade, supplanting Pasai as a favored port. Javanese merchants operate in Malacca, embrace Islam and attract Muslim trade from Java and elsewhere in Asia.

1429–1478: Succession of Majapahit rulers.

1478: Possible conquest of Majapahit by the Islamic state of Demak; new research suggests that Majapahit continues as late as 1486, and possibly later.

Early 16th century: Islamic ruler of Demak, Raden Patah (reigns 1500–1518) conquers Majapahit and establishes an empire on Java and Sumatra that eventually extends over much of the former Majapahit realm and turns conquered territories into Muslim states.

1511: Muslim traders ousted by the Portuguese conquest of Malacca resettle in northern Sumatra and other Muslim ports such as Banten and Brunei.

1522: After failure to take the Sumatran port of Pasai, Portugal focuses attention on the Moluccas, in eastern Indonesia, where the Spice Islands Ternate and Tidore are located. Ternate becomes a Portuguese-dominated port.

The way of the ancient kings
Was to know the limits of
Structured authority.

A structure of rule/allusion that is
hidden/expressed
Has authority to see and be seen
Such is the meaning of excellence true.

Babad Jaka Tingkir, 16th-century court history

1524: Aceh overcomes Pasai in north Sumatra. Under Ali Mughayat Syah (reigns *c.* 1514–1530), Aceh becomes a powerful maritime state with lucrative trade in pepper and Indian cloth, and engages in territorial expansion.

1546: The Battle of Panarukan results in severe losses for Demak and leads to a rapid decline of its influence.

1575: Sultan Baab Ullah (reigns 1570–1583) founds an Islamic state on Ternate after the expulsion of the Portuguese.

1580s–1600: Although the actual details are lost in legend and myth, it appears that Panembahan Senapati Ingalaga (reigns *c.* 1584–1601) may have conquered the region in central Java known as Mataram. In any case, Mataram emerges as a military force that expands northward and eastward and becomes the major power in central Java.

1607–1636: Sultan Iskandar Muda extends Aceh sovereignty into central Sumatra and expands into Malaya.

1614–1619: Under Sultan Agung (reigns 1613–1645), a grandson of Senapati, Mataram attacks coastal ports and destroys centers of sea trade in an attempt to stem disunity in Java.

1622: Agung establishes authority over Sukadana, in southwest Borneo, causing Dutch and English enterprises to withdraw.

1625: Agung takes Surabaya on northeast coast of Java after an eleven-year struggle.

1628–1629: Mataram forces under Agung launch attack but fail to take the Dutch East India Company's station at Batavia.

1630: Bali repulses an attempt to introduce Islam by Agung and maintains ties with remaining Hindu states in east Java.

Late 1640s: Process of Dutch territorial acquisition begins with Mataram cessions of large sections of territory in exchange for support. Banten is also subordinated to the Dutch.

1667: The Dutch take Makasar, a major Islamic center in southwest Sulawesi (Celebes), and also subdue Aceh and Palembang.

1682: The English are expelled from Banten, and their presence is limited to Benkulu and other areas of western Sumatra. Dutch influence here brings the end of the independence of another Islamic state.

THE EUROPEAN PRESENCE: 1511–1942

Beginning in the sixteenth century, European companies in the so-called Spice Islands of eastern Indonesia expand the production and export of native products, while local kingdoms seek to maintain territorial control. Portugal and England vie for a share of the spice and sugar trade, while Holland succeeds in establishing a colonizing foothold in Indonesia. At this time, Mataram, centered in east Java and the last of the great Muslim kingdoms, continues to expand.

By the late eighteenth century the Dutch control most of Java. An increase in agricultural production leads to population growth on Java in the nineteenth century, yet while the export economy expands, the local economy suffers. Cultivation remains under local control, and profits go to the Dutch (the government once the Dutch East India Company is dissolved in 1800). The Dutch extend their colonization throughout the archipelago; piracy increases.

By the early twentieth century, popular sentiment in Holland is leaning toward the cessation of exploitation in its colonies, but provisions for greater local governmental authority through decentralization fall short, as does a welfare system that provides health and education for the indigenous population. These policies fail to serve a rapidly growing population; however, an educated elite class of native Indonesians becomes the foundation for nationalism that emerges in the twentieth century. That nationalist movement, which is divided by Islamic and secular ideologies, as well as those of Communist and other competing organizations, is strengthened by the Japanese invasion.

1511: Portuguese explorers capture the port of Malacca, erect a fort there, and settle in, but Portuguese corruption and disorganization soon lead to the loss of sea-trade control of Malacca and to the rise of Sumatran maritime trade centers.

1521: The North Sumatran kingdom of Aceh repulses Portuguese attempt to take the Pasai kingdom. Portugal focuses attention on the Moluccas, in eastern Indonesia, where the Spice Islands of Ternate and Tidore are located.

1522: Portugal establishes a fortress at Ternate; eventually the local king is deposed.

1546–1547: Francis Xavier (1506–1552), the Spanish Jesuit priest based at Malacca (1545–1549), personally carries his mission to the Moluccas.

1560s: A small Catholic population develops in the Moluccas around the missionaries left by Francis Xavier.

1575: The Portuguese are ousted from Ternate and an Islamic state is founded under Sultan Baab Ullah (reigns 1570–1583).

1578: Portugal establishes a fortress at Tidore while maintaining a major port at Malacca; the center of trade in Indonesia is on the island of Ambon in the Moluccas. Meanwhile, Portugal is shifting its focus of trade to China and Japan.

1595–1598: First expeditions to the East Indies by competing Dutch trade companies.

1602: The Dutch East India Company is formed with a merger of the competing companies. England also enters the spice trade.

1605: The Dutch East India Company occupies Ambon and establishes its headquarters.

1606: Spanish fleet takes Ternate and Tidore.

1618–1619: Armed forces of Agung, ruler of Mataram from 1613–1645, and the Dutch East India Company engage in hostilities in their attempts to dominate the sea trade in Java. In 1619, Jan Pieterszoon Coen (governor of the Indies, 1618–1629), conquers the city of Batavia (present-day Jakarta) and moves the Dutch East India Company headquarters there. Batavia becomes a thriving commercial city and involves Holland in internal politics and defense against Banten and Mataram.

1623: The Dutch massacre the English on Ambon to discourage rival trade; after continued struggle to compete with Dutch trading, the English eventually shift their attention to India while keeping a presence in Indonesia.

1625: Mataram takes Surabaya on northeast coast of Java after an eleven-year struggle.

1628–1629: The Dutch East India Company resists an attack on Batavia by Agung.

1630: Bali repulses Agung's attempt to introduce Islam; ties are maintained with remaining Hindu states in east Java.

1635–1646: Mataram's rulers, realizing that they cannot defeat the increasing numbers of Europeans moving throughout Indonesia, gradually cease hostilities with the Dutch East India Company and try to cooperate with the Dutch. The Dutch trading companies are interested in establishing trade monopolies rather than in proselytizing or desire for territorial expansion. Initially, local administration on Java and in Dutch-controlled areas elsewhere is left in the hands of indigenous rulers who have often agreed to allow the Dutch East India Company exclusive access to specific local products. By the late seventeenth century there is concerted effort to control crop production on Java and eastern Indonesia to maximize profits on the European market.

1659: The Dutch destroy Palembang in southern Sumatra, Mataram's last ally outside Java.

1666–1669: Under Governor Johan Maetsuycker (1653–1678), the Dutch take Makasar, an Islamic center and major port of southwest Sulawesi (Celebes).

1682: The Dutch East India Company takes Banten; the English are expelled from Banten and their presence is limited to Benkulu and other areas of western Sumatra. Dutch influence brings the end of independence of another Islamic state.

1704–1708: The First Javanese War of Succession is fought by claimants for the Mataram throne; in exchange for protection, the Dutch East India Company expands its territorial acquisition and trade control. Throughout the eighteenth century Dutch territorial interests on Java increase. The policy of enforced delivery of crops at fixed prices makes for a stagnant local economy, and the class of coastal Javanese traders is ruined. The Dutch East India Company gradually restricts royal authority, but administrative control remains limited to that necessary for commercial purposes. The impact of Dutch economic domination on domestic subsistence agriculture or commerce, as well as customs and social structure, is minimal at this time.

1719–1723: The Second Javanese War of Succession is actually a rebellion against the Dutch East India Company's vassal ruler. The opposition is quashed after four years of conflict.

1746–1757: The Third Javanese War of Succession results in Mataram's division into two principalities in 1755, Surakarta and Yogjakarta, thus furthering the kingdom's disintegration and strengthening the Dutch trade monopoly. The administrative organization, in which petty princes are accountable to a ruler, remains unchanged, as do most customs at the aristocratic and village levels.

1784: The Anglo-Dutch Treaty assures the English rights of passage and free trade throughout the area, breaking the Dutch monopoly.

January 1, 1800: The Dutch East India Company is formally dissolved and its territory and operations are taken over by the Dutch government. For the Indonesians there is little change, inasmuch as many of the same personnel and policies remain in place.

1810: Governor of Java Herman Daendels builds fortifications against the British, including a road system, and attempts to introduce liberal administrative policies favorable to the local population; however, his reforms are based on centralization of power.

1811–1816: Control of Java passes to Britain during the Napoleonic Wars. Governor of Java Thomas Stamford Raffles (1781–1826) establishes closer administrative controls over local authority. At the same time, Raffles introduces extensive economic and social reforms and abolishes the forced delivery system almost entirely.

1816: Dutch sovereignty is restored; Raffles's liberalized policies are detrimental to the deteriorating Dutch economy, and it becomes necessary to make greater demands of the peasant labor force to ensure Dutch supplies to the European market. There is considerable local opposition.

1817: Raffles returns to Indonesia as governor of Benkulu, a small Sumatran trading post on the southwest coast.

1824: The Treaty of London is signed by England and Holland to end their rivalries in Southeast Asia. England cedes Benkulu and its interests in Sumatra and pledges no future interests in the area. Aceh remains independent; Borneo and other contested areas remain unresolved.

1825–1830: The Java War, sparked by Dutch interference in a dynastic conflict and flamed by resistance to Dutch authority, is led by the Javanese prince, Diponegoro. It takes a heavy toll on Javanese lives and on the Dutch treasury. The Muslim reform movement (*wahhabi*) spreads throughout the Islamic world and plays a role in the Javanese rebellion. These events put an end to the liberal policies introduced by Raffles.

1830: To increase crop production in Java, Governor Van den Bosch (1830–1833) introduces the "Culture System." This is an intensification of the forced delivery system; one-fifth of a peasant's crops are appropriated as a tax. Stricter controls lead to subsequent social changes in village life, including population growth. Van den Bosch uses the earlier system in which local rulers provide administrative functions to oversee village production, and profits climb.

1858: Treaty with Sumatran state of Siak provides that principalities on northeast coast of Sumatra come under Dutch authority.

1860: Eduard Douwes Dekker (1820–1887) (under the pen name of Multatuli), a former Dutch East India Company official, publishes a novel, *Max Havelaar*, which exposes the oppressive and corrupt ways of the Dutch in Indonesia. It will be cited by those who seek to reform or even eliminate Dutch rule.

1867: The Dutch parliament assumes financial responsibility for all its territorial interests.

1870: The Agrarian Law removes all cash crops from the Culture System except sugar and coffee, which are the bulk of export crops. Gradually the Culture System is abandoned entirely. The law also extends eligibility to lease land to virtually all Dutch subjects.

1870s: The Dutch in Batavia (Jakarta) establish firmer control over Borneo (Kalimantan), Celebes (Sulawesi), the Moluccas, and the Lesser Sundas and extend their colonization throughout the archipelago.

1871: The Sumatra Treaty is signed with Britain, through which Dutch control of Sumatra, excluding Aceh, is sanctioned in exchange for commercial concessions to Britain.

1871: The first oil well is drilled in northern Sumatra, but full-scale commercial production will not begin for another twenty years.

1873–1908: War with Aceh results in its subordination to Holland.

August 1883: The volcano on the island of Krakatoa erupts and explodes; much of the island collapses, creating a *tsunami* (tidal wave) that washes over the shores of nearby islands and kills some 36,000 people; its ash drifts around the upper atmosphere and affects the world's climate for several years.

1900: Founding of the Kartini School for Girls based on principles promoted by feminist and political activist Raden Adjeng Kartini (1879–1904). By this time rubber, copra, and tin are added to the crops that are the principal export products. Sumatra has become a focus of economic expansion, and firmer control is extended to outer islands; the spice trade in the Moluccas, on the decline since the late eighteenth century, is regulated. Towns are built, partially modeled on those in Holland, and road and communications systems are installed. Social and ethnic divisions become more pronounced, and a ruinous credit system develops.

1901: The Ethical Policy is implemented by the Dutch parliament in response to a change in popular attitude. The policy provides for health and education expenditures for the indigent and for greater local autonomy in its colonies.

1903: The Decentralization Law creates a local governing autonomy while maintaining complete Dutch authority over the Indonesian governor.

1906: The Village Regulation Act provides local autonomy but is subject to governmental interference; no real transfer of power takes place.

1908: Dr. Wahidin Soedirohoesodo (1857–1914) founds the Budi Utomo (High Endeavor) organization dedicated to establishing a national school system based on Western guidelines.

We know that we are impregnated with European ideas and feelings—but the blood, the Javanese blood that flows live and warm through our veins, can never die. We feel it in the smell of incense and in the perfume of flowers, in the tops of the cocoa-nut trees, the cooing of the turtle doves, the whistling of the fields of ripened rice, the pounding of the haddi-blokken at the time of the rice harvest.

Letters of a Javanese Princess, by Raden Adjeng Kartini (1911)

1911–1912: The Sarekat Dagang Islam (Islamic Commercial Union) movement promotes economic nationalism and a return to traditional Islam as a foundation for a national identity. In 1912 it drops the name to emphasize its appeal to broader elements in Indonesia.

1911: E. F. E. Douwes Dekker (1879–1950), of Indonesian-Dutch parentage, founds the Indies Party, proclaiming nationalism and calling for independence. The government refuses to recognize the party, and in 1913 its leaders are exiled.

1912: Kyai Haji Ahmad Dahlan (1868–1923) founds the Muhammadiyah (Way of Mohammed), a Muslim party dedicated to counteracting the spread of Christian missionary work by dedication to educational and welfare works as well as teaching a more authentic Islam with ties to Mecca. This movement slowly grows to become a major religious and educational force throughout Indonesia.

May 1918: The Volksraad, or People's Council, meets in Jakarta to facilitate communications between the government and the Dutch, Indonesian, and Asian populations. This attempt at decentralization fails to provide significant legislative power at the local level.

1920: A Communist splinter group of Sarekat Islam forms the Perserikatan Kommunist di India (PKI), which is aligned ideologically with Moscow in its opposition to Islam as well as Western domination. (In 1924 it will change its name to Partai Kommunis Indonesia.)

1925: A constitution is drafted to provide a decentralized system of provincial government, but it gives little power to Indonesian local authorities.

1927: Under the leadership of (Ahmad) Sukarno (1901–1970), Perserikatan Nasional Indonesia (PNI) is founded to unite nationalist groups in pacifist noncooperation.

1928: The All-Indonesia Youth Congress adopts Malay, the traditional language of traders, as Bahasa Indonesian, the language of Indonesia.

1929: Sukarno is arrested; the PNI is banned and absorbed by the Independent People's Party (PRI), which seeks independence through cooperation with the Dutch.

1933: Publication of literary journal *Poedjangga Baroe* (New Poet) begins; in its pages, national literary standards and cultural identity are explored by modernist writers. Amir Hamzah (1911–1946) is a prominent poet whose works are published in this journal.

1936: The Volksraad requests a discussion of steps to be taken toward self-government; Holland's agreement to do so is superseded by war in Europe.

1941: Douwes Dekker, who has become an officer of the Japanese Chamber of Commerce, is arrested along with other nationalist leaders.

August 1941: In retaliation for the Japanese invasion of Indochina, the Dutch freeze all Japanese assets in the Dutch East Indies and cancel all oil deals.

January 11, 1942: Japan invades Indonesia.

March 8, 1942: The Dutch in Java surrender to Japan and the governor-general is arrested.

WORLD WAR II AND INDEPENDENCE: 1942–1998

The Japanese invasion destroys Dutch power in Indonesia. Although the Indonesian people endure great hardships during the occupation years, Japan's policies serve to unify the nationalist movement. Immediately following the surrender of Japan to the Allied powers, the independence of Indonesia is declared so that by the time the Dutch return to reclaim Indonesia, revolutionary forces are in place. A ruined economy, population increases and peasant impoverishment, lack of capital and trained personnel, and overstaffed and undertrained administrative systems are among the problems facing the new nation. As head of state, Sukarno, although charismatic, is autocratic and fails to grasp financial realities; to make matters worse, he is at odds with the Muslim Masjumi party and supports the Communists, aligning himself with Moscow. Inflation, military interference, political upheaval and corruption, and expansionism into Kalimantan (Borneo) and Irian Jaya (West New Guinea) all contribute to the growing instability under Sukarno.

After a military coup, possibly instigated by Communist factions, and the ensuing anticommunist massacres, power shifts to General (Thojib) Suharto. Over the decades, stability, economic development, and support for social welfare characterize Suharto's regime, although there is increasing protest against his autocratic rule and financial corruption in Suharto's inner circle. In particular, the issue of the status of East Timor remains.

Oil and gas, wood products, rubber, and coffee are the principal export products. By the end of the twentieth century Indonesia is a predominantly Muslim country of 180,000,000, composed of about three hundred ethnic groups who speak Bahasa Indonesian as well as more than five hundred dialects. The country's rich artistic heritage is diverse and regional. Buddhist and Hindu temples are found on Java, Asmat woodcarvings are distinctive to Irian Jaya, Java is known for *batik*, a dyed cloth, while the elaborately dyed patterned cloth known as *chat* weaving is a product of Bali and Sumba. Javanese musical and dramatic arts, such as the predominantly percussion *gamelan* orchestras and the *wayang* puppet plays, have spread throughout the archipelago to become national expressions.

April 1942–May 1945: During the occupation, many Indonesians collaborate with the Japanese but some of them also secretly plan for independence; one of the lessons they have learned is that their former Western masters can be defeated. The Japanese gradually impose harsher and harsher measures including enforced labor and strict rationing; they also try to enlist the support of the Indonesian people by promising independence (formally on September 7, 1944). As the Japanese are clearly losing the war in the Pacific, they realize that the best they can hope for is to grant independence and so prevent the Dutch from taking back Indonesia, but the end of the war comes too abruptly.

June 1, 1945: Sukarno proclaims his Pancasila, the Five Principles of Unity that become the foundation for Indonesian nationalism.

August 10, 1945: The Japanese surrender and accept terms of the Potsdam Agreement, under which British forces will temporarily occupy Indonesia to protect the Dutch and other Allies.

August 17, 1945: Sukarno declares the independence of a new republic that represents predominantly Javanese interests, with himself as head of state. This is the date that Indonesians will continue to celebrate as their independence day.

September–October 1945: Indonesians begin to move as though they are already an independent state, but the British troops begin to arrive by the latter half of September. Meanwhile, Japanese forces still in Indonesia decide to reinforce control and by early October there is open warfare that will continue for several weeks. Gradually the British troops are present in large enough numbers and they decide to enforce control.

October 28–November 10, 1945: British Indian troops fight Indonesian resistance troops at Surabaya. On November 10 (now commemorated as Heroes' Day), the British start a major sweep through Surabaya that ends three weeks later with some six thousand Indonesians dead.

1946: Throughout this year Indonesia is in turmoil as various Indonesians compete to take control of the revolution while the Dutch try to reassert control. Sukarno is only one of several competing leaders, but he slowly emerges as the only one who commands enough respect to stop the violence.

November 12, 1946: At Linggadjati, Java, the Dutch agree to recognize Sukarno's Republic, composed of Java, Sumatra, and Madura, but only as a member of a federal United States of Indonesia that would leave the Dutch in control of the rest of Indonesia. Many Indonesians reject such an arrangement, and there is increasing turmoil throughout Indonesia.

July 20–August 4, 1947: The Dutch recommence military operations, but stop at the command of a United Nations resolution.

January 17, 1948: An agreement signed aboard the American warship USS *Renville* states that Dutch sovereignty will continue until a United States of Indonesia is established; the admission of states outside the republic, which is predominantly Indonesian, would be submitted to popular vote.

January–December 1948: Turmoil continues throughout much of Indonesia, as various factions compete for power: constant demonstrations, strikes, even open warfare. In particular, the Indonesian Communists find themselves fighting Sukarno and his allies.

Finally, on December 18 the Dutch mount another of their so-called police actions; they end up occupying Yogjakarta, the republican capital, imprisoning the government leaders, and imposing Dutch rule over several regions.

January–December 1949: Having accepted a UN call for a cease-fire, the Dutch now find themselves facing a guerrilla war while the several Indonesian factions continue to quarrel. Meanwhile, the United States is taking the lead in calling for the Dutch to grant full independence to Indonesia.

December 27, 1949: Following the Round Table Conference at the Hague (August–November 1949) Indonesia is established a sovereign independent federation of sixteen states in cooperation with the Netherlands-Indonesian Union. Sukarno is president and Mohammed Hatty is prime minister. Full independence is to be granted when social and political stability is achieved.

1950: Sukarno replaces the Round Table Agreement with a centralized government, in which West New Guinea is excluded. Some groups feel that this arrangement ignores regional interests outside of Java, and there is also apprehension about expansion of communist power.

1952: Contention begins over West New Guinea (Irian Jaya) and the Moluccas; the Dutch halt negotiations. Hostilities escalate, resulting in heavy losses on both sides over the next years.

July 1956: Hatty, a moderate, submits his resignation (effective December 1) over differences with Sukarno.

1956: Rebels establish regional councils on Sumatra.

1957: East Indonesia and Kalimantan (Borneo) establish local authority.

1957: Dutch assets are appropriated, personnel depart, and production and export decline.

March 1957: Sukarno abolishes multiparty cabinet and implements "guided democracy," a militarily supported civil government with himself as central figure.

February 1958: Revolutionary government is established at Padding in central Sumatra but gains little public support.

July 5, 1959: Sukarno dissolves the Constituent Assembly to form a presidential government with an appointed parliament. He reinstates the constitution of 1945, which gives him greater power. On July 9 a new cabinet is installed with Sukarno as its prime minister.

1960s: Large reserves of natural gas are found in the Banda Aseh province of Sumatra; by the 1970s Indonesia will prosper in the global oil boom.

March 5, 1960: Sukarno suspends the parliament and effectively rules as the sole authority in Indonesia. He proceeds to sever relations with Holland and abolish the Masjumi and Socialist parties.

August 15, 1962–May 1, 1963: In an agreement with the Netherlands on August 15, a cease-fire between Dutch and Indonesian troops on West New Guinea goes into effect on August 17. On October 1, 1962, West New Guinea comes under interim UN administration; on May 1, 1963, it is turned over to the administration of Indonesia.

1964: Ever since the Federation of Malaysia was established in 1963, Indonesia has complained that it was really under control of the British colony, who had also forced North Borneo and Sarawak to join it. During this year, Sukarno sends small military units into Malaysia to try to stir up trouble, but the British aid the Malaysians in resisting these Indonesians.

January 1965: Sukarno, to express his continuing opposition to the newly created Federation of Malaysia, withdraws Indonesia from the United Nations.

September 30–November 1965: A group of army officers, calling itself the 30 September Movement, assassinates six generals and attempts to seize the government. General (Thojib) Suharto (1921–1999) takes control

of the military and suppresses the coup by October 2. The rebels are accused of being procommunist; army leaders allow mobs of civilians and soldiers to massacre any they regard as Communists or even leftists.

January 1966: During the past few months, the government-tolerated violence leaves an estimated 250,000 dead. (Some claim as many as 750,000.) The PKI, Indonesia's Communist party, is virtually destroyed.

March 11, 1966: Sukarno gives Suharto authority to restore order; power shifts to Suharto, who breaks ties with China and adopts a pro-West policy of economic reform, returning appropriations and encouraging foreign investment.

March 1967: The MPRS (Provisional People's Consultative Assembly) places Sukarno under house arrest for the remainder of his life and names Suharto acting president.

August 1967: ASEAN (Association of Southeast Asian Nations) is formed to establish terms of cooperation among Indonesia, Malaysia, Singapore, Thailand, and the Philippines.

1969: After several years of turmoil, Suharto ends the conflict with Malaysia, rejoins the United Nations, and, with the support of the army, restores stability. The MPRS declares Suharto permanent president.

July–September 1969: Under the provisions of the August 15, 1962, agreement with the Netherlands, in what the Indonesian government calls an "act of free choice," the population of West New Guinea votes through a series of assemblies. On August 17, President Suharto declares that the majority has voted to remain within Indonesia. In September, West New Guinea becomes a province of Indonesia under the name of West Irian.

March 3, 1973: West Irian's name is formally changed to Irian Jaya. "Irian" is most likely an indigenous word for "volcanic islands," while "Jaya" is an Indonesian word for "glorious."

January 1974: Suspicion that Japan, in collusion with the government, is exploiting the economy leads to rioting.

1975: With the departure of the Portuguese from East Timor, civil war breaks out in this largely Catholic former Portuguese colony; the radical Front of Independent East Timor triumphs and declares that it does not intend to join West Timor as a part of Indonesia. Indonesia invades East Timor; heavy civilian casualties provoke international outrage.

July 17, 1976: East Timor is incorporated into Indonesia. The rebellion by the East Timorese, however, continues and in the next twenty years some 200,000 are said to have died in the civil war and of the disease and famine it causes.

January 1978: Student riots protesting government corruption are suppressed.

November 1991: A massacre at Dili, East Timor, leaves at least fifty peaceful East Timorese demonstrators dead when the army opens fire during the funeral of a man allegedly slain by the army. The international outcry pressures Indonesia to set up an investigative commission and take disciplinary measures.

March 10, 1993: Suharto wins a sixth consecutive five-year term in uncontested election in the People's Consultative Assembly. Suharto promises to ease the government's "iron grip."

March 11, 1993: A resolution passed by the UN Commission on Human Rights is critical of Indonesian human rights policies in East Timor.

June 21, 1994: Three magazines critical of the government are banned, reversing the recent easing of curbs on free speech. On June 27 protesters demonstrate in Jakarta.

December 7, 1995: On the twentieth anniversary of the invasion of East Timor, protesters storm the Dutch and Russian embassies in Jakarta and stage sit-ins. The government says those involved in the protest are free to seek asylum in Portugal, joining more than forty other protesters who had recently done so.

September 18, 1996: After postponement of an earlier sale in protest against Indonesian suppression of political dissent, the Clinton administration announces the sale of nine F-16 fighter jets to Indonesia.

September 26, 1997: An Indonesian airliner crashes on Sumatra and all 234 people aboard are killed; it is believed that the airliner lost its way in the thick haze that has settled over much of the country and adjacent areas of Malaysia due to the uncontrolled forest fires raging since June. The fires are deliberately set in Borneo and Sumatra for clearing land, but this year they are believed to have been flamed by drought brought on by the periodic warming of ocean waters known as El Niño. The smoke causes respiratory ailments throughout Indonesia and Malaysia; it is also responsible for automobile accidents and a falling off in tourism.

October 1997: In the wake of the collapse of Thailand's and Malaysia's currencies and financial structures, Indonesia's currency, the *rupiah*, and financial structures are also declining drastically. The international financial community begins to call for President Suharto to move swiftly against the country's shaky financial institutions, many of which are controlled by his own widespread family, but the aging Suharto seems unable or unwilling to do so.

January 1998: By now the Indonesian *rupiah* has fallen as much as 80 percent against the U.S. dollar and many both abroad and in Indonesia are calling for Suharto to resign. Instead, he announces that he intends to run for another term as president in the March 1998 elections. Under pressure from the International Monetary Fund, however, Suharto does agree to certain strict reforms of the nation's finances.

March 10, 1998: Suharto is reelected president (for his seventh five-year term) by the one hundred-member People's Consultative Assembly, dominated by Suharto loyalists. He promises to introduce reforms, but the international community and his domestic critics remain skeptical.

May 15–21, 1998: Since Suharto's reelection

as president, there has been increasing unrest, demonstrations, and violence in the
main cities of Indonesia. Protesting the hardships inflicted by the collapse of their economy and the resultant demands made by the
international financial community, mobs
riot, burn, and pillage in Jakarta; in particular, people take their resentment out on the
Chinese community, which comprises only
3 percent of Indonesia's population but is
said to control almost 50 percent of its economy. At least five hundred people are killed
by the police and army. Calls for Suharto's
resignation have now come to a climax, and
on May 21 he resigns, appointing his vice
president Bacharuddin Yusuf Habibie to fill
out his five-year term. Although Habibie
promises reforms, it is clear that the army
remains the power behind these developments.

July 29–August 6, 1998: In an effort to demonstrate Jakarta's commitment to a peaceful
resolution of the fate of East Timor, on July
29 the government begins to withdraw one
thousand troops. This still leaves at least
eleven thousand troops behind. On August
6 Indonesia and Portugal agree on the broad
outlines of plans for East Timor, allowing it
a measure of self-government.

September 1998: Indonesia remains on the
verge of economic and social collapse. Its
currency has lost almost all its value, most
of its 240 banks are insolvent, and its people
lack even the most basic foods.

Laos

PREHISTORIC LAOS: 10,000 B.C.–A.D. 1353

Little is known about the prehistory of this small landlocked country, isolated by its geography and yet strongly linked to events occurring within in its more powerful neighbors. As elsewhere in what would become known as the Indochina peninsula, although early hominids (*Homo erectus*) stray into and through the land (*Homo erectus* remains and a chopper tool said to date to 500,000 B.C. are reported), there are no solid traces of occupation until *Homo sapiens* settles down—in Laos, about 10,000 B.C. The first inhabitants of Laos may be the ancestors of some of the tribal groups that still inhabit the remote mountains in the twentieth century; long disparagingly called Kha (slaves) by other Lao people, they are now more formally known as Lao Theung (Lao of the mountainsides). During the ensuing millennia, several waves of people will make their way into Laos, all—except for the occasional few from India—of Mongoloid extraction. These residents of Laos share a fairly common culture with many people living throughout Southeast Asia and southern and central China—conducting a basic subsistence economy but gradually diversifying their food sources and toolkit as they pass through the Neolithic, Bronze, and Iron ages. Through these many millennia, the people living in Laos tend to be recipients of and reactors to more advanced cultures in the lands around them. Not until the first millennium A.D. do Tai people begin to move into the land to be known as Laos, but Laos continues to be exposed to its more dynamic neighbors, particularly Thailand and Cambodia. Contributing to this lack of a cohesiveness is the fact that Laos is divided into a number of small city-states or principalities (known as *muang*), often at war with one another. Not until the fourteenth century will there begin the long process of unification that will eventually lead to modern Laos.

10,000–3000 B.C.: Scattered throughout parts of Laos are small groups of hunters-gatherers who appear to share the Hoabinhian culture first found in Vietnam. This is characterized by the tools made of river pebbles, flaked usually on only one side in Laos.

3000–1500 B.C.: People in what is now Laos begin to adopt the Neolithic culture that includes agriculture (eventually rice), domesticated animals (pigs, cattle, fowl), and pottery.

1500 B.C.: By this time, the indigenous peoples are adding metallurgy to their repertoire of skills, thus entering into the Bronze Age. These people are probably being influenced by the more advanced culture of Thailand as in such places as Ban Chiang.

1000–100 B.C.: It is about this time that people in northern Laos begin to develop a society that is regarded as a Bronze Age/megalithic culture. Known mainly by its burial structures and practices, the first phase lasts from about 1000 to 500 B.C.; the people bury their dead in underground burial chambers marked by upright stone slabs, or menhirs. Starting about 500 B.C. they shift to cremating their dead and placing the ashes in large stone jars, averaging some five feet in height, the largest weighing an estimated fifteen tons. It is these that have given this region, Xiang Khouang, the name by which it is known today, the Plain of Jars. Little is known about these people, but judging from the rich grave goods—pottery, bronze artifacts, and glass beads—they prospered, probably by controlling the trade in salt and eventually iron.

500–1 B.C.: Laotians continue to be under the influence of neighboring cultures. Bronze work of this period, such as axes and bracelets found in the Luang Prabang area of Laos, reflects the influence of the Dong Son culture of Vietnam. Bronze drums of this period found in Laos also suggest direct contact with Yunnan, southwestern China, the homeland of some Tai people. Iron also begins to be worked.

Engineers lead water,
fletchers make arrows,
carpenters form the wood,
wise men master themselves.

Dhammapada (The Way of the Doctrine), ancient Pali poem

A.D. 500: Possibly under pressure from Chinese and Vietnamese, the first identifiable Tai-speaking people from southeastern China begin to move into the remote mountains of northeastern Laos.

400–800: Some of the Mon-Khmer tribal people in Laos begin to fall under the influence, if not control, of the Khmer in Cambodia.

600–850: Some Mon people in northern Laos come under the influence of Dvaravati, the strongly Buddhist culture that appears to spread across northern Thailand from the trade routes linking India to Southeast Asia.

800–900: The Nan-chao kingdom of southwestern China exerts some power over northern Laos. (Some accounts suggest that the Nan-Chao people had peripheral contacts with the Tai.)

800–1000: The Tai people who are the most immediate ancestors of modern Laotian Tai people begin to move farther into Laos from southeastern China (although some may be coming by way of northern Vietnam). Many of these people also move into lands that will become Thailand and Burma.

850–1200: The Khmer empire centered at Angkor, Cambodia, exercises considerable influence in Laos. Monks begin to spread Theravada Buddhism in Laos.

1100–1250: By now more organized than the original inhabitants of Laos, some Tai in Laos establish various principalities known as *muang.* Elsewhere across Southeast Asia—in fact, all the way from Assam in northeastern India—other groups of Tai establish similar small principalities.

About the year 1200, the Lao alphabet begins to come into existence.

1250–1350: Tai people continue to move into Laos (and elsewhere in northern Southeast Asia); some scholars believe they may to some extent be under pressure from the Mongols who have moved down and taken southern China including the kingdom of Nan-chao. Various Tai *muang* contest for power in Laos; the most powerful of these seems to be based in northern Laos and is known as Muang Sua (and later as Luang Prabang).

THE KINGDOM OF LAN XANG: 1353–1707

During these 350 years, the foundations of what would become the modern nation-state of Laos are effectively laid down. It is not known as Laos but as Lan Xang; its boundaries are not the same as modern Laos but are sometimes larger and sometimes smaller; it is neither a completely independent nor truly centralized state; and most of its inhabitants probably never move beyond a feudal society and basic subsistence economy. But between the reigns of its founder, Fa Ngum, and its last and greatest ruler, Souligna Vongsa, Lan Sang achieves a certain unity and status that later Laotians would regard as their great moment on the stage of history. (It is from the outset of this period that the golden statue of the Buddha known as the Prabang becomes the palladium of Laos, the sacred symbolic image of national identity and security.) Most of its inhabitants are Southern Mongoloids who speak Tai languages, and although some of the kings try to impose Buddhism as the official religion, many of the people adhere to their traditional animistic religion. Two forces gradually work against the stability of Lan Xang: one involves the occasional disputes among leaders over succession to the throne, and the other involves relations with neighboring states. In the end, these two forces combine to break up Laos and postpone its ultimate unification and independence for another 275 years.

c. **1345–1352:** Fa Ngum (1316–1374) is the descendant of a Tai family forced into exile from Muang Sua, the region of northern Laos it has long ruled. After being raised at the court of Angkor, Cambodia, where he marries a Cambodian princess, he embarks on a campaign to regain Muang Sua. After a series of military campaigns, Fa Ngum not only regains the kingdom but also extends his control over territory to the east and south.

As if she had descended to this earth from the sky,
The beauty of her form fitting for Prince Cheuang,
Surrounded by her serving girls,
The most beautiful of the children of Khom.

Thao Hung, medieval epic poem

1353–1373: In 1353 Fa Ngum is crowned ruler of the extended kingdom he calls Lan Sang (Kingdom of the Million Elephants). During the next twenty years Fa Ngum promotes Theravada Buddhism as the state religion. He sends a mission to Angkor that brings back a golden statue of the standing Buddha known as the Prabang and has it placed in a special pagoda in his capital in Muang Sua. During these twenty years he extends his power over much of Laos and well into Thailand.

1373: Evidently because of certain excesses, Fa Ngum is driven into exile by his ministers. He dies in 1374 and is succeeded by his son Oun Hueun, who rules as Sam Sen Thai.

1374–1417: Sam Sen Thai presides over a relatively peaceful period. He develops an administrative system that will survive in Laos until the twentieth century; at its core is an absolute monarchy with princes of royal blood overseeing most activities. He also erects many temples, and these become the center of Laotian community life.

1417: On the death of Sam Sen Thai, Lan Kham Deng becomes king. In 1421 he sends Laotian forces to aid the Vietnamese in their fight against the Chinese, but the Laotians defect to the Chinese; the Vietnamese will take revenge in 1478.

1428: Lan Kham Deng dies. There follows a succession of kings, many of whom die prematurely, suggesting internal strife over succession to the throne.

1478–1480: Vietnamese emperor Le Thanhtong invades Lan Sang, sacks Muang Sua, and seizes some territory for about a year; the Vietnamese may have left on their own will, but Laotians claim that they are expelled by Laotian forces commanded by a prince who assumes the throne under the name of Suvanna Banlang.

1480–1520: A period of relative peace. The major ruler during this period (1507–1520) is Visoun (Lightning Bolt).

1520–1548: Phothisarat reigns over Lan Sang and encourages Buddhism; in 1527 he issues a decree banning the sacrifices to local spirits (*phi*).

1548–1572: Setthathirat, the eldest son of Phothisarat, succeeds his father and unifies the kingdom of Lan Sang with the kingdom to its west, Lan Na; after three years, however, he loses control over Lan Na. In 1560 Setthathirat moves the capital from Muang Sua south to Vieng Chan (modern Vientiane); he builds the Wat Keo to enshrine the Pra Keo, a green jasper carving of the Buddha, and the That Luang, a shrine to house Buddhist relics. He also makes a treaty of alliance with Ayudha, a Tai kingdom to the southwest. It is in 1563 that the capital and kingdom of Muang Sua are renamed Luang Prabang (in honor of the gold Buddha that remains there).

1550–1650: The *Sin Xay*, the Laotian epic poem by Thao Pangkham but based on traditional Hindu themes, is written down during this time.

1563–1578: Burma invades Laotian territory on three occasions: 1563, 1569–1570, and 1574. After the last invasion, the Burmese effectively reduce Lan Sang to a vassal state. It will be 1603 before Lan Sang is able to renounce all tributary ties to Burma.

1621–1637: A period of struggle for the throne of Lan Sang ends with succession of Souligna Vongsa in 1637. During his long reign (until 1694), he will strengthen his kingdom's borders by signing treaties with Thailand and Vietnam. He promotes Buddhism and the arts, and his reign is regarded as a "golden age" of Laotian history.

1641–1642: Gerrit van Wuysthoff, agent for the Dutch East India Company, visits Vieng Chan, the capital of Lan Sang.

Ye muses and ye gods and goddesses of the four horizons, come help me tell how this monarch despaired, bereaved of his beloved sister. Life became such a burden to him that he, King of millions of men, abdicated in favor of his wife and became a monk. Then he set out in search of his sister.

Sin Xay, epic poem by Pangkham (17th century)

1642–1647: Jesuit Father Giovanni Maria Leris is in Vieng Chan trying to convert the Laotians to Christianity, but he has no success.

1694–1700: Souligna Vongsa dies, leading to a dispute over succession. In 1700, Sai Ong Hue, a nephew living in Vietnam, and backed by the Vietnamese, captures the capital, Vieng Chan, and claims the throne under the name of Setthathirat II, but he is effectively a vassal of the southern Vietnamese.

1705–1707: The contest for the rule of Lan Sang continues. Setthathirat II removes the Prabang, the standing Buddha, from Luang Prabang to Vieng Chan.

1707: Kitsarat, a grandson of Soulingna Vongsa, captures Luang Prabang. Lan Sang is effectively divided in two, with Setthathirat II ruling the south from Vieng Chan but basically under Vietnamese suzerainty.

DIVIDED AND CONQUERED: 1707–1893

With the split of the kingdom of Lan Sang into two—and then soon into three—Laos enters a long period of internal strife and foreign interventions. Although this has little impact on most of the inhabitants of Laos—until they are forced into the various military expeditions or they fall prey to foreign invaders—Laos reaches a nadir, becoming essentially a vassal state of foreign powers—the Siamese of Thailand, the Khmer of Cambodia, the Burmese of Myanmar, and the Vietnamese. By the nineteenth century Laos effectively ceases to exist and its several parts are merely pawns in the conflicts among the other Southeast Asian states. Meanwhile, the French and British are also competing for territory and influence in this part of the world; after Britain gains control of Burma (1824–1885) and France gets control of Vietnam (1858–1883), the British encourage the Siamese to occupy Laos in order to impede French access to the upper Mekong River valley. Thailand sends troops into northern Laos to repel marauding bandits, then proceeds to occupy all of northern Laos and establish outposts in northern Vietnam. The French explorer Auguste Pavie gains the confidence of Laotian rulers and almost single-handedly persuades them to accept French protection. By 1893, Thailand accepts the Mekong River as its eastern boundary, leaving France in control of Laos.

1713: Another nephew of Souligna Vongsa, Soi Sisamout, breaks away the southern region of Vieng Chan to form his own kingdom of Champassak. He relies so heavily on support from neighboring Siamese (in Thailand) and Khmer (in Cambodia) that Champassak is effectively a vassal state of Bangkok.

1713–1771: Laos is now divided into three kingdoms—Luang Prabang in the north, Vieng Chan in the center, and Champassak in the south. The leaders continue to threaten and invade each other's territories and capitals with the aid of Vietnamese, Burmese, and Siamese warriors.

1778–1779: The Siamese seize the thrones of Champassak and Vieng Chan; after sacking the Vieng Chan capital, they take the royal family along with the Prabang, the statue of the standing Buddha, to Bangkok.

1781: The Siamese place a vassal king, Chao Nanthasen (reigns 1781–1792) on the throne in Vieng Chan and allow him to take the Prabang Buddha back.

1792: Nanthasen invades Luang Prabang but because the Siamese have a treaty of alliance with Luang Prabang, Nanthasen is deposed as king of Vieng Chan and replaced by a younger brother, Chao In (reigns 1792–

1805). The major regions of Laos come effectively under the control of Bangkok.

1805–1828: Anuvong (or Chao Anou), brother of Chao In, succeeds to the throne of Vieng Chan; he has fought alongside the Siamese and is effectively a vassal king, but he cultivates closer relations with the newly united Vietnamese state. In 1819, he persuades Bangkok to place his son, Chao Nho, on the throne in Champassak, and in 1827 the two kings decide to revolt against the Siamese. Anuvong leads their combined forces toward Bangkok; the Siamese defeat Anuvong (who flees to Vietnam), sack Vieng Chan, and again carry off the Prabang Buddha to Bangkok. In 1828, Anuvong returns to Vieng Chan with the backing of the Vietnamese but is defeated and dies in captivity (1835). The Siamese largely destroy the capital and reduce the former kingdom of Vieng Chan to an administrative province of Siam, even moving the bulk of its population into Thailand.

1817–1836: In Luang Prabang of this time, King Manta Tourat tries to maintain neutrality with both the Siamese in Thailand and the Vietnamese, but Laos remains a vassal state of Thailand.

1832: The Vietnamese emperor annexes

Xieng Khouang, the small province lying east of Vieng Chan and Luang Prabang.

1846–1885: The Siamese send troops into several parts of Laos in order to deter the Vietnamese from expanding. By 1858, however, the French are moving into Vietnam; by 1883 they are effectively in control of all of Vietnam and they are beginning to turn their attention to Laotian affairs.

1850s: Since at least the mid-1700s, the Hmong (sometimes known as the Meo or Miao) and the Mien (Yao) peoples from southern China have moved south into Laos. Living in isolated villages and surviving with a slash-and-burn type of agriculture, they are distinguished by the fact that they will not live at altitudes less than three thousand feet.

1861: Henri Mouhot, the French naturalist who was the first European to see the splendid ruins at Angkor in Cambodia, dies of malaria near Luang Prabang.

1867: As a gesture of goodwill, King Mongkut of Thailand allows the Prabang Buddha to be returned to Luang Prabang (where it remains to this day).

1886–1887: An agreement between Thailand and France allows the French to establish a vice-consulate in Luang Prabang. The first vice-consul, Auguste Pavie, arrives in February 1887. Pavie has been supervising the laying of telegraph lines for the French in Indochina but has taken a strong personal interest in the region and its cultures.

July 1887: Some six hundred Chinese and so-called Black Tai marauders capture and sack the city of Luang Prabang. August Pavie flees with the aging King Oun Kham and his family in a canoe, thereby suggesting that the French will make better protectors of Laos than the Siamese, who still regard themselves as sovereign over much of Laos.

1887–1895: Auguste Pavie leads three ambitious exploratory expeditions (1887–1889, 1889–1891, 1892–1895) in Laos; his contacts will help to establish the French presence. His massive reports are published as the *Mission Pavie* (1898–1919).

April–October 3, 1893: The French have continued to challenge the Siamese in Laos, and, after a series of incidents, in April French troops move to occupy Laotian territories east of the Mekong River. The Siamese kill a French officer, and so the French send warships up the Chaophraya River to Bangkok. In July the French ships fight their way past the defenses at Paknam and arrive at Bangkok. Emboldened by their success, the French increase their demands; effectively blockaded by the French and unable to obtain any international support, the Siamese capitulate and on October 3 sign a treaty formally giving up all claims to Laos east of the Mekong River. Although not explicitly stated, this effectively cedes control of Laos to the French.

FRENCH PROTECTORATE: 1893–1953

Auguste Pavie boasts that the French takeover of Laos is a "conquest of the hearts" and that officially Laos is only a protectorate, but the end effect is another case of Western colonialism. It does not happen instantly—it is by a series of steps over several years that France asserts control. The sixty years of the French protectorate are not without problems and protests; in particular, French attempts to impose heavy taxes and forced labor inspire a series of rebellions. But by and large the French are able to rule with a relatively light hand (and small staff), in part because they allow many of the traditional rulers, elites, and cultural practices to remain in place. The French abolish slavery but they make little effort to educate most Laotians and they do not install much of an industrial economy; in fact, Laos does not have many natural resources of great value to the French. On the other hand, they do introduce some improvements—in matters of governmental administration, health and sanitation, and public works. Above all, the French unify the various territories and "assemble" and preserve a land that emerges eventually as an independent Laos. But this will occur only after Laos undergoes the occupation of the Japanese during World War II and several years of struggle against the French attempt to reassert control.

1893: Although the French will resort to various administrative reshufflings in the years ahead—claiming that part of Laos is only a protectorate, dividing Laos into two major regions, and so on—Laos is in fact incorporated into France's Indochinese Union, set up in 1887 to include Vietnam and Cambodia.

1895: Kham Souk is installed under the name Zakarine as king (reigns 1895–1904) of Luang Prabang.

September 30, 1895; November 30, 1896: The French issue two decrees on the administration and enforcement of law in Laos.

January 16, 1896: Britain and France reach an agreement, making the Mekong River the border between their respective colonial possessions, Burma and Laos.

1900: The French rename the city of Vieng Chan as Vientiane and make it the administrative capital of their protectorate in Laos. Luang Prabang is allowed its traditional royal family, but the French basically administer it.

1901–1907: The Kha, the indigenous people of the Bolovens Plateau in southern Laos, are aroused by some of their leaders, in particular a messianic religious leader Phou Mi Boun (also known as Bac My), to rebel against the French; their rebellion goes on for several years but is eventually put down.

1902–1907: Between these years, the French and Thailand agree to settle boundaries that allow Laos some limited territory on the west bank of the Mekong River. The result is that Laos is now larger and more unified than it has perhaps ever been.

We must put up with the mud to eat the eels in it.

Traditional Laotian proverb

1904: King Zakarine is succeeded by his eldest son, Sisavang Vong; he will reign until 1959.

1914–1916: In northern Laos, the Lu people, led by Chao Fa Pha Ong Kham, a disgruntled Lu chieftain, rebel along with Chinese Tai people; the French eventually restore order.

1918–1922: A revolt that begins among the Hmong people in southern China and northern Vietnam spreads into northeastern Laos under the leadership of Tiao Pha Patchay but is eventually suppressed.

1923: The French establish an elected Indigenous Consultative Assembly for Laos, which first meets on August 30, but its role is strictly advisory.

1934–1936: Another period of unrest among the Kha people on the Bolovens Plateau.

1940: With the fall of France to the Germans in June, the Japanese reach an understanding with the Vichy regime in France that they can move unhindered into the former French possessions in Indochina. Along with wanting the natural resources of the region, the Japanese want to prevent the Allies from having access to the Nationalist Chinese forces.

November 1940–January 1941: Japan has already signed a treaty of friendship with Thailand, and now the Japanese permit Thailand to seize those parts of Laos west of the Mekong River that Thailand had been forced to cede to France back in 1904. The Treaty of Tokyo formalizes this on May 9, 1941.

July 29, 1941: By now the Japanese are effectively in control of all of French Indochina; on this day the Japanese and Vichy French sign a treaty recognizing this. Most Laotians are not particularly upset or even affected by this new state of affairs, but some go underground to resist the Japanese.

August 29, 1941: Vichy France and King Sisavang Vong of Luang Prabang sign a treaty that places various provinces and regions under a centralized government to be nominally headed by the king; Prince Petsarath becomes prime minister. During the ensuing years the Japanese allow the French flag to fly throughout Indochina, and many Vichy French continue to administer most internal Laotian affairs, but many Laotians are well aware of the weakness of their former French "protectors."

December 22–23, 1944: With most of France now liberated from the Germans and with General Charles de Gaulle now in charge, Free French commandos begin to parachute into northern Laos to establish that the French are going to take a role in resisting the Japanese.

March–August 1945: Worried about the way the war is going, the Japanese on March 9 declare an end to cooperation with the Vichy French collaborators in Laos and intern all the French they can apprehend. Now determined at least to end the role of the French in Indochina, the Japanese encourage the Laotian leaders to declare independence. King Sisavang Vong and his son, Crown Prince Savang Vatthana, however, are pro-French, and it is April 8 before they declare independence. When the crown prince calls for an uprising against the Japanese, the Japanese send him to Saigon and allow Prime Minister Prince Petsarath to run the country. Meanwhile, a struggle for power in postwar Laos comes to the surface; thousands of Vietnamese—long resident in Laos, where the French had recruited them to fill administrative positions—appear to be ready to make a bid for power; many Laotians are ready to side with the Free French forces; other Laotians who have been in exile in Thailand during the war want an independent Laos free of both French and Vietnamese influence.

August 14–18, 1945: The Japanese surrender leads to a number of disturbances in Laos. The Japanese are supposed to retain order until Chinese and British forces replace them, but before these latter can get there some French began to reassert control. On August 18 Prince Petsarath reaffirms the independence of Laos from the French. He appoints a committee made up of members of his family, other elite Laotians, and some Vietnamese who have held positions in Laos; the problem is that some of these people are definitely anti-French, but others still feel that Laos can best obtain its independence with the aid of the French.

Late August–October 10, 1945: At the end of August, small French military units parachute into Laos; they free French colonial officials still interned by the Japanese, move into the capital of Vientiane and the city of Luang Prabang, and make it clear that they intend to reimpose French rule. On August 30 King Sisavang Vong announces that he accepts the resumption of the French protectorate. After Prince Petsarath on September 15 declares the independence and unity of Laos, the king dismisses him from his office as prime minister on October 10.

October 8–30, 1945: Prime Minister Petsarath's younger half-brother Prince Souphanouvong has been living in Vietnam, where he has become a supporter of Ho Chi Minh, the Communist Vietnamese leader, who declared an independent Vietnam in September and who is determined to prevent the French from reasserting their control in Indochina. On October 8 Souphanouvong arrives back in Laos and installs himself as the president of a Committee for Independent Laos and commander of the Laotian liberation army; on October 12 the committee proclaims a provisional constitution and assembly for an independent Laotian government; on October 20, when the king refuses to endorse this, the provisional assembly votes to depose him. On October 30 Souphanaouvong signs an agreement with representatives of Ho Chi Minh that allows units of the Communist Vietminh guerrilla forces to operate in Laos.

November 1945–April 23, 1946: Laos is

plunged into a period of disarray as all the various factions — Vietnamese, Hmong, pro- and anti-communists, royalists, pro-French, genuine pro-independence Laotians, French military–compete for control. The French commit ever larger military forces and gradually push back the Laotians fighting for independence and their Communist Vietnamese supporters. On March 21, 1946, at Thakkek, central Laos, Souphanouvong with his Communist Vietnamese force fights a losing battle against French forces with their tanks and airplanes; he is wounded but survives. The French occupy the major cities, and many of the educated elite who had hoped to govern an independent Laos flee into Thailand, where Prince Petsarath establishes a government-in-exile. Recognizing that he has no other support, Sisavang Vong accepts the new constitution of the assembly and is reinstalled as king, but the country effectively remains a French protectorate.

August 27, 1946: France and Laos sign an agreement worked out by a joint commission that establishes Laos as a constitutional monarchy with a constituent assembly.

November 17, 1946: France and Thailand sign an agreement under which Thailand returns the Lao territories that the Japanese had given to Thailand.

May 11, 1947: The new constitution produced by the assembly is promulgated by the king.

July 19, 1949: France and Laos sign a new agreement that confirms the autonomy of Laos within the French Union and grants Laos greater independence in foreign affairs. The prominent Laotians who have been claiming to be the government-in-exile in Thailand formally disband; many of the leaders return to Laos to enter the new government, but Prince Souphanouvong, now choosing to seek a Communist-led revolution, does not.

August 13–15, 1950: Souphanouvong has moved his headquarters to northern Vietnam where he announces formation of a resistance government, Pathet Lao (Lao Country). Meeting somewhere in the remote border region with Laos, he has himself elected prime minister.

November 21, 1951: Souvanna Phouma's, half brother of Souphanouvong, becomes prime minister of Laos. From now until Souphanouvong is named president in 1975, these two will struggle to determine the future of their country.

April 1953: Vietminh forces from Vietnam invade Laos. The French Air Force flies Laotian troops to the front and the Viet Minh soon retreat back into Vietnam.

October 22, 1953: France signs a treaty recognizing Laos as a sovereign state, although still within the French Union. Moreover, France retains one important right: "the means and the direction of policy proper to the preparation and the assurance of . . . defense."

INDEPENDENT LAOS: 1953–1998

The next forty-five years of Lao history divide into two halves: the first dominated by a Communist-led rebellion, the second by the imposition of a Communist state. The independence granted by the French in 1953 leaves Laos facing crushing economic, political, and military demands. During the first twenty-two years Laos is split by what is essentially a civil war, although it is fought mainly by political maneuvers. When the Communists do finally take power in December 1975, continuing crises involve relations with their neighbors. Underlying all of Laos's problems is the fact that it remains a poor country, with an economy still basically dependent on agriculture (rice in particular); although there are potentially valuable natural resources — gypsum, lead, silver, tin, zinc, and teak and other valuable woods — they have never been fully developed. The most recent Communist leaders struggle to bring their country into the twenty-first century, trying to accommodate their economic and ideology with the traditional Buddhism that still dominates the culture and social life of the mass of Laotians.

December 1953: After the failure of their first invasion, Communist Vietminh forces from Vietnam move into northern Laos and dislodge the small French and Laotian units. This time, the Vietminh are accompanied by the Pathet Lao, who set up their "government" in Sanneua, in northeastern Laos. In the ensuing months, the Pathet Lao make some incursions into central Laos.

May 8–July 20, 1954: An international conference has been meeting at Geneva, Switzerland, to try to resolve conflicts in Korea and Indochina. The Indochinese phase begins on May 8, one day after the French suffer their worst defeat in the war in Vietnam by surrendering at Dien Bien Phu. The agreement finally reached on July 20 means the recognition by the major powers of an independent Laos but left the two northeastern provinces of Laos, Sanneua and Phongsaly, as "regrouping zones" for the Pathet Lao until elections can be held in 1955. The central government is supposed to administer these provinces, but the Pathet Lao will resist all their efforts and actually continue to attack government military outposts.

January 1955: As called for by the Geneva Conference, the International Control Commission (ICC) begins to try to get the warring parties in Laos to come to some agreement.

December 25, 1955: Elections for the National Assembly are held throughout Laos, but the Pathet Lao boycotts them. Instead, the Pathet Lao forces the government of Souvanna Phouma into a continual round of negotiations.

November 2 and 12, 1957: The Vientiane Agreements call for the integration of 1,500 Pathet Lao soldiers into the royal army, the formation of a coalition government, and the return of the two northern provinces to royal control.

July 20–23, 1958: Souphanouvong and one of his aides are now in the coalition cabinet and Pathet Lao members sit in the National Assembly, so the International Control Commission formally adjourns itself on July 20. The government of Souvanna Phouma has been so charged with corruption and mismanagement of finances that he resigns on July 23.

August 18, 1958–October 29, 1959: By this time the Communist North Vietnamese are moving men and arms down through Laotian territory—the Ho Chi Minh Trail—to aid the Vietminh fighting for control of South Vietnam; it is quite clear, too, that the North Vietnamese are supporting the Pathet Lao. A right-wing government takes over in Laos on August 18, 1958, and excludes all former Pathet Lao from its cabinet; when the government arrests Pathet Lao leaders in May 1959, fighting between the Communists and the pro-government forces renews in July. The United States supplies military equipment and Special Forces troops to aid the Laotian government. A United Nations inspection team arrives in mid-September 1959, and King Sisavang Vong dies in October, to be succeeded by his son Savang Vatthana on October 29.

December 31, 1959–December 1960: A group of frustrated politicians and military leaders carry out a coup at the end of December 1959. The king oversees the formation of an interim government until elections are held in April 1960, when the right-wing gains power again; although the new young leaders pledge an end to corruption and nepotism, they will not allow the Pathet Lao to share power. A coup by neutralists led by Captain Kong Le on August 8–9, 1960, overthrows this government and turns it over to Souvanna Phouma, but right-wing General Phoumi Nosavan leads a counter-coup. For several months, Laos is split by several factions, and on December 13–16 General Phoumi actually captures Vientiane, the capital, using U.S.-supplied arms.

January 1961–April 1963: Laos is now torn by civil war, with the Communist North Vietnamese backing one faction and the United States backing another. A cease-fire goes into effect on May 3, leading to a new Geneva Conference (commencing on May 16); the competing Laotian leaders, meeting on the Plain of Jars, finally reach an agreement, a coalition government forms on June 23, and on July 23 the Geneva Agreements declare the neutrality of Laos. The coalition collapses on April 1, 1963.

April 1963–February 1973: Laos spends this decade torn by a civil war marked not just by frequent battles but also by coups and countercoups, charges and countercharges, questionable negotiations and failed agreements; among other results is that one-sixth of the population become refugees. The events in Laos are both parallel and linked to events in Vietnam. The United States not only supplies money and arms to its favored faction, the royalist/conservative government, but also in May 1964 commences bombing of Pathet Lao targets in Laos. Meanwhile, the North Vietnamese and Soviet Union are supplying the Pathet Lao; in fact, the North Vietnamese Communists are effectively directing the revolution. In February 1971, the South Vietnamese military's Operation Lam Son 719 moves into Laos to cut off the Ho Chi Minh Trail, but it ends with their retreat. Finally the negotiations that commence in October 1972 lead to a cease-fire on February 22, 1973, which launches the final stage of the civil war.

September 14, 1973: The cease-fire of February 1973 has been broken by both sides—including bombings by U.S. B-52s. But now a true cease-fire is attained, when Souvanna Phouma agrees to form a coalition government with the Pathet Lao.

The Americans had taught the bandits, and the latter had taught Lao Bi in turn, that any Miao who happened to fall in the hands of the Pathet Lao would be tortured to death in every imaginable manner. One had better commit suicide than let oneself be captured. The Americans' words prove to be more noxious than poisonous leaves.

"Rains in the Jungle," short story by Thao Boun Lin
(1967)

April 1974–November 1975: With the embrace of the two half-brothers, Souvanna Phouma and Souphanouvong, the new coalition government takes office on April 5, 1974. The last U.S. military operations in Laos come on June 4. By this time Souphanouvong and his fellow Pathet Lao Communists are working from within to take over complete power. In conjunction with the final Communist offensive in Vietnam, the Pathet Lao forces recommence military operations against the Royal Laotian Army in February 1975; elements of the North Vietnamese Army move into Laos and position themselves along the borders with Cambodia and Thailand. By August 1975, the Pathet Lao "Revolutionary Administration" takes control of the capital; in the next few weeks the Communists move to control local elections. King Savang Vatthana abdicates on November 29.

December 1–2, 1975: At a secret meeting in Vientiane, the Pathet Lao Communists form the Lao People's Democratic Republic, with Souvanouvong as president and Kaysone Phomvihan (1920–1992) as prime minister. Souvanna Phouma is reduced to being a figurehead "adviser." The Communist takeover of Laos is now complete.

1975–1979: Among those Laotians who have most stoutly resisted the Communist Pathet Lao are the Hmong people, the people who had migrated into Laos from southern China in the eighteenth century. After their defeat by the Pathet Lao in the spring of

1975, some 25,000 Hmong flee into Thailand. Another 60,000 remain in the mountains south of the Plain of Jars. In 1977, Laotian and Vietnamese forces start a campaign to wipe out these Hmong, employing every means including bombing raids and poisons; by the end of 1979, almost all surviving Hmong have fled to Thailand and from there are being resettled in foreign countries; eventually some 150,000 Hmong and other Laotians will settle in the United States.

July 1977–November 23, 1988: Laotian and Vietnamese delegates sign a twenty-five-year Treaty of Friendship and Cooperation on July 18, 1977. It allows for Vietnamese military and civilian "advisers" to take an active part in running Laos; in effect, Laos becomes virtually an adjunct of Vietnam. This results in Laos supporting Vietnam when the latter invades Cambodia in December 1978 and when in turn Vietnam is invaded by China in February-March 1979; this leads to poor relations between Laos and China. Not until the Laotian government announces on November 23, 1988, that all Vietnamese troops have left is Laos free of Vietnam's heavy hand.

June 6, 1984–March 11, 1991: Laos and Thailand have been engaging in an ongoing series of quarrels over their disputed borders for many years—centuries, in fact—and fighting breaks out again on June 6, 1984. This latest dispute leads to on-again, off-again talks between the two countries and occasional open hostilities. On March 11, 1991, the two countries agree to withdraw their forces from disputed villages and this leads to at least a temporary end of hostilities.

February 1985: The first joint U.S.-Lao mission begins what will become an on-going search for U.S. personnel missing in action during the Vietnam-Laos conflict.

November 30, 1987: After a decade of hostile relations, Laos and China agree to restore diplomatic relations.

December 10, 1989: General Vang Pao, leader of the Hmong resistance who is at this time based in Thailand, announces the formation of United Laotian National Liberation Front as a government-in-exile. In ensuing years he will attempt to mount several operations but with no success (and eventually he settles in the United States).

August 13–15, 1991: A new constitution is ratified by the Supreme People's Assembly. Kaysone Phomvihan is elected president to replace the ailing Souphanouvong, thus marking a new phase in the history of Laos.

August 16, 1993: A joint Norwegian-Swedish group signs an agreement to construct the largest and most expensive public works project ever in Laos, the Nam Theun II dam and hydroelectric project; to be located in the highlands of eastern Laos, it is expected to generate enough electricity to earn the equivalent of three-quarters of Laos's total annual imports. However, in the years that follow, the project proves so controversial, primarily because of its impact on the environment, that its construction continues to be postponed.

April 8, 1994: The Friendship Bridge linking Laos and Thailand is officially opened; spanning the Mekong River, it links with Laos nine miles east of Vientiane. It is expected to greatly stimulate Laos's economy, which remains strongly dependent on Thailand.

May 18, 1995: The United States announces an end to its twenty-year-old trade embargo on Laos. Many of the Hmong and Laotians living in the United States protest this on the grounds that the government of Laos represses the popular will and abuses human rights.

July 1996: In an attempt to pacify the ongoing unrest among various elements of their population, government leaders in Vientiane call on Buddhist monks to cooperate in promoting "a cultural renaissance." This is part of a general shift among Lao leaders to deemphasize rigid communism and promote nationalism and traditional culture.

July 23, 1997: Laos joins the Association of Southeast Asian Nations (ASEAN).

August–December 1997: With the collapse of Thailand's currency and the general economic crisis sweeping through Southeast Asia, Laos's own currency, the *kip*, also declines greatly (60 percent since 1996) and its already shaky economy is further weakened.

December 21, 1997: Laos holds a general election—its fourth since the Communists took over in December 1975—for the 99 members of its National Assembly. A 99 percent turnout of voters is reported. There is only one legal party in Laos, the Lao People's Revolutionary Party.

February 23–26, 1998: Laos's newly elected National Assembly meets and elects Khamthay Sipohandone as the country's new president and Sisavant Keobuphan as the new prime minister.

Malaysia

PREHISTORIC MALAYSIA: 75,000 B.C.–A.D. 200

During what geologists call the Pleistocene epoch (approximately 1,800,000–8000 B.C.), Malaysia and its offshore islands are joined by a continental shelf (known as the Sunda Shelf) to the Indochinese peninsula and the islands of Indonesia. During these hundreds of thousands of years, as the earth's sea level alternately rises and lowers, Malaysia's coastal lands are intermittently covered or exposed. Although hominids of the *Homo erectus* species apparently made their way across the Sunda Shelf to the Indonesian islands of Java and Sumatra, no fossils of this early species are known in Malaysia. (There have been a few finds of stone tools at Koto Tampan in peninsular Malaysia that some scholars date to as far back as 73,000 B.C., but most date this site closer to 30,000 B.C.) It is not until about 38,000 B.C. that the first hominid remains appear in Malaysia, and by then they are of the species *Homo sapiens*. Although the origins of these first Malaysians are uncertain, they are almost certainly Australoids (Australo-Melanesians), ancestors of the several mixed-Mongoloid peoples who live to this day throughout Southeast Asia and the Pacific. In Malaysia these people are known as the *orang asli* (indigenous people); to anthropologists the most populous group are known as the Negritos (formerly called the Semang); they are generally characterized by their dark coloring, small stature, and tightly curled hair. By about 6000 B.C. the sea level has essentially receded for the last time, leaving the land forms of Malaysia and most of the rest of Southeast Asia much as they are to this day. Starting about 2000–1500 B.C. a major change begins to occur with the arrival of two groups of Mongoloid peoples in the Malay Peninsula. The first group are most likely from southern China and/or Thailand; they will remain largely in the interior as agriculturists. The second group are from islands to the east and north (possibly Borneo and the Philippines); linguistically these new Malaysians are considered Austronesians, relatives of the people who, starting about 3000 B.C., moved out from Taiwan to settle throughout much of the Philippines, Indonesia, New Zealand, many of the Pacific islands, and Madagascar. As various Mongoloid peoples make their way into Malaysia, becoming more numerous and possibly more active, the Australoids are in general being isolated or pushed to the interior of the region; gradually, however, there will be considerable intermixture of the two peoples, leading to the modern Malays. During some two thousand or so years, Malaysia passes through several cultural stages that reveal increasingly closer ties between the new Malaysians and the cultural phases of the rest of Southeast Asia.

38,000–2000 B.C.: At the Niah Caves in Sarawak (north central Borneo, now part of the Malaysia Federation) a long sequence of stone tools, animal bones, and human burials reflects continuous habitation here. The earliest find, however, is simply a human skull.

26,000–16,000 B.C.: Stone tools unique to Southeast Asia of this period are found near Tingkayu in eastern Sabah, Borneo (now part of the Malaysia Federation).

12,000–5000 B.C.: During this period, humans are buried in the Niah Caves. Some are accompanied by apparently prized objects (such as a rhinoceros bone "pillow" and a shell with red ochre).

11,000–1000 B.C.: The Hoabinhian stone tool industry (so named after Hoa Binh, the site in Vietnam where the first of its distinctive flaked pebble tools have been found) appears in Malaysia. The Hoabinhian people of Malaysia appear mostly to inhabit inland rock shelters (although some large shell middens along the coast also have Hoabinhian tools). The major sites include Gua Cha (where the people bury twenty-seven of their dead over several thousand years), Kota Tongkat, Gua Gunung Runtuh, Gua Peraling, and Gua Chawas. The Hoabinhian people of Malaysia, Australo-Melanesians, are hunters and food gatherers and do not practice agriculture; however, they may encourage the growth of plants such as yams by using their tools to prune away unwanted vegetation.

8000–5000 B.C.: Hunters occupy the Madai Caves in eastern Sabah, Borneo; they make stone tools, eat large amounts of shellfish, and hunt such animals as the orangutan, cattle, and rhinoceros.

2000–1000 B.C.: Starting in the late third millennium, a new phase of Neolithic culture emerges in northern and central Malay Peninsula; known as the Ban Kao culture (from the site in Thailand with especially rich remains), its material assemblage includes pottery (distinctive tripod vessels and bell-mouthed jars), adzes, bark-cloth beaters, and bracelets; the people cultivate some plants, possibly including rice. It is generally believed that this culture is introduced by people coming into the Malay Peninsula from somewhere in southern China or mainland Southeast Asia (most likely Thailand); they are a Mongoloid people who speak some variety of an Austroasiatic language (related to the Mon-Khmer languages). However, this Ban Kao culture may not depend entirely on new migrants but may be developed among settled people; in any case it is not uniform throughout Malaysia. One site in Malaysia with especially striking remains of this Ban Kao culture is Gua Cha, also a site of the preceding Hoabinhian culture; its Neolithic remains date to about 1500–1000 B.C. As these Mongoloid people establish settlements, they begin to displace the hunter-gatherer Australoids (Australo-Melanesians). Some of these *orang asli* (indigenous people) will gradually pull back into the forested, mountainous interior of the Malaysian peninsula; at least one group of these Australoids apparently mixes with the new Mongoloid peoples to produce the ancestors of the present-day Senoi people who inhabit the interior of Malaysia. In any case, most of the people who inhabit the interior of the Malay peninsula will remain speakers of Austroasiatic languages.

2000–500 B.C.: At the caves of Niah and Lubang Angin at Sarawak, Borneo (now part of the Malaysia Federation), people—many wrapped in bamboo strips or bark cloth, some in log coffins—are buried in shallow pits; along with the bodies are quite elaborate pottery and (from the end of this period) even some textiles, glass beads, and iron fragments.

1500–500 B.C.: Overlapping the settlement of the Malay Peninsula by the Austroasiatic peoples from the mainland, another Southern Mongoloid people move into the Malay Peninsula. They are descendants of people probably originally from southern China but who, having spent many hundreds of years on Taiwan and probably on other Southeast Asian islands such as the Philippines and Borneo, are now moving into the Malay Peninsula. (These people were sometimes known as the Proto-Malays but today are more generally called Austronesians.) Some at least bring with them a Neolithic culture based on agriculture; it is most likely that these people introduce the cultivation of dry rice and millet into Malaysia. Unlike the previous inhabitants of the Malay Peninsula, however, they are a sea-oriented people, more open to movement and trade.

1000–300 B.C.: Pottery, shell ornaments, fish bones, and the expected stone tools of this period attest to occupation of the Bukit Tengkorak rock shelter in Sabah, Borneo. Also found here is obsidian, volcanic stone that may have been imported all the way from the island of Fiji; this and other finds at Bukit Tengkorak suggest a maritime-based economy.

300 B.C.–A.D. 200: The Austronesian Mongoloids who have settled in the Malay Peninsula appear to come to the fore, at least around the coastal regions. Although there may be some new migrants, most are probably descendants of the earlier migrants and are now simply making more contacts with their Asian neighbors. It is also possible that these new people are beginning to adopt the cultivation of wet rice. In any case, bronze and iron technology is introduced into Malaysia at this time, and thus the main sites are regarded as belonging to the Dong Son culture of Southeast Asia; so named after its prime site in northern Vietnam, the Dong Son culture is characterized by its use of copper and bronze, high-status burials, and the first appearance of iron in Southeast Asia. In particular, the Dong Son culture is distinguished by its bronze drums; some are miniatures but others are as big as forty inches in diameter; they are highly decorated with both geometric and representational figures; they were apparently used for ceremonial-religious purposes. It appears that most of the bronze drums found in Malaysia are imported from Vietnam, but the local Malaysians do begin to make various tools, weapons, ornaments, bells, and other artifacts from bronze.

In the later years of this Dong Son culture in Malaysia—at least by A.D. 1–200—iron also is being used to make axes, knives, sickles, spearheads, and other artifacts. The technology also appears to have been imported from Vietnam, but the actual objects are being made by local Malaysian ironsmiths. Contemporary with the ironmaking of this period in Malaysia are graves lined with stone slabs; in addition to the iron tools found in these graves, there are glass beads and jewelry, bronze bowls, and pottery.

EARLY KINGDOMS: A.D. 200–1400

During the first centuries of this period, local evidence of happenings in Malaysia comes mostly from archaeological finds. But the Malay Peninsula, with its abundance of natural resources, is located on maritime routes that at least by the fifth century are used by traders going back and forth between China and India. Thus, in the absence of court chronicles and remains such as are found in other parts of Asia, information on the early history of Malaysia is based on accounts of maritime trade travelers and Buddhists on pilgrimage to India. Although Chinese, Indian, and Arab chronicles provide a wealth of accounts, these must be carefully scrutinized for chronological and historical accuracy.

During this period, cultural influences from India in particular are adapted to local custom in the trade centers and courts, where elements of Hinduism and Buddhism are assimilated. From the eighth to the twelfth centuries the Srivijaya trading state, based in Palembang on Sumatra, is believed to have spread its influence over the Malay Peninsula, although records of this are scant. It will not be until the rise of Islamic Malacca (c. 1400) that the better documented history of Malaysia begins.

3d century A.D.: The prevailing material culture in Malaysia remains the Dong Son type; both bronze and iron are used. Malaysian trade links with India are by now well established, and Indian merchants are appearing in the north of the peninsula.

5th century: There are records of Chinese Buddhist pilgrims making their way by sea to India and some presumably put in at Malaysia. Chinese chronicles offer evidence of shell trade on the Malay Peninsula. Evidence also suggests that Malaysian tin is being exported to India.

7th century: There is evidence of the export of iron and gold from Sarawak, Borneo, to other areas of Southeast Asia.

8th–12th centuries: In southeastern Sumatra, a group of towns, centered around Palembang, conduct the trading "empire" of Srivijaya. (670 is usually the date given for its founding.) It appears that some coastal towns in western Malaysia are linked to these trading operations but there is little hard evidence.

9th century: At Kedah, in northwestern Malaysia, a monastery and temple monuments dating from some time in this century show Indian influence.

12th century: The increase of Chinese shipping in the Malacca Straits disperses Malay authority as independent ports established in the peninsular Malay states negotiate directly with the Chinese.

Late 13th century: Chieftains from southern Siam control states in northern Malay Peninsula.

1351: The rise of the Ayudhya Kingdom in Siam brings greater pressure on northern Malayan states to pay homage, beginning a conflict that continues for centuries.

Late 14th century: Stone inscription found at Trengganu is the earliest Islamic document found on the Malay Peninsula.

1390: Paramesvara (?—1413/14), possibly a Sumatran prince fleeing Palembang, leaves Temasek (modern-day Singapore) where he has founded a settlement, and reestablishes himself on the Malay Peninsula.

While you carry the Raja's burden on your head, don't forget to keep your own bundle under your arm.

Malayan proverb

RISE OF MALAY STATES: 1400–1824

The founding of Malacca may have occurred as early as 1400; although reliable historical records of this powerful Malay center are sparse, the state's heritage and accomplishments are described in Tomé Pires's Portuguese treatise *Suma Oriental* (1563) and extolled in the stories of the Malay literary chronicle, the *Sejarah Melayu*. Malacca sends tribute to China, to the Majapahit in Java, and to the Ayudhya in Siam, in exchange for protection and assistance. Efficient states-manship and the prestige of rulers of exalted, if mythical, lineage contribute to the hegemony achieved by Malacca. Islam is adopted in the early fifteenth century; Malacca becomes a center of Islamic learning and a model of Muslim prosperity to the rest of the archipelago. Kite-flying is a favorite pastime in the sultanates that develop.

After the fall of Malacca to Portugal, the court is reestablished at Johor. The Malaccan sultanate of Perak, which is rich in tin deposits, arises on the western coast of the peninsula. Malayan states on the northern peninsula are under vassalage to the Siamese Ayudhya kingdom, which provides protection and patronage; conflict inevitably ensues. At the same time, Malay culture expands throughout these kingdoms, and a common language, tradition, and belief system are maintained. Johor's principal enemies in the early seventeenth century are the Aceh and the Portuguese, resulting in an alliance with the Dutch, who begin their trading ventures in the area at this time. Johor's assistance in the Dutch assault on Malacca is rewarded with trade privileges and protection, and soon the state replaces Dutch Malacca as an international trade center. However, Johor feels the strain of Dutch trade restrictions, as well as pressure from Siam; a regicide further weakens the kingdom.

Early 15th century: Paramesvara is credited with founding the port of Malacca under the protection of China; the center of maritime power in the area shifts from Sumatra to Malacca. About 1414, Megat Iskandar Syah assumes power, ruling to 1424. [He was probably the son of Paramesvara but some regard him to be Paramesvara and a convert to Islam.] Whoever is in charge, Malacca's borders, economy, and influence greatly expand.

c. 1446—c. 1459: Reign of Sultan of Malacca Muzaffar Syah, who succeeds in repulsing attacks from Siam and extends Malacca's boundaries.

1456–1498: Tun Perak is *bendahara* (chief minister) under whose leadership Siamese invasion is repulsed and Malacca becomes an empire, controlling Pahang, the area from Perak to Johor on the west coast, Riau-Lingga, Singapore, and areas of coastal Sumatra.

1460: Mansur Syah (dies 1477), second Sultan of Malacca, marries a Chinese princess

who brings to Malacca a large court. Through Chinese and Malay intermarriage, subsequent generations create a prospering and educated society based in Malacca and combining Chinese and Malay cultural traditions.

1488–1530: Reign of Sultan Mahmud Syah, who is ousted by the conquering Portuguese. The lineage is reestablished in Johor and Perak.

1511: Portuguese conquest of Malacca; Sultan Mahmud and his son Ahmad flee to Bentan on Riau Archipelago; Mahmud has his son killed and reestablishes the sultanate. Bentan becomes a successful port.

1526: Portuguese destroy the sultanate at Bentan; Mahmud flees to Sumatra, where he dies two years later.

1528?–1549?: Reign of Sultan Muzaffar Syah, Sultan of Perak. A son of Sultan Mahmud, this Malaccan prince creates a court reflecting that of the former Malaccan kingdom.

1530–1536: Sultan Alauddin Riayat Syah succeeds his father Mahmud; he reestablishes the Malaccan dynasty and thriving port at Johor.

1549?–1577?: Reign of the Sultan of Perak, Mansur Syah, who had been raised at the court at Johor until his father Muzaffar's death. The kingdom prospers from its wealth in tin deposits.

1613–1620: The Sumatran kingdom of Aceh under Sultan Iskandar Muda (reigns 1607–1636) sacks Malayan states. The Aceh offer tin contracts in Perak to the Dutch Trading Company (VOC).

1640–1641: The Dutch seize Malacca to control trade in the Straits and in the Malayan tin-producing states. Abdul Jalil, Sultan of Johor, assists in ousting the Portuguese from Malacca. The port fails to recover its former prosperity.

1641: Dutch mediate a treaty of nonaggression between Johor and Aceh.

1641: The VOC demands exclusive rights to tin purchase in Perak, setting off a period of strife between the Dutch and Aceh.

1673: Johor is destroyed by the Sumatran kingdom of Jambi; Sultan Abdul Jalil (1623–1677) relocates to Pahang, just to the northeast. Laksamana Tul Abdul Jalil, the sultan's minister, reestablishes Johor and develops a powerful family position in the sultanate.

1699: Sultan Mahmud, a youthful tyrant lacking leadership, is murdered by his nobles, ending a probably mythical lineage that was claimed to have direct ties to Alexander the Great. The regicide severs links with the former glory of Malaccan lineage and ends unity in the kingdom.

Late 17th century: Mingankabau, a matrilineal and agricultural people from Sumatra, migrate to unpopulated areas of the southern Malay Peninsula.

c. 1700: Selangor, on the west coast, has a Buginese sultan, from the seafaring tribe originally from Sulawesi (Celebes).

1704: The Sultan of Brunei cedes most of present-day Sabah to the Sultan of Sulu, the island kingdom to the north, in exchange for assistance in quelling a rebellion in the area.

1715: In a conflict over compensation for assistance in a succession dispute in Kedah, on the northwestern coast of the peninsula, Buginese migrants invade and pillage Kedah.

1718: Raja Kecil, claiming to be the murdered Sultan Mahmud's son, captures Johor and proclaims himself ruler; the Bugis soon recapture Johor and in 1721 install Malay Prince Sulaiman as figurehead ruler while a Bugi is made heir to the throne. Raja Kecil retreats to Siak (Sumatra) where he launches unsuccessful attacks on Bugis.

1743: Selangor, Lingii, and Kelang come under control of the Riau Bugis, who competed with other Buginese groups for these areas rich in tin.

1746: The VOC concludes an agreement with the state of Perak, which is divided by succession conflicts between Sultan Muzaffar and Raja Iskandar. A small outpost with Dutch troops to oversee tin distribution is established.

1750–1760: Sultan Mansur (1741–1793) of Trengganu, in the eastern central coast of the peninsula, resides in Riau-Johor to lead opposition to Bugis; upon his return to Trengganu Mansur promotes Malay unity.

1752–1765: The Sultanate of Perak, who renews the agreement with the VOC, guaranteeing protection from external attack as well as internal threat. Peace and prosperity ensue. Raja Iskandar, now sultan of Perak, adopts the name Iskander Zul-karnain (Alexander the Great), recalling the claim to that lineage.

1779: Death of Sultan Muhammad Jiwa, ruler of Kedah, who establishes an organized administration based on Islamic codes of law and traditional custom.

1784: Bugis ambitions for dominance in the area end with a failed attack on Riau.

1786: British establish a trading post at Penang off the northwest coast of the peninsula, under Captain Francis Light.

1794: Malacca comes under British rule.

1818: The British governor of Malacca, Colonel William Farquhar, signs a trade treaty with the sultan in Riau.

1819: Thomas Stamford Raffles signs an agreement with Singapore's minister Temenggong Abdul Rahman, establishing a trading port on Singapore for the British East India Company, ending the possibility of Malay commercial dominance in the area.

EUROPEAN PRESENCE: 1824–1957

In the face of growing European competition and pressure from the Straits Settlements, British colonialism in Malaysia becomes formalized with the Treaty of Pangkor, in which it gains control over local governments. These are administered by the Residential System, under which local customs are respected, and the cooperation of the ruling class is enlisted to fulfill British goals of export trade profitability. By the early twentieth century, Britain secures its financial interests with a colonial authority that enforces the law, a communications and transportation system, a Western-style administrative system, and an immigration policy that provides the manpower needed for the export industries. Chinese workers are dominant in tin mining and commerce, whereas rubber production is assigned to Indians. Racial divisions are to be key in the formation of a unified independent state out of the prosperous colony of British Malaya.

1824: The Treaty of London divides the colonized areas between England and Holland; England controls Penang, Malacca, and Singapore, while Holland controls parts of Indonesia, including Beng Kulu in Sumatra. The Johor-Riau kingdom is divided between Holland and England. Riau becomes the Sultanate of Lingga, and Temenggong Abdul Rahman becomes a leading Malay power.

1824: High-grade ore is discovered in Sarawak; Brunei chieftains oversee Dayak workers.

1826: Formation of the Straits Settlements, comprising the island of Penang, Singapore, and Malacca under the administrative control of the British in Calcutta.

1830: Dayak workers rebel against Pangiran Makota, the Bruneian chieftain overseeing ore mining in Sarawak.

1839: James Brooke arrives in Sarawak; the sultan of Brunei requests his assistance in quashing the Dayak rebellion. In return, Brooke requests the governorship of Sarawak.

September 1841: Brunei cedes Sarawak and its dependencies to James Brooke, who proclaims himself raja in 1846.

1862–1895: Temenggong Abu Bakar, Maharajah, and Sultan bring progressive rule to Johor, developing its agricultural economy and attracting European investments.

1867: The Straits Settlements become Crown colonies under administrative control of London's Colonial Office.

1873: Britain declares the western Malay states protectorates.

1874: The Treaty of Pangkor establishes the Residential System under which administrative power at the district level is in the hands of British officials.

1875: The Malay Revolt and other uprisings in Perak protesting the Residential System are quashed. The First Resident of Perak, J. W. W. Birch, who had been at odds with the sultan, is murdered; British troops execute three chiefs and exile Sultan Abdullah.

1877: Much of present-day Sabah in North Borneo is leased from the Sultan of Sulu by Anglo-Austrian business interests to establish trading posts.

1880: Britain takes over North Borneo trading interests, founds the British North Borneo Company, establishes sovereignty over the area, and levies taxes on the indigenous population. This policy incites rebellions.

1887: Raja Yusuf is proclaimed Sultan of Perak by Britain.

1891: Abdul Rahman (Datuk Bahaman) spearheads the opposition known as the Pahang War, a series of rebellions in that state set off by new Resident policies, particularly those that limit the regional chieftains' ability to collect revenues.

July 1896: In an attempt to centralize British power in Malaya, Britain forms the Federated Malay States, bringing Perak, Selangor, Negeri Sembilan (Nine States), and Pahang under British control. A Resident-General oversees the Residents and governs in consultation with Malay State Councils, whose role is advisory.

1909: Kedah, Perlis, Kelantan, and Terengganu reject subordination to Siam and accept British advisors, forming the Unfederated States.

1914: Johor joins the Federated Malay States.

1926: Kesatuan Melayu Singapura (KMS), the Singapore Malay Union, is formed and gains support in the Straits Settlements.

April 1930: The Malayan Communist Party (MCP) is formed.

1938: The Kesatuan Melayu Mulu (Union of Young Malays), a nationalist left-wing splinter group of KMS, is formed.

1939: KMS holds pan-Malayan conference.

December 8, 1941: Japan begins invasion of Malaya through Kedah and Kelantan in the north. The rapid advance and conquest undermines Britain's role as protector. Chinese, Communists, and other groups form the Malayan People's Anti-Japanese Army, a guerrilla group supported by the British army.

February 15, 1942: The Allies capitulate in Singapore. Japan unites the Malay Peninsula with Sumatra in the Greater East Asia Co-Prosperity Sphere, interning British officials and abolishing its administrative systems.

August 1943: The Unfederated States are ceded to Thailand by Japan as a reward for declaring war on the Allies. They are returned to their pre-war status in August 1945.

August 15, 1945: Japanese surrender to Allies; British return to administer Malaysia.

January 1946: Presentation of the Malaya Union Plan, formed to bring the Malay states and immigrant populations under a unified administration under British sovereignty, with equal rights for all races, and maintaining sultanates' rule.

March 1946: The United Malays National Organization is formed at the Pan-Malayan congress in Kuala Lumpur. Datuk Onn Ja'afar, Chief Minister of Johor, its elected president, opposes the colonial regime.

April 1, 1946: The Malaya Union Plan is inaugurated.

Mid-1946: Sabah becomes a British crown colony.

February 1, 1948: Anglo-Malay negotiations revoke the Malaya Union Plan and establish Federation of Malaya; a strong federal government and executive council are to govern a unified and integrated society in which the sovereignty of sultans over states is recognized. Citizenship is restricted to Malays and non-Malays who have been residents for a minimum of fifteen years and speak either Malay or English. Chinese and Indian populations are not represented in the negotiations.

June 18, 1948: The Malayan Communist Emergency is declared as a result of guerrilla actions and violence against Europeans by the Malayan Communist Party, which is supported by trade unions and by the Chinese working class who feel betrayed by the citizenship laws of the Federation.

February 1949: The Malayan Chinese Association (MCA) is formed under leadership of Tan Cheng Lock.

1949: The British governor of Sarawak is assassinated.

1951: Anthony Brooke abandons claim to Sarawak; as a British colony, Sarawak prospers in oil and timber trade, and health and education services are improved.

Datuk Onn Ja'afar resigns from UMNO to form Independence of Malaya Party. Tunku

Abdul Rahman takes over UMNO leadership and forms electoral alliance with MCA.

October 6, 1951: British High Commissioner Sir Henry Gurney is murdered by MCP guerrillas.

1954: The Malayan Indian Congress joins the UNMO Alliance.

1955: The Alliance wins a federal election and calls for independence.

August 15, 1957: Merdeka (Independence) Constitution is ratified; on August 31 independence is declared. A constitutional monarchy is formed, with Tunku Abdul Rahman as prime minister; a king is to be chosen every five years from among the nine sultans. The eleven states have their own elected governments and elected representatives to the national *Dewan Negara* (Senate) and *Dewan Rakyat* (People's House). Malay would become the national language within ten years.

Rest in peace, my son
Although our rice-fields are flooded,
The rain comes from God,
A blessing pours down in deluge.

And day comes, as if it does not bring light,
Listen,
The toads have ceased to call,
To-morrow will bring sunshine,
And our padi will flourish again.

"Dialogue," poem by Kassim Ahmad (mid-20th century)

INDEPENDENCE: 1957–1998

Unity in the ethnically, economically, and politically diverse new nation is predicated on achieving racial balance and goodwill (*muhibbah*) between the races. Tensions between Malays and Chinese populations, and the rise of fundamentalism among the Malays, who are predominantly Muslim, as well as tensions between Malay and Indian communities, are challenges that the government seeks to overcome with reforms of the New Economic Policy. An abundance of natural resources, as well as a booming tourist industry and foreign investment in manufacturing, are the bases for a thriving economy that promotes social stability.

Malay culture is a distinctive synthesis of influences, with roots in indigenous traditions, Hinduism, Islam, and Western culture. The principal art forms on the peninsula, besides music, dancing and literature, are the decorative arts. Characteristic Malay artistry is expressed in rattan and basket weaving, batik cloth, woodcarving, and work in silver.

1957: Britain grants Malaya independence.

1958: MCP guerrillas surrender in large numbers, succumbing to pressure from security forces.

July 31, 1960: With the ending of the Communist threat, the Communist Emergency is lifted.

September 16, 1963: Singapore, Sarawak, and Sabah (British North Borneo) are incorporated into Malaya to form the Federation of Malaysia, with the intention of bringing political and economic unity to the area. The inclusion of Sarawak and Sabah triggers a conflict (*Konfrontasi*) with Indonesia, which has an interest in North Borneo.

1965: Riots in Singapore result from racial tension with the peninsular states.

August 5, 1965: A constitutional amendment is passed allowing Singapore to secede from the Federation of Malaysia. Singapore's opposition movement and its large Chinese population, which affect the racial balance of the new nation, had undermined Malaysian stability.

August 1966: Agreement with Indonesia in which Sabah and Sarawak are to decide by election to join the Federation, thus ending Konfrontasi.

August 1967: Association of Southeast Asian Nations (ASEAN) is formed with Malaysia, Singapore, Indonesia, the Philippines, and Thailand to assert regional neutrality and co-operation.

1967: Sabah holds its first state election, bringing the Sabah Alliance party into power.

May 13, 1969: In the wake of national elections, in which the Alliance loses its majority, racial tensions between Chinese and Malay populations erupt into violence in Kuala Lumpur. A national emergency is declared and all opposition to the UMNO suppressed.

January 1970: The National Consultative Council is formed to represent all segments of society in decision making by consensus (*muafakat*).

August 31, 1970: A new coalition of parties, the Barisan Nasional (National Front), is formed under Tun Abdul Razak. A statement of national unity, *Rukunegara*, is proclaimed.

1970: New Economic Policy is introduced to improve economic conditions for *bumiputras*, the Malay and indigenous populations, through plans for development that include racial quotas and financial assistance over a period of twenty-five years. This special treatment to Malays arouses resentment among other racial groups, particularly Chinese and Indian; by its conclusion in 1990, the policy fails to reach its goal of 30 percent Malay participation in the economy, but has been successful in creating a class of Malay businessmen by the mid-1990s.

February 1971: Parliamentary rule is restored; constitutional amendments prohibit public discussion of the status of the Malay population or of Islam as the national religion. Minimum quotas are set for Malay and indigenous students in professional schools.

1974: Barisan Nasional wins landslide victory in national elections, giving popular support

to policies aimed at creating unity in Malaysia.

1975: Berjaya, a multiracial opposition party, wins the state election in Sabah with the support of UMNO, and joins the Barisan.

January 14, 1976: At the death of Tun Razak, Datuk Hussein Onn takes over the government, with Dr. Mahathir Mohamad as deputy prime minister. Hussein Onn asserts central control over state policy by removing from office the chief ministers of Perak, Malacca, and Kelantan.

1981: Dr. Mahathir Mohamad becomes president of UMNO and succeeds as prime minister.

1982 and 1986: Mahathir, a medical doctor, wins landslide victories for Barisan Nasional coalition. In his years in office, he will lead Malaysia to unprecedented levels of prosperity and provide the various groups who comprise Malaysia—ethnic Malays, Chinese, and Indians—a new sense of national identity and union.

1987: Government fear of opposition and racial tension leads to arrests under the Internal Security Act.

1991: The New Development Policy replaces the patronage of the New Economic Policy with business incentives to promote industry while maintaining the goal of 30 percent Malay ownership of national wealth.

May 1992: Malaysia Mining Corporation, a major producer of tin, announces that it will discontinue tin mining operations due to low prices on the global market and rising production costs.

February 4, 1994: The nine sultans who rule Malaysia choose former diplomat Sultan Jaafar bin Abdul Rahman as the tenth king, replacing Azlan Shah of Perak, for the rotating five-year position established at independence.

December 18, 1995: Malaysia, as a member of the Association of Southeast Asian Nations, signs a pact declaring the area from Myanmar to Indonesia a nuclear-free zone. This is an effort to prevent southeast Asian nations from acquiring or producing their own nuclear weapons.

July 1997: Malaysia's currency, the *ringgit*, and its financial institutions are moving into a serious decline in the wake of the collapse of Thailand's economy. Malaysian Prime Minister Mahathir Mohamad, in public and international forums, tries to blame the crisis on foreign money speculators, but he is roundly criticized by the international community. The fact is that Malaysia's economy, like those of many of the Asian nations, is based on too many questionable loans and shaky financial policies.

January 1998: After months of a collapsing currency and economy, the Malaysian government agrees to austerity measures laid down by the International Monetary Fund.

September 1, 1998: Prime Minister Mahathir, in an effort to insulate Malaysia from the currency crisis sweeping the global economy, initiates capital controls to protect the *ringgit*.

September 2, 1998: Mahathir dismisses (as of September 3) his deputy and finance minister, Datuk Seri Anwar Ibrahim, who has been charging Mahathir with mishandling the nation's economy. This leads to a mounting series of protests and demonstrations by Anwar and his supporters.

September 20, 1998: After leading some 35,000 of his supporters through the streets of Kuala Lumpur, Anwar is arrested at his home and taken to jail. He will later claim that he was beaten by the police.

October 5, 1998: Anwar, appearing in court with a neck brace (which he claims is needed because of beatings by the police), is denied bail. He is to be tried on November 2 for charges of corruption and sodomy.

Myanmar (Burma)

PREHISTORIC MYANMAR: 400,000–200 B.C.

Myanmar's prehistoric phase of many thousands of years presents a special challenge because relatively little is known about it, there having been scant archaeological work in recent years. It is agreed that early hominids (*Homo erectus*) were present in Myanmar as early as 400,000 B.C., but there is then a large gap—at least in present knowledge—before the appearance of *Homo sapiens* and an identifiable late Paleolithic culture in Myanmar. At least by 10,000 B.C., however, Myanmar does seem to be participating in the cultural developments that pass throughout Southeast Asia—what are generally characterized as Neolithic and Bronze Age cultures. Not until about 200 B.C. will a recognizably distinctive society emerge in this region. Up to this time, however, one element seems clear: the Irrawaddy River is already the backbone of what will one day be known as Myanmar.

400,000–10,000 B.C.: This long period, the Middle and Upper Pleistocene of geologists, the Paleolithic of archaeologists, is known as the Anyathian period in Myanmar. The main sites are along the Irrawaddy River but there are also sites in the Kachin Hills in the north and the Shan region to the south and east. At least until the final phase, the hominids who make the stone (and fossil wood) tools of the basic chopper and hand-adze variety are *Homo erectus*; the limited finds at present do not allow for demonstrating much development of these tool types across the millenniums. By about 100,000 B.C. archaic *Homo sapiens* and then modern *Homo sapiens* move in, but their tools are also relatively basic.

10,000–3000 B.C.: Tools made of unifacial (one-sided) flaked river pebbles suggest that Myanmar is sharing in the culture complex widespread throughout much of Southeast Asia, the Hoabinhian culture (so named after its prime site in northern Vietnam). A variety of stone tools begin to appear at various sites, most still along the Irrawaddy River Valley but also in other regions of Myanmar. By the final stage, a full-scale Neolithic culture is in place with people practicing at least limited food cultivation, making pottery, and weaving rope and mats.

One of the best known of the late-Neolithic sites is the Padah-lin Caves (in central Myanmar on the western margin of the Shan Plateau), which seem to house a workshop for stone implements. In addition to the many stone tools, potsherds, bones, and other finds, one of the caves has fine paintings on the rock walls; done in red ochre, they are similar to cave paintings known from the Upper Paleolithic caves in Europe.

1500 B.C.: In the Shan region, people are making socketed weapons and implements and bronze adzes, wedges, and spear points. Although metals are increasingly used in Myanmar, most of the inhabitants continue to use stone and other materials for their tools and implements.

500 B.C.: A Tibeto-Burman Mongoloid people, traditionally known as Pyu, enter the upper part of the Irrawaddy River valley. In the next few centuries they gradually move southward, gaining control over the valley as they establish their settlements.

300 B.C.: Some people in Myanmar seem to be participating in the Dong Son culture (so named after its prime site in northeastern Vietnam); its most distinctive and striking production are bronze drums decorated with incised geometric and representational (animals, humans) designs. Dong Son-style drums, almost certainly imported, are found at sites in Myanmar.

200 B.C.: The Pyu people's settlements begin to suggest an emergent "urban" culture in Myanmar. They are using iron as well as bronze for various implements.

FORMATIVE PERIOD: 200 B.C.–A.D. 1044

During this period, there is still not a clear line between stone age, bronze age, and iron age cultures—literally, all three materials are being used for tools and implements and all three stages of culture exist simultaneously in many parts of Myanmar. Typical of Southeast Asia of this period, small settlements/villages occasionally cooperate but frequently contest with one another. First to take center stage are the many Pyu cities that appear in central and northern Myanmar; although by no means as large or complex as cities such as ancient Rome, some are surprisingly ambitious. They have solid outer walls, fortifications, "palaces," temples, monasteries, and extensive dwellings; brick is a common building material. Although there are legendary allusions to Pyu "dynasties" of this period, little specific is known of this urban society, but it must have been fairly well organized to support these cities. (Many of these cities remain inhabited for many centuries beyond this period and in fact prefigure Myanmar cities of the centuries right to the present.) Surviving inscriptions from these sites preserve the Pyu Tibeto-Burman language, but almost always they record traditional Indian texts. This confirms the strong influence of Hindu, Buddhist, and Jain cultures of India; in particular, Theravada Buddhism is prominent in these cities, memorialized in the *stupas* (domed temples) and monasteries. Some evidence, too, suggests that Myanmar is part of the trade route that links Rome with Southeast Asia. Meanwhile, other peoples appear on the stage of Myanmar: the Tai Shan; the Mon; the Nan-chao from Yunnan, China; the Khmer from Cambodia; and finally the Burmans of Pagan. Over several centuries, some of these people come into conflict, but by 1044 one kingdom, centered at Pagan, emerges as the dominant presence in Myanmar.

200 B.C.–A.D. 850: One of the oldest known of the Pyu cities is Mongmao (also Mongmai) in central Myanmar; it has remains of city walls 1.5 miles in diameter and of a stupa. Typical of the Pyu cities are such finds as beads, relief carvings, funeral urns, and bricks. In nearby sites, fine silver objects are found.

100 B.C.–A.D. 850: One of the model urban centers in Myanmar is Beikthano—which includes fortifications, city walls eight miles in perimeter, impressive gateways with sentry niches and wooden gates, *stupas*, monasteries, and dwellings. The ashes of the dead are buried in urns. Many ceramic vessels, some decorated with traditional Indian motifs including the swastika, a sun symbol.

A.D. 450–650: This is the peak period of the Pyu city of Sri Ksetra on the Irrawaddy, some 180 miles north of present-day Rangoon. Most impressive is its circular city wall—some 8.5 miles in circumference and rising to fifteen feet at places. Writing (found on stone, gold plates, silver vessels, burial urns) records the Pyu Tibeto-Burman language in several Indian scripts including Pali and Sanskrit; most inscriptions are verses derived from classical Indian texts. Among the remains of many structures are Buddhist stupas, the domed temples, and Buddhist monasteries, decorated with carvings depicting traditional episodes in Buddha's life. Bronze figurines and coins also have traditional Indian motifs.

600–1000: Tai peoples living in southwest China and northeastern Laos, apparently under some pressure from neighboring people, move to the south and west. Those who end up in northeastern Myanmar are known as the Shan. (They will retain to modern times their own dialect of the Tai language and certain cultural traditions that distinguish them from other inhabitants of Myanmar.) Other Tai peoples move into the highlands of Myanmar and contemporary Thailand; they will eventually dominate the plains of central Thailand.

750–900: In the southwestern Chinese region of Yunnan, the provincial military state of Nan-chao gains some autonomy from the Chinese government and begins to exert its own pressure on its neighbors including the various peoples in Myanmar. For the most part Nan-chao simply mounts raids, although in 835 Nan-chao warriors seem to undertake a major invasion of Myanmar. These attacks do not seem to achieve much permanent political success in Myanmar, but the Nan-chao presence does open lines of communication and trade between China and India; as a Buddhist state, Nan-chao also advances the role of Buddhism in Myanmar.

800–1000: Hamsavati is a Mon state along the coast of the Gulf of Martaban in west central Myanmar and centered on the cities of Pegu and Thaton. Probably through their trading contacts with Ceylon and India, the Hamsavati Mon serve to advance the transmission of Buddhism into Southeast Asia.

850–1044: Burman people based in the irrigated rice fields around Mandalay in central Myanmar, have been moving into the territory hitherto dominated by the Pyu and Mon. By about 1000, these Burmans are establishing their own state, centered on the city of Pagan. At first Pagan is only one of many competing kingdoms in Myanmar but by 1044 Anawrahta, a new ruler of Pagan, commences more assertive and expansive policies.

UNITED AND DIVIDED KINGDOMS: 1044–1825

The First Myanmar Empire is founded at Pagan and thrives under established political, economic, and administrative systems. Pagan rulers attempt to achieve unity and stability from the Irrawaddy (Ayeyarwady) River Valley to the Tenasserim peninsula through territorial expansion and cultural assimilation of conquered peoples. The monarchs patronize Theravada Buddhism, which is believed to have arrived from India in the first millennium A.D., and engage in large-scale temple building projects. By the mid-thirteenth century the Buddhist *sangha* (church or religious community) is at the center of a cultural "golden age" during which monumental art, scholarly literature, and poetry flourish under generous state patronage. The toll of such patronage on the state's economy contributes to the weakening of the empire, which falls to Mongol invasion, and is followed by two centuries of fragmentation under the warring rulers of the various states. For today's archaeologists, Pagan is a site rich with the ruins of some five thousand religious monuments.

The Second Myanmar Empire is ruled by the Toungoo dynasty, which is centered in Pegu, just northeast of present-day Rangoon, and later moves to Ava (Inwa), near Mandalay. Although this era is characterized by impressive military successes and territorial expansion, there is instability and fragmentation under Toungoo rule. Rivalries among the ruling elite as well as internal revolt and raids from neighboring states bring the fall of this dynasty, making way for the Third Empire and reunification under the Konbaung dynasty in the eighteenth century. At this time the British and French are vying for bases in Myanmar, where British shipping interests in the Bay of Bengal are under close watch by the two hostile European nations. Myanmar annexation of Rakhine extends the state's boundaries to the border with India; the ensuing border conflicts result in war with Britain, and the eventual loss of sovereignty.

1044: Anawrahta (reigns 1044–1077), known as the founder of the First Myanmar Empire, succeeds as king of Pagan. Anawrahta expands the kingdom with a strengthened army and fortified defenses, and increases agricultural production with new irrigation works.

1057: Anawrahta gains hegemony over Thaton, center of the Mon court in Lower Myanmar, and secures the port cities. He returns to Pagan with a large supply of laborers who fill a manpower shortage, as well as priests, scribes, scholars, and artisans who bring Mon cultural influences to the kingdom. Theravada Buddhism is patronized with the prosperity brought by conquest and by the expansion of agriculture and trade; construction begins on the Shwezigon pagoda, to house a copy of the sacred Tooth of Buddha relic.

1083: Anawrahta's young son, Sawlu, who has succeeded him, is taken prisoner and executed by a group of Mon rebels led by his governor.

1084–1111: Kyansittha, king of Pagan, follows a policy of reconciliation with the Mon that includes religious tolerance and cultural assimilation of Theravada Buddhism with folk beliefs; Mon is the language of the court, where Mon scholars and artisans are patronized.

1112: Myazedi stone inscriptions dating from this time are the earliest preserved literary evidence in Burmese language; their texts provide valuable historical information.

1113–1167: Alaungsithu succeeds his grandfather Kyansittha. His reign is noted for dedication to cultural unification, which is legitimized by construction of religious structures, such as the Thatbinnyu temple at Pagan and the Shwegugyi pagoda; there are attempts to put Burmese into written form.

1173–1210: After a series of parricides and fratricides, Narapatisithu takes the throne; he engages in territorial conquests that increase the available labor force, agricultural production, and the construction of religious monuments. This is also a time of cultural flowering; the clergy produce scholarly works written in Burmese, which has replaced the Mon, Pali, and Sanskrit languages at court.

1210–1234: Reign of Nadaungmya, last of the kings of the expansionist era during which temple-building and lavish patronage of the *sangha*, the monastic community, flourishes.

1234–1249: Reign of Kyaswa, who attempts

through confiscation of lands to take control of an economy which has been depleted by overspending. By this time imperial power is dissipated and the *sangha* has become the focus of political and economic power.

1249–1254: Reign of Uzana, who fails to revive imperial authority.

1254–1287: Reign of Narathihapati, last of the Pagan kings. Narathihapati engages in temple construction to legitimize his reign; economic loss to the church continues and Pagan decline accelerates.

1271: Incident in which Mongol envoys seeking tribute from Pagan disappear, increasing tensions.

1273: Taking advantage of Mongol threat to Pagan kingdom from the north, Mon of Lower Burma launch rebellion.

1286: Myanmar diplomatic mission arrives in Bejing to negotiate peace with Khubilai Khan; Narathihapati retreats during negotiations and is killed in 1287 by his son.

1287: Mongol forces invade and reach Pagan.

1289: Kyawswa, heir to Pagan throne, is established as king but is effectively subject to the Mongols. He is supported by three brothers, often referred to as the Shan, who are perhaps royal princes.

1293: Pagan regains control over Lower Burma.

1298: The Shan brothers take Pagan and execute Kyawswa the following year.

1303: Mongols withdraw from Myanmar; the Shan brothers divide central Myanmar among themselves, and rule from their courts at Pinya, Sagaing and Myinzaing.

c. 1312–1324: Sihasu, a Shan brother, builds a new capital at Pinya and establishes the Pagan genealogy through marriage to Pagan queens.

1364: A capital is built at Ava (Inwa, near present-day Mandalay) by Thadominbya, descendent of Sihasu, establishing the Shan-Bamar (Burmese) dynasty which succeeds in uniting central and northern Myanmar.

1367–1400: Swasake, king of Ava, makes peace with the Mon and repairs irrigation systems, bringing stability and prosperity to the kingdom.

1385–1423: Reign of Razadarit, Mon king of Pegu, who engages in war against Ava's ruler Minkhaung (reigns 1401–1422); the latter is also at war with the Shan.

1453–1472: Reign of Shinsawbu, daughter of Razadarit and Mon queen of Pegu; under her rule towns in southern Myanmar develop as trade centers; Shinsawbu promotes Pegu as a center of Buddhism, and much work is added to the Shwedagon temple (begun in 585 B.C.).

1459: Arakan (Rakhine) acquires Chittagong, in present-day Bangladesh.

1472–1492: Reign of Mon king Dhammazedi, a monk whose effective administration promotes peace and the spread of Theravada Buddhism as far as Ava.

1531: Tabinshwehti becomes first king of the Second Myanmar Empire, which is ruled by the Toungoo dynasty; Tabinshwehti conquers the Mon and moves his capital from Toungoo to Pegu.

There is great profit in bringing rice and lac and all the rest of it from Pegu to Malacca.

Suma Oriental, by Tomé Pires (1512–1515)

1550: Tabinshwehti is murdered by Mon rebels; Bayinnaung (reigns 1551–1581) takes the throne and brings much of present-day Myanmar as well as areas of Manipur, Yunnan, Laos, and Thailand under Burmese control.

1568–1569: Bayinnaung subdues neighboring Ayudhya.

1581–1599: Nandabayin, the last king of the first Toungoo dynasty, subdues Mon rebellions; in 1599, Tai and rebel Toungoo armies sack Pegu. Following Nandabayin's death at the hand of his conquerors, the empire breaks up into petty states, some of which come under Portuguese and Thai rule.

1606: Second Toungoo dynasty established by

Anaukpetlun (reigns 1606–1628). Anaukpetlun gains control of a large part of northern Myanmar, as well as coastal areas to the south that had fallen to the Portuguese.

1629–1648: Reign of Thalun, who moves the Toungoo capital from Pegu to Ava in 1634. Thalun restores peace and order, reorganizes the administration, updates irrigation systems in the central plains, and promotes foreign trade relations. In 1638 the first tax survey is taken. Minister Kaingsa Manu compiles the first Burmese lawbook, the *Maharaja Dhammathat*.

1666: Arakan loses control of Chittagong.

1709: English merchants open a dockyard at Thanlyin (Syriam), a center of foreign trade on the Hlaing River.

1729: The French open a dockyard at Thanlyin (Syriam).

1750: A Mon embassy is sent to the French viceroy in India, French ambassador de Bruno arrives in Thanlyin, and an English embassy arrives at the Mon court in Pegu.

1752–1760: Reign of the first king of the Konbaung dynasty, Alaungpaya (1711–1760) who had been a chieftain at Moksobo (Shwebo) in northern Myanmar. Alaungpaya is a leader in the rebellion against Mon rule and succeeds in unifying Myanmar, heralding in the Third Myanmar Empire. In 1756 and 1757 Alaungpaya takes the port of Thanlyin and Pegu. In 1760 Alaungpaya invades Siam, is wounded at Ayudhya, and dies as the Myanmar army retreats.

1753: The British East India Company occupies the island of Negrais in order to check French military activity in the Bay of Bengal until 1759, when the Burmese destroy the British settlement there.

1763–1776: Reign of the Konbaung King Hsinbyushin, which is characterized by military success. Between 1766 and 1769 the Burmese succeed in invading Siam and sacking Ayutthaya, and repulse a series of attacks from China. Under Hsinbyushin the Burmese invade Manipur and Vientiane (in modern-day Laos) as well as the Chiang Mai province in Siam.

1782–1819: Reign of King Bodawpaya, who secures the throne by massacring all possible rivals and their families. He moves the capital from Inwa to Amarapura, seven miles away.

At the place where the white canopy bowed down, a large pagoda named Htilominlo was erected. When Nandaungmya was established as king, he set the other four princes to rule Pagan kingdom. There were four rulers of the land, four governors, four secretaries, and four judges; these duties were fulfilled by the four brothers as they ordered their quarters.

Maniyadanabon, by Shin Sandalinka (late 18th century)

1784–1785: Myanmar under Bodawpaya attacks and annexes Rakhine (Arakan), a fragmented state on the west coast bordering Bangladesh; this expansion brings Myanmar to the frontier of British India. At this time the Myanmar invasion of Siam is repulsed, and by 1802 its forces retreat from Siamese-held Vientiane and Chiang Mai. Bodawpaya engages in temple building on a large scale; his projects require a large labor force that is conscripted from the countryside, causing disruption of village life.

1794: Insurrections at Rakhine result from Bodawpaya's conscription policy. Large numbers of rebels flee to British-held Bangladesh.

1795 and 1802: Britain sends envoy Michael Symes as representative of the Indian government to establish a commercial treaty for the British East India Company; to resolve border issues at Rakhine; and to assure that France would not establish bases in Myanmar against British shipping in the Bay of Bengal.

1811: Forces under Chinbyan, a Rakhinese leader in British Raj territory, invade Rakhine and take the ancient capital of Mrohaung. Rebellion continues until the death of Chinbyan in 1815.

1819: Bagyidaw succeeds his grandfather Bodawpaya to the throne; border skirmishes continue, and by 1822 Myanmar asserts authority over Manipur and Assam. The expansionist goals of both Britain and Myanmar lead to the First Anglo-Burmese War.

FOREIGNERS RULE: 1824–1948

The border conflicts between Myanmar and British India, as well as British concern over Myanmar's relations with France, lead to war and Myanmar's loss of its two large coastal provinces, Rakhine and Tenasserim. Further losses in two subsequent wars cause humiliation at the court at Ava (Inwa). Although Britain grants the annexed territories a certain amount of administrative autonomy, upper level officials filling executive and judicial roles are drawn from the Indian Civil Service, and a new and alien court system is imposed on the population. In 1886 Britain annexes the entire country to India, bringing commercial and strategic advantages to the British empire and undermining French influence in the area. The imposition of Western education and exposure to printing brings a group of writers that includes U Kui, U Lat, and Pi Mo Nin to explore the new literary form of the Myanmar novel.

Along with a stable government and growing economy under British rule, Myanmar is subjected to social and cultural dislocations that inspire resistance to authority, and nationalist sentiment grows. Britain pursues a policy of regional division that places ethnic areas under individual systems of government. Economic hardship is aggravated by Britain's involvement in World War I; Burmese resentment of Indian and other Asians in government service and business increases. An early manifestation of nationalist unity comes in the form of Buddhist associations' demands that the custom of removing shoes at Buddhist sites be honored by the British, who have a tradition of disregarding this show of respect. Politicization of religious and cultural grievances paves the way for the political unrest that takes root in the 1920s, and later for the organization of nationalist fronts that emerge during the Japanese occupation. Accompanying this move toward political independence, writers such as Thakin Kodaw Hmaing and Maha Swe revive traditional Myanmar literary forms to explore contemporary themes, while the *Khitsan* literary movement is an influential proponent of modernist Burmese writing. Authors take up the theme of life under Japanese occupation (Maung Htin's novel *Nga Ba* stands out among these works). Not long after the end of World War II, a weakened Britain recognizes the inevitable and agrees to Burmese independence.

March 5, 1824: The First Anglo-Burmese War breaks out over border conflicts in Rakhine.

February 24, 1826: Treaty of Yandabo; accepting Britain's terms for peace as British troops reach Yandabo, near (Ava) Inwa, Myanmar agrees to cede the maritime provinces of Rakhine and Tenasserim as well as Assam and Manipur, pay heavy war indemnities, exchange diplomatic envoys, and negotiate a trade treaty.

1830: Henry Burney arrives as first permanent British Resident at Amarapura; he faces issues pending from the Yandabo Treaty.

1837: Bagyidaw, having gone insane, is deposed by his brother Tharrawaddy, who does not recognize the Treaty of Yadabo and rearms his troops. An uneasy peace ensues until Tharrawaddy, who is also going insane, dies in 1846. Chaos under the rule of his successor Pagan Min leads to acceleration of conflict with Britain.

April 1852–June 1853: Second Anglo-Burmese War breaks out as Dalhousie intervenes in a commercial dispute. British capture Rangoon (April 12, 1852), then Pegu and Prome (October 1852), finally annexing Lower Burma (December 1852).

February 1853: Prince Mindon Min (reigns 1853–1878), a son of Tharrawaddy, replaces Pagan Min as king and attempts to regain occupied territories through peaceful means. A devout Buddhist, Mindon relocates the capital to Mandalay, where he creates a center of culture and religion; he takes steps toward modernizing the administrative system.

1862: Pegu, Tenasserim, and Rakhine are annexed to Britain as the province of British Burma, with its capital at Rangoon (Yangon).

1866: A palace coup (also known as Myingun Rebellion), led by Mindon's sons, is a result of disagreement over concessions made to Britain.

1875: British authorities in the Indian government instruct their Resident at Mandalay not to remove his shoes when entering the Burmese king's presence, as is customary; this arrogance destroys the envoy's line of communication with the king.

1878: Thibaw (reigns 1878–1885), last king of the Konbaung dynasty, is placed on the throne by agreement of ministers, who intend to wield power under a weakened monarchy; in fact his queen, Supayalat, and her entourage wield the power.

1882: In an effort to establish contacts in Europe and to benefit from British and French rivalry, Thibaw sends a Myanmar embassy to France.

August 1885: The Hluttaw rules against the Bombay Burma Trading Corporation in a court case concerning irregularities at its timber mills. This judgment leads to the Third Anglo-Burmese War and the occupation of Mandalay by British forces. Thibaw surrenders in November, bringing an end to the Third Myanmar Empire.

January 1886: Myanmar is annexed to British territories in southern Burma and declared a British colony; in February all of Burma is proclaimed a province of India.

1886–1895: Burmese wage guerrilla war in the north against the British.

1906: The Young Men's Buddhist Association (YMBA) is formed in Rangoon supporting Buddhism as the national religion.

December 1920: First Rangoon (Yangon) University strike.

January 1923: The Dyarchy, or dual government, constitution is implemented to provide reform in the legislative council. Although this allows some self-government to the Burmese, this legislation does not apply to states lying outside central Burma where Britain maintains direct control.

1930: The nationalist Do Bama Asi Ayon (Our Burma) party is founded in Rangoon. Members refer to themselves as *thakin* (masters). The party calls for modernization and organization of Burmans, and founds the All Burma Youth League.

1930–1931: The Saya San (Tharrawaddy) peasant rebellion breaks out in southern Myanmar, where low rice prices have affected the peasant population. Under nationalist leader Saya San, the rebels demand a return to traditional social and political order, and form an army to attack and defeat the British. By late 1931 the rebellion's leaders are captured and executed.

1936: Second Rangoon University strike under leadership of U Aung San (1915–1946).

April 1, 1937: Under the Government of Burma Act of 1935, the British separate the province of Burma from India and place it under a British governor responsible to Great Britain. Dr. Ba Maw (1893–1977) is Burma's first prime minister.

August 15, 1939: The Communist Party of Burma (CPB) is formed.

December 13, 1941: Japanese troops come from Thailand and invade Burma. They need the natural resources of Burma (oil, tin, rice) and want to cut off the Burma Road, the chief supply route of the Allies to China.

December 28, 1941: The Burma Independence Army (BIA), a volunteer army trained by Japan, is formed in Bangkok under the command of Aung San to join Japan in the campaign against the British in Myanmar. Members of the Nationalist Thakin provide administrative assistance in areas under BIA control. By July 1942 Japan has control of most of Myanmar and the British retreat into India; the BIA is disbanded and replaced with the Burma Defense Army, which provides border defense.

August 1, 1943: Japan grants nominal independence to what is in fact a puppet state of Burma. Dr. Ba Maw is head of state, Aung San is minister of defense, and members of the independence movement hold cabinet positions.

1943–1945: The mass of Burmese soon become disillusioned and deprived under Japanese rule and the chief collaborators realize that they must turn against the Japanese if they are to have a role in their nation's future.

March 27–August 12, 1945: In March, the Burma National Army (BNA), organized in August 1943 out of the Burma Defense Army, launches armed rebellion against the Japanese. The Anti-Fascist People's Freedom League (AFPFL), a coalition of resistance groups founded in August 1944 under the leadership of Aung San, also leads resistance forces. By May the Allies, joined by the BNA and AFPFL, have reconquered most of Myanmar; Japan surrenders on August 12.

October 4, 1946: Aung San is Deputy Chairman of the new Executive Council of the British Governor; the Aung San-Atlee Agreement of January 1947 gives the interim government full ministerial authority.

July 19, 1947: Assassination of Aung San and other members of the interim government, after which the provisional government is established, with U Thalin Nu as prime minister. The KNU (Karen National Union), a rebel group founded in April 1947, now forms the Karen National Defense Organization (KNDO) as its military arm.

October 17, 1947: Nu-Atlee Treaty is signed in London, recognizing Myanmar's independence. On December 10, 1947, the Burmese Independence Bill is passed by British Parliament.

January 4, 1948: The Constitution of the Union of Burma, based on principles of parliamentary democracy and providing for separate systems of government in each state, comes into effect, since observed as Myanmar's independence day. The KNU does not recognize the Union of Burma, demanding independence and large areas of southern and central Myanmar. Prime Minister U Nu proclaims Buddhism the national religion.

INDEPENDENT MYANMAR: 1948–1998

The constitution of the Union of Burma adopted in 1948 provides for a federated republic in which states, which are divided largely by ethnic groupings, maintain a certain degree of autonomy. But the goal of national unity is compromised by ethnic unrest, in particular the demand of Karen minorities for separate statehood. Civil strife and insurrections also arise from disagreement between opposition groups over the terms of the Nu-Atlee Treaty. Ten years after independence a split within the ruling AFPFL creates dissension and chaos, weakening Prime Minister U Nu's leadership and opening the way for military takeover of the government in 1958. For the next thirty years the military-dominated Burma Socialist Programme Party rules a single-party socialist state through the unicameral Pyithu Hluttaw (People's Assembly), the legislative branch that is elected every four years. The Assembly loses its legislative power following a military takeover in 1988 by the State Law and Order Restoration (SLORC) junta and the return to a nominal multiparty system. In 1997 the military regime reorganizes as the State Peace and Development Council but continues to rule under a program based on Marxist-style and authoritarian state control while appealing to national identity by emphasizing Buddhist ethics and deeply rooted cultural and religious traditions.

1948: The Land Nationalization Act redistributes arable land from the landlords to the cultivators, who receive financial assistance from the government.

March 27, 1948: Civil war breaks out as Communist Party instigates armed uprisings; Islamic *mujahids* (insurgents) from Rakhine follow with antigovernment rebellions; hostilities continue for several years before the government regains authority.

January 1949: The KNDO rebellion breaks out; the rebels succeed in controlling large sections of Myanmar until the following year, when they retreat to rural areas in the southeast.

December 1949: Chinese Guomindang (Nationalist) forces invade Shan state in northeast Myanmar to establish bases for attacks on Yunnan.

1951: The Anti-Fascist People's Freedom League (AFPFL) wins a landslide victory in the first parliamentary elections held under the constitution drafted in 1947.

August 1952: The Pyidawtha, an eight-year welfare, economic growth, and industrialization plan, is adopted.

In the blast of the whirlwind,
A leaf caught up, spinning;
Whirling and eddying,
And floating in the wind.

"A Leaf in the Whirlwind," poem by Dagon Taya (1950s)

May 1954: Prime Minister U Nu convenes the Sixth Great Buddhist Synod at Rangoon on the grounds of the Kaba Aye (World Peace) Pagoda, where the International Institute for Advanced Buddhist Studies is also located. The council, composed of Buddhist scholars from around the world, will spend two years codifying and editing the traditional sacred texts of the *Tripitaka*.

1956: AFPFL again wins in parliamentary elections; the newly formed National Unity Front (NUF) wins over 30 percent of the vote.

May 1958: AFPFL party splits into two factions, creating political confusion. In October the caretaker government under General (Bogyoke) U Ne Win takes control of the government to maintain stability until free elections are held. Key administrative positions are held by military officials; NUF leaders are jailed.

February 1960: U Nu's Pyidaungsu Party returns to power in parliamentary elections. U Nu's plan to establish a strong economy under a democratic system is hindered by dissension within his party as well as demands for autonomy from Kachin and Shan states. Buddhism is made state religion by parliamentary decree.

March 2, 1962: A military coup brings Gen. U Ne Win's Revolutionary Council (RC) to power, ending the parliamentary era and ushering in a period of military rule which is to last until 1974. U Nu is placed under detention, not to be released until 1966. On July 4 the Burma Socialist Programme Party (BSPP), which is to be the single political party from 1964 to 1988, is founded.

February 1963: Banks and the timber trade are nationalized.

March 28, 1964: All legal political parties and organizations except the BSPP are banned.

April 1964: Export trade and commodity distribution operations are nationalized.

August 1969: In Bangkok, Thailand, former Prime Minister U Nu founds the Parliamentary Democracy Party to challenge the Revolutionary Council.

August 1971: State visit of U Ne Win to People's Republic of China to establish political relations.

January 23, 1974: New constitution creates the Socialist Republic of the Union of Burma; it provides for a one-house legislature and replaces the parliamentary law established in the constitution of 1947 (which in any case has been inactive under the military government since 1962). The BSPP under U Ne Win remains in power.

May–June 1974: Food shortages cause workers' strikes.

December 1974: Students and Buddhist monks demonstrate against the government in Yangon (Rangoon) over the issue of former statesman and UN Secretary General U Thant's burial in what is considered a disrespectful manner.

May 1980: Buddhist monks convene in Rangoon; at this meeting with government officials, the monastic community (*sangha*) is brought under government authority and the clergy are issued identification cards.

May 28, 1980: Government grants general amnesty; U Nu returns from exile.

August 1980: Ne Win announces retirement from presidency; in November BSPP leader U San Yu is elected president (1980–1988).

October 1982: Hluttaw passes the new Burma Citizenship Law, creating three classes of citizens and in effect limiting the participation of foreign residents in military and political activity.

March 1988: Student demonstrations at Rangoon University begin; protest spreads to other campuses and all schools are closed in June.

July 23, 1988: A BSPP emergency Congress convenes. U San Yu and U Nu resign from the party; martial law is declared in Rangoon on August 3. Martial law is lifted on August 24 after strikes and demonstrations leave many dead.

September 9, 1988: U Nu proclaims an interim government with himself as prime minister.

September 18, 1988: A military coup overthrows the government; the State Law and Order Restoration Council (SLORC), a military junta headed by General Saw Maung, comes to power.

September 24, 1988: The National League for Democracy (NLD) is founded and becomes the major opposition party to SLORC.

September 26, 1988: The BSPP is reorganized as the National Unity Party (NUP).

October 26, 1988: Political Parties Registration Law permits registered political organizations to function.

November 1988: The All Burma Students' Democratic Front, an underground group seeking to restore democracy, and the umbrella group Democratic Alliance of Burma are formed at this time.

April 17, 1989: Ethnic conflict within the Communist Party of Burma, which controls border areas in Shan and Kachin, causes its breakup and ends forty-one years of insurgency.

May 27, 1989: Burma is renamed Myanmar, an ancient name for Burma and a deliberate appeal to a national pride and tradition.

May 27, 1990: The National League for Democracy (NLD), the chief opposition party, gains 60 percent of the vote in the general election, and the NUP gains 21 percent of the vote, but the SLORC does not honor the election; NLD members and elected candidates are arrested, others flee to the Thai border. In December, a National Coalition Government is declared by the NLD at party headquarters at Manerplaw near the Thai border.

October 14, 1991: Daw Aung San Suu Kyi, daughter of Aung San (assassinated on July 19, 1947) and NLD party leader who has been under house arrest since 1989, is awarded the Nobel Peace Prize.

April 23, 1992: General Saw Maung resigns as chairman of SLORC and is succeeded by vice-chairman General Than Shwe, who also becomes prime minister.

August 24, 1992: Universities and institutions of higher education reopen; primary and middle schools have opened earlier.

July 10, 1995: Aung San Suu Kyi is freed from six years of house arrest; she vows to continue efforts to foster democracy in Myanmar. In November she announces the NLD's boycott of talks to draft a new constitution, claiming the convention is not pursuing democracy.

January 1, 1996: Government troops seize a drug operation on Thai border through a negotiated surrender of Khun Sa, who had run what is considered to be one of the world's largest heroin-trafficking rings. The operation is run by the private, heavily armed Mong Tai Army, which also leads the ongoing Shan independence insurgency.

November 15, 1997: In an attempt to legitimize the military regime, a group of younger, better educated army officers remove some of the older officers; they then announce that they have reorganized the governing body as the State Peace and Development Council.

May 31, 1997: The Association of Southeast Asian Nations (ASEAN) announces that it is going to admit Myanmar (in July) as a member in defiance of demands by the United States and human rights activist groups that Myanmar be excluded.

March 22, 1998: About thirty armed men from Myanmar cross the border into Thailand and burn a camp holding some 8,700 refugees from Myanmar; most of these people belong to the Karen ethnic group of Myanmar, 100,000 of whom have taken refuge in Thailand in an attempt to gain some autonomy for their people.

July 24–29, 1998: Aung San Suu Kyi, in defiance of the government order restricting her to the capital, sets out with two supporters to visit leaders of her National League for Democracy party in a town one hundred miles away. Her vehicle is stopped by police on the edge of Yangon, and she chooses to sit in the car for almost six days, despite protests from the international community. On July 29 the police forcibly return her to her home.

August 9–14, 1998: On August 9 the government arrests eighteen foreign activists, including six Americans, for handing out leaflets to call attention to the tenth anniversary of the failed attempt to establish democracy. After their trial on August 14 they are sentenced to five years of hard labor, but the sentences are immediately suspended and they are put on planes and deported.

August 12–24, 1998: Aung San Suu Kyi sets out again to visit party leaders outside Yangon, and her car is again blocked. With her health greatly deteriorating, she finally agrees to return to her home on August 24.

Philippines

PREHISTORIC PERIOD: 38,000 B.C.–A.D. 700

During the Pleistocene (approximately 1.75 million years ago to 10,000 B.C.), the lowering and rising of the world's sea levels have left the Philippine Islands alternately connected to and isolated from the nearby islands and via them to the mainland of Southeast Asia. Although some scientists claim to find stone tools made by *Homo erectus* as early as 500,000 B.C., most scholars believe that the first humans to move into the Philippines are *Homo sapiens* who come no earlier than about 38,000 B.C. For many thousands of years, these first Filipinos probably live somewhat isolated, their basic culture that of the hunters-gatherers and stone tools of this period. Then, starting about 3000–2800 B.C., new migrants begin to link the Philippines with developments in East and Southeast Asia, and the Philippines participate in the evolving cultural phases of Southeast Asia—the Neolithic, Bronze Age, and eventually the Iron Age. However, the first written references to the Philippines are not found until the eighth century A.D. and the coming of the first Chinese and Japanese.

38,000–28,000 B.C.: People regarded as the ancestors of the present-day Negritos move into the Philippines. (It is assumed that they walk across land bridges from the southwest, accessible due to the low sea level.) Their exact origin is not known, but these people are distinguished by their relatively short stature, dark skin, and tightly curled hair; they are probably related to the peoples who are also settling the Melanesian Islands in this era. (The Negritos still live in coastal and inland locales in parts of the Philippines where they include such tribes as the Aeta; their most immediate modern relatives seem to be the Negritos of peninsular Malaysia.)

28,000–3000 B.C.: The inhabitants of the Philippines probably do not differ much from the peoples and cultures elsewhere in Southeast and East Asia (although when the sea rises to its present level, between about 13,000 and 6000 B.C., the islands are physically isolated). They are primarily hunters, fishers, and food-foragers, with little material culture beyond their flaked stone tools; they do not weave textiles nor make pottery; they move about rather than maintain villages; and they have little social organization beyond the family. The main sites for finds include the Tabon Caves on Palawan, the Musang Cave in northern Luzon, and the Balabok shelter in the Sulu Archipelago. By the end of this period, some of the early Filipinos are making blade tools; they chew the betel nut; they probably cultivate root crops such as the taro and yam.

2800–1500 B.C.: By this time Southern Mongoloid people classed as Austronesians are moving into the Philippines; the first to come are probably traders or fishermen who have gained skill and confidence with their boats. The prevailing theory is that they come from Taiwan to the north, but some believe they come up from the Southeast Asian islands to the southwest; there may well be a continuation of movements back and forth between several of these regions. (Still another theory is that the ensuing developments are not due to a major migrant group but to cultural evolution among the resident Filipinos.) In any case, these Austronesians settle and spread around the Philippines; others appear on the islands to the south and west. These Austronesians are not the ancestors of the modern Han Chinese but are probably related to Mongoloid people already inhabiting parts of southern China. They bring a culture that includes basic agriculture (millet and rice), domestic dogs and pigs, pottery, stone adzes, and a special competence with canoes and sailing.

1500–500 B.C.: There is probably some mixing and intermarriage among the aboriginal Negritos and the newer Mongoloid Austronesians, but for the most part these two peoples go their own way. (The Negritos do eventually adopt the language of the Austronesians.) The Austronesian Filipinos maintain their own basic economy, culture, and society: they cultivate old foods and add new ones to their diet; they weave textiles, make pottery, construct simple wooden houses; they live in small villages but have little social stratification. By now trade brings increasing contacts with the other peoples of Southeast Asia, and Filipinos adopt some of their new material culture such as special adzes, jade, and copper/bronze. Meanwhile the Filipinos also transfer back to their relatives in Taiwan such new foods as coconuts, bananas, and breadfruit from the tropical regions.

500 B.C.–A.D. 700: During these centuries, the Filipinos adopt some of the material culture of the world around them: copper, bronze and (after *c.* 200 B.C.) iron for tools, weapons, and ornaments; glass jewelry and jade ear pendants; burial jars; the blowgun (while the Negritos keep their bow and arrow.) One of the best known of the Filipino cultures of the period (at least from A.D. 1–700) is the Kalanay (after the excavations in Kalanay Cave on Masbate Island. Most notably, in northern Luzon prosperous families begin to make elaborate mountain terraces to support intensive wet-rice cultivation. Their society remains rooted in villages, but burials reveal some stratification by wealth and status. Maritime trade brings them into contact not only with their immediate neighbors but also with those such as Indians who are moving into Southeast Asia. It will be the sixteenth century before there is evidence of an indigenous writing system, but by the seventh century A.D. Chinese and Japanese writings are beginning to refer to the Philippines.

EMERGENT PHILIPPINES: A.D. 750–1521

Because there is no evidence of literacy before the end of the sixteenth century, Philippine recorded history of this time is based primarily on Spanish accounts of cultural traditions, as well as transcriptions of oral epic poems and myths. The Philippines are populated by linguistically diverse cultures who speak a variety of Austronesian languages, and live in widely scattered, self-sufficient kinship groups. The settlements, known as *barangays* after the sail boats that brought early Malay family groups to the Philippines, are administered by *datus*, or chieftains. The stratified society consists of chieftains, the nobility who serve them, a class of freemen, and the hereditary "dependent" class of sharecroppers, debt peons, and war captives. Although little substantive evidence remains, it is believed that various religious cults practice rituals to placate the wrath of the many gods and goddesses as well as give offerings to the *anitos* and *diwatas*, the large population of spirits. Nature and ancestor worship are practiced; there is no evidence of human sacrifice or cannibalism. Spanish chronicles describe carved wooden figures dating from this time.

10th century: Arab trade routes pass through the Philippines.

11th century: Records show that Chinese towns are established along coastal areas of the archipelago during China's Song dynasty.

14th century: Trade contacts expand as Indochinese, Siamese, and Vietnamese begin to trade with the Philippines.

15th century: Ming emperor Yung Lo sends expeditions to the Philippines and trading posts are established; a mixed Filipino-Chinese population develops.

Late 15th century: Islam has become established on the large island of Mindanao and on the Sulu archipelago to the south; by the early sixteenth century, Islam is also apparently taking hold in the Manila area.

FOREIGN PRESENCE: 1521–1946

The geographic fragmentation of the archipelago of over seven thousand mountainous islands as well as the decentralization inherent in the social structure of *barangay* units facilitate Spanish colonization. The Spanish state and Catholic church share common objectives and function interdependently, although not always without conflict over methods of securing their goals. Remote hill communities resist paying tribute, reject the new faith, and do not acknowledge Spanish sovereignty. The indigenous culture remains embedded in Philippine society and in many areas Christianity is filipinized.

During the seventeenth century shipping trade flourishes with the Manila galleons, which make annual voyages to Acapulco, Mexico, carrying silks and luxury items from China, and return with silver, provisions, personnel, and mail. The Chinese come to dominate retail trade and crafts; their agricultural skills increase production. Hostility to the Chinese population results in a series of anti-Chinese riots and massacres, but this does not stop the emergence of a wealthy Chinese *mestizo* class through intermarriage with Filipinos. The *ilustrados* (illustrious ones) form the ruling elite that includes the new business class of affluent, educated Filipinos, the Chinese *mestizo* community, island-born Spanish, and some Spanish *mestizos*. By the late nineteenth century, criticism of Spanish rule becomes more overt; a desire for reform and opposition movements develops and comes to a climax in the 1890s.

Following the defeat of the Spanish in the Spanish-American War and the subsequent defeat of the Filipinos, the Americans establish a commonwealth administration. Unlike Spanish colonialists, the Americans separate church functions from state administration. The Americans promote some social programs and reforms but basically leave the power with the *ilustrados*, the landed, educated, and business classes. Economic conditions of the peasantry worsen as the vast estates and large-scale agricultural production thrive, encouraging left-wing resistance. But the demands for change and independence are temporarily put on hold by the Japanese invasion and occupation during World War II.

March 1521: Ferdinand Magellan (1480–1521) arrives in the Philippines and claims the area for Spain. He is killed in the Battle of Mactan off the island of Cebu.

On this island of Zubu [Cebu] there are several towns, and each one yielded food and tribute. And near this island of Zubu, there is one called Mattan [Mactan], and the port and the town have the same name as the island, Mattan. The chieftains are named Zula, Cilapulapu, and the town that we burned was on this island, and was called Bulaia.

The Voyage of Magellan, by Antonio Pigafetta (1525)

1543: Ruy de Villalobos reaches the islands of Samar and Leyte in the Visayas and names the area Felipinas for Crown Prince Philip II of Spain, but makes no attempt to settle the area.

February 1565: Miguel Lopez de Legaspi (1511–1572) arrives in Cebu with his crew, troops, and Augustinian friars; he establishes himself as governor of the Visayas, the group of islands in the central Philippines. Legaspi is commissioned by King Philip II of Spain to colonize the area for the purpose of Christianization and trade, and is given instructions to adhere to principles of peaceful occupation.

1570–1571: Legaspi sends troops north to claim the area that will be known as Manila, on the island of Luzon, and they are met with some Muslim resistance. With the arrival of reinforcements, Legaspi leaves the Visayas for Manila to establish a settlement at the port that has been frequented by Chinese traders. As the "Manila galleon" trade with the Americas develops, a large Chinese population involved with this lives in an area known as the Parian (marketplace) quarter outside the Manila city walls.

June 3, 1571: Manila is attacked by the Spanish; local chieftains capitulate and acknowledge Spanish sovereignty. With Manila under Christian rule, the spread of Islam on Luzon is checked; Mindanao and Sulu remain Moslem. However, Christianity never takes much hold in the south.

1578–1606: In 1578 fifteen Franciscan friars arrive in Cavite to join the Augustinians; in 1581 Jesuits arrive; Dominican friars arrive in 1587, followed by Recollects in 1606. The various Catholic priestly orders, under the direction of the Spanish crown, are assigned to specific areas for proselytizing; after an area's conversion has been secured, it is to be handed over to secular governors. In practice, the priestly orders often resist relinquishing power and come to own a large percentage of cultivated land, producing the income needed for missionary work through concessions to the *inquilino* (lessee), who sublets the land to sharecroppers who pay him a hefty commission. Under the policy of resettlement of native populations, the *barangay* family units are removed from ancestral lands and relocated to *pueblos*, or villages, which are constructed around a central plaza featuring a town hall and a church. Friars are parish priests who, along with Spanish provincial governors, oversee the administration of *pueblos* (villages) although the people continue to recognize the *barangay* system. Manila becomes the center of commerce and residence of the majority of Spaniards; primarily priests and government officials reside in the provinces.

1600: A Dutch fleet under Oliver van Noort plunders Chinese and Filipino ships in Manila Bay, beginning a long series of Dutch attempts to wrest the Philippines from Spain. Van Noort is defeated by the Spanish at the Battle of Mariveles.

1601: The College of Santo Tomás is founded by the Dominican order in Manila.

1609–1648: The Hispano-Dutch war puts a strain on Philippine resources. Manila Bay is subject to continued attacks from Dutch fleets. Local labor and tribute taxes become the principal economic support of the Spanish colonial regime. Filipinos are drafted as laborers to provide ship building and other services for the military. The Spanish imposes *vandala*, or quotas of goods to be sold at a fixed price by villagers, but the government often does not pay.

January 1621–May 1622: A joint Anglo-Dutch blockade of Manila Bay immobilizes trade in the port.

1642: Prohibition of Spanish residency in the provinces is relaxed; it is further relaxed in 1696.

1648: The Treaty of Muenster halts Dutch attacks on the Philippines; raiding of ships continues. Spain's success in defending their colony can be in part attributed to the support of their Filipino subjects.

1657: Tax on Filipino villagers to provide rice for laborers is abolished, while other taxes continue to be imposed.

1744: The Dagohoy Revolt, led by Francisco Dagohoy, breaks out in Bohol. Dagohoy, whose brother is refused a Christian burial following his death in the service of the church, gathers a large following and declares war on Catholicism. The revolt gives voice to widespread grievances against Spanish colonization; it ends after twenty years with amnesty for the rebels.

October 1762–May 1764: Britain occupies Manila at the time of the Seven Years' War. As Spanish military prestige is compromised, Filipino opposition to Spain spreads and rebellions break out in the provinces. European trading companies take an interest in Philippine commercial potential.

December 14, 1762–September 29, 1763: The Ilokos Revolt is led by Diego Silang (1730–1763) who offers to provide troops to fight the British and demands abolition of tribute; when his demands are not met by the Spanish, he establishes an independent government in Vigan. Silang is assassinated on May 28, 1763; his wife Gabriela takes his place but is captured and hanged on September 29.

1763: Rebellion in the provincial capital of Binalatongan led by Palaris, who is captured and killed in 1765.

February 26, 1768: The Ordinances of Good Government are proclaimed by the Spanish in a policy aimed at protecting the authority of the central government from abuse by provincial governors and parish priests.

Late 18th century: Tobacco and sugar are introduced as cash crops by governor José de Basco y Vargas.

1782: Colonial government establishes a tobacco monopoly by restricting its cultivation to assigned locations.

1782 or 1784: The first shipment of tobacco and indigo is sent to Spain, giving rise to agriculture as a commercial industry.

1789: The Port of Manila is opened to shipping of all nations carrying goods of Asian origin. Trade in European goods is forbidden, although this rule is not strictly enforced.

April 1815: Manila galleon shipping to Acapulco, Mexico, is abandoned as unprofitable.

1823: The Novales Mutiny, in protest against racial discrimination in the military, fails in its attempt to seize Manila.

1834: The Port of Manila is opened to unrestricted trade and foreign investment.

1863: The Educational Reform decree seeks

to improve educational standards and promote Spanish and other skills; the system remains under clerical control and little change is implemented.

1867: Law is passed limiting government appointments to those who know Spanish. After December 20, 1868, no non-Spanish-speaking Filipino is to be appointed to any office. This law is not enforced by the clergy, who are in charge of education in the provinces and fear that Spanish can provide a tool of resistance to colonization and Christianization; Spanish fails to take hold as the local language.

1870s: The Propaganda Movement is organized by Filipinos exiled in Spain who call for cultural nationalism as well as political rights and freedoms.

July 1878: The Sultan of Sulu acknowledges Spanish sovereignty, ending active Muslim resistance to Spanish rule there.

1884: The tribute tax is abolished in favor of the *cédula personal*, or head tax, collected from all adults, including the *principalia* of the pueblos and others previously excluded. This tax increases revenues for the colonial regime; a small fraction of the revenues is allocated to public services for Filipinos.

1887: Banned writer José Rizal (1861–1896), a member of the Propagandist Movement, publishes *Noli me Tangere* in Berlin. Rizal brings this novel, which criticizes Spanish colonialism in the Philippines, into the country but returns to Europe so as not to endanger his family.

Farewell, dear Fatherland, clime of the sun
  caressed,
Pearl of the Orient seas, our Eden lost,
Gladly now, I go to give thee this faded life's
  best
And were it brighter, fresher, or more blest
Still I would give it to thee, nor count the cost.

  "The Lost Eden," by José Rizal (1896)

1892: After his second novel, *El Filibusterismo*, is published in Ghent, José Rizal returns from abroad and founds the Liga Filipina, a peaceful association advocating reform. He is immediately arrested and banished to Mindanao.

July 1892: Andrés Bonifacio (1863–1897), member of the Liga Filipina, founds Kataastaasan Kagalanggalangan Katipunan ng Mga Anak ng Bayan (Highest and Most Respectable Society of the Sons of the People). This secret brotherhood advocates Filipino unity and independence through revolution.

August 1896: Governor Ramón Blanco banishes Filipino insurgents, and hundreds are killed or imprisoned in Manila. The Katipunan society is discovered by the government and its leaders are persecuted; Bonifacio sets up revolutionary government in Tejeros.

October 31, 1896: Leadership of the revolt passes to Emilio Aguinaldo (1869–1964) who addresses the Filipino people, giving this name to a people previously identified by their dialect or region, or simply as *indios* by the Spanish. Aguinaldo leads a revolt in his home province of Cavite. Blanco is recalled to Spain and replaced by Camilio García de Polavieja.

December 30, 1896: Charged by the Spanish with fomenting revolution, José Rizal is executed after brief trial and his family is persecuted.

March 1897: Bonifacio is replaced by Aguinaldo, who is proclaimed president of the revolutionary government; Bonifacio attempts to form a rival regime at Limbon, but he and his followers are captured and executed by the Spanish. Spain installs Fernando Primo de Rivera as governor of Philippines, replacing Polavieja.

December 1897: The Pact of Biyak na Bato is signed between Aguinaldo's government and Spanish authorities; under this agreement, which is soon broken by both sides, revolutionaries are to be exiled in Hong

Kong and receive financial compensation in exchange for surrender of arms.

Early 1898: General Francisco Makabulos establishes a new revolutionary government in central Luzon.

May 1, 1898: The Spanish fleet is defeated in the Battle of Manila Bay by U.S. forces under Commodore George Dewey. At an earlier meeting in Hong Kong with Aguinaldo, Dewey has promised that the United States will support independence in return for support against the Spanish. On about May 15 Aguinaldo returns to the Philippines.

June 12–23, 1898: On June 12 Aguinaldo declares independence in Manila; on June 23 he declares himself president of the revolutionary government. Provincial leaders acknowledge Aguinaldo's leadership.

August 13, 1898: After a sham battle to protect Spain's honor by having put up a fight, Manila falls to U.S. forces under Dewey.

December 10, 1898: Under the Treaty of Paris that formally concludes the Spanish-American War, Spain cedes the Philippines to the United States. Meanwhile, the U.S. government has decided that it is not going to recognize Aguinaldo and an independent Philippines. The United States is already organizing its military in the Philippines to challenge the Filipinos.

January 23, 1899: The Philippine Republic is proclaimed with Aguinaldo as president.

February 4, 1899: Hostilities with the United States break out and Aguinaldo gradually retreats to northern Luzon to wage guerrilla warfare. For the next three years, the U.S. government will commit some 100,000 men to suppressing this revolt.

December 1900: The Federalista Party, advocating statehood, is formed.

March 23, 1901: Emilio Aguinaldo is captured in Palanan, Isabela Island.

April 19, 1901: Aguinaldo takes an oath of loyalty to the United States, which has promised independence in the near future, and calls on his countrymen to negotiate a peace. The war drags on, however, for another year.

July 4, 1901: William H. Taft is established as governor of an entirely civilian government.

1901: The Sedition Act bars nationalist parties from forming and prohibits advocating independence or displaying the Philippine flag.

July 1, 1902: The U.S. Congress passes the Philippine Government Act, providing for the Philippines to be governed by a five-man commission appointed by the U.S. president. Executive power will be in the hands of the American governor-general, but there will a bicameral legislature, with an elected lower house and an appointed upper house. Two Filipino delegates are to sit in the U.S. Congress but do not have a vote. A Supreme Court based on the American model is established with a Filipino chief justice.

March 1907: The Sedition Act is lifted for a national election of representatives to the Philippine Assembly, the first elected legislature in Asia.

July 1907: The Partido Nacionalista under Manuel Quezon (1878–1944) wins a decisive victory in the Philippine Assembly. Nacionalista leader Sergio Osmeña (1878–1961) is first speaker of the assembly.

1913: Governor Francis Burton Harrison (1913–1921), appointed by President Woodrow Wilson, pursues a policy of "Filipinizing" the civil service; appointments are made to Filipino bureaucrats in an effort to progress toward self-government.

1914: The Partido Democrata is founded but dissolves in 1933 after a series of electoral defeats.

1916: The U.S. Congress passes the Jones Act, which allows an elected Filipino Senate to replace the American commission.

1922: The Nacionalista Party splits and Manuel Quezon establishes the Partido Nacionalista Colectivista, defeating Sergio Osmeña in an upper house election.

July 1923: Filipino leaders Manuel Quezon, president of the Senate, and Manuel Roxas

(1892–1948), speaker of the House, resign along with department heads protesting Governor Leonard Wood's use of veto power over legislation.

1925: The Nacionalistas under Osmeña and the Colectivistas under Quezon reunite and win majority seats in the Assembly and Senate elections.

1930: In response to acute poverty in central Luzon, the area surrounding Manila, the Philippine Communist Party (PCP) is founded, and draws from urban and agrarian reform movements. The Lava brothers, Vicente, José and Jesus, members of a wealthy land-owning family, are the party's leaders.

December 1931: Osmeña and Roxas leave for Washington to negotiate an independence bill, sponsored by Representative Harry Hawes of Missouri; the bill is vetoed by Hoover, passed by Congress, and rejected by the Filipino legislature.

1932: Labor leader Crisanto Evangelista is arrested and the Communist Party banned; its leaders are imprisoned.

1933: The League of Poor Workers, Aguman Ding Maldang Talapagobra, is formed in the Pampanga area of rice and sugar haciendas.

1933: Benigno Ramos, former editor of *Sakdal* (To Strike), a small newspaper promoting social reform and independence, forms the Sakdal Party. The party gains a strong following and the following year wins seats in the House elections.

March 24, 1934: The U.S. Congress passes the Philippine Independence Act (Tydings-McDuffie Act), creating an interim period from 1935 to 1946 for a semi-autonomous government, with complete independence to be achieved on July 4, 1946. The act is accepted by the Philippine legislature.

May 1935: Sixty people are killed in the Sakdal Revolt, in which more than sixty thousand demonstrators protest government attempts to suppress this growing popular movement.

September 17, 1935: Manuel Quezon (1935–1944) is elected president and Sergio Osmeña is vice president of the newly established Commonwealth of Philippines, which is inaugurated on November 15. The Philippines is now almost self-governing, with the United States handling defense and foreign affairs. General Douglas MacArthur is appointed military adviser to the Philippine government.

1938: President Manuel Quezon implements the "social justice" policy by freeing imprisoned Communist leaders, who join with Socialists to form a new Communist party under Crisanto Evangelista. Communist party fails to raise significant opposition to Nacionalistas in the elections of this year.

1940: President Quezon proclaims Tagalog the national language of the Philippines.

December 8, 1941: Following the attack on Pearl Harbor, the Japanese bomb military sites in the Philippines and the first small Japanese units land north of Luzon Island. The main invasion by the Japanese begins on December 10.

January 2, 1942: Japanese forces take Manila; the occupation regime instates Jorge Vargas as head of Philippine executive commission. Defeated forces organize large-scale guerrilla warfare to fight Japanese occupation.

March 29, 1942: Communists form guerrilla group Hukbalahap (People's Anti-Japanese Army) in Pampanga, on Luzon, under leadership of Luis Taruc (b. 1913). "Huks" fight occupation collaborators at the hacienda and barrio level, and also join noncommunist resistance groups loyal to the commonwealth government. On June 2, 1942, the Japanese execute Communist leader Crisanto Evangelista.

October 14, 1943: Nacionalista statesman José Laurel (1891–1959) is installed as president of the puppet government by the occupying Japanese. Manuel Quezon establishes an exile government in the United States to pave the way for independence.

August 1, 1944: Sergio Osmeña takes over the government in exile upon Quezon's death.

October 20, 1944: U.S. forces led by General Douglas MacArthur and Filipino forces led by Sergio Osmeña land on Leyte to commence the campaign to liberate the Philippines.

January 9–March 3, 1945: The Battle for Manila leaves the city in ruins.

February 27, 1945: Commonwealth government is reestablished.

July 5, 1945: The liberation of the Philippines is declared by General Douglas MacArthur.

September 3, 1945: The Japanese formally surrender all their forces on the Philippines to General MacArthur.

INDEPENDENT REPUBLIC OF PHILIPPINES: 1946–1998

The end of the war leaves the Philippines in a state of physical disarray; famine and epidemics devastate the population, but it is eager for the independence that finally comes in 1946. Among the problems faced by the new nation are communism and the Huk and agrarian rebellions, which are fueled by landlord exploitation of tenant farmers. The democracy that develops, modeled on the western legislative and judicial systems, is uniquely Filipino, and primarily benefits the ruling class until Ramon Magsaysay addresses the socioeconomic problems that give rise to antigovernment activity. By offering reform and assistance at the village level, Magsaysay brings an era of peace and confidence in government; after his death in an airplane crash, his programs are abandoned by subsequent administrations. Throughout the 1960s and 1970s, President Ferdinand Marcos's government freezes the political process and suppresses individual freedoms through referenda and constitutional amendments, actions that again give rise to opposition. The indigenous Moro people seeking autonomy or secession revive their struggle at this time. Under pressure from the Reagan administration to control communist insurgency through political, social and economic reform, Marcos calls for an early presidential election to reaffirm his power. After much public protest against Marcos's claim of victory, Corazón Aquino, who represents the nation's opposition to the dictatorship that had developed under Marcos, declares herself president. Marcos is offered asylum in Hawaii in exchange for a peaceful transition to a new government under Aquino. The new democracy continues to struggle against poverty and governmental inefficiency and relations with other Asian nations improve, but the economic crisis that grips much of Southeast Asia in the mid-1990s casts a shadow across the Philippines' economy and social progress.

Early 1946: The Communist Congress of Labor Organizations and the new National Peasants' Union (Pambansang Kaisahan ng mga Magbubu Kid) unite to support opposition to Manuel Roxas, leader of the Liberal Party. Opposition is led by Sergio Osmeña's Nacionalistas in a coalition with the Democratic Alliance, which includes among its leaders communists and Luis Taruc, chief of Hukbalahap.

April 23, 1946: The Liberal party wins the elections and the six Alliance candidates elected to the House, including Taruc, are denied their seats.

July 4, 1946: The Philippine Republic attains full independence and Manuel Roxas is inaugurated as its first president (governs 1946–1948). Elpidio Quirino is vice president.

1946: The Hukbalahap Rebellion against the Roxas administration is carried out by guerrillas who raid haciendas and towns under landlord control. By 1950 rebels establish bases from central and southern Luzon to Panay Island in the Visayas.

1946: The Philippine Trade Act (Bell Act) is passed by the U.S. Congress, easing tariffs on Philippine imports to the United States and providing for American exploitation of

Philippine natural resources. At this time, the Philippine Rehabilitation Act (Tydings Act) provides for war damages.

March 17, 1947: The Military Bases Agreement is concluded, granting ninety-nine-year leases for U.S. military bases in the Philippines.

January 1948: Roxas declares a general political amnesty.

March 6, 1948: Roxas outlaws the Hukbalahap guerrilla movement.

April 15, 1948: Manuel Roxas dies and is replaced by vice president Elpidio Quirino (governs 1949–1953) who fails to negotiate a truce with Luis Taruk and the Hukbalahap.

November 1949: Quirino wins a national election using what are widely believed to be unscrupulous methods.

1949–1950: Philippine delegate to the United Nations Carlos P. Romulo is elected president of the General Assembly; he is the first Asian to hold that position.

1950: Former guerrilla leader Ramon Magsaysay (1907–1957) is appointed defense minister and launches a successful campaign against the Huk, which renames itself the Hukbong Mapagpalaya ng Bayan (People's Liberation Army). By October the Huk movement goes underground.

1951: The National Movement for Free Elections (NAMFREL), a citizen's group fighting electoral corruption, polices the senatorial elections with support of Defense Secretary Ramon Magsaysay, and opposition Liberal Party members win legislative seats.

August 1951: The Mutual Security Treaty is signed with the United States to affirm its defense commitment.

1953: Magsaysay breaks with the Liberal Party and wins the presidential election for the Nacionalista Party, defeating the incumbent Elpidio Quirino; President Magsaysay institutes reforms and promotes policy of rural development.

1954: The Philippines participates in the establishment of the Southeast Asia Treaty Organization (SEATO) to develop Asian con-

tacts and expand the nation's focus of international relations beyond Washington.

February 17, 1954: Meeting between Benigno Aquino (1932–1983), a Manila journalist, and Luis Taruc, the Huk leader.

May 1954: Luis Taruc surrenders.

December 15, 1954: José Laurel is the principal architect of the Laurel-Langley Trade Agreement, giving the Philippines more favorable trade conditions.

March 18, 1957: Magsaysay is killed in a plane crash; vice president Carlos P. Garcia (1896–1971) is sworn in. The former Magsaysay for President Movement (MPM) regroups as the Progressive Party of the Philippines to challenge the two-party system and chooses Manuel Manahan as its presidential candidate. Progressives fail to provide significant opposition.

November 12, 1957: Carlos Garcia of the Nacionalista Party wins the election. Diosdado Macapagal (1910–) of the Liberal Party is vice president.

June 1958: Taruk is given a life sentence for his guerrilla activities.

1959: The Grand Alliance is formed by Nacionalistas and some Liberal Party members and wins senate seats.

December 14, 1961: The Grand Alliance joins the Liberal Party to become the majority party in the legislature. The Liberal Party's Macapagal wins the presidency; the Grand Alliance's Emmanuel Palaez is vice president.

1961: Philippines joins Malaysia and Thailand in the Association of Southeast Asia (ASA) to promote economic and cultural cooperation.

August 8, 1963: Land Reform Code abolishes sharecropping tenancy and provides government assistance to new farm owners.

1964: The U.S. Congress passes Philippines war-damages claims laws.

November 9, 1965: Liberal Party leader and Senate president Ferdinand Marcos (1914–1989) defeats Macapagal in the presidential election; he will remain in office until 1986.

September 1966: The United States agrees to

reduce military base leases to twenty-five years, and offers a $45 million aid package.

August 1967: Philippines joins the Association of Southeast Asian Nations (ASEAN).

September 11, 1968: Marcos grants amnesty to Huk leader Luis Taruc and another 165 prisoners.

December 26, 1968: The New Communist Party of the Philippines is founded.

November 11, 1969: Marcos defeats Sergio Osmeña, Jr., to become the first reelected president.

1970: Anti-American rioting in Manila during March and April. A general strike is proclaimed on April 7, protesting increases in oil and transportation prices. Students and workers demand Marcos's resignation.

November 27, 1970: Assassination attempt on Pope Paul VI in Manila.

August 1971: Marcos invokes emergency measures in response to terrorist act at opposition party rally, attributing the attack to communists and accusing Benigno Aquino of aiding subversives.

November 7, 1971: The Senate election is marred by violence in which two hundred are killed; opposition Liberal Party wins six of eight Senate seats contested in this election.

September 1972: Marcos declares martial law; demonstrations are banned, curfews are imposed, all news media are closed, and opposition politicians, including Benigno Aquino, are arrested.

October 20, 1972: A new constitution provides for Marcos's continued rule. Arrests mount and violence escalates.

January 17, 1973: Marcos extends martial law. There is little response to his offer of amnesty to Communists; some political detainees are released.

July 1973: Marcos eases free speech restrictions and lifts curfews; under a new constitution, his presidency is overwhelmingly approved by national referendum rather than national election. Further referenda extend his powers and term of office.

January 1975: The Catholic church calls for a boycott of the national referendum, doubting the possibility of honesty. The first anti-government demonstration takes place since the imposition of martial law.

April 4, 1975: Benigno Aquino begins a forty-day hunger strike.

June 1975: Marcos visits Beijing and announces the normalization of relations with China.

January 1976: Marcos suspends all national elections for the immediate future.

November 7, 1977: A report released on this date estimates that fifty thousand civilians have been killed over the past five years in the fighting between Muslim rebels and the government.

November 25, 1977: A military tribunal sentences Aquino to death; international criticism forces Marcos to reopen the trial. In 1980, Aquino will be allowed to go into exile.

June 12, 1978: Marcos is instated as premier, in addition to his position as president; his wife Imelda is appointed to the cabinet.

July 1979: Imelda Marcos visits Beijing and several trade links are signed. Agreement includes provision for an air link between Manila and Beijing, and for Philippine construction of tourist hotels in Beijing.

May 10, 1979: A revised trade treaty with Japan attempts to correct the imbalance in Japan's favor.

January 17, 1981: Marcos ends nine years of martial law.

June 16, 1981: Marcos is elected to another six-year term.

August 7, 1982: Marcos appoints his wife Imelda to the executive council, which is given presidential powers in the event of his death.

August 21, 1983: Benigno Aquino is shot to death at Manila airport upon his return from self-imposed exile; Marcos denies government involvement in the shooting. Violent protests ensue.

October 23, 1984: A commission concludes that the Philippine military is responsible for Aquino's death.

1985: Chief of Staff General Fabian C. Ver and twenty-five others are charged with assassination of Aquino on January 23. On December 2, a three-man civilian court acquits all the accused, and Ver is reinstated as chief of staff; the verdict is denounced as a mockery of justice.

December 3, 1985: Corazón Aquino (born 1933), Benigno Aquino's wife, announces her candidacy for the presidency.

February 7, 1986: Election-day violence claims at least thirty lives; the following day Aquino claims victory over Marcos, who calls for a state of emergency.

February 24, 1986: The Reagan administration offers the Marcos family political asylum; they are transported to Hawaii two days later. Switzerland freezes all their bank accounts, which are said to hold assets worth US$6 billion.

November 23, 1986: Aquino dismisses her defense minister Juan Ponce Enrile, who considers her policy toward the leftist New People's Army too lenient; he then becomes leader of the newly formed Grand Alliance for Democracy (GAD).

February 2, 1987: Voters approve a draft constitution providing for a single six-year presidential term; the legislature is to have a say on the status of U.S. military bases.

May 11, 1987: Aquino supporters gain a majority in legislative elections.

August 28, 1987: Former Aquino ally Colonel Gregorio Honasan attempts a military coup and is arrested.

October 17, 1988: The United States signs an interim agreement under which it will pay US$481 million for military bases for the next two years.

October 22, 1988: Imelda and Ferdinand Marcos are indicted by a grand jury in New York on charges of defrauding American banks and embezzling Philippine funds in the purchase of Manhattan real estate.

September 28, 1989: Ferdinand Marcos dies in Honolulu; Aquino denies him burial in the Philippines. Marcos loyalists demonstrate in Manila.

December 1, 1989: President Bush gives U.S. air support to government forces in an attempted military coup in the Philippines. Rebels surrender on December 5.

July 1990: Imelda Marcos is acquitted of charges in New York; she is embroiled in civil cases and a lawsuit in Switzerland.

September 1991: The Philippine Senate votes against extension of the U.S. lease of Subic Bay Naval Station; Aquino supports the base and calls for a referendum. In December the United States is ordered to leave by the end of 1992.

January 1992: Imelda Marcos campaigns for the presidency; she is arrested on fifty-three criminal charges.

June 23, 1992: Former defense secretary and Aquino ally General Fidel V. Ramos wins presidential election and is sworn in on June 30.

February 1992: Imelda Marcos agrees to bury her husband near the family home in the northern province of Ilocos, which had been his stronghold, rather than in Manila.

June 30, 1992: President Ramos takes office and grants amnesty to Communist insurgents as well as right-wing coup leaders.

November 1992: The U.S. naval base at Subic Bay closes; it will be converted into an industrial park and international port.

January 1994: The government signs a ceasefire with Muslim separatists.

November 1994: Hundreds of Filipino children abandoned by American fathers, mainly servicemen, seek U.S. entry visas by lottery.

May 1995: Imelda Marcos wins a seat in the Philippine House of Representatives.

September 1996: Government and Muslim rebels sign formal peace agreement ending a twenty-six-year insurgency; rebels accept increased autonomy rather than statehood.

July 1997: The Philippines, along with other fast-growing nations of South and Southeast Asia, is shaken by a currency crisis that has spread from Thailand; Manila is granted a $1 billion loan through the International Monetary Fund to help shore up the Philippine peso.

January 29, 1998: The U.S. Supreme Court reverses the 1990 decision of the New York court and finds Imelda Marcos guilty of fraud and embezzlement; she continues to maintain a strong political presence in the Philippines.

January 15, 1998: The United States and the Philippines reach an agreement that will allow U.S. fleet visits and joint military exercises in the Philippines. It will be signed on February 10 in Manila.

May 11, 1998: In elections for a new president, Joseph E. Estrada emerges as the winner, although his rivals will not fully concede until May 29. Estrada, a college dropout and onetime B-movie actor, has been opposed by former presidents Ramos and Aquino, but he has appealed to many Filipinos for his populist stance.

September 23, 1998: Philippine Airlines, the national carrier, suspends all service at midnight. The immediate cause is a labor dispute, but the airline has been running up large financial losses for years, and its demise at this time is but one of a number of signs that the Philippines economy is suffering from the general economic woes of Asia.

Singapore

PRECOLONIAL PERIOD: 13TH CENTURY–1819

In the late thirteenth century, Marco Polo refers to a thriving port that is possibly Temasek; archaeological evidence dating from the late fourteenth century suggests that Temasek is engaged in prosperous commerce. However, these histories conflict with Chinese chronicles from this time, in which piracy and violence in a small outpost are described. The stories in the *Sejarah Melayu* (Malay Annals), which are intended to establish a venerable Malaccan lineage, describe a great trading city destroyed by Srivijaya. The island is referred to as Singapura, or the "Lion City," which has led historians to propose a variety of interpretations, inasmuch as there are no lions on the island. The Portuguese traveler Tomé Pires's account, written just after the fall of Malacca in 1511, describes Singapore as consisting of nothing more than a few villages that are engaged in war and piracy. The picture of a small port lying off the main trade route, at times tied to an empire and at times surviving on piracy, emerges from these disparate sources.

13th century: Temasek (Sea Town) is likely the site of a small Srivijayan port on what is now Singapore.

1365: The Javanese epic poem *Nagarakertagama* describes a settlement on Singapore as Temasek.

Early 14th century: A Chinese trader's chronicle describes Temasek as a port with Chinese inhabitants and some two hundred to three hundred pirate boats.

By 1365: Majapahit (Javanese) lays claim to Temasek as vassal state.

c. **1390:** According to Malay legend, Sumatran prince Paramesvara rebels against Majapahit and is driven out by the Javanese. He establishes himself as ruler on Singapore.

c. **1398:** Singapore is attacked by invading Majapahit and Ayudhya (Siamese) empires. According to tradition, Paramesvara leaves for Malacca on Malay Peninsula and founds a sultanate. Singapore remains a minor port, with a small population of *orang laut* (sea people), under vassalage to Malacca.

1613: Date of burning down of a port, possibly Singapore, by the Portuguese after seizing Malacca.

Early 19th century: Temenggong (chief) of Johor Abdul Rahman establishes a town on the former site of Singapore. It is populated by a small number of Chinese and Malays, as well as the *orang laut* tribes.

COLONIAL PERIOD: 1819–1959

When Sir Thomas Stamford Raffles (1781–1826), arrives on Singapore as a government administrator and a representative of the British East India Company, he finds little evidence of former settlement. Raffles leases the port without authorization of the British Foreign Office, and with strong objections from the Dutch, during the Anglo-Dutch peace negotiations in Europe. The small population of Malays and *orang laut* are soon outnumbered by a large influx of Chinese who are brought to build the new colony; within a few years the port becomes a thriving international town attracting prosperous merchants from Europe, America, as well as Asia. The *orang laut* communities disperse; their populations diminish and become absorbed into the growing populations of immigrant Malays. To these are added Chinese and Indian groups; small numbers of Europeans and Arabs are also attracted to the exotic and thriving international port. By the end of the nineteenth century Singapore is the commercial center of the Malayo-Muslim world, as well as a center for Muslim religious publications.

February 6, 1819: Sir Thomas Stamford Raffles formalizes a trade agreement for the British East India Company with Sultan Husain Syah and Temenggong Abdul Rahman, establishing a British trading port on the island in return for yearly tribute. The port is governed by Colonel William Farquhar.

1823: Raffles quarrels with Farquhar and replaces him as Resident. Raffles then strips Farquhar of his rank of colonel.

1823: Raffles agrees to buy land rights and judicial powers of Sultan Husain and the Temenggong Abdul Rahman. He prohibits gambling and discourages drinking and prostitution, prohibits the slave trade, and puts other restrictions on slavery. Raffles lays the foundation for the Singapore Institution, a center for higher education financed through private funding.

1823–1826: Administration of Singapore is handed to Dr. John Crawford upon Raffles's retirement.

1824: Singapore becomes a British possession under the Anglo-Dutch Treaty of London, and the Treaty of Friendship and Alliance between the British East India Company and the Sultan Husain and Temenggong Abdul Rahman.

1826: Singapore joins Penang and Malacca to form the Straits Settlements under administration of the British East India Company,

in order to service and defend Britain's monopoly of trade with China. Penang is the administrative center.

1833: The British East India Company loses its trade monopoly in China and therefore reduces its involvement in the Straits Settlements.

1841: The Dutch lift trade restrictions imposed to limit Singapore's trade with Indonesia, and Singapore's economy expands.

1859: Telegraph service between Singapore and Batavia, on Java, is installed, and the first dry-dock facility opens.

Many of our people from the Fukien province were born and gathered together on this island. If we do not educate them, how could they be expected to appreciate the righteous path of our sages?

Inscription on Chinese Free School in Singapore (1861)

1864: Tanjong Pagar Dock Company, which will become the leading docking company by the end of the century, is formed.

April 1, 1867: Singapore becomes a Crown Colony along with the other Straits Settlements, ending the administration by the British East India Company. Sir Henry St. George Ord is the first governor.

1905: The Tanjong Pagar Dock Company is appropriated by the government in order to modernize port facilities; it is renamed the Tanjong Pagar Dock Board.

1910: The government takes over the manufacture and sale of opium in order to control its use.

1926: Mohammed Eunos bin Abdullah (born 1876), journalist and legislative leader, is the first president of the Kesatuan Melayu Singapura (Singapore Malay Union).

1933: The Aliens Ordinance establishes quotas for male immigrants and imposes fees on aliens; this law is aimed at stemming the growth of the Chinese population.

December 8, 1941: Japanese mount an air raid on Singapore.

February 1942: Governor Shenton Thomas orders the destruction of industrial and communications facilities in the face of the Japanese invasion. Britain surrenders on February 15 in what Churchill calls "the worst disaster and largest capitulation in British history." Japan sets up a colonial government and renames the country Syonan. *Sook ching* (purification campaign) is waged against Singaporean Chinese, who are massacred in large numbers.

September 12, 1945: Japan surrenders to the Allies; in compensation for atrocities committed during the occupation, Japan will extend considerable financial assistance to Singapore.

Late 1945: Singapore is under British military rule.

December 1945: The Malay Democratic Union, the first indigenous political party, is formed. The party supports a Malayan Union in which Singapore is included.

April 1946: Singapore's status as separate Crown Colony is reinstated. Singapore is excluded from the Malayan Union and, in 1948, from the Federation of Malaya, which replaces it.

1948: A Malayan emergency crackdown on left-wing activities affects Singapore's trade unions and radical political groups, leaving the Legislative Council in the hands of moderates.

1951: The Progressive Party wins six of nine seats in the Legislative Council.

1953: Britain appoints Sir George Rendel to head a commission to review the constitution and take steps toward self-government.

October 1954: The People's Action Party under Lee Kuan Yew is formed.

April 1955: The Rendel constitution is implemented; David Marshall, leader of the Labor Front, becomes chief minister.

June 1956: Marshall resigns as chief minister after failing to negotiate independence; Communist uprisings ensue under chief minister Lim Yew Hock.

INDEPENDENCE: 1959–1998

British withdrawal from Singapore leaves the small city-state with a tangible infrastructure of shipping and other technological installations, schools, hospitals, recreational facilities, as well as an effective parliamentary government. Under the PAP's unopposed leadership, political stability is assured. English is promoted as the language for development in business, technology, and government, while ethnic mother tongues are valued for maintaining morality and cultural richness. Since independence, Singapore develops into a prosperous nation and leading world port with one of the highest living standards in Asia.

May 30–June 5, 1959: On May 30 the People's Action Party wins forty-three of the fifty-one seats in the first Legislative Assembly. On June 3 Britain grants limited self-government under a new constitution; Britain remains responsible for defense and foreign affairs. On June 5 Lee Kuan Yew becomes prime minister and the new government seeks inclusion in the Federation; Malaysia resists incorporating Singapore's left-leaning Chinese majority.

June 1961: The left-wing faction of the PAP opposes Lee's proposal to be included in the Federation of Malaysia; dissenters form the United People's Party under Ong Eng Guan.

July 1961: PAP dissenters form the Barisan Sosialis (Socialist Front) under Lim Chin Siong.

February 1963: Communists, trade union leaders, student activists, and members of the BS are arrested.

July 9–September 16, 1963: The Malaysia Agreement includes the Federation of Malaya, Singapore, Sarawak, and North Borneo (Sabah) in the Federation of Malaysia. In signing this, Britain agrees to an independent Singapore, but the agreement is not implemented until September 16.

August 31, 1963: Singapore unilaterally declares independence from Britain. PAP wins legislative victory and restricts left-wing activities. Lee Kuan Yew will effectively rule as a dictator until 1990, imposing his own political and social views on the people of Singapore, who acquiesce because of the economic prosperity he brings.

September 1963: Indonesia objects to the Federation of Malaysia and initiates attacks that are to last two years, causing considerable damage to Singapore's trade facilities.

Mid-1964: Racial riots and political tensions in Singapore jeopardize alliance with Malaysia.

August 9, 1965: Singapore reluctantly leaves the Federation of Malaysia and on December 22 becomes the independent Republic of Singapore within the Commonwealth of Great Britain; Malay remains a national language.

December 1965: First meeting of Parliament; minor administrative changes are made and the constitution is retained.

1967: The City and State Project gives the government power to acquire lands for development of new towns as well as for urban renewal projects.

1968: The Environmental Health Act is passed to control pollution and enhance the health and well-being of citizens.

November 1971: The last British troops are withdrawn.

1973: An international sports complex is opened; Singapore hosts the Southeast Asia Peninsular Games.

1974: The Newspaper and Printing Presses Act supervises government criticism by the press.

1986: The Urban Development Authority is formed to restore ethnic neighborhoods and preserve colonial heritage amid the proliferation of modern development.

May 1987: The Internal Security Act is invoked to arrest dissidents.

1987: English is adopted as the first language in educational institutions.

November 26, 1990: Lee Kuan Yew resigns and becomes a senior cabinet minister. Goh Chok Tong becomes prime minister, promising a more open, less restrictive political atmosphere.

1991: Japanese Prime Minister Toshiki Kaifu formally apologizes for crimes committed during the occupation of Singapore.

1992: Singapore announces a decision partly to privatize the nation's mass transit, telecommunications, and port facilities, as well as gas and electric utilities, by offering shares to Singapore citizens.

But there are those who stay to root
that in the greening of Singapore
(of course they know it can be greener)
they may shelter under the shade
of trees they have planted
(they know that some are instant)
and pluck the fruits of trees
seeded years ago.

"Opting Out of Singapore," poem by Robert Yeo
(20th century)

September 1, 1993: Ong Teng Cheong, a deputy prime minister and former PAP chairman, is sworn in for a six-year term as

Singapore's first directly elected president; although the position is largely ceremonial, since 1991 the president has some veto powers in cabinet elections as well as influence over budgetary decisions.

May 5, 1994: An eighteen-year old American, Michael Fay, is punished with flogging for incidents of vandalism committed in Singapore in October 1993. He is also fined and held in prison for four months. Singapore responds to international criticism by pointing to Singapore's low crime rate. Fay is released on June 21.

September 23, 1994: When Dutch engineer Johannes van Damme is hanged on narcotics charges, he becomes the first Westerner to be executed under Singapore's 1975 drug law mandating the death penalty.

December 18, 1995: Singapore, as a member of the Association of Southeast Asian Nations, signs a pact declaring the area from Myanmar to Indonesia a nuclear-free zone. This is an effort to prevent Southeast Asian nations from acquiring or producing their own nuclear weapons.

December 1996: Prime minister Goh Chok Tong is declared reelected when no rival is nominated in his district.

January 2, 1997: The ruling PAP captures all but two seats in the eighty-three-seat Parliament. Prime Minister Goh claims his election constitutes a rejection of Western-style liberal democracy.

January 1998: Singapore has been relatively free of the economic storms buffeting its Asian neighbors, but there are signs that it is also being affected, as in recent months its stock market index has declined 340 points and its currency (the Singapore dollar) has declined to a seven-year low.

June 1998: Singapore's economy, still better off than that of most other Asian nations, is showing further signs of strain. One of the world's major manufacturers of computer parts, which make up 45 percent of its locally produced exports, it has experienced a 17 percent decline in such exports within the last year. Retail sales within Singapore itself have declined 25 percent. In place of the thousands of wealthy Asians who have for years flocked to Singapore to spend their money, many more thousands of poor Indonesians and Malaysians are trying to sneak illegally into Singapore to find jobs. On June 30 the government announces it intends to spend S$2 billion to stimulate the economy, making for the first budget deficit in over a decade.

August 23, 1998: Prime Minister Goh speaks out against the increasing claims by Malaysians and Indonesians that Singapore is trying to capitalize on its two neighbors' economic troubles. Goh points out that Singapore holds billions of Malaysian *ringgit* and is leaving several trillion *rupiah* deposited in Indonesia's banks; Singapore also has some S$14 billion invested in the two countries, so it has nothing to gain from a decline in their economies.

September 23, 1998: In 1996 Singapore's government announced it is commencing "Singapore One–One Network for Everyone": installing an ultra-fast fiber-optic network that would eventually link every household, school, and office in Singapore. By now some S$200 million in government and private funds has been spent and the network is available to some 2,800,000 people, but only 300,000 people are known to be making use of it.

Thailand

PREHISTORIC THAILAND: 36,000 B.C.–A.D. 100

Although there may have been early hominids who strayed into and through the land that would become Thailand, there are no known traces of human occupation until about 36,000 B.C. By this time, these people are modern *Homo sapiens* who share a fairly common culture with many people living throughout Southeast Asia and southern and central China. However, they are not the direct ancestors of most modern inhabitants of Thailand; during the ensuing millennia, different peoples will make their way into Thailand, all—except for those from India—probably of Mongoloid extraction. By about 10,000 B.C. the inhabitants of Thailand are participating in the general cultural developments of Southeast Asia, conducting a basic subsistence economy but diversifying their food sources and toolkit; starting about 2500 B.C. they begin to adopt agriculture (most especially rice), domesticate animals (pigs, cattle, fowl), and make pottery; by at least 1500 B.C. they are adding metallurgy to their repertoire of skills. During the next 1,500 or so years, the inhabitants of Thailand develop an economy that appears to be heavily dependent on wet-land cultivation of rice, which in turn leads to a more complex society, but what is lacking is evidence of political organization.

36,000–26,000 B.C.: At Lang Rongrien, a rock shelter in southern Thailand, simple stone tools indicate human occupation; nothing more is known of these people nor of other contemporary sites in Thailand. At this site, there is then apparently a complete break in occupation until the Hoabinhian culture phase.

21,000–2500 B.C.: In northern and central Thailand there are indications that some sites remain inhabited continuously to the Neolithic period.

10,000–2500 B.C.: During this period, the Hoabinhian culture phase (so named after its prime site in northern Vietnam, Hoa Binh) is found in several parts of Thailand. The culture is distinguished by its particular type of flaked pebbles used as tools. The people also use many wooden and bamboo tools, including the blowgun, and they make fishtraps and baskets. There are indications (as at Spirit Cave, northwestern Thailand) that these people gather edible fruits, legumes, and roots, but there is as yet no firm evidence for systematic cultivation.

3600–2500 B.C.: There are claims that even as early as 3600 B.C. people in northeastern Thailand (at the sites of Non Nok Tha and Ban Chiang) are making copper and bronze tools. This would make these people the earliest known users of such metallurgy in the world. This claim is disputed by most experts, for they find none of the supporting context for metallurgy as found elsewhere in the world; most experts feel that metallurgy did not begin in Thailand until about 1500 B.C., and they redate the finds at Non Nok Tha and Ban Chiang to this later period.

2500–1000 B.C.: This is regarded as the Neolithic period for much of Thailand. There are different manifestations at different sites, but some shared features—a variety of stone and bone tools, pottery, agriculture, domesticated animals. One particular culture of this period is that named after the Ban Kao site in the Kwae Noi River valley, northwest of Bangkok; eventually the Ban Kao culture extends all the way down into peninsular Malaysia. Ban Kao people make shouldered adzes, stone bracelets, bone fishhooks, cloth-beaters, and spindle whorls; they erect houses raised on posts; they make cord-marked pottery, often with tripod supports; although it is not clear whether they cultivate rice, they have stone reaping knives; they bury their dead with considerable grave goods.

2000–1400 B.C.: By 2000 B.C. at the latest, dry-land rice is being cultivated in central Thailand. In southern Thailand, strong ag-riculturally based communities are emerging. At Khok Phanom Di, about thirty miles east of Bangkok, a large burial site indicates a major community; they fish with harpoons and hooks and eat a wide variety of seafood; they have domesticated dogs and fowl and possibly the domesticated pig; they have fine pottery vessels, distinctively decorated with incised zones filled with stamped impressions. Their burial sites suggest some people are able to afford considerable possessions.

1500–500 B.C.: It is at the outset of this period, most experts believe, that metallurgy based on copper and bronze begins in Thailand. (Still uncertain, however, is the relationship of this development to metallurgy in China at this time.) The full-fledged Bronze Age culture does not begin until about 1000 B.C. with the use of metals for tools (axes, fishhooks), weapons (spearheads and arrowheads), and jewelry (bracelets). Thailand proves to have plentiful amounts of copper and tin.

500–1 B.C.: Although isolated iron artifacts have been made in Thailand in previous centuries, it is during this time that iron begins to be used more widely there. It is also the time when wet-land rice cultivation is adopted in Thailand, advanced in some cases by the construction of moats, reservoirs, and canals to direct water to rice fields. Such projects probably require more complex village societies in terms of specialized individual skills and organized community labor; they probably also lead to some concentration of wealth and power, but aside from elaborate burials, little is known of the people who inhabited Thailand during this time. By the second half of this period, there are increasing signs of trade from India passing through Thailand.

MON COMMUNITIES AND TAI MUANG: A.D. 100–1000

During the early centuries of the first millennium, life in Thailand proceeds much as it has for the previous one thousand or more years. There is some increase in village activities, however, as measured by irrigation projects, metallurgy, trade, and elaborate burials. The people in Thailand at this time are probably speaking a Mon-Khmer language, linking them with other Austroasiatic peoples from southern Burma, Cambodia, and northern Vietnam. At least by about A.D. 500, it is believed that Indian traders who are in contact with some of these Mon people are introducing Hinduism and Buddhism; in particular, Mon communities from west-central to eastern Thailand develop a society and economy and culture with a strong Buddhist element: this complex is known as Dvaravati. Meanwhile, somewhere in the region of northern Vietnam and southern China, people known as Tai are living in valleys and lowlands; their culture, generally similar to that of other peoples in Southeast Asia and southern China, shares some distinctive elements: houses on piles above ground, tattooing, higher social status of women. In particular, the Tai language differs considerably from that spoken by their neighbors, the Chinese, Vietnamese, Burmese, Cambodians, and Malaysians. Certainly by about the year 700 Tai people are moving into Thailand from northern Vietnam and southeastern China. With their distinctive sociopolitical arrangement known as *muang*, these Tai people begin to establish the social-political underpinnings of historical Thailand by about the year 1000.

A.D. 1–700: Possibly under pressure from the more expansive Chinese, during the early centuries of the Christian era, small numbers of Tai people from southern China and/or northern Vietnam apparently begin to move across northern Vietnam, then into Laos, and possibly into northern Thailand.

500–900: During this period a network of settlements develops across west-central Thailand eastward and northeastward into what is now Laos. These settlements appear to be on trade routes linking the region to southern Burma (and ultimately India) to the west, Cambodia and the Gulf of Siam to the southeast, and Vietnam and China to the northeast. Thriving on trade, these settlements grow into fairly ambitious towns, with earth ramparts and moats; however, there is no evidence that this is anything like an organized or centralized empire. It is believed that these towns are the work of Mon people linked to fellow Mon in Burma who have long come under the influence of the Hindu and Buddhist culture of India. In any case, these towns in Thailand have a strong Buddhist presence, including monasteries, sculptures made of terracotta or stucco, and

inscriptions; the culture complex is obviously imported from India, as is reflected by its name given to these towns and their culture complex—Dvaravati. Not clear is exactly what relationship this Buddhist culture has with the Tai people who are now moving into this region.

700–900: During this period, some Tai people move still farther into Thailand, into Burma, even into northeastern India. They apparently bring with them some of their social institutions, specifically the *chao* (lord), a warlord or chieftain who exerts authority over an area with several villages—probably more a mutual defense arrangement than actual conquest: this distinctive sociopolitical arrangement is called a *muang* in the Tai language. Meanwhile, between about 730 and 900, inhabitants of Yunnan, the southwestern region of China, set up a kingdom known as Nan-chao (southern lord); Nan-chao and its leaders seem to be fairly aggressive and even move into northern Thailand. It is not known exactly what their relations are with the Tai of the regions they conquer, but it is possible that Nan-chao both pushes some Tai deeper into Thailand

and inspires other Tai to adopt its more organized and assertive style.

900–1100: Nan-chao loses much of its external power by the early 900s, but the Tai in Thailand now find themselves pretty much hemmed in by the newly liberated (from China) Vietnamese to the northeast, the Champa kingdom along Vietnam's central coast, the kingdoms in Burma to the west, and the Khmer kingdom in Cambodia and central Thailand to the south. By the end of the eleventh century the Tai people in Thailand are beginning to define themselves apart from their neighbors and yet to interact with these people.

EMERGING TAI STATES: 1000–1351

Initially the classical empires dominate Southeast Asia. In the west, the Pagan empire of Burma holds sway. In the south central region, the Khmer empire ruled by Angkor administers widespread provinces and principalities headed by governors or princes. Following a resurgence of Theravada Buddhism, the Tai peoples in the north begin an advance southward. They assimilate indigenous peoples, inhabit provinces at the fringes of the empires, and start to act independently. Notable are the Tai kingdoms of Lan Na and Phayao which arise in the north, Lopburi to the south, and Nakhon Si Thammarat on the Malay Peninsula. In the center is Sukhothai, which achieves impressive dimensions in political prestige, geographical influence, and artistic accomplishment. This is viewed as the cradle of Tai civilization. As their founding rulers die, the early Tai states recede in power and importance.

c. **1000:** In northern Thailand, or Lan Na (Yonok region), Theravada Buddhism sweeps through Tai peoples. They will begin to inhabit lowland plains to south, suitable for irrigated cultivation of rice, and to build urban centers.

1000–1200: The Khmer empire establishes dominance over central area, including Mon-Buddhist-Dvaravati cultural regions.

1001: Lopburi, a fringe province of the Khmer empire, seeks to assume independent role by sending diplomatic mission to China. It sends further missions in 1115 and 1155, during periods of instability in Khmer empire.

c. **1050:** In Burma, the Pagan empire arises and expands southward to take over Mon states of Pegu and Thaton.

c. **1100:** The Shan of northeastern Burma come to rule northern Burma and southwestern China. According to chronicle accounts, the Shan also conquer Lao *muang* states in the Lan Sang and Yonok regions of northern Thailand.

c. **1150:** A bas relief sculpture at Angkor Wat depicts a detachment of armed Syam Kuk (Siamese) soldiers, led by a Khmer commander riding on an elephant.

Late 1100s: Chronicles suggest that Nan-Chao allows independent Tai *muang* in southern Yunnan, one of which is Lan Na, possibly as a buffer against the Pagan empire.

1240s: Following defeat of the Khmer stronghold in the central region, Sri Indraditya (reigns 1240s–1270s) becomes the first Tai king of Sukhothai.

c. **1250:** Lopburi becomes independent of the Khmer empire; it will send diplomatic missions to Mongol court from 1280 until 1299.

1250: By now the principality of Nakhon Si Thammarat on the Malay Peninsula, a center of international shipping and trade, is in Tai hands after two centuries of Khmer, Malay, Burmese, Mon, and South Indian rivalry for power on the peninsula.

c. **1250–1350:** The Tai gradually overrun the central region heretofore controlled by the Pagan and Khmer empires, establishing a series of Tai *muang* from the northern uplands to the Malay peninsula.

1253: Khubilai Khan leads Mongol armies in the capture of Nan-Chao and eventually of Song China. Mongols begin pacification of the "southern barbarians," including Shan and Tai groups, who begin to send tribute to Mongol rulers in China.

1259: In the north, Mangrai (reigns 1259–1317) becomes ruler of Chiang Saen principality. He quickly absorbs neighboring Tai principalities, creating Lan Na kingdom and establishing alliances with neighboring Tai princes. On April 18, 1296, he begins construction of the new capital city of Chiang Mai.

c. 1279: Ramkhamhaeng (reigns 1279?–1298) becomes the third king of Sukhothai. By exercising military strength and moral prestige, and by forming alliances and vassal-overlord relationships with other principalities and dependencies, he creates an empire throughout central Thailand and the Malay Peninsula.

Late 1200s: Chinese chronicles refer to Sukhothai as Siem, or Siam. It is this name, Siam, that Westerners will come to assign to all of Thailand in the ensuing centuries.

1283: King Ramkhamhaeng of Sukhothai claims to invent an accessible script form of the tonal Tai language. Siamese Tai becomes the language of politics and status.

1287: Leaders of three major Tai states—Mangrai of Lan Na, Ngam Muang of Phayao, and Ramkhamhaeng of Sukhothai—form an alliance against the Mongols.

1296: A Chinese envoy visits Angkor and reports war with the Siamese (probably Sukhothai); he also mentions a silkworm industry run by Siamese settlers.

> *There is fish in the water and rice in the fields. The lord of the realm does not levy toll on his subjects for traveling the roads; they lead their cattle to trade or ride their horses to sell. . . . When any commoner or man of rank dies, his estate—his elephants, wives, children, granaries, rice, retainers and groves of areca and betel—is left in its entirety to his son.*
>
> From an inscription attributed to Ramkhamhaeng, king of Sukhothai (1292)

1296: Chinese Mongols recapture the rebellious Chiang Hung, and Mangrai quickly retakes the principality. Major Chinese invasions in 1301 of northern Tai region prove unsuccessful.

1298: After the death of King Ramkhamhaeng, the Sukhothai empire begins to falls apart as smaller principalities struggle for independence. By 1320 Sukhothai is reduced to a kingdom of only local influence.

c. 1309–1311: Chiang Hung and Chiang Mai conduct a series of raids into Chinese territory. After China turns to diplomacy, Chiang Mai sends tribute missions to Chinese court (1315–1347).

1317: Mangrai's death leads to a dynastic power struggle in the kingdom of Lan Na, resulting in six kings in eleven years. Finally his great-grandson Kham Fu (reigns 1328–1337) restores stability to diminished Lan Na. He establishes the new administrative city of Chiang Saen northeast of Chiang Mai.

AYUDHYA KINGDOM: 1351–1767

This period, named after the kingdom's new capital city, encompasses the centuries that see the foundation of a sophisticated, cosmopolitan, and resilient Siam as the leading power in Southeast Asia. The growth of a central administration, tied to an intricate hierarchy, is facilitated by the implementation of civil and criminal legal codes. Trade, especially rice export, becomes an essential source of revenue. Despite close and eventually disruptive commercial and diplomatic involvement with Europeans, Ayudhya is able to maintain its autonomy. Periodic internal instability occurs with often violent succession struggles. Militarism plays a key role as the kingdom is surrounded by aggressive foes — other Tai states, Cambodians, Vietnamese, and the Burmese who eventually destroy Ayudhya.

March 4, 1351: According to chronicle accounts, Lopburi U Thong, or King Ramathibodi I (reigns 1351–1369), founds a new capital city of Ayudhya north of mouth of Chaophraya River, which empties into the Gulf of Siam.

1353: After capturing the capital city of Luang Prabang with the help of the Khmer army, Fa Ngum (reigns 1353–1373) ascends the throne of the Kingdom of Lan Sang.

1369: King Ku Na (reigns 1355–1385) of Lan Na invites the Sukhothai Buddhist monk Venerable Sumana to establish the Singhalese sect in Lamphun. Over the following centuries, Lan Na kings offer patronage to the sect, which becomes a leading religious and cultural influence on northern Tai people.

1370s: After a Ming restriction is imposed on Chinese export ceramics, production of ceramics as a commercial venture begins in Sukhothai. Export of Tai wares into other regions of Southeast Asia continues into the sixteenth century.

1378: King Borommaracha I (reigns 1370–1388) forces Sukhothai to submit to Ayudhya domination, then goes on to wage war against the kingdom of Lan Na.

Late 1300s: The kings of Ayudhya set up formal codes of civil and criminal law. In 1397 Ayudhya imposes its legal system on Sukhothai.

1400: Sukhothai King Mahathammarcha III (reigns 1398–1419) captures Nakhon Sawan from Ayudhya, blocking its river traffic from the north, and gains influence over the principalities of Nan and Phrae.

1404–1405: Lan Na, with an army of some 300,000, beats back an invasion from Chinese Yunnan.

c. 1412: Ayudhya installs a chief resident in Sukhothai, reduces Mahathammarcha III to vassal ruler. In 1438 Sukhothai is incorporated as a province of the kingdom of Ayudhya.

1431–1432: An Ayudhya military expedition seizes Angkor, loots the capital, and installs a vassal ruler.

1442: Ayudhya begins a century of warfare against Lan Na. To accommodate the campaign, King Borommatrailokanat (reigns 1448–1488) temporarily moves the capital north to Phitsanulok, systematizes state administration, and extends control over manpower.

1448–1488: Ayudhya King Borommatrailokanat issues the Laws of Civil Hierarchy and of Military and Provincial Hierarchies, outlining a complex social structure based on specific status assigned to each individual.

c. 1450: At this time three major Tai states exist — Ayudhya, Lan Na, and Lan Sang in the northeast, with its capital at Luang Prabang.

1451: A Lan Na army unsuccessfully attempts to win back Sukhothai for its hereditary prince.

1456–1457: The Ayudhya kingdom unsuccessfully tries to seize the Lan Na cities of Phrae and Lampang.

1478: In Lan Sang, the Vietnamese capture the capital of Luang Prabang. King Suvanna Banlang (reigns 1479–1486) reorganizes troops, ousts the Vietnamese, and recaptures Luang Prabang. Victory results in two centuries of peace between Vietnam and Lan Sang.

1507: Conflict between the Lan Na and Ayudhya kingdoms resumes in the Sukhothai region, where the Lan Na forces are defeated. In 1515 Ayudhya captures and loots Lampang, but pulls back again.

1511: After seizing Malacca, the Portuguese send their first mission to Ayudhya to forge a pact granting the Portuguese trading rights and rights of residence and religious freedom in Siam (as Thailand is now known to Westerners), in exchange for Portuguese firearms and ammunition.

1515: A Lan Na army from Chiang Mai invades Ayudhya but is driven back. King Ramathibodi II (reigns 1489–1529) counterattacks and defeats the Chiang Mai army at the Battle of Me Wang River.

1525: Late in the reign of Lan Na king Müang Kaeo (reigns 1495–1526), the Pali-language chronicle *Jinakalamali* is written to memorialize acts of religious merit performed by the king and his steady patronage of the Singhalese Buddhist sect.

1545: The capital city, Ayudhya, burns, losing some ten thousand buildings.

1545: Assassination of King Ket Chettharat (reigns 1526–1538, 1543–1545) marks the abrupt decline of Lan Na that started with his reign.

1549: Following political unrest, Ayudhya is attacked by a large Burmese army from the north and by Khmer from the east. King Chakkraphat (reigns 1548–1569) successfully defends his empire but begins a military reorganization and fortification in order to withstand future Burmese attacks.

1558: Burmese take the city of Chiang Mai and establish a military garrison there to guard Lan Na, now a Burmese vassal state. Lan Na becomes a base for Burmese campaigns against Ayudhya and Lan Sang. During the next eleven years the Burmese continue to attack Tai territory and cities.

1569: Ayudhya falls to the Burmese, who loot the city, install a vassal king, and take away thousands of war captives. They leave behind a small military garrison. Over the next two decades, as Khmer invade six times, the Burmese allow the Ayudhya kingdom to upgrade its defense forces and fortifications so that it can be responsible for its own protection.

1575: Ayudhya sends diplomatic missions to China seeking a replacement for the royal seal of office, which the Burmese destroyed. This signals China's recognition of Siamese autonomy.

June 1590: Naresuan (reigns 1590–1605) becomes king of Ayudhya, after defying Burmese and repulsing several Burmese punitive expeditions from 1585 to 1587. He makes crucial changes to strengthen central government.

October 1592: After hearing of Japan's invasion of Korea, King Naresuan offers help to China by sending a Siamese navy against Toyotomi Hideyoshi's forces. In February 1593 China rejects the Siamese offer.

January 18, 1593: In a major offensive, the Burmese army attacks Ayudhya and is defeated in the epic Battle of Nong Sarai. The Siamese victory, led by King Naresuan atop a war elephant, puts an end to three decades of Burmese aggression. Naresuan goes on to pursue successful campaigns against Cambodia and the southern Burmese coastal provinces of Tenasserim and Tavoy; this opens the way to trade in the Bay of Bengal.

Being an indentured servant you will lead a dog's life. . . . They will tattoo your wrist and force you into the corvée,
> *You will suffer all the time. . . .*
> *Dragging heavy logs around*
> *With a fragile body like yours, you won't*
stand a chance

"Khun Chang Khun Phaen," Thai folk tale

1598: Following a series of military campaigns against Burma, which virtually collapses in 1599, Ayudhya gains suzerainty over Lan Na. In the same year, King Naresuan signs a treaty with the Spanish based in the Philippines. Other trading partners of Ayudhya include Portugal, China, Japan, and the Ryukyu Kingdom.

1602: Dutch traders obtain Ayudhya permission to open a trading post at Pattani, followed by one in Ayudhya in 1608. Dutch influence increases when in 1617 they gain a monopoly over the export of Siamese hides. In 1632, they assist King Prasat Thong (reigns 1630–1656) in suppressing conspiracy of Japanese mercenaries led by Yamada Nagamasa. Later relations between Dutch and the court deteriorate, and Dutch close Ayudhya post in 1663. A new treaty in 1664 brings Dutch back to Ayudhya.

1608: King Ekathotsarot (reigns 1605–1610/11) sends the first Siamese European diplomatic mission to the Netherlands after sending one to Portuguese Goa in 1606.

1612: English ships of East India Company arrive in Ayudhya and establish factories (trading stations) at Ayudhya and Pattani. Competition with the Dutch leads the English to withdraw from Siam by 1623. They return in the 1660s.

1630s–1640s: King Prasat Thong (reigns 1629–1656) enhances the position of the throne within the state by reducing the power of nobles and by encouraging Dutch cooperation.

1662: In order to finance ongoing wars against Lan Na and Burma, King Narai (reigns 1656–1688) imposes a royal monopoly on all trade.

French Jesuit missionaries arrive in Ayudhya; they offer technical expertise in constructing fortifications and palaces and are allowed to open a seminary. In 1673, a French ecclesiastical mission brings letters from Pope Clement IX and Louis XIV. The Ayudhya court sends a 1684 mission to France requesting an alliance; the French mission that returns in 1685–1686, however, is interested primarily in converting King Narai to Christianity.

July 14, 1687: In the Mergui Massacre, some sixty British are killed at Tenasserim coastal port after a breakdown of relations between the English East India Company and the Siamese over privateering. After local authorities open fire on the English, the Ayudhya

kingdom later calls in the French, with a military presence, to govern Mergui.

September 1687: In six large warships, a French mission of diplomats, Jesuits, and artisans, headed by the director of the French East India Company, arrives in Ayudhya. The mission concludes a new commercial treaty with Siam on December 11, 1687.

June 5, 1688: Constantine Phaulkon (1647–1688) is executed for treason. The Greek adventurer had arrived in Ayudhya in 1678, ingratiated himself with King Narai, and rapidly rose to a position of prominence. Phaulkon's advocacy of closer relations with France, favoritism toward particular traders, and numerous other machinations provoke opposition into action against him, as the king lies dying. Known as the Revolution of 1688, the uprising is motivated by abuse of power and by Siamese insecurity about the game of international politics. In consequence, French troops are ousted from Bangkok garrison and Mergui; French missionaries are imprisoned temporarily and Catholics are persecuted. After an attempt to play off the French against the Dutch and contact with European intrigue, the Siamese court keeps interaction with Westerners to a minimum for the next 150 years.

1720: A Siamese land and sea expeditionary force unsuccessfully attempts to restore the ousted Cambodian king. Cambodians agree to pay regular tribute to the Ayudhya kingdom.

c. **1720s:** Exports of Siamese rice to China increase and now are handled by Chinese rather than Dutch merchants. Chinese enter official service in the Ayudhya court to conduct trade on its behalf. Thus local Chinese community becomes more fully integrated into the economic, social, and political life of Ayudhya.

January 1733: The death of King Thai Sa (reigns 1709–1733) leads to typically violent succession dispute, carried on this time by opposing armies of thousands. King Borommakot (reigns 1733–1758) emerges victorious and, to prevent such future struggles, he fragments state control of manpower by diffusing the functions of central administration to the provinces.

1744–1745: Following a Burmese initiative, Ayudhya opens diplomatic relations with Burma.

1751: A mission from Ceylon asks for Ayudhyan help in restoring Singhalese Buddhism, in decline after Portuguese and Dutch rule. Ayudhya sends eighteen Siamese monks to reordain Singhalese monks and to found an order of Siamese monks in Ceylon. This request marks Siam's importance as an international center of Buddhism.

April 1760: Hostilities resume as a Burmese invasion force besieges an unprepared Ayudhya. The Burmese retreat after their leader is killed accidentally in an explosion.

1763: After a six-month siege Burmese forces capture Chiang Mai and Lamphun. Soon all Lan Na is under Burmese control.

April 7, 1767: Following the siege, Burmese capture Ayudhya, destroy the capital, and take thousands of prisoners, including nobility and royal family members, back to Burma.

Some wandered about, starving, searching for food. They were bereft of their families, their children and wives, and stripped of their possession and tools. . . . They had no rice, no fish, no clothing. . . . They found only the leaves of trees and grass to eat. . . . Afflicted with a thousand ills, some died and others lived on.

From an account of life after the Burmese sack of Ayudhya (late 18th century)

BANGKOK ERA: 1767–1932

Siam's new capital is founded at Bangkok by King Rama I, the first of the Chakri dynasty (which is still on the throne). From a small kingdom with loose control over local hereditary rulers and warlords, Siam eventually becomes an integrated nation administered by a large central bureaucracy. Production of rice and other commodities for the export market, as well as trade, first with Asian partners and then with the West, lead to economic growth and make Bangkok a leading port city. Siam avoids colonization by playing off Western powers against each other and by making territorial concessions to England and France. Reform and modernization of the religious, legal, educational, and military establishments complete the era.

October 1767: Sino-Thai leader Taksin seizes the port of Thonburi, defeats Burmese forces in the region, and establishes the new Siamese capital there. He begins rule (reigns 1767–1782) and gradually recaptures Ayudhyan territories.

1774: Lan Na forces sent by Burmese against Taksin's army instead join the Siamese. After a Burmese counterattack, Siamese troops retake Chiang Mai in late 1776.

April 6, 1782: Following a rebellion against the increasingly cruel and irrational Taksin, Chaopraya Chakri accepts the throne as

Rama I (reigns 1782–1809). He soon moves the capital across the Chaophraya River to Bangkok, where a new royal palace, Buddhist monasteries, and dwellings for officials and aristocracy are constructed along a network of canals.

February 1785–early 1786: Five Burmese armies totaling more than 100,000 soldiers invade Siam in the north and south but are repulsed.

August 27, 1785: To win Britain as an ally against the Siamese and Burmese, the sultan of Kedah grants the port and island of Penang to the East India Company. In 1800, the British will gain the territory on Malay Peninsula that they name Province Wellesley.

1785: Rama I requires all freemen to perform corvée (forced labor); to ensure compliance, all are to be tattooed with the names of their master and town.

1788–1789: Rama I calls a council to formulate the definitive text of the Pali-language Buddhist scriptures, the *Tripitaka*, and issues laws to reform religion.

1797: Thailand's literary classic *Ramakian*, the Siamese version of the Indian *Ramayana* epic, is set to verse. Other appropriated Asian classics of the era include the Chinese *Romance of Three Kingdoms*, the Mon chronicle *Rachathirat*, the Javanese *Palang* and *Inao*, *Unarut* from the Indian *Mahabharata*, the Persian *Duodecagon*, and the Pali *Mahavamsa*.

1805: Rama I appoints a commission to organize a definitive legal code. This Three Seals Law, based on earlier Ayudhyan and traditional Indian law, remains in effect throughout the nineteenth century.

1821: British representative John Crawfurd arrives in Bangkok seeking diplomatic and commercial relations, following a Siamese invasion of Kedah that disturbs Penang trade. The Siamese agree to recognize only British control of Penang and rebuff other overtures.

1824–1830: Rama III (reigns 1824–1851) abolishes almost all royal monopolies except the sugar trade. The government withdraws from active participation in trade and turns to raising revenue from monetary taxes on production and trade.

December 1825: British emissary Captain Henry Burney arrives in Bangkok to pursue diplomatic relations and commercial concessions. When the British defeat the Burmese, the Siamese enter negotiations and conclude a treaty with the British in June 1826. The Siamese position in Kedah, Kelantan, Terengganu, and Pattani is recognized, as are borders between British Burma and Siam. Procedures are set for trade and disputes, and Siamese duties on trade are reduced, resulting in increased international trade and contacts with the West.

January–May 4, 1827: In the Anu Rebellion, Lao troops from Vientiane and Champassak invade Siam. After defeating the Lao, the Siamese occupy Vientiane and destroy it in 1829.

1834–1846: More than a decade of competition and warfare with Vietnam over Cambodia leads Siam to negotiate terms with Vietnam whereby Cambodia is to be tributary state of Siam, with lesser tribute due to Vietnam.

1840s: Trade with China, Siam's main trading partner, lessens because of the opium wars and colonization in China. As a result, Siam further encourages European trade. The government abandons effort to use corvée labor for public works projects and turns to Chinese immigrant wage labor.

April 3, 1851: Rama III dies and is succeeded by his brother Mongkut as Rama IV (reigns 1851–1868). As a leading monk, Mongkut reformed Buddhist practices, supervised Buddhist education programs, and studied English and Latin, as well as Western science and mathematics, as did a small Siamese elite of the era. As king, Mongkut attempts legal reforms, improves the condition of slaves, and permits women some choice in marriage. He rules with help from hired foreign advisors.

1855: With the Bowring Treaty, British get residence, extraterritoriality, and trading rights. The pact removes privileges of Chinese trading companies, seeks to regularize import and export duties, and maximizes British and Siamese profits from opium trade. With concessions therein, Siam avoids gunboat diplomacy and over next seven years concludes similar pacts with the United States, France, Denmark, Portugal, the Netherlands, and Germany.

Trade with larger and more efficient European ships leads to an increase in Thai exports of rice, sugar, tobacco, indigo, pepper, and other spices. The cultivation of coffee and rubber is introduced.

1863: New Cambodian King Norodom agrees to French protection while still secretly recognizing Siamese suzerainty.

1866: A Siamese court rules that certificates for payment of land tax may be regarded as proof of land ownership, thus providing the basis for tenants and squatters to challenge superior rights of nobles and royalty to land. This judgment is revoked in 1896.

1866–1868: The French Lagrée-Garnier Expedition travels up the Mekong River, through mostly Siamese territory.

1867: Siam recognizes the French protectorate over Cambodia.

October 1, 1868: King Mongkut dies, leaving as heir his fifteen-year-old son Chulalongkorn (reigns 1868–1910), who has been taught Western subjects by English governess Anna Leonowens. (A century later this episode will gain worldwide attention through the American musical *The King and I*.) The regent rules until Chulalongkorn is crowned Rama v in November 1873. He immediately attempts modernizing reforms of legal, economic, and administrative systems, but opposition forces delay. In 1892, inauguration of his initiatives includes educational and military reform.

1874: A royal decree mandates that children born after 1868 to *that* (indentured servants or slaves) will be free on reaching the age of twenty-one.

1883: Construction of telegraph lines begins.

1885: Chulalongkorn appoints Prince Devawongse (1858–1923), who skillfully heads the ministry of foreign affairs for the next thirty-eight years.

July 1893: In the Paknam Incident, French warships are fired upon by Siamese acting in self-defense; the French proceed upriver to blockade Bangkok. France uses this crisis to force Siam to grant France, in a treaty of October 1893, jurisdiction over Siamese territory east of the Mekong River.

1897: The government creates a provincial police force to control general lawlessness resulting from tenant-landlord disputes. In the 1890s a series of military expeditions is sent out to control banditry and riots in the countryside.

1902: Several rebellions resist centralization of provincial administration and modernization.

1904: In the Treaty of 1904, Siam cedes to France two more Lao provinces west of the Mekong. France receives three western Cambodian provinces in the Treaty of 1907.

March 10, 1909: In the Anglo-Siamese Treaty, Britain gets control of four Malay states of Perlis, Kedah, Terengganu, and Kelantan. It also will supervise construction of a railroad linking Singapore and Bangkok.

March 1–2, 1912: A planned coup against King Vajiravudh (Rama VI, reigns 1910–1925) is cut short by the arrests of ninety-six junior army officers. The plot forces the king to assume a new role in government. He introduces surnames, redesigns the flag, encourages monogamy, improves status of women, promotes nationalism, and establishes Chulalongkorn University in 1916.

July 22, 1917: After remaining neutral since the outbreak of World War I, Siam declares war against Germany and its allies. In June 1918, Siam sends a 1,300-man expeditionary force to aid France. This grants Siam a seat at the Versailles peace conference, where it seeks to end unequal treaties with Western powers. The United States concedes in 1920, France and Britain in 1925, and other countries in 1926. New treaties do away with extraterritoriality and restore tariff autonomy.

1921: Compulsory education law requires all children, ages seven to fourteen, to attend school.

1928–1929: The first modern Thai novels appear. Authors Kulap Saipradit, Prince Akatdamkoeng, and "Dokmai Sot" (M. L. Buppha Kunjara Nimmanhemin) explore cultural conflicts between the West and Siam and examine the effects of modernization.

1930–1932: Severe economic depression strikes as rice prices drop by two-thirds, land values plummet, and a financial crisis results from an initial decision to maintain gold as the basis of currency.

THE MODERN ERA: 1932–1997

The new age begins with the overthrow of the absolute monarchy in favor of representative government. Nevertheless, this so-called constitutional era is characterized largely by a succession of military coups and authoritarian regimes. The nationalism of the 1930s ends in cooperation with the Japanese during World War II. In the following decades, the United States is a strong ally and Thailand's economy booms during the Korean and Vietnam wars. Communist insurgents, conflicts in neighboring countries, and overwhelming numbers of refugees create serious problems. In the 1970s Japanese investment begins to pervade the region. Despite strong agricultural, manufacturing, tourism, and trade sectors, internal problems multiply in the 1980s and 1990s, with inflation, population growth, unemployment, and finally an unprecedented financial crisis.

June 23, 1932: A bloodless military coup against King Prajadhipok (Rama VII, reigns 1925–1935) overthrows absolute monarchy, initiates constitutional representative government.

December 20, 1932: A new constitution takes effect. The king is to keep his throne but abstain from political activity. All citizens are to be equal under the law, with religious freedom guaranteed.

April 2, 1933: The king issues martial law, dissolves parliament, and sets aside the constitution to govern with a twenty-member council. Move is overturned by military coups of June 15 and 30.

November 1933: Less than 10 percent vote in the first elections for half of the members of the legislature. The first direct elections are in November 1937, with 26 percent voting. By 1938, seventy provincial assemblies represent democracy at lower levels.

March 2, 1935: King Prajadhipok abdicates, opposing the undemocratic nature of the military regime, and is succeeded by ten-year-old Prince Ananda Mahidol (Rama VIII, reigns 1935–1946), who serves under regency.

Mid 1930s–1940s: Government starts indus-tries as full or partial owner; these include railways, electricity, waterworks, and consumer goods.

1937: During the Sino-Japanese War, Siam's populous Chinese community organizes anti-Japanese boycotts, damaging the nation's economy and foreign relations. Growing anti-Chinese sentiment is further provoked by large sums of money sent to relatives in China, hurting finances. This leads to restrictions on Chinese immigration and economic activity.

December 26, 1938: Military officer Luang Phibunsongkhram (1897–1964) heads the government in his first term as prime minister (1938–1944). Also serving as minister of defense and of the interior, he inaugurates a policy of militant nationalism.

July 4, 1939: Phibun officially changes the name of Siam to Thailand (*Muang Thai,* or Land of the Free); this policy seeks to unite all Tai-speaking peoples, including those in neighboring lands. He also adopts the Western calendar.

September 8, 1939: As World War II begins, Thailand proclaims neutrality. On June 12, 1940, Thailand signs five-year treaty of friendship with Japan.

November 1940: Following the German victory over France, Thailand invades French territory west of the Mekong and in western Cambodia. The Japanese mediate a settlement whereby Thais take back Lao Sayaboury, western Champassak, and Cambodian Battambang and Siem Reap.

December 8, 1941: Japanese invade Thailand to establish a base for the planned conquest of British Malaya, Singapore, and Burma. Thailand agrees to allow Japanese occupation in return for Japanese assurances of Thai independence. Thai are subjected to numerous British and U.S. air raids along with Japanese requisitions of goods and labor.

January 25, 1942: Emboldened by Japanese military successes, Phibun contracts a military alliance with Japan and declares war against the United States and Britain. Thailand's Washington emissary M. R. W. Seni Pramoj holds the declaration to be illegal, refuses to deliver it to the U.S. government, and begins organizing, with U.S. and British help, the Free Thai movement of students stranded abroad. Trained recruits are secretly returned to Thailand to join the local Free Thai underground, organized by Pridi Phanomyong (1900–1983), to aid the Allied war effort. Free Thai activism will help the treatment of Thailand by the Allies after the war.

February 9, 1942: Chinese forces defeat Thai troops in a clash near the Indochina frontier. On March 17 near the Burmese border, Chinese soldiers defeat a three hundred-man Thai force, killing one hundred.

May 1942: Thai troops overrun the Shan region of northeast Burma.

July 5, 1943: Japan grants Malay and Burmese areas to Thailand in return for war cooperation. The Treaty of August 1943 confirms Thai acquisition of the Shan region and Kelantan, Terengganu, Perlis, and Kedah.

July 24, 1944: The national assembly forces Phibun's resignation, as the Free Thai Movement infiltrates the countryside and government.

August 14, 1945: King Ananda Mahidol voids the declaration of war on the United States and Britain. Fearing British invasion, Thais make an offer to the Allies to turn the regular army and Free Thai guerrilla forces against Japan. They promise to return annexed Burma and Malay areas to Britain; this becomes effective on September 8.

September 9, 1945–May 1949: The name Siam is restored.

January 1, 1946: Siam, India, and Britain sign a peace treaty in Singapore.

April 1946: The Thai high court halts war-crimes prosecution of Phibun and associates on grounds of constitutionality, thus exonerating them from charges of collaboration with Japan. Phibun returns to power (1948–1957) in a coup.

June 9, 1946: Under mysterious circumstances, King Ananda Mahidol apparently is assassinated. Mishandling of this affair weakens the new government. He is succeeded by King Bhumibol Adulyadej (Rama IX, reigns 1946–).

October 15, 1946: Under military and political pressure from the French in Indochina, Siam agrees to return to France areas of Cambodia and Laos annexed during the war.

December 12, 1946: Siam's application for UN membership is unanimously approved; Siam is seated on April 28, 1947.

1950–1953: The Korean War stimulates an economic boom as Thai exports of rice, rubber, and tin rise. Thailand is first Asian nation to send troops to fight with UN forces in Korea. As important ally, Thailand receives from the United States from 1951 to 1957 $149 million in economic aid and $222 million in military aid. This further increases the political power and personal wealth of military leaders.

September 1954: The Southeast Asia Treaty Organization (SEATO), with headquarters in Bangkok, is founded to defend against communist aggression in region. (It is disbanded on June 30, 1977.)

September 17, 1957: Amid fraud and scandal, Phibun is ousted in a bloodless coup; he flees to exile in Japan.

July 1, 1958: Field Marshal Sarit Thanarat orders a huge bonfire of opium pipes in front of the Royal Palace. On October 20 he declares martial law and abolishes the constitution, seeking a return to traditional Thai values and restoring the monarchy to an active but ceremonial role. As premier (1959–1963), he promotes irrigation, rural electrification, and other development projects.

March 6, 1962: In the secret Rusk-Thanarat agreement, the United States promises to protect Thailand against direct communist aggression. On May 15, the United States orders four thousand troops to Thailand, bringing the total to five thousand, to protect against communist infiltration from Laos. The pact is the basis for the U.S. military presence during the Vietnam War.

1964–1975: The Vietnam War produces an economic boom from U.S. dollars for the construction of roads, U.S. military bases, and airstrips; these developments expose all, not just the elite, to Western culture and media; this leads to a rise in tourism, prostitution, and corruption. Thailand's direct participation in the war includes deployment of a Royal Thai Air Force contingent to South Vietnam in 1964, a naval contingent in 1965, and ground combat units, totalling over 11,000 by 1969. By July 1966 25,000 U.S. troops are stationed in Thailand as an "aerial second front" for the Vietnam War.

1965–1974: With U.S. funding, Thailand begins a secret war in Laos, pitting up to five thousand troops on the side of the monarchy against the Pathet Lao Communist insurgency there.

October 14, 1973: Dr. Sanya Dharmasakti, the first civilian premier (1973–1975) since 1957, takes over. Premier Thanom Kittikachorn (1963–1973) is forced to resign after a series of demonstrations, beginning in June, by some 200,000 to 500,000 students calling for the release of political prisoners and a new constitution. They clash with police, but the army refuses to send troops against civilian mobs. This brings an end to one-man authoritarian rule but not to the role of the military, which is forced to share political power more widely.

[The candidates] say they can solve all kinds of
   problems . . .
There will be lots of roads and canals
You won't have to raise buffaloes
Because we will provide you with tractors
We are all so pleased at this news
But they have become MPs for many years now
We are still using buffaloes . . .
And they have become very rich

   From a Thai *luk thung* (country music) song (1970s)

July 20, 1976: The United States completes withdrawal of its military forces from Thailand, at Thailand's request.

October 6, 1976: A military coup violently ends student demonstrations. Mass arrests and repression of dissidents and press follow, ending the brief democratic experiment.

February 1, 1981: On a four-day visit to Bangkok, Chinese Premier Zhao Ziyang indicates that China will no longer support communist insurgency movements in Southeast Asia. On December 1, 1982, a thousand communist rebel troops surrender to the Thai army in northeast Thailand.

1981–1983: Financial woes resulting from the second oil crisis lead Thailand to borrow a record amount from the World Bank and to seek huge standby credits from International Monetary Fund (IMF). Required institutional and policy reforms are not implemented. By 1980s, Japan is source of two-thirds of all Thai foreign aid. By 1988, spurred by quasi-capitalist export industries, Thailand is most rapidly growing economy in region.

January 20, 1992: A UN regional conference

reports 400,000 Thai infected with the AIDS virus and 2 million expected to die by the year 2000. A UN report of March 8, 1993, cites Thailand for slavery, with poor families sometimes selling children into bondage to factories, restaurants, private households, and brothels that serve foreigners on "sex tours."

May 17–19, 1992: Violent military "Black May" crackdown leaves hundreds dead. Protesters call for the resignation of the corrupt military government, amendment of the constitution, and for the premier to be an elected official.

April 5, 1995: Thailand, Cambodia, Laos, and Vietnam sign the Mekong River water-use pact.

June 9, 1996: Celebration of the fiftieth anniversary of King Bhumibol Adulyadej, the world's longest-serving living monarch. He has helped to resolve recent political conflicts.

July 2, 1997: Thailand's economy has been slipping for several months and there are increasing indicators of fundamental financial problems such as bad loans and inflated real estate as well as revelations of Thai banking mismanagement and fraud. Because Thailand's currency, the *baht*, is becoming the target of international currency speculators, the government announces that it is doing away with controls and letting it float in the international money exchanges. This effectively devalues the *baht*, and in turn this causes the currencies of the Philippines, Malaysia, and Indonesia to plunge. In August, the International Monetary Fund and Japan pledge $17.2 billion in loans to Thailand to help stabilize the economy.

September 27, 1997: Parliament approves a new constitution, the sixteenth since 1932, but the first drafted through a process of public debate and review: it seeks to eliminate pervasive political corruption, and to institute a new system of proportional representation and Thailand's first bill of rights.

November 3–14, 1997: Prime Minister Chavalit Yongchaiyudh, blamed by many for Thailand's economic woes, resigns on November 3. After negotiations among the opposition parties, a coalition chooses Chuan Leekpai, and he is sworn in on November 14.

June 1998: By this time Thailand's deepening recession has forced some four thousand companies to close, and the rate of unemployment is 8.4 percent of the workforce. The *baht* has sunk to about 35 percent of its value against the U.S. dollar and other solid currencies.

September 1998: Despite its many financial and economic problems, experts in international finance are beginning to give high marks to Thailand's efforts to reform its economy. For one thing, even though the *baht* has regained some of its value, Thailand's exports are the most competitive in Southeast and East Asia. In August Thailand announces that it is closing four of the country's fifteen banks and is creating up to $7.2 billion in domestic bonds to help refinance the remaining banks. Various foreign companies are beginning to return to investing in operations in Thailand.

Vietnam

PREHISTORIC PERIOD: 21,000 B.C.–A.D. 43

Although hominids dating back as far as 1,800,000 B.C. have been found in China to the north and in Indonesia to the south, there have been no such finds in the land that will become Vietnam. Neither are there any finds reported of early (150,000–50,000 B.C.) *Homo sapiens* in Vietnam, although inasmuch as they were present in southern China some may have lived in Vietnam. Almost certainly by 20,000 B.C., the late Upper Paleolithic, *Homo sapiens* are living in parts of Vietnam and beginning to develop some distinctive cultural traditions in response to local environment and resources. (Because the sea level has risen greatly since then, it may well have wiped out early coastal sites of these people.) In particular, Vietnam lies in a tropical climate zone, one subject to the monsoon—the annual rainy season alternating with a dry season. Water is plentiful in terms of surrounding ocean, rivers, and annual rainfall. The rainfall also supports a dense forest cover and eventually supports rice cultivation. Not until the Late Paleolithic is a culture known to emerge in Vietnam. For some twenty thousand years, a series of cultural phases would develop in Vietnam; although there is not total agreement on the exact dates, the sequence is generally agreed on. It is also agreed that there will eventually be a mixture of the original Australo-Melanesian inhabitants of Vietnam and the later arriving Mongoloids. The Vietnamese cultures produce several distinctive achievements, yet eventually the more populous and expansive Chinese will move in and take control of Vietnam. Although at this time there is neither a border nor much distinction between "China" and "Vietnam" in this region, the earliest references to the people of Vietnam distinguish them as the *Lac*. During the third century B.C. the Chinese name for the region and people of southeastern China becomes *Yueh*, and the name for those still further south becomes *Nan Yueh*; eventually the order is reversed and the region and people and place are called *Yueh Nan*; to the people who will become the Vietnamese, *Yueh* is pronounced *Viet* and *Nan* is pronounced *Nam*, and thus Viet Nam.

21,000–9,000 B.C.: The earliest tools found in Vietnam are from Sonvi, in northern Vietnam; they are mainly end- and side-flaked pebbles. Nothing else is known about the people who make these, but some at least will continue to do so during the following Hoabinhian culture period.

16,000–1000 B.C.: The earliest known culture in Vietnam takes its name from the first site where it was discovered, Hoa Binh, in northern Vietnam. Eventually the Hoabinhian culture will be found across much of Indonesia and Malaysia, west to Burma, and north into southern China and possibly to Taiwan. The characteristic tools are flat river pebbles of varying shapes but usually about fist size, flaked on one or both sides but with cutting edges around their entire circumference. Over the millennia, there are numerous variations, but the other parts of the material culture often include stone mortars and pounders, bone points, and flexed burials (sometimes dusted with red ocher). The Hoabinhians, at least for most of this time, almost certainly forage and hunt for most of their food; although not agriculturists, they may take some trouble to encourage such native plants as yams, taro, and Job's tears (seeds from a grass, *Coix lacryma-jobi*). Eventually at least some Hoabinhian people in Vietnam adopt the Neolithic culture with its pottery and agriculture.

9000–6000 B.C.: During this time, the Bac Son culture of Vietnam overlaps with the Hoabinhian; it is more like a variant industry of the Hoabinhian, the main difference being that the edges of the stone tools are ground rather than flaked.

During this time, it is possible that some Vietnamese began to domesticate the water buffalo, and that the first Vietnamese pottery is made by about 7000 B.C.

6000–3000 B.C.: At Thanh Hoa province in northern Vietnam, remains from a shell mound reveal what is called the Da But culture, suggesting a transition to a Neolithic culture. Its tools are mainly of the Hoabin-hian or Bacsonian types but they also make polished stone adzes. These people are mostly foragers but they fish and gather shellfish. They appear to have domesticated the pig and fowl. They also cultivate fiber plants.

At least by 4500 B.C. some Vietnamese are making simple pottery. Southern Mongoloid people may have been making their way at least into northern Vietnam, where they mixed with some of the Australo-Melanesian peoples living there: Quynh Van in northern Vietnam (*c.* 4000 B.C.) is one site with evidence of such a mixture.

Some claim that bronze working is developed in Southeast Asia by the end of this period and that it spreads from here to China, but most experts reject both these claims.

3000–1500 B.C.: There is a definite influx of Southern Mongoloid people into Vietnam. Relatively large communities begin to emerge. In the delta of the Red River, the site of Phung Nguyen provides the name for the distinctive Neolithic culture of Vietnam during the years 2500–1500 B.C., with settlements on slightly elevated terrain above stream valleys, stone adzes and bracelets, and pottery with incised bands or zones filled with stamped impressions. By the end of this period, the first bronze-working in Vietnam begins to appear at Dong Dau. Also by the end of this period, dry rice may be cultivated in Vietnam; it is debated whether this was introduced from China or began in Southeast Asian lands such as Vietnam and then spread to what is now China.

1500–500 B.C.: Imported Chinese Shang-style bronze vessels, bells, and weapons appear in Vietnam. By about 1000 B.C. copper and bronze begin to be more widely worked in northern Vietnam; iron will also be worked by at least the final centuries of this period. This suggests some control of natural resources (copper, tin, iron), new skills and technology, and possibly some concentration of wealth and power in the hands of a few chiefs and a supporting hierarchy.

600–1 B.C.: In the Bac Bo region of the delta of the Red River in northern Vietnam there is evidence of casting copper to make axes, fishhooks, projectile points, and bracelets. These are used alongside basic stone tools and weapons, but the new metal tools (iron is also being worked by the end of this period) allow for clearing more forests to plant crops and to raise livestock. By this time, some Vietnamese are cultivating wet rice in rain-fed or irrigated fields; they use plows and water buffalo.

It is near the outset of this period that the classic Dong Son culture of Vietnam (so named after its prime site in north central Vietnam) comes into being. Its most distinctive and striking production are bronze drums: Ranging in size from miniatures to some with drumheads forty inches in diameter, they are decorated with incised geometric and representational (animal, human) designs. Dong Son-style drums, some imported, some locally made, will be found at many sites in Southeast Asia and southern China.

As the size and complexity of the bronze and other metal products increase during this time, there are undoubtedly both more and larger networks for exchanging goods, food, and products of all kinds. Increased craft skills and food production also support a new, more stratified society. This leads to some concentration of power in the hands of new elites and the development of more centralized, hierarchical societies, although these are still relatively small communities, with chiefs rather than kings. The elites indulge in quite elaborate burials, in which they deposit their bronze objects along with other prized possessions.

During this same period (or beginning perhaps as early as 1000 B.C.), at Sa Huynh, along the coast of southeastern Vietnam, another culture emerges. These people are Austronesian-speakers who will become known as the Chams; they may have settled here from peninsular Malaysia or Borneo, or they may be indigenous people who borrowed much of the Austronesian culture. The Sa Huynh culture will spread throughout a large part of southern Vietnam, over into the Mekong Delta region. The Chams appear to be influenced by the metalworking industries of northern Vietnam, but use more iron than bronze. Their culture is particularly noted for its burials in jars and special earrings. Gradually the Chams will establish a kingdom of their own known as Champa.

300–210 B.C.: By the outset of this period, Chinese from the north are increasing their dealings with the inhabitants of southern China and the northern Vietnamese, who share a common and undefined border. By the last third of the century, these northern Chinese (led by the Qin dynasty, 221–206 B.C.) are invading the region of southeastern China known as Ou and apparently some of the Ou elite flee down into the region of northern Vietnam dominated by Vietnamese known as Lac. Then according to a mixture of legend and history, a certain An Duong (his true name is Thuc Phan) becomes king of the new region in northern Vietnam now known as Au Lac (*au* being the Vietnamese version of the Chinese *ou*).

208–136 B.C.: After the death of the Qin emperor in China, another (at least to some extent) legendary leader, Chao T'o (Trieu Da in Vietnamese), a commissioner for the Chinese Qin dynasty in the region around Canton, controls southeastern China. Then about 185 B.C. Chao T'o moves down and invades the Au Lac region, deposing King An Duong. Chao T'o establishes his own capital near Canton and proclaims himself emperor of Nan Yueh (Land of the Southern Yueh). He claims territory as far south as Danang, Vietnam. Later Vietnamese will honor Chao T'o as someone who defends local interests against the Han dynasty that assumes power in China about 202 B.C.

136–111 B.C.: With Chao T'o's death in 136 B.C. the region he ruled gradually loses power to the more assertive Han dynasty. Finally, in 111 B.C. the Han Chinese seize and burn the Nan Yueh capital and annex the entire kingdom of Nan Yueh, reducing it to a province named Chiao-chih (Giao Chi in Vietnamese).

110 B.C.–A.D. 9: During this period, the Han Chinese assign governors and some small military forces to the region that will become northern Vietnam but are basically interested in exploiting its natural resources and trade potential. Although the Chinese allow the old indigenous oligarchy of northern Vietnam to maintain some of its powers, these so-called Lac lords are turned into tribute-paying administrators.

A.D. 9–23: Wang Mang, a high official at the Han court, seizes power; his disruptive policies send thousands of Chinese fleeing southward and many end up in Vietnam. Some of these Han Chinese introduce Chinese ways into Vietnam, from more advanced agricultural practices to Chinese marriage and family traditions.

40–43: The Lac lords along with other Vietnamese are becoming restive under Chinese administration. Trung Trac is the daughter of a Lac lord and, according to later accounts, in A.D. 40 takes control of her father's region; she quickly abolishes Chinese taxes and extends her authority over much of northern Vietnam. Unwilling to allow this, in the year 41 the Han Chinese send General Ma Yuan with thousands of troops to dispose of Trung Trac and her younger sister Nhi. When Ma Yuan moves with his overpowering force into the territory of the Lac lords, many of the Vietnamese become discouraged. In 42 Trung Trac battles the Chinese but is defeated; thousands of her supporters are captured and beheaded; by the end of the year, Trung Trac and Nhi suffer the same fate (and their heads are sent to the Han court. In some accounts they commit suicide.) During the year 43 Ma Yuan continues to quell Vietnamese resistance and imposes more direct control by the Han Chinese and their laws. By the time he leaves in 44, Ma Yuan has laid the basis for the distinctive Chinese-Vietnamese society that endures in northern Vietnam for almost a thousand years.

CHINESE DOMINATION: A.D. 43–939

The immediate effect of the conquest of northern Vietnam by General Ma Yuan is to introduce a fair number of Han Chinese into the region. They soon begin to intermarry with the local inhabitants and create a certain mixed Chinese-Viet population. Although various Chinese practices are forced upon the locals and the Chinese language becomes the official language, and although the Lac lords lose their full powers, elements of the indigenous culture remain and to some extent predominate. The Chinese-Viet elite also continues to oversee the land, the basis of the agricultural economy. By the second century Han power is being challenged throughout much of its empire and there are several uprisings in northern Vietnam. With the end of the Han dynasty in 220, China itself moves into a period of disarray (known as the period of Six Dynasties), during which northern Vietnam is often in rebellion against the Chinese. Meanwhile, central Vietnam is essentially an independent kingdom known as Champa while southern Vietnam is also a rather amorphous region known as Funan. Under China's Tang dynasty, Chinese authority is reasserted over northern Vietnam, renamed Annam; Champa remains independent, but Funan is largely absorbed by the Khmer of Cambodia. Northern Vietnam, however, remains in constant turmoil until finally in 939 Chinese forces are defeated and the Vietnamese assert their independence.

50–200: More than a hundred brick tombs in northern Vietnam of this period contain a variety of material goods: ceramic vessels, lamp stands, model farms, bronze vessels, glass ornaments, iron swords, coins, game boards, musical instruments, and mirrors. These tombs confirm the existence of a prosperous ruling-class who draw on the Han Chinese culture but appear to be solidly rooted in Vietnam.

2d century: At several times throughout this century, Vietnamese and Chinese-Vietnamese rise up and attack Han Chinese officials and authority in northern Vietnam. Sometimes with armed force, sometimes with threats, sometimes with concessions, the Chinese manage to put down these rebellions. Meanwhile the central government of the Han dynasty is itself in turmoil and gradually loses its ability to hold its far-flung empire together.

100–600: In southern Vietnam around the Mekong Delta is a region known to the Chinese as Funan. Its major center is Oc Eo along the coast, with canals, pools, and brickworks. From the second century on, objects (coins, statues, and so on) from India and even from Rome attest to the fact that this is a prominent trading port. By the mid-fourth century, Funan is adopting the Brahman religion and Sanskrit writing system from India. About 500, however, Funan goes into decline and by the year 600 much of its territory falls under control of the Khmer in Cambodia.

***c.* 180–226:** About 180, Shih Hsieh, a Chinese, is appointed prefect of a region that includes much of northern Vietnam; he is able to take advantage of the increasingly ineffective Han dynasty to become the de facto ruler, which the Han court officially recognizes in 205. His rule is characterized by generally peaceful cooperation with the local Vietnamese; he does not attempt to suppress local Vietnamese culture or traditions. Contacts and trade with India thrive; in particular, Buddhism prospers and Buddhist temples are built. When the Han dynasty ends in 220 and China is split into three kingdoms, Shih Hsieh allies himself with the Wu dynasty that is based in Nanking. By the time of Shih Hsieh's death in 226, various prosperous landowning families are increasingly coming to dominate Vietnam's economic, social, and political life, but the Wu court continues to intervene in Vietnam.

192: South of the region where these events have been occurring, in what will centuries later become central Vietnam, the people known as the Cham have been conducting their own affairs somewhat isolated from their northern neighbors, although they do trade with them. In 192 Ou Lien, son of a district official in this region, kills the district's Chinese magistrate and proclaims himself king of Lin-I. This is regarded by some as the beginnings of the Cham kingdom, or Champa (which will persist as an independent kingdom into the seventeenth century).

248: Lin-I (Cham) forces invade northern Vietnam and seize some of the bordering territory controlled by the Wu dynasty of China. In the unrest that accompanies this invasion, several Vietnamese lead rebellions against the oppressive Wu Chinese; the most admired of these is a young woman named Lady Trieu, who is soon defeated and killed. A highly legendary person, she will be revered by the Vietnamese in ensuing centuries.

4th–6th centuries: Although the Cham kingdom and northern Vietnam continue to fight, the border between these two regions becomes relatively stabilized. The Chinese continue to exert authority in northern Vietnam, but the divisiveness in China itself weakens its power in Vietnam. Traders, scholars, and monks from India contribute to the spread of Buddhism, although most Vietnamese do not abandon traditional belief in the spirits that inhabit natural forms.

541–547: Ly Bi, a descendant of a Chinese

family that settled in northern Vietnam in the first century, leads a revolt against the Chinese authorities; in 544 he proclaims himself emperor of Nam Viet and establishes his capital near modern Hanoi, but this falls to the Chinese in 546, and Ly Bi is killed in 547. Northern Vietnamese leaders continue to resist the Chinese for several decades.

618–907: During this period, the Tang dynasty in China reasserts Chinese authority in northern Vietnam and suppresses most overt opposition. In 679 China changes the name of the province of Giao Chi—essentially northern Vietnam—to Annam (pacified South) and places it under an official called the protector-general. (Although the Chinese change the name again in 758 to Tran Nam [guarded south], this never takes hold.) There are several serious rebellions (in 687, 722, and 782) and in 767 An Nam suffers greatly from a seaborne invasion by islanders of Southeast Asia (possibly from Java). Each time the Chinese reassert authority, but slowly the Tang authority weakens. Most Vietnamese continue to retain much of their culture, including their language and the habit of chewing betel.

782–791: Phung Hung and his brother Phung Hai, Vietnamese who trace their ancestry to legendary Vietnamese kings, seize control of northern Vietnam. Hung dies in 789 and is briefly succeeded by Hai, but Hung's son An pushes Hai out; in 791 Phung An surrenders meekly to envoys from an invading Chinese army.

820: An aged Chinese Buddhist monk, Vo Ngon Thong comes to Vietnam and founds a new sect that adopts his name; he dies in 826 but his sect remains a force in Vietnam until the thirteenth century. Buddhism in general continues to play a prominent role in Vietnam society.

823–867: Armies from the Nan-chao kingdom, in the remote Chinese region known as Yunnan, northwest of Vietnam, attack and plunder Annam in 823–824 and then again in 858–863. In 867 the Chinese general Kao P'ien (Gao Pian) defeats the last of the Nan-chao forces and their Vietnamese allies. Kao P'ien proceeds to rebuild the capital at Dai La (near present-day Hanoi).

906–930: As the Tang dynasty begins to disintegrate in China, its authority in Vietnam weakens; among other signs, Chinese military units are withdrawn to fight more serious threats elsewhere on China's borders. In 906 the Khuc family emerges as a power in the Red River delta of Annam, but in 930 an army from southern China seizes Dai-la and takes the leader of the Khuc family back to China.

931–937: Duong Dinh Nghe, a Vietnamese general from the province of Ai (Thanh Hoa), along the coast south of the Red River delta, leads an army against the capital, Dai La. He drives the Chinese protector-general out and assumes that post, ruling over northern Vietnam until he is assassinated in 937.

938: Ngo Quyen is a young general under Duong Dinh Nghe, who gives Ngo Quyen one of his daughters as a wife and puts him in command of Ai province. When Duong Dinh Nghe is assassinated, Ngo Quyen leads a force to Dai La and assumes leadership of the resistance against the Chinese. When the Chinese forces come up the Bach Dang River, near present-day Haiphong, Ngo Quyen defeats them. The Chinese withdraw from Vietnam.

939: Ngo Quyen drops the Chinese title of protector-general and names himself king of his land. This year is regarded as the end of Chinese rule and the beginning of independent Vietnam.

INDEPENDENT VIETNAM: 939–1883

For the next nine centuries—with one brief interruption by Chinese rule—Vietnam is an independent land. In the first four centuries, it is an increasingly powerful Buddhist polity within mainland Southeast Asia. Then, following a major transformation in the fifteenth century, Dai Viet falls victim to warfare among strong clans. Underlying these hostilities is the subtext of the rivalry between the northern homeland and southern borderlands, while parallel to this phenomenon are two continual motifs of this long period: holding off interventions by China in the north and expansion of the south farther into adjacent lands. The Vietnamese are not always successful in either, but in general they attain both goals. Meanwhile, the Vietnamese maintain and develop their own culture—its language, both spoken and written, their religion, their common traditions and customs; the "classic" age of Vietnamese literature falls within this period. In the end, though, what overwhelms them is the totally foreign power of the French.

939–963: Ngo Quyen rules northern Vietnam but even though he has pushed Chinese out, he maintains many of the traditions of Chinese government. After his death in 944, a period of anarchy follows: Relatives, rival families, warlords, and just about anyone else who chooses to claim some power or territory—all keep northern Vietnam in a state of constant turmoil.

963–979: A Vietnamese of rustic background named Dinh Bo Linh, after a series of victories over competing leaders, manages to establish peace across much of northern Vietnam. He tries to ensure unity by intermarriages between his family and the still powerful Ngo family. In 966 he proclaims himself emperor to assert equality with the Chinese but in fact he has to engage in diplomatic maneuvers to get the Chinese to accept Vietnamese independence. Among his many appointments is that of the Buddhist monk Ngo Chan Luu as "Great Teacher for Correcting and Sustaining Viet." (Ngo Chan Luu's writings are among the oldest extant from Vietnam.) In 979 Dinh Bo Linh is assassinated but he has laid the groundwork for the Vietnamese kings who will follow.

10th–12th centuries: Buddhism flourishes in Vietnam as seen in the hundreds of pagodas erected, the many monks, and the great numbers of Buddhist texts.

Wood contains the essence of fire,
And the fire sometimes is reborn.
Why say that fire does not reside there,
If it flashes forth when one bores into the wood?

"The Wood and the Fire," Buddhist *ke*, or chant, by
Ngo Chan Luu (959–1011)

1009–1225: Ly Cong Uan, commander of the palace guard, assumes the throne and establishes the Ly dynasty that rules until 1225. He moves the capital back to Dai-la on the site of present-day Hanoi and renames it Thang Long (which remains the capital until 1802). In 1054 his grandson renames the country Dai Viet ("Great Viet"). Culminating a series of attacks on Champa, in 1069 the Vietnamese capture the Cham king and as a price for his release take over three provinces from Champa. In 1076 the Vietnamese turn back an invasion by Song dynasty forces from China.

1145–1220: The kingdom of Champa has long been subject to Cambodian threats, and in 1145 Cambodia invades Champa and seizes its capital, Vijaya; the Cambodians are driven out in 1150, and in 1177 a Cham fleet sails up the Mekong River and attacks Angkor, killing the king. In 1190 the Cambodians defeat Champa and annex much of it in 1203. Around 1220, however, the Cambodians leave Champa and restore the throne to a Cham prince.

1225–1400: Tran Thu Do marries his nephew to the Ly emperor's daughter and controls the throne to establish the Tran dynasty. The Tran rulers do effect various domestic reforms and projects, but they also spend much of their energies attacking Champa. During the Tran dynasty, Confucianism comes to rival Buddhism as a major guiding philosophy of life, at least among upper-class Vietnamese. The Tran dynasty comes to an end in 1400 as the court official and regent Ho Quy Ly seizes power after intermarrying his family with the Tran.

1257–1288: The Mongols take over China and are determined also to control Vietnam. The Mongols first attack in 1258 and burn the capital Thang Long but soon withdraw. In 1282 a Mongol sea expedition against Champa also takes its capital but is unable to suppress Cham resistance. In 1284 the Mongols attack Dai Viet and again capture the capital, but they are forced out in 1285. In 1287 Mongol land and sea forces invade Vietnam but in 1288 are thoroughly defeated at a battle at the Bach Dang River.

1406–1428: Claiming that they want to restore the Tran dynasty to power, the Chinese invade and take over Vietnam. The Chinese require that their orthodoxy be taught in the schools and used by Vietnamese literati; women must wear Chinese style clothing, and everyone must carry an identification card. Chinese Confucianism tends to take hold alongside the Buddhism that has long dominated Vietnamese society. In 1418 Le Loi, a local Vietnamese landowner, begins a guerrilla war and soon gains support from many Vietnamese. In 1421, Laotian troops sent to aid the Vietnamese defect to the Chinese; the Vietnamese will not soon forget this. In 1426 the Vietnamese, led by Le Loi, soundly defeat the Chinese at the Battle of Tot Dong (west of present-day Hanoi). In 1427 the Vietnamese lay siege to the Chinese holed up in the capital Thang Long and also block two Chinese relief armies. In 1428 Le Loi proclaims himself emperor of Dai Viet and concludes a peace with the Ming dynasty; although still admitting to some submission to China, Le Loi gains recognition of an independent Vietnam that he and his descendants will rule until 1787. Le Loi establishes his capital at Thang Long, also called Dong Kinh (which will become Tonkin to Western ears), present-day Hanoi.

1428: To celebrate the entry of the triumphant Vietnamese forces into Hanoi, Nguyen Trai (1380–1442) composes his best known poem, "Proclamation on the Pacification of the Ngo." Trai is chief adviser to Le Loi when they oust the Ming Chinese; he is also a poet and philosopher. After the Chinese defeat, he retires from public life, then becomes a victim of intrigue as he and his entire family are executed by political rivals. Nguyen Trai's literary works are suppressed until the 1960s. They are among the oldest in the demotic Vietnamese and its *nom* script to have survived.

Emperor by the grace of heaven, I proclaim:
Only a just war bears happiness.
We want the soldiers to deliver the people,
to disarm violence.
Our country is Dai [Great] Vietnam.
It is an ancient and beautiful nation.
It has its rivers, its mountains,
its frontiers in all regions.
It has its traditions and customs.

"The Proclamation on the Pacification of the Ngo," poem by Nguyen Trai (1428)

1446–1471: The Vietnamese invade Champa and take its capital, Vijaya, almost immediately but then withdraw. It is 1471 before Le Thanh-tong, regarded as the most effective king of the Le dynasty, completes the conquest. Le Thanh-tong (reigns 1460–1497) systematizes the laws and regulations, centralizes the administration, reorganizes the army, and institutes numerous reforms and projects. Underlying much of Le Thanh-tong's work is the Confucian goal of maintaining order and respect. Le Thanh-tong, himself a scholar, promotes learning and literature, and his reign sees the composition of several of Vietnam's classic histories and anthologies.

1478–1480: In retaliation for the defection of the Laotian forces in 1421, the Vietnamese invade the Laotian kingdom of Lan Sang and capture and sack its capital, Luang Prabang. The Vietnamese leave Lan Sang in 1480.

16th century: Starting about 1505, Vietnam is almost continually engulfed by disputes among individuals and families and their supporters who are trying to gain power. The Mac dynasty (1528–1592) gains power and continues the Le administration but ultimately the Trinh and the Nguyen clans defeat the Mac, with the Le kings as little more than figureheads. Intellectuals and writers employ the demotic *nom* to express their dissatisfaction with the state of affairs.

1535: The first Western trading post in Vietnam is established by the Portuguese Captain Antonio da Faria at Faifo, south of present-day Danang.

1615–1627: In 1615 an Italian Jesuit missionary, Father Francis Buzomi, organizes the construction of the first Catholic church in Vietnam, near Danang. In 1627 a French Jesuit, Alexandre de Rhodes, adapts the Vietnamese language to the Roman alphabet; this script is known as *quoc ngu*. Until his death in 1660, de Rhodes will work ceaselessly both to advance Christianity in Vietnam and to convince the French of the possibility of establishing a Christian empire in Asia.

1626–1673: What is effectively a civil war continues as the Nguyen clan governs the southern border region independent of the Trinh clan in the north. The Nguyen clan extends its power south from the present-day city of Hue. The two clans fight a series of battles, with the Nguyen eventually enlisting the aid of the Portuguese and the Trinh enlisting the Dutch. The Trinh reestablish the Le civil administration, and in 1673 the two clans agree to a truce and accept the Linh River as the boundary between their territories. (As it happens, this is near the 17th parallel, which will be used to divide Vietnam by the Geneva Conference in 1954.)

1680: French traders establish their first trading station in Vietnam, but it soon fails.

18th century: Three celebrated women poets are active during this century: Doan Thi Diem (1705–1748), Ho Xuan Huong (at its end), and the one known only as "Wife of the Chief of Thanh Quan District."

1717–1749: In various combinations, all the powers in the Indochina Peninsula—Vietnam, Laos, Cambodia, and Thailand—have long been contesting territory. After a major conflict in 1717 the Vietnamese take advantage of Cambodia's war with Thailand and take over some provinces of Cambodia's on the southern coast. In 1739 the Cambodians commence a campaign to regain this territory, but after ten years the Vietnamese end up taking over even more land around the Mekong Delta.

To marry and have a child—how banal!
But to be pregnant without the help of a
  husband—what merit!

Poem by Ho Xuan Huong (late 18th century)

1772–1787: The mass of Vietnamese peasants have long been suffering (and occasionally rebelling) under the rule of various prominent clans such as the Nguyen. In 1772 three brothers from a family in southern Vietnam lead a revolt against the Nguyen; they call their movement Tay Son (after their native highland village). By 1775 they have conquered most of southern Vietnam. After introducing various reforms that benefit the peasants, they then march against the Trinh clan in northern Vietnam. (In 1784 the Tay Son have to retake Saigon from a member of the Nguyen clan, Nguyen Anh.) By 1787 the Tay Son army has overthrown the Trinh in northern Vietnam. The youngest brother assumes the name of Quang Trung and the title of emperor.

1788–1789: In 1788, claiming to aid the Le ruler, a Chinese army invades Vietnam and occupies Hanoi. In 1789 Quang Trung launches a surprise attack during the Tet season and forces the Chinese out of Vietnam: the Vietnamese will regard this as one of the finest military victories in their history. (And despite constant threats, China will not invade Vietnam again until 1979.)

1789–1802: Nguyen Anh, who has assumed command of the defeated Nguyen clan forces, commences a successful campaign in the south against the Tay Son supporters. Nguyen Anh has by now obtained the support of French traders and mercenaries, organized by the Catholic missionary Pigneau de Béhaine. In 1799 a Vietnamese army under Nguyen Anh's son, Canh, defeats the Tay Son forces at Quinhon. This is the beginning of the end for the Tay Son movement, and in 1802 Nguyen Anh becomes emperor under the name Gia Long. He proclaims a united Viet Nam (his new name for all the territories) and establishes the new capital at Hue.

1802–1819: Emperor Gia Long takes an active role in hostilities involving Cambodia, Thailand, and Laos. In 1811 he sends a force that fights Thai forces. When he dies in 1819, he is succeeded by one of his sons, Minh Mang, who unlike Gia Long is strongly Confucian and distrusts dealings with the French or other Westerners who are increasingly more active throughout Southeast Asia.

***c.* 1810:** Publication of *Truyen Thuy Kieu*, the romantic epic poem that remains the best-known literary work in Vietnam. It is composed by Nguyen Du, regarded as probably the greatest classical poet of Vietnam. *Kieu* is based on a Chinese poem, but Nguyen Du has created his own work; it tells of the trials and sufferings of a beautiful and intelligent young woman, Thuy Kieu, who finds herself constantly victimized by the patriarchal society of her time. Many of its 3,254 lines (in the demotic *nom*) are still memorized and quoted by Vietnamese of all walks of life.

A hundred years—in this life span on earth,
how apt to clash, talent and destiny!
Men's fortunes change even as nature shifts—
the sea now rolls where mulberry fields grew.
One watches things that make one sick at heart.
This is the law: no gain without a loss,
and heaven hurts fair women for sheer spite.

   Truyen Thuy Kieu, epic poem by Nguyen Du (*c.* 1810)

1825–1832: Emperor Minh Mang has refused to receive a British envoy (1822) and in 1825 he issues an edict banning any more Catholic missionaries from entering Vietnam. Minh Mang increasingly centralizes power in the capital. In 1832 he orders that all Catholic missionaries be arrested and he has a French missionary strangled to death as punishment for involvement in a southern rebellion. During the next seven years, ten more foreign missionaries will be executed.

1833–1845: During these years, Vietnam and Thailand compete and on occasion fight openly to control Cambodia. In 1845 Vietnam and Thailand agree to share power over Cambodia.

1847: Following the arrest of a French missionary by the Emperor Thieu Tri, French warships fire on Danang harbor defenses, sink three Vietnamese ships, and kill hundreds of Vietnamese.

1848: The new emperor, Tu Duc, announces that he plans to remove Christianity in all its forms from Vietnam. He proceeds to persecute both Vietnamese and French Christians.

1856: A French warship arrives at Danang with a message for the emperor. When the Vietnamese refuse to deliver it, the French destroy the harbor defense again and then occupy the citadel. A second French warship arrives a few weeks later but the French, finding themselves short of supplies, depart.

August 30, 1858: The emperor orders the decapitation of the Spanish bishop of Tonkin (northern Vietnam), upon which a French fleet of fourteen warships bombards Danang on August 30. Then some 2,500 French and 500 Spanish troops occupy the town. In the ensuing weeks, the Vietnamese continue to fight, and the French and Spanish troops become drastically weakened from various diseases.

1859–1861: The French leave a force of nearly one thousand men at Danang and proceed in their warships to assault Saigon on February 17, 1859. Unable to capture Saigon completely, they leave a small Franco-Spanish force there and return to Danang. The emperor lays siege to Saigon in March 1860, but a French relief force defeats the Vietnamese in February 1861 and by July the French have raised the siege. During the next four months the French gain control of three adjacent provinces, but Vietnamese guerrillas continue to harass the French in the years ahead.

June 5, 1862: Emperor Tu Duc signs the Treaty of Saigon, giving the French various political, economic, and religious rights. The French are also allowed to make Saigon and the three adjacent provinces a protectorate, which they call Cochinchina, and Catholic missionaries are allowed to proselytize.

1863: The French appoint Admiral Pierre Benoît de la Grandière governor of Cochinchina, and he immediately begins to extend French rule throughout Indochina.

1866–1868: A French team of explorers, led by Captain Doudart de Lagrée, travels up the Mekong River to see if it might serve as a trade route with China. Lagrée dies and Lt. Francis Garnier assumes command; on returning to Saigon he reports that the Mekong is not suitable as a water route. His *Voyage d'Exploration* (1873), however, fires French interest in Vietnam and promotes the notion that the Red River in northern Vietnam is the route for trade with China.

1867: The French and Thai sign a treaty under which Thailand recognizes France's taking Cambodia as a protectorate. Admiral Grandière also takes three more provinces of southern Vietnam into Cochinchina, which now embraces all southern Vietnam; Cochinchina is effectively a French colony. The Vietnamese governor of these three provinces is so humiliated by this that he commits suicide.

1873: A French merchant-adventurer, Jean Dupuis, seizes part of Hanoi, raises the French flag, and asks for aid from the French in Cochinchina. The French dispatch a force that is allowed to proceed because the emperor believes it will oust Dupuis. Instead, the French force joins Dupuis and issues orders that the Red River be open to foreign trade. When the Vietnamese object, the French take the citadel and proceed to conquer the region between Hanoi and the Gulf of Tonkin (although the commander Lt. Francis Garnier is killed in the fighting).

1874: The French governor of Cochinchina arranges for a treaty with the emperor, under which the French evict Dupuis from Hanoi and withdraw their forces from Tonkin. The emperor meanwhile confirms French control of Cochinchina and opens the Red River to foreign trade. The emperor, however, proceeds to persecute Vietnamese Catholics and encourages Chinese mercenaries known as the Black Flags in northern Vietnam, believing they will sooner or later help get rid of the French.

1881: A major typhoon hits Indochina, causing the deaths of an estimated 300,000, many of them in Vietnam.

1882: The French have for some time been claming that they should act to prevent other foreign powers from taking over northern Vietnam. They send a force of some seven hundred men to take over Hanoi again and then the area between Hanoi and the harbor town of Haiphong. They also seize the coal mines at Hongay.

May–August 1883: In May, the Black Flag Chinese kill the commander of the French forces in Tonkin in an ambush near Hongay. When Emperor Tu Duc dies with no heir, a struggle for succession ensues. In August a French fleet arrives in the Perfume River near Hue and proceeds to inflict heavy ca-

sualties on the Vietnamese. The Vietnamese are forced to negotiate.

August 25, 1883: Under the Treaty of Protectorate, the Vietnamese agree to accept Tonkin (northern Vietnam) and Annam (central Vietnam) as protectorates of France, while Cochinchina remains a French colony. Vietnam ceases to exist as a name for a unified country as it is effectively a land under French governance.

FRENCH RULE: 1883–1954

The French move in and treat Vietnam as three separate regions—Tonkin (northern), Annam (central), and Cochinchina (southern)—while at the same time trying to join it to their larger Indochinese Union (which also includes Cambodia and Laos). Although the French only occasionally resort to force of arms, they have many ways of exploiting the people and resources of Vietnam. Meanwhile, they confront almost continual resistance, usually led by intellectuals and often based in remote regions: the French control the cities and the puppet emperor but not the people. (It should also be recognized that many Vietnamese do become Roman Catholics and adopt France and its culture.) With World War II, Vietnam falls under the rule of Japan but as soon as the war ends, the French move back in. An armed struggle against the French is led by Ho Chi Minh and his fellow Communists and finally proves so costly to the French that they withdraw in 1954.

August 1883–June 9, 1885: The Chinese do not accept the French claim to rule in Indochina, and in August they send troops into northern Vietnam. During December the French launch a major assault against the Chinese; fighting continues for the next two years. On June 9, 1885, the French and Chinese sign the Treaty of Tientsin, under which China recognizes that France controls the protectorates of Tonkin and Annam.

1885–1888: The first relatively unified resistance to the French is led by Ton That Thuyet, a relative of the royal family. Since 1883 he has been gathering arms and supplies at a base north of Hue. In July 1885 he provokes the French into sacking the city of Hué for three days. The thirteen-year-old emperor Ham Nghi flees with Ton That Thuyet to the remote base; before leaving, Ham Nghi issues a proclamation known as

the *Can Vuong* (Loyalty to the Emperor) in which he urges all Vietnamese to sacrifice everything to keep their country from the foreigners. In decades to follow this document will inspire many Vietnamese. Ton That Thuyet soon goes to China, and in late 1888 the French capture Ham Nghi and deport him to Algeria. The movement collapses, but other guerrilla leaders fight on.

1887: The French form the Indochinese Union, administered by a governor general under the Ministry of Colonies in Paris. The Union includes Tonkin, Annam, Cochinchina (which already includes parts of Cambodia), and Cambodia proper. (Laos will be included in the union in 1893.)

1888–1896: One of the most notable resistance leaders is Phan Dinh Phung, a highly refined man who has been serving at the imperial court. Although he did not approve of

Ton That Thuyet's ways, he too organizes a guerrilla army and bases himself on a mountain outside Hatinh, a town on the coast of north central Vietnam. Phan Dinh Phung organizes his followers into twelve districts, trains his forces, and manufactures his own arms and ammunition. In the end, though, the French forces prove too much, and when Phan Dinh Phung dies of dysentery in 1896, the movement collapses. This effectively ends overt armed resistance to the French, who have not hesitated to use the most brutal and repressive means to crush all opposition.

1897–1902: A former journalist and a deputy in the French parliament, Paul Doumer serves as governor-general of Indochina. Although a liberal in French terms, in Vietnam he sets the pattern for French exploitation of the Vietnamese. He imposes strict controls to extract taxes from the Vietnamese, essentially forcing them to pay for their own occupiers. He centralizes the administration and gets rid of all pretense that the Vietnamese emperor has any power. He encourages policies that allow French and Vietnamese speculators to acquire land owned by Vietnamese peasants. And as a final blow, he creates an official monopoly to produce and market opium, leading to such consumption by Vietnamese and local Chinese that the opium business eventually pays for one-third of France's costs of administering Vietnam.

1905–1925: With Japan's victory over Russia in 1905, Asians are inspired to realize they need not remain subservient to Western nations. One such in Vietnam is Phan Boi Chau, an intellectual who has become increasingly upset by his countrymen's situation under the French. He conceives of a plan to rally the Vietnamese around a constitutional monarch, and selects Prince Cuong De to fill that role. Phan Boi Chau goes to Japan, where he is influenced by Sun Yat-sen, the Chinese revolutionary. Phan Boi Chau eventually abandons his plan for a monarchy and adopts the goal of establishing a republic. He organizes the Viet Nam Duy Tan Hoi, or Association for the Modernization of Vietnam, hoping to appeal to middle-class Vietnamese. He also helps form the East Asian United League to unite Asians in a common struggle against their foreign occupiers. Phan Boi Chau constantly moves throughout Asia to evade French agents, but he is caught in Shanghai in 1925. Tried in Hanoi for sedition, he is placed under house arrest in Hue, where he dies in 1940.

1905–1926: Phan Chu Trinh, once an official at the imperial court, accompanies Phan Boi Chau to Japan in 1905. Trinh, however, almost immediately rejects the idea of relying on Japan and establishing a constitutional monarchy for Vietnam. He returns to Vietnam and embarks on his own program: appealing to the French to extend to the Vietnamese the same liberal ideals and humane behavior they profess to endorse. He starts a school to provide young Vietnamese with a modern liberal education but the French close this. In 1908 the French arrest him during a roundup of nationalists; condemned to death, he is saved by protests of supporters in France. After three years in prison, he is released but must go to Paris. In the early 1920s he is finally allowed to return to Vietnam, where he dies in 1926.

1908–1915: Vietnam is racked by revolts protesting the taxes mandated by the French; Vietnamese in the French army mutiny; guerrillas carry on in the countryside. By 1915 the French have suppressed all such threats to their rule.

February–April 1916: Vietnamese resistance leaders plan for the young emperor Duy Than, who supports the revolutionaries, to lead an uprising of Vietnamese troops scheduled to be sent to France to fight against Germany. Word of the plan reaches the French, and they disarm the soldiers. Unaware of this, the leaders and various partisan units outside Hue and Danang revolt. The

French quickly subdue them, execute the leaders, and depose and banish Duy Than.

August–December 1917: Again hoping to take advantage of the resentment among Vietnamese troops in the French colonial army, Luong Ngoc Quyen, a follower of Phan Boi Chau, organizes a revolt in Thai Nguyen province northeast of Hanoi. The soldiers and revolutionaries succeed in taking control briefly of Hanoi and parts of the province, but the French soon drive them back into the mountains. Luong is killed in the fighting, and the revolt comes to nothing.

1919: At the Paris Peace Conference following World War I, several Vietnamese residing in Paris draw up an eight-point program for their country's independence. They send a printed copy to the conference secretariat, and one of the leading initiators, Nguyen Ai Quoc (Nguyen the Patriot) tries to meet personally with President Woodrow Wilson, whose famous Fourteen Points manifesto calls for self-determination for all peoples. Quoc is turned away, and the eight points are never officially recognized. Quoc's real name is Nguyen Sinh Cung, who many years later will become known under another of his adopted names, Ho Chi Minh. He has been wandering throughout much of the world since 1911, in part to escape the French dominance of his homeland, in part to see how the rest of the world lives.

1919: The Cao Dai is founded by Ngo Van Chieu, a mystic. Appealing to the Vietnamese people's belief in the supernatural, this sect draws on Buddhism, Confucianism, Daoism, and Christianity and mixes it with a strain of secularism. Within twenty years Cao Dai counts some 300,000 adherents, and after World War II it will become even more numerous and play an active role in the political life of Vietnam.

1920–1925: Living in Paris, Nguyen Ai Quoc moves from being a socialist to favoring communism, but only because he believes that the new USSR is capable of carrying out an anticolonial revolution that will liberate Vietnam. He goes to Moscow for much of 1924, then on to Canton, China, where he becomes involved with various communists. In 1925 he founds the Thanh Nien Cach Mang Dong Chu Hoi, the Revolutionary Youth League of Vietnam, the first Marxist organization of Indochinese.

1925: The twelve-year-old Bao Dai becomes emperor of Vietnam. For the next thirty years he will serve as an ineffectual pawn of the French.

1925–1926: The first major student activism and demonstrations are set off by the arrest and trial of Phan Boi Chauu and the death of Phan Chu Trinh.

1929–1930: René Bazin, a Frenchman who recruits Vietnamese for virtually slave labor, is assassinated by an agent of the Viet Nam Quoc Dan Dang (VNQDD), the party of nationalists opposed to the communists. Many VNQDD members are arrested by the French. In 1930 VNQDD activists incite Vietnamese soldiers at Yenbay to mutiny against their French officers; the French quickly put down the revolt, execute many soldiers, and also about a dozen VNQDD leaders.

1930: In Kowloon, Hong Kong, Nguyen Ai Quoc founds the Viet Nam Cong San Dang, the Vietnam Communist Party, which becomes the Indochinese Communist Party. But with the Hong Kong police on his trail, Quoc sets off once more on years of wandering. It will be 1941 before he resurfaces in Vietnam.

1931–1936: The depression that spreads throughout the world leaves the Vietnamese people worse off than ever. Prices of their two prime income producers, rice and rubber, collapse; unemployment and hunger follow; strikes and unrest ensue. In 1936 the Popular Front government of France introduces some fairly liberal reforms in Vietnam, such as French domestic labor laws, but these prove ineffectual and short-lived.

1932: Emperor Bao Dai returns to Vietnam after being educated in France. At first it appears the French are going to allow him to take an active role in a more liberal regime. In practice the French do not give him much power, and he soon turns to indulging himself in his personal interests. The French continue to dominate and exploit Vietnam, while various nationalistic and dissenting Vietnamese, abroad as well as in Vietnam, try unsuccessfully to change the situation.

September 22, 1940: France's Vichy government, collaborating with the Nazis, concludes an agreement to permit Japan to station troops and use facilities in Tonkin. In spite of this, Japanese troops invade Vietnam from China. The French order an end to all resistance. The Japanese leave the French colonial administration in place but gradually take over full control. By the end of 1941 and the full-scale war in the Pacific, Japan is treating Vietnam as its colony.

May 10, 1941: Earlier this year, Nguyen Ai Quoc has made his way back into Vietnam. On this day, he meets with various communist leaders and they form the Viet Nam Doc Lap Dong Minh, the Vietnam Independence League. This is an effort to unite all Vietnamese in the fight against the Japanese and French. It will soon become known as the Vietminh, while Nguyen Ai Quoc will adopt his best-known pseudonym, Ho Chi Minh ("Ho the Enlightened One").

The ancients pleased themselves by singing of nature;
Rivers, mountains, smoke, snow, moon, and wind.
It is necessary to add steel to the verses of our time.
The poets must also know how to fight!

"On Reading the Anthology of 1,000 Poets," poem by Ho Chi Minh (c. 1942)

1942–1943: Ho Chi Minh goes to China intending to get Chiang Kai-shek and his Nationalists to aid the Vietnamese in their fight against the Japanese. Instead, Chiang Kaishek has him imprisoned for thirteen months. (In prison he writes a number of poems that will become well known to Vietnamese in later years.) He finally convinces his captors that he will work for their goals and, adopting his new name, is allowed to slip back into Vietnam.

1943–1944: During this time, supported by the Chinese and Americans, Ho and his supporters sabotage Japanese facilities, rescue downed Allied fliers, and generally keep the Japanese off balance. Through all this, however, he is working to advance his own communist cause.

December 22, 1944: With Ho Chi Minh's support, Vo Nguyen Giap sets up an armed brigade of thirty-four Vietnamese; within days they begin to attack French outposts in northern Vietnam. This marks the beginning of the Vietminh's armed struggle against the French.

March 9, 1945: Realizing that they are losing the war across the Pacific, the Japanese imprison the French authorities and grant independence to Vietnam. They reinstall Bao Dai as head of state, but he never gains much support for what is in fact a puppet government.

August 16–29, 1945: After the Japanese surrender to the Allies, Ho Chi Minh and his People's Congress create a National Liberation Committee to form a provisional government. On August 18 the Japanese transfer power to the Vietminh, intending thereby to thwart the French. On August 23 Bao Dai abdicates. On August 29 the Vietminh and the People's Congress establish a provisional government, with Bao Dai as "supreme advisor."

September 2, 1945: In Hanoi, Ho Chi Minh proclaims the independent Democratic Republic of Vietnam. Officers of the U.S. Office of Strategic Services (OSS) stand by as Ho quotes the American Declaration of Independence.

September 9, 1945: Nationalist Chinese troops move into northern Vietnam and within two days are occupying Hanoi. The Allies have agreed to this with the goal of ousting the Japanese, but the Vietnamese regard it as an invasion by their traditional enemy.

September 12–24, 1945: On September 12 British troops arrive in Saigon to accept the surrender of Japanese forces. However, there is so much fighting among the various Vietnamese factions hoping to gain control that on September 21 the British command declares martial law and allows Japanese troops to help in restoring order. The British also arm 1,400 French troops who immediately turn on the Vietminh. By September 24, when the new French military commander arrives in Saigon, Vietnam is torn by violence.

January 6, 1946: Elections in northern Vietnam for a National Assembly give an overwhelming majority to Vietminh candidates, but by earlier arrangement with the occupying Chinese commander the Nationalists also are allowed to share power.

February–April 1946: French Foreign Legion troops arrive in southern Vietnam and battle the Vietminh.

February 28, 1946: China and France sign a treaty under which the Chinese agree to leave Vietnam and the French give up all territorial claims in China.

March 6–September 12, 1946: On March 6 Ho Chi Minh signs an agreement with France that recognizes the Democratic Republic of Vietnam as a free state within an Indochinese Federation and French Union. On June 1 the French High Commissioner for Indochina violates this treaty by announcing that Cochinchina is to remain an autonomous state, thus splitting Vietnam in two. On September 12 the French and Vietnamese end negotiations to resolve their differences, with the Vietminh agreeing to a cessation of hostilities.

November 20–December 7, 1946: A French patrol boat seizing a Chinese boat in Haiphong harbor exchanges shots with Vietnamese troops onshore. This leads to fighting between the French and Vietnamese. On November 23 a French cruiser, supported by artillery and aircraft, bombards Haiphong, killing some one thousand people. During the next two weeks, French forces move throughout Haiphong attacking Vietminh positions.

December 19, 1946: Disturbed by the actions of the French, the Democratic Republic of Vietnam declares war on them. The Vietminh blow up the power station in Hanoi, and resistance breaks out in several major Vietnamese cities.

January–February 19, 1947: The Vietminh place Hue under siege but it is lifted by the French on February 10. By February 19 the French also relieve their garrison in Hanoi.

October 1947: The French army launches a major offensive against the Vietminh forces in northern Vietnam.

December 7, 1947–June 8, 1948: In December 1947, on a French warship off Haiphong, Emperor Bao Dai signs an agreement with the French that gives Vietnam limited independence. In June 1948 the French force the Vietnamese to accept General Nguyen Van Xuan as their prime minister; the general is a naturalized French citizen who can hardly speak Vietnamese.

March 8–December 30, 1949: In March, Emperor Bao Dai signs the Elysée Agreement with the French, under which Vietnam becomes an "associated state" of the French Union. France retains control of Vietnam's defense, foreign affairs, and finances. In April, an assembly votes to end Cochinchina's colonial status and unite it with the rest of Vietnam. The new state is established in Saigon on June 14; on June 28, Cochinchina is united with the rest of Vietnam. The French do not grant full sovereignty to the state of Vietnam until December 30.

1949–1950: The People's Republic of China gains control of all China, down to the border with Vietnam, and the Communists link up with the Vietminh.

January 14, 1950: Ho Chi Minh declares that the Democratic Republic of Vietnam established by his Vietminh movement is the true legal government. The USSR and Communist China recognize this, but the United States, Great Britain, and several other Western nations recognize Bao Dai's state and its status within the French Union.

May–November 1950: The Vietminh conduct a major campaign against the French in northern Vietnam. The Vietminh succeed in taking five provincial capitals and costing the French some six thousand casualties.

May 28–June 20, 1951: The Vietminh conduct another major campaign against the French in northern Vietnam, but this time the Vietnamese gain little and suffer heavy casualties.

January–February 1953: The French conduct a combined land-sea campaign against Vietminh forces in southern Vietnam.

April 11–20, 1953: Hoping to distract the French forces in Vietnam, the Vietminh invade Laos. Linking up with the Communist Pathet Lao, they advance to the outskirts of the capital, Luang Prabang, then withdraw back into Vietnam.

November 20, 1953: In November, French troops parachute into the area of a mountain valley at Dien Bien Phu in northwestern Vietnam. The French have decided that this sits at a strategic location and are determined to hold it at all costs. Eventually some 16,500 French troops are holed up here.

March 12–May 7, 1954: The siege of Dien Bien Phu begins with an artillery bombardment by the Vietminh. As the weeks pass, the Vietminh gradually take all the outer forts and the French become isolated. The operation catches the attention of the world and becomes a symbol of the doomed French cause. On April 1, President Dwight Eisenhower announces that the United States will not provide military force to help the French; in fact, the United States is by now paying for about 75 percent of the French war in Indochina, and it is on this occasion that Eisenhower refers to the "domino theory," according to which the fall of one Southeast Asian country to communists will lead to a succession of such falls. After fifty-six days the French surrender: the French count some 5,400 killed, and half of the 10,000 who surrender are wounded.

April 26–July 20, 1954: With the siege of Dien Bien Phu clearly casting its shadow, an international conference on Far Eastern affairs commences in Geneva, Switzerland. On July 20 the Geneva Accords are signed, calling for a cease-fire in Vietnam, Laos, and Cambodia; all three states are recognized as independent. (The cease-fire does not take full effect until August.) The United States and Emperor Bao Dai's government refuse to sign. In Vietnam, a provisional demarcation line is drawn at the 17th parallel until North and South Vietnam can hold elections in July 1956.

INDEPENDENT VIETNAM: 1954–1998

The line drawn between North and South Vietnam is only the most literal indication of a deeply divided Vietnam. Ho Chi Minh and the communists are able to impose a rigid unity in the north (in part because so many dissenters flee). In the south, conservative-rightist-nationalists (which includes most Roman Catholics and the pro-French military) are pitted against both communist-nationalists and neutral Buddhists. Southern Vietnamese return to infiltrate the South and are soon leading the fight against the Saigon government, itself torn by internecine strife. Meanwhile, the United States gradually moves from financial and arms aid to military advisers to protective forces to combat troops. By 1965 both the United States and North Vietnam commit themselves to an all-out war that proves horribly destructive to the Vietnamese people and their cities and countryside. Eventually, this war proves so costly in terms of money and lives to the United States that it quits in 1973; two years later Communist forces from North Vietnam take over South Vietnam. A united Vietnam continues for some years to fight against its traditional enemies in the Indochina Peninsula and China to the north. By the 1990s Vietnam finally seems free of its age-old external threats and is being accepted into the international community, while its Communist leaders try to work out new ways to deal with its internal problems of poverty and economic underdevelopment.

July 7, 1954: Emperor Bao Dai installs Ngo Dinh Diem as prime minister of South Vietnam. A Catholic who has been in self-imposed exile since 1950, Diem moves quickly to impose his rule.

October 8–11, 1954: On October 8 French troops begin to leave North Vietnam; the French acknowledge some 93,000 killed in Indochina since 1946. Meanwhile, the flight from North Vietnam to South Vietnam is underway; eventually 1 million Vietnamese, most of them Catholics, will flee. On October 11 the Vietminh take over North Vietnam, which is renamed the Democratic Republic of Vietnam.

January 1955: The U.S. government pledges more military assistance to South Vietnam and supports a French offer to supply a French general to oversee the organizing and training of the South Vietnamese army.

March 1955: This month sees the beginning of open fighting between Ngo Dinh Diem's government and various parties, sects, and factions within South Vietnam. Although it will vary in its levels of openness and violence, this infighting really never stops until the Communists take over twenty years later.

July 16, 1955: Ngo Dinh Diem announces that he will not participate in the elections called for by the Geneva Accords because his government did not sign them.

October 26, 1955: After defeating Emperor Bao Dai in an election for president, Ngo Dinh Diem proclaims the new Republic of Vietnam.

April 28, 1956: With the departure of the last French soldier, the U.S. Military Assistance Advisory Group (USMAAG) takes over the training of the South Vietnamese armed forces.

October 27–November 11, 1956: In October, the government of Ho Chi Minh admits that it has made terrible mistakes in trying to impose land reform in North Vietnam. Since taking over in October 1954, the Communists have killed an estimated fifteen thousand North Vietnamese by this and other of their reforms. Even this apology does not stop the protests; between November 8 and 11 protesting farmers and Roman Catholics in North Vietnam rise up and fight the North Vietnam army; hundreds are killed and some two thousand executed after the army restores order.

1957–1959: Diem cracks down hard on all opposition, labeling everyone Communists; in particular he attacks any remnants of the Vietminh he can find in South Vietnam. Meanwhile, he has been antagonizing the peasants by refusing to introduce meaningful land reform; the nepotism and corruption of his regime is also turning many non-Communists against him. Aware of this growing discontent, the leaders in Hanoi give orders in October 1957 that the Communists in South Vietnam should begin to organize thirty-seven armed companies to operate in the Mekong Delta.

May 5–19, 1957: During his visit to the United States, President Diem assures President Eisenhower that the Communist opposition in South Vietnam has been eliminated. Eisenhower in turn assures him of American support.

1959: This year sees a major stepping up of the Communist insurgency in Vietnam. In May, North Vietnam forms Group 559 to infiltrate personnel and arms into South Vietnam along the Truong Son Strategic Supply Route—what becomes widely known as the

Ho Chi Minh Trail. In September North Vietnam forms Group 959 to supply Communist forces operating in Laos. North Vietnam also establishes its air force and navy. U.S. military "advisers" also begin going into the field with South Vietnamese infantry regiments; on July 8, the first two American combat fatalities occur when Communist guerrillas attack Bienhoa, some twenty miles northeast of Saigon. In August, Diem promulgates a law calling for complete repression of the Communists in South Vietnam.

November 11–12, 1960: Some military units attempt a coup against Diem, but other troops rally and suppress it. This turns out to be only the first of many such attempted and sometimes successful coups that will weaken South Vietnam during the next fifteen years.

December 20, 1960: Hanoi announces the formation of the National Front for the Liberation of the South; this will become known as the Vietcong ("Vietnamese Communists").

October 1961: Admitting that the Communists within South Vietnam are becoming increasingly more powerful, President Diem declares a state of emergency but then uses his new powers to arrest his political opponents.

February 8, 1962: The U.S. Military Assistance Command, Vietnam (MACV) is installed in Saigon as the United States recognizes that it is becoming fully involved in the war.

January 2, 1963: At Ap Bac in the Mekong Delta, some 2,500 South Vietnamese army troops, armed with advanced and heavy equipment and supported by U.S. helicopters, trap a force of some three hundred Vietcong. But the South Vietnamese suffer some 160 casualties and the United States loses three helicopter pilots while the Vietcong escape. This will turn out to be the pattern in the years ahead: South Vietnamese and U.S. forces "win" the battle but at a heavy cost, while the Communists, whatever their losses, slip away until the next confrontation.

May 8–August 1963: While celebrating the birthday of the Buddha, South Vietnamese Buddhists are fired on and killed by government troops. Buddhists make up some 70 percent of the population of South Vietnam but they are almost completely dominated by Diem's Catholic supporters. A series of protests by Buddhists ensues, including numerous self-immolations. (The first by a Buddhist monk is on June 11.) In August, government troops attack Buddhist temples and arrest over one thousand monks and nuns.

The United States is beginning to make known its displeasure with Diem's handling of this and related matters.

November 1–2, 1963: Dissident army officers besiege the presidential palace but Ngo Dinh Diem and his brother Nhu, head of the hated secret police, escape to a Catholic church. On November 2 they negotiate with the officers, who promise to spare their lives; picked up in an armored personnel carrier, they are executed. General Duong Van Minh becomes the effective head of the government.

January 30, 1964: Major General Nguyen Khanh leads a coup that overthrows General Duong Van Minh and his government.

February–July 1964: The Vietcong increase their attacks both as a guerrilla army and as terrorists, inflicting increasingly high casualties on Vietnamese and U.S. personnel.

The villager regards me
agonized and fearless;
he answers willingly,
"I hate both sides
I follow neither,
not Communist nor anti-Communist,
I only want to go
where they will let me live
and help me in my living."
O life? What resignation,
what shame, what pity!

"Experience," poem by Thich Nhat Hanh (1960s)

August 2–7, 1964: On August 2 the USS *Maddox*, an electronic monitoring ship in the Tonkin Gulf, is attacked by three North Vietnamese patrol boats; the U.S. ship, aided by planes from a nearby U.S. aircraft carrier, sinks one of the boats and cripples the others. At first the U.S. government orders the navy simply to take steps to maintain their "right of freedom to the seas." But on the night of August 4 the *Maddox* reports that it is attacked again by patrol boats; in fact, it is determined almost immediately that this is a false alarm. This time, however, President Johnson authorizes a military reprisal. On August 5 planes from U.S. carriers bomb installations over a hundred-mile strip of North Vietnam along the Gulf of Tonkin. On August 7 the U.S. Congress authorizes Johnson "to take all necessary measures." Known as the Tonkin Gulf Resolution, with no formal declaration of war this will be employed by presidents Johnson and Nixon in the years ahead to maintain the fighting in Vietnam.

February 19–22, 1965: After months of unrest and various reshufflings of his government, General Nguyen Khanh is overthrown in a coup by other dissident officers. He goes into permanent exile, but most of his government's leaders remain in power.

March 8–9, 1965: Two battalions of U.S. Marines land near Danang. Although the U.S. government claims they are simply there as a protective force, they turn out to be the first of many thousands of U.S. combat troops sent to Vietnam.

June 12–19, 1965: In another coup, General Nguyen Van Thieu and Air Vice-Marshal Nguyen Cao Ky take over as the ninth government in twenty months.

March–June 1966: With the war raging both in the countryside and cities, South Vietnam continues to be wracked by riots, strikes, and unrest, much of it instigated by the Buddhists. During this period, South Vietnamese army troops in Danang also revolt against the Saigon government. By June 22, however, the government has pretty much suppressed the revolts.

September 3, 1967: Elections in South Vietnam retain Nguyen Van Thieu as president, with Marshal Ky as vice president.

December 1967: The war continues to rage throughout Vietnam; its cities, villages, and countryside are becoming devastated. The United States now has almost 500,000 troops there and has committed massive air forces to bombing North Vietnam. Casualties among all groups—military and civilian—are mounting into the hundreds of thousands.

January 30–February 10, 1968: The Vietnamese New Year, known as Tet, is understood to be a truce period but in the early hours of the first day, the Vietcong and North Vietnamese army launch their largest and best coordinated offensive of the war. They attack all major cities in South Vietnam and many military installations; a nineteen-man suicide squad of Vietcong seizes a part of the U.S. embassy compound in Saigon for several hours. By February 10 the offensive is largely crushed (although it will take almost another month before the Communist forces are driven out of Hue). Although the U.S. and South Vietnamese forces can claim a victory, the impact on the American home front and government is one of disillusion and dismay over the war in Vietnam.

March 16, 1968: An American army platoon kills between two hundred and five hundred unarmed villagers in My Lai. There is no report of this at the time. Later this will become a national scandal as "the My Lai massacre," and several American officers will be charged with murder.

May 10, 1968: North Vietnamese and American negotiators meet in Paris to commence peace talks. Little progress is made during the first six months.

January 16, 1969: An agreement is reached in Paris to allow delegates of the South Vietnamese and the National Liberation Front to participate in the peace talks.

August 4, 1969: Henry Kissinger, chief American delegate at the Paris peace talks, begins the first of many secret meetings with North Vietnamese delegates.

September 2, 1969: Ho Chi Minh dies at age seventy-nine.

October 3, 1971: Nguyen Van Thieu is re-elected president in a controversial one-man contest, allegedly receiving 94 percent of the votes. The war drags on as do the peace talks in Paris.

March–September 1972: The North Vietnamese and Vietcong launch a major offensive at the end of March, and for the next six months continue to press their attack. By May 1 they have taken the major northern provincial capital of Quang Tri; it will be September 15 before the South Vietnamese retake it.

April 10–October 20, 1972: Frustrated by a lack of progress in Paris and the renewed Communist aggression in Vietnam, the United States begins to bomb targets in North Vietnam on April 10, the first time since November 1967. On April 16 U.S. bombers begin bombing targets near the North Vietnamese cities of Hanoi and Haiphong. The bombing continues with the goal of forcing the Communists to come to terms in Paris. On October 20, President Nixon calls for a halt to bombing north of the 20th parallel.

August 11, 1972: The last U.S. ground combat unit in Vietnam is deactivated, but the bombing of North Vietnam continues.

October–December 16, 1972: Negotiations in Paris are leading to an agreement between the United States and North Vietnam, but South Vietnam's President Thieu continues to reject any suggestion that the Communists might have any presence in South Vietnam. On October 22 a U.S. negotiator personally meets with Thieu in Saigon but cannot get him to concede. Kissinger returns to negotiations in Paris but on December 16 he announces in Washington that the talks have failed. Each side blames the other.

December 18, 1972–January 15, 1973: The United States recommences B-52 bombing of North Vietnam above the 20th parallel, including Hanoi for the first time. On December 24–25 there is a thirty-six-hour Christmas pause. With the prospect of renewing the peace talks shortly, the United States stops bombing above the 20th parallel on December 31. On January 15, 1973, bombing, mining, and all other offensive actions in North Vietnam cease.

January 8–27, 1973: On January 8 peace negotiations start again. On January 23 it is announced that the chief negotiators have initialed an agreement. The formal agreement is signed on January 27. All foreign troops must withdraw but Communist forces may remain in place in South Vietnam and the country remains divided at the 17th parallel. President Thieu refuses to sign this agreement. The cease-fire is supposed to go into effect on January 28, but in fact there are continuous violations; the agreement serves as nothing more than a cover for the United States to leave Vietnam.

January 4, 1974: President Thieu announces that the war has "restarted."

May–August 1974: North Vietnamese troops and the Vietcong are on the attack throughout much of South Vietnam. By August Communist troops are only fifteen miles from Saigon.

March 1975: North Vietnamese troops commence a major offensive that almost at once turns into a rout of the South Vietnamese military. On March 14 President Thieu orders the South Vietnam army to withdraw from the northern provinces and central highlands. By March 25 Hue is being abandoned. Thousands of civilians and army deserters are streaming southward.

April 1975: The Communists launch their final offensive. From April 8 to April 21 South Vietnamese troops fight one final battle to defend Saigon, but in the end they retreat. On April 25 President Thieu flees Vietnam. On April 30 the Communists move through

Saigon and take over the governmental buildings. General Duong Van Minh, who had led the overthrow of Ngo Dinh Diem in November 1963, formally surrenders South Vietnam to the Communists. Thousands of Vietnamese flee by land and sea; this flight will begin again in 1978 and continue for several years. The Communists soon announce that they are changing the name of Saigon to Ho Chi Minh City.

July 2, 1976: The National Assembly, elected in April, proclaims the unification of Vietnam as the Socialist Republic of Vietnam, with Hanoi as the capital.

September 20, 1977: Vietnam is admitted into the United Nations.

December 1977–January 6, 1978: Vietnamese forces attack Cambodia after Cambodian forces had raided Vietnam. They temporarily withdraw from Cambodia on January 6, 1978.

March–July 1978: Following the nationalization of all private businesses in March, thousands of Chinese flee Vietnam. In July, China retaliates by cutting off all aid to Vietnam.

November 3, 1978: Vietnam and the USSR sign a twenty-five-year pact of mutual aid and friendship. China calls the pact a threat to the security of Southeast Asia.

December 14, 1978–January 7, 1979: In December 1978 Vietnam invades Cambodia. On January 7, 1979, the Vietnamese take the capital Phnom Penh and the government of Pol Pot falls. The Vietnamese will occupy Cambodia until September 1989. Pol Pot and his Khmer Rouge supporters, however, continue to fight on.

February 17–March 5, 1979: In retaliation for Vietnam's invasion of Cambodia, China invades northern Vietnam. Both sides suffer heavy casualties, and China withdraws its troops by March 5.

June 23–25, 1980: Vietnamese troops cross into Thailand, claiming that Cambodian refugees are using Thailand as a base from which to maintain their fight against the

Vietnamese-backed government in Cambodia. Vietnam and Thailand will continue to exchange charges and occasional hostilities in the years ahead.

February–July 1984: Vietnam and China continue to accuse each other of shelling their territory. In July 1984 the two countries engage in open fighting near their border. This conflict goes on intermittently for many years, flaring up with various incidents (such as China's shooting down of a Vietnamese airplane in October 1987, or skirmishes in March 1988 over the disputed Spratly Islands in the South China Sea).

July 10, 1986: Le Duan, the leader of the Communist Party of Vietnam, dies. At the Sixth National Congress of the Party in December, a policy of "renewal" is adopted.

June 22, 1988: Do Muoi is elected prime minister; he will turn out to be more open to promoting economic policies that break from a rigid communism.

September 1989: Vietnam claims that its troops have left Cambodia, ending an eleven-year occupation, but Vietnam continues to claim a role in any final resolution of affairs in Cambodia. (There are constant reports that some Vietnamese forces remain in Cambodia.)

July 1990: In line with a general move toward improving its economy through foreign investment, the government amends its laws to allow private individuals to negotiate with foreign companies.

August 9, 1991: Do Muoi is replaced as prime minister by Vo Van Kiet, known to favor even more liberal economic policies.

June 4, 1992: The government announces that it has released all former South Vietnamese officials who have been held in detention camps.

October 19, 1993: Vietnam and China sign a preliminary agreement to resolve peacefully their border disputes.

February 3, 1994: The United States removes its nineteen-year-old trade embargo with the understanding that the Vietnamese will make greater effort to locate some 1,600 Americans still missing in action from the war.

July 11, 1995: President Clinton announces normalization of diplomatic relations between the United States and Vietnam. On August 6 the United States officially changes its liaison office in Hanoi to an embassy.

1997: Vietnam's three major exports during this year are crude oil (US$1.4 billion), textiles and garments (US$1.3 billion), and shoes, sandals, and leatherware (US$1.1 billion). There are increasing calls for Vietnam to be granted more favorable trade arrangements with the United States, but American government officials insist there are still too many questions about the Vietnam economy, in particular, a bureaucracy that appears to interfere with truly free trade.

June–November 1997: In Thai Binh province in northern Vietnam, peasants rebel against local leaders, closing the marketplace and disrupting the rice harvest to protest corruption, high taxes, and the unresponsiveness of the government to their needs. When officials dispatch police and government officials to quiet things down, they are taken hostage. The standoff ends peaceably when the government in Hanoi promises to take action.

September 21–27, 1997: During the opening session of the National Assembly, the Communist Party replaces much of Vietnam's now aging and ill leadership. The most prominent of these is the election of Phan Van Khai as the new prime minister.

May 13–20, 1998: On May 13 Philip Knight, chief executive of Nike footwear, announces a sweeping series of reforms in its factories in Vietnam and elsewhere in Asia; this comes in response to a campaign that has been underway for over a year to expose the wages and working conditions in Nike's Asia factories. On May 20 an interfaith group of Americans, who inspected factories in Vietnam, Indonesia, and China during a twelve-day tour in March, criticizes working conditions they found in Nike's factories.

September 18–21, 1998: On September 18 Nike, the footwear manufacturer, announces that it is suspending plans to increase its investment in Vietnam. On September 21 Nike also confirms that it has recently laid off at least 2,700 workers in Vietnam because of the worldwide downturn in sales.

PART FOUR

Central Asia

Mongolia

EARLY HISTORY: 200,000 B.C.–A.D. 1125

There is no evidence as yet that early hominids settled in Mongolia, most likely because of the inhospitable terrain and climate. Most of Mongolia is high above sea level; much of the western, northern, and central part is mountainous; the rest is taken up by the Gobi Desert. It is a dry climate, with extremely cold, windy winters; parts of Mongolia experience hot summers. About 200,000 B.C., perhaps earlier, some archaeological evidence indicates human (probably archaic *Homo sapiens*) presence in the Gobi Desert in southern Mongolia. Thereafter the evidence of human settlement in Mongolia is scant, but clearly *Homo sapiens* have moved into this region; there are many finds of stone tools dating from 50,000 B.C. on. Eventually these people establish the nomadic way of life that will prevail even to the end of the twentieth century: it is based on following herds of various animals such as sheep, goats, and yaks while living in their portable felt tents *(ger)*. Probably during the second millennium B.C. these early Mongolians are among the first to domesticate horses for their own uses; later they also adopt the camel. Not until the third century B.C. do Chinese sources begin to refer to a consistently identifiable culture in the region of the Mongolian steppes. For the next fourteen centuries, various groups of people rise and fall in power in the region that today comprises Mongolia and the bordering provinces of northern China (including the vast region now called Inner Mongolia). Some of these peoples are from Mongolia and neighboring Manchuria, some are Turks from the west. In the early seventh century A.D. Chinese of the Tang dynasty commence a series of campaigns and by 744 have driven out the Turks, but then another Turkic people, the Uyghurs, become the dominant force in this region. The Uyghurs' power collapses about 840 and a period of relative anarchy ensues, with tribesmen from Manchuria, first the Khitan and then the Jurchen, becoming the main power. It is not until about 1125 that the people who will become known in history as the Mongols begin to emerge as the major force in this region.

200,000 B.C.: Archaic *Homo sapiens* may begin human habitation of the Gobi desert in southern Mongolia.

324?–c. 206 B.C.: The three major states of China's Warring States period (403–221 B.C.), Qin (Ch'in), Jiao (Chao), and Yan (Yen), construct defensive barriers in their northern borders, in part to protect themselves from the nomadic peoples of the Mongolian steppes, referred to as the Xiongnu or Hsiaung-nu. When the Qin emerge as the sole rulers (221–206 B.C.) they particularly strengthen these fortifications, which become the nucleus of the Great Wall of China.

Late 3d century B.C.: Two Donghu (Tung-hu, eastern barbarians) peoples, the Xianbei (Hsien-pi) and the Wuhuan, control territory stretching from the southern part of Inner Mongolia to southern Manchuria. They make frequent attacks on the Xiongnu to the west.

212 B.C.: The Qin, who had unified China in 221 B.C., begin to take control of the territory in the Ordos desert from the Xiongnu people. Later that year the Qin complete construction of a section of the Great Wall of China. Although weakened, the tribal confederation of the Xiongnu begin to move toward some solidarity.

209 B.C.: The great Xiongnu leader Motun comes to power. By the end of the third century B.C. he defeats the Donghu and the Yuezhi (Yeh-chih), from whom he assumes command of the important Gansu corridor. He also reclaims Xiongnu territory in the Ordos Desert from the weakened Qin.

198 B.C.: Liu Bang, the ruler (206–195 B.C.) of the Early (or Western) Han Dynasty, negotiates the first of the so-called *he-qin (ho-ch'in)* peace treaties with the Xiongnu. By the terms of the treaty Han is to send a princess and other gifts to the ruler of the Xiongnu. In return the Xiongnu vow not to invade Han.

134 B.C.: Suffering under the increasingly unequal terms of the *he-qin* treaties (there are ten negotiated between 198 B.C. and 135

B.C.), Han plots to trick Xiongnu troops into an ambush. The Xiongnu leader discovers the plot and severs diplomatic relations.

129 B.C.: Han launches a full-scale offensive against the Xiongnu.

127 B.C.: Han drives the Xiongnu from the Ordos.

121 B.C. and 119 B.C.: The Xiongnu suffer two decisive defeats in their struggle with the Han. They move their capital north of the Gobi and abandon both territories west of the Gansu corridor and the pastures of the Qilian and Yanzhi mountains.

115–60 B.C.: Han and the Xiongnu vie for control of the region surrounding the important Tarim Basin. The struggle centers on Jushi, which the Xiongnu lose in 60 B.C.

53 B.C.: The Xiongnu leader, Hu-han-yeh, agrees to become part of the Han tributary system.

A.D. 18–46: Reign of Xiongnu leader Hu-tu-erh-shih. The Xiongnu enjoy a brief period of renewed prosperity as China becomes preoccupied with civil wars. They reclaim lost territory in the Tarim Basin region and exert influence over the Donghu tribes. However, the Xiongnu court had lost its ability to centralize authority over local potentates. After Hu-tu-erh-shih's death in A.D. 46 the Xiongnu split permanently into southern and northern factions.

A.D. 50: The eight tribes of the Southern Xiongnu reenter the Chinese tributary system.

Spring 73: The Later Han (or Eastern Han, A.D. 25–220) dynasty begins a decisive campaign against the North Xiongnu, wresting from them regions they controlled in the Tarim Basin.

87: The Xianbei (Hsien-pi), a tribal division of the Donghu, mount a successful offensive against the Northern Xiongnu. Their victory marks the beginning of their dominance of the regions west and north of the Later Han. The Xianbei assume the formerly Xiongnu-dominated area of Outer Mongolia as their base of power.

2d century–4th century: As the power of Later Han diminishes, various nomadic peoples assume control of China's outlying territories. The Xianbei dominate. The Wuhuan and the Toba (To-pa), a subgroup of the Xianbei, are also important. All these peoples are Donghu in origin. China north of the Yangtze becomes a region of political chaos, and is entirely overrun by nomadic peoples by 317.

220: The Later Han falls.

c. **Early 4th century:** The so-called Xiongnu Distich, a two-line verse attributed to an anonymous Xiongnu author, is recorded in the Chinese source *Zhoushu*. The text, conveyed phonetically with Chinese characters and translated into the Chinese language, has been used by linguists to trace the Turkic origins of the Xiongnu language.

338?–376?: The Toba emerge to control the vast region between the Yangtze River and the Gobi Desert. Their center of power is the present-day Shanxi province of China. They found the semi-sinicized state of Dai.

386: Dai fully assumes a state structure based on the Chinese model and becomes the Northern Wei dynasty (386–534).

c. **5th century:** The Ruanruan (Juan-Juan) emerge concurrently with the Northern Wei in China. Their origin is obscure, but they appear to be a nomadic Mongol people based in the steppes north of the Altai Mountains. They defeat the remnants of the Northern Xiongnu, who retreat to the Ural Mountains and the Caspian Sea from whence, some scholars hypothesize, they migrate to Europe to eventually become the infamous Huns. By the end of the fifth century the Ruanruan control an empire that is roughly equivalent in size to Northern Wei. It stretches north of China along the Mongolian steppes.

438: Wei launches the first of several campaigns against the Ruanruan. However, the Ruanruan leader, Wu-ti (429–444), avoids engagement with the Chinese troops who having exhausted their supplies, retreat. Another Wei campaign in 443 similarly fails.

448: Wei mounts a successful attack on the Ruanruan, who thereafter turn their attention away from Chinese territory and toward the Tarim Basin.

460: The Ruanruan attack Qocho and vanquish the Quju (Chu-chu) dynasty, which had been a powerful force in the regions west of present-day Xian.

471: The Ruanruan assume control over the city-state of Khotan, an important location on the lucrative east-west trading routes.

520: The Ruanruan Khaghan Chounu (Chou-nu) is murdered, perhaps by the mandate of his own mother. His younger brother A-na-kui ascends to the throne, but partisans of Chounu dispute the legitimacy of his claim. As A-na-kui seeks asylum in the Wei court, his uncle Brahman assumes the title of Khaghan. The Ruanruan never recover from this factional strife.

546?–552: The Turks, a people of obscure ethnic origin who may have had no more commonality than their vassalage as manufacturers of metal instruments, rebel against their Ruanruan masters. Bumin, who led the rebellion, died shortly after their victory.

553: The establishment of the First Turk khaghanate. Ishtemi, the brother of Bumin, rules the western parts of the empire roughly divided by the Altai Mountains, while Muhan, the son of Bumin, rules the more dominant eastern parts which stretch south of Lake Baikal extending beyond the Gobi into parts of Manchuria, and include the Tukn Forest, the locus of Turk national consciousness. The empire is further divided into four administrative divisions, the central, eastern, western, and western frontier. Each region had its own khaghan with the ruler of the central region presiding over all as the Great Khaghan.

557–561: Ishtemi, the khaghan of the western frontier region, acting in concert with the Persians, vanquishes the Hephthalites.

568: Through emissaries sent from the western frontier region to Constantinople, the Turks establish diplomatic contact with Byzantium. At least one other Turk delegation (in 563) was sent to Constantinople, but the fruits of this initial mission are unclear.

576: Turk and allied troops capture Bosporus, a Byzantine city in Crimea. Diplomatic relations suffer.

581–583: Succession struggles lead to the breakup of the empire into Eastern Turk and Western Turk domains.

598: Tardu becomes khaghan of the Eastern Turk. He attempts to reunify the Turks, but fails.

601: Tardu leads an attack on the Sui dynasty (581–618) capital of Chang'an (present-day Xian). Sui, however, is able to resist the offensive.

603: Tardu dies.

619–630: Reign of the Western Turk Khaghan Tong Yabghu. An able diplomat, Tong forges alliances with the Tang in China and with Constantinople. After his death, no strong ruler emerges and the Western Turk empire becomes embroiled in factional strife which hastens its disintegration.

630: Emperor Taizong of the Tang dynasty (618–906) in China launches a decisive offensive against the Eastern Turk. The defeated Eastern Turk Khaghan Xieli is taken prisoner and dies in captivity in 634.

657: Helu, the last ruler of the Western Turks is taken prisoner by Tang. Some factions of Turks continue to resist Chinese hegemony.

692–716: Rule of Kapghan, khaghan over the Turk khaghanate. He defeats the Khitan and establishes diplomatic relations with Tang.

742: The Uyghur ruler, Guli peiluo (Ku-li pei-lo), leads an alliance of Uyghur, Karluk, and Basmil forces against the Turks.

744: Having defeated the Turks, Guli peiluo turns against his allies. He establishes an Uyghur empire in the Mongolian steppes with its capital at Karabalghasun on the Orkhon River.

747–759: Reign of Uyghur Khaghan Moyanchuo (Mo-yen-cho).

755–763: The Uyghurs give military assistance to the Tang government in its efforts to suppress the powerful An Lushan rebel-

lion. This begins a long-standing Tang dependence on Uyghur military might.

759–779: Reign of Uyghur Khaghan Mouyu.

762: Mouyu travels to China, supporting Tang efforts to put down the An Lushan rebellion. While in China he converts to Manichaeism, which he later imposes as the state religion in the Uyghur empire. The Uyghur state becomes the only East Asian state to officially adopt Manichaeism.

Late 8th century: Uyghur power declines.

?795–?808: A powerful khaghan whose name is unknown but who ruled under the lengthy title *Tngrid ijlijg bulmosh alp kutlugh ulugh bilg Khaghan* (the Khaghan based on the authority of Heaven) briefly restores the power of the Uyghur empire.

820: Taking advantage of the weakening condition of the Uyghurs, the Kirghiz begin raids on Uyghur territory.

840: Kirghiz forces supported by loyal Karluks invade Uyghur territory and kill the khaghan. The Uyghur people flee south to the Tarim Basin, eventually to establish a kingdom in the Turpan region (present-day Turkestan).

916: Taking advantage of the collapse of the Tang dynasty in China, Abaoji (A-pao-chi; 872–926), leader of the Khitan, founds the Liao dynasty (916–1125). The Khitan, a Mongolian people originally inhabiting the forested region along the upper course of the Liao River, have been expanding their territories since the collapse of the Uyghurs in 840. The collapse of the Tang dynasty in 906 further enables their aggressive expansion policy. By 925 they control territories ranging from eastern Mongolia to the Korean peninsula north of the Koryo kingdom.

c. 1000: The Mongol tribes, which are referred to in Chinese atlases, appear to occupy the mountainous regions of Manchuria northeast of Mongolia and the regions east of Lake Baikal.

1114: War erupts between the Khitan and the Jurchens, a rebellious vassal people who had formed an alliance with the Song dynasty in China.

1124: Fleeing the Jurchen, a remnant of the Khitan army allies itself with the Uyghurs in the Tarim Basin and establishes the prosperous state of Khara-Khitai, also called the Western Liao dynasty (1124–1218). In time, Khara-Khitai dominates Transoxiana, the region east of the Oxus River (now called the Amu Darya).

1125: The last Khitan emperor is captured by the Jurchen.

CHINGGIS KHAN AND THE FIRST MONGOL CONQUESTS: 1125–1264

The Mongols, a confederation of nomadic tribes and clans inhabiting areas of Manchuria northeast of present-day Mongolia, emerge by a combination of luck and military skill as the dominant force in the Mongolian steppes. Several strong clan leaders vie for supremacy among the Mongols, but in 1206 Temujin prevails. (He will become known as Chinggis Khan, traditionally spelled Ghengis Khan: *qa'an* is a word of Turkic origin meaning "ruler.") He consolidates and reorganizes Mongol society, and then in a brilliant series of military campaigns amasses an empire that stretches from parts of northern China in the east to the Caspian Sea in the west. After Chinggis Khan's death in 1227, a brief but relatively nonviolent power struggle ensues until a compromise is reached, and the khanate is divided among his descendants, with one to be recognized as the Great Khan. (This policy will be generally followed throughout Mongol history.) The various khans proceed to advance their control over several new territories—northern China, southern Russia, Persia, across West Asia and even thrusting into Europe as far as Hungary and Poland. By 1260, however, the empire begins to fragment. Khubilai Khan's ascension to Great Khan is hotly contested, particularly by the Chaghadai khanate, which becomes permanently alienated from the Great Khan. Conflict between the Ilkhanate and the Golden Horde, which had been intensifying for several years, erupts into war in 1261.

1148: Led by Kabul Khan, the increasingly powerful Mongols impose a tribute on the Jurchen state of Jin.

Mid-12th century: War between the Tartars and the Mongols begins. Yesugei, the father of Temujin (later to become Chinggis Khan), distinguishes himself in the conflict.

1161: The Jurchen army comes to the aid of the retreating Tartars and soundly defeats the Mongols. The Tartars become the dominant power in eastern Mongolia.

1162: Traditional date for birth of Temujin. Scholars generally regard the mid-1160s as more likely for the birth of the future khan.

Mid-1170s: Yesugei is killed by Tartars, a victim of the power struggles within the clan. Temujin and his family are abandoned in the desert. Temujin, however, survives, and by the end of the twelfth century is a leading figure among the Mongol tribes.

At the moment when [Chinggis Khan] was born, he was born holding in his right hand a clot of blood the size of a knuckle bone. Such was the manner in which one gave him the name Temujin, saying, "He was born at the moment when one brought Temujin Uge of the Tatar". . . . [When his father asked a man to offer his daughter to marry Chinggis Khan], the man answered: "I, this night, dreamed a dream. A white gyrfalcon, holding both sun and moon, flew hither and is lighted in my hand. . . . I saw this my dream at the moment when thou wast leading thy son hither. . . . What dream is it? A good omen of you Kiyad people is come and hath foretold [thy coming hither].

The Secret History of the Mongols, by an unknown author, possibly 13th century

1194: The Jin emperor calls on Temujin and the leaders of other Mongol tribes, notably Jamukha of the Kereyid, to help defeat the Tartars, whom the Jurchen now view as a threat to national security. The alliance vanquishes the Tartars.

1200–1205: Leaders of various Mongol tribes vie for supremacy in a united Mongol empire. The principal rivals to the position of supreme khan prove to be Jamukha and Temujin. Through a combination of luck, strategy, and brutal policies of retribution, Temujin prevails.

1204: Realizing the necessity of written language for effective government, Temujin orders a prisoner by the name of Ta-t-a Tung-a to adapt the Uyghur script to the Mongol language.

And so in the Year of the Tiger, having set in order the lives of all the people whose tents are protected by skirts of felt, the Mongol clans assembled at the head of the Onon. They raised a white standard of nine tails and proclaimed Chinggis Khan the Great Khan.

The Secret History of the Mongols, by an unknown author, possibly 13th century

---

1206: Temujin calls for a *khuriltai*, an official meeting of Mongol tribes, on the Onon River in northeast Mongolia. The *khuriltai* proclaims him to be Chinggis Khan (probably Oceanic Ruler), and portions out the territories in his control to various generals who in return pledge loyalty to the Khan.

1208: Chinggis defeats the Naiman prince Kuchlug, an important rival who flees to the territories of Khara-Khitai in Central Asia. He finds the former empire in a much diminished state and is able to gain control of its government.

1209: The Uyghurs accept Mongol rule.

1209: Chinggis leads a successful campaign against the Western Xia (Hsi-Hsia), or Tangut peoples, in northern China.

1211: The Mongols begin their campaign against the Jurchen Jin dynasty in China. They meet with some success but are frustrated in their attempts to capture major cities by China's extensive system of fortifications. Chinggis in turn consults Mongol engineers to devise the most effective besieging methods the world had yet to see. This was to become an essential aspect of the Mongol war machine.

1213: Chinggis penetrates China south of the Great Wall.

1215: Chinggis takes Beijing (Yanjing). The Jin move their capital to Kaifeng.

1218: Chinggis dispatches the general Jebe to dispose of Kuchlug, who still controlled Khara-Khitai territories. The predominantly Muslim people of these regions, whose faith had been persecuted by Kuchlug, side with the Mongols who assume control over the region almost entirely without struggle.

Spring 1218: Chinggis sends a trade delegation to Utrar, a city on the eastern shore of the Syr Darya controlled by Ala al-Din Muhammad, ruler of Khwarazm. The governor of the region, Inalchug, condemns all but a few of the travelers to death. The massive Mongolian western campaign begun the following year was in part retribution for this event.

1219: Chinggis leads a sudden and violent campaign to regions across Tien Shan west of Turkestan. The Mongols use the territory they had recently acquired from Khara-Khitai as springboard for their offensive against Khwarazm. Chinggis concentrates his attack first on Transoxiana, a region roughly equivalent to Uzbekistan. The Khwarazm forces are overwhelmed. Muhammad flees to an island in the Caspian, where he dies in 1221.

Early or mid-13th century: *The Secret History of the Mongols* is compiled. It is the only extant Mongolian source of their own early history. As it was completed in the Year of the Rat, scholars generally propose either 1220 or 1240 as the completion date, although it appears to have been emended and added to in ensuing years. Another

Mongolian history, the *Altan Debter* (Golden Book), has been lost.

February 1220: The city of Bukhara falls to the Mongols. Samarkand also falls within a month.

1220–1223: The Mongols split into divisions led by different commanders and venture into parts of India, Afghanistan, Persia, Anatolia, and Russia. Although they vanquish any opposition they face, including a Russian army numbering eighty thousand men, the Mongols do not ultimately incorporate all this territory into their empire. The mission serves more as reconnaissance for the campaigns of a decade later. They do, however, establish a protectorate over most of Central Asia and Afghanistan.

1224: The general Subetei leads his troops back from their reconnaissance of the Russian steppes and rejoins the Mongol army.

Late 1226: Chinggis leads an attack against the Western Xia, who had failed to provide support for his Central Asian campaigns. The two armies clash on the frozen Yellow River. Although outnumbered, the Mongols defeat the Tangut forces of Western Xia. They drive the armies of the Jin and Western Xia southeast to Sichuan province. Western Xia surrenders late in 1127.

1227: Chinggis dies.

1229: Chinggis's son Ogodei (1186–1241) is confirmed as Great Khan in accordance with the wishes of Chinggis. His brother Chaghadai (c. 1185–1242) receives the territories of Central Asia, another brother Tolui (c. 1190–1232) North China and the Mongolian steppes, his nephew Batu the westernmost lands and control of the Golden Horde, which is ultimately to conquer Russia.

1231: The Mongols invade the Korean peninsula.

1234: Ogdei drives the Jurchen back into Manchuria. Mongols occupy all of Northern China.

1235: Ogdei erects a city wall around the capital Karakoram.

1236: The Mongol army led by Batu and Subetei defeat the Bulghars.

1237–1238: Mongol forces, numbering as many as 600,000 and led by Batu and Subetei, cross the Volga River. They strike quickly and effectively, holding Riazan, Moscow, and Vladimir-Suzdal by March 1238.

1239: The Koryo dynasty, which governs Korea, capitulates to the Mongols. Despite swearing fealty to the Khan, the Korean court maintains a degree of autonomy.

1239: Mongol forces led by Kden enter Tibet.

November 1240: The Mongol army crosses the Dnieper River in the Ukraine.

December 6, 1240: Kiev falls to the Mongols.

Spring 1241: Batu drives storms through Eastern Europe, taking Cracow (March 18), Liegnitz (April 9), and Pest (April).

Late 1241: The Mongols cross the Danube and begin raids near Vienna.

December 11, 1241: Ogdei dies. The apparently invincible Mongol forces in Europe withdraw to the Russian steppe. Under the law set down by Chinggis, Batu returns toward Mongolia to take part in the election of a new khan.

1243: The Seljuk sultanate of Rum in Anatolia submits to Mongol rule after suffering defeat to the Mongol forces led by Baiju at the Battle of Kse Dagh.

1246: Giovanni da Piano del Carpine (John of Plano Carpini), an Italian Franciscan missionary sent by Pope Innocent IV, reaches Karakoram. He later publishes an account of his travels called *Ystoria Mongolorum*. Later emended editions came to be known as *The Tartar Relation*.

Summer 1246: Ogdei's son Guyuk is elected Khan at a *khuriltai*. Batu strongly contests the election.

1247–1318: Life of Rashid ad-Din, the great Persian historian. Ilkhan Ghazan (reigns 1295–1304) commissions him to write *Jami-al-Tavarikh*, an illustrated history of the Mongols.

1248: Guyuk dies.

c. 1250–1280: A number of public debates are

held between Daoists and Buddhists. After the Mongols conquer Tibet in 1252, Tibetan Buddhists exert an increasingly dominant influence on the Mongol court. Khubilai Khan himself comes to favor Buddhism, promoting Phags-pa lama (1235–1280), a high Buddhist monk, to an important position within the government. This begins a long and fruitful relationship between Tibetan Buddhists and the Mongols.

1251: Mngke, son of Tolui and brother of the future Khubilai Khan, is elected Khan on the strength of Batu's nomination (Batu himself declined the election). In gratitude for Batu's support, Mngke grants Batu relative autonomy in his governance of the Golden Horde situated on the Russian steppe. Mngke then plans an offensive against the Song dynasty, which controls China's southern regions (1127–1279). His brother Khubilai is elevated to a rank nearly equal to Mngke himself. The two brothers assume command of the Mongol forces marshaled for the China offensive.

1252: Mongol troops, under orders from Mngke, invade Tibet and quickly subdue all resistance.

1253: Hulegu begins his campaigns in the Middle East. His primary objective is to subdue the Ismailis, who terrorize the region with their ruthless army known as the Assassins.

1254: William of Rubruck, a French Franciscan missionary, reaches Karakoram. He later publishes an account of travels called *Itinerarium*, editions of which are extant.

1255: Batu, first Khan of the Golden Horde, dies.

1256: Hulegu succeeds in vanquishing the Assassins. He remains in Persia and establishes the Ilkhanate (1256–1335).

1257: Berke becomes Khan of the Golden Horde; he later becomes the first Mongol ruler to convert to Islam. However, it is not until the reign of Ozbeg (reigns 1313–1341) that Islam becomes the official religion of the Golden Horde.

1257: Thang Long (modern Hanoi), Vietnam, falls to the Mongols.

1258: Hulegu seizes Baghdad and conquers the Abbasid caliphate, executing the Abbasid caliph. This action angers Berke, Khan of the Golden Horde, who had converted to Islam.

August 1259: Mngke dies, probably of dysentery, while campaigning in China.

1260: In Palestine at the Battle of Ain Jalut, a Mamluk army led by Baibars defeats the Ilkhanate forces of the Mongols. It is the first significant defeat any Mongol division has suffered in more than seventy years.

May 5, 1260: A *khuriltai* convenes in Kaifeng and elects Khubilai Great Khan. The legitimacy of Khubilai is hotly contested, particularly by his brother Arigh Bke.

June 1260: A rival faction to Khubilai elects Arigh Bke Great Khan. Civil war erupts.

1260–1268: The brothers Nicolo and Maffeo Polo of Venice become among the first Western traders to venture into Mongol territory all the way to the capital near modern Beijing. They meet Khubilai, who invites them to visit China again.

1261: War between the Golden Horde and the Ilkhanate erupts. This begins a long and damaging rivalry between the two khanates.

1264: Arigh Bke surrenders to Khubilai.

THE MONGOL EMPIRE: 1264–1368

After subduing all opposition to his ascension as Great Khan, Khubilai moves to complete his conquest of China. In 1279 he defeats the last of the Song troops and proclaims the beginning of the Yuan dynasty. In his reign as Great Khan, Khubilai becomes increasingly preoccupied with the governance of China and less concerned with other realms in the expansive Mongol empire. Other khanates likewise become more autonomous. The lifestyle intrinsic to the administration of vast territories excludes nomadic traditions, and the Mongols living outside the steppes gradually become integrated into the realms under their control. The Ilkhanate by the time of its dissolution in 1355 is almost entirely Islamic in character. The Golden Horde and the Chaghadai Khanate, on the other hand, reign over territories conducive to the nomadic way of life. Both the Golden Horde and the Ilkhanate convert to Islam in the late thirteenth and early fourteenth centuries. In general, however, each of the khanates tends to be relatively tolerant of religious diversity. Khubilai, furthermore, encourages trade in a way that no past Chinese emperor had. This leads to a tremendous confluence of cultures along the Silk Road and in China proper. The most famous cultural ambassador is Marco Polo, who resides in Khubilai's court (1275–1292). Khubilai's successors, however, lack his political savvy. The Yuan court grows increasingly out of touch with its administrative responsibilities. A series of plagues and natural disasters exacerbate internal dissension in China as the Yuan court remains embroiled in the sort of factional strife that seems so endemic to Mongol regimes. Large-scale rebellions erupt in the 1340s. In 1368 Zhu Yuanzhang proclaims himself first emperor of the Ming dynasty.

1265: Hulegu, khan of the Ilkhanate, dies. Arbqa (reigns 1265–1282) assumes the title of Ilkhan. During Arbqa's rule the capital of the Ilkhanate is fixed at Tabriz.

1267: Khubilai begins construction on a winter capital in Dadu (present-day Beijing). He maintains a summer palace at Shangdu (Xanadu) north of the Great Wall.

1268: Khubilai initiates a new offensive against the Song dynasty.

1269: A new alphabet intended to replace Uyghur script in transcribing the Mongolian language is promulgated. The script is often referred to as the Phags-pa script, after its creator, a Buddhist monk employed by Khubilai.

1271: Khubilai founds the Yuan ("first") dynasty (1271–1368) of China. He assumes the title Zhiyuan (the greatest of the Yuan).

1271–1292: The Polo brothers initiate a second trading mission. They are joined by Nicolo's son Marco. In 1274 they arrive at Khubilai's summer palace at Shangdu, and Marco quickly gains favor with Khubilai. They remain in Asia until 1292, and Marco often serves in the employ of Khubilai's court.

1274: Khubilai mounts an unsuccessful invasion of Japan.

Proceeding three days' journey in a northeasterly direction, you arrive at a city called Shandu, built by the grand khan Kublai, now reigning. In this he caused a palace to be erected, of marble and other handsome stones, admirable as well for the elegance of its design as for the skill displayed in its execution.

The Travels of Marco Polo, 13th century

1276: Mongol troops led by Bayan capture Hangzhou, the Song capital.

1279: The last remnants of the Song army are destroyed in a naval battle in Guangzhou Bay.

1281: Khubilai mounts a second invasion of Japan. Again he is unsuccessful.

1284–1291: Reign of Ilkhan Arghun. He is notable for his adherence to Buddhism.

1292–January 1293: Khubilai's forces invade and conquer Java, but are soon driven off the island by a former Javanese ally. This expedition, in addition to the two failed Japanese invasions, puts a serious financial strain on Khubilai's empire.

February 18, 1294: Khubilai Khan dies.

May 10, 1294: Chengzong, a grandson of Khubilai, is enthroned as emperor of the

Yuan dynasty. He issues an edict calling for the veneration of Confucius.

1295: Ghazan becomes Ilkhan. He declares Islam the official religion, orders all Buddhist buildings to be destroyed, and exiles all Buddhist monks.

1299: Marco Polo's famous account of his travels throughout the Mongol empire, known in English as *The Travels of Marco Polo*, begins to circulate in Europe.

1299–1300: Ilkhanate forces invade Syria. After occupying the territory for less than a year they withdraw.

1304: Ilkhan Ghazan dies.

1304–1316: Reign of Ilkhan Oljetu.

1313: Ascension of Ozbeg to Khan of the Golden Horde. Mongols of the Golden Horde convert to Islam.

1316–1335: Reign of Ilkhan Abu Said.

1322: The Ilkahns and the Mamluks agree to peace.

1323: Yuan emperor Shidebala is assassinated. Ten years of factional strife follow. The Yuan dynasty never recovers stability.

1333: Toghon Temur ascends to the throne of Great Khan at the age of thirteen.

November 1335: Ilkhan Abu Said dies. No Chinggisid successor is chosen. This marks the end of the Ilkhanate.

1340s: Various large-scale rebellions erupt in Mongol-controlled southern China. From the many competing rebel factions, Zhu Yuanzhang, a former bandit, emerges as the most dominant leader. He will later become the first Ming emperor.

1346: Outbreak of bubonic plague among Mongol troops besieging Kaffa in the Crimea. The disease quickly spreads to Europe.

1353–1354: Plague erupts in China.

1347–1363: Reign of Tughluq Temur, khan of the Chaghadai khanate.

1368: Zhu Yuanzhang drives the last of the nine successors of Khubilai from Dadu. He establishes the Ming dynasty (1368–1644).

INTERNECINE STRIFE: 1369–1691

The Ming dynasty supplants the Yuan, and the Mongols of the Great Khanate flee into the Mongolian steppes. The Ilkhanate dissolves, and the Chaghadai khanate becomes a mere puppet state of Tamerlane (possibly a descendant of Chinggis Khan). By the end of the fourteenth century only the Golden Horde remains in control of the territories it acquired during the Mongol conquests of 1125–1368. Yet even the Golden Horde proves to have tenuous hold on its base of power. Meanwhile on the Mongolian steppes, various clans vie for supremacy. A number of charismatic leaders aspire to unite the Mongols and revive the empire of Chinggis Khan, but inevitably, upon the death of a given leader, succession disputes lead once again to chaos. The lack of unity among the clans makes the Mongols susceptible to Manchu invasion, and in late seventeenth century the Manchus conquer Mongolia and assimilate it into the Qing dynasty, the empire founded on the Chinese state in 1644. Zanabazar, the first Bogdo Gegen (Living Buddha), is born in 1635. The Bogdo Gegen becomes the head of the Mongolian Buddhists, and a symbol of Mongolian national identity. Zanabazar also excels as a sculptor and becomes Mongolia's most significant patron of the arts.

1369: Tamerlane conquers Transoxiana. He establishes his capital in Samarkand and exacts a pledge of loyalty from Tughluq Temur Khan of the Chaghadai khanate. Temur abandons Transoxiana to his son, a mere puppet of Tamerlane, and establishes control over Moghulistan to the east.

1370: Toghun Temur, the last Yuan emperor, dies in Karakoram.

1370–1378: Toghun Temur's son Ayurshiridhara assumes the title Great Khan, but is unable to reverse the course of the royal institution's disintegration.

1376–1395: Reign of Tokhtamish as Khan of the Golden Horde.

1378–1388: Reign of Toquz Temur as Great Khan. His authority is increasingly disrespected. When Ming troops mount a successful offensive against the Mongols in 1388, he is assassinated. A centralized Mongol state becomes a fiction, as tribal leaders reclaim authority.

1380: Muscovite forces defeat the Golden Horde at Kulikovo Polye.

1388: Ming troops vanquish Karakoram, destroying the city and taking more than seventy thousand prisoners.

1391: Tamerlane invades the Eurasian steppes controlled by the Golden Horde. The Golden Horde retreats.

1395: Tamerlane's troops overrun the Caucasus and Southern Russia. The Golden Horde is driven from its central base of power.

Early 15th century: Mongol clans divided roughly into the Western Mongols, of which the most powerful group is the Oirats of the Altai region, and the Eastern Mongols, later known as the Khalkha, vie for supremacy of the Mongolian steppes.

1409–1424: Ming forces invade the territory of the Eastern Mongols and suffer a resounding defeat. The Ming emperor, Yongle, assumes command of the campaign against the Eastern Mongols, but a series of offensives fail to yield the total submission of either the Eastern Mongols or the Oirats.

1430: Haji Girei, formerly a member of the Golden Horde, founds the khanate of the Crimea. This is the first of several splinterings of the Golden Horde, which ultimately lead to its dissolution in 1502.

1445: Ulu Mohammed and his son, Mahmudek, found the Kazan khanate and proclaim themselves independent of the Golden Horde, of which they were formerly members.

1449: Esen, leader of the Oirat Mongols, defeats and captures the Ming emperor.

1453: Esen proclaims himself Khan of the Mongols, explicitly evoking the legacy of Chinggis Khan, despite the fact that he bore no relation to the Chinggsid line. This proves to be his downfall as conservative elements in his court defect. The following year he is assassinated in a rebellion.

1466: Prince Qasim founds the Astrakhan khanate, further dividing the Golden Horde.

1470: Dayan Khan, a descendent of Khubilai, is named khan of the Eastern Mongols at the age of five.

1491: Dayan Khan leads the Eastern Mongols to victory over their Oirat rivals. He establishes a confederation that stretches from the Ural Mountains to Lake Baikal.

Early 16th century: The Uzbeks rise to power in Central Asia. They rule over a vast territory that includes regions of the former Chaghadai khanate.

16th century: The Mongol clans solidify their positions, dividing the regions north of the Great Wall of China into spheres of influence that, excepting periodic surges of one clan or another, continue until Manchu domination in the eighteenth century. The Chahar Mongols reign in Inner Mongolia; the Eastern Mongols, who come to be known as the Khalkhas dominate the modern independent state of Mongolia; the Ordos occupy much of the area south of the Gobi, particularly the fertile land within the great loop of the Yellow River; while the Tumed reign just north of the Ordos.

1502: Ivan III dispatches an army of Crimean Mongols and Muscovites against the Golden Horde. Mengli Girei, khan of the Crimea, leads the offensive. He sacks Sirai, dealing the final blow to the Golden Horde.

1543: Dayan Khan dies. No clear successor to his throne is named, as the influence of the Eastern Mongols elapses.

1543–1583: Reign of Altan Khan of the Tumed. Like Esen and Dayan Khan, he seeks to reestablish a true Mongol state. His attention to the practical affairs of government, however, brings him much closer to realizing this aspiration than his predecessors. He builds a capital in Hohhot, recruits experienced Chinese administrators, and ultimately establishes Tibetan Buddhism as the state religion.

1540s: Altan Khan leads a number of devastating attacks on China's northern frontier, concentrating on the province Shanxi. His aim is to force the Ming rulers into opening trade with the Mongols.

1550: Altan Khan leads his troops to the gates of Beijing. The Ming court agrees to grant trading rights to Mongols along the border, but later reneges on its word, which in turn leads to more attacks by Altan Khan.

1552: Ivan the Terrible conquers the Kazan khanate.

1554: Ivan the Terrible conquers the Astrakhan khanate.

1554–1588: Reign of Abadai Khan of the Khalkha Mongols. He does much to promote Buddhism within Khalkha territory.

1571: After decades of bloody conflict, Altan Khan and Ming officials agree on terms of peace. Commerce between the Mongols and China opens.

1577: Altan Khan meets with the Tibetan lama Sonam Gyatso at Hohhot and converts to Buddhism.

1586: Abadai Khan of the Khalkha Mongols establishes Erdeni Zuu, the first lamaist monastery in Mongolia. The monastery is built near the ruins of the old Mongol capital Karakoram.

1594–1655: Reign of Gombodorji as Khan of the Tusheets, the most significant of the Eastern Mongol clans (Khalkhas). The domain of the Tusheets stretches during Gombodorji's reign from the Gobi to the area south of the Siberian village Kiakhta, and includes the city of Urga (founded in 1639).

1599–1662: Life of Zaya Pandita. He creates a script for Oirat Mongolian and translates Buddhist works.

Early 17th century: The Zunghars, a Western Mongolian clan situated along the Emil River, attempt to foster a more sedentary existence by promoting agriculture, endorsing Buddhism, and building towns around palaces.

1604–1634: Reign of Ligdan Khan of the Chahar Mongols. Like Altan Khan and Abadai Khan, he seeks to give legitimacy to his rule by promoting Buddhism. He commissions a Mongol translation of the *Kanjur*, the Tibetan Buddhist canon.

1618: A tribe of Western Mongols known as the Kalmyks begin to migrate to the Volga Valley in Russia. This migration continues throughout the century.

1632: The Jin dynasty of the Manchus initiate a campaign against the Chahar Mongols of Ligdan Khan. The Manchus score a series of easy defeats, as Ligdan Khan retreats into Tibet, where he contracts smallpox and dies.

1635: Ligdan Khan's successor submits to Manchu rule. The land of the Chahars is integrated into the Manchu Jin dynasty. The Manchus organize this territory as part of their military reserve, marking the beginning of the administrative concept of Inner Mongolia.

1638–1639: Leading figures amongst the Khalkhas accept Zanabazar (1635–1723), the son of Tusheet Khan Gombodorji, as the Bogdo Gegen (or Jebtsundamba Khutuktu in Tibetan, meaning Living Buddha). This begins a long line of ecclesiastical leaders who assume the same title, the last of which dies in 1924. This creation of this office was the brainchild of Tusheet Khan Gombodorji as part of his drive to unite the Khalkha khanates. The figure would function much like the Dalai Lamas of Tibet, concentrating national sentiment on a single religious leader.

1639: The city of Urga (present-day Ulaanbaatar) is founded. The Bogdo Gegen establishes his residency there. The city grows to be the commercial and artistic center of Mongolia.

1640: The Khalkhas and leaders of the Western Mongols meet to forge a stronger union. Despite agreeing to recognize the religious authority of the Bogdo Gegen, the leaders fail to agree on a platform for a united Mongolian state.

1640: Gushi Khan of the Khoshuts, a subclan of the Oirats, defeats the King of Tibet, ending secular power in the Buddhist country. The Khoshuts become protectors of the Dalai Lama's authority.

1641–1652: The Russians conquer the Buryat Mongols and establish control of the area surrounding Lake Baikal.

1644: The Manchus establish the Qing dynasty (1644–1911) in China.

1646: The Qing dynasty, overwhelming the disunited Mongol forces, exact a tribute from the Khalkha khanates.

1654: Gushi Khan of the Khoshuts dies. The Dalai Lama becomes the sole power in Tibet.

1655: The Kalmyks in the Volga Valley make peace with the Russians. They are later used as cavalrymen in Russian campaigns in the Crimea.

1657: Zanabazar introduces the Maitreya Festival (Maidari) at Erdeni Zuu. The day-long festival has is origins in Tibet and celebrates the Buddha of the Future (Maitreya).

1671: Galdan Khan returns from Lhasa to avenge the murder of his brother, the Zunghar khan. He quickly assumes power over the Zunghars, a Western Mongol clan continuing to resist Manchu domination.

Chinggis Khan said to his son: "If you do not know how to organize some part of the people you will not be powerful. The Bayurci (chief cook) is a man who knows the apportioning of food; with the people who attend a gathering, he does not come too late, during the feast there is never any scarcity, and he himself finds an opportunity to get drunk. Thus it is the same to organize a great people as it is to manage ready food."

From *Altan toboi* (Golden Button), a chronicle by Lubsan Dandzan, 17th–18th century

---

1679: Galdan, with the support of the Dalai Lama in Tibet, conquers much of Turkestan (present-day Xinjiang).

1688: Galdan leads a large-scale offensive against the Khalkhas. He reaches deep into Khalkha territory, occupying and destroying part of the Erdeni Zuu monastery. Galdan had earlier sought the support of Zanabazar, the Bogdo Gegen, in his effort to unify the Mongols. Zanabazar refused his support, enraging the desperate Galdan.

1689: Having agreed to peace with Russia under the Treaty of Nerchinsk (1689) the Qing dynasty concentrates its efforts on vanquishing Galdan.

May 29–June 3, 1691: Leaders of the Khalkha Mongols, including Zanabazar, the Bogdo Gegen, meet with Manchu authorities in Dolonnor, formerly the site of Khubilai Khan palace Shangdu (Xanadu), and submit formally to Qing rule.

MANCHU RULE: 1691–1911

Having seduced the Khalkha leaders by guaranteeing their aristocratic position, the Manchus set about vanquishing remaining Mongolian opposition to their rule. Galdan, the powerful Zunghar leader, is defeated in 1696, but resistance continues among some Western Mongols. Full-scale rebellion erupts in 1757, but lack of organization and inferior manpower doom the Mongol insurgents, and Qing authority in 1759 is more secure than ever. The Manchus continue to rule Mongolia for another century and half. During this time, there is no serious threat to

Manchu domination. Qing policies of administering the territory without attention to traditional khanate boundaries, forbidding one of Mongol birth to become the Bogdo Gegen (the principal religious leader in Mongolia), and allowing Chinese monopolization of the caravan trade effectively circumvent a flowering of nationalistic sentiment and stagnate the economy. However, the arts continue to flourish during this period following the inspiration of Zanabazar, the first Bogdo Gegen who dies in 1723.

1696: Qing forces defeat Galdan Khan. He dies the next year. Tsewang Rabtan, Galdan's nephew, continues to lead raids on the Chinese borderland into the mid-eighteenth century.

Early 18th century: The Manchus seek to minimize the risk of Mongol uprising by administering the country without attention to traditional khanate boundaries.

18th–19th century: Chinese merchants, traditionally forbidden to enter Mongol territory, bypass laxly enforced Qing regulations and begin to dominate caravan trade inside Mongolia. The merchants are notorious for lending Mongolians money at tremendously high rates. This contributed significantly to Mongolia's impoverishment as it entered the twentieth century.

1705: Backed by the Qing court, Lha-bzang, khan of the Khoshuts, marches on Lhasa. The move is promoted by the Manchus in order to deny the Zunghars led by Tsewang Rabtan to gain control of the symbolically important Tibet.

1717–1720: Tsewang Rabtan leads the Zunghars into Tibet. The Zunghars defeat the Khoshuts and occupy Lhasa until 1720. Their pillaging is so severe, however, that when Manchu troops invade the city in 1720 they are regarded as rescuers.

1723: Zanabazar, the first Bogdo Gegen and Mongolia's most illustrious artist, dies in Beijing.

1724–1757: Life of Losang Tenbey Drnmey, second Bogdo Gegen.

1727: Tsewang Rabtan dies. Galdan Tsering assumes leadership of the Zunghars. Qing mounts an offensive hoping to capitalize on Zunghar disorganization. The attack fails.

1732–1734: The Zunghars penetrate into Khalkha territory as far as Erdeni Zuu, but, finding themselves overextended, retreat.

1745: The Zunghars make peace with the Manchus. Galdan Tsering dies.

1755–1757: An anti-Manchu rebellion erupts, led by Amarsanaa (1718–1757) and Chingunjav. Preying on the lack of Mongol unity, the Manchus quickly suppress the rebel forces.

1757: Concerned that the Bogdo Gegen may prove to be a rallying point for nationalistic sentiment, the Qing court declares the Bogdo Gegen will no longer be discovered in Mongolia. Henceforth the Bogdo Gegen is discovered in Tibet.

1758–1773: Life of Yeshe Tenbey Nyima, third Bogdo Gegen.

Winter 1770–January 1771: Massive numbers of Kalmyks migrate eastward, returning to Mongolian territory where they are granted grazing land by the Manchus.

1775–1813: Life of Losang Tupten Wongchuk, fourth Bogdo Gegen.

1783: Catherine the Great dispatches Potemkin to the Crimea, where he deposes Shahin Girai, khan of Crimea and the last reigning descendant of Chinggis Khan. Russia annexes the territory.

1809: Fourth Bogdo Gegen builds the Gandan monastery at Urga.

1811: The first *tsam* dances in Khalkha. This ritual dance theater took place in the course of day-long festivals. The purpose of the dance is to exorcise the enemies of the Buddhist religion. The stories often incorporate age-old epic folktales.

1815–1842: Lifespan of Losang Tsultrim Jikmay, fifth Bogdo Gegen.

1820–1836: The Maidar Temple, dedicated to the Future Buddha (Maidar or Maitreya), is built in Urga.

1842–1849: Life of Losang Palden Tenpa, sixth Bogdo Gegen.

Mid-19th century: Injanashi writes *Kke Sudur* (Blue Chronicle), a fictional account of Mongol history, and *Nigen dabkhur asar*, a romantic novel. Both books are heavily influenced by Chinese models.

1850–1868: Life of Ngawang Chkyi Wongchuk Trinley Gyatsho, seventh Bogdo Gegen.

1851–1864: The Taiping Rebellion in China. Mongol volunteers led by Prince Senggelin-qin assist Qing forces in defeating the rebel forces.

1870–1924: Lifespan of Ngawang Losang Chkyi Nyima Tenzin Wongchuk, eighth and final Bogdo Gegen.

1880: An anti-Manchu mutiny erupts within a Qing garrison stationed in Uliasutai.

1903: Ayuussh founds an anti-Manchu liberation movement in Khalkha.

1908: A Mongolian newspaper, *Mongolyn Sonin Bichig*, is first published in Harbin.

1911: The Qing dynasty falls.

TWENTIETH-CENTURY MONGOLIA: 1911–1998

After the dissolution of the Manchu empire in 1911, a movement for Mongol independence emerges led by the Bogdo Gegen (the Living Buddha). True autonomy, however, is not forthcoming, as Mongolia becomes subject to the power struggle between China and Russia over supremacy in Asia. With Russia embroiled in a civil war, China opportunistically seizes Outer Mongolia, only to be driven out in 1921 by the mercenary Baron von Ungern-Sternberg. Later that year, Soviet backed revolutionaries establish a new regime in Ulaanbaatar (the renamed city of Urga). In 1924 the People's Republic of Mongolia is founded, but policy continues to be dominated by the influence of Moscow. During World War II Inner Mongolia is occupied by the Japanese, but a Soviet-Mongol alliance staves off Japanese attempts to push forward into Outer Mongolia. Under the terms of an agreement between Chiang Kai-shek and the other members of the Yalta Conference, a plebiscite is held after the war in which the Mongol people support absolute independence as opposed to autonomous status within China. China, however maintains its claim to Inner Mongolia. Relations between the People's Republic of China and the Mongolian People's Republic are amiable from 1950 until the onset of the Sino-Soviet split of the late 1950s and early 1960s, when Mongolia sides with the Soviets. In 1961 the United Nations recognizes the Mongolian People's Republic. Yumjaagiyin Tsedenbal, longtime leader of the Communist Party, resigns in 1984, which clears the way for a series of reforms. These reforms culminate in the new constitution of 1992 and the abandonment of the precepts of the old Mongolian People's Republic for a more democratic government.

December 1, 1911: With the collapse of the Manchu-Qing dynasty in China, some Mongolian princes proclaim Outer Mongolia's independence from China. They proceed to drive the last of the Chinese forces out of Outer Mongolia.

December 28, 1911: A Buddhist priest, the Eighth Bogdo Gegen, becomes the ruler of a theocratic government. The capital is established at Urga. Russian military advisors are sent from Moscow to create and train a national army.

July 1912: Russia and Japan convene in the last of a series of secret meetings and agree to recognize their respective spheres of influence in Mongolia and Manchuria.

November 3, 1912: A Russo-Mongol agreement is reached on the question of Mongol independence. Unwilling to support the total independence of an unstable country on its border, and at the same time fearful of Chinese domination, Russia supports the euphemistically phrased "autonomy within China."

November 5, 1913: Russia signs a declaration recognizing Chinese suzerainty in Outer Mongolia. In exchange China recognizes Mongolia's political autonomy in its own affairs.

May 25, 1915: China, Russia, and Mongolia sign the Treaty of Kyakhta, which formalizes Outer Mongolia's autonomy in internal affairs.

February and March 1919: A conference is held in Chita, Siberia, concerning the unification of Inner and Outer Mongolia as well as Buryatia (conquered by the Russians in the mid-seventeenth century). A provisional government is formed, but the pan-Mongolian effort falters on account of the lack of support within the Outer Mongolian government, and the increased efforts of the Chinese to reestablish suzerainty in Outer Mongolia.

October 1919: Led by one of its virtually independent warlords a Chinese army invades Outer Mongolia and wrests an acknowledgment of Chinese suzerainty from the Bogdo Gegen government.

March 1920: Mongolia's two principal revolutionary groups join forces to form the Mongolian People's Party under the leadership of Sukhe Bator (1893–1923).

October 1920–January 1922: With civil war raging in Russia, units of Russia's White Army led by Baron von Ungern-Sternberg invade Outer Mongolia. Using often brutal methods, they oust the Chinese, but in the process incur the resentment of the Mongolians. A combined force of Mongolian revolutionaries and Communist Soviet troops eventually captures von Ungern-Sternberg (August 1921) and vanquishes the remaining White Russian troops (January 1922).

July 11, 1921: Mongolia declares itself an independent state. (July 11 becomes the recognized and currently celebrated date of Mongolian independence.) The Bogdo Ge-

gen retains his religious position but loses most real power as the People's Party names Dogsomyn Bodoo premier and foreign minister. The capital is established in the recently captured city of Urga. Soviet troops remain in virtual occupation.

February 22, 1923: The revolutionary hero Sukhe Bator dies prematurely. A trained soldier, he became a communist and led the forces that laid the foundation of the new Mongolia.

1924: The Mongolian National Bank is established as a joint Mongolian-Soviet company. It introduces the *tugrik* as the new national currency.

May 20, 1924: The Bogdo Gegen dies. No successor is found and the institution dissolves.

November 25, 1924: A Soviet-style constitution is promulgated and the Mongolian People's Republic is formally proclaimed. Urga is renamed Ulaanbaatar.

March 1925: Soviet troops withdraw.

October 23–December 10, 1928: At the Seventh Party Congress, a heated debate between leftist and rightist elements in the Mongolian government takes place. The leftists emerge victorious as the former party chairman, a rightist, is exiled to Moscow.

December 1928: The leftists, led by Choybalsan, begin to restructure Mongolian government along more revolutionary lines. The state assumes control of all property that had previously belonged to land owners or to religious groups and organizes stockbreeders and farmers into collectives. Conservative officials are purged from the government ranks. A five-year economic plan is adopted.

1931–1932: The severe economic plan and rapid communization of a people with a long history of nomadism proves disastrous. In western Mongolia anti-Communist uprisings threaten to escalate into civil war. Ultimately, Soviet troops are called in to quell the discontent. The radical policies are eased, and a more gradual socioeconomic reform policy, called the New Turn Policy, is accepted.

November 27, 1934: The Soviets and the Mongolians reach an agreement on military cooperation to provide against the threat of Japanese expansion.

January 1935: Soviet troops reenter Mongolia.

1935–1939: The Mongolian government's policy of religious persecution intensifies. In 1937 and 1938, approximately two thousand monks and abbots are executed. Buddhism is all but eradicated as a public institution.

March 12, 1936: The terms of the Soviet-Mongolian mutual defense agreement of 1934 are renegotiated as the Mongolian-Soviet Treaty of Friendship.

May 1939–September 16, 1939: Armed conflict erupts between the Japanese forces in Manchukuo, the puppet state in Manchuria, and Soviet-Mongolian forces. Fighting is centered on the Khalhyn Gol, a river in northeast Mongolia. The Japanese sustain heavy losses. On September 16 the Japanese sign a peace agreement with the Soviets.

March–April 1940: The Tenth Party Congress convenes. Yumjaagiyin Tsedenbal is elected general secretary, but Choybalsan remains the preeminent party member. A new constitution is promulgated which contains no substantial changes from the first constitution drafted in 1924.

April 13, 1941: Japan and the Soviet Union sign the Soviet-Japanese Neutrality Pact, a provision of which is to recognize Mongolia's territorial integrity.

1942: Choybalsan University, later renamed Mongolian State University, is established in Ulaanbaatar.

August 10, 1945: Mongolia declares war on Japan and joins the Soviet invasion force as it quickly overruns Inner Mongolia and Manchuria.

August 14, 1945: By the terms of the Sino-Soviet Treaty of Friendship and Alliance, China agrees to recognize Mongolia's independence after years of stubbornly insisting on Mongolia's status as an autonomous region of China. The treaty calls for a plebiscite to substantiate the Mongolian determination for such independence. The referendum is held on October 20, 1945. The electorate unanimously votes for independence.

January 15, 1945: China recognizes Mongolian independence.

February 1946: Mongolia promotes the use of the Cyrillic alphabet in the military and in schools.

1947: A large-scale literacy program is adopted to meet the growing need of modernization.

Late 1947: Efforts to achieve total communization are reinstituted. Private ownership of anything, including livestock, is outlawed.

December 1947: The Eleventh Party Congress inaugurates the First Five-Year Plan (1948–1952).

October 1949: Mongolia recognizes the People's Republic of China.

January 26, 1952: Choybalsan dies. Tsedenbal assumes the title of prime minister while remaining the party's general secretary.

1952: A ten-year Sino-Mongolian Agreement on Economic and Cultural Cooperation is reached between China and Mongolia. The agreement is indicative of improvements in Sino-Soviet relations. When the Soviet Union and China begin again to differ on important policy matters in the 1960s, relations between Mongolia and China concomitantly weaken, evidence of Mongolia's continuing dependence on the USSR.

November 1953: The Twelfth Party Congress convenes and approves the Second Five-Year Plan, which emphasizes the necessity of an increase in grain production as well as continued development of livestock. Dashiyn Damba is elected general secretary.

1956: The party Central Committee condemns the excesses of Choybalsan, accusing the dead leader of Mongolia of having constructed a personality cult. This resembles the Soviet condemnation of Stalin around the same time.

March 1958: The Thirteenth Party Congress adopts a Three-Year Plan for the transformation of its livestock economy into a agricultural-industrial economy. Mining, electric power, construction are emphasized.

July 6, 1960: A third constitution for the Mongolian People's Republic is promulgated. Like the 1940 constitution, however, it does not differ substantially from the original constitution drafted in 1924.

October 1961: Mongolia is admitted to the United Nations.

June 1962: Mongolia joins the Council for Mutual Economic Assistance (COMECON), an economic organization of Soviet-bloc countries founded in 1949.

January 1966: Leonid Brezhnev, the Soviet leader, pays an official visit to Ulaanbaatar. A new twenty-year Treaty of Friendship, Cooperation and Mutual Assistance replaces the previous treaty of 1946. An important aspect of the new agreement is a renewed commitment to defense.

June 1966: A fourth Five-Year Plan (1966–1970) is adopted at the Fifteenth Party Congress. Again the plan focuses on transforming the nomadic economy into an agricultural-industrial economy.

1971: After severe economic setback on account of the weather and the generally unrealistic aims of the previous Five-Year Plans, the Soviets agree to increase their role in financing a Fifth Five-Year Plan (1971–1975). The objective of transforming Mongolia's nomadic economy remains the same. A period of relative prosperity follows.

June 1974: Tsedenbal resigns as prime minister and becomes chairman of the People's Great Hural. Jambyn Batmonh becomes premier. Tsedenbal, however, remains in control of the government.

October 1976: Brezhnev and other top Soviet officials meet with Tsedenbal and Batmonh. Soviets renew their commitment to eco-

nomic aid. A Sixth Five-Year Plan (1976–1980) is subsequently adopted.

1980: Chinese officials are expelled from Mongolia.

August 23, 1984: While Tsedenbal is visiting Moscow, the People's Great Hural meets and announces his retirement.

December 1984: Batmonh becomes chairman of the People's Great Hural.

March 7, 1989: The Kremlin announces that it will withdraw 75 percent of the fifty thousand Soviet troops stationed in Mongolia.

December 1989–March 1990: Several large-scale demonstrations erupt in Ulaanbaatar calling for reforms and multiparty elections.

March 12, 1990: General Secretary Batmonh and the entire Politburo offer their resignations.

March 14, 1990: A committee selects Gombojauyn Ochirbat as new General Secretary of the Mongolian People's Revolutionary Party and selects a new Politburo.

July 29, 1990: Mongolia holds its first free elections. The Mongolian People's Revolutionary Party wins 343 out of 430 Great Hural seats and about 60 percent of the fifty-three-seat Small Hural.

September 3, 1990: Ochirbat is elected president.

April 20, 1991: Tsedenbal dies in Moscow at the age of seventy-four.

June 28, 1991: The Council for Mutual Economic Assistance (COMECON), an economic organization of Soviet-bloc countries that Mongolia joined in 1962, disbands.

1992: A new, more democratic constitution is promulgated.

February 2, 1992: Mongolia's first stock exchange opens in Ulaanbaatar.

June 28, 1992: Elections are held for the unicameral Great Hural, which replaces the bicameral Great Hural and Small Hural. The Mongolian People's Revolutionary Party sweeps the elections.

June 6, 1993: Promising economic reforms, Ochirbat is reelected president.

June 25, 1993: The International Monetary

Fund approves a $57 million loan to boost the failing Mongolian economy.

June 30, 1996: The Democratic opposition coalition wins a decisive victory over the formerly Communist Mongolian People's Revolutionary Party in elections for the unicameral Great Hural.

July 19, 1996: Mendsayhany Enkhsaikhan, a liberal economist and member of the Mongolian Social Democratic Party, is elected premier.

May 18, 1997: Natsagiyn Bagabandi, chairman of the Mongolian People's Revolutionary Party, defeats incumbent Ochirbat in the presidential election.

September 1997: The government announces plans to auction off nearly all state-controlled businesses during the next two years.

October 7, 1997: Members of the Mongolian Assistance Group, an international body pledged to help Mongolia develop its economy, promises US$250 million in aid to support the liberal economic reforms of the Bagabandi government.

April 23, 1998: Tsahiagiyin Elbegdorj is elected prime minister. He is president of the Mongolian National Democratic Party and chairman of the ruling Democratic Union coalition.

July 24, 1998: Prime Minister Elbegdorj and his government resign after he loses a vote of confidence.

October 2, 1998: Sanjaasuregiin Zorig, a popular leader who played a major role in the democratic revolution of 1990 and was expected to become the next prime minister, is found axed and stabbed to death in his home. The motive for his murder is not known.

Central Asian Republics

PRE-ISLAMIC CENTRAL ASIA: 70,000 B.C.–A.D. 652

Much of the early history of Central Asia is unknown. Because the geography of the region is not generally conducive to agriculture, the early inhabitants adopt a nomadic way of life and leave behind no written records. Various tribal confederations rise in dominance and establish an empire of sorts over the important oases and trade cities. These tribal confederations inevitably prove fragile, however, as internal strife and inadequate means of governance lead to the dissolution of power. Early examples of this sort of "nomadic empire" are the Scythians and Samartians, both of Iranian origin, and the Xiongnu, a Turkic-Mongol people who are most active in the Mongolian steppes, but who also come to control the Tarim Basin. Parthia, the great empire that was to dominate Mesopotamia in the third century B.C., had its origins on the southern steppes of present-day Turkmenistan. The Persians, the Chinese Han, the Indian king Kanishka, and the Macedonian armies of Alexander the Great all make inroads into Central Asia, contributing to the great confluence of culture still to be found in the region. However, the most significant events in terms of defining the ultimate cultural character of the region are the conquests of the Turkish khaghanate in the sixth century, and the ascendancy of Islam in the seventh through the tenth centuries.

70,000–55,000 B.C.: The first settlements in Central Asia appear in the Ferghana Valley (present-day Uzbekistan) and in the Tien Shan range near Issyk-Kol.

5,000–3,000 B.C.: Evidence from an archaeological site north of Ashgabat in Turkmenistan indicates that the Neolithic Jeitun civilization becomes one of the first cultures in Central Asia to make use of agriculture.

2000 B.C.: Settlements typical of the Bronze Age Abdronovo appear throughout Kazakhstan. In the Amu Darya (Oxus) valley and near the Aral Sea Indo-Iranian tribes begin to settle the areas later known as Khorezm and Sogdiana.

1200 B.C.: A Late Bronze Age people known as the Cimmerians settle in the Volga, the southern part of the Russian steppe.

Late 8th century B.C.: The Scythians supplant the Cimmerians in the Ukraine. The Scythians are of uncertain origin. Many scholars believe that they are similar ethnically to the Cimmerians. After establishing themselves between the lower Dnieper and the lower Bug, the Scythians begin a series of violent campaigns to the south, invading the Caucasus, Asia Minor, Armenia, Media, and the Bosporan kingdom.

550 B.C.: Cyrus the Great of Persia (559–530 B.C.) vanquishes the Median empire. This marks the beginning of Achaemenid empire, the territorial extent of which is not clear, but seems to have extended from the Jaxartes River to the Indus, and included the Central Asian provinces of Bactria and Sogdiana, both of which are located in present-day Tajikistan.

530 B.C.: Cyrus, the Persian conqueror, dies in combat with the Massagetae tribal confederation.

522–486 B.C.: Rule of Darius the Great (Darius I) over the Achaemenid empire.

512–514 B.C.: Darius I leads an unsuccessful campaign to subdue the Scythians.

c. 5th century B.C.: Minusinsk, a town on the upper Yenisei near the Altai mountain range, becomes the primary Central Asian center for metallurgy. Production changes from bronze to silver c. 330–220 B.C.

496 B.C.: Scythians invade Thrace.

486–465 B.C.: Reign of Xerxes over the Achaemenid empire.

480 B.C.: Xerxes leads a Persian campaign against Greece. Troops from the Central Asian provinces participate.

c. 350–250 B.C.: Scythian culture in the southern Russian steppes reaches its zenith. Trade with the Greek colonies of the Black Sea area flourishes.

330–327 B.C.: Alexander the Great marches with his troops beyond the Caspian Sea. The Achaemenid king Darius III is killed in combat with Alexander. Alexander conquers Bactria in the Amu Darya valley, Sogdiana to the east of the Amu Darya, and then pushes south into the Indian subcontinent.

323 B.C.: Alexander the Great dies. Many Greek colonists in Bactria and Sogdiana mutiny and return to Greece.

Mid-3d century B.C.: Turkmenistan is incorporated into the Parthian empire. It remains governed by Parthia until the Sassanian conquests of the fourth century A.D.

Late 3d century B.C.: The Samartians, a nomadic group, like the Scythians of Iranian origin, cross the Volga and drive the Scythians back to the Crimea. Celts and Thracians likewise harass the Scythians from the west.

209–174 B.C.: Reign of Motun of the Xiongnu. By the end of the third century B.C. he defeats the Donghu and the Yuezhi (Yueh-chih) from whom he assumes command of the important Gansu corridor.

2d century B.C.: According to Chinese sources, the Yuezhi (or the Tokharians) reach the Amu Darya valley, having been driven out of the Tarim Basin by the Xiongnu. The Yuezhi are thought to speak an early form of the Indo-European language.

115–60 B.C.: The Han and the Xiongnu vie for control of the region surrounding the important Tarim Basin. The struggle centers on Jushi, which the Xiongnu lose in 60 B.C.

1st century B.C.: The Yuezhi force the Scythian tribes out of the Amu Darya and into lands held by the Parthian empire. The Parthians move to subdue the Scythians, but meet with several defeats that prove critical to Parthian control of its eastern frontier.

A.D. 18–46: Reign of Xiongnu leader Hu-tu-erh-shih. The Xiongnu enjoy a brief period of renewed prosperity as China becomes preoccupied with civil wars. They reclaim lost territory in the Tarim Basin region and exert influence over the Donghu tribes. However, the Xiongnu court has lost its ability to centralize authority over local potentates. After Hu-tu-erh-shih's death in A.D. 46 the Xiongnu split permanently into southern and northern factions.

Spring 73: Later Han (or Eastern Han, A.D. 25–220) begins a decisive campaign against the North Xiongnu, wresting from them regions they controlled in the Tarim Basin.

Late 1st century: The Later Han general Ban Chao (Pan Ch'ao, 32–102) leads his troops into Central Asia as Han reasserts its control over the Tarim Basin and reopens the Silk Road.

Mid-1st century: It is hypothesized that the first sculptures of the Gandhara School are carved in Taxila and in the Peshawar Vale. These iconic Buddhist images, which spread along the Silk Road throughout Central Asia and into China, contribute significantly to the spread of Buddhism.

Early 2d century: Kanishka, a Yuezhi prince from Kashgar, establishes a massive empire, often called the Kushan or Kusana empire, that includes almost the entire region of the former Soviet republics of Central Asia, Afghanistan, Pakistan, all of northern India, and parts of eastern and central India. He assumes the Buddhist title Devaputra (son of Divine Being) and does much to further the spread of Buddhism throughout Central Asia. The Kushan empire declines in the late second century and submits to the Sassanid dynasty of Persia in c. 260.

224: Ardashir I conquers Parthia and founds the Sassanid dynasty, which governs Persia until 652 when it is defeated by the Arabs.

Mid–late 5th century–Mid 6th century: The Hephthalites, a vassal tribe to the Ruanruan originating in the Altai region and settling in Turkmenistan, rise to power in the Amu Darya region formerly ruled by the Yuezhi. The Hephthalites then extend their authority to the regions north and south of the Hindu Kush, and in the sixth century to Sogdiana, Kashgar, Khotan, and Qocho.

c. 5th century: The Ruanruan (Juan-Juan) emerge concurrently with the Northern Wei in China. They are a nomadic proto-Mongol people based in the steppes north of the Altai Mountains. They defeat the remnants of the Northern Xiongnu, who retreat to the Ural Mountains and the Caspian Sea from

whence, some scholars hypothesize, they migrate to Europe eventually to become known as the infamous Huns.

460: The Ruanruan attack Qocho and vanquish the Quju (Chu-chu) dynasty, which had been a powerful force in the region west of present-day Xian.

471: The Ruanruan assume control over the city-state of Khotan, an important location on the lucrative east-west trading routes.

546–552?: The Turks, a people of obscure ethnic origin who may have had no more commonality than their vassalage as manufacturers of metal instruments, rebel against their Ruanruan masters. Bumin, who led the rebellion, dies shortly after their victory.

553: The first Turk khaghanate is established. Ishtemi, the brother of Bumin, rules the western parts of the empire roughly divided by the Altai Mountains, while Muhan, the son of Bumin, rules the more dominant eastern parts.

557–561: The Turk general Ishtemi and the Persian king Anushirvan mount a simultaneous attack on Hepthalite territories. The Hepthalite empire collapses, and it is not referred to again in Chinese or Persian annals.

568: Through emissaries sent from the western frontier region to Constantinople, the Turks establish diplomatic contact with Byzantium. At least one other Turk delegation (in 563) was sent to Constantinople, but the fruits of this initial mission are unclear.

570–632: Life of Muhammad, prophet of Islam.

619–630: Reign of the Western Turk Khaghan Tong Yabghu. An able diplomat, Tong forges alliances with the Tang in China and with Constantinople. After his death no strong ruler emerges, and the Western Turk empire becomes embroiled in factional strife that hastens its disintegration.

651: Herat falls to the Arabs.

652: The Sassanian empire crumbles under Arab pressure. The Arabs establish protectorates in Iran and Afghanistan, but do not immediately venture into Amu Darya valley.

THE RISE OF ISLAM, THE MONGOLIAN EMPIRE, AND THE KAZAKHS AND UZBEKS: 652–1771

The Arabs establish a presence in Central Asia in the late seventh century, and in the early eighth century the Umayyad dynasty incorporates the territories of the Amu Darya valley and Transoxiana (Mawarannahr) into the Islamic empire. Under the Abbasid caliphate, which supplants the Umayyad dynasty in 750, Islam spreads rapidly, drastically altering the cultural character of the region. The spread of Islam reaches the nomadic Turkic tribes of the northeast, which become the heirs to the region as the presence of the Persian dynasties wanes. The Mongols conquer the territories in the early thirteenth century and establish the Chaghadai khanate, which governs much of Central Asia until the early fourteenth century, when the state begins to fragment. The Uzbeks rise to power in the sixteenth century and remain a strong presence even as Russia begins to encroach on the Kazakh steppes. By the end of the eighteenth century, however, Russia has firmly established its hold on Kazakhstan and much of Uzbekistan and Turkestan.

Late 7th century: The Arabs expand their eastern border, taking prominent towns in the Amu Darya valley such as Samarkand and Bukhara. Full-scale campaigns into Central Asia do not begin, however, until the reign of al-Walid, caliph of the Umayyad dynasty, which supplants the Sassanians in 661.

661: The caliph Muawiyah I establishes the Umayyad dynasty of the Islamic empire.

705–715: Reign of caliph al-Walid of the Umayyad dynasty. His policy of expansion brings the Islamic empire into Central Asia.

742: The Uyghur ruler, Guli peiluo (Ku-li p'ei-lo), leads an alliance of Uyghur, Karluk, and Basmil forces against the Turks.

750: Abbasids defeat the Umayyads and establish a new dynasty over the Islamic empire. Their rule is characterized by a tolerance of non-Arab peoples. This tolerance contributes to a firmer administrative hold on outlying regions such as Central Asia, and consequentially a wider acceptance of Islam and Arab customs. The capital moves from Damascus to Baghdad.

751: Arab and Tibetan forces defeat the Chinese in battle at the Talas River, checking Chinese encroachment into Central Asia. According to tradition, Chinese papermakers captured at Samarkand at this time taught the Arabs how to make paper; Arabs then spread this technique throughout much of the Arab word during the next fifty years.

When high above the blue sky and down below the brown earth had been created, betwixt the two were created the sons of men. And above the sons of men stood my ancestors, the kaghans Bumin and Ishtemi. Having become master of the Turk people, they installed and ruled its empire and fixed the law of the country.

The Orkhon inscriptions, anonymous, c. 8th century

759–779: Reign of Uyghur Khaghan Mouyu (Mou-yu). Mouyu travels to China, supporting Tang efforts to put down the An Lushan rebellion. While in China he converts to Manichaeism, which he later imposes as the state religion in the Uyghur empire. The Uyghur state becomes the only East Asian state to officially adopt Manichaeism.

755–797: Reign of Khri-srong-Ide-btsan over the Tibetan empire. During his reign the Tibetans assume control of the Tarim Basin.

Late 8th century: Uyghur power declines.

820: Taking advantage of the weakening condition of the Uyghurs, the Kirghiz, probably a Siberian people originally inhabiting the regions of the upper Yenisei River valley, begin raids on Uyghur territory.

840: Kirghiz forces supported by loyal Karluks invade Uyghur territory and kill the khaghan. The Uyghur people flee south to the Tarim Basin, eventually to establish a kingdom in the Turpan region (present-day Turkestan).

875: The Samanids, a ruling house of native Iranians, assume control of Transoxiana ostensibly as governors within the Abbasid caliphate. However, like many local rulers within the Islamic empire at this time, they enjoy a large degree of autonomy.

Early 10th century: Satuq Bughra Khan (dies 955?) establishes the Karakhanid state in Transoxiana. He later converts to Islam. The Karakhanid territory is peopled mostly by Turkish tribes of the Karluk tribal confederation, formerly centered in the Chu valley.

992: The Karakhanids defeat the Samanids at Bukhara and briefly occupy the city. Their leader, Harun, becomes ill, however, and the troops withdraw.

999: The Karakhanids take Bukhara again. This time they hold the city. The Karakhanids establish a firm hold on territories north of the Amu Darya. South of the Amu Darya is the Ghaznavid empire, nominally under Samanid suzerainty.

1040: The Seljuks, a group of nomadic Turkish warriors, defeat the Ghaznavid empire near Merv. They gradually assume control of the crumbling Samanid empire and establish the Great Seljuk Sultanate in the mid-eleventh century. Although the empire briefly includes Bukhara and Samarkand, the eastern border generally remains west of the Amu Darya.

1124–1141: Led by Yelu Dashi (Yeh-lu Tashih) the Khitan of the vanquished Liao dynasty flee west. They cross the Tarim Basin and invade the steppes east of the Tien Shan mountains. The Khitan conquer the Karakhanid empire in Transoxiana and then defeat the Seljuk general Sanjar on the Qat-

wan steppe. The empire established by Yelu Dashi becomes known as the Khara-Khitai (Black Kitans).

1206: Chinggis Khan unites the Mongol tribes.

1208: Kuchlug, a defeated rival of Chinggis Khan, flees to the territories of Khara-Khitai. He finds the former empire in a much diminished state and is able to gain control of its government.

1209: The Uyghurs accept Mongol rule.

Hoja borrowed a large cauldron from a neighbor. On returning it, Hoja also gave him a small pot inside it. "What is this?" asked the neighbor. Hoja said, "Your cauldron gave birth to a small pot." The neighbor gratefully accepted it. Some time later, Hoja borrowed the cauldron again. Weeks passed and he did not return it. The neighbor went to ask what had become of his cauldron. "I'm sorry," said Hoja, "but your cauldron died." The furious neighbor shouted, "a cauldron cannot die!" But Hoja replied, "You believed it gave birth, so you must accept that it died."

Central Asian folktale, ascribed to Nasreddin Hoja,
11th–14th centuries

1218: Chinggis Khan dispatches troops to Khara-Khitai. The predominantly Muslim people of these regions, whose faith had been persecuted by Kuchlug, side with the Mongols, and Chinggis assumes control over the region almost entirely without a struggle.

Spring 1218: Chinggis sends a trade delegation to Utrar, a city on the eastern shore of the Syr Darya controlled by Ala al-Din Muhammad, ruler of Khorezm (Khwarazm). The governor of the region, Inalchug, condemns all but a few of the travelers to death. The massive Mongolian western campaign begun the following year was in part retribution for this event.

1219: Chinggis leads a sudden and violent campaign to regions across Tien Shan west of Turkestan. The Mongols use the territory they have recently acquired from Khara-Khitai as springboard for their offensive against Khorezm. Chinggis concentrates his attack first on Transoxiana. The Khorezm forces are overwhelmed. Muhammad flees to an island in the Caspian where he dies in 1221.

February 1220: The city of Bukhara falls to the Mongols. Samarkand also falls within a month.

Samarkand is a noble city, adorned with beautiful gardens, and surrounded by a plain, in which are produced all the fruits that man can desire. The inhabitants, who are partly Christians and partly Mahometans, are subject to the dominion of a nephew of the grand khan, with whom, however, he is not upon amicable terms, but on the contrary there is perpetual strife and frequent wars between them.

The Travels of Marco Polo, 13th century

1229: Ogodei (1186–1241) is proclaimed Great Khan of the Mongols. His brother Chaghadai (c. 1185–1242) receives the territories of Central Asia as his *ulus* and establishes the Chaghadai khanate, which governs much of Central Asia until the early fourteenth century when the state begins to fragment. Territories stretch from the Altai in the upper Irtysh to the Aral Sea and the Amu Darya.

1369: Tamerlane conquers Transoxiana. He establishes his capital in Samarkand and exacts a pledge of loyalty from Tughluq Temur Khan of the Chaghadai khanate. Temur abandons Transoxiana to his son, a mere puppet of Tamerlane, and establishes control over Moghulistan to the east.

1389: Unable to manage a forceful reconstruction of the Chaghadai khanate, Tamerlane recognizes the autonomy of Moghulistan and concentrates his energies on his northern frontier.

1391: Tamerlane invades the Eurasian steppes controlled by the Golden Horde. The Golden Horde retreats.

1395: Tamerlane's troops overrun the Caucasus and southern Russia. The Golden Horde is driven from its central base of power.

February 1405: Tamerlane dies.

1428–1447: Abu'l-Khayr, khan of the Uzbek khanate, unifies the nomadic tribes inhabiting the steppes of present-day Kazakhstan and leads a campaign against the Timurid empire. He manages to take Khorezm and the regions around the Syr Darya. His hopes to unify his holdings into a stable empire fail as several of princes defected to the Esenbuqa, the Chaghatai Khan of Moghulistan (c. 1465). These defectors and their followers became known as Kazakhs (meaning "independent" or "vagabond").

1456–1457: The Oirat Mongols of Western Mongols begin a series of raids into the Uzbek territories of Abu'l-Khayr.

1468: The Kazakh clans defeat the Abu'l-Khayr and assume dominance over the former Uzbek khanate.

1476–1539: Life of the Uzbek ruler Ubaydullah. He expels the last of the Timurids from Transoxiana, but his efforts to expand the Uzbek territories into Iran fail. He is remembered as a patron of the arts and is reputed to have been an excellent poet himself.

Her tint like the silver-colored white jonquil
Her figure like a bud made of silver.
Her every eyelash the point of a pen,
Having blackened the warrant for death [of a man].

"Farha wa Shirin," poem by Mir Ail Shir Nawaiy, 1484

1500: The grandson of Abu'l Khayr, Muhammad Shaybani conquers Bukhara and Samarkand, and establishes the Shaybanid dynasty in the territories formerly constituting the Timurid empire (roughly Turkmenistan and western Uzbekistan).

1509–1518: Reign of Kasym, khan of the Kazakhs, and height of Kazakh power in the steppes. After his death the empire is fraught with internecine strife.

1538–1580: Reign of Haq Nazar of the Kazakhs. During his reign the Kazakh factions form into three distinct groups: The Great, Middle, and Lower Hordes.

Early 17th century: The Torguts, a tribe of the Oirats of western Mongolia, sweep across Kazakh territory. Defeating any resistance to their migration they finally settle between the Ural River and the Volga. They become known as the Kalmyk Horde.

1680–1718: Reign of Kazakh Khan Tauke. He codifies tribal practice into formal laws for the Kazakh state.

1681–1684: Oirat armies under Galdan invade Central Asia. Galdan establishes a protectorate over Kashgaria in 1678, and conquers Moghulistan. His armies make numerous raids into the Syr Darya region.

1698–1757: The Oirats repeatedly raid the Kazakh territories. The results are often devastating for the Kazakhs. It is not until the Manchus defeat the Oirat empire in 1757 that these raids cease. During this century of violence the Kazakhs become increasingly dependent on Russia for protection.

1723: The Kalmyks capture the Talas River valley, forcing the Kazakhs to abandon their livestock and flee north, thus making them more vulnerable to Russian authority.

1731: Abu Khayr, khan of the Kazakh Lesser Horde, swears fealty to Russia in exchange for military protection.

1771: The Kazakh khans swear fealty to the Manchus. In essence the lands of Kazakhstan split into a protectorate of Russia in the west and a protectorate of Manchu China in the east.

RUSSIAN RULE AND INDEPENDENCE: 1771–1998

In the nineteenth century Russia slowly, but deliberately, establishes its control of the Kazakh steppes and Transoxiana. The last Turkmen territories are taken in 1881, completing the Russian conquest of Central Asia. Russians gradually replace natives in positions of authority, and Russian peasants migrate in large numbers to the uncultivated land of the steppes, which is often cheaply sold or simply given away. After defeating the White Army in 1920, the Bolsheviks are quick to establish control of the Central Asian territories. Joseph Stalin divides the territories into five constituent soviet socialist republics of the Soviet Union: the Kazakh SSR, Uzbek SSR, Tajik SSR, Kirghiz SSR, and Turkmen SSR. The nomadic way of life gradually becomes all but extinct under Soviet administration. Particularly damaging are Stalin's forced collectivization campaign (1929–1933), and Khrushchev's Virgin Lands Campaign (1953–1965). As the Soviet Union crumbles, the constituent republics declare their independence and set up so-called democratic republics, which for the most are nothing more than autocratic regimes. Tajikistan becomes embroiled in a power struggle that results in a five-year civil war. A peace treaty is signed in 1997. New wealth promises to enter the region at the end of the twentieth century as foreign companies look to tap into Central Asia's substantial oil and natural gas reserves.

Late 18th–early 19th century: Russia assumes more active control over the territories of Kazakhstan, discouraging nomadism and encouraging Russian migration and the establishment of farms. Rebellions led by Pugachev (1773–1775) and by Kenisary Qasimov (1837–1844), and riots in the Mansysh-

lak region in 1867 are ineffective and only lead to an increase in Russian supervision.

1854: The Russians organize the eastern Kazakh steppe into the *oblasts* (provinces) of the Siberian Kyrgyz, with its capital at Omsk, and Semipalatinsk, with its capital at the town of Semipalatinsk.

1859: The Russians organize the western Kazakh steppe into the *oblast* of Orenburg Kyrgyz.

1864: The Russians annex the Syr Darya region.

1869: The Russians found the port of Krasnovodsk on the eastern coast of the Caspian Sea.

1876: Russian troops defeat the Uzbek khanate of Kokand and seize the Alay valley, bringing Kirghiz under its control.

Late 19th century: A group of Central Asian intellectuals known as *jadids* address what they perceive as the backwardness of Central Asia by starting schools and a printing press and advocating modernization. The Russians, however, suppress the movement and, although it continues to function underground, its teachings are not widely disseminated.

If you but observe this Russian:
He reconnoitered, the land he took
The dark gray, born from the mare, he took,
Fat, wealthy men he took.
Every hiding place he took.

From "Tar zaman" (A Bad Time), poem by Kirghiz
poet Aristanbekuulu (1840–1882)

1880–1888: Construction of the Trans-Caspian Railroad.

1881: The Russians defeat the army of Turkmen rebels at Gokdepe.

1891: Promulgation of the so-called Steppe Statute, which dictates that the "excessive land" of the Kazakh steppe be sold or given outright to Russian peasants for agricultural purposes.

1899: The Russians establish a governate-general of Turkistan, with its capital at Tashkent.

1916: Hundreds of thousands of men from the Central Asian states are drafted into the Russian army. This touches off widespread uprisings. Sympathy with the Bolsheviks increases.

November 1917: Islamic leaders gather in the city of Kokand and create a provisional government calling for the autonomy of Central Asia. The Red Army quickly suppresses the movement in February 1918.

April 1918: The Bolsheviks establish the Turkistan Autonomous Soviet Socialist Republic (ASSR).

1918–1920: The Social Revolutionary Transcaspian Provincial Government holds out against the Bolsheviks in Turkmenistan, holding Ashgabat until July 1919 and Krasnovodsk until February 1920.

August 26, 1920: The Soviets establish the Kirghiz Autonomous Republic, which includes Kazakhstan and parts of Kyrgyzstan. The region, minus the lands of the Kirghiz *oblast* (created in 1924), becomes the Kazakh ASSR in 1925.

October 1920–1924: The Soviets take control of the vassal states of the Emirate of Bukhara and the Khanate of Khiva, establishing the Soviet Republics of Bukhara and Khorezm respectively. In 1924 these republics are assimilated into the Uzbek SSR.

1922–1923: The Basmachi rebellion erupts in Bukhara. The Soviets remain in control, but rebel bands continue to operate under Ibrahim Bek until 1931.

1924: The Soviets establish the Turkmen SSR (Soviet Socialist Republic) and the Uzbek SSR, which includes the Tajik ASSR.

1926: The Soviets establish the Kirghiz ASSR.

1926–1956: B. G. Gafurov leads the Communist Party in the Tajik ASSR (after 1929 the Tajik SSR). Also a historian, Gafurov succeeds in creating national sentiments among the Tajik people.

1927: The Soviets begin a policy of colonization in Kazakhstan and intensify efforts to obliterate nomadic ways of life.

December 5, 1929: The Soviets establish the Tajik SSR.

November 1929–1933: Stalin begins his campaign of forced collectivization in Central Asia. Exact numbers are unknown, but it is estimated that millions die of overwork and starvation.

1936: The Kazakh ASSR and the Kirghiz ASSR become constituent republics of the Soviet Union.

My jewel, my sun, Stalin,
Like musk your scent has spread around.
Your mine of intellect and thought
The limitless sea has encompassed.

From "Stalin," poem by Kazakh poet Omirzaq-aqin,
1937

1941–1945: During World War II the Soviet Union increases economic output in Central Asia. Northern Kazakhstan is rapidly industrialized, and coal mines are established in Kyrgyzstan.

1953–1965: As part of the Virgin Lands Campaign inaugurated by Nikita Khrushchev, vast amounts of former grazing lands are plowed up and replaced with grain fields.

1959–1986: Kazakh Dinmukhamed Kunayev holds the post of first secretary of the Communist Party of Kazakh SSR. He is the only Kazakh to become a member of the Soviet Politburo. When he is forced to retire in 1986 and replaced by the non-Kazakh Gennadi Koldin, riots erupt in Alma-Atay.

1959–1983: Sharaf Rashidov holds the post of first secretary of the Communist Party of Uzbek SSR.

August–December 1991: The Soviet Union disintegrates, and one by one its constituent republics declare their independence. Kyrgyzstan and Uzbekistan declare theirs on August 31, Tajikistan on September 9, Turkmenistan on October 27, and Kazakhstan on December 16.

December 21, 1991: The five Central Asian republics apply to join the Commonwealth of Independent States (CIS), the loose association of twelve former constituent republics of the Soviet Union formed initially by Russia, Belarus, and Ukraine to advance economic and military cooperation.

1990s: Foreign companies compete to negotiate contacts for oil and natural gas explorations and pipelines in the newly independent countries of Central Asia.

March 2, 1992: The five newly independent republics of Central Asia are accepted into the United Nations.

April 1992–June 27, 1997: In Tajikistan, what commences as protests by people opposed to the conservative-communist government of Rahman Nabiyev soon becomes a full-scale civil war. The rebel forces are primarily pro-Islamic, opposed to the largely secular, and increasingly autocratic, state being imposed by the communists. Although the Tajikistan government claims to be a noncommunist state, there is no question that it depends heavily on Russia for support.

May 9–10, 1992: The leaders of Kazakhstan, Kyrgyzstan, Turkmenistan, and Uzbekistan (Tajikistan does not attend because of its ongoing civil war) meet with the leaders of Iran, Pakistan, and Turkey and adopt a statement agreeing to expand economic and political cooperation; in particular, they agree to initiate discussions on transport links and gas pipelines.

May 18, 1992: Turkmenistan adopts a new constitution, leaving the communists in power as the Democratic Party. President Saparmurad Niyazov will gradually assert his authority until he becomes a virtual dictator.

May 23, 1992: Kazakhstan—along with Ukraine and Belarus one of three former Soviet republics with nuclear weapons in its territory—signs a protocol to the Strategic Arms Reduction Treaty (START); all three countries pledge to eliminate nuclear weapons by the end of the decade.

September 7, 1992: In Tajikistan, Rahman Nabiyev is forced out of office as prime minister and replaced by Imamoli Rakhmanov; in the ensuing years, he will become the virtual dictator of Tajikistan.

September 30, 1992: With the situation in Tajikistan deteriorating, Russian troops take control of the airport of its capital, Dushanbe.

January 3–4, 1993: The leaders of the five Central Asian states meet at Tashkent to discuss increasing cooperation; they complain that they are being treated as "younger brothers" by the other members of the Commonwealth of Independent States.

January 28, 1993: Kazakhstan's parliament adopts its new constitution; its stress on making Kazakh the official language bothers Russia, inasmuch as almost 40 percent of the population are ethnic Russians.

March 3, 1993: As the civil war threatens to ravage Tajikistan, the first troops from other CIS states arrive as a peacekeeping force. One of the concerns of Russia and the other states is that civil war threatens to become a war between Tajikistan and Afghanistan, where the pro-Islamic rebels are known to be able to take refuge.

May 5, 1993: Kyrgyzstan adopts its new constitution.

January 15, 1994: In Turkmenistan, voters overwhelmingly endorse an extension of Saparmurad Niyazov's term beyond 1997.

April 29–30, 1994: Kazakhstan, Kyrgyzstan, and Uzbekistan formally establish an economic union to compete with what they feel are the unfair tactics of other members of the CIS.

September 18 and October 23, 1994: In Tajikistan, the government and the rebels agree to cease-fires, but neither holds up for much more than a day. As the civil war rages, casualties on both sides continue to mount.

January 20–23, 1995: President Nursultan Nazarbayev of Kazakhstan signs an agreement with President Yeltsin of Russia to establish joint armed forces. On January 23 the two leaders agree to cooperate in exploring for oil and gas resources in the Caspian Sea.

March 26, 1995: In Uzbekistan, voters overwhelmingly back a proposal to postpone elections until the year 2000, effectively granting full powers to President Islam Karimov.

August 30, 1995: In Kazakhstan, the voters give overwhelming support to the new constitution; it effectively grants total powers to President Nazarbayev.

December 24, 1995: In Kyrgyzstan, Askar Akayev is reelected (with some 72 percent of the vote) for his second five-year term as president.

February 10, 1996: In Kyrgyzstan, a referendum grants the president sweeping new powers, further consolidating the rule of Askar Akayev.

July 21–August 15, 1996: In Tajikistan, the United Nations tries to maintain a cease-fire while peace talks proceed with government and the Islamic opposition, but the effort collapses.

December 3, 1996: At a meeting in Moscow, President Imamoli Rakhmanov of Tajikistan and Sayed Abdullah Nuri, leader of the Islamic Renaissance Party and now the spokesman for the rebel forces, sign a preliminary peace agreement.

December 11–12, 1996: Following an agreement signed in Moscow, a UN-sponsored cease-fire between the government and pro-Islamic forces comes into effect. It lasts only a day.

May 21, 1997: In Kyrgyzstan, since 1992 President Akayev has transferred some 60 percent of the former state-owned industries to the private sector; now he announces that he is suspending this privatization because the prices being paid are too low.

June 25, 1997: Kazakhstan and China sign a contract, projected to be worth billions of dollars, under which China is to exploit and develop three oil fields in Kazakhstan.

June 27, 1997: In Moscow, Tajikistan's President Rakhmanov and Islamic leader Sayed Abdullah Nuri sign a Final Peace and National Reconciliation Accord.

July 7–10, 1997: The first session of the Tajik National Reconciliation Commission meets in Moscow; it elects Sayed Abdullah Nuri chairman. Both sides agree to a policy of "mutual forgiveness." President Rakhmanov orders a 30 percent reduction of the nation's armed forces.

July 24–August 19, 1997: Colonel Mahmud Khudoberdiyev, commander of the Tajik army's First Brigade, based in southern Tajikistan, objects to the peace agreement that grants full recognition and rights to the pro-Islamic forces. On July 24 he declares that he is taking control of southern and central Tajikistan. On August 10, he moves his forces to within twenty miles of the capital, Dushanbe. Government troops move against him, and on August 19 the government announces that they are victorious; Khudoberdiyev and some fifty of his supporters flee to the mountains along the border with Uzbekistan. (He will be accused of leading an attack on the presidential guard in Dushanbe on October 12, but this is never proven.)

September 11, 1997: Sayed Abdullah Nuri, leader of the Islamic Renaissance Party, arrives in the capital after a five-year exile and meets with President Rakhmanov. The two discuss the schedule for implementing the peace agreement.

November 8, 1997: President Nazarbayev officially declares Akmola, in northern Kazakhstan, as the new capital. (Alma-Atay had been the capital.)

December 4, 1997: Government ministers from twenty countries attend a meeting of the Asian Mutual Relations and Trust Conference in Kazakhstan.

March 24, 1998: Kyrgyzstan Prime Minister Apas Jumagulov resigns and is immediately replaced by Kubanychbek Zhumaliyev.

April 23, 1998: After a meeting at the White House in Washington, President Niyaszov of Turkmenistan and President Clinton issue a statement agreeing to expand cooperation between their two countries through both governmental and private sector partnerships.

May 20, 1998: At a gold-refining plant in Kyrgyzstan owned by a Canadian company, Cameco Corp., a truck crashes and spills about two tons of sodium cyanide into a river that flows into Lake Issyk-Kol, Kyrgyzstan's most famous symbol and the heart of its tourist industry. In the weeks that follow, despite the company's claims that scientific tests show that the cyanide is not killing any lakes or poisoning food, agriculture and tourism in the region are drastically cut back as the Kyrgyz people express their frustration with the increasing presence of such foreign-owned industrial enterprises in their midst.

July 17, 1998: The daughter of Kazakhstan's president Nazarbayev marries the son of Kyrgyzstan's president Akayev, thereby further consolidating close relations between the two countries.

August 24, 1998: Russia announces that by the end of the year it will have withdrawn the three thousand Russians who have been guarding the borders of Kyrgyzstan. Russia says that this is due strictly to its current financial crisis.

Tibet

The oldest past of Tibet is obscure. The terrain is so inhospitable that some of it has yet to be explored, and there has been little archaeological investigation. Presumably the earliest inhabitants practice an animistic, shamanistic religion known to precede Buddhism in Tibet, where it is called the Bon religion. Meanwhile, trade routes through Tibet link India, China, and Central Asia. Tibet does not truly emerge as a historical entity until the seventh century A.D., when Buddhism and centralized rule, two of Tibet's most enduring institutions, are established. By the thirteenth century, the two are firmly combined by monastic rule. The first Dalai Lama is named in the sixteenth century. Hundreds of years of Lamaism, the Tibetan form of Mahayana Buddhism, create in Tibet a peaceful, devout community devoted to learning and meditation.

Tibet (Tibetan *Bod*) has close cultural ties with India, with which it shares its long southern border. By contrast, conflict and occupation mark Tibet's history with its northern neighbors. Over many centuries the Mongols, and later the Manchus, repeatedly invade and subjugate China and thereby control the Dalai Lama. By the end of the nineteenth century the British are taking an active role in Tibet's affairs, and by the early decades of the twentieth century China is asserting its claims on Tibet. In 1950 the People's Republic of China invades and in 1959 annexes Tibet. Designated the Xizang Autonomous Region of China, Tibet falls victim to a Chinese campaign to disperse the Tibetans and destroy their culture. A persistent Tibetan rebellion is suppressed, while the Dalai Lama, exiled in India, keeps Tibetan traditions alive on foreign soil.

416 B.C.: King Nyatri Dzenpo, the first recorded Tibetan king, founds a dynasty in the Yarlung valley. He builds the first fortress in Tibet at Yambulhakang.

C. A.D. 570–620: Tribal chief Namri Songzen attempts unification of the region.

620: Namri Songzen's son Songzen Gampo, first emperor of Tibet, begins his reign (620–

649). He conquers the kingdoms of Nepal to the west and Kamarupa to the south, unifying a large empire and establishing his capital at Lhasa. His marriage to a Tang princess establishes a dynastic tie with China.

7th century: The presence of Buddhist missionaries in Tibet challenges the indigenous Bon religion. Songzen Gampo sends scholar

Thonmi Sambhota to Kashmir to collect Buddhist texts. Thonmi Sambhota's translation of Buddhist scriptures into Tibetan stabilizes the language, and Tibetan script develops from the alphabetical Gupta script of the original Sanskrit texts.

Mid- to late 8th century: Indian Buddhist mystics Santarakshita and Padmasambhava visit Tibet. Padmasambhava (Lotus-born), also called Guru Rimpoche (Precious Teacher), introduces Tantric Buddhism (Vajrayana) and founds first monastic order. The Nyingma (ancient) or Red Hat Buddhism of Padmasambhava's followers is the first of the great Tibetan Buddhist orders. He is traditionally credited as the author of the *Tibetan Book of the Dead*, a sacred text containing the ritual for dying (attributed by modern scholars to Kar-ma Ling-pa in the fifteenth century), and with institution of the Tibetan tradition of *terma*, the practice of burying religious texts.

755–797: Emperor Trisong Dezen reigns at the height of the empire.

791: Completion of first Buddhist monastery in Tibet at Samye in the eastern region. Buddhist clergy begin to rise to political power during the reign of king Ralpachen (c. 815–838).

8th–9th centuries: Bhautta rule in western Tibet.

c. 800–1000: Starting early in the ninth century, Tantrism, an esoteric strand of Hinduism and Jainism as well as Buddhism, is introduced into Tibet when Tantric texts are brought from India. Tantrism includes *mantras* (sacred syllables), *mandalas* (ritual diagrams), *tanghkas* (religious scroll paintings), and explanations of Tantra, the sacred texts; Tantrism also involves strict discipline, including yoga and other practices to attain mastery over oneself and physical phenomena. Tantrism becomes a strong influence on Tibetan Buddhism and reaches its peak *c.* 1000.

832: The first treaty with China ("of uncle

and nephew"), intended to reduce military conflict, is signed.

1042: Indian Buddhist *pandit* (teacher and scholar) Atisa (982–1054) visits central Tibet and revitalizes declining Buddhist practice. Many monasteries are built during a second great wave of Buddhism (10th–12th centuries); they accumulate land holdings, establish armies, and assume political power.

1073: Konchok Gyalpo, breaking with Nyingma order, founds Sakya (gray earth) monastery. Sakya is the second of the four great orders of Tibetan Buddhism.

1123: Death of the ascetic Milarepa (cotton-clad Mila), through whom the teachings of his master, Marpa (1012–1096), and Marpa's teacher, the Indian *yogi* Naropa (956–1040), are transmitted. Codified by Gampopa (1079–1153), these texts become the foundation of Kagyu (oral transmission), the third great order of Tibetan Buddhism.

1193: Death of Dusum Chempa (1110–1193), first head of the Karmapa (Black Hat) sect of Kagyu Buddhism. The Karmapas are one of the first orders to identify their head lamas by means of reincarnation.

13th century: Completion of Tibetan translation of the 4,569 works of the Buddhist canon.

1204: Invasion by the Muslim Indian Iktiar ud-Din Muhammad is rebuffed.

1251: Death of Kunga Gyaltsen (1182–1251), Sakya *pandit* and author of the earliest history of Tibet.

1251: Mongols invade Tibet. Khubilai Khan is converted to Lamaism by the abbot of the Sakya lamasary, who is installed as the first priest-king of Tibet (reigns 1270–1340). The Sakya dynasty lasts until 1358. The Mongols continue to exercise considerable influence over Tibet for almost four hundred years.

c. 1322: Scholar and teacher Buton (1290–1364) completes a history of Buddhism in Tibet. He classifies the Tibetan Buddhist canon into *Kanjur* (Buddha's words) and *Tenjur* (commentaries and treatises).

15th century: At some point during this period lived Kar-ma Ling-pa, one of Tibet's most revered *Ter-tons* (treasure revealers), individuals who reveal mystical texts ascribed to paranormal origin. Modern scholars credit him with writing down the *Bar-do-tho-dol*, widely known in the West as *The Tibetan Book of the Dead*. *Bardo* refers to the intermediate stage Tibetan Buddhists believe a person goes through between death and rebirth, and this text is designed to be read as part of the rituals that ease a person's way through this stage.

O son of noble family, when your body and mind separate, the dharmata [essence of reality] will appear, pure and clear yet hard to discern, luminous and brilliant, with terrifying brightness, shimmering like a mirage on a plain in spring. Do not be afraid of it, do not be bewildered. This is a natural radiance of your own dharmata, therefore recognize it.

Bar-do-tho-dol ("liberation from bardo [the intermediate state] by hearing," known in the West as the *Tibetan Book of the Dead*), ascribed to Kar-ma Ling-pa, 15th century

---

1409: The first Gelugpa (Yellow Hat) monastery is founded at Ganden, near Lhasa, by religious reformer Tsong Khapa (1357–1419). Gelugpa is the last of the four great orders of Tibetan Buddhism (and destined to become the largest); monasteries are built nearby at Drepung (1416) and Sera (1419). Gelugpas observe strict monastic discipline and institutionalize the practice of identifying religious leaders by recognizing reincarnations of past leaders.

1578: After his conversion to Buddhism, Mongol prince Altan Khan bestows the honorific title Dalai Lama (priest with ocean-like wisdom) on Sonam Gyatso (1543–1588), abbot of Drepung monastery. The title is posthumously applied to his predecessors Gedung Truppa (1391–1474) and Gedung Gyatso (1475–1542), henceforth regarded as the first and second Dalai Lamas.

1642–1720: The Mongols reassert their authority over Tibet. The Mongols do not themselves rule Tibet, instead investing temporal authority in the fifth Dalai Lama, Ngawang Lobzang Gyatso ("the Great Fifth," 1617–1682), who defeats the rival Karmapa sect, creates a monastic administration, and raises Gelugpas to political power. Successive Dalai Lamas continue to exercise both spiritual and temporal rule.

Nine or ten months later in the Tiger Year a son was begotten in the womb of Kun bZang Ma. At this event, flowers came down like rain. A rainbow like a tent of light and similar auspicious signs appeared gain and again. At good times the unusual sight of a white robed goddess, coming from the sky and showering the queen with water, was clearly seen by all.

From gCung Po Don Yod (The Younger Brother Don Yod), a popular Tibetan folktale and play, 17th century(?)

Mid-17th century: The Dalai Lama predicts the reincarnation of Panchen Lama Chokyi Gyaltsen (1570–1662), the second-highest spiritual authority in Tibet. He thus becomes the first in a reincarnated line of Panchen Lamas. The Chinese emperor grants sovereignty over western Tibet to the second Panchen Lama (1663–1737); he and his successors rule from Tashilhunpo monastery near Shigatse in western Tibet.

1720–1795: The Qing dynasty of China claims sovereignty over Tibet after a Manchu army expels the Mongols from Lhasa.

If one looks always at the faults of others,
One does not notice that one's every moment
Passes in blindness to one's own faults.
One parts from hope for any spiritual progress.

From *Songs of Spiritual Change*, by Gyalwa Kalzang Gyats'o, Seventh Dalai Lama (1708–1757)

1727–1728: Civil war. The Chinese dispatch fifteen thousand troops across the border and force the Dalai Lama into exile. Two Chinese representatives *(ambans)* take up residence in the capital. Under Sino-Tibetan policy, Tibet is closed to foreigners, including the British in India, until the late nineteenth century.

1774–1775: George Bogle, on a commercial embassy from Indian governor-general Warren Hastings, fails to secure an overland British trade route through Tibet to China. Later trade missions similarly fail.

1788–1792: Gurkha invasions from Nepal are repulsed by the Chinese army. The *ambans'* power is increased by a Sino-Tibetan treaty of 1792.

1795: Taking advantage of the weakness of failing Qing dynasty, Tibet liberates itself from Chinese rule.

1841–1842: A Kashmiri invasion is repulsed.

1854–1856: A Gurkha invasion leads to war. The Manchus do not intervene to support Tibet.

1879, 1881: Bengali schoolteacher Saratchandra Das visits Lhasa. He learns Tibetan, compiles a Tibetan-English dictionary (1902), and writes the first English-language account of Tibetan monks.

1887: Unsuccessful Tibetan invasion of Sikkim. The Tibet-Sikkim border is delineated in the Sino-British Calcutta Convention (1890) confirming Sikkim's status as a British protectorate.

July 1903: Indian viceroy Lord Curzon authorizes the invasion of Tibet in order to counter perceived Russian influence. A British expeditionary force led by Col. Francis Younghusband reaches Khama Dzong (July 7, 1903), defeats Tibetan forces, and reaches Lhasa (August 2, 1904). Younghusband exceeds his mandate by imposing terms opening Tibetan trade to Britain and prohibiting extension of commercial privileges to Russia.

April 27, 1906: An Anglo-Chinese agreement is signed confirming Chinese sovereignty over Tibet. An Anglo-Russian agreement (August 18, 1907) similarly acknowledges China's sovereignty.

December 1911: Tibetans take advantage of revolution in China to begin to expel the Chinese after a two-year occupation; the last Chinese leave Tibet in January 1913.

1913: The Tibetan National Assembly and the thirteenth Dalai Lama (1875–1933) declare Tibetan independence. China disregards their claim.

October 13, 1913–July 3, 1914: British, Chinese, and Tibetan delegates convene for the first round of the Simla Conference (which actually holds its initial sessions in Delhi, India). Sir Henry McMahon, Britain's foreign secretary for India, is chosen to preside. The major issue is to clarify the status of Tibet, to which China lays absolute claim while the Tibetans claim absolute independence. Britain proposes a compromise of recognizing an Inner Tibet, over which China will retain political sovereignty (while allowing Tibetans to retain their traditional religious authority), and an Outer Tibet, which will be completely independent. McMahon draws the boundaries for these two zones on a map, and much of the debate during the ensuing months involves adjusting these boundaries. On April 27, the British and Tibetans believe they have reached an agreement with China after the Chinese delegate initials the draft, but his government repudiates it. The delegates return to their meetings and continue to readjust the boundaries. On July 3 Britain and Tibet agree to a final version of the boundary and sign the Simla Convention. China refuses to sign; it never will. The boundary becomes known as the McMahon Line and has since been regarded as quite arbitrary, with little regard for the geographic, ethnographic, or traditional factors in this region of the Himalayas. It is generally agreed that the Simla Convention really only satisfies Britain's goal of obtaining trading privileges in Tibet.

1918: Tibetans overthrow Chinese rule and

govern independently during the following decades of political upheaval and revolution in China and Russia. The period is turbulent in Tibet, too, particularly in the eastern region of Kham.

1940: Tenzin Gyatso (1935–) is enthroned as the fourteenth Dalai Lama.

May 22, 1950: The newly declared People's Republic of China offers autonomy if Tibet embraces Communism.

October 7, 1950: China invades with eighty thousand troops and annexes Tibet, known in China as Xizang province. The Dalai Lama is kept as a figurehead and attempts to mediate between his people and the Chinese. A Tibetan appeal to the United Nations (November 10) and several years of armed revolt are unavailing.

May 23, 1951: Tibet's integration with China is formalized in a seventeen-point treaty signed in Beijing. China pledges regional autonomy. The Dalai Lama accepts the agreement in 1953.

October 26, 1951: The Chinese army occupies Lhasa.

Mid-1954: Chinese troops kill an estimated forty thousand Tibetan rebels.

April 29, 1954: A Sino-Indian Agreement recognizes China's right to "the Tibet region of China."

1956–1959: Tibetans are subjected to forced labor and deportations. China resettles millions of ethnic Chinese in Tibet in an effort to destroy Tibetan culture.

March 10–27, 1959: A rebellion in Lhasa against Chinese rule is crushed; an estimated 87,000 Tibetans are killed and many more jailed.

March 31, 1959: The Dalai Lama flees to India, where he accuses the Chinese of genocide. He will eventually be joined by seventy thousand followers who are granted political asylum in India. They establish a government in exile at Dharmsala, thirty-five miles from the Tibetan border.

1960: The Panchen Lama's monastery, Tashilhunpo, is sacked by the Chinese; four thousand monks are killed or sent to labor camps. The seventh Panchen Lama, Chokyi Gyaltsen, denounces China's invasion of Tibet; he is jailed in 1964 for fourteen years.

March 9, 1961: The Dalai Lama appeals to the United Nations to restore Tibetan independence. He will campaign for decades to come for condemnation of Chinese occupation; although he gains great respect and a large following for his person and his message, he receives little support from the world's governments.

1965: China absorbs Tibet as Xizang Zizhiqu Autonomous Region.

1966–1976: Six thousand Tibetan monasteries and temples are demolished during the Cultural Revolution in China, their artwork and libraries destroyed, and monks dispersed. Religious activity is banned, as is traditional Tibetan dress. More than a million Tibetans are thought to have been killed during the years of the Cultural Revolution in China.

Great compassion is the root of all forms of worship.

Teachings of the Fourteenth Dalai Lama (1935–), late 1970s

1980–1982: The Dalai Lama sends four delegations to Tibet to investigate conditions there; negotiations continue through the early 1980s for his own return to his country.

October 1, 1987: Ten days of violent anti-Chinese demonstrations begin in Lhasa. The city is sealed. Further major demonstrations occur March and December 1988, March 1989, September 1990, and May 1993. Martial law is imposed on Lhasa from March 1989 to May 1990.

February 1988: An Asia Watch report documents China's human rights violations in Tibet. During the following years, the United Nations and many other independent human rights groups report the Chinese authorities' arbitrary arrest and torture of Tibetan dissidents and their ongoing campaign to destroy Buddhism. The European Economic Community (1992) and Germany (1996), among others, pass resolutions condemning these violations.

March 5–7, 1989: Anti-Chinese violence breaks out in Lhasa. China declares martial law in an effort to forestall demonstrations on the thirtieth anniversary of the 1959 uprising.

October 5, 1989: The Dalai Lama is awarded the Nobel Peace Prize for his nonviolent campaign to expel the Chinese from Tibet. China denounces the award. The prize adds to public awareness of the Dalai Lama's international campaign against Chinese occupation of and suppression of human rights in Tibet. Western governments treat the Dalai Lama with wary respect, not wanting to jeopardize their relations with China.

1990: A census records Tibet's population at nearly 2.2 million.

1991: People around the world dedicated to winning more freedom for Tibet, its inhabitants, and its culture, observe the "Year of Tibet," which the Dalai Lama called for to counter China's official celebrations for the fortieth anniversary of its annexation of Tibet (May 23, 1951).

1992: China targets Tibet for industrial development by naming it a Special Economic Zone.

May 14, 1995: The Dalai Lama selects six-year-old Gedhun Choeklyi Nyima as the eleventh Panchen Lama. China arrests the boy and installs its own candidate, Gyaincain Norbu (December 8, 1995). The incident causes an international outcry.

March 3, 1997: Communist Chinese leaders deny claims that China is moving thousands of ethnic (Han) Chinese into Tibet; they claim that only 3.3 percent of Tibet's population of some 2,400,00 are Chinese and that this is actually a decline from 3.7 percent in 1990. International visitors to Tibet, however, report a growing Chinese presence and influence, especially in Lhasa.

July 22, 1997: Gyaincain Norbu, the head of Tibet's local government, says that China will never grant Tibet the kind of autonomy just recently allowed to Hong Kong.

June 27, 1998: During his visit in China, at a joint press conference with President Jiang Zemin in Beijing, U.S. President Clinton directly invites Jiang Zemin to meet with the Dalai Lama to discuss the situation in Tibet. Zemin says that if the Dalai Lama acknowledges that Tibet is an inseparable part of China, "then, as far as I see it, the door to negotiation is open." This is widely reported; given less publicity is the fact that Clinton agreed that Tibet is Chinese territory and that the Dalai Lama must acknowledge this.

July 10, 1998: The Dalai Lama announces that he is postponing his long-planned return visit to Tibet to avoid provoking China.

September 25, 1998: In a meeting with visiting French President Lionel Jospin, President Jiang Zemin of China repeats that he is willing to meet with the Dalai Lama if he will recognize China's rule over Tibet.

National/Independence Days

BANGLADESH

March 26: Independence Day. On this date in 1971, a group of Bengali nationalists made a radio broadcast calling for East Pakistan to become independent from Pakistan. On April 17, leaders of the breakaway East Pakistan openly and more formally declared independence as Bangladesh. After the war that ensued, the West Pakistan army was forced to surrender to the forces of India on December 16, 1971, and this day is observed in Bangladesh as Victory (or National) Day. East Pakistan thus became Bangladesh, although Pakistan did not formally recognize this status until February 22, 1974.

BHUTAN

December 17: National Day. On this date in 1907, the powerful warlord Ugyen Wangchuk declared himself first king of Bhutan. Although technically an independent land for all of its history, Bhutan had in fact long been under the rule of Tibet and then to some degree under China. By the nineteenth century, Great Britain, through its governance of India, had also begun to take control of Bhutan's affairs, and Britain continued to exercise considerable control over Bhutan's affairs even after Wangchuk's declaration. Finally on August 2, 1935, Britain gave Bhutan autonomy from British India's princely states. On August 8, 1949, India began to assume responsibility for Bhutan's foreign affairs, defense, and economy.

BRUNEI

February 23: Independence Day. On this date in 1984, the Sultanate of Brunei formally proclaimed its independence at ceremonies witnessed by some seventy leaders from around the world. Brunei had been a British protectorate since September 17, 1888; Britain began to withdraw from Brunei's internal affairs in 1959, maintaining a role only in defense and foreign affairs. Britain itself had in fact granted Brunei its independence as of January 1, 1984.

CAMBODIA

November 9: Independence Day. On this date in 1953, King Norodom Sihanouk, having returned to the capital from his self-imposed exile, proclaimed full independence from France. On November 8, 1949, France had recognized Cambodia as an independent state but only within the French Union. On July 20, 1954, as part of the Geneva Accords, France formally reiterated Cambodia's independence.

CENTRAL ASIAN REPUBLICS

The five republics observe the dates they declared their independence from the USSR:

Kyrgyzstan (Kirghiz): August 31, 1991
Uzbekistan: August 31, 1991
Tajikistan (Tadzhikistan): September 9, 1991
Turkmenistan: October 27, 1991
Kazakhstan: December 16, 1991

CHINA

October 1–2: National Days. On these dates in 1949, the People's Republic of China was founded by the victorious Communists. Although China had been led by various non-Han Chinese at times across the centuries, it has always been an independent nation. On October 10, 1911, the Chinese revolution began with mutinies of army units. On December 20, 1911, Sun Yat-sen was elected president of the united provinces of China; he took office on January 8, 1912, as president of the provisional Republic of China. China did not become a republic until the last emperor abdicated on February 12, 1912.

HONG KONG

July 1. On this date in 1997, Hong Kong gained its independence from Great Britain under terms of the treaty signed by China and Great Britain on September 26, 1984. On this same day, Hong Kong became a Special Administrative Region of China.

INDIA

August 15: Independence Day. At midnight on August 14–15, 1947, India became an independent nation, although it retained dominion status within the British Commonwealth of Nations.

INDONESIA

August 17: Independence Day. On this date in 1945, as Japan formally surrendered at the end of World War II, Indonesian nationalist leaders unilaterally declared their independence from their former Dutch rulers. The Dutch refused to recognize complete independence until December 27, 1949. West New Guinea became the province of West Irian on August 17, 1969; it changed its name to Irian Jaya on March 3, 1973.

JAPAN

February 11: National Foundation Day; May 3: Constitution Memorial Day. The first of these observes the date in 660 B.C. when, according to Japanese tradition, the first human emperor Jimmu Tenno ascended to the throne. First designated as a national holiday in 1872 when it was called Empire Day, it was abolished after World War II; it was revived with its new name in 1966. The second holiday commemorates the date in 1947 when the constitution of post–World War II Japan was adopted.

KOREA

South Korea

March 1: Independence Day; October 3: National Foundation Day. The first of these observes the date in 1919 when demonstrations broke out in Seoul against the Japanese occupation of Korea. A declaration of independence was read at a public rally, and before the demonstrations ended, an estimated 32,000 Koreans were killed or wounded by the Japanese. Although independence was not gained until August 15, 1945, with the surrender of Japan, this event in 1919 is recognized as inspiring the independent movement (known as *samil-jol*).

The second of these dates observes Tangun Day, the date in 2333 BC when according to legend Tangun Wanggom (Sandalwood King) founded the Korean nation.

North Korea

August 15: Liberation Day; September 9: Independence Day. The first of these observes the date in 1945 when, with the surrender of Japan at the end of World War II, Korea was given its independence. Korea almost immediately became divided between the Russian-dominated north and the American-dominated south.

The second date observes the date in 1948 when the Communists in northern Korea founded the Democratic People's Republic of Korea.

LAOS

July 19: Independence Day; December 2: Republic Day. The first of these observes the date in 1949 that France recognized Laos as a sovereign state. It was on October 12, 1945, in the aftermath of Japan's surrender, that prominent Laotians proclaimed their country's independence; however, the French moved in and reimposed their rule. Even after July 19, 1949, Laos remained within the French Union; on October 22, 1953, France took another step and formally recognized Laos as an independent state but still within the French Union. On July 20, 1954, as a result of the Geneva Accords, France finally gave up all claims to Laos.

The second of these observes the date in 1975 when the current Lao People's Democratic Republic was proclaimed.

MACAU

December 20: Independence Day. On this date in 1999 Macau attained full independence from Portugal and returned to China. Although the Portuguese had had nominal control of Macau since 1557, in fact the Chinese had long dominated political life.

MALAYSIA

August 31: National Day. This observes the date in 1957 when Malaysia—then known as the Federation of Malaya—gained its independence (or *merdeka*) from Great Britain. The Federation of Malaysia was formed on September 16, 1963.

MALDIVES

July 26: Independence Day; November 11: Republic Day. The first observes the date in 1965 when the Maldives were granted independence from Great Britain, which had been in control since 1887. The second observes the date in 1968 when the Maldives became a republic.

MONGOLIA

July 11: Revolution Day. This observes the date in 1921 when Mongolia declared itself an independent state. China and Russia had been competing for control of Mongolia for centuries. In 1911, with the collapse of the Manchu dynasty in China, some Mongolian princes drove the Chinese forces out and asked for Russia's support. Legally, however, Mongolia remained Chinese territory, and the Chinese and Russians continued to fight over it. In July 1921, Mongolia was declared an independent state but a monarchy. On March 13, 1924, under the influence of its Russian-backed Communist leaders, the Mongolian People's Republic was formed. China did not recognize Mongolia's independence until August 14, 1945.

MYANMAR (BURMA)

January 4: Independence Day. This observes the date in 1948 when, breaking with the British Commonwealth, Burma declared itself the independent Union of Burma. On May 27, 1989, it renamed itself Myanmar.

NEPAL

January 11: Unity Day; February 18: National Democracy Day; November 8: Constitution Day. The first observes the occasion in 1768 when a number of hill states were unified under Prithvi Narayan Shah as the Kingdom of Gorkha and separated itself from India and Tibet. The British in fact moved in during the nineteenth century and effectively governed Nepal, but recognized its independence in 1923 with a Treaty of Friendship.

The second observes the date in 1951 when King Tribhuvan was restored to the throne and ended the century-long monopoly of power by the Rana family.

The third observes the date in 1990 when the modern constitution was adopted.

PAKISTAN

August 14: Independence Day. This observes the date in 1947 when at midnight (August 14–15) Pakistan declared itself an independent state. It deliberately observes August 14 in order to establish its independence also from India, which celebrates its independence on August 15. Pakistan was then made up of two separated sections, West Pakistan and East Pakistan; East Pakistan broke away in 1971 and became independent Bangladesh. March 23 is also observed as Pakistan Day in recognition of the day in 1956 when Pakistan adopted its first constitution.

PHILIPPINES REPUBLIC

June 12: Independence Day. This observes the date in 1898 when Emilio Aguinaldo declared the islands independent. At that time, the Philippines were under control of Spain, which was engaged in a war with the United States. After defeating the Spanish, the United States took possession of the Philippines. The Philippines became a commonwealth within the United States on November 15, 1935, but on July 4, 1946, the United States granted full independence. Until 1962, the Philippines observed that as their independence day, but President Diosdado Macapagal changed the date to June 12.

SINGAPORE

August 9: Independence Day. This observes the date in 1965 when Singapore broke away from the Federation of Malaysia and declared itself a fully independent state. Britain had granted Singapore limited self-government on June 2, 1959, but maintained a role in its defense and foreign affairs. Singapore declared itself independent of Britain on August 31, 1963, but on September 16, 1963, it joined the Federation of Malaysia.

SRI LANKA (CEYLON)

February 4: Independence and National Day. This observes the date in 1948 when Ceylon gained its independence from Great Britain (under Britain's Ceylon Independence Act of 1947) Ceylon reverted to its older name, Sri Lanka, on May 22, 1972.

TAIWAN

October 10: National Day (Double Tenth Day). This observes the date (10/10) in 1911 when the revolution began that overthrew the Qing dynasty in China. At that time, Taiwan had been under the control of the Japanese since 1895. Upon the defeat of Japan in August 1945, Taiwan unofficially returned to the possession of China; on October 2, 1945, Taiwan was officially made a part of the Republic of China. (Under the peace treaty signed in San Francisco on September 8, 1951, Japan abandoned any claims to Taiwan and the nearby Pescadores Islands.) On December 8, 1949, the Nationalists (Guomindang), having lost mainland China to the Communists, claimed Taiwan as their territory and soon took over its government. Communist China still claims Taiwan as its legal territory, but to maintain a sense of independence Taiwan observes different national holidays than does the Communist mainland.

THAILAND

April 16: Chakri Day. This observes the date in 1782 when Chaopraya Chakri was enthroned, founded Bangkok as his capital, and established the Chakri dynasty. The dynasty still rules Thailand, although the absolute monarchy ended on June 24, 1932. Although it has occasionally been occupied by other Asians (such as the Japanese in World War II) and its borders have changed over the centuries, Thailand has always been an independent country. (It claims 1238 as the traditional founding date.) On January 15, 1896, reflecting the competition between the two countries throughout Asia, Britain and France signed an accord guaranteeing the independence of Thailand.

TIBET

Tibetans observe many holy days based on the various occasions in the Buddhist calendar, not holidays based on secular events. Although the Tibetans had been ruled by their own Dalai Lama since the 1600s, the land fell under the control of China during the early 1700s. After the Chinese Revolution in 1911, Tibet gained a measure of independence although China continued to claim it as one of its territories. The Chinese Communists invaded Tibet in 1950 and on May 23, 1951, announced signing an agreement under which Tibet surrendered its sovereignty to China while retaining its right to self-government. However, this was followed by such resistance by the Tibetans that in 1965 the Communists made Tibet an autonomous region within China. In practice, however, China completely rules Tibet.

VIETNAM

September 2: Independence Day. This observes the date in 1945 when Ho Chi Minh declared the country's independence from France in the aftermath of World War II. France went to war to reestablish its dominance. On July 1, 1949, France proclaimed the independence of a united Vietnam but only within the French Union. It was July 20, 1954, before France signed the Geneva Accords that granted Vietnam full independence. However, the accords recognized a divided Vietnam at the 17th parallel, with the Communists taking control to the north and the anti-Communists taking control to the south. On October 11, 1954, the Communists took over North Vietnam and renamed it the Democratic Republic of Vietnam. On October 26, 1955, those in control of South Vietnam named it the Republic of Vietnam. After the Communists triumphed in the war they unified Vietnam and on July 26, 1976, named it the Socialist Republic of Vietnam.

Scientific-Technological Achievements in Asia

Beginning in prehistoric times, peoples and individuals who would come to be known as Asians (as defined in this volume) made many original and significant contributions to applying science and technology. Many of these are the first known, or among the first known, in the entire world. This pattern of Asian invention and innovation continued throughout the early millennia of recorded history—roughly 3000 to 1 B.C. By the last centuries of this period, Asians were not just applying science and technology, but they had also begun to articulate original insights and concepts in areas such as mathematics, astronomy, mechanical engineering, and chemistry. For the next thousand years, (c. A.D. 1–1000) Asians continued to make many more important scientific advances and technological inventions; in some instances, they may have drawn on work done by Middle Easterners or Greeks, for by this time contacts between these peoples were increasing. By about the year 1200, in fact, a slowly reviving Europe, drawing at times on the prior knowledge and work of the Asians, began to assert itself in all areas, including science and technology. By about the year 1600, the West had completely usurped Asia's role as the major originator and innovator in these fields. There are many and complex reasons for this, but among them was the fact that Asians tended to be bound to traditional ways so that their early successes ended by becoming confining; also, with the arrival of more aggressive or at least assertive Westerners in their midst, Asians tended to be overwhelmed by the new science and technology (some of which in fact drew on earlier Asian discoveries). In any case, it would be the twentieth century before Asians would once again begin to make crucial contributions in the sciences and technology, but by this time, these fields have become truly international enterprises in their concepts, inventions, institutions, and individual contributors. The chronology that follows, therefore, cuts off with the 1500s.

Note: * = oldest known or among the oldest known in the world

*2,000,000–1,800,000 B.C.: Among the earliest known stone tools are some flaked stones found at Riwat, Pakistan (former date) and some pointed tools found at Xihoudu, Shanxi, northern China (latter date).

*1,800,000 B.C.?: Also at the site of Xihoudu, Shanxi, northern China, is what some claim is the earliest evidence of controlled fire; this claim is not generally accepted.

500,000 B.C.: Inhabitants of caves at Zhoukoudian, China, are using a variety of stone tools; although it has long been claimed that these people also have controlled fire, in 1998 it was revealed that there is no evidence to support this.

350,000 B.C.: The oldest evidence for the use of ocher in Asia comes from Hunsgi, Karnataka, India.

*58,000–43,000 B.C.: Circumstantial evidence of the oldest known use of watercraft in the world comes from the signs of human settlements in Australia (first date) and New Guinea (by latter date) of this time. These people almost certainly set out from the islands of southeast Asia and must have rafts or crude boats.

39,000 B.C.: The oldest known gathering of shellfish (almost certainly for food) in Asia is found at Niah Caves, Borneo. This same site also has the oldest known evidence in Asia for fishing.

34,000 B.C.: Some of the oldest known bone awls in Asia are those found at Shuidonggou, northern China.

33,000–28,000 B.C.: The oldest known stone axes in Asia are being used in parts of Borneo and Japan.

28,000 B.C.: Possibly the oldest known evidence of the grinding of the edges of stone to produce more efficient axes and adzes is at Narita, Japan.

The oldest known remains of a watercraft in Asia are found on Okinawa.

26,000 B.C.: The oldest known stone with a bored hole in Asia is a graphite disk, probably a pendant, found near Shanxi province in northern China.

*24,000 B.C.: A bone needle, the oldest known evidence of sewing, is found at Shiyu, northern China.

22,000 B.C.: Among the oldest signs of fishing in Asia are fish bones found in the Zhoukoudian caves, China.

20,000 B.C.: Among the oldest known examples of the use of plant fiber to make mats or cords or baskets are those found at Leang Burung in Sulawesi, Indonesia. (The only older are found at sites in Australia and Lespugue, France.)

18,000 B.C.: The oldest known evidence from Asia that people are extracting minerals for decorative purposes is some jade from the Arts Bogd area of Mongolia.

*15,000 B.C.: Among the oldest evidence of the keeping of canids—that is, wolf ancestors of dogs—is an isolated find of bones from Sokchangni in South Korea.

The oldest known barbed bone points in Asia are found at Belan Valley, Uttar Pradesh, India.

*12,000 B.C.: Among the oldest known pottery in the world is that found in Japan (at the Fakui Cave) and Liyuzui, Guangxi, China: this means these are the locales of among the oldest known evidence of vessels used for holding liquids. (Still older pottery has been found in eastern Siberia.)

8000 B.C.: The oldest known instance in Asia of keeping ruminants (sheep) is found at Sarai-Nahar Rai, Uttar Pradesh, India.

*7,000 B.C.: Among the oldest known suggestions of deliberate cultivation of plants is that found at Spirit Cave in Thailand (probably beans or other legumes) and at Lake Jih-yueh T'an on Taiwan (probably gourds).

The oldest known cultivated cereal grasses (barley, wheat) in Asia are found at Mehrgarh, Pakistan.

At this same time, the oldest known rectangular dwellings in Asia are found at Mehrgarh, Pakistan.

It is about this time that the water buffalo is being domesticated in southern China and the fowl (chicken) is being domesticated in Southeast Asia.

It is about this time that in parts of Asia kilns are being used for firing ceramics.

The earliest known fish hooks found in Asia are from the site of Natsushima, Honshu, Japan.

Also from Natsushima, Honshu, Japan, is the earliest known evidence in Asia of the making of textiles.

6000 B.C.: The earliest evidence of cultivated cereal grasses in East Asia is the foxtail millet found in northern China, probably domesticated from the green bristlegrass found in the Yellow River valley.

Also by this time it is believed that rice, at least its wild forebears, is being cultivated in central China.

Also from this time comes the earliest evidence of rectangular dwellings in Japan at Sozudai, Kyushu.

5000 B.C.: The earliest known domesticated dogs in South Asia are found at Adamgarh, Madhya Pradesh, India.

*Among the oldest known evidence for the keeping of nonruminant animals are finds from the site of Zengpiyan, Guangxi, in southern China (pigs) and Cishan, Hebei, China (pigs and chickens).

4500 B.C.: The earliest known evidence for the keeping of ruminants in East Asia are bones of small and probably domesticated cattle from sites in northern China.

***4500–4000 B.C.:** Possible period when the blowgun is invented, most likely in Indonesia, probably in Borneo; whenever and wherever, the blowgun appears to be an invention of Southeast Asia.

4000 B.C.: A primitive form of a plow, the ard, is being used in China.

Possibly the oldest known use of metal (copper) in Asia is found at Mehrgarh, Pakistan.

3500 B.C.: The earliest potter's wheel in Asia is found in India. It is also about this time that people in India and China begin to use the wheel for transport.

***c. 2850–2650 B.C.:** The oldest known fragments of silk cloth are found in China and dated to this time.

2600–2000 B.C.: In the Harappan culture of northern India, weights and linear measures are standardized; accurate balances, scales, and measuring instruments are employed throughout the widespread Harappan civilization. Weights are graded cubes of chert employing a binary-cum-decimal system; standard measures are based on the "Indus

inch" of 355 mm and a larger unit of 67.6 cm.

2500 B.C.: Earliest known evidence of bronze in Asia is bronze slag and a cast bronze knife from Linjia, northern China.

2300 B.C.: Chinese are able to predict the equinoxes and solstices.

2255–2208 B.C.: According to Chinese legend, the principles of both herbal medicine and acupuncture are said to be originated at this time by Emperor Shun (but there is no physical evidence for this).

2208–2195 B.C.: Chinese tradition attributes to reign of legendary Emperor Yu a magic square that involves some knowledge of mathematics.

***2200 B.C.:** The Chinese appear to be among the first to show knowledge of how to mill grain.

1800 B.C.: Copper is used at Non Pa Wai, Thailand.

1600 B.C.: Bronze plows are being used in Vietnam.

***1500 B.C.:** By now the Chinese are beginning to breed silkworms in some quantities, although it will be several centuries before silkmaking becomes a major process.

1500 B.C.: The Chinese use horse-drawn vehicles, the first to do so in East Asia.

Chinese texts refer to brewing of beer.

The soybean is being cultivated in Manchuria.

1350 B.C.: Shang oracle bones of this period in China have inscriptions that suggest a decimal place-value numeration system.

12th century B.C.: In India, Lagadha writes *Vedanga Jyotisa* (Vedic Astronomical Auxiliary), astronomical computations for the Vedic ritual calendar. The need for accurate calendars to time Brahamanical rituals propels the development of astronomy into a major Indian science.

1122 B.C.: Legendary date for the first Chinese map of all of China.

***1000 B.C.:** The Chinese are among the first to cut ice and store it for refrigeration purposes.

By this time the outrigger canoe has probably been developed in the islands of Southeast Asia; as people move out to Madagascar and Easter Island, they almost certainly have something more seaworthy than dugout canoes.

1000–200 B.C.: It is during this period that the Chinese develop the technique of acupuncture as a method of physical therapy.

850 B.C.: A Chinese author, Fan-Li, discusses the cultivation of fish.

800–500 B.C.: The *Sulvasutras* (Cord Rules), part of the Hindu texts known as the *Vedas*, although not strictly speaking mathematical texts (they are manuals for preparing sacrificial altars), indicate some awareness of and/or ability to use the zero, positive integers, negative numbers, fractions, and powers of ten. The *Sulvasutras* also reveal knowledge of what is known as the Pythagorean theorem, calculating square roots, and measuring a circle.

8th–3d centuries B.C.: During these centuries the basic texts of the *I Ching* (Book of Changes) are probably collected; important appendices and commentaries are added during the ensuing centuries. The *I Ching* is an elaborate system of symbols based on ancient omens and divination practices; it has a profound effect on the development of Chinese science.

781 B.C.: The first Chinese record of an eclipse.

*600 B.C.: Chinese employ fumigation of houses to rid them of pests. In the centuries that follow, Chinese scholars fumigate libraries to keep down the bookworms.

What will eventually become China's Grand Canal is begun during this century. When largely finished in 1327, it extends almost 1,100 miles from Beijing to Hangzhou (in eastern China).

c. 600 B.C.?: Possibly the time of a somewhat legendary figure in Indian medicine, Susruta. (Others date him anywhere from 1000 B.C. to A.D. 900.) He is said to have taught medicine at Varanasi, India, where he specialized in surgery and operated on cataracts. He is credited with having either composed or edited the *Susrutasamhita*, the oldest and the seminal book on surgery in early India (although the extant written versions date from many centuries later). Amazingly modern in some of the instruments, diagnoses, and procedures it describes, it is also one of the major texts of the Indian school of Ayurvedic medicine. *Ayurveda* means "the science of [living to an old] age" and is the name applied to the traditional science of holistic medicine practiced in India for thousands of years. It is also about this time that a collection of hymns known as the *Atharvaveda* is compiled; most of this text are spells, many of them designed to cure diseases, thereby revealing Indians' belief that illness is caused by evil spirits.

6th century B.C.: The oldest known Chinese text revealing knowledge of fairly advanced mathematics, the *Zhoubi suanjing* (*Chou pei suan ching*) (Arithmetical Classic of the Zhou Dynasty Gnomons) may have been composed during this time, although some of its material is believed to draw on mathematics known as far back as 1105 B.C. (The oldest extant text dates only from A.D. 1213.) Basically a work on the calendar and astronomy, it draws on a knowledge of fractions, extraction of square roots, and geometry, including something akin to the Pythagorean theorem.

513 B.C.: First mention in China of the smelting and casting of iron.

500 B.C.: Iron begins to come into use in China; its use will soon spread throughout Asia.

The Chinese are now making glass beads; it is assumed that they learned of glassmaking from contacts with Mesopotamia, where glass has been made from about 2900 BC.

Humped cattle from India are introduced into the Mediterranean world.

Hindus appear to use plastic surgery.

*Chinese farmers are planting crops in rows, applying manure, and hoeing away weeds, some two thousand years before these practices are widespread in Europe.

500 B.C.–A.D. 500: During this period, a series of medical texts will be compiled in India; taken together, they set forth the basic principles and practices of India's traditional Ayurvedic school of medicine.

4th century B.C.: A Chinese text refers to using smoke in battles and sieges as both a toxic substance and as a smokescreen.

Starting during this century, Chinese astronomers begin to compile star catalogues in considerable and correct detail.

352 B.C.: The first recording of a nova, an explosion of a star. From this point until A.D. 1604, the Chinese will record at least seventy-five novas and supernovas (which they call "guest stars").

325 B.C.: References to sugar cane as used in India begin to appear in writings.

*300 B.C.: The Chinese invent a horse harness that pushes against the chest rather than throat. (By about 100 B.C. the Chinese will refine this to make a collar harness, still the most efficient type of harness.)

*The Chinese invent cast iron and use bellows to make it. About this time, too, Chinese invent a form of the bellows that produces a continuous stream of air.

*A Chinese text has earliest known reference to a lodestone's alignment to the earth's magnetic field; it is not used to find directions but for divination.

*A Chinese text refers to the use of poison gas in battle.

300 B.C.: In a Hindu text, the *Bhagabati Sutra*, a Jain mathematician reveals a sense of infinite and what modern mathematicians know as combinatories.

300–210 B.C.: Various northern Chinese warlords begin to construct what will become the Great Wall. By about 210, Chinese convicts and conscripted laborers have completed a major segment of Great Wall. When completed (1644) it will extend some 1,500 miles.

3d century B.C.: A Chinese treatise on the calendar, *Master Lu's Spring and Autumn Annals*, describes years in terms of twelve lunar months.

At least by this century, the Chinese have devised a technique for cupellating, or refining, silver from lead.

Two of China's legendary physicians are said to have been flourishing during this century: Chang Chung-kung, famous for his treatise on fevers, and Hua-tu, famous as a surgeon said to have employed anesthesia.

At least by this time, the Chinese have been setting up hospitals for the ill.

c. 269–233 B.C.: In India, the symbols for first nine numbers of the Brahmi system are appearing in decrees of King Ashoka. These digits will become basis of modern Western numerals, evolving first in India, then being picked up by Muslims (probably in the eighth century A.D.), appearing in Spain (due to Arabs) in the ninth century and then in Italy and Western Europe by the fifteenth century.

270 B.C.: Some interpret the *Yavanajataka*, an Indian work on astrology, as the oldest extant Indian work with the decimal place-value system with a symbol (a dot) for zero.

*2d century B.C.: A Chinese medical text of this time, the *Su Wen*, indicates an awareness that blood circulates through the blood vessels. Other ancient Chinese texts during the next few centuries also refer to this phenomenon, which will not be recognized in the West until described by William Harvey in 1628.

Also by this time the Chinese have a clear awareness of the movement of the tides and their link to the moon.

*140 B.C.: Chinese may have invented paper by this time, although they do not use it to write on.

*100 B.C.: The Chinese invent the crank handle for turning wheels.

100 B.C.–A.D. 100: The oldest extant Chinese text with systematic mathematical knowledge, and possibly the oldest such extant in the world, the *Sunzi Suanjing* (*Sun tsu suan* *ching*) (Master Sun's Mathematical Manual) is probably composed during this time, although some of its material is undoubtedly centuries older. It shows some knowledge of number theory and the problem of divisibility.

*1st century B.C.: A set of Chinese counting rods from this period is the oldest known computing device (although they are mentioned in Chinese documents of the second century B.C.). It is certain that for many centuries the Chinese have been using such rods on counting boards to perform various calculations and operations; small (four-inch) bamboo rods are manipulated in various rows and columns. Such counting boards probably influenced the early development of the decimal place-value system.

Some Chinese recognize that fossils are the remains of ancient living creatures.

*90 B.C.: Ssuma Ch'ien's *Historical Records* has the first known reference to a parachute.

*c. A.D. 1: The Chinese invent methods for drilling deep wells to obtain salt water and natural gas.

*The Chinese build suspension bridges of cast iron.

*A Chinese text indicates that the Chinese have invented the belt drive.

*The oldest known depiction of a ship's rudder is made in China.

By this time the *Ayurveda*, the basic Hindu text that draws on centuries of traditional medicine, has been set down.

1st century A.D.: The *Jiuzhang suanshu* (*Chiu chang suan shu*) (Computational Prescriptions in Nine Chapters), a classic Chinese mathematical text, was probably compiled during this time although it undoubtedly draws on older works. A collection of 246 word problems, it draws on a knowledge of the Pythagorean theorem and triples, linear and quadratic equations, calculating volume of a pyramid, extracting square and cube roots, and fractions; it also shows an awareness of negative numbers. By the ninth century this will be one of several

Chinese works imported into Japan, where it will influence that country's mathematics.

*Chinese artisans have a sliding caliper with decimal graduations to measure their work.

1st–2d centuries: King Kanishka's court physician Caraka revises ancient Vedic medical texts, which then become known as the *Caraka Samhita*, the oldest classical Ayurvedic medical text still in present-day use.

1st–4th centuries: Chinese alchemists, working within a centuries-old Daoist tradition, seek not to make gold but to identify the materials and methods that will prolong human life. Among the best known of these are Li Shao-Chun, Ko Hung, and Sun Szu-Mo.

*30: Chinese invent a water-powered bellows to use in making cast iron.

78–139: Lifespan of Zhang Heng, a notable Chinese inventor. He invents a type of seismograph to indicate the direction of an earthquake; he combines a water clock with an armillary to make a device that can track the position of stars; he develops a method of using a grid to locate points on a map. He also notes the nonuniformity of the sun's motion.

80: A Chinese text describes a spoon made from a magnetic iron that always aligns north-south; it is used for divination. (This may date to as early as the second century B.C. The magnetic properties of lodestone, or magnetite, have been known to various ancient peoples at least since 500 B.C.)

A Chinese text describes a chain pump that raises water from lakes or rivers.

90: Chinese invent a device to winnow grain by using a rotating fan to separate wheat from the chaff.

*100: Chinese discover advantages of hitching one horse in front of another.

*Chinese discover the oldest known insecticide: dried powdered chrysanthemum, which contains pyrethrum.

2d–4th centuries: During this time Hindu scientists compile treatises on astronomy known as *Siddhantas* (systems). From the late fourth century, *Surya Siddhanta* (System of the Sun) survives intact. Another of the same period is *Paulisha Siddhanta* (Pauline System).

2d–6th centuries: Some Chinese show awareness that mountains have been elevated from land that was once below the sea.

*c. 180: Ting Huan, Chinese inventor and mechanic, invents a system of suspending an object by linked and pivoted rings to hold it horizontal. In the 1600s Girolamo Cardano will "invent" such a device, which the West will call "Cardan's suspension."

*c. 190: *Shu Shu Chi I*, Chinese text describing a "ball arithmetic" device, may be oldest account of an abacus. (See entry for A.D. *c.* 570.)

200: The Chinese are developing porcelain.

*The Chinese invent the whippletree, the bar that allows two oxen to pull a single cart.

By now the Chinese have improved the ways to manufacture rag paper, and they will begin to use it more widely in the century that follows.

3d century: Liu Hui is a major mathematician of this century. His major work is a commentary on the *Jiuzhang suanshu*, but he composes his own, *Haidao suanjing* (Sea Island Mathematical Manual), which deals with surveying problems. In his commentary, Liu Hui refines the value of π to 3.141024.

229–271: Lifespan of Pei Hsiu, noted Chinese cartographer and geographer.

c. 270: Chinese may have invented a magnetic compass to locate south. (Up to now magnetic lodestones have been used for divination or magical demonstrations.)

300: The Chinese begin to use coal instead of wood as fuel to make cast iron.

Chinese may be using the abacus, although the first solid reference is not until *c.* 570.

4th century: At least by this time, the Chinese have invented a still with which to distill and then condense materials.

At least by this time the Chinese have quarantine regulations for certain diseases.

c. 340: A Chinese text describes the use of ants that are hung in orange groves to keep down insect pests.

c. 350–400: The *Surya Siddhanta*, an Indian work on astronomy, now uses sexagesimal fractions. It includes references to trigonometric functions. The work is revised during succeeding centuries, taking its final form in the tenth century. It forms the foundation of medieval Indian astronomy and is the basis for the calendar developed in Nepal.

c. 400: The Chinese begin to make a type of steel by combining cast iron and wrought iron.

*The Chinese invent the umbrella.

Early 5th century: Another early Indian work containing trigonometry, the *Paitamahasiddhanta*, deals with astronomical problems.

429–500: Lifespan of Zu Chongzhi, who writes the (lost) Chinese text, *Zhuishu*; it was said to have contained a derivation of the approximation of π as 3.1415926, the most accurate until Islamic mathematicians work it out.

Late 5th–early 6th centuries: Lifespan of Aryabhata the Elder, an Indian who writes an astronomy text known as the *Aryabhatiya*, the oldest datable Indian work by an identifiable author that contains mathematics. (His text is lost to sight until 1864 but known through many commentaries.) He shows an ability to use geometry, trigonometry, and some algebra; his work shows a knowledge of quadratic equations and indeterminate linear equations; he also arrives at a close value for π, 3.1416. His astronomical discoveries include the earth's rotation on its axis and the length of the solar year. His work inspires Indian astronomy and mathematics for the next five hundred years.

6th century: The Chinese establish leper colonies.

Famous Chinese mathematicians of this century include Chon Luan, Chang Kiukien, and Hsia-hou yang.

*500: Possibly the Chinese or Koreans have invented the stirrup by this time.

c. 505–587?: Possible lifespan of Hindu mathematician and astronomer Varahamihira. He is the author of the *Pancasiddhantika*, a compendium of astronomical systems; he uses zero as a number. Hindu mathematics of this period also recognizes irrational and negative numbers.

530: Chinese invent a water-powered machine that can produce a back-and-forth shaking motion that can be used to sift flour.

550: Emperor Yuan's *Book of the Golden Hall Master* describes land vehicles driven by wind in their sails.

c. **550:** Indian mathematician and astronomer Varahamihira recognizes zero. Sixth-century Indian mathematics also recognizes irrational and negative numbers. Mathematics flourishes under the Guptas.

c. **570:** Commentary by Chen Luan on *Shu Shu Chi I* (see A.D. 190) may in fact be the first account of an abacus. In any case, device has been used in China for many centuries.

c. **575:** An inscription in Gujarat, India, is the earliest recorded appearance of the mathematical notational system of nine digits and a sign (dot) for zero to indicate place value.

*577: The Chinese are said to have invented some type of match.

589–618: The Great Wall of China is extended.

598–?: Lifespan of Brahmagupta (also known as Bhillamalacarya), the noted Hindu mathematician and astronomer. At age thirty he composed his major work, the *Brahmasphutasiddhanta* (Corrected Brahma System). Most of the book is on astronomy, but he devotes two chapters to mathematics; he uses fractions, progressions, and algebra. He writes about the special properties of zero, indeterminate equations, and negative numbers.

c. **600:** Bhaskara I, a prominent Indian mathematician, is active at this time.

Also probably dating from about this time is the Bakhshali Manuscript, the oldest extant Sanskrit mathematical manuscript.

601: Indian physicians compile the *Vaghbata*, a medical text.

608–615: A major section of China's Grand Canal is completed during the reign of Emperor Yangdi.

610: The first segmental-arch bridge is built by Li Chun in China.

615: Japanese use "burning water," apparently petroleum.

618–907: During the Tang dynasty, China codifies its mathematics in the *Tang liudian*, an educational program designed to train professional mathematicians. It will become the model for Korean and Japanese mathematics in centuries to come.

*620: The first authenticated Chinese porcelain is produced.

c. **650:** Chinese use lampblack ink to take rubbings; will eventually lead to wood-block printing.

*650–950: During the Tang dynasty, the Chinese probably discover the declination of magnetic needle—that is, that magnetic north and south do not always coincide with geographic north and south.

659: An imperial decree commissions the first great Chinese pharmacopoeia, *Hsin Hsiu Pen Ts'ao* by Su Jing.

670–936: During the Silla period in Korea, the study of mathematics is encouraged to fulfill administrative needs. There is an official curriculum and mathematics is incorporated into codes of laws and ethics. This tradition will survive through Korea's subsequent history.

*682–727: Lifespan of I-Hsing (Yi Xing), a Tantric Buddhist monk, mathematician, and astronomer. Early in the eighth century he and Lyang Lingdzan, an engineer, invent a hydromechanical clock that includes a water-wheel linkwork escapement. I-hsing also devises a more accurate calendar.

683: The earliest dated inscriptions outside India using the decimal place-value system including zero are made in Cambodia. (They use the Indian system.) The same system will be adopted in China sometime thereafter and will appear in a Chinese astronomical work of 718.

c. **700:** About this time the Koreans and Japanese adopt counting rods and counting boards from the Chinese.

8th century: Chinese (as well as some in the Islamic world) are experimenting with the camera obscura; it has probably been known in China for a thousand years.

701: Emperor Monbu of Japan establishes a university system; its mathematical curriculum adopts ten Chinese classic treatises.

704–750: The oldest wood-block printing known is an example from Korea, but it is probable that Chinese use woodblocks for printing by this time.

718: China's Tang dynasty brings in Indian scholars; led by Chutan Hsita, they prepare an astronomical work, *Chiu-chih li* (Nine Planets), based on Indian sources.

c. 723: Under the guidance of I-Hsing, the Chinese conduct a geodetic survey to calculate the meridian arc along terrain of some 1,700 miles from the borders of Indochina to Mongolia. This would almost certainly be the most ambitious such scientific expedition up to this time.

748: The first printed newspaper appears in Beijing, China.

751: Chinese papermakers captured at Samarkand enable its manufacture to spread throughout the Arab world in the next fifty years.

c. 773: An Indian scholar visiting the court of al-Mansur in Baghdad brings a copy of Brahmagupta's *Brahmasphutasiddhanta* and thereby introduces the Hindu decimal system; the Arabs translate this (by about 820) and then quickly spread it throughout the Islamic world.

c. 775: Chinese are using block-printing. Pictorial block-printing used in Japan.

c. 780–850: Lifespan of Muhammad Ibn Musa al-Khwarizmi, probably from the area now part of Uzbekistan and Turkmenistan, composes one of the earliest Islamic algebra texts, *Al-kitab al-muhtasar fi hisab al-jabr wal-muqabala.* (In fact, the *al-jabr* in his title becomes the word algebra in the West.) In addition to his significant works on mathe-

matics, he writes an important work on geography in which he develops a map of the Islamic world. he probably also wrote *Art of Hindu Reckoning*, which when translated into Latin introduced Hindu numerals into Europe, which then became known as "Arabic numerals."

810–900: About 810, the Chinese government issues paper bank drafts (ancestor of paper money). By c. 900 paper money is being used in Sichuan province, China.

c. 825: A Chinese text refers to mixing charcoal, sulfur, and potassium nitrate (saltpeter); this produces a primitive form of gunpowder, but the Chinese at first use it only for ceremonies.

c. 850: Period of activity of Mahavira, the Hindu mathematician; his major work, the *Ganitasarasangraha*, shows a clear ability to make use of the zero, square and cube roots, fractions, and quadratic equations.

*868: Chinese print the earliest known complete book, *The Diamond Sutra*, an Indian text.

Arabs perfect the astrolabe.

900–1200: Chinese develop more advanced techniques for making iron and steel.

*919: A Chinese text refers to the use of a form of gunpowder to ignite a flamethrower.

940: Chinese astronomer Qian Lo-Zhih, draws up a detailed star map based on what the West will later call the Mercator projection.

945–1003: Lifespan of Gerbert d'Aurillac, who will become Pope Sylvester II in 999; as a young man he evidently was introduced to Muslim mathematics while studying in Spain. He will establish a school of mathematics and his own work has the first appearance in the Christian West of Hindu-Arabic numerals.

c. 950: The Chinese invent the fire-lance (*huo chiang*), a device in which a rocket composition is enclosed in a bamboo tube and then fired in close combat.

960–1279: During the Song dynasties, true porcelain pottery is made in China. The

Chinese also improve a stoneware with a pale green glaze (celadon).

976: Chinese invent a chain drive for a mechanical clock.

980: Chinese invent a lock canal.

A Chinese text of this time refers to steam-washing the clothes of people suffering from certain diseases so that others in the family will not be infected.

11th century: The *Kalacakratantra*, a traditional Indian Buddhist text, is set down about this time; it will have a major effect on Tibetan astronomy.

1006: The Chinese emperor establishes granaries for emergency famine relief.

c. 1010: Chinese are drilling wells by using heavy pointed weights at the end of ropes.

1035: A Chinese painting depicts a spinning wheel.

c. 1041–1048: The Chinese Pi Cheng, a commoner about whom nothing else is known, is evidently the first to employ printing from movable type (he uses clay blocks). The Chinese begin to print some books with movable type soon afterward. (Pi Cheng's work is first described by Shen Kuo in 1080.)

*1044: The first formula or recipe for true gunpowder is published in the Chinese text, *Wu Ching Tsung Yao*. It will be 1285 at the earliest before the West appears to know about gunpowder.

1068: Wang Anshi, prime minister of Chinese emperor Shenzong, nationalizes agricultural production and distribution.

1080: The Chinese text, *Meng Chi Pi Than*, by Shen Kuo, is the first known text clearly to describe the magnetic needle compass and movable type. This is a century before the first written reference in Europe to such a compass.

1083: Chinese print mathematical books.

1094: The *Hsin I Hsiang Fa Yao* by Su Sung Jung describes the erection (in 1088) in Beijing of a forty-foot-high tower with elaborate machinery that, powered by a water wheel, operates an orrery, armillary, and a clock with an escapement.(He credits the mech-

anism to the eighth-century Chinese monk-engineer Lyang Lingdzan.) Although used for astronomical devices, not to tell time, this would be the first escapement mechanism known; the first in Europe dates from the 1300s.

c. 1100: By this time, some Chinese judges are said to be using magnifying lenses of rock crystal to decipher illegible documents and dark eyeglasses to hide their reactions from litigants.

1102: The *Ying Tsao Fa Shih*, a classic work on Chinese architecture, appears.

1107: Chinese invent multicolor printing, primarily for making money.

1110–1150: The Chinese are employing the fire-lance (*huo chiang*) in battles.

1114–1185: Lifespan of Bhaskara II, the noted Indian astronomer and mathematician. His major work is the *Siddhantasiromani*, a four part-work; the last two parts deal with astronomy, but the first, the *Lilavati*, and the second, the *Bijaganita*, deal with geometry and algebra.

*1119: The first printed reference to the use of a magnetic compass for navigation appears in Chu Yu's *P'ingcho Table Talk*; it is assumed that the Chinese have been using it for some time before this.

1161: Chinese may have used bombs that produce shrapnel in battle. Certainly by 1230 the Chinese are using explosive devices in warfare.

1190: The oldest known depiction of a fishing reel in China.

1232: Chinese use kites to send messages behind enemy lines during siege by Mongols.

1234: This is the date traditionally claimed for using movable metal (bronze) type to print the *Kogum Sangjong Yemun* on an island off the coast of Korea. The first extant book using movable metal type, however, dates only to the early fifteenth century.

1247: Qin Jiushao (*c.* 1202–1261) publishes *Shushu jiuzhang*, which includes among other innovations a method for solving systems of linear congruences and systems for solving polynomial equations.

1261: Yang Hui writes *Methods of Computation*, in which appears what the West will eventually know as "Pascal's triangle." He also shows innovative way of solving equations.

*c. 1270: Guo Shou Zhing (1231–1316) invents an instrument with an equatorial mounting that allows an astronomer to view the motion of celestial bodies while moving the viewing instrument in only one direction—a device not invented in the West for another three centuries.

1275–1292: Marco Polo serves under Khubilai Khan. His account of his travels to China and his time there will describe many of China's technological developments. (However, it is not true that he reports that the Chinese have eyeglasses to improve vision.)

1279–1368: During the Yuan dynasty in China, the *Yu Du* (Great Atlas) is produced by Zhu Si Ben. An astronomical observatory is also established in Beijing.

*c. 1280: Metal-barrel firearms, small cannons, are probably being used by the Chinese. By this time, too, the Chinese are almost certainly using rocket arrows—arrows launched by the recoil effect of the explosion of gunpowder in the fire-lance. It is believed that it was about this time that Europeans first learned of gunpowder and its application in weapons.

*1281: The Yuan government adopts the calendar of astronomer Guo Shou Zhing, the world's most accurate at this time. Guo determines that 365.2425 days make up a year.

*1288: Chinese use small cannons to propel shells.

*1297: First authentic record of Chinese using a magnetic marine compass.

1299: A Chinese text, Zhu Shijie's *Suanxue qimeng* (Introduction to Mathematical Studies), will eventually be translated into Korean and then be introduced into Japan in the 1590s. There it becomes one of the basic texts of traditional Japanese mathematical

knowledge known as *wasan* (Japanese arithmetic).

14th century: This is the century of two of the most influential Tibetan astronomers: Buston Rin-chen grub (1290–1344) and Rangbyung rdo-rje (1284–1339). They use a certain amount of mathematics as a basis for their astronomical calculations.

c. 1313: Wang Zhen (fl. 1290–1333) develops new printing techniques and makes sixty thousand Chinese characters out of hardwood; these become the first practical movable wooden type and he uses them to print a treatise on agriculture, the *Nung Shu*.

c. 1340–1425: Lifespan of Madhava of Sangamagrama, Indian astronomer, mathematician, and founder of Kerala school Indian mathematics. His best known work is the *Venvaroha*, a handbook for calculating lunar positions; some of his calculations involve infinite series, unknown in Europe until the seventeenth century.

15th century: Although it will not be until the end of the century that reliable Chinese books refer to eyeglasses, other testimony makes it quite clear that the Chinese have eyeglasses at least by the first decades of this century. (Eyeglasses were known and used in Italy at least by 1300; it is possible that the Chinese learned of them through Mongol intermediaries.)

1405–1433: A Muslim Chinese sea captain, Zheng He, conducts seven officially sponsored sea expeditions that take him to Southeast Asia, India, Africa, and eventually all the way to Mecca. This is one of the few occasions where the Chinese reach out and show interest in the outside world.

1418–1450: Korea's King Sejong establishes a Bureau of Mathematics and an Agency for Calendars. He reforms the educational system so that the sons of nobility study mathematics and sends Korean scholars to China to learn more advanced mathematics. He is credited with establishing the Korean musical scale.

*1436: The earliest illustration of a modern abacus appears in a Chinese text, *Hsin Pien*

Tui Hsiang Ssu Yen. This book is also famous as the oldest illustrated children's primer in any langauage.

1440s: Ulugh-Beg, Turkmeni prince and grandson of Tamerlane, builds an astronomical observatory at Samarkand with an astrolabe allowing fairly precise observations of stars and planets.

1490s: Chinese apparently invent the modern type of toothbrush, with pig bristles at right angle to the handle.

Late 1400s: The first books printed with movable metal type (usually bronze) are appearing in China and Korea.

c. 1505: Wan Hu, a Chinese scientist, is said to have tied gunpowder rockets to a chair in attempt to build a "flying machine"; his device explodes in a test and Wan Hu is killed.

*1585: Zhu Zai-Yu of China works out an "equal temperament scale" based on sound vibrations; it is possible that his work influences the Western scale.

1596: In Korea, Admiral Yi Sunsin (Visunsin) develops the first ironclad ship.

1515–1596: Lifespan of Li Shi-Zhen, China's great botanical writer. About 1583 he compiles a vast pharmacopoeia *Ben Zao Gang Mu,* which contains descriptions of one thousand plants and eight thousand prescriptions.

APPENDIX 3

Asian History: A Chronological Overview

HISTORY	ARTS, CULTURE, THOUGHT, AND RELIGION
Paleolithic–Neolithic: 2,000,000–3000 B.C.	*Paleolithic–Neolithic: 2,000,000–3000 B.C.*
2,000,000–600,000 B.C.: Two million years ago the first hominids appear in a few parts of continental Asia, including today's Pakistan and China; probably descendants of the hominids that first appeared in Africa, their scientific name is *Homo erectus*. Possibly by 1.8 million and certainly by 1.2 million years ago, some make their way across the large land mass known as the Sunda Shelf that links the mainland of Malaysia to the islands of Southeast Asia, including Java and Sumatra.	**2,000,000–600,000 B.C.:** Nothing remains from this period to suggest the presence of arts or intellectual culture.
600,000–100,000 B.C.: Hominids (probably the same *Homo erectus* species) continue to inhabit parts of continental Asia and its attached islands. The best-known site is at the Zhoukoudian Caves, thirty miles southwest of Beijing (600,000–210,000 B.C.). By about 260,000 B.C., archaic *Homo sapiens* appears at sites in China and then elsewhere in Asia.	**600,000–100,000 B.C.:** No signs of cultural artifacts other than tools. Care may be given to injured/sick and to disposal of the dead. Speech probably begins to emerge during this period.
100,000–35,000 B.C.: Fossil finds from northeast-central Java appear to be *Homo erectus*, but some may be *Homo sapiens*. As with earlier hominids, scholars disagree whether they are direct descendants of immigrants from Africa or whether they evolved independently in Asia. In various parts of the Indian subcontinent and on Sri Lanka, stone tools and other signs testify to the presence of human beings. In central Asia, the first settlements appear between 70,000 and 55,000 B.C. Some experts believe that people migrating from the Mongolian region and Lake Baikal in southern Siberia move across to Japan *c.* 65,000 B.C.	**100,000–35,000 B.C.:** Some signs of careful burials, suggesting a belief in the afterlife.

SCIENCE-TECHNOLOGY, ECONOMICS, AND EVERYDAY LIFE	THE WORLD

Paleolithic–Neolithic: 2,000,000–3000 B.C.

Paleolithic–Neolithic: 2,000,000–3000 B.C.

2,000,000–600,000 B.C.: Some early hominids in Asia make flaked stone tools or pointed tools, but most make crude stone chopping tools. They do little more than gather and scavenge food for survival.

2,000,000–600,000 B.C.: The first known hominids in Europe appear near the end of this period, probably *Homo erectus* (upright man) descended from African hominids.

600,000–100,000 B.C.: Hominids in Asia are still making basic stone tools, but with some regional and temporal variants. They hunt small animals with wooden spears. By the end of this period, some hominids are controlling fires in hearths.

600,000–100,000 B.C.: Hominids inhabit parts of Europe; eventually they combine features of both *Homo erectus* and archaic *Homo sapiens* who also probably wandered up from Africa. By *c.* 200,000 B.C. these have evolved into Neanderthals, a relation (but not ancestor) of modern *Homo sapiens*. They make a variety of stone tools and live in caves or huts of branches; they make fires, gather food, hunt, and fish. Most authorities agree that no hominids of any kind yet live in the Western Hemisphere.

100,000–35,000 B.C.: Archaic *Homo sapiens* in Asia are making more specialized stone tools.

100,000–35,000 B.C.: Modern humans (*Homo sapiens sapiens*) appear in Europe, most likely having wandered up from Africa. By the end of this period they have either wiped out or absorbed Neanderthals. Some archaeologists claim that finds in North America date to 100,000 B.C.; if so, these would probably be archaic *Homo sapiens*, not ancestors of later Indians.

HISTORY

Paleolithic–Neolithic: 2,000,000–3000 B.C.

35,000–12,000 B.C.: By this time, modern *Homo sapiens* is clearly settling throughout much of Asia—including Korea, Japan, Indonesia, Sri Lanka, the Philippines—possibly having evolved from the local archaic *Homo sapiens* but more likely having emigrated from Africa across central Asia. Beginning *c.* 30,000 B.C., apparently several groups of people from northeastern and central Asia have moved through Korea and across the land bridge that connects the continent to Japan and Okinawa; by 16,000 B.C., the rising sea level has isolated the islands of Japan (including Okinawa) and stranded the people there.

16,000–3000 B.C.: The Hoabinhian culture—taking its name from the first site where its tool assemblage was first discovered, Hoa Binh, in northern Vietnam—spreads across much of Indonesia and Malaysia, west through parts of Thailand to Burma, and north into southern China.

10,000–3000 B.C.: The first Taiwanese may come from the Chinese mainland opposite or from the Malay Peninsula or Indonesia, but little definite is known about them or how they got there.

ARTS, CULTURE, THOUGHT, AND RELIGION

Paleolithic–Neolithic: 2,000,000–3000 B.C.

35,000–12,000 B.C.: People may exercise aesthetic decisions in making artifacts, but these artifacts are made of degradable materials such as wood or fiber.

20,000 B.C.: Figurines found in Japan and Korea are the oldest known figurines made in Asia. Those from Korea suggest the people had some animistic faith.

17,000 B.C.: Rock engravings found at Sokchangni, Korea, are the oldest known in East Asia.

11,000–10,000 B.C.: Earliest pottery fragments found in Japan. By *c.* 10,500 B.C. the Jomon culture of Japan, with its distinctive cord pottery, begins to emerge.

10,000–3000 B.C.: The Padah-lin Caves, in central Myanmar, are the site of fine paintings made in red ocher on the rock walls, similar to cave paintings known from Upper Paleolithic caves in Europe.

10,000–3000 B.C.: Some of the people of the Hoabinhian culture, which is spreading across much of Southeast Asia, practice flexed burials, with the corpses sometimes dusted with red ocher.

SCIENCE-TECHNOLOGY, ECONOMICS, AND EVERYDAY LIFE

Paleolithic–Neolithic: 2,000,000–3000 B.C.

35,000–12,000 B.C.: Modern *Homo sapiens* are now widespread throughout Asia and making even more versatile and sophisticated stone tools.

25,000–21,000 B.C.: People in Japan are making pebble tools and large flake tools, including axlike tools with edge grinding (signs of repair) and knifelike tools of obsidian (volcanic glass). Dwelling sites, often on natural terraces near streams, yield remains of hearths, post holes, storage pits, and crude circles of small stone, possibly used to secure temporary animal-skin shelters.

16,000–3000 B.C.: The Hoabinhian culture—named from the first site where its tool assemblage was first discovered, Hoa Binh, in northern Vietnam—spreads across much of Southeast Asia, into southern China, and possibly to Taiwan (by 10,000 B.C.). The Hoabinhians forage and hunt for most of their food but may take some trouble to encourage native plants. The people also use many wooden and bamboo tools, including the blowgun, and they make fish traps and baskets. Large shell middens (refuse heaps) on Sumatra suggest some people also maintain a coastal culture.

12,000–3,000 B.C.: During this period, most people in Asia continue to obtain nourishment by hunting, fishing, and food gathering. They still depend on a fairly specialized stone toolkit, but also make weapons, implements, and gear of all kinds from wood and fiber. By the middle of the period, in several parts of Asia *Homo sapiens* begins to develop the Neolithic culture: polished and specialized stone tools, pottery, weaving, cultivated crops, domesticated animals (dogs, pigs, sheep, cattle), and simple settlements.

THE WORLD

Paleolithic–Neolithic: 2,000,000–3000 B.C.

35,000–12,000 B.C.: Modern *Homo sapiens* quickly takes over across much of Europe and develops Upper Paleolithic culture with a variety of tools and weapons, carved figurines, artful cave paintings, and hints of magical-ceremonial life. Possibly by 35,000 B.C., and certainly by 12,000 B.C., modern human beings are moving from northeast Asia across a land bridge at the Bering Strait into the Americas; most are related to the Mongoloid peoples of East Asia and northeastern Siberia, but some may be of Caucasian stock.

13,000 B.C.: Gradual environmental warming trend begins. At end of Paleolithic era, excavated sites indicate that nomadic bands are beginning to settle in hunting camps. Burial sites with grave offerings, skilled stone toolmaking technologies, and far-reaching trade networks suggest high population density, relative complexity of social organization, and cultural exchanges between Europe and the Middle East and Asia.

12,000–3000 B.C.: Peoples across Europe develop a diverse Mesolithic culture (varied materials, simple boats, new food sources). About 7500 B.C. various Europeans are developing a Neolithic culture based on cultivated crops, domesticated animals, and pottery. At least two more major waves of migrants from Asia move into and throughout the Americas. By at least 5000 B.C. some peoples in Mexico, Peru, and the southwestern United States begin to cultivate plants (among them squash, maize, and beans) and to domesticate a few animals (such as fowls, guinea pigs, and llamas). This encourages permanent settlements and more complex societies. By 3400 B.C. the foundations of advanced civilizations are being laid in Mesopotamia and Egypt.

HISTORY

Paleolithic–Neolithic: 2,000,000–3000 B.C.

7000–3500 B.C.: At Mehrgarh (now in west-central Pakistan), people develop the earliest agricultural and pastoral community known in South Asia.

5000–3000 B.C.: Evidence from an archaeological site north of Ashgabat in Turkmenistan indicates that the Neolithic Jeitun civilization is one of the first cultures in Central Asia to make use of agriculture.

4500–3000 B.C.: Throughout Asia, peoples with varying external physical characteristics are developing distinctive cultures that will provide the foundations for the societies of ensuing millennia.

ARTS, CULTURE, THOUGHT, AND RELIGION

Paleolithic–Neolithic: 2,000,000–3000 B.C.

7000–3500 B.C.: At Mehrgarh, in west-central Pakistan, people at first make baskets for containers; by *c.* 5500 B.C. they are making crude pottery, some with painted designs, as well as terracotta figurines. Next to their houses they bury their dead with elaborate beaded ornaments.

6000–5000 B.C.: Neolithic peoples in Korea make a simple pottery that is either completely undecorated or adorned with short strips of clay affixed to the vessel's body. Pottery of this type is also found in Manchuria and Japan.

5000–2000 B.C.: In China, the Yangshao culture (5000–3000 B.C.) and Lungshan culture (4000–2000 B.C.) make distinctive pottery.

4500–2500 B.C.: Some inhabitants of Macau possess a painted pottery of a type familiar from Hong Kong during this time (where it is known as the Chung Hom Wan type). In the later phase, incised pottery of the type found in Hong Kong and known as the Sham Wan phase of the Middle Neolithic is also found in Macau.

3500–2600 B.C.: Craftsmen at Mehrgarh are making painted pottery with the potter's wheel and high-temperature kilns. Regional variations in cultures are emerging throughout Asia, as indicated by various painted designs on pottery and different types of clay figurines.

SCIENCE-TECHNOLOGY, ECONOMICS, AND EVERYDAY LIFE	THE WORLD

Paleolithic–Neolithic: 2,000,000–3000 B.C.

Paleolithic–Neolithic: 2,000,000–3000 B.C.

7000–3500 B.C.: At Mehrgarh (now in west-central Pakistan), people make mud-brick houses with storage areas. At least by about 5000 B.C. they cultivate barley and wheat and make small stone querns to grind grains; they also shift from hunting wild game to raising sheep, goats, and humped zebu, a species of cattle. Possibly the oldest known use of metal—copper—in Asia is also found at Mehrgarh c. 4000 B.C. By 3500 B.C. the potter's wheel is introduced in India and specialized crafts appear in many places. People in India and China use the wheel for transport.

6000 B.C.: Dry rice cultivation may have begun in China.

5000–3000 B.C.: Chinese sites show signs of keeping nonruminant animals such as pigs and chickens. From northern China comes the oldest known evidence in East Asia for possibly domesticated ruminants, namely the bones of small cattle.

4500–2500 B.C.: Southern Mongoloid people make their way to Taiwan in canoes or small boats. They carry over the Neolithic culture that has been developing on the mainland. Although mainly relying on hunting, fishing, and gathering available wild foods, they may also engage in some agriculture, for by this time many Chinese are cultivating millet and rice.

3000 B.C.: There is now a recognizable difference between the food sources of northern (millet) and southern (rice) China. People in Thailand are cultivating dry rice and legumes.

HISTORY

Ancient Times: 3000 B.C.–A.D. 499

3000–1500 B.C.: Some Austronesian people on Taiwan begin to move outward, first to the Philippines and eastern Indonesia; by 1500 B.C. Austronesians are moving on to western Indonesia and Malaysia and eastward to the Micronesian islands of the Pacific.

3000–1700 B.C.: In the Indus Valley of northwest India, one of the most advanced societies of the ancient world emerges, with ambitious cities at Harappa and Mohenjo-Daro; this so-called Harappan culture declines by about 1700 B.C.

1750–1040 B.C.: In China, the Bronze Age Shang is the first of China's historic dynasties. Political structures take root and society stratifies into a peasantry and an aristocracy of landowners and warriors.

1700–1000 B.C.: Nomads from the Eurasian steppes, speaking Indo-European languages and traditionally called "Aryans," move down across the northern Indian subcontinent; their military superiority enables the Indo-Europeans to impose their culture, diet, and beliefs.

ARTS, CULTURE, THOUGHT, AND RELIGION

Ancient Times: 3000 B.C.–A.D. 499

3000–2600 B.C.: People of the Harappan culture of the Indus Valley make seals with geometric symbols; they probably press them on soft clay to declare ownership or for decoration. Potters also mark their wares with symbols.

2600–2000 B.C.: Harappan culture inscriptions on seals, pottery, and household goods employ the earliest form of distinctive Indus script. Religion pervades Harappan culture, as seen in many mother-goddess figurines, ritual baths, and burials.

2000–1700 B.C.: Chinese people develop a basic writing system.

1700–1600 B.C.: China's Shang period produces the area's first bronze vessels, often used in sacrifices and burials.

1700–900 B.C.: Indo-European, or Aryan, people who have moved into northern India develop their Vedic religion, or Brahmanism, with its music, dance, and central rite of fire sacrifice.

1500–1000 B.C.: Chinese people develop an ambitious writing system, the basis of later classical Chinese script.

1500–1000 B.C.: In India, several collections of religious texts known as the *Rig Vedas* are composed by Aryan priests and passed down by oral tradition (until these are written down *c.* 600 B.C.).

1384–1111 B.C.: Chinese of the Shang period use "oracle bones"—inscribed cattle shoulder bones and turtle shells—for divination. They are the earliest known written form of the Chinese language.

1200 B.C.?–A.D. 300: At some time during this long period carvings are made on rocks in Hong Kong and Macau. The carvings are probably associated with rituals and religious beliefs.

SCIENCE-TECHNOLOGY, ECONOMICS, AND EVERYDAY LIFE

Ancient Times: 3000 B.C.–A.D. 499

3000–1500 B.C.: People in what is now Laos begin to adopt the Neolithic culture that includes agriculture (eventually rice), domesticated animals (pigs, cattle, fowl), pottery, and sophisticated stone tools.

2600–2000 B.C.: The Harappan culture in northern India uses standardized weights and linear measures.

2500 B.C.: Most experts believe that bronzemaking in Asia begins in China *c.* 2500 B.C.

2000 B.C.: Tea, bananas, and apples are cultivated in India.

2000–1700 B.C.: The Lungshan culture of China develops simple bronze metallurgy and domesticates wheat.

2000–500 B.C.: In various Indonesian islands *c.* 2000 B.C. the first signs of the Neolithic cultural complex appear: cultivated plants (rice possibly by 2500 B.C., then possibly millet by 2000 B.C.), tubers (such as taro), fruit-bearing trees (such as bananas), pig husbandry, and pottery.

1500 B.C.: By this time, although individuals throughout Asia are adding metallurgy to their repertoire of skills, most people continue to use stone and other materials for their tools and implements.

Shang dynasty Chinese make increasingly more sophisticated bronze vessels, weave silk, use horse-drawn vehicles and the potter's wheel, and domesticate the water buffalo.

1500–500 B.C.: At the outset of this period, most experts believe, metallurgy based on copper and bronze begins in Thailand. The full-fledged Bronze Age culture of Thailand does not begin until *c.* 1000 B.C., with the use of metals for tools (axes, fishhooks), weapons (spearheads and arrowheads), and jewelry (bracelets). Thailand proves to have plentiful amounts of copper and tin. By *c.* 1000 B.C. copper and bronze begin to be more widely worked in northern Vietnam and Cambodia. In India, copper- and bronze-workers produce weapons and tools.

THE WORLD

Ancient Times: 3000 B.C.–A.D. 499

3000–1500 B.C.: In the Middle East, the Sumerian civilization is developing in the valleys of the Tigris and Euphrates rivers. The Sumerians develop the cuneiform system of writing, employ animal-drawn wheeled vehicles, irrigate desert lands, and construct large ceremonial structures. In Egypt, the great pyramids are erected (2980–2800 B.C.) and pharaohs rule over a centralized and hierarchical society. Judaism appears to be developing as a religion among the Israelites.

In Western Europe (including the British Isles, France, Spain, and Denmark) megalithic cultures emerge, Stonehenge being the best-known material survival. Another culture thrives in the Danube/Balkans region.

Around the Mediterranean, advanced cultures develop, particularly in the Aegean area, which includes the Minoan culture of Crete and the Greek-speaking Helladic culture of the mainland.

Agriculture is changing the cultures of Central America and Mexico (maize) and Peru (potatoes and sweet potatoes), supporting settled communities and permanent structures.

1500–1100 B.C.: Mycenaean Greeks take over Crete and exert influence throughout the eastern Mediterranean (taking Troy *c.* 1190?), but by 1100 eastern Mediterranean society goes into decline.

The pharaohs unite Upper and Lower Egypt and extend Egypt's power over many of the neighboring lands, including Mesopotamia to the east. Amenhotep IV, as Ikhnaton, imposes monotheism on Egypt (1374–1358 B.C.).

HISTORY

Ancient Times: 3000 B.C.–A.D. *499*

1040–256 B.C.: In China, the Zhou dynasty rules during a period of general political disorder and turbulence. Zhou society evolves steadily from the feudal form, with its hereditary warrior nobility, toward an independent, centralized state with armies drawn from a landed peasantry.

1000–600 B.C.: The Indo-Aryan society and Hindu caste system, centered in the Ganges region, evolves.

ARTS, CULTURE, THOUGHT, AND RELIGION

Ancient Times: 3000 B.C.–A.D. *499*

1000 B.C.: The Chinese written vocabulary reaches three thousand characters. The first known Chinese poetry is believed to date from this time.

1000–100 B.C.: People in northern Laos begin to develop a society that is regarded as a Bronze Age/megalithic culture. In the first phase (1000 to 500 B.C.), people bury their dead in underground burial chambers marked by upright stone slabs (menhirs). About 500 B.C. they shift to cremating their dead and placing the ashes in large stone jars.

SCIENCE-TECHNOLOGY,
ECONOMICS, AND EVERYDAY LIFE

Ancient Times: 3000 B.C.–A.D. *499*

1500–500 B.C. *(continued)*: In the Philippines, the Austronesian Filipinos maintain their own basic economy, culture, and society: they cultivate old foods and add new ones to their diet; they weave textiles, make pottery, and construct simple wooden houses. By now trade brings increasing contacts with the other peoples of Southeast Asia, and Filipinos adopt some of their new material culture such as special adzes, jade, and copper/bronze. Meanwhile the Filipinos also transfer back to their relatives in Taiwan such new foods as coconuts, bananas, and breadfruit from the tropical regions.

1200–1100 B.C.: Iron technology is introduced into northern India; it will spread southward and eastward.

12th century B.C.: In India, the need for accurate calendars for religious observances calls for accurate astronomical calculations and thus leads to development of science of astronomy.

1000–750 B.C.: The Chinese advance their knowledge of astronomy and predict an eclipse (781).

9th century B.C.–4th century B.C.: Korea enters the Bronze Age with an agricultural people using bronze daggers and bronze mirrors. These people are the first Koreans to cultivate rice.

800–500 B.C.: The earliest known works of Indian mathematics, the *Sulbasutras*, make use of plane geometry and algebra.

THE WORLD

Ancient Times: 3000 B.C.–A.D. *499*

1100–750 B.C.: The Assyrians emerge as the major power in the Middle East. King David rules Judea (1005–961 B.C.); King Solomon (961–933 B.C.) builds the Great Temple and expands Jerusalem. Much of eastern Mediterranean seems to slip into a cultural "dark age," but influences from Middle East gradually begin to bring it back into light.

1000–750 B.C.: Indians of what is now the eastern United States cultivate plants. Cities are emerging in Middle America.

1000 B.C.–A.D. 350: Nubia, eastern Africa (modern Sudan), has been controlled by Egyptians for a thousand years, but now its main kingdom, Kush, begins to develop; between about 750 and 670 B.C., Nubians actually rule Egypt. The Kushites discover iron and develop technology for making iron tools and weapons.

900–500 B.C.: The Etruscan people develop a sophisticated culture in central Italy; they rule Rome until in 509 the Romans rebel and form their own republic. In 494, Rome forms the Latin League in central Italy.

HISTORY

Ancient Times: 3000 B.C.–A.D. 499

600 B.C.–A.D. 300: In north India, the numerous warring groups and families are now replaced by unstable states that rise and disappear during centuries of constant warfare. But by the end of this period, India is actively engaging—through trade, religious missions, and military encounters—with Greece and Rome, West Asia and Central Asia, Southeast Asia, and China.

500–200 B.C.: At least by the end of this period, people known as Khmer are moving into modern Cambodia. Nothing certain is known of their origins, but it appears they are moving south from Thailand's Khorat Plateau. They speak a Mon-Khmer language that is closely related to the languages then spoken by most Vietnamese and at least some peoples in Laos, Thailand, Burma, Malaysia, and India.

403–221 B.C.: In China, this era is known as the Warring States period; seven major rivals jockey for supremacy and the Zhou dynasty no longer dominates. Population growth and urbanization characterize the period.

ARTS, CULTURE, THOUGHT, AND RELIGION

Ancient Times: 3000 B.C.–A.D. 499

700–500 B.C.: In India, reaction against orthodox Vedic Brahmanism is seen as more mystical and meditative elements replace strict rituals. This is also the period when the *Upanishads*, more abstract and philosophical works, are composed.

6th century B.C.: By tradition, the *Dao De Jing* (also known as the *Classic of the Way and Its Power*) appears. Ascribed to the possibly legendary Laozi, it is regarded as the founding document of Daoism (Taoism).

563–483 B.C.: Probable lifespan of Siddhartha Gautama, the Buddha; after achieving enlightenment, he lives as an itinerant preacher and rejects Vedic and Brahmanic authority.

551–499 B.C.: Lifespan of Kung Ch'iu; eventually the Chinese will refer to him as Kung-fu-tzu (Great Master Kung), known to the West as Confucius. He promotes a humanistic and ethical approach to life and society.

540–468 B.C.: Lifespan of Vardhamana Mahavira, founder of Jainism, a branch of Hinduism that emphasizes *ahimsa* (non-harming), asceticism, fasting, and vegetarianism.

468–376 B.C.: Lifespan of Mozi, a Chinese philosopher of the Warring States period and an early rival of Confucius. A utilitarian philosopher, he is interested in practical economic matters and criticizes extravagant funeral practices and other elaborate rituals.

SCIENCE-TECHNOLOGY, ECONOMICS, AND EVERYDAY LIFE

Ancient Times: 3000 B.C.–A.D. 499

600–1 B.C.: Near the outset of this period the classic Dong Son culture of Vietnam (named after its prime site in north-central Vietnam) comes into being. The Dong Son culture is characterized by its use of copper and bronze—in particular, by its bronze drums. Dong Son-style drums, some imported, some locally made, will be found at many sites in Southeast Asia and southern China.

6th century B.C.: The *Zhoubi suanjing*, a work on the calendar and astronomy, is the oldest known Chinese text revealing knowledge of fairly advanced mathematics; it may have been composed during this period.

500–1 B.C.: Although isolated iron artifacts have been made in Southeast Asia and East Asia before this time, it is during these centuries that iron-making begins to be more widely adopted. Copper and bronze (including bronze casting) are still more common. The new metal tools of this period allow for clearing more forests to plant crops and to raise livestock.

By this time, some Vietnamese are cultivating wet rice in rain-fed or irrigated fields; they use plows and water buffalo. It is also the time when wetland rice cultivation is adopted in Thailand, advanced in some cases by the construction of moats, reservoirs, and canals to direct water to rice fields.

THE WORLD

Ancient Times: 3000 B.C.–A.D. 499

776 B.C.: The first Olympic Games are held in Greece.

750–500 B.C.: The epic poems about the Greeks' past, *Iliad* and *Odyssey*, are written down and attributed to a poet called Homer. In Greece, a distinctive civilization emerges, with writing and coinage, new types of pottery and sculpture, and intellectual works.

750–500 B.C.: Across central and western Europe, various peoples are now using iron.

581–497 B.C.: Lifetime of Pythagoras, the Greek philosopher/mathematician.

550–330 B.C.: The Persians create an empire that dominates much of the Middle East until defeated by Alexander the Great.

500–325 B.C.: After the Greeks defeat the Persians at Marathon (490), Salamis (480) and Plataea (479), Greek civilization flourishes, centered in Athens and producing such giants as Pericles, Sophocles, Plato, Demosthenes, and Aristotle.

447–433 B.C.: The Parthenon is constructed in Athens.

HISTORY

Ancient Times: 3000 B.C.–A.D. 499

400 B.C.: Yayoi people, most likely coming from Korea, move into Japan; they soon absorb or supplant Jomon people (who are enclaved on islands, including Okinawa).

4th century B.C.: In Korea, various tribal states are emerging, but by the end of century the northern Chinese state of Yan invades Korea.

321–297 B.C.: Chandragupta Maurya founds the Mauryan empire, which rules much of India until 184 B.C.

327–303 B.C.: Northwest India is conquered by Alexander the Great, but after his death (323 B.C.) his successors are driven out in 303.

325–256 B.C.: The state of Qin in North China gradually subdues its various rival states in China.

ARTS, CULTURE, THOUGHT, AND RELIGION

Ancient Times: 3000 B.C.–A.D. 499

400–100 B.C.: India's *Ramayana* is composed, the first literary poem in Sanskrit.

400 B.C.–A.D. 400: The *Mahabharata*, India's great folk epic and world's longest poem, is composed.

c. 370–c. 300 B.C.: Lifespan of Mengzi, known in the Western world as Mencius, the first important successor to Confucius in the same tradition.

361 B.C.: In China, Gongsun Yang (Lord Shang) is the supposed author of one of the two surviving treatises of the Legalist School of government.

SCIENCE-TECHNOLOGY, ECONOMICS, AND EVERYDAY LIFE	THE WORLD

Ancient Times: 3000 B.C.–A.D. 499

Ancient Times: 3000 B.C.–A.D. 499

500 B.C.–A.D. 500: On Sri Lanka, sophisticated engineering, particularly the discovery of outlet-valve technology, underpins the development of one of the world's greatest ancient hydraulic civilizations. Kings Panduwasa and Pandukabhaya are two of the earliest builders of massive earthen "tanks" linked by canals. This monumental irrigation system allows the cultivation of rice in the arid northern and southern plains.

In India, a series of medical texts are compiled; they set forth the basic principles and practices of India's traditional Ayurvedic school of medicine.

500 B.C.–A.D. 700: During these centuries, the Filipinos adopt some of the material culture of the world around them: copper, bronze, and (after *c.* 200 B.C.) iron for tools, weapons, and ornaments; glass jewelry and jade ear-pendants; burial jars; and the blowgun (while the Negritos keep their bow and arrow.)

4th century B.C.: In Korea, iron rapidly replaces bronze in the making of weapons and tools, particularly among members of the emergent ruling class. A unique heating system, called the *ondol*, is also developed around this time: It consists of flues running under the floor bearing heat from a fire on one side of the house to a chimney on the other.

390 B.C.: Gauls from northern Italy sack Rome.

359–338 B.C.: Philip becomes king of Macedonia and leads Macedonians to take over Greece.

336–323 B.C.: Alexander the Great dominates most of Greece and leads the Greeks to conquer the Persian empire and other lands into India until his death.

323–283 B.C.: Lifetime of Euclid, the Greek mathematician.

323–30 B.C.: The so-called Hellenistic Age in eastern Mediterranean, which ends with the Roman conquest of Egypt.

HISTORY

Ancient Times: 3000 B.C.–A.D. 499

300 B.C.–A.D. 200: The Dong Son culture, so named after its primary site in northern Vietnam, spreads throughout parts of Southeast Asia.

c. 269–233 B.C.: Chandragupta's grandson Ashoka rules at height of Mauryan imperial power and encourages spread of Buddhism in India.

221–206 B.C.: The Qin state forcibly unifies China. Qin administrators impose standards in various areas, build highways, irrigation systems, canals, and start the Great Wall of China. Emperor Qin Shi's public works, military projects, and lavish burial deplete imperial resources. Upon his death the empire begins to break apart.

202 B.C.–A.D. 220: Four years of civil war in China end with the establishment of the Han dynasty. The Early Han emperors extend the bureaucracy and government monopolies. Landed estates increase in extent, impoverishing a part of the peasantry. Trade increases. Military initiatives push China's borders outward.

108 B.C.: China's Han dynasty Emperor Wudi establishes Chinese outposts in northern Korea. The Chinese do not abandon their last outpost until A.D. 313, and Korea is heavily influenced by Chinese culture.

100 B.C.–A.D. 107: In Japan's Middle Yayoi period, Chinese material culture (bronze mirrors, etc.) begins to appear.

57 B.C.: In Korea, three warring kingdoms emerge; they will continue their competition until Korea is unified in A.D. 668.

1st century A.D.: Central Asian tribes known as Yuezhi or Tokharians, based in Afghanistan, expand their power across Central Asia and migrate to northwestern India. Kadphises I (reigns c. 15–65), leader of one of their clans, the Kushans, founds the Kushan dynasty.

ARTS, CULTURE, THOUGHT, AND RELIGION

Ancient Times: 3000 B.C.–A.D. 499

300 B.C.–A.D. 200: The Dong Son culture is particularly distinguished by its bronze drums. Highly decorated with both geometric and representational figures, they are apparently used for ceremonial-religious purposes.

3d century B.C.: Buddhism, established in the Kathmandu Valley of Nepal, introduces elements that become central to Nepalese culture, including architectural forms such as *stupas* (domed temples) and such ideas as the king as upholder of cosmic law.

c. 269–233 B.C.: After Indian emperor Ashoka converts to Buddhism, he builds stupas and monasteries, starts tradition of erecting stone pillars inscribed with Buddhist texts, and begins carving chambers in rock for religious meditation. Ashoka also inscribes his edicts on rocks and caves.

SCIENCE-TECHNOLOGY, ECONOMICS, AND EVERYDAY LIFE

Ancient Times: 3000 B.C.–A.D. 499

300 B.C.–A.D. 200: The Austronesian Mongoloids who have settled in the Malay Peninsula appear to come to the fore, at least around the coastal regions. It is possible that these new people are beginning to adopt the cultivation of wet rice. In any case, bronze and iron technology is introduced into Malaysia at this time.

c. 269–233 B.C.: In India, the first nine numbers of Brahmi are used in the decrees of King Ashoka; these digits will become the basis of modern Western numerals.

221–210 B.C.: Chinese convicts and conscripted laborers begin to build a major segment of the Great Wall and a highway system.

2d century B.C.: Bronze and copper artifacts (numerous drums, a statuette, a lidded vessel) of the Dong Son style appear in Java, Sumatra, and the southern Moluccas; most likely these are imported from Vietnam, although some may have been made locally. There are indications of an advancing maritime technology during this century.

A Chinese medical text of this time indicates an awareness that blood circulates through blood vessels.

115 B.C.: China establishes state monopolies for salt and iron.

100 B.C.: Water clocks are in use in China.

THE WORLD

Ancient Times: 3000 B.C.–A.D. 499

287?–212 B.C.: Lifetime of Archimedes, the Greek mathematician.

264 B.C.: First public combats of gladiators in Rome. (Gladiatorial combat will be banned in A.D. 325.)

260–202 B.C.: Rome is at war with Carthage.

200 B.C.: In what is now the southwestern United States, the Hohokam Indian culture begins to emerge; it will thrive by constructing an elaborate network of irrigation ditches.

197–146 B.C.: Romans conquer Greece. Power throughout the Mediterranean now shifts to Rome.

100 B.C.: In Mexico, Indians have by now built extensive cities at Monte Albán and Teotihuacan. They have a writing system, a counting system, and a calendar.

71 B.C.: In Italy, a revolt of slaves and gladiators under Spartacus is crushed.

60–44 B.C.: After his victories in Spain, Julius Caesar returns and is elected consul (60 B.C.). After conquering Gaul (51 B.C.), he returns to Italy (49 B.C.) and triumphs in civil war in Italy (46 B.C.) but is assassinated (44 B.C.).

31 B.C.–A.D. 14: Octavius Caesar defeats fleets of Antony and Cleopatra at Actium; the latter two commit suicide. In 27 B.C., Octavius, now Augustus Caesar, establishes the Roman Empire.

HISTORY

Ancient Times: 3000 B.C.–A.D. 499

A.D. 43–939: The Chinese conquer northern Vietnam, and many Han Chinese move into the region. They soon begin to intermarry with the local inhabitants and create a mixed Chinese-Viet population; although various Chinese practices are forced on the locals and the Chinese language becomes the official language, elements of the indigenous culture remain and even predominate.

Late 1st–Early 2d centuries: Reign of Kanishka, third and greatest Kushan king. He conquers a huge territory that includes almost the entire region of the later Soviet Republics of Central Asia, Afghanistan, Pakistan, all of northern India, and parts of eastern and central India. The Kushan empire declines in the late second century and submits to the Sassanian dynasty of Persia *c.* 260.

ARTS, CULTURE, THOUGHT, AND RELIGION

Ancient Times: 3000 B.C.–A.D. 499

250 B.C.–A.D. 100: Buddhism spreads throughout India, Sri Lanka, Indonesia. Starting about 100 B.C. Mahayana (Great Wheel) Buddhism begins to split off from the earlier Theravada (Hinayana) tradition; although their doctrines differ in some ways, the two schools coexist throughout Asia.

200 B.C.–A.D. 200: In India, numerous cave temples are excavated from rock cliffs for retreats and meditation. Often with elaborate carvings and paintings, they become a major art form in India.

100 B.C.: In Japan, distinctive reddish-orange Yayoi pottery replaces Jomon ware.

1st century B.C.–1st century A.D.: The *Bhagavad Gita*, a major Hindu text of devotion and social ethics, is composed.

1st–2d centuries B.C.: The earliest anthropomorphic representations of Buddha appear; they include many physical details that have since become conventional. These iconic Buddhist images, which spread along the Silk Road throughout Central Asia and into China, contribute significantly to the spread of Buddhism.

SCIENCE-TECHNOLOGY,
ECONOMICS, AND EVERYDAY LIFE

THE WORLD

Ancient Times: 3000 B.C.–A.D. *499*

Ancient Times: 3000 B.C.–A.D. *499*

HISTORY

Ancient Times: 3000 B.C.–A.D. 499

ARTS, CULTURE, THOUGHT, AND RELIGION

Ancient Times: 3000 B.C.–A.D. 499

A.D. 1: By now the Chinese are making fine lacquerware.

A.D. 50–200: More than one hundred brick tombs in northern Vietnam contain a variety of material goods that confirm the existence of a prosperous ruling class that draws on Han Chinese culture but appears to be solidly rooted in Vietnam.

SCIENCE-TECHNOLOGY, ECONOMICS, AND EVERYDAY LIFE

Ancient Times: 3000 B.C.–A.D. 499

1st century A.D.: The *Jiuzhang suanshu*, a classic Chinese mathematical text, is probably compiled during this time. It draws on knowledge of the Pythagorean theorem, linear and quadratic equations, and square and cube roots.

A.D. 80: A Chinese text describes a spoon made of magnetic iron that always aligns north-south; it is used for divination.

THE WORLD

Ancient Times: 3000 B.C.–A.D. 499

1 B.C.–A.D. 212: Rome begins this era by dominating all of the Mediterranean and much of Europe. Romans conquer much of Britain (43–180) and Germany (by 96). Although Rome extends citizenship to every free-born subject (212), peoples on fringes of empire continue to make trouble for the Romans.

64: Great fire in Rome is blamed on Christians; Peter and Paul are executed. Christians will be persecuted intermittently until Constantine issues the Edict of Milan in 313.

79: Pompeii destroyed by an eruption of the volcano Vesuvius.

HISTORY

Ancient Times: 3000 B.C.–A.D. 499

100–550: By about A.D. 100 the kingdom of Funan is asserting its rule over much of southern Cambodia in the general area of the Mekong basin and along the coast of the Gulf of Siam. Funan is probably a loose confederation of principalities, or chiefdoms, without a fixed political or ritual center, but the coastal city of Oc Eo appears to be a large and thriving city, strategically situated at the junction of important maritime trading routes between China and India. Oc Eo goes into decline during the fourth century; in the late sixth century, Funan disappears from Chinese records and is replaced by the region called Chenla by Chinese historians.

108–150: Tibetan and Xiongnu raiders force millions of Chinese to quit the northwest and move southward into Sichuan and Yunnan. Trade along the Silk Road is disrupted.

220–589: The end of the Han dynasty in China leads to the period known as the Three Kingdoms (220–265) and Six Dynasties (317–589); these centuries are marked by turmoil. The political and social fragmentation is the longest period of disunion in Chinese history.

220–939: With the end of the Han dynasty (220) and China's disarray, northern Vietnam is often in rebellion against the Chinese. Meanwhile, central Vietnam becomes a nearly independent kingdom known as Champa, while southern Vietnam belongs to the amorphous region known as Funan.

225: Southern India breaks up into various kingdoms.

250: Japan is now being overrun by powerful warring chiefs.

Early 4th century: Waves of nomadic peoples sweep into China from the north and northwest. They establish a series of brief dynasties; warfare is constant in the north for most of the century and leads to a mass migration to the safer south. These intruders intermarry, adapt to Chinese ways, and rule in collaboration with the established aristocratic families.

ARTS, CULTURE, THOUGHT, AND RELIGION

Ancient Times: 3000 B.C.–A.D. 499

2d century: Chinese sculptors fashion fine bronze three-dimensional representations of familiar Han scenes.

100–220: In Hong Kong, a brick chamber-tomb on the Kowloon peninsula is the oldest and strongest evidence of the Chinese presence or influence.

100–600: In southern Vietnam around the Mekong Delta is a region known to the Chinese as Funan. Its major center is Oc Eo. From the second century onward objects such as coins and statues from India and even from Rome attest that this is a prominent trading port. By the mid-fourth century Funan adopts the Brahman religion and Sanskrit writing system from India.

150–250: Period of the Gandharan, or Indo-Greek, school of art in India's northwest; it combines largely Buddhist subjects with classical Greco-Roman modeling and clothing.

166: The cult of the Buddha is formally introduced at China's imperial court in Luoyang.

250–500: In Japan great grave mounds, surrounded by moats, are erected.

4th century: In a time of upheaval in China, Buddhism spreads rapidly. Although Confucian ideas continue to shape the views of the elite on politics, society, ethics, and etiquette, Buddhism appeals in its offering of consolations and magical powers. Non-Chinese invaders who settle permanently among the Chinese also accept Buddhism.

SCIENCE-TECHNOLOGY, ECONOMICS, AND EVERYDAY LIFE

Ancient Times: 3000 B.C.–A.D. 499

105–300: The traditional date in China for the invention of rag paper; it is unlikely that this was invented at one moment, but the Chinese may well have been developing paper based on wood or fibers for some time. In any case, rag paper comes into widespread use by 300.

3d century: The prevailing material culture in Malaysia remains the Dong Son type; both bronze and iron are used. Malaysian trade links with India are by now well established, and Indian merchants are appearing in the north of the peninsula.

c. 270: The Chinese may have invented the magnetic compass.

320–600: In India, the Gupta period includes advances in astronomy, mathematics, and medicine.

c. 350–400: The *Surya Siddhanta*, a seminal Indian astronomical work, uses trigonometric functions. It forms the foundation of medieval Indian astronomy and is the basis for the Hindu calendar.

THE WORLD

Ancient Times: 3000 B.C.–A.D. 499

c. 100–178: Lifetime of Ptolemy, astronomer, mathematician, and geographer.

180: With the death of Marcus Aurelius, Rome enters into a period of strife, with twenty-four emperors reigning in next hundred years.

247–268: Goths move against the Roman Empire, taking Romania (257) and sacking Athens (268).

285–312: Diocletian partitions the Roman Empire into Western and Eastern empires; Constantine reunites it (312).

300–1000: The Hopewell culture in what is now the eastern United States builds large burial mounds and ceremonial centers.

c. 325: In central Mexico, Teotihuacan emerges as a major city and ceremonial center.

361: Christianity has been spreading throughout the Roman Empire, but the emperor Julian tries to revive paganism.

HISTORY

Ancient Times: 3000 B.C.–A.D. 499

c. 320: Chandragupta I (reigns *c.* 320–335) founds Gupta dynasty (*c.* 320–647) in Ganges Valley and Maghada; he sets the stage for India's classical age. North and north-central India are united for 250 years under Gupta rule, the first major empire since the Mauryas.

386: The Toba Turks, a Tartar people from eastern Mongolia, found the Northern Wei dynasty with their capital at Luoyang; they are able to hold North China together for a century and a half. The regional dynasties of the South, one succeeding another, are at peace most of the time.

5th century: Militarily aggressive south Indian (Tamil) states begin repeated attacks on Sri Lanka, at times ruling island kingdoms. The kingdoms of India and Sri Lanka become politically entwined over the following centuries, and south India profoundly influences Sinhalese art and architecture.

c. 400–750: The first Nepalese state is ruled by the Licchavi dynasty, descended from north Indian clan.

457: Skandagupta (reigns 454–467) defeats invading Hunas, a Turko-Mongolian people from Central Asia, but their repeated invasions from the northwest fatally weaken Guptas.

Middle Ages: 500–1499

500–550: Hunas from Central Asia overrun northern India, ending the Gupta dynasty's classical age. Although Hindu princes defeat the Hunas (*c.* 550), other Central Asian tribesmen move into northern India, and India in general spends the next six centuries torn by internal strife.

550–1220: Nomadic Turkish tribes assert loose control over the vast territory of Central Asia stretching from Manchuria in the east to the Persian frontier in the west. By the early 13th century the Mongols have taken full control.

ARTS, CULTURE, THOUGHT, AND RELIGION

Ancient Times: 3000 B.C.–A.D. 499

4th–6th centuries: Gupta sculpture, with its elegance and simplicity, is the classical period of plastic art in India.

c. 400–750: Golden age of Nepalese culture under the Licchavis is heavily influenced by north Indian Kushan models. Sanskrit is the official administrative and literary language. Monasteries, *stupas*, *lingam* shrines (phallic representations of Siva), palaces, *stelae* (pillars), and fountains are constructed. This practice spreads to Tibet.

400: The earliest examples of Japanese writing are from this time. It will be another two centuries before historical documents are recorded.

450–650: In Myanmar, writing in Indian scripts and with verses derived from classical Indian texts (found on stone, gold plates, silver vessels, burial urns), bronze figurines, coins with traditional Indian motifs, and stupas and monasteries attest to the strong influence of the Hindu, Buddhist, and Jain cultures of India.

Late 5th century: Gupta Buddhist cave paintings flourish in India, with those of Ajanta entering their final phase until the seventh century.

c. 496: In Sri Lanka, the "cloud maidens" are painted in the caves of Sigiriya.

Middle Ages: 500–1499

6th–9th centuries: *Bhakti*, a personal mystical-devotional movement within Hinduism, spreads from south India, carried by wandering teachers and seers.

538 (or 552): According to tradition, Buddhism is introduced in Japan from Korea and soon wins official support. Shinto, the indigenous religion of Japan, with its cults of sacred places and spirits, will survive.

Early 6th century: According to tradition, Chan (in Japanese, Zen) Buddhism is introduced to China through Bodhidharma, an Indian sage.

SCIENCE-TECHNOLOGY, ECONOMICS, AND EVERYDAY LIFE

Ancient Times: 3000 B.C.–A.D. 499

c. 400: The Chinese begin to make a type of steel by combining cast iron and wrought iron.

Late 5th–Early 6th centuries: Lifespan of Aryabhata, an Indian who writes the *Aryabhatiya*; he shows an ability to use geometry, trigonometry, and some algebra; he arrives at the value for π, 3.1416.

Middle Ages: 500–1499

550: Indian mathematicians recognize zero and irrational and negative numbers.

570: From China comes the first solid reference to the abacus; it is believed that the Chinese were using an early form at least two centuries previously.

589–618: The Sui dynasty in China launches ambitious projects to enlarge the Great Wall and to build canals.

595: An inscription in Gujarat, India, is the earliest recorded appearance of the mathematical notation system of nine digits and a sign (dot) for zero to indicate place value.

THE WORLD

Ancient Times: 3000 B.C.–A.D. 499

364: The Roman Empire is again divided into Western and Eastern empires, rejoined in 392, and divided again in 395.

395–476: Visigoths, Vandals, Huns, and Goths begin to move into Italy and various Roman provinces. Visigoths sack Rome (410). Vandals sack Rome (455). Goths set up kingdom in Italy (476).

433–453: Attila leads Huns on a series of campaigns into France and Italy. In 468, Huns withdraw from Europe following Attila's death in battle near what is now Venice.

449: Jutes, Angles, and Saxons from northern Europe invade Britain. Rome has effectively abandoned Britain.

476: The Roman Empire in the West comes to an end with the ascent of the Saxon leader Odoacer.

481: Clovis becomes king of France and defeats the Romans (486) and the Alemanni (496).

499: Across Europe new and distinctive societies are emerging; based on old tribal groupings, they form the basis of the European nation-state.

Middle Ages: 500–1499

500: The Mayan centers of Copan and Tikal thrive. Monte Albán flourishes under the Zapotecs in central Mexico. In the Peruvian Andes the Tiahuanaco and Huari states begin to emerge. In southeastern Colorado, Anasazi Indians begin to settle at Mesa Verde.

c. 500–540: Reign of the legendary King Arthur in Britain.

527–565: Justinian is emperor at Constantinople. He issues a law code (529), constructs the basilica of the Hagia Sophia (532–537), and introduces the silk industry from China (552).

HISTORY

Middle Ages: 500–1499

600–710: Asuka period, Japan's first historical period (because of the surviving written documentation).

612–647: China's five attempts to conquer Korea all fail.

618–907: The Tang dynasty rules China. Tang emperors consolidate and expand the imperial state; prosperity allows them to encourage both public works and the arts. Chinese assert authority over northern Vietnam—renamed Annam—but it remains in constant turmoil.

620–649: Songzen Gampo, the first emperor of Tibet, conquers the kingdoms of Nepal to the west and Kamarupa to the south, unifying a large empire and establishing his capital at Lhasa.

645: In Japan, a coup d'état overthrows oppressive Soga rulers. Successful plotter and clan chief Nakatomi no Kamatari is rewarded with the new family name of Fujiwara. For five hundred years, Fujiwara remains the most influential family at the imperial court.

668–889: China's Tang dynasty has attempted several invasions of Korea, but not until Chinese forces combine with Silla Korean forces do Chinese gain control of Korean territories. The Silla Koreans, however, drive the Chinese out (676) and assert their dominance on the peninsula. Silla attempts to gain more control in 889 but fails when the country erupts in peasant rebellions.

8th–9th centuries: Tibet and China often engage in warfare over disputed territories. In 832 Tibet signs a treaty with China intended to reduce military conflict. By 850 Tibet's power is collapsing; in 879 Nepal gains independence from Tibet.

710–794: The Nara period in Japan. Although Japanese culture develops, violent power struggles in court often threaten to destroy government authority and destabilize the nation.

ARTS, CULTURE, THOUGHT, AND RELIGION

Middle Ages: 500–1499

7th century: In east India, rise of Sakti cult within Hinduism revives the worship of the mother goddess from old fertility cults.

7th–8th centuries: the first great age of Indian Hindu temples includes such as those at Mamallapuram, Elephanta, and Ellora.

604: In Japan, the Code of Shotoku Taishi (sage virtue) effectively establishes Buddhism as the state religion.

607: In Japan, Horyo-ji Temple is erected. It apparently burns down about 670 but is rebuilt in 750. It remains the oldest surviving wooden building in the world.

618–907: Under the Tang dynasty arts flourish in China. Buddhism makes a significant contribution, both as an inspiration to artists and as a subject of devotional works of art.

620: Although the Chinese have long been making early forms of porcelain, this is the earliest date for authentic porcelain.

638: The form of Christianity known as Nestorianism has spread into China from the Middle East. The first Nestorian temple is built in Chang'an (Xian).

651: Arab mission introduces Islam to China.

8th–11th centuries: Tantric Buddhism—an esoteric strand of Hinduism and Jainism as well as Buddhism—spreads across India into Nepal, Tibet, Southeast Asia, China, and Japan. Tantrism includes *mantras* (sacred syllables), *mandalas* (ritual diagrams), *tanghkas* (religious scroll paintings), and explanation of Tantra, the sacred texts; tantrism also involves strict discipline, including yogic and other practices to attain mastery over oneself and physical phenomena.

SCIENCE-TECHNOLOGY, ECONOMICS, AND EVERYDAY LIFE

Middle Ages: 500–1499

604: Japan adopts the Chinese calendar.

605: In China, the first stretch of the Grand Canal is completed.

608–615: A major section of China's Great Wall is constructed.

615: The Japanese use "burning water," actually petroleum.

618–907: During the Tang dynasty China codifies its mathematics and establishes a program to educate professional mathematicians. It will become the model for Korea and Japan in centuries to come.

628: Brahmagupta composes the *Brahmasphutasiddhanta*, a major Indian text on astronomy and mathematics.

***c.* 650:** The Chinese use lampblack ink to take rubbings; it is believed that this eventually leads to woodblock printing

650–950: At some time during this period the Chinese evidently discover the declination of the magnetic needle.

704–750: The oldest wood-block printing is an example from Korea.

734–805: Lifespan of Lu Yu, author of the Chinese *Book of Tea*, which discusses cultivation of tea bushes and tea processing in detail. During this time, tea drinking begins to become popular in China; it will spread to Japan in the ninth century.

THE WORLD

Middle Ages: 500–1499

***c.* 540–604:** Pope Gregory I (reigns 590–604) organizes Catholic rituals and systematizes sacred chants.

567: Franks divide their kingdom into what will become Belgium, Germany, and France.

622: Muhammad flees from Mecca to Medina (the Hegira).

635–641: Muslims conquer Damascus and overthrow Syria's Persian rulers. By 641 they have conquered Egypt.

711–718: Muslim Arabs conquer much of Spain. The Muslim empire now extends from the Pyrenees to China.

***c.* 715:** *Beowulf,* the Old English epic poem, is composed.

732: Charles Martel stops the advance of Muslims at Poitiers (Tours), France.

771–814: King of the Franks since 768, Charlemagne rules over the Western Roman Empire.

HISTORY

Middle Ages: 500–1499

711–715: Muslim Arabs invade and conquer the Indus Valley, then proceed to establish the first Islamic state in South Asia.

730–900: In Yunnan, the southwestern region of China, rises a kingdom known as Nan-chao (southern lord). Nan-chao seems to be fairly aggressive, probably pushing some Tai deeper into Thailand and possibly inspiring other Tai to adopt its more organized and assertive style.

751: Arab forces defeat a Chinese expeditionary army at the battle of the Talas near Samarkand. This marks the high point of Chinese expansion into Central Asia.

Late 8th–12th centuries: Various kingdoms based in Java and Sumatra vie for power in the Indonesian archipelago.

c. 770–1295: A succession of Khmer kings establishes and extends Khmer rule over Cambodia.

ARTS, CULTURE, THOUGHT, AND RELIGION

Middle Ages: 500–1499

Early 8th century: A succession of Japanese embassies to China brings elements of Chinese culture—including calligraphy and Buddhist and Confucian thought—back to influence Japanese society.

712–755: Emperor Xuanzong reigns in what will be recalled as the golden age of the Tang dynasty. The era is particularly noteworthy for the poetry known as *shi*; strict rules of rhyme and meter govern this form of short lyric poetry, which often has a strong emphasis on nature. Its best-known practitioners are Wang Wei (669–759), Li Bo (701–762), Du Fu (712–770), and Pai Chui (772–846). Xuanzong is a patron of Daoism as well.

712: The oldest extant literary work in Japan, a compilation of legends and history known as *Kojiki*, is written on scrolls.

Mid- to late 8th century: Indian Buddhist mystics Santarakshita and Padmasambhava visit Tibet. Padmasambhava introduces Tantric Buddhism (Vajrayana) and founds the first monastic Buddhist order. He is traditionally credited as the author of the *Tibetan Book of the Dead*, a sacred text containing the ritual for dying (attributed by modern scholars to Kar-ma Ling-pa in the fifteenth century). Bhutan also becomes a Buddhist kingdom in the eighth century.

c. 770–1295: During these centuries, a succession of Khmer kings rules in Cambodia. In addition to extending the state's power, they build a succession of monumental "temple mountains" and shrines in or around the capital cities of Yasodharapura and Angkor. The great temples, the most famous of which is Angkor Wat (completed c. 1150), perform the double function of honoring the Hindu deities and legitimizing their reigns. By the eleventh century, some temples and monasteries are also dedicated to Buddhism.

788–820: In India, Shankara develops Vedanta philosophy, a synthesis of Hinduism and Buddhism.

SCIENCE-TECHNOLOGY, ECONOMICS, AND EVERYDAY LIFE	THE WORLD
Middle Ages: 500–1499	*Middle Ages: 500–1499*

735–737: In Japan, a great smallpox epidemic kills possibly 30–40 percent of the population. In the centuries that follow, epidemics, famine, and natural disasters continually tear the nation's social fabric and contribute to lawlessness and violence.

751: Chinese papermakers captured by Arabs at Samarkand enable the manufacture of paper to spread throughout the Arab world over the next fifty years.

c. 773: The Hindu decimal system and numerals are introduced to Baghdad. The Hindu numerals spread throughout the Arab world. When adopted by Europeans *c.* 1200 they become known as "Arabic numerals."

775: The Chinese are using block-printing; the Japanese use only pictorial block-printing.

786: Haroun-al-Raschid, a noted benefactor of the arts and sciences, ascends the throne of Baghdad.

HISTORY

Middle Ages: 500–1499

794–1185: The Heian period in Japan is regarded as the golden age of Classical Japan. The emperor fades into the background as rival courtier families strive for supremacy. Fujiwara family dominance is complete when Fujiwara no Yoshifusa installs his grandson as Emperor Seiwa (reigns 858–876), with himself ruling as regent.

907–960: With the end of the Tang dynasty, China enters the brief Epoch of the Five Dynasties as short-lived dynasties rule the north China plain. The overlapping Ten Kingdoms rule different regions of South China. The north is beset with conflict and economic dislocation, but South China is comparatively peaceful. Disunion stimulates economic development.

918–1231: In Korea, Wang Kon founds the kingdom of Koryo. By 936 he has extended his power throughout the peninsula. A period of prosperity follows the defeat of the Khitans in 1018. In 1170 discontented military officers stage a series of rebellions, and a succession of military dictatorships follows.

939: Northern Vietnamese defeat Chinese forces and assert their independence.

960–1125: In China, the period of the Northern Song dynasty. The Chinese excel in technical innovation, political theory, culture, and the arts, but invaders from inner Asia gradually assert political control over large sections of northern China.

967–1068: At the height of Japan's Heian era, Fujiwara regents exercise power while emperors are kept busy with ritual and ceremonies.

ARTS, CULTURE, THOUGHT, AND RELIGION

Middle Ages: 500–1499

Late 8th century–late 9th century: The Buddhist kingdom of Sailendra flourishes in Java until the mid-9th century. Borobudur, the Mahayana Buddhist temple complex known for its immense *stupa*, is built by Sailendra rulers near Jogakarta in central Java. The temple represents a synthesis of Buddhist belief and indigenous ancestor worship.

868: The earliest extant printed book, the *Diamond Sutra*, is produced at Dunhuang, China.

***c.* 900:** Beginning of gradual end of close ties of Japan with cultural and political life in China; Japanese language begins to replace Chinese as the language of culture; the Japanese develop cursive signs to record Japanese sounds.

10th century: Zoroastrian refugees from religious persecution in Persia begin to settle in India; they are ancestors of the modern Parsis.

10th–12th centuries: Buddhism flourishes in Vietnam as seen in the hundreds of pagodas erected, the many monks, and the great numbers of Buddhist texts.

960–1280: This period in China produces the familiar scholar/gentleman, who carries on such cultural traditions as calligraphy, landscape painting, literature, and philosophical speculation. This is also period of great watercolor artists and fine pottery in China.

SCIENCE-TECHNOLOGY, ECONOMICS, AND EVERYDAY LIFE

Middle Ages: 500–1499

c. **825:** Muhammad ibn Musa Al-Khwarizmi, from Uzbekistan or Turkmenistan, composes an important work of mathematics; the *al-jabr* in its title is romanized as "algebra." The Arabic word means "bone-setting."

A Chinese text describes a chemical mixture that is a primitive form of gunpowder but it is used only for ceremonies.

c. **870:** Arabs develop the astrolabe.

c. **877–889/890:** In Cambodia, Indravarman I begins the practice of constructing vast irrigation projects, including reservoirs, necessary for wet-rice cultivation as well as for supplying temple moats.

10th century: Middle Eastern and Chinese traders are regular visitors to the Maldives. The economy is trade-dependent; Maldives imports grain and textiles that islands cannot produce in exchange for fish (especially dried "Maldive fish" exported to Ceylon), coconuts, ambergris, and the cowrie shells used as currency throughout Asia.

900–1200: The Chinese develop advanced techniques for making iron and steel.

950: The Chinese invent a fire-lance, a device in which an explosive rocket composition is enclosed in a bamboo tube and then fired in combat.

980: The Chinese invent a lock canal.

THE WORLD

Middle Ages: 500–1499

800s: The Norse, or Vikings, move out from Scandinavia to attack and settle parts of northern Europe and North Atlantic (and eventually southern Europe). In 862, Vikings seize power in territory that becomes part of Russia.

c. **850:** Classic Mayan culture in the central Yucatan collapses.

871–899: Alfred the Great rules much of England.

900–950: Toltecs begin to dominate more of Middle America; they develop a city at Tula. The Teotihuacan center is partially destroyed. In Peru, the Chimu kingdom begins to emerge. The Anasazi Indians move into Chaco Canyon in northern New Mexico; the Hohokam culture thrives in southern Arizona.

c. **930:** The Benedictine monastery of Cluny (built in 914) extends reforms throughout France.

980: Vikings begin attacks on England.

998–1016: Danes move into England; Danish king Canute is king of England (1016–1035).

982–*c.* 1000: Erik the Red establishes the first Viking colony in Greenland. His son Leif Erikson establishes a settlement at L'Anse aux Meadows in Newfoundland.

HISTORY

Middle Ages: 500–1499

1021–1192: In India the Ghaznavids, Muslim Turks, establish a Muslim principality over Lahore (now east-central Pakistan). In 1186 they are replaced by Ghurids, also Muslims from Afghanistan, who rule from here until moving to Delhi in 1192.

1044-1287: Burman people, originally based in the irrigated rice fields in central Myanmar, establish their own state, centered on the city of Pagan. By 1044, Anorahta, a new ruler of Pagan, commences more assertive and expansive policies. Pagan will dominate Myanmar until its power begins to decline in 1287.

1102–1142: Jurchen tribes—farmers, herders, and hunters originally from the mountain forests of eastern Manchuria—raid Khitan Liao frontiers and by 1125 launch full-scale war against the Song dynasty. In 1127 the Jurchens take the Song capital, Kaifeng, and force the Song to abandon all of North China. By 1142 the Jurchen Jin dynasty rules much of northern China.

1113–1150: Khmers dominate Malaysia, Thailand, and Champa (central Vietnam).

1127–1279: China's Song dynasty, driven from the north by Jurchens, sets up a new court and capital at Hangzhou and establishes the Southern Kingdom. For most of their long rivalry, commerce between the Southern Song and the Jin of the north is uninterrupted, to both states' advantage.

1185–1333: During the Kamakura period in Japan, the Minamoto family gains power under the emperor and establishes the shogunate. This is the first of a series of shogunates that will rule Japan until the middle of the nineteenth century, leaving the emperor a figurehead.

ARTS, CULTURE, THOUGHT, AND RELIGION

Middle Ages: 500–1499

11th–12th centuries: Bronze sculptures of India's Chola kingdom reach the height of elegance.

1000–1250: The new genre of miniature paintings spreads across much of India; many illustrate Hindu, Buddhist, and Jaina manuscripts.

***c.* 1002:** The Japanese classic *Makuran-Soshi* (The Pillow Book), the diary of a woman's thoughts and experiences at court, is written.

***c.* 1002–1019:** *Genjii Monogatari* (Tale of Genji) is written by a Japanese woman, Murasaki Shikibu. It is now regarded as one of the world's earliest novels.

1053: In Japan, a gilded wooden Buddha is regarded as a masterpiece of Jocho, the greatest sculptor of the age.

***c.* 1082:** First Japanese scroll paintings of narrative scenes.

1122–1146: Reign of Injong in Korea. He does much to advance the system of education. A number of eminent scholars emerge from the schools established by Injong, most notably the Confucian scholar Kim Pusik (1075–1151), who is commissioned to compile the *Samguk sagi* (Historical Records of the Three Kingdoms), the oldest extant record of Korea's history.

Mid-12th century: In Korea, Koryo ceramists develop the technique of *sanggam*, a process for delineating designs using inlaying as opposed to carving or incising. The celadon porcelain of this time is generally considered among the finest ceramic art ever produced in the world. It is characterized by the simple elegance of its form and the delicacy of its colors due to the mineral nephrite, a particularly light-green variety of jade.

1153: In the Maldives, the last Buddhist king is converted to Sunni Islam and founds a sultanate that endures until 1932. The Maldives never institutes a secular legal system, but enforces *sharia* (Islamic law).

1191: With the return of Eisai from China, Zen Buddhism is introduced into Japan. With its stress on personal discipline, it will appeal to the warrior class; it takes hold throughout the next century.

SCIENCE-TECHNOLOGY, ECONOMICS, AND EVERYDAY LIFE

Middle Ages: 500–1499

c. 1041: A Chinese commoner, Pi Cheng, is evidently the first to employ printing from movable type (clay blocks).

1050: In Japan, artisans, up to now under the patronage of the court and government, begin to produce goods on their own and sell them in the public marketplace; this leads to the formation of *za*—crafts or trade guilds of artisans.

1050–1250: Song China is the world's first society to make widespread use of the printed book. Paper is made from plant fibers; printing is done with wooden blocks.

1088: Chinese in Beijing construct a water-powered clock that has the first known escapement mechanism. (It will be described in exact detail in a Chinese text of 1094.)

1100: Some Chinese judges are said to be using magnifying lenses of rock crystal to decipher documents and dark eyeglasses to hide reactions from litigants.

1110–1150: Chinese are using the fire-lance in battle.

1119: The first printed reference to using the magnetic compass for navigation appears in China.

Mid-12th century: On Sri Lanka, Parakrama Samudra, a massive artificial lake and the greatest irrigation work on the island, is completed during reign of Parakramabahu I "the Great" (reigns 1153–1186).

1161: The Chinese use bombs that produce shrapnel in battle.

THE WORLD

Middle Ages: 500–1499

1000: Toltecs from central Mexico move into the Mayan realm; the revived center of Chichén Itzá shows their influence. In eastern North America, the Mississippian temple mound culture now thrives, centered at Cahokia in southwestern Illinois.

1055–1076: The Seljuk Turks, Muslims from Central Asia and western Mongolia, have been extending their power for several decades. In 1051 they seize Baghdad; in 1071, they defeat the Byzantine army at the Battle of Manzikert (Turkey); in 1076 they capture Jerusalem and Damascus.

1066: William of Normandy defeats the Saxon king Harold at the Battle of Hastings; England falls under Norman rule.

1094: St. Mark's Basilica in Venice is completed.

1096–1099: The First Crusade ends in disaster, but some Christian knights end up capturing Jerusalem (1099) and establishing Latin states along the east coast of the Mediterranean.

1100: In Peru, Cuzco begins to emerge as the chief Inca center.

1100s: Many Gothic cathedrals are built throughout Europe. In Paris, Notre Dame is begun in 1163; that of Chartres is begun in 1194.

Arabic works in science and math are translated into Latin and influence European thought.

1148: Normans take Tunis and Tripoli; by 1160 the Normans will be driven from North Africa.

1147–1149: The Second Crusade ends with the Christian defeat at Damascus. The Latin states of the eastern Mediterranean come under Muslim attack.

1150: The Anasazi culture in Chaco Canyon (New Mexico) collapses.

1163–1193: The Muslim warrior Saladin becomes leader of Egypt, captures Jerusalem (1187), and extends rule over Syria and Mesopotamia.

1189–1192: The Third Crusade ends with stalemate; Saladin negotiates with Richard the Lion-Hearted to let Christian pilgrims enter Jerusalem.

HISTORY

Middle Ages: 500–1499

1205–1227: The Mongols, the new great power on the steppe, launch their first raid into Xia territory (1205). In 1211 Chinggis (Ghengis) Khan leads the Mongols in invading China, capturing the city on the site of Beijing (1214); by 1227, when Chinggis dies, his empire spreads from the Pacific Ocean to the Caspian Sea.

1206–1526: The Islamic Delhi sultanate rules over much of India.

1231–1368: A Mongolian army invades Korea; by 1270 Mongol domination is largely accepted. After the Mongols proclaim the Yuan dynasty in China (1271) they extract from Koryo a vow of loyalty. When the Mongols are driven from China and the Ming dynasty is proclaimed (1368), Korea's king sends envoys to Beijing to establish congenial diplomatic relations.

c. **1250–1350:** The Tai gradually overrun the central region of Southeast Asia heretofore controlled by the Pagan and Khmer empires, establishing a series of Tai city-states from the northern uplands to the Malay Peninsula. As their founding rulers die, the early Tai states recede in power and importance.

1251: Mongols invade Tibet. Khubilai Khan is converted to Lamaism by the abbot of the Sakya lamasary, who is installed as the first priest-king of Tibet (reigns 1270–1340). The Sakya dynasty lasts until 1358. The Mongols continue to exercise considerable influence over Tibet for the next five hundred years.

1253: Khubilai Khan leads Mongol armies in capture of Nan-chao. Mongols begin the pacification of the "southern barbarians," who begin to send tribute to Mongol rulers in China.

1258–1288: The Mongols launch attacks (1258, 1281, 1284, 1287–1288) against Vietnam. Although they are able to take capital cities, they are unable to hold much territory, and in 1288 the Mongols are thoroughly defeated at a battle at the Bach Dang River.

ARTS, CULTURE, THOUGHT, AND RELIGION

Middle Ages: 500–1499

1197, 1203: The Ghurid Turks' sacking of Buddhist monasteries in India contributes to decline of Buddhism in India. Buddhism has been declining due to a loss of royal patronage and the assimilation of Buddhism into Hinduism.

1198: Quwwat al-Islam, the oldest extant Muslim mosque in India, is completed in Delhi; with the declaration of the Sultanate of Delhi in 1201, Muslim influence in Indian culture spreads.

1200–1500: The three major orders of Islamic mysticism known as Sufism are brought into India from Iraq and Persia.

13th–14th centuries: The Urdu language, developed by Ghurid Turks to deal with local Hindus, is based on Turkish, Persian, and Hindi. It will become widespread in northern India and later develop into a literary language.

1200–1660s: Gujarati manuscript painting thrives in India.

Early 13th century: The devotional-mystical *bhakti* movement spreads through northern India.

Early or mid-13th century: *The Secret History of the Mongols* is compiled. It is the only extant Mongolian source of their own early history.

Mid-13th century: Fleeing the advancing Mongols in Central Asia, many Muslim scholars, writers, artists, and holy men move down into India.

c. **1250–1280:** After the Mongols conquer Tibet in 1252, Tibetan Buddhists exert an increasingly dominant influence on the Mongol court. Khubilai Khan himself comes to favor Buddhism.

SCIENCE-TECHNOLOGY, ECONOMICS, AND EVERYDAY LIFE

Middle Ages: 500–1499

13th century: Muslim immigrants into India include many scientists who introduce Arabic texts, instruments, and methods, some with ancient Greek origins. Indians adopt and adapt some of these Greco-Arabic scientific contributions.

White paper is first manufactured in India.

1234: The traditional date claimed for using movable metal (bronze) type to print a book in Korea.

THE WORLD

Middle Ages: 500–1499

1200: Proto-Aztec culture rises in central Mexico. The Mixtecs are influential in southern Mexico.

1200s: The decimal system and Arabic numerals are introduced into Europe by mathematicians such as Leonardo Fibonacci (*c.* 1170–1250).

1201–1204: The Fourth Crusade takes Constantinople and divides up much of the eastern Mediterranean among European warlords.

1215: English barons force King John to sign the Magna Carta.

1225–1274: Lifespan of Thomas Aquinas, philosopher and theologian.

1242: Alexander Nevsky defeats Teutonic knights on frozen Lake Peipus.

1265–1321: Lifespan of Dante Alighieri, Italian poet.

1271–1292: The Polo brothers of Venice initiate a second trading mission. They are joined by Nicolo Polo's son Marco. In 1274 they arrive at Khubilai Khan's summer palace at Shangdu. The Polos remain in Asia until 1292, and Marco serves in the employ of Khubilai's court. After Marco returns to Italy (1295), his account begins to circulate in manuscript.

HISTORY

Middle Ages: 500–1499

1264–1279: Khubilai, grandson of Chinggis Khan, becomes Great Khan of the Mongols. He moves his capital from Karakoram in Mongolia to Beijing; by 1279, the Mongols have defeated the last of the loyal Song forces.

1274 and 1281: Khubilai Khan's two attempts to invade Japan end in disaster.

1279–1368: With the murder of the heir to the Song dynasty, Khubilai Khan establishes the Mongol Yuan dynasty, which will rule China until 1368. China is now wholly occupied for the first time in its history.

1287–1303: Mongol forces invade and reach Pagan, in Myanmar, and establish a puppet king; the Shan brothers lead the resistance and overthrow the king, and in 1303 the Mongols withdraw from Myanmar.

1291–1292: The Mongols move into Java but are soon driven off.

1293–1500: The Hindu kingdom of Majapahit, based in Java, controls much of Indonesia and holds power throughout Southeast Asia.

1333–1573: In Japan, the Hojo regency is overthrown, leading to the Muromachi period (also known as the Ashikaga period). Civil wars, rebellions, and a general breakdown of the public order are accompanied by extraordinary achievements in the arts.

1351–1767: After power struggles in Siam, the Ayudhya kingdom gains sway and King Borommatrailokanat (reigns 1448–1488) lays the foundations of a Thai state that will last into the twentieth century. Although a cosmopolitan and resilient Siam emerges as the leading power in Southeast Asia, periodic internal instability occurs with often violent succession struggles.

1351–1388: Firuz Shah rules the Delhi sultanate; although he restores rule over northern India, most of India is torn by wars.

1353–1373: In what will become Laos, Fa Ngum is crowned ruler of the extended kingdom he calls Lan Sang (Kingdom of the Million Elephants). During these twenty years he extends his power over much of Laos and well into Siam.

ARTS, CULTURE, THOUGHT, AND RELIGION

Middle Ages: 500–1499

1271: Khubilai Khan, in establishing the Yuan dynasty in China, adopts a new legal code, incorporating some Mongol customs. He also restores traditional Confucian court rituals, promotes translation of the Confucian classics into Mongolian, and makes overtures to Buddhist and Daoist religious groups as well.

1339: In Kyoto the first Zen dry garden is laid out, using sand and rocks.

Mid-14th–mid-15th centuries: In southern India, the city of Vijayanagar emerges as a capital city of considerable wealth, a center of fine architecture, learning, and art.

1350–1434: Japanese *noh* drama is pioneered by the priest Kan'ami and his son, the actor-dramatist Motokiyo Zeami.

1351–1388: Firuz Shah Tughluq, the Islamic ruler of the Delhi Sultanate, launches a major building program in northern India.

1353–1371: In Laos, Fa Ngum promotes Theravada Buddhism as the state religion. He sends a mission to Angkor that brings back a golden statue of the standing Buddha known as the Prabang and has it placed in a special pagoda in his capital in Muang Sua.

1368–1644: China's Ming dynasty produces rich silks and beautiful porcelain that are in demand all over the world.

1397: Kyoto's Golden Pavilion, a pagoda, is completed.

SCIENCE-TECHNOLOGY,
ECONOMICS, AND EVERYDAY LIFE

Middle Ages: 500–1499

14th–15th centuries: Japan sees the introduction of paper manufacture, silk brocade, and cotton cloth.

THE WORLD

Middle Ages: 500–1499

1288: Ottoman Empire founded by Osman I, a Muslim Turk; during the next century the Ottomans extend their rule over Turkey and into Greece.

1291: With the fall of Acre to Muslims, Christian rule in the Middle East ends.

1296–1434: The cathedral of Florence is erected.

c. **1300–1700:** Benin, a city in modern Nigeria, rules over a powerful and sophisticated kingdom; it sends its own ambassador to Portugal and produces remarkable works in carved ivory and cast bronze.

c. **1325:** Foundation of the Aztec center at Tenochtitlan (later Mexico City).

1328: After centuries of fighting the Scottish clans, England recognizes Scotland's independence with Robert the Bruce as its king.

1337–1453: The Hundred Years' War between France and England.

1340–1400: Lifespan of Geoffrey Chaucer, English poet.

1347–1352: Bubonic plague, the "Black Death," spreads from Asia and kills a quarter of Europe's population.

1382–1400: The Black Death reappears in Europe and kills an estimated 75 million people.

1389: At the Battle of Kosovo, the Ottoman Turks defeat a coalition of Serbs, Bosnians, and Albanians and extend their rule over much of the Balkans.

HISTORY

Middle Ages: 500–1499

1353 and 1431: Thais sack the Khmer capital of Angkor in Cambodia.

1363–1405: Timur the Lame (Tamerlane), a Mongol conqueror, assembles his empire: Persia (1381–1387), the Golden Horde (1388–1391), Mesopotamia (1393–1394), Russia (1395), India (1398–1399), Syria (1400), and Anatolia (1402). When he dies in 1405, he is preparing to invade China.

Late 14th century: In Korea various factions within Koryo vie with one another to fill the vacuum of power left by the Mongols, whose empire rapidly declines by this time. In 1392 Yi Song-gye emerges to initiate the Yi dynasty that rules Korea until 1910.

1368–1372: In China, Zhu Yuanzhang, a commoner, drives out the Mongols and as Hongwu (or Taizu) establishes the Ming dynasty, which rules until 1644.

1404–1406: Civil wars in Indonesia undermine Majapahit stability and allow for the emergence of the state of Malacca on the Malay Peninsula, which comes to control the strait and international trade.

1406–1428: Claiming that they want to restore the Tran dynasty to power, the Chinese invade and take over Vietnam and impose their Confucian society. After defeating the Chinese in 1427, Le Loi, a Vietnamese landowner, proclaims himself emperor of Dai Viet (1428) and concludes a peace with the Ming dynasty. Although still admitting to some submission to China, Le Loi gains recognition of an independent Vietnam that he and his descendants will rule until 1787.

1451–1526: On breakup of Tamerlane's empire, India is ruled by Afghan Lodi dynasty.

1467–1568: In Japan, the Warring States period begins with a shogunal succession dispute. Anarchy continues for a century as warlords, adventurers, religious sects, and even villages struggle for supremacy and survival.

ARTS, CULTURE, THOUGHT, AND RELIGION

Middle Ages: 500–1499

1397–1422: High point of southern Islamic culture in India, centered on Firuzabad; many fine buildings are constructed.

15th century: At some point during this period lived Kar-ma Ling-pa, one of Tibet's most revered *Ter-tons* (treasure revealers), individuals who reveal mystical texts ascribed to paranormal origin. Modern scholars credit him with writing down the *Bar-do-tho-dol*, widely known in the West as *The Tibetan Book of the Dead*.

1402–1435: Chinese produce fine examples of carved red lacquerware and red porcelain.

Late 15th century: In the Philippines, Islam has become established on the large island of Mindanao and on the Sulu Archipelago to the south; by the early sixteenth century Islam is also apparently taking hold in the Manila area.

SCIENCE-TECHNOLOGY, ECONOMICS, AND EVERYDAY LIFE	THE WORLD
Middle Ages: 500–1499	*Middle Ages: 500–1499*

Early 15th century: In Bhutan *Shabdrung* (spiritual ruler) Thangtong Gyalpo builds iron chain-suspension bridges that help to link major valleys into a trade network.

1405–1433: A Muslim Chinese sea captain, Zheng He, carries out a series of officially sponsored sea expeditions that take him to southeast Asia and eventually all the way to Mecca. This is one of the few occasions when the Chinese reach out and show interest in the outside world.

1440s: Ulugh-Beg, a Tamerlane prince and grandson of Timur, builds an astronomical observatory at Samarkand.

Late 1400s: The first books printed with movable metal type appear in China and Korea.

1400s: Portuguese conduct voyages of discovery into the Atlantic, down the African coast, and eventually to India and South America.

1440–1469: Under Montezuma I, the Aztecs impose their rule over much of central Mexico.

1428: Joan of Arc leads French against English; in 1431 she is burned as a witch.

1434: African slaves are brought to Portugal, the first of some twenty million to be brought to Europe and the New World in the next four hundred years.

1434–1492: The Medici family—particularly Cosimo (1389–1464) and Lorenzo (1449–1492)—dominates Florence and supports the arts and culture.

1438–1499: The Inca conquer tribes in Peru and along the western coast of South America to build their empire.

1452–1519: Lifespan of Leonardo da Vinci, Italian artist and engineer.

1453: The fall of Constantinople to the Ottoman Turks ends the Eastern Roman Empire; the Turks take Athens in 1458.

1455–1485: The Wars of the Roses in England ends with Henry VII's defeat of Richard III, which begins the Tudor dynasty in England.

HISTORY

Middle Ages: 500–1499

ARTS, CULTURE, THOUGHT, AND RELIGION

Middle Ages: 500–1499

Early Modern Times: 1500–1899

1505–1639: The Portuguese begin to move into Sri Lanka in 1505; by the end of the century they will control much of Sri Lanka.

1511–1606: In 1511 Portuguese explorers capture the port of Malacca on the Malay Peninsula, erect a fort, and settle in. The Portuguese soon focus attention on the Moluccas in eastern Indonesia, the so-called Spice Islands of Ambon, Ternate, and Tidore. In 1512 the Portuguese move onto Ambon and then establish forts on Ternate and Tidore. In 1606 a Spanish fleet takes Ternate and Tidore, but Portugal has been shifting its focus of trade to China and Japan.

1526: Babur, a Muslim from Afghanistan, becomes the first Mughul ruler of India.

Early Modern Times: 1500–1899

1526–1530: The Mughal empire is founded in India during the reign of Babur, a Turkish prince and descendant of Chinggis Khan and Tamerlane. He introduces Turkish language and culture into India.

1542–1549: Francis Xavier (1506–1552), the Spanish Jesuit priest, founds his mission at Goa, on the coast of India (1542), then moves on to Malacca (1545), from which he carries his mission to the Moluccas. In 1549 he lands in Japan, where he is at first welcomed in the hope that trade will follow. In fact, Jesuit missionaries follow and some Japanese begin to convert to Christianity. Xavier dies of fever in 1552 while attempting to enter China.

SCIENCE-TECHNOLOGY, ECONOMICS, AND EVERYDAY LIFE

Middle Ages: 500–1499

THE WORLD

Middle Ages: 500–1499

1492: Christopher Columbus's first voyage to the Americas begins movement of Europeans to New World. King Ferdinand and Queen Isabella expel Muslims and Jews from Spain.

1495: First recorded outbreak of syphilis (in Naples) launches debate over whether it was introduced from the New World. (By the twentieth century it was recognized that syphilis had probably been in the Old World for many centuries.)

1497–1508: Anglo-Italian sailors John and Sebastian Cabot discover Labrador, Newfoundland, Nova Scotia, and the Hudson Bay.

1498: The Dominican friar Savonarola is hanged and then burned in Florence because of his criticism of the Pope and the Roman Catholic church.

1499: Amerigo Vespucci sails along the coast of Venezuela; he will later claim he first discovered South America in 1497. In any case, his Latinized name is assigned to the New World by the German mapmaker Martin Waldseemueller in 1507.

Early Modern Times: 1500–1899

1515–1596: Lifespan of Li Shi-Zhen, China's first great botanical writer. He compiles a pharmacopoeia that contains descriptions of one thousand plants and eight thousand prescriptions.

1540–1545: Sher Shah, ruler of India, introduces a standard silver rupee. He also builds an extensive network of roads in northern India.

1556: A mammoth earthquake devastates large areas of Shanxi province in China.

Late 16th century: Akbar introduces into India the Persian techniques for weaving pile carpets.

This period sees a rapid expansion of India's trade with Europe and the Middle East.

1571–1639: During these years, first the Portuguese, then the English, Spanish, and Dutch begin to start trading operations in Japan. When the Japanese see the effects of the ever-increasing presence and activities on their society, they ban all Westerners except the Dutch.

Early Modern Times: 1500–1899

1500–1550: Flowering of Italian Renaissance arts under Leonardo, Michelangelo, Raphael, Bellini, Giorgione, and Titian. Northern European art is also flourishing under Dürer, Cranach the Elder, the Holbeins, Gruenewald, and Altdorfer.

1508–1549: Spanish adventurers explore and conquer the Americas. Ponce de León, Balboa, and others discover and explore Central America and southeast coast of North America; Cortés conquers the Aztec empire in Mexico (1519–1524); Pizarro takes Peru (1531–1533). Coronado leads an expedition into the American Southwest (1540); the first Jesuit missionaries arrive in South America (1549). Jacques Cartier claims land in Canada for France (1534–1541).

HISTORY

Early Modern Times: 1500–1899

1553–1600: The Portuguese reach an agreement with the Chinese that allows them to establish a trading base in the area of Macau. By 1557 Macau has become an important Portuguese entrepôt linking the lucrative trade routes between Europe and East Asia and enabling the Portuguese virtually to monopolize Western trade with China.

1555–1605: Akbar the Great proceeds to conquer much of India, the climax of Mughul rule in India.

1567–1598: In Japan, Nobunaga deposes the shogunate and reigns supreme; he is succeeded in 1582 by Hideyoshi, who continues to end feudal power; in 1592 Hideyoshi invades Korea but is turned back; in 1596 he makes peace with China; his second invasion of Korea (1597–1598) fails.

1573: In the Maldives, a popular revolt expels the Portuguese. In the centuries that follow, although governments occasionally pay tribute to Sri Lanka, the Dutch, and the British, the Maldives remain governed locally and under Islamic rule.

1580s–1594: During this period, the Thais seize a major part of Cambodia. For the next 270 years, the Thais and the Vietnamese dominate Cambodia.

1595–1669: In 1595 Dutch trading companies make their first expeditions to the East Indies. By 1669 the Dutch are the dominant European trading power in the Indonesian archipelago.

1598: At the death of Hideyoshi, Ieyasu Tokugawa restores the shogunate and in 1603 makes himself supreme ruler of Japan; the Tokugawa family rules Japan until 1868.

ARTS, CULTURE, THOUGHT, AND RELIGION

Early Modern Times: 1500–1899

Mid-16th–late 17th centuries: Mughal rulers of India introduce a strong Persian element into Indian culture, particularly poetry, painting, and architecture. Golconda, in southeast India, becomes a major city under its sultans; distinctive styles of painting develop there. Mughal painting reaches its peak under Emperor Jahangir in the early seventeenth century.

1565: The first Catholic missionaries, Augustinian friars, arrive in the Philippines. After the Spanish take Manila they strongly promote Christianity; the Franciscans arrive in 1578. The spread of Islam on Luzon is checked, but Christianity never takes much hold in the south.

1570s: Japan's emperor Nobunaga takes steps to eliminate the political and military influence of the Buddhist sects. He also builds a great castle at Azuchi and commissions the era's greatest painter, Kano Eitoku, to decorate it. (The castle burns down in 1582.)

1582: Akbar, the Mughal emperor of India, promulgates his new syncretistic faith, drawing on religions of Hindus, Jains, Parsis, Buddhists, and Christians. Orthodox Muslims reject this as heresy. It does not survive Akbar's death in 1605.

1583–1598: Japan's ruler Hideyoshi commissions a number of magnificent buildings—including the castle at Osaka, the great Buddha Hall at Kyoto, and Fushimi Castle—and repairs many religious structures. But alarmed by Jesuit influence, Hideyoshi denounces Christianity and orders expulsion of all Jesuits (1587). In 1597 he orders that twenty-six Japanese converts to Christianity and foreign missionaries be crucified.

1593: Chu-tsai-ya of China develops the twelve equal-temperament tones in an octave.

1602: The Dutch begin large-scale importation of Chinese porcelain. Ming kilns are best known for polychrome pieces with a blue underglaze. Such pieces are in great demand in Europe and Asia; by 1682 the Dutch East India Company will have shipped twelve million pieces to Europe.

SCIENCE-TECHNOLOGY, ECONOMICS, AND EVERYDAY LIFE

Early Modern Times: 1500–1899

1573: When China's government lifts its ban on trading with Europeans (1567), Chinese merchants make contact with the Spanish in the Philippines. Within a few years, trade flourishes between China and the Americas, with Chinese silks and porcelain exchanged in vast quantities for New World silver. Much of this commerce flows through Manila, the Spanish trading center in the Philippines. Along with silver, new plants such as sweet potatoes, peanuts, and maize are introduced to China.

1592–1598: During Korea's Imjin War against the Japanese, Korean admiral Yi Sunsin achieves a number of decisive victories at sea by employing armored ships of his own invention called *kobukson* (turtle ships); these ships are thought to be the first ironclads ever used in battle.

17th century: India's cotton cloth finds a global market.

1601–1610: Matteo Ricci, an Italian Jesuit missionary, works in China. A linguist, mathematician, and scientist, he learns Chinese. He will maintain contact with Europe and introduce the West's scientific developments to the Chinese.

THE WORLD

Early Modern Times: 1500–1899

1517–1541: Martin Luther's protests against the Catholic Church launch what becomes the Protestant Reformation; Henry VIII marries Anne Boleyn (1533) and takes England out of the Roman Church; John Calvin establishes Protestant government in Geneva, Switzerland (1541).

1520–1571: The Ottoman Empire has been extending its rule around the Mediterranean. Under Emperor Suleiman I "The Magnificent" (reigns 1520–1566) the Ottomans continue their expansion. By 1526 the Turks have conquered much of Hungary but are turned back at Vienna (1529), and a combined European fleet defeats the Turks at the naval Battle of Lepanto (1571).

1545–1598: The Catholic Church calls the Council of Trent (1545–1563) to launch the Counter-Reformation. Protestants and Catholics wage bloody wars across Europe; in 1572 Protestants in France are massacred by Catholics on St. Bartholomew's Eve. In 1598 Henry IV's Edict of Nantes extends tolerance to French Protestants.

1558–1603: Elizabeth I rules England; during the vibrant Elizabethan Age the arts flourish, particularly the theater, led by William Shakespeare.

1581–1588: Spain attempts to expand its empire, but in 1581 the Netherlands proclaims independence from Spain; in 1588 the Spanish Armada fails in an attempt to invade England.

1592–1640: A scientific revolution is led by men such as Brahe, Galileo, Kepler, Bacon, Harvey, Torricelli, and Descartes.

1600–1690: The Baroque period in European art, with painters such as Caravaggio, Rubens, Van Dyck, Velasquez, and Rembrandt; architects such as Boromini; sculptors such as Bernini; and musicians such as Monteverdi, Schuetz, Buxtehude, and Lully.

HISTORY

Early Modern Times: 1500–1899

1616–1629: Ngawang Namgyal (1594–1651), a Tibetan monk, arrives in Bhutan in flight from the Dalai Lama. After defeating rival religious leaders, he assumes the title *shabdrung* (this office, the spiritual head of government, is sometimes called *dharma raja*). He is Bhutan's first great national figure.

1623–1682: England enters the spice trade and moves into the Moluccas. In 1623, the Dutch massacre the English on Ambon to discourage rival trade; after continued struggle to compete with Dutch trading, the English eventually shift their attention to India while keeping a token presence in Indonesia.

1638–1639: Japanese massacre Christians and close Japan to all foreigners except some Chinese and Dutch traders.

1639–1640: Dutch defeat Portuguese to win control of east and west coasts of Sri Lanka. The Dutch control Sri Lanka until they lose it to the English in 1796.

1640–1641: The Dutch oust the Portuguese from Malacca.

1644–1912: The Ming emperor Chongzhen hangs himself; the Manchu general Wu Sangui founds the Qing (Ch'ing) dynasty, which rules China until 1912.

1658–1707: Aurangzeb deposes Shah Jahan, conquers much of India, and rules as the Great Mughul.

1687: England's East India Company, already in possession of the Indian Trade Monopoly, is granted monopoly over trade with China by the British government.

1691–1911: The Manchu/Qing dynasty ruling China effectively controls much of Mongolia.

1707–1893: Laos enters a long period of internal strife and foreign intervention. Divided into several parts, it becomes a pawn in the conflicts among Thailand, Cambodia, Myanmar, and Vietnam.

1727–1795: Tibet falls under Chinese rule, but breaks free in 1795.

ARTS, CULTURE, THOUGHT, AND RELIGION

Early Modern Times: 1500–1899

1614–1638: The true leader of Japan, Tokugawa Ieyasu, calls in 1614 for the prohibition of Christianity in Japan and the expulsion of all remaining missionaries. Persecution of Christians escalates as dozens are executed.

1631–1651: During last twenty years of his rule in Bhutan, Ngawang Namgyal constructs dozens of *dzongs* (fortified monasteries) in the western valleys of Bhutan; these massive sloping stone structures serve both as monastic communities and civil administrative centers. His legal code, *Tsa Yig*, is based on Buddhist *dharma* (religious law) and remains in force until the 1960s.

1632–1647: The Taj Mahal is erected at Agra, India, as a tomb for Shah Jahan's favorite queen, Mumtaz Mahal.

1644–1694: Lifespan of Matsuo Basho, Japan's most famous poet; he is especially noted for his *haiku*, a seventeen-syllable poetic form employing natural imagery.

1658–1707: Reign of Mughal emperor Aurangzeb. A devout Muslim, he enforces Islamic law, destroys Hindu temples, and maintains Mughal tradition in construction of mosques such as the Badshahi Mosque at Lahore.

1665: *Ukiyo monogatari* (Tale of the Floating World), a Japanese classic by Asai Ryoi, is published; its title refers to the world of courtesans and actors, which becomes a popular subject for Japanese writers and artists in ensuing centuries.

SCIENCE-TECHNOLOGY, ECONOMICS, AND EVERYDAY LIFE

Early Modern Times: 1500–1899

1602: The Dutch East India Company is formed with a merger of competing companies. The market for spices in Europe propels much of the trade and ensuing economic and political developments in Southeast Asia.

1609–1648: War between Spain and the Netherlands puts strain on Philippine resources. Filipinos are drafted as laborers to build ships and provide other services to the Spanish military. The Spanish government imposes *vandala*, or quotas of goods to be sold at fixed price by villagers, but the government often does not pay.

1623: India exports its first tobacco, a crop introduced by the Portuguese in the late 16th century. Cotton, sugar cane, opium, and indigo are India's major cash crops.

Late 17th century: Vast amounts of tea are being imported to Britain and are paid for with silver bullion, creating a trade imbalance in China's favor.

1720: After the Japanese government ends the ban on Dutch scientific and technical books and allows their translation, Japanese scholars flock to Nagasaki to study Western science and technology. The first complete Japanese translation of a Western anatomical text will appear in 1774.

1720: China ships 400,000 pounds of tea annually to England.

THE WORLD

Early Modern Times: 1500–1899

1607–1630: The English commence their colonization of northeastern America at Jamestown (1607), Plymouth (1620), and Boston (1630).

1618–1648: The Thirty Years' War rages across Europe.

1650–1700: The scientific revolution continues, now led by such scholars as von Guericke, Malpighi, Boyle, Newton, Halley, van Leeuwenhoek, Hooke, Leibnitz, and Huyghens.

1643–1715: The four-year-old Louis XIV inherits the throne of France; eventually his court at Versailles dominates the French state and culture.

1683: Vienna is again besieged by Ottoman Turks but is relieved by John Sobieski.

1689–1754: A series of wars involving European states (among them England, France, Austria, Spain) spreads to North America, where they become known as the French and Indian Wars.

c. 1700: The Ashanti people of west Africa (modern Ghana) form a confederation with neighboring states; they continue to extend their power until they are defeated in 1896 after a series of wars with the English.

HISTORY

Early Modern Times: 1500–1899

1741–1754: The French introduce the European arms trade to the Indian subcontinent. Their military successes lead Indian princes to pay for French training for their own troops; *sepoys* (European-trained and-led Indian infantrymen) become a staple of both European and Indian armies.

1744–1763: The French and English in India fight three wars, two of them extensions of European wars. When the third war ends, England is left the uncontested colonial power on the subcontinent. The French East India Company is dissolved in 1769, and France's role in India effectively ends.

1757: The English solidify their rule in India by defeating Indian forces at the Battle of Plassey.

1759: The Chinese promulgate trading restrictions to ensure that Western traders do not expand into other areas of China. These rules are gradually tightened, to the frustration of the foreigners.

1771–1881: The lands of Central Asia gradually become protectorates and then conquered possessions of Czarist Russia. Russians gradually replace natives in positions of authority, and Russian peasants migrate in large numbers to the uncultivated land of the steppes, which is often cheaply sold or simply given away.

1782: The Chakri dynasty is founded in Siam (Thailand); it continues to rule through the twentieth century.

1794: Malacca comes under British rule.

1796–1798: The British seize Dutch possessions in Sri Lanka. Formal cession under the Peace of Amiens (1801) makes the island Britain's first Crown colony (until 1948). The British also take over governing the Maldives.

ARTS, CULTURE, THOUGHT, AND RELIGION

Early Modern Times: 1500–1899

Mid-17th century–18th century: In Korea, the Sirhak, or Practical Learning, school of thought flourishes. Sirhak thinkers, like their counterparts in Europe's Enlightenment, generally eschew metaphysical concerns in pursuit of a pragmatic scholarship founded upon explicit verification. They produce a vast body of encyclopedic work on subjects as disparate as farming and Chinese classical scholarship.

1692: China's emperor Kangxi issues an edict extending toleration to Christian converts so long as they continue to perform ancestral rites. He rescinds the edict, however, when a Vatican envoy rules against allowing Chinese Christians to perform the ancient rites.

18th century: In Japan, the great masters of woodblock prints emerge, including Harunobu (1724–1770), Kiyonobu (1752–1815), and Utamaro (1754–1806).

   With the decline of the Mughal empire, northern Indian artists, musicians, and poets disperse to other courts. Urdu replaces Persian as India's major literary language among Muslims.

1724: China's emperor Yongzheng bans Christianity; Jesuits are permitted only in Beijing. He orders, however, that the ban not be enforced with violence.

1764: The Golden Temple at Amritsar, holiest shrine of the Sikhs, is rebuilt.

1780s–1800: In India, with the growing prominence of the British and their East India Company, English-language newspapers appear; the English also sponsor colleges to teach Indians their traditional culture and found the Asiatic Society of Bengal to promote research and knowledge of India's past among Westerners. This is not a completely altruistic undertaking, inasmuch as the British want to win over the Indians and to educate them for the civil service.

1792: *The Dream of the Red Chamber,* China's greatest novel, incomplete at author Cao Xueqin's death in 1763, is published. It follows the fortunes of the Jia family from wealth and power to gradual decline and final collapse.

SCIENCE-TECHNOLOGY, ECONOMICS, AND EVERYDAY LIFE

Early Modern Times: 1500–1899

1729: England exports two hundred chests of opium, each holding 130 to 160 pounds of the drug, into China. The opium trade grows as the West tries to right the balance of trade with China: the Chinese are far less interested in Western products (except for weapons and medical technology) than Westerners are in China's silks, porcelain, and tea. Opium is one import the Chinese buy avidly.

1724–1735: Sawai Jai Singh II, maharaja of Jaipur, builds five astronomical observatories across northern India. These are huge precision and masonry instruments of his own design, and he employs dozens of astronomers.

1750: Cotton and tobacco culture are widespread in northeast China. This is a region of small-holdings, with the average family plot running to 2.5 acres and holdings greater than twenty acres uncommon. Elsewhere, American and African crops such as the sweet potato, Irish potato, maize, and peanut are spreading and improving the Chinese diet.

1770s: The British continue to bring opium from India into China in an attempt to regularize the balance of trade with China. By the early 19th century, opium is second only to land taxes as the East India Company's source of revenue in India.

1796: In China an imperial edict bans the opium trade, which nonetheless continues to expand illegally.

THE WORLD

Early Modern Times: 1500–1899

1700–1780: The Enlightenment flourishes in Western Europe, led by men such as Locke, Voltaire, Rousseau, Hume, Montesquieu, Diderot, and the French Encyclopedists.

1720–1790: European classical music flourishes under Bach, Vivaldi, Handel, Glück, Haydn, and Mozart.

1775–1789: American colonists revolt against England and end up gaining their independence. After a constitution is adopted in 1787, George Washington is elected the first president of the United States in 1789.

1789–1799: French commoners rise up against the monarchy, declare a republic (1792), and execute King Louis XVI (1793). The "reign of terror," after two years of violence and chaos, is succeeded by years during which France, led by Napoleon, makes wars against much of Europe.

1791–1833: Europeans had been trading slaves from Africa to the Americas since 1501; the British outlawed slavery at home in 1772; Friends (Quakers) established first American abolition society in 1775. The Englishman William Wilberforce leads the campaign to bring England finally to outlaw slavery in its colonies in 1833.

HISTORY

Early Modern Times: 1500–1899

Early 19th century: European powers begin to force trade onto China and in so doing bring in opium.

1811–1816: During the Napoleonic Wars, Java falls under British rule and Sir Thomas Stamford Raffles reforms the administration.

1824: The Treaty of London is signed by England and Holland to end their rivalries in Southeast Asia by dividing up the colonized areas of Indonesia.

1824–1885: Britain gains control of Burma.

1839–1842: James Brooke, a retired British army officer, arrives in Sarawak and in 1840 he assists Brunei's chieftain in quashing a rebellion. In return, in 1842 Brooke is ceded part of Sarawak and its dependencies, to be inherited by his descendants.

1839–1842: In 1839 the Chinese government demands immediate surrender of all opium, which is then publicly destroyed. As tensions mount, the British fire at a Chinese junk, thus starting the First Anglo-Chinese War, known also as the First Opium War. The war ends with the Treaty of Nanking, under which China gives Hong Kong to Great Britain and opens five major Chinese ports to British trade.

1856–1860: After the Second Anglo-Chinese War (Second Opium War), the Treaty of Peking forces China to give Britain territory adjacent to Hong Kong, Kowloon, and Stonecutters Island.

1850s: After Britain takes over Hong Kong, Macau is relegated to a minor commercial role. However, the introduction of licensed gambling in the 1850s provides a new source of revenue.

1851–1864: During the Taiping Rebellion in China, millions of Chinese die. Many Western mercenaries participate, but in general European powers support the reigning Qing dynasty in order to preserve their own trading rights.

ARTS, CULTURE, THOUGHT, AND RELIGION

Early Modern Times: 1500–1899

1797: Thailand's literary classic *Ramakian*, the Siamese version of the Indian *Ramayana* epic, is set to verse.

19th century: Japan's second generation of great woodblock print artists includes Hosukai (1760–1849) and Hiroshige (1797–1858).

c. 1810: Publication of *Truyen Thuy Kieu*, the romantic epic poem that remains the best known literary work in Vietnam. It is composed by Nguyen Du, regarded as probably the greatest classical poet of Vietnam. *Kieu* is based on a Chinese poem, but Nguyen Du has created his own work; it tells of the trials and sufferings of a beautiful and intelligent young woman, Thuy Kieu, who finds herself constantly victimized by the patriarchal society of her time. Many of its 3,254 lines (in the demotic *nom*) are still memorized and quoted by Vietnamese of all walks of life.

1815–1830: The Bengal Renaissance commences, promoting Bengali as a literary language and the Bengali traditions and culture. Bengali soon comes into use to write India's first major modern vernacular literature. Calcutta emerges as the intellectual center of India.

1835: After a British government report recommending that Western education be promoted in India and that English be established as the language of higher education, English replaces Persian as the official language of government and the courts. English is also adopted as the major language at Indian universities.

1850s: The Taiping Rebellion sweeps China, drawing strength from Chinese popular religion with its ghosts, spirits and admixtures of Daoism, Buddhism, and, in the case of the Taiping leader Hong Xiuquan, Christianity.

1860: Eduard Douwes Dekker (1820–1887) (under the pen name Multatuli), a former Dutch East India Company official, publishes a novel, *Max Havelaar*, that exposes the oppressive and corrupt ways of the Dutch in Indonesia. It will be cited by those who seek to reform or even eliminate Dutch rule.

SCIENCE-TECHNOLOGY,
ECONOMICS, AND EVERYDAY LIFE

Early Modern Times: 1500–1899

1800: Imports of opium from British India reach four thousand chests a year. An addiction problem becomes evident in some parts of China; by the 1820s, enough opium enters the country to feed the habits of one million addicts.

1827–1834: In 1827 the British introduce coffee cultivation into India. Coffee replaces spices as major export commodity; migrant Tamil laborers are recruited from Tamil Nadu in south India to work plantations. Cultivation reaches its peak in the 1870s before a blight in the 1890s destroys the industry; it does not recover for fifty years. Meanwhile, in 1834 the British import tea seeds and specialist labor from China and initiate Indian cultivation of tea on government-owned plantations in Assam (1836). Tea plantations extend beyond Assam and Bengal into south India. Exports to Britain begin in the late 1830s; tea exports nearly triple from 1875–1885 as India displaces China as Britain's major supplier of tea.

1854: The first mechanized jute mill in India opens. Exported since 1838, jute becomes a major industry with development of large-scale production to replace Russian supplies interrupted by the Crimean War. The first modern cotton mill also dates from this year, and cotton production becomes a major industry for India.

1859: Telegraph service between Singapore and Batavia, on Java, is installed, and the first drydock facility opens.

1868: The first Japanese contract workers arrive in Hawaii to work on sugar plantations.

1869: The Suez Canal opens, reducing passage between India and Britain from three months to three weeks. All of Asia will gradually be brought into closer contact with Western cultural and economic influences.

1871: The first oil well is drilled in northern Sumatra, but full-scale commercial production will not begin for another twenty years.

THE WORLD

Early Modern Times: 1500–1899

1799–1815: Napoleon Bonaparte returns to France after years of military successes, overthrows the government (1799), crowns himself as emperor (1804). He continues fighting other European states until he is finally defeated at Waterloo and exiled to St. Helena.

1800–1830: European writers, musicians, and artists, with a new emphasis on the individual and feelings, create what is labeled the Romantic movement: Wordsworth, Shelley, Keats, Byron, Goethe, Schiller, Beethoven, Schubert, Weber, Chateaubriand, Constant, Turner, and Gericault.

1812–1815: The United States engages in a brief but intense series of battles against the British from Canada to New Orleans.

1815: Meeting at the Congress of Vienna as a result of the defeat of Napoleon, diplomats of Western Europe—principally Britain, Russia, France, and Austria—draw the boundaries for Europe and set in place a peace that will by and large last a century.

1815–1876: Almost ceaseless scientific and technological advances—steamboats, railroads, metals processing, telegraph, photography, electric light bulbs, telephone, elevators—transform daily life.

1816–1828: In southeast Africa, Chief Shaka of the Zulus leads his well-trained army in conquests of neighboring people.

1820–1890: Opera flourishes in Europe with such composers as Donizetti, Bellini, Rossini, Berlioz, Wagner, Gounod, Massenet, and Verdi.

1835–1880: The golden age of the novel in Europe: Dickens, the Brontes, Trollope, Eliot, Gogol, Dosteovsky, Tolstoy, Turgenev, Sand, Hugo, Dumas, Balzac, and Flaubert.

HISTORY

Early Modern Times: 1500–1899

1853–1858: Japan has been effectively cut off from the West for more than two hundred years and even kills foreigners who come ashore accidentally. In 1853 the U.S. government sends Commodore Matthew Perry to force Japan to open diplomatic and trade relations. In 1854 the shogunate signs a treaty of friendship with the United States, then signs similar treaties with Britain, Russia, and the Netherlands. By 1858 Japan has signed commercial treaties with many European powers and opened its ports to foreign trade. This leads the Japanese government to purge those within it who are opposed to reopening Japan to the West.

1857–1858: The Sepoy Mutiny in India leads the British government to abolish the East India Company and to take control of India.

1858–1883: France gains control of Vietnam.

1863: A delegation of French naval officers concludes a treaty with King Norodom, and Cambodia becomes a French protectorate.

1864–1865: After decades of border raids and tensions, the British army invades and in five months defeats Bhutan. Under the Treaty of Sinchula (1865), Bhutan becomes a quasi-protectorate of Great Britain.

1867: Japan's Emperor Mutsuhito regains power from the Tokugawas, ending the shogun period and restoring imperial control under the Meiji dynasty. He begins modernization of the country, adopting a new constitution in 1869. With modernization of the legal system, by 1899 foreigners are willing to renegotiate commercial treaties with Japan.

1876–1890: Korea has been known as the "Hermit Kingdom" because of its strict isolation. In 1876, Japan forces Korea to open some ports to trade and to allow Japanese to settle in Korea. During the 1880s, the United States, Russia, and several European countries sign commercial treaties with Korea.

ARTS, CULTURE, THOUGHT, AND RELIGION

Early Modern Times: 1500–1899

1860–1941: Lifespan of Rabindranath Tagore, who leads a modern Indian literary renaissance; he wins the Nobel Prize for Literature in 1913.

1875: In growing reaction to the English influence in India, the Arya Samaj association is founded in Bombay to promote a revival of Hinduism. It will count a million members by 1931.

Late 19th century: Central Asian intellectuals known as *jadids* address what they perceive as the backwardness of Central Asia by starting schools and a printing press and advocating modernization. The Russians, however, suppress the movement; although it continues to function underground, its teachings are not widely disseminated.

1867: Publication of the first Japanese-English dictionary, the work of the American missionary and physician James Hepburn.

1868–1870: Japan's government decrees (1868) the separation of Shinto and Buddhism. In 1870 Shinto becomes the state religion.

1873: As part of the modernization being promoted by the Meiji dynasty, Japan abolishes old edicts banning Christianity, but freedom of religion is not specifically granted.

1889: The first Japanese movie premieres in Tokyo.

1890: Protestant missionaries are established in fifteen of China's sixteen provinces. By 1900, there are five hundred Protestant mission stations in the country.

1892: After his second novel, *El Filibusterismo*, is published in Ghent, José Rizal returns to the Philippines from abroad and founds the Liga Filipina, a peaceful association advocating reform. He is immediately arrested and banished to Mindanao.

SCIENCE-TECHNOLOGY, ECONOMICS, AND EVERYDAY LIFE

Early Modern Times: 1500–1899

1872: A railroad connecting Tokyo and Yokohama is completed. Public telephone service between the two cities is introduced in 1890.

1873: Japan adopts the Gregorian calendar of the West.

1875: Tokyo Meteorological Observatory is founded; Japan's National Astronomical Observatory is founded in 1878.

1876: China's first railway opens near Shanghai. Conservative Chinese regard railroads as disruptive and inharmonious. The provincial governor, disapproving, orders the track torn up in 1877.

1877: An American zoologist organizes Tokyo University's zoology department and introduces Darwinian theory to Japanese students.

1880s: China develops national cable and telegraph communications systems.

***c.* 1880–1910:** On Sri Lanka, three major cash crops—tea, rubber, and coconuts—come to dominate the plantation system of agriculture introduced by the British in the 1830s. (They remain the mainstay of Sri Lanka's present-day economy.) British recruit a large number of resident Tamils as a permanent labor force on tea and rubber plantations.

1883: The volcano on the island of Krakatoa erupts and explodes; much of the island collapses, creating a *tsunami* (tidal wave) that washes over the shores of nearby islands and kills some 36,000 people; its ash drifts around the upper atmosphere and affects the world's climate for several years.

1890s: Bombay has eighty power cotton mills by the early 1890s. By 1900, Bombay and Ahmadabad, emerging as industrial cities, are centers of this important export commodity.

1896: China has 300 miles of railroad, compared to 2,300 miles in Japan, 21,000 miles in Great Britain, and 182,000 miles in the United States.

1897: Japanese inventor and industrialist Toyoda Sakichi designs the first Japanese power loom; in 1924 he will design the most advanced automated power loom, allowing Japan to dominate the world's silk trade.

THE WORLD

Early Modern Times: 1500–1899

1836–1890: With the Whitmans' crossing of the Continental Divide and their settlement in the Pacific Northwest, Americans begin to move ever more westward; at first they settle along the Pacific coast but eventually they settle the Great Plains. Wherever they go they displace and defeat the native Indians.

1845–1870: From Massachusetts to New York, writers create a golden age of American literature: Emerson, Thoreau, Poe, Fuller, Alcott, Hawthorne, Melville, Dickinson, and Whitman.

1848–1849: Many Europeans have become restless under their archaic and autocratic rulers, and there are uprisings in Berlin, Budapest, Milan, Naples, Prague, Rome, Vienna, and Venice. Within a year these revolts are largely repressed and many of the leaders and supporters go into exile.

1859–1899: Darwin, Pasteur, Mendel, Maxwell, Mendeleyev, Roentgen, J. J. Thomson, Curie, and others come forth with a series of scientific discoveries that will transform the modern world.

1861–1865: With slavery as the central issue, Americans of the North engage the newly proclaimed Confederacy of the South in a bloody civil war. In 1863, Lincoln proclaims that slaves are to be freed; slavery is not formally abolished until the Thirteenth Amendment of 1866. Lincoln's assassination (1865) ends what might have been a true resolution of the issue.

1869: After an exhibition in Paris where paintings are labeled "impressionist," a school of painting flourishes: Monet, Manet, Renoir, Degas, Morisot, Pissarro, Sisley, Cassatt, Hassam, and others.

1875–1895: In the United States, an age of prosperity and expansiveness is led by such industrialists as Carnegie and Frick, financiers as Gould and Morgan, and transportation giants as Vanderbilt and Harriman.

1880s–1920: During the 1880s, European nations—Belgium, France, Germany, Great Britain, Italy, and Spain—begin to divide up Africa until by 1920 all of Africa (except Ethiopia and Liberia) is under colonial rule.

HISTORY

Early Modern Times: 1500–1899

1893: Thailand sends troops into northern Laos to repel marauding bandits, then proceeds to occupy all of northern Laos and establish outposts in northern Vietnam. When the French step in to protect Laos, Thailand accepts the Mekong River as its eastern boundary, leaving France in control of Laos.

1894–1895: Japan and China compete to gain control over Korea. Their rivalry culminates in the Sino-Japanese War (1894–1895); Japan emerges victorious and China repudiates its suzerainty over Korea. Japan moves at once to exercise authority over Korea's government.

1895: Under the Treaty of Shimonoseki, China cedes Taiwan and the Pescadores Islands to Japan in perpetuity. Local leaders in Taiwan immediately proclaim independence and attempt to establish Asia's first republic. After five months of "pacification," the Japanese crush the new republic.

1897–1899: Seeing that after the war against the Japanese China is greatly weakened, Germany, Russia, Britain, and France rush to seize Chinese territory for themselves. In 1898–1899 the United States tries to inaugurate an "Open Door" policy for China; with limited success, the initiative seeks to arrest the Great Powers' dividing of China into "spheres of influence."

1898–1899: The secret society of the Harmonious Fists emerges in China. Known in the West as The Boxers, the society blames all China's ills on foreigners and steps up attacks on Chinese Christian converts. Foreign missionaries call on imperial forces to quell the outbreaks.

1899–1902: Filipinos, having seen the replacement of their Spanish rulers by the United States, rise in revolt; 4,234 Americans and at least 20,000 Filipinos die.

ARTS, CULTURE, THOUGHT, AND RELIGION

Early Modern Times: 1500–1899

SCIENCE-TECHNOLOGY,
ECONOMICS, AND EVERYDAY LIFE

THE WORLD

Early Modern Times: 1500–1899

Early Modern Times: 1500–1899

1896: The first modern Olympics is held in Athens, Greece.

1898: After an explosion on the USS *Maine* in the harbor of Havana, Cuba, the United States goes to war against Spain; it ends with the United States taking over Puerto Rico, the Philippines, and Guam. The United States also annexes Hawaii.

1899–1902: The Boer War is fought in South Africa. Although the Boers lose the war to the British, the Republic of South Africa will be established in 1910.

HISTORY

The Twentieth Century: 1900–1998

1900–1901: In China, the Boxer Rebellion spreads as armed men kill foreign missionaries and engineers and lay siege to the foreign legations quarter in Beijing. In August 1900 a multinational force of twenty thousand troops from Japan, Russia, Britain, the United States, and France lifts the siege and loots the city. Under the treaty signed in 1901, China surrenders many rights.

1901–1911: China's Manchu rulers' attempts at reforms are too little, too late. By 1905 several revolutionary republican groups in China combine to form the United League, headed by Sun Yatsen. They conduct a series of armed attacks on Manchu forces, and by the end of 1911 most of the southern and central provinces have revolted against the Manchus.

1904–1905: Japan and Russia are increasingly confrontational over Manchuria and Korea. In 1904 Japan declares war on Russia. After a year of hard fighting, the two warring nations sign a treaty arranged by U.S. president Theodore Roosevelt. Having defeated Russia, Japan suddenly emerges as major player on the world stage.

1910: Japan takes complete control of Korea and rules it until the end of World War II.

1911–1946: With the end of the Manchu dynasty in China, a movement for Mongol independence emerges. In 1924 the People's Republic of Mongolia is founded, but policy continues to be dominated by Moscow. A plebiscite is held in 1945 in which the Mongolian people support absolute independence; China recognizes this in 1946 but maintains its claim to Inner Mongolia.

1912–1922: The Republic of China is established with Sun Yat-sen as president. However, former Manchu military official Yuan Shi-kai seizes power and makes himself virtual dictator. A period of turmoil ensues.

1914–1918: As World War I rages in Europe, Japan declares war against Germany but does not send any forces, instead simply takes over Germany's colonial holdings in China and several islands in the Pacific.

ARTS, CULTURE, THOUGHT, AND RELIGION

The Twentieth Century: 1900–1998

1900–1903: Japanese women begin to emerge as a political force when the first Japanese woman who studied abroad founds the Tokyo Women's English School (1900); the feminist poet Yosano Akiko issues volume of poems of passion and sensuality (1901); and the first women's magazine in Japan, *Fujin no tomo* (Women's Friend) is published (1903).

1909: A copy of the Cambodian translation of sacred Buddhist writings is deposited at a temple at Angkor Wat. For the next sixty years Cambodian monarchs frequently visit the site and sponsor religious ceremonies there.

1913: India produces its first feature movie. Its first talkie is produced in 1931.

1915: Chen Duxiu (1879–1942), Dean of Letters at Beijing University, founds the periodical *New Youth*, which attacks traditional Chinese thought. In keeping with this, the magazine will abandon classical Chinese and publish in the vernacular.

***c.* 1916:** The first animated movies are produced in Japan.

SCIENCE-TECHNOLOGY, ECONOMICS, AND EVERYDAY LIFE

The Twentieth Century: 1900–1998

1905: After a decade of foreign capital infusion and construction, China's railroad network is around 4,000 miles.

1911: India's first steel mill opens. Largely spurred by Allied military requirements during World War I, it becomes the British Empire's largest steelmaking complex. The steel industry undergoes enormous growth during and after World War I.

1914: Young Chinese scientists trained in the United States establish the Science Society. The society's journal will become influential.

1916: China's government sets up the Geological Survey of China. It sponsors the paleontological research that leads to the discovery of Peking Man in 1929.

1916–1925: Cambodia enters a period of increased economic prosperity; the first Cambodian rice mills are inaugurated, and the country begins exporting high-quality rubber. Roads and railways are built, but the profits fail to trickle down to the peasantry, and constant rural rebellion and disorder mark the period.

THE WORLD

The Twentieth Century: 1900–1998

1900: Publication of Sigmund Freud's *The Interpretation of Dreams,* the first of Freud's works that bring his theories and insights into common currency.

1903: Exercising gunboat diplomacy, the United States oversees the breakaway of Panama from Colombia and then signs a treaty granting the United States the right to construct a canal across the isthmus (1907–1914).

Guglielmo Marconi sends the first readable transatlantic wireless radio message. The Wright brothers make the first sustained manned flights in a gasoline-powered aircraft.

1905: Russians rise up in a revolt before the Winter Palace in Leningrad and on the cruiser *Potemkin.* After making certain concessions, the tsar withdraws them and dissolves the Duma in 1906.

Albert Einstein publishes three scientific papers that revolutionize modern physics and the understanding of the universe.

1912: The SS *Titanic* strikes an iceberg in the North Atlantic and sinks within two and a half hours, with the loss of 1,513 lives.

1912–1913: Two wars in the Balkans result in the loss of much of the Ottoman Turkish Empire's territory in Europe.

1914–1918: The assassination of Archduke Franz Ferdinand leads the powers of Europe to choose sides and World War I is fought for over four years. The United States enters the war officially in April 1917, but its troops do not go into action until October.

1917: Russian troops mutiny and force the end of the Romanov dynasty. Lenin and his Bolsheviks lead a revolution in October and take control of Russia. Tsar Nicholas and his family are executed in 1918.

HISTORY

The Twentieth Century: 1900–1998

1918: Tibetans overthrow Chinese rule and govern independently during the following decades of political upheaval and revolution in China and Russia.

1918–1929: In Russia, when the Bolsheviks come to power, they start incorporating the Central Asian states as Soviet Socialist Republics. The nomadic way of life gradually becomes all but extinct under Soviet administration.

With the end of World War I and the Paris peace conference (1919), U.S. president Woodrow Wilson calls for self-determination for colonial lands, but Europeans (and Japan) hold on to their possessions throughout Asia. Thus new revolutionaries begin to take the lead in their Asian lands; many are or become Communists and must at first operate from exile. Among them is the Vietnamese revolutionary Ho Chi Minh.

1922–1928: China is embroiled in a civil war as northern warlords try to take power. Sun Yat-sen reemerges as the leader of a Nationalist Party, and Communists are encouraged to support it. After Sun Yat-sen dies in 1925, Chiang Kai-shek takes command of the Nationalists, defeats the northern warlords, then turns against the Communists. By 1928 he has taken Beijing and gained control over most of China. The Communists retreat to remote parts of China.

1934–1935: To avoid pressure from the Nationalist forces, Mao Zedong, the leading Chinese Communist, leads a small band of followers on the "long march" to Shaanxi in northwest-central China.

1935: The Commonwealth of Philippines is inaugurated. The Philippines is now almost self-governing, with the United States handling defense and foreign affairs. General Douglas MacArthur is appointed military adviser to the Philippine government.

ARTS, CULTURE, THOUGHT, AND RELIGION

The Twentieth Century: 1900–1998

1919: Beijing University librarian Li Dazhao (1889–1927) publishes an introduction to Marxist theory in *New Youth*. He organizes a Marxist study group at the university in 1921; its attendees include Mao Zedong, a young student from rural Henan.

1923: Sir Muhammad Iqbal (1877–1938) publishes *Bang-i-Dira*, a collection of his poems in Urdu. He soon after embarks on a long and distinguished political career that will lead to an independent Pakistan.

1926: Japanese art historian Yannagi Muneyoshi coins the term *mingei* (folk craft) and starts a movement to promote traditional decorative arts. In 1936 he helps to found Japan Folk Craft Museum.

1927: Suzuki Daisetzu (1870–1966) begins publication of *Essays in Zen Buddhism* and helps to spread Zen Buddhism around the world.

1928–1929: The first modern Thai novels appear. Authors Kulap Saipradit, Prince Akatdamkoeng, and "Dokmai Sot" (M. L. Buppha Kunjara Nimmanhemin) explore cultural conflicts between the West and Thailand, and the effects of modernization.

1933: In Indonesia, publication of literary journal *Poedjangga Baroe* (New Poet) begins; in its pages, national literary standards and cultural identity are explored by modernist writers. Amir Hamzah (1911–1946) is a prominent poet whose works are published in this journal.

1936: The first Khmer-language newspaper, *Nagarra Vatta* (Angkor Wat), appears. For the first time, Cambodians can read about world events in their own language. The paper provides a focus for an increasing sense of nationalism.

SCIENCE-TECHNOLOGY, ECONOMICS, AND EVERYDAY LIFE

The Twentieth Century: 1900–1998

1920: Some 1,700 Chinese-owned industrial enterprises employ 500,000 workers. China's railroad network totals 7,000 miles, modest for a country of such great size; China's national system, with around 3,800 miles of track, employs 73,000 workers.

India's Meghnad Saha publishes a pioneering work on thermal ionization in interstellar atmosphere that will become the basis of modern astrophysics.

1922: Forty-nine new cotton mills open in China. Large modern flour mills are established around Shanghai; cigarette and paper industries flourish in the Guangzhou area. North China collieries employ fifty thousand miners.

1924: Method of quantum statistical mechanics by Satyendra Nath Bose (1894–1974), a Calcutta physicist, is published by Albert Einstein. It becomes known as "Bose-Einstein statistics." The subatomic particle "boson" is later named for him.

1929–1933: Joseph Stalin begins his campaign of forced collectivization in Central Asia. Exact numbers are unknown, but it is estimated that millions die of overwork and starvation.

The British Malayan Oil Company, a subsidiary of Royal Dutch Shell, finds oil at the Seria field.

1930: India's Sir Chandrasekhara Venkata Raman wins the Nobel Prize for physics for his 1928 discovery of the "Raman effect," changes in light wavelengths on which spectroscopy technology is based. He founds the Indian Academy of Sciences (1934).

THE WORLD

The Twentieth Century: 1900–1998

1919: The Paris Peace Conference assigns Germany sole responsibility for World War I; U.S. President Woodrow Wilson's idealistic agenda is virtually ignored and his own country will refuse to join the League of Nations.

1921: The Irish Free State is formally proclaimed, but the six northern counties vote to remain within the United Kingdom.

1921–1932: A series of disarmament conferences is held in various cities (among them Washington, London, and Geneva) in an attempt to get the major powers at least to limit their armed forces, but none of the agreements hold up.

1923: Adolf Hitler fails at the so-called Beer Hall *Putsch* in Munich, Germany; he will spend nine months in prison where he writes *Mein Kampf*, laying out his plans for world conquest.

Benito Mussolini, having forced the king of Italy to let him form a government in 1922, imposes his fascist dictatorship.

Kemal Ataturk becomes president of the Republic of Turkey and proceeds to lead his country into the modern secular world.

1924–1927: Lenin dies (1924), and within three years Joseph Stalin will effectively take control of the Soviet Union.

1928: The Pact of Paris, better known as the Kellogg-Briand Pact, is signed by fifteen nations (and eventually by forty-seven more), agreeing to outlaw war as an instrument of national policy.

1929–1932: The crash of the New York stock market in October 1929 soon leads to the collapse of European and world credit and banking systems. Germany cannot keep up its heavy reparations payments. World trade declines and tariffs rise. By 1932, millions in the industrialized nations are unemployed and the world is mired in a major depression.

1933: In January, Adolf Hitler becomes chancellor of Germany, although his Nazi Party does not hold a majority; in March Hitler is granted the right to rule by decree. He wastes no time in cracking down on all opposition, and by April he is already attacking the Jews.

HISTORY

The Twentieth Century: 1900–1998

1937–1938: In Japan, militarists have gained control. The Japanese launch a major attack on China. By the end of 1938, Japan controls most of eastern China. For the next seven years China will be engaged in a continuous war with Japanese occupation forces.

1940: Japan's government repeats claim that its only goal is "a new order in Greater East Asia." This becomes known as the "Greater East Asia Co-Prosperity Sphere," which Japan intends to exploit to become the dominant power in Asia. Japan makes its first move after France surrenders to Germany (June 1940); Japan invades French Indochina and leaves the Vichy French in administrative control.

1940–1943: Thailand signs a "treaty of friendship" with Japan, then allows Japanese troops to enter in return for Japanese assurances of Thai independence. Thailand attacks French positions in Laos and Cambodia, regaining control of much of northwestern Cambodia. In 1943, Japan grants Malay and Burmese areas to Thailand in return for war cooperation. All these lands are given back at the end of the war.

1941: After months of negotiations with the United States, on December 7 Japan launches a surprise air attack on the U.S. naval base at Pearl Harbor, Hawaii, and the islands of Guam and Wake. On December 8, Japan bombs U.S. bases in the Philippines and lands a small force on Bataan. During the rest of December, the Japanese also land at Malaya, Thailand, Hong Kong, Borneo, and Burma. Hong Kong surrenders on December 25; Manila is declared an open city on December 27.

ARTS, CULTURE, THOUGHT, AND RELIGION

The Twentieth Century: 1900–1998

1942: Mao Zedong convenes the Yan'an Forum on Literature and Art, part of the Communists' ideological Rectification Campaign of 1942–1943. The forum lays down the party line on the forms and purposes of literature. The life of the people is "the sole and inexhaustible source of processed literature and art," Mao declares. He disdains traditional forms of high art, whether Chinese or foreign.

SCIENCE-TECHNOLOGY, ECONOMICS, AND EVERYDAY LIFE

The Twentieth Century: 1900–1998

1933–1940: The economic depression that spreads throughout the world inevitably affects Asia, but to the extent that most of its inhabitants are already living at such a basic level and do not participate in high-level industrial-financial operations, the mass of people find their lives more exposed to traditional problems such as famines and floods.

1940–1945: As World War II sweeps across East and Southeast Asia, its industries, trade, and technological development become overwhelmed by Japanese invasion and eventual Allied campaigns. Brunei, for example, is invaded by Japan troops; Britain had destroyed oilfield and port installations to deny Japan oil facilities; Japan drills new wells and develops a naval base. India's economy, however, booms during World War II. It is a period of rapid industrial growth, especially of steel, cotton, paper, and cement, though much of the output of war industries and the agricultural sector is swallowed up by Allied armies and inflation. Pharmaceutical, chemical, and light engineering sectors are developed. Domestic manufacture of bicycles, railroad engines, and automobiles begins.

1947: In China, bubonic plague kills thirty thousand in the Manchurian industrial city of Harbin. The outbreak is traced to the Japanese release in August 1945 of flea-infested rats army researchers had used in germ warfare experiments.

THE WORLD

The Twentieth Century: 1900–1998

1933 *(continued):* In March, Franklin Delano Roosevelt is inaugurated U.S. president; he moves quickly to restore confidence in the banks, then launches his New Deal, with a series of government programs designed to put the country back to work.

1933–1938: Hitler defies the Versailles Treaty and international opinion, rearms Germany, takes over the Rhineland (1936), Austria (1938), and the Sudetenland of Czechoslovakia (1938).

1939–1945: Invading Poland in September 1939, the Germans begin World War II; it will soon spread around the globe as nation after nation becomes involved; when the Japanese bomb Pearl Harbor in December 1941, the United States will join in. Germany surrenders in May 1945.

1945–1948: Even before the war ends, nations are meeting in San Francisco (April) to draw up the charter of the United Nations. It goes into effect on October 24.

1946–1949: In February 1946 Stalin declares that the division of the world into two camps is inevitable so long as capitalism survives; in March, Winston Churchill declares that "an iron curtain has descended across the Continent." The Cold War is under way. In 1947 the Soviets fail to agree with other Allies on unified Germany and Communists take over in Poland. In 1947 the United States proposes the Marshall Plan for European recovery. In 1949 the North Atlantic Treaty Organization (NATO) forms.

1948: The Organization of American States (OAS) forms. The independent state of Israel is created. South Africa adopts *apartheid* policy.

HISTORY

The Twentieth Century: 1900–1998

1942–1945: Part of the costliest war in all history is fought across Pacific and much of Asia, although most of the Indian subcontinent is untouched. Japan occupies almost all of Southeast Asia and East Asia. Trade comes to a standstill in the region and food becomes scarce; the Japanese occupation is often extremely harsh. In April 1942 the United States carries out a small bombing raid on Tokyo, but serious raids on Japan do not commence until 1944, climaxing with the dropping of two atomic bombs on Japan in August 1945, leading to Japan's immediate surrender.

1945–1946: Taking advantage of Japan's defeat and the weakened European forces in Asia, several of the former colonial lands claim their independence. Thus Ho Chi Minh declares for Vietnam, Sukarno for Indonesia, and Prince Souphanouvong for Laos. As the Europeans quickly move in to reassert their control, rebellions begin to spread; as the Communists are often the best organized and motivated, they take the lead in several of these rebellions.

1945–1952: After signing the instrument of surrender in September, Japan faces the Allied occupation with over 2 million war dead and many cities and factories destroyed. While leaving the emperor as a figurehead, the United States forces Japan to become a modern democratic nation by reforming the nation's political and economic structure.

1946: The Philippine Republic attains full independence.

1946–1949: A civil war rages in China between the Nationalist forces of Chiang Kai-shek and Communist armies led by Mao Zedong. The Communists take over northern China and push the Nationalists into smaller and smaller enclaves. In October 1949 Mao takes over Beijing and declares the People's Republic. In December Chiang Kai-shek and his Nationalist forces and supporters move their capital to Taiwan and impose their rule as the Republic of China. Hong Kong and Macau are left alone.

ARTS, CULTURE, THOUGHT, AND RELIGION

The Twentieth Century: 1900–1998

SCIENCE-TECHNOLOGY,
ECONOMICS, AND EVERYDAY LIFE

THE WORLD

The Twentieth Century: 1900–1998

The Twentieth Century: 1900–1998

HISTORY

The Twentieth Century: 1900–1998

1946–1954: Vietnamese of various political persuasions rise up against the French and commence a war that will go on for eight years.

1947: India becomes independent; simultaneously, Pakistan breaks away to form its own Islamic state. Britain also grants Sri Lanka independence.

1950–1961: In 1950 China invades Tibet with 80,000 troops and annexes Tibet. (In 1965 China absorbs Tibet as Xiyang Zizhiqu Autonomous Region.) During the ensuing decades, China kills and deports hundreds of thousands of Tibetans while imposing ever more strict rule. China also resettles millions of ethnic Chinese in Tibet in an effort to destroy Tibetan culture. In 1959 the Dalai Lama flees to India, where he will eventually be joined by many thousands of Tibetans. He will campaign for decades to come to end the Chinese occupation.

1950–1953: Unable to agree on a unified Korea after the end of World War II, the United States, the Soviet Union, and China allow it to be divided into a Communist North and an anti-Communist South. In June 1950 North Korean troops invade South Korea. U.S. forces, soon joined by those of other United Nations members, enter on behalf of South Korea; the war rages up and down the peninsula, and eventually Chinese forces enter to support North Korea. Negotiations to end the war commence in July 1951, but the fighting continues until an armistice is signed in July 1953.

1951: With rising violence against foreign rule, Anthony Brooke abandons all claims of his family to Sarawak, which becomes a British colony.

1952: The occupation of Japan formally ends and the U.S.-Japan Security Treaty takes effect: the United States maintains forces in Japan, while Japan contributes financially. The U.S.-Japan Mutual Defense Assistance Agreement (March 1954) will reinforce the treaty. Japan also signs a peace treaty with China in 1952.

ARTS, CULTURE, THOUGHT, AND RELIGION

The Twentieth Century: 1900–1998

1951: *Rashomon*, a movie directed by Kurosawa Akira, wins the grand prize at the Venice Film Festival; this will lead to the opening of Western movie theaters to Japanese movies.

1955: Japan's government commences designating outstanding men and women as National Living Treasures.

China's government dismisses the writer Hu Feng from the writer's union and other posts for "bourgeois and idealist thinking." He resists the primacy of Marxist theory in art criticism. Arrested in July and tried in secret, Hu is held in prison for most of the next twenty-four years.

1957: Mao Zedong launches his "Hundred Flowers Campaign" in April to encourage criticism of the Communist Party and government. It quickly gets out of control, and by June he cancels it. During the rest of 1957 the Communist Party instead conducts an Anti-Rightist campaign; 300,000 people are branded as rightists and subjected to various forms of persecution, including exile to hard labor in the countryside and jail. Writers and artists are particular targets. The journalist Liu Binyan (born 1925) is among the younger victims. Older, established writers are not overlooked during the Hundred Flowers Campaign. Ding Ling (1904–1985), author of the ideologically correct, Stalin Prize-winning work of "proletarian" literature, *The Sun Shines Over the Sanggan River*, calls for the lifting of government controls on literature. In the aftermath, she is stripped of her party jobs and sent to work as a laborer on a farm near the Siberian frontier.

1958: Seiji Ozawa from Japan wins first prize at French conductors' competition; he will go on to become the conductor and music director of the Boston Symphony Orchestra.

SCIENCE-TECHNOLOGY,
ECONOMICS, AND EVERYDAY LIFE

The Twentieth Century: 1900–1998

1950–1964: In 1950 Taiwan, with U.S. aid, launches a highly successful land reform program that increases agricultural production and paves the way for Taiwan's industrialization. In 1964, U.S. aid to Taiwan is officially terminated. Taiwan's economy takes off to become one of the world's fastest growing economies over the next two decades.

1958: In April, as part of China's Great Leap Forward, the government initiates a new collectivization drive, moving to abolish private agricultural plots and merge rural collectives (production brigades and teams) into larger and larger communes. By December, the Communist Party Central Committee claims that 740,000 cooperatives have merged into 26,000 communes with 120 million households. Great Leap Forward mismanagement causes massive disruption in the countryside; poor harvests and government requisitions of food trigger three years of famine that claims at least 20 million lives.

THE WORLD

The Twentieth Century: 1900–1998

1950–1954: Anticommunism pervades American society, highlighted by such events as the conviction (1950) of Alger Hiss, Senator Joseph McCarthy's speech (1950) claiming he has a list of many known Communists in the State Department, and the execution of Ethel and Julius Rosenberg (1953). "McCarthyism" will not end until McCarthy is condemned by the Senate in 1954.

1953: Francis Crick, an Englishman, and James Watson, an American, announce that they have discovered the structure of DNA; this will lead to a new field, molecular biology, with unending impact on knowledge of and applications to all forms of life.

1956: The Soviet Union sends in troops to put down uprisings in Poland and Hungary.

1957: The Soviet Union launches Sputnik I, the first manmade earth satellite.

The Treaty of Rome establishes the European Economic Community, a major step on the way to a European Union and the Eurodollar.

HISTORY

The Twentieth Century: 1900–1998

1954: The major powers hold a Far Eastern Conference in Geneva, Switzerland. On July 20 France, in addition to ending its war in Vietnam, agrees to recognize the absolute independence of Cambodia and Laos as well as of Vietnam.

In September, SEATO (the Southeast Asia Treaty Organization) is formed as a mutual security organization; it includes the United States, France, the Philippines, Thailand, Pakistan, Australia, and New Zealand. It disbands in 1976.

1962: War breaks out between India and China over rival claims to borderland territory. Chinese troops advance before unilaterally withdrawing. An informal truce follows; China retains selected frontier areas, and borders remain undefined.

1964–1973: At least since 1955 the United States has been supplying military advisers and support to South Vietnam's government in its war against Communists. In 1964 the United States starts committing its own combat forces and soon moves into a full-scale war in Vietnam; eventually it expands into Laos and Cambodia. It takes a tremendous toll of lives on all sides and devastates much of South and North Vietnam. Neither side's leaders seem willing to compromise, but after the United States starts pulling out its forces in 1970, South Vietnam is forced to accept negotiations.

1966–1968: With encouragement from Mao Zedong and his wife Jiang Qing, radical university students in Beijing and elsewhere rise against their faculty and administration, triggering what Mao dubs the Great Proletarian Cultural Revolution. For two years, China is torn apart by zealots who try to wipe out every vestige of China's pre-Communist past and traditions. Finally in 1968 Mao Zedong orders an end to Red Guard violence to stave off a civil war. The People's Liberation Army gradually restores order, but the Cultural Revolution continues in the form of censorship and control of all areas of Chinese society.

ARTS, CULTURE, THOUGHT, AND RELIGION

The Twentieth Century: 1900–1998

1964: *The East Is Red*, a historical poem with music and dancing, is staged in Beijing. It will become the best known of the Communist operas.

1966–1968: During China's Great Proletarian Cultural Revolution, the goal is to attack bourgeois, liberal, and revisionist ideas in the party, government, army, and the culture. During June and July tens of thousands of students leave school to join the Red Guards. Writers and artists once again become special targets. Red Guards publicly humiliate the author Ba Jin, whose novel *Family* had been a bestseller in the 1930s; radicals force Ba's wife to work as a street cleaner. Red Guards drive the distinguished novelist Lao She to suicide. After a year of such excesses, party moderates try unsuccessfully to control the students through "work teams" sent onto the campuses and by forming their own Red Guard units in the hope of coopting the movement.

1966–2000: There is a striking flowering of Indian writers, many of whom compose their works in English and thereby gain an international public. Among them are R. K. Narayan, V. S. Naipaul (born in Trinidad), Anita Desai, and Salman Rushdie.

SCIENCE-TECHNOLOGY,
ECONOMICS, AND EVERYDAY LIFE

The Twentieth Century: 1900–1998

Late 1960s: As part of the "Green Revolution," high-yield crops are introduced through much of Asia, among them dwarf Indica rice, Mexican wheat, and Taiwanese and Philippine rice. Crop yields double in some places, but chemical fertilizers used with the new seeds eventually present environmental problems.

1964: China explodes its first atomic bomb.

1964–1975: Throughout much of Southeast Asia, the Vietnam War produces an economic boom from U.S. dollars for the construction of roads, military bases, and airstrips; these developments expose all, not just the elite, to Western culture and media; this leads to a rise in tourism, prostitution, and corruption.

1966: Taiwan inaugurates its Export Processing Zones. Designed to encourage Western investment by reducing red tape and providing economic incentives, the zones are later emulated by other Asian countries, including China.

1967: China explodes its first fusion or hydrogen bomb.

THE WORLD

The Twentieth Century: 1900–1998

1959–1961: Fidel Castro enters Havana, Cuba, in triumph after the dictator Batista flees. At first he calls his revolution "humanistic" but in 1961, after the disastrous failure of the U.S.-supported invasion at the Bay of Pigs, he will declare himself a Marxist-Leninist.

1962: The U.S. discovery that Russia has nuclear missiles on Cuba produces the October missile crisis; after several tense days it is resolved with Russia's agreement to remove them in return for a secret U.S. agreement to withdraw its nuclear missiles in Turkey.

1963: President John F. Kennedy is assassinated in Dallas.

1963–1968: Since helping to organize the boycott of the buses in Montgomery, Alabama, the Rev. Martin Luther King Jr. has become the leader of the civil rights struggle by African-Americans. His assassination in 1968 is but one of a series of events this year that profoundly unsettle American society.

1964: Charged by South African authorities with sabotage and subversion, Nelson Mandela is sentenced to life imprisonment. He is released in 1990; in 1994 he is elected president of South Africa.

1969: U.S. astronaut Neil Armstrong becomes the first man to walk on the moon (July 21).

HISTORY

The Twentieth Century: 1900–1998

1967: ASEAN (the Association of Southeast Asian Nations) is formed to establish terms of cooperation among Indonesia, Malaysia, Singapore, Thailand, and the Philippines.

1971: In April, Nationalist leaders in East Pakistan declare independence as the state of Bangladesh. A nine-month civil war ensues, killing 300,000 people; some 10 million refugees cross the border to India. In December the Third Indo-Pakistani War coincides with the final stage of the Bangladeshi war of independence. Superior Soviet-equipped Indian forces defeat Pakistani forces and on December 17 a cease-fire is declared. East Pakistan achieves independence as the state of Bangladesh.

1971: Taiwan, the Republic of China, is expelled from the United Nations. The People's Republic of China is admitted to hold the China seat.

1972: Richard Nixon visits China, marking the opening of the West to China and China to the West.

1973–1976: The Paris Agreements on "ending the war and restoring peace in Vietnam" are signed by opposing sides in January 1973. But the North and South Vietnamese continue to fight until the Communists enter Saigon in April 1975. In July 1976 the Communists proclaim the unified Socialist Republic of Vietnam. The Communists who have taken control in Laos have proclaimed the People's Democratic Republic of Laos in December 1975.

1975–1989: Cambodia's Republican army formally surrenders to the Khmer Rouge, who proceed to massacre unknown numbers—perhaps as many as two million—of their countrymen. In 1977, Vietnam, alarmed by the Democratic Kampuchea-Beijing alliance, launches a major offensive into Cambodia. By January 1979 Phnom Penh is abandoned to the Vietnamese forces. The Khmer Rouge retreats to the Thai border and set up resistance bases. Vietnam forces will remain in Cambodia until 1989.

ARTS, CULTURE, THOUGHT, AND RELIGION

The Twentieth Century: 1900–1998

1968: Kawabata Yasunari wins Japan's first Nobel Prize in Literature.

1970: Japanese writer and right-wing militarist Mishima Yukio commits suicide.

1970s: Among the signs of increasingly more widespread interactions between the West and East, there is a great interest in Japanese martial arts such as karate, especially in the United States. Zen Buddhism and various Indian meditation disciplines are practiced in the West; the *Tibetan Book of the Dead and* the Chinese *I Ching* gain a new public; young Westerners begin to visit Nepal, and Katmandu, its capital, becomes a major tourist destination.

1974: After the Vienna Philharmonic and the Philadelphia Orchestra tour China in 1973, an editorial in the *People's Daily* attacks Beethoven, Schubert, and other European composers as "bourgeois."

1977: As China's Cultural Revolution begins to be dismantled, college entrance examinations are restored. Decision-making is restored to academics; ideological supervision is reduced; and quality over quantity is sought in the schools. The latter leads to a restoration of the two-track system favoring talented students, which, as Mao feared, tends to favor students of educated or high-status background.

SCIENCE-TECHNOLOGY, ECONOMICS, AND EVERYDAY LIFE

The Twentieth Century: 1900–1998

1970: China launches its first satellite into space.

1974: India conducts its first underground test of a nuclear device.

1975: The first Indian satellite, named *Aryabhata* after the fifth-century astronomer, is launched.

1975–1998: Vietnam emerges from thirty years of war with much of its land, infrastructure, and industries devastated. Laos is in a similar situation. Both countries' new Communist leaders persist in imposing their centralized policies but are unable to move their countries forward; Vietnam even fails to produce enough rice, long a commodity it exported. By the 1990s, Vietnam begins to invite foreign investment, but Laos is less open to the outside world.

THE WORLD

The Twentieth Century: 1900–1998

1972–1974: The Watergate affair begins with a bungled burglary at the Watergate apartment complex on June 17, 1972, and ends with President Richard Nixon's resignation on August 9, 1974.

HISTORY

The Twentieth Century: 1900–1998

1978–1980: Deng Xiaoping wins a power struggle and emerges as China's paramount leader. Deng's market-oriented economic policies trigger a boom.

1983–1986: Benigno Aquino, the Filipino leader of the opposition to the dictatorship of Ferdinand Marcos, is shot to death at Manila airport upon his return from self-imposed exile; in 1984 a commission concludes the Philippine military is responsible for Aquino's death. In 1986 Corazón Aquino, Benigno's widow, defeats Marcos in a presidential election. Marcos calls for a state of emergency, but protests force him to back down. The Reagan administration provides the Marcos family political asylum in Hawaii.

1984: Brunei becomes an independent nation ruled by Sultan Hassanal Bolkiah as its "democratic" monarch. Gurkha troops of the British army remain to guard Brunei's valuable oil fields.

1984: The Sino-British Joint Declaration is signed by British and Chinese Prime Ministers. The British agree to return the whole of the Hong Kong region to Chinese control in 1997.

1984: Sikhs occupy the Golden Temple in Amritsar, India, and demand constitutional recognition of Sikhs and special status for their holy city. An Indian army attack on the Golden Temple leaves hundreds dead and destroys some of the temple buildings. In October, Indira Gandhi is assassinated in her garden by two of her Sikh bodyguards seeking revenge for the assault on the Golden Temple. Hindus avenging Mrs. Gandhi's death attack Sikhs and their properties before the army is finally called out.

1986–1987: Formal negotiations between Portugal and China on the future of Macau produce the Sino-Portuguese Joint Declaration (April 1987). Under the terms of the declaration, China assumes sovereignty of Macau on December 20, 1999.

ARTS, CULTURE, THOUGHT, AND RELIGION

The Twentieth Century: 1900–1998

1985: China's government issues a new charter for the Chinese Writers Association that promises freedom of expression—so long as members follow party and Marxist-Leninist guidelines.

1987: Okamoto Ayako becomes the first Japanese architect to win the Pritzker Prize, regarded as the "Nobel Prize for architects." In 1993, Maki Fumihiko will also win the Pritzker.

1988: China's first exhibit of nude paintings opens in Beijing.

SCIENCE-TECHNOLOGY, ECONOMICS, AND EVERYDAY LIFE

The Twentieth Century: 1900–1998

1980s: Industrial growth throughout much of Asia continues at an astonishing rate, fueled by foreign investments and purchases. Japan, South Korea, Singapore, and Hong Kong are among those that prosper the most through manufacturing technical wares such as electronic goods and automobiles. Thailand, the Philippines, and Malaysia prosper more from manufacturing such items as clothing and toys. Indonesia and Brunei prosper through their rich oil deposits. India's economy prospers through its educated class, which develops a more broad-based intellectual and industrial output. But not all countries participate. Bangladesh in particular remains the "basket case" of Asia. Aside from the problems presented by its expanding population, a number of horrendous floods, a major cyclone, and a tidal wave leave millions of people homeless or without food and millions of houses and other structures destroyed.

1980: China announces the successful launch of an ICBM with warhead delivery capability.

1982–1992: Under China's new policy of encouraging enterprising manufacturers to deal with the West, the mainland province of Guangdong opposite Hong Kong becomes a major industrial zone. For example, all but a few of British Hong Kong's 3,200 toy factories relocate to mainland Guangdong, where labor costs are low and profits high.

1984: China's Central Committee issues Document Number 1, which acknowledges the virtual dismantling of the system of collectivized farming and establishes what is known as the "responsibility system." In return for negotiated payments to the state, farmers may grow what they choose and keep whatever is left after they make their agreed-to deliveries. Plot assignments may be sold or inherited, though nominally the state still owns the land. The committee also extends special economic zone status to fourteen additional coastal cities and Hainan Island.

THE WORLD

The Twentieth Century: 1900–1998

1979–1981: After almost thirty-eight years in power and after a year of increasing unrest, the Shah of Iran flees into exile. The Ayatollah Khomeini returns from exile and assumes control and begins to impose strict Islamic controls. In November, Iranians seize the U.S. embassy in Teheran, taking sixty-six hostages; fifty-one are held until the moment Ronald Reagan is sworn in as U.S. president on January 20, 1981.

1982: The public begins to be informed of a new disease that is killing increasing numbers of mostly male homosexuals and drug users—the Acquired Immune Deficiency Syndrome, or AIDS. In the years that follow, millions of people of both sexes and all persuasions around the world will acquire the usually fatal virus.

1983–1987: President Reagan calls for a "Strategic Defense Initiative" that is quickly dubbed "Star Wars" because of its high-tech nature. The Russians attack it as an escalation of the arms race, but when Mikhail Gorbachev assumes leadership of the Soviet Union in 1985, he does agree to speed up arms control negotiations. In December 1987 Reagan and Gorbachev sign a treaty calling for the reduction of their nations' nuclear arsenals.

1987–1991: Gorbachev calls for both economic reforms (*perestroika*) and a more open society (*glasnost*) in the Soviet Union. In doing so, he unleashes forces that he cannot control. By 1989, former Soviet-dominated states of East Europe are throwing off their Communist leaders; this culminates with the destruction of the Berlin Wall in November. As the Soviet economy begins to collapse, Boris Yeltsin emerges as the most outspoken critic of Gorbachev's reformist ways, although he takes the lead in putting down an attempted coup in August 1991. On December 25, 1991, Gorbachev formally proclaims the end of the USSR and resigns; Yeltsin becomes president of a new confederation headed by Russia.

HISTORY

The Twentieth Century: 1900–1998

1989: In April Chinese students mass in Beijing's Tiananmen Square to protest conditions at local universities but soon turn to demanding political reforms. This leads to escalating protests until an estimated 100,000 students rally in Beijing to mark the seventieth anniversary of the 1919 demonstrations that launched the May Fourth Movement. As students gain international publicity and domestic support, on June 3–4 troops and armored vehicles move against the Tiananmen Square protesters. Estimates of the dead range from one thousand to ten thousand; hundreds of student leaders are arrested but some manage to escape into exile abroad.

1991: The Soviet Union disintegrates, and one by one its constituent republics declare their independence. This includes Kyrgyzstan, Uzbekistan, Tajikistan, Turkmenistan, and Kazakhstan. On December 21, the five Central Asian republics apply to join the Commonwealth of Independent States (CIS), the loose association of twelve former constituent republics of the Soviet Union formed initially by Russia, Belarus, and Ukraine to advance economic and military cooperation.

1997: Britain's lease expires at midnight on June 30, and Hong Kong becomes a Special Administrative Region of China.

1997–1998: After Thailand devalues its currency in July 1997, the so-called Asian flu begins to weaken the economies and financial structures of many nations throughout Asia. The International Monetary Fund tries to prop up some of these countries with loans, but unemployment spreads. Japan is especially hard hit and seems unable to respond quickly. In Indonesia, the hard times bring social unrest that leads to the overthrow of the Sukarno regime.

ARTS, CULTURE, THOUGHT, AND RELIGION

The Twentieth Century: 1900–1998

1990: Wealthy Japanese have for some time been buying up Western art at high prices; at auctions in New York, Ruyoei Saito, president of a paper manufacturing company, pays record-setting prices for a Van Gogh and a Renoir.

1993: In Bangladesh, Islamic extremists threaten to put on trial Taslima Nasreem for her book *Lajja* (*Shame*), which they claim includes blasphemous elements such as depicting Muslims attacking a Hindu family. When the government files a case charging her with blasphemy in 1994, she flees; on returning in September 1998, the government puts out a warrant for her arrest.

1994: Chinese authorities ban the film *The Blue Kite*, a story of family suffering during the political upheavals of the 1950s and 1960s.

SCIENCE-TECHNOLOGY, ECONOMICS, AND EVERYDAY LIFE

The Twentieth Century: 1900–1998

1984 *(continued)*: Gaining its independence from Britain, Brunei proceeds to thrive on its oil and natural gas reserves, which comprise a major share of Brunei's export earnings; it is the world's second largest producer of liquefied natural gas. On a much smaller scale, there is an industry of brass workers practicing traditional lost-wax casting techniques to produce cannons, guns, and gongs for ceremonial and decorative use.

1986: Some 400,000 small- and medium-sized businesses produce 40 percent of China's industrial output. Most firms are collectively owned, but a growing number are in private hands. Both types of ownership operate increasingly on market principles.

1992: A UN regional conference cites 400,000 Thai infected with AIDS virus and two million expected to die by the year 2000.

1993: A joint Norwegian-Swedish group signs an agreement to construct the largest and most expensive public works project ever in Laos, the Nam Theun II dam and hydroelectric project; to be located in the highlands of eastern Laos, it is expected to generate enough electricity to earn the equivalent of three-quarters of Laos's total annual imports. However, in the years that follow, the project proves so controversial, primarily because of its impact on the environment, that its construction continues to be postponed.

Bhutan and India agree to joint construction of one of Asia's largest dams on the Sankosh River, a $760 million project.

1994: Construction begins on the long-planned Three Gorges Dam project on the Yangtze. Cost estimates range upwards of $100 billion for what will be the largest hydroelectric project in history, creating a 400-mile-long reservoir that will inundate 160 towns and force the relocation of 1.3 million people. Critics say it will severely damage the Yangtze environment.

The Friendship Bridge linking Laos and Thailand is officially opened; spanning the Mekong River, it links with Laos nine miles east of Vientiane. It is expected to greatly stimulate Laos's economy, which remains strongly dependent on Thailand.

THE WORLD

The Twentieth Century: 1900–1998

1991: After Iraq takes over Kuwait in August 1990, the United States leads a coalition of thirty-four nations whose military expedition drives Iraq's forces out of Kuwait in a ground war that lasts only one hundred hours in February.

Croatia and Slovenia declare their independence from the former Yugoslavia, thus triggering what will become a bloody civil war that will rack Yugoslavia for years to come.

1992–1993: The civil war in Yugoslavia spreads to Bosnia-Herzogovina. Sarajevo, the capital, finds itself besieged by Serb forces who slowly destroy its buildings and infrastructure with their artillery fire; in 1993 Serb forces comply with a NATO ultimatum and withdraw their heavy artillery from Sarajevo.

1993: Troops loyal to Boris Yeltsin put down a rebellion by hardline Communists.

U.S. president Bush and Russian president Yeltsin sign the second Strategic Arms Reduction Treaty.

The Maastricht Treaty goes into effect, a major step toward the European Union.

1994: In Rwanda, a civil war leaves some 500,000 massacred in only a few months.

Russia invades the republic of Chechnya and embarks on a frustrating war.

HISTORY

The Twentieth Century: 1900–1998

ARTS, CULTURE, THOUGHT,
AND RELIGION

The Twentieth Century: 1900–1998

SCIENCE-TECHNOLOGY, ECONOMICS, AND EVERYDAY LIFE

The Twentieth Century: 1900–1998

1995: Floods devastate the grain crop in North Korea, leaving at least 100,000 homeless and causing billions of dollars in damage.

ASEAN members sign a pact declaring the area from Myanmar to Indonesia a nuclear-free zone. This is an effort to prevent Southeast Asian nations from acquiring or producing their own nuclear weapons.

1996–1997: Long lagging behind the rest of its Asian neighbors, North Korea's economy deteriorates and its food crisis grows worse in 1996; it is believed that a serious famine now threatens North Korea. Not until February 1997 does North Korea publicly admit that it has only about half the grain it needs to feed its people; by April it reaches a new agreement with the United States, which will supply much of the grain needed.

1997: Forest fires raze thousands of acres in Indonesia and cast a blanket of thick smog over much of Indonesia, Brunei, and Malaysia. The fires are deliberately set in Borneo and Sumatra for clearing land, but this year they are believed to have been flamed by drought brought on by the periodic warming of ocean waters known as El Niño. The smoke causes respiratory ailments and smoke inhalation throughout Indonesia and Malaysia; it is also responsible for automobile accidents and a falling off in tourism. In September, an Indonesian airliner crashes on Sumatra and all 234 people aboard are killed; it is believed that the airliner lost its way in the thick haze that has settled over much of the country.

1997–1998: With Thailand's devaluation of its currency in July, the domino effect sets in: at first it hits the countries of Southeast Asia—Malaysia, Singapore, Indonesia, the Philippines, Vietnam—but very quickly it also hits East Asia, including Hong Kong, Korea, and Japan. Currencies are weakened, stock markets crash, banks collapse, property values decline; as Asians begin to hold back on their own purchases from abroad, international trade declines and soon Asian factories are closing. Careless banking procedures,

THE WORLD

The Twentieth Century: 1900–1998

1995: The presidents of Bosnia-Herzogovina, Serbia, and Croatia sign a treaty (in Dayton, Ohio) that ends the four-year-old civil war.

After months of negotiations, Israel's prime minister Itzhak Rabin and the Palestinian leader Yasir Arafat sign a historic peace accord in Washington in September. In December, Rabin is assassinated by a right-wing Israeli youth.

1996: Russian president Yeltsin and U.S. president Clinton are both reelected. Kofi Annan of Ghana is elected secretary general of the United Nations, the first African to hold this office.

1997–1998: In mid-November 1997, Saddam Hussein bans UN inspectors from checking out his armaments; after the United States threatens to bomb Iraq in February 1998, Iraq signs a new agreement to let the inspectors back. In November 1998, Hussein again refuses to allow the inspectors to do their work but again he backs down.

El Niño, a meteorological condition derived from warmer waters in the Pacific, begins to affect the world's weather.

1998: An uprising in the Kosovo province of the former Yugoslavia escalates, and Serbia moves in its troops who apply increasing force; when NATO threatens to commence bombing the Serbs, they pull their troops out in October.

Protestants and Catholics in Northern Ireland reach a major accord in April; it is approved by the voters in May.

The economic crisis that began in Southeast Asia in July 1997 begins to spread throughout the world. Russia finds itself in extreme trouble, with its economy and finances virtually collapsing and President Yeltsin appearing increasingly more erratic and isolated.

HISTORY

The Twentieth Century: 1900–1998

ARTS, CULTURE, THOUGHT, AND RELIGION

The Twentieth Century: 1900–1998

SCIENCE-TECHNOLOGY,
ECONOMICS, AND EVERYDAY LIFE

The Twentieth Century: 1900–1998

THE WORLD

The Twentieth Century: 1900–1998

1997–1998 *(continued)*: risky investment practices, nepotism, corruption, and outright criminal behavior endemic in many of these countries only aggravate the situation. Typical is what happens to Singapore's economy: One of the world's major manufacturers of computer parts, which make up 45 percent of its locally produced exports, it experiences a 17 percent decline in such exports during this first year of the crisis. Retail sales within Singapore itself have declined by 25 percent. In place of the thousands of wealthy Asians who have for years flocked to Singapore to spend their money, many more thousands of poor Indonesians and Malaysians are trying to sneak illegally into Singapore to find jobs. On June 30, 1998, the government announces it intends to spend US $2 billion to stimulate the economy, making for the first budget deficit in over a decade.

1998: It is reported that by the end of 1997, foreign-invested companies employ some 11 percent of China's nonagricultural workforce and account for some 14 percent of the country's total annual industrial output.

Boeing, the American-based largest producer of aircraft in the world, announces that China has bought one-tenth of the firm's aircraft in the past three years, that one of the world's largest spare-parts centers been established by Boeing in Beijing, and that more than one-third of the 8,500 Boeing aircraft flying around the world are equipped with parts made in China.

In April, Pakistan conducts the first successful test of the surface-to-surface Ghauri missile, capable of penetrating deep into Indian territory. In mid-May India conducts five underground nuclear tests; two weeks later Pakistan announces it has tested five nuclear devices, thus making its the world's seventh nuclear power.